CODES & CHEATS

SPRING 2008 EDITION

Prima Games

A Division of Random House, Inc.

3000 Lava Ridge Court, Suite 100

Roseville, CA 95661

www.primagames.com

The Prima Games logo is a registered trademark of Random House, Inc., registered
in the United States and other countries. Primagames.com is a registered trademark
of Random House, Inc., registered in the United States.

Product Manager: Jason Wigle

Editor: Kate Abbott

Interior Layout & Design: Winter Graphics North

Manufacturing Contact: Suzanne Goodwin

All products and characters mentioned in this book are trademarks of their respective companies.

Please be advised that the ESRB Ratings icons, "EC," "E," "E10+," "T," "M," "AO," and "RP"
are trademarks owned by the Entertainment Software Association, and may only be used with
their permission and authority. For information regarding whether a product has been rated by the
ESRB, please visit www.esrb.org. For permission to use the Ratings icons, please contact the ESA
at esrblicenseinfo.com.

Important:

Prima Games has made every effort to determine that the information contained in this book is
accurate. However, the publisher makes no warranty, either expressed or implied, as to the
accuracy, effectiveness, or completeness of the material in this book; nor does the publisher
assume liability for damages, either incidental or consequential, that may result from using the
information in this book. The publisher cannot provide information regarding gameplay, hints
and strategies, or problems with hardware or software. Questions should be directed to the
support numbers provided by the game and device manufacturers in their documentation. Some
game tricks require precise timing and may require repeated attempts before the desired result is
achieved.

ISBN: 978-0-7615-5665-7

Library of Congress Catalog Card Number: 2007940357

Printed in the United States of America

08 09 10 11 HH 10 9 8 7 6 5 4 3 2 1

Table of Contents - DS

Age of Empires: The Age of Kings

Unlockables

Unlockable	How to Unlock
Agincourt	250 empire points
Archipelago Large	200 empire points
Asia Major	300 empire points
Bridges Large	100 empire points
Castles	150 empire points
France	100 empire points
Hannibal's Crossing	250 empire points
Hastings	250 empire points
Khyber Pass	250 empire points
King of the Mountain	300 empire points
Outremer	150 empire points
Skirmish—Desert	250 empire points
Skirmish—Plains	250 empire points
Swamplands	150 empire points
Valley	100 empire points
Dark Ram	150 empire points
Dopple-handers	100 empire points
Genoese Crossbowmen	100 empire points
Knights of the Round Table	200 empire points
Mons Meg	150 empire points
Swiss Pikemen	100 empire points
War Wolf	150 empire points
Welsh Bowmen	100 empire points

Tabs (left margin): DS, GBA, PSP, PS2, PS3, Wii, Xbox, Xbox 360, Index

Alex Rider: Stormbreaker

Enter the password screen from the main menu and input the following.

Password	Effect
JESSICA PARKER	Allows you to purchase black belt
6943059	Allows you to purchase disk 6 after completing game
VICTORIA PARR	Allows you to purchase M16 badge
RENATO CELANI	Allows you to purchase the fugu
SARYL HIRSCH	Allows you to purchase the sunglasses
9785711	Allows you to select level HARD
4298359	Everything at shop is at half price!
9603717	Gallery is added to Secret mode
5204025	Get 10,000 spy points
6894098	Outfit change is added to Secret mode

Animaniacs: Lights, Camera, Action!

To activate a cheat, pause the game and enter the code, then un-pause the game.

Cheat Codes

Code	Effect
⒧, ⒭, ←, ←, ↑, ↑	Disable Time
→, →, →, ←, ←, ←, ⒭, ⒧	Kingsize Pickups
⒧, ⒧, ⒭, ⒭, ↓, ↓	Skip Level
Wakko, Wakko, Wakko, Wakko, Wakko	Level 1
Dot, Yakko, Brain, Wakko, Pinky	Level 2
Yakko, Dot, Wakko, Wakko, Brain	Level 3
Pinky, Yakko, Yakko, Dot, Brain	Level 4
Pinky, Pinky, Yakko, Wakko, Wakko	Level 5
Brain, Dot, Brain, Pinky, Yakko	Level 6
Brain, Pinky, Wakko, Pinky, Brain	Level 7
Brain Pinky, Pinky, Wakko, Wakko	Level 8
Dot, Dot, Yakko, Pinky, Wakko	Level 9
Brain, Dot, Brain, Yakko, Wakko	Level 10
Akko, Yakko, Pinky, Dot, Dot	Level 11
Pinky, Pinky, Brain, Dot, Wakko	Level 12
Yakko, Wakko, Pinky, Wakko, Brain	Level 13
Pinky, Wakko, Brain, Wakko, Yakko	Level 14
Dot, Pinky, Wakko, Wakko, Yakko	Level 15

Balls of Fury

Unlockables

Unlockable	How to Unlock
Karl Wolfschtagg	Win 20 matches
Master Wong	Beat Arcade mode on Easy
Young Randy	Beat Story mode on Easy

DS

GBA

PSP

PS2

PS3

Wii

Xbox

Xbox 360

Index

DS
GBA
PSP
PS2
PS3
Wii
Xbox
Xbox 360
Index

Burnout Legends

Unlockables

Unlockable	How to Unlock
Assassin Compact	Awarded at 15 Takedowns
Compact Cop	Awarded for Gold in Silver Lake or Airport Pursuit
Custom Compact	Awarded for Gold in Harbour Town Race
Dominator Compact	Awarded at 10,000 Burnout Points
DX Compact	Awarded for Gold in Airport Eliminator
Legend Compact	Awarded for Gold in Palm Bay Legend Face-Off
Legend Gangster	Awarded for Gold in Interstate Legend Face-Off
Legend Special	Awarded for 13 Gold Medals
Modified Compact	Awarded for Gold in Interstate Race
Prototype Compact	Awarded at start of Compact Series
Tuned Compact	Awarded at start of Compact Series
Assassin Coupe	Awarded at 60 Takedowns
Coupe Cop	Awarded for Gold In Vineyard or Palm Bay Pursuit
Custom Coupe	Awarded for Gold in Riviera Race
Dominator Coupe	Awarded at 40,000 Burnout Points
DX Coupe	Awarded for Gold in Big Surf Shores Eliminator
Legend Pickup	Awarded for Gold in Vineyard Legend Face-Off
Legend Special	Awarded for 41 Gold Medals
Legend SUV	Awarded for Gold in Airport Legend Face-Off
Modified Coupe	Awarded for Gold in Silver Lake Race
Prototype Coupe	Awarded for Unlocking Coupe Series
Tuned Coupe	Awarded for Unlocking Coupe Series
4WD Heavy Duty	Awarded for 300,000 Crash Dollars
4WD Racer	Awarded for 2 Crash Golds in Compact
B-Team Van	Awarded for 2 Crash Golds in Muscle
City Bus	Awarded for 2 Crash Golds in Sports
Delivery Truck	Awarded for 400,000 Crash Dollars
Firetruck	Collect all Crash Golds
Heavy Pickup	Awarded for 100,000 Crash Dollars
Longnose Cab	Awarded for 2 Crash Golds in Coupe
SUV Deluxe	Awarded for 200,000 Crash Dollars
Tractor Cab	Awarded for 500,000 Crash Dollars
Trash Truck	Awarded for 2 Crash Golds in Super
Assassin Muscle	Awarded at 30 Takedowns
Custom Muscle	Awarded for Gold in Downtown Race
Dominator Muscle	Awarded at 25,000 Burnout Points
DX Muscle	Awarded for Gold in Palm Bay Eliminator
Legend Classic	Awarded for Gold in Riviera Legend Face-Off
Legend J-Muscle	Awarded for Gold in Big Surf Shores Legend Face-Off
Legend Special	Awarded for 27 Gold Medals
Modified Muscle	Awarded for Gold in Big Surf Shores Race

Burnout Legends *(continued)*

Muscle Cop	Awarded for Gold in Downtown or Dockside Pursuit
Prototype Muscle	Awarded for Unlocking Muscle Series
Tuned Muscle	Awarded for Unlocking Muscle Series
Classic Hot Rod	Collect all Takedown Trophies
Euro Racer	Collect all Postcards
Gangster Boss	Collect Gold in all Legend Face-Off Events
Ultimate Coupe	Collect all Signature Takedowns
US Racer	Awarded for Gold in Super GP
World Racer	Awarded for Gold in Special GP
Assassin Sports	Awarded at 90 Takedowns
Custom Sports	Awarded for Gold in Airport Race
Dominator	Awarded at 60,000 Burnout Points
DX Sports	Awarded for Gold in Downtown Eliminator
Legend Racer	Awarded for Gold in Downtown Legend Face-Off
Legend Roadster	Awarded for Gold in Silver Lake Legend Face-Off
Legend Special	Awarded for 55 Gold Medals
Modified Sports	Awarded for Gold in Island Paradise Race
Prototype Sports	Awarded for Unlocking Sports Series
Sports Cop	Awarded for Gold in Golden City or Island Paradise Pursuit
Tuned Sports	Awarded for Unlocking Sports Series
Assassin Super	Awarded at 120 Takedowns
Custom Super	Awarded for Gold in Dockside Race
Dominator Super	Awarded at 80,000 Burnout Points
DX Super	Awarded for Gold in Silver Lake Eliminator
Legend Hot-Rod	Awarded for Gold in Dockside Legend Face-Off
Legend Special	Awarded for 70 Gold Medals
Legend Super Car	Awarded for Gold in Harbour Town Legend Face-Off
Modified Super	Awarded for Gold in Golden City Road Rage
Prototype Super	Awarded for Unlocking Super Series
Super Cop	Awarded for Gold in Riviera or Big Surf Pursuit
Tuned Super	Awarded for Unlocking Super Series

Bust a Move DS

Enter this code at the Main menu.

Unlockable	Code
Sound Test	SELECT, Ⓐ, Ⓑ, ←, →, Ⓐ, SELECT, →

Cartoon Network Racing

Cheats

Go to options, then go to the nickname option. Enter these codes at the nickname screen. WARNING: Use of any of these codes deactivates saving for as long as they are in effect.

Password	Effect
AAARGH	Enables all hazards and pickups in time trial
STONEME	Rockets turn non-invulnerable opponents into stone
IMACOPTER	Top-down view

Cartoon Network Racing (continued)

ROCKETMAN	Unlimited dumb rockets
SPINACH	Unlimited superpower energy
GIMMIE	Unlock everything

Unlockables

Unlockable	How to Unlock
Bonus Game A: CN Sketchbook	Beat Cowardly Championship and buy for 1,000 Toon Coins
Bonus Game B: Kart Kurling	Beat Pork Butt Championship and buy for 10,000 Toon Coins
Cartoon A: Dexter's Rival	Beat Booger Championship and buy for 5,000 Toon Coins
Cartoon B: Telephonies	Beat a Record in Time Trial and buy for 10,000 Toon Coins
Cartoon C: Black Sheep	Beat Flipped-Out Cowardly Championship and buy for 25,000 Toon Coins
Booger Championship	Beat Cowardly Championship
Chemical-X Championship	Beat Pork Butt Championship
Flipped-Out Booger Championship	Beat Flipped-Out Cowardly Championship
Flipped-Out Chemical-X Championship	Beat Flipped-Out Pork Butt Championship
Flipped-Out Cowardly Championship	Beat Soupered-Up Chemical-X Championship
Flipped-Out Pork Butt Championship	Beat Flipped-Out Booger Championship
Pork Butt Championship	Beat Booger Championship
Souped-Up Booger Championship	Beat Souped-Up Cowardly Championship
Souped-Up Chemical-X Championship	Beat Souped-Up Pork Butt Championship
Souped-Up Cowardly Championship	Beat Chemical-X Championship
Souped-Up Pork Butt Championship	Beat Souped-Up Booger Championship
Soupered-Up Booger Championship	Beat Soupered-Up Cowardly Championship
Soupered-Up Chemical-X Championship	Beat Soupered-Up Pork Butt Championship
Soupered-Up Cowardly Championship	Beat Soupered-Up Chemical-X Championship
Soupered-Up Pork Butt Championship	Beat Soupered-Up Booger Championship
Blossom Souped-Up Upgrade	Beat Chemical-X Championship and buy for 500 Toon Coins
Blossom Soupered-Up Upgrade	Beat Souped-Up Chemical-X Championship and buy for 1,000 Toon Coins
Bubbles Souped-Up Upgrade	Beat Chemical-X Championship and buy for 500 Toon Coins
Bubbles Soupered-Up Upgrade	Beat Souped-Up Chemical-X Championship and buy for 1,000 Toon Coins
Bunny Bravo Souped-Up Upgrade	Unlock Bunny Bravo and buy for 500 Toon Coins
Bunny Bravo Soupered-Up Upgrade Coins	Unlock Bunny Bravo and buy for 1,000 Toon
Buttercup Souped-Up Upgrade	Beat Chemical-X Championship and buy for 500 Toon Coins
Buttercup Soupered-Up Upgrade	Beat Souped-Up Chemical-X Championship and buy for 1,000 Toon Coins
Chicken Souped-Up Upgrade	Beat Chemical-X Championship and buy for 500 Toon Coins
Chicken Soupered-Up Upgrade	Beat Souped-Up Chemical-X Championship and buy for 1,000 Toon Coins

Cartoon Network Racing (continued)

Courage Souped-Up Upgrade	Beat Chemical-X Championship and buy for 500 Toon Coins
Courage Soupered-Up Upgrade	Beat Souped-Up Chemical-X Championship and buy for 1,000 Toon
Cow Souped-Up Upgrade	Beat Chemical-X Championship and buy for 500 Toon Coins
Cow Soupered-Up Upgrade	Beat Souped-Up Chemical-X Championship and buy for 1,000 Toon Coins
Dee Dee Souped-Up Upgrade	Unlock Dee Dee and buy for 500 Toon Coins
Dee Dee Soupered-Up Upgrade	Unlock Dee Dee and buy for 1,000 Toon Coins
Dexter Souped-Up Upgrade	Beat Chemical-X Championship and buy for 500 Toon Coins
Dexter Soupered-Up Upgrade	Beat Souped-Up Chemical-X Championship and buy for 1,000 Toon Coins
Eustace Souped-Up Upgrade	Unlock Eustace and buy for 500 Toon Coins
Eustace Soupered-Up Upgrade	Unlock Eustace and buy for 1,000 Toon Coins
Him Souped-Up Upgrade	Unlock Him and buy for 500 Toon Coins
Him Soupered-Up Upgrade	Unlock Him and buy for 1,000 Toon Coins
I.M. Weasel Souped-Up Upgrade	Beat Chemical-X Championship and buy for 500 Toon Coins
I.M. Weasel Soupered-Up Upgrade	Beat Souped-Up Chemical-X Championship and buy for 1,000 Toon Coins
I.R. Baboon Souped-Up Upgrade	Unlock I.R. Baboon and buy for 500 Toon Coins
I.R. Baboon Soupered-Up Upgrade	Unlock I.R. Baboon, beat Souped-Up Chemical-X Championship, and buy for 1,000 Toon Coins
Johnny Bravo Souped-Up Upgrade	Beat Chemical-X Championship and buy for 500 Toon Coins
Johnny Bravo Soupered-Up Upgrade	Beat Souped-Up Chemical-X Championship and buy for 1,000 Toon Coins
Mandark Souped-Up Upgrade	Unlock Mandark and buy for 500 Toon Coins
Mandark Soupered-Up Upgrade	Unlock Mandark and buy for 1,000 Toon Coins
Mojo Jojo Souped-Up Upgrade	Unlock Mojo Jojo and buy for 500 Toon Coins
Mojo Jojo Soupered-Up Upgrade	Unlock Mojo Jojo, beat Souped-Up Chemical-X Championship, and buy for 1,000 Toon Coins
Muriel Souped-Up Upgrade	Unlock Muriel and buy for 500 Toon Coins
Muriel Soupered-Up Upgrade	Unlock Muriel, beat Souped-Up Chemical-X Championship, and buy for 1,000 Toon Coins
Professor Utonium Souped-Up Upgrade	Unlock Professor Utonium and buy for 500 Toon Coins
Professor Utonium Soupered-Up Upgrade	Unlock Professor Utonium and buy for 1,000 Toon Coins
Suzy Souped-Up Upgrade	Unlock Suzy and buy for 500 Toon Coins
Suzy Soupered-Up Upgrade	Unlock Suzy, beat Souped-Up Chemical-X Championship, and buy for 1,000 Toon Coins
The Red Guy Souped-Up Upgrade	Unlock The Red Guy and buy for 500 Toon Coins
The Red Guy Soupered-Up Upgrade	Unlock The Red Guy and buy for 1,000 Toon Coins

DS
GBA
PSP
PS2
PS3
Wii
Xbox
Xbox 360
Index

DS

GBA

PSP

PS2

PS3

Wii

Xbox

Xbox 360

Index

Cartoon Network Racing (continued)

Bunny Bravo	Beat Soupered-Up Chemical-X Championship and buy for 10,000 Toon Coins
Dee Dee	Beat Soupered-Up Booger Championship and buy for 5,000 Toon Coins
Eustace	Beat Soupered-Up Cowardly Championship and buy for 5,000 Toon Coins
Him	Beat all Records in Normal Time Trial and buy for 50,000 Toon Coins
I.R. Baboon	Beat Chemical-X Championship and buy for 1,000 Toon Coins
Mandark	Beat Souped-Up Chemical-X Championship and buy for 5,000 Toon Coins
Mojo Jojo	Beat Souped-Up Pork Butt Championship and buy for 2,000 Toon Coins
Muriel	Beat Souped-Up Cowardly Championship and buy for 2,000 Toon Coins
Professor Utonium	Beat Soupered-Up Pork Butt Championship and buy for 10,000 Toon Coins
Suzy	Beat Souped-Up Booger Championship and buy for 2,000 Toon Coins
The Red Guy	Beat Flipped-Out Chemical-X Championship and buy for 25,000 Toon Coins
New Theme A	Beat Flipped-Out Chemical-X Championship and buy for 10,000 Toon Coins
New Theme B	Beat all Records in Time Trial in all four Championships and buy for 10,000 Toon

Castlevania: Dawn of Sorrow

Unlockables

Unlockable	How to Unlock
Death's Robe	Finish Boss Rush Mode under 6 minutes
Nunchakus	Finish Boss Rush Mode under 7 minutes
Potion	Finish Boss Rush Mode with any time
RPG	Finish Boss Rush Mode under 5 minutes
Terror Bear	Finish Boss Rush Mode under 8 minutes
Boss Rush	Beat the game with best ending (All bosses)
Julius Mode	Finish the game with the bad ending
New Game +	Beat the game with best ending (All bosses)
Sound Test Mode	Complete the game with the best ending and the Sound Test mode will appear on the Main Menu

Castlevania: Portrait of Ruin

Unlockables

Unlockable	How to Unlock
Alternate Vincent Portrait	Clear Hard Mode
Boss Rush Course 2 and 3	Obtain Good Ending
Sound Mode	Obtain Good Ending
Astral Ring	Clear Course 1 in 1 minute
Illusion Fist	Clear Course 2 in 5 minutes
Invisible Cape	Clear Course 1 in 3 minutes

Castlevania: Portrait of Ruin (continued)

Record 1	Clear Course 2 in 3 minutes
Record 2	Clear Course 3 in 3 minutes
Scout Armor	Clear Course 3 in 5 minutes
Konami Man and +50 Strength	Defeat Hard Mode with Level 1 Cap
Twin Bee and +50 Intelligence	Defeat Hard Mode with Level 25 Cap
Vic Viper and +50 Luck	Defeat Hard Mode with Level 50 Cap
Richter Mode	Beat the whip memory at the end of the game and defeat Dracula
Sisters Mode	Beat the whip memory and defeat Dracula
The Magus Ring	Complete all of Wind's quests

Charlotte's Web

Unlockables Minigames

Each minigame is unlocked by finding a hidden icon within the game. Grabbing the icons unlocks the minigame. The following is where each icon is located and which game it unlocks.

Unlockable	How to Unlock
Aeronauts	Secret room located in level 4
Apple Masher	Secret Room on top of the haystacks in level 3
Bale Out	Secret Room in Zuckerman's barn
Bounce	Enter the hole in the tree and search in the branches in level 8
Bumper Cars	Ledge outside of the circus tent in level 13
Food Catch	Enter the tires and the icon will be on the tire pile in level 10
Ring Toss	Secret Room outside of the circus tent in level 14
Snacktime for Templeton	Enter the tires and the icon will be on the tire pile in level 9
Spree Ball	On top of the Information Booth in level 14
Water Fun	Enter the hole in the tree and search the branches in level 5
Webbing Crashers	Secret room next to the water wheel in level 6

The Chronicles of Narnia: The Lion, The Witch, and The Wardrobe

Enter these codes at the Main menu.

Unlockable	Code
Acquire Armor	Ⓐ, Ⓧ, Ⓨ, Ⓑ, ↑, ↑, ↑, ↓
All Blessings	←, ↑, Ⓐ, Ⓑ, →, ↓, Ⓧ, Ⓨ
All Skills at Maximum	Ⓐ, ←, →, Ⓑ, ↓, ↑, Ⓧ, Ⓧ
Extra Money	↑, Ⓧ, ↑, Ⓧ, ↓, Ⓑ, ↓, Ⓑ
Invincibility	Ⓐ, Ⓨ, Ⓧ, Ⓑ, ↑, ↑, ↓, ↓
Maximum Attributes	←, Ⓑ, ↑, Ⓨ, ↓, Ⓧ, →, Ⓐ
Restore Health	←, →, ↑, ↓, Ⓐ, Ⓐ, Ⓐ, Ⓐ
Stronger Attacks	Ⓐ, ↑, Ⓑ, ↓, Ⓧ, Ⓧ, Ⓨ, Ⓨ

DS

GBA

PSP

PS2

PS3

Wii

Xbox

Xbox 360

Index

Disney's Kim Possible Kimmunicator

Enter these codes while playing—do not pause. You must hold down L+R to enter these codes.

Unlockable	Code
9,999 parts	Y, Y, X, B, A, Y
99 lives	A, A, A, Y, X, Y, B, A
Don't lose lives	Y, Y, Y, X
Extra Life	A, A, A, Y, X, Y
Full Health	A, A, A, Y
Invincibility	Y, Y, Y, X, A, B
Unlock all gadgets	Y, Y, X, B, A, Y, Y, A
Unlock all missions	X, Y, X, A, X, B
Unlock all outfits	B, A, X, Y, A, B

Dragon Ball Z: Supersonic Warriors 2

Unlockables

Unlockable	How to Unlock
Increases your DP by 1	Complete 5~6 levels
Increases your DP by 1	Complete the Novice mode
Increases your DP by 2	Complete the Hard mode
Increases your DP to infinite	Complete the Mania Mode
Android #18	Beat Krillin's "Differences in Experience" stage
Androids #16 and #17	Beat Android #18's "16's Agitation" stage
Babidi	Beat Vegeta's "Evil Discovered" stage
Bardock(SP)	Complete the 2 Bardock levels in Goku's story
Broly	Beat the map where you fight Broly in Goku's story
Buu (Good)	Beat Gotenks's "Super Buu Has Emerged!" stage
Cell (Complete)	Beat Cell's Complete Body: Successful!" stage
Cell (Second Form)	Beat Dr. Gero's "18, Activate" stage
Cell Jr.	Beat Cell (Second Form)'s "Cell Jr." stage
Cooler	Beat Frieza's "A Battle of Blood Relations" stage
Dabura	Beat Buu's "The Gate to the Other World" stage
Dende	Beat Piccolo's "Cooler's Armored Squad" stage
Dr. Gero	Beat Gohan's "Ambition" stage
Frieza	Beat Goku's "Enraged Warriors" stage
Ginyu	Beat Vegeta's "Battle of Namek" stage
Gohan (Teen)	Beat Kid Gohan's "Golden Warrior" stage
Goku (Super Saiyan)	Beat Goku's "Showdown: Core/Cooler" stage
Hercule	Beat Buu's "Best Friend" stage
Infinite Dragon Power	Beat every mode
Majin Vegeta	Have SSJ Vegeta and Babidi on the same team
Maximum Mode	Beat one round of Z Battle
Maximum Mode (Hard)	Complete Maximum mode (Novice)
Maximum Mode (Mania)	Complete Maximum mode (Hard)
Mecha Frieza	Beat Frieza's "Time in the Other World" stage
Mecha Frieza(DP3)	Complete last level of Frieza's story

Dragon Ball Z: Supersonic Warriors 2 (continued)

Metal Cooler	Beat Cooler's "Big Gette Star" stage
Shenron	Beat Ginyu's "That Hurts, Shenron!" stage
Super Buu	Beat Buu's "Best Friend" stage
Super Saiyan 2 Gohan(DP6)	Complete last level of Gohan's story
Super Saiyan 3 Gotenks(DP7)	Complete last level of Gotenks's story
Tien and Yamcha	Beat Krillin's "Revived! The Ginyu Force" stage
Trunks (Super Saiyan)	Beat Trunks's "Time Machine" stage
Vegeta (Evil)	Beat all three ranks in Maximum mode
Vegeta (Super Saiyan)	Beat Vegeta's "Vegeta vs. Android 18" stage
Zarbon and Dodoria	Beat Frieza's "Frieza's Irritation" stage

Dragon Booster

At the Main menu, select Password to enter these cheats.

Unlockable	Password
999,999 Dracles	8, 9, 7, 10, 5, 13
Blue Energy Bolt Gear Obtained	9, 2, 13, 8, 1, 12
Draculim Bars are replaced by sushi in All City Race/Free Run	7, 8, 13, 12, 10, 10
Dragon Booster and Legendary Beau are unlocked	12, 6, 12, 10, 13, 3
Dragon-Human Duel vs. Reepyr	1, 9, 3, 6, 5, 2
Green Charging Gear Obtained	5, 12, 13, 5, 8, 11
Shadow Booster and Shadow Dragon are unlocked	2, 5, 4, 11, 6, 2
Skills Competition vs. Wulph	13, 9, 8, 12, 10, 1
Sprint Meter can't be recharged	1, 7, 5, 3, 2, 11
Take Super Damage from obstacles and opponents in All City Race/Free Run	11, 11, 11, 11, 11, 11
Unlimited sprint meter	9, 13, 6, 5, 5, 12

FIFA 07

Unlockable	Code
Additional Chant FX	Win 10 games outside of Career mode
Challenge Mode	Win five games
Classic Team	Complete Challenge mode
Dribbling Mini Game	Win 5 games in a row, in Career mode
Giant Team Flag	Win a match in Career mode
Goalkeeper Mini Game	Remain unbeaten in five games, in Career mode
Home Stadium Upgrade 1	Win a blowout in Career mode
Home Stadium Upgrade 2	Move into first place in the league, while playing Career mode
Home Stadium Upgrade 3	Win the league in Career mode
Home Stadium Upgrade 4	Win your domestic cup in Career mode
Home Stadium Upgrade 5	Win your domestic cup twice, in Career mode
Home Stadium Upgrade 6	Win the league twice, in Career mode
Interception Mini Game	Win 10 games in Career mode

DS

GBA

PSP

PS2

PS3

Wii

Xbox

Xbox 360

Index

GoldenEye: Rogue Agent

Unlockables

Unlockable	How to Unlock
EM Hack	Beat VT Mission One
Magnetic Field	Beat VT Mission 5
MRI Vision	Beat Campaign Mission 1
Polarity Shield	Beat VT Mission 3
Atlantis	Virtual Training 2
Bath House	Beat Hong Kong on Hard mode
Bore Tunnel	Beat Hard Campaign Mission 1
Carver's Press	Virtual Training 6
Funhouse	Virtual Training 1
Goldengate	Virtual Training 4
Mining Pit	Get All the Rogue Bonuses on one Campaign File
Moonraker	Virtual Training 3
Uplink	Virtual Training 5
Goldeneye Mode	Beat Virtual Training 6 on Normal Campaign
MRI Vision Only Mode	Beat Mission 1 on Normal difficulty
Auric Goldfinger Skin	Beat Hard Campaign Mission 2
Dr. No Skin	Beat Mission 5 on Hard Campaign
Francisco Scaramanga Skin	Beat Virtual Training 1 on Normal Campaign
Goldeneye Skin	Beat Easy Campaign
OddJob Skin	Beat Hard Campaign Mission 1
Pussy Galore Skin	Beat Virtual Training 4 on Normal Difficulty
Xenia Onatopp Skin	Beat Mission 4 on Normal Campaign
Goblin Mine	Beat Hong Kong on Hard Mode
Golden Gun	Beat Virtual Training 1 in Hard Campaign
MK2 Detonator	Beat Virtual Training 2 in Hard Campaign
Omen XR	Beat Mission 6 on Hard Campaign
Venom 200mL	Beat Auric Enterprises on Normal difficulty
Atlantis Stage	Beat Virtual Mission 2
Carver's Press Stage	Beat Virtual Training 6
Golden Gate Stage	Beat Virtual Training 4
Hack ability	Beat Virtual Mission 1
Moonraker Stage	Beat Virtual Training 3
Polarity Shield	Beat Virtual Training 3
Uplink Stage	Beat Virtual Training 5
Virtual Mission 2	Beat Virtual Mission 1
Virtual Training 4	Beat Virtual Training 3
Virtual Training 6	Beat Virtual Training 5
You Only Live Once Mode	Complete Campaign Mode on Hard

LEGO Star Wars II: The Original Trilogy

Enter this password in the Cantina.

Unlockable	Password
10 extra studs	4PR28U

Madden NFL 2005

Codes

Touch the small spot in the middle of the main menu to display the cheat entry box. Then enter one of the following codes to activate the corresponding cheat function:

Code	Effect
SMASHMOUTH	Harder hits
SUPERSLICK	More fumbles
BADPASS	More interceptions
SAD SACK	More sacks
SHORTTIME	Opponent gets 3 downs
LONGTIME	You get 5 downs

Mega Man Battle Network 5: Double Team

Codes

Highlight the corresponding program from the list and hold down the right button. Then push the following buttons to compress them by one block. To uncompress them, just repeat the above process again.

Code	Effect	Code	Effect
BLBABLBBAA	Air Shoes	BBRALBLARR	Giga Virus
RBBARBRARB	Anti-Damage	ALRABLRALR	Hub Batch
LLLRRBARBL	Attack MAX	ABLARABLRL	Humor
RLRLRBBRAB	Auto Recover	LRLABLBBLA	Jungle
AABRABRLLR	Battery	LABBLBAALL	Mega Folder +2
ABBRAABRBR	Beat	BBABBRRLAR	Mega Folder+1
BARABRLRRA	Body Pack	AABLARBLAA	Mega Virus
BABLABRLRB	Bug Stop	RLRARRLLLR	Millions
LLRARLBLAR	Buster Pack	LBRARLABLB	Oil Body
ALAARBRBAR	Charge MAX	LLRBLLAALB	Reflect
RRBBRBRBAA	Chivalry	RBLRBRLLRL	Rush
BRALARBAAB	Collect	ABARALRBBA	Shield
AARLBABALB	Custom+1	RLLALLBABB	Sneak Run
BARLLRALBR	Custom+2	RARLLRRABA	Speed MAX
RLABBARALR	First Barrier	RABRALLRBA	Super Armor
BABALRARAA	Fish	LBLABLABAL	Tango
ALLBRLAAAL	Float Shoes	ARBBRLRALA	Undershirt
RRLBLLARBL	Giga Folder +1		

Mega Man Battle Network 5: Double Team (continued)

Prize Codes

Go to the numberman machine in Higsby's shop when it is placed there, and enter the passwords to get your prize. These codes can only be used for the DS version, they won't work on the GBA versions.

Code	Effect	Code	Effect
99428938	Area Steal	76820385	P.Attack+3
91182599	Dark Recovery	48582829	P.Chip+50
78234329	DoroTsunamiBall	28475692	P.HP+100
01285874	Leaders Raid L	53891756	P.HP+50
39285712	Lord of Chaos X	29486933	Super Kitakaze
29387483	MagmaSeed	12495783	Sword
64836563	NumberBall	85375720	TP Chip
22323856	P. Battle Pack 1	19283746	Tsunami Hole
66426428	P. Battle Pack 2	15733751	Unlocker

Numberman Navi Customizer Program Codes

Enter these codes in the Numberman Lotto Number to get a Navi customizer program

Password	Effect	Password	Effect
25465278	Anti Aqua*	48785625	HP+300 (Pink NCP)
35607360	Anti Elec*	13926561	HP+300 (White NCP)
73877466	Anti Fire*	03419893	HP+400 (Pink NCP)
05068930	Anti Navi V	45654128	HP+400 (Yellow)
44213168	Anti Recovery P	31084443	HP+50 NCP
10386794	Anti Sword R	50906652	HP+500 (Pink)
10133670	Anti Wood*	72846472	HP+500 (White NCP)
63231870	Attack MAX (Yellow NCP)	29789661	Lock Enemy
79877132	BeatSupport NCP	97513648	Mega Folder 2 NCP
30112002	BodyPack (Green)	18746897	Recovery 300 Y
50364410	Bug Fix*	09609807	Rush (Yellow)
80246758	BusterPack NCP	64892292	Sneakrun
87412146	Charge MAX (White NCP)	28256341	SoulT+1 (Yellow)
15595587	Custom 2	36695497	Speed MAX (Pink NCP)
07765623	Custom Bolt 3 G	12541883	Spin Blue
68799876	Dark Invis*	78987728	Spin Green
52052687	Death Match 3 V	30356451	Spin Red
91098051	DjangoSP D	48958798	Static S
83143652	Fast Gauge*	54288793	Tango (Green)
12118790	Full Energy	73978713	Unlocker
90914896	Full Energy	28706568	Unlocker
68942679	Grab Revenge P	64664560	Unlocker
35321321	Gun Del Sol 3 O	00798216	Untrap
90630807	HP +200 (Pink NCP)		

Unlockable prizes

Every time a Liberation Mission is completed, you get a prize depending on the number of phases you completed it in.

Unlockable	How to Unlock
AntiNavi M	Beat Liberation 4 in 9–10
Anubis A	Beat Liberation 9 in 14 or less
BlackWing W	Beat Liberation 7 in 10 or less
BlizzardMan B	Beat Liberation 1 in 6–7
BlizzardManSP B	Beat Liberation 1 in 5 or less
CloudMan C	Beat Liberation 3 in 8–9
CloudManDS B	Beat Liberation 8 in 13–14
CloudManSP C	Beat Liberation 3 in 7 or less
Colonel C	Beat Liberation 6 in 9–10 (Colonel version only)
CosmoMan C	Beat Liberation 5 in 8–9
CosmoManDS	Beat Liberation 9 in 15–16
CosmoManSP C	Beat Liberation 5 in 7 or less
FullCust *	Beat Liberation 4 in 8 or less
Muramasa M	Beat Liberation 8 in 12 or less
ProtoMan B	Beat Liberation 6 in 9–10 (ProtoMan version only)
ShadeMan S	Beat Liberation 2 in 8–9
ShadeManDS S	Beat Liberation 7 in 11–12
ShadeManSP S	Beat Liberation 2 in 7 or less
Z-Saber Z	Beat Liberation 6 in 8 or less

Mega Man Star Force: Dragon

Passwords

Compose a mail by pressing "X" in the mail screen, and send it to yourself. Type "Cipher" in the subject, then type the code in the body of the email. Send the email, and exit back to the main screen (Map screen). If you entered it correctly, it should give you a card.

Password	Effect
Let's combine our strength!	Brave Sword 3 Card
Dec. 17, 1986	ChainBubble3
ISNBDUBO	Cloaker
ILABCLERSAS	D. Energy
SIXGAME-O	D.Energy SubCard
CENCARLEBBUB	D.Eye Mega Weapon
KNIGSPIAREM	FlickrKck3
NGYNGIWCUS	GhostPulse2 B. Card
Legendary SP Card Master Shin	Grants DragonSky
ROHNATPE	Heatball3
Star Force, the ultimate power!	LeoKingdm SP
KMALEETZCP	M. Breath (Mega Weapon) 1/2/1 Charge may Freeze or Bubble target
Ride On the Wave Road!	MopLance3
Go On Air battle card to trade info with friends.	PegasusMagic SP
Wave Change!	Porcupine Needle Mega Weapon, AT1|SP3|CH1 Geo Stellar, On The Air!!
Brother Action RPG	QnOphiucaSP Card

DS

GBA

PSP

PS2

PS3

Wii

Xbox

Xbox 360

Index

Mega Man Star Force: Dragon (continued)

Password	Effect	Password	Effect
AURIEFRUTS	Recovery 50 B. Card	Get stronger through BrotherBands!	Unlocks GrndWave3
PREOBCOPB	SearchEye SubCard		
LAREBARAON	TimeBomb1 B. Card	Only you can protect the Wave Road!	Unlocks JetAttack3
Let's form a BrotherBand!	TimeBomb3		
ALPTUNZLA	Unlocker	Win big with a Star Force Big Bang!	Unlocks PlasmaGun3
NRQSIMAMSTU	Unlocker SubCard		
DWOWOOLFS Subcard	Unlocks Cloaker	Mega Man 20th Anniversary Game	Unlocks Stikyrain3
Fly away for CygnusWingSP skies unknown!	Unlocks	I love Battle Network!	Unlocks SyncHook1
NGAMEMA RESCAFROT	Unlocks D. Energy	IPHAUEOEUNQC	Unlocks TailBurner3
Transers are FireBazooka3 really useful!	Unlocks	Store info in TaurusFireSP your Transer!	Unlocks
How many more until you have all the cards?	Unlocks Freezenukle	Time to bust some EM viruses!	Unlocks WideWave3
Pegasus, Leo, Dragon - which is for you?	Unlocks Gatling3	OSLEGRATE	You get Heavy Cannon
Check out the Mega Man website!	Unlocks GhstPulse3		

Naruto: Ninja Council 3

Unlockables

Unlockable	How to Unlock
Gaara	Beat "Secret Technique" with Chidori
Gallery 1	Beat the three rows of missions
Gallery 2	Beat all missions
Itachi	Beat "Revenge!" with Sasuke
Jiraiya	Beat "Teach him a lesson"
Jirobo	Beat "Chubby's Pride"
Kabuto	Beat "The Way of the Ninja" with anybody
Kakashi	Beat "Secret Technique Training"
Kankuro	Beat "I'll Handle This" with Parasitic Insect Jutsu
Kidomaru	Beat "Pinpoint Blindspot!"
Kisame	Beat "Kisame's Counterattack"
Might Guy	Beat Taijutsu Training" with no techniques
Orochimaru	Beat the all missions
Sakon	Beat "Combo!"
Tayuya	Beat "Calculated"
Temari	Beat "What a Drag..." with Shadow Possession Jutsu
The Third Hokage	Beat "Find the Glowing Scroll" Note: The Third Hokage is ONLY a support character
Tsunade	Beat "The Famous Kunoichi!"

Need for Speed Underground 2

Unlockables

While playing "Underground" mode and the game offers you a mini-game, or when selecting them from the Bonus Events menu, score points to unlock the bonuses.

Unlockable	How to Unlock
Brakes Bonus	Beat 7,500pts in Pressure Tuning 2
Chassis Bonus	Beat 5,000pts in Pressure Tuning 1
Controls Bonus	Beat 5,000pts in Engine Tuning 3
Drivetrain Bonus	Beat 50pts in Dyno Run1
Engine Bonus	Beat 100pts in Nitrous Tuning 1
Exhaust Bonus	Beat 2000pts in Engine Tuning 1
Nitrous Bonus	Beat 175pts in Nitrous Tuning 3
Suspension Bonus	Beat 100pts in Dyno Run2
Turbo Bonus	Beat 150pts in Nitrous Tuning 2
Wheels Bonus	Beat 4,000pts in Engine Tuning 2

Puyo Pop Fever

To enter this code, go into Options, then Gallery, then highlight Cutscene Viewer.

Unlockable	Code
Unlock all characters and cutscenes	Hold ⊗ and press ↑, ↓, ←, →

Robots

Unlockables

Minigames available at main menu.

Unlockable	How to Unlock
Bonus Transit Challenge Courses	Complete the 5 transit courses throughout the game
BWI Transit	Complete the transit course on Bigweld industries
Chop Shop Transit	Complete the transit course on Chop Shop
Jack Hammer's Oil Rush	Aid Jack with the customers on the bar
Mansion Transit	Complete the transit course on Bigweld's Mansion
Outmode Transit	Complete the transit course on Outmode
Transit System	Enter a Transit System for the first time
Uppercity Transit	Complete the transit course on Uppercity
Zip Line Course	After finding Bigweld in his mansion, you go through a stage in a Zip Line, hitting dominoes; complete the course

Tom Clancy's Splinter Cell Chaos Theory

Unlockables

Unlockable	How to Unlock
Argus Mercenary Costume	In Machi Akko, go to the bar and use the microphone. Look behind you for a keycard. Go back to the hallway with three doors, and use it on the closet.
Camouflage Sam Costume	In the Lighthouse level, snipe the man on the roof, but don't rappel down. On the high right corner is the costume.
Displace Mercenary Costume in Display Level	Go to floor three. Use the optic cable to see which room has the green package. Enter the room, and use keypad code 5800

DS
GBA
PSP
PS2
PS3
Wii
Xbox
Xbox 360
Index

DS

GBA

PSP

PS2

PS3

Wii

Xbox

Xbox 360

Index

Tom Clancy's Splinter Cell Chaos Theory (continued)

Unlockable	How to Unlock
Displace Suit	Room next to the room where you have a last chance to save, code is 5800.
Masked Sam Costume	In the Penthouse level, go to Zherkezhi's apartment, and go to the first room on the top floor. Go down the long, dark hall and type 5698 in the pad.
National Guard Costume	In the Manhattan Streets level, go to the open area before the penthouse. Climb the pipe, jump left, and go down to the next platform, in the corner.
Shadownet Agent Costume	In Kokubo Sosho, go down the elevator, where lasers are at the bottom. Find a ladder to climb back up. The room will have lasers and the costume.
Short Sleeved Sam Costume in Bank Level	Go to the small vault left of the computer and use the lockpick.
Snow Guard Costume in Battery Level	Get the wrench, and go to the U-shaped room. Enter the keycard room, take out the guard, climb on the crate, and bash next crate.
Thermal Suit Costume in Hokkaido Level	Find the wrench, and find the man who is shooting on the roof, get to him and fall through the vent, exiting the room, and bash the door.
Full Equipment Mode (infinite ammo etc.)	Beat the game at least once.

Tony Hawk's American Sk8land

Unlockables

Unlockable	How to Unlock
Always Special	Beat Classic mode 9 times
Crate-a-Skater	Beat Classic mode once
First Person Camera	Beat Classic mode 6 times
Giant Mode	Beat Classic mode 4 times
Hoverboard	Beat Classic mode 11 times
Lip Balance	Beat Classic mode twice
Manual Balance	Beat Classic mode twice
Matrix Mode	Beat Classic mode 5 times
Nearly Always Ribbon	Beat Classic mode 12 times
Ninja Skater	Beat Classic mode with all characters (13 times)
Paper Tony	Beat Classic mode 10 times
Rail Balance	Beat Classic mode twice
Replay Cam	Beat Classic mode 7 times
Tiny Mode	Beat Classic mode 3 times
Turbo Mode	Beat Classic mode 8 times

Transformers: Autobots

Unlockables

Unlockable	How to Unlock
Funky Bus	Connect to the Allspark Wars server for the first time
Gunner	750 WiFi Tokens
Infinite Energy Cheat	1,000 WiFi Tokens
Infinite Energy Cheat	Get 100% completion
Longhorn	250 WiFi Tokens

Transformers: Autobots (continued)

Maintenance	Beat the game
Psycho Cars Cheat	500 WiFi Tokens
SkyDive	2,500 Wi-Fi Points
Skydive	Download at Target
Super Jump Cheat	2,000 WiFi Tokens
Top/Down View Cheat	3,000 WiFi Tokens
Transport	1,500 WiFi Tokens

The Urbz: Sims in the City

Unlockables

Unlockable	How to Unlock
Magic Lamp	Beat the Artsies rep mission while being an Artsie and buying the magic lamp xizzle
Magic Lamp	Invite Crystal to your house and she might give you the magic lamp
Candy Cane	Play for 120 days
Jack-o-Lantern	Play for 60 days
Mardi Gras Mask	Play for 30 days
Pilgrim Gnome	Play for 90 days
Bod-Mod Booth	Earn full rep meter with the Artsies and talk to Roxie Moxie
Mad Skillz Cerebral Data Infuser	Earn full rep meter with the Nerdies and talk to Polly Nomial
Ultimate MP-DEE Stereo System	Earn full rep meter with the Streeties and talk to Darius
Sensory Deprivation Tank	By earning full rep with the Richies you can unlock the BEST item in the game, which refills ALL your motive bars when you use it
'98 Adder Bumper	Invite Luthor L. Bigbucks over
3-Card Monte Table	Invite Berkeley Clodd over
Blind Justice Statue	Invite Lily Gates over
Burning Spoke Sign	Invite Dusty Hogg over
Comedy & Tragedy Masks	Invite Prichard Locksley over
Flaming Hoop	Invite Roxanna Moxie over
Go Board	Invite Futo Maki over
Golden Mop Award	Invite Kris Thistle over
Key to the City	Invite Daddy Bigbucks over
Khroniton Reactor	Invite Polly Nomial over
Lawn Flamingo	Invite Phoebe Twiddle over
Lottie Cash Statue	Invite Lottie Cash over
Megalodon Tooth	Invite Sharona Faster over
Miss Urbverse Trophy	Invite Misty Waters over
Movie Standee	Invite Theresa Bullhorn over
Music Stand	Invite Cannonball Coleman over
Orange Pedestal	Invite Giuseppi Mezzoalto over
Periodic Table of Elements	Invite Dr. Maximillian Moore over
Prehistoric Ficus	Invite Mokey/Dr. Mauricio Keyes over

Sidebar tabs: DS | GBA | PSP | PS2 | PS3 | Wii | Xbox | Xbox 360 | Index

The Urbz: Sims in the City (continued)

Punk T-Shirt	Invite Busta Cruz over
Safe	Invite Detective Dan D. Mann over
Traffic Light	Invite Ewan Watahmee over
Typewriter	Invite Lincoln Broadsheet over
Uncle Suede's Cane	Invite Darius over
Voodoo Dan Doll	Invite Mambo Loa over
Garbage Can (near entrance to Club Xizzle in Glasstown)	100% relationship with Phoebe Twiddle
Hole Behind Poster in Jail	100% relationship with Detective Dan De Mann
Lost cave in Sim quarter	100% relationship with Ewan Watahmee
Old broken down school bus (near thrift shop)	100% relationship with Giuseppi Mezzoalto
Projection booth (near door behind the snack counter of the cinema in Glasstown)	100% relationship with Theresa Bullhorn

Yu-Gi-Oh! GX: Spirit Caller

Card Passwords

Enter the card passwords into the password machine to be able to purchase the card. You can only get cards you already have, or have a pack list with the card in it.

Password	Effect	Password	Effect
83994646	4-Starred Ladybug of Doom	25345186	After the Struggle
23771716	7 Colored Fish	16135253	Agido
24140059	A Cat of Ill Omen	18036057	Airknight Parshath
06850209	A Deal with Dark Ruler	48202661	Aitsu
49140998	A Feather of the Phoenix	06150044	Alkana Knight Joker
68170903	A Feint Plan	99785935	Alpha the Magnet Warrior
21597117	A Hero Emerges	21070956	Altar for Tribute
00295517	A Legendary Ocean	91869203	Amazon Archer
51351302	A Man with Wdjat	67987611	Amazoness Archers
05728014	A Rival Appears!	67987611	Amazoness Archers
28596933	A Wingbeat of Giant Dragon	73574678	Amazoness Bowpiper
13026402	A-Team: Trap Disposal Unit	29654737	Amazoness Chain Master
89718302	Abare Ushioni	47480070	Amazoness Paladin
27744077	Absolute End	94004268	Amazoness Swords Woman
49771608	Absorbing Kid from the Sky	10979723	Amazoness Tiger
18318842	Abyss Soldier	95174353	Amoeba
00001755	Abyssal Designator	67371383	Amphibian Beast
21323861	Acid Rain	64342551	Amphibious Bugroth MK-3
41356845	Acid Trap Hole	00303660	Amplifier
47372349	Acrobat Monkey	23927567	An Owl of Luck
62325062	Adhesion Trap Hole	93221206	Ancient Elf
53828396	Adhesive Explosive	31557782	Ancient Gear

Yu-Gi-Oh! GX: Spirit Caller (continued)

Password	Effect	Password	Effect
10509340	Ancient Gear Beast	88236094	Aswan Apparition
80045583	Ancient Gear Cannon	87340664	Atomic Firefly
92001300	Ancient Gear Castle	63689843	Attack and Receive
67829249	Ancient Gear Drill	91989718	Attack Reflector Unit
83104731	Ancient Gear Golem	37970940	Aussa the Earth Charmer
56094445	Ancient Gear Soldier	71453557	Autonomous Action Unit
54912977	Ancient Lamp	99284890	Avatar of the Pot
43230671	Ancient Lizard Warrior	84914462	Axe Dragonute
17092736	Ancient Telescope	40619825	Axe of Despair
15013468	Andro Sphinx	48305365	Axe Raider
02204140	Ante	11901678	B. Skull Dragon
13250922	Anteatereatingant	15317640	B.E.S. Covered Core
65064143	Anti-Aircraft Flower	22790789	B.E.S. Crystal Core
53112492	Anti-Spell	44954628	B.E.S. Tetran
09156135	Apprentice Magician	88819587	Baby Dragon
09156135	Apprentice Magician	47453433	Back to Square One
48539234	Appropriate	82705573	Backfire
85639257	Aqua Madoor	36280194	Backup Soldier
40916023	Aqua Spirit	40633297	Bad Reaction to Simochi
55001420	Arcane Archer of the Forest	07165085	Bait Doll
50287060	Archfiend of Gilfer	00242146	Ballista of Rampart Smashing
18378582	Archlord Zerato	61528025	Banisher of the Light
53153481	Armaill	41925941	Bark of Dark Ruler
90374791	Armed Changer	81480460	Barrel Dragon
00980973	Armed Dragon LV 3	10963799	Barrier Statue of the Torrent
46384672	Armed Dragon LV 5	46145256	Barrier Statue of the Heavens
73879377	Armed Dragon LV 7	89091579	Basic Insect
59464593	Armed Dragon LV 10	61181383	Battery Charger
09076207	Armed Ninja	63142001	Batteryman AA
84430950	Armed Samurai—Ben Kei	19733961	Batteryman C
07180418	Armor Axe	48094997	Battle Footballer
79649195	Armor Break	05053103	Battle Ox
36868108	Armored Glass	18246479	Battle Steer
15480588	Armored Lizard	55550921	Battle Warrior
17535588	Armored Starfish	94463200	Battle-Scarred
20277860	Armored Zombie	40133511	Bazoo the Soul-Eater
69296555	Array of Revealing Light	46009906	Beast Fangs
42364374	Arsenal Bug	35149085	Beast Soul Swap
55348096	Arsenal Robber	99426834	Beastking of the Swamps
85489096	Arsenal Summoner	16899564	Beautiful Headhuntress
62633180	Assault on GHQ	32452818	Beaver Warrior
37053871	Astral Barrier	16255442	Beckoning Light
02134346	Asura Priest	49522489	Beelze Frog

Yu-Gi-Oh! GX: Spirit Caller (continued)

Password	Effect	Password	Effect
20374520	Begone, Knave	02204140	Book of Life
22996376	Behemoth the King of All Animals	14087893	Book of Moon
		91595718	Book of Secret Arts
33731070	Beiige, Vanguard of Dark World	76532077	Bottomless Shifting Sand
85605684	Berserk Dragon	16507828	Bracchio-raidus
39168895	Berserk Gorilla	87910978	Brain Control
39256679	Beta the Magnet Warrior	20101223	Breath of Light
25655502	Bickuribox	82878489	Bright Castle
61127349	Big Bang Shot	24294108	Burning Land
95472621	Big Burn	18937875	Burning Spear
14148099	Big Core	80163754	Burst Breath
16768387	Big Eye	27191436	Burst Return
53606874	Big Insect	17655904	Burst Stream of Destruction
42129512	Big Koala	78193831	Buster Blader
65240384	Big Shield Gardna	04861205	Call of the Mummy
51562916	Big Wave Small Wave	11384280	Cannon Soldier
59380081	Big-Tusked Mammoth	72892473	Card Destruction
58696829	Bio-Mage	57953380	Card of Safe Return
45547649	Birdface	00062121	Castle of Dark Illusions
41426869	Black Illusion Ritual	44209392	Castle Walls
55761792	Black Luster Ritual	95727991	Catapult Turtle
72989439	Black Luster Soldier—Envoy of the Beginning	36468556	Ceasefire
		90101050	Celtic Guardian
65169794	Black Pendant	01248895	Chain Destruction
38670435	Black Tyranno	51449743	Chain Detonation
87564352	Blackland Fire Dragon	79323590	Chain Energy
39507162	Blade Knight	25050038	Chain Healing
58268433	Blade Rabbit	64599569	Chimeratech Overdragon
97023549	Blade Skater	81380218	Chorus of Sanctuary
28470714	Bladefly	21888494	Chosen One
89041555	Blast Held By a Tribute	22479888	Clay Charge
21051146	Blast Magician	06967870	Cliff the Trap Remover
98239899	Blast with Chain	92667214	Clown Zombie
21466326	Blasting the Ruins	40240595	Cocoon of Evolution
05464695	Blazing Inpachi	60682203	Cold Wave
30653113	Blessings of the Nile	07565547	Collected Power
32015116	Blind Destruction	10375182	Command Knight
25880422	Block Attack	93889755	Crass Clown
23995346	Blue Eyes Ultimate Dragon	67494157	Crawling Dragon
20871001	Blue Medicine	38289717	Crawling Dragon #2
80906030	Blue-Eyes White Dragon	46696593	Crimson Sunbird
89631139	Blue-Eyes White Dragon	57728570	Crush Card Virus
89631139	Blue-Eyes White Dragon (SDK-001 Version)	66742250	Curse of Anubis
		28279543	Curse of Dragon

DS GBA PSP PS2 PS3 Wii Xbox Xbox 360 Index

Yu-Gi-Oh! GX: Spirit Caller (continued)

Password	Effect	Password	Effect
12470447	Curse of Fiend	76922029	Don Zaloog
02926176	Curse of Royal	67464807	Dora of Fate
94377247	Curse of the Masked Beast	50045299	Dragon Capture Jar
70095154	Cyber Dragon	01435851	Dragon Treasure
80316585	Cyber Harpie Lady	66672569	Dragon Zombie
63224564	Cyber Shield	55991637	Dragon's Gunfire
48766543	Cyber-Tech Alligator	54178050	Dragon's Rage
40418351	Cyberdark Dragon	32437102	Dragonic Attack
77625948	Cyberdark Edge	13215230	Dream Clown
41230939	Cyberdark Horn	00473469	Driving Snow
03019642	Cyberdark Keel	12493482	Dunames Dark Witch
05494820	Cyclon Laser	51228280	Dungeon Worm
81866673	D Hero—Dasher	31476755	Dust Barrier
40591390	D Hero—Dreadmaster	59820352	Earth Chant
70074904	D. D. Assailant	42578427	Eatgaboon
37043180	D.D. Warrior	97342942	Ectoplasmer
28378427	Damage Condenser	69954399	Ekibyo Drakmord
72520073	Dark Artist	37820550	Electro-Whip
32344688	Dark Chimera	90219263	Elegant Egotist
01804528	Dark Coffin	30314994	Element Dragon
70231910	Dark Core	21844576	Elemental Hero Avian
04614116	Dark Energy	79979666	Elemental Hero Bubbleman
90980792	Dark Jeroid	84327329	Elemental Hero Burstinatrix
99789342	Dark Magic Curtain	84327329	Elemental Hero Clayman
40609080	Dark Magician	35809262	Elemental Hero Flame Wingman
40737112	Dark Magician of Chaos	47737087	Elemental Hero Rampart Blaster
99261403	Dark Rabbit		
92377303	Dark Sage	25366484	Elemental Hero Shining Flare Wingman
40933924	Dark Scorpion Burglars		
20858318	Dark Scorpion Combination	20721928	Elemental Hero Sparkman
93599951	Dark Spirit of the Silent	40044918	Elemental Hero Stratos
45895206	Dark-Piercing Light	61204971	Elemental Hero Thunder Giant
80168720	Darkness Approaches		
95286165	De-Fusion	39897277	Elf's Light
19159413	De-Spell	28649820	Embodiment of Apophis
69122763	Deal of Phantom	30531525	Enchanting Fitting Room
39719977	Delta Attacker	98045062	Enemy Controller
93747864	Desert Sunlight	94716515	Eradicating Aerosol
94212438	Destiny Board	56606928	Eternal Draught
05616412	Destruction Punch	95051344	Eternal Rest
84257639	Dian Keto the Cure Master	63749102	Exarion Universe
22959079	Dimensionhole	26725158	Exile of the Wicked
74701381	DNA Surgery	74131780	Exiled Force

DS
GBA
PSP
PS2
PS3
Wii
Xbox
Xbox 360
Index

DS
GBA
PSP
PS2
PS3
Wii
Xbox
Xbox 360
Index

Yu-Gi-Oh! GX: Spirit Caller (continued)

Password	Effect
97687912	Fairy Meteor Crush
17653779	Fairy's Hand Mirror
19394153	Feather Shot
71060915	Feather Wind
41392891	Feral Imp
77456781	Fiend Kraken
18591904	Final Destiny
73134081	Final Flame
66788016	Fissure
60862676	Flame Cerebrus
34460851	Flame Manipulator
40502030	Flame Swordsman
98252586	Follow Wind
81439173	Foolish Burial
74923978	Forced Requisition
87430998	Forest
24094653	Fusion Gate
26902560	Fusion Sage
56594520	Gaia Power
66889139	Gaia the Dragon Champion
06368038	Gaia the Fierce Knight
37313786	Gamble
14977074	Garoozis
25833572	Gate Guardian
30190809	Gear Golem the Moving Fortress
69140098	Gemini Elf
24668830	Germ Infection
41762634	Giant Flea
13039848	Giant Soldier of Stone
42703248	Giant Trunade
36354007	Gilford the Lightning
04149689	Goblin Fan
11868825	Goblin's Secret Remedy
67959180	Goddess of Whim
53493204	Goddess with the Third Eye
15367030	Gokibore
27408609	Golden Homunculus
52648457	Gorgon's Eye
79571449	Graceful Charity
74137509	Graceful Dice
02906250	Grappler
82542267	Gravedigger Ghoul

Password	Effect
25262697	Gravekeeper's Assailant
16762927	Gravekeeper's Servant
63695531	Gravekeeper's Spear Soldier
33737664	Graverobber's Retribution
85742772	Gravity Bind
14141448	Great Moth
13429800	Great White
41172955	Green Gadget
53829412	Griffore
90502999	Ground Collapse
40659562	Guardian Sphinx
73079365	Gust
55321970	Gust Fan
31122090	Gyakutenno Megami
88789641	Hallowed Life Barrier
76812113	Harpie Lady
91932350	Harpie Lady 1
27927359	Harpie Lady 2
54415063	Harpie Lady 3
12206212	Harpie Lady Sisters
18144506	Harpie's Feather Duster
52040216	Harpie's Pet Dragon
35762283	Heart of the Underdog
19613556	Heavy Storm
54493213	Helios—the Primordal Sun
80887952	Helios Duo Megistus
17286057	Helios Tris Megiste
76052811	Helpoemer
52584282	Hercules Beetle
22020907	Hero Signal
81167171	Hero Spirit
46130346	Hinotama
76184692	Hitotsu-Me Giant
69669405	Horn Imp
38552107	Horn of Light
64047146	Horn of the Unicorn
75830094	Horus the Black Flame Dragon Lv. 4
11224103	Horus the Black Flame Dragon Lv. 6
48229808	Horus the Black Flame Dragon Lv. 8
15083728	House of Adhesive Tape

Yu-Gi-Oh! GX: Spirit Caller (continued)

Password	Effect	Password	Effect
61740673	Imperial Order	20394040	Lava Battleguard
52684508	Inferno Fire Blast	00102380	Lava Golem
12247206	Inferno Reckless Summon	07902349	Left Arm of the Forbidden One
94163677	Infinite Cards	44519536	Left Leg of the Forbidden One
54109233	Infinite Dismissal	61854111	Legendary Sword
79575620	Injection Fairy Lily	03136426	Level Limit—Area B
03492538	Insect Armor with Laser Cannon	62867251	Light of Intervention
23615409	Insect Barrier	55226821	Lightning Blade
96965364	Insect Imitation	23171610	Limiter Removal
16227556	Inspection	81777047	Luminous Spark
36261276	Interdimensional Matter Transporter	17658803	Luster Dragon #2
98374133	Invigoration	25769732	Machine Conversion Factory
21770260	Jam Breeding Machine	46700124	Machine King
21558682	Jam Defender	30241314	Macro Cosmos
83968380	Jar of Greed	83746708	Mage Power
14851496	Jellyfish	62279055	Magic Cylinder
77585513	Jinzo #7	59344077	Magic Drain
15401633	Jirai Gumo	77414722	Magic Jammer
30113682	Judge Man	53119267	Magic Thorn
55256016	Judgment of Anubis	96008713	Magic-Arm Shield
24068492	Just Desserts	81210420	Magical Hats
76634149	Kairyu-Shin	31560081	Magician of Faith
12829151	Kanan the Swordmistress	93013676	Maha Vailo
62340868	Kazejin	09074847	Major Riot
88979991	Killer Needle	99597615	Malevolent Nuzzler
79853073	Kinetic Soldier	40374923	Mammoth Graveyard
69455834	King of Yamimakai	54652250	Man-Eater Bug
60519422	Kishido Spirit	44287299	Masaki the Legendary Swordsman
01184620	Kojikocy	82432018	Mask of Brutality
67724379	Koumori Dragon	28933734	Mask of Darkness
76512652	Krokodilus	20765952	Mask of Dispel
37390589	Kunai with Chain	29549364	Mask of Restrict
97590747	La Jinn the Mystical Genie of the Lamp	56948373	Mask of the Accursed
		57882509	Mask of Weakness
66526672	Labyrinth of Nightmare	10189126	Masked Sorcerer
99551425	Labyrinth Tank	22046459	Megamorph
67284908	Labyrinth Wall	48642904	Mesmeric Control
87756343	Larvae Moth	44656491	Messenger of Peace
77007920	Laser Cannon Armor	75646520	Metal Detector
90330453	Last Day of Witch	68339286	Metal Guardian
85602018	Last Will	68540058	Metalmorph
87322377	Launcher Spider	50705071	Metalzoa

DS
GBA
PSP
PS2
PS3
Wii
Xbox
Xbox 360
Index

Yu-Gi-Oh! GX: Spirit Caller (continued)

Password	Effect	Password	Effect
90660762	Meteor Black Dragon	39019325	Order to Smash
64271667	Meteor Dragon	74191942	Painful Choice
33767325	Meteor of Destruction	42035044	Panther Warrior
64274292	Meteorain	50152549	Paralyzing Potion
37580756	Michizure	62762898	Parrot Dragon
32012841	Millennium Shield	24433920	Pendulum Machine
07489323	Milus Radiant	36039163	Penguin Knight
37520316	Mind Control	93920745	Penguin Soldier
01918087	Minor Goblin Official	48579379	Perfectly Ultimate Great Moth
44095762	Mirror Force	58192742	Petit Moth
93108433	Monster Recovery	90669991	Pineapple Blast
74848038	Monster Reincarnation	24094653	Polymerization
97612389	Monster Tamer	70828912	Premature Burial
58074572	Mooyan Curry	00549481	Prevent Rat
33508719	Morphing Jar	51371017	Princess of Tsurugi
50913601	Mountain	43711255	Prohibition
70307656	Mucus Yolk	29155212	Pumpking the King of Ghosts
46657337	Muka Muka	76754619	Pyramid Energy
22493811	Multiplication of Ants	77044671	Pyramid Turtle
40703222	Multiply	94905343	Rabid Horseman
14181608	Mushroom Man	12580477	Raigeki
68191243	Mustering of the Dark Scorpions	56260110	Raimei
54098121	Mysterious Puppeteer	66719324	Rain of Mercy
68516705	Mystic Horseman	51267887	Raise Body Heat
18161786	Mystic Plasma Zone	07625614	Raregold Armor
49251811	Mystic Probe	33066139	Reaper of the Cards
15025844	Mystical Elf	86445415	Red Gadget
36607978	Mystical Moon	38199696	Red Medicine
05318639	Mystical Space Typhoon	36262024	Red-Eyes B. Chick
63516460	Mystical Wind Typhoon	74677422	Red-Eyes Black Dragon
14315573	Negate Attack	64335804	Red-Eyes Black Metal Dragon
17955766	Neo-Spacian Aqua Dolphin	32807846	Reinforcement of the Army
58775978	Nightmare's Steelcage	17814387	Reinforcements
19230407	Offerings to the Doomed	51482758	Remove Trap
79335209	Ojama Black	08951260	Respect Play
12482652	Ojama Green	99518961	Restructer Revolution
90140980	Ojama King	27174286	Return from the Different Dimension
42941100	Ojama Yellow	77622396	Reverse Trap
19523799	Ookazi	70903634	Right Arm of the Forbidden One
63120904	Orca Mega-Fortress of Darkness	08124921	Right Leg of the Forbidden One
39537362	Ordeal of a Traveler		
78986941	Order to Charge		

DS
GBA
PSP
PS2
PS3
Wii
Xbox
Xbox 360
Index

Yu-Gi-Oh! GX: Spirit Caller (continued)

Password	Effect	Password	Effect
83555666	Ring of Destruction	76103675	Sparks
20436034	Ring of Magnetism	31553716	Spear Dragon
70344351	Riryoku Field	42598242	Special Hurricane
88279736	Robbin' Goblin	38275183	Spell Shield Type-8
68846917	Rock Ogre Grotto #1	18807108	Spellbinding Circle
91939608	Rogue Doll	49328340	Spiral Spear Strike
93382620	Rope of Life	94772232	Spirit Message "A"
51452091	Royal Decree	31893528	Spirit Message "I"
26378150	Rude Kaiser	30170981	Spirit Message "L"
70046172	Rush Recklessly	67287532	Spirit Message "N"
15303296	Ryu-Kishin	92394653	Spirit's Invitation
24611934	Ryu-Kishin Powered	15866454	Spiritualism
66602787	Saggi the Dark Clown	94425169	Spring of Rebirth
32268901	Salamandra	81385346	Stamping Destruction
25955164	Sanga of the Thunder	65810489	Statue of the Wicked
26202165	Sangan	13599884	Steel Scorpion
11760174	Sasuke Samurai #2	02370081	Steel Shell
50400231	Satellite Cannon	83225447	Stim-Pack
02792265	Servant of Catabolism	63102017	Stop Defense
03819470	Seven Tools of the Bandit	98434877	Suijin
30778711	Shadow Ghoul	70781052	Summoned Skull
58621589	Shadow of Eyes	85520851	Super Conductor Tyranno
56830749	Share the Pain	27770341	Super Rejuvenation
52097679	Shield & Sword	40453765	Swamp Battleguard
59560625	Shift	13069066	Sword Arm of Dragon
73665146	Silent Magician LV 4	37120512	Sword of Dark Destruction
72443568	Silent Magician LV 8	98495314	Sword of the Deep-Seated
01557499	Silver Bow and Arrow	05372656	Sword of the Soul-Eater
90357090	Silver Fang	72302403	Swords of Revealing Light
08131171	Sinister Serpent	50005633	Swordstalker
73752131	Skilled Dark Magician	18895832	System Down
00126218	Skull Dice	43641473	Tailor of the Fickle
98139712	Skull Invitation	41142615	The Cheerful Coffin
06733059	Skull Lair	30606547	The Dark Door
63035430	Skyscraper	92408984	The Dragon's Bead
78636495	Slate Warrior	68400115	The Emperor's Holiday
00596051	Snake Fang	42829885	The Forceful Sentry
86318356	Sogen	84136000	The Grave of the Enkindling
41420027	Solemn Judgment	81820689	The Inexperienced Spy
35346968	Solemn Wishes	66926224	The Law of the Normal
47852924	Soul of the Pure	25109950	The Little Swordsman of Aile
05758500	Soul Release	49064413	The Masked Beast
92924317	Soul Resurrection	16430187	The Reliable Guardian
97362768	Spark Blaster	43434803	The Shallow Grave

DS GBA PSP PS2 PS3 Wii Xbox Xbox 360 Index

DS
GBA
PSP
PS2
PS3
Wii
Xbox
Xbox 360
Index

Yu-Gi-Oh! GX: Spirit Caller (continued)

Password	Effect	Password	Effect
29491031	The Snake Hair	22056710	Vampire Genesis
06285791	The Wicked Worm Beast	53839837	Vampire Lord
41462083	Thousand Dragon	95220856	Vengeful Bog Spirit
05703682	Thousand Energy	50259460	Versago the Destroyer
63519819	Thousand-Eyes Restrict	39774685	Vile Germ
91781589	Thunder of Ruler	15052462	Violet Crystal
40907090	Tiger Axe	14898066	Vorse Raider
80987696	Time Machine	12607053	Waboku
71625222	Time Wizard	63162310	Wall Shadow
82003859	Toll	90873992	Warrior Elimination
59383041	Toon Alligator	23424603	Wasteland
42386471	Toon Gemini Elf	85066822	Water Dragon
89997728	Toon table of contents	38992735	Wave Motion Cannon
80813021	Torike	15150365	White Magical Hat
53582587	Torrential Tribute	77754944	Widespread Ruin
35686187	Tragedy	87796900	Winged Dragon, Guardian of the Forest #1
64697231	Trap Dustshoot	57116033	Winged Kuriboh
04206964	Trap Hole	98585345	Winged Kuriboh LV 10
46461247	Trap Master	49417509	Wolf
46918794	Tremendous Fire	12253117	World Suppression
02903036	Tribute Doll	62651957	X-Head Cannon
79759861	Tribute to the Doomed	02111707	XY-Dragon Cannon
03149764	Tutan Mask	91998119	XYZ-Dragon Cannon
94119974	Two-Headed King Rex	99724761	XZ-Tank Cannon
83887306	Two-Pronged Attack	65622692	Y-Dragon Head
72842870	Tyhone	25119460	YZ-Tank Dragon
21237481	Type Zero Magic Crusher	59197169	Yami
94568601	Tyrant Dragon	13834120	Yellow Gadget
80604091	Ultimate Offering	04542651	Yellow Luster Shield
15894048	Ultimate Tyranno	64500000	Z-Metal Tank
22702055	Umi	30090452	Zanki
82999629	Umiiruka	69123138	Zera the Mant
70368879	Upstart Goblin	24311372	Zoa
01784619	Uraby	31339260	Zombie Warrior
06007213	Uria, Lord of Searing Flames		

Yu-Gi-Oh! GX: Spirit Caller (continued)

Unlockables

Unlockable	How to Unlock
Acrobat Monkey	Defeat Kagemaru
Adhesive Explosive	Starter at well
Babycerasaurus	After finalists are decided in tournament
Batteryman C	Finish game
Batteryman D	Finish game
Beelze Frog	After finalists are decided in tournament
Blast Asmodian	After finalists are decided in tournament
Dragon Capture Jar	Finish game
Ebon Magician Curran	After abandoned dorm events
Hane-Hane	Defeat Bastion for the second time
Jerry Beans Man	Starter at well
Oscillo Hero #2	Starter at well
Skelengel	Defeat Kagemaru
Soitsu	After abandoned dorm events
Star Boy	Defeat Bastion for the second time
White Magician Pikeru	Finish game
Alchemy Disk	Defeat Prof. Banner until he gives it to you
Amazonness Disk	Defeat Tania until she gives it to you
Cheap Duel Disk	Get from linking with Nightmare Troubadour
Gorgeous Disk	Defeat Admiral until he gives it to you
Kaibaman Disk	Deafeat Kaibaman until he gives it to you
Pharaoh Disk	Defeat Abidos until he gives it to you
Vampire Disk	Defeat Camula until she gives it to you
Academy Jersey	Defeat Fonda until she gives it to you
Black Uniform	Defeat Chazz until he gives it to you
Blue Uniform	Defeat Dark Zane until he gives it to you
Duel Coat	Defeat Crowler until he gives it to you
Hawaiian Shirt	Defeat Atticus until he gives it to you
Kaibaman Coat	Defeat Kaibaman until he gives it to you
North Academy Uniform	Defeat Chazz until he gives it to you
Stuffy Collared Shirt	Get from linking with Nightmare Troubadour
Suit	Duel Chumley until he gives it to you
Titan Coat	Defeat Titan until he gives it to you
Yellow Uniform	Defeat Professor Sartyr until he gives it to you

DS

GBA

PSP

PS2

PS3

Wii

Xbox

Xbox 360

Index

Table of Contents - GBA

DS
GBA
PSP
PS2
PS3
Wii
Xbox
Xbox 360
Index

Advance GTA

Unlockable	Objective
Formula 1 Mode	To access the extra Formula 1 mode, play through the Championship mode and beat all four of the classes with a first place in each race. You get a new car (Formula 1 racecar) after the last race. At the Menu screen, the Extra 2 option will be available.

Advance Rally

Unlockable	Objective
Co-Driver Mode	Win first place in all races in World Rally mode.
Hidden Track	Win first place in Co-Driver mode.

Aggressive Inline

Unlockable	Objective
All Levels	At the Title screen, press ↑,↓,↑,↓,←,→,Ⓑ,Ⓒ
All Levels Up to Deadman's Sewer	At the Title screen, press Ⓛ,Ⓑ,Ⓡ,Ⓑ
All Skaters	Ⓛ,Ⓛ,Ⓑ,Ⓑ,Ⓡ,Ⓡ,Ⓛ,Ⓡ

Alex Rider: Stormbreaker

Passwords

Password	Effect
6894098	Bugs can't detect you
9785711	Chase passthrough
4298359	Dizzy enemies
6943059	Enemies have extra health
9603717	Extra enemy damage
SARYL HIRSCH	Fast downtimer
5204025	Guards can't detect you
VICTORIA PARR	One hit K.O.
RENATO CELANI	Slow bullets
JESSICA PARKER	Unlimited health

American Idol

Enter the following codes as a password.

Unlockable	Code
Last Three Practice Songs	Z999&6QR
More Costumes	HTH4&6CK

Back to Stone

Passwords

Password	Effect
CREDITSSSS	Ending credits
THEENDSSSS	Last Part of the story

Backyard Baseball 2007

Unlockables

Unlockable	How to Unlock
Unlock Paul Konerko	Type Grand Slam as a code
Area 51	Make it to the World Series
Bobby Abreau	Earn 15 season home runs with one person
Derek Jeter	Turn 2 double plays in one game
Derrick Lee	Get 30 season hits
Dontrelle Willis	Earn 45 strikeouts during the season
Johan Santana	Pitch a shut-out against any team
Monstrous Stadium	Make the playoffs
Paul Konerko	Hit a grand slam in a game

Backyard Basketball 2007

Unlimited Turbo

Unlockable	How to Unlock
Unlimited Turbo	At the match up screen, enter ↑, ↑, ←, →, Ⓑ, ↓

Ballistic: Ecks vs. Sever 2

Enter the following words in the Password screen:

Unlockable	Code		Immobilized Enemies	COLDFEET
All Weapons	TOOLEDUP		Invincibility	DEATHWISH
Alternate Sounds	HORNBLOW		Invisibility	DOYOUCME
Huge Explosions	ACMEBANGS		Rapid Fire	MYBIGUN
Unlimited Ammo	BIGPOCKET			

Level	Ecks Code	Sever Code		Seven	LITTERBUG	STINGER
Two	SMOKEY	RAVEN		Eight	MUSTANG	NAIL
Three	BUTTERFLY	FIREFLY		Nine	SPECTRE	ZORRO
Four	COVEY	BULLDOG		Ten	NIMROD	XRAY
Five	TIGER	DRAGON		Eleven	SPOOKY	REDDOG
Six	HORNET	LOUDMOUTH				

Barbie in The 12 Dancing Princesses

Passwords

Password	Effect
cat, cat, slippers, prince	Level 2-A
cat, old lady, bird, monkey	Level 2-B
old lady, slippers, slippers, slippers	Level 3-A
blonde girl, blonde girl, monkey, blonde girl	Level 3-B
old lady, brunette girl, cat, brunette girl	Level 4-A
monkey, prince, blonde girl, bird	Level 4-B
old lady, bird, slippers, monkey	Level 5-A

Barbie in The 12 Dancing Princesses (continued)

Password	Effect
brunette girl, bird, blonde girl, old lady	Level 5-B
prince, monkey, blonde, old lady	Level 6-A
brunette girl, cat, old lady, slippers	Level 6-B
blonde girl, brunette girl, prince, old lady	Level 7-A
monkey, cat, blonde girl, old lady	Level 7-B
blonde girl, blonde girl, prince, brunette girl	Level 8

Batman: Rise of Sin Tzu

Enter the following codes at the Main menu while holding ⒧+ⓡ.

Unlockable	Code
All Rewards	←,↓,←,→,←,←,↓,→
All Upgrades	↓,↑,↓,←,↓,↓,↑,↓
God Mode	↑,→,↑,←,↓,←,↓,→
Unlimited Combo Meter	←,→,↓,↑,↑,↓,→,←

Battle B-Daman: Fire Spirits

Passwords

Password	Effect
FEROCIOUS WOLF!	Assault Beast and Storm Chimera
THE SWIFT WINGS	Blitz Eagle
THE RAZING FIRE	Crimson Saber
STRONG RED GALE	Drive Body (Chrome Harrier)
REVIVAL OF EVIL	Labyrinth
DEVILISH FIGURE	Motor DHB Core (Mega Diabros)
LET'S B-DAFIRE!	Revolver Heaven
GIFT FROM ATLUS	Stream Pegasus
MONGREL FANG!	Berserk Ogre
A BLOODY BODY	Blood Shark
GLEAMING FANG	Gao Tiger
SHADOWY ARMOR	Kokuryu-oh
GUST OF WIND!	Oak Raven
GOLDEN ARMOR!	Ohryu-oh
TONS OF BALLS	Saber Loader and Load Wing Trigger
VENOMOUS TAIL	Venom Sting
YOKUSAIMARU!	Yokusaimaru
GO YAMATO!	1,500 B-daBucks
HEY TOMMI!	2,000 B-daBucks
B-DAFIRING	3,000 B-daBucks
B-DAFIRING	3,000 B-daBucks
HARD TEETH	Cheesy Mouse
SHOOT IT!!	Saber Barrel and L/R Shield Stand

DS

GBA

PSP

PS2

PS3

Wii

Xbox

Xbox 360

Index

DS

GBA

PSP

PS2

PS3

Wii

Xbox

Xbox 360

Index

Battle B-Daman: Fire Spirits (continued)

Passwords

Enter these codes at the Parts Shop once you have gained the Bronze Pass, which you start the game with. (Note: Each letter set represents the corresponding katakana symbol. Lowercase letters mean the small version of the symbol, and "-" means the long line that represents a held vowel.)

Password	Effect
DA I WA YA MA TO	1,500 Biiro (Money)
TA ME GO RO - !	2,000 Biiro (Money)
BI - FU a I A	3,000 Biiro (Money)
TSU YO I MA E BA	Hamburger (Hamster) B-daman set
PE tsu TO BO TO RU	Pet Bottle Magazine II
NE RA I U TE !	Saber Barrel, and L + R Stand Shields (or money if you have them already)

Passwords

Enter these codes at the Parts Shop once you have gained the Silver Pass, which is obtained at the beginning of the Winners Tournament. If you have the parts that a Zero Code unlocks, you receive the cost in biiro (money) instead. (Note: Each letter set represents the corresponding katakana symbol. Lowercase letters mean the small version of the symbol, and "-" means the long line that represents a held vowel.)

Password	Effect
JI yu U JI N NO KI BA	Berserk Ogre B-daman Set
CHI MA MI RE NO KA RA DA	Blood Shark B-daman Set
YA MI NI HI KA RU KI BA	GaoTiger B-daman Set
A N KO KU NO YO RO I	KokuRyuuOh B-daman Set
O U GO N NO YO RO I	OuRyuuOh B-daman Set
BI - DA MA TA KU SA N	Saber Loader Magazine and Long Trigger Wing (one part)
MO U DO KU NO SHI tsu PO	Venom Sting B-daman Set
TO BE YO KU SA I MA RU	Yokusaimaru B-daman Set

Bionicle: The Game

Enter these passwords in the Passwords menu.

Unlockable	Password
All Toa missions complete	FD555B
All Toa Symbols	3QQQGC
Complete Onua's Level	WLBQBB
Takanuva	J+B%%%
Unlock Lewa	MVCVBB
Unlock Lewa and Onua	3GLBZB
Unlock Lewa, Tahu, Kopaka, and Gali	YVVWFV

Boxing Fever

To enter these passwords, go into the Setup menu, then enter the Passwords menu.

Unlockable	Password
Boxor	H7649DH5
Boxor2	2GG48HD9
Boxor3	8G3D97B7
Byclop	G51FF888
E.Byclop	B3G58318

Britney's Dance Beat

Unlockable	Code
Activate Cheat Mode (All levels and bonuses)	Enter HMNFK as a password.

Capcom Classics Mini Mix

Passwords

Password	Level
AAIA AAAA AAIA	01
BCJB BBNB NBAB	02
CEOC KCOC OCMC	03
DGPD LDBD BDAD	04
HLDJ PIGH GHCH	05
HLDJ DIGH GHGH	06
HLEJ DIGH GHHH	07
INHK GJHI HILI	08
JPIL HKIB IBMJ	09
CJBE ADBO BONC	10
BJAP PEAN ANOB	11
DMCC BGCP CPOD	12

Cars

Codes

Enter the following at the "Press Start" screen. An engine noise confirms correct code entry.

Unlockable	How to Unlock
90 Bolts and All Levels Unlocked	↑,↑,↓,↓,←,→,←,→,Ⓑ,↓
Unlock All Car Colors	↑,↑,←,→,→,←,↓,↓
Unlock All Cars	→,↓,→,Ⓑ
Unlock All Screenshots at the Drive-In	←,↓,→,↓
Unlock Radiator Cap Secret Circuit	←,←,→,→,Ⓑ,Ⓑ,↓

DS

GBA

PSP

PS2

PS3

Wii

Xbox

Xbox 360

Index

DS

GBA

PSP

PS2

PS3

Wii

Xbox

Xbox 360

Index

Castlevania: Aria of Sorrow

Description	Code/Objective
Don't Use Items	Enter "NOUSE" as your name.
Don't Use Souls	Enter "NOSOUL" as your name.
Get Best Ending	Collect all of the ancient books and beat Graham. You will then be taken to a fight against Chaos.
Boss Rush Mode	Beat the game to unlock Boss Rush mode.
Unlock Hard Mode	Beat the game and earn the good ending to unlock Hard Mode.
Julius Belmont	Beat the game once with Soma, then begin a new game and use the name "Julius."

Castlevania: Circle of the Moon

Description	Objective
Get the Shining Armor	Beat the Battle Arena in the chapel tower.
Unlock Fighter Mode	Beat the game twice (the second time in Magician mode). Your stats are higher then usual, but there are no DSS cards to collect.
Unlock Magician Mode	After you beat the game, enter the name "FIREBALL" at the Data screen. You will begin the game with all DSS Cards available right away.

Castlevania: White Night Concerto

Unlockable	Code
Boss Rush Mode	Complete the game. There are three levels (easy, normal, and hard) that must be unlocked by playing each in succession, starting with easy.
Classic Simon	Unlock Boss Rush mode, then press ↑, ↑, ↓, ↓, ←, →, ←, →, Ⓑ, Ⓐ, ⓈⒺⓁⒺⒸⓉ at the Konami logo. Select Boss Rush mode to play as the NES version of Simon.
Hard Mode	Enter HARDGAME as a name after completing the game at least once. A voice at the start of the introduction confirms correct code entry.
No Magic	Enter NO MAGIC as a name after completing the game at least once.
Play as Maxim Kischine	Enter MAXIM as a name after completing the game at least once. He is faster and jumps higher than Belmont.
Sound Test Mode	Complete the game with the good ending (where you rescue Maxim and Lydie).

Charlotte's Web

Unlockables

Unlockable	How to Unlock
Aeronauts	Find the icon in a secret room level 4
Bumper Cars	Find the icon in level 13
Food Catch	Find the icon in level 10
Snacktime to Templeton	Find the icon in level 9
Storybook Page 1	Complete level 1
Storybook Page 2	Find all 20 goose eggs in level 2
Storybook Page 3	Complete level 4
Storybook Page 4	Find all 10 logs in level 5
Storybook Page 5	Find all goslings in level 6
Storybook Page 6	Complete level 6

Charlotte's Web (continued)

Unlockable	How to Unlock
Storybook Page 7	Find all 20 apples in level 8
Storybook Page 8	Save all 10 rats in level 9
Storybook Page 9	Save all 11 rats in level 10
Storybook Page 10	Save all 10 rats in level 11
Storybook Page 11	Complete level 12
Storybook Page 12	Find all 10 tickets in level 13
Storybook Page 13	Find all 10 tickets in level 14
Storybook Page 14	Complete level 15
Storybook Page 15	Complete level 16
Webbing Crashers	Find the icon in level 6

Chu Chu Rocket

Unlockable	Objective
Hard Mode	Complete Normal mode.
Mania Mode	Complete Special mode.
Special Mode	Complete Hard mode.

Contra Advance: The Alien Wars EX

Enter passwords in the passwords menu.

Unlockable	Password
Level 2 with 99 lives	Y4HC1B L5P212 34ZWF1
Level 3 with 99 lives	WXJD1Z JHSJ1Q KKNCY1
Level 5 with 99 lives	G3421N TDN51N C3BV2C
Level 6 with 99 lives	W3MJ1S J4VP1N YY24BD
Novice Level 2	11111N TYLH1Z FCS5H1
Novice Level 3	111113 TYLH1W BHZXZ1
Novice Level 4	11111B TYLH1T XLGHSB
Normal Level 2	111111 TYLH1S 35MYH1
Normal Level 3	11111H TYLH1X QTTH1B
Normal Level 4	11111J TYLH1Z MY1RSB
Normal Level 5	11111V TYLH13 2D21LC
Normal Level 6	11111M TYLH1V CFDJDD

Crash Bandicoot: The Huge Adventure

Unlockable	Objective
Bonus level	Finish the game with a 100 percent completion. Play again and fight the final boss. Win the battle to play a level featuring mutated bosses.
Double Jump	Defeat N. Gin on the boss stage on the second floor to get the Double Jump.
Super Belly Flop	Get all the items.
Tornado Spin	Defeat Tiny on the boss stage on the third floor.
Turbo	Complete the game to unlock the ability to run faster in subsequent games. Hold Ⓛ during gameplay to move faster.

DS

GBA

PSP

PS2

PS3

Wii

Xbox

Xbox 360

Index

DS

GBA

PSP

PS2

PS3

Wii

Xbox

Xbox 360

Index

Crash Bandicoot Purple: Ripto's Rampage

In the Mode menu press L + R, and enter the following codes.

Unlockable	Code
100 Wumpa	CR4SH
200 Wumpa	G3CK0
500 Wumpa	C0FF33
All Intermission Sequences	CVTZ
Grenades	STR4WB3RRY or SVNB1R. Press the R to throw grenades
Green Pants	K1LL4Z
Kickin' It Old Skool! (Gray Game)	R3S3NTZ
Mayan Jungle Card	WH1STL3
Orange Pants	BR3NT
Orangilicious Mode	L4MPP0ST
Purple Fever	WVMP4FR00T
Sewers Card	PH0N3T4G

> **TIP**
>
> ### Spyro Party USA Mini-Game
>
> *Hold L + R while powering up the Game Boy Advance.*

Crash Nitro Kart

Unlockable	Code
Crash Party USA	Hold both trigger buttons when turning on the game to access the mini game.

Crazy Taxi

Unlockable	Objective
City 2	Get a Crazy License ($10,000+) in City 1 on normal rules.

CT Special Forces

Unlockable	Code
Level 2	1608
Level 3	2111
Final Level	1705
Unlock Special Characters	0202

Curious George

Passwords

Password	Effect
GPSDGHQP	Access to Level 5 with 4 Golden Clocks
GQSDBHSP	Access to Level 6 with 5 Golden Clocks
BGSDBHGP	Access to Level 7 with 6 Golden Clocks
GCMJBHFP	Access to Level 8 with 7 Golden Clocks
TNTDBHNQ	Level 2
TNTDBHBQ	Level 3
PSTDHHSS	Level 6
TNSDBHAG	Level 8

Danny Phantom: The Ultimate Enemy

Enter these passwords at the Passwords menu.

Unlockable	Password
Boss Rush mode	Rush
Dash's Haunted Locker	Dash
Easy and Hard Difficulty	Vlad
Hindin' Ghost Seek	Seek
Levitation	Jazz
Sam's X-ray Ecto Detector	Ecto

Doom

To access the following unlockables, press (START) to pause gameplay, hold (L)+(R), then enter code.

Unlockable	Code
All Weapons, Items and Keys	(A), (B), (B), (A), (A), (A), (A), (A)
Berserk Mode	(B), (A), (B), (A), (A), (A), (A), (A)
Computer Map	(B), (A), (A), (A), (A), (A), (A), (A)
Disable God Mode	(A), (A), (B), (A), (B), (B), (B), (B)
God Mode	(A), (A), (B), (A), (A), (A), (A), (A)
Invulnerability	(B), (B), (B), (A), (A), (A), (A), (A)
Level Skip (Use only in single-player games.)	(A), (B), (A), (A), (B), (B), (B), (A)
Radiation suit	(B), (B), (A), (A), (A), (A), (A), (A)
Turn Off God Mode	(A), (A), (B), (A), (B), (B), (B), (B)
Warp 10 Levels	(A), (B), (A), (A), (B), (B), (A), (A)
Warp to Next Level	(A), (B), (A), (A), (B), (B), (B), (A)

Double Dragon Advance

In the Options screen, hold (SELECT) and enter the following codes.

Unlockable	Code
10 Credits	(L),(R),↓,(L),(R),↓,(L),(R),→
Background Music Select	(R),(L),(R),(L)
Expert Mode	↑,↑,↓,↓,←,→,←,→

DS

GBA

PSP

PS2

PS3

Wii

Xbox

Xbox 360

Index

DS

GBA

PSP

PS2

PS3

Wii

Xbox

Xbox 360

Index

Dragon Ball: Advanced Adventure

Unlockables

Unlockable	How to Unlock
Boss Mode	Collect all 54 items found in Story and Extra mode stages
Boss Mode	Finish the game with both Goku and Krillin
King Piccolo	Finish the game with Goku
Open Red Doors in Action Stages	Red doors are automatically open in "Extra" Game
Piccolo	Finish the game with Krillin
Play as Juckie Chun, Taopaipai, Son (Grandpa) Gohan, and Tenshinhan in Free Battle Mode	Beat them in the Story mode Free Battles
Play as Krillin	Finish the game with Goku
Rock Breaking Minigame	Finish the game with Goku
Sound Test	Beat Boss mode
Sound Test (In Options Menu)	Beat Boss Rush mode
Unlock Cyborg Taopaipai for Tournament Mode	Beat him in the final level of Tournament mode
Unlock Extra Mode	Beat Story mode with Goku
Unlock Juckie Chun for Tournament Mode	Beat him with Goku in Story mode
Unlock Minigame Mode (Rock Breaking, Korin's Tower)	Finish the game with Goku
Unlock Piccolo for Tournament Mode	Finish the game with Krillin
Unlock Son Gohan (Goku's grandfather) for Tournament Mode	Beat him with Goku in Story mode
Unlock Survival Mode in Free Battle Mode	Beat Story mode with Goku
Unlock Taopaipai for Tournament Mode	Beat him with Goku in Story mode
Unlock Tenshinhan for Tournament Mode	Beat him with Goku in Story mode
Use Cyber Taopaipai in Free Battle Mode	Beat Cyber Taopaipai in Survival mode after unlocking Piccolo
Use Piccolo in Free	Finish the Game with Goku and Krillin Battle Mode
Use the Characters Fought in VS Mode in Extra Mode (Except Piccolo and Cyborg Taopaipai)	Find and collect all Dragon Balls and collect their respective portraits in Extra mode

Dragon Ball Z: The Legacy of Goku

Unlockable	Code
Invincibility	↑, ↓, ←, →, Ⓑ, Ⓐ

Dragon Ball Z: Legend of Goku II

Unlockable	Objective
Alternative Ending	Unlock Mr. Satan and go to Level 50, then go to West City and break down the Level 50 door to ZZTV.
Gohan's Trophy	Go to Level 50 with Gohan, then go to the "50" gate outside Gingertown to collect the trophy.
Goku's Trophy	Finish the game.
Piccolo's Trophy	Go to Level 50 with Piccolo, then go to the "50" gate at Namek planet to collect the trophy.
Play as Hercule	Go to Level 50 with Gohan, Piccolo, Vegeta, and Trunks, then go to the character-specific "50" gates to collect trophies.
Trunks' Trophy	Go to Level 50 with Trunks, then go to the "50" gate at West City to collect the trophy.
Unlock Mr. Satan (Hercule)	Get everyone but Goku to Level 50, then go through each character's Level 50 Area and collect their Character Trophies. Then beat the game and you'll get Goku's Trophy, with a message telling you that Mr. Satan is now playable.
Vegeta's Trophy	Go to Level 50 with Vegeta, then go to the "50" gate at Northern Mountains to collect the trophy.

Dragon Ball Z: Supersonic Warriors

Unlockable	Objective
Secret Final Battles	Complete story mode without losing once, then wait until after the credits. Note: Not all characters have a final battle.

Drake and Josh

Passwords

Password	Effect
6731	Level 1-1
6165	Level 1-2
7475	Level 1-3
8636	Level 1-4
7716	Level 2-1
5725	Level 2-2
3576	Level 3-1
8285	Level 3-2
7546	Level 4-1
7621	Level 4-2
2875	Level 4-3
5147	Level 5-1
5285	Level 6-1
8273	Level 6-2
2548	Episode 6, Final Level: Stage Fright Arcade, All Guitars, No Essay Papers
7576	Minigame: Cafeteria Panic
5688	Minigame: Soda Pop Blues
2548	Minigame: Stage Fright

DS
GBA
PSP
PS2
PS3
Wii
Xbox
Xbox 360
Index

DS
GBA
PSP
PS2
PS3
Wii
Xbox
Xbox 360
Index

Duke Nukem Advance

Unlockable	Code
Cheat Mode	At anytime during the game, pause and enter ←, ↑, Ⓐ, ↑, ←, Ⓐ, (START), (SELECT)

Extreme Ghostbusters

Level	Password
Big Building Boss	8G20S86SC
Carnivorous and Hungry	WSFKP6WT3
Closer to the Underworld	MD*XN7KTJ
Ethereal Ball	MD2TK4XTK
In the Wings	MDZ9KK/T8
On Stage	WS0PJ6LTC
Racing 2	30J82JBMB
Racing 3	VD*PJKFTS
Racing 4	LDK9K6HTC
The Botanical Museum Final Boss	VSFPPMHT8
The Broadway Star Theater	VS31JL9TW
The Corridors	5PMDTF/K2
The Crypt	V8JNNVGLC
The Final Confrontation	MS29P7JTW
The Hall	HGBNL14VJ
The Offices	21QSR9JTS
The Main Aisle	BNKN34SMW

Final Fight One

Unlockable	Code
Alpha Cody and Alpha Guy (Alpha Cody is bigger, and Alpha Guy is stronger.)	Press ← or → at the Character Selection screen to choose these fighters.
Change Control Settings	Pause gameplay and hold Ⓛ+Ⓡ+Ⓑ+Ⓐ.

Finding Nemo

Unlockable	Code	Unlockable	Code
Level 2	Password: HZ51	Level 7	Password: 73P1
Level 3	Password: ZZ51	Level 8	Password: 8MN2
Level 4	Password: 8061	Level Select and Access All Gallery Images	Password: M6HM
Level 5	Password: QHP1		
Level 6	Password: 8BP1		

Gekido Advance: Kintaro's Revenge

Chapter	Code
Chapter 2 The Three Seals	SACCO
Chapter 3 The Ancient Book	TAPPO
Chapter 4 Searching for Koji	TEMPO
Chapter 5 The Final Battle	BECCO

Grand Theft Auto Advance

Unlockable	Code
Location Coordinates	During gameplay, press and hold START + Ⓐ + Ⓑ.

Guilty Gear X

Unlockables	Code
Alternate Costumes	Press START or SELECT when choosing a fighter at the Character Selection screen.

Gundam Speed Battle Assault

Enter this code at the Password menu.

Unlockable	Code
Aegis's story complete, Cgue unlocked	CL3RRSD0J
All stories complete, all Mobile Suits unlocked, Very Hard mode unlocked	WLJK7SD0S
Astray and Forbidden's story complete	?DNWRSD0J
Blitz's story complete, Astray unlocked	DVNYRSD00
Cgue's story complete	XL4GRSD0J
Strike's story complete	C2KQRSD0J

Harlem Globetrotters: World Tour

Passwords

Password	Effect
XCTXJK	2 Teams Beaten
XNSXHD	3 Teams Beaten
XYRXGT	4 Teams Beaten
X7QXFL	5 Teams Beaten
XHQXXG	6 Teams Beaten
XSPXWD	7 Teams Beaten
XZNXVS	8 Teams Beaten
X4LX9L	10 Teams Beaten
XDLXRH	11 Teams Beaten
XPKXQJ	12 Teams Beaten
XZJXPM	13 Teams Beaten
X8HXNQ	14 Teams Beaten
XTGX3H	15 Teams Beaten

Unlockables

Unlockable	How to Unlock
Anthony Greenup	Get 300 points
Dwayne Rogers	Get 750 points
Eugene Edgerson	Get 1,150 points
Globie	Get 1,200 points
Herbert Lang	Get 500 points
Jefferson Sobral	Get 950 points
Jimmy Twyman	Get 1,100 points
Keiron Shine	Get 850 points
Kevin Daley	Get 100 points
Larry House	Get 350 points

DS

GBA

PSP

PS2

PS3

Wii

Xbox

Xbox 360

Index

DS

GBA

PSP

PS2

PS3

Wii

Xbox

Xbox 360

Index

Harlem Globetrotters: World Tour (continued)

Unlockable	How to Unlock
Lincoln Smith	Get 900 points
Matt Jackson	Get 400 points
Maurice Shaw	Get 800 points
Michael Lee	Get 550 points
Michael Wilson	Get 150 points
Mike St. Julien	Get 1,000 points
Nate Lofton	Get 600 points
Otis Key	Get 450 points
Paul Gaffney	Get 250 points
Reggie Phillips	Get 700 points
Robert Turner	Get 1,050 points
Scooter McFadgon	Get 650 points
Sterling Forbes	Get 200 points

Hot Wheels Velocity X

Unlockable	Code
All Cars	496-93-993
Everything	723-83-462

Iridion 3D

Unlockable	Code
All Levels	Go to the Password screen and enter S3L3CT0N, press OK, then return to the Password screen from the main menu and enter SH0WT1M3, then press OK.

James Bond 007: Nightfire

During gameplay, pause the game and input the following codes. A voice will confirm correct code entry.

Unlockable	Code
500 Bullets	R, ←, L, →, ↑, SELECT, →
All Levels	R, ←, L, →, ↑, SELECT, R
Invincibility	R, ←, L, →, ↑, SELECT, ←

Jet Grind Radio

Unlockable	Objective
Hear the Sega Scream	Tap Ⓐ as the game boots.
Noise Tanks	Beat the Benten-Cho levels earning a Jet ranking.
Poison Jam	Beat the Kogane-Cho levels earning a Jet ranking.
Prof. K	Beat the game.
The Love Shockers	Beat the Shibuya-Cho levels earning a Jet ranking.

Jimmy Neutron: Boy Genius

Go to Enter Code in the Main menu and enter the following passwords.

Unlockable	Easy Mode Code	Hard Mode Code
Asteroid Field	WM5DR5H3MCLB	2040YL61TT0T
Dungeon	N?+94T1?DJXW	456N$DWBWM?F
Ending Scene	3L!VPH26V7$8	+CLT3LD1TTSF
King Goobot	BD5VVRDF3GXV	—
Poultra	939BSYT41N0Z	XZ16F2F8NS$!
Yokian Moon	KVZQG3Q50LZG	GGP6WCC273-3
Yokus	—	2H?-!L81TT0K
Yokian Palace	MMS-KXBVC4FS	+R6H!L91TT0F

Justice League Heroes: The Flash

Enter at the title screen while holding Ⓑ.

Unlockable	Code
All heroes	↑, ↓, ←, →, →, ←, ↓, ↑, (START)
All lives	↑, ↓, ↑, ↑, ↓, ↓, ↑, ↓, (START)
Larger enemies	↑, ↑, ↓, ↓, ←, →, ←, →, (START)
Smaller enemies	↓, ↓, ↑, ↑, →, ←, →, ←, (START)
Flash is larger	←, ↑, →, ↓, ←, ↑, →, ↓, (START)
Flash is smaller	↓, ↓, ↓, ←, ↑, ↑, →, →, (START)

Konami Collector's Series: Arcade Advanced

Unlockable	Code
Frogger (Enhanced graphics)	↑,↑,↓,↓,←,→,←,→,Ⓑ,Ⓐ, (START)
Gyruss (Enhanced graphics)	↑,↑,↓,↓,←,→,←,→,Ⓑ,Ⓐ, (START)
Rush'n Attack (Two extra lives)	↑,↑,↓,↓,←,→,←,→,Ⓑ,Ⓐ, (START)
Scramble (Enhanced graphics)	↑,↑,↓,↓,←,→,←,→,Ⓑ,Ⓐ, (START)
Time Pilot (Extra stage)	↑,↑,↓,↓,←,→,←,→,Ⓑ,Ⓐ, (START)
Yie Ar Kung Fu (Extra fighters in Vs. mode)	↑,↑,↓,↓,←,→,←,→,Ⓑ,Ⓐ, (START)

Lilo and Stitch

Use the following icon combinations as passwords to skip to specific levels.

Unlockable	Code
Beach	Stitch, Stitch, Stitch, Stitch, Stitch, Stitch, Stitch.
End	Pineapple, Pineapple, Pineapple, Pineapple, Stitch, Stitch, Stitch.
Escape!	Stitch, Scrump, UFO, Gun, Rocket, Scrump, UFO.
Final Challenge	Lilo, Pineapple, Flower, Pineapple, Gun, Gun, Stitch.
Junkyard Planet	UFO, Rocket, Stitch, Rocket, Rocket, Scrump, Stitch.
Mothership	UFO, Scrump, Stitch, Rocket, UFO, Stitch, UFO.
Rescue	Flower, Scrump, UFO, Gun, Gun, Gun, UFO. .
Space Cruiser	Lilo, Rocket, Stitch, Rocket, Rocket, Scrump, Stitch.

DS

GBA

PSP

PS2

PS3

Wii

Xbox

Xbox 360

Index

The Lord of the Rings: The Return of the King

Unlockable	Objective
Smeagol	Complete the game with 2000 or more kills.

Medal of Honor: Underground

Unlockable	Code
God Mode	Go to Options and enter "MODEDEDIEU" as a password.

Unlockable	Easy Mode Level Passwords	Medium Mode Level Passwords	Hard Mode Level Passwords
Level 1	TRILINGUE	IRRADIER	DOSSARD
Level 2	SQUAME	FRIMAS	CUBIQUE
Level 3	REVOLER	ESCARGOT	CHEMIN
Level 4	FAUCON	DEVOIR	BLONDEUR
Level 5	UNANIME	COALISER	BLESSER
Level 6	ROULIS	BASQUE	AVOCAT
Level 7	RELAVER	ROBUSTE	AFFINER
Level 8	POUSSIN	SOYEUX	LAINE
Level 9	PANOPLIE	TERRER	MESCLUN
Level 10	NIMBER	VOULOIR	NORME
Level 11	NIAIS	COUVERT	ORNER
Level 12	KARMA	VOYANCE	PENNE
Level 13	INCISER	PIGISTE	QUELQUE
Level 14	GADOUE	NOMMER	REPOSE
Level 15	FUSETTE	JETER	SALIFIER
Level 16	EXCUSER	ENJAMBER	TROPIQUE
Level 17	ENRICHIR	MORPHE	VOTATION

Mega Man Battle Network 6 Cybeast Falzar

Compress Navi Customizer Programs

To compress program pieces in the navi customizer, open up the navi customizer screen, and highlight the piece you wish to shrink. Hold Right on the D-pad and press the corresponding set of buttons to shrink the piece. To decompress the piece, repeat the process.

Code	Effect
ARBABRRBAL	AirShoes
LBRBABLBAL	AttackMAX
BRBBBBBARR	BatteryMode
LRBBALRABA	BeatSupport
RLABLRLAAB	BodyPack
BAABBBALBA	BoosterPack
AAABRLBAAL	BugStopper
LLALLBABBB	ChargeMAX
ALABBAAABA	Collector's Eye
LBBRBAALRR	Custom1
RALLAABRBA	Custom2
BBARABLARR	First Barrier
RALABLBBRB	Float Shoes
ABLRRBRLBA	FolderBack1

Mega Man Battle Network 6 Cybeast Falzar (continued)

Code	Effect
BBARBLARBL	FolderBack2
BLBRLLLABA	GigaFolder1
LLABLBABLL	HumorSense
ARAABARRBA	I'm Fish
ALARBRARLB	JungleLand
BLALBRALBA	KawarimiMagic (AntiDmg)
ARLALALLAB	MegaFolder1
LALRBLRLRA	MegaFolder2
RBARALBBBL	Millionaire
AAALAABLRA	NumberOpening
LRABARBBLR	OilBody
AALABRALBA	RapidMAX
BABARRLLAB	RathmicalPoem
LAABRRLRLR	Reflect
RLBAABALLR	RushSupport
RRABLRARLA	Search Shuffle
BBBAABAABB	SelfRecovery
RBBBAAABRL	Shield
BBBABBAARB	ShinobiDash
ALAAALLABR	SlipRunner
ABLLAALRBA	SuperArmor
BRBRRABBRA	TangoSupport
RRALLRAABB	UnderShirt

Lottery Chip Machine Codes

Once you can enter the chip shop in Central Town, go inside to find a green machine on the right side. Press A in front of the machine, and enter the following numbers to receive bonus items.

Password	Effect
71757977	AirWheel3 O
51702791	AquaMan *
69544569	BambooLance *
24616497	BlastMan *
97049899	BlizzardBall H
28271002	Body Pack (Pink NCP)
19790420	Buster Pack (Red NCP)
92070765	ChargeMan *
51378085	CircleGun V
44892547	ColonelArmy *
23722234	CountBomb3 M
38116449	DeathMatch *
32310827	DiveMan *
60884138	DrillArm M
79814666	DustMan *
30424514	ElecMan *
08789369	ElementWrap *

DS

GBA

PSP

PS2

PS3

Wii

Xbox

Xbox 360

Index

DS

GBA

PSP

PS2

PS3

Wii

Xbox

Xbox 360

Index

Mega Man Battle Network 6 Cybeast Falzar (continued)

Password	Effect
45566783	Full Energy SubChip
39345472	Full Energy SubChip
87341489	Get "Full Energy"
04789479	Get "Unlocker"
54654618	Get NCP "HP+300"
10414878	GroundMan *
14212857	GunDelSol3 W
12404002	HeatMan *
49951337	HP+100 (White NCP)
08749780	HP+400 (Green NCP)
55031325	HP+500 (White NCP)
84387543	KillerMan *
68008194	Lock Enemy SubChip
37495453	Lock Enemy SubChip
16336487	Lock Enemy SubChip
98766899	Lock Enemy SubChip
88674125	MegaBoomerang M
70741543	Program for Beat
32132348	Program for Rush
12046210	Rapid MAX (Green NCP)
59485971	Receive an Untrap SubChip
94305487	Receive ChargeMAX Navi Cust program
24823665	Receive HP+200 Navi Cust program
37889678	Receive HP+50 Navi Cust program
09256524	Receive SpinGreen
77837421	Receive SpinRed
41976910	Receive SpinYellow
75641392	Recovery300 Y
15511679	Shinobi Dash SubChip
74198795	Shinobi Dash SubChip
79459146	Shinobi Dash SubChip
55910601	SlashMan *
69548756	Tango Support (Green NCP)
00297421	TenguMan *
67520179	TomahawkMan *
97403000	Uninstall G
04789479	Unlocker SubChip
41161139	Unlocker SubChip
82564319	Unlocker SubChip
99910954	Unlocker SubChip
09000465	Untrap SubChip
22812406	Untrap SubChip

Mega Man Battle Network 6 Cybeast Falzar (continued)

Giga Chips

Unlockable	How to Unlock
BassAnly/ForteAnother F	Defeat Bass/Forte SP in Graveyard Area
BugThunder V	Buy it from a Bugfrag Dealer in Sky Area1 for 100 Bugfrags
CrossDiv D	Buy it from a Punk navi in Graveyard Area for 30,000 Zenny
HubBatch/SaitoBatch J	Defeat Bass/Forte BX in Underground2
MetrKnuk N	Receive from E-Mail when you first enter Graveyard Area

Items from Net Cafe Owners

In each of the Net areas (excluding the ACDC and Green Areas), there is a Net Cafe where you can buy coffee for 10z a cup. Each time you buy a cup, the owners give you a small piece of information. After you buy enough coffee, they recognize you as a regular customer and give you an item.

Unlockable	How to Unlock
AntiSwrd *	GreenArea2 Net Cafe
BugStop (Yellow NCP)	CentralArea1 Net Cafe
HP Memory	SkyArea1 Net Cafe

Secret Bosses

There are secret bosses in the game that require having a certain amount of chips or having a certain Title Screen Icon.

Unlockable	How to Unlock
Bass/Forte BX	Obtain the Bass/Forte Icon
Bass/Forte SP	Collect all 200 Standard Chips
Falzar Beast Megaman/Rockman SP	Obtain the Bass/Forte Icon
Falzar SP	Collect all Title Screen Icons
Protoman/Blues FZ	Complete all 35 Requests on the Request BBS

Title Screen Icons

Unlockable	How to Unlock
"GIGA COMP" Icon	Collect all 5 Giga Chips
"MEGA COMP" Icon	Collect all 39 (45 in JP Version) Mega Chips
"P.A. COMP" Icon	Activate all 30 Program Advances
"STD COMP" Icon	Collect all 200 Standard Chips
Beast Link Gate Icon (JP Only)	Defeat Forte SP at Graveyard Area 2 with all 5 Falzar Link Navis installed through their respective Navi Data Chips through a Beast Link Gate device
Blues [Protoman] Icon	Using the 10 Event Cards off Modification Card Part 2 e+ Cards that unlock the 10 Extra Missions, complete them and then defeat Blues [Protoman] FZ
Faltzer Icon	Beat the game
Forte [Bass] Icon	Defeat Forte [Bass] SP
Starred "S" Icon	Collect all 17 Secret Chips

DS
GBA
PSP
PS2
PS3
Wii
Xbox
Xbox 360
Index

DS

GBA

PSP

PS2

PS3

Wii

Xbox

Xbox 360

Index

Monster House

Unlockables

Unlockable	How to Unlock
Doom Bringer 3000	Beat Skull's high score of 50,000 in the Thou Art Dead arcade game
Hard Mode	Beat the game once
Ruby Key	Beat the game once

Mortal Kombat: Tournament Edition

Description	Objective
Bo' Rai Cho Fatality	Beat Tag Team Mode with every character (except Noob Saibot & Sektor).
Cyrax Fatality	Defeat ten opponents in Survival Mode with Cyrax.
Drahmin	Beat 1P Tag Team mode on Normal+ difficulty with any team.
Drahmin Fatality	Purchase in the Krypt.
Hsu Hao	Beat 1P Arcade Mode on Normal+ difficulty.
Hsu Hao Fatality	Purchase in the Krypt.
Johnny Cage Fatality	Purchase in the Krypt.
Mavado Fatality	Purchase in the Krypt.
Nitara Fatality	Purchase in the Krypt.
Noob Saibot	Beat both 1P Arcade and Tag Team modes with every other character (except Sektor). Then beat 1P Arcade mode on Hard difficulty with Scorpion with his "Reaper Scorpion".
Noob Saibot Fatality	Beat Tag Team mode with a team of Noob Saibot and Scorpion.
Quan Chi Fatality	Beat Tag Team mode with a team of Quan Chi and Sareena.
Raiden Fatality	Defeat ten opponents in Survival Mode with Raiden.
Reptile	Beat 1P Arcade Mode with every character (except for Sektor and Noob Saibot) on Normal+ difficulty.
Reptile Fatality	Purchase in the Krypt.
Sareena Fatality	Purchase in the Krypt.
Scorpion Fatality	Defeat ten opponents in Survival Mode with Scorpion.
Sektor	Link to MK:DA.
Sektor Fatality	Beat Tag Team mode with a team of Sektor and Cyrax.
Shang Tsung Fatality	Beat Tag Team mode with a team of Shang Tsung and Quan Chi.

Nancy Drew: Haunted Mansion

Level	Password
Briefcase	Sheep, Tiger, Horse, Ox
Chinese Room	Ox, Horse, Tiger, Sheep
Chinese Room 2	Rooster, Boar, Rabbit, Dragon
Entry Door	Dragon, Rabbit, Boar, Rooster
Hallway Door	Snake, Monkey, Dog, Rat
Peep Hole	Rat, Dog, Monkey, Snake

Open Season

Codes

At any time during the game, press Start to pause and then hold Ⓛ. The words "Cheat Mode" appear on the screen. Continue to hold Ⓛ and enter any of these passwords for the desired effect. You can use only three cheat codes per save file and you must be on a level to skip it. The words "Cheat Mode" flash green if the code was entered correctly.

Unlockable	How to Unlock
30 Woo-Hoo Bars	↑, →, ↓, ←, ↑, (SELECT), ◎
Skip "Beaver Land"	◎, (SELECT), Ⓑ, ↓, →
Skip "Duck Land"	◎, (SELECT), Ⓑ, ↓, ←
Skip "Rabbit Land"	◎, (SELECT), Ⓑ, ↓, ↑
Skip "Skunk Land"	◎, (SELECT), Ⓑ, ↓, ↓
Skip "Squirrel Land"	◎, (SELECT), Ⓑ, ↓, Ⓑ
Three Extra Lives	↑, ↑, ↓, ↓, ←, →, ←, →, Ⓑ, ↓, ◎
Change Boog into a Polar Bear	At any time in a level, bring up the Pause screen, hold Ⓛ, and press ↓, ↑, ↓, Ⓑ, ↓

Over the Hedge: Hammy Goes Nuts

Unlockables

Unlockable	How to Unlock
Challenge Mode	Beat the Story mode
Penny	Beat level "Try, Try Again" of the Story mode, and then buy her for 140 nuts
Stella	Beat level "Depelter Turbo" of the Story mode, and then buy her for 70 nuts
Backyard Cup	Beat "FANtastic" in the Story mode and then buy for 210 nuts
Sound Test	Beat the "Ozzie's Trek" level of the Story mode

Pac-Man Collection

Here are the passwords for the last five levels of Pac Attack.

Unlockable	Code	Unlockable	Code
Level 96	YLW	Level 99	CHB
Level 97	PNN	Level 100	LST
Level 98	SPR		

Pirates of the Caribbean: The Curse of the Black Pearl

From the Main menu, choose Continue Game and enter any of the following passwords.

Unlockable	Code
Enemies Are More Aggressive/Harder	G3N1VS
Game Credits	CR3D1TS
Infinite Lives	1MM0RT4L
Picture of a Baby	L1TTLVN
Start With Triple Cannons, Sabre and Pistol	G00D13S
Soldiers and Pirates Become Sheep	SH33P
Unlimited Cannonballs and Bullets	BVLL1TZ

DS

GBA

PSP

PS2

PS3

Wii

Xbox

Xbox 360

Index

DS

GBA

PSP

PS2

PS3

Wii

Xbox

Xbox 360

Index

Polarium Advance

Unlockables

Unlockable	How to Unlock
3 Special Puzzles	Complete all puzzles in Polarium Reference

Extra Tile and Cursor Sets

Complete Daily Polarium for at least two "full" months. (Your first month does not count unless you start on the first day of any month.) You unlock either a tile or cursor set on the first day of the following month, depending on the month (see below). The last set is unlocked when you finish a year in *Daily Polarium*. Note that you don't need to complete the secondary objectives to unlock these. Once unlocked, you can choose these in the Option menu.

Unlockable	How to Unlock
Cursor Set	On 1st of March, July, and November
Tile Set	On 1st of January, May, and September
Tile Set #5	Beat 75 puzzles
Tile Set #6	Beat 195 puzzles

Unlockables

Unlockable	How to Unlock
Sudden Death Mode	Beat the first rank time in both Easy and Hard mode
Unlock Extra Tile Set	Insert your copy of *Polarium Advance* into the DS GBA Slot when playing *Actionloop (Magnetica)*

Princess Natasha: Student Secret Agent

Passwords

Password	Effect
OLEGSGIZMO	All Gadgets
SMASHROBOT	Extra Levels
CRUSHLUBEK	Infinite Lives

R-Type III

Enter these codes at the Password menu.

Unlockable	Code
Level 2	5bdgb
Level 3	5hhlq
Level 4	5mglt
Level 5	5rflx
Level 6	5wdl0

Rampage Puzzle Attack

Enter this password in the Password menu.

Unlockable	Password
All levels beaten	GQJTMHKBHF

Ratatouille

Passwords

Password	Effect
X4V!3RJ	Invincibility
3R1CQRR	Unlock all bonus pictures
H3L!X3!	Unlock all levels (Press Ⓛ or Ⓡ at chapter select screen)
JV4ND1Z	Unlock all minigames

Rayman 3: Hoodlum Havoc

Unlockable	Objective
Unlock Bonus Levels with Link to Nintendo GameCube	Once you have collected at least 100 orbs, link your GBA to your GCN to purchase bonus levels.

Ready 2 Rumble Boxing: Round 2

Enter the following codes at the Main menu.

Unlockable	Code
Michael Jackson	Highlight the Arcade option, then press ←, ←, →, →, ←, ←, Ⓛ+Ⓡ. You'll hear a cheering noise if you entered the code correctly.
Shaquille O'Neal	Highlight the Survival option, then press ←, ←, ←, →, →, →, ←, ←, →, Ⓛ+Ⓡ.

Ripping Friends

Enter this code in the Password screen.

Unlockable	Code
Level Select	→, Ⓛ, ↑, ↓, Ⓑ, ←, ←, →, ←

River City Ransom EX

Enter the following case sensitive codes in the Name Change screen under the Status menu.

Unlockable	Name
$999,999	PLAYA
Custom Char	XTRA0
Custom Move	XTRA2
Custom Self	XTRA1
Delete Saved Games	ERAZE
Maximum Stats	DAMAX

Robotech: The Macross Saga

Enter these codes in the Title screen. There will be a chicken clucking if the code is entered correctly.

Unlockable	Code
All Characters	↓, ↓, ↓, ↓, ↓, Ⓡ, Ⓡ
Level Select	↑, ↓, ↑, ↓, Ⓛ, Ⓡ, Ⓛ, Ⓡ
Max Upgrades	↑, →, ↓, ←, Ⓡ, Ⓛ, Ⓛ, Ⓛ
Unlimited Lives	→, →, →, ↑, ↑, Ⓛ, Ⓛ

DS

GBA

PSP

PS2

PS3

Wii

Xbox

Xbox 360

Index

DS

GBA

PSP

PS2

PS3

Wii

Xbox

Xbox 360

Index

Rock 'Em Sock 'Em Robots

Passwords

Password	Effect
3CTNKS	Game Finished
LSTL2B	Unlock Black Bruiser
B5T32J	Unlock Blue Bomber
J[]T7KH	Unlock Brown Bully
NMTZKQ	Unlock Green Grappler
2XT9KN	Unlock Orange Oppressor
6QT1KK	Unlock Pink Pummeller
02TX2T	Unlock Purple Pyro
GZTV2K	Unlock Silver Stretcher
W8T52Q	Unlock Yellow Yahoo

Scooby-Doo!

Enter the following codes as passwords.

Unlockable	Code
Coliseum Level	MXP#2VBL
Ocean Chase Level	CHBB5VBX
Prehistoric Jungle Level	5S@C7VB8

Scooby-Doo and the Cyber Chase

Enter these codes in the passwords menu.

Unlockable	Code (Level Passwords)
Coliseum	LCW72VBL
Ocean Chase	2XF74WS9
Prehistoric Jungle	BTV@S7F#
Snow Chase	V3Z9R7T3
Boardwalk	X@X#V7FF

Scooby-Doo 2: Monsters Unleashed

Unlockable	Code
Final Level: Scooby vs. Masked Guy	5DBY3MT8

Scourge: Hive

Unlockables

Unlockable	How to Unlock
Boss Rush	Complete the game on Hard difficulty
Costume	Complete game on Normal difficulty
Hard Difficulty	Complete the game on Normal difficulty
Insane Difficulty	Complete the game on Hard difficulty
Ultra Mode	Complete the game on Insane difficulty

Serious Sam Advance

Level	Easy Mode Password	Normal Mode Password	Hard Mode Password
Amon Thule	HEXMODE	OPEE	WOLF
Baths of Diocletian	NEED	OWL	LIMO
Caesar's Palace	WAFTY	MOOPAY	MOCKNEY
Gladiator School	COINAGE	FRYUP	MADEUP
Praetorian Fort	NORTHERN	FILLY	MIRROR
Pyramid Entrance	BADDUN	BETTERER	CHIPPER
Slave Compound	BOBBINS	PILCH	FORREST
Slave Quarters	TOAST	BEVIL	BEAK
The Forum of Mars	GAMES	DUCKAROO	FOZZER
Temple of Herkat Lower	MNIP	KIPPAGE	TITHES
Tomb of Ramses	MEGAMUNT	HORSE	EYE

The Simpsons: Road Rage

Unlockable	Code
All Cars, Levels and Bonuses	Maggie, Willy, Bart, Chief Wiggum, Apu, Moe, Krusty, Barney
All Characters	Bart, Bart, Lisa, Lisa, Marge, Marge, Barney, Barney

Shining Soul II

Enter these codes as a name.

Unlockable	Code
Atlus Ring	Vjum
Resist Fire +30 bonus	Iyoku
Resist Poison +30 bonus	Hachi
Resist Ice +30 bonus	Mizupin
Resist Dark +30 bonus	Montaka
Dream Hat	Nindri
Vitality +5 bonus	Taicho

Sonic Advance

Description	Objective
Hidden Sound Test Mode Songs	To get more than the 39 default songs in Sound Test mode, complete The Moon Zone, Extra mode, or unlock the Super Sonic Ending. Three additional songs will be available.
Moon Zone	Collect all seven Emeralds for all characters. Complete the game as Sonic to unlock the Moon Zone.
Tails as Partner (Tails will follow you during the game, but can't be controlled.)	Highlight Sonic at the character selection screen and press ↑. Next, highlight Tails and press ↓. Then, highlight Knuckles and press Ⓛ. Finally, highlight Amy and press Ⓡ. Now you can highlight Sonic and press Ⓐ to select him.

DS

GBA

PSP

PS2

PS3

Wii

Xbox

Xbox 360

Index

DS

GBA

PSP

PS2

PS3

Wii

Xbox

Xbox 360

Index

Sonic Adventure 2

Unlockable	Objective
Amy	Beat the game and get all seven Chaos Emeralds with Cream, Knuckles, Sonic, and Tails.
Bonus Level	Beat the game and collect all of the Chaos Emeralds with Amy, Cream, Sonic, Tails and Knuckles.
Boss Option in Time Attack	Beat the game and collect all Chaos Emeralds with three characters.
Cream	Finish the Leaf Forest level as Sonic.
Knuckles	Finish the Sky Canyon level as Sonic.
Sound Test	Beat the game and collect all Chaos Emeralds with two characters.
Tails	Finish the Music Plant level as Sonic.
Tiny Chao Garden	Beat the game and collect all Chaos Emeralds.

Spider-Man

Description	Objective
Ending Bonus	Complete the game to unlock the level select option at the Main menu. Press START during gameplay to choose a new level.
Movie Clips	Take pictures on every level to unlock all movie clips.
Unlock Cheat Mode	Complete the game, collecting all of the small red spiders and taking the pictures on each stage to unlock the cheats (armor upgrade, strength enhancement, and level cheat) in the Secrets menu.

Sports Illustrated for Kids Baseball

Select Season mode, pick a team and in Team Management choose Cheat Code. Enter the following codes to unlock the specified players.

Player	Code
Eddie Penn (2B)	SIKSTAR
George Stocks (P)	TARGETPLYR
Keith Fisher (3B)	GAMESTOP
Mark Modesto (RF)	GOCIRCUIT
Michael Quince (1B)	BESTBUYSTR
Nateo Geooni (CF)	EBRULES
Riley Waters (SS)	BAMSTAR
Tecumseh Brown (LF)	SIKPOWER

Sports Illustrated for Kids Football

Select Season mode, pick a team and choose Cheat Code. Enter the following codes to unlock the specified player.

Player	Code
Eddie Brown (LRB/ROLB)	ERPI AYFR
Hal Church (LG/LOLB)	RZONESTAR
Mac Marshall (RRB/FS)	BAMPLYR
Mark Haruf (QB/SS)	CIRCUITFUN
Rob Lewis (LRB/ROLB)	SIKPOWER
Ryan Hunter (RRB/SS)	TARGETSTAR

Sports Illustrated for Kids Football (continued)

Player	Code
Sammy Rivera (LE/RILB)	TOUCHDOWN
Sandy Sanders (RE/LOLB)	SIKSTAR
Wayne Selby (C/RT)	BESTBUYPWR

Spy Hunter

Description	Code
Arcade Mode	Enter EDACRA as a name.
Super Agent Mode	Complete the game with all Primary Objectives and Secondary Objectives.

Spyro Orange: The Cortex Conspiracy

At the Game Mode menu, press the Ⓛ + Ⓡ buttons together to activate the code entry screen, then enter the following codes.

Unlockable	Code
100 Gems	V1S10NS
200 Gems	T4P10C4
Enemies are sheep	SH33P
Gray Game	G3MZ
Hidden Card	V4N1LL4
Hidden Card	S0YB34N
Orange Game	SP4RX
Orange Spyro	SPYR0
Purple Game	P0RT4L
Spyro's flame is replaced with sheep	B41S0KV

TIP

Crash Party USA Mini-Game

Hold Ⓛ + Ⓡ while powering up the Game Boy Advance.

Spyro: Season Of Ice

Enter the following codes at the Title screen when "Press Start" appears.

Description	Code
99 Lives	←,→,→,→,↓,↑,→,↑,Ⓐ
Unlimited Health in Sparx Worlds	↓,↑,↑,↓,←,→,→,←,Ⓐ
Unlimited Weapons in Sparx Worlds	↓,→,↑,←,←,↑,→,↓,Ⓐ
Unlock All Levels	↓,↓,↑,↑,←,→,↑,↓,Ⓐ
Warp	←,→,→,←,↑,←,←,→,Ⓐ
Warp Unlock All Levels	↓,↑,↓,←,→,↑,←,↑,Ⓐ

For extra Sparkx weapons, press →,↑,→,←,↓,↑,←,↓,Ⓐ at the Title screen. Then, use one of the following commands during gameplay in Sparx worlds.

Unlockable Weapons	Code
Homing Bombs	↓+SELECT
Invincibility Shield	↑+SELECT
Rapid Fire	←+SELECT
Smart Bomb	→+SELECT

DS

GBA

PSP

PS2

PS3

Wii

Xbox

Xbox 360

Index

Star Wars: Flight of the Falcon

Unlockable	Code
All Levels and Bonus Game	4?6C
Bonus Level	RRV2
Episode IV	TGHK
Episode V	8TV2
Episode VI	TSB2

Street Fighter Alpha 3

Unlockable	Code
Play as Shin Akuma	Hold (START) when selecting Akuma
Fight Shin Akuma in Final Battle mode	Hold (A) + (B) when selecting a speed

Stuart Little 2

Level	Code	Level	Code
Level 1	1377	Level 7	5688
Level 2	1487	Level 8	6678
Level 3	2278	Level 9	6588
Level 4	6366	Level 10	6216
Level 5	6787	Level 11	7614
Level 6	5778	Level 12	7421

Super Dodgeball Advance

Unlockable	Objective
Dream Team A: the Shooters	Win Special Championship for the second time.
Dream Team B: the Rockets	Win Championship mode once.
Dream Team C: Iron Men	Win Special Championship mode once.
Special Championship	Beat the Rocket team in the finals of Championship mode.

TIP

Rank Climbing Tip

To climb the ranks quickly during Championship mode, always challenge the top team. If you win, you'll move halfway up the list each time. In four matches, you could be playing for Number One!

Super Monkey Ball Jr.

Enter these codes at the Title screen.

Unlockable	Code
Enable All	↓, ↓, ↑, ↑, ←, →, ←, →, (B), (A)
Super Blocky Mode	←, ←, →, →, ↓, ↓, (A)
Super Nice Try Mode	↑, ↑, ↓, ↓, ←, →, ←, →, (B), (A)

Super Puzzle Fighter II Turbo

Secret Character	Code
Play as Akuma	Highlight Morrigan, hold (SELECT), and press ↓,↓,↓,←,←,←,(A).
Play as Anita	Highlight Morrigan, press (SELECT), and move the pointer to highlight Donovan and press (A).
Play as Dan	Highlight Morrigan, hold (SELECT), and press ←,←,←,↓,↓,↓,(A).
Play as Hsien-Ko paper Talisman	Highlight Morrigan, press (SELECT), move the pointer to highlight Hsien-Ko, and press (A).
Select Devilot	Highlight Morrigan, hold (SELECT), and press ←,←,←,↓,↓,↓,(A) as the timer hits 10.

Super Robot Taisen: Original Generation

Unlockables

Unlockable	How to Unlock
Gespenst Mk-II S	Destroy the R-GUN on stage 30 on Ryusei's path
Gespenst-R	On the Kyosuke Route, make sure Guilliam is at least level 23 by stage 19
Graviton Launcher	Make sure your opposite main character (Ryusei or Kyosuke) has at least at least 55 kills by stage 32
Grungust	Destroy the R-GUN on stage 30 on Kyosuke's path without getting the Huckebein 008L
Guarlion	Destroy it with either Task or Rai on stage 24
Hero Symbol	Daitetsu (Ryusei Route) or Lefina (Kyosuke Route) must be at least level 35 by stage 35
Huckebein 008L	Have Ingram be at level 32 before stage 30 (Ryusei Route) or Villeta at level 23 by stage 19 on the Kyosuke Route
Kai	Take the Kyosuke Route
Keep the Ability to Combine into SRX	Take the Ryusei Route
Lion-F	Take the Ryusei path
R-GUN	Destroy it on stage 30
Shishio Blade	On Hard difficulty, make sure your main character has at least 50 kills by stage 26 and destroy Zengar on stage 26
Soul of Metal	Daitetsu (Kyosuke Route) or Lefina (Ryusei Route) must be at least level 38 by level 38
Valcion Kai	On stage 28, reduce the HP of the Valcion Kai below 10% without destroying it

Super Robot Taisen: Original Generation 2

Unlockables

Unlockable	How to Unlock
Huckebein Mk.III R	Make sure Retzal has at least 35 kills by the end of stage 18. Make sure Leona, Bullet, Rio, Ryoto, Task, and Kushua have a combined total of at least 185 levels by the end of stage 33. Get the skill point on stage 30.

Lamia's Secret Robots

For both of these, make sure Lamia moves onto the square Echidna retreated on during stage 10/13 (depending on which path you took) and that she has a total of 55 kills before the end of stage 24. She will join you with one of them on stage 28.

Unlockable	How to Unlock
Ash Saver	Make sure Lamia has 2 (and only 2) battle encounters with Axel on stage 19
Vysaga	Playing on a New Game+ and make sure Lamia has only 1 battle encounter with Axel on stage 19
Boost Hammer	Let Arado kill all the initially placed enemies in Chapter 16 within 4 turns, and it'll be available after the chapter
Ex Hard Mode	Finish the Story mode

DS

GBA

PSP

PS2

PS3

Wii

Xbox

Xbox 360

Index

DS

GBA

PSP

PS2

PS3

Wii

Xbox

Xbox 360

Index

Super Robot Taisen: Original Generation 2 (continued)

Unlockable	How to Unlock
G Impact Stick and New Chaguramu Shooter	Don't use Daigenguard to kill any enemy in chapter 30 (but Gungrest Type 3 can)
Gespenst Mk.II S	Make sure Kai has at least 55 kills and is level 33 before the end of stage 33
Gravition Launcher	Let Viletta kill all the enemies in chapter 6 except Seolla, Yuuki, and Carla. It'll appear on Viletta's MkII-R in Chapter 15
Keeping the Wild Wuerger L	On stage 27, make sure Mai gets at least 5 kills with the Wild Wuerger L
Second Soul of Steel and Second Mark of Brave	Before the end of chapter 33, both captain's levels are over 33
Shishioh Blade	Bullet's kill count is more than 45 before the end of chapter 14 and it's available before the beginning of chapter 17
Soul of Steel, Mark of Brave, High-tech AI, Second Shishioh Blade, Second G Impact	Defeat all 3 bosses in chapter 15, making sure to defeat Graterkin (upper position) last
Sound Test	After beating the game once, highlight "change BGM" while in the Battle menu, and ↓, ↑, ←, →, ←, →
Special Mode	Beat EX Hard mode once
Special Stage Scenario	Earn at least 35 or more skill points before the end of Scenario 42 to access the final stage
Stealth Wing 1	Stay in Easy mode by getting very few skill points and when you get to Scenario 16, Gilliam's Gespent will have it equipped
Stealth Wing 2	Kill Carla in any of the first stages and when she joins you she'll have it equipped on the Randgrith
Wild Wuerger L	On stage 19, make sure Arad destroys at least 4 Gespents before moving him next to Zeora and make sure he has at least 55 kills before stage 24

Teenage Mutant Ninja Turtles 2: Battle Nexus

Unlockable	Battle Mode Passwords	Race Mode Passwords
Course 16	DDRSMSR	RDLDSMD
Course 17	SMRDLML	MDSMSDM
Course 18	LMSLSRS	SRMLDDR

At the Title screen, press ↑, ↑, ↓, ↓, ←, →, ←, →, Ⓑ, Ⓐ. This displays "COWABUNGA" when players clear the Story mode.

Tekken

Unlockable	Code
Alternate Costumes	Press Ⓛ, Ⓡ, or (START) at the character selection screen.
Fight as Heihachi	Complete the game with all nine characters. Heihachi will appear next to Hworang and Paul at the character selection screen.
Team Battle Modes	Complete Arcade mode as Heihachi to unlock the Versus Team Battle options.

Thunderbirds

Enter these codes at the Password screen.

Unlockable	Code	Unlockable	Code
Level 2	BCD	Level 4	H3D
Level 3	THM		

Tom and Jerry Tales

Passwords

Password	Effect
6 P L 4 G	BACK YARD—PASSAGE TO DINING ROOM
6 8 L Q T	BACK YARD—SAVE AT LVL 1
R N F F 7	BACK YARD—SAVE AT LVL 2
G L 4 6 R	BACK YARD—SAVE AT LVL 3
T R 9 N Z	BACK YARD—SAVE AT LVL 4
J G W S D	BEDROOM—PASSAGE TO BACK YARD
K 7 Z C L	BEDROOM—SAVE AT LVL1
B N Y 4 3	BEDROOM—SAVE AT LVL2
P H 4 5 N	BEDROOM—SAVE AT LVL3
8 L V 3 H	BEDROOM—SAVE AT LVL4
S F 2 K 8	DINING ROOM—SAVE AT LVL 1
8 T K Y T	DINING ROOM—SAVE AT LVL 2
X L X G L	DINING ROOM—SAVE AT LVL 3
M 9 M Y F	GAME ROOM—PASSAGE TO BEDROOM
3 F 2 B H	GAME ROOM—SAVE AT LVL1
F 8 5 T F	GAME ROOM—SAVE AT LVL2
B B R 5 R	GAME ROOM—SAVE AT LVL3
H L 8 B R	GAME ROOM—SAVE AT LVL4
P L Z 9 8	KITCHEN—PASSAGE TO LIVING ROOM
X H 2 J 6	KITCHEN—SAVE AT LVL1
C L 2 W R	KITCHEN—SAVE AT LVL2
M F 9 T H	KITCHEN—SAVE AT LVL3
X H U B F	KITCHEN—SAVE AT LVL4
Q X H 6 7	LIVING ROOM—PASSAGE TO GAME ROOM
X L X S L	LIVING ROOM—SAVE AT LVL1
M P S 9 9	LIVING ROOM—SAVE AT LVL2
C R 5 4 D	LIVING ROOM—SAVE AT LVL3
Q Z 6 5 W	LIVING ROOM—SAVE AT LVL4

Tom Clancy's Splinter Cell

Unlockable	Objective
Extra Missions	Link to the Nintendo GameCube version of Splinter Cell to download extra missions.
Unlock Another Bonus Mission	Find all the safes in missions one through nine.
Unlock Bonus Mission	Beat levels one to five with a completion rate of 60% or higher.

DS

GBA

PSP

PS2

PS3

Wii

Xbox

Xbox 360

Index

DS

GBA

PSP

PS2

PS3

Wii

Xbox

Xbox 360

Index

Tomb Raider: Legend

Bulletproof Lara and Infinite Ammo

At any time during gameplay, hold Ⓛ and input the codes below.

Unlockable	How to Unlock
Bulletproof Lara	Ⓑ,Ⓡ,Ⓑ,↓,↓,↓
Infinite Ammo	↓,Ⓑ,↓,Ⓡ,↑,←

Tony Hawk's Downhill Jam

Boards

Unlockable	How to Unlock
Asma's Long Board	Finish in first place in the Championship in Steps of Morocco
Brogan's Short Board	Finish in first place in the Championship in Castle of Edinburgh
Corrina's Short Board	Finish in first place in the Championship in Tour of Rome
Hugh's Mountain Board	Finish in first place in the Championship in Vail Mountain
Janica's Long Board	Finish in first place in the Championship in Rio de Janeiro
Joe's Short Board	Finish in first place in the Championship in San Francisco
Lian Zi's Long Board	Finish in first place in the Championship in Lights of Hong Kong
Marie's Short Board	Finish in first place in the Championship in Montmartre
Mirim's Mountain Board	Finish in first place in the Championship in Ruins of Machu Picchu
Tony Hawk's Final Board	Finish in first place in the Championship in Hawaii
Tony Hawk's Short Board	Complete the last Training Course within the time limit

Appearance

Unlockable	How to Unlock
Baggy Green	Beat the second challenge in San Francisco
Jeans Baggy 1	Beat the third challenge in Tour of Rome
Jeans Baggy 2	Beat the second challenge in Steps of Morocco
Jeans Tight	Beat the second challenge in Castle of Edinburgh
Leather	Beat the second challenge in Vail Mountain
Long Black	Beat the third challenge in Castle of Edinburgh
Long Blonde	Beat the second challenge in Rio de Janeiro
Long Brown	Beat the second challenge in Tour of Rome
Longsleeved 2	Beat the third challenge in San Francisco
Longsleeved 3	Beat the first challenge in Tour of Rome
Sandals	Beat the third challenge in Vail Mountain
Short Brown 3	Beat the third challenge in Steps of Morocco
Short Brown 4	Beat the third challenge in Lights of Hong Kong
Shorts	Beat the third challenge in Rio de Janeiro
Shortsleeved 1	Beat the first challenge in Steps of Morocco
Shortsleeved 2	Beat the first challenge in Castle of Edinburgh
Shortsleeved 3	Beat the first challenge in Vail Mountain
Shortsleeved 4	Beat the first challenge in Rio de Janeiro
Sneakers Red	Beat the first challenge in San Francisco
Tanktop Red	Beat the first challenge in Lights of Hong Kong

Tony Hawk's Downhill Jam (continued)

White	Beat the second challenge in Lights of Hong Kong

Stages

Unlockable	How to Unlock
Castle of Edinburgh	Finish third or better in the Championship in San Francisco
Hawaii	Finish third or better in the Championship in all 9 other Championships
Lights of Hong Kong	Finish third or better in the Championship in Rio de Janeiro
Montmartre	Finish third or better in the Championship in Tour of Rome
Rio de Janeiro	Finish third or better in the Championship in Steps of Morocco
Ruins of Machu Picchu	Finish third or better in the Championship in Vail Mountain
Steps of Morocco	Finish third or better in the Championship in San Francisco
Tour of Rome	Finish third or better in the Championship in Castle of Edinburgh
Vail Mountain	Finish third or better in the Championship in Castle of Edinburgh

Tricks

Unlockable	How to Unlock
360 Flip Street	Beat the third Trick Course in Tour of Rome
360 Shove It	Beat the third Trick Course in San Francisco
Airwalk Special	Beat the third Trick Course in Steps of Morocco
Benihana	Beat the third Trick Course in Castle of Edinburgh
Double Hardflip Special	Beat the third Trick Course in San Francisco
Fingerlip	Beat the third Trick Course in Ruins of Machu Picchu
FS 360 Shove It	Beat the third Trick Course in Lights of Hong Kong
Japan Air	Beat the third Trick Course in Rio de Janeiro
Ollie Airwalk	Beat the third Trick Course in San Francisco
Pop Shove It BS	Beat the third Trick Course in Vail Mountain

Ultimate MUSCLE

Description	Objective
Sgt. Kinnikuman	Beat Survival mode on Hard difficulty.
Young Buffaloman	Beat Survival mode on Normal difficulty.
Young King Muscle	Beat Story mode once on Easy difficulty without losing.
Young Ramenman	Beat 3 on 3 mode on Normal difficulty.

Unfabulous

Change Addie's Outfit

Stand in front of Addie's wardrobe and press Ⓑ. A password entry screen appears, and you can change Addie's outfit by entering the following passwords.

Password	Effect
4B20C5	Outfit 1
N5J8HZ	Outfit 2
Z16DB5	Outfit 3
M519FH	Outfit 4

DS

GBA

PSP

PS2

PS3

Wii

Xbox

Xbox 360

Index

DS

GBA

PSP

PS2

PS3

Wii

Xbox

Xbox 360

Index

Level Passwords

Select continue from the main menu and enter these passwords to get to different stages.

Password	Effect
Ben, Geena, Addie, Brandywine	"Addie's Dream"
Geena, Zach, Zach, Brandywine	"Wild Style Performance"
Brandywine, Geena, Geena, Zach	Addie discovers the punch is spiked
Addie, Geena, Addie, Ben	Addie gets into a disagreement about the talent show
Ben, Addie, Zach, Brandywine	Addie plays with the Roundabouts
Brandywine, Geena, Addie, Ben	Addie prepares for a party
Brandywine, Zach, Brandywine, Geena	Addie receives the flyer for the talent show
Brandywine, Addie, Addie, Zach	Addie teams up with Cranberry and Maris
Zach, Brandywine, Addie, Addie	End of the game
Ben, Zach, Ben, Addie	Minigame
Geena, Ben, Addie, Ben	View the credits

Van Helsing

Enter these codes at the Password menu.

Unlockable	Code
Traveling by Train level	3X9 M12 111
Carriage Battle level	9C1 P!W LC1
KC1 Escape from Castle level	8P$ 7D8
On the Trail of the Werewolf level	65M 5HL 611
St. Peter's Basilica level	2S5 M12 111
Valken the Werewolf level	54! 5DV 411
Vaseria Village level	4H@ 5DH 311
Dracula's Children level	7BQ *24 8C1
Dracula's Castle level	BF1 8KF MC1
Dracula Final level	CG5 B78 *M1

Wild Thornberrys: The Movie

Enter the following as a password.

Unlockable	Code
Level Select	HB5F

Wing Commander: Prophecy

Enter the following codes at the Start screen.

Description	Code
Invincibility	↑,↓,Ⓐ,Ⓑ,←,→,Ⓛ,Ⓛ,Ⓡ,Ⓡ,Ⓑ,Ⓐ
Mission Select	↑,↑,Ⓛ,Ⓡ,↓,↓,Ⓐ,Ⓐ,Ⓑ,Ⓐ
View Alien Ships in Tactical Database	Ⓡ,Ⓛ,Ⓐ,Ⓐ,Ⓐ,Ⓑ,↑,←,↓,→,↑,Ⓐ

Wolfenstein 3D

For the following unlockables, press (START) to pause gameplay, hold
(L)+(R), then enter code.

Description	Code
Advance to Boss Level	Press (A),(B),(A),(A),(B),(B),(A),(A). The sound of a siren confirms correct code entry. When the game is resumed, you start at the current boss.
All Weapons, Keys, Ammo, and Health	Press (A),(B),(B),(A),(A),(A),(A),(A). A shout confirms correct code entry. All weapons and keys are unlocked and your health and ammunition are restored.
God Mode	Press (A),(A),(B),(A),(A),(A),(A),(A). A sound confirms correct code entry.
Skip Level	Press (A),(B),(A),(A),(B),(B),(B),(A). The sound of a door opening confirms correct code entry. When the game is resumed, you start on the next level.

TIP

If you use the Skip Level code on Level 1, you go to the secret floor!

X2: Wolverine's Revenge

Description	Code
Double jumps	Hold (L) at the slot Select screen and press (SELECT),←,↑,↓,↓,↑,↓.
Invincibility	Hold (L) at the slot Select screen and press ↓,↑,↓,↓,↑,↑,↓,(SELECT).
Regenerate with Claws Extended	Hold (L) at the slot Select screen and press →,↑,↓,→,→,←,(SELECT),(SELECT).

XXX

Description	Code
Completion Bonuses (Options for infinite health and ammunition are unlocked.)	After defeating Yorgi in Level 12, the credits appear. At the end of the credits, go to "Extras."

Yggdra Union

Completion Bonuses
These must be done before completing the game.

Unlockable	How to Unlock
Card Illustrations	Have the Revelations of Pantheon from level BF47
Character Illustrations	Have the Hand Mirror of Utsmi from level BF18
Item Picture Book	Have the Item Book from level BF39
Sound Mode	Have the Old Music Box from level BF28
Yggdra Game Records	Have the Lithography of Mesara from level BF44

Extra Contents—English Version

Unlockable	How to Unlock
Cards Section in Extra Contents	Steal the Rev. of the Gods item in BF47
Characters Section in Extra Contents	Pick up the Mirror of Truth item in BF18
Credits Section in Extra Contents	View any ending
Extra Contents Section	View any ending
Items Section in Extra Contents	Pick up the Item Manual item in BF39
Sound Section in Extra Contents	Pick up the Old Music Box item in BF28
War Chronicles Section in Extra Contents	Pick up the Mesala's Tablet item in BF44

DS

GBA

PSP

PS2

PS3

Wii

Xbox

Xbox 360

Index

Sidebar tabs: DS | GBA | PSP | PS2 | PS3 | Wii | Xbox | Xbox 360 | Index

Yu-Gi-Oh! The Duelist of the Roses

Unlockable	Code	Unlockable	Code
Ancient Tree of Enlightenment	EKJHQ109	Harpy's Feather Duster	8HJHQPNP
Aqua Dragon	JXCB6FU7	Horn of the Unicorn	S14FGKQ1
Barrel Dragon	GTJXSBJ7	Left Arm of the Forbidden One	A5CF6HSH
Beast King of the Swamp	QXNTQPAX	Magician of Faith	GME1S3UM
Birdface	N54T4TY5	Meteor Dragon	86985631
Blast Sphere	CZN5GD2X	Mimicat	69YDQM85
Change of Heart	SBYDQM8B	Mirror Wall	53297534
Crush Card	SRA7L5YR	Mystical Capture Chains	N1NDJMQ3
Dark Hole	UMJ10MQB	Robotic Knight	S5S7NKNH
Dragonseeker	81EZCH8B	Royal Decree	8TETQHE1
EarthShaker	Y34PN1SV	Seiyaryu	2H4D85J7
Elf's Light	E5G3NRAD	Serpentine Princess	UMQ3WZUZ
Exodia: The Forbidden One	37689434	Slate Warrior	73153736
Fairy King Truesdale	YF07QVEZ	Swordsman From A Foreign Land	CZ81UVGR
Fairy's Gift	NVE7A3EZ	SwordStalker	AH0PSHEB
Goblin Fan	92886423	Tactical Warrior	054TC727
Gravity Bind	0HNFG9WX		
Greenkappa	YBJMCD6Z		

Yu-Gi-Oh! Eternal Duelist Soul

Enter these passwords in the Password menu.

Enter the following passwords for Exodia Pieces

33396948	08124921
44519536	70903634
07902349	08058240

The following passwords are for cards.

Card	Password	Card	Password
Ancient Elf	93221206	Great White	13429800
Ansatsu	48365709	Magical Ghost	46474915
Beaver Warrior	32452818	Mammoth Graveyard	40374923
Blue Eyes White Dragon	89631139	Man-Eating Bug	54652250
Book of Secret Arts	91595718	Man-Eating Treasure Chest	13723605
Celtic Guardian	91152256	Monster Reborn	83764718
Change of Heart	04031928	Mystical Elf	15025844
Claw Reacher	41218256	Neo the Magic Swordsman	50930991
Curse of Dragon	28279543	Reinforcements	17814387
Dark Magician	46986414	Silver Fang	90357090
Doma the Angel of Silence	16972957	Summoned Skull	70781052
Dragon Zombie	66672569	The Stern Mystic	87557188
Feral Imp	41392891	Trap Hole	04206964
Fissure	66788016	Waboku	12607053
Gaia	06368038	Winged Dragon	87796900
Giant Soldier of Stone	13039848	Witty Phantom	36304921

Yu-Gi-Oh! The Falsebound Kingdom

Unlockable	Objective
Armored Zombie	Use Call of the Grave on Zanki.
B. Skull Dragon	Red-Eyes B. Dragon+Summoned Skull
Black Luster Soldier	Use Black Luster ritual on Gaia the Fierce Knight.
Blue-Eyes Ultimate Dragon	Three Blue Eyes
Chimera the Flying Mythical Beast	Berformat+Gazelle
Cosmo Queen	Dark Elf+Mystical Elf
Crimson Sunbird	Mavelus+Winged Eagle
Dragon Zombie	Use Call of the Grave on Crawling Dragon.
Gaia the Dragon Champion	Gaia the Fierce+Curse of Dragon
Gate Guardian	Kazejin+Suijin+Sanga
Magician of Black Chaos	Use Black Luster ritual on Dark Magician.
Metalzoa	Use Metal Morph on Zoa.
Meteor B. Dragon	Meteor Dragon+ Red Eyes Black Dragon
Rabid Horseman	Battleox+Mystic Horseman
Red Eyes Black Metal Dragon	Use Metal Morph on Red Eyes Black Dragon.
Thousand Dragon	Baby Dragon+Time Wizard
Twin Headed Thunder Dragon	Two Headed King Rex+Thunder Dragon
Valkyrion	Alpha+Beta+Gamma

TIP

To get some free money, enter this code while playing on a Black Piece of land: ↑,↑,↓,↓,←,→,←,→,Ⓑ,Ⓐ. The game will laugh and say "Yu, Yu". You will then be rewarded with 537 gold.

Yu-Gi-Oh! Reshef of Destruction

Enter the following codes as passwords.

Unlockable	Code	Unlockable	Code
7 Colored Fish	23771716	Amphibious Bugroth	40173854
Abyss Flower	40387124	Ancient Brain	42431843
Acid Crawler	77568553	Ancient Elf	93221206
Acid Trap Hole	41356845	Ancient Jar	81492226
Air Marmot Of Nefa	75889523	Ancient One of the Forest	14015067
Akakieisu	38035986		
Akihiron	36904469	Ancient Sorcerer	36821538
Alinsection	70924884	Ancient Tool	49587396
All-Seeing Goddess	53493204	Blue Eyes White Dragon	89631139
Alligator's Sword	64428736		
Alpha The Magnet Warrior	99785935	Dark Magician	46986414
		Dragon Zombie	66672569
Amazon Of The Seasons	17968114	Harpie Lady	76812113
Amazon Sword Women	94004268	Life Eater	52367652
Ameba	95174353	Lisark	55210709
Unlockable	Code	Mushroom Man	14181608

DS

GBA

PSP

PS2

PS3

Wii

Xbox

Xbox 360

Index

Yu-Gi-Oh! Reshef of Destruction (continued)

Unlockable	Code	Unlockable	Code
Mystical Elf	15025844	Puts Dark Magician Knight in Grandpa's Shop	50725996
Penguin Knight	36039163		
Summoned Skull	70781052	Puts Harpie's Feather Duster in the Shop	18144506
Sword Arm of Dragon	13069066		
Witty Phantom	36304921	Puts Knight's Title in Grandpa's Shop	87210505
Puts Beta The Magnet Warrior in the Shop	39256679		

Yu-Gi-Oh! World Championship

Unlockable	Code
Blue Millennium Booster	Beat Rare Hunter 10 times
Blue Premium Booster	Beat Yami Yugi 20 times
Blue/Green Millennium Booster	Beat String 10 times
Dark Ruler Hades Booster	Beat Bandit Keith 10 times
Gold Millennium Booster	Beat Odion 10 times
Green Premium Booster	Beat Simon 20 times
Guardian Sphinx Booster	Beat Pegasus 10 times
Jinzo Booster	Beat Weevil 10 times
Orange Premium Booster	Beat Yami Marik 20 times
Pink Premium Booster	Beat Yami Bakura 20 times
Purple Millennium Booster	Beat Umbra and Lumis 10 times
Purple Premium Booster	Beat the Duel Computer 20 times
Red Millennium Booster	Beat Arkana 10 times
Relinquished Booster	Beat Rex Raptor 10 times
The Masked Beast Booster	Beat Maku Tsunami 10 times
Thousand Eyes Restricted Booster	Beat Bonz 10 times
Toon Summoned Skull Booster	Beat Espa Roba 10 times
Yamata Dragon Booster	Beat Joey Wheeler 10 times
Zombrya the Dark Booster	Beat Mai Valentine 10 times

Yu-Gi-Oh! World Championship (Cards)

Enter these codes in the passwords menu.

Unlockable	Code	Unlockable	Code
30,000-Year White Turtle	11714098	Alligator's Sword Dragon	3366982
4-Starred Ladybug of Doom	83994646	Alpha the Magnet Warrior	99785935
7 Colored Fish	23771716	Amazon Archer	91869203
7 Completed	86198326	Amazon of the Seas	17968114
Abyss Flower	40387124	Ameba	95174353
Acid Crawler	77568553	Amphibian Beast	67371383
Acid Trap Hole	41356845	Amphibious Bugroth	40173854
Air Eater	8353769	Ancient Brain	42431843
Air Marmot of Nefariousness	75889523	Ancient Elf	93221206
Akakieisu	38035986	Ancient Jar	81492226
Akihiron	36904469	Ancient Lizard Warrior	43230671
Alinsection	70924884	Ancient One of the Deep Forest	14015067
Alligator's Sword	64428736	Ancient Sorcerer	36821538

Yu-Gi-Oh! World Championship (Cards) (continued)

Unlockable	Code	Unlockable	Code
Ancient Telescope	17092736	Beautiful Headhuntress	16899564
Ancient Tool	49587396	Beaver Warrior	32452818
Ancient Tree of Enlightenment	86421986	Behegon	94022093
Ansatsu	48365709	Bell of Destruction	83555666
Anthrosaurus	89904598	Berfomet	77207191
Anti Raigeki	42364257	Beta the Magnet Warrior	39256679
Anti-Magic Fragrance	58921041	Bickuribox	25655502
Appropriate	48539234	Big Eye	16768387
Aqua Chorus	95132338	Big Insect	53606874
Aqua Dragon	86164529	Big Shield Gardna	65240384
Aqua Madoor	85639257	Binding Chain	8058240
Aqua Snake	12436646	Bio-Mage	58696829
Aqua Spirit	40916023	Bio Plant	7670542
Arlownay	14708569	Bite Shoes	50122883
Arma Knight	36151751	Black Dragon Jungle King	89832901
Armaill	53153481	Black Illusion Ritual	41426869
Armed Ninja	9076207	Black Luster Ritual	N/A
Armored Glass	36868108	Black Luster Soldier	N/A
Armored Lizard	15480588	Black Pendant	65169794
Armored Rat	16246527	Blackland Fire Dragon	87564352
Armored Starfish	17535588	Bladefly	28470714
Armored Zombie	20277860	Blast Juggler	70138455
Attack and Receive	63689843	Blast Sphere	26302522
Axe of Despair	40619825	Blind Destruction	32015166
Axe Raider	48305365	Block Attack	25880422
Baby Dragon	88819587	Blocker	34743446
Backup Soldier	36280194	Blue-Eyed Silver Zombie	35282433
Banisher of the Light	61528025	Blue-Eyes Toon Dragon	53183600
Baron of the Fiend Sword	86325596	Blue-Eyes Ultimate Dragon	23995346
Barox	6840573	Blue-Eyes White Dragon	80906030
Barrel Dragon	81480460	Blue Medicine	20871001
Barrel Lily	67841515	Blue-Winged Crown	41396436
Barrel Rock	10476868	Boar Soldier	21340051
Basic Insect	89091579	Bolt Escargot	12146024
Bat	72076281	Bolt Penguin	48531733
Battle Ox	5053103	Bombardment Beetle	57409948
Battle Steer	18246479	Bone Mouse	21239280
Battle Warrior	55550921	Boneheimer	98456117
Bazoo the Soul-Eater	40133511	Boo Koo	68963107
Beaked Snake	6103114	Book of Secret Arts	91595718
Bean Soldier	84990171	Bottom Dweller	81386177
Beast Fangs	46009906	Boulder Tortoise	9540040
Beast of Gilfer	50287060	Bracchio-Raidus	16507828
Beastking of the Swamps	99426834	Brave Scizzar	74277583
Beastly Mirror Ritual	N/A	Breath of Light	20101223
Beautiful Beast Trainer	29616941	Bright Castle	82878489
		B. Skull Dragon	N/A

Side tabs: DS, GBA, PSP, PS2, PS3, Wii, Xbox, Xbox 360, Index

DS

GBA

PSP

PS2

PS3

Wii

Xbox

Xbox 360

Index

Yu-Gi-Oh! World Championship (Cards) (continued)

Unlockable	Code	Unlockable	Code
Bubonic Vermin	6104968	Crush Card	57728570
Burglar	6297941	Cure Mermaid	85802526
Burning Land	24294108	Curse of Dragon	28279543
Burning Spear	18937875	Curse of Fiend	12470447
Buster Blader	78193831	Curse of the Masked Beast	94377247
Call of the Dark	78637313	Curtain of Black Magic	99789342
Call of the Grave	16970158	Curtain of the Dark Ones	22026707
Call of the Haunted	97077563	Cyber Commander	6400512
Candle of Fate	47695416	Cyber Falcon	30655537
Cannon Soldier	11384280	Cyber Harpie	80316585
Card Destruction	72892473	Cyber Jar	34124316
Card of Safe Return	57953380	Cyber Saurus	89112729
Castle of Dark Illusions	62121	Cyber Shield	63224564
Castle Walls	44209392	Cyber Soldier	44865098
Catapult Turtle	95727991	Cyber Soldier of Darkworld	75559356
Ceasefire	36468556	Cyber-Stein	69015963
Celtic Guardian	91152256	Cyber-Tech Alligator	48766543
Ceremonial Bell	20228463	Cyclon Laser	5494820
Chain Destruction	1248895	Dancing Elf	59983499
Chain Energy	79323590	Dancing Fairy	90925163
Chakra	N/A	Dark Artist	72520073
Change of Heart	4031928	Dark Assailant	41949033
Change Slime	18914778	Dark Bat	67049542
Charubin the Fire Knight	37421579	Dark Chimera	32344688
Chimera the Flying Mythical Beast	4796100	Dark Elf	21417692
Chorus of Sanctuary	81380218	Dark Energy	4614116
Chosen One	21888494	Dark-Eyes Illusionist	38247752
Claw Reacher	41218256	Darkfire Dragon	17881964
Clown Zombie	92667214	Darkfire Soldier #1	5388481
Cockroach Knight	33413638	Darkfire Soldier #2	78861134
Cocoon of Evolution	N/A	Dark Gray	9159938
Cold Wave	60682203	Dark Hole	53129443
Collected Power	7565547	Dark Human	81057959
Commencement Dance	N/A	Dark King of the Abyss	53375573
Confiscation	17375316	Dark Magic Curtain	99789342
Copy Cat	26376390	Dark Magic Ritual	N/A
Corroding Shark	34290067	Dark Magician	46986414 or 40609080
Cosmo Queen	N/A	Dark Magician Yami	36996508
Crab Turtle	N/A	Dark Magician Girl	N/A
Crass Clown	93889755	Dark Necrofear	31829185
Crawling Dragon	67494157	Darkness Approaches	80168720
Crawling Dragon #2	38289717	Dark Plant	13193642
Crazy Fish	53713014	Dark Prisoner	89558090
Crimson Sentry	28358902	Dark Rabbit	99261403
Crimson Sunbird	46696593	Dark Sage	92377303
Crow Goblin	77998771	Dark Shade	40196604

Yu-Gi-Oh! World Championship (Cards) (continued)

Unlockable	Code	Unlockable	Code
Dark Spirit of the Silent	93599951	Dust Tornado	60082869
Dark Titan of Terror	89494469	Earthbound Spirit	67105242
Dark Witch	35565537	Earthshaker	60866277
Darkworld Thorns	43500484	Eatgaboon	42578427
Dark Zebra	59784896	Ekibyo Drakmord	69954399
Deal of Phantom	69122763	Eldeen	06367785
Deepsea Shark	28593363	Electric Lizard	55875323
Deepsea Warrior	24128274	Electric Snake	11324436
De-Fusion	95286165	Electro-Whip	37820550
Delinquent Duo	44763025	Elegant Egotist	90219263
De-Spell	19159413	Elf's Light	39897277
Destiny Board	94212438	Embryonic Beast	64154377
Destroyer Golem	73481154	Emperor of the Land and Sea	11250655
Destruction Punch	5616412	Empress Judge	15237615
Dharma Cannon	96967123	Empress Mantis	58818411
Dian Keto the Cure Master	N/A	Enchanted Javelin	96355986
Dice Armadillo	69893315	Enchanting Mermaid	75376965
Dig Beak	29948642	Eradicating Aerosol	94716515
Dimensional Warrior	37043180	Eternal Draught	56606928
Dimensionhole	22959079	Eternal Rest	95051344
Disk Magician	76446915	Exchange	05556668
Dissolverock	40826495	Exile of the Wicked	26725158
Djinn the Watcher of the Wind	97843505	Exodia the Forbidden One	33396948
DNA Surgery	74701381	Eyearmor	64511793
Dokuroizo the Grim Reaper	2588288 i	Fairy Box	21598948
Dokurorider	N/A	Fairy Dragon	20315854
Dokuroyaiba	30325729	Fairy Guardian	22419772
Doma the Angel of Silence	16972957	Fairy Meteor Crush	97687912
Doron	756652	Fairy of the Fountain	81563416
Dorover	24194033	Fairy's Gift	68401546
Dragon Capture Jar	50045299	Fairy's Hand Mirror	17653779
Dragoness the Wicked Knight	70681994	Fairywitch	37160778
Dragonic Attack	32437102	Faith Bird	75582395
Dragon Piper	55763552	Fake Trap	03027001
Dragon Seeker	28563545	Feral Imp	41392891
Dragon Statue	28563545	Fiend Kraken	77456781
Dragon Treasure	1435851	Fiend Reflection #1	68870276
Dragon Zombie	66672569	Fiend Reflection #2	2863439
Dream Clown	13215230	Fiend's Hand	52800428
Drill Bug	88733579	Fiend's Mirror	N/A
Driving Snow	473469	Fiend Sword	22855882
Droll Bird	97973387	Final Destiny	18591904
Drooling Lizard	16353197	Final Flame	73134081
Dryad	84916669	Fire Eye	88435542
Dunames Dark Witch	12493482	Firegrass	53293545
Dungeon Worm	51228280	Fire Kraken	46534755

DS
GBA
PSP
PS2
PS3
Wii
Xbox
Xbox 360
Index

Yu-Gi-Oh! World Championship (Cards) (continued)

Unlockable	Code	Unlockable	Code
Fire Princess	64752646	Gate Deeg	49258578
Fire Reaper	53581214	Gate Guardian	25833572
Fire Sorcerer	27132350	Gatekeeper	19737320
Firewing Pegasus	N/A	Gazelle the King of Mythical Beasts	5818798
Fireyarou	71407486		
Fissure	66788016	Gearfried the Iron Knight	423705
Flame Cerebrus	60862676	Gemini Elf	69140098
Flame Champion	42599677	Genin	49370026
Flame Dancer	12883044	Germ Infection	24668830
Flame Ghost	58528964	Ghoul with an Appetite	95265975
Flame Manipulator	34460851	Giant Flea	41762634
Flame Swordsman	45231177 or 40502030	Giant Germ	95178994
		Giant Mech-Soldier	72299832
Flame Viper	2830619	Giant Rat	97017120
Flash Assailant	96890582	Giant Red Seasnake	58831685
Flower Wolf	95952802	Giant Scorpion of the Tundra	41403766
Flying Fish	31987274	Giant Soldier of Stone	13039848
Flying Kamakiri #1	84834865	Giant Trunade	42703248
Flying Kamakiri #2	3134241	Giant Turtle Who Feeds on Flames	96981563
Flying Penguin	5628232		
Follow Wind	98252586	Gift of the Mystical Elf	98299011
Forced Requisition	74923978	Giganto	33621868
Forest	87430998	Giga-tech Wolf	8471389
Fortress Whale	N/A	Giltia the D. Knight	51828629
Fortress Whale's Oath	N/A	Girochin Kuwagata	84620194
Frenzied Panda	98818516	Goblin Attack Force	78658564
Frog the Jam	68638985	Goblin Fan	4149689
Fungi the Musk	53830602	Goblin's Secret Remedy	11868825
Fusion Gate	33550694	Goddess of Whim	67959180
Fusionist	1641882	Goddess with the Third Eye	53493204
Fusion Sage	26902560	Gokibore	15367030
Gadget Soldier	86281779	Golgoil	7526150
Gaia	6368038	Gorgon Egg	11793047
Gaia Power	56594520	Graceful Charity	79571449
Gaia the Dragon Champion	66889139	Graceful Dice	74137509
Gaia the Fierce Knight	06368038 or 00603060	Gradius	10992251
		Grand Tiki Elder	13676474
Gale Dogra	16229315	Grappler	2906250
Gamble	37313786	Gravedigger Ghoul	82542267
Gamma the Magnet Warrior	11549357	Gravekeeper's Servan	16762927
Ganigumo	34536276	Graverobber	61705417
Garma Sword	90844184	Graverobber's Retribution	33737664
Garma Sword Oath	78577570	Graveyard and the Hand of Invitation	27094595
Garnecia Elefantis	49888191		
Garoozis	14977074	Gravity Bind	85742772
Garuda the Wind Spirit	12800777	Great Bill	55691901
Garvas	69780745	Great Mammoth of Goldfine	54622031

Unlockable	Code	Unlockable	Code
Great White	13429800	Humanoid Worm Drake	5600127
Greenkappa	61831093	Hungry Burger	N/A
Green Phantom King	22910685	Hunter Spider	80141480
Griffore	53829412	Hurricail	15042735
Griggle	95744531	Hyo	38982356
Ground Attacker Bugroth	58314394	Hyosube	2118022
Ground Collapse	90502999	Hyozanryu	62397231
Gruesome Goo	65623423	Hysteric Fairy	21297224
Gryphon Wing	55608151	Ice Water	20848593
Guardian of the Labyrinth	89272878	Illusionist Faceless Mage	28546905
Guardian of the Sea	85448931	Ill Witch	81686058
Guardian of the Throne Room	47879985	Imperial Order	61740673
Gust	73079365	Infinite Cards	94163677
Gust Fan	55321970	Infinite Dismissal	54109233
Gyakutenno Megami	31122090	Insect Armor with Laser Cannon	3492538
Hamburger Recipe	N/A	Insect Barrier	23615409
Hane-Hane	7089711	Insect Imitation	96965364
Haniwa	84285623	Insect Queen	91512835
Happy Lover	99030164	Insect Soldiers of the Sky	7019529
Hard Armor	20060230	Inspection	16227556
Harpie Lady	76812113	Invader from Another Dimension	28450915
Harpie Lady Sisters	12206212	Invader of the Throne	3056267
Harpie's Brother	30532390	Invigoration	98374133
Harpie's Feather Duster	18144506	Invitation to a Dark Sleep	52675689
Harpie's Pet Dragon	52040216	Island Turtle	4042268
Hayabusa Knight	21015833	Jam Breeding Machine	21770260
Headless Knight	5434080	Jam Defender	21558682
Heavy Storm	19613556	Jar of Greed	83968380
Hercules Beetle	52584282	Javelin Beetle	N/A
Hero of the East	89987208	Javelin Beetle Pact	N/A
Hibikime	64501875	Jellyfish	14851496
High Tide Gyojin	54579801	Jigen Bakudan	90020065
Hinotama	46130346	Jinzo	77585513
Hinotama Soul	96851799	Jinzo #7	32809211
Hiro's Shadow Scout	81863068	Jirai Gumo	94773007
Hitodenchak	46718686	Job-Change Mirror	55337339
Hitotsu-Me Giant	76184692	Jowgen the Spiritualist	41855169
Holograh	10859908	Judge Man	30113682
Horn Imp	69669405	Just Desserts	24068492
Horn of Heaven	98069388	Kagemusha of the Blue Flame	15401633
Horn of Light	38552107	Kageningen	80600490
Horn of the Unicorn	64047146	Kairyu-Shin	76634149
Hoshiningen	67629977	Kaiser Dragon	94566432
Hourglass of Courage	43530283	Kamakiriman	68928540
Hourglass of Life	8783685	Kaminari Attack	9653271
House of Adhesive Tape	15083728		
Humanoid Slime	46821314		

Yu-Gi-Oh! World Championship (Cards) (continued)

Unlockable	Code	Unlockable	Code
Kaminarikozou	15510988	Lesser Dragon	55444629
Kamionwizard	41544074	Light of Intervention	62867251
Kanan the Swordmistress	12829151	Lightforce Sword	49587034
Kanikabuto	84103702	Liquid Beast	93108297
Kappa Avenger	48109103	Little Chimera	68658728
Karate Man	23289281	Little D	42625254
Karbonala Warrior	54541900	Lord of D	17985575
Kattapillar	81179446	Lord of the Lamp	99510761
Kazejin	N/A	Lord of Zemia	81618817
Key Mace	1929294	Luminous Spark	81777047
Key Mace #2	20541432	Lunar Queen Elzaim	62210247
Killer Needle	88979991	Mabarrel	98795934
King Fog	84686841	Machine Conversion Factory	25769732
King of Yamimakai	69455834	Machine King	46700124
Kiseitai	4266839	Mage Power	83746708
Kojikocy	1184620	Magic Cylinder	62279055
Korogashi	32569498	Magic Jammer	77414722
Kotodama	19406822	Magic Thorn	53119267
Koumori Dragon	67724379	Magical Ghost	46474915
Krokodilus	76512652	Magical Hats	81210420
Kumootoko	56283725	Magical Labyrinth	64389297
Kunai with Chain	37390589	Magic-Arm Shield	96008713
Kurama	85705804	Magician of Faith	31560081
Kuriboh	40640057	Maha Vailo	93013676
Kuwagata A	60802233	Maiden of the Moonlight	79629370
Kwagar Hercules	95144193	Major Riot	9074847
Kycoo the Ghost Destroyer	88240808	Malevolent Nuzzler	99597615
La Jinn the Mystical Genie of the Lamp	97590747	Mammoth Graveyard	40374923
		Man Eater	93553943
Labyrinth Tank	99551425	Man-Eater Bug	54652250
Lady of Faith	17358176	Man-Eating Black Shark	80727036
LaLa Li-oon	9430387	Man-Eating Plant	49127943
Larvae	94675535	Man-Eating Treasure Chest	13723605
Laser Cannon Armor	77007920	Manga Ryu-Ran	38369349
Last Day of Witch	90330453	Marie the Fallen One	57579381
Last Warrior from Another Planet	86099788	Marine Beast	29929832
Last Will	85602018	Marine the Fallen One (1700/1200)	57579381
Laughing Flower	42591472	Masaki the Legendary Swordsman	44287299
Launcher Spider	87322377 or 80703020		
		Mask of Brutality	82432018
Lava Battleguard	20394040	Mask of Darkness	28933734
Left Arm of the Forbidden One	7902349	Mask of Dispel	20765952
Left Leg of the Forbidden One	44519536	Mask of Restrict	29549364
Legendary Sword	61854111	Mask of the Accursed	56948373
Leghul	12472242	Masked Sorcerer	10189126
Leogun	10538007	Master & Expert	75499502

DS
GBA
PSP
PS2
PS3
Wii
Xbox
Xbox 360
Index

Yu-Gi-Oh! World Championship (Cards) (continued)

Unlockable	Code	Unlockable	Code
Mavelus	59036972	Mystic Box	25774450
Mechanical Snail	34442949	Mystic Clown	47060154
Mechanical Spider	45688586	Mystic Horseman	68516705
Mechanicalchaser	7359741	Mystic Lamp	98049915
Meda Bat	76211194	Mystic Plasma Zone	18161786
Mega Thunderball	21817254	Mystic Probe	49251811
Megamorph	22046459	Mystic Tomato	83011277
Megazowler	75390004	Mystical Capture Chain	63515678
Meotoko	53832650	Mystical Elf	15025844
Mesmeric Control	48642904	Mystical Moon	36607978
Messenger of Peace	44656491	Mystical Refpanel	35563539
Metal Detector	75646520	Mystical Sand	32751480
Metal Dragon	9293977	Mystical Sheep #1	30451366
Metal Fish	55998462	Mystical Sheep #2	83464209
Metal Guardian	68339286	Mystical Space Typhoon	5318639
Metalmorph	68540058	Needle Ball	94230224
Metalzoa	50705071	Needle Worm	81843628
Millennium Golem	47986555	Negate Attack	14315573
Millennium Shield	32012841	Nekogal #1	1761063
Milus Radiant	7489323	Nekogal #2	43352213
Minar	32539892	Nemuriko	90963488
Minomushi Warrior	46864967	Neo the Magic Swordsman	50930991
Mirror Force	44095762	Nimble Momonga	22567609
Mirror Wall	22359980	Niwatori	7805359
Misairuzame	33178416	Nobleman of Crossout	71044499
Molten Destruction	19384334	Nobleman of Extermination	17449108
Monster Egg	36121917	Numinous Healer	2130625
Monster Eye	84133008	Octoberser	74637266
Monster Reborn	83764718	Ocubeam	86088138
Monster Tamer	97612389	Offerings to the Doomed	19230407
Monstrous Bird	35712107	Ogre of the Black Shadow	45121025
Moon Envoy	45909477	One-Eyed Shield Dragon	33064647
Mooyan Curry	58074572	Ooguchi	58861941
Morinphen	55784832	Ookazi	19523799
Morphing Jar	33508719	Orion the Battle King	2971090
Morphing Jar #2	79106360	Oscillo Hero	82065276
Mother Grizzly	57839750	Oscillo Hero #2	27324313
Mountain	50913601	Painful Choice	74191942
Mountain Warrior	4931562	Pale Beast	21263083
Mr. Volcano	31477025	Panther Warrior	42035044
Muka Muka	46657337	Paralyzing Potion	50152549
Mushroom Man	14181608	Parasite Paracide	27911549
Mushroom Man #2	93900406	Parrot Dragon	62762898
Musician King	56907389	Patrol Robo	76775123
M-Warrior #1	56342351	Peacock	20624263
M-Warrior #2	92731455	Pendulum Machine	24433920 or 20404030
Mysterious Puppeteer	54098121		

DS
GBA
PSP
PS2
PS3
Wii
Xbox
Xbox 360
Index

Yu-Gi-Oh! World Championship (Cards) (continued)

Unlockable	Code	Unlockable	Code
Penguin Knight	36039163	Robbin' Goblin	88279736
Penguin Soldier	93920745	Rock Ogre Grotto #1	68846917
Petit Angel	38142739	Rock Spirit	82818645
Petit Dragon	75356564	Rocket Warrior	30860696
Petit Moth	58192742	Rogue Doll	91939608
Polymerization	24094653	Root Water	39004808
Pot of Greed	55144522	Rose Spectre of Dunn	32485271
Power of Kaishin	77027445	Royal Decree	51452091
Pragtical	33691040	Royal Guard	39239728
Premature Burial	70828912	Rude Kaiser	26378150
Prevent Rat	549481	Rush Recklessly	70046172
Princess of Tsurugi	51371017	Ryu-Kishin	15303296
Prisman	80234301	Ryu-Kishin Powered	24611934
Prohibition	43711255	Ryu-Ran	2964201
Protector of the Throne	10071456	Saber Slasher	73911410
Psychic Kappa	7892180	Saggi the Dark Clown	66602787
Pumpking the King of Ghosts	29155212	Salamandra	32268901
Punished Eagle	74703140	Sand Stone	73051941
Queen Bird	73081602	Sangan	26202165
Queen of Autumn Leaves	4179849	Sea Kamen	71746462
Queen's Double	5901497	Sea King Dragon	23659124
Raigeki	12580477	Seal of the Ancients	97809599
Raimei	56260110	Sebek's Blessing	22537443
Rain of Dark Magic	27827272	Sectarian of Secrets	15507080
Rainbow Flower	21347810	Senju of the Thousand Hands	23401839
Raise Body Heat	51267887	Seven Tools of the Bandit	3819470
Rare Fish	80516007	Shadow Specter	40575313
Ray & Temperature	85309439	Share the Pain	56830749
Reaper of the Cards	33066139	Shield & Sword	52097679
Red Archery Girl	65570596	Shining Abyss	87303357
Red Medicine	38199696	Shining Fairy	95956346
Red-Eyes Black Dragon	74677422	Shovel Crusher	71950093
Red-Eyes Black Metal Dragon	64335804	Silver Bow and Arrow	1557499
Reinforcements	17814387	Silver Fang	90357090
Relinquished	64631466	Sinister Serpent	8131171
Remove Trap	51482758	Skelengel	60694662
Respect Play	8951260	Skelgon	32355828
Restructer Revolution	99518961	Skull Dice	126218
Reverse Trap	77622396	Skull Lair	6733059
Revival Jam	31709826	Skull Mariner	5265750
Rhaimundos of the Red Sword	62403074	Skull Red Bird	10202894
Right Arm of the Forbidden One	70903634	Skull Servant	32274490
Right Leg of the Forbidden One	8124921	Skull Stalker	54844990
Ring of Magnetism	20436034	Skullbird	8327462
Riryoku	34016756	Slate Warrior	78636495
Rising Air Current	45778932	Sleeping Lion	40200834
Roaring Ocean Snake	19066538	Slot Machine	3797883

Unlockable	Code	Unlockable	Code
Snake Fang	596051	Swordsman of Landstar	3573512
Snakeyashi	29802344	Swordstalker	50005633
Snatch Steal	45986603	Tailor of the Fickle	43641473
Sogen	86318356	Tainted Wisdom	28725004
Solemn Judgment	41420027	Takriminos	44073668
Solemn Wishes	35346968	Takuhee	3170832
Solitude	84794011	Tao the Chanter	46247516
Solomon's Lawbook	23471572	Temple of Skulls	732302
Sonic Bird	57617178	Tenderness	57935140
Sonic Maid	38942059	Terra the Terrible	63308047
Sorcerer of the Doomed	49218300	The 13th Grave	32864
Soul Hunter	72869010	The Bewitching Phantom Thief	24348204
Soul of the Pure	47852924	The Bistro Butcher	71107816
Soul Release	5758500	The Cheerful Coffin	41142615
Sparks	76103675	The Drdek	8944575
Spear Cretin	58551308	The Eye of Truth	34694160
Spellbinding Circle	18807108	The Flute of Summoning Dragon	43973174
Spike Seadra	85326399	The Forceful Sentry	42829885
Spirit Message A	94772232	The Furious Sea King	18710707
Spirit Message I	31893528	The Immortal of Thunder	84926738
Spirit Message L	30170981	The Inexperienced Spy	81820689
Spirit Message N	67287533	The Legendary Fisherman	3643300
Spirit of Flames	13522325	The Little Swordsman of Aile	25109950
Spirit of the Books	14037717	The Masked Beast	49064413
Spirit of the Harp	80770678	The Regulation of Tribe	296499
Stain Storm	21323861	The Reliable Guardian	16430187
Star Boy	8201910	The Shallow Grave	43434803
Steel Ogre Grotto #1	29172562	The Snake Hair	29491031
Steel Ogre Grotto #2	90908427	The Stern Mystic	87557188
Steel Scorpion	13599884	The Thing That Hides in the Mud	18180762
Steel Shell	2370081	The Unhappy Maiden	51275027
Stim-Pack	83225447	The Wandering Doomed	93788854
Stone Armadiller	63432835	The Wicked Worm Beast	6285791
Stone Ogre Grotto	15023985	Thousand Knives	63391643
Stop Defense	63102017	Three-Headed Geedo	78423643
Stuffed Animal	71068263	Three-Legged Zombies	33734439
Succubus Knight	55291359	Thunder Dragon	31786629
Summoned Skull	70781052	Tiger Axe	49791927 or 40907090
Supporter in the Shadows	41422426		
Swamp Battleguard	40453765	Time Machine	80987696
Sword Arm of Dragon	13069066	Time Seal	35316708
Sword Hunter	51345461	Time Wizard	71625222
Sword of Dark Destruction	37120512	Toad Master	62671448
Sword of Deep-Seated	98495314	Togex	33878931
Sword of Dragon's Soul	61405855	Toll	82003859
Swords of Revealing Light	72302403	Tomozaurus	46457856
Swordsman from a Foreign Land	85255550	Tongyo	69572024

DS

GBA

PSP

PS2

PS3

Wii

Xbox

Xbox 360

Index

DS

GBA

PSP

PS2

PS3

Wii

Xbox

Xbox 360

Index

Yu-Gi-Oh! World Championship (Cards) (continued)

Unlockable	Code	Unlockable	Code
Toon Alligator	59383041	Waboku	12607053
Toon Mermaid	65458948	Wall of Illusion	13945283
Toon Summoned Skull	91842653	Warrior Elimination	90873992
Toon World	15259703	Warrior of Tradition	56413937
Torike	80813021	Wasteland	23424603
Tornado Wall	18605135	Water Element	3732747
Torrential Tribute	53582587	Water Girl	55014050
Total Defense Shogun	75372290	Water Magician	93343894
Trakadon	42348802	Water Omotics	2483611
Trap Hole	4206964	Waterdragon Fairy	66836598
Trap Master	46461247	Weather Control	37243151
Trent	78780140	Weather Report	72053645
Trial of Nightmare	77827521	Whiptail Crow	91996584
Tribute to the Doomed	79759861	White Hole	43487744
Tripwire Beast	45042329	White Magical Hat	15150365
Turtle Tiger	37313348	Wicked Mirror	15150371
Twin Long Rods #2	29692206	Widespread Ruin	77754944
Twin-Headed Fire Dragon	78984772	Windstorm of Etaqua	59744639
Twin-Headed Thunder Dragon	54752875	Wing Egg Elf	98582704
Two-Headed King Rex	94119974	Winged Cleaver	39175982
Two-Mouth Darkruler	57305373	Winged Dragon, Guardian of the Fortress #1	87796900
Two-Pronged Attack	83887306		
Tyhone	72842870	Wings of Wicked Flame	92944626
Tyhone #2	56789759	Wingweaver	31447217
Type Zero Magic Crusher	21237481	Witch of the Black Forest	78010363
UFO Turtle	60806437	Witch's Apprentice	80741828
Ultimate Offering	80604091	Witty Phantom	36304921
Umi	22702055	Wodan the Resident of the Forest	42883273
Umiiruka	82999629		
Unfriendly Amazon	65475294	Wood Remains	17733394
United We Stand	56747793	World Suppression	12253117
Unknown Warrior of Fiend	97360116	Wow Warrior	69750536
Upstart Goblin	70368879	Wretched Ghost of the Attic	17238333
Uraby	1784619	Yado Karu	29380133
Ushi Oni	48649353	Yaiba Robo	10315429
Valkyrion the Magna Warrior	75347539	Yamatano Dragon Scroll	76704943
Vermillion Sparrow	35752363	Yami	59197169
Versago the Destroyer	50259460	Yaranzo	71280811
Vile Germs	39774085	Zanki	30090452
Violent Rain	94042337	Zoa	24311372
Violet Crystal	15052462	Zombie Warrior	31339260
Vishwar Randi	78556320	Zombyra the Dark (2100/500)	88472456
Vorse Raider	14898066	Zone Eater	86100785

Yu-Gi-Oh! Worldwide Edition: Stairway to the Destined Duel

To access these cheats, go to the main map, press Ⓡ, then go to the Misc menu. Select Password and enter these codes to unlock the corresponding card for your deck.

Card	Code
30,000-Year White Turtle	11714098
4-Starred Ladybug of Doom	83994646
7 Colored Fish	23771716
7 Completed	86198326
Abyss Flower	40387124
Acid Crawler	77568553
Acid Trap Hole	41356845
Air Eater	08353769
Air Marmot of Nefariousness	75889523
Akakieisu	38035986
Akihiron	36904469
Alinsection	70924884
Alligator's Sword	64428736
Alligator's Sword Dragon	03366982
Alpha the Magnet Warrior	99785935
Amazon Archer	91869203
Amazon of the Seas	17968114
Ameba	95174353
Amphibian Beast	67371383
Amphibious Bugroth	40173854
Ancient Brain	42431843
Ancient Elf	93221206
Ancient Jar	81492226
Ancient Lizard Warrior	43230671
Ancient One of the Deep Forest	14015067
Ancient Sorcerer	36821538
Ancient Telescope	17092736
Ancient Tool	49587396
Ancient Tree of Enlightenment	86421986
Ansatsu	48365709
Anthrosaurus	89904598
Anti Raigeki	42364257
Anti-Magic Fragrance	58921041
Appropriate	48539234
Aqua Chorus	95132338
Aqua Dragon	86164529

Card	Code
Aqua Madoor	85639257
Aqua Snake	12436646
Aqua Spirit	40916023
Arlownay	14708569
Arma Knight	36151751
Armaill	53153481
Armed Ninja	09076207
Armored Glass	36868108
Armored Lizard	15480588
Armored Rat	16246527
Armored Starfish	17535588
Armored Zombie	20277860
Attack and Receive	63689843
Axe of Despair	40619825
Axe Raider	48305365
Baby Dragon	88819587
Backup Soldier	36280194
Banisher of the Light	61528025
Baron of the Fiend Sword	86325596
Barox	06840573
Barrel Dragon	81480460
Barrel Lily	67841515
Barrel Rock	10476868
Basic Insect	89091579
Bat	72076281
Battle Ox	05053103
Battle Steer	18246479
Battle Warrior	55550921
Bazoo the Soul-Eater	40133511
Beaked Snake	06103114
Bean Soldier	84990171
Beast Fangs	46009906
Beast of Gilfer	50287060
Beastking of the Swamps	99426834
Beautiful Beast Trainer	29616941
Beautiful Headhuntress	16899564
Beaver Warrior	32452818
Behegon	94022093
Bell of Destruction	83555666
Berfomet	77207191

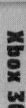

DS
GBA
PSP
PS2
PS3
Wii
Xbox
Xbox 360
Index

Yu-Gi-Oh! Worldwide Edition: Stairway to the Destined Duel (continued)

Card	Code	Card	Code
Beta the Magnet Warrior	39256679	Buster Blader	78193831
Bickuribox	25655502	Call of the Dark	78637313
Big Eye	16768387	Call of the Grave	16970158
Big Insect	53606874	Call of the Haunted	97077563
Big Shield Gardna	65240384	Candle of Fate	47695416
Binding Chain	08058240	Cannon Soldier	11384280
Bio-Mage	58696829	Card Destruction	72892473
Bio Plant	07670542	Card of Safe Return	57953380
Bite Shoes	50122883	Castle of Dark Illusions	00062121
Black Dragon Jungle King	89832901	Castle Walls	44209392
Black Illusion Ritual	41426869	Catapult Turtle	95727991
Black Pendant	65169794	Ceasefire	36468556
Blackland Fire Dragon	87564352	Celtic Guardian	91152256
Bladefly	28470714	Ceremonial Bell	20228463
Blast Juggler	70138455	Chain Destruction	01248895
Blast Sphere	26302522	Chain Energy	79323590
Blind Destruction	32015166	Change of Heart	04031928
Block Attack	25880422	Change Slime	18914778
Blocker	34743446	Charubin the Fire Knight	37421579
Blue-Eyed Silver Zombie	35282433	Chimera the Flying Mythical Beast	04796100
Blue-Eyes Toon Dragon	53183600		
Blue-Eyes Ultimate Dragon	23995346	Chorus of Sanctuary	81380218
Blue-Eyes White Dragon	80906030	Chosen One	21888494
Blue Medicine	20871001	Claw Reacher	41218256
Blue-Winged Crown	41396436	Clown Zombie	92667214
Boar Soldier	21340051	Cockroach Knight	33413638
Bolt Escargot	12146024	Cold Wave	60682203
Bolt Penguin	48531733	Collected Power	07565547
Bombardment Beetle	57409948	Confiscation	17375316
Bone Mouse	21239280	Copy Cat	26376390
Boneheimer	98456117	Corroding Shark	34290067
Boo Koo	68963107	Crass Clown	93889755
Book of Secret Arts	91595718	Crawling Dragon	67494157
Bottom Dweller	81386177	Crawling Dragon #2	38289717
Boulder Tortoise	09540040	Crazy Fish	53713014
Bracchio-Raidus	16507828	Crimson Sentry	28358902
Brave Scizzar	74277583	Crimson Sunbird	46696593
Breath of Light	20101223	Crow Goblin	77998771
Bright Castle	82878489	Crush Card	57728570
Bubonic Vermin	06104968	Cure Mermaid	85802526
Burglar	06297941	Curse of Dragon	28279543
Burning Land	24294108	Curse of Fiend	12470447
Burning Spear	18937875	Curse of the Masked Beast	94377247

DS

GBA

PSP

PS2

PS3

Wii

Xbox

Xbox 360

Index

Yu-Gi-Oh! Worldwide Edition: Stairway to the Destined Duel (continued)

DS
GBA
PSP
PS2
PS3
Wii
Xbox
Xbox 360
Index

Card	Code	Card	Code
Curtain of the Dark Ones	22026707	Deepsea Shark	28593363
Cyber Commander	06400512	Deepsea Warrior	24128274
Cyber Falcon	30655537	De-Fusion	95286165
Cyber Harpie	80316585	Delinquent Duo	44763025
Cyber Jar	34124316	De-Spell	19159413
Cyber Saurus	89112729	Destiny Board	94212438
Cyber Shield	63224564	Destroyer Golem	73481154
Cyber Soldier	44865098	Destruction Punch	05616412
Cyber Soldier of Darkworld	75559356	Dharma Cannon	96967123
Cyber-Stein	69015963	Dice Armadillo	69893315
Cyber-Tech Alligator	48766543	Dig Beak	29948642
Cyclon Laser	05494820	Dimensional Warrior	37043180
Dancing Elf	59983499	Dimensionhole	22959079
Dancing Fairy	90925163	Disk Magician	76446915
Dark Artist	72520073	Dissolverock	40826495
Dark Assailant	41949033	Djinn the Watcher of the Wind	97843505
Dark Bat	67049542	DNA Surgery	74701381
Dark Chimera	32344688	Dokuroizo the Grim Reaper	25882881
Dark Elf	21417692	Dokuroyaiba	30325729
Dark Energy	04614116	Doma the Angel of Silence	16972957
Dark-Eyes Illusionist	38247752	Doron	00756652
Darkfire Dragon	17881964	Dorover	24194033
Darkfire Soldier #1	05388481	Dragon Capture Jar	50045299
Darkfire Soldier #2	78861134	Dragoness the Wicked Knight	70681994
Dark Gray	09159938	Dragonic Attack	32437102
Dark Hole	53129443	Dragon Piper	55763552
Dark Human	81057959	Dragon Seeker	28563545
Dark King of the Abyss	53375573	Dragon Statue	28563545
Dark Magic Curtain	99789342	Dragon Treasure	01435851
Dark Magician	46986414	Dragon Zombie	66672569
Dark Necrofear	31829185	Dream Clown	13215230
Darkness Approaches	80168720	Drill Bug	88733579
Dark Plant	13193642	Driving Snow	00473469
Dark Prisoner	89558090	Droll Bird	97973387
Dark Rabbit	99261403	Drooling Lizard	16353197
Dark Sage	92377303	Dryad	84916669
Dark Shade	40196604	Dunames Dark Witch	12493482
Dark Spirit of the Silent	93599951	Dungeon Worm	51228280
Dark Titan of Terror	89494469	Dust Tornado	60082869
Dark Witch	35565537	Earthbound Spirit	67105242
Darkworld Thorns	43500484	Earthshaker	60866277
Dark Zebra	59784896		
Deal of Phantom	69122763		

Yu-Gi-Oh! Worldwide Edition: Stairway to the Destined Duel (continued)

Card	Code	Card	Code
Eatgaboon	42578427	Fire Sorcerer	27132350
Ekibyo Drakmord	69954399	Fireyarou	71407486
Eldeen	06367785	Fissure	66788016
Electric Lizard	55875323	Flame Cerebrus	60862676
Electric Snake	11324436	Graveyard and the Hand of Invitation	27094595
Electro-Whip	37820550		
Elegant Egotist	90219263	Gravity Bind	85742772
Elf's Light	39897277	Great Bill	55691901
Embryonic Beast	64154377	Great Mammoth of Goldfine	54622031
Emperor of the Land and Sea	11250655		
		Great White	13429800
Empress Judge	15237615	Greenkappa	61831093
Empress Mantis	58818411	Green Phantom King	22910685
Enchanted Javelin	96355986	Griffore	53829412
Enchanting Mermaid	75376965	Griggle	95744531
Eradicating Aerosol	94716515	Ground Attacker Bugroth	58314394
Eternal Draught	56606928	Ground Collapse	90502999
Eternal Rest	95051344	Gruesome Goo	65623423
Exchange	05556668	Gryphon Wing	55608151
Exile of the Wicked	26725158	Guardian of the Labyrinth	89272878
Exodia the Forbidden One	33396948	Guardian of the Sea	85448931
Eyearmor	64511793	Guardian of the Throne Room	47879985
Fairy Box	21598948		
Fairy Dragon	20315854	Gust	73079365
Fairy Guardian	22419772	Gust Fan	55321970
Fairy Meteor Crush	97687912	Gyakutenno Megami	31122090
Fairy of the Fountain	81563416	Hane-Hane	07089711
Fairy's Gift	68401546	Haniwa	84285623
Fairywitch	37160778	Happy Lover	99030164
Faith Bird	75582395	Hard Armor	20060230
Feral Imp	41392891	Harpie Lady	76812113
Fiend Kraken	77456781	Harpie Lady Sisters	12206212
Fiend Reflection #1	68870276	Harpie's Brother	30532390
Fiend Reflection #2	02863439	Harpie's Feather Duster	18144506
Fiend's Hand	52800428	Harpie's Pet Dragon	52040216
Fiend Sword	22855882	Hayabusa Knight	21015833
Final Destiny	18591904	Headless Knight	05434080
Final Flame	73134081	Heavy Storm	19613556
Fire Eye	88435542	Hercules Beetle	52584282
Firegrass	53293545	Hero of the East	89987208
Fire Kraken	46534755	Hibikime	64501875
Fire Princess	64752646	High Tide Gyojin	54579801
Fire Reaper	53581214	Hinotama	46130346
		Hinotama Soul	96851799

Yu-Gi-Oh! Worldwide Edition: Stairway to the Destined Duel (continued)

Card	Code
Hiro's Shadow Scout	81863068
Hitodenchak	46718686
Hitotsu-Me Giant	76184692
Holograh	10859908
Horn Imp	69669405
Horn of Heaven	98069388
Horn of Light	38552107
Horn of the Unicorn	64047146
Hoshiningen	67629977
Hourglass of Courage	43530283
Hourglass of Life	08783685
House of Adhesive Tape	15083728
Humanoid Slime	46821314
Humanoid Worm Drake	05600127
Hunter Spider	80141480
Hurricail	15042735
Hyo	38982356
Hyosube	02118022
Hyozanryu	62397231
Hysteric Fairy	21297224
Ice Water	20848593
Illusionist Faceless Mage	28546905
Ill Witch	81686058
Imperial Order	61740673
Infinite Cards	94163677
Infinite Dismissal	54109233
Insect Armor with Laser Cannon	03492538
Insect Barrier	23615409
Insect Imitation	96965364
Insect Queen	91512835
Insect Soldiers of the Sky	07019529
Inspection	16227556
Invader from Another Dimension	28450915
Invader of the Throne	03056267
Invigoration	98374133
Invitation to a Dark Sleep	52675689
Island Turtle	04042268
Jam Breeding Machine	21770260
Jam Defender	21558682
Jar Of Greed	83968380
Jellyfish	14851496

Card	Code
Jigen Bakudan	90020065
Jinzo	77585513
Jinzo #7	32809211
Jirai Gumo	94773007
Job-Change Mirror	55337339
Jowgen the Spiritualist	41855169
Judge Man	30113682
Just Desserts	24068492
Kagemusha of the Blue Flame	15401633
Kageningen	80600490
Kairyu-Shin	76634149
Kaiser Dragon	94566432
Kamakiriman	68928540
Kaminari Attack	09653271
Kaminarikozou	15510988
Kamionwizard	41544074
Kanan the Swordmistress	12829151
Kanikabuto	84103702
Kappa Avenger	48109103
Karate Man	23289281
Karbonala Warrior	54541900
Key Mace	01929294
Key Mace #2	20541432
Killer Needle	88979991
King Fog	84686841
King of Yamimakai	69455834
Kiseitai	04266839
Kojikocy	01184620
Korogashi	32569498
Kotodama	19406822
Koumori Dragon	67724379
Krokodilus	76512652
Kumootoko	56283725
Kunai with Chain	37390589
Kurama	85705804
Kuriboh	40640057
Kuwagata A	60802233
Kwagar Hercules	95144193
Kycoo the Ghost Destroyer	88240808
La Jinn the Mystical Genie of the Lamp	97590747
Labyrinth Tank	99551425

DS
GBA
PSP
PS2
PS3
Wii
Xbox
Xbox 360
Index

DS
GBA
PSP
PS2
PS3
Wii
Xbox
Xbox 360
Index

Yu-Gi-Oh! Worldwide Edition: Stairway to the Destined Duel (continued)

Card	Code	Card	Code
Lady Assailant of the Flames	90147755	Mage Power	83746708
Lady of Faith	17358176	Magic Cylinder	62279055
Lady Panther	38480590	Magic Jammer	77414722
LaLa Li-oon	09430387	Magic Thorn	53119267
LaMoon	75850803	Magical Ghost	46474915
Larvas	94675535	Magical Hats	81210420
Laser Cannon Armor	77007920	Magical Labyrinth	64389297
Last Day of Witch	90330453	Magic-Arm Shield	96008713
Last Warrior from Another Planet	86099788	Magician of Faith	31560081
Last Will	85602018	Maha Vailo	93013676
Laughing Flower	42591472	Maiden of the Moonlight	79629370
Launcher Spider	80703020	Major Riot	09074847
Lava Battleguard	20394040	Makiu	27827272
Left Arm of the Forbidden One	07902349	Malevolent Nuzzler	99597615
Left Leg of the Forbidden One	44519536	Mammoth Graveyard	40374923
Legendary Sword	61854111	Man Eater	93553943
Leghul	12472242	Man-Eater Bug	54652250
Leogun	10538007	Man-Eating Black Shark	80727036
Leo Wizard	04392470	Man-Eating Plant	49127943
Lesser Dragon	55444629	Man-Eating Treasure Chest	13723605
Lightforce Sword	49587034	Manga Ryu-Ran	38369349
Lightning Blade	55226821	Marie the Fallen One	57579381
Lightning Conger	27671321	Marine Beast	29929832
Limiter Removal	23171610	Maryokutai	71466592
Liquid Beast	93108297	Masaki the Legendary Swordsman	44287299
Lisark	55210709	Mask of Brutality	82432018
Little Chimera	68658728	Mask of Darkness	28933734
Little D	42625254	Mask of Dispel	30765952
Living Vase	34320307	Mask of Restrict	29549364
Lord of the Lamp	99510761	Mask of the Accursed	56948373
Lord of Zemia	81618817	Mask of Weakness	57882509
Luoky Trinket	03985011	Masked Clown	77581312
Luminous Spark	81777047	Masked Sorcerer	10189126
Lunar Queen Elzaim	62210247	Master & Expert	75499502
Mabarrel	98795934	Mavelus	59036972
Machine Attacker	38116136	Mech Bass	50176820
Machine Conversion Factory	25769732	Mech Mole Zombie	63545455
Machine King	46700124	Mechaleon	94412545
Mad Sword Beast	79870141	Mechanical Snail	34442949
Madjinn Gunn	43905751	Mechanical Spider	45688586
		Mechanicalchaser	07359741
		Meda Bat	76211194

Yu-Gi-Oh! Worldwide Edition: Stairway to the Destined Duel (continued)

Card	Code
Mega Thunderball	21817254
Megamorph	22046459
Megasonic Eye	07562372
Megazowler	75390004
Megirus Light	23032273
Melchid the Four-Face Beast	86569121
Meotoko	53832650
Mesmeric Control	48642904
Messenger of Peace	44656491
Metal Detector	75646520
Metal Dragon	09293977
Metal Fish	55998462
Metal Guardian	68339286
Metalmorph	68540058
Metalzoa	50705071
Michizure	37580756
Midnight Fiend	83678433
Millennium Golem	47986555
Millennium Shield	32012841
Milus Radiant	07489323
Minar	32539892
Minomushi Warrior	46864967
Minor Goblin Official	01918087
Miracle Dig	06343408
Mirror Force	44095762
Mirror Wall	22359980
Misairuzame	33178416
Molten Destruction	19384334
Mon Larvas	07225792
Monster Egg	36121917
Monster Eye	84133008
Monster Reborn	83764718
Monster Recovery	93108433
Monster Tamer	97612389
Monstrous Bird	35712107
Monsturtle	15820147
Moon Envoy	45909477
Mooyan Curry	58074572
Morinphen	55784832
Morphing Jar	33508719
Morphing Jar #2	79106360
Mother Grizzly	57839750

Card	Code
Mountain	50913601
Mountain Warrior	04931562
Mr. Volcano	31477025
Muka Muka	46657337
Multiply	40703222
Muse-A	69992868
Mushroom Man	14181608
Mushroom Man #2	93900406
Musician King	56907389
M-Warrior #1	56342351
M-Warrior #2	92731455
Mysterious Puppeteer	54098121
Mystery Hand	62793020
Mystic Box	25774450
Mystic Clown	47060154
Mystic Horseman	68516705
Mystic Lamp	98049915
Mystic Plasma Zone	18161786
Mystic Probe	49251811
Mystic Tomato	83011277
Mystical Capture Chain	63515678
Mystical Elf	15025844
Mystical Moon	36607978
Mystical Refpanel	35563539
Mystical Sand	32751480
Mystical Sheep #1	30451366
Mystical Sheep #2	83464209
Mystical Space Typhoon	05318639
Neck Hunter	70084224
Necrolancer the Timelord	61454890
Needle Ball	94230224
Needle Worm	81843628
Negate Attack	14315573
Nekogal #1	01761063
Nekogal #2	43352213
Nemuriko	90963488
Neo the Magic Swordsman	50930991
Night Lizard	78402798
Nightmare Scorpion	88643171
Nightmare's Steelcage	58775978
Nimble Momonga	22567609
Niwatori	07805359

DS

GBA

PSP

PS2

PS3

Wii

Xbox

Xbox 360

Index

Yu-Gi-Oh! Worldwide Edition: Stairway to the Destined Duel (continued)

Card	Code
Nobleman of Crossout	71044499
Nobleman of Extermination	17449108
Numinous Healer	02130625
Nuvia the Wicked	12953226
Obese Marmot of Nefariousness	56713552
Octoberser	74637266
Ocubeam	86088138
Offerings to the Doomed	19230407
Ogre of the Black Shadow	45121025
One-Eyed Shield Dragon	33064647
One Who Hunts Souls	03606209
Oni Tank T-34	66927994
Ooguchi	58861941
Ookazi	19523799
Orion the Battle King	02971090
Oscillo Hero	82065276
Oscillo Hero #2	27324313
Overdrive	02311603
Painful Choice	74191942
Pale Beast	21263083
Panther Warrior	42035044
Paralyzing Potion	50152549
Parasite Paracide	27911549
Parrot Dragon	62762898
Patrol Robo	76775123
Peacock	20624263
Pendulum Machine	20404030
Penguin Knight	36039163
Penguin Soldier	93920745
Petit Angel	38142739
Petit Dragon	75356564
Petit Moth	58192742
Phantom Dewan	77603950
Phantom Ghost	61201220
Polymerization	24094653
Pot of Greed	55144522
Pot the Trick	55567161
Power of Kaishin	77027445
Pragtical	33691040
Premature Burial	70828912
Prevent Rat	00549481

Card	Code
Princess of Tsurugi	51371017
Prisman	80234301
Prohibition	43711255
Protector of the Throne	10071456
Psychic Kappa	07892180
Pumpking the King of Ghosts	29155212
Punished Eagle	74703140
Queen Bird	73081602
Queen of Autumn Leaves	04179849
Queen's Double	05901497
Raigeki	12580477
Raimei	56260110
Rain of Mercy	66719324
Rainbow Flower	21347810
Rainbow Marine Mermaid	29402771
Raise Body Heat	51267887
Rare Fish	80516007
Ray & Temperature	85309439
Reaper of the Cards	33066139
Red Archery Girl	65570596
Red Medicine	38199696
Red-Eyes B. Dragon	74677422
Red-Eyes Black Metal Dragon	64335804
Red-Moon Baby	56387350
Reinforcements	17814387
Relinquished	64631466
Remove Trap	51482758
Respect Play	08951260
Restructer Revolution	99518961
Return of the Doomed	19827717
Reverse Trap	77622396
Revival Jam	31709826
Rhaimundos of the Red Sword	62403074
Right Arm of the Forbidden One	70903634
Right Leg of the Forbidden One	08124921
Riryoku	34016756
Riryoku Field	70344351
Rising Air Current	45778932
Roaring Ocean Snake	19066538

Yu-Gi-Oh! Worldwide Edition: Stairway to the Destined Duel (continued)

Card	Code
Robbin' Goblin	88279736
Rock Ogre Grotto #1	68846917
Rock Ogre Grotto #2	62193699
Rock Spirit	82818645
Rocket Warrior	30860696
Rogue Doll	91939608
Root Water	39004808
Rose Spectre of Dunn	32485271
Royal Command	33950246
Royal Decree	51452091
Royal Guard	39239728
Rude Kaiser	26378150
Rush Recklessly	70046172
Ryu-Kishin	15303296
Ryu-Kishin Powered	24611934
Ryu-Ran	02964201
Saber Slasher	73911410
Saggi the Dark Clown	66602787
Salamandra	32268901
Sand Stone	73051941
Sangan	26202165
Science Soldier	67532912
Scroll of Bewitchment	10352095
Sea Kamen	71746462
Sea King Dragon	23659124
Seal of the Ancients	97809599
Sebek's Blessing	22537443
Sectarian of Secrets	15507080
Senju of the Thousand Hands	23401839
Serpent Marauder	82742611
Seven Tools of the Bandit	03819470
Shadow Ghoul	30778711
Shadow of Eyes	58621589
Shadow Specter	40575313
Shadow Spell	29267084
Share the Pain	56830749
Shield & Sword	52097679
Shining Abyss	87303357
Shining Fairy	95956346
Shining Friendship	82085619
Shovel Crusher	71950093
Silver Bow and Arrow	01557499

Card	Code
Silver Fang	90357090
Sinister Serpent	08131171
Skelengel	60694662
Skelgon	32355828
Skull Dice	00126218
Skull Invitation	98139712
Skull Lair	06733059
Skull Mariner	05265750
Skull Red Bird	10202894
Skull Servant	32274490
Skull Stalker	54844990
Skullbird	08327462
Sky Dragon	95288024
Slate Warrior	78636495
Sleeping Lion	40200834
Slot Machine	03797883
Snake Fang	00596051
Snakeyashi	29802344
Snatch Steal	45986603
Sogen	86318356
Solemn Judgment	41420027
Solemn Wishes	35346968
Solitude	84794011
Solomon's Lawbook	23471572
Sonic Bird	57617178
Sonic Maid	38942059
Sorcerer of the Doomed	49218300
Soul Hunter	72869010
Soul of Purity and Light	77527210
Soul of the Pure	47852924
Soul Release	05758500
Souls of the Forgotten	04920010
Sparks	76103675
Spear Cretin	58551308
Spellbinding Circle	18807108
Spherous Lady	52121290
Spike Seadra	85326399
Spikebot	87511987
Spiked Snail	98075147
Spirit Elimination	69832741
Spirit Message "A"	94772232
Spirit Message "I"	31893528
Spirit Message "L"	30170981

Yu-Gi-Oh! Worldwide Edition: Stairway to the Destined Duel (continued)

Card	Code	Card	Code
Spirit Message "N"	67287533	Tao the Chanter	46247516
Spirit of Flames	13522325	Tatsunootoshigo	47922711
Spirit of the Books	14037717	Temple of Skulls	00732302
Spirit of the Breeze	53530069	Tenderness	57935140
Spirit of the Harp	80770678	Tentacle Plant	60715406
Spirit of the Mountain	34690519	Terra the Terrible	63308047
Spirit of the Winds	54615781	That Which Feeds on Life	52367652
Spiritualism	15855454	The 13th Grave	00032864
St. Joan	21175632	The All-Seeing White Tiger	32269855
Stain Storm	21323861	The Bewitching Phantom Thief	24348204
Star Boy	08201910	The Bistro Butcher	71107816
Steel Ogre Grotto #1	29172562	The Cheerful Coffin	41142615
Steel Ogre Grotto #2	90908427	The Dark Door	30606547
Steel Scorpion	13599884	The Drdek	08944575
Steel Shell	02370081	The Earl of Demise	66989694
Stim-Pack	83225447	The Emperor's Holiday	68400115
Stone Armadiller	63432835	The Eye of Truth	34694160
Stone D.	68171737	The Fiend Megacyber	66362965
Stone Ghost	72269672	The Forceful Sentry	42829885
Stone Ogre Grotto	15023985	The Forgiving Maiden	84080938
Stop Defense	63102017	The Furious Sea King	18710707
Stuffed Animal	71068263	The Gross Ghost of Fled Dreams	68049471
Succubus Knight	55291359		
Summoned Skull	70781052	The Immortal of Thunder	84926738
Summoner of Illusions	14644902	The Inexperienced Spy	81820689
Supply	44072894	The Judgment Hand	28003512
Supporter in the Shadows	41422426	The Last Warrior from Another Planet	86099788
Swamp Battleguard	40453765		
Sword Arm of Dragon	13069066	The Legendary Fisherman	03643300
Sword Hunter	51345461	The Little Swordsman of Aile	25109950
Sword of Dark Destruction	37120512		
Sword of Deep-Seated	98495314	The Masked Beast	49064413
Sword of Dragon's Soul	61405855	The Melting Red Shadow	98898173
Swords of Revealing Light	72302403	The Portrait's Secret	32541773
Swordsman from a Foreign Land	85255550	The Regulation of Tribe	00296499
		The Reliable Guardian	16430187
Swordsman of Landstar	03573512	The Rock Spirit	76305638
Swordstalker	50005633	The Shadow Who Controls the Dark	63125616
Synchar	75646173		
Tailor of the Fickle	43641473	The Shallow Grave	43434803
Tainted Wisdom	28725004	The Snake Hair	29491031
Takriminos	44073668	The Statue of Easter Island	10262698
Takuhee	03170832	The Stern Mystic	87557188
		The Thing That	18180762

Yu-Gi-Oh! Worldwide Edition: Stairway to the Destined Duel (continued)

Card	Code
Hides in the Mud	
The Unfriendly Amazon	65475294
The Unhappy Maiden	51275027
The Wandering Doomed	93788854
The Wicked Worm Beast	06285791
Thousand Knives	63391643
Thousand-Eyes Idol	27125110
Thousand-Eyes Restrict	63519819
Three-Headed Geedo	78423643
Three-Legged Zombies	33734439
Thunder Dragon	31786629
Tiger Axe	49791927
Time Seal	35316708
Time Wizard	71625222
Toad Master	62671448
Togex	33878931
Toll	82003859
Tomozaurus	46457856
Tongyo	69572024
Toon Alligator	59383041
Toon Mermaid	65458948
Toon Summoned Skull	91842653
Toon World	15259703
Torike	80813021
Tornado Bird	71283180
Tornado Wall	18605135
Torrential Tribute	53582587
Total Defense Shogun	75372290
Trakadon	42348802
Trap Hole	04206964
Trap Master	46461247
Tremendous Fire	46918794
Trent	78780140
Trial of Nightmare	77827521
Tribute to the Doomed	79759861
Tripwire Beast	45042329
Turtle Bird	72929454
Turtle Raccoon	17441953
Turtle Tiger	37313348
Turu-Purun	59053232
Twin Long Rods #1	29692206
Twin Long Rods #2	78984772
Twin-Headed Fire Dragon	78984772
Twin-Headed	54752875

Card	Code
Two-Headed King Rex	94119974
Two-Mouth Darkruler	57305373
Two-Pronged Attack	83887306
Tyhone	72842870
Tyhone #2	56789759
Type Zero Magic Crusher	21237481
UFO Turtle	60806437
Ultimate Offering	80604091
Umi	22702055
Umiiruka	82999629
Unfriendly Amazon	65475294
United We Stand	56747793
Unknown Warrior of Fiend	97360116
Upstart Goblin	70368879
Uraby	01784619
Ushi Oni	48649353
Valkyrion the Magna Warrior	75347539
Vengeful Bog Spirit	95220856
Vermillion Sparrow	35752363
Versago the Destroyer	50259460
Vile Germs	39774685
Violent Rain	94042337
Violet Crystal	15052462
Vishwar Randi	78556320
Vorse Raider	14898066
Waboku	12607053
Wall of Illusion	13945283
Warrior Elimination	90873992
Warrior of Tradition	56413937
Wasteland	23424603
Water Element	03732747
Water Girl	55014050
Water Magician	93343894
Water Omotics	02483611
Waterdragon Fairy	66836598
Weather Control	37243151
Weather Report	72053645
Wetha	96643568
Whiptail Crow	91996584
White Dolphin	92409659
White Hole	43487744
White Magical Hat	15150365
Wicked Dragon with the Ersatz Head	02957055
Wicked Mirror	15150371

DS

GBA

PSP

PS2

PS3

Wii

Xbox

Xbox 360

Index

Yu-Gi-Oh! Worldwide Edition: Stairway to the Destined Duel (continued)

Card	Code
Widespread Ruin	77754944
Wilmee	92391084
Windstorm of Etaqua	59744639
Wing Eagle	47319141
Wing Egg Elf	98582704
Winged Cleaver	39175982
Winged Dragon, Guardian of the Fortress #1	87796900
Winged Dragon, Guardian of the Fortress #2	57405307
Winged Egg of New Life	42418084
Wings of Wicked Flame	92944626
Wingweaver	31447217
Witch of the Black Forest	78010363
Witch's Apprentice	80741828
Witty Phantom	36304921
Wodan the Resident of the Forest	42883273
Wolf	49417509
Wood Clown	17511156

Card	Code
Wood Remains	17733394
World Suppression	12253117
Worm Drake	73216412
Wow Warrior	69750536
Wretched Ghost of the Attic	17238333
Yado Karu	29380133
Yaiba Robo	10315429
Yamadron	70345785
Yamatano Dragon Scroll	76704943
Yami	59197169
Yaranzo	71280811
Yashinoki	41061625
Yormungarde	17115745
Zanki	30090452
Zarigun	10598400
Zoa	24311372
Zombie Warrior	31339260
Zombyra the Dark	88472456
Zone Eater	86100785

Unlockable Character	Objective
Duke Devlin	Defeat the following characters at least one time: Yugi Moto, Tea, Joey, Bakura, Seto Kaiba, Ishizu, Rex, Weevil, Solomon, Mai, Espa Roba, Mako, Mokuba, Bandit Keith, Maximillion Pegasus, Seeker/Rare Hunter, Strings, Odion, Umbra & Lumis, Arkana, Marik, and Shadi.
Mokuba	You have to lose 5 duels. It doesn't matter which duelist you lose to.
Pegasus	Obtain a Toon World card. Search around Battle City and he shows up as a duelist you haven't fought yet.
Shadi and the Rare Hunters	Complete Marik's little Phantom Pyramid.

Unlockable	Code
100 Lives	Hold Ⓛ at the slot Select screen and press →,→,→,→,→,→,→,→.
All Power-Ups	Hold Ⓛ at the slot Select screen and press →,←,→,←,→,←,→.
Free Mode (No restrictions)	Beat all the limitation duels once.
Ghost Hideout	Beat all of the Ghosts (i.e. Rare Hunter, Strings, Arkana) at least once. After you beat the last Ghost, there is a cutscene with Grandpa Yugi and Tea. Tea leads you, possessed, to the Ghosts Hideout where you duel. After that, you duel with other Ghosts/Rare Hunters until you get to the final stage where you face Marik. After you complete the Ghosts Hideout, you unlock all of the Ghosts/Rare Hunters to challenge and play freely.

DS
GBA
PSP
PS2
PS3
Wii
Xbox
Xbox 360
Index

Table of Contents - PSP

300: March to Glory

Enter this code while the game is paused.

Unlockable	Code
25,000 Kleos	⇩, ⇦, ⇩, ⇦, ⇧, ⇦

Ace Combat X: Skies of Deception

Unlockables

Unlockable	How to Unlock
Air Guardian	Keep losses of the allied helicopters heading for Sachana Air Base to a minimum
Bronze Ace	Destroy 200 enemies
Bronze Defender	Maintain command of the skies for over 5 minutes in Air Superiority
Bronze Star of Victory	Win 10 Multiplayer battles
Conqueror	Finish the campaign while taking part in all missions (17)
Expert Marksman	Destroy 50 aircraft with guns
Eye of the Storm	Defeat the Gleipnir
Freedom Tower	Liberate Griswall
Gold Ace	Destroy 1,000 enemies
Land Guardian	Keep allied casualties at Stand Canyon to a minimum
Mark of the Vioarr	Defeat the Fefnir
Marksman	Destroy 5 aircraft with guns

DS

GBA

PSP

PS2

PS3

Wii

Xbox

Xbox 360

Index

Ace Combat X: Skies of Deception (continued)

Sea Guardian	Keep damage to the allied fleet at Terminus Island to a minimum
Sharpshooter	Destroy 15 aircraft with guns
Silver Ace	Destroy 500 enemies
Swift Hunter	Finish campaign with the fewest missions (10)
Apalis: Earth Shaker / Cockpit / $34,200	S-rank mission 03A with Apalis
Cariburn: Sylph Wing / Wing / $55,600	S-rank mission 01 with Cariburn
Falken: Laser Extender / Weapon / $69,800	S-rank mission 10A with Falken
Forneus: Diffusion Coat / Armor /$49,600	S-rank mission 09A with Forneus
Fregata: Hydra Engine / Engine/ $51,600	S-rank mission 02 with Fregata
X-02: Long Range MSSL / Weapon / $45,100	S-rank mission 13A with X-02
XFA-27: Scarface MBS / Weapon / $76,500	S-rank mission 04B with XFA-27
ADF-01 FALKEN	Complete SP stage
SP Stage "Operation X"	Complete all missions and mission branches
Stage 03B "Captive City"	Complete 05 or 06 before going to 04
Stage 07C "Time Limit"	07->09->11->07C
Stage 12C "Wild Card"	07->08->10->09->12C

Ape Escape Academy

Unlockable Minigames

Unlockable	How to Unlock
Ape Ping-Pong Minigame	Get 40 Specter Emblems
Ape Ping-Pong Minigame Bonus Characters	Complete the Ape Ping-Pong Minigame
Jake Attacks Minigame	Get 30 Specter Emblems
Snowkidz Snowboarding Minigame	Get 10 Specter Emblems
Specter Boxing Minigame	Get 20 Specter Emblems
Specter Boxing Minigame Bonus Characters	Complete the Specter Boxing Minigame
Survival Mode in Spector Boxing	Complete Spector Boxing

Alien Syndrome

Unlock Extra Difficulties

Unlockable	How to Unlock
Unlock Hard Difficulty	Beat the game on Normal difficulty
Unlock Expert Difficulty	Beat the game on Hard difficulty

DS

GBA

PSP

PS2

PS3

Wii

Xbox

Xbox 360

Index

Armored Core: Formula Front

Manual Controlled Tricks

Use during a manually controlled battle.

Code	Effect
✤ and ✤ Simultaneously	Drop Extensions
✤ and ● Simultaneously	Drop Left Arm Weapon
✤ and ■ Simultaneously	Drop Right Arm Weapon
Boost Forward on the ground and press ●	Fire Energy Wave

Unlockable Features

For *Armored Core: Formula Front International* version only.

Unlockable	How to Unlock
50 Exhibition Matches	Beat Formula Regular League
Ending Credits (movie attachment)	Beat all 50 Exhibition Matches

ATV Offroad Fury Blazin Trails

To enter these passwords go to the Options menu, select the Player Profile menu, and then enter the Cheat menu.

Unlockable	Code
1,500 Credits	$MONEYBAG$$
All Music Videos	BILLBOARDS
All Rider Gear	DUDS
Unlock Everything (except the Fury Bike)	ALL ACCESS
Unlock Rims	DUBS

Blitz: Overtime

Password

In the main menu in the "extras" option, input these codes to unlock the following.

Password	Effect
ONFIRE	Ball trails always on. Only affects Quick Play mode.
BOUNCY	Beach Ball. Only affects Quick Play mode.
PIPPED	Double unleash icons. Only affects Quick Play mode.
CHAMPS	In Campaign mode, highlight a team but do not select it. Stay on the menu and press ■, ■, ▲, Triangle to instantly win against the selected team.
NOTTIRED	Stamina disabled. Only affects Quick Play mode.
CLASHY	Super Clash mode. Only affects Quick Play mode.
BIGDOGS	Super Unleash Clash mode. Only affects Quick Play mode.
CHUWAY	Two player co-op mode.

Call of Duty: Roads to Victory

Survival! Mode

It only works if you select Hardened or Veteran difficulty. It will not work on Green. Once you do this, your original save is gone.

Unlockable	How to Unlock
Survival! Mode	Play and beat the game on Veteran mode, then it will ask if you want to switch to Survival! mode. Select yes.

Unlockables

Complete the following tasks to unlock the corresponding cheats.

DS

GBA

PSP

PS2

PS3

Wii

Xbox

Xbox 360

Index

DS
GBA
PSP
PS2
PS3
Wii
Xbox
Xbox 360
Index

Call of Duty: Roads to Victory (continued)

Unlockable	How to Unlock
Infinite Ammunition	Complete the game on Green, or complete the game with all Bronze medals
Infinite Grenades	Complete the game on Veteran, or complete the game with all Silver medals
Infinite Health	Complete the game on Hardened, or complete the game with all Gold medals

Capcom Classic Collection Remixed

Enter this code at the Press Start screen.

Unlockable	Code
Arts, Tips, and Sound Tests for Every Game	Press ⇦, ⇨ on D-pad, ⇦, ⇨ on Analog stick, ■, ●, ⇧, ⇩

Coded Arms

Unlockables

Unlockable	How to Unlock
Blast Helm	Defeat lvl 50 boss—Enforcer
Copperhead	Beat Sector 2 Ruins Boss—Mantis
Inferno	Beat Sector 2 Base boss—Colossus
Infinity	Finish Story mode Once
Judgement	Beat Sector 2 City boss—Enforcer
Neutron Gun	Beat the boss on Infinity mode level 30
Onslaught	Beat the boss on Infinity mode level 10
Surge Helm	Defeat lvl 40 boss—Mantis
Trident	Beat the boss on Infinity mode level 60
Vulcan	Beat the boss on Infinity mode level 20

Death Jr.

To enter these codes, pause the game and hold ⓛ+ⓡ.

Unlockable	Code
All Weapons and Weapon Upgrades	⇧, ⇧, ⇩, ⇩, ⇦, ⇨, ⇦, ⇨, ✕, ●
Ammo Refilled	▲, ▲, ✕, ✕, ■, ●, ■, ●, ⇩, ⇨
Assist Extender	⇧, ⇧, ⇩, ⇩, ▲, ▲, ✕, ✕, ▲, ▲
Attacks Have Different Names	⇧, ⇧, ⇩, ⇦, ▲, ▲, ■, ✕, ●, ■
Big Heads	▲, ●, ✕, ■, ▲, ⇧, ⇨, ⇩, ⇦, ⇧
Big Scythe	▲, ■, ✕, ●, ▲, ⇧, ⇦, ⇩, ⇨, ⇧
Bullet Holes Become Pictures	⇧, ⇨, ⇩, ⇦, ⇧, ▲, ●, ✕, ■, ▲
Eyedoors Don't Require Souls to Open	⇧, ⇩, ⇦, ⇨, ⇧, ▲, ■, ✕, ●, ■
Fill Pandora's Assist Meter	⇧, ⇨, ⇩, ⇦, ⇩, ⇨, ⇩, ⇦, ✕, ✕
Free All Characters and Unlock All Levels (Must be entered in the stage and re-entered in the museum)	⇧, ⇧, ⇧, ⇧, ⇩, ⇩, ⇩, ⇩, ✕, ✕
Free Seep	⇦, ⇦, ⇨, ⇨, ⇨, ⇨, ⇦, ⇦, ✕, ✕
Increased Health and Stamina	⇧, ⇧, ⇩, ⇩, ✕, ●, ▲, ■, ✕, ✕
Invincibility	⇧, ⇧, ⇩, ⇩, ⇦, ⇨, ⇨, ■, ▲
Monsters Are Different Colors and Scythe Has Trails	⇩, ✕, ⇩, ✕, ⇩, ✕, ⇩, ✕, ⇩, ✕
Odd Monsters and Scythe Has Trails	▲, ⇧, ●, ⇨, ✕, ⇩, ■, ⇦, ▲, ⇧

Death Jr. (continued)

Unlockable	Code
Unlimited Ammo	▲, ▲, ×, ×, ■, ●, ■, ●, ⇨, ⇩
Warp to Advanced Training Stage	⇩, ×, ⇩, ×, ⇩, ×, ⇩, ×, ⇩, ■
Warp to Basic Training Stage	⇧, ▲, ⇧, ×, ⇩, ×, ⇩, ×, ⇩, ×
Warp to Big Trouble in Little Downtown Stage	⇧, ▲, ⇩, ×, ⇩, ×, ⇩, ×, ⇩, ×
Warp to Bottom of the Bell Curve Stage	⇩, ×, ⇩, ×, ⇩, ×, ⇩, ×, ⇩, ▲
Warp to Burn it Down Stage	⇩, ×, ⇧, ▲, ⇩, ×, ⇩, ×, ⇩, ×
Warp to Final Battle Stage	⇩, ×, ⇩, ×, ⇩, ×, ⇩, ▲, ⇧, ×
Warp to Growth Spurt Stage	⇩, ×, ⇩, ×, ⇩, ×, ⇩, ×, ⇩, ×
Warp to Happy Trails Insanitarium Stage	⇩, ×, ⇩, ▲, ⇩, ×, ⇩, ×, ⇩, ×
Warp to Higher Learning Stage	⇩, ×, ⇩, ×, ⇩, ×, ⇩, ▲, ⇩, ×
Warp to How a Cow Becomes a Steak Stage	⇩, ×, ⇩, ×, ⇩, ▲, ⇩, ×, ⇩, ×
Warp to Inner Madness Stage	⇩, ×, ⇩, ×, ⇧, ▲, ⇩, ×, ⇩, ×
Warp to Into the Box Stage	⇩, ×, ⇩, ×, ⇩, ×, ⇧, ▲, ⇩, ×
Warp to Moving on Up Stage	⇩, ▲, ⇧, ×, ⇩, ×, ⇩, ×, ⇩, ×
Warp to My House Stage	⇩, ×, ⇩, ▲, ⇩, ×, ⇩, ×, ⇩, ×
Warp to Seep's Hood Stage	⇩, ▲, ⇩, ×, ⇩, ×, ⇩, ×, ⇩, ×
Warp to Shock Treatment Stage	⇩, ×, ⇩, ×, ⇩, ×, ⇧, ×, ⇩, ×
Warp to The Basement Stage	⇩, ×, ⇩, ×, ⇩, ×, ⇩, ×, ⇧, ▲
Warp to The Burger Tram Stage	⇩, ×, ⇩, ×, ⇩, ×, ⇧, ×, ⇩, ×
Warp to The Corner Store Stage	⇩, ×, ⇩, ×, ⇩, ×, ⇩, ×, ⇩, ×
Warp to The Museum	⇧, ×, ⇩, ×, ⇩, ×, ⇩, ×, ⇩, ×
Warp to Udder Madness Stage	⇩, ×, ⇩, ×, ⇧, ×, ⇩, ×, ⇩, ×
Weapons Have Different Names	⇩, ⇩, ⇧, ⇧, ⇦, ⇨, ⇦, ⇨, ■, ▲
Widget	⇨, ⇧, ⇩, ⇧, ▲, ⇧, ⇨, ■, ▲, ⇨

Death Jr. II: Root of Evil

Enter these codes while the game is paused.

Unlockable	Code
All Weapon Upgrades	Hold L2 and press ⇧, ⇧, ⇩, ⇩, ⇦, ⇨, ⇦, ⇨, ×, ●
Invincibility	Hold L2 and press ⇧, ⇧, ⇩, ⇩, ⇦, ⇨, ⇦, ⇨, ■, ▲
Refill Ammunition	Hold L2 and press ▲, ▲, ×, ×, ■, ●, ■, ●, ⇩, ⇨
Unlimited Ammunition	Hold L2 and press ▲, ▲, ×, ×, ■, ●, ■, ●, ⇨, ⇩

Def Jam: Fight for NY-The Takeover

Enter these passwords in the Cheats menu under extras.

Unlockable	Password	Unlockable	Password
After Hours by Nyne	LOYALTY	*Original Gangster* by Ice-T	POWER
Anything Goes by C-N-N	MILITAIN	*Poppa Large* by Ultramagnetic MC's	ULTRAMAG
Blindside by Baxter	CHOPPER		
Bust by Outkast	BIGBOI	*Seize the Day* by Bless	SIEZE
Comp by Comp	CHOCOCITY	*Take a Look at my Life* by Fat Joe	CARTAGENA
Dragon House by Masa Mix	AKIRA		
Get It Now by Bless	PLATINUMB	*Walk with Me* by Joe Budden	PUMP
Koto by Chiang's Mix	GHOSTSHELL	Add 100 reward points	REALSTUFF
Lil Bro by Ric-A-Che	GONBETRUBL	Add 100 reward points	GOUNDRGRND
Man Up by Sticky Fingaz	KIRKJONES	Add 100 reward points	THEEMCEE
Move! by Public Enemy	RESPECT	Add 100 reward points	BULLETPROOF

DS
GBA
PSP
PS2
PS3
Wii
Xbox
Xbox 360
Index

DS

GBA

PSP

PS2

PS3

Wii

Xbox

Xbox 360

Index

Def Jam: Fight for NY–The Takeover (continued)

Unlockable	Password	Unlockable	Password
Add 100 reward points	DASTREETS	Add 200 reward points	DRAGONHOUSE
Add 200 reward points	REAL STYLE	Add 300 reward points	NEWYORKCIT
Add 200 reward points	SUPER FREAK		

Disgaea: Afternoon of Darkness

Etna Mode

Disgaea contains a hidden mode called Etna mode. Normally you have to get this mode by going through the game and reading Etna's diary every chapter, but you can unlock it instantly by entering the following code during the title screen, with the pointer on "New Game." If you're successful, you'll hear Etna's voice.

Effect	Code
Unlock Etna Mode (US)	▲, ■, ●, ▲, ■, ●, ✕

Extra Classes

Unlockable	How to Unlock
Angel	Female Cleric, Knight, and Archer all at level 100 or higher.
Archer	Level 3 or higher in Bow Weapon Mastery.
EDF Soldier	Level 30 or higher Gun Weapon Mastery.
Galaxy Mage	Level a Prism Mage to Level 50.
Galaxy Skull	Level a Prism Skull to Level 50.
Knight	Female Warrior and Female Mage each at level 10 or higher.
Majin	Male Warrior, Brawler, Ninja, Rogue, and Scout all at level 200 or higher.
Ninja	Male Fighter and Male Warrior with a total level of 10 or higher.
Prism Mage	Level a Star Mage to Level 35.
Prism Skull	Level a Star Skull to Level 35.
Rogue	Both Fighter and Warrior, Males or Females, each at level 5 or higher.
Ronin	Female Warrior and Female Fighter with a total level of 10 or higher.
Scout	Two Fighters/Warriors, Males or Females, each at level 5 or higher.
Star Mage	Get one Fire, Ice, and Wind Mage and level all three of them to level 5.
Star Skull	Get one Fire, Ice, and Wind Skull and level all three of them to level 5.

Dragon Ball Z: Shin Budokai

Unlockables

You must complete every fight quickly and with most of your health.

Card Sheet	How to Unlock
No. 10	Finish all fights in Chapter 5
No. 13	Z rank on all fights for Chapter 1
No. 14	Z rank on all fights for Chapter 2
No. 15	Z rank on all fights for Chapter 3
No. 16	Z rank on all fights for Chapter 4
No. 17	Z rank on all fights for Chapter 5
No. 24	Z rank on all fights for Dragon Road

Unlockable Characters

Defeat the specified characters in Dragon Road mode.

Unlockable	How to Unlock
Adult Gohan—Mystic Form	Defeat Vegeta in Chapter 4-A-B 5
Adult Gohan—Super Saiyan 2 Form	Defeat Broly in Chapter 2-6
Adult Gohan—Super Saiyan Form	Defeat Frieza in Chapter 1-8
Broly—Legendary Super Saiyan Form	Defeat Frieza in Chapter 4-A-B 6

Dragon Ball Z: Shin Budokai (continued)

Cell—Super Perfect Form	Defeat Cell in Chapter 2-5
Cooler—Final Form	Defeat Pikkon in Chapter 4-B-A 5
Frieza—100% Full Power Form	Defeat Frieza in Chapter 3-2
Future Trunks—Super Saiyan Form	Defeat Gotenks in Chapter 4-2
Goku—Kaioken Form	Defeat Krillin in Chapter 1-2
Goku—Super Saiyan 2 Form	Defeat Fake Goku in Chapter 2-2
Goku—Super Saiyan 3 Form	Defeat Vegeta in Chapter 3-7
Goku—Super Saiyan Form	Defeat Janemba in Chapter 1-9
Goku SS3	Beat Majin Vegeta in Chapter 3
Gotenks	Defeat Gotenks in Chapter 1-4
Gotenks—Super Saiyan 3 Form	Defeat Cell in Chapter 3-A-4
Gotenks—Super Saiyan Form	Defeat Gotenks in Chapter 1-5
Janemba	Beat Story Mode
Krillin—Unlock Potential Form	Defeat Goku in Chapter 5-1
Piccolo—Fuse with Kami Form	Defeat Cell in Chapter 2-1
Pikkon	Defeat Janemba in Chapter 2- 9
Teen Gohan—Super Saiyan 2 Form	Defeat Teen Gohan in Chapter 3-9
Teen Gohan—Super Saiyan Form	Defeat Cell in Chapter 3-8
Vegeta—Majin Form	Defeat Vegeta in Chapter 4-7
Vegeta—Super Saiyan 2 Form	Defeat Janemba in Chapter 2-7
Vegeta—Super Saiyan Form	Defeat #18 in Chapter 2-3
Vegetto and Gogeta	Beat the last chapter choosing either path
Vegetto—Super Saiyan Form	Defeat Kid Buu in Chapter 5–B-9

Exit

In order to use these codes, you must complete the first situation level.

Unlockable	Code
Unlocks Situation 8	L, R, ⇐, ⇒, ■, ●, ✕, ▲
Unlocks Situation 9	▲, ⇩, ●, ⇐, ✕, ⇧, ■, ⇒
Unlocks Situation 10	⇒, ⇩, ⇧, ⇐, ●, ✕, R, L

Full Auto 2: Battlelines

Enter these codes in the codes section under features.

Unlockable	Code
All Cars	⇧, ⇧, ⇧, ⇧, ⇐, ⇩, ⇧, ⇒, ⇩, ⇩, ⇩, ⇩
All Events	START, ⇐, SELECT, ⇒, ⇒, ▲, ✕, ■, START, R, ⇩, SELECT

Ghost Rider

Unlockable	Code
Charge Link Infinite	End the game in Normal difficulty
First Mortal Blow	End the game in Normal difficulty
Infinite Spirit	End the game in Normal difficulty
Invincibility	End the game in Normal difficulty
Mode Turbo	End the game in Normal difficulty

Grand Theft Auto: Liberty City Stories

Enter these codes during gameplay. Do not pause the game.

Unlockable	Code
$250,000	L, R, ▲, L, R, ●, L, R

DS

GBA

PSP

PS2

PS3

Wii

Xbox

Xbox 360

Index

Side tabs: DS · GBA · PSP · PS2 · PS3 · Wii · Xbox · Xbox 360 · Index

Grand Theft Auto: Liberty City Stories (continued)

Aggressive Drivers	■, ■, R, ×, ×, L, ●, ●
All Green Lights	▲, ▲, R, ■, ■, L, ×, ×
All Vehicles Chrome Plated	▲, R, L, ⇩, ⇩, R, R, ▲
Black Cars	●, ●, R, ▲, ▲, L, ■, ■
Bobble Head World	⇩, ⇩, ⇩, ●, ●, ×, L, R
Cars Drive On Water	●, ×, ⇩, ●, ×, ⇧, L, L
Change Bike Tire Size	●, ⇨, ×, ⇧, ⇨, ×, L, ■
Clear Weather	⇧, ⇩, ●, ⇧, ⇩, ■, L, R
Commit Suicide	L, ⇩, ⇦, R, ×, ●, ⇧, ▲
Destroy All Cars	L, L, ⇦, L, L, ⇨, ×, ■
Display Game Credits	L, R, L, R, ⇧, ⇩, L, R
Faster Clock	L, L, ⇦, L, L, ⇨, ●, ×
Faster Gameplay	R, R, L, R, R, L, ⇩, ×
Foggy Weather	⇧, ⇩, ▲, ⇧, ⇩, ×, L, R
Full Armor	L, R, ●, L, R, ×, L, R
Full Health	L, R, ×, L, R, ■, L, R
Have Girls Follow You	⇩, ⇩, ⇩, ▲, ▲, ●, L, R
Never Wanted	L, L, ▲, R, R, ×, ■, ●
Overcast Weather	⇧, ⇩, ×, ⇧, ⇩, ▲, L, R
Pedestrians Attack You	L, L, R, L, L, R, ⇧, ▲
Pedestrians Have Weapons	R, R, L, R, R, L, ⇨, ●
Pedestrians Riot	L, L, R, L, L, R, ⇦, ■
Perfect Traction	L, ⇧, ⇦, R, ▲, ●, ⇩, ×
Rainy Weather	⇧, ⇩, ■, ⇧, ⇩, ●, L, R
Raise Media Attention	L, ⇧, ⇨, R, ▲, ■, ⇩, ×
Raise Wanted Level	L, L, ■, L, L, R, ▲, L, R
Random Pedestrian Outfit	L, L, ⇦, L, L, ⇨, ■, ▲
Slower Gameplay	R, ▲, ×, R, ■, ●, ⇦, ⇨
Spawn Rhino	L, L, ●, L, L, ●, ⇩, L
Spawn Trashmaster	▲, ●, ⇩, ▲, ●, ⇧, L, L
Sunny Weather	L, L, ●, R, R, ■, ▲, ×
Upside Down Gameplay	⇩, ⇩, ⇩, ×, ×, ■, R, L
Upside Up	▲, ▲, ▲, ⇧, ⇧, ⇩, L, R
Weapon Set 1	⇧, ■, ■, ⇩, ⇦, ■, ■, ⇨
Weapon Set 2	⇧, ●, ●, ⇩, ⇦, ●, ●, ⇨
Weapon Set 3	⇧, ×, ×, ⇩, ⇦, ×, ×, ⇨
White Cars	×, ×, R, ●, ●, L, ▲, ▲

Grand Theft Auto: Vice City Stories

Enter any of these codes while playing.

Unlockable	Code
25% of MP Content	⇧, ⇧, ⇧, ■, ■, ▲, R, L
50% of MP Content	⇧, ⇧, ⇧, ●, ●, ×, L, R
75% of MP Content	⇧, ⇧, ⇧, ⇧, ×, ×, ■, R, L
100% of MP Content	⇧, ⇧, ▲, ▲, ●, L, R
All Cars Are Black	L, R, L, R, ⇦, ●, ⇧, ×
Armor	⇧, ⇩, ⇦, ⇨, ■, ■, L, R
Cars Avoid You	⇧, ⇧, ⇨, ⇦, ▲, ●, ●, ■

98

Grand Theft Auto: Vice City Stories (continued)

Unlockable	Code
Chrome Cars	⇨, ⇧, ⇦, ⇩, ▲, ▲, L, R
Clear Weather	⇦, ⇩, R, L, ⇨, ⇧, ⇦, ✕
Commit Suicide	⇨, ⇨, ●, ●, L, R, ⇩, ✕
Destroy All Cars	L, R, R, ⇦, ⇨, ■, ⇩, R
Faster Clock	R, L, L, ⇩, ⇧, ✕, ⇩, L
Faster Gameplay	⇦, ⇦, R, R, ⇧, ▲, ⇩, ✕
Foggy Weather	⇦, ⇩, ▲, ✕, ⇨, ⇧, ⇦, L
$250,000	⇧, ⇩, ⇦, ⇨, ✕, ✕, L, R
Guys Follow You	⇨, L, ⇩, L, ●, ⇧, L, ■
Health	⇧, ⇩, ⇦, ⇨, ●, ●, L, R
Lower Wanted Level	⇦, ⇨, ▲, ▲, ⇩, ⇩, ✕, ✕
Nearest Ped Gets in Your Vehicle (Must Be in a Car)	⇩, ⇧, ⇨, L, L, ■, ⇧, L
Overcast Weather	⇦, ⇩, L, R, ⇨, ⇧, ⇦, ■
Peds Attack You	⇩, ▲, ⇧, ✕, L, R, L, R
Peds Have Weapons	⇧, L, ⇩, R, ⇦, ●, ⇨, ▲
Peds Riot	R, L, L, ⇩, ⇦, ●, ⇩, L
Perfect Traction	⇩, ⇦, ⇧, L, R, ▲, ●, ✕
Rainy Weather	⇦, ⇩, L, R, ⇨, ⇧, ⇦, ▲
Raise Wanted Level	⇧, ⇨, ■, ■, ⇩, ⇦, ●, ●
Slower Gameplay	⇦, ●, ●, ⇩, ⇩, ⇧, ▲, ✕
Spawn Rhino	⇧, L, ⇩, R, ⇦, L, ⇨, R
Spawn Trashmaster	⇩, ⇧, ⇨, ▲, L, ▲, L, ▲
Sunny Weather	⇦, ⇩, R, L, ⇨, ⇧, ⇦, ●
Upside Down Mode 1	■, ■, ■, L, L, R, ⇦, ⇨
Upside Down Mode 2	⇦, ⇦, ⇦, R, R, R, L, ⇩, ⇦
Weapon Set 1	⇦, ⇨, ✕, ⇧, ⇩, ■, ⇦, ⇨
Weapon Set 2	⇦, ⇨, ■, ⇧, ⇩, ▲, ⇦, ⇨
Weapon Set 3	⇦, ⇨, ▲, ⇧, ⇩, ●, ⇦, ⇨

Gretzky NHL

At the Gretzky Challenge Unlockables screen, press START to bring up the cheat entry.

Unlockable	Password
Get One Gretzky Point	CANADIAN DOLLAR
RoboEnforcer Model-44	ROBO CHECKS
Unlock 1910 Montreal Canadians Uniform	THE HABS
Unlock 1924 Montreal Canadians Uniform	LE HABITANT
Unlock 1927 Detroit Red Wings Uniform	BEEP BEEP
Unlock 1928 Boston Bruins Uniform	WICKED HAAAAAHD
Unlock 1929 Ottawa Senators Uniform	THE SENANATOR
Unlock 1930 Toronto Maple Leafs Uniform	NORTH OF THE BORDER
Unlock 1967 Pittsburgh Penguins Away Uniform	POPPIN TALK
Unlock 1970 Minnesota North Stars Uniform	TWIN STARS
Unlock 1975 Kansas City Scouts Uniform	YOU LITTLE DEVIL
Unlock 1976 New York Rangers Away Uniform	NEW YORK NEW YORK
Unlock 1977 Calgary Flames Away Uniform	FLAME ON
Unlock 1977 Colorado Rockies Uniform	DEVIL MADE ME DO IT

DS
GBA
PSP
PS2
PS3
Wii
Xbox
Xbox 360
Index

Gretzky NHL (continued)

Unlockable	Password
Unlock 1977 Vancouver Canucks Home Uniform	GREAT WHITE NORTH
Unlock 1977 Washington Capitals Away Uniform	CONGRESSIONAL WISDOM
Unlock 1978 New York Islanders Away Uniform	ORDWAY MADE ME DO IT
Unlock 1979 Edmonton Oilers Away Uniform	A SCARY SIGHT TO THE HOME CROWD
Unlock 1979 Edmonton Oilers Home Uniform	THREADS OF CHAMPS
Unlock 1979 St. Louis Blues Away Uniform	A BLUE NOTE
Unlock 1979 St. Louis Blues Home Uniform	MARDI GRAS
Unlock 1980 Quebec Nordiques Uniform	FRENCH FOR CANADIAN
Unlock 1983 Edmonton Oilers Away Uniform	ALL HAIL WAYNE
Unlock 1988 Pittsburgh Penguins Away Uniform	STEEL TOWN
Unlock 1989 Los Angeles Kings Away Uniform	KING GRETZKY
Unlock 1989 Los Angeles Kings Home Uniform	KING WAYNE
Unlock 1990 Winnipeg Jets Away Uniform	PORTAGE AND MAIN
Unlock 1990 Winnipeg Jets Home Uniform	MIDDLE OF CANADA
Unlock 1993 San Jose Sharks Away Uniform	SHARK BAIT
Unlock 1995 St. Louis Blues Away Uniform	VINTAGE BLUES
Unlock 1999 New York Rangers Home Uniform	UPPER WEST SIDE
Unlock Alternate Anaheim Mighty Ducks Uniform	FLYING VEE
Unlock Alternate Atlanta Thrashers Uniform	THRASHED TO THE MAX
Unlock Alternate Boston Bruins Uniform	NOMAR STILL RULES
Unlock Alternate Buffalo Sabers Uniform	IN THE SNOW BELT
Unlock Alternate Calgary Flames Uniform	THREE ALARM BLAZE
Unlock Alternate Chicago Blackhawks Uniform	WINDY CITY
Unlock Alternate Colorado Avalanche Uniform	SNOW DRIFTS
Unlock Alternate Columbus Blue Jackets Uniform	BLUE SHOES
Unlock Alternate Dallas Stars Uniform	HOCKEY IN TEXAS
Unlock Alternate Edmonton Oilers Uniform	PUMPIN OIL
Unlock Alternate Florida Panthers Uniform	SOUTH BEACH
Unlock Alternate Los Angeles Kings Uniform	IT IS GOOD TO BE THE KING
Unlock Alternate Minnesota Wild Uniform	COLD AS HECK
Unlock Alternate Nashville Predators Uniform	ALIEN VS NASHVILLE
Unlock Alternate New York Islanders Uniform	LAWNG ISLAND
Unlock Alternate New York Rangers Uniform	GREAT WHITE WAY
Unlock Alternate Ottawa Senators Uniform	MAJORITY RULE
Unlock Alternate Philadelphia Flyers Uniform	FANATICAL
Unlock Alternate San Jose Sharks Uniform	GET A BIGGER BOAT
Unlock Alternate Toronto Maple Leafs Uniform	HEY TERRANCE
Unlock Alternate Vancouver Canucks Uniform	WEST COAST EH
Unlock Big Boards Checking Option	ALL ABOARD
Unlock Everything	SHOENLOC
Unlock No Skate Fatigue Option	CAFFEINATED
Unlock Perfect Aim Option	THREAD THE NEEDLE
Unlock Perfect Slap Shots Option	SLAP THAT PUCK
Wayne Gretzky 1979	UNSTOPPABLE GREATNESS
Wayne Gretzky 1987	GLORY DAZE
Wayne Gretzky 1994	WEST COAST WAYNE
Wayne Gretzky 1999	A LEGEND ON ICE

DS

GBA

PSP

PS2

PS3

Wii

Xbox

Xbox 360

Index

Gretzky NHL 06

At the Main menu, select Features. Next, select "Gretzky Challenge" and unlockables. At the unlockables screen, press ⟨START⟩ to bring up the Password Entry menu.

Unlockable	Password
Earn one Gretzky point	CULKY NETC
Unlock all alternate uniforms	NNIADOUAMFM
Unlock all vintage uniforms	DLEONG ARE
Unlock all Wayne Gretzkys	TEH ESATGRTE NOES
Unlock big boards checking	LAL ABRAOD
Unlock bigger players	ARGLE NI RAGECH
Unlock everything	CONHEOSL
Unlock no skater fatigue	EFDTAFEACIN
Unlock perfect aim mode	TADHRE TEH EDNELE
Unlock perfect slap shots	SAPL TATH CUKP
Unlock RoboEnforcer Model-44	OBOR SKHECC
Unlock smaller players	IGHTMY UOSEM
Unlock Stanley Cup Championship video	VINIOS FO LYRGO

Harry Potter and the Goblet of Fire

Unlockable Levels

Unlockable	How to Unlock
Defense Against the Dark Arts (Lesson 1)	Finish the opening level
Moody's Challenges	Complete the "Forbidden Forest" level

Unlockable Minigames

Unlockable	How to Unlock
Dugbog Bulb Raid	Get 5 Tri-wizard Shields
Exploding Snap	Get 2 Tri-wizard Shields
Niffler Time Challenge	Get 8 Tri-wizard Shields
Wizard Pairs	Beat the first level of the game

Hot Shots Golf Open Tee

Unlockable	Code
Easy Loyalty	To gain loyalty much quicker than playing an entire round of golf, start a match play game under challenge mode. Give up on the first three holes by pressing Select then Start to forfeit. After the match you will still gain loyalty for your character.

LEGO Star Wars II: The Original Trilogy

Passwords

Enter the following codes at the Mos Eisley Cantina to unlock the character for purchase in Free Play mode.

Unlockable	How to Unlock	Unlockable	How to Unlock
Beach Trooper	UCK868	Gamorean Guard	YZF999
Ben Kenobi's Ghost	BEN917	Gonk Droid	NFX582
Bespin Guard	VHY832	Grand Moff Tarkin	SMG219
Bib Fortuna	WTY721	Han Solo with Hood	YWM840
Boba Fett	HLP221	IG-88	NXL973
Death Star Trooper	BNC332	Imperial Guard	MMM111
Emperor	HHY382	Imperial Officer	BBV889
Ewok	TTT289	Imperial Shuttle Pilot	VAP66

DS

GBA

PSP

PS2

PS3

Wii

Xbox

Xbox 360

Index

LEGO Star Wars II: The Original Trilogy (continued)

Unlockable	How to Unlock	Unlockable	How to Unlock
Imperial Spy	CVT125	Snow Trooper	NYU989
Lobot	UUB319	Stormtrooper	PTR345
Palace Guard	SGE549	TIE Fighter	HDY739
Rebel Pilot	CYG336	TIE Fighter Pilot	NNZ316
Rebel Trooper from Hoth	EKU849	TIE Interceptor	QYA828
Red Noses on All Characters	NBP398	Ugnaught	UGN694
Santa Hat and Red Clothes	CL4U5H	White Beard Extra	TYH319
Skiff Guard	GBU888		

Unlockable Characters

Complete challenge by collecting 10 Blue Minikits within the time limit allowed per level.

Unlockable	How to Unlock
R4-P17, PK Droid	Episode 4, Chapter 2
Battle Droid, B. D. (Security), B. D. (Geonosis), B. D. (Commander)	Episode 4, Chapter 4
Chancellor Palpatine, General Grievous, Grievous' Bodyguard	Episode 6, Chapter 5
Clone (Episode III, Pilot)	Episode 4, Chapter 6
Clone (Episode III, Swamp)	Episode 5, Chapter 4
Clone, Clone (Episode III), Commander Cody, Clone (Episode III Walker)	Episode 6, Chapter 3
Disguised Clone, Boba Fett (Boy)	Episode 6, Chapter 1
Droideka	Episode 4, Chapter 5
Geonosian	Episode 5, Chapter 3
Jango Fett	Episode 6, Chapter 2
Luminara, Ki-Adi-Mundi, Kit Fisto, Shaak Ti	Episode 5, Chapter 1
Mace Windu, Mace Windu (Episode 3)	Episode 6, Chapter 6
Padmé (Battle), Padmé (Clawed), Padmé (Geonosis)	Episode 5, Chapter 2
Padmé, Anakin Skywalker (boy)	Episode 4, Chapter 3
Queen Amidala, Royal Guard, Captain Panaka	Episode 5, Chapter 6
Super Battle Droid	Episode 5, Chapter 5
TC-14	Episode 4, Chapter 1
Wookiee, Jar Jar Binks	Episode 6, Chapter 4

Madden NFL 07

Passwords

Enter these names in the password section to get the Madden cards.

Password	Effect	Password	Effect
B57QLU	1958 Colts Gold card	COAGI4	1981 Chargers Gold card
1PL1FL	1966 Packers Gold card	WL8BKI	1982 Redskins Gold card
MIE6WO	1968 Jets Gold card	H0EW7I	1983 Raiders Gold card
CL2TOE	1970 Browns Gold card	M1AM1E	1984 Dolphins Gold card
NOEB7U	1972 Dolphins Gold card	QOETO8	1985 Bears Gold card
YOOFLA	1974 Steelers Gold card	ZI8S2L	1986 Giants Gold card
MOA11I	1976 Raiders Gold card	SP2A8H	1988 49ers Gold card
C8UM7U	1977 Broncos Gold card	2L4TRO	1990 Eagles Gold card
VIU0O7	1978 Dolphins Gold card	J1ETRI	1991 Lions Gold card
NLAPH3	1980 Raiders Gold card	W9UVI9	1992 Cowboys Gold card

Madden NFL 07 (continued)

Password	Effect	Password	Effect
DLA3I7	1993 Bills Gold card	WROA0R	QB on Target card
DR7EST	1994 49ers Gold card	WROA0R	Quarterback 100% Accuracy for one half
F8LUST	1996 Packers Gold card	RLA9R7	Super Bowl XLI Gold card
FIES95	1998 Broncos Gold card	WRLUF8	Super Bowl XLII Gold card
S90USW	1999 Rams Gold card	NIEV4A	Super Bowl XLIII Gold card
YI8P8U	Aloha Stadium Gold card	M5AB7L	Super Bowl XLIV Gold card
5LAW00	Lame Duck card	5LAQ00	Your opponent will have to throw Lob Passes for one half
XL7SP1	Mistake Free card		
XL7SP1	Mistake Free card, effective for one half		

MediEvil Resurrection

To enter this code, pause the game.

Unlockable	Code
Invincibility and All Weapons	Hold Ⓡ, then press ⇩, ⇧, ■, ▲, ▲, ●, ⇩, ⇧, ■, ▲

Metal Gear Acid

Enter the following in the Passwords menu through the Main menu.

Card	Password
Gives Card No. 173 - Viper	Viper
Gives Card No. 178 - Mika Slayton	Mika
Gives Card No. 182 - Karen Houjou	Karen
Gives Card No. 184 - Jehuty	Jehuty
Gives Card No. 199 - XM8	Xmeight
Gives Card No. 200 - Kosaka Yuka	Kobe
Gives Card No. 201 - Asaki Yoshida	umeda
Gives Card No. 202 - Yu Saito	YEBISU
Gives Card No. 203 - Shibuya Eri	Roppongi

Metal Gear Acid 2

Enter these passwords at the password screen. You'll obtain them as you load your saved games.

Password	Effect
Ronaldsiu	Banana Peel Card
Dcy	Card No. 203—Decoy Octopus
SONOFSULLY	Card No. 291—Jack
Vrs	Card No. 046—Strain (JP Version only)
Cct	Card No. 099—Gijin-san (JP Version only)
Konami	Card No. 119—Reaction Block
Viper	Card No. 161—Viper
Mika	Card No. 166—Mika Slayton
Karen	Card No. 170—Karen Houjou
Jehuty	Card No. 172—Jehuty
Xmeight	Card No. 187—XM8
Signt	Card No. 188—Mr. Sigint
Sgnt	Card No. 188—SIGINT (JP Version only)
Hrrr	Card No. 197—Sea Harrier (JP Version only)
Dcyctps	Card No. 203—Decoy Octopus (JP Version only)

DS
GBA
PSP
PS2
PS3
Wii
Xbox
Xbox 360
Index

DS

GBA

PSP

PS2

PS3

Wii

Xbox

Xbox 360

Index

Metal Gear Acid 2 (continued)

Password	Effect
Rgr	Card No. 212—Roger McCoy (JP Version only)
Xx	Card No. 281—Hinomoto Reiko (JP Version only)
Kinoshitaa	Card No. 285—Kinoshita Ayumi (JP Version only)
Shiimeg	Card No. 286—Ishii Meguru (JP Version only)
Nonat	Card No. 287—Sano Natsume (JP Version only)
No Place	Card No. 288—MGS4 (JP Version only)
Snake	Card No. 294—Solid Snake (MGS4)
Otacon	Card No. 295—Otacon (MGS4)
shrrr	Card No. 197 Sea Harrier (US version)
Ginormousj	Emma's Parrot Card
Gekko	Gekko (US Version)
NEXTGEN	Get MGS4 card
shinta	Gives you card Gijin-san
nojiri	Gives you card Strand
mgr	Ishii Meguru
aym	Kinoshita Ayumi
mk2	Metal Gear MK. II (MGS4) Card unlocked
smoking	No Smoking card (US Version)
thespaniard	Possessed Arm card
gcl	Reaction Block 119 (Japanese version only)
tobidacid	Solid Eye card (US/UK Version)
ntm	Unlocks Natsume Sano Card an Solid Eye Video
Hnmt	Unlocks Reiko Hinomoto card
Mccy	Unlocks the Roger McCoy card

Card Pack Upgrades

Complete the game once. Load your finished game save and play through the game again. At the points where you received the card packs, they will be upgraded into newer versions.

Unlockable	How to Unlock
Chronicle Unlimited Pack	Upgrade Chronicle Pack
MGS1 Integral Pack	Upgrade MGS1 Pack
MGS2 Substance Pack	Upgrade MGS2 Pack
MGS3 Subsistence Pack	Upgrade MGS3 Pack

Unlockable Cards

Complete the game on any difficulty and get a certain rare card.

Unlockable	How to Unlock
"E-Z Gun" Card	Beat 6 levels in Arena mode on Easy setting
"G36C" Card	Beat 6 levels in Arena mode on Extreme setting
"Stealth Camo" Card	Beat 6 levels in Arena mode on Normal setting
Metal Gear RAY	Beat Campaign mode twice
Metal Gear Rex	Complete game on Normal
MGS4	Complete game on Easy
Running Man Card	Complete 6 rounds in the Arena on Hard setting

Midnight Club Racing 3: Dub Edition

Go into the Options menu, then into the Cheats menu to enter these passwords.

Unlockable	Password
Max Nitro	fillmeup
Unlock All Cities in Arcade Mode	crosscountry
Unlocks Atlanta & Detroit	roadtrip
Vehicles Take No Damage	ontheroad

MLB 07: The Show

Codes

Code	Effect
All Pitches Have Max Break	Pause during a game and enter: ⇨, ✦, ✦, ✦, ✦, ✦, ✦, ✦
All Pitches Have Max Speed	Pause during a game and enter: ⇧, ✦, ✦, ✦, ✦, ✦, ✦, ✦
Silver Era Team and Gold Era Team Unlocked	At the main menu: ⇦, ✦, ✦, ✦, ✦, ✦, ✦, ✦

MVP Baseball

Under the "My MVP" menu, create a player named "Dan Carter." Once you do this, there will be a message indicating that the code was successful.

NBA Ballers Rebound

Enter these passwords in the Phrase-ology under Inside Stuff.

Unlockable	Password
All Alternate Gear, Players, and Movies	NBA Ballers True Playa
Allen Iverson's Recording Studio	The Answer
Alonzo Mourning Alternate Gear	Zo
Ben Gordon's Yacht	Nice Yacht
Chris Weber's Alternate Gear	24 Seconds
Clyde Drexler's Alternate Gear	Clyde The Glide
Dikembe Mutumbo's Alternate Gear	In The Paint
Emanuel Ginobli Alternate Gear	Manu
Jerry Stackhouse Alternate Gear	Stop Drop And Roll
Julius Irving Alternate Gear	One On One
Kevin McHale Alternate Gear	Holla Back
Lebron James' Alternate Gear	King James
Magic Johnson Alternate Gear	Laker Legends
Nene's Hilarios Alternate Gear	Rags To Riches
Pete Maravich's Alternate Gear	Pistol Pete
Rasheed Wallace Alternate Gear	Bring Down The House
Rick Hamilton's Alternate Gear	Rip
Stephon Marbury's Alternate Gear	Platinum Playa
Steve Francis Alternate Gear	Ankle Breaker
Steve Francis' Alternate Gear	Rising Star
Tim Duncan Alternate Gear	Make It Take It
Wilt Chamberlain's Alternate Gear	Wilt The Stilt

DS

GBA

PSP

PS2

PS3

Wii

Xbox

Xbox 360

Index

DS

GBA

PSP

PS2

PS3

Wii

Xbox

Xbox 360

Index

Need for Speed Carbon: Own the City

Unlockable Cars

Beat the following bosses to unlock these cars:

Unlockable	How to Unlock
911 Carrera S	Beat MK
Aston Martin DB9	Beat Jenna
Carrera GT and Lamborghini Gallardo	Beat Clutch
Chevy Cobalt SS and VW Golf GTI	Beat Marcus
Chrysler 300 and Pontiac GTO	Beat Layla 1
Firebird, Toyota MR2, and '67 Mustang	Beat Poorboy
Lotus Elise and Mustang GT	Beat Steve
Mercedes SL65, Corvette, and Ford GT	Beat Scotty
Mitsubishi Eclipse	Beat Sly
Nissan 350Z	Beat Daemon
Pontiac Solstice	Beat Striker
RX-7, Skyline GTR, and WRX STI	Beat Buddy
RX-8, Toyota Supra, and Audi TT	Beat Layla 3

NFL Street 2 Unleashed

Enter the following in the Cheats menu.

Unlockable	Codes
AFC East All Stars	EAASFSCT
AFC North All Stars	NAOFRCTH
AFC South All Stars	SAOFUCTH
AFC West All Stars	WAEFSCT
EA Field	EAField
Fumble Mode (Other team fumbles)	GreasedPig
Gargantuan Players	BIGSmash
Max Catch	MagnetHands
NFC East All Stars	NNOFRCTH
NFC North All-Stars	NNAS66784
NFC South All Stars	SNOFUCTH
NFC West All Stars	ENASFSCT
No Fumble Mode	GlueHands
Reebok Team	Reebok
Unlimited Turbo	NozBoost

Pac-Man World 3

Enter this code at the main menu.

Unlockable	Code
Unlock levels and mazes	⇐, ⇒, ⇐, ⇒, ●, ⇧

Pinball Hall of Fame

Enter these passwords on the Password screen.

Unlockable	Password	Unlockable	Password
999 Credits	JAT	Unlocks Aces High for freeplay	UNO
Freeplay on Big Shot	UJP	Unlocks Central Park for freeplay	NYC
Freeplay on Black Hole	LIS	Unlocks custom balls in Options	CKF
Freeplay on Goin' Nuts	PHF	Unlocks freeplay on Strikes 'N Spares	PBA
Freeplay on Love Meter	HOT		
Freeplay on Tee'd Off	PGA	Unlocks optional tilt in Options	BZZ
Freeplay on Xolten	BIG	Unlocks Play Boy table for freeplay	HEF
Unlocks Payout mode	WGR		

Power Stone Collection

Unlockables

Finish the game with certain characters to get "their" item.

Unlockable	How to Unlock
Amenomurakuno	Beat the game with Ryoma
Crystal Ball	Beat the game with Rouge
Decoy Bomb	Beat the game with Ayame
Giant Boots	Beat the game with Gunrock
Maches Chainsaw	Beat the game with Jack
Soccer Ball	Beat the game with Falcon
Stone Sweeper	Beat the game with Julia
Thunderbolt Rider	Beat the game with Accel
Totem Hammer	Beat the game with Galuda
Turbo Helmet	Beat the game with Pete
Twin Potion	Beat the game with Wang-Tang
Wok Gun	Beat the game with Gourmand

Characters (for Power Stone 2)

These character unlocks are exclusively for *Power Stone 2*.

Unlockable	How to Unlock
Kraken	Beat the game as Falcon in 1 vs. 3 mode
Mel	Beat the game as Pride in 1 vs. 3 mode
Pride	Beat the game as Falcon in 1 vs. 3 mode
Valgas	Beat the game as Kraken in 1 vs. 3 mode

Unlock Bosses—Power Stone 1

Unlockable	How to Unlock
Final Form Valgas	Complete the game with Valgas
Kraken	Complete the game with all characters (except *PS2* characters)
Valgas	Complete the game with Kraken

Unlock Original Special Weapons from PS1

Complete the game once with any character to unlock all the original secret weapons from *Power Stone 1*.

Unlockable	How to Unlock
Machine Gun	Beat game once
Nyoi-Bo	Beat game once

DS

GBA

PSP

PS2

PS3

Wii

Xbox

Xbox 360

Index

DS

GBA

PSP

PS2

PS3

Wii

Xbox

Xbox 360

Index

Power Stone Collection (continued)

Unlockable	How to Unlock
Power Shield	Beat game once
Ray Gun	Beat game once

Unlockable Characters

This is only for *Power Stone 1*.

Unlockable	How to Unlock
Accel	Beat the game with Gourmond
Gourmond	Beat the game with Julia
Julia	Beat the game with Pete
Pete	Beat the game once with any character

Ratatouille

Codes

Select "Options" at the main menu, then "Extras," and finally "Cheats." Enter one of the following codes to activate the corresponding cheat function. A sound confirms correct code entry. Make sure you enter the codes in lowercase.

Code	Effect
saycheese	9,999 Cheese
anyonecancook	All recipes
gusteauvid	All videos
itscake	Any health restored to full
boingspawn	Bouncy cheese
skycan	Can all blue cheese
pieceocake	Easy enemies
myhero	Enemies cause no damage
deepfryer	Hard enemies

Ridge Racer

Unlockables

Unlockable	How to Unlock
AGE Type-R tune-up kit for the PROPHETE and ABEILLE	Complete Tour 27 (EX Tour)
AGE Type-Z tune-up kit for the PROPHETE	Complete Tour 28 (EX Tour)
ASSOLUTO Type-R tune-up kit for the FATALITA and BISONTE	Complete Tour 16 (Pro Tour)
ASSOLUTO Type-Z tune-up kit for the FATALITA	Complete Tour 32 (EX Tour)
Class 2 ABEILLE Type-S	Complete Tour 1 (Basic Tour)
Class 2 BISONTE Type-S	Complete Tour 3 (Basic Tour)
Class 2 ESPERANZA Type-S	Complete Tour 2 (Basic Tour)
Class 3 EO Type-S	Complete Tour 5 (Basic Tour)
Class 3 FATALITA Type-S	Complete Tour 4 (Basic Tour)
Class 3 RAGGIO Type-S	Complete Tour 6 (Basic Tour)
Class 4 BAYONET Type-S	Complete Tour 9 (Basic Tour)
Class 4 FIERA Type-S	Complete Tour 8 (Basic Tour)
Class 4 PROPHETE Type-S	Complete Tour 7 (Basic Tour)
Class 5 ABEILLE Type-S	Complete Tour 10 (Pro Tour)

Ridge Racer (continued)

Unlockable	How to Unlock
Class 5 BISONTE Type-S	Complete Tour 12 (Pro Tour)
Class 5 ESPERANZA Type-S	Complete Tour 11 (Pro Tour)
Class 6 EO Type-S	Complete Tour 13 (Pro Tour)
Class 6 FATALITA Type-S	Complete Tour 14 (Pro Tour)
Class 6 RAGGIO Type-S	Complete Tour 15 (Pro Tour)
Credits/Ending Movie	Complete PRO Tour 18
Crimsonrock Pass Reverse	Complete Tour 3 (Basic Tour)
Crystal Coast Highway Reverse	Complete Tour 13 (Pro Tour)
Crystal Coast Highway	Complete Tour 6 (Basic Tour)
DANVER Type-R tune-up kit for the BAYONET	Complete Tour 26 (EX Tour)
DANVER Type-Z tune-up kit for the BAYONET	Complete Tour 31 (EX Tour)
Diablo Canyon Road Reverse	Complete Tour 6 (Basic Tour)
Diablo Canyon Road	Complete Tour 4 (Basic Tour)
Downtown Rave City Reverse	Complete Tour 19 (Pro Tour)
Downtown Rave City	Complete Tour 12 (Pro Tour)
Ending Movie (under "View Prizes")	Complete Tour 18 (Pro Tour)
GNADE Type-R tune-up kit for the ESPERANZA	Complete Tour 24 (EX Tour)
GNADE Type-Z tune-up kit for the ESPERANZA	Complete Tour 29 (EX Tour)
Greenpeak Highlands Reverse	Complete Tour 9 (Basic Tour)
HIMMEL Type-R tune-up kit for the EO	Complete Tour 17 (Pro Tour)
HIMMEL Type-Z tune-up kit for the EO	Complete Tour 30 (EX Tour)
Kamata Angelus (a.k.a. Angel)	Beat Pro Tour 20 "Angelus Duel"
KAMATA Type-R tune-up kit for the FIERA	Complete Tour 25 (EX Tour)
KAMATA Type-Z tune-up kit for the FIERA	Complete Tour 22 (Pro Tour)
Lakeside Parkway Reverse	Complete Tour 7 (Basic Tour)
Lakeside Parkway	Complete Tour 3 (Basic Tour)
Machine Design Collection 1 (under "View Prizes")	Complete Tour 37 (EX Tour)
Machine Design Collection 1	Complete EX Tour 37
Machine Design Collection 2 (under "View Prizes")	Complete Tour 38 (EX Tour)
Machine Design Collection 2	Complete EX Tour 38
Machine Design Collection 3 (under "View Prizes")	Complete Tour 39 (EX Tour)
Machine Design Collection 3	Complete EX Tour 39
Midtown Expressway Reverse	Complete Tour 7 (Basic Tour)
Rage Racer Opening Movie (under "View Prizes")	Complete Tour 34 (EX Tour)
Rave Racer Arcade Intro Movie	Complete EX Tour 36
Rave Racer Demo Movie (under "View Prizes")	Complete Tour 36 (EX Tour)
Ridge City Highway Reverse	Complete Tour 5 (Basic Tour)
Ridge City Highway	Complete Tour 2 (Basic Tour)
Ridge Racer 2004 E4 Movie (under "View Prizes")	Complete Tour 35 (EX Tour)
Ridge Racer 4 Intro Movie	Complete EX Tour 33
Ridge Racer 5 Intro Movie	Complete EX Tour 34
Ridge Racer Type-4 Opening Movie (under "View Prizes")	Complete Tour 33 (EX Tour)
Ridge Racers 2004 E3 Demo Movie	Complete EX Tour 35

DS

GBA

PSP

PS2

PS3

Wii

Xbox

Xbox 360

Index

Ridge Racer (continued)

Unlockable	How to Unlock
Seaside Route 765 Reverse	Complete Tour 4 (Basic Tour)
Silvercreek Dam Reverse	Complete Tour 13 (Pro Tour)
Silvercreek Dam	Complete Tour 10 (Pro Tour)
SOLDAT Type-R tune-up kit for the RAGGIO	Complete Tour 18 (Pro Tour)
SOLDAT Type-Z tune-up kit for the RAGGIO	Complete Tour 23 (Pro Tour)
Special Class KAMATA ANGELUS ("Angel")	Complete Tour 20 (Pro Tour)
Special Class NAMCO PACMAN ("Pac-Man")	Complete Tour 21 (Pro Tour)
Special Class New Rally-X Car	Achieve a score of 50,000 pts in New Rally-X and complete Tour 18 (Pro Tour)
Special Class SOLDAT CRINALE ("Devil")	Complete Tour 19 (Pro Tour)
Sunset Drive Reverse	Complete Tour 2 (Basic Tour)
Union Hill District Reverse	Complete Tour 9 (Basic Tour)

Ridge Racer 2

Special Cars

You can earn the Special Cars in Pro Tour. You must race the car and beat it in a set number of races in order to earn it.

Unlockable	How to Unlock
Angelus	Beat the Pro #27 Races
Angelus Kid	Beat the Pro #29 Races
Crinal	Beat the Pro #28 Races
Crinal Kid	Beat the Pro #30 Races
Digdug Hijack	Beat the Pro #25 Races
Dragonsaber Wild Gang	Beat the Pro #26 Races
Pack-Man	Beat the Pro #31 Races
Yamasa Raggio	Beat the Pro #32 Races

SOCOM: U.S. Navy SEALs Fireteam Bravo 2

Unlockables

Sync with *SOCOM: Combined Assault* for these multiplayer unlockables.

Unlockable	How to Unlock
Jester	Complete the *Socom: Combined Assault* campaign at the rank of Admiral
Killjoy	Complete *Socom: Combined Assault* campaign at the rank of Commander or higher
Simple	Complete *Socom: Combined Assault* at the rank of Ensign or higher
Specter	Automatically unlocked

Unlockables for Multiplayer

To unlock some of this gear, you need a certain number of CE points.

Unlockable	How to Unlock	Unlockable	How to Unlock
Backpack Black	1,000 CE points	Boonie Black Up	500 CE points
Backpack Desert	1,000 CE points	Boonie Desert Side	500 CE points
Biohazard Bag	5,000 CE points	Boonie Desert Up	500 CE points
Black Baseball Back	1,000 CE points	Boonie Green	1,000 CE points
Black Baseball	1,000 CE points	Boonie Jungle Side	500 CE points
Boonie Black Side	500 CE points	Boonie Jungle Up	500 CE points

DS

GBA

PSP

PS2

PS3

Wii

Xbox

Xbox 360

Index

SOCOM: U.S. Navy SEALs Fireteam Bravo 2 (continued)

Unlockable	How to Unlock	Unlockable	How to Unlock
Camera	100 CE points	Ninja	30,000 CE points
Desert Tiger	10,000 CE points	Ninja	30,000 CE points
Desert Tiger	8,000 CE points	Pack Desert	500 CE points
Digital Desert	4,000 CE points	Pack Green	500 CE points
Digital Desert	4,000 CE points	Shades Gold	5,000 CE points
Fate	15,000 CE points	Shades Orange	1,000 CE points
Flak Helmet Black	1,000 CE points	Shades Red	1,000 CE points
Gloom	15,000 CE points	Shades Small	1,000 CE points
Hawaiian	20,000 CE points	Ski Goggles Black	100 CE points
Hazmat	100 CE points	Ski Goggles Orange	1,000 CE points
Helmet Black Small	1,000 CE points	Ski Goggles Red	1,000 CE points
Helmet Black	1,000 CE points	Tiger Stripe	1,000 CE points
Helmet Desert Small	1,000 CE points	Tiger Stripe	1,000 CE points
Helmet Desert	1,000 CE points	Undercover	1,000 CE points
Helmet Green Small	1,000 CE points	Undercover	1,000 CE points
Helmet Green	1,000 CE points	Urban	10,000 CE points
Helo Black Dark	6,000 CE points	Urban	8,000 CE points
Helo Black Shade	6,000 CE points	Winter	1,000 CE points
Helo Black	5,000 CE points	Winter	1,000 CE points
Lensflare	1,000 CE	Yellow Baseball Back	1,000 CE points
Nemesis	15,000 CE points	Yellow Baseball	1,000 CE points

Unlockable Weapons and Items for Single-Player Campaign via Command Equity (CE)

To unlock these weapons and items for use in the single-player campaign at any time, you must expend the CE points that you have earned from missions.

Unlockable	How to Unlock
AT-4 Rocket Launcher	500 CE
Body Armor	100 CE
GMP Submachine Gun	300 CE
Heavy Suppressor Rifle Attachment	200 CE
HK7 Submachine Gun	600 CE
L96AW Rifle	800 CE
Laser Sight Rifle Attachment	100 CE
M8 Rifle	1,500 CE
M8-62 Shotgun Rifle Attachment	100 CE
M87ELR Rifle	1,500 CE
MM-1 MultiLauncher Grenade Launcher	2,800 CE
R 303 Rifle	500 CE
Red Dot Scope Rifle Attachment	200 CE
SCFR-HW Rifle	2,000 CE
SCFR-LW Rifle	1,200 CE

SOCOM: U.S. Navy SEALs Fireteam Bravo 2 (continued)

Unlockable	How to Unlock
SPZ-15 Shotgun	200 CE
Thermal Scope Rifle Attachment	600 CE
Variable Scope Rifle Attachment	800 CE

Unlockable Weapons and Items for Single-Player Campaign via Local Influence (LI)

To unlock these weapons and items for use in the single-player campaign at any time, you must increase your LI rating from Low to these preset levels.

Unlockable	How to Unlock
9mm Sub Submachine Gun	Increase LI rating to Average
AK-47 Rifle	Increase LI rating to Average
ATS-86G Rifle	Increase LI rating to Good
Crossbow	Increase LI rating to Average
F90 Submachine Gun	Increase LI rating to Superb
GS-1 Frag Rifle Attachment	Increase LI rating to Good
M1 Rifle	Increase LI rating to Average
M1918 Machine Gun	Increase LI rating to Average
M1928 Submachine Gun	Increase LI rating to Average
PMN Mines	Increase LI rating to Average
Repeating Crossbow	Increase LI rating to Superb
RPG-7 Rocket Launcher	Increase LI rating to Average
RTK-74 Machine Gun	Increase LI rating to Good
SAS-R Rifle	Increase LI rating to Average
SG-7 Shotgun	Increase LI rating to Good
SK.61 Submachine Gun	Increase LI rating to Good
SR-22 Rifle	Increase LI rating to Superb
STG-77 Rifle	Increase LI rating to Good
VSV-39 Rifle	Increase LI rating to Good

Sonic Rivals

Unlock New Cups

To unlock new cups (as well as obtain Chaos Emerald cards) for Cup Circuit mode, you have to complete Easy, Medium, and Hard challenges in specific zones in Challenge mode as follows:

Unlockable	How to Unlock
Blue Chaos Cup	Complete all challenges for Death Yard Zone
Cyan Chaos Cup	Complete all challenges for Colosseum Highway Zone
Green Chaos Cup	Complete all challenges for Forest Falls Zone
Grey Chaos Cup	Complete every challenge in the game
Purple Chaos Cup	Complete all challenges for Meteor Base Zone
Red Chaos Cup	Complete all challenges for Sky Park Zone
Yellow Chaos Cup	Complete all challenges for Crystal Mountain Zone

Unlock Skins

To unlock certain skins you must complete Story mode with certain characters.

Unlockable	How to Unlock
Knuckles Skin	Complete Story mode with Knuckles
Metal Sonic Skin	Unlock Metal Sonic
Shadow Skin	Complete Story mode with Shadow
Silver Skin	Complete Story mode with Silver
Sonic Skin	Complete Story mode with Sonic

Spider-Man 2

Go to Options, Special, and Cheats on the Main menu, and then type in the following passwords.

Unlockable	Password
All Levels Unlocked	WARPULON
All Moves Purchased	MYHERO
All Movies Unlocked	POPPYCORN
Enemies Have Big Heads and Feet	BAHLOONIE
Infinite Health	NERGETS
Infinite Webbing	FILLMEUP
Spidey Has Big Head and Feet	HEAVYHEAD
Tiny Spider-Man	SPIDEYMAN
Unlock All Production Art	SHUTT
Unlock Storyboard Viewer	FRZFRAME

Star Wars Battlefront 2

Pause the game and enter this code.

Unlockable	Code
Invincibility	⇧, ⇧, ⇧, ⇦, ⇩, ⇩, ⇩, ⇦, ⇧, ⇧, ⇧, ⇦, ⇨

Tony Hawk's Underground 2 Remix

Go to Game Options, then Cheat Codes and enter the following codes.

Unlockable	Code
Perfect Rail Balance	Tightrope
Unlock Tony Hawk from Tony Hawk Pro Skater 1	Birdman

Teenage Mutant Ninja Turtles

Codes

Enter this in the Mission Briefing screens.

Code	Effect
✧, ✧, ✧, ✧, ✧, ✧, ✧, ✧, ✧, ✕	Unlocks a Fantasy Costume

DS

GBA

PSP

PS2

PS3

Wii

Xbox

Xbox 360

Index

DS
GBA
PSP
PS2
PS3
Wii
Xbox
Xbox 360
Index

Test Drive Unlimited

Unlockables

Unlockable	How to Unlock
Aston Martin DB4 GT Zagato	Beat the Aston Martin series
AC 289	Win all Rookie series races
Cadillac XLR-V	Come in 1st in all races
Caterham CSR 260	President of Clubman Car Club
Chevrolet Corvette Stingray 69	President of Classic Car Club
Ford Shelby Cobra Concept	President of Club Stripe
Ford Shelby GR-1 Concept	Come in 1st in all Touring Car League races
Jaguar Type E Coupe	President of Club d'Elegance
Koenigsegg CC8S	Beat the Master Challenge Series
Lamborghini Countach 25th Anniversary	Earn 1,000,000 points
Lamborghini Miura P400SV	Lamborghini GP Challenge
Lotus Esprit V8	Beat the Laenani Collection races
Mercedes-Benz CLK DTM AMG	President of German Car Club
Own All the Houses	Win all the Viaggio Grande races
Shelby Cobra Daytona Coupe	Earn 500,000 points
Spyker C8 Spyder T	President of Accolade Ala Moana Club

Thrillville

Codes

Enter these while in a park. You hear a chime if it worked.

Unlockable	How to Unlock
Add $50,000	■, ●, ▲, ■, ●, ▲, ✕
Mission Complete	■, ●, ▲, ■, ●, ▲, ●
Unlock All Parks	■, ●, ▲, ■, ●, ▲, ■
Unlock All Rides in Park	■, ●, ▲, ■, ●, ▲, ▲

Tiger Woods PGA Tour 06

Unlockables

Unlockable	How to Unlock
Big Bertha Blue	Callaway Golf Sponsorship
Big Bertha Red	Callaway Golf Sponsorship
Big Mo's Lumber	Complete the tournament on Kim Furyk Rivals challenge board
Blue R	Grafalloy Sponsorship
Blue S	Grafalloy Sponsorship
Blue X	Grafalloy Sponsorship
Can you beat me?	Win the "Aces Wild" trophy ball
Cleveland Launcher Gold S Flex	Cleveland Sponsorship
CPR Extra Stiff Flex	Nike Sponsorship
CPR Stiff Flex	Nike Sponsorship
Diamond Driver Shafts	Beat Jim Furyk's quick challenge in Rivals mode
Dynamic Gold R300	True Temper Sponsorship
Dynamic Gold S300	True Temper Sponsorship
Dynamic Gold X100	True Temper Sponsorship

Tiger Woods PGA Tour 06 (continued)

Unlockable	How to Unlock
EA 1-Under Edition Shafts	Win the birdie streak trophy ball
EA Custom Colour Shafts	Beat Colin Montgomerie's Quick Challenge
EA Custom Colour Shafts	Beat Colin Montgomerie's Rivals Challenge
EA Custom Colour Shafts	Defeat Justin Rose in Rivals mode match play
EA Custom Colour Shafts	Defeat Justin Rose in Rivals mode match play
EA Custom Colour Shafts	Defeat Justin Rose in Rivals mode match play
EA Dark Wood Shafts	Play 10 head-to-head games
EA Double-Eagle Ball	Win the "My First Double Eagle" trophy ball
EA Full Spin	Complete Colin Montgomerie's putting frenzy
EA LDC Trophy Ball	Win the "Long Drive Challenge" Trophy Ball
EA Light Wood Shafts	Defeat Charles Howell III in Rivals mode match play
EA Medium Wood Shafts	Play 10 head-to-head games
EA Power Boost Ball	Win Stuart Appleby's bonus skins event
EA Sports XXX Flex	Win 10 trophy balls
Eagle Series Shafts	Win the "My first eagle" trophy ball
Gold Collection Spinnerz	Complete Adam Scott's quick challenge in Rivals mode
Golden Collection Edition Shafts	Win Stuart Appleby's Bonus Skins Event
Hx Hot	Callaway Sponsorship
Hx Red	Callaway Sponsorship
HX Tour	Callaway Golf Sponsorship
Legend Edition Shafts	Complete Adam Scott's Rivals mode
Legend Tour Series Ball	Complete Retief Goosens tournament in Rivals mode
Loco Bite	Dunlop Sponsorship
Loco Pro Ht	Dunlop Sponsorship
M.A.S.2 Low Torque Flex S	Taylormade Sponsorship
M.A.S.2 Low Torque Flex X	Taylormade Sponsorship
M.A.S.2 Mid Torque Flex S	Taylormade Sponsorship
M.A.S.2 Mid Torque Flex X	Taylormade Sponsorship
Nike Ignite S Flex	Nike Sponsorship
Nike Ignite X Flex	Nike Sponsorship
Nike Mojo	Nike Sponsorship
Nike One Black	Nike Sponsorship
Nike One Gold	Complete Mike Weir's Tournament
Nike One TW Spec	Play 10 head-to-head games
PING SI3 S	Ping Sponsorship
PING SI3 X	Ping Sponsorship
PING TFC 100 S	Ping Sponsorship
PING TFC 100 X	Ping Sponsorship
Pro Launch R	Grafalloy Sponsorship
Pro Launch S	Grafalloy Sponsorship
Pro Launch X	Grafalloy Sponsorship
RCH 65W Firm Flex	Callaway Sponsorship
RCH 65W Regular Flex	Callaway Sponsorship

DS

GBA

PSP

PS2

PS3

Wii

Xbox

Xbox 360

Index

Tiger Woods PGA Tour 06 (continued)

Unlockable	How to Unlock
RCH System 55 Firm Flex	Callaway Sponsorship
RCH System 55 Regular Flex	Callaway Sponsorship
Super Loco	Dunlop Sponsorship
TA2 LNG	Nike Sponsorship
TA2 SPN	Nike Sponsorship
Tigers Nike One	Play 10 head-to-head games
TX-90 R	True Temper Sponsorship
TX-90 S	True Temper Sponsorship
TX-90 S	True Temper Sponsorship
Warbird	Callaway Sponsorship

Tom Clancy's Splinter Cell Essentials

Bonus Mission Codes

Enter the following at the bonus mission screen (you have to enter the code each time you want to play the mission).

Unlockable	How to Unlock
Unlock the Heroin Refinery Mission	Hold Select and press $\boxed{L}$+$\boxed{R}$ three more times
Unlock the Paris-Nice Mission	Hold Select and press $\boxed{L}$+$\boxed{R}$ 12 more times
Unlock the Television Free Indonesia Mission	Hold Select and press $\boxed{L}$+$\boxed{R}$ three times

Tomb Raider: Legend

Codes

Enter these codes while playing a level, but they only work once you have unlocked them.

Code	Effect
Bulletproof	Hold $\boxed{L}$, then: ✕, $\boxed{R}$, ▲, $\boxed{R}$, ■, $\boxed{R}$
Draw Enemy Health	Hold $\boxed{L}$, then: ■, ●, ✕, $\boxed{R}$, $\boxed{R}$, ▲
Infinite Assault Rifle Ammo	Hold $\boxed{L}$, then: ✕, ●, ✕, $\boxed{R}$, ■, ▲
Infinite Grenade Launcher	Hold $\boxed{L}$, then: $\boxed{R}$, ▲, $\boxed{R}$, ●, $\boxed{R}$, ■
Infinite Shotgun Ammo	Hold $\boxed{L}$, then: b, ●, ■, $\boxed{R}$, ■, ✕
Infinite SMG Ammo	Hold $\boxed{L}$, then: ●, ▲, $\boxed{R}$, $\boxed{R}$, ✕, ●
One Shot Kill	Hold $\boxed{L}$, then: ▲, ✕, ▲, ■, $\boxed{R}$, ●
Wield Excalibur	Hold $\boxed{L}$, then: ▲, ✕, ●, $\boxed{R}$, ▲, $\boxed{R}$
Wield Soul Reaver	Hold $\boxed{L}$, then: ✕, $\boxed{R}$, ●, $\boxed{R}$, $\boxed{R}$, ■

Unlockable Cheats

These cheats are only unlocked when you clear the game or meet the following criteria.

Unlockable	How to Unlock
Bulletproof Lara	Clear England under 27:00 in Time Trials
Infinite Grenade Launcher Ammo	Clear Kazakhstan under 27:10 in Time Trials
Infinite MG415 Ammo	Clear Peru under 21:30 in Time Trials
Infinite RC650 Ammo	Clear Japan under 12:15 in Time Trials
Infinite shotgun Ammo	Clear Ghana under 20:00 in Time Trials
One Hit Deaths	Clear Bolivia (stage 8) under 4:15 in Time Trials
Show Enemy Health	Clear Bolivia under 12:30 in Time Trials

Tomb Raider: Legend (continued)

Unlockable	How to Unlock
Textureless Mode	Clear the game on any difficulty
Unlock Excalibur	Clear Nepal under 13:40 in Time Trials
Unlock the Soul Reaver	Clear the game and complete all time trials

Unlockables

Unlockable	How to Unlock
Alister Fletcher	Collect 90% of all bronze rewards
Amanda Evert	Collect 70% of all bronze rewards
Anaya Imanu	Collect 30% of all bronze rewards
Biker, Brown Jacket Outfit	Complete Bolivia on the Medium setting in Treasure Hunt mode
Bolivia Redux—100% of all object models	Collect all silver rewards in Bolivia (level 8)
Bolivia	Collect all bronze rewards from Bolivia
Bolivia—100% of all object models	Collect all silver rewards in Bolivia
Bronze Gallery	In Tomb trials, finish all levels in Treasure Hunt mode on Easy difficulty
Croft Manor—100% of all object models	Collect all silver rewards in Croft Manor
England	Collect all bronze rewards from England
England—100% of all object models	Collect all silver rewards in England
Ghana	Collect all bronze rewards from Ghana
Ghana—100% of all object models	Collect all silver rewards in Ghana
Gold Gallery	In Tomb trials, finish all levels in Treasure Hunt mode on Hard difficulty
Increased Accuracy	50% of silver and bronze rewards
Increased Damage	75% of silver and bronze rewards
Increased Magazine Capacity	25% of silver and bronze rewards
James Rutland	Collect 50% of all bronze rewards
Japan	Collect all bronze rewards from Japan
Japan—100% of all object models	Collect all silver rewards in Japan
Kazakhstan	Collect all bronze rewards from Kazakhstan
Kazakhstan—100% of all object models	Collect all silver rewards in Kazakhstan
Lara Croft	Collect 10% of all bronze rewards
Legend, Camo Shorts	Beat Bolivia on the Hard setting in Treasure Hunter mode
Nepal	Collect all bronze rewards from Nepal
Nepal—100% of all object models	Collect all silver rewards in Nepal
Peru	Collect all bronze rewards from Peru
Peru—100% of all object models	Collect all silver rewards in Peru
Shogo Takamoto	Collect 60% of all bronze rewards
Silver Gallery	Complete Bolivia, Croft Manor, and Fiery Maze on the Easy setting in Treasure Hunt mode
Silver Gallery	In Tomb trials, finish all levels in Treasure Hunt mode on Medium difficulty
Special	Collect all bronze rewards from Croft Manor
Toru Nishimura	Collect 40% of all bronze rewards

DS

GBA

PSP

PS2

PS3

Wii

Xbox

Xbox 360

Index

DS

GBA

PSP

PS2

PS3

Wii

Xbox

Xbox 360

Index

Tomb Raider: Legend (continued)

Unlockable	How to Unlock
Unknown Entity	Collect 100% of all bronze rewards
Winston Smith	Collect 80% of all bronze rewards
Zip	Collect 20% of all bronze rewards

Twisted Metal Head On

Input these codes during gameplay.

Unlockable	Code
Invulnerability	→, ←, ↓, ↑ and finally press L1 + R1
Infinite Weapons	▲, ▲, ↓, ↓, L1 + R1

Virtua Tennis World Tour

Enter these codes at the Main menu while holding L3.

Unlockable	Code
All Racquets and Clothing Available in the Home Screen	⇨, ⇦, ⇨, ⇨, ⇧, ⇧, ⇧
Begin World Tour mode with $1,000,000	⇧, ⇩, ⇦, ⇩, ▲, ▲, ▲
Earn $2000 Every Week in World Tour mode	⇧, ⇩, ⇨, ⇩, ▲, ■, ▲
Unlock All Stadiums	⇧, ⇩, ⇦, ⇨, ■, ■, ■
Unlock the players King & Queen	⇧, ⇩, ⇧, ⇩, ■, ▲, ■

WRC: FIA World Rally Championship

Enter these passwords as Profile names.

Unlockable	Password
Bird camera	dovecam
Enables Supercharger cheat	MAXPOWER
Extra avatars	UGLYMUGS
Ghost car	SPOOKY
Reverses controls	REVERSE
Time trial ghost cars	AITRIAL
Unlock everything	PADLOCK

X-Men Legends II: Rise of Apocalypse

These codes must be entered on the pause screen.

Unlockable	Code
1-Hit Kills with Punches	⇦, ⇦, ⇨, ⇦, ⇨, ⇧, START
God Mode	⇩, ⇧, ⇩, ⇧, ⇨, ⇩, ⇨, ⇦,
Super Speed	⇧, ⇧, ⇧, ⇩, ⇩, ⇩, START
Unlimited XTreme Power	⇦, ⇩, ⇨, ⇩, ⇩, ⇧, ⇧, ⇩, START

Enter these at Forge or Beast's equipment screen.

Unlockable	Code
100,000 techbits	⇧, ⇧, ⇧, ⇩, ⇨, ⇨, START

Enter these codes at the team management screen.

Unlockable	Code
All Characters	⇨, ⇦, ⇦, ⇨, ⇧, ⇧, ⇧, START
All Character Skins	⇩, ⇧, ⇦, ⇨, ⇧, ⇧, START
All Skills	⇦, ⇨, ⇦, ⇨, ⇩, ⇧, START
Level 99 Characters	⇧, ⇩, ⇧, ⇩, ⇦, ⇧, ⇦, ⇨, START

Enter these in the Review menu.

Unlockable	Code
All Comic Books	⇨, ⇦, ⇨, ⇨, ⇧, ⇧, ⇧, ⇨, START
All Concept Art	⇦, ⇨, ⇦, ⇨, ⇧, ⇧, ⇩, START
All Game Cinematic	⇦, ⇨, ⇦, ⇨, ⇩, ⇩, ⇦, START

Enter this in the Danger Room.

Unlockable	Code
All Danger Room Courses	⇨, ⇨, ⇦, ⇦, ⇧, ⇩, ⇧, ⇩, START

Table of Contents - PS2

Side tabs: DS, GBA, PSP, PS2, PS3, Wii, Xbox, Xbox 360, Index

DS

GBA

PSP

PS2

PS3

Wii

Xbox

Xbox 360

Index

.hack//Part 2: Mutation

Unlockable	Code
DVD EASTER EGG	On the companion DVD, from the Title Menu—select Data, highlight Gallery, press →, then enter/confirm your selection.

.hack//Part 4: Quarantine

Unlockable	Objective
Parody Mode	Complete the game once.

007: Agent Under Fire

Unlockable	Objective
Alpine Guard Skin in Multiplayer Mode	Complete the Streets of Bucharest level with a "Platinum" rank and all 007 icons.
Calypso Gun in Multiplayer Mode	Complete the Fire and Water level with a Platinum" rank and all 007 icons.
Carrier Guard Multiplayer Skin	Complete the Evil Summit level with a "Platinum" rank and all 007 icons.
Cyclops Oil Guard Skin in Multiplayer Mode	Complete the Poseidon level with a "Platinum" rank and all 007 icons.
Full Arsenal in Multiplayer Mode	Complete the Forbidden Depths level with a "Platinum" rank and all 007 icons.
Golden	Complete the Forbidden Depths level with a "Gold" rank.
Golden Accuracy Power-Up (Enables greater auto-aim.)	Complete the Bad Diplomacy level with a "Gold" rank.
Golden Bullet Power-Up	Complete the Poseidon level with a "Gold" rank.
Golden CH-6 (Gives you unlimited rockets.)	Complete the Precious Cargo level with a "Gold" rank.
Golden Clip Power-Up	Complete the Cold Reception level with a "Gold" rank.
Golden Grenade Power-Up	Complete the Night of the Jackal level with a "Gold" rank.
Golden Gun (Unlocks the Golden P2K with special silencer.)	Complete the Trouble in Paradise level with a "Gold" rank.
Golden Gun in Multiplayer Mode	Complete the Precious Cargo level with a "Platinum" rank and all 007 icons.
Gravity Boots in Multiplayer Mode	Complete the Bad Diplomacy level with a "Platinum" rank and all 007 icons.
Guard Skin in Multiplayer Mode	Complete the Cold Reception level with a "Platinum" rank and all 007 icons.
Lotus Esprit Car	Complete the Streets of Bucharest level with a "Gold" rank.
Poseidon Guard Skin in Multiplayer Mode	Complete the Mediterranean Crisis level with a "Platinum" rank and all 007 icons.
Rapid Fire Power-Up	Complete the Fire and Water level with a "Gold" rank.
Regenerative Armor Power-Up	Complete the Mediterranean Crisis level with a "Gold" rank.
Rocket Manor Multiplayer Level (This cheat unlocks a new multiplayer level. It is a large, open area. The map settings allow only rockets.)	Complete the Trouble in Paradise level with a "Platinum" rank and all 007 icons.
Stealth Bond	Complete the Dangerous Pursuit level with a "Platinum" rank and all 007 icons.

DS
GBA
PSP
PS2
PS3
Wii
Xbox
Xbox 360
Index

007: Agent Under Fire (continued)

Unlockable	Objective
Unlimited Car Missiles	Complete the Dangerous Pursuit level with a "Gold" rank.
Unlimited Golden Gun Ammunition	Complete the Evil Summit level with a "Gold" rank.
Viper Gun in Multiplayer Mode	Complete the Night of the Jackal level with a "Platinum" rank and all 007 icons.

007: Nightfire

For the following codes, select the "Codenames" option at the main menu. Select your character and enter one of the following codes at the Secret Unlocks screen. Save your Codename after entering the code. Then exit your Codename and begin gameplay.

Unlockable	Code
All Gadget Upgrades	Q LAB
All Multiplayer Options	GAMEROOM
Alpine Escape Level	POWDER
Camera Upgrade	SHUTTER
Chain Reaction Level	MELTDOWN
Bigger Clip for Sniper Rifle	MAGAZINE
Countdown Level	BLASTOFF
Decrypter Upgrade	SESAME
Deep Descent Level	AQUA
Double-Cross Level	BONSAI
Enemies Vanquished Level	TRACTION
Equinox Level	VACUUM
Golden P2K	AU P2K
Golden PP7	AU PP7
Grapple Upgrade	LIFTOFF
Island Infiltration Level	PARADISE
Laser Upgrade	PHOTON
Level Select	PASSPORT
Multiplayer Bond Spacesuit	ZERO G
Multiplayer Mode All Characters	PARTY
Multiplayer Mode Assassination Option	TARGET
Multiplayer Mode Baron Samedi	VOODOO
Multiplayer Mode Bond Tuxedo	BLACKTIE
Multiplayer Mode Christmas Jones	NUCLEAR
Multiplayer Mode Demolition Option	TNT
Multiplayer Mode Drake	NUMBER 1 (Note: Don't forget the space in the code.)
Multiplayer Mode Elektra King	SLICK
Multiplayer Mode Explosive Scenery Option	BOOM
Multiplayer Mode GoldenEye Strike Option	ORBIT
Multiplayer Mode Goldfinger	MIDAS
Multiplayer Mode Jaws	DENTAL
Multiplayer Mode Max Zorin	BLIMP
Multiplayer Mode Mayday	BADGIRL
Multiplayer Mode Nick Nack	BITESIZE
Multiplayer Mode Oddjob	BOWLER

DS

GBA

PSP

PS2

PS3

Wii

Xbox

Xbox 360

Index

DS

GBA

PSP

PS2

PS3

Wii

Xbox

Xbox 360

Index

007: Nightfire (continued)

Unlockable	Code
Multiplayer Mode Protection Option	GUARDIAN
Multiplayer Mode Pussy Galore	CIRCUS
Multiplayer Mode Renard	HEADCASE
Multiplayer Mode Scaramanga	ASSASSIN
Multiplayer Mode Team King of the Hill Option	TEAMWORK
Multiplayer Mode Uplink Option	TRANSMIT
Multiplayer Mode Wai Lin	MARTIAL
Multiplayer Mode Xenia Onatopp	JANUS
Night Shift Level	HIGHRISE
P2K Upgrade	P2000
Phoenix Fire Level	FLAME
Rifle Scope Upgrade	SCOPE
Stunner Upgrade	ZAP
Vanquish Car Missile Upgrade	LAUNCH
Tranquilizer Dart Upgrade	SLEEPY

The following codes can be entered during gameplay.

Unlockable	Code
Berserk Racing	While racing on the Paris Prelude, Enemies Vanquished, Island Infiltration, or Deep Descent levels, press START to pause gameplay, hold L1, press →, ▲, ▲, ■, ▲, ●, then release L1.
Bonus Race in Alps	While racing on the Enemies Vanquished level, press START to pause gameplay, hold L1, press ●, ●, ■, ■, ▲, then release L1.
Double Armor during Racing	While racing on the Paris Prelude, Enemies Vanquished, Island Infiltration, or Deep Descent levels, press START to pause gameplay, hold L1, press ■, ▲, ●, ■, ■, then release L1.
Drive a Shelby Cobra	Begin gameplay on the Enemies Vanquished level. Press START to pause gameplay, hold L1, press →, →, ■, ←, ←, ↑, then release L1. You can now use the Shelby Cobra from the Paris Prelude level in the race through the Alps.
Drive an SUV	While racing on the Enemies Vanquished level, press START to pause gameplay, hold L1, press ■, ●, ▲, ■, ▲, then release L1.
Frantic Racing	While racing on the Paris Prelude, Enemies Vanquished, Island Infiltration, or Deep Descent levels, press START to pause gameplay, hold L1, press ■, ▲, ●, ■, ▲, ●, then release L1.
Quadruple Armor during Racing	While racing on the Paris Prelude, Enemies Vanquished, Island Infiltration, or Deep Descent levels, press START to pause gameplay, hold L1, press ■, ▲, ●, ■, ■, ■, ■, ■ then release L1.
Super Bullets during Racing	While racing on the Paris Prelude, Enemies Vanquished, Island Infiltration, or Deep Descent levels, press START to pause gameplay, hold L1, press ●, ●, ●, ● then release L1. (You can also do this when you fly the plane with Alura.)
Trails during Racing	While racing on the Paris Prelude, Enemies Vanquished, Island Infiltration, or Deep Descent levels, press START to pause gameplay, hold L1, press ■, ●, ●, ■, then release L1.
Triple Armor during Racing	While racing on the Paris Prelude, Enemies Vanquished, Island Infiltration, or Deep Descent levels, press START to pause gameplay, hold L1, press ■, ▲, ●, ■, ■, ■ then release L1.

18 Wheeler American Pro Trucker

Unlockable	Code
Extra Truck	At the Start screen, hold any button and press START.

50 Cent Bulletproof

To enter these passwords, pause the game. Go into Options, then enter the Cheat menu.

Unlockable	Password
Action 26	orangejuice
All Music Tracks	GrabAllThat50
All Music Videos	HookMeUp50
All Weapons	GotThemRachets
Bloodhound Counterkill	gunrunner
Bulletproof aka Invincible	ny'sfinestyo
Empty n' Clips Counterkill	workout
"G'd Up" Counterkill	GoodDieYoung
"Guillotine" Counterkill	GettingDropped
Infinite Ammo	GrizzSpecial
Mike Mode	the hub is broken
My Buddy video	sayhellotomylittlefriend
So Seductive video	yayoshome Tony Yayo
"Wanksta" Counter-Kill	AintGotNothin

Ace Combat 04: Shattered Skies

Alternate Colors

To unlock the alternate colors for the planes, you must find and shoot down an ace placed in each mission. Here are the planes and locations for each mission.

Mission	Ace Locations
1	F-5, just north of the allied airbase
2	A-10, north of the enemy airbase
3	F-16, south of the second radar station (the westernmost one)
4	Mirage 2000, northwest of the westernmost radar jamming plane
5	MIG-29, south of the far western pumping station on the map
6	F-14, north of the northenmost group of enemies on the map
7	TND-IDS, north of the solar tower
8	F-18, after refueling during the mission, the ace appears east of the main combat area
9	F-15C, north of the center beach combat area
10	RF-01, map's far northwest corner, northwest of the sub base
11	SU-35, the ace appears with about 90 seconds left during this mission
12	F-2, north of the Stonehenge gun base
13	F-15E, after clearing the radar balloons, enemy fighters appear; the ace is in the northeast
14	F-22, ace is in the northeast
15	EF-2000, ace is in the map's center when the mission starts (between the two southern combat zones)
16	F-117, ace is northwest of the westernmost combat zone (hard to find due to stealth;, head 2 grids north and 1 west)

DS
GBA
PSP
PS2
PS3
Wii
Xbox
Xbox 360
Index

Ace Combat 04: Shattered Skies (continued)

Mission	Ace Locations
17	F-15A, ace is in the map's far northwestern corner, past the city
18	S-37, ace is north of megalith

Unlockables

Unlockable	How to Unlock
Expert Difficulty	Beat the game under hard difficulty.
Get All Three X-02	First, beat the game on Normal with S ranks in all missions for the gray X-02. Do the same on Hard for the black X-02, and the same on Expert for the white X-02.
Secret Modes	Get Secret modes by defeating the game. Finish the game in any difficulty to aquire Special Continue, Trial missions, FMV sequences, 36 music tracks from the game, and the ablity to change the color of your aircraft.
Unlock All Aircraft	Complete the game on normal and get an S rank for every mission to unlock all the aircraft, including the X-02 Multirole fighter, which is perfect for just about any mission.
View the FMV Opening with Selected Plane	You can do this with all planes and different colors. First go to the start mission and select the plane, after that you'll see the weapon menu. Exit the start mission and go to the title.
X-02 Color Schemes	To get the first color scheme for the bonus aircraft, the X-02, get S Rankings on all missions on Hard difficulty, either in Story or Free Mission mode. For the second color, play through the game and get S Rankings on all missions on the Expert difficulty.

Ace Combat V: The Unsung War

Unlocking AC5: UW Medals can be done in Campaign mode or Free Mission mode.
SP Color Schemes: All planes must be bought before obtaining color. Can be done in Free Mission mode.

Unlockable	Objective
Bronze Ace Medal	Destroy 200 enemy targets.
Bronze Shooter Medal	Down 5 enemy planes (cumulative) with ONLY machine gun fire from your aircraft.
Bronze Wing Medal	Earn S Ranks on all 32 missions on "Normal" handicap.
Desert Eagle Medal	Aid friendlies in Missions 16A or 16B, and no more than 3 can bite the dust.
Gold Ace Medal	Destroy 1000 enemy targets.
Gold Anchor Medal	Protect the Kestral and fleet in Mission 3: Narrow Margin.
Gold Shooter Medal	Down 50 enemy planes (cumulative) with ONLY machine gun fire from your aircraft.
Gold Wing Medal	Earn S Ranks on all 32 missions on "Expert" handicap.
Grand Falcon Medal	Annihilate all 16 named planes in second play-through on "Normal" or higher handicaps.
Guardian Medal	Down 10 enemy aircraft who have a missile lock on your wingmen's six.
Lightning Hammer Medal	Protect all 8 armored tanks on ground, and not even one can be destroyed.
Needle's Eye Medal	Get "Perfect" phrases from AWACS in all 6 landings and 2 refuelings stages.
Silver Ace Medal	Destroy 500 enemy targets.
Silver Shooter Medal	Down 15 enemy planes (cumulative) with ONLY machine gun fire from your aircraft.
Silver Wing Medal	Earn S Ranks on all 32 missions on "Hard" handicap.

Ace Combat V: The Unsung War (continued)

Unlockable	By Shooting Down
EA-18G	ABELCAIN (Mission 16B)
EA-6B	DUNE (Mission 10)
F-14D	ZIPANG (Mission 3)
F-2A	CYPHER (Mission 18)
F-4G	MINDRIPPER (Mission 4)
FB-22	PROTEUS (Mission 17)
Hawk	GIGANTOR (Mission 1)
MIG-1.44	REPLICATOR (Mission 27+)

Unlockable	By Shooting Down
MIG-21-93	SWORDKILL (Mission 23)
MIG-31M	COSM (Mission 16A)
MIR-2000D	ZAHARADA (Mission 6)
Rafale B	DECODER (Mission 26)
SU-37	YELLOW (Mission 27)
TND-ECR	TWICE DEAD (Mission 18+)
X-29A	DAREDEVIL (Mission 15)
YA-10B	DISTANT THUNDER (Mission 25)

Unlockable	How to Unlock
F-22A	Complete Arcade Mode
Falken	Complete Expert with all S Ranks
X-02	Complete Hard mode earning all "S" rankings

Activision Anthology

Unlockable	How to Unlock
Atlantis: Disco Mode	Score at least 30,000 points in the game.
Barnstorming Commercial	Get a time of less than 34 seconds on game 1.
Beamrider	Score 2,500 points on game 8.
Boxing	Score more than 70 in a match to defeat the CPU.
Brainstorming	Get a time of less than 55 seconds on game 3.
Chopper Command Commercial	Score at least 4,000 points.
Chopper Command: Motion Blur Mode	Score at least 6,000 points.
Chopper Command Patch	Score at least 8,000 points.
Crackpots	Score at least 17,500 points.
Crackpots: Bungee Mode	Score at least 25,000 points.
Decathlon: Bronze Patch	Score at least 8,000 points in a single-player game.
Decathlon: Gold Patch	Score at least 9,400 points in a single-player game.
Decathlon: Silver Patch	Score at least 9,000 points in a single-player game.
Dolphin	Score at least 15,000 points.
Dolphin: Secret Society Patch	Score at least 25,000 points.
Dolphin: Warped Mode	Score at least 10,000 points.
Dragster	Reset the game 20 times, either by winning or blowing an engine.
Enduro	Drive at least 250 miles.
Fishing Derby: Distortion Mode	Win a game against the CPU.
Freeway Commercial	Score at least 30 points on game 1.
Freeway Patch	Score at least 10 points on game 3 or 7.
Frostbite	Score at least 12,000 points.
Frostbite: Vertical Hold Mode	Score at least 4,000 points.
Grand Prix Commercial	Get a time under 45 seconds in game 1.
Grand Prix Patch	Get a time under 2:30 in game 4, under 1:30 in game 3, under 1:00 in game 2, or under 0:35 in game 1.

DS

GBA

PSP

PS2

PS3

Wii

Xbox

Xbox 360

Index

DS

GBA

PSP

PS2

PS3

Wii

Xbox

Xbox 360

Index

Activision Anthology (continued)

Unlockable	How to Unlock
H.E.R.O.	Score at least 75,000 points.
Kabobber Commercial	Score at least 10,000 points.
Kaboom Commercial	Score at least 150 points.
Kaboom Patch	Score at least 200 points.
Keystone Kapers	Score at least 10,000 points.
Laser Blast Commercial	Lose all lives.
Laser Blast Patch	Score at least 10,000 points.
Laser Blast: 1,000,000 Patch	Score at least 100,000 points.
Megamania	Score at least 15,000 points.
Megamania: Starfield Mode	Score at least 5,000 points.
Pitfall Commercial	Score 12,000 points.
Pitfall Patch	Score 20,000 points.
River Raid	Score at least 8,000 points.
Skiing	Win game 1 with a time under 35 seconds.
Stampede	Score at least 1,000 points in game 3.
StarMaster	Unlocked when the timer reaches 300 seconds on the Ensign level.
Tennis	Win 6 games (1 match) against the CPU.

Aeon Flux

Outfits

Enter these codes into the Cheat menu.

1. In the Extras menu (press ● when at the main menu) pick Cheats.

2. In game, pause the game, go to Cheats, and then enter.

You will see the in game Cheats in the Cheat menu.

Password	Effect
ALPHA ROMEO MIKE SIERRA	(Arms) Unlock Revelation OutFits (Extras)
BRAVO ALPHA GOLF MIKE ALPHA NOVEMBER	(Bagman) Action Movie (In Game)
BRAVO ALPHA YANKEE OSCAR UNIFORM	(Bayou) Unlock All Replay Episodes (Extras)
BRAVO LIMA UNIFORM ROMEO	(Blur) Unlock War OutFits (Extras)
BRAVO UNIFORM CHARLIE KILO FOXTROT SIERRA TANGO	(Buckfst) One Strike Kills (In Game)
CHARLIE LIMA OSCAR NOVEMBER ECHO	(Clone) Unlimited Health (In Game)
CHARLIE LIMA OSCAR TANGO HOTEL ECHO SIERRA	(Clothes) Unlock Monican Freya/Hostess Judy/Una/Fashion Una OutFits (Extras)
CHARLIE UNIFORM TANGO INDIA OSCAR NOVEMBER ECHO	(Cutione) Free Fatalities (In Game)
FOXTROT UNIFORM GOLF	(Fug) Unlimited Ammo (In Game)
GOLF ROMEO ALPHA YANKEE	(Gray) Unlock Fame OutFit (Extras)
HOTEL ECHO ALPHA LIMA MIKE ECHO	(Healme) Restore Health (In Game)
JULIET ALPHA CHARLIE KILO ECHO TANGO	(Jacket) Unlock Bomber Jacket OutFit (Extras)
LIMA CHARLIE VICTOR GOLF	(Lcvg) Unlimited Power Strikes (In Game)
MIKE OSCAR VICTOR INDIA ECHO	(Movie) Unlock Seed OutFits (Extras)
PAPA INDIA XRAY ECHO SIERRA	(Pixes) Unlock All Slideshows (Extras)

Aeon Flux (continued)

Password	Effect
TANGO ROMEO INDIA ROMEO OSCAR XRAY	(Trirox) God Mode (In Game)
UNIFORM KILO GOLF ALPHA MIKE ECHO ROMEO	(Ukgamer) Action Movie (In Game)
UNIFORM ROMEO BRAVO ALPHA NOVEMBER	(Urban) Unlock Seed OutFits (Extras)
WHISKEY HOTEL INDIA TANGO ECHO	(White) Unlock Mrs. Goodchild OutFits (Extras)

Aero Elite Combat

Unlock the following fighters by completing the listed task.

Fighter	Objective
A-10	Do all ground training objectives in Training Mode.
Blue Impulse F-86 Fighter	On the island map, grab the Blue Impulse logo during Free Flight Mode.
Blue Impulse T2 Trainer	On the bay map, grab the Blue Impulse logo under the bridge during Free Flight Mode.
C1	Beat maneuver objectives at Aero Meet.
F-104J fighter	Reach Mach 2.0.
F-105 Drone	Fly 50,000 feet in Training Mode.
F-14B Test Bed	Beat Reconnaissance Mission 2.
F-15 Aggressor 1	Log 50 kills.
F-15 Aggressor 2	Log 100 kills.
F-15C	Finish ACM objectives at Aero Meet.
F-15J	Finish 10 scrambles.
F-2B	Finish 50 scrambles.
F-86 Fighter	Log one hour of playing time in Training Mode.
Oh-6	Finish helicopter training.
Su-27 Fighter	Beat Reconnaissance Mission 3.

Agassi Tennis Generation

Unlockable	Code
All Players	In the Main menu, press R2, L2, L3, ●, ✕, ●.

Age of Empires II: The Age of Kings

Passwords

Enter on password menu:

Password	Effect
CHEESE STEAK JIMMY'S	1,000 Food
ROBIN HOOD	1,000 Gold
ROCK ON	1,000 Stone
LUMBERJACK	1,000 Wood
NATURAL WONDERS	Control nature (lose control of men)
RESIGN	Defeat yourself
BLACK DEATH	Destroy all the enemies
WIMPYWIMPYWIMPY	Destroy yourself
FURIOUS THE MONKEY BOY	Get a Furious Monkey Boy
HOW DO YOU TURN THIS ON	Gives a "cobra" car
TO SMITHEREENS	Gives a saboteur
I LOVE THE MONKEY HEAD	Gives a VDML

Age of Empires II: The Age of Kings (continued)

Password	Effect
AEGIS	Immediate building
TORPEDOx	Kills opponent x
POLO	Remove shadow
MARCO	Reveal map
WOOF WOOF	Turns birds into super dogs

Aggressive Inline

Enter the following codes at the Cheat screen.

Unlockable	Code
All Bonus Characters	↓, →, →, ↓, ←, ←, ↓, →, →, →
All Keys	S, K, E, L, E, T, O, N
Juice Bar Is Always Full (Your juice bar will remain full, even if you crash.)	B, A, K, A, B, A, K, A
Juice Regeneration	←, ←, →, →, ←, →, ↓, ↑, ↑, ↓, A, I
Level Select, All Park Editor Objects, Full Stats	↑, ↑, ↓, ↓, ←, →, ←, →, B, A, B, A
Low Gravity Wallride	↑, ↓, ↑, ↓, ←, →, ←, →, A, B, A, B, S
Master Code	P, L, Z, D, O, M, E
Never Die	K, H, U, F, U
Perfect Grinds	B, I, G, U, P, Y, A, S, E, L, F
Perfect Handplants	J, U, S, T, I, N, Space, B, A, I, L, E, Y
Perfect Manuals	Q, U, E, Z, D, O, N, T, S, L, E, E, P
Super Spin	←, ←, ←, ←, →, →, →, →, ←, →, ←, →, ↑
FMV Sequences	Complete the normal challenges in a level to unlock its FMV sequence.

Alien Hominid

Use the following passwords to unlock additional hats. Sound confirms correct entry.

Hat Description	Code	Hat Description	Code
Flowers Hat	Grrl	Afro Hat	Superfly
Abe Lincoln Hat	Abe	Slick Hair Hat	Goodman
Hunting Hat	Cletus	Crazy Hair Hat	Tomfulp
Blonde Wig Hat	April	Tiara Hat	Princess

Altered Beast

Unlockables

Unlockable	How to Unlock
18th Cinematic	Complete the game under Hard difficulty setting.
All Boss Fights	Complete the game once.
All Cinematics	Complete the game once.
Grizzly	Complete "Elevator Of Doom" mode.
U.W.H.	Beat all the bosses in Boss Time Attack mode under the target time.
Weretiger	Find and view all Enemy Data (including Bosses and Uniques).

DS
GBA
PSP
PS2
PS3
Wii
Xbox
Xbox 360
Index

Alter Echo

Enter the following codes during gameplay.

Unlockable	Code
Restore Health	↑, ↑, ↓, ↓, ←, →, ←, →, L3+→
Restore Time Dilation	↑, ↑, ↓, ↓, ←, →, ←, →, L3+↑

Amplitude

Unlockable	Code
Blurry Mode	Press R3, R3, R3, R3, L3, L3, L3, L3, R3.
Scramble Gem Positions	Press ✕, ✕, ←, ←, R3, R3, →, →.
Tunnel Mode	Press L3, L3, L3, R3, R3, R3, L3, R3, L3. Repeat the code for a different view.
Turn Notes into Monkey Heads	Press L3, L3, L3, L3, R3, R3, R3, R3, L3.

Unlock Freq Parts and Prefabs: Beat the Boss Song of any level to unlock extra Freq pieces. In addition, you can finish the Bonus Song on each level to gain new Freq parts and Prefabs.

Ape Escape 2

Unlockable	Code
Unlock Spike	Beat the game, collecting 297 monkeys in the process.
Use Spike	At the Main menu, highlight New Game, and press L2+START to use him.

Arc the Lad: Twilight of the Spirits

Unlockable	Objective
Choco	Beat the 30-round arena trial in Rueloon with Darc's party.
Diekbeck	Beat the 20-round arena trial in Cathena with Kharg's party.
New Game+ (This option lets you begin the game as Kharg.)	Complete the game to unlock the option New Game+.

Arctic Thunder

Enter these codes at the Mode Select screen

Unlockable	Code
Start Invisible	■, ●, ■, R2, ●, ●, START
Atomic Snowballs	■, ■, ■, L1, ●, START
Boost Mode	●, R1, R1, ●, R2, START
Catch Up	●, ■, ●, ●, ■, START
Clone Mode	L1, L2, L2, ●, L1, ●, START
Grappling Hooks	●, ●, L2, ●, ●, L1, START
No Drones	■, ■, ●, ●, L1, R1, START
No Power Ups	■, ■, ●, ■, R2, ■, START
Random Power Up Locations	R1, R2, ■, ●, R1, R2, START
Rooster Mode	R1, R2, L2, L1, ■, START
Snow Bombs	●, ●, R1, R2, START
Super Boosts	●, L1, ■, R2, ■, L2, START

DS GBA PSP PS2 PS3 Wii Xbox Xbox 360 Index

DS

GBA

PSP

PS2

PS3

Wii

Xbox

Xbox 360

Index

Armored Core 2

Human Plus Cheats: Drop to -50,000 credits and an experiment will be done on you. Do this multiple times to get the full benefits of this code. Each time you do this code you restart your game. Do this code multiple times to unlock various cheats described below.

Unlockable	Code
First Human Plus Cheat	Perform the Human Plus Cheats code once to unlock an automatic radar.
Second Human Plus Cheat	Perform the Human Plus Cheats code twice to unlock the ability to throw the laserblade.
Third Human Plus Cheat	Perform the Human Plus Cheats code three times to have heat taken away from attacks.
Fourth Human Plus Cheat	Perform the Human Plus Cheats code four times to gain the ability to walk while shooting back weapons.
Fifth Human Plus Cheat	Perform the Human Plus Cheats code five times to use half of the energy.
Sixth Human Plus Cheat	Perform the Human Plus Cheats code six times to have double energy.
First-Person Angle	Hold START + ■ + ▲ during gameplay. The game will pause. Now press START to resume the game.
Set Camera Angle	Hold START + ● + ✕ during gameplay and the game will pause. Press START to resume playing. The camera is now fixed at the pre-location.
Use Overweight Cores	Beat Mission mode and let the credits finish.

Armored Core 3

Unlockable	Code
Add Defeated AC Emblems	Press SELECT + START when viewing a defeated AC at the Victory screen to add the defeated AC's emblem to the list. A sound confirms correct code entry.
Drop Parts	Hold L1 + L2 + R1 + R2 + ▲ to drop your R arm weapon, Back Unit, and Inside parts. Hold L1 + L2 + R1 + R2 + L3 to drop Extension parts. Hold L1 + L2 + R1 + R2 + ● to drop L arm weapons.
First-Person View	Insert a memory card with saved game files from Armored Core 2 or Armored Core 2: Another Age. After saving and resuming in Armored Core 3 from that memory card, pause gameplay, then press L1 + R2 + ✕ + ■ + Dir for a first-person view of the current screen. The screen returns to normal when you resume the game.

Armored Core: Silent Line

Unlockable	Code
Get Bonus Parts	Get an A or S on any mission.
Get Defeated AC Emblems	Press START and SELECT when the victory slogan appears.

Army Men: Air Attack 2

Level	Password
Level 2	↑, ✕, ▲, →, ←, ■, ●, ✕
Level 3	▲, ●, ↓, ←, ■, ■, ↑, ↑
Level 4	✕, →, ←, ✕, ●, ■, ■, ▲
Level 5	↓, ↓, ●, ■, ●, ■, →, ✕
Level 6	▲, ✕, ↑, ←, →, ←, ●, ▲
Level 7	←, ■, →, ↓, ●, ✕, ✕, →
Level 8	▲, →, ■, ■, ●, ↓, ↓, ✕

Army Men: Air Attack 2 (continued)

Level	Password
Level 9	↑, ×, ■, ←, →, ●, ←, ←
Level 10	▲, ↑, ●, ×, ■, ↓, ↓, ↓
Level 11	●, ●, ↑, ←, →, ×, ▲, ■
Level 13	←, ←, ▲, ●, ×, ×, ↓, →
Level 15	←, →, ●, ×, ■, ↓, ↓, ●
Level 16	▲, ●, ×, →, →, ●, ■, ↓
Level 18	●, ×, →, ▲, ■, ↑, ×, ×
Level 20	↑, ×, ●, ↑, ←, ■, ●, ×

Army Men: Sarge's Heroes 2

To enter Passwords, go to the Levels selection at the main menu. At the Input Code screen, insert the following codes.

Unlockable	Code
All Levels	FREEPLAY
All Weapons	GIMME
Bed	COT
Boot Camp	BOOTCAMP
Bridge	OVERPASS
Cashier	EXPRESS
Castle	CITADEL
Desk	ESCRITOIRE
Dinner Table	DINNER
Graveyard	NECROPOLIS
Immortal	NODIE
Invisible	NOSEEUM
Mini Mode	SHORTY
Pinball Machine	BLACKKNIGHT
Plasticville	BLUEBLUES
Pool Table	EIGHTBALL
Refrigerator	COOLER
Revenge	ESCAPE
Rocket Base	NUKEM
Super Sized	IMHUGE
Tan Base	MOUSE
Test Info	THDOTEST
Toy Shelf	BUYME
Toy Train Town	LITTLEPEOPLE

ATV Offroad Fury

To access the following unlockables, select Pro-Career mode and enter code. You will then return to the Main menu and begin gameplay.

Unlockable	Code
2 ATVs	CHACHING
All Tracks	WHATEXIT
Tougher A.I.	ALLOUTAI

DS

GBA

PSP

PS2

PS3

Wii

Xbox

Xbox 360

Index

DS

GBA

PSP

PS2

PS3

Wii

Xbox

Xbox 360

Index

ATV Offroad Fury 2

Go to Profile Editor, Unlock Items, Cheats, and enter the following:

Unlockable	Code
1,000 Profile Points	GIMMEPTS
Aggressive AI	EATDIRT—Re-enter the code to deactivate it.
All ATVs	SHOWROOM
All Mini-Games	GAMEON
All Equipment	THREADS
All Tracks	TRLBLAZR
All Championship Events	GOLDCUPS
Disable Wrecks	FLYPAPER Re-enter the code to deactivate it.
San Jacinto Isles	GABRIEL
Unlock Everything	IGIVEUP
Widescreen Mode	WIDESCRN

ATV Offroad Fury 3

At the Main menu, go to Options. Select Player Profile, then select Enter Cheat.

Unlockable	Code
Everything Except Fury Bike	!SLACKER!

ATV Quad Power Racing 2

Enter the following codes as your player name.

Unlockable	Code
All Riders	BUBBA
All Tracks	ROADKILL
All Vehicles	GENERALLEE
All Challenges	DOUBLEBARREL
All Tricks	FIDDLERSELBOW
Max Stats	GINGHAM
Champ	REDROOSTER

Auto Modellista

Unlockable	Objective
Tamiya Kagegawa Circuit (Remote controlled car racing level)	Complete all 7 mountain based tracks.

B-Boy

Passwords

Enter the codes to unlock hidden stuff.

Password	Effect
93665	Crazy legs
26939	Disable all codes
41549	Disable HUD in battles
15483	Have maxim hype anytime (your opponent as well)
56239	Hide beat markers
35535	Play as Host 1

B-Boy (continued)

Password	Effect
61275	Play as Rack
83083	Red Bull king of the ring
20014	Unlock all clothes
85363	Unlock all Jam mode characters
92750	Unlock all Jam mode levels
34589	Unlock all Jam mode levels, characters, and music
85872	Unlock all Jam mode music
39572	Unlock all Livin' Da Life mode moves, music, and clothes
50361	Unlock all moves
43649	Unlock all moves for both Livin' Da Life and Jam mode
78727	Unlock all music
17345	Unlock Club level
11910	Unlock Pro level

Unlockable Characters

Unlockable	How to Unlock
Crazy Legs in Arcade Mode	Win survivor battle on Easy, Medium, and Hard with Kmel.
Crumbs in Arcade Mode	Win survivor battle on Easy, Medium, and Hard with Ivan.
Host 1 in Arcade Mode	Win survivor battle on Easy, Medium, and Hard with Lilou.
Kazuhiro in Arcade Mode	Win survivor battle on Easy, Medium, and Hard with Hong 10.
Kmel in Arcade Mode	Win survivor battle on Easy, Medium, and Hard with Ruen.
Lilou in Arcade Mode	Win survivor battle on Easy, Medium, and Hard with Mouse.
Mellow D in Arcade Mode	Win survivor battle on Easy, Medium, and Hard with Rosa Roc.
Physicx in Arcade mode	Win survivor battle on Easy, Medium, and Hard with Darkness.
Rack in Arcade Mode	Win survivor battle on Easy, Medium, and Hard with Physicx.
Sonic in Arcade Mode	Win survivor battle on Easy, Medium, and Hard with Benny.

Unlockable Enviroments (Stages)

Unlockable	How to Unlock
Battle of the Year Cypher	Win survivor battle on Easy and Medium with Ivan.
City Park Night	Win survivor battle on Easy and Medium with Rack.
Downtown Night	Win survivor battle on Easy and Medium with Host 1.
FSS Korea	Win survivor battle on Easy and Medium with Physicx.
FSS USA	Win survivor battle on Easy and Medium with Rosa Roc.
Grand Jam	Win survivor battle on Easy and Medium with Mouse.
IBE	Win survivor battle on Easy and Medium with Benny.
Red Bull: King of the Ring	Win survivor battle on Easy and Medium with Sonic.
Rock Steady Anniversary	Win survivor battle on Easy and Medium with Crazy Legs.
South Side Harbour Night	Win survivor battle on Easy and Medium with Lilou.
Stormdrain Night	Win survivor battle on Easy and Medium with Kmel.
Street Final	Win survivor battle on Easy and Medium with Ruen.
The Jam Down	Win survivor battle on Easy and Medium with Mellow D.
The Tower Night	Win survivor battle on Easy and Medium with Kazuhiro.
UK Champs	Win survivor battle on Easy and Medium with Hong 10.
Urban Games	Win survivor battle on Easy and Medium with Darkness.
Urban Outlaws	Win survivor battle on Easy and Medium with Crumbs.

DS
GBA
PSP
PS2
PS3
Wii
Xbox
Xbox 360
Index

Bad Boys: Miami Takedown

Unlockable	Code
Cheat Mode	At the Title screen, press ●,↑,■,▲,→,↓.

Baldur's Gate: Dark Alliance

Enter the following codes during gameplay, then press START.

Unlockable	Code
Invulnerability and Level Warp	L1 + R2 + ▲ + ←
Level 20 Character	L1 + R2 + ←

Baldur's Gate: Dark Alliance II

Unlockable	Code
Invulnerability and Level Warp	During gameplay, hold L1 + R1 + ▲ + ■ + ● + ✕ and press START.
Level 10	During gameplay, hold L1 + R1 + ▲ + ■ + ● + ✕ and press L2.
Level Warp and Infinite Health	During game play press and hold L1 + R1 + ▲ + ■ + ● + ✕ then, while still holding these buttons, press START. A menu should appear.

The Bard's Tale

During gameplay, hold L1 + R1 and press the following buttons:

Unlockable	Code
Can't Be Hurt	→,←,→,←,↑,↓,↑,↓
Can't Be Struck	←,→,←,→,↑,↓,↑,↓
Damage X100	↑,↓,↑,↓,←,→,←,→
Everything On	↑,↑,↓,↓,←,→,←,→
Full Health and Mana	←,←,→,→,↑,↓,↑,↓

Batman: Rise of Sin Tzu

At the "Press Start" screen, hold L1 + L2 + R1 + R2 and enter the following codes.

Unlockable	Code
All Characters at 100%	↑,↑,←,←,→,→,↓,↓
All Rewards	↓,↑,↓,↑,←,→,←,→
All Upgrades	↑,↑,←,←,→,→,→,↓,↓
Everything	↓,↑,↓,↑,←,→,←,→
Infinite Combo Bar	←,→,↑,↓,→,←,↓,↑
Infinite Health	↑,→,↓,←,↑,←,↓,→

Batman Vengeance

At the Main menu, enter the following codes.

Unlockable	Code
All Cheats	L2, R2, L2, R2, ■, ■, ●, ●
Infinite Batcuffs	■, ●, ■, ●, L2, R2, R2, L2
Infinite Bat Launcher	●, ■, ●, ■, L1, R1, L2, R2
Infinite Electric Batarangs	L1, R1, L2, R2

Battle Engine Aquila

Use these passwords as name profiles. You must have a memory card or it will not prompt you to enter a Profile. (Note: case sensitive).

Unlockable	Password
All Bonuses	105770Y2
God Mode	B4K42
Level Select	!EVAH!

DS

GBA

PSP

PS2

PS3

Wii

Xbox

Xbox 360

Index

Battlestar Galactica

Enter in the Extras Menu. A sound will confirm successful code entry.

Unlockable	Code
Unlock Everything	↑, ↓, ↓, ←, ←, ←, ←, →, →, ←, ←, ↑, ↑, ←, ←, ↓, ←, →
Production Stills and Artwork	←, ↑, ←, ←, ↓, ←, ↑, ↓
Production Stills and Artwork	↑, ↑, ↓, ↓, →, ↑, →, ↓
Production Stills and Artwork	↑, ←, ↑, →, ↑, ←, ↑, →
Production Stills and Artwork	→, →, ↑, ↑, ←, ←, ↑, ↑
Production Stills and Artwork	↓, ↓, ↓, ←, ←, ←, ←, ←
Production Stills and Artwork	↓, ↑, ↑, ↓, ↓, ↓, ←, →

Big Mutha Truckers

Enter the cheats in caps below on the Cheats screen of the Options menu.

Unlockable	Code
Automatic Nav	USETHEFORCE
Diplomatic Immunity	VICTORS
Everything	CHEATINGMUTHATRUCKER
Evil Truck	VARLEY
Fast Truck	GINGERBEER
Infinite Time	PUBLICTRANSPORT
Level Select	LAZYPLAYER
Small Pedestrians	DAISHI
Toggle Damage	6WL
Tons of Cash	LOTSAMONEY

Unlockable	Objective
Bottomless Cash Account (This only works in a new game.)	On the Main menu, press ●, ●, ■, ●, ●, SELECT.
Extra Rig	Play the 60 day version of "Trial By Truckin'" and win the race to Big Mutha Trucking HQ to unlock a new rig.

Big Mutha Truckers 2

To enter these passwords, highlight "Trial by Trucking" and press ●.

Unlockable	Password
$115,000	CASH
Add Lots of Bikers	BIKERS
Add Lots of Cops	COPS
Invincible	NODAMAGE
Opens All Bridges	BRIDGE
Pays Off the Next Juror	PJ
Removes All Cops	NOCOPS
Unlock All Gallery Images	GALLERY
Unlock All Missions	MISSIONS

Black and Bruised

Go into the Setup menu and select the Codes menu. Press START, enter the code, then press START again.

Unlockable	Code
Second Skin	×, R1, ●, ■
All Boxers	×, ●, ■, ■, R1, R1, ■, ●, ×
All Boxer's Life	×, ■, ●, R1, ×, ■, ●, R1
Constant Power-Ups	×, ●, ×, ●, ×, ●, ■, ■, ■
Conversation Mode	R1, ×, ●, ■, R1, R1, R1
Double Speed	R1 10 times
Invincible Mode	×, ×, ●, ●, R1, R1, ■, ■
Scrap Yard Arena	●, R1, ●, R1, ×, ×

Blade II

Go to the Main menu (Blade II Logo), hold L1, and press enter code.

Unlockable	Code
All Weapons	■,●,↓,←,●,●,▲
All Missions	↓,↑,←,●,●,→,↓,■
Daywalker Difficulty	←,●,↑,↓,■,●,✕

During gameplay, pause the game. Hold L1 and enter code.

Unlockable	Code
Invulnerability for Friendlies	■,●,▲,✕,■,●,▲,✕
Unlimited Ammo	←,●,→,■,↑,▲,↓,✕
Unlimited Health	▲,■,▲,■,▲,●,▲,●
Unlimited Rage	←,↓,←,↓,→,↑,→,↑

Blitz: The League

From the Main menu, go to "Extras," then "Codes" and enter the following passwords.

Unlockable	Password
Ball Trail Always On	ONFIRE
Beach Ball	BOUNCY
Double Unleash Icons	PIPPED
Stamina Off	NOTTIRED
Super Clash	CLASHY
Super Unleash Clash	BIGDOGS
Two Player Co-op	CHUWAY

BloodRayne

Under "Options" on the Cheat menu, enter the following codes to unlock the corresponding cheat.

Unlockable	Code
Enemy Freeze	DONTFARTONOSCAR
Fill Bloodlust	ANGRYXXXINSANEHOOKER
God Mode	TRIASSASSINDONTDIE
Gratuitous Dismemberment Mode	INSANEGIBSMODEGOOD
Juggy Mode	JUGGYDANCESQUAD
Level Select	ONTHELEVEL
Restore Health	LAMEYANKEEDONTFEED
Show Weapons	SHOWMEMYWEAPONS
Time Factor Mode	NAKEDNASTYDISHWASHERDANCE

BloodRayne 2

Enter code phrase in the Cheats Section.

Unlockable	Code
1,000 carnage points	Cargo Fire Imp Kak
1,000 gun points	Late Nurture Qweef Super
All powers	Blank Ugly Pustule Eater
Fill bloodlust	Naked Juggy Resistance Pacy
Freeze enemies	Blue Green Purple Imp
God mode	Uber Taint Joad Durf Kwis
Enemies explode	Dodge This Moist Pimp

BloodRayne 2 (continued)

Unlockable	Code
Overload mode	This Dark Distorted Reality
Refill Ammo	Whack This Molested Ninja
Restore Health	Nurture Happy Pustule Erasure
Time Factor	Quantum Lament Distorted Doting
Unlimited Ammo	Ugly Dark Heated Orange Quaff
Unlimited Health	Terminal Reality Super Uber XXX Vacate
Unlimited Rage	Pimp Reap Dark Dark Muse
All Combos	Bone This Curry Vote
All Guns	Whiskey Fake Kablow Shoot
All Levels	Anomalies Are Juan Insulated
All Movies	Pension Reap Super Vulgar
All Slideshows	Ardent Hungry Naked Ninja
All Outfits	Whack Lick Erotic Cunningly
Hidden Message	Rayne Rules
Hidden Message	Majesco Rules
Hidden Message	Terminal Reality Rules

Bloody Roar 3

Unlockable	Code
Debug Mode (Import Version)	From the Main menu, enter the Options menu. After you're at the Options menu, press and hold L2 and hit the ● button.
High Speed Mode	Win 100 battles in Survival with a single character, then record your name in the records.
Hyper Beast Mode	Win 10 fights with a single character in Arcade mode and record your name.
Kohryu	Win four rounds in Arcade mode without continuing, then defeat Kohryu in round five.
No Blocking Mode	Gain first place in Arcade mode
One Fall Mode (The first to fall will lose, but he or she will be invincible to all other attacks.)	Win 20 rounds in Survival mode with a single character.
One Hit Knockdowns	Get first place in Sudden Death mode.
Sudden Death Survival	Survive through nine fights in Survival mode.
Super Difficulty	Complete Arcade mode once without continuing.
Uranus	Complete Arcade mode without continuing once, then Uranus appears. Defeat him to play as him.

Blow Out

During gameplay, pause the game and choose Cheats. Enter the following:

Unlockable	Code
All Weapons	CHARLIEHUSTLEOVERDRESSEDROMEO
Big Feet Mode	DEADREDPARTYSHOES
Big Head	BUTTCHEATCANSURPRISE
Clear Map	YESTERDAYYOURZEBRADIE
Frozen Enemies	CHARLIEOSCARLIMADELTA
God Mode	NOPAINNOCANE
Level Select	COOLLEVELCHEATCODE

DS

GBA

PSP

PS2

PS3

Wii

Xbox

Xbox 360

Index

DS

GBA

PSP

PS2

PS3

Wii

Xbox

Xbox 360

Index

Blow Out (continued)

Unlockable	Code
Level Up Weapons	FRIENDLIESTGODINGALAXY
Restore Health	CANEREADYTOROCK
Time Factor	CHARLIEALPHANOVEMBERECHO
Unlimited Ammo	FISHINABARREL
Unlock Doors	ANYANDALLCODE

BMX XXX

TIP

Remove the game cover from the case to see a more revealing picture on the reverse side.

Enter the following codes at the Cheat menu.

Unlockable	Code
All Bikes	65 SWEET RIDES
All FMV Sequences	CHAMPAGNE ROOM
Amish Boy's Bikes	AMISHBOY1699
Bonus Movie 1 FMV Sequence	THISISBMXX
Bonus Movie 2 FMV Sequence	KEEPITDIRTY
Dam 1 FMV Sequence	BOING
Dam 2 FMV Sequence	THONG
Final Movie FMV Sequence	DDUULRRLDRSQUARE
Fire Bullets	BRONXCHEER—Begin a level, stop your rider, then move the right analog stick to First-Person mode. Press ✕ to shoot people and cars.
Ghost Control Mode (This mode allows you to steer ghost-ridden bikes.)	GHOSTCONTROL
Green Skin Mode (Now you can choose a green skin tone in the custom rider creator.)	MAKEMEANGRY
Happy Bunny Mode (This mode allows you to get more air.)	FLUFFYBUNNY
Hellkitty's Bikes	HELLKITTY487
Itchi's Bikes	ITCHI594
Joyride's Bikes	JOYRIDE18
Karma's Bikes	KARMA311
La'tey's Bikes	LATEY411
Las Vegas 1 FMV Sequence	HIGHBEAMS
Las Vegas 2 FMV Sequence	TASSLE
Las Vegas Level	SHOWMETHEMONEY
Launch Pad 69 1 FMV Sequence	IFLINGPOO
Launch Pad 69 2 FMV Sequence	PEACH
Launch Pad 69 Level	SHOWMETHEMONKEY
Level Select	XXX RATED CHEAT
Manuel's Bikes	MANUEL415
Mika's Bikes	MIKA362436
More Speed	Z AXIS
Night Vision Mode (Objects appear greenish.)	3RD SOG
Nutter's Bikes	NUTTER290

BMX XXX (continued)

Unlockable	Code
Park Editor	BULLETPOINT—See Caution
Play as Amish Boy	ELECTRICITYBAD or I LOVE WOOD
Rampage Skatepark 2 FMV Sequence	BURLESQUE
Rampage Skatepark Level	IOWARULES
Random Introduction Sequence (Now the introduction sequence is various FMV sequences you already unlocked.)	XXXINTRO
Rave's Bikes	RAVE10
Roots Level	UNDERGROUND
Sheep FMV Sequence	ONEDOLLAR
Sheep Hills 2 FMV Sequence	69
Sheep Hills Level	BAABAA
Skeeter's Bikes	SKEETER666
Stage Select	MASS HYSTERIA
Super Crash Mode (This mode makes your character extra bouncy when you crash.)	HEAVYPETTING
Syracuse 1 FMV Sequence	FUZZYKITTY
Syracuse 2 FMV Sequence	MICHAELHUNT
Syracuse Level	BOYBANDSSUCK
The Bronx, NYC, 1 FMV Sequence	LAPDANCE
The Bronx, NYC, 2 FMV Sequence	STRIPTEASE
The Bronx, NYC, 3 FMV Sequence	FREESAMPLE
The Dam Level	THATDAMLEVEL
Tripledub's Bikes	TRIPLEDUB922
Twan's Bikes	TWAN18
UGP Roots Jam 2 FMV Sequence	BOOTYCALL
Visible Gap Mode	PARABOLIC

CAUTION

Park Editor Caution!

This crashes the game. It is not known at this time if you can correctly enable this feature.

Bombastic

Unlockable	Objective
Advanced Mode	Beat Quest Mode.
Challenge 1	Password: BbrMjXSbnB3
Classic Mode	Get a high score in Trial or Quest Mode.
Second Quest Mode	Earn all Perfects in Quest Mode.
Theatre Mode	Beat Quest Mode.
Time Attack Mode	Earn all Perfects in Quest Mode.

Bond 007: Everything or Nothing

Unlockable	Code	Unlockable	Code
Cistern	30 Points	Egypt Guard	180 Points
Baren Samedi	50 Points	South Commander	210 Points
Odd Job	70 Points	Moscow Guard	230 Points
Egypt Commander	90 Points	Le Rouge	260 Points
Hazmat Guard	110 Points	003	290 Points
Mya	130 Points	Katya Jumpsuit	320 Points
Test Lab	160 Points	Serena	350 Points

DS GBA PSP PS2 PS3 Wii Xbox Xbox 360 Index

Bond 007: Everything or Nothing (continued)

Unlockable	Code		Production Stills 6	7 Gold
Burn Chamber	370 Points		Serena	8 Gold
Diavolo Moscow	400 Points		Production Stills 7	9 Gold
Serena	430 Points		Tank Upgrade	10 Gold
Miss Nagai	450 Points		Underworld	11 Gold
Golden Gun	1 Platinum		Cayenne Upgrade	12 Gold
Improved Traction	3 Platium		Production Stills 8	13 Gold
Improved Battery	5 Platium		Mya	14 Gold
Double Ammo	7 Platium		Vanquish Upgrade	15 Gold
Double Damage	9 Platium		Production Stills 9	16 Gold
Full Ammo	11 Platium		Miss Nagai	17 Gold
Cloak	13 Platium		Production Stills 10	18 Gold
Full Battery	15 Platium		Production Stills 11	19 Gold
All Weapons	17 Platium		Katya	20 Gold
Unlimited Battery	19 Platium		Triumph Upgrade	21 Gold
Unlimited Ammo	23 Platium		Production Stills 12	22 Gold
Slow Motion Driving	25 Platium		Production Stills 13	23 Gold
Platium Gun	27 Platium		Nanotank Upgrade	24 Gold
Production Stills 1	1 Gold		Production Stills 14	25 Gold
Production Stills 2	2 Gold		Gallery	27 Gold
Production Stills 3	3 Gold		MI6 Combat Simulator	Complete all Missions
Production Stills 4	4 Gold		MI6 Survival Test	Complete all Missions
Production Stills 5	5 Gold			
Helicopter Upgrade	6 Gold			

The Bouncer

Complete the game to unlock more characters each time.

Unlockable	Code
Alternate Costumes	Four different costumes for use in any mode other than Story are available for each character. To use one of these costumes, hold R1, R2, L1, or L2 while selecting the character of your choice.
Black-Hooded Sion	Access Sion's black hooded costume in Versus and Survival mode after you complete Survival mode once by holding L1+L2+R1+R2 when selecting Sion.
Leann Caldwell	Play through the entire game as Kou (you can't switch to any other character at any time).
Low Speed Mode	To move in slow motion, gain a ranking with each character in Arcade mode.
MSF Kou	Play through the game as Kou, until he is infiltrating the Mikado building as a MSF soldier. Save your game and you can use that costume in Survival and Versus modes by holding L1+L2+R1+R2 when selecting Kou in those modes.
Wong Leung	Play through the game as any character. Battle Kaldea (the battle right before the final fight), with any character other than Sion. Then, use Sion to complete the game.

Bratz: Rock Angelz

Passwords

Once you have access to the Bratz Office, go to the Cheat computer and input the following codes for special results.

Password	Effect
STYLIN	Changes Camerron
MEYGEN	Changes Dylan
PRTPRN	Changes Koby
BLINGZ	Changes London Boy
ROCKIN	Changes Paris Boy
YASMIN	Gives you 1,000 Blingz
PHOEBE	Gives you 2,000 Blingz
DANCIN	Gives you 2,100 Blingz
WAYFAB	Gives you 3,000 Blingz
HOTTIE	Gives you 6,000 Blingz
KOOLKT	Unlocks party jewelry
MODELS	Unlocks party outfit
BLAZIN	Unlocks ringtone 12
BNYBOO	Unlocks ringtone 14
FIANNA	Unlocks ringtone 15
ANGELZ	Unlocks ringtone 16

Brian Lara International Cricket 2005

Enter these passwords in the Cheat menu.

Unlockable	Password
Unlock All Classic Matches	BOWLEDHIM
Unlock All Teams	GOODLENGTH
Unlock All the Classic Players	GONEFORADUCK
Unlock All Trophys	DOLLY
Unlock the Classic XI Challenge	STUMPED
Unlock the Picture Gallery	SLEDGING

Brothers in Arms: Road to Hill 30

Unlockable	Code
All levels and difficulties	Create a profile with the name BAKERSDOZEN

Buffy the Vampire Slayer: Chaos Bleeds

Unlockable	Objective
Abominator	Finish Mission 10 with Professional rating
Amber Benson Interview	Complete Mission 2
Amber Benson Voice Over Session	Complete Mission 8
Anthony Stewart Interview	Cqmplete Mission 1
Anthony Stewart Voice Over Session	Complete Mission 7
Bat Beast	Finish Mission 4 with Professional rating
Cemetery	Finish Mission 2 with Slayer rating
Chainz	Finish Mission 10 with Slayer rating
Chaos Bleeds Comic Book	Complete Mission 5
Chris	Finish Mission 12 with Slayer rating
Faith	Finish Mission 8 with Professional rating
Female Vampire	Finish Mission 1 with Slayer rating

Buffy the Vampire Slayer: Chaos Bleeds (continued)

Unlockable	Objective
Initiative	Finish Mission 8 with Slayer rating
James Marsters Voice Over Session	Complete Mission 6
Joss Whedon	Finish Mission 12 with Professional rating
Joss Whedon Voice Over Session	Complete Mission 11
Kakistos	Finish Mission 9 with Slayer rating
Male Vampire	Finish Mission 1 with Professional rating
Materani	Finish Mission 5 with Professional rating
Nicholas Brendan Interview	Complete Mission 3
Nicholas Brendon Voice Over Session	Complete Mission 9
Out-Takes	Complete Mission 12
Psycho Patient	Finish Mission 6 with Professional rating
Quarry	Finish Mission 11 with Slayer rating
Robin Sachs Interview	Complete Mission 4
Robin Sachs Voice Over Session	Complete Mission 10
S&M Mistress	Finish Mission 7 with Slayer rating
S&M Slave	Finish Mission 7 with Professional rating
Sid the Dummy	Finish Mission 6 with Slayer rating
Tara	Finish Mission 3 with Slayer rating
Zombie Demon	Finish Mission 3 with Professional rating
Zombie Devil	Finish Mission 4 with Slayer rating
Zombie Gorilla	Finish Mission 11 with Professional rating
Zombie Skeleton	Finish Mission 2 with Professional rating
Zombie Soldier	Finish Mission 9 with Professional rating

Bully

To enter these codes you must have a second controller. Enter these codes while playing. Do not pause on controller two.

Unlockable	Code
All Clothes	L1, L1, R1, L1, L1, L1, R1, R1
All Gym	Hold L1 and press ⇧, ⇦, ⇩, ⇨, ▲, ■, ✕, ✕
All Hobo Fighting Moves	Hold L1 and press ⇧, ⇦, ⇩, ⇨, ▲, ■, ✕, ●
Full Health	Hold L1 and press R2, R2, R2
All Weapons	Hold L1 and press ⇧, ⇧, ⇧, ⇧
Infinite Ammo Toggle	Hold L1 and press ⇧, ⇩, ⇧, ⇩
Massive Money Gain	Hold L1 and press ▲, ■, ●, ✕
Refill Ammo	Hold L1 and press ⇧, ⇧
5 Punch Combo	Find transistor 4 and bring to the hobo
Leg Sweep	Find transistor 2 and bring to the hobo
Overhead Punch	Find transistor 6 and bring to the hobo
Roundhouse Kick	Find transistor 5 and bring to the hobo
Side Kick	Find transistor 3 and bring to the hobo
Uppercut	Find transistor 1 and bring to the hobo
#1 Paper Boy Ribbon	Finish level 4 Paper Route
Aluminum Trophy	Complete "Racing the Vale"
Artist's Set	Finish class 5 Art
BMX Frame	Finish class 5 Shop
Boxing Gloves	Finish mission "Dishonorable Fight"
Bullworth Golden Shield	Complete "Total Mayhem"

Bully (continued)

Unlockable	How To
Burned School Banner	Complete the mission "The Gym Is Burning" in Chapter V
Character Sheets	Complete "Character Sheets"
Dodgeball	Finish class 5 Gym
Football Jersey	Complete Chapter IV
Girlie Girl Poster	Buy at Carnival for 10 Tickets
Girl's Panties	Complete "Panty Raid"
Gnome	Destroy all Gnomes
Greaser Jacket	Complete Chapter III
Grim Reaper	Complete the mission "Funhouse Fun" in Chapter IV
Picture of Beatrice	Complete the mission "That ***ch" in Chapter I
Picture of Lola	Complete the mission "The Tenements" in Chapter III
Picture of Lola Kissing Gordo	Complete the mission "Jealous Johnny" in Chapter III
Picture of Mandy	Complete the mission "Discretion Assured" in Chapter IV
Picture of Ms. Phillips	Finish class 5 Photography
Picture of Pinky	Complete the mission "Carnival Date" in Chapter II
Picture of Zoe	Complete the mission "Smash It Up" in Chapter V
Pumpkin	Destroy all Pumpkins
Rat in a Jar	Complete the mission "Rats in the Library" in Chapter V
Rock Band Poster	Buy at Carnival for 10 Tickets
Russell's Shirt	Complete Chapter I
Teddy Bear	Complete the mission "Carnival Date" in Chapter II
Tombstone	Destroy all Tombstones
Trophy on Windowsill	Finish mission "Beach Rumble"
V Is for Victory Poster	Complete "The Campaign"
Various Chem Plant Signs	Complete both part of the mission "Busting In" in Chapter V
Venus Flytrap Head	Complete the mission "Weed Killer" in Chapter II
Wrestling Headgear	Finish class 3 Gym
Bike Helmet	Beat any bike race
Bike Shorts	Travel 100K on a bike
Black Cowboy Hat	Give a homeless guy some spare change in Bullworth
Black Ninja Outfit	Fill up your yearbook completely
Black Skate Shoes	Travel at least 50.00km on foot
BMX—Basic	Finish Shop class 1
BMX—Retro	Finish Shop class 2
BMX—Green	Finish Shop class 3
BMX—Blue	Finish Shop class 4
BMX—Red	Finish Shop class 5
BMX Champion	Complete one of the bike races
Boxing Outfit	Beat either "Boxing Challenge" or "Prep Challenge" in Chapter 2
Camera—Black and White Camera and Small Photo Album	Finish Photography class 1

Bully (continued)

Unlockable	How To
Camera—Colored Digital Camera	Finish Photography class 4
Camera—Large Photo Album	Finish Photography class 3
Camera—Yearbook	Finish Photography class 2
Carton of Eggs in Jimmy's dorm	Finish mission "The Eggs"
Cheerful Reindeer Sweater	Pick it up in the school office, during winter
Communication—Advanced Taunting	Finish English class 4
Communication—Basic Apologies	Finish English class 1
Communication—Improved Taunting	Finish English class 2
Communication—Police Apologies	Finish English class 5
Communication—Prefect and Teacher Apologies	Finish English class 3
Crash Helmet	Place 1st in the Kart Race at the Carnival
Dunce Cap	Fail three classes in a row
Edna Mask	Destroy 19 Tombstones during Halloween
Fast Food	Complete the Burger Joint errand found in Bullworth Vale
Firecracker in Chem Set	Complete Chemistry 1
Firefighter's Helmet	Pull the Fire Alarm 20 times
Free Soda from Soda Machines	Buy 100 Sodas
Gnome Costume	Smash all garden gnomes
Go Kart	Beat all Go Kart races
Gold Suit	Buy all clothing in the game
Graduation Hat	Beat all five levels of all of your classes
Green Ninja Outfit	Hit stuff with projectiles (eggs, etc.) 1,000 times
Grotto Master	Collect all G&G cards
Incognito Hat	Complete errand #21 (near City Hall)
Jimmy's Skeleton Halloween Costume	Beating the mission "The Candidate" opens up the mission "Halloween," which unlocks the costume
Orderly Uniform	Complete "Finding Johnny Vincent" in Chapter 5
Pirate Hat	Beat up pirate on island near Beach House
Prison Uniform	Beat all the detention mini games at least once
Pumpkin Head	Destroy all the 27 pumpkins during "Halloween Event"; they are around the school and inside the main building
Red Ninja Outfit	During Halloween at Bullworth Academy, complete the Big Prank task
Rubber Band Ball	Collect all 75 Rubber Bands
Running Shorts	Run/Walk 40 KM ingame
School Mascot	Beat "Nice Outfit" in Chapter 4
Soda Hat	Drink 500 Sodas

DS
GBA
PSP
PS2
PS3
Wii
Xbox
Xbox 360
Index

Bully (continued)

Unlockable	How To
Stink Bombs	Complete Chemistry 2
Tiny Swimsuit	At the Beach House location, find the Preppie with a blue mission on the beach and beat his swimming time
Viking Helmet	Obtain all collectables
Werewolf Mask	Found in a school locker after picking the lock
Wrestling Uniform	Beat Gym 1
x2 Carnival Prize Tickets per Win	Finish Photography class 5
Beatrice As a Girlfriend	Complete the mission "That ***ch" in Chapter I
Lola As a Girlfriend	Complete the mission "The Tenements" in Chapter III
Mandy As a Girlfriend	Complete the mission "Discretion Assured" in Chapter IV
Pinky As a Girlfriend	Complete the mission "Carnival Date" in Chapter II
Zoe As a Girlfriend	Complete the mission "Smash It Up" in Chapter V

Bujingai

Unlockable	Objective
All CGs and Credit Scenes	Complete the game.
Hard Mode	Complete the game.
High Score Display	Complete the game.
Opening Demo	Complete the game.
Stage Select	Complete the game.
Super Mode	Complete the game in Hard Mode.

Burnout: Revenge

Have a *Madden NFL 06* and *Burnout 3: Takedown* saved before starting a new game. You will unlock two special cars for Crash mode.

Unlockable	Code
Dominator Assassin	Burnout 3 Save
Madden Challenge Bus	Madden 06 Save

Cabela's Big Game Hunter

Unlockables

Unlockable	How to Unlock
Bonus Hunters	Complete an area in Career mode. Save the game and exit. Then load the game and start a new career to get a new hunter. With each area completed, a new hunter will be unlocked.
X-Ray Scope	Get all the tags in a level. Then play that level again in "Quick Hunt" mode. Press ⇩ while using the scope to see through the animals.

Call of Duty Big Red One

To enter this code, go into the Chapter Selection menu.

Unlockable	Code
Level Select	Hold L1 + R1 and press ⇧, ⇧, ⇩, ⇩, ⇦, ⇦, ⇨, ⇨, ■, ⇨, ■, ⇨, ■

Call of Duty: Finest Hour

Unlockable	Code
All levels	Hold up on controller two at the level select and enter with Start, Select, Select, Square with controller one.

DS

GBA

PSP

PS2

PS3

Wii

Xbox

Xbox 360

Index

DS

GBA

PSP

PS2

PS3

Wii

Xbox

Xbox 360

Index

Call of Duty 3

Enter this code in the Chapter Select screen.

Unlockable	Code
Unlock All Levels	Hold t and press ⇨, ⇨, ⇦, ⇦, ■, ■

Capcom Classic Collection

Enter this code at the title screen.

Unlockable	Code
Unlock Everything	L1, R1, Up Right Analog, Down Right Analog, L1, R1, Up Left Analog, Down Left Analog, L1, R1, ⇧, ⇩

Capcom Classic Collection Vol. 2

Enter this code at the Press Start screen.

Unlockable	Code
Cheats, Tips, Arts, and Sound Tests for Every Game	⇦, ⇨, ⇧, ⇩, L1, R1, L1, R1

Carmen Sandiego: The Secret of the Stolen Drums

Unlockables

Unlockable	How to Unlock
Bonus Mode	Finish the game once

Cars

To enter these passwords, select Options, then select Cheat Codes.

Unlockable	Password
All cars	YAYCARS
All character skins	R4MONE
All tracks and mini games	MATTL66
Fast start	IMSPEED
Infinite boost	VROOOOM
Unlock art	CONC3PT
Unlock Master's speedy circuit and Master's countdown cleanup	TRGTEXC
Unlocks movie clips	WATCHIT

CART Fury: Championship Racing

From the Main menu, go to Options, then Cheats and enter the following:

Unlockable	Code
All Cars	▲, ✕, ▲, ■, L2, ▲— Go to the Driver Select screen and press L1 to access them.
All Movies	L1, ●, R2, ✕, L2, ▲— Go to the Danny Sullivan Theater to access them.
All Tracks	▲, ✕, ✕, R2, R1
Big Heads	▲, ■, ■, L2, L1, R2
Unlockable	Code
Death Cars	L2, ■, L1, R2, R2, ✕
Death Wall	✕, ■, R2, ▲, R1, R2
Extra Drivers	Press R1 at the Driver Select screen.

CART Fury: Championship Racing (continued)

Unlockable	Code
Extra Vehicles	Press L1 at the Driver Select screen.
Infinite Turbo	✕, ✕, ■, ■, L2, L2
Infinite Continues	L1, L2, L1, ■, ▲, ●
Low Gravity	R2, R1, ■, ■, L1, L1
Night Drive	✕, ●, ▲, L2, R2, L1
Playable Death Car	L1, ■, R1, R2, L2, L1
Rocket Wheels	L1, R2, ▲, ■, ■, ▲
Thick Fog	R2, R1, ✕, ■, ■, ●
Unlimited Time	■, L1, R2, ●, ▲, R1

Catwoman

Unlockable	Code
Hidden Galleries	In the Vault Code Screen, enter 1940.

Champions of Norrath

Enter this code during gameplay.

Unlockable	Code
Instant Level 20 Character	Start a new character, and as soon as you have control of him or her, press L1+R2+▲+R2.

Champions of Norrath: Realms of Everquest

Unlockable	Code
Level 20 Character	During gameplay, press and hold L1+R2+▲+R2. This allows your character to unlock 75,000 coins, 999 skill points, and Level 20.

Chaos Legion

Unlockable	Objective
Level Select	Beat the boss at the end of Stage Nine to acquire the Map Selector, which allows you to choose levels.
New Enemies in Old Levels	Beat the Stage Ten boss then select Change Appearance.
Play as Arcia	Beat the game once to play as Arcia.
Hard Mode	Beat the game once.
Super Mode	Beat the game on Hard.
Ultimate Legion	Collect all of the Thanatos Chips scattered throughout the stages.

Chicken Little

At the Main menu, select Extras. Then select Cheat Codes to enter these passwords.

Unlockable	Password
Big Comb Mode	Ball, Bat, Bat, Ball
Big Feet	Hat, Glove, Glove, Hat
Big Head	Hat, Helmet, Helmet, Hat
Feathers Fly Off When Running	Bat, Shirt, Shirt, Ball

DS

GBA

PSP

PS2

PS3

Wii

Xbox

Xbox 360

Index

DS
GBA
PSP
PS2
PS3
Wii
Xbox
Xbox 360
Index

Chicken Little (continued)

Unlockable	Password
Invincibility	Ball, Ball, Ball, Shirt
Paper Pants	Bat, Bat, Hat, Hat
Sunglasses	Glove, Glove, Helmet, Helmet
Underwear	Hat, Hat, Shirt, Shirt

The Chronicles of Narnia: The Lion, The Witch, and The Wardrobe

To enter these codes, you must be at the title screen. Hold both L1+R1 simultaneously and press ↓, ↓, →, ↑. The words "Please Press Start" should turn green. You will now be able to enter any of the following codes.

Unlockable	Code
Automatically Complete Level	While in-game hold L1 and press ↓, ←, ↓, ←, ↓, →, ↓, →, ↑
Fill Combo Meter	While in-game hold L1 and press ↑, ↑, →, ↑
Receive 10,000 Coins	While in-game hold L1 and press ↓, ←, →, ↓, ↓
Restore All Children's Health	While in-game hold L1 and press ↓, ←, ←, →
Unlock All Abilities in Inventory	While in-game hold L1 and press ↓, ←, →, ←, ↑
Open All Levels	While on the Wardrobe screen hold L1 and press ↑, ↑, →, →, ↑, →, ↓
Unlock All Bonus Levels	While on the Bonus Drawer hold L1 and press ↓, →, →, →, ↓, →, ↑

City Crisis

Unlockable	Code
Chase Mode	Earn an A rating on all missions and an S on the Bus Chase.
Disaster Mode	Achieve an S rating in Final Rescue Mode.
Final Rescue Mode	Earn an S rating with the Sports Car.

Clock Tower 3

Unlockable	Objective
Cinema Theater	Beat the game once. You can press R1 at the Theater screen to view in-game art.
New Costumes	Beat the game once, and you'll receive a key. Start a new game using the same save, and use the key to unlock Alyssa's closet. Five new outfits will be available.

Conflict: Desert Storm-Back to Baghdad

In the Main menu, press L1, L1, R1, R1, ■, ■, ▲, ▲, ●, ●. During gameplay, pause the game, then go to Options to access Cheats.

Conflict: Global Terror

Enter this code at the Main menu.

Unlockable	Code
Cheat Menu is activated	L1, R1, L1, R1, ●, ●, ●, ●

Conflict: Vietnam

Unlockable	Code
Cheat Menu	In the Main menu, press L1, R1, L1, R1, ■, ▲, ●, ▲, ■, ●. Go to the Options screen to access the cheats.

Conflict Zone

Pause gameplay, then enter the following codes.

Unlockable	Code
100 Population	✕, →, →, ←, ↑
Access to All Missions in Replay Mode	✕, ↑, ↑, ←, →, ←
Faster Building	✕, ↓, ↓, ↑, ←, →
Money Cheat	✕, ←, →, ↑, ←

Constantine

Press SELECT to open your journal and enter these codes.

Unlockable	Codes
Big Headed Demons	R2, ⇦, ⇨, ⇦, ⇦, ⇨, ⇦, R2.

Contra: Shattered Soldier

Unlockable	Objective
Contra vs. Puppy	Complete the game with an "S" rank.
Database Option	Complete the game with a "B" or "C" rank under the Normal difficulty setting.
Final Boss Battle in Training Mode	Defeat the final boss under Normal difficulty setting.
Gallery Option	Complete the game with an "A" rank under the Normal difficulty setting.
In-Game Reset	Hold L1+L2+R1+R2+START+SELECT during gameplay.
Level 5 in Training Mode	Complete Level 5 during the game under Normal difficulty setting.
Level 6	Complete Level 5 with an "A" rank.
Level 6 in Training Mode	Complete Level 6 under Normal difficulty setting.
Level 7	Complete Level 6 with an "A" rank.
Level 7 in Training Mode	Complete Level 7 under Normal difficulty setting.
Return	Complete Level 7 up to the credits with an "A" rank.
Satellite Weapon	Complete Level 5 with a "B" or "C" rank.
Theater Option	Complete the game under the Normal difficulty setting. Your rank determines how much of the theater unlocks.
Thirty Lives (Only affects your first credit)	Press ↑, ↑, ↓, ↓, L1, R1, L2, R2, L3, R3 on controller two at the title screen. A sound confirms correct code entry. See Note.
Triumphant Return	Complete Level 7, including after the credits, with an "A" rank.

Corvette

Unlockable	Code
All Cars and Courses	Go to Options, then Game Options and select "Change Name." Enter XOPENSEZ.

Crazy Taxi

Unlockable	Code
Another View	Begin a game. While the game is in progress, press and hold L1 and R1, then press ● to enter first-person driving mode. Press ▲ (while holding L1 and R1) to show things from a wider angle.
Expert Mode	Press and hold L1 and R1, then press START before you see the character selection screen. "Expert" appears onscreen if done properly.

DS · GBA · PSP · PS2 · PS3 · Wii · Xbox · Xbox 360 · Index

DS

GBA

PSP

PS2

PS3

Wii

Xbox

Xbox 360

Index

Crazy Taxi (continued)

Unlockable	Code
Taxi Bike	At the character select screen, hit L1+R1 three times quickly. You can also gain access to the bike after you beat all Crazy Box challenges. Press ↑ at the select screen to get it.
Turn Off Arrow	Hold R1 and press START before you see the character selection screen. "No Arrows" appears on the screen if entered correctly.
Turn Off Destination Mark	Press and hold, then press START before you see the character selection screen. "No Destination" appears on screen if done correctly.
Unlock Another Day	Press and hold R1. Keep holding it until you choose a taxi driver. After you do, "Another Day" appears onscreen, indicating correct code entry.

Crimson Sea 2

Unlockable	Objective
Diez in Multiplayer	Complete the Diez Woman Warrior Mission with an S ranking.
Shami in Multiplayer	Complete the Princess Shami Mission with an S ranking.

Cy Girls

Unlockable	Objective
Benigumo	Complete Aska's game.
X	Complete Ice's game on any difficulty.

The Da Vinci Code

Codes

Go to codes at the Options menu then type the code in.

Code	Effect
Et In Arcadia Ego	All bonuses unlocked
Apocrypha	All visual database entries unlocked
Sacred Feminine	Double health
Vitruvian Man	God mode (infinite health)
Clos Luce 1519	Level select
Phillips Exeter	One hit fist kill
Royal Holloway	One hit weapon kill

Dance Summit 2001 Bust-a-Move

Unlockable	Objective
Disco Estrus Team and Muscle Stadium Stage	Beat the game twice.
Far East Commanders Team and Iga Base Stage	Beat the game four times.
Galaxy 4 Team and Disco 21 Stage	Beat the game in Team mode.
Jumbo Max Team and 79 Street Stage	Beat the game three times

Dave Mirra Freestyle BMX 2

Input the following codes at the Main menu.

Unlockable	Code
All Bikes	↑, ←, ↓, →, ↓, ↓, →, ↓, ↓, ←, ■
Amish Boy	↑, ←, ↓, →, →, ←, ←, ↑, ↑, ←, ■
Colin Mackay's Competition Outfit	↑, ↓, →, ↓, ↑, →, →, ↑, ■
Dave Mirra's Competition Outfit	↑, ↓, ↑, ↓, →, ←, ↑, ↑, ■
Joey Garcia's Competition Outfit	↑, ↓, ↑, ←, ↓, →, ↓, →, ■

Dave Mirra Freestyle BMX 2 (continued)

Unlockable	Code
Kenan Harkin's Competition Outfit	↑, ↓, ←, ↓, ←, ↑, ↓, ↑, ■
Leigh Ramsdell's Competition Outfit	↑, ↓, ↓, ←, ↓, ↓, ↓, ←, ■
Luc-E's Competition Outfit	↑, ↓, ←, ↓, ←, →, ←, ←, ■
Mike Dias	↑, ←, ↓, →, →, ←, ↑, ↓, ↑, →, ■
Mike Laird's Competition Outfit	↑, ↑, ↓, ↓, ←, →, ↓, ←, ■
Rick Moliterno's Competition Outfit	↑, ↓, ↑, ↑, ↑, ↑, ←, ↑, ■
Ryan Nyquist's Competition Outfit	↑, ↓, ↓, ←, ↓, ↑, ↑, ↓, ■
Scott Wirch's Competition Outfit	↑, ↓, →, ↓, ↑, →, →, ↑, ■
Tim Mirra's Competition Outfit	↑, ↓, →, ←, ←, ↑, ↓, ↑, ■
Todd Lyons' Competition Outfit	↑, ↓, ↓, →, ↑, ←, ←, ↓, ■
Troy McMurray's Competition Outfit	↑, ↓, ←, ↓, →, ←, ↑, ←, ■
Zack Shaw's Competition Outfit	↑, ↓, ←, →, ↓, ↓, →, ↓, ■

Dead or Alive 2

Unlockable	Objective
Ayane C3 Costume	Complete Story mode with Ayane on any setting.
Ayane C4 Costume	Complete Story mode with Ayane and without Continuing on default settings or higher. Or complete Story mode using Ayane five times on any setting.
Ayane C5 Costume	Earn 1.5 million points with Ayane in Survival mode on default settings or higher. Or play as Ayane more than 25 times.
Ayane C6 Costume	Beat more than 50 stages with Ayane in Survival mode on any setting. Or play as Ayane more than 50 times.
Ayane C7 Costume	Complete Time Attack mode with Ayane and in less than 4:15 on any setting. Or play as Ayane more than 100 times.
Ayane C8 Costume	Get the "Tiara" item with Ayane in Survival mode on any setting. Or play as Ayane more than 200 times.
Bass C3 Costume	Complete Story mode with Bass on any setting.
Bass C4 Costume	Complete Story mode with Bass and without Continuing on default settings or higher. Or complete Story mode using Bass five times on any setting.
Bass C5 Costume	Get the "Championship Belt" item with Bass in Survival mode on any difficulty setting. Or play as Bass more than 50 times.
Bayman	Beat Story mode with every character. Or complete Story mode using any combination of characters 30 times.
Bayman C3 Costume	Play as Bayman more than 10 times.
Bayman C4 Costume	Get the "Bayman's Missile" item with Bayman in Survival mode on any setting. Or play as Bayman more than 30 times.
Deluxe Credit Ending	Beat the game with every character in Very Hard mode.
Ein C3 Costume	Complete Story mode with Ein on any setting.
Ein C4 Costume	Complete Story mode with Ein and without Continuing on default settings or higher. Or complete Story mode using Ein five times on any setting.
Ein C5 Costume	Get the "Scrolls" item with Ein in Survival mode on any setting. Or play as Ein more than 50 times.
Gen Fu C3 Costume	Complete Story mode with Gen on any setting.
Gen Fu C4 Costume	Complete Story mode with Gen and without Continuing on default settings or higher. Or complete Story mode using Gen five times on any setting.
Gen Fu C5 Costume	Earn 1 million points with Gen in Survival mode on default settings or higher. Or play as Gen more than 30 times.

DS
GBA
PSP
PS2
PS3
Wii
Xbox
Xbox 360
Index

DS

GBA

PSP

PS2

PS3

Wii

Xbox

Xbox 360

Index

Dead or Alive 2

Unlockable	Objective
Gen Fu C6 Costume	Win 48 matches in Survival mode on default settings or higher. Or play as Gen more than 75 times.
Gen Fu C7 Costume	Get the "Mah Jong Counter" item with Gen in Survival mode. Or play as Gen more than 100 times.
Helena C3 Costume	Complete Story mode with Helena on any setting.
Helena C4 Costume	Complete Story mode with Helena and without Continuing on default settings or higher. Or complete Story mode using Helena five times on any setting.
Helena C5 Costume	Earn 2 million points with Helena in Survival mode on default settings or higher. Or play as Helena more than 30 times.
Helena C6 Costume	Complete Time Attack mode with Helena in less than 4:15 on default settings or higher. Or play as Helena more than 75 times.
Helena C7 Costume	Get the "Rocket" item with Helena in Survival mode on any setting. Or play as Helena more than 150 times.
Jann Lee C3 Costume	Complete Story mode with Jann Lee on any setting.
Jann Lee C4 Costume	Complete Story mode with Jann Lee and without Continuing on default settings or higher. Or complete Story mode using Jann Lee five times on any setting.
Jann Lee C5 Costume	Earn 1 million points with Jann Lee without Continuing on default settings or higher. Or play as Jann Lee more than 50 times.
Jann Lee C6 Costume	Get the "Dragon" item with Jann Lee in Survival mode on any setting. Or play as Jann Lee more than 100 times.
Kasumi C3 Costume	Complete Story mode with Kasumi on any setting.
Kasumi C4 Costume	Complete Story mode with Kasumi and without Continuing on default settings or higher. Or complete Story mode using Kasumi three times on any setting.
Kasumi C5 Costume	Complete Story mode with Kasumi and without Continuing on default settings or higher. Or complete Story mode using Kasumi five times on any setting.
Kasumi C6 Costume	Earn 2 million points with Kasumi in Survival mode on default settings or higher. Or play as Kasumi more than 50 times.
Kasumi C7 Costume	Complete more than 50 stages with Kasumi in Survival mode on default settings or higher. Or play as Kasumi more than 100 times.
Kasumi C8 Costume	Get the "Cherry" item with Kasumi in Survival mode on any setting. Or play as Kasumi more than 200 times.
Lei Fang C3 Costume	Complete Story mode with Lei Fang on any setting.
Lei Fang C4 Costume	Complete Story mode with Lei Fang and without Continuing on default settings or higher. Or complete Story mode using Lei Fang three times on any setting.
Lei Fang C5 Costume	Earn 1 million points with Lei Fang in Survival mode on default settings or higher. Or complete Story mode five times with Lei Fang.
Lei Fang C6 Costume	Complete Tag Battle mode with Lei Fang in a C5 costume and partnering with Jann Lee in a C5 costume. Or play as Lei Fang more than 50 times.
Lei Fang C7 Costume	Complete Time Attack mode with Lei Fang in less than 4:15 on default settings or higher. Or play as Lei Fang more than 100 times.
Lei Fang C8 Costume	Get the "Decoration Cake" item with Lei Fang in Survival mode on any setting. Or play as Lei Fang more than 200 times.
Leon C3 Costume	Complete Story mode with Leon on any setting.

Dead or Alive 2

Unlockable	Objective
Leon C4 Costume	Complete Story mode with Leon and without continuing on default settings or higher. Or complete Story mode using Leon three times on any setting.
Leon C5 Costume	Get the "Missile" item with Leon in Survival mode on any setting. Or play as Leon more than 50 times.
Ryu Hayabusa C3 Costume	Complete Story mode with Ryu on any setting.
Ryu Hayabusa C4 Costume	Complete Story mode with Ryu and without Continuing on default settings or higher. Or complete Story mode using Ryu five times on any setting.
Ryu Hayabusa C5 Costume	Earn 1 million points with Ryu in Survival mode on default settings or higher. Or play as Ryu more than 50 times.
Ryu Hayabusa C6 Costume	Get the "Green Tea" item with Ryu in Survival mode on any setting. Or play as Ryu more than 100 times.
Tengu	Collect 10 stars in Survival mode.
Tina C3 Costume	Complete Story mode with Tina on any setting.
Tina C4 Costume	Complete Story mode with Tina and without Continuing on default settings or higher. Or complete Story mode using Tina five times on any setting.
Tina C5 Costume	Earn 1.5 million points with Tina in Survival mode on default settings or higher. Or play as Tina more than 30 times.
Tina C6 Costume	Complete Time Attack mode with Tina in less than 4:15 on default settings or higher. Or play as Tina more than 75 times.
Tina C7 Costume	Get the "Roast Chicken" item with Tina in Survival mode on any setting. Or play as Tina more than 100 times.
Zack C3 Costume	Complete Story mode with Zack on any setting.
Zack C4 Costume	Complete Story mode with Zack and without Continuing on default settings or higher. Or complete Story mode using Zack five times on any setting.
Zack C5 Costume	Earn 1 million points with Zack in Survival mode on default settings or higher. Or play as Zack more than 50 times.
Zack C6 Costume	Get the "Parfait" item with Zack in Survival mode on any setting. Or play as Zack more than 100 times.

Dead or Alive 2: Hardcore (DOA2)

Unlockable	Objective
Bayman	Beat Story mode with every character on the Easy Difficulty setting. Bayman becomes unlocked in all modes except for Story mode.
Bonus Options	Pause the game. Press ▲+✕.
CG Gallery	Beat Team mode with five characters.
Longer Credits	Beat the Story mode with all the characters on Very Hard Difficulty.
More Bounce	Go into the Options menu. Change your age between 13 and 99. The higher you set your age, the more bounce you will see from the female characters.

Dead to Rights

Enter the follwing codes at the New Game screen, just after "Press Start" appears. After entering the following codes listen for a message that confirms correct code entry.

Unlockable	Code
10,000 Bullets Mode (unlimited ammo)	Hold L1+L2+R1+R2 and press ↑,←,↓,→,●.
Bang Bang Mode	Hold L1+L2+R1+R2 and press ●,▲,■,●,→.

DS

GBA

PSP

PS2

PS3

Wii

Xbox

Xbox 360

Index

Dead to Rights (continued)

Unlockable	Code
Boomstick Mode (unlimited shotguns)	Hold L1+L2+R1+R2 and press →,●,●,●,■.
Chow Yun Jack Mode (You receive a pair of double guns at the beginning of the level, even if you would normally have none.)	Hold L1+L2+R1+R2 and press ▲,●,↑,↑,↑.
Double Melee Attack Damage	Hold L1+L2+R1+R2 and press ●,●,↑,↑,■.
Enemies Disarmed	Hold L1+L2+R1+R2 and press →,■,←,●,▲.
Enemies More Accurate	Hold L1+L2+R1+R2 and press ▲,■,←,←,●.
Hard-Boiled Mode (increases the challenge level significantly)	Hold L1+L2+R1+R2 and press ▲,■,←,←,●.
Invisible Character (Enemies can still see you, but you can only see your own shadow.)	Hold L1+L2+R1+R2 and press ▲,▲,↑,↑,▲.
Lazy Mode (all levels, minigames, and FMV sequences)	Hold L1+L2+R1+R2 and press ↓,←,↓,▲,↓.
One-Hit Wonder Mode	Hold L1+L2+R1+R2 and press ▲,●,●,●,←.
Powered-up Punches and Kicks	Hold L1+L2+R1+R2 and press ↓,●,←,←,←.
Precursor Mode (turns off all targeting cursors)	Hold L1+L2+R1+R2 and press ↑,↑,↓,↓,↑.
Sharpshooter Mode	Hold L1+L2+R1+R2 and press ■,■,■,↓,→.
Super Cop Mode (harder difficulty)	Hold L1+L2+R1+R2 and press ■,▲,←,↑,→.
Time to Pay Mode (all disarms)	Hold L1+L2+R1+R2 and press ■,●,●,●,→.
Unlimited Adrenaline	Hold L1+L2+R1+R2 and press ←,→,←,●,■.
Unlimited Armor	Hold L1+L2+R1+R2 and press ↑,↑,↑,■,↓.
Unlimited Dual Guncons	Hold L1+L2+R1+R2 and press ▲,●,↑,↑,↑.
Unlimited Human Shields	Hold L1+L2+R1+R2 and press ■,▲,●,▲,■.
Unlimited Shadow Stamina	Hold L1+L2+R1+R2 and press ●,■,▲,●,↓.
Wussy Mode (less accurate enemies)	Hold L1+L2+R1+R2 and press ■,←,▲,↑,↓.

Def Jam Vendetta

Enter the following codes on any non-Story mode character select screen.

Unlockable	Code
Arii	Hold L2 + L2 + R1 + R2 and press ✕, ■, ▲, ●, ■.
Briggs	Hold L2 + L2 + R1 + R2 and press ✕, ▲, ●, ■, ●.
Briggs (alternate costume)	Hold L2 + L2 + R1 + R2 and press ✕, ▲, ■, ✕, ●.
Carla	Hold L2 + L2 + R1 + R2 and press ✕, ■, ✕, ✕, ✕.
Chukklez	Hold L2 + L2 + R1 + R2 and press ■, ■, ▲, ✕, ●.
Cruz	Hold L2 + L2 + R1 + R2 and press ●, ▲, ▲, ✕, ●.
D-Mob	Hold L2 + L2 + R1 + R2 and press ■, ▲, ●, ✕, ●.
D-Mob (alternate costume)	Hold L2 + L2 + R1 + R2 and press ■, ■, ▲, ■, ■.
Dan G	Hold L2 + L2 + R1 + R2 and press ✕, ●, ✕, ●, ■.
Deebo	Hold L2 + L2 + R1 + R2 and press ●, ●, ✕, ✕, ▲.
Deja	Hold L2 + L2 + R1 + R2 and press ●, ■, ●, ●, ✕.
DMX	Hold L2 + L2 + R1 + R2 and press ●, ✕, ●, ▲, ■.
Drake	Hold L2 + L2 + R1 + R2 and press ▲, ■, ●, ✕, ✕.
Drake (alternate costume)	Hold L2 + L2 + R1 + R2 and press ✕, ▲, ▲, ●, ●.
Funkmaster Flex	Hold L2 + L2 + R1 + R2 and press ●, ▲, ●, ●, ■.

Def Jam Vendetta (continued)

Unlockable	Code
Headache	Hold L2 + L2 + R1 + R2 and press ▲, ▲, ▲, ■, ●.
House	Hold L2 + L2 + R1 + R2 and press ▲, ✕, ▲, ●, ■.
Iceberg	Hold L2 + L2 + R1 + R2 and press ■, ▲, ●, ■, ●.
Ludacris	Hold L2 + L2 + R1 + R2 and press ●, ●, ●, ■, ■.
Manny (alternate costume)	Hold L2 + L2 + R1 + R2 and press ●, ■, ●, ■, ●.
Masa	Hold L2 + L2 + R1 + R2 and press ✕, ●, ▲, ■, ■.
Method Man	Hold L2 + L2 + R1 + R2 and press ■, ●, ✕, ▲, ●.
Moses	Hold L2 + L2 + R1 + R2 and press ▲, ▲, ■, ■, ✕.
N.O.R.E.	Hold L2 + L2 + R1 + R2 and press ●, ■, ▲, ✕, ●.
Nyne	Hold L2 + L2 + R1 + R2 and press ■, ●, ✕, ✕, ▲.
Omar	Hold L2 + L2 + R1 + R2 and press ●, ●, ■, ▲, ▲.
Opal	Hold L2 + L2 + R1 + R2 and press ●, ●, ■, ■, ▲.
Peewee	Hold L2 + L2 + R1 + R2 and press ✕, ✕, ■, ▲, ■.
Peewee (alternate costume)	Hold L2 + L2 + R1 + R2 and press ▲, ▲, ■, ▲, ●.
Penny	Hold L2 + L2 + R1 + R2 and press ✕, ✕, ✕, ▲, ●.
Pockets	Hold L2 + L2 + R1 + R2 and press ▲, ■, ●, ■, ✕.
Proof (alternate costume)	Hold L2 + L2 + R1 + R2 and press ✕, ■, ▲, ▲, ●.
Razor	Hold L2 + L2 + R1 + R2 and press ▲, ■, ▲, ●, ✕.
Razor (alternate costume)	Hold L2 + L2 + R1 + R2 and press ■, ●, ✕, ▲, ▲.
Redman	Hold L2 + L2 + R1 + R2 and press ●, ●, ■, ▲, ✕.
Ruffneck	Hold L2 + L2 + R1 + R2 and press ✕, ■, ✕, ▲, ●.
Ruffneck (alternate costume)	Hold L2 + L2 + R1 + R2 and press ■, ●, ▲, ✕, ■.
Scarface	Hold L2 + L2 + R1 + R2 and press ●, ■, ✕, ▲, ■.
Sketch	Hold L2 + L2 + R1 + R2 and press ▲, ▲, ●, ■, ✕.
Snowman	Hold L2 + L2 + R1 + R2 and press ▲, ▲, ✕, ✕, ●.
Spider (alternate costume)	Hold L2 + L2 + R1 + R2 and press ■, ▲, ✕, ■, ●.
Steel	Hold L2 + L2 + R1 + R2 and press ●, ■, ●, ●, ▲.
T'ai	Hold L2 + L2 + R1 + R2 and press ●, ●, ▲, ✕, ●.
Zaheer	Hold L2 + L2 + R1 + R2 and press ▲, ▲, ■, ✕, ✕.

Destroy All Humans

To activate these codes, pause the game and hold L1, then enter the code and release L1.

Unlockable	Code
Ammo-A-Plenty	⇐, ●, R2, ⇒, R1, ■
Aware Like a Fox	⇒, ■, R2, R1, ⇒, R2
Bulletproof Crypto	■, ●, ⇐, ⇐, ●, ■
Deep Thinker	R1, R2, ●, ⇒, R2, ●
Mmmm...Brains!	R1, R1, R2, R2, ⇐, ⇒, ⇐, ⇒, R2 This code increases DNA. (You must be on the Mothership.)
More Upgrades	■, ●, ⇐, ⇐, ●, ■ (You must be on the Mothership.)
Nobody Loves You	⇒, R2, R1, ■, ⇒

Deus Ex: Conspiracy Theory

Activate Cheats: Enter the Goals/Notes/Images screen. Press L2, R2, L1, R1, START (3) to display another tab on this screen with the following cheats that you can turn on and off: God, Full Health, Full Energy, Full Ammo, Full Mods, All Skills, Full Credits, and Tantalus.

DS
GBA
PSP
PS2
PS3
WII
Xbox
Xbox 360
Index

Devil Kings

Unlockables

Unlockable	How to Unlock
Fight Your Own Army	Beat all 12 Conquest modes

Playable Characters

Complete required task, and these new characters appear under Characters in the Gallery menu.

Arslan	Finish Landing at Nanvia
Azure Dragon	Achieve Total Conquest with Azure Dragon
Bramble	Finish Divide & Conquer Faylinn
Devil King	Achieve Total Conquest with Devil King
Etc	Achieve Total Conquest with any character
Frost	Achieve Total Conquest with Frost
Hornet	Achieve Total Conquest with Hornet
Irdene	Finish Storm on the Great Plains
Iron OX	Achieve Total Conquest with Iron OX
Kahz	Finish Flooding Giuthas Nam
Lady Butterfly	Achieve Total Conquest with Lady Butterfly
Lark	Finish Divide & Conquer Faylinn
Muri	Finish Ambush at Shadow Gorge
Orwik	Finish Siege of Dark Spire
Puff	Achieve Total Conquest with Puff
Q-Ball	Achieve Total Conquest with Q-Ball
Reaper	Finish Crossing the River Styx
Red Minotaur	Achieve Total Conquest with Red Minotaur
Scorpio	Achieve Total Conquest with Scorpio
Talon	Achieve Total Conquest with Talon
Venus	Achieve Total Conquest with Venus
Zaan	Finish Leveling Kushk

Movies

Complete required task, and these new movies appear under Movies in the Gallery menu.

Anime Opening—Tokyo City	Achieve Total Conquest with any character
Archrival	Finish Battle at Riverglen with Red Minotaur or Scorpio
Azure Dragon-Ending	Achieve Total Conquest with Azure Dragon
Azure Dragon—Opening	Finish any stage with Azure Dragon
Battle at Deadwood	Finish Deadwood Counterattack with Devil King or Lady Butterfly
Battle at Great Plains	Finish Storm on the Great Plains with Red Minotaur or Scorpio
Devil King Army—Opening	Finish any stage with Devil King or Lady Butterfly
Devil King-Ending	Achieve Total Conquest with Devil King
Dragon VS Devil King	Finish Fall of the High Temple with Azure Dragon
Fight for Love	Finish Arctica Rebellion with Q-Ball or finish Pilgrimage to Cathedral City with Puff
Frost Army—Opening	Finish any stage with Venus

Devil Kings (continued)

Movies

Frost—Ending	Achieve Total Conquest with Frost
Hornet—Ending	Achieve Total Conquest with Hornet
Iron OX—Ending	Achieve Total Conquest with Iron OX
Iron OX—Opening	Finish any stage with Iron OX
Lady Butterfly—Ending	Achieve Total Conquest with Lady Butterfly
Mutual Respect	Finish Leveling Kush with Iron OX
Puff—Ending	Achieve Total Conquest with Puff
Puff—Opening	Finish any stage with Puff
Q-Ball—Ending	Achieve Total Conquest with Q-Ball
Q-Ball—Opening	Finish any stage with Q-Ball
Reaper's Betrayal	Finish Twisted High Temple with Devil King or Lady Butterfly
Red Minotaur Army—Opening	Finish any stage with Red Minotaur or Scorpio
Red Minotaur—Ending	Achieve Total Conquest with Red Minotaur
Scorpio—Ending	Achieve Total Conquest with Scorpio
Talon—Ending	Achieve Total Conquest with Talon
Venus—Ending	Achieve Total Conquest with Venus

Movies

Complete required task, and these new tracks appear under Music in the Gallery menu. Tracks 01 to 04 are unlocked by default.

Music Track 05—The Upper Hand	Finish Arctica Rebellion
Music Track 06—Adrenaline Rush	Finish Deadwood Counterattack
Music Track 07—Half of the Battle	Finish Border Patrol
Music Track 08—Beachhead	Finish Flooding Giuthas Nam
Music Track 09—Double Trouble	Finish Landing at Nanvia
Music Track 10—Tropical Storm	Finish Leveling Kush
Music Track 11—Fight to the Death	Finish Landing at Nanvia
Music Track 12—Bramble's Scramble	Finish Divide & Conquer Faylinn
Music Track 13—Enlightenment	Finish Pilgrimage to Cathedral City
Music Track 14—Theme of Riverglen	Finish Battle at Riverglen
Music Track 15—Tide of Battle	Finish Assault on Bloomdale
Music Track 16—Pursuing Love	Finish Assault on Bloomdale
Music Track 17—Frostbite	Finish Arctica Rebellion
Music Track 18—Rumble of Valor	Finish Siege of Dark Spire
Music Track 19—Riding High	Finish Siege of Dark Spire
Music Track 20—Might and Steel	Finish Storm on the Great Plains
Music Track 21—Betrayal	Finish Fall of the High Temple
Music Track 22—Storm Ride	Finish Chase at the Tablelands
Music Track 23—The Thorn	Finish Deadwood Counterattack
Music Track 24—The Downpour	Finish Ambush at Shadow Gorge
Music Track 25—Tuonela	Finish Crossing the River Styx
Music Track 26—Back Against the Wall	Finish Crossing the River Styx
Music Track 27—Staccato Dream	Finish Battle at Riverglen
Music Track 28—Albatross	Finish Leveling Kush

DS
GBA
PSP
PS2
PS3
Wii
Xbox
Xbox 360
Index

DS

GBA

PSP

PS2

PS3

Wii

Xbox

Xbox 360

Index

Devil Kings (continued)

Music Track 29—No Return	Finish Crossing the River Styx
Music Track 30—Little Big Heart	Finish Arctica Rebellion
Music Track 31—Burning Butterfly	Finish Battle at Riverglen
Music Track 32—The Abyss	Finish Fall of the High Temple
Music Track 33—Thunderbolt	Finish Chase at the Tablelands
Music Track 34—Boiling Point	Finish Divide & Conquer Faylinn
Music Track 35—Divine Love	Finish Pilgrimage to Cathedral City

Devil May Cry 2

Unlockable	Objective
Alternate Dante Costume	Complete the game with Dante at Normal difficulty.
Alternate Devil May Cry 1 Costume for Dante	Complete the game in Dante Must Die mode.
Alternate Costumes for Lucia	Complete the game with Lucia to unlock her alternate costume. Complete the game with Lucia under the Hard difficulty setting to unlock another costume.
Bloody Palace Mode	Complete the game with Dante and Lucia.
Dante Must Die Mode	Complete the game with Dante and Lucia under the Hard difficulty setting.
Dante's Diesel Bonus Level and Costume	Play Dante's Mission 1, then save the game. Reset the PlayStation2, and wait for the "Press Start button" message to reappear. Press L3, R3, L1, R1, L2, R2, L3, R3. A sound confirms correct code entry. Press START to return to the Main menu. Choose the "Load game" option, press L3 or R3 to access the new costume, and load a game to play the bonus level.
Dante's Diesel Costume	Press R1, R1, ▲, ■, R2, R2 during gameplay.
Hard Difficulty Setting	Complete the game with Dante and Lucia.
In-Game Reset	Press START + SELECT during gameplay to return to the title screen.
Level Select	Complete the game as either character under any difficulty setting.
Lucia's Arius bod	Complete the game in Lucia Must Die mode.
Lucia Must Die Mode	Complete the game with Lucia under the Hard difficulty setting.
Lucia's Diesel Bonus Level and Costume	Play Lucia's Mission 1, then save the game. Reset the PlayStation2, and wait for the "Press Start button" message to reappear. Press L3, R3, L1, R1, L2, R2, L3, R3. A sound confirms correct code entry. Press START to return to the Main menu. Choose the "Load game" option, press L3 or R3 to access the new costume, and then load a game to play the bonus level.
Lucia's Diesel Costume	Press L1, L1, ▲, ■, L2, L2 during gameplay.
Play as Trish	Complete the game with Dante under the Hard difficulty setting. Trish has Dante's stats and items and starts with the Sparda.

Completion Bonuses: Use the following to unlock the completion bonuses by only playing Dante's game. Switch from Disc 1 to 2 anytime during Dante's game. Complete the game to unlock Level Select mode, Hard difficulty, Bloody Palace mode, and the credits. If you change from Disc 1 to 2 before completing the game in Hard mode, you unlock Trish and other bonuses.

Devil May Cry 3

Enter at the Main menu.

Unlockable	Code
Unlock Everything	Hold down L1, L2, R1, R2 and rotate the left analog stick until you hear Devil May Cry.

Disney's Extreme Skate Adventure

Go to Options, select Cheat Codes, then enter the following codes.

Unlockable	Code
All Create-a-Skaters	sweetthreads
All Skaters	friendsofbob
All Levels	extremepassport
Filled Special Meter	supercharger
Lion King Video	savannah
Tarzan Video	nugget
Toy Story Video	marin

Disney Golf

Unlockables

Unlockable	How to Unlock
Expert Mode	Win 3 matches at Beginner class to unlock this (still relatively easy) "Expert" difficulty setting
Mortimer	Unlock by beating 3 expert modes with 1 character, then beat preliminary match against him
Pete	Beat him in the Long Drive challenge, Expert Class
Unlock Daisy	Beat her in Challenge Mode, Beginner Class
Unlock Drake	Beat him in the Nearest to Pin Challenge, Expert Class
Unlock European Golf Course	Beat Mortimer in a Skins Match at Expert Class
Unlock Max	Beat him in Combination Play, Expert Class
Unlock Midair Matchup	Beat the Mickey Cup to unlock this somewhat unorthodox style of golfing
Unlock Sky Course	Beat Morty in a Midair Match
Unlock the Mickey Cup	Win at least 3 matches at Expert Class difficulty

Disney's Tarzan Untamed

Unlockable Characters

Complete the following tasks to unlock extra characters for the skiing and surfing challenges:

Unlockable	How to Unlock
Jane	Complete the Terk challenges in world 1
Porter	Complete the Terk challenges in world 2
Terk	Complete all the Terk challenges

Dog's Life

Unlockable	Code
Enable Cheat menu	■, ■, ■ hold ■ (till the dog growls), hold ■ (till the dog growls), hold ■ (till the dog growls), ←, →, ↓

Downhill Domination

During your run, you must use the unlock code (↑,▲,↓,✕,←,●,→,■) first before trying any of the others.

Unlockable	Code	Unlockable	Code
Adrenaline Boost	↓,←,←,→	Energy Restore	↓,→,→,←,←
Always Stoked	↓,■,■,←,●	Extra Smack Time	←,→,↓,↓
Anti-Gravity	↓,▲,■,■,↑	Infinite Bottles	↑,✕,←,←,●,●
Combat Upgrade	↑,↓,←,←,→	Mega Flip	→,↑,↑,→,→,■

DS

GBA

PSP

PS2

PS3

Wii

Xbox

Xbox 360

Index

Downhill Domination (continued)

Unlockable	Code	Unlockable	Code
More $$$	→,↑,↑,●,●,■	Super Bounce	←,■,✕,↑,▲
No Combat	←,■,●,■,←	Super Bunny Hop	↑,✕,←,■,↑
Speed Freak	↓,▲,→,→,■	Upgrade to Bottle	↑,↓,←,←,→,→
Stoke Trick Meter	↓,←,←,→,→		

Dr. Muto

Enter the following as codes.

Unlockable	Code	Unlockable	Code
All Gadgets	TINKERTOY	Go Anywhere	BEAMMEUP
Invincibility (This has no effect when you fall from high places.)	NECROSCI	Never Take Damage	CHEATERBOY
		Secret Morphs	LOGGLOGG
		Super Ending	BUZZOFF
All Morphs	EUREKA	View FMV Sequences	HOTTICKET

Dragon Ball Z

Unlockable	Objective
Android #16	Complete the "Aim for Perfect Form" episode.
Cell, Android #17, and Teen Gohan	Play through "The Androids Saga" at any level.
Dodoria	Defeat Recoome with Vegeta.
Freiza, Ginyu, and Recoome	Play through "The Namek Saga" at any level.
Mr. Satan (Hercule)	Win a World Match Tournament at the Adept level.
Radditz, Vegeta, and Nappa	Play through "The Saiyan Saga" at any level
Saiyaman (Gohan's Alter Ego)	Win a World Match Tournament at the Advanced level.
Super Saiyan Ability (Goku Only)	Play through "The Namek Saga" at any level.
Super Saiyan Ability (Vegeta Only)	Play through "The Androids Saga" at any level.
Super Vegeta	Complete the "Vegeta's Confidence" episode.
Trunks	Complete the "Perfect Form Cell Complete" episode.
Yamcha	Complete the "Aim for Perfect Form" episode.
Zarbon	Complete the "Vegeta's Attack" episode.
Alternate Appearance	Press ■ or ● at the Character Selection screen. Your character may have different clothes or colors. See Tip.
View Alternate Costumes	Press R1 and R2 at the Capsule Change screen to view the character's alternate costumes. Press L1 and L2 to zoom in and out. Use the left analog stick to rotate the characters.

TIP

Alternate Appearance Tip!
Try this with Trunks and make him go Super Saiyan!

Dragon Ball Z: Budokai

Unlockable	Objective
1-Star Dragonball	Super-Rare—if the desired Dragonball isn't the Recommended Capsule, exit and re-enter Mr. Popo's shop until it's displayed.
2-Star Dragonball	Super-Rare—same as above.
3-Star Dragonball	Super-Rare—same as above.
4-Star Dragonball	You get this free when starting a new game. Note: if you have a second memory card, you can get this by starting a game and trading.
5-Star Dragonball	Super-Rare—same as Dragonballs 1-3.

Dragon Ball Z: Budokai (continued)

Unlockable	Objective
6-Star Dragonball	Super-Rare—same as Dragonballs 1-3.
7-Star Dragonball	Super-Rare—same as Dragonballs 1-3.
Android 16	Defeat Android 16 in story mode as Cell.
Android 17	Defeat Android 17 in story mode as Picollo.
Android 18	Defeat Android 18 in story mode as Vegeta.
Android 19	Defeat Android 19 in story mode as Vegeta.
Captain Ginyu	Defeat Ginyu in Story Mode after he takes over Goku's body.
Cell	Defeat Cell in story mode.
Dodoria	Defeat Frieza with Vegeta in Story Mode.
Frieza	Defeat Frieza in story mode.
Hercule	Beat the adept mode of the World Tournament.
Nappa	Defeat Nappa in story mode.
Raditz	Defeat Raditz in story mode.
Recoome	Defeat Recoome in story mode.
Teen Gohan	Defeat Cell as Gohan in story mode.
The Great Saiyaman	Beat the advanced mode of the World Tournament.
DrTrunks	Beat Perfect Form Cell Complete.
DragVegeta	Defeat Vegeta in story mode.
Yamcha	Beat A Cold-Blooded Assasin.
Zarbon	Defeat Zarbon in story mode as Vegeta.

Dragon Ball Z: Budokai 2

Unlockable	Objective
Adept World Tournament	Unlock 16 Characters, then buy it from Bulma.
Advanced World Tournament	Unlock all 29 Characters, then buy it from Bulma.
Android 16	Beat Android 16 with Goku.
Android 17	Beat Android 17 with Piccolo.
Android 18	Beat Android 18 with Krillen.
Android 20	Beat Android 20 with Goku.
Babidi's Ship	Collect All 7 Dragon Balls and Wish for it from Shenron.
Breakthroughs	Wish for them on the Dragon Balls.
Bulma's costumes 2-6	Wish for them on the Dragon Balls.
Cell	Beat Cell with Goku.
City Street Stage	Beat Super Buu with Gohan in Stage 8 without being defeated.
Dabura	Get 100 kili on Babidi's Spaceship.
Frieza	Beat Frieza with Goku.
Future Trunks	Beat Vegeta on Namek with Kid Trunks.
Ginyu	Beat Ginyu on Namek with Vegeta.
Gokule (Capsule)	Get both Breakthroughs of Goku and Hercule.
Gotenks (Capsule)	Enter Stage 7.
Hercule	Beat Majin Buu as Gt.Saiyaman in Stage 6.
Hercule	Beat Fat Buu with Saiyaman.
Kabitoshin (Potara)	Collect seven Dragon Balls and wish for the capsule from the Dragon.
Kid Buu	Get 3600 kili in Babidi's Spaceship.
Kid Buu	Get 4600 kili.
Majin Buu	Get 1200 kili in Babidi's Spaceship.
Majin Buu	Get 2500 kili.
Majin Vegeta	In Dragon World, Stage 5, defeat any Majin character to get the Capsule that allows you to get Majin Vegeta. Note: Dabura does not count.
Nappa	Beat Nappa with Vegeta (can only be done when you unlock Vegeta and start Dragon mode again).
Raditz	Beat Raditz with Goku.

Dragon Ball Z: Budokai 2 (continued)

Unlockable	Objective
Recoome	Beat Recoome with Goku.
Saiyaman	Beat Cell with Gohan (adult) only.
Silver Membership Card	Have a Budokai 1 save on your memory card when you start a New Game.
SSJ2 Gohan (adult)	Defeat Majin Vegeta before Majin Buu kills Babidi in Stage 6 (the area with the large ring).
Super Buu	Get 2400 kili in Babidi's Spaceship.
Super Buu	Get 3170 kili.
Super Buu's Absorbtion Technique	Get 10,000 kili.
Super Saiyan 2 (Goku)	Beat Cell in Stage 4 with Goku.
Super Saiyan 2 (Vegeta)	Beat Super Buu (Gohan) as Vegeta Stage in 8.
Super Saiyan 3 (Goku)	Beat Majin (Fat) Buu in Stage 6 with Goku.
Super Saiyan (Goku)	Let Krillen die in Stage 3 .
Supreme Kai	Beat Supreme Kai with Goku.
Teen Gohan	Beat Cell for the last time on Supreme Kai's planet with Gohan (adult).
Tiencha(Capsule)	Get both breakthoughs of Tien and Yamcha.
Tourdement Adept	Unlock 16 characters and buy it.
Tourdement Advance	Unlock all 29 characters and buy it.
Vegeta	Beat Vegeta with Goku on Namek.
Vegeto (Capsule/Goku)	Get Goku to Surpreme Ki then to Vegeta in Stage 8
Vegeto (Capsule/Vegeta)	Wish for it on the Dragon Balls.
Vegetto (Potara with Vegeta)	Collect seven Dragon Balls and wish for the capsule from the Dragon.
Videl	Beat Super Buu (Gohan) as Hercule in Stage 8.
Yamcha	Beat Nappa with Tien.

Dragon Ball Z: Budokai Tenkaichi

Unlockables

Unlockable	How to Unlock
Attack+6	Fuse Attack+3 + Attack+3
Defence+6	Fuse Defence+3 + Defence+3
Favourite Technique+6	Fuse favourite technique+3 + favourite technique+3
Finishing Move+6	Fuse finishing move+3 + finishing move+3
Health+6	Fuse Health+3 + Health+3
Ki+6	Fuse Ki+3 + Ki+3
Speed+6	Fuse Speed+3 + Speed+3
Super Finishing Move+6	Fuse super finishing move+3 + Super finishing move+3
Android 16	Beat Cell with him in Z Battle Gate
Android 17	Beat him with Piccolo in Z Battle Gate
Android 18	Beat her with SSJ Vegeta in Z Battle Gate
Android 19	Beat him with SSJ Vegeta in Z Battle Gate
Android 20 (Dr. Gero)	Beat him with Piccolo in Z Battle Gate
Base Long Haired Trunks	Successfully complete Z Battle Gate to unlock Base Long Haired Future Trunks.
Burter	Beat him with Goku in Z Battle Gate

Dragon Ball Z: Budokai Tenkaichi (continued)

Unlockable	How to Unlock
Captain Ginyu	Defeat Captain Ginyu with Goku to unlock him
Cell Jr.	Beat him with Super Saiyan Teen Gohan
Dabura	Beat him with Gohan in Z Battle Gate
Dodoria	Beat him with Vegeta in Z Battle Gate
Frieza 2nd Form	Beat him with Kid Gohan in Z Battle Gate
Frieza 3rd	Beat him with Vegeta in Z Battle Gate
Frieza Final Form	Beat him with Vegeta in Z Battle Gate
General Tao	Collect the 7 Dragon Balls in Z Battle Gate
Ginyu	Beat him with Goku in Z Battle Gate
Goten	Beat Adult Gohan with him in Z Battle Gate
Gotenks	Beat Super Buu with SSJ Gotenks in Z Battle Gate
Guldo	Beat him with Chaozu in Z Battle Gate
Hercule	Beat Perfect Cell with him in Z Battle Gate
Jeice	Beat him with Vegeta in Z Battle Gate
Kid Buu	Beat him with Goku in Z Battle Gate
Kid Goku	Collect the 7 Dragon Balls in Z Battle Gate
Kid Trunks	Beat Vegeta with him in Z Battle Gate
Majin Buu	Beat Super Buu Gohan with Vegitoin Z Battle Gate
Master Roshi	Collect the 7 Dragon Balls in Z Battle Gate
Monster Zarbon	Defeat Monster Zarbon with Vegeta
Nappa	Beat him with Goku in Z Battle Gate
Oozaru	Collect the 7 Dragon Balls in Z Battle Gate
Perfect Cell	Beat him with SSJ2 Gohan in Z Battle Gate
Raditz	Beat him with Piccolo in Z Battle Gate
Recoome	Beat him with Goku in Z Battle Gate
Saibaman	Beat Saibaman with Krillin
Saibamen	Successfully complete Raditz Saga 100%
Semi Perfect Cell	Defeat Semi Perfect Cell with SSJ2 Gohan
SSJ Adult Gohan	Defeat Buu to unlock
SSJ Long Haired Future Trunks	Successfully complete Z Battle Gate
SSJ Teen Gohan	Successfully complete Z Battle Gate
SSJ2 Adult Gohan	Defeat Buu
SSJ2 Teen Gohan	Successfully complete Z Battle Gate
SSJ2 Vegeta	Stay alive for 2 minutes against Kid Buu in Z Battle Gate
SSJ4 Vegeta	Defeat Broly with USSJ Vegeta
Super Buu	Defeat Super Buu in the fight absorbed Gohan
Super Saiyan 2 Goku	Beat Perfect Cell in Z Battle Gate
Super Saiyan 3 Goku	Beat Majin Buu with him in Z Battle Gate
Super Saiyan 4 Goku	Beat Super Android 17 with him in Z Battle Gate
Super Saiyan 4 Vegeta	Beat Super Saiyan 2 Vegeta with Broly
Super Saiyan Future Trunks	Beat Mecha Frieza with him in Z Battle Gate
Super Saiyan Goku	Beat Frieza with him in Z Battle Gate
Super Saiyan Goten	Beat him with Kid Trunks in Z Battle Gate
Super Saiyan Gotenks	Beat Super Buu with SSJ3 Gotenks in Z Battle Gate

DS
GBA
PSP
PS2
PS3
Wii
Xbox
Xbox 360
Index

Dragon Ball Z: Budokai Tenkaichi (continued)

Unlockable	How to Unlock
Super Saiyan Kid Trunks	Beat Hercule with Kid Trunks in Z Battle Gate
Super Saiyan Vegeta	Beat Android 18 with him in Z Battle Gate
Ultra Super Saiyan Vegeta (Super Vegeta)	USSJ Vegeta vs Kid Buu (Let timer run out)
USSJ Vegeta	Beat Perfect Cell with USSJ Vegeta in Z Battle Gate
Vegito	Majin Buu vs Kid Buu (Let timer run out)
Videl	Hercule vs Kid Buu (Let timer run out)
Baby Vegeta	Tuffles + Artificial Bruits Waves
Bardock	Kakarot + Hatred of Saiyans
Bojack (Post Transformation)	Galactic Warriors + Seal Release
Broly	Super Saiyan + Broly
Cooler Final Form	Frieza's Older Brother + Super Transformation
Frieza Final Form (Full Power)	Frieza Final Form + Super Transformation
Great Saiyaman	Gohan + Transforming Hero set
Janemba	Psyche Orge + People's Maliciousness
Majin Buu (Gotenks Absorbed)	Super Saiyan 3 Gotenks + Absorption
Majin Buu (Pure Evil)	Majin Buu (Good) + Wicked Person's Bullet
Majin Buu (Ultimate Gohan Absorbed)	Ultimate Gohan + Absorption
Majin Vegeta	Super Saiyan 2 Vegeta + Babidi
Mecha Frieza	Frieza Final Form (Full Power) + Reconstruction Surgery
Perfect Cell (Perfect Form)	Super Saiyan Goku + Cell Perfect Form
Super 17	Android 17 + Android 17
Super Saiyan 3 Gotenks	Super Saiyan + Super Saiyan Gotenks
Super Saiyan 4 Gogeta	SS4 Goku's fusion + SS4 Vegeta's fusion
Super Saiyan Gogeta	Goku's Fusion + Vegeta's Fusion
Super Saiyan Super Trunks	Super Saiyan + Super Saiyan Trunks
Super Vegito	Super Saiyan + Vegito
Ultimate Gohan	Super Saiyan 2 Gohan + Elder Supreme Kai
Vegeta (Scouter)	Vegeta + Scouter

Dragon Ball Z: Budokai Tenkaichi 2

Unlockables

Unlockable	How to Unlock
100% Full Power Frieza	Super Transformation + Final Form Frieza
Android 13	Computer + Hatred
Android 13 Fusion	Android 13 + Parts of #14/#15
Baby Vegeta	Baby + Vegeta (second form)
Bardock	Defeat Super Namek Lord Slug with Z-fighters (Lord Slug saga)
Bojack	Unsealed + Galactic Warrior
Broly	Son of Paragus + Hatred of Goku
Broly Legendary Super Saiyan	Super Saiyan Broly + Breakthrough Limit
Broly Super Saiyan	Broly + Super Saiyan
Burter	Defeat Burter and Jeice with Goku (Frieza Saga)
Cell 1st Form	Defeat Cell with 17 and Piccolo (Android Saga)

Dragon Ball Z: Budokai Tenkaichi 2 (continued)

Unlockable	How to Unlock
Cell 2nd Form	Defeat Cell 2nd Form with Trunks and Super Saiyan Vegeta (Android Saga)
Cell Jr	Defeat 5x Cell Jr with Super Saiyan Teen 2 Gohan (Android Saga)
Cell Perfect	Self Destruction + Cell Perfect Form
Cell Perfect Form	Defeat Cell Perfect Form with Super Saiyan Teen 2 Gohan (Android Saga)
Cooler	Frieza's Brother + Hatred of Goku
Cui	Vegeta's rival + Frieza's soldier
Demon King Dabura	Defeat Demon King Dabura with Z-Fighters (Buu Saga)
Dodoria	Beat him in Dragon Adventure
Dr. Gero	Defeat Dr. Gero with Krillin (Android Saga)
Evil Buu	Evil Human Cannonball + Majin Buu
Final Form Cooler	Super Transformation + Cooler
Frieza	Beat him in story mode
Frieza 2nd Form	Defeat Frieza 2nd Form with Vegeta, Krillin, and Kid Gohan (Frieza Saga)
Frieza 3rd Form	Defeat Frieza 3rd Form with Piccolo, Krillin, and Kid Gohan (Frieza Saga)
Frieza Final Form	Defeat Frieza Final Form with Goku (Frieza Saga)
Full Power Bojak	Ultimate Transformation + Bojack
Garlick Jr.	Demonic Star + Dead Zone
General Tao	Bros. of Crane Hermit + Memorial Campaign
Giant Lord Slug	Slug + Giant Form
Ginyu	Defeat Goku (Ginyu) and Jeice with Vegeta, Krillin, and Kid Gohan (Frieza Saga)
Gohan Super Buu	Gohan Absorbed + Evil Buu
Gotenks	Defeat Buu (Pure Evil) with Majin Buu and Hercule (Buu Saga)
Gotenks Super Buu	Gotenks Absorbed + Evil Buu
Grandpa Gohan	Master Roshi's pupil + Fox mask
Great Ape	Defeat Vegeta with Goku (Destined Rivals Saga)(last Match)
Great Ape Baby	Super Baby 2 + Artificial Blutz Wave
Great Ape Bardock	Power Ball + Bardock
Great Ape Nappa	Power Ball + Nappa
Great Ape Raditz	Power Ball + Raditz
Great Ape Turles	Power Ball + Turles
Great Ape Vegeta	Power Ball + Vegeta (Scouter)
Great Saiyaman	Defeat Zangya and Bojack with Teen Gohan (Bojack Unbound Saga)
Great Saiyaman 2 (Saiyawoman)	Defeat Broly with Goten and Adult Gohan (Broly:2nd Coming)
Guldo	Defeat Guldo with Vegeta, Gohan, and Krillin(Frieza Saga)
Hercule	Defeat Perfect Cell with Super Trunks (Android Saga)
Hirudegarn	Hildegarn's top half + Hildegarn's lower half
Janemba	Saike demon + People's bad energy
Jeice	Defeat Goku (Ginyu) and Jeice with Vegeta, Krillin, and Kid Gohan (Frieza Saga)

DS

GBA

PSP

PS2

PS3

Wii

Xbox

Xbox 360

Index

DS

GBA

PSP

PS2

PS3

Wii

Xbox

Xbox 360

Index

Dragon Ball Z: Budokai Tenkaichi 2 (continued)

Unlockable	How to Unlock
Kibitoshin	Kibito + Supreme Kai
Kid Buu	Defeat Kid Buu with Goku and Vegeta(Buu Saga)
Kid Goku	Beat Grandpa Gohan in the free event in the Destined Rivals Saga when you first take control of Goku
Lord Slug	Namekian + Mutation
Majin Buu (Pure Evil)	Human gunman's gun + Majin Buu
Majin Vegeta	Defeat Majin Buu with Supreme Kai and Adult Gohan (Buu Saga)
Majuub	Defeat Super Baby 2 with Pan and Ubb (Baby, The Avenger)
Master Roshi	Defeat Raditz with Goku
Master Roshi Full Power	Master Roshi + Seriousness
Mecha Frieza	Reconstructive Surgery + 100% Full Power Frieza
Metal Cooler	Big Gete Star + Cooler
Monster Zarbon	Broken Seal + Zarbon
Nappa	Beat him in Story
Omega Shenron	Syn Shenron + Ultimate Dragon Ball
Pan	Defeat Hirudengarn with Tapion and Kid Trunks (2nd Time) (Wrath of the Dragon)
Perfect Cell	Cell Saga
Pikkon	Beat him in Dragon Adventure
Recoome	Defeat Recoome with Goku and Vegeta (Frieza Saga)
Salza	Coolers soldier + Armored Cavalry
Sauzer	Armored Troopers + Cooler's Henchmen
SSJ 2 Goku	Defeat Majin Vegeta
SSJ 3 Goku	Defeat Fat Buu
SSJ Adult Gohan	History of trunks
SSJ Goku	Defeat Freeza as SSJ Goku
SSJ trunks (with sword)	History of trunks
Super Android #17	HFIL fighter #17 + Android 17
Super Baby 1	Baby Vegeta + Lower class Saiyan
Super Baby 2	Super Baby 1 + Power from lower class
Super Buu	Defeat Super Buu with Ultimate Gohan (Buu Saga)
Super Buu Gohan Absorbed	Absorb Gohan + Super Buu
Super Buu Gotenks Absorbed	Absorb Gotenks + Super Buu
Super Garlick Jr.	Giant Form + Garlick Jr.
Super Gogeta	Defeat Janemba (Final Form) with Pikkon (Fusion Reborn)
Super Gotenks	Defeat Buu (Pure Evil) with Majin Buu and Hercule (Buu Saga)
Super Gotenks 3	Defeat Super Buu with Goten, Kid Trunks, and Piccolo (Buu Saga)
Super Janemba	Janemba + Ultimate Transformation
Super Perfect Cell	Suicide Bomb + Perfect Cell
Super Saiyan 2 Adult Gohan	Defeat Android 18 with Hercule (Buu Saga)
Super Saiyan 2 Goku	Defeat Majin Buu with Supreme Kai and Adult Gohan (Buu Saga)
Super Saiyan 2 Vegeta	Defeat Super Buu (Gotenks Absorbed) with Goku (Buu Saga)

Dragon Ball Z: Budokai Tenkaichi 2 (continued)

Unlockable	How to Unlock
Super Saiyan 3 Goku	Defeat Majin Buu with Majin Vegeta (Buu Saga)
Super Saiyan 4 Gogeta	Defeat Omega Shenron with Super Saiyan 4 Goku and Super Saiyan 4 Vegeta (Evil Dragon Saga)
Super Saiyan 4 Goku	Defeat Super Baby 2 with Majubb (Baby, The Avenger)
Super Saiyan 4 Vegeta	Defeat Omega Shenron with Super Saiyan 4 Goku (Evil Dragon Saga)
Super Saiyan Adult Gohan	Defeat Adult Gohan with Future Trunks (History of Trunks Saga)
Super Saiyan Goku	Defeat Frieza Final Form with Piccolo, Krillin, and Kid Gohan (Frieza Saga)
Super Saiyan Goten	Defeat General Tao with Videl and Great Saiyaman (Buu Saga)
Super Saiyan Kid Trunks	Defeat General Tao with Videl and Great Saiyaman (Buu Saga)
Super Saiyan Teen 2 Gohan	Survive the Matach against 5x Cell Jr with Z-fighters (Android Saga)
Super Saiyan Teen Gohan	Defeat Perfect Cell with Super Trunks (Android Saga)
Super Saiyan Trunks	Defeat Cell 2nd Form with Tien (Android Saga)
Super Saiyan Trunks (Sword)	Defeat Androids 17 and 18 with Super Saiyan Adult Gohan (History of Trunks Saga)
Super Saiyan Vegeta	Defeat Metal Cooler with Super Saiyan Goku (Return of Cooler Saga)
Super Saiyan Vegeta (2nd form)	Defeat Vegeta with Super Saiyan Teen Trunks (Buu Saga)
Super Trunks	Defeat Perfect Cell with Super Vegeta (Android Saga)
Super Vegeta	Defeat Cell 2nd Form with Tien (Android Saga)
Super Vegetto	Defeat Super Buu (Gohan Absorbed) with Goku and Vegeta (Buu Saga)
Super Yi-Shin-Long	Syn Shenron + Ultimate Dragon Ball
Supreme Kai	Defeat Android 18 with Hercule (Buu Saga)
Syn Shenron	Evil Dragon + Negative Energy
Tapion	Beat him in Dragon Adventure
Turles	Lower-Class Saiyan Soldier + Fruit of the Gods
Ultimate Gohan	Defeat Buu with Super Gotenks 3 or Piccolo (Buu Saga)
Uub	Defeat Hirudengarn with Super Saiyan 3 Goku (Wrath of the Dragon)
Vegeta (Android Saga)	Metal-Cooler Movie/Android Saga
Vegeta (Post Namek)	Defeat Metal Cooler with Super Saiyan Goku (Return of Cooler Saga)
Vegeta (2nd Form)	Defeat Vegeta with Super Saiyan Teen Trunks (Buu Saga)
Vegito	Defeat Super Buu (Gohan Absorbed) with Goku and Vegeta (Buu Saga)
Videl	Defeat Zangya and Bojack with Piccolo and Teen Gohan (Bojack Unbound Saga)
Yajirobe	Beat Great Ape Gohan with Piccolo (Saiyan Saga)
Zangya	The Flowers of Evil + Galactic Warrior
Zarbon (normal form)	Beat him in Dragon Adventure
Zarbon Post Transformation	Unsealed + Zarbon
Beautiful Treachery	Defeat Dodoria with Gohan and Krillin in mission 01 of the Frieza Saga "A Pursuer Who Calls Death"
Destined Rivals	Defeat Gohan with Goten in mission 01 of the Majin Buu Saga "Training With Goten"

DS
GBA
PSP
PS2
PS3
Wii
Xbox
Xbox 360
Index

Dragon Ball Z: Budokai Tenkaichi 2 (continued)

Unlockable	How to Unlock
Fateful Brothers	Defeat Raditz with Piccolo in mission 00 of the Saiyan Saga "Mysterious Alien Warrior"

Dragon Ball Z: Budokai Tenkaichi 3

Unlockable Moves

Unlockable	How to Unlock
I Give You a Romantic	Dragon History Cleared
Super Survivor (Instrumental, Full)	Dragon World Tour, Cell Game, Difficulty 2 Victory
Super Survivor (Instrumental, Short)	Dragon World Tour, World Tournament, Difficulty 2 Victory
Super Survivor (Vocal, Full)	Dragon World Tour, Otherworld Tournament, Difficulty 3 Victory
Super Survivor (Vocal, Short)	Dragon World Tour, Super World Tournament, Difficulty 3 Victory

Unlocking Characters

Unlockable	How to Unlock
Akkuman	Dragon History IF saga "Unexpected Messiah" cleared
Android 08 (Hatchan in Japanese)	Dragon History IF saga "Kindhearted Android" cleared
Arale	Dragon History IF saga "Dream Match" cleared
Babidi	Dragon History Buu saga "Good bye Proud Warrior" cleared
Chi-Chi	Red Shenron's Wish
Cyborg Tao-Pai-Pai	Otherworld Tournament level 2 victory
Dr. Wheelo	Dragon History special saga "Dr. Wheelo" cleared
Fasha (Seripa in Japanese)	Yamcha Game level 3 victory
General Blue	Dragon History Dragon Ball saga "Searching in Penguin Village" cleared
Gohan (Future)	Shenron's Wish
Goku(GT)	Dragon History GT saga "Undead Monster!?" cleared
King Cold	Cell Game level 3 victory
King Piccolo	Dragon History Dragon Ball saga "Revenge of Goku" cleared
King Vegeta	Dagon History IF saga "Galaxy Battle" cleared
Nail	Dragon History Frieza saga "Super Saiyan!?" cleared
Nam	Dragon History Dragon Ball saga "Dreadful Tenku Peke Ji Ken" cleared
Nova Shenron	Dragon History GT saga "Warrior of Sun" cleared
Pilaf Machine	Super World Tournament level 2 victory
Spopovich	World Tournament level 3 victory
Tambourine	Dragon History Dragon Ball saga "Revenge of Goku" cleared

Unlocking Stages

Unlockable	How to Unlock
Desert (Day)	Shenron's Wish
Desert (Evening)	Yamcha game level 2 victory
Desert (Night)	Cell game level 2 victory
Janemba Hell	Dragon History special saga "Janemba" cleared

Dragon Ball Z: Budokai Tenkaichi 3 (continued)

Unlockable	How to Unlock
King Castle	Red Shenron's Wish
Mt. Paozu	Shenron's Wish
Muscle Tower	Dragon History Dragun Ball saga "Decisive Battle in Holy Place" cleared
Penguin Village	Red Shenron's Wish

Dragon Ball Z: Sagas

Pause the game and go into the Controller screen, then enter these codes.

Unlockable	Code
All Upgrades	⇧, ⇦, ⇩, ⇨, SELECT, START, ■, ✕, ●, ▲
Invincibility	⇩, ✕, SELECT, START, ⇨, ■, ⇦, ●, ⇧, ▲

Drakengard

Unlockable	Objective
Fly on a Jet	Complete the Free Mission at Shinjuku and this will unlock the Jet. On any sky mission where you chose which Dragon to take, highlight Chaos Dragon. Select it and start your mission while riding a Jet.

Driv3r

In the Main menu, enter the following cheats. Go to the Options menu and select Cheats to enable or disable them.

Unlockable	Code
All Missions	L1, R1, L1, L2, ■, ■, ●
All Vehicles	L1, L1, ■, ●, L1, R1, ●
All Weapons	R1, L2, ■, ●, R1, R2, L2
Immunity	●, ●, L1, L2, R1, R2, ■
Invincibility (Take a Ride)	■, ■, L1, R1, L2, R2, R2
Unlimited Ammo	R1, R2, R1, R2, ■, ●, ■

Driver Parallel Lines

Enter these passwords in the Cheat menu.

Unlockable	Password
All Vehicles	CARSHOW
All Weapons in Your Time Zone	GUNRANGE
Indestructible Cars	ROLLBAR
Infinite Ammunition	GUNBELT
Infinite Nitro	ZOOMZOOM
Invincibility	IRONMAN
Weaker Cops	KEYSTONE
Zero Cost	TOOLEDUP

Duel Masters

Enter these codes while in a duel.

Unlockable	Code
Add One Shield to Player One	Hold R1 and press ✕, ■, ▲
Add One Shield to Player Two	Hold R1 and press ✕, ●, ▲
Break One of Player One's Shields	Hold R1 and press ▲, ■, ✕
Break One of Player Two's Shields	Hold R1 and press ▲, ●, ✕
Player One Wins Instantly	Hold R1 and press L1, R1, L1
Player Two Wins Instantly	Hold R1 and press R1, L1, R1

DS
GBA
PSP
PS2
PS3
Wii
Xbox
Xbox 360
Index

Dynasty Warriors

Unlockable	Objective
Different Intro Sequence	Beat Mosou mode with any character.
Editing Mode	Beat Mosou mode with all the characters except for Diao Chan, Dong Zhuo, Yuan Shao, Lu Bu, and Zhang Jiao.
Free Health	Find a save point even if you don't have a memory card. The game asks if you want to save. It doesn't matter if you save or not. When you return to your game all of your health will be restored.
Cao Cao	Beat Mosou mode with Dian Wei, Xiahou Dun, Xiahou Yuan, Xu Zhu, Zhang Liao, and Sima Yi.
Dong Zhuo, Diao Chan, Yuan Chao, and Zhang Jiao in Free Mode	Beat Mosou mode with one member of each kingdom.
Liu Bei	Beat Mosou mode with Zhao Yun, Huang Zhong, Guan Yu, Zhang Fei, Ma Chao, Jiang Wei, and Zhuge Liang.
Lu Bu in Free Mode	Complete Stage 2, Hulao Gate, in Musou mode with at least 1,000 KOs.
Lu Meng, Taishi Ci, and Gan Ning	Beat Mosou mode with Lu Xun, Zhou Yu, or Sun Shang Xiang.
Ma Chao, Huang Zhong, and Jiang Wei	Beat Mosou mode with Zhao Yun, Zhang Fei, or Guan Yu.
Side Selection and BGM Option	Beat Mosou mode with one member of each kingdom.
Sima Yi	Beat Mosou mode with Dian Wei, Xiahou Dun, and Xu Zhu.
Sun Quan and Sun Jian	Beat Mosou mode with Lu Xun, Sun Shang Xiang, Zhou Yu, Lu Meng, Taishi Ci, and Gan Ning.
Zhang Liao and Xiahou Yuan	Beat Mosou mode with Dian Wei, Xiahou Dun, or Xu Zhu.

Dynasty Warriors 3

After inputting the following codes, listen for the cheer that confirms correct code entry.

Unlockable	Code
All FMV Sequences	Highlight the Free Mode icon at the main menu. Press ▲, L1, ▲, R1, ▲, ■, L2, ■, R2, ■.
All Generals	Highlight the Free Mode icon at the main menu. Press R2, R2, R2, L1, ▲, L2, L2, L2, R1, ■.
All Items	Go to the "Options" in the main menu and highlight "Open Screen." Press R1, ■, R1, ▲, R1, L1, ■, L1, ▲, L1.
All Shu Generals	Highlight the Free Mode icon at the main menu. Press L1, ■, ▲, R2, L1, L2, L2, R1, ■, L1.
All Wei Generals	Highlight the Free Mode icon at the main menu. Press ▲, ▲, L1, ■, R1, R2, L1, L2, L2, L2.
All Wu Generals	Highlight the Free Mode icon at the main menu. Press L2, L1, ■, ▲, L1, L2, R1, R2, L1, L2.
Bonus FMV Sequence	Highlight the "Replay" option at the Opening Edit screen, hold R1+L1+R2+L2, then press ✕. Alternately, hold R1+L1+R2+L2 and press START. You see all the people from the gray army dancing.
Control Loading Screen	Press ● to increase the wind as the level name flutters on the loading screen before a battle. Press ✕ to decrease the wind speed.

Dynasty Warriors 3 (continued)

Unlockable	Code
Free Mode Side Selection	Highlight the Free Mode icon at the main menu. Press R1, R2, L2, L1, ■, L1, L2, R2, R1, ▲.
In-game Reset	Press SELECT + START during gameplay.
Opening Edit Option	Highlight the Free Mode icon at the main menu. Press R1, ■, R1, ▲, R1, L1, ■, L1.

TIP

Start the game with a memory card with a saved game from Dynasty Warriors 2 and some characters unlocked in Dynasty Warriors 2 are available in your new game!

Eagle Eye Golf

Unlockables

Unlockable	How to Unlock
ACCESSORIES	
Air Glove	Win the Amateur Tournament (Amateur event)
Blue Necklace	Win the Scorpio Cup (Pro-Ams event)
Camel Shoes	Win the Challenge Cup (Pro-Ams event)
Crystal Badge	Win 30 consecutive Survival matches
Draw Chain	Win Diamond League (World Pros event)
Garnet Ring	Win Victoria Cup (Tour Pro event)
Green Necklace	Win Eden Tradition (World Pros event)
Heated Glove	Win Southern Cross (Senior Pros event)
Heavy Shoes	Complete Mission Level 1
Light Shoes	Win Vesper Cup (Tour Pro event)
Middle Chain	Complete Mission Level 5
Natala	Win 100 consecutive Survival matches
Smart Glove	Win Master's Cup (World Pros event)
Smart Shoes	Win Gold Cup (Senior Pros event)
Upper Chain	Win Bronze Cup (Senior Pros event)
BALLS	
Air Ball	Win Country Cup (Tour Pro event)
Air Spin Ball	Win Eagle Cup (Junior Pro event)
Bone Ball	Win Avalon's Survival (Special event)
Cyber Ball	Win 50 consecutive Survival matches
Edge Ball	Win British Cup (Senior Pro event)
Grass Ball	Win Dream Cup (Junior Pro event)
Hermit Ball	Win 80 consecutive Survival matches
Light Ball	Win the Open Nights (Pro-Ams event)
Smart Ball	Win Platinum League (World Pro event)
Spin Ball	Win the Hiyodori Cup (Amateur event)
Star Ball	Win Owl Cup (Junior Pro event)
Super Ball	Win 20 consecutive Survival matches
Wide Ball	Win Castle League (Tour Pro event)
CHARACTERS	
Baron	Beat him in Avalon's Survival (Special event)

Sidebar tabs: DS, GBA, PSP, PS2, PS3, Wii, Xbox, Xbox 360, Index

DS
GBA
PSP
PS2
PS3
Wii
Xbox
Xbox 360
Index

Eagle Eye Golf (continued)

Unlockable	How to Unlock
Burman	Beat him in Eden Tradition (World Pros event)
Diego	Beat him in Avalon's Survival (Special event)
Erica	Beat her in the World Tournament (Senior Pros event)
Freddie	Beat him in Avalon's Survival (Special event)
Joshy	Win 70 consecutive Survival matches
Karen	Beat her in the Junior Tour (Junior Pros event)
Katrea	Beat her in Avalon's Survival (Special event)
Ricardo	Beat him in Avalon's Survival (Special event)
Sharon	Beat her in the Victoria Cup (Tour Pro event)
Tom	Beat him in the Sakura Cup (Amateur event)
Vera	Beat her in Avalon's Survival (Special event)
CLUBS	
Air Club	Complete Mission Level 3
Antique Club	Win Winter Open (World Pro event)
Carbon Club	Win the Sakura Cup (Amateur event)
Control Club	Win Junior Tour (Junior Pro event)
Custom Club	Win Amapro Tournament (Pro-Am event)
Edge Club	Win 10 consecutive Survival matches
Flying Club	Win Azalea Tournament (Senior Pro event)
Force Club	Win The Emperors (Special event)
Grass Club	Win Dead Leaf Tour (World Pro event)
Master Club	Win Crystal Open (Junior Pro event)
Metal Bat	Win 60 consecutive Survival matches
Metal Club	Win the Challenge Cup (Pro-Ams event)
Persimmon Club	Complete Mission Level 2
Power Club	Win Classic Open (Junior Pro event)
Princess Club	Win National League (World Pro event)
Rock Club	Win 40 consecutive Survival matches
Sand Club	Win Japan Cup (Senior Pro event)
Spin Club	Win World Tournament (Senior Pro event)
Steel Club	Win the Desert Open (Amateur event)
Avalon's Hill	Complete all Senior Pro tournaments
Crystal Park	Complete all Junior Pro tournaments
Eden's Garden	Complete all Tour Pro tournaments
Premium Nights	Complete all amateur tournaments

EndGame

Enter these codes at the Main menu. The numbers represent how many times you shoot the screen. One shot is the letter "A," two shots are "B," and so forth. In between each letter you reload.

For example: 3-15-4-5 ("code") means you shoot three times, reload, shoot 15 times, reload, shoot four times, reload, and then shoot five times.

Unlockable	Code
All Mighty Joe Jupiter Mode	13-9-7-8-20-9-5-18 ("MIGHTIER")
All Specials	13-5-2-9-7-3-8-5-1-20 ("MEBIGCHEAT")

EndGame (continued)

Unlockable	Code
Arcade Mode	2-12-1-13 ("BLAM")
Country Challenges	1-2-18-15-1-4 ("ABROAD")
Unlock the Jukebox	12-5-20-19-2-15-15-7-9 ("LETSBOOGIE")

Enter the Matrix

Enable Cheats: Enter the hacking system and enter cheat.exe from the A prompt. Then you can enter the codes below.

Warning! The game can crash with cheats enabled.

Unlockable	Code
All weapons	0034AFFF
Blind Enemies	FFFFFFF1
Bonus level	13D2C77F
Deaf Enemies	4516DF45
Faster Logos	7867F443
Faster Logos	7867F443
Infinite ammo	1DDF2556
Infinite focus	69E5D9E4
Infinite Health	7F4DF451
Invisibility	FFFFFFF1
Low gravity	BB013FFF
Multiplayer	D5C55D1E
Recover Focus Fast	FFF0020A
Taxi Driving	312MF451
Turbo mode	FF00001A

ESPN NFL 2K5

Change VIP Profile name to the following and access the specified unlockable.

Unlockable	VIP Pofile Name
1,000,000 Crib Credits	"PhatBank"
All Crib items	"CribMax"
All Milestones complete (full trophy room)	"MadSkilz"

ESPN NHL 2K5

Unlockable	Code
Everything in the Skybox	Create a profile with the name LuvLeafs.

ESPN NHL Hockey

Enter this code at the Game Modes screen.

Unlockable	Code
Unlock everything	R1, R1, L1, ←, ←, ↓, ●, R1, ●, L1, ↑, →, ●, ↓, ←, ←, ●, R1, ↓, ↑

Evil Dead: Fistful of Boomstick

Unlockable	Objective
Arcade Levels	The levels you beat in story mode will be available in Arcade mode.
Production Art	Once you've beaten a level, you can see the production artwork for the game from the Extras menu.

DS

GBA

PSP

PS2

PS3

Wii

Xbox

Xbox 360

Index

DS

GBA

PSP

PS2

PS3

Wii

Xbox

Xbox 360

Index

Evolution Skateboarding

After entering the following codes, listen for the sound to confirm correct entry.

Unlockable	Code
All Characters and Alt skins	↑, ↓, ←, →, ↑, ↓, ←, →, ↑, ↓, ←, →, ●
All Stages	L2, R2, ←, →, ←, →, ←, →, ↓, ↓, ↑, ↑, ↓, ↑

F1 Career Challenge

Description	Hint
No Stop/Go Penalty	In Multiplayer mode you can enter the pits at any speed and from any direction without the normal stop/go penalty.

Family Guy

Stewie's Arsenal

To upgrade to new ray gun options, you need to collect a certain number of components. The first option is the straight shot, and the second option is the special shot.

Unlockable	How to Unlock
Hyper Plasma Ball Lvl 1/Plasma Artillery Lvl 2	Collect 300 components
Hyper Plasma Ball Lvl 2/Shock Wave Lvl 1	Collect 400 components
Plasma Ball Lvl 1/Spread Shot Lvl 2	Collect 100 components
Plasma Ball Lvl 2/Plasma Artillery Lvl 1	Collect 200 components
Ray Gun/Spread Shot Lvl 1	Collect 20 components
Rocket Launcher Lvl 1/Shock Wave Lvl 2	Collect 500 components
Rocket Launcher Lvl 2/ Heat Seekers	Collect 700 components

Fantastic Four

Enter these codes quickly at the Main menu. You will hear a sound to confirm a correct entry.

Unlockable	Code
Barge Arena Level and Stan Lee Interview #1	■, ●, ■, ⇩, ⇩, ⇩, ⇧
Bonus Level Hell	⇨, ⇨, ■, ●, ⇦, ⇧, ⇩
Infinite Cosmic Power	⇧, ■, ■, ■, ⇦, ⇨, ●

FantaVision

Description	Objective
Bonus Option 1	Beat and save the game under the Normal difficulty setting.
Bonus Option 2	Beat and save the game under the Hard difficulty setting.

Fatal Frame II: Crimson Butterfly

Unlockables

Unlockable	How to Unlock
Unlock alternate ending and two more costumes	Complete the game under Nightmare difficulty
Unlock Feel and Expand camera abilities	Complete the game under Easy or Nomal difficulty
Unlock Hard mode, two alternate costumes, and Mio's glasses	Complete the game under Normal difficulty
Unlock maid costume for Mayu	Complete all missions in Mission Mode
Unlock Mission mode, Gallery, Ghost List options	Complete the game under Easy or Nomal difficulty
Unlock Set-Up Information	Complete the Ghost List

Fatal Frame II: Crimson Butterfly (continued)

Unlockable	How to Unlock
Unlock two alternate costumes	Complete all missions in Mission Mode with a "S" ranking
View the alternate ending, unlock Nightmare mode, Album mode, true ending sequence, and two more costumes	Complete the game under Hard difficulty
View the first ending	Complete the game under Easy or Normal difficulty

Fatal Frame III: The Tormented

Unlockables

Unlockable	How to Unlock
Equipped Function: Fs	Clear all missions with S rank
Equipped Function: In	Complete the game in Nightmare mode
Equipped Function: Sn	Complete the game in Normal mode
Equipped Function: Zm	Complete the game in Normal mode and capture 100 or more ghosts
Kei—Browband	Complete the game in Normal mode
Kei—Fox ears	Complete the game in Hard or 3 times in Normal mode
Kei—Glasses	Complete the game twice in Hard or Nightmare mode
Kei—Glasses (white)	Complete the ghost list
Kei—Yukata (navy)	Complete the game in Normal mode
Kei—Yukata (orange)	Complete the game twice in Hard or Nightmare mode
Miku—Barrette	Complete the game in Normal mode
Miku—Cat ears	Complete the game in Hard or 3 times in Normal mode
Miku—Glasses	Complete the game twice in Hard or Nightmare mode
Miku—Headband	Complete the ghost list
Miku—Pinafore dress	Complete the game in Nightmare mode or clear all missions
Miku—Yukata (blue)	Complete the game in Normal mode
Miku—Yukata (pink)	Complete the game twice in Hard or Nightmare mode
Miku—Zero costume	Complete the game in Hard or 3 times in Normal mode
Rei—Cat ears	Complete the game in Hard or 3 times in Normal mode
Rei—Glasses	Complete the game twice in Hard or Nightmare mode
Rei—Hair ornament	Complete the game in Normal mode
Rei—Headband	Complete the ghost list
Rei—Pinafore dress	Complete the game in Nightmare mode or clear all missions
Rei—Suit	Complete the game in Hard or 3 times in Normal mode
Rei—Yukata (black)	Complete the game in Normal mode
Rei—Yukata (red)	Complete the game twice in Hard or Nightmare mode
Ruri—Bell	Complete the game in Hard or 3 times in Normal mode
Ruri—Ribbon	Complete the game in Normal mode
The concept	Complete the game in Normal mode and capture 50 or more ghosts
Trailer	Complete the game in Normal mode and capture 50 or more ghosts
Trailer Images	Complete the game in Normal mode and capture 50 or more ghosts

DS | GBA | PSP | PS2 | PS3 | Wii | Xbox | Xbox 360 | Index

DS

GBA

PSP

PS2

PS3

Wii

Xbox

Xbox 360

Index

Fatal Frame III: The Tormented (continued)

Unlockable	How to Unlock
Upgraded Lens (Crush)	Complete the game in Normal mode and capture 150 or more ghosts
Upgraded Lens (Serial)	Clear all missions
Upgraded Lens (Stop)	Complete the game in Normal mode

FIFA 05

Unlockable	Code
Go to Career Mode, Practice Mode, Jukebox, Set Pieces Section, Tournament Mode, and Create Tournament	1,000 points
Become a 5-Star Manager, Win EFA and Champions League	10,000 points
Five-Game Winning Streak, Beat a 5-Star Team, Get a Clean Sheet	2,000 points
Qualify for Europe Career Mode, Play Online	4,000 points
Win a Tournament, Create a Player, Get a Promotion, Score a Hat-Trick, Win a Penalty Shootout, Win an International Game, Win by More Than 5 Goals	6,000 points
Complete a Career	8,000 points

FIFA 07

Unlockable	Code
AC Milan 3rd Kit	1,250 points
Accrington Stanley 3rd Kit	500 points
Adidas Fevernova 2002 Football	750 points
Adidas Telstar 1974 Football	750 points
Adidas Tricolore 1990 Football	750 points
Ajax 3rd Kit	750 points
Arsena 3rd Kit	1,250 points
Celtic 3rd Kit	750 points
F.A. Premier League Season Highlights	1,500 points
German Bundesliga Season Highlights	1,500 points
Liverpool 3rd Kit	1,250 points
Real Madrid 3rd Kit	1,250 points

FIFA Street

Unlockable	Codes
Mini Players	Pause the game and hold L1+▲ and press ⇧,⇦,⇩,⇩,⇨,⇩,⇧,⇦.
Normal Size Players	Pause the game and hold L1+▲ and press ⇨,⇨,⇧,⇦,⇩,⇩,⇦,⇦.
All Apparel	At the main menu hold L1+▲ and press ⇨,⇨,⇦,⇧,⇧,⇧,⇩,⇦.

FIFA Street 2

Enter this code at the Main menu while holding L1 + ▲.

Unlockable	Code
All stages unlocked	⇦, ⇧, ⇧, ⇨, ⇩, ⇩, ⇩, ⇩

Fight Club

Unlockable	Code
Play as a skeleton	Create a fighter and name him Skeleton

Fight Night 2004

Enter the following codes at the Main Menu.

Unlockable	Code
All Venues	←,←,←,→,→,→,←,←,→
Big Head	←,→,←,→,←,→,←
Small Fighter	Highlight "Play No8," then press ←,←,←,→,→,→,←,✕
Fight as Big Tigger	Select My Corner, Record Book, Most Wins-Boxer, and press ↑,↑.

Fight Night Round 2

Unlockable	Code
Mini Fighters	At the choose Venue screen hold ↑ until you hear a bell ring.
Unlock Fabulous	Create a character with the first name GETFAB then cancel out and Fabulous will be available for Play Now and Career mode.
All Venues Unlocked	At the game mode selection screen hold ← until you hear a bell.

Final Fantasy XII

Unlockable	How To
Ashe	Awarded for having the average party level over 50
Ba'Gamnan	Awarded for completing the hunt catalog
Balthier	Awarded for attacking 300 times
Basch	Awarded for killing 500 foes
Belias	Awarded for obtaining every esper
Carrot	Awarded for defeating the monster, Carrot
Chocobo	Awarded for walking 50,000 steps
Crystal	Awarded for obtaining every character's magics
Dalan	Awarded for completing every map
DeathGaze	Awarded for defeating the monster, Death Gaze
Fafnir	Awarded for defeating the monster, Fafnir
Fran	Awarded for using magic 200 times
Gabranth	Awarded for initiating every fusion technique
Gilgamesh	Awarded for defeating the monster, Gilgamesh
Gurdy	Awarded for using/spending 1,000,000 gil
Hell Wyrm	Awarded for defeating the monster, Devil Dragon
King Behemoth	Awarded for defeating the monster, King Behemoth
Migelo	Awarded for selling 1,000 loot
Mimic	Unlock and buy all Monographs and Canopic Jar, also create and buy several Bazaar items to unlock
Montblanc	Awarded for attaining (monster) chain level 50
Penelo	Awarded for getting 100,000 gil
Rasler	Awarded for mastering all character's license board
Reks	Awarded for earning 500,000 clan points
Trickster	Awarded for defeating the monster, Trickster
Ultima	Awarded for defeating the esper, Ultima
Vaan	Awarded for stealing 50 times from enemies
Vayne	Awarded for using techniques 100 times
Vossler	Awarded for obtaining every character's techniques
Yazmat	Awarded for defeating the monster, Yazmat
Zodiac	Awarded for defeating the esper, Zodiac

DS

GBA

PSP

PS2

PS3

Wii

Xbox

Xbox 360

Index

DS
GBA
PSP
PS2
PS3
Wii
Xbox
Xbox 360
Index

Final Fantasy XII (continued)

Unlockable	How To
Master Den	Fish up Cactoid Crest in the Secret Reaches
Middle Reaches	Get 5 perfect fishing in the Lower Reaches
Secret Reaches	Fish up Cactoid Bond in the Upper Reaches with Matamune
Taikou Chest (treasure)	Get 9 perfect fishing in the Master Den
Upper Reaches	Get 5 perfect fishing in the Middle Reaches

Finding Nemo

Unlockable	Code
Credits	▲,■,●,▲,▲,■,●,▲,●,▲,■,●,▲,●,▲,■,●,●,▲,●,▲,■,●
Invincibility	▲,■,■,●,●,●,▲,▲,■,■,●,●,■,▲,●,●,■,▲,●, ●,■,●,●,▲,●,■,●,●,▲
Level Select	▲,▲,▲,■,■,●,■,▲,■,▲,■,▲,●,▲,▲
Secret Level	▲,■,●,●,■,▲,▲,■,●,●,■,▲,▲,●,■,▲,■,●,●,■,▲

FlatOut

Create a profile using these passwords.

Unlockable	Code
Lots of Cash	GIVECASH
Unlocks Everything	GIVEALL
Use the Shift Up Button to Launch the Driver	Ragdoll

FlatOut 2

Enter these passwords in the Cheats menu under extras.

Unlockable	Password	Unlockable	Password
All Cars and 1 Million Credits	GIEVEPIX	Lots of Money	GIVECASH
		Mob Car	BIGTRUCK
All Tracks	GIVEALL	Pimpster Car	RUTTO
Big Rig	ELPUEBLO	Rocket Car	KALJAKOPPA
Flatmobile Car	WOTKINS	School Bus	GIEVCARPLZ

Freaky Flyers

Description	Objective
Gremlin (Race Mode)	On the Thugsville board, notice the two elevated train tracks on either side of the map. Follow the right track to a tunnel. Once you are inside, take the left fork.
Pilot X	On the last level in Adventure mode, beat Pilot X by destroying his robot.

Freedom Fighters

Enter these codes during gameplay.

Unlockable	Code	Unlockable	Code
Blind AI	▲,✕,■,●,●,←	Slow Motion	▲,✕,■,●,●,→
Nail Gun	▲,✕,■,●,✕,←	Unlimited Ammo	▲,✕,■,●,✕,→

Freestyle Metal X

Unlockable	Code	Unlockable	Code
$1,000,000	sugardaddy	All riders	dudemaster
All posters and photos	seeall	All songs	hearall
All bike parts	garageking	All special stunt slots	fleximan
All costumes	johnnye	All videos	watchall
All levels and events	universe		

Frogger Ancient Shadow

These codes can be entered in the Code menu from the Main menu.

Unlockable	Code
Art 1	Frogger, Frogger, Frogger, Frogger
Art 2	Finnus, Finnus, Finnus, Finnus
Art 3	Berry, Berry, Berry, Berry
Bird Nest Wig	Lily, Lily, Lily, Lily
Dev Picture 1	Wani, Frogger, Wani, Frogger
Dev Picture 2	Berry, Berry, Berry, Wani
Lobster Wig	Finnius, Wani, Lumpy, Frogger
Programmer Art 1	Wani, Wani, Wani, Wani
Programmer Art 2	Lumpy, Frogger, Berry, Lily
Programmer Art 3	Wani, Frogger, Lily, Finnius
Sail Boat Wig	Lumpy, Lumpy, Lumpy, Lumpy
Skull Wig	Frogger, Lumpy, Lily, Frogger

Fugitive Hunter: War on Terror

Unlockable	Code
Cheat Menu	On the Title Screen, press ●,●,●,●,●,■,■,■,■,■. A chime will sound. Select Special Features to access the Cheat menu.
Some enemies as Bin Laden	In the Afghanistan-Pakistan Border mission, pause the game and press ●,●,●,■,■,■,■,R2.

Full Spectrum Warrior

Enter these codes in the Cheat menu under Options.

Unlockable	Code
All bonuses	LASVEGAS
All chapters	APANPAPANSNALE9
All enemies displayed on GPS	CANADIANVISION
Authentic mode	SWEDISHARMY
Big Head Mode	NICKWEST
Cloak Stealth Mode	BULGARIANNINJA
Opfors will have no cover	NAKEDOP4
Unlimited Ammo	MERCENARIES
Unlimited Rockets & Grenades	ROCKETARENA

Futurama

Press and hold down L1 + L2 while playing and enter the following codes to jump to that level.

Level	Code
Bogad's Swamp	↓, ■, ▲, ↓, ■, ▲, ■, ▲, ←, ↑, SELECT
Canyon	↓, ■, ▲, ↓, ■, ▲, ■, ▲, →, ↑, SELECT
Inner Temple	↓, ■, ▲, ↓, ■, ▲, ■, ▲, ↓, ▲, SELECT
Junkyard 1	↓, ■, ▲, ↓, ■, ▲, ■, ▲, →, ←, SELECT
Junkyard 2	↓, ■, ▲, ↓, ■, ▲, ■, ▲, →, ▲, SELECT
Junkyard 3	↓, ■, ▲, ↓, ■, ▲, ■, ▲, →, ●, SELECT
Left Wing	↓, ■, ▲, ↓, ■, ▲, ■, ▲, ↓, →, SELECT
Market Square	↓, ■, ▲, ↓, ■, ▲, ■, ▲, ↓, ↑, SELECT
Mine	↓, ■, ▲, ↓, ■, ▲, ■, ▲, →, →, SELECT
Mine Tunnel	↓, ■, ▲, ↓, ■, ▲, ■, ▲, →, ↓, SELECT
Mom's HQ—Bender	↓, ■, ▲, ↓, ■, ▲, ■, ▲, ▲, ↑, SELECT

DS
GBA
PSP
PS2
PS3
Wii
Xbox
Xbox 360
Index

Futurama (continued)

Mom's HQ—Fry	↓, ■, ▲, ↓, ■, ▲, ■, ▲, ▲, ↓, SELECT
Mom's HQ—Leela	↓, ■, ▲, ↓, ■, ▲, ■, ▲, ▲, →, SELECT
New New York	↓, ■, ▲, ↓, ■, ▲, ■, ▲, ↑, ×, SELECT
Old New York	↓, ■, ▲, ↓, ■, ▲, ■, ▲, ↑, ←, SELECT
Planet Express	↓, ■, ▲, ↓, ■, ▲, ■, ▲, ↑, ↑, SELECT
Red Light District	↓, ■, ▲, ↓, ■, ▲, ■, ▲, ↑, ▲, SELECT
Right Wing	↓, ■, ▲, ↓, ■, ▲, ■, ▲, ↓, ↓, SELECT
Sewers	↓, ■, ▲, ↓, ■, ▲, ■, ▲, ↑, →, SELECT
Subway	↓, ■, ▲, ↓, ■, ▲, ■, ▲, ↑, ↓, SELECT
Temple Courtyard	↓, ■, ▲, ↓, ■, ▲, ■, ▲, ↓, ←, SELECT
Uptown	↓, ■, ▲, ↓, ■, ▲, ■, ▲, ↑, ●, SELECT

Future Tactics: The Uprising

Codes

Code	Effect
↑, ←, ↓, ←, ↓, ↑, ↑, ←	Big Heads
L1, ←, L1, ←, R1, →, R1, →	Disco Mode
↑, ↑, ↑, ↑, ↑, ↑, ↓, →, ↑	Low Gravity

Unlockables

Unlockable	How to Unlock
Custom	Get two 100% head shot statuses in a row
Defeat Leader	Have all team members beat an episode with 100%
Humans and Creatures	In Single Player mode, have a character upgrade a weapon. Also, do not have any character miss during the level.
Level Select	Beat the game twice
Team Power	Get two head shots in a row

Gallop Racer 2003

Description	Hint
Free Horse	If you don't have any money, go to the next month and try to get a 0-point horse.

Gauntlet: Dark Legacy

Enter the codes in the spot where you name new characters. You can only utilize one special character or game mode at a time. Choose the character type (i.e. Dwarf, Valkyrie, etc.), as well as naming that character according to the code. Use special game modes (i.e., Unlimited Supershot, Unlimited Invulnerability) with any character type.

Unlockable	Code
$10,000 Gold per level	10000K
9 Keys and 9 Potions Per Level	ALLFUL
Battle General (Knight)	BAT900
Castle General (Warrior)	CAS400
Chainsaw Jester	KJH105
Cheerleader (Valkyrie)	CEL721
Created By Don (Knight)	ARV984
Desert General (Wizard)	DES700
Dwarf General	ICE600

Unlockable	Code
Employee Stig (Knight)	STG333
Ex-Employee Chris (Knight)	CSS222
Football Dude (Knight)	RIZ721
Happy Face Jester	STX222
Karate Steve (Knight)	SJB964
Manager Mike (Knight)	DIB626
Mountain General (Warrior)	MTN200
Ninja (Knight)	TAK118
Punkrock Jester	PNK666
Rat Knight (Warrior)	RAT333

Gauntlet: Dark Legacy

Unlockable	Code	Unlockable	Code
Regular Garm (Wizard)	GARM99	Unlimited Invisibility	000000
S & M Dwarf	NUD069	Unlimited Invulnerability	INVULN
School Girl (Valkyrie)	AYA555	Unlimited Play As Pojo	EGG911
Sickly Garm (Wizard)	GARM00	Unlimited Rapid Fire	QCKSHT
Sky General (Wizard)	SKY100	Unlimited Reflective Shot	REFLEX
Sumner (Wizard)	SUM224	Unlimited Shrink Enemy and Growth	DELTA1
Town General (Valkyrie)	TWN300		
Unlimited 3 Way Shot	MENAGE	Unlimited Supershot	SSHOTS
Unlimited Extra Speed	XSPEED	Unlimited X-Ray Glasses	PEEKIN
Unlimited Full Turbo	Purple	Waitress (Knight)	KAO292
Unlimited Halo and Levitate	1ANGLI		

Genji: Dawn of the Samurai

Unlockables

Unlockable	How to Unlock
BGM Test	Beat the game on Normal
Continue Mode	Beat the game on Normal
Movie Gallery	Beat the game on Normal
Voice Test	Beat the game on Normal
Character Art	Beat Hard mode
Enemy Art	Beat Hard mode
Stage Art	Beat Hard mode

The Getaway

During the opening movie, press the following buttons to access these cheats:

Unlockable	Code
Armored Car Weapon	↑,↓,←,→,■,▲,●
Double Health	↑,↑,←,←,→,→,●,●,↓
Free Roam Mode and Credits	▲,▲,▲,←,■,▲,▲,▲,←,●
Unlimited Ammo	↑,↓,←,→,▲,↑,↓,←,→,■

Ghost Rider

Unlockable	Code
Blade	Beat the game on Easy mode
Classic Ghost Rider	Beat the game on Extreme mode
Extreme Mode	Beat the game on Easy mode
Ghost Rider 2099	Beat the game on Easy mode
Infinite Link Charge	Beat the game on Easy mode
Infinite Spirit	Beat the game on Easy mode
Invincibility	Beat the game on Easy mode
One-Hit-Kill	Beat the game on Easy mode
Turbo Mode	Beat the game on Easy mode
Ultimate Ghost Rider	Beat the game on Easy mode
Vengeance	Beat the game on Easy mode

DS

GBA

PSP

PS2

PS3

Wii

Xbox

Xbox 360

Index

DS
GBA
PSP
PS2
PS3
Wii
Xbox
Xbox 360
Index

Ghosthunter

Description	Code
Increase damage	Hold right on d-pad while pressing L3 for 5 seconds, then press ●
Laz never dies	Hold right on d-pad while pressing L3 for 5 seconds, then press ▲

Gladius

At school, pause the game and enter the following codes.

Unlockable	Code
Equip Anything	→, ↓, ←, ↑, ←, ←, ←, ←, ▲, ▲, ▲
More Experience	→, ↓, ←, ↑, ←, ←, ←, ←, ▲, →
More Money	→, ↓, ←, ↑, ←, ←, ←, ←, ▲, ←

Goblin Commander: Unleash the Horde

Press and hold L1 + R1 + ▲ + ↓ for three seconds, then enter the following codes.

100 Gold	L1, R1, R1, R1, R1, L1, ▲, L1, L1, L1
God Mode	R1, R1, R1, L1, L1, L1, R1, L1, ▲, R1
Souls	R1, L1, L1, L1, L1, R1, ▲, R1, R1, R1
Win Level	R1, R1, L1, L1, L1, R1, R1, ▲, ▲, ▲

The Godfather

These codes can be entered on the pause screen.

Unlockable	Code	Unlockable	Code
$5,000	■, ●, ■, ■, ●, L3	Full Health	⇦, ■, ⇨, ●, ⇨, L3
Full Ammo	●, ⇦, ●, ⇨, ■, L3		

Enter this code on the Join Family menu.

Unlockable	Code
Unlock All Movies	●, ■, ●, ■, ■, L3

Golden Eye: Rogue Agent

Enter these codes while the games is paused.

Unlockable	Code
All Eye Powers	L1, L1, R2, R2, R1, R2, L1, L2
Full Health and Armor	R1, R1, R2, L2, R2, R1, L1, R2
Fully Charge Eye power	L1, R1, L1, L2, L2, R2, R1, L2

Enter these codes at the Extras Screen.

Unlockable	Code
No Eye powers in multiplayer mode	⇧, ⇧, ⇩, ⇦, ⇨, ⇨, ⇦, ⇩
One-Life mode	⇦, ⇩, ⇧, ⇨, ⇧, ⇨, ⇦, ⇩
Unlock all levels	⇩, ⇨, ⇩, ⇨, ⇧, ⇧, ⇧, ⇦

Gran Turismo 3 A-Spec

Complete the races listed to unlock the corresponding automobiles.

Objective	Car
4WD Challenge	Mitsubishi Lancer Evolution VII GSR
4WD Challenge	Mitsubishi Lancer Evolution VII Rally Car Prototype
4WD Challenge	Suzuki Alto Works, Suzuki Sports Limited
80's Sports Car Cup	Mazda Savanna RX7 Infini III
80s Sports Car Cup	Nismo Skyline GT-R S-tune

Gran Turismo 3 A-Spec (continued)

Objective	Car
All Golds on A License	Mazda RX8
All Golds on B License	Mazda Miata RS
All Golds on IA License	Aston Martin Vanqish
All Golds on IB License	Nissan Z Concept Car
All Golds on Rally License	Subaru Impreza Rally Car Prototype
All Golds on S License	Dodge Viper GTS-R Concept Car
All Japanese GT Championship	Honda Arta NSX JGTC, Denso Supra Race Car
Altezza Championship Race	Tom's X540 Chaser, Toyota Vitz RS 1.5
Altezza Race	Toyota Celica SS-II
American Championship	Subaru Impreza Sedan WRX STi Version VI, Chevy Camaro Race Car, Audi TT 1.8T Quattro, Mazda RX7 Type RS
Amateur 4WD Challenge	Titanium Mitsubishi Lancer Evolution
Amateur Evolution Meeting	Mitsubishi Lancer Evolution VI Rally Car
Amateur Race of Turbo Sports	White Mine's Lancer Evolution VI
Beginner FR Challenge series	Nissan Silvia K's 1800cc
Beginner GT World Championships	Tan Nissan Skyline GT-R V-spec II
Beginner MR Challenge	Blue Toyota MR-S S Edition.
Beginner Race of Turbo Sports	Silver Daihatsu Mira TRXX Avanzato R
Beginner Race of NA Sports series	Silver Honda CRX Del Sol SiR
Beginner Type R Meeting	Yellow Honda Civic SiR.
Beetle Cup	Volkswagen New Beetle Rsi
Boxer Spirit	Subaru Legacy Blitzer B4
British GT Car Cup	Aston Martin Vanquish
Clubman Cup	Mazda Eunos Roadster
Deutsche Tourenwagen Challenge	Volkswagen Lupo Cup Car, Volkswagen Beetle Cup Racer, Astra Touring Car, RUF 3400S
Dream Car Championship	Mitsubishi FTO LM Race Car, Mazda RX7 LM Race Car
Dream Car Championship	Toyota GT1, Panoz Esperante GTR, FTO LM Race Car, F090/s
European Championship	Lotus Elise 190, Nissan GTR V-Spec, Gillet Vertigo Race Car, Mini Cooper 1.3i
Evolution Meeting	Mitsubishi Lancer Evolution IV GSR
Evolution Meeting	Mitsubishi Lancer Evolution VI Rally Car
FF Challenge	Celica TRD Sports M
FF Challenge	Toyota Vitz RS 1.5
FR Challenge	Nissan Silvia K's 1800cc
FR Challenge	Toyota Sprinter Trueno GT-Apex Shigeno Version
Get All Golds	Mitsubishi Lancer Evolution V GSR
Get All Golds	Suzuki Escudo Pikes Peak Version

DS

GBA

PSP

PS2

PS3

Wii

Xbox

Xbox 360

Index

DS
GBA
PSP
PS2
PS3
Wii
Xbox
Xbox 360
Index

Gran Turismo 3 A-Spec (continued)

Objective	Car
Get All Golds	Team ORECA Dodge Viper GTSR
Gran Turismo All-Stars	Mine's GT-R-N1 V-spec, Raybrig NSX
Gran Turismo World Championship	Nissan C-West Razo Silvia, Nissan Z Concept car, Toyota GT1 Road Car, Mazda RX8
Gran Turismo World Championship	Toyota Celica GT-Four, Mitsubishi Lancer Evolution VI GSR, Mazda Miata, Nissan Skyline GTR V-spec II
Japanese Championship	Mazda RX7 Type RZ, Mitsubishi Evolution IV GSR, FTO GP Version R, Subaru Impreza WRX Sti Version VI Wagon
Legend of Silver Arrow	Mercedes Benz CLK Touring Car (D2 AMG Mercedes)
Legend of Silver Arrow	Mercedes SLK 230 Kompressor
Lightweight K Cup	Mini Cooper 1.3i
Like the Wind	Mazda 787B
MR Challenge	Honda NSX Type S Zero
MR Challenge	Tommy Kaira ZZII
MR Challenge	Toyota MR-S S Edition
NA Race of NA Sports	Honda CRX Del Sol SiR
NA Race of NA Sports	Mazda RX8 Turbo
Race of Red Emblem	Nismo 400R
Race of Turbo Sports	Mines Lancer Evolution VI GSR
Smokey Mountain II	Mitsubishi Lancer Evolution VI Rally Car
Smokey Mountain Rally	Ford Focus Rally Car
Spider & Roadster Championship	Shelby Cobra
Spider and Roadster cup with gold medals across the board	Mazda Roadster RS
Spider/Roadster Cup	Mazda Miata Roadster RS
Stars & Stripes Grand Championship	Spoon Sports S2000 Race Car
Stars & Stripes Grand Championship	Chevrolet Camaro SS
Sunday Cup	Toyota Sprinter, Trueno GT-Apex (AE-86 Type I)
Super Special Route 5 Wet	Citroen Xsara Rally Car
Super Special Route 5 Wet II	Subaru Impreza Rally Car Prototype
Super Speedway 150 Miles	Chevrolet Corvette C5R, Tickford Falcon XR8 Race Car, F090/S
Swiss Alps	Peugeot 206 Rally Car
Swiss Alps II	Mitsubishi Lancer Evolution VII Rally Car Prototype
Tahiti Challenge of Rally	Toyota Celica Rally Car
Tahiti Challenge of Rally II	Toyota Corolla Rally Car
Tahiti Maze	Ford Escort Rally Car
Tahiti Maze II	Impreza Rally Car
Tourist Trophy	Audi S4

Gran Turismo 3 A-Spec (continued)

Objective	Car
Tourist Trophy Audi TT Race	Audi TT 1.8T Quattro
Turbo Race of Turbo Sports	Daihatsu Mira TR XX Avanzato R
Type R Meeting	4 cars, Honda NSX Type-R
Type R Meeting	Honda Civic SiR-II VII GSR
Vitz Race	4 cars, Toyota Vitz RS 1.5
Cupman Cup with gold medals in each of the three races	Eunos Roadster
Sunday Cup with gold medals in each of the three races	Toyota Sprinter Truendo GT-Apex

TIP

To unlock tracks in Arcade mode beat each tier of tracks on easy mode, and you unlock the next tier of tracks.

The following table lists each tier with its tracks.

Tier 1	Tier 2	Tier 3
Super Speedway	Smokey Mountain II	Swiss Alps II,
Midfield Raceway	Tokyo R146	Trial Mountain II
Smokey Mountain	Grand Valley Speedway	Deep Forest Raceway II
Swiss Alps	Laguna Seca Raceway	Special Stage Route 5
Trial Mountain	Rome Circuit	Seattle Circuit
Midfield Raceway II	Tahiti Circuit	Test Course

Gran Turismo 4

Arcade Tracks

Play through X number of days to unlock listed track in Arcade mode.

Unlockable	How to Unlock
Apricot Hill Raceway	Days Completed = 169
Autumn Ring	Days Completed = 281
Cathedral Rocks Trail I	Days Completed = 239
Chamonix	Days Complete = 309
Circuit de la Sarthe 1	Days Completed = 267
Circuit de la Sarthe 2 (Unchicaned)	Days Complete = 351
Costa di Amalfi	Days Completed = 253
Cote d Azur	Days Completed = 183
Deep Forest Raceway	Days Completed = 15
Fuji Speedway 2005 F	Days Complete = 323
Fuji Speedway 2005 GT	Days Completed = 141
Fuji Speedway 80s	Days Completed = 43
George V Paris	Days Completed = 225
Grand Valley Speedway	Days Completed = 99
Hong Kong	Days Completed = 113
Ice Arena	Days Completed = 155
Infineon Raceway Stock Car Course	Days Completed = 309
Opera Paris	Days Completed = 29
Special Stage Route 5	Days Completed = 57
Suzuka Circuit	Days Completed = 71

DS

GBA

PSP

PS2

PS3

Wii

Xbox

Xbox 360

Index

Gran Turismo 4 (continued)

Unlockable	How to Unlock
Suzuka Circuit West Course	Days Completed = 127
Tahiti Maze	Days Completed = 197
Tsukuba Circuit Wet	Days Complete = 337
Twin Ring Motegi Road Course	Days Completed = 211
Twin Ring Motegi Road Course East Short	Days Completed = 85

Unlockable Vehicles

Unlockable	How to Unlock
Acura DN-X '02	A License—All Silver or better (US Version)
Acura HSC '04	Win Type R Meeting at Honda in the Japanese Showroom
Alfa Romeo 155 2.5 V6 TI Race Car '93	Win Italian Festival
Alfa Romeo Giulia Sprint GTA 1600 '65	Win GTA Cup at Alfa Romeo in the Italian showroom
Alfa Romeo Giulia Sprint Speciale '63	Win 1000 Miles
Alpine A110 1600S '73	Win Renault Alpine Cup at Alpine in the French Showroom
Alpine A310 1600VE '73	Win George Paris
Aston Martin DB9 Coupe '03 (Super Gold - Special Color)	Win Aston Martin Carnival at Aston Martin in the British showroom
Audi Abt Audi TT-R Touring Car '02	Win Nurburgring 4 Hours Endurance
Audi Le Mans quattro '03	Win Tourist Trophy at Audi in the German showroom
Audi Nuvotari Quattro '03	Complete 25% of game
Audi Pikes Peak quattro '03	Win A3 Cup at Audi in the German showroom
Audi R8 '01	Win Sarthe Circuit 24 Hours I
Auto Union V16 Type C Streamline	Win Grand Valley Speedway 300Km
Autobianchi A112 Abarth '79	Get all gold in all the races for the Sunday Cup
Autobianchi A112 Abarth '79	Win the Sunday Cup
Bentley Speed 8 Race Car '03	Win Sarthe Circuit 24 Hours II
BMW 2002 Turbo '73	Win 1 Series Trophy at BMW in the German Showroom
BMW M3 GTR '03	Win Club "M" at BMW in the German Showroom
BMW M3 GTR Race Car '01	Win Schwarzwald League A
BMW MacLaren F1 GTR Race Car '97	Win Gran Turismo All Stars
Cadillac Cien '02	Win Rally d' Umbria
Chaparral 2D Race Car ('67)	Win Nurburgring 4 Hours Endurance
Chevrolet Camaro IROC-Z Concept '88 American Showroom.	Win Camaro Mooting at Chevrolet in the American Showroom.
Chevrolet Camaro LM Race Car '01	Stars and Stripes (American Hall)
Chevrolet Camaro LM Race Car '01	Win Stars and Stripes
Chevrolet Chevelle SS 454 '70 (American Hall)	American Muscle Car Championship
Chevrolet Chevelle SS 454 '70	Win American Muscle Car Championship
Chevrolet Corvette Convertible (C1) '54	American Championship (American Hall)
Chevrolet Corvette Convertible (C1) '54	Win American Championship

Gran Turismo 4 (continued)

Unlockable	How to Unlock
Chevrolet Corvette Stingray Coupe (C2) '63	Corvette Festival (Chevrolet Dealership)
Chevrolet Corvette Z06 (C2) Race Car '63	Win Vette! Vette! Vette! at Chevrolet in the American Showroom
Chevrolet Silverado SST Concept '02	Win the Sport Truck Race
Chrysler Prowler '02	Win the Spider and Roadster
Citroen 2CV Type A '54 (Peche—Special Color)	Win 2HP—2CV Classics at Citroen in the French Showroom
Citroen 2CV Type-A '54	Win French Championship
Cizeta V16T '94	Win Supercar Festival
Clio Renault Sport Trophy V6 24V Race Car '00	Win Clio Trophy at Renault in the French Showroom
Daihatsu Midget '63	Win Midget II Race at Daihatsu in the Japanese Showroom
Daihatsu Storia X4 '00 (Special Color—Emerald Green Metallic)	Win Copen Race at Daihatsu in the Japanese Showroom
Dmc DeLorean S2 '04	Complete Missions 1-10
Dodge Charger Super Bee 426 Hemi '71	Win New York 200 Miles
Dodge Viper GTSR Concept '00	Win Crossfire Trophy at Chrysler in the American Showroom
Dome Zero '78	Get All Gold in International A License
Ford Escort Rally Car '98	Win Tahiti
Ford GT '05	Win Premium Sports Lounge
Ford GT Concept '02	Win Tsukuba Circuit
Ford GT LM Edition '02	Win Infineon World Sport Car Trophy
Ford GT LM Edition Spec-II '04	Win Gran Turismo World Championship
Ford GT40 Race Car '69	Win Laguna Seca 200 Miles
Ford Model T Tourer '15	Get All Golds in Super License
Ford RS200 '84	Win Grand Canyon
Ford RS200 Rally Car '85	Win Rally d' Capri
Ginetta G4 '64	Win the Light Weight K Cup
Honda Dualnote '01	Get All Silver in Domestic A License (Japanese Version)
Honda HSC (Honda Sports Concept) '03	Win Type R Meeting at Honda in the Japanese Showroom (U.S Version)
Honda Life Step Van '72	Win Japanese Compact Car Cup
Honda Mugen Motul Civic Si Race Car '87	Win Civic Race at Honda in the Japanese Showroom
Honda NSX-R Concept '01	Win Race of NA Sports
Honda NSX-R LM Edition Race Car '02	Win Super Speedway 150 Miles
Honda NSX-R LM Edition Road Car '02	Win Motegi 8 Hours Endurance
Honda S500 '63	Get All Golds in Domestic B License
Honda S800 RSC Race Car '68	Win World Compact Car Race
Hyundai Clix '01	Win Hyundai Sports Festival at Hyundai in the Korean Showroom
Hyundai HCD6 '01	Win Cathedral Rocks (Trail II)
Infiniti FX45 Concept '02	Win Chamoni

DS
GBA
PSP
PS2
PS3
Wii
Xbox
Xbox 360
Index

Gran Turismo 4 (continued)

Unlockable	How to Unlock
Isuzu 117 Coupe '68 (Special Color—Maple Orange)	Win Isuzu Sports Classics at Isuzu in the Japanese Showroom
Jaguar E-Type Coupe '61	Win British GT Cup
Jaguar XJ220 LM Edition '01	Win European Championship
Jaguar XJ-R9 Race Car	Complete 50% of the game
Jay Leno Tank Car '03	Complete Missions 11-20
Jensen Healey Interceptor Mk.III '74	Get All Gold in International B License
Lancia Delta HF Integrale Rally Car '92	Win Rally d' Umbria
Lancia Delta S4 Rally Car '85	Win Rally d' Umbria
Lancia Stratos Rally Car '77	Win Chamoni
Land Rover Range Stormer Concept '04	Win Cathedral Rocks (Trail I)
Lister Storm V12 Race Car '99	Win Suzuka 1000km
Lotus Elan S1 '62	Win Lotus Classics at Lotus in the British showroom
Lotus Elise Type 72 '01	Win Elise Trophy at Lotus in the British showroom
Lotus Esprit Turbo HC '87	Win the MR Challenge
Lotus Europa Special '71	Win British Light Weight Car Race
Mazda 110S (L10A) '67	Win Club "RE" at Mazda in the Japanese Showroom
Mazda 6 Concept '01	Win the FF Challenge (U.S Version)
Mazda 6 Touring Car '02	Win Tsukuba Circuit (U.S Version)
Mazda Atenza Concept '01	Win the FF Challenge
Mazda Atenza Touring Car '02	Win Tsukuba Circuit
Mazda BP Falken RX-7 (D1GP) '03	Win Race of Turbo Sports
Mazda Kusabi '03	Get All Silver in Domestic B License
Mazda Mazdaspeed 6 '05	Win Clubman Cup (U.S Version)
Mazda Mazdaspeed Atenza '05	Win Clubman Cup
Mazda MX-Crossport '05 Japanese Showroom	Win NR-A Roadster Cup at Mazda in the
Mazda RX-7 LM Race Car '01	Win Roadster 4 Hours Endurance
Mazda RX-8 Concept (Type-I) '01	Win Tsukuba Circuit
Mazda RX-8 Concept (Type-II) '04	Get All Silver in International B License
Mazda RX-8 Concept LM Race Car '01	Win NR-A RX-8 Cup at Mazda in the Japanese Showroom.
Mercedes Sauber C 9 Race Car '89	Win Formula GT World (US version)
Mercedes-Benz AMG 190E 2.5 16V Evolution II (DTM) '92	Win Schwarzwald League B
Mercedes-Benz AMG CLK-GTR Race Car '98	Win German Touring Car Championship
Mercedes-Benz Benz Patent Motor Wagen '1886	Win European Classic Car Championship
Mercedes-Benz CLK Touring Car '00	Win Legends of the Silver Arrow at Mercedez-Benz in the German Showroom
Mercedes-Benz Daimler Motor Carriage 1886	Win World Classic Car Series
Mercedez-Benz 300 SL Coupe '54	Win SL Challenge at Mercedez-Benz in the German Showroom

Gran Turismo 4 (continued)

Unlockable	How to Unlock
Mercury Cougar XR-7 '67	Complete Super License
MGF '97 (Yellow—Special Color)	Win the MG festival at MG in the British showroom
Mini Marcos GT '70	Get gold in Mini Mini Sports Meeting
Mistubishi Lancer 1600 GSR Rally Car '74	Win Evolution Meeting at Mitsubishi in the Japanese Showroom
Mitsubishi CZ-3 Tarmac '01	Win Swiss Alps
Mitsubishi CZ-3 Tarmac Rally Car '02	Win Grand Canyon
Mitsubishi FTO Super Touring Car '97	Win Tokyo R246 300km
Mitsubishi HSR-II Concept '89	Win Japanese 80's Festival
Mitsubishi '03	Win Mirage Cup at Mitsubishi in the Japanese Showroom
Mitsubishi Lancer Evolution IV Rally Car'97	Win Ice Arena
Mitsubishi Pajero Evolution Rally	Win Cathedral Rocks (Trail II)
Mitsubishi Pajero Rally Raid Car '85	Win Tahiti
Mitsubishi Straion 4WD Rally Car '84	Win Grand Canyon
Nike One 2022	Complete International B License
Nike One 2022	Win Saleen S7 Club at Saleen in the American Showroom
Nismo 270R '94 (S14)	Complete International A License
Nismo 400R (R33) '96	Win Japanese 90's Challenge
Nismo GT-R LM Road Going Version '95	Win Race of the Red "R" Emblem at Nissan in the Japanese Showroom
Nismo Skyline GT-R LM Road Going Version	Win the Race of the Red Emblem
Nissan 240ZG (HS30) '71	Win Club "Z" at Nissan in the Japanese Showroom
Nissan Bluebird 1600SSS Rally Car (510) '69	Win Ice Arena
Nissan Fairlady Z Concept LM Race Car '02	Win Japanese Championship
Nissan Gran Turismo Skyline GT-R (PaceCar) '01	Win Real Circuit Tours
Nissan GT-R Concept '01	Get All Silver in International A License
Nissan GT-R Concept LM Race Car '02	Win Dream Car Championship
Nissan mm-R Cup Car '01 Japanese Showroom	Win March Brothers at Nissan in the
Nissan Motul Pitwork Z (JGTC) '04	Win Japanese GT Championship
Nissan Option Stream Z '04	Win Tuning Car Grand Prix
Nissan R89C Race Car '89	Complete Missions 30-34
Nissan R92CP Race Car '92	Win Fuji 1000km
Nissan Silvia 240RS Rally Car '85	Win Swiss Alps
Nissan Skyline 2000GT-B '67	Win the FR Challenge
Nissan Skyline GT-R '01	Get All Golds in Domestic A License
Nissan Skyline GT-R Race Car (CALSONIC) '93	Win Tsukuba 9 Hours Endurance
Nissan Skyline Hard Top 2000GT-R (KPGC10) '70	Win Japanese 70's Classic
Opel Calibra Touring Car '94	Win Speedster Trophy at Opel in the German showroom

Gran Turismo 4 (continued)

Unlockable	How to Unlock
Opera Performance S2000 '04	Win Polyphony Digital Cup
Pagani Zonda Race Car '01	Complete Missions 21-24
Peugeot 205 Turbo 16 Evolution 2 Rally Car '86	Win George Paris
Peugeot 205 Turbo 16 Rally Car e85	Win 206 Cup at Peugeot in the French showroom
Plymouth Super Bird '70	Classic Muscle Car Championship (American Hall)
Plymouth Super Bird '70	Win Classic Muscle Car Championship
Polyphony Formula Gran Turismo 04 (Black Version)	Complete 100% of Gran Turismo Mode
Polyphony Formula Gran Turismo '04	Win Formula GT World (Japanese version)
Polyphony Formula Gran Turismo '04	Win Nurburgring 24 Hours Endurance
Pontiac Solstice Coupe Concept '02	Get All Silver in Super License
Pontiac Sunfire GXP Concept '02	Complete Domestic A License
Renault 5 Maxi Turbo Rally Car '85	Win George Paris
Renault 5 Turbo '80	Win Tahiti
Renault AVANTIME '02 (Special Color—Jaune)	Win Megane Cup at Renault in the French Showroom
Ruf CTR Yellow Bird '87	Win Boxer Spirit
Shelby Mustang G.T. 350R '65	Win Shelby Cobra Cup at Shelby in the American Showroom
SILEIGHTY '98	Win Silvia Sisters at Nissan in the Japanese Showroom
Subaru Impreza Rally Car '01	Win Chamoni
Subaru Impreza Rally Car '99	Win Cathedral Rocks (Trail I)
Subaru Impreza Rally Car Prototype '01	Win Rally d' Capri
Subaru Impreza Super Touring Car '01	Win Stars of Pleiades at Subaru in the Japanese Showroom
Subaru Subaru 360 '58 (WR Blue Mica—Special Color)	Win Subaru 360 Race at Subaru in the Japanese Showroom
Suzuki Concept-S2 '03	Win Suzuki K-Car Cup at Suzuki in the Japanese Showroom
Suzuki Escudo Dirt Trial Car '98	Win Cathedral Rocks (Trail I)
Suzuki GSX-R/4 '01	Win Suzuki Concepts at Suzuki in the Japanese Showroom
Toyota 7 Race Car '70	Complete Missions 25-29
Toyota Altezza Touring Car '01	Win Altezza Race at Toyota in the Japanese Showroom
Toyota Celica GT-FOUR Rally Car (ST185) '95	Win Cathedral Rocks (Trail II)
Toyota Celica GT-FOUR Rally Car (ST205) '95	Win Swiss Alps
Toyota Motor Triathlon Race Car '04	Win the 4WD Challenge
Toyota RSC '01	Win Ice Arena
Toyota RSC Rally Raid Car '02	Win Rally d' Capri
Toyota Vitz RS Turbo '02 (Special Color—Orange Metallic)	Win Vitz Race at Toyota in the Japanese Showroom
Toyota 88C-V Race Car (MINOLTA) '89	Win El Captain 200 Miles

Gran Turismo 4 (continued)

Unlockable	How to Unlock
Triumph Spitfire 1500 '74 (Special Color—Maroon Metallic)	Win the Spitfire Cup at the Triumph dealer.
TVR Cerbera Speed 12 '00 (Chameleon—Special Color)	Win Black Pool Racers at TVR in the British showroom
Volkswagen Beetle 1100 Standard (Type-11) '49	Win Beetle Cup at Volkswagen in the German Showroom
Volkswagen Golf I GTI '76	Win GTi Cup at Volkswagen in the German Showroom
Volkswagen Karmann Ghia Coupe (Type-1) '68	Win Lupo Cup at Volkswagen in the German Showroom
Volkswagen Lupo 1.4 '02	Complete Domestic B License
Volkswagen W12 Nardo Concept '01	Win Like the Wind
Volvo 240 GLT Estate '88	Win European Hot Hatch Car Championship

Grand Prix Challenge

Description	Code	Description	Code
Ace difficulty	REDJOCKS	All tracks	TEAMPEEP
All Grand Prix Challenges	IMHRACING		

Grand Theft Auto 3

Enter all of the following codes during gameplay. After doing so, wait for the message to confirm correct code entry.

Description	Code
All Weapons	Press R2, R2, L1, R2, ←, ↓, →, ↑, ←, ↓, →, ↑. See Tip.
Better Driving Skills	Press R1, L1, R2, L1, ←, R1, R1, ▲. Press L3 or R3 to jump while driving.
Destroy All Cars	Press L2, R2, L1, R1, L2, R2, ▲, ■, ●, ▲, L2, L1.
Different Costume	Press →, ↓, ←, ↑, L1, L2, ↑, ←, ↓, →.
Faster Gameplay	Press ▲, ↑, →, ↓, ■, L1, L2. Repeat this code to increase its effect.
Flying Car (Low Gravity)	Press →, R2, ●, R1, L2, ↓, L1, R1. Accelerate and press ↑ to fly.
Fog	Press L1, L2, R1, R2, R2, R1, L2, ✕.
Full Armor	Press R2, R2, L1, L2, ←, ↓, →, ↑, ←, ↓, →, ↑.
Full Health	Press R2, R2, L1, R1, ←, ↓, →, ↑, ←, ↓, →, ↑. See Note.
Invisible Cars	Press L1, L1, ■, R2, ▲, L1, ▲.
More Money	Press R2, R2, L1, L1, ←, ↓, →, ↑, ←, ↓, →, ↑.
Normal Weather	Press L1, L2, R1, R2, R2, R1, L2, ▲.
Overcast Skies	Press L1, L2, R1, R2, R2, R1, L2, ■.
Rain	Press L1, L2, R1, R2, R2, R1, L2, ●.
Slower Gameplay	Press ▲, ↑, →, ↓, ■, R1, R2 This cheat also continues the effect of an adrenaline pill.
Speed Up Time	Press ●, ●, ●, ■, ■, ■, ■, ■, L1, ▲, ●, ▲. Repeat this code to increase its effect.
Tank (Rhino)	Press ●, ●, ●, ●, ●, ●, R1, L2, L1, ▲, ●, ▲. This may be repeated as many times as needed.

DS
GBA
PSP
PS2
PS3
Wii
Xbox
Xbox 360
Index

Grand Theft Auto 3 (continued)

NOTE

Better Driving Skills Note

Saving the game allows your car to never tip. Also, every car will have hydraulics that enable it to jump 15 feet in the air over other cars. After this code is enabled, any time you roll your car, press ■ + ✕ to flip back over. This works as long as your car is not on its roof.

TIP

All Weapons Code Tip

Repeat this code for more ammunition. To get unlimited ammunition, enable the "All Weapons" code continuously until whatever you want is at 9999 shots. The next time your clip runs out, it will reload automatically, but the magazine (9999) will stay the same. Note: If you are busted, your weapons will disappear and this code will have to be repeated.

NOTE

Full Health Code Note

If this code is enabled during a mission where there is damage on your car, the meter will reset to zero. If your vehicle is on fire, enable the "Full Health" code to extinguish it. This code also repairs your car. You can't see the repairs, but it acts like a new car. If you're on a mission where you need a mint-condition car, sometimes enabling the "Full Health" code will fulfill the requirements.

CAUTION

Warning!

Saving the game after inputting the following codes will make them permanent.

Description	Code
All Pedestrians Have Weapons	Press R2, R1, ▲, ✕, L2, L1, ↑, ↓. See Caution Below.
Higher Wanted Level	Press R2, R2, L1, R2, ←, →, ←, →, ←.
Increased Gore	Press ■, L1, ●, ↓, L1, R1, ▲, →, L1, ✕. No confirmation message will appear. See Note.
No Wanted Level	Press R2, R2, L1, R2, ↑, ↓, ↑, ↓, ↑, ↓.
Pedestrians Attack You	Press ↓, ↑, ←, ↑, ✕, R1, R2, L1, L2.
Pedestrians Riot	Press ↓, ↑, ←, ↑, ✕, R1, R2, L2, L1.

NOTE

With this code enabled, you can shoot off pedestrians' arms, legs, and heads with some weapons (sniper rifle, assault rifle, explosives) with an increase in the overall amount of blood left behind.

CAUTION

Be careful after entering this code, some pedestrians will throw bombs or shoot at you if you steal their car.

Grand Theft Auto Liberty City Stories

Enter these codes during game play—do not pause.

Unlockable	Code
$250,000	L1, R1, ▲, L1, R1, ●, L1, R1
Aggressive Drivers	■, ■, R1, ✕, ✕, L1, ●, ●
All Green Lights	▲, ▲, R1, ■, ■, L1, ✕, ✕
All Vehicles Chrome Plated	▲, R1, L1, ⇩, ⇩, R1, R1, ▲

Grand Theft Auto Liberty City Stories (continued)

Unlockable	Code
Black Cars	●, ●, R1, ▲, ▲, L1, ■, ■
Big Heads	⬇, ⬇, ⬇, ●, ●, ✕, L1, R1
Cars Drive On Water	●, ✕, ⬇, ●, ✕, ⬆, L1, L1
Change Bike Tire Size	●, ➡, ✕, ⬆, ➡, ✕, L1, ■
Clear Weather	⬆, ➡, ●, ⬆, ⬇, ■, L1, R1
Commit Suicide	L1, ⬇, ⬅, R1, ✕, ●, ⬆, ▲
Destroy All Cars	L1, L1, ⬅, L1, L1, ➡, ✕, ■
Display Game Credits	L1, R1, L1, R1, ⬆, ⬇, L1, R1
Faster Clock	L1, L1, ⬅, L1, L1, ➡, ●, ✕
Faster Gameplay	R1, R1, L1, R1, R1, L1, ⬇, ✕
Foggy Weather	⬆, ➡, ▲, ⬆, ⬇, ✕, L1, R1
Full Armor	L1, R1, ●, L1, R1, ✕, L1, R1
Full Health	L1, R1, ✕, L1, R1, ■, L1, R1
Never Wanted	L1, L1, ▲, R1, R1, ✕, ■, ●
Overcast Weather	⬆, ⬇, ✕, ⬆, ⬇, ▲, L1, R1
Peds Attack You	L1, L1, R1, L1, L1, R1, ⬆, ▲
Peds Have Weapons	R1, R1, L1, R1, R1, L1, ➡, ●
Peds Riot	L1, L1, R1, L1, L1, R1, ⬅, ■
People Follow You	⬇, ⬇, ⬇, ▲, ▲, ●, L1, R1
Perfect Traction	L1, ⬆, ●, R1, ▲, ●, ⬇, ✕
Rainy Weather	⬆, ⬇, ■, ⬆, ⬇, ●, L1, R1
Raise Media Attention	L1, ⬆, ●, R1, ▲, ■, ⬇, ✕
Raise Wanted Level	L1, R1, ■, L1, R1, ▲, L1, R1
Slower Gameplay	R1, ▲, ✕, R1, ■, ●, ⬅, ➡
Spawn a Rhino	L1, L1, ⬅, L1, L1, ➡, ▲, ●
Spawn a Trashmaster	▲, ●, ⬇, ▲, ●, ⬆, L1, L1
Sunny Weather	L1, L1, ●, R1, R1, ■, ▲, ✕
Upside Down Gameplay	⬇, ⬇, ⬇, ✕, ✕, ■, R1, L1
Upside Down Gameplay2	✕, ✕, ✕, ⬇, ⬇, ■, L1, R1
Upside Up	▲, ▲, ▲, ⬆, ⬆, ➡, L1, R1
Weapon Set 1	⬆, ■, ■, ⬇, ⬅, ■, ■, ➡
Weapon Set 2	⬆, ●, ●, ⬇, ⬅, ●, ●, ➡
Weapon Set 3	⬆, ✕, ✕, ⬇, ⬅, ✕, ✕, ➡
White Cars	✕, ✕, R1, ●, ●, L1, ▲, ▲

Grand Theft Auto: San Andreas

Description	Code
250,000 & full health and armor	R1, R2, L1, ✕, ⬅, ⬇, ➡, ⬆, ⬅, ⬇, ➡, ⬆
4 star wanted level	R1, R1, ●, L1, ⬆, ⬇, ⬆, ⬇, ⬆, ⬇
Aggressive Traffic	R2, ●, R1, L2, ⬅, R1, L1, R2, L2
All Traffic Lights Stay Green	➡, R1, ⬆, L2, L2, ⬅, R1, L1, R1, R1
All Vehicles Invisible (Except Motorcycles)	▲, L1, ▲, R2, ■, L1, L1
Attain 2 star wanted level	R1, R1, ●, ⬅, ➡, ⬅, ➡
Black Traffic	●, L2, ⬆, R1, ⬅, ✕, R1, L1, ⬅, ●
Cars on Water	➡, R2, ●, R1, L2, ■, R1, R2

DS GBA PSP PS2 PS3 Wii Xbox Xbox 360 Index

DS

GBA

PSP

PS2

PS3

Wii

Xbox

Xbox 360

Index

Grand Theft Auto: San Andreas (continued)

Description	Code
Commit Suicide	→, L2, ↓, R1, ←, ←, R1, L1, L2, L1
Destroy Cars	R2, L2, R1, L1, L2, L2, ■, ▲, ●, ▲, L2, L1
Faster Cars	→, R1, ↑, L2, L2, ←, R1, L1, R1, R1
Faster Clock	●, ●, L1, ■, L1, ■, ■, ■, L1, ▲, ●, ▲
Faster Gameplay	▲, ↑, →, ↓, L2, L1, ■
Flying Boats	R2, ●, ↑, L1, →, R1, →, ↑, ■, ▲
Fog	R2, ✕, L1, L1, L2, L2, L2, ✕
Get a Bounty on your head	↓, ↑, ↑, ↑, ✕, R2, R1, L2, L2
Lower Wanted Level	R1, R1, ●, R2, ↑, ↓, ↑, ↓, ↑, ↓
Morning	R2, ✕, L1, L1, L2, L2, L2, ■
Night	R2, ✕, L1, L1, L2, L2, L2, ▲
Overcast	R2, ✕, L1, L1, L2, L2, L2, ■
Pedestrian Attack (can't be turned off)	↓, ↑, ↑, ↑, ✕, R2, R1, L2, L2
Pedestrian Riot (can't be turned off)	↓, ←, ↑, ←, ✕, R2, R1, L2, L1
Pedestrians have weapons	R2, R1, ✕, ▲, ✕, ▲, ↑, ↓
Perfect Handling	▲, R1, R1, ←, R1, L1, L2, L1
Pink Traffic	●, L1, ↓, L2, ←, ✕, R1, L1, →, ●
Play as Wuzi	L2, R2, L1, L2, L2, L2, L1, L1, L1, L1, ▲, ▲, ●, ●, ■, L2, L2, L2, L2, L2, L2
Raise Wanted Level	R1, R1, ●, R2, →, ←, →, ←, →, ←
Romero	↓, R2, ↓, R1, L2, ←, R1, L1, ←, →
Slower Gameplay	▲, ↑, →, ↓, ■, R2, R1
Spawn a Ranger	↑, →, →, L1, →, ↑, ■, L2
Spawn A Rhino	●, ●, L1, ●, ●, ●, L1, L2, R1, ▲, ●, ▲
Spawn a Stretch	R2, ↑, L2, ←, ←, R1, L1, ●, →
Spawn Bloodring Banger	↓, R1, ●, L2, L2, ✕, R1, L1, ←, ←
Spawn Caddy	●, L1, ↑, R1, L2, ✕, R1, L1, ●, ✕
Spawn Hotring Racer #1	R1, ●, R2, →, L1, L2, ✕, ✕, ■, R1
Spawn Hotring Racer #2	R2, L1, ●, →, L1, R1, →, ↑, ●, R2
Spawn Rancher	↑, →, →, L1, →, ↑, ■, L2
Spawns jetpack	L1, L2, R1, R2, ↓, ↓, ←, right, L1, L2, R1, R2, ↑, ↓, ←, →,
Storm	R2, ✕, L1, L1, L2, L2, L2, ●
Trashmaster	●, R1, ●, R1, ←, ←, R1, L1, ●, →
Weapons 1	R1, R2, L1, R2, ←, ↓, →, ↑, ←, ↓, →, ↑
Weapons 2	R1, R2, L1, R2, ←, ↓, →, ↑, ←, ↓, ↓, ←
Weapons 3	R1, R2, L1, R2, ←, ↓, →, ↑, ←, ↓, ↓, ↓

Grand Theft Auto: Vice City

Enter all of the following codes during gameplay. After doing so, wait for the message to confirm correct code entry.

Description	Code
Aggressive Traffic	Press R2, ●, R1, L2, ←, R1, L1, R2, L2
Armor	Press R1, R2, L1, ✕, ←, ↓, →, ↑, ←, ↓, →, ↑
Better Driving Skills	Press ▲, R1, R1, ←, R1, L1, R2, L1. Press L3 or R3 to jump while driving.
Bikini Women with Guns (The women drop guns when they die.)	Press →, L1, ●, L2, ←, ✕, R1, L1, L1, ✕
Black Traffic	Press ●, L2, ↑, R1, ←, ✕, R1, L1, ←, ●
Bloodring Banger (Style 1)	Press ↑, →, →, L1, →, ↑, ■, L2.
Bloodring Banger (Style 2)	Press ↓, R1, ●, L2, L2, ✕, R1, L1, ←, ←
Caddy	Press ●, L1, ↑, R1, L2, ✕, R1, L1, ●, ✕

Grand Theft Auto: Vice City (continued)

Description	Code
Candy Suxxx Costume	Press ●, R2, ↓, R1, ←, →, R1, L1, ×, L2.
Car Floats on Water	Press →, R2, ●, R1, L2, ■, R1, R2. See Note.
Change Wheel Size (The wheels of some vehicles become larger, while others become smaller.)	Press R1, ×, ▲, →, R2, ■, ↑, ↓, ■. Repeat this code to increase its effect.
Destroy Cars	Press R2, L2, R1, L1, L2, R2, ■, ▲, ●, ▲, L2, L1
Dodo Car (Flying)	Press →, R2, ●, R1, L2, ↓, L1, R1. Accelerate and press the analog stick back to glide.
Extended Wanted Level Status	Press R2, ●, ↑, L1, →, R1, →, ↑, ■, ▲. A box will appear under your felony stars showing how long you have had a felony and how close the cops are.
Faster Game Clock	Press ●, ●, L1, ■, L1, ■, ■, ■, L1, ▲, ●, ▲
Faster Gameplay	Press ▲, ↑, →, ↓, L2, L1, ■
Foggy Weather	Press R2, ×, L1, L1, L2, L2, L2, ×
Health	Press R1, R2, L1, ●, ←, →, ↑, ↓, ←, →, ↑, ↑
Hilary King Costume	Press R1, ●, R2, L1, →, R1, L1, ×, R2
Hotring Racer (Style 1)	Press R1, ●, R2, →, L1, L2, ×, ×, ■, R1
Hotring Racer (Style 2)	Press R2, L1, ●, →, L1, R1, →, ↑, ●, R2
Increase Your Vehicle's Top Speed	Press →, R1, ↑, L2, L2, ←, R1, L1, R1, R1
Ken Rosenberg Costume	Press →, L1, ↑, L2, L1, →, R1, L1, ×, R1
Lance Vance Costume	Press ●, L2, ←, ×, R1, L1, ×, L1
Love Fist Limousine	Press R2, ↑, L2, ←, ←, R1, L1, ●, →
Love Fist Musician 1 Costume	Press ↓, L1, ↓, L2, ←, ×, R1, L1, ×, ×
Love Fist Musician 2 Costume	Press R1, L2, R2, L1, →, R2, ←, ×, ■, L1
Lower Wanted Level	Press R1, R1, ●, R2, ↑, ↓, ↑, ↓, ↑, ↓
Mercedes Costume	Press R2, L1, ↑, L1, →, R1, →, ↑, ●, ▲
Normal Weather	Press R2, ×, L1, L1, L2, L2, L2, ↓
Overcast Skies	Press R2, ×, L1, L1, L2, L2, L2, ■
Pedestrian Costume	Press →, →, ←, ↑, L1, L2, ←, ↑, ↓, → Repeat this code to cycle through the various pedestrian costumes.
Pedestrians Attack You	Press ↓, ↑, ↑, ↑, ×, R2, R1, L2, L2 You cannot disable this code.
Pedestrians from "Thriller"	Press ■, L1, ▲, R2, ■, L1, L1 No confirmation message appears.
Pedestrians Have Weapons	Press R2, L1, ×, ▲, ×, ▲, ↑, ↓ You cannot disable this code.
Pedestrians Riot	Press ↓, ←, ↑, ←, ×, R2, R1, L2, L1 You cannot disable this code.
Phil Cassady Costume	Press →, R1, ↑, R2, L1, →, R1, L1, →, ●.
Pink Traffic	Press ●, L1, ↓, L2, ←, ×, R1, L1, →, ● or ×.
Police Return from Dead	Press ●, L1, ↓, L2, ←, ×, R1, L1, →, ×.
Rainy Weather	Press R2, ×, L1, L1, L2, L2, L2, ●.
Raise Wanted Level	Press R1, R1, ●, R2, ←, →, ←, →, ←, →.
Rhino Tank	Press ●, ●, L1, ●, ●, ●, L1, L2, R1, ▲, ●, ▲.
Ricardo Diaz Costume	Press L1, L2, R1, R2, ↓, L1, R2, L2.
Romero's Hearse	Press ↓, R2, ↓, R1, L2, ←, R1, L1, ←, →.
Sabre Turbo	Press →, L2, ↓, L2, L2, ×, R1, L1, ●, ←.
Slower Gameplay	Press ▲, ↑, →, ↓, ■, R2, R1.
Sonny Forelli Costume	Press ●, L1, ●, L2, ←, ×, R1, L1, ×, ×.

Sidebar tabs: DS, GBA, PSP, PS2, PS3, Wii, Xbox, Xbox 360, Index

DS
GBA
PSP
PS2
PS3
Wii
Xbox
Xbox 360
Index

Grand Theft Auto: Vice City (continued)

Description	Code
Suicide	Press →, L2, ↓, R1, ←, ←, R1, L1, L2, L1.
Sunny Weather	Press R2, ✕, L1, L1, L2, L2, L2, ▲.
Tommy Groupies	Press ●, ✕, L1, L1, R2, ✕, ✕, ●, ▲.
Trashmaster	Press ●, R1, ●, R1, ←, ←, R1, L1, ●, →.
Weapons (Tier 1)	Press R1, R2, L1, R2, ←, ↓, →, ↑, ←, ↓, →, ↑ The least powerful weapons in each category are unlocked.
Weapons (Tier 2)	Press R1, R2, L1, R2, ←, ↓, →, ↑, ←, ↓, ↓, ←.
Weapons (Tier 3)	Press R1, R2, L1, R2, ←, ↓, →, ↑, ←, ↓, ↓, ↓.

> **NOTE**
>
> *After enabling this code while driving on the water, repeat the code to deactivate it. The car you drive goes directly to the bottom of the water and keeps going without losing any health. You soon hit a piece of land and either end up stuck in the ground or can drive again. You do not lose any health during the entire time.*

Grand Theft Auto: Vice City Stories

Enter these codes while playing.

Unlockable	Code
Acquire Weapon Set 1	⇦, ⇨, ✕, ⇧, ⇩, ■, ⇦, ⇨
Acquire Weapon Set 2	⇦, ⇨, ■, ⇧, ⇩, ▲, ⇦, ⇨
Acquire Weapon Set 3	⇦, ⇨, ▲, ⇧, ⇩, ●, ⇦, ⇨
All Green Lights	⇧, ⇩, ▲, ✕, L1, R1, ⇦, ●
Cars Avoid You	⇧, ⇧, ⇨, ⇩, ▲, ●, ●, ■
Clear Weather	⇦, ⇩, R1, L1, ⇨, ⇧, ⇦, ✕
Destroy Cars Near You	L1, R1, R1, ⇦, ⇨, ■, ⇩, R1
Foggy Weather	⇦, ⇩, ▲, ✕, ⇩, ⇧, ⇦, L1
Full Armor	⇧, ⇩, ⇦, ⇨, ■, ■, L1, R1
Full Health	⇧, ⇩, ⇦, ⇨, ●, ●, L1, R1
$250,000	⇧, ⇩, ⇦, ⇨, ✕, ✕, L1, R1
Guy Magnet	⇨, L1, ⇩, L1, ●, ⇧, L1, ■
Never Wanted (turns off after rampages)	⇧, ⇨, ▲, ▲, ⇩, ⇦, ✕, ✕
No Traction	⇩, ⇦, ⇧, L1, R1, ▲, ●, ✕
Overcast Weather	⇦, ⇩, L1, R1, ⇨, ⇧, ⇦, ■
Pedestrians Attack You	⇩, ▲, ⇧, ✕, L1, R1, L1, R1
Pedestrians Have Weapons	⇧, L1, ⇩, R1, ⇦, ●, ⇨, ▲
Pedestrians Riot	R1, L1, L1, ⇩, ⇦, ●, ⇩, L1
Rainy Weather	⇦, ⇩, L1, R1, ⇨, ⇧, ⇦, ▲
Raise Wanted Level	⇧, ⇨, ■, ■, ⇩, ⇦, ●, ●
Slow Down Game	⇦, ⇦, ●, ●, ⇩, ⇧, ▲, ✕
Spawn Rhino Tank	⇧, L1, ⇩, R1, ⇦, L1, ⇨, R1
Spawn Trashmaster Truck	⇩, ⇧, ⇨, ▲, L1, ▲, L1, ▲
Speed Up Clock	R1, L1, L1, ⇧, ⇩, ✕, ⇩, L1
Speed Up Game	⇦, ⇦, R1, R1, ⇧, ▲, ⇩, ✕
Sunny Weather	⇦, ⇩, R1, L1, ⇨, ⇧, ⇦, ●

Grand Theft Auto: Vice City Stories (continued)

Unlockable	How To
Color Changed to Black (Except for Cop Cars)	L1, R1, L1, R1, ⇦, ●, ⇧, ✕
Vehicles Color Changed to Chrome	⇨, ⇧, ⇦, ⇩, ▲, ▲, L1, R1
Wasted! (Commit Suicide)	⇨, ⇨, ●, ●, L1, R1, ⇩, ✕
Infinite Ammo	100% Completion
Watch Mission Cutscenes at Clymenus Suite	100% Completion
AK-47	Collect 50 Balloons
Armor	Collect 60 Balloons
Equalizer (Pistol with Scope)	Collect 80 Balloons
Flamethrower	Collect 70 Balloons
M249 Machine Gun	Collect 99 Balloons
Molotov Cocktails	Collect 40 Balloons
Pistol	Collect 10 Balloons
Scorpion (SMG)	Collect 20 Balloons
Sniper Rifle	Collect 90 Balloons
Stubby Shotgun	Collect 30 Balloons
All Taxis have "Jump" feature (L3)	Complete 50 fares on Taxi missions
Armor Boost	Beat all 15 levels of the "Vigilante" side mission
Become Fireproof	Beat all 15 levels of the "Firefighter" side mission
Bulletproof Empire Vehicles	Take over all 30 Empire Businesses
Free Pay N Spray	Deliver all 32 cars to the Impound Yard
Health Boost	Beat all 15 levels of the "Air Ambulance" side mission
Infinite Sprinting	Beat all 15 levels of the "Paramedic" side mission
Infinite Swimming Strength	Beat all 15 levels of the "Beach Patrol" side mission
Army Fatigues	Beat the mission "Over the Top"
Casual Clothes	Beat the mission "Conduct Unbecoming"
Cuban Clothes	Beat all of Umberto's missions
Hired Muscle Clothes	Purchase a "High Roller" Protection Racket building
Hood Clothes	Purchase a "High Roller" Robbery building
Leisure Clothes	Purchase a "High Roller" Prostitution building
Mr. Repo Clothes	Purchase a "High Roller" Loan Shark building
Pastel Suit	Beat the mission "Brawn of the Dead"
Smart Suit	Complete all Empire side missions
Smuggler Clothes	Purchase a "High Roller" Smuggling building
Track Suit	Purchase a "High Roller" Drug Dealer building
Trailer Trash Clothes	Beat the mission "D.I.V.O.R.C.E"
Wetsuit	Complete all 8 Jetski races at the Film Studio
Winner Outfit	Beat the mission "Last Stand"
Bovver '64	Complete "White Lies" (behind third safehouse)

DS
GBA
PSP
PS2
PS3
Wii
Xbox
Xbox 360
Index

Grand Theft Auto: Vice City Stories (continued)

Unlockable	How To
Bulletproof BF Injection	Complete "Beach Patrol" (Sunshine Autos)
Bulletproof Sanchez	Complete "Conduct Unbecoming" (First safehouse)
Bulletproof Stretch	Complete "Kill Phil" (Sunshine Autos)
Bulletproof Ventoso	Complete "To Victor, the Spoils" (King Knuts, Downtown)
Jetski	Complete "From Zero to Hero" (south of Stadium)
Little Willie	Complete "From Zero to Hero" (On roof of third safehouse)
Marquis	Complete "From Zero to Hero" (opposite first safehouse)
Quad Bike	Complete "When Funday Comes" (Sunshine Autos)
Skimmer	Complete "From Zero to Hero" (Behind third safehouse)
SPLITZ-6 ATV	Complete "From Zero to Hero" (Second safehouse)
Squallo	Complete "From Zero to Hero" (near second safehouse and junkyard)

Great Escape

Press the following button combinations at the Main menu.

Unlockable	Code
All Movies	L2, L2, ■, ●, ●, R2, R1, ■, ■, ●, L2, R1
Level Select	■, L2, ■, R1, ●, R2, ●, L2, L2, R2, ●, ■
Unlimited Ammo	■, ●, L2, R1, R2, L2, ●, ■, L2, R1, L2, R1

Gretzky NHL 2005

To enter this password, go to the Unlockables screen and press START.

Unlockable	Password
Unlock Everything	SHOENLOC

Guitar Hero

Enter these codes on Game Mode selection screen.

Unlockable	Code
Crowd has Monkey Heads	Blue, Orange, Yellow, Yellow, Yellow, Blue, Orange
Crowd has Skull Heads	Orange, Yellow, Blue, Blue, Orange, Yellow, Blue, Blue
Character uses Air Guitar	Orange, Orange, Blue, Yellow, Orange
Rock meter will always stay green	Yellow, Blue, Orange, Orange, Blue, Blue, Yellow, Orange
Unlock Everything	Yellow, Orange, Blue, Blue, Orange, Yellow, Yellow
Unlocks Hero Guitar	Blue, Orange, Yellow, Blue, Blue
Venue Disappears	Blue, Yellow, Orange, Blue, Yellow, Orange

Guitar Hero 2

Enter codes at the main menu.

Unlockable	Code
Air Guitar	Yellow, Yellow, Blue, Orange, Yellow, Blue
Crowd Has Eyeball Heads	Blue, Orange, Yellow, Orange, Yellow, Orange, Blue
Crowd Has Monkey Heads	Orange, Blue, Yellow, Yellow, Orange, Blue, Yellow, Yellow
Flaming Head	Orange, Yellow, Orange, Orange, Yellow, Orange, Yellow, Yellow
Horse Head	Blue, Orange, Orange, Blue, Orange, Orange, Blue, Orange, Orange, Blue
Hyper Speed	Orange, Blue, Orange, Yellow, Orange, Blue, Orange, Yellow
Performance mode	Yellow, Yellow, Blue, Yellow, Yellow, Orange, Yellow, Yellow

DS

GBA

PSP

PS2

PS3

Wii

Xbox

Xbox 360

Index

Guitar Hero Encore: Rocks the 80s

At the main menu, enter a code to get the desired effect.

G: Press the Green fret button.

R: Press the Red fret button.

Y: Press the Yellow fret button.

B: Press the Blue fret button.

O: Press the Orange fret button.

Code	Code Effect
Y,B,Y,O,B,B	Air Guitar
Y,B,O,O,O,B,Y	Crowd Has Eyeball Heads
B,B,O,Y,B,B,O,Y	Crowd Has Monkey Heads
Y,O,Y,O,Y,O,B,O	Flame Head
B,O,O,B,Y,B,O,O,B,Y	Horse Head
Y,B,O,O,B,Y,Y,O	Hyperspeed Activate/De-Activate
B,B,O,Y,Y,B,O,B	Performance Mode
B,O,Y,R,O,Y,B,Y,R,Y,B,Y,R,Y,B,Y	Unlock Everything

Unlockable Guitars

Complete the following to be able to buy the guitar in the shop.

Unlockable	How to Unlock
Axe Guitar	Beat Expert Career
Casket Guitar	Beat Medium Career
Eyeball Guitar	Five star every song on Hard Career
Fish Guitar	Beat Easy Career
Snaketapus Guitar	Beat Hard Career
The LOG Guitar	Five star every song on Expert Career
USA Guitar	Five star every song on Easy Career
Viking Guitar	Five star every song on Medium Career

Gun Griffon Blaze

Description	Hint
Start With Different Weapons	Which country your pilot is from determines which set of weapons your mech is outfitted with. Change your pilot's origin to equip your mech with different weapons. From the Main menu select Create New Pilot. From here, you can rename your pilot and change other statistics.

Half-Life

Go to Options, then Cheat Codes, and enter the following:

Unlockable	Code
Alien Mode	↑,▲,↑,▲,↑,▲,↑,▲
Infinite Ammo	↓,×,←,●,↓,×,←,●
Invincibility	←,■,↑,▲,→,●,↓,×
Invisibility	←,■,→,●,←,■,→,●
Slow Motion	→,■,↑,▲,→,■,↑,▲
Xen Gravity	↑,▲,↓,×,↑,▲,↓,×

DS

GBA

PSP

PS2

PS3

Wii

Xbox

Xbox 360

Index

Harry Potter and the Chamber of Secrets

Unlockables

Unlockable	How to Unlock
Nimbus 2000 Broomstick	On the second day of school, go to the Quidditch practice and complete the training with a B or better rank.

Harry Potter and the Order of the Phoenix

Unlockable Trophies in the Room of Rewards

Perform the following tasks to unlock new trophies in the Room of Rewards:

Unlockable	How to Unlock
Architecture Cup	Uncover all the 12 hidden Hogwarts symbols
Characters Cup	Meet all 58 characters in Hogwarts
Defence Against the Dark Arts Cup	Cast all defensive spells in six duels
Exploding Snap Cup	Beat all 2 Exploding Snap champions
Explorer Cup	Find all known areas of Hogwarts
Famous Witches and Wizards Cup	Find the 15 hidden wizard plaques around Hogwarts
Friends of the Year Cup	Finish the story, find 5 Luna's lost belongings
Golden Gobstone Cup	Beat all 4 Gobstones champions
Grandmasters Cup	Beat all 3 wizard chess champions
Homework Cup	Complete all 3 teacher mini-quests
House Ghost Cup	Find all four House Ghosts
Nature Trail Cup	Find all animal footprints
Ornithology Cup	Find all the 5 flying creatures of Hogwarts
Portrait Password Cup	Find all 12 portrait passwords in Hogwarts
School Pride Cup	Complete all 66 Hogwarts chores
Secret Statue Cup	Find the 12 secret wizard chess statues of Hogwarts
Smugglers Cup	Find 12 Fred and George's hidden parcels around Hogwarts
Studious Success Cup	Get an 'O' (Outstanding) in all lessons.

Haunted Mansion

While playing hold right on the d-pad and enter these codes.

Unlockable	Code
God Mode	■, ●, ●, ●, ■, ●, ▲, ✕
Level Select	●, ●, ■, ▲, ▲, ■, ●, ✕
Upgrade Weapon	■, ■, ▲, ▲, ●, ●, ●, ✕

Headhunter

Description	Code
Activate Cheat Mode	Hold R1 + ■ and press START during gameplay.

Heroes of the Pacific

Enter these codes at the Main menu. Note that you will disable game-saving when these codes are entered.

Unlockable	Code
Cheat Menu	L1, R2, L2, R3, R1, L3

Heroes of the Pacific (continued)

Unlockable	Code
Unlock all planes and missions	Right Analog stick up, Right Analog stick down, Right Analog stick left, R2, L1, Right Analog stick right
Unlock Japanese Planes	●, R2, L1, L2, ⇦, ⇧
Upgrade planes	L1, Right Analog stick left, R2, Right Analog stick right, ⇨, ⇩

Hitman: Blood Money

On the Opera House mission, in the basement at the back part of the stage, there is a room that leads to staircases to bathrooms on the first floor. After heading down the stairs, enter a room, kill the three rats on the ground, and check the bench at the end of the room. There is a keycard for the rat club. Head to the second level where you collect the lightroom keycard. There is a door that cannot be opened. Use the rat club keycard and in there are rats boxing and gambling.

Hitman: Contracts

Unlockable	Code
Complete Level	During gameplay, press R2, L2, ↑, ↓, X, L3, ●, X, ●, X
Level Select	In the Main menu, press ■, ▲, ●, ←, ↑, →, L2, R2

Hitman 2: Silent Assassin

Enter the following codes during gameplay.

Description	Code
All Weapons	R2, L2, ↑, ↓, X, ↑, ■, X
Bomb Mode	R2, L2, ↑, ↓, X, ↑, L1
Full Heal	R2, L2, ↑, ↓, X, ↑, ↓
God Mode	R2, L2, ↑, ↓, X, R2, L2, R1, L1
Lethal Charge	R2, L2, ↑, ↓, X, R1, R1
Level Skip	R2, L2, ↑, ↓, X, L3, ●, X, ●, X Enable this code immediately after starting a level to complete it with a Silent Assassin rank.
Megaforce Mode	R2, L2, ↑, ↓, X, R2, R2 Restart the level to remove its effect.
Nailgun Mode (Weapons pin people to walls.)	R2, L2, ↑, ↓, X, L1, L1
Punch Mode	R2, L2, ↑, ↓, X, ↑, ↑
Slow Motion	R2, L2, ↑, ↓, X, ↑, L2
SMG and 9mm Pistol SD	L2, R2, ↑, ↓, X, ↑, R2, R2
Toggle Gravity	R2, L2, ↑, ↓, X, L2, L2
Level Select	R2, L2, ↑, ↓, ■, ▲, ●

Hot Shots Golf 3

Description	Code
In-Game Reset	Press L1 + R1 + L2 + R2 + START + SELECT during gameplay.
Left-Handed Golfer	Press START when selecting a golfer.

DS
GBA
PSP
PS2
PS3
Wii
Xbox
Xbox 360
Index

Hot Shots Golf FORE!

In the Options menu, go into the Password screen to enter these passwords.

Unlockable	Password
Capsule 1	WXAFSJ
Capsule 2	OEINLK
Capsule 3	WFKVTG
Capsule 4	FCAVDO
Capsule 5	YYPOKK
Capsule 6	GDQDOF
Capsule 7	HHXKPV
Capsule 8	UOKXPS
Capsule 9	LMIRYD
Capsule 10	MJLJEQ
Capsule 11	MHNCQI
Price Reduction	MKJEFQ
Tourney Rank Down	XKWGFZ
Unlock 100t Hammer Club	NFSNHR
Unlock All Golfers	REZTWS
Unlock Aloha Beach Resort	XSREHD
Unlock Bagpipe Classic	CRCNHZ
Unlock Beginner's Ball	YFQJJI
Unlock Big Air Club	DLJMFZ
Unlock Bir Air Ball	CRCGKR
Unlock Blue Lagoon C.C.	WVRJQS
Unlock Caddie Clank	XCQGWJ
Unlock Caddie Daxter	WSIKIN
Unlock Caddie Kayla	MZIMEL
Unlock Caddie Kaz	LNNZJV
Unlock Caddie Simon	WRHZNB
Unlock Caddie Sophie	UTWIVQ
Unlock Dream G.C.	OQUTNA
Unlock Everybody's CD - Voice Version	UITUGF
Unlock Extra Pose Cam	UEROOK
Unlock Extra Swing Cam	RJIFQS
Unlock Extra Video	DPYHIU
Unlock Heckletts	DIXWFE
Unlock HSG Rules	FKDHDS
Unlock Infinity Ball	DJXBRG
Unlock Infinity Club	RZTQGV

Unlockable	Password
Unlock Landing Grid	MQTIMV
Unlock Menu Character Brad	ZKJSIO
Unlock Menu Character Phoebe	LWVLCB
Unlock Menu Character Renee	AVIQXS
Unlock Mike Costume	YKCFEZ
Unlock Mini-Golf 2 G.C.	RVMIRU
Unlock Nanako Costume	BBLSKQ
Unlock Phoebe Costume	GJBCHY
Unlock Pin Hole Ball	VZLSGP
Unlock Replay Cam A	PVJEMF
Unlock Replay Cam B	EKENCR
Unlock Replay Cam C	ZUHHAC
Unlock Sidespin Ball	JAYQRK
Unlock Silkroad Classic	ZKOGJM
Unlock Suzuki Costume	ARFLCR
Unlock Turbo Spin Ball	XNETOK
Unlock United Forest G.C.	UIWHLZ
Unlock Wallpaper Set 2	RODDHQ
Unlock Western Valley C.C.	LIBTFL
Unlock Wild Green C.C.	YZLOXE
Upgrade 100t Hammer Club to mid-level	BVLHSI
Upgrade Big Air Club from mid-level to top level	JIDTQI
Upgrade Big Air Club to mid-level	TOSXUJ
Upgrade Infinity Club from mid-level to top level	EIPCUL
Upgrade Infinity Club to mid-level	WTGFOR
Upgrade Pin Hole Club from mid-level to top level	RBXVEL
Upgrade Pin Hole Club to mid-level	TTIMHT
Upgrade Turbo Spin Club from mid-level to top level	DTIZAB
Upgrade Turbo Spin Club to mid-level	NIWKWP

Hot Wheels Velocity X

Unlockable	Code
All Cars and Tracks	In the Main menu, hold $L1$ + $R1$ and press ●, ■, ■, ▲, ✕

DS
GBA
PSP
PS2
PS3
Wii
Xbox
Xbox 360
Index

DS
GBA
PSP
PS2
PS3
Wii
Xbox
Xbox 360
Index

The Hulk

From Options, select Code Input and enter the following. When done, go to Special Features and select Cheats to activate them.

Unlockable	Code
Double Hulk HP	HLTHDSE
Full Rage Meter	ANGMNGT
Half Enemies HP	MMMYHLP
Invulnerability	GMMSKIN
Puzzle Solved	BRCESTN
Regenerator	FLSHWND
Reset High Score	NMBTHIH
Unlimited continues	GRNCHTR
Unlock all levels	TRUBLVR
Wicked Punch	FSTOFRY

Enter the following codes at the Code Terminal.

Unlockable	Code
Play as Gray Hulk	"JANITOR"
Desert Battle Art	"FIFTEEN"
Hulk Movie FMV Art	"NANOMED"
Hulk Transformed Art	"SANFRAN"
Hulk vs. Hulk Dogs Art	"PITBULL"

Ice Age 2

Pause the game to enter these codes.

Unlockable	Code
Unlimited Energy	⇩, ⇦, ⇨, ⇩, ⇩, ⇨, ⇦, ⇩
Unlimited Health	⇧, ⇨, ⇩, ⇧, ⇩, ⇩, ⇨, ⇦
Unlimited Pebbles	⇩, ⇩, ⇦, ⇧, ⇧, ⇨, ⇧, ⇩

I-Ninja

To enter the following codes, pause the game and enter code.

Unlockable	Code
Big Head	Hold R1 and press ▲,▲,▲,▲. Release R1, hold L1, and press ▲,▲. Hold R1+L1, and press ▲,●,▲.
Level Skip	Hold R1 and press ■,■,■,●. Release R1, hold L1, and press ▲,▲. Release L1, hold R1, and press ■,■.
Sword Upgrade	Hold L1+R1 and press ●,■,●,▲,▲,■,●,■.

The Incredible Hulk: Ultimate Destruction

At the Code Input screen, enter the following codes.

Unlockable	Code
5,000 Smash Points	SMASH5
10,000 Smash Points	SMASH10
15,000 Smash Points	SMASH15
Abomination (must complete Story mode first)	VILLAIN
All Vehicles Become Taxis	CABBIES
American Flag Shorts	AMERICA
Black and White Graphics	RETRO
Canadian Flag Shorts	OCANADA
Cow Missiles	CHZGUN
Double Hulk's Damage Abilities	DESTROY
Double Value of Health Pickups	BRINGIT

DS

GBA

PSP

PS2

PS3

Wii

Xbox

Xbox 360

Index

The Incredible Hulk: Ultimate Destruction (continued)

Unlockable	Code
French Flag Shorts	DRAPEAU
German Flag Shorts	DEUTSCH
Gorilla Invasion Mode	KINGKNG
Gray Hulk (without suit)	CLASSIC
Grey Hulk Mr. Fix It	SUITFIT
Italian Flag Shorts	Mutanda
Japanese Flag Shorts	FURAGGU
Low Gravity	PILLOWS
Mass Transit On/Off	TRANSIT
Sepia Mode	HISTORY
Spanish Flag Shorts	BANDERA
Union Jack Flag Shorts	FSHNCHP
Wild Traffic	FROGGIE

The Incredibles

Some of these codes only work on certain levels and certain characters. Pause the game, choose Secrets, and enter the following:

Unlockable	Code
Blurry Game	LOSTGLASSES
Credits	YOURNAMEINLIGHTS
Ethereal View	EMODE
Eye Laser	GAZERBEAM
Fast Motion Game	SASSMODE
Game 20% Easier	BOAPLACE
Giant Head	EINSTEINIUM
Heads up Display	BHUD
Heavy Iron Logo	HI
Henchmen Bounce More	SPRINGBREAK
Infinite Incredi-Power for Elastigirl	FLEXIBLE
Inverts Aiming Controls for Turrets	INVERTURRET
Inverts Camera Control on the X-axis	INVERTCAMERAX
Inverts Camera Control on the Y-axis	INVERTCAMERAY
Invincible Dash (Damage and Collisions)	GILGENDASH
Mr. Incredible Glows When Swimming	TOWNIE
Mr. Incredible Lights Plants on Fire	PINKSLIP
One Hit Kills	KRONOS
Refill 30 Health	UUDDLRLRBAS
Slow Motion	BWTHEMOVIE
Tiny Head	DEEVOLVE
Unlimited Incredi-Power (Limited Time)	DANIELTHEFLASH
Violet has Infinite Invisibility Power (Limited Time)	TONYLOAF
Weakens Bomb Damage	LABOMBE

The Incredibles: Rise of the Underminer

To enter these codes, pause the game. Press o to open the menu, then select Secrets to enter a password.

Unlockable	Password
All of Frozone's moves upgraded	FROZMASTER
All of Mr. Incredible's moves upgraded	MRIMASTER

The Incredibles: Rise of the Underminer (continued)

To enter these codes, pause the game. Press o to open the menu, then select Secrets to enter a password.

Unlockable	Password
Frozone's Super Move	FROZBOOM
Give Frozone 1,000 Experience Points	FROZPROF
Give Mr. Incredible 1,000 Experience Points	MRIPROF
Mr. Incredible's Super Move	MRIBOOM

Jak II

Unlockables

Do the following tasks during gameplay to unlock these items.

Unlockable	How to Unlock
Alt. Scrap Book	Collect 200 orbs
Big Head	Collect 30 orbs
Hero Mode	Collect 200 orbs
Invunerability	Collect 175 orbs
Jak's Goatee	Collect 5 orbs
Level Select	Collect 145 orbs
Mirror World	Collect 15 orbs
Peace Maker Gun Course	Collect 105 orbs
Reverse Races	Collect 135 orbs
Scene Player Act 1	Collect 65 orbs
Scene Player Act 2	Collect 95 orbs
Scene Player Act 3	Collect 125 orbs
Scrap Book	Collect 55 orbs
Small Head	Collect 45 orbs
Unlimited Ammo	Collect 155 orbs
Unlimited Dark Jak	Collect 165 orbs
Vulcan Fury	Collect 75 orbs

Jak 3

Secrets

Buy these in the Secret menu.

Unlockable	How to Unlock
Audio Commentary	5 Precursor Orbs after buying scene players 1-3
Bad Weather	5 Precursor Orbs after Act 1-1
Big Head Mode	3 Precursor Orbs after Act 1-1
Blaster Damage Upgrade	6 Precursor Orbs after Act 1-9
Dark Jak Invisibility	25 Precursor Orbs after Act 3-11
Fast Movies	5 Precursor Orbs after Act 1-1
Hero Mode	5 precursor orbs, after finishing the game
Increased Blaster Gun Ammo Capacity	4 Precursor Orbs after Act 1-17
Increased Peace Maker Ammo Capacity	4 Precursor Orbs after Act 2-19
Increased Scatter Gun Ammo Capacity	4 Precursor Orbs after Act 1-17
Increased Vulcan Fury Ammo Capacity	4 Precursor Orbs after Act 1-24

DS

GBA

PSP

PS2

PS3

Wii

Xbox

Xbox 360

Index

DS

GBA

PSP

PS2

PS3

Wii

Xbox

Xbox 360

Index

Jak 3 (continued)

Invulnerability	100 Precursor Orbs after Act 3-11
Jak 3 Model Viewer	2 Precursor Orbs after Act 3-11
Jak and Daxter Model Viewer	2 Precursor Orbs after Act 1-24
Jak II Model Viewer	2 Precursor Orbs after Act 2-25
Level Select: ACT 1	5 Precursor Orbs, buy it after Act 1

Level Select: ACT 2 5 Precursor Orbs, buy it after Act 2		**Peace Maker Increased Radius** 6 Precursor Orbs after Act 2-19	
Level Select: ACT 3 5 Precursor Orbs, buy it after Act 3		**Rachet and Clank Gun Courses** 6 Precursor Orbs after Act 2-12	
Mega Scrap Book 2 Precursor Orbs after Act 3-11		**Scatter Gun Rate-Of-Fire Upgrade** 6 Precursor Orbs after Act 1-9	
Mirror World 5 Precursor Orbs after Act 1-1		**Scene Player Act 1** 2 Precursor Orbs after Act 1	

Scene Player Act 2	2 Precursor Orbs after Act 2
Scene Player Act 3	2 Precursor Orbs after Act 3
Scrap Book	2 Precursor Orbs after Act 1-24
Slow Movies	5 Precursor Orbs after Act 1-1
Small Head Mode	3 Precursor Orbs after Act 1-1
Toggle Jak's Goatee	2 Precursor Orbs after Act 1-1
Unlimited Ammo	50 Precursor Orbs after Act 3-11
Unlimited Dark Jak	50 Precursor Orbs after Act 3-11
Unlimited Light Jak	50 Precursor Orbs after Act 3-11
Unlimited Vechicle Turbos	30 Precursor Orbs after Act 2-25
Upgrade Vechicle Toughness	15 Precursor Orbs after Act 2-14
Vulcan Fury Damage Upgrade	6 Precursor Orbs after Act 1-17

James Bond 007: Everything or Nothing

Cheats are unlocked depending on how many platinum 007s you've earned. To activate a cheat once it is unlocked, pause the game and enter the code listed underneath the cheat.

Platinum	Cheat	Code
1	Golden Gun	●, ▲, ✕, ●, ▲
3	Improved Traction	●, ✕, ✕, ■, ▲
5	Improved Battery	●, ■, ●, ■, ▲
7	Double Ammo	●, ●, ✕, ●, ▲
9	Double Damage	●, ▲, ▲, ■, ●
11	Full Ammo	●, ●, ▲, ■, ■
13	Cloak	●, ▲, ✕, ▲, ■
15	Full Battery	●, ▲, ▲, ✕, ●
17	All Weapons	●, ▲, ✕, ✕, ●
19	Unlimited Battery	●, ■, ●, ■, ▲
23	Unlimited Ammo	●, ✕, ■, ✕, ●
25	Slow Motion Driving	●, ■, ▲, ✕, ▲
27	Platinum Gun	●, ■, ■, ●, ✕

Unlockable	Objective	Unlockable	Objective
All Weapons	17 Platinum	Cayenne Upgrade	12 Gold
Baron Samedi	50 Points	Cistern	30 Points
Burn Chamber	370 Points	Cloak	13 Platinum

James Bond 007: Everything or Nothing (continued)

Unlockable	Objective	Unlockable	Objective
Diavolo Moscow	400 Points	Production Stills 1	1 Gold
Double Ammo	7 Platinum	Production Stills 2	2 Gold
Double Damage	9 Platinum	Production Stills 3	3 Gold
Egypt Commander	90 Points	Production Stills 4	4 Gold
Egypt Guard	180 Points	Production Stills 5	5 Gold
Full Ammo	11 Platinum	Production Stills 6	7 Gold
Full Battery	15 Platinum	Production Stills 7	9 Gold
Gallery	27 Gold	Production Stills 8	13 Gold
Golden Gun	1 Platinum	Production Stills 9	16 Gold
Hazmat Guard	110 Points	Production Stills 10	18 Gold
Helicopter Upgrade	6 Gold	Production Stills 11	19 Gold
Improved Battery	5 Platinum	Production Stills 12	22 Gold
Improved Traction	3 Platinum	Production Stills 13	23 Gold
Katya	20 Gold	Production Stills 14	25 Gold
Katya Jumpsuit	320 Points	Serena	350 Points
Le Rouge	260 Points	Serena	430 Points
Moscow Guard	230 Points	Serena	8 Gold
MI6 Combat Simulator	Complete all Missions	Slow Motion Driving	25 Platinum
		South Commander	210 Points
MI6 Survival Test	Complete all Missions	Tank Upgrade	10 Gold
Miss Nagai	450 Points	Test Lab	160 Points
Miss Nagai	17 Gold	Triumph Upgrade	21 Gold
Mya	130 Points	Underworld	11 Gold
Mya	14 Gold	Unlimited Ammo	23 Platinum
Nanotank Upgrade	24 Gold	Unlimited Battery	19 Platinum
Odd Job	70 Points	Vanquish Upgrade	15 Gold
003	290 Points		
Platinum Gun	27 Platinum		

Jaws Unleashed

Enter these passwords as Profile names.

Unlockable	Password	Unlockable	Password
1 Million Points	Blooood	Unlock all Bonuses	Shaaark

Jeremy McGrath Supercross World

Enter the following codes at the Main menu.

Unlockable	Code
Unlimited Turbo Boost	R2, L1, ■, ●, ●, ●
Weird Gravity	⇧, ⇧, ⇧, ⇧, R2, ■, ●

Juiced

Enter this password in the Password menu.

Unlockable	Password
All Cars in Arcade Mode	PINT

Justice League Heroes

To enter these codes, pause the game and hold L1, L2, R1, R2

Unlockable	Code
Gives 20 points to shields	⇧, ⇧, ⇩, ⇩
Gives 25 Random Boosts	⇦, ⇨, ⇦, ⇨

DS

GBA

PSP

PS2

PS3

Wii

Xbox

Xbox 360

Index

Justice League Heroes (continued)

Invincibility	⇦, ⇩, ⇨, ⇧, ⇦, ⇩, ⇨, ⇧
Maxes out abilities	⇨, ⇩, ⇨, ⇩
Unlimited Energy	⇩, ⇩, ⇨, ⇨, ⇧, ⇧, ⇦, ⇦
Unlock everything	⇩, ⇦, ⇧, ⇧, ⇨

Karaoke Revolution Volume 2

Enter the following codes at the main title screen.

Unlockable	Code
GMR (Aneeka)	→, ←, R3, ←, ↑, ↑, L3, ↓, ●, ■
Harmonix (Ishani)	L3, ●, ↑, ●, ■, L3, ↓, ↓, R3
Konami (Dwyane)	→, R3, →, R3, ■, →, ●, ■, ↓, ←

Kelly Slater's Pro Surfer

To enter the following codes select the "Extras" option, and then choose "Cheats." Enter each code for the desired unlockable. An "Unlocked" message confirms correct code entry.

Unlockable	Code	Unlockable	Code
All Boards	6195554141	Select	3285554497
All Objectives Completed	8565558792	Master Code	7145558092
		Maximum Stats	2125551776
All Suits	7025552918	Perfect Balance	2135555721
All Surfers	9495556799	Play as Freak	3105556217
All Tricks	6265556043	Play as Rainbow	8185555555
First-Person View	8775553825 Pause gameplay and choose the "Camera Settings" option to change the view.	Play as Tiki God	8885554506
		Play as Tony Hawk	3235559787
		Play as Travis Pastrana	8005556292
Higher Jumps	2175550217	Trippy Graphics	8185551447

Killzone

Enter these codes at the Main menu.

Unlockable	Code
Big Head Enemies	Hold L1 and press ●, ■, ✕, ●, ●
More Powerful Weapons	Hold L1 and press ●, ▲, ●, ▲, ✕
Unlock All Levels and Characters	Enter Shooterman as a profile name
Unlocks All Movies	Hold L1 and press ●, ■, ▲, ●, ■

King of Route 66

Description	Objective
Tornado Truckers for VS Battle	Win Rival Chase 5 times in a row to unlock all of the Tornado Truckers for VS Battle mode.

> **NOTE**
>
> *Each win will unlock the Tornado Truckers in this order: Bigfoot, Lizard Tail, Luna Queen, Danny Edge, and Mr. Crown.*

Kingdom Hearts

Unlockables

Unlockable	How to Unlock
Adamant Shield	For sale at the Item Shop in Traverse Town
Aero	Defeat Opposite Armor in Traverse Town
Aeroga	Find all 99 Dalmations
Aerora	Located in the room behind a Yellow Trinity in Neverland
Blizzaga	Defeat Behemoth in the Hades Cup
Blizzara	Defeat Jafar (normal form) in Agrabah
Blizzard	Find all 4 pieces of evidence in Wonderland
Crabclaw	Seal Atlantica
Cura	Defeat Shadow Sora in Neverland
Curaga	Talk to Aerith in the library in Hollow Bastion
Cure	Defeat Clayton in the Deep Jungle
Defender	A rare item dropped by Defenders in Hollow Bastion
Diamond Dust (only available in Final Mix)	Beat Ice Titan in the Gold Cup
Divine Rose	Talk to Belle in the Hollow Bastion Library
Dream Rod	Acquire every spell and visit Merlin
Dream Shield	This can be found after obtaining all seven spell arts items from white mushrooms and then talking to Merlin
Fairy Harp	Seal Neverland
Fira	Defeat Jafar (genie form) in Agrabah
Firaga	Receive during chat with princesses in Hollow Bastion
Fire	Defeat Guard Armor in Traverse Town
Genji Shield	Beat Yuffie in the Hades Cup
Gigas Fist	For sale at the Item Shop in Traverse Town
Gold Match	Complete the Hades Cup
Golem Shield	For sale at the Item Shop in Traverse Town
Grand Mallet	For sale at the Item Shop in Traverse Town
Graviga	Defeat Hades in the Hades Cup
Gravira	Defeat Oogie Boogie(second form)
Gravity	Finish the Phil Cup
Gummi Collection	Retrieve all 99 Dalmatian Puppies, then you will get the entire Gummi Collections from Pongo and Perdita, along with an Aero Spell Upgrade
Hades Cup	Seal Hollow Bastion keyhole and unlock all other tournaments
Herc's Shield	Beat the Hercules Cup
Hercules Cup	Seal Halloween Town and Neverland keyhole
Jungle King	Seal the Deep Jungle
Lady Luck	In a white trinity mark in Wonderland
Lionheart	Beat Leon and Cloud in the Hades Cup
Lord Fortune	Get every summon and visit the Fairy Godmother
Magus Staff	For sale at the Item Shop in Traverse Town
Metal Chocobo	Defeat Cloud in the Hercules Cup
Morning Star	For sale at the Item Shop in Traverse Town

Kingdom Hearts (continued)

Unlockable	How to Unlock
Mythril Shield	For sale at the Item Shop in Traverse Town
Oathkeeper	Talk to Kairi in the Secret Waterway in Traverse Town
Oblivion	In a chest in Hollow Bastion's Grand Hall
Olympia	Complete all the cup tournaments at the coliseum
One Winged Angel (only available in Final Mix)	Beat Sephiroth in Platinum Match
Onyx Shield	For sale at the Item Shop in Traverse Town
Pegasus Cup	Complete Monstro
Phil Cup	Seal Traverse Town keyhole
Platinum Match	Seal Hollow Bastion keyhole
Pumpkinhead	Seal Halloween Town
Save the King	Beat the Hades Cup time attack
Save the Queen	Beat the Hades Cup solo
Shooting Star	For sale at the Item Shop in Traverse Town
Silver Mallet	For sale at the Item Shop in Traverse Town
Smasher	For sale at the Item Shop in Traverse Town
Spellbinder	Speak to Merlin after getting all first level (Fire, Blizzard, etc.) magic
Stop	Defeat Parasite Cage in Monstro
Stopga	Defeat the optional boss, Phantom, in Neverland
Stopra	Finish the "Pooh's Swing" minigame in 100 Acre Woods
Stout Shield	For sale at the Item Shop in Traverse Town
Three Wishes	Seal Agrabah
Thundaga	Defeat Cerberus the second time in the Hades cup
Thundara	Defeat Ursula (large form)
Thunder	Finish the barrel smashing training in the coliseum
Ultima Weapon	Synthesize all the items at the Moogles Workshop, and it will be an item you can synthesize
Violetta	White Trinity in Olympus Coliseum
Warhammer	For sale at the Item Shop in Traverse Town
Wisdom Staff	For sale at the Item Shop in Traverse Town
Wishing Star	Save Pinnochio from Monstro, and Geppetto gives it to you in his house in Traverse Town
Wizard's Relic	A rare item dropped by Wizards in Hollow Bastion

Summons

Unlockable	How to Unlock
Bambi	Receive the Naturespark Gem by playing Pooh's Hunny Hunt, then give it to the Fairy Godmother
Dumbo	Obtain the Watergleam Gem from a chest in Monstro's Mouth, then give it to the Fairy Godmother
Genie	Seal Agrabah's keyhole
Mushu	Defeat Dragon-Maleficent to obtain Fireglow Gem, then give it to the Fairy Godmother
Simba	Speak to Leon early at Secret Waterway then go to Merlin's house and talk to Fairy Godmother
Tinker Bell	Seal Neverland's Keyhole

DS · GBA · PSP · PS2 · PS3 · Wii · Xbox · Xbox 360 · Index

Kingdom Hearts (continued)

Unlockable	How to Unlock

Torn Pages

After completing the second Traverse Town quest, an old book appears in Merlin's House. Specifically, it's a copy of Winnie-the-Pooh, although it's missing a few pages. To restore the different locations to Pooh's world, and in the process unlock a wide selection of mini-games and hidden items, find the following Torn Pages.

Unlockable	How to Unlock
Torn Page 1	Traverse Town: Rescue 51 Dalmatians
Torn Page 2	Agrabah: Dark Chamber in the Cave of Wonders
Torn Page 3	Monstro: Chamber 6
Torn Page 4	Halloweentown: The bookcase in the Doctor's Lab
Torn Page 5	Atlantica: Ariel's Grotto

Unlockable Weapons

Unlockable	How to Unlock
Save The King (Goofy)	Complete the Hades Cup in time limit mode
Save The Queen (Donald)	Complete the Hades Cup alone (just with Sora)
Ultima Weapon (Sora)	Synthesize all 24 items in the item workshop and the Ultima Weapon will be avaiable to synthesize

Unlocking All of the Abilities

Here's how to unlock Sora's many special attacks.

Unlockable	How to Unlock
Ars Arcanum	Beat Captain Hook
Cheer	Obtained by collecting certain items in Hundred Acre Wood
Dodge Roll	Obtained from Goofy after beating Guard Armor
Ragnarok	Beat Riku the second time in Hollow Bastion
Sonic Blade	Obtained from Cloud after beating Cerberus
Strike Raid	Beat the Pegasus Cup
Trinity Limit	Beat the Hades Cup

Klonoa 2

Description	Objective
Hidden Levels	In each stage are six stars. If you collect all six, you gain a doll that appears on the R1 screen. Collect eight dolls to unlock the first hidden level, and all sixteen for the second.
Music Box	Complete both hidden levels to unlock the Music Box sound test. The first hidden level gives you the first 27 tracks, while the second one gives you the remaining songs.
Pictures in Image Gallery	Each stage has 150 little gems scattered about. If you collect all 150, you'll open up more images in the special image gallery.

L.A. Rush

Enter codes while playing. Do not pause.

Unlockable	Code
$5,000	⇧, ⇩, ⇦, ⇨, ●, ⇦, R2, ⇧
Disable Police	⇩, ⇦, ⇨, R2, ■, ⇨, R1, ⇦
Fast Traffic	⇧, ⇩, ⇨, ⇨, ■, ⇨, ●, ⇦
No Catching Up on Races	Enter C-VHARD as a profile name.
Unlimited N20	⇧, ⇩, ⇦, ⇨, ■, ⇧, ⇩, ●, ⇧

DS

Le Mans 24 Hours

Enter the following codes as your name at the Championship mode name screen.

Unlockable	Code
All Cars	ACO
All Championships	NUMBAT
All Tracks	SPEEDY
Le Mans	WOMBAT
See the Credits	HEINEY

GBA

Legacy of Kain: Defiance

Pause gameplay to enter the following codes.

Unlockable	Code
All Bonuses	R2, ↓, L2, R1, ←, L2, ↓, L1, ▲
All Combo Moves	→, ↓, ↑, ↓, ↓, R1, ▲, ●, ↓
All Dark Chronicles	R1, ↓, R2, L1, →, R2, ▲, ↓, L1
All Power Ups	←, ←, ↑, ↑, L1, R2, ●, ↓, ▲
Cartoon Version	↑, ↓, ↑, ↓, R1, R2, ↓, ●, ▲
Full Health and Reaver Charge	←, →, ←, →, R1, L1, ●, ▲, ↓
No Textures	L1, ↓, R2, →, R2, ↑, ▲, L1, ↓
Tube Reaver	↑, ↓, ←, →, R2, L2, ▲, ↓, ●
Unlimited Reaver Charge and Balance Emblem	↓, ↓, ↑, ←, R1, R2, ↓, ▲, ●
Wireframe	L1, ↓, L1, ↑, R1, L2, L1, ↓, ▲

PSP
PS2

The Legend of Spyro: A New Beginning

Enter these codes while the game is paused.

Unlockable	Code
Infinite Breath	⇧, ⇧, ⇩, ⇩, ⇦, ⇨, ⇦, ⇨, L1, R1, L1, R1
Infinite Health	⇧, ⇧, ⇩, ⇩, ⇦, ⇨, ⇦, ⇨, L1, L1, R1, R1

PS3

Legends of Wrestling 2

To access the Cheats menu, select Career mode and choose any wrestler. During Career mode, enter one of each of the match types. Either finish the match or immediately exit. After you enter all match types, a message stating that you can now purchase the cheats in the shop appears.

Description	Obective
Andy Kaufman	Select Career mode and choose Jerry Lawler as your wrestler. Defeat Andy Kaufman to unlock him at the shop.
Big John Studd	Select Career mode and choose any wrestler. Defeat Big John Studd to unlock him at the shop.
British Bulldog	Select Career mode and choose Dynamite Kid. Successfully complete Career mode to unlock British Bulldog at the shop.
Bruno Sammartino	Select Career mode and choose Hulk Hogan. Successfully complete Career mode to unlock Bruno Sammartino at the shop.
Owen Hart	Select Career mode and choose Bret Hart. Successfully complete Career mode to unlock Owen Hart at the shop.
Unlimited Green Coins	Successfully complete Career mode with all wrestlers to get unlimited Green Coins.

Wii
Xbox
Xbox 360
Index

LEGO Racer 2

Enter these codes at the Main menu.

Unlockable	Code
Mars Tracks	⇦, ⇦, ⇨, ⇨, ⇦, ⇦, ⇨, ⇦, ⇩, ⇦, ⇨
Martian	⇨, ⇦, ⇩, ⇧, ⇩, ⇦, ⇨, ⇧, ⇧
Wide Angle	⇦, ⇨, ⇨, ⇨, ⇨, ⇧, ⇧, ⇧, ⇩, ⇩, ⇩, ⇦, ⇦, ⇦, ⇨, ⇨

LEGO Star Wars

In Dexter's Diner, go to Codes and enter the following. This will unlock characters for purchase in Free Play mode.

Character	Code	Character	Code
Battle Droid	987UYR	Grievous' Bodyguard	ZTY392
Battle Droid (Commander)	EN11K5	Invincibility	4PR28U
Battle Droid (Geonosis)	LK42U6	Jango Fett	PL47NH
Battle Droid (Security)	KF999A	Ki-Adi Mundi	DP55MV
Big Blasters	IG72X4	Kit Fisto	CBR954
Boba Fett	LA811Y	Luminara	A725X4
Brushes	SHRUB1	Mace Windu (Episode III)	MS952L
Classic Blasters	L449HD	Minikit Detector	LD116B
Clone	F8B4L6	Moustaches	RP924W
Clone (Episode III, Pilot)	BHU72T	Padme	92UJ7D
Clone (Episode III, Swamp)	N3T6P8	PK Droid	R840JU
Clone (Episode III, Walker)	RS6E25	Princess Leia	BEQ82H
Clone (Episode III)	ER33JN	Purple	YD77GC
Count Dooku	14PGMN	Rebel Trooper	L54YUK
Darth Maul	H35TUX	Royal Guard	PP43JX
Darth Sidious	A32CAM	Shaak Ti	EUW862
Disguised Clone	VR832U	Silhouettes	MS999Q
Droideka	DH382U	Silly Blasters	NR37W1
General Grievous	SF321Y	Super Battle Droid	XZNR21
Geonosian	19D7NB	Tea Cups	PUCEAT
Gonk Droid	U63B2A		

LEGO Star Wars II: The Original Trilogy

Enter these passwords in the Cantina.

Unlockable	Password	Unlockable	Password
Beach Trooper	UCK868	IG-88	NXL973
Ben Kenobi (Ghost)	BEN917	Imperial Guard	MMM111
Bespin Guard	VHY832	Imperial Officer	BBV889
Bib Fortuna	WTY721	Imperial Shuttle Pilot	VAP664
Boba Fett	HLP221	Imperial Spy	CVT125
Death Star Trooper	BNC332	Jawa	JAW499
Ewok	TTT289	Lobot	UUB319
Gamorrean Guard	YZF999	Palace Guard	SGE549
Gonk Droid	NFX582	Rebel Pilot	CYG336
Grand Moff Tarkin	SMG219	Rebel Trooper (Hoth)	EKU849
Greedo	NAH118	Sandtrooper	YDV451
Han Solo (Hood)	YWM840	Skiff Guard	GBU888

DS

GBA

PSP

PS2

PS3

Wii

Xbox

Xbox 360

Index

DS

GBA

PSP

PS2

PS3

Wii

Xbox

Xbox 360

Index

LEGO Star Wars II: The Original Trilogy (continued)

Unlockable	Password	Unlockable	Password
Snowtrooper	NYU989	Tie Fighter Pilot	NNZ316
Stormtrooper	PTR345	Tie Interceptor	QYA828
The Emperor	HHY382	Tusken Raider	PEJ821
Tie Fighter	HDY739	Ugnaught	UGN694

Life Line

Unlockable	Objective
Extra Costume	Complete the game once and save, then start a new game with that game save.

The Lord of the Rings: The Return of the King

Accessing the video clips depends on how far you've gone in the game. Here's a table showing what you can find and what level you must complete to find it. For example, you can't see the game concept art slide show until you've successfully completed Paths of the Dead.

Unlockable Video Features

Video Title	Must Complete
Andy Serkis Interview	The Crack of Doom
Billy Boyd Interview	The Crack of Doom
Christopher Lee Interview	The Road to Isengard
David Wenham Interview	The Crack of Doom
Dom Monaghan Interview	The Crack of Doom
Elijah Wood Interview	Shelob's Lair
Film Concept Art	Helm's Deep
Film Production Stills	The Southern Gate
Game Concept Art	Paths of the Dead
Hobbits on Gaming	Helm's Deep
Ian McKellen Interview	Minas Tirith—Top of the Wall
Sean Astin Interview	Escape from Osgiliath

For the following codes:

1. Pause the game so the Options menu appears.
2. Hold down all shoulder buttons at once.
3. Enter the code with shoulder buttons still depressed.

   When you've entered the code correctly you'll hear a sound that indicates success.

> **TIP**
>
> *If you want to enter more than one code, release the shoulder buttons, then hold them down again before entering each code.*

Code	Usage	Character	PS2 Combo
+1,000 Experience Points	one-time use	Gimli	●, ●, ▲, ✕
+1,000 Experience Points	one-time use	Gandalf	●, ▲, ↑, ↓
+1,000 Experience Points	one-time use	Merry	↓, ↓, ■, ✕
+1,000 Experience Points	one-time use	Frodo	↓, ▲, ↑, ↓
+1,000 Experience Points	one-time use	Faramir	■, ▲, ↑, ■
+1,000 Experience Points	one-time use	Aragorn	↑, ■, ▲, ✕
+1,000 Experience Points	one-time use	Sam	▲, ✕, ↓, ✕
+1,000 Experience Points	one-time use	Pippin	▲, ✕, ■, ✕

The Lord of the Rings: The Return of the King (continued)

Code	Usage	Character	PS2 Combo
+1,000 Experience Points	one-time use	Legolas	✕, ▲, ↑, ✕
3 Hit Combo for	on/off	Gandalf	↓, ✕, ▲, ↓
3 Hit Combo for	on/off	Aragorn	■, ↓, ●, ↑
3 Hit Combo for	on/off	Frodo	■, ↓, ▲, ■
3 Hit Combo for	on/off	Faramir	■, ▲, ↑, ▲
3 Hit Combo for	on/off	Legolas	■, ▲, ▲, ●
3 Hit Combo for	on/off	Sam	■, ✕, ●, ■
3 Hit Combo for	on/off	Gimli	↑, ■, ●, ■
3 Hit Combo for	on/off	Pippin	↑, ↑, ■, ●
3 Hit Combo for	on/off	Merry	▲, ✕, ↑, ▲
4 Hit Combo for	on/off	Frodo	↓, ■, ↓, ●

Secret Codes

Code	Usage	Character	PS2 Combo
4 Hit Combo for	on/off	Gandalf	↓, ▲, ↑, ●
4 Hit Combo for	on/off	Merry	■, ✕, ■, ■
4 Hit Combo for	on/off	Sam	↑, ↓, ▲, ▲
4 Hit Combo for	on/off	Aragorn	↑, ■, ▲, ↓
4 Hit Combo for	on/off	Gimli	▲, ■, ↑, ✕
4 Hit Combo for	on/off	Legolas	✕, ●, ▲, ■
4 Hit Combo for	on/off	Faramir	✕, ■, ↑, ✕
4 Hit Combo for	on/off	Pippin	✕, ✕, ↓, ●
All Actor Interviews	one-time use	Special Features	✕, ■, ✕, ↑
All Experience you get, your buddy gets	on/off	Co-op	↓, ✕, ✕, ✕
All Health you get, your buddy gets	on/off	Co-op	▲, ↑, ■, ■
All Upgrades	one-time use	Any Character	↑, ↓, ▲, ■
Always Devastating	on/off	Any Character	▲, ↑, ▲, ↓
Infinite Re-spawns for Co-op	on/off	All	●, ■, ↑, ●
Infinite Missiles	on/off	Any Character	■, ■, ↓, ●
Invulnerable	on/off	Any Character	■, ●, ■, ↑
Level 2 Skills	on/off	Merry	●, ↓, ■, ■
Level 2 Skills	on/off	Aragorn	●, ▲, ✕, ▲
Level 2 Skills	on/off	Sam	●, ✕, ●, ▲
Level 2 Skills	on/off	Gandalf	↓, ▲, ✕, ▲
Level 2 Skills	on/off	Pippin	↓, ✕, ↓, ↑
Level 2 Skills	on/off	Legolas	■, ■, ●, ■
Level 2 Skills	on/off	Gimli	↑, ●, ■, ■
Level 2 Skills	on/off	Frodo	▲, ↑, ↓, ●
Level 2 Skills	on/off	Faramir	✕, ■, ✕, ↓
Level 4 Skills	on/off	Legolas	↓, ↓, ✕, ✕
Level 4 Skills	on/off	Aragorn	↓, ■, ●, ■
Level 4 Skills	on/off	Merry	■, ✕, ●, ↓
Level 4 Skills	on/off	Sam	↑, ↓, ■, ✕

DS
GBA
PSP
PS2
PS3
Wii
Xbox
Xbox 360
Index

The Lord of the Rings: The Return of the King (continued)

Code	Usage	Character	PS2 Combo
Level 4 Skills	on/off	Gimli	▲, ■, ↓, ↑
Level 4 Skills	on/off	Frodo	▲, ↑, ●, ↓
Level 4 Skills	on/off	Gandalf	▲, ↑, ■, ✕
Level 4 Skills	on/off	Pippin	✕, ↓, ↓, ↓
Level 4 Skills	on/off	Faramir	✕, ✕, ■, ■
Level 6 Skills	on/off	Pippin	●, ▲, ●, ▲
Level 6 Skills	on/off	Aragorn	●, ▲, ■, ■
Level 6 Skills	on/off	Legolas	↓, ●, ↑, ↓
Level 6 Skills	on/off	Merry	↓, ↓, ■, ▲
Level 6 Skills	on/off	Sam	↓, ↓, ↑, ↑
Level 6 Skills	on/off	Frodo	↓, ↓, ✕, ▲
Level 6 Skills	on/off	Gimli	↓, ▲, ↓, ■
Level 6 Skills	on/off	Gandalf	▲, ▲, ✕, ↑
Level 6 Skills	on/off	Faramir	▲, ✕, ↓, ●
Level 8 Skills	on/off	Frodo	●, ●, ↓, ↓
Level 8 Skills	on/off	Sam	●, ●, ▲, ▲
Level 8 Skills	on/off	Faramir	●, ↓, ↓, ↓
Level 8 Skills	on/off	Gandalf	●, ■, ↓, ↓
Level 8 Skills	on/off	Merry	↓, ▲, ✕, ■
Level 8 Skills	on/off	Legolas	■, ↑, ↑, ↓
Level 8 Skills	on/off	Pippin	■, ↑, ↑, ●
Level 8 Skills	on/off	Aragorn	↑, ■, ▲, ↑
Level 8 Skills	on/off	Gimli	✕, ●, ↓, ■
Perfect Mode	on/off	Any Character	●, ↓, ▲, ✕
Restore Health	one-time use	Any Character	■, ■, ●, ●
Restore Missiles	one-time use	Gimli	●, ●, ●, ✕
Restore Missiles	one-time use	Merry	■, ●, ●, ▲
Restore Missiles	one-time use	Pippin	↑, ●, ↓, ■
Restore Missiles	one-time use	Gandalf	▲, ↓, ✕, ■
Restore Missiles	one-time use	Aragorn	▲, ■, ■, ▲
Restore Missiles	one-time use	Faramir	▲, ↑, ✕, ✕
Restore Missiles	one-time use	Legolas	▲, ▲, ▲, ↓
Restore Missiles	one-time use	Frodo	▲, ▲, ▲, ●
Restore Missiles	one-time use	Sam	✕, ✕, ●, ✕
Targeting Indicator Mode	on/off	Any Character	↓, ●, ↑, ■
Unlock Secret Character	one-time use	Frodo	▲, ●, ●, ●
Unlock Secret Character	one-time use	Frodo	●, ■, ■, ✕
Unlock Secret Character	one-time use	Pippin	▲, ●, ■, ↓
Unlock Secret Character	one-time use	Merry	✕, ↓, ↓, ✕
Unlock Secret Character	one-time use	Faramir	✕, ✕, ▲, ▲
Unlock Special Abilities for	on/off	Gimli	●, ■, ✕, ●
Unlock Special Abilities for	on/off	Aragorn	↓, ●, ▲, ▲
Unlock Special Abilities for	on/off	Pippin	■, ✕, ●, ▲
Unlock Special Abilities for	on/off	Sam	↑, ●, ✕, ●

The Lord of the Rings: The Return of the King (continued)

Code	Usage	Character	PS2 Combo
Unlock Special Abilities for	on/off	Gandalf	↑, ↓, ▲, ●
Unlock Special Abilities for	on/off	Faramir	↑, ■, ●, ↑
Unlock Special Abilities for	on/off	Merry	↑, ▲, ●, ●
Unlock Special Abilities for	on/off	Legolas	▲, ●, ✕, ●
Unlock Special Abilities for	on/off	Frodo	▲, ✕, ↓, ✕

The Lord of the Rings: The Two Towers

To access the unlockable, pause gameplay, hold L1+L2+R1+R2, and enter the required button combinations.

Description	Code	Description	Code
Add 1,000 Experience Points	Press ✕, ↓, ↓, ↓.	Level 5 Skills	Press ✕, ✕, ↓, ↓.
		Level 6 Skills	Press ■, ←, ■, ←.
Level 2 Skills	Press ●, →, ●, →.	Level 8 Skills	Press ✕, ✕, ↓, ↓.
Level 3 Skills	Press ▲, ↑, ▲, ↑.	Restore Ammunition	Press ✕, ↓, ▲, ↑.
Level 4 Skills	Press ▲, ↑, ▲, ↑.	Restore Health	Press ▲, ↓, ✕, ↑.

The following codes require that you first complete the game before enabling the code. To access the unlockable, pause gameplay, hold L1+L2+R1+R2, and and enter the required button combinations.

Unlockable	Code
All Combo Upgrades	Press ▲, ●, ▲, ●.
All Skills	Press ▲, ●, ▲, ●.
Devastating Attacks	Press ■, ■, ●, ●. Hold ▲ during battles to do devastating attacks.
Invincibility	Press ▲, ■, ✕, ●.
Slow Motion	Press ▲, ●, ✕, ■.
Small Enemies	Press ▲, ▲, ✕, ✕.
Unlimited Missile Weapons	Press ■, ●, ✕, ▲.

Madagascar

Enter these codes while playing.

Unlockable	Code
All power-ups	●, ✕, ✕, ●, ▲, L1, ■, R1, L1
Invincibility	⇧, ⇩, ✕, ✕, R1, L1, R2, L2, ▲, ■, ●
Level select	R1, R1, ●, L2, L1, ✕, ▲, R1, ▲

Madden NFL 2004

Description	Objective
1990 Eagles Classic Team	Earn Level 4 EA Sports Bio
Bingo! Cheat	Earn Level 2 EA Sports Bio
Steve Spurrier Coach	Earn Level 6 EA Sports Bio

Madden NFL 2005

From My Madden menu, go to Madden Cards, Madden Codes, and enter the following:

Card	Password	Card	Password
Aaron Brooks Gold Card	_J95K1J	Ahman Green Gold Card	T86L4C
Aaron Glenn Gold Card	Q48E9G	Al Wilson Gold Card	G72G2R
Adewale Ogunleye Gold Card	C12E9E	Alan Faneca Gold Card	U32S9C
		Amani Toomer Gold Card	Z75G6M

Madden NFL 2005 (continued)

Card	Password	Card	Password
Andre Carter Gold Card	V76E2Q	Dom Capers Gold Card	B97I6R
Andre Johnson Gold Card	E34S1M	Domanick Davis Gold Card	L58S3J
Andy Reid Gold Card	N44K1L	Donnie Edwards Gold Card	E18Y5Z
Anquan Boldin Gold Card	S32F7K	Donovin Darius Gold Card	Q11T7T
Antoine Winfield Gold Card	A12V7Z	Donovon McNabb Gold Card	T98J1I
Bill Cowher Gold Card	S54T6U	Donte Stallworth Gold Card	R75W3M
Brad Hopkins Gold Card	P44A8B	Dre Bly Gold Card	H19Q2O
Bret Favre Gold Card	L61D7B	Drew Bledsoe Gold Card	W73M3E
Brian Billick Gold Card	L27C4K	Dwight Freeney Gold Card	G76U2L
Brian Dawkins Gold Card	Y47B8Y	Edgerrin James Gold Card	A75D7X
Brian Simmons Gold Card	S22M6A	Ed Reed Gold Card	G18Q2B
Brian Urlacher Gold Card	Z34J4U	Eric Moulds Gold Card	H34Z8K
Brian Westbrook Gold Card	V46I2I	Flozell Adams Gold Card	R54T1O
Bubba Franks Gold Card	U77F2W	Fred Taylor Gold Card	I87X9Y
Butch Davis Gold Card	G77L6F	Grant Wistrom Gold Card	E46M4Y
Byron Leftwich Gold Card	C55V5C	Herman Edwards Gold Card	O19T2T
Carson Palmer Gold Card	O36V2H	Hines Ward Gold Card	M12B8F
Casey Hampton Gold Card	Z11P9T	Jack Del Rio Gold Card	J22P9I
Chad Johnson Gold Card	R85S2A	Jake Delhomme Gold Card	M86N9F
Chad Pennington Gold Card	B64L2F	Jake Plummer Gold Card	N74P8X
Champ Bailey Gold Card	K89O9E	Jamie Sharper Gold Card	W27I7G
Charles Rogers Gold Card	E57K9Y	Jason Taylor Gold Card	O33S6I
Charles Woodson Gold Card	F95N9J	Jason Webster Gold Card	M74B3E
Chris Hovan Gold Card	F14C6J	Jeff Fisher Gold Card	N62B6J
Corey Simon Gold Card	R11D7K	Jeff Garcia Gold Card	H32H7B
Courtney Brown Gold Card	R42R75	Jeremy Newberry Gold Card	J77Y8C
Curtis Martin Gold Card	K47X3G	Jeremy Shockey Gold Card	R34X5T
Dallas Coach Gold Card	O24U1Q	Jerry Porter Gold Card	F71Q9Z
Damien Woody Gold Card	F78I1I	Jerry Rice Gold Card	K34F8S
Dante Hall Gold Card	B23P8D	Jevon Kearse Gold Card	A78B1C
Dat Nguyen Gold Card	Q86I2S	Jim Haslett Gold Card	G78R3W
Daunte Culpepper Gold Card	O62O9K	Jim Mora Jr. Gold Card	N46C3M
Dave Wannstedt Gold Card	W73D7D	Jimmy Smith Gold Card	I22J5W
David Boston Gold Card	A25I9F	Joe Horn Gold Card	P91A1Q
David Carr Gold Card	C16E2Q	Joey Harrington Gold Card	Z68W8J
Dennis Erickson Gold Card	J83E3T	John Fox Gold Card	Q98R7Y
Dennis Green Gold Card	C18J7T	Jon Gruden Gold Card	H6I18A
Derrick Brooks Gold Card	P93I9Q	Josh McCown Gold Card	O33Y4X
Derrick Mason Gold Card	S98P3T	Julian Peterson Gold Card	M89J8A
Deuce McAllister Gold Card	D11H4J	Julius Peppers Gold Card	X54O4Z
Dexter Coakley Gold Card	L35K1A	Junior Seau Gold Card	W26K6Q
Dexter Jackson Gold Card	G16B2I	Kabeer Gbaja-Biamala Gold Card	U16I9Y
Dick Vermeil Gold Card	F68V1W	Keith Brooking Gold Card	E12P4S

Card	Password
Keith Bulluck Gold Card	M63N6V
Kendrell Bell Gold Card	T96C7J
Kevan Barlow Gold Card	A23T5E
Kevin Mawae Gold Card	L76E6S
Kris Jenkins Gold Card	W63O3K
Kyle Boller Gold Card	A72F9X
Kyle Turley Gold Card	Y46A8V
LaDainian Tomlinson Gold Card	M64D4E
LaVar Arrington Gold Card	F19Q8W
Laveranues Coles Gold Card	R98I5S
Lawyer Milloy Gold Card	M37Y5B
La'Roi Glover Gold Card	K24L9K
Lee Suggs Gold Card	Z94X6Q
Leonard Davis Gold Card	H14M2V
Lovie Smith Gold Card	L38V3A
Marc Bulger Gold Card	U66B4S
Marcel Shipp Gold Card	R42X2L
Marcus Stroud Gold Card	E56I5O
Marcus Trufant Gold Card	R46T5U
Mark Brunell Gold Card	B66D9J
Marshall Faulk Gold Card	U76G1U
Marty Booker Gold Card	P51U4B
Marty Schottenheimer Gold Card	D96A7S
Marvin Harrison Gold Card	T11E8O
Marvin Lewis Gold Card	P24S4H
Matt Hasselback Gold Card	R68D5F
Michael Bennett Gold Card	W81W2J
Michael Strahan Gold Card	O66T6K
Michael Vick Gold Card	H67B1F
Mike Alstott Gold Card	D89F6W
Mike Brown Gold Card	F12J8N
Mike Martz Gold Card	R64A8E
Mike Mularkey Gold Card	C56D6E
Mike Rucker Gold Card	K89O6S
Mike Shanahan Gold Card	H15L5Y
Mike Sherman Gold Card	F84X6K
Mike Tice Gold Card	Y31T6Y
New England Coach Gold Card	N24L4Z
Nick Barnett Gold Card	X95I7S
Norv Turner Gold Card	F24K1M
Olin Kreutz Gold Card	R17R2O

Card	Password
Orlando Pace Gold Card	U42U9U
Patrick Surtain Gold Card	H58T9X
Peerless Price Gold Card	X75V6K
Peter Warrick Gold Card	D86P8O
Peyton Manning Gold Card	L48H4U
Plaxico Burress Gold Card	K18P6J
Priest Holmes Gold Card	X91N1L
Quentin Jammer Gold Card	V55S3Q
Randy Moss Gold Card	W79U7X
Ray Lewis Gold Card	B94X6V
Reggie Wayne Gold Card	R29S8C
Rex Grossman Gold Card	C46P2A
Rich Gannon Gold Card	Q69I1Y
Richard Seymour Gold Card	L69T4T
Ricky Williams Gold Card	P19V1N
Rod Smith Gold Card	V22C4L
Rodney Harrison Gold Card	O84I3J
Ronde Barber Gold Card	J72X8W
Roy Williams Gold Card	J76C6F
Rudi Johnson Gold Card	W26J6H
Sam Madison Gold Card	Z87T5C
Samari Rolle Gold Card	C69H4Z
Santana Moss Gold Card	H79E5B
Seattle Coach Gold Card	V58U4Y
Shaun Alexander Gold Card	C95Z4P
Shaun Ellis Gold Card	Z54F2B
Shawn Rogers Gold Card	J97X8M
Shawn Springs Gold Card	Z28D2V
Simeon Rice Gold Card	S62F9T
Stephen Davis Gold Card	E39X9L
Steve Mariucci Gold Card	V74Q3N
Steve McNair Gold Card	S36T1I
Steve Smith Gold Card	W91O2O
Takeo Spikes Gold Card	B83A6C
Tedy Bruschi Gold Card	K28Q3P
Terence Newman Gold Card	W57Y5P
Terrell Suggs Gold Card	V71A9Q
Tiki Barber Gold Card	T43A2V
T.J. Duckett Gold Card	P67E1I
Todd Heap Gold Card	H19M1G
Tom Brady Gold Card	X22V7E
Tom Coughlin Gold Card	S71D6H
Tony Dungy Gold Card	Y96R8V

Madden NFL 2005 (continued)

Card	Password	Card	Password
Tony Gonzalez Gold Card	N46E9N	Walter Jones Gold Card	G57P1P
Torry Holt Gold Card	W96U7E	Washington Coach Gold Card	W63V9L
Travis Henry Gold Card	F36M2Q	Will Shields Gold Card	B52S8A
Trent Green Gold Card	Y46M4S	Zach Thomas Gold Card	U63I3H
Ty Law Gold Card	F13W1Z		

Secret Teams

Team	Password	Team	Password
1958 Colts	_P74X8J	1978 Dolphins	G97U5X
1966 Packers	G49P7W	1980 Raiders	K71K4E
1968 Jets	C24W2A	1981 Chargers	Y27N9A
1970 Browns	G12N1I	1982 Redskins	F56D6V
1972 Dolphins	R79W6W	1983 Raiders	D23T8S
1974 Steelers	R12D9B	1984 Dolphins	X23Z8H
1976 Raiders	P96Q8M	1985 Bears	F92M8M
1977 Broncos	O18T2A		

Secret Teams

Team	Password	Team	Password
1986 Giants	K44F2Y	1991 Lions	I89F4I
1988 49ers	F77R8H	1992 Cowboys	I44A1O
1990 Eagles	G95F2Q	1993 Bills	Y66K3O

Secret Stadiums

Stadium	Password	Stadium	Password
Pro Bowl Hawaii '05	G67F5X	Super Bowl XLII	T67R1O
Super Bowl XL	O85P6I	Super Bowl XXXIX	D58F1B
Super Bowl XLI	P48Z4D		

Pump Up and Cheerleader Cards

Card	Password	Card	Password
49ers Cheerleader	_X61T6L	Jets Pump Up Crowd	S45W1M
Bears Pump Up Crowd	K17F2I	Lions Pump Up Crowd	C18F4G
Bengals Cheerleader	Y22S6G	Packers Pump Up Crowd	K26Y4V
Bills Cheerleader	F26S6X	Panthers Cheerleader	M66N4D
Broncos Cheerleader	B85U5C	Patriots Cheerleader	O59P9C
Browns Pump Up Crowd	B65Q1L	Raiders Cheerleader	G92L2E
Buccaneers Cheerleader	Z55Z7S	Rams Cheerleader	W73B8X
Cardinals Cheerleader	Q91W5L	Ravens Cheerleader	P98T6C
Chargers Cheerleader	Q68S3F	Redskins Cheerleader	N19D6Q
Chiefs Cheerleader	T46M6T	Saints Cheerleader	R99G2F
Colts Cheerleader	M22Z6H	Seahawks Cheerleader	A35T8R
Cowboys Cheerleader	J84E3F	Steelers Pump Up Crowd	C98I2V
Dolphins Cheerleader	E88T2J	Texans Cheerleader	R74G3W
Eagles Cheerleader	Q88P3Q	Titans Cheerleader	Q81V4N
Falcons Cheerleader	W86F3F	Vikings Cheerleader	E26H4L
Giants Pump Up Crowd	L13Z9J		
Jaguars Cheerleader	K32C2A		

DS
GBA
PSP
PS2
PS3
Wii
Xbox
Xbox 360
Index

DS

GBA

PSP

PS2

PS3

Wii

Xbox

Xbox 360

Index

Madden NFL 2005 (continued)

Card	Description	Code
3rd Down	For one half, your opponent has 3 downs to get a first down.	_Z28X8K
5th Down	For one half, you will have 5 downs to get a first down.	P66C4L
Bingo!	Your defensive interceptions increase by 75% for the game.	J33I8F
Da Bomb	You will receive unlimited pass range for one half.	B61A8M
Da Boot	You will receive unlimited field goal range for one half.	I76X3T
Extra Credit	Awards 4 points for every interception and 3 points for every sack.	M89S8G
1st and 15	Requires your opponent to get 15 yards to reach a first down for one half.	V65J8P
1st and 5	Your first down yards to go will be set to 5 for one half.	O72E9B
Fumblitis	Your opponent's fumbles will increase by 75% for the game.	R14B8Z
Human Plow	Your Broken Tackles will increase by 75% for the game.	L96J7P
Lame Duck	Your opponent will throw a lob pass for one half.	D57R5S
Mistake Free	You can't fumble or throw an interception for one half.	X78P9Z
Mr. Mobility	Your QB can't get sacked for one half.	Y59R8R
Super Dive	Your diving distance increases by 75% for the game.	D59K3Y
Tight Fit	Your opponent's uprights will be made very narrow for one half.	V34L6D
Unforced Errors	Your opponent will fumble every time he tries to juke for one half.	L48G1E

Madden NFL 06

To enter this code, go into My Madden, select Madden Cards, then select Enter Code.

Unlockable	Code	Unlockable	Code
1st and 5 Bronze	2Y7L8B	Extra Credit Bronze	3D3Q3P
1st and 15 Bronze	2W4P9T	Human Plow Bronze	3H3U7F
3rd Down Bronze	3F9G4J	Super Dive Bronze	3H8M5U
5th Down Bronze	3E9R4V	Tight Fit Bronze	3D8X6T
Da Boot Bronze	3J3S9Y	Unforced Errors Bronze	2Z2F4H
Donovan McNabb Gold Card (alternate)	8Q2J2X		

Madden NFL 07

Under Madden Cards, select Madden Codes to enter these passwords. Passwords are case sensitive.

Unlockable	Password
When this card is played, you can't fumble or throw interceptions for one half	XL7SP1
When this card is played, your opponent will throw a lob pass for one half	5LAWO0
When this card is played, your QB accuracy will be 100% for one half	WROA0R

Mafia

Unlockable	Objective
Car Selection	Learn to break into cars during missions. This will allow you to use it in Free Ride.
City Selection	Progress through story mode to unlock more areas for Free Ride.
Monster Truck	Take first place in all of the races in Racing Championship mode.

DS

GBA

PSP

PS2

PS3

Wii

Xbox

Xbox 360

Index

Mafia (continued)

Unlockable	Objective
Time of Day	Progress through story mode to unlock a Day/Night option for Free Ride.

Magic Pengel: Color

Description	Objective
Kiba's Letter 1 Page	Get 1,000,000 gold gems.

Major League Baseball 2K5: World Series Edition

Create a new profile and enter the following names.

Unlockable	Code
Unlock All Cheats	Ima Cheater
Unlock All Classic Teams	Old Timers
Unlock All Extras	Gimme Goods

Major League Baseball 2K7

To enter these codes, select My 2K7. Then select Enter Cheat Code.

Unlockable	Code
Boosts a team's power rating by 25% for 1 inning	mightymick
Boosts the hitting of the 3, 4, 5 hitters in the lineup by 50% for 1 game	triplecrown
Boosts your ability to hit home runs during the game just like The Mick	m4murder
Mickey will pinch hit	phmantle
Unlocks everything	Derek Jeter
Unlocks Mickey Mantle in free agency	themick

Manhunt

Unlockable	Code
God Mode	After finishing the game on Fetish mode, enter ↓,↓,●,↑,■,▲,■, R2,↑,↑,L1,▲ at the Title Screen.

Marc Ecko's Getting Up: Contents Under Pressure

Enter these passwords in the Cheats menu under Options.

Unlockable	Password	Unlockable	Password
All Art	SIRULLY	All Movies	DEXTERCROWLEY
All Black Book	SHARDSOFGLASS	All iPod Songs	GRANDMACELIA
All Characters in Versus Mode	STATEYOURNAME	All Versus Arenas	WORKBITCHES
All Combat Upgrades	DOGTAGS	Infinite Health	MARCUSECKOS
All Legends	NINESIX	Infinite Skills	FLIPTHESCRIPT
All Levels	IPULATOR	Max Health	BABYLONTRUST
		Max Skills	VANCEDALLISTER

The Mark of Kri

Enter the following codes at the Title Screen (where it says "Press Start"). If you enter them correctly, you will hear Rau give a vocal cue.

Unlockable	Code
All Enemies Tougher	×, ●, ■, ■, ×, ■, ●, ●, ×, ●, ●, ×
Invincible Rau	■, ●, ×, ■, ●, ■, ×, ●, ×, ■, ●, ×
Stronger Health Pickups	×, ×, ×, ×, ■, ■, ■, ■, ●, ●, ●, ●
Turn off Arena A.I.	×, ●, ●, ●, ×, ■, ■, ■, ×, ●, ■, ×
Unlimited Arrows	×, ●, ■, ■, ×, ■, ●, ●, ×, ■, ■, ×
Wimpy Enemies	×, ●, ●, ■, ×, ■, ■, ●

Marvel Nemesis: Rise of the Imperfects

To enter these passwords, go into the Options menu and select Cheats.

Unlockable	Password
Elektra swimsuit model card	THEHAND
Solara swimsuit model card	REIKO
Storm swimsuit model card	MONROE
Unlocks all Fantastic Four comics	SAVAGELAND
Unlocks all Tomorrow People comics	NZONE

Marvel Ultimate Alliance

Enter these codes while playing.

Unlockable	Code
God Mode	⇧, ⇩, ⇧, ⇩, ⇧, ⇦, ⇩, ⇨, START
Super Speed	⇧, ⇦, ⇧, ⇨, ⇩, ⇨, START
Touch of Death	⇦, ⇨, ⇩, ⇩, ⇨, ⇦, START

Enter these codes at the Team menu.

Unlockable	Code
100K	⇧, ⇧, ⇩, ⇩, ⇨, ⇦, START
All Characters	⇧, ⇧, ⇩, ⇩, ⇦, ⇦, ⇨, START
All Costumes	⇧, ⇩, ⇧, ⇩, ⇧, ⇨, ⇦, ⇨, ⇧, ⇩, START
All Powers	⇦, ⇨, ⇩, ⇧, ⇧, ⇧, ⇩, ⇦, ⇨, START
Level 99	⇧, ⇦, ⇧, ⇧, ⇩, ⇨, ⇩, ⇩, START
Unlocks Daredevil	⇦, ⇦, ⇨, ⇨, ⇦, ⇨, ⇦, START
Unlocks Silver Surfer	⇩, ⇩, ⇧, ⇧, ⇨, ⇦, ⇩, ⇦, START

Enter these codes at the Review menu.

Unlockable	Code
All Cinematics	⇧, ⇦, ⇦, ⇦, ⇨, ⇨, ⇧, START
All Comics	⇦, ⇩, ⇨, ⇦, ⇧, ⇧, ⇨, START
All Concept Art	⇩, ⇩, ⇩, ⇨, ⇨, ⇦, START
All Wallpapers	⇧, ⇩, ⇨, ⇦, ⇦, ⇧, ⇩, START

Mat Hoffman's Pro BMX 2

Quickly press the following buttons when "Press Start" appears. A sound confirms correct code entry.

Unlockable	Code
All Music Tracks	L1, ←, ←, →, →, →, ×, ×
Big Foot's FMV Sequences	R1, ↑, ↓, ←, ×, ×, ×, R1
BMX Costume	●, ▲, ←, →, ←, ●

DS

GBA

PSP

PS2

PS3

Wii

Xbox

Xbox 360

Index

DS
GBA
PSP
PS2
PS3
Wii
Xbox
Xbox 360
Index

Mat Hoffman's Pro BMX 2 (continued)

Unlockable	Code
Boston Level in Road Trip Mode	■, ↑, ↓, ↓, ↑, ■
Chicago Level in Road Trip Mode	■, ↑, ▲, ↑, ▲, ■
Cory Nastazio's FMV Sequences	R1, ■, ●, ●, ■, ■, ■, R1
Day Smith's FMV Sequences	R1, ●, ←, ←, ■, →, →, R1
Elvis Costume	●, L1, L1, ↑, ↑
Fiery Hands and Feet	↓, ▲, ▲, ✕, ✕, R1, R1
Invisible Bikes	↓, ↑, ←, ↓, →, ↓, ←, ↑
Joe Kowalski's FMV Sequences	R1, ↑, ✕, ▲, ↓, R1
Kevin Robinson's FMV Sequences	R1, ✕, ▲, ↓, ↑, R1
Kid's Bike	✕, ←, ←, L1, R1, ← Alternately, after you release the Medi-vac chopper and save the downed biker in Chicago, go to the location of the ambulance to find the bike.
Las Vegas Level in Road Trip Mode	■, R1, ←, L1, →, ■
Los Angeles Level in Road Trip Mode	■, ←, ▲, ▲, ←, ■
Mat Hoffman's FMV Sequences	R1, ←, ●, ←, ●, ←, R1
Level Select	■, →, →, ▲, ↓, ■ See Note.
Mike Escamilla's FMV Sequences	R1, ●, ✕, ✕, ●, ✕, ✕, R1
Nate Wessel's FMV Sequences	R1, ↓, ▲, ●, ↓, ▲, ●, R1
New Orleans Level in Road Trip Mode	■, ↓, →, ↑, ←, ■
Perfect Balance	↓, ↑, ●, ↓, ↑, ●, ↓, ↑, ●
Play as Big Foot	▲, →, ↑, →, ↑, ■
Play as Day Smith	▲, ↑, ↓, ↑, ↓, ■
Play as the Mime	▲, ←, →, ←, →, ← Alternately, find all the gaps in the game.
Play as Vanessa	▲, ↓, ←, ←, ↓, ■
Play as Volcano	▲, ↑, ↑, ✕, ↑, ↑, ✕
Unlockable	Code
Portland Level in Road Trip Mode	■, ✕, ✕, ▲, ▲, ■
Rick Thorne's FMV Sequences	R1, L1, →, R1, ←, R1
Ruben Alcantara's FMV Sequences	R1, ←, →, ←, →, ←, →, R1
Seth Kimbrough's FMV Sequences	R1, ↑, ↑, ●, ●, ●, R1
Simon Tabron's FMV Sequences	R1, L1, L1, R1, L1, L1, R1
Special Meter Always Full	↓, ✕, ✕, ✕, R1, R1, R1
Tiki Battle Mode	L1, L1, ↓, R1, ✕, L1

TIP

To disable the codes, quickly enter almost any code when "Press Start" appears, and add an extra R1 at the end. A different sound confirms correct code entry.

NOTE

Level Select Note

This code does not unlock all levels in Road Trip mode; only in Freeride, Session, and Multiplayer modes.

The Matrix: Path of Neo

Unlockables

Unlockables for the "Making Of..." Section of Extras

Unlockable	How to Unlock
Storyboard Sequence 1	Found on "Redpill Rescue: The Key"; to unlock, clear the stage without using weapons

DS

GBA

PSP

PS2

PS3

Wii

Xbox

Xbox 360

Index

The Matrix: Path of Neo (continued)

Unlockable	How to Unlock
Storyboard Sequence 2	Found on "The Frenchmen" Stage; to unlock, at the end of the dungeon hallway, take a right and follow the passage to a briefcase that's near a gate
Storyboard Sequence 3	Found on "Distorted Dimension" Stage; to unlock, on "Face 2" area with three doors, focus+move the block and open gate to center door, find briefcase
Storyboard Sequence 4	Found on "Distorted Dimension" Stage; to unlock, on "Face 3" move straight ahead from entrance, drop a couple levels down, find briefcase in a niche
Storyboard Sequence 5	Found on "Distorted Dimension" Stage; to unlock, follow steps above, find big stained glass window, wall run up the side, follow ledge to briefcase
View Hand-to-Hand Combo's	Found on "Distorted Dimensions" Stage; to unlock, on "Face 1" wall run up the wall with windows, focus jump to focus pack, look left, jump to briefcase
View Staff Combos	Found on "Kung Fu Training"; to unlock, execute 3 silent takedowns on all 3 enemies in the tool shop to get a briefcase
View Sword Combos	Found on "Sword Training" Stage; to unlock, smash the pot behind the waterfall to reveal a briefcase

Unlock Special Combos

Unlockable	How to Unlock
Machine Gun Kick (Strike x5, Focus+Strike, Special Attack+Strike, rapidly tap Strike)	Found on "The Chase: I Need an Exit Stage"; to unlock, find the briefcase in the corner of the market area behind the fruit stands
Quick Kicks (Strike x4, Focus+Strike, Special Attack+Strike)	Found on "Storming the Drain" Stage; to unlock, in the second to last room, use the ledges along the wall to reach both of the top two platforms
The Beginning of the End (Strike x4, Focus+Strike, Special Attack+Strike, Focus+Special Attack, rapidly tap Strike)	Found on "Seraph's Apology" Stage; to unlock, once you return to the teahouse from the theatre, destroy all 8 columns and a table to get a briefcase
The Code Breaker (Focus+Special Attack, rapidly tap Strike, Special Attack, rapidly tap Strike)	Found on Weapon's Training Stage; to unlock, find the briefcase among the Operator's secret stash in a dark upstairs room
The One (Strike x5, Focus+Strike, Special+Strike, rapidly tap Strike, Focus+Special, rapidly tap Strike, Special, tap Strike, Jump, 360 at peak)	Found on "The Burly Brawl" Stage; to unlock, defeat 30 Smiths before the level ends to make a briefcase appear in the center of the level and claim it
Ultimate Hyper Strike (Strike x4, Focus+Strike, Special Attack+Strike, Focus+Special Attack, Strike)	Found on "Redpill Rescue: Security Gaurd" Stage; to unlock, defeat the 5 members of SWAT by the stairs in 30 seconds, use frag grenade

Max Payne

Unlockable	Code
All Weapons and Full Ammo	Pause the game and press L1, L2, R1, R2, ▲, ●, ✕, ■.
Infinite Health	Pause the game and press L1, L1, L2, L2, R1, R1, R2, R2.
Level Select	Finish the first chapter of the Subway. Return to the Main Menu and press ↑, ↓, ←, →, ↑, ←, ↓, ●.
Slow Motion Sounds	Pause the game and press L1, L2, R1, R2, ▲, ■, ✕, ●.
Unlimited Bullet Time	Pause the game and press L1, L2, R1, R2, ▲, ✕, ✕, ▲.

DS

GBA

PSP

PS2

PS3

Wii

Xbox

Xbox 360

Index

Max Payne 2

Unlockable	Objective
Second Ending	Complete game on Dead on Arrival mode.

Maximo

Unlockable	Objective
Gallery Mode	Collect the Sorceress kiss at the end of each level. Seat each of the four kisses to a power-up position. Once the game is completed, the art gallery will be unlocked.
Mastery Mode	Have a 100 percent mastery ranking at the end of the game for all levels except those in the Hub. To master a level, you must kill every enemy and find every hidden chest.

Maximo vs. Army of Zin

Unlockable	Objective	Unlockable	Objective
Art Gallery 1	Master The First Strike	Art Gallery 11	Master Perilous Path
Art Gallery 2	Master Into the Fire	Art Gallery 12	Master The Under hive
Art Gallery 3	Master No Sanctuary	Art Gallery 13	Master Old Wounds
Art Gallery 4	Master The House Crasher	Art Gallery 14	Master The Great Vault
Art Gallery 5	Master Forest of Fear	Art Gallery 15	Master Drained Depths
Art Gallery 6	Master Gallows Gorge	Art Gallery 16	Master Sunken City
Art Gallery 7	Master Sinister Stones	Art Gallery 17	Master Guardian of the Deep
Art Gallery 8	Master Cyclocks	Art Gallery 18	Master The Soulcrusher
Art Gallery 9	Master Down with the Ship	Art Gallery 19	Master Tinker's Rescue
Art Gallery 10	Master Rad to Hawkmoor	Art Gallery 20	Master The Master of the Zin

Medal of Honor: European Assault

To unlock the ability to enter cheats, go to the Pause menu and enter the Activate Cheat Entry code.

Unlockable	Code
Active Cheat Entry	Hold L1+R1 then press ●,●,←,▲,●,✕
Player Suicide (SP only)	✕,▲,●,→,▲,●
Hide HUD	●,↓,●,↑,▲,●
Kill Nemesis	↓,L2,R2,↑,■
Pickup OSS Document	↑,✕,R2,R1,↑,■
Disable Shellshock	L2,R1,L2,▲,▲,▲

Medal of Honor: Frontline

Enter the following codes at the Enigma Machine. Green lights will confirm correct code entry. Select the "Bonus" option under the Enigma Machine to enable or disable the cheat.

Description	Code
Achilles' Head mode (Nazis can be killed only with a headshot when this cheat is active.)	GLASSJAW
Bullet Shield Mode (Bullets will not damage you.)	BULLETZAP
Complete Current Mission with Gold Star	MONKEY
Complete Previous Mission with Gold Star	TIMEWARP
Invisible Enemies (You will see only your enemies' guns and helmets.)	WHERERU
Making of D-Day FMV Sequence	BACKSTAGEO
Making of Needle in a Haystack FMV Sequence	BACKSTAGER
Making of Rolling Thunder FMV Sequence	BACKSTAGEI

Medal of Honor: Frontline (continued)

Description	Code
Making of Several Bridges Too Far FMV Sequence	BACKSTAGEF
Making of Storm in the Port FMV Sequence	BACKSTAGET
Making of The Horten's Nest FMV Sequence	BACKSTAGES
Master Code	DAWOIKS
Men with Hats (Characters will have various objects on their heads.)	HABRDASHR
Mission 2 (A Storm in the Port)	ORANGUTAN
Mission 3 (Needle in a Haystack)	BABOON
Mission 4 (Several Bridges Too Far)	CHIMPNZEE
Mission 5 (Rolling Thunder)	LEMUR
Mission 6 (The Horten's Nest)	GORILLA
Mohton Torpedoes (Your bullets will change into "photon torpedoes.")	TPDOMOHTON
Perfectionist (Nazis kill you with one shot.)	URTHEMAN
Rubber Grenade Mode	BOING
Silver Bullet Mode (Silver Bullet mode allows enemies to be killed with one shot.)	WHATYOUGET
Snipe-O-Rama Mode (All guns can zoom like a sniper rifle.)	LONGSHOT

Enter the following codes while the game is paused. The game will automatically resume after correct code entry.

Unlockable	Code
Invincibility	■, L1, ●, R1, ▲, L2, SELECT, R2
Unlimited Ammunition	●, L2, ■, L1, SELECT, R2, ▲, SELECT

 TIP

To get the EA LA Medal of Valor, complete the game with a Gold Star in every mission.

Medal of Honor: Rising Sun

Go to the Options screen and select Password. Enter the following codes. You will hear a chime to confirm code entry.

Unlockable	Code
All Missions	BUTTERFLY—Go to Mission Select and pick the desired level.
Invisible Soldiers	TRIGGER
Unlimited Ammo	GOBY

Mega Man Anniversary Collection

Unlockable	Code
Atomic Planet Credits	Defeat the first 3 bosses of Mega Man 1.
G4TV Interview/Retrospective	Complete Mega Man 8.
Homage to Mega Man Song	Complete Mega Man 2.
Mega Man 2: All energy tanks	A5 B1 B3 C4 D2 D3 E1 E4 E5
Mega Man 2: All weapons, items, and 4 energy tanks	A5 B2 B4 C1 C3 C5 D4 D5 E2
Mega Man 2: The Power Fighters	Complete Mega Man 7.
Mega Man 3: All weapons, items, 9 energy tanks, and no Dr. Wily Robots	Blue: A3 B5 D3 F4 Red: A6
Mega Man 4: All weapons and items	A1 A4 B5 E2 F1 F3
Mega Man 5: All weapons and items	Blue: B4 D6 F1 Red: C1 D4 F6
Mega Man 6: All weapons and items	B6 D4 F2 F4 F6

Sidebar tabs: DS, GBA, PSP, PS2, PS3, Wii, Xbox, Xbox 360, Index

DS

GBA

PSP

PS2

PS3

Wii

Xbox

Xbox 360

Index

Mega Man Anniversary Collection (continued)

Unlockable	Code
Mega Man 7: R.U.S.H., super rocket arm, 999 bolts, 4 Birds, 4 energy & weapon tanks, SP tank, energy bolt, exit, all weapons, shield, robot screw, all bosses dead	7853 5842 2245 7515
Mega Man Drum & Bass Song	Defeat the first three bosses of Mega Man 8.
Mega Man Power Fighters	Complete Mega Man 3.
Mega Man Radio Cut song	Complete Mega Man 7.
Mega Man: The Power Battles	Complete Mega Man 3.
Picture Set 1	Complete Mega Man 2.
Picture Set 2	Complete Mega Man 4.
Picture Set 3	Complete Mega Man 8.
Plant Man remix song	Defeat Plant Man in Mega Man 5.
Power Battle	Defeat Needle Man in Mega Man 3.
Power Fighters	Defeat Junk Man in Mega Man 7.
Protoman Song	Complete Mega Man 4.
Select Jungle Remix	Complete Mega Man 7
Unlock Interview	Make your way to Wily's Tower in Mega Man 8.
Wily Vs Bass Song	Complete Mega Man 4.
Wily's Revenge Song	Complete Mega Man 2.

Men in Black II: Alien Escape

Enter these codes at the Title Screen. The screen will flash when code entry is successful. If codes are entered, you will not be able to save your game or unlock features.

Unlockable	Code
Agent Data	↑, ↓, ●, R2, ←, L2, →, ×, R2, ■, ↑, R1
Alien Data	■, L1, ●, L2, ↓, ▲, R1, →, ×, ←, R2, ▲
All CST	■, ↑, L2, ←, ▲, ×, R2, ●, →, R1, ■, ●
All Levels	R2, ▲, ←, ●, ■, L2, ←, ↑, ×, ↓, L2, ■
All Weapons at Full Power	↑, ↓, ×, ■, R1, ▲, ▲, ←, ●, L1, L1, →
Boss Mode	R1, ▲, ↓, ↓, ×, L2, ←, ■, →, ▲, R2, L1
Don't Drop Pickups When Hit	↓, ↑, ×, ■, ↓, ↑, ×, ■, L1, L2, ■, ●
Invincibility	→, ×, R1, ▲, ↑, L2, ×, ←, L1, ●, ×, R2
Full Powerup on Bolt Weapons	←, →, ↑, ↓, L1, ●, ▲, R2, ←, ↓, ■, ■
Full Powerup on Spread Weapons	L2, R1, ●, L2, ↓, ↑, L1, →, ←, ×
Full Powerup on Homing Weapon	←, ↑, ■, L1, ←, ←, L1, ←, ●, ←
Full Powerup for Plasma Weapon	←, ●, ▲, →, L1, ■, ←, R1, R1, ▲
Full Powerup on Area Effect Weapon	←, ×, ▲, ↑, ▲, ■, L2, ←, R2
Making Of	●, R2, L2, ●, ▲, ↓, ■, ×, →, L1, ×, ↑

Men in Black II: Alien Escape (continued)

Unlockable	Objective
Big Otasi Easter Egg (N.Y. Streets, Stage 2, Section 6)	After killing Shark Guy and the two teleporters, the barrier in front of the Subway stairs will explode and you can proceed to the next stage. Instead of going down the Subway stairs, walk to the building doorway that is behind the stairs. Stand next to the doorway for twenty seconds or so, then walk left to the line of cars that stretch across the street. Look past the cars to see a giant Otasi running across the street. It is purely a visual thing—you don't get any bonuses—but what a sight!

Metal Gear Solid 2: Substance

Description	Objective
Alternate Ending	Clear "A Snake Tale" to unlock the M9. Then use it to stun all the Bosses instead of killing them.
Boss Survival Mode	Clear the game on any difficulty.
Casting Theater	Clear the game on any difficulty.
Digital Camera	Complete the game to unlock the camera. The digital camera is at Strut E Shell 1.
MGS Snake	Clear 100% of the VR missions as Snake, Pliskin, Tuxedo Snake, Raiden, Ninja Raiden and Raiden X.
Ninja Raiden	Clear 50% of the VR missions using Raiden. Ninja Raiden is only available on VR Missions.
Photograph Mode	Clear Bomb Disposal mode, "Hold-up" mode, and Eliminate mode. Photograph mode is in the VR Missions only.
Pliskin	Clear 50% of the VR missions using Snake.
Raiden X	Clear 100% of the VR missions using Raiden and Ninja Raiden.
Sunglasses	Complete the game twice, then Snake and Raiden will be wearing sunglasses.
Tuxedo Snake	Clear 100% of the VR missions using Pliskin.

Micro Machines

Unlockable	Objective
Big Head Mode	Collect all three Star Tokens in This Ol' House GP.
Birds-Eye View Camera	Collect all three star tokens in Perilous Places GP.
Micro Marble	Collect all three Star Tokens in 911: Emergency GP.
Color Tint Edit	Collect all three Star Tokens in Hicksville HoeDown GP.
Concept Art	Collect all three Star Tokens in Jungle Jamboree GP.
Hovercar Vehicle	Win the Platinum Cup in challenge mode.
Micro Soccer Mode	Find the three hidden Star Tokens located in the Beachside GP in single player mode.

Midnight Club: Street Racing

Description	Code
Bonus Cars	Keep an eye out for red circles that appear on levels. Stop your car on the circle until you hear a gurgling sound. That unlocks a new car. There are red circles on London and New York, but there could be a lot more from other levels.
Dune Buggy Car	Use a memory card that has some saved data from the Smugglers Run game.

DS

GBA

PSP

PS2

PS3

Wii

Xbox

Xbox 360

Index

Midnight Club II

Enter the following codes from the Cheat menu.

Unlockable	Code
All Cars	theCollector
All Game Modes	dextran
All Locations	Globetrotter
All Locations and Cars (Arcade mode only)	pennyThug
Better Control in the Air	carcrobatics
Change Difficulty Levels	howhardcanitbe0 (easiest)
Change Difficulty Levels	howhardcanitbe1
Change Difficulty Levels	howhardcanitbe2
Change Difficulty Levels	howhardcanitbe3
Change Difficulty Levels	howhardcanitbe4
Change Difficulty Levels	howhardcanitbe5
Change Difficulty Levels	howhardcanitbe6
Change Difficulty Levels	howhardcanitbe7
Change Difficulty Levels	howhardcanitbe8
Change Difficulty Levels	howhardcanitbe9 (hardest)
Infinite Nitrous	greenLantern
Invincibility	gladiator
Machine Gun and Rocket Code	savethekids
LAPD car in Arcade Mode	Beat all five circuit races for LA in Arcade mode.
Paris Cop Car	Beat all 6 of the Paris arcade circuit tracks.
SLF450X	Complete 100% of the game.
The Veloci	Beat all of the World Champion's races.
Tokyo Cop Car	Beat all 7 Tokyo arcade circuit tracks.

Midnight Club 3 Dub Edition

Enter these case sensitive passwords in the Cheats section under Options.

Unlockable	Password
All cities in arcade mode	crosscountry
Bunny ears	getheadl
Chrome Body	haveyouseenthisboy
Faster pedestrians/All cities in arcade mode	urbansprawl
Flaming Head	trythisathome
Increase car mass in arcade mode	hyperagro
No damage	ontheroad
Pumpkin Heads	getheadk
Skull head	getheadn
Snowman head	getheadm
Special move Agro	dfens
Special move Roar	Rjnr
Special move Zone	allin
Unlock all cities	roadtrip
Yellow Smile	getheadj

Mike Tyson Heavyweight Boxing

Enter the following codes at the Title Screen

Unlockable	Code	Unlockable	Code
Big Head Mode	■,●,↑,↓	Small Head Mode	■,●,↓,↑
Codies Credits	×,▲,■,●	Square 2D/flat Mode	↓,↑,●,■
Custom boxer textures	L1,R1,×,×,▲,×	Super Mutant Mode	■,←,↑,▲
Platinum Unlock (All boxers, arenas, and game modes)	■,●,L2,R2		

Minority Report

Enter the following as codes.

Description	Code	Description	Code
All Combos	NINJA	Maximum Ammunition	MRJUAREZ
All FMV Sequences	DIRECTOR	Maximum Damage	SPINACH
All Weapons	STRAPPED	Pain Arenas	MAXIMUMHURT
Armor	STEELUP	Play as Clown	SCARYCLOWN
Baseball Bat	SLUGGER	Play as Convict	JAILBREAK
Bouncy Men	BOUNZMEN	Play as GI	GNRLINFANTRY
Cluttered Locations	CLUTZ	Play as Lizard	HISSSS
Concept Art	SKETCHPAD	Play as Moseley	BIGLIPS
Dramatic Finish	STYLIN	Play as Nara	WEIGHTGAIN
Ending Sequence	WIMP	Play as Nikki	HAIRLOSS
Extra Health	BUTTERUP	Play as Robot	MRROBOTO
Free Aim	FPSSTYLE	Play as Superhero	SUPERJOHN
Invincibility	LRGARMS	Play as Zombie	IAMSODEAD
Level Select	PASSKEY	Rag Doll	CLUMSY
Level Skip	QUITER	Slow Motion Button	SLIZOMIZO

Mister Mosquito

Enter these codes on the Selection menu. Hold L2 will entering the codes.

Unlockable	Code
Doctor Mosquito	⇧,⇨,⇦,⇩, ■, ■, R2, R2, R2
Mama Mosquito	⇧,⇨,⇦,⇩, ■, ■, R1, R1, R1

MLB 2004

The game must be paused for these codes to work. You will feel the controller vibrate if you entered the codes correctly.

Unlockable	Code
Big Ball	L2, L2, L2, L2, ↑, →, ↓, ←
Big Body Mode	↑, ↓, ←, →, L2, L2, R2, R1
Big Head Mode	↑, ←, ↓, →, ↑, →, ↓, ←
Faster Players	←, →, →, ←, L2, R1, R1, L2
Invisible Body Mode	R1, R2, R1, R2, ↑, ↓, ←, →
Programmer Names	R1, R2, →, →, ←, ←, L2, L2
Slower Players	←, ←, →, →, R2, R2, L2, L2
Tiny Head Mode	↑, ↓, ↑, ↓, R1, R1, L2, L2

DS

GBA

PSP

PS2

PS3

Wii

Xbox

Xbox 360

Index

MLB 2005

Enter the following codes in the Main menu:

Unlockable	Code	Unlockable	Code
All Players	←,↑,←,→,↓,→,←,↑	Black and White	↑,↑,↓,↓,←,→,←,→
All Stadiums	↓,↑,←,→,↑,↑,→,↓	Faster Runners	←,→,←,→,←,→,↑,↑
All Teams	←,→,→,↓,↓,←,↑,↑	Slow Runners	→,←,→,←,→,←,↓,↓
All Uniforms	↑,↓,←,→,←,↓,↑,↓	Small Head	↑,↓,↑,↑,→,→,→,←
Beans (Flatulent Ballplayers)	→,→,→,→,→,→,←,↓	Super Pitch Break	→,←,→,←,→,←,↑,↑
Big Ball	↑,↑,→,←,↑,↑,→,←	Super Pitch Speed	↑,↑,↑,←,←,←,←,→
Big Head	←,→,←,→,↑,↑,↑,↓	Super Six Pitches	↓,↑,↓,→,→,→,→,←

MLB 2006

Pause the game to enter this code.

Unlockable	Code
Fart Mode	⇧,⇧,⇩,⇩,⇦,⇨,⇦,⇨

MLB Slugfest 2003

Enter these codes in the "Today's Match-Up" screen. The first number is the number of times you press ■, the second is the number of times you press ▲, and the third is the number of times you press ●.

Unlockable	Code	Unlockable	Code
16" Softball	2 4 2 ↓	No Fatigue	3 4 3 ↑
Big Heads	2 0 0 →	Pinto Team	2 1 0 →
Eagle Team	2-1-2 →	Rocket Park Stadium	3 2 1 ↑
Extra Time After Plays	1 2 3 ↑	Roman Coliseum Stadium	3 3 3 ↑
Horse Team	2 1 1 →	Rubber Ball	2 4 2 ↑
Lion Team	2 2 0 →	Terry Fitzgerald Team	3 3 3 →
Log Bat	0 0 4 ↑	Tiny Heads	2 0 0 ←
Mace Bat	0 0 4 ←	Todd McFarlane Team	2 2 2 →
Max Batting	3 0 0 ←	Tournament Mode	1 1 1 ↓
Max Power	0 3 0 ←	Unlimited Turbo	4 4 4 ↓
Max Speed	0 0 3 ←	Wiffle Ball Bat	0 0 4 →
No Contact Mode	4 3 3 ←		

MLB Slugfest 2004

Cheat Mode: Press ■, ▲, and ● to change the icons in the first, second, and third boxes respectively at the match-up screen. The numbers in the following list indicate the number of times you press each button. After the icons change, press the D-pad in the indicated direction to enable the code. For example, to enter 1-2-3 ←, press ■, ▲, ▲, ●, ●, ●, ←.

Description	Code	Description	Code
16" Softball	2, 4, 2, ↓	Dolphin Team	1, 0, 2, ↓
Alien Team	2, 3, 1, ↓	Dwarf Team	1, 0, 3, ↓
Atlantis Stadium	3, 2, 1, ←	Eagle Team	2, 1, 2, ↓
Big Head	2, 0, 0, →	Empire Park Stadium	3, 2, 1, →
Blade Bat	0, 0, 2, ↑	Evil Clown Team	2, 1, 1, ↓
Bobble Head Team	1, 3, 3, ↓	Extended Time for Codes	3, 0, 3, ↑
Bone Bat	0, 0, 1, ↑	Forbidden City Stadium	3, 3, 3, ←
Casey Team	2, 3, 3, ↓	Gladiator Team	1, 1, 3, ↓
Cheats Disabled	1, 1, 1, ↓	Horse Team	2, 1, 1, →
Coliseum Stadium	3, 3, 3, ↑	Ice Bat	0, 0, 3, ↑

MLB Slugfest 2004 (continued)

Description	Code	Description	Code
Lion Team	2, 2, 0, →	Pinto Team	2, 1, 0, →
Little League	1, 0, 1, ↓	Rivera Team	2, 2, 2, ↑
Log Bat	0, 0, 4, ↑	Rocket Park Stadium	3, 2, 1, ↑
Mace Bat	0, 0, 4, ←	Rodeo Clown	1, 3, 2, ↓
Max Batting	3, 0, 0, ←	Rubber Ball	2, 4, 2, ↑
Max Power	0, 3, 0, ←	Scorpion Team	1, 1, 2, ↓
Max Speed	0, 0, 3, ←	Spike Bat	0, 0, 5, ↑
Midway Park Stadium	3, 2, 1, ↓	Team Terry Fitzgerald	3, 3, 3, →
Minotaur Team	1, 1, 0, ↓	Team Todd McFarlane	2, 2, 2, →
Monument Stadium	3, 3, 3, ↓	Tiny Head	2, 0, 0, ←
Napalitano Team	2, 3, 2, ↓	Unlimited Turbo	4, 4, 4, ↓
Olshan Team	2, 2, 2, ↓	Whiffle Bat	0, 0, 4, →

MLB Slugfest Loaded

Enter the following codes at the Versus screen.

Unlockable	Code	Unlockable	Code
Big Head Mode	■, ■, →	Softball Mode	■, ■, ▲, ▲, ▲, ▲, ●, ●, ↓
Max Batting	■, ■, ■, ←		
Max Power	▲, ▲, ▲, ←	Tiny Head Mode	■, ■, ←
Max Speed	●, ●, ●, ←	Unlimited Turbo	■, ■, ■, ■, ▲, ▲, ▲, ▲, ●, ●, ●, ●, ↓
Rubber Ball Mode	■, ■, ▲, ▲		

Mobile Suit Gundam: Journey to Jaburo

Description	Code
Tactics Battle Mode	Complete Story Mode.

Mortal Kombat: Deadly Alliance

Unlockable	Code
Random Character Select	Highlight "Shang Tsung" (for player one) or "Quan Chi" (for player two) at the Character Selection screen, and then hold ↑ + START.
Versus Mode Stage Select	Press R1 before either player chooses a character to get a screen with a screenshot of a stage. Press ← or → to change to the desired stage.
Versus Mode Skill Select	Press L2 before either player chooses a character.

Fatalities!

You can do fatalities from anywhere on screen! Press L1 at the Finish Him/Her screen to change into your fatality stance, or you have to figure out the distance range.

Fatality	Button Combination
Bo Rai Cho (Belly Flop)	Press Away (x3), ↓, ●.
Cyrax (Smasher)	Press Toward (x2), ↑, ▲.
Drahmin (Iron Bash)	Press Away, Toward (x2), ↓, ✕.
Frost (Freeze Shatter)	Press Toward, Away, ↑, ↓, ■.
Hsu Hao (Laser Slice)	Press Toward, Away, ↓, ↓, ▲.
Jax (Head Stomp)	Press ↓, Toward (x2), ↓, ▲.
Johnny Cage (Brain Ripper)	Press Away, Toward (x2), ↓, ▲.
Kano (Heart Grab)	Press Toward, ↑ (x2), ↓, ■.
Kenshi (Telekinetic Crush)	Press Toward, Away, Toward, ↓, ✕.

DS · GBA · PSP · PS2 · PS3 · Wii · Xbox · Xbox 360 · Index

Mortal Kombat: Deadly Alliance (continued)

Fatality	Button Combination
Kitana (Kiss of Doom)	Press ↓, ↑, Toward (x2), ▲.
Kung Lao (Hat Throw)	Press ↓, ↑, Away, ✕.
Li Mei (Crush Kick)	Press Toward (x2), ↓, Toward, ●.
Mavado (Kick Thrust)	Press Away (x2), ↑ (x2), ■.
Nitara (Blood Thirst)	Press ↑ (x2), Toward, ■.
Quan Chi (Neck Stretch)	Press Away (x2), Toward, Away, ✕.
Raiden (Electrocution)	Press Away, Toward, Toward (x2), ✕.
Reptile (Acid Shower)	Press ↑ (x3), Toward, ✕.
Scorpion (Spear)	Press Away (x2), ↓, Away+●.
Shang Tsung (Soul Steal)	Press ↑, ↓, ↑, ↓, ▲.
Sonya (Kiss)	Press Away, Toward (x2), ↓, ▲.
Sub Zero (Spine Rip)	Press Away, Toward (x2), ↓, ✕.

Moto GP

Description	Objective
Alex Barros	Get one lap under 1'54"000 at Motegi stage in Time Trial mode on any difficulty.
Alex Criville	Place first at Jerez in Arcade mode on Normal difficulty.
Carlos Checa	Get one lap under 1'24"000 at Paul Ricardo stage in Time Trial mode on any difficulty setting.
Gun Koma	Complete one season under Season mode on Easy difficulty.
Haruchika Aoki	Beat 24"000 in Challenge mode on any difficulty setting.
Jean Michel Bayle	Beat 8"280 in Challenge mode on any difficulty setting.
Jerez Reverse	Place first at Jerez in Arcade mode on Hard difficulty.
John Kocinski	Place first at Paul Ricard in Arcade mode on Normal difficulty.
Jose Luis Cardoso	Beat 20"300 in Challenge mode on any difficulty setting.
Juan Borja	Beat 22"200 in Challenge mode on any difficulty setting.
Jurgen Vd Goorbergh	Beat 13"600 in Challenge mode on any difficulty setting.
K1	Get three laps under 1'22"500 in Time Trial mode on any difficulty setting.
Kenny Roberts	Place first at Motegi in Arcade mode on Normal difficulty.
Klonoa	Beat 21"000 in Challenge mode on any difficulty setting.
Max Biaggi	Get one lap under 2'12"000 at Suzuka stage in Time Trial mode on any difficulty setting.
Mick Doohan	Get first overall at the end of five seasons in Season mode on Hard difficulty.
Mike Hale	Beat 22"000 in Challenge mode on any difficulty setting.
Motegi Reverse	Place first at Motegi in Arcade mode on Hard difficulty.
Nobuatsu Aoki	Beat 20"000 in Challenge mode on any difficulty setting.
Norick Abe	Place first at Suzuka in Arcade mode on Normal difficulty.
Paul Ricard Reverse	Place first at Paul Ricard in Arcade mode on Hard difficulty.
Photo	Beat 20"500 in Challenge mode on any difficulty setting.
Photo	Bcot 24"000 in Challonge mode on any difficulty setting.
Photo	Beat 25"200 in Challenge mode on any difficulty setting.
Photo	Beat 28"500 in Challenge mode on any difficulty setting.
Photo	Beat 29"500 in Challenge mode on any difficulty setting.
Photo	Beat 31"000 in Challenge mode on any difficulty setting.
Photo	Beat 31"700 in Challenge mode on any difficulty setting.
Photo	Beat 33"000 in Challenge mode on any difficulty setting.
Photo	Beat 33"600 in Challenge mode on any difficulty setting.
Photo	Beat 34"500 in Challenge mode on any difficulty setting.
Photo	Beat 35"200 in Challenge mode on any difficulty setting.

DS · GBA · PSP · PS2 · PS3 · Wii · Xbox · Xbox 360 · Index

Moto GP (continued)

Description	Objective
Photo	Beat 36"700 in Challenge mode on any difficulty setting.
Photo	Beat 56"200 in Challenge mode on any difficulty setting.
Photo	Complete all races in one season under Season mode on any difficulty setting.
Photo	Complete all races in one season under Season mode on Normal or Hard difficulty.
Photo	Complete every race over five seasons in Season mode on hard difficulty where the laps are set to full.
Photo	Complete three consecutive laps where all the lap times are under 2'10"000 in Time Trial mode on any difficulty setting.
Photo	Get a Bronze or Silver on all the challenges above in Challenge mode on any difficulty setting.
Photo	Get a Gold on all the challenges above in Challenge mode on any difficulty setting.
Photo	Pass 10 or more bikes in one lap in Arcade mode on any difficulty setting.
Photo	Place first at Suzuka in Arcade mode on any difficulty setting. You must not touch another or go off road at any time.
Photo	Race with all 12 teams in Season mode on Hard difficulty.
Photo	Race with all 12 teams in Season mode on Normal difficulty.
Photo	Use a Level C or D team and finish first overall at the end of one season in Season mode on Hard difficulty.
Photo	Using all three Level A teams, place first on every circuit in Arcade mode on any difficulty setting.
Regis Laconi	Beat 24"000 in Challenge mode on any difficulty setting.
Sete Gibernau	Get one lap under 1'47"000 at Jerez stage in Time Trial mode on any difficulty setting.
Simon Crafar	Place first at Donington in Arcade mode on Normal difficulty.
Suzuka Reverse	Place first at Suzuka in Arcade mode on Hard difficulty.
Tadayuki Okada	Get one lap under 1'36"000 at Donington stage in Time Trial mode on any difficulty setting.
Takuma Aoki	Beat 35"500 in Challenge mode on any difficulty setting.
Tetsuya Harada	Complete all five seasons in Season mode on Hard difficulty

Motor Mayhem

Description	Code
Buzzsaw as a playable character	Beat the Deathmatch, Endurance, and Eliminator modes with the same character on either Hard or Very Hard difficulty.

MTX Mototrax

Go to the Options menu and select Cheats. Enter the following:

Unlockable	Code	Unlockable	Code
All Tracks	BA7H	Officer Dick	BADG3
Butterfingers Gear	B77393	Sky Camera	HIC
Fast Acceleration	JIH345	Slipknot Maggot	86657457
Left Field Gear	12345	Slipknot Movie	23F7IC5
Max Air	BFB0020	SoBe Gear	50B3
Nokia Trickbot	HA79000	Speed Demon	773H999

DS

GBA

PSP

PS2

PS3

Wii

Xbox

Xbox 360

Index

DS

MTX vs. ATV Unleashed

Enter in the Cheats menu.

Unlockable	Code
50cc Bikes	Minimoto
Unlock all freestyle tracks	Huckit
Unlock Everything	Toolazy

MVP Baseball 2003

Description	Code
16:9 Anamorphic View	Press and hold the L2 and R2 triggers for more than 3 seconds. Then, press ← on the directional pad to enable. Press → on the directional pad to disable.
Broken Bats	Create a player named Keegn Patersn, Jacob Patersn, or Ziggy Patersn.
Home Run Cheat	Create a player named Erik Kiss.

MVP Baseball 2004

Enter the following names in the Create a Player screen:

Name	Unlockable
John Prosen	Huge Hat
Jacob Paterson	Huge Bat
Kenny Lee	Bone Scaling Cheat
Erik Kiss	Bad Player

MVP Baseball 2005

Create a character with these names.

Unlockable	Name
Player has a huge bat	Keegan Paterson
Player has a huge bat	Jacob Paterson
Player has a huge bat	Isaiah Paterson
Unlock Everything	Katie Roy

MX Unleashed

Go to Options and select Cheat Codes. Pick the cheat you want and press ● to enter the code.

Unlockable	Code	Unlockable	Code
500cc Bikes	BIGDOGS	Expert A.I.	OBTGOFAST
50cc Bikes	SQUIRRELDOG	Freestyle Tracks	BUSTBIG
A.I. Bowling	WRECKINGBALL	National Tracks	ECONATION
All Bonuses/Completion	CLAPPEDOUT	Pro Physics	SWAPPIN
All Machines	MINIGAMES	Supercross Tracks	STUPERCROSS

My Street

Description	Code
Custom Body Parts	Beat Story Mode once.

Nano Breaker

Enter code during game.

Unlockable	Code
Mini Map Shooter	⇑, ⇑, ⇓, ⇓, ⇐, ⇒, ⇐, ⇐, ⇒, ✕, ●

GBA
PSP
PS2
PS3
Wii
Xbox
Xbox 360
Index

Narc

Enter these codes while playing. Do not pause the game.

Unlockable	Code
All Drugs	Repeatedly press L1 + R1 + L3
All Weapons	Repeatedly press L1 + R1 + R3
Infinite Ammo	Repeatedly press L1 + R1 + ⇧ (Only for the weapon you have equipped.)
Invincibility	Repeatedly press R1 + L1 + ✕
Show all Drug Stashes	Repeatedly press L1 + R1 + ⇦

Naruto: Ultimate Ninja 2

Enter these codes in Naruto's House selection.

Unlockable	Code
1,000 Ryo	Water Rat Rooster Boar
1,000 Ryo	Water Rat Monkey Rooster
1,000 Ryo	Water Rat Rat Monkey
1,000 Ryo	Water Horse Rat Ram
1,000 Ryo	Water Horse Hare Dragon
1,000 Ryo	Water Horse Horse Horse
1,000 Ryo	Fire Rat Snake Dragon
1,000 Ryo	Fire Rat Dragon Dog
1,000 Ryo	Water Ram Horse Dog
1,000 Ryo	Water Ram Rooster Monkey
1,000 Ryo	Water Hare Monkey Monkey
1,000 Ryo	Earth Snake Snake Snake
5,000 Ryo	Water Snake Rooster Horse
5,000 Ryo	Water Tiger Dragon Tiger
Get Ninja Card (Tactics 66)	Earth Dragon Rat Dragon
Ninja Info Card (Jutsu-63)	Fire Ox Tiger Dog
Ninja Info Card (Jutsu-86)	Fire Ox Hare Hare
Ninja Info Card (Tactics 46)	Fire Ox Dog Snake
Ninja Info Card (Tactics-157)	Fire Rat Dragon Hare
Ninja Info Card (tactics-87)	Lightning Rat Rat Horse
Sexy Jujitsu Ninja Info Card	Lightning Rat Ox Tiger
Unlock "Fiery Duo's Challenge"	Wind Dog Monkey Ram
Unlock All Characters	Lightning Snake Rat Dragon

NASCAR 2001

Unlockable	Objective
Black Box Classic Car	Win the Short Track Challenge.
Black Box Exotic Car	Win the Half Season.
EA Sports Car	Win the Road Course Challenge.
EA.com Car	Win the Superspeedway Shootout at Veteran or Legend difficulty.
Treasure Island Track	Under Veteran difficulty, win a season.

DS
GBA
PSP
PS2
PS3
Wii
Xbox
Xbox 360
Index

DS

NASCAR 2005: Chase for the Cup

In the Edit Driver Screen, enter the following names to access cheats (the names are case-sensitive):

Unlockable	Password
$10,000,000	Walmart NASCAR
All Bonuses	Open Sesame
Dale Earnhardt	The Intimidator
Fantasy Track	Walmart Exclusive
Mr. Clean Pit Crew	Clean Crew

GBA

NASCAR 06: Total Team Control

In Fight to the Top mode, go to the Edit Driver screen and enter the following passwords as your first and last names. (Note: case sensitive)

Unlockable	Password
$10,000,000	Walmart Money
Dale Jarett in the UPS "Big Brown Truck"	Race TheTruck
Max Fan Level	Super Star
Max Prestige	MeMyself AndI
Max Team Prestige	All ForOne
Unlock All Chase Plates	Gimme Gimme
Unlocks Dale Sr.	The Intimidator
Walmart Raceway, Walmart Cars, and Walmart Sponsorship for Custom Car	Walmart Exclusive

PSP

PS2

NASCAR Heat 2002

Unlockable	Objective
Unlock Hardcore Realism Mode	To unlock Hardcore Realism Mode, earn a 100 point rating on any track. The Hardcore Realism will be unlocked for the track on which you earned the rating.
Unlock Richard Petty	Complete all of the Heat Challenges and earn at least a Bronze rating on each to unlock the legendary Richard Petty.

PS3

NASCAR Thunder 2002

Go to Create-a-Car and enter any of these names to unlock a new car in Driver Select:

Dave Alpern	Troi Hayes	Dave Nichols
Buster Auton	Crissy Hillsworth	Ken Patterson
Scott Brewer	Traci Hultzapple	Dick Paysor
Audrey Clark	Rick Humphrey	Beeny Persons
Rick Edwards	Kristi Jones	Tom Renedo
Michelle Emser	Joey Joulwan	Chuck Spicer
Katrina Goode	Cheryl King	Sasha Soares
Diane Grubb	Mandy Misiak	
Jim Hannigan	Josh Neelon	

Wii

Xbox

Xbox 360

Index

NASCAR Thunder 2003

Enter the following codes at the Create-a-Car screen.

Unlockable	Code
Get Dale Earnhardt	Dale Earnhardt
Get Fantasy Drivers	Extra Drivers

NASCAR Thunder 2004

Go to Features and select Create-A-Car. Enter Seymore Cameos as the driver name to unlock a cool Thunder Plate.

NBA 2K6

From the Main menu, go to "Features," then "Codes" to enter the following codes.

Unlockable	Code
2005-2006 Pacers Uniform	31andonly
2K Sports Team	2ksports
Nike Up Tempo Pro Shoes	anklebreakers
Nike Zoom Kobe 1 Shoes	kobe

From the Main menu, go to "Features," then "THE CRIB." Go to the PowerBar vending machine and enter the following codes.

Unlockable	Code
+10 Bonus for Defensive Awareness	lockdown
+10 Bonus for Offensive Awareness	getaclue
Max Durability	noinjury
Powerbar Tattoo	pbink
Unlimited Stamina	nrgmax
Unlock All Items	criball

NBA Ballers

Enter these codes in the "VS" screen. The first number is the number of times you press ■, the second is the number of times you press ▲, and the third is the number of times you press ●.

Unlockable	Code	Unlockable	Code
2X Juice Replenish	431	Perfect Free Throws	327
Alley-Oop Ability	725	Play As Afro Man	517
Alternate Gear	123	Play As Agent	557
Baby Ballers	423	Play As BiznezMan-A	537
Back-In Ability	122	Play As BiznezMan-B	527
Back-In Ability	317	Play As Coach	567
Big Head Mode	134	Play As Secretary	547
Expanded Move Set	512	Put Back Ability	313
Fire Ability	722	Pygmy	425
Good Handling	332	R2R Mode	008
Half House Meter	367	Rain	222
Hot Spot	627	Random Moves	300
Kid Ballers	433	Shows Shot Percentage	012
Legal Goal Tending	756	Snow	333
No Weather	112	Speedy Players	213
Paper Ballers	354	Stunt Dunk Ability	374

DS
GBA
PSP
PS2
PS3
Wii
Xbox
Xbox 360
Index

NBA Ballers (continued)

Unlockable	Code	Unlockable	Code
Super Back-Ins	235	Super Steals	215
Super Blocks	124	Tournament Mode	011
Super Push	315	Young Ballers	443

Go to "Inside Stuff" and select "Phrase-ology." Enter the following codes to unlock goodies:

Unlockable	Code
Allen Iverson's Alternate Gear	killer crossover
Allen Iverson's Studio	the answer
Alonzo Mourning	zo
Amare Stoudamire	rising sun
Baron Davis	Stylin & Profilin
Ben Wallace's alternate outfit	radio controlled cars
Bill Russell	celtics dynasty
Bill Walton	towers of power
Chris Webber	24 seconds
Clyde Drexler	clyde the glide
Darryl Dawkins	rim wrecker
Dikembe Mutumbo	in the paint
Dominique Wilkins	dunk fest
Elton Brand	rebound
George Gervin	the ice man cometh
Jalen Rose	bring it
Jason Kidd	pass the rock
Jason Williams	give and go
Jerry Stackhouse's Alt. Gear	Stop Drop and Roll
John Stockton	court vision
Julius Erving	one on one
Karl Malone	special delivery
Karl Malone's Devonshire Estate	ice house
Kevin Garnett's alternate outfit	boss hoss
Kevin McHale	holla back
Kobe Bryant's Alt. Gear	Japanese steak
Larry Bird	hoosier
Latrell Sprewell	spree
Lebron James	king james
Magic Johnson	laker legends
Manu Ginobili gear	manu
Michael Finley	student of the game
Nene Hilario	rags to riches
Oscar Robertson's Alt. Gear	Ain't No Thing
Pete Maravich	pistol pete
Rashard Lewis	fast forward
Rasheed Wallace	bring down the house
Ray Allen	all star

NBA Ballers (continued)

Unlockable	Code
Reggie Miller's Alt. Gear	From Downtown
Richard Hamilton	rip
Robert Parrish's Alt. Gear	The Chief
Scottie Pippen	playmaker
Scottie Pippen's Yacht	nice yacht
Shaq's alternate outfit	diesel rules the paint
Special Movie #1	juice house
Special Movie #2	nba showtime
Special Shoe #1	dub deuce
Stephon Marbury	platinum playa
Steve Francis	ankle breaker
Steve Francis's Alt. Gear	Rising Star
Steve Nash	hair canada
Tim Duncan	make it take it
Tony Parkers Alternative outfit	run and shoot
Tracy McGrady	living like a baller
Wally Szczerbiak	world
Walt Frazier	Penetrate and Perpetrate
Wes Unseld	old school
Willis Reed	hall of fame
Wilt Chamberlain	wilt the stilt
Yao Ming	center of attention
Yao Ming's Grade School	prep school

NBA Hoopz

At the Versus screen, use the following buttons to change the numbers for code entry: ■ to change the first number, ✕ to change the second number, and ● to change the third number. Then use the D-Pad to enter the direction. If you entered the code correctly you'll see the name of the code displayed on the screen.

Unlockable	Objective	Unlockable	Objective
ABA Ball	1-1-1 →	No Goaltending	4-4-4 ←
Away Uniform	0-2-4 →	No Hotspots	3-0-1 ↑
Beach Court	0-2-3 ←	Play As Dr. Atomic	5-4-4 ←
Big Heads	3-0-0 →	Show Hotspot	1-1-0 ↓
Granny Shots	1-2-1 ←	Show Shot Percent	0-1-1 ↓
Home Uniform	0-1-4 →	Street Court	3-2-0 ←
Infinite Turbo	3-1-2 ↑	Tiny Heads	3-3-0 ←
No Fouls	2-2-2 →	Tiny Players	5-4-3 ←

NBA Jam

Create a new profile using these names.

Unlockable	Code
Unlock Everything	-LPP-
Unlock the NBA Jam Development Team	CREDITS

DS · GBA · PSP · PS2 · PS3 · Wii · Xbox · Xbox 360 · Index

DS

GBA

PSP

PS2

PS3

Wii

Xbox

Xbox 360

Index

NBA Live 2001

Unlockable	Objective
Creating a Dream Team	Go into Season mode, hit ● to bring up the menu bar, and select "Roster" from the bar. From here, select "Create Player." When creating a player, load him up with maximum stats and save him into the Free Agent pool. Then, return to the menu bar, select "Roster" and Sign the player you've just made. If his rating is over 90, you can trade him for any player in the league (including Shaq and Allen Iverson). Repeat this process until you have all the talent you want.
Make a Super Star Even Better	At the Main menu, press ● to open the Active menu. Select "Roster," then select "Edit Player." A Super Star loads up if your Create-a-Player list is empty. Make the player's stats better (3 pointers, strength, dunking, etc.) by hitting [R2] at the Edit Player screen. If you want a different player, go back to the empty Create-a-Player list by pressing [L1]. Press [START] and change someone else.

NBA Live 2003

Go to Create-a-Player and enter the following names as the last name (if done correctly, a message will appear):

Unlockable	Name	Unlockable	Name
B-Rich	DOLLABILLS	Fabolous	GHETTOFAB
Busta Rhymes	FLIPMODE	Hot Karl	CALIFORNIA
DJ Clue	MIXTAPES	Just Blaze	GOODBEATS

NBA Live 2004

Unlockable	Code	Unlockable	Code
15,000 NBA Store Points	87843H5F9P	All NBA Gear	ERT9976KJ3
All Hardwood Classic Jerseys	725JKUPLMM	All Shoes	POUY985GY5
		All Team Gear	YREY5625WQ

For the following codes, go to Roster Management from Team Management. Create a player with any of the following last names listed.

Unlockable Player	Name	Unlockable Player	Name
Aleksander Pavlovic	WHSUCPOI	Nedzad Sinanovic	ZXDSDRKE
Andreas Glyniadakis	POCKDLEK	Paccelis Morlende	QWPOASZX
Carlos Delfino	SDFGURKL	Remon Van de Hare	ITNVCJSD
James Lang	NBVKSMCN	Rick Rickert	POILKJMN
Jermaine Dupri	SOSODEF	Sani Becirovic	ZXCCVDRI
Kyle Korver	OEISNDLA	Sofoklis Schortsanitis	IOUBFDCJ
Malick Badiane	SKENXIDO	Szymon Szewczyk	POIOJIS
Mario Austin	POSNEGHX	Tommy Smith	XCFWQASE
Matt Bonner	BBVDKCVM	Xue Yuyang	WMZKCOI

To enter the next two tables of codes, go to NBA Live and select NBA Codes.

Unlockable Shoes	Code
Air Bounds (Black/White/Blue)	7YSS0292KE
Air Bounds (White/Black)	JA807YAM20
Air Bounds (White/Green)	84HHST61QI
Air Flight 89 (Black/White)	FG874JND84
Air Flight 89 (White/Black)	63RBVC7423
Air Flight 89 (White/Red)	GF9845JHR4
Air Flightposite (White/Black/Gray)	74FDH7K94S

NBA Live 2004 (continued)

Unlockable Shoes	Code
Air Flightposite (White/Black)	6HJ874SFJ7
Air Flightposite (Yellow/Black/White)	MN54BV45C2
Air Flightposite 2 (Blue/Gray)	2389JASE3E
Air Foamposite 1 (Blue)	OP5465UX12
Air Foamposite 1 (White/Black/Red)	DOD843HH7F
Air Foamposite Pro (Black/Gray)	3245AFSD45
Air Foamposite Pro (Red/Black)	DSAKF38422
Air Foamposite Pro (Blue/Black)	DG56TRF446
Air Force Max (Black)	F84N845H92
Air Force Max (White/Black/Blue)	985KJF98KJ
Air Force Max (White/Red)	8734HU8FFF
Air Hyperflight (White)	14TGU7DEWC
Air Hyperflight (Blue/White)	A0K374HF8S
Air Hyperflight (Yellow/Black)	JCX93LSS88
Air Hyperflight (Black/White)	WW44YHU592
Air Jordan 11 (White)	HG76HN765S
Air Jordan 11 (White/Black)	A2S35TH7H6
Air Jordan 11 (Black/Red/White)	GF64H76ZX5
Air Jordan 11 (Black/Varsity Royal/ White)	HJ987RTGFA
Air Jordan 11 (Cool/Grey)	GF75HG6332
Air Jordan 3 (Black/White/Gray)	CVJ554TJ58
Air Jordan 3 (White)	G9845HJ8F4
Air Jordan 3 (White/Clay)	435SGF555Y
Air Jordan 3 (White/Fire Red)	RE6556TT9O
Air Jordan 3 (White/True Blue)	FDS9D74J4F
Air Max2 CB (Black/White)	87HZXGFIU8
Air Max2 CB (White/Red)	4545GFKJIU
Air Max2 UPTEMPO (Black/White/Blue)	NF8745J87F
Air Max Elite (Black)	A4CD54T7TD
Air Max Elite (White/Black)	966ERTFG65
Air Max Elite (White/Blue)	FD9KN48FJF
Air Zoom Flight (Gray/White)	367UEY6SN
Air Zoom Flight (White/Blue)	92387HDO77
Air Zoom Generation (White/Red/Black)	23LBJNUMB1
Air Zoom Generation (Black/Red/White)	LBJ23CAVS1
Nike Blazer (Black)	XCV6456NNL
Nike Blazer (Khaki)	W3R57U9NB2
Nike Blazer (Tan/White/Blue)	DCT5YHMU9O
Nike Blazer (White/Orange/Blue)	4G66JU99XS
Nike Shox BB4 (Black)	WE424TY563
Nike Shox BB4 (White/Black)	23ERT85LP9
Nike Shox BB4 (White/Light Purple)	668YYTRB12
Nike Shox BB4 (White/Red)	424TREU777
Nike Shox VCIII (Black)	SDFH764FJU
Nike Shox VCIII (White/Black/Red)	5JHD367JJT

DS

GBA

PSP

PS2

PS3

Wii

Xbox

Xbox 360

Index

DS

NBA Live 2005

Go to My NBA Live, EA Sports Lounge, NBA Codes to enter these codes.

Unlockable	Code
50,000 Dynasty Points	YISS55CZ0E
All Classics Hardwood Jerseys	PRYI234N0B
All Shoes	FHM389HU80
All Team Gear	1NVDR89ER2
Unlockable Shoes	**Code**
Nike Air.Huarache	VNBA60230T
Nike BG Rollout	0984ADF90P
Nike Shox Elite	2388HDFCBJ
Nike Air Unlimited	XVLJD9895V
Zoom Lebron II Shoes	1KENZO23XZ
Zoom Generation Low	234SDJF9W4
Unlockable Team	**Code**
Atlanta Hawks 2004-05 Alternate	HDI834NN9N
Boston Celtics 2004-05 Alternate	XCV43MGMDS
Dallas Mavericks 2004-05 Alternate	AAPSEUD09U
Golden State Warriors 2004-05 Alternate	NAVNY29548

NBA Live 06

Go to "My NBA Live," then "NBA Codes" to enter the following codes.

Unlockable	Code
Adidas A3 Garnett 3 Shoes	DRI239CZ49
S. Carter III LE Shoes	JZ3SCARTVY
TMac5 Black Shoes	258SHQW95B
TMac5 White Shoes	HGS83KP234P

NBA Live 07

To enter these passwords, select My NBA Live, then NBA Codes.

Unlockable	Code
Charlotte Bobcats secondary road uniform	JKL846ETK5
New Jersey Nets secondary road uniform	NB79D965D2
Utah Jazz secondary road uniform	228GG7585G
Washington Wizards secondary road uniform	PL5285F37F

NBA Shootout 2004

Unlockable	Code
All-Time Greats	At any screen in the All-Time Greats menu hold L1 + R1 + L2 + R2 and press ● + ■ to unlock selected players.

NBA Street

After entering one of the following icon codes, press Enter on the D-Pad to complete code entry.

Unlockable	Code
ABA Ball	Basketball, Turntable, Turntable, Basketball
ABA Socks	Microphone, Microphone, Microphone, Microphone
Athletic Joe "The Show"	Turntable, Shoe, Basketball, Turntable
Authentic Uniforms	Basketball, Basketball, Turntable, Turntable

NBA Street (continued)

Unlockable	Objective
Beach Ball	Basketball, Turntable, Turntable, Shoe
Big Heads	Microphone, Turntable, Shoe, Turntable
Captain Quicks	Backboard, Basketball, Shoe, Turntable
Casual Uniforms	Turntable, Turntable, Basketball, Basketball
Disable All Cheats	Turntable, Turntable, Turntable, Turntable
EA Big Ball	Basketball, Turntable, Microphone, Basketball
Easy Distance Shots	Shoe, Turntable, Backboard, Basketball
Explosive Rims	Turntable, Shoe, Microphone, Basketball
Harder Distance Shots	Shoe, Shoe, Backboard, Basketball
Less Blocks	Backboard, Turntable, Shoe, Backboard
Less Gamebreakers	Turntable, Backboard, Microphone, Shoe
Less Steals	Backboard, Turntable, Microphone, Basketball
Mad Handles	Backboard, Shoe, Turntable, Basketball
Medicine Ball	Basketball, Turntable, Turntable, Backboard
Mega Dunking	Backboard, Basketball, Turntable, Basketball
More Gamebreakers	Turntable, Microphone, Backboard, Shoe
No Alley-oops	Backboard, Microphone, Turntable, Shoe
No Auto Replays	Turntable, Shoe, Turntable, Turntable
No Dunks	Backboard, Basketball, Turntable, Shoe
No Gamebreakers	Turntable, Microphone, Microphone, Shoe
No HUD Display	Turntable, Microphone, Turntable, Shoe
No Player Indicators	Microphone, Basketball, Basketball, Microphone
No Shot Clock	Microphone, Microphone, Basketball, Backboard
No Shot Indicator	Microphone, Backboard, Shoe, Microphone
No Turbo	Turntable, Microphone, Microphone, Backboard
No Two-pointers	Backboard, Backboard, Basketball, Backboard
NuFX Ball	Basketball, Turntable, Backboard, Basketball
Player Names	Basketball, Turntable, Shoe, Backboard
Soccer Ball	Basketball, Shoe, Turntable, Basketball
Springtime Joe "The Show"	Turntable, Turntable, Basketball, Turntable
Sticky Fingers	Backboard, Microphone, Turntable, Basketball
Summertime Joe "The Show"	Turntable, Basketball, Basketball, Turntable
Super Swats	Backboard, Backboard, Turntable, Basketball
Tiny Heads	Microphone, Shoe, Basketball, Shoe
Tiny Players	Microphone, Basketball, Microphone, Basketball
Ultimate Power	Backboard, Turntable, Turntable, Backboard
Unlimited Turbo	Shoe, Basketball, Backboard, Basketball
Volleyball	Basketball, Turntable, Turntable, Microphone
WNBA ball	Basketball, Turntable, Shoe, Basketball
All Courts	In Hold the Court mode, go to the screen where you choose your court. Hold R2 and press ↑,↓,←,→,→,←,↓,↑. While still holding ↑, press ✕.
Biggs and Beacon Hill Court	Play the City Circuit and reach the Region 1 City Challenge. Defeat Biggs' team to unlock him as a selectable player and unlock the Beacon Hill court.
Bonafide and Broad Street Court	Play the City Circuit and reach the Region 2 City Challenge. Defeat Bonafide's team to unlock him as a selectable player and unlock the Broad Street court.
Created Player Pieces	Complete the Hold the Court challenges to unlock more pieces and development points for created players.

DS
GBA
PSP
PS2
PS3
Wii
Xbox
Xbox 360
Index

DS
GBA
PSP
PS2
PS3
Wii
Xbox
Xbox 360
Index

NBA Street (continued)

Unlockable	Objective
DJ and Venice Beach Court	Play the City Circuit and reach the Region 4 City Challenge. Defeat DJ's team to unlock him as a selectable player and unlock the Venice Beach court.
Drake and the Yard Court	Play the City Circuit and reach the Region 3 City Challenge. Defeat Drake's team to unlock him as a selectable player and unlock The Yard court.
More Player Creation Points	Note: This code can only be used for new players. Hold L1+✓ and press ←,↓,→, then press ■,▲,● at the Create Player menu.
NBA Superstars	Play the City Challenge and defeat an NBA team to unlock a player from their roster.
Stretch and Rucker Park Court	Play the City Circuit and reach the Region 2 City Challenge. Defeat Stretch's team to unlock him as a selectable player and unlock the Rucker Park court.
Takashi and Yakatomni Plaza Court	Play the City Circuit and reach the Region 5 City Challenge. Defeat Takashi's team to unlock him as a selectable player and unlock the Yakatomni Plaza court.

For the following unlockables, enter the "Enter User ID" screen and go to the User Record box (displays either a user ID's record information, or "no user record").

Unlockable	Code
NYC Legends Team	Hold L2 and press ↓,↓,↓,←,X. Alternately, get 30 wins in any mode.
Team 3LW	Hold R1 and press ←,←,→,↓,X. Alternately, get 20 wins in any mode.
Team Big	Hold L2 and press ↑,↓,↓,←,X. Alternately, get 10 wins in any mode.
Team Dream	Hold R1, then press ↑,↑,→,→,X. Alternately, win (complete all the objectives) Hold the Court mode to unlock a team that includes Graylien Alien, Magma Man, and Yeti Snowman.
Team Street Legends	Hold R1, then press →,←,↑,↓,X. Alternately, win the City Circuit to unlock the Street Legends team. This team includes Biggs, Bonafide, Drake, DJ, Takashi, Stretch, and Michael Jordan.

NBA Street Vol 2

For the following unlockables, hold ✓, then enter code.

Unlockable	Code	Unlockable	Code
All Jerseys	■,▲,●,●	Hard 2-Pointers	▲,■,●,▲
All Quicks	▲,●,▲,■	No Counters	▲,▲,●,●
Always Legend Trails	▲,▲,▲,■	Street Kids	▲,▲,●,■
Big Heads	●,■,■,●	Turbo	■,■,▲,▲
Easy 2-Pointers	▲,●,■,▲	Unlimited Turbo	■,■,▲,▲
Easy Shots	▲,●,■,▲	Unlock All Legends	■,▲,▲,●
Explosive Rims	●,●,●,▲	WNBA Ball	●,▲,▲,●

Unlockable	Objective
"Chocolate Thunder" and "The Glide" Boss Moves	Beat the Broad Street Challenge in Be a Legend mode.
'85 Jordan	Beat NBA challenge, Street School, and Be a Legend.
All Courts	Beat Be a Legend and NBA Challenge.
Biggie Little	Beat the Foster Beach Tournament in Be a Legend mode.
Bill Russell's Jersey	Beat the Northwest region with no losses.
Bill Walton's Jersey	Score over 1,000,000 trick points in a game.
Bobbito	Spend 250 Reward points to unlock him or win 10 games in Pick Up mode.

NBA Street Vol 2 (continued)

Unlockable	Objective
Bonafide	Beat the tournament in Rucker Park in Be a Legend.
Boss Move "Big Dipper"	Beat the Foster Beach Street Challenge in Be a Legend.
Boss Move "Biggie Little"	Beat the Foster Beach Tournament in Be a Legend.
Boss Move "Bonafide"	Beat the Rucker Park Tournament in Be a Legend.
Boss Move "Droppin' Dimes"	Beat the Lincoln College Tournament in Be a Legend.
Boss Move "Jordan"	Beat the Rucker Park '78 Street Challenge in Be a Legend mode.
Boss Move "Magic"	Beat the Lincoln College Street Challenge in Be a Legend mode.
Boss Move "Nique"	Beat the Mosswood Tournament in Be a Legend.
Boss Move "Stretch"	Beat the Soul in the Hole Tournament in Be a Legend.
Boss Move "The Doctor"	Beat the Mosswood Street Challenge in Be a Legend.
Boss Move "The Legend"	Beat the Greenlake Street Challenge in Be a Legend.
Boss Move "The Oz"	Beat the Mosswood Tournament in Be a Legend.
Boss Move "The Pistol"	Beat the Soul in the Hole Street Challenge in Be a Legend mode.
Boss Move "Whitewater"	Beat the Greenlake Tournament in Be a Legend.
Clyde Drexler's Jersey	Reach Reputation Level 1 in Be a Legend mode.
Connie Hawkins' Jersey	Win a game and get 20 blocks.
Darryl Dawkins' Jersey	Beat the Broad Street Challenge in Be a Legend mode.
David Thompson's Jersey	Reach Reputation Level 1 in Be a Legend mode.
Dime	Beat the tournament held at the Lincoln College in Los Angeles in the Be A Legend mode.
Dominique Wilkins, James Worthy, and Moses Malone	Beat the Southwest Region.
Dominique Wilkins' Jersey	Reach Reputation Level 4 in Be a Legend mode.
Earvin "Magic" Johnson's Jersey	Beat the Lincoln College Street Challenge in Be a Legend mode.
Elgin Baylor Jersey	Shutout the opponent.
George Gervin's Jersey	Reach Reputation Level 5 in Be a Legend mode.
James Worthy's Jersey	Beat the Northeast region with no losses to unlock the jersey.
Jerry West Jersey	Win a game without getting blocked.
Julius Erving's Jersey	Beat the Mosswood Street Challenge in Be a Legend.
Julius Erving, Connie Hawkins, and Earl Monroe	Beat the Rucker Park '78 Street Challenge in Be a Legend mode.
Just Blaze	Beat the Rucker Park '78 Street Challenge in Be a Legend mode.
Larry Bird's Jersey	Beat the Greenlake Street Challenge.
Larry Bird, Clyde Drexler, and Isiah Thomas	Beat the Central Region.
Michael Jordan's Jersey	Beat the Rucker Park '78 Street Challenge in Be a Legend mode.
MJ Throwback Jersey	Play Pick-up Game mode in each of the scoring rule categories.
Moses Malone's Jersey	Max out your created baller's stats and then win a game with him.
Nelly and the St. Lunatics	Get 750 reward points and buy their card.
Oscar Robertson's Jersey	Beat the Southwest Region with no losses.

DS

GBA

PSP

PS2

PS3

Wii

Xbox

Xbox 360

Index

NBA Street Vol 2 (continued)

Unlockable	Objective
Osmosis	Beat the tournament held in Mosswood in Oakland in the Be A Legend mode.
Pete Maravich, David Thompson, and George Gervin	Beat the Northwest Region.
Rucker Park '78	Beat Be a Legend mode to get Rucker park '78.
Street Champ Clothes	Beat Be a Legend mode to unlock the clothes.
Stretch	Win the Soul in the Hole Tournament to unlock Stretch.
Tiny Archibald Throwback Jersey	Beat street school without messing up.
Walt Frazier's Jersey	Beat the Central region with no losses.
Whitewater	Win the Greenlake Tournament to unlock whitewater.
Wilt Chamberlain's Jersey	Beat the Foster Beach Street Challenge in Be a Legend mode.

NCAA Football 2004

Unlockable	Code	Unlockable	Code
2002 All-American Team	Level 18	Rose Bowl Pennant	Level 2
Butter Fingers Pennant	Level 4	Tostitos Bowl Pennant	Level 12
Orange Bowl Pennant	Level 8		

For the following unlockables, score a touchdown, then enter code.

Unlockable	Objective	Unlockable	Objective
Bow	L2+▲	Kick Ball Into Crowd	R2+●
Display Ball	R2+▲	Spike Ball	L2+■
Dunk Over Goal Post	R2+■	Spike ball, then Shrug	L2+●
Heisman Pose	L2+✕	Throw Ball Into Crowd	R2+✕

NCAA Football 2005

Go to "My NCAA". Choose "Pennant Collection" and press Select to enter these codes.

Unlockable	Code	Unlockable	Code
1st and 15	THANKS	2003 All-Americans	FUMBLE
Baylor Ratings Boost	SIC EM	Alabama All-Time Team	ROLL TIDE
Blink (ball is spotted short for opponent)	FOR	Arizona Mascot Team	BEAR DOWN
Boing (opponent drops more passes)	REGISTERING	Arkansas All-Time Team	WOOPIGSOOIE
Butter Fingers	WITH EA	Auburn All-Time Team	WAR EAGLE
Crossed The Line	TIBURON	Badgers All-Time Team	U RAH RAH
Cuffed Cheat	EA SPORTS	Clemson All-Time Team	DEATH VALLEY
Illinois Ratings Boost	OSKEE WOW	Colorado All-Time Team	GLORY
Jumbalaya	HIKE	Florida All-Time Team	GREAT TO BE
Molasses	HOME FIELD	Florida State All-Time Team	UPRISING
Ouch	BLITZ	Georgia All-Time Team	HUNKER DOWN
Quarterback Dud	ELITE 11	Georgia Tech Mascot Team	RAMBLINWRECK
Stiffed	NCAA	Iowa All-Time Team	ON IOWA
Take Your Time	FOOTBALL	Iowa State Mascot Team	RED AND GOLD
Texas Tech Ratings Boost	FIGHT	Kansas Mascot Team	ROCK CHALK
Thread The Needle	2005	Kansas State All-Time Team	VICTORY
What A Hit	BLITZ	Kentucky Mascot Team	ON ON UK

NCAA Football 2005 (continued)

Unlockable	Code	Unlockable	Code
LSU All-Time Team	GEAUX TIGERS	Pittsburgh All-Time Team	LETS GO PITT
Miami All-Time Team	RAISING CANE	Purdue All-Time Team	BOILER UP
Michigan All-Time Team	GO BLUE	South Carolina Mascot Team	GO CAROLINA
Michigan State Mascot Team	GO GREEN	Syracuse All-Time Team	ORANGE CRUSH
Minnesota Mascot Team	RAH RAH RAH	Tennessee All-Time Team	BIG ORANGE
Mississippi State All-Time Team	HAIL STATE	Texas A&M All-Time Team	GIG EM
Missouri Mascot Team	MIZZOU RAH		
Nebraska All-Time Team	GO BIG RED	Texas All-Time Team	HOOK EM
North Carolina All-Time Team	RAH RAH	UCLA All-Time Team	MIGHTY
		USC All-Time Team	FIGHT ON
North Carolina State Mascot Team	GO PACK	Virginia All-Time Team	WAHOOS
Notre Dame All-Time Team	GOLDEN DOMER	Virginia Tech All-Time Team	TECH TRIUMPH
NU Mascot Team	GO CATS		
Ohio State All-Time Team	KILLER NUTS	Wake Forest Mascot Team	GO DEACS GO
Oklahoma All-Time Team	BOOMER	Washington All-Time Team	BOW DOWN
Oklahoma State All-Time Team	GO POKES	Washington Sate Mascot Team	ALL HAIL
Ole Miss Mascot Team	HOTTY TOTTY	West Virginia Mascot Team	HAIL WV
Oregon All-Time Team	QUACK ATTACK		
Penn State All-Time Team	WE ARE		

NCAA March Madness 06

Enter "My NCAA" and go into the Lounge. In the Lounge select Cheat Codes to enter these passwords.

Unlockable	Password	Unlockable	Password
Air Jordan III Shoes	39N56BXC4S	All Historic Teams	PSDF9078VT
First Air Jordans	2J9UWAS44L		

Need for Speed Carbon

Enter at the main menu.

Unlockable	Code
Extra Money	⇩, ⇧, ⇦, ⇩, ⇩, ⇧, ■, ▲
Infinite Crew Charge	⇩, ⇧, ⇧, ⇨, ⇦, ⇦, ⇨, ■
Infinite NOS	⇦, ⇧, ⇦, ⇩, ⇦, ⇨, ■
Infinite SpeedBreaker	⇩, ⇨, ⇨, ⇩, ⇨, ⇧, ⇩, ■
Need For Speed Carbon Logo Vinyls Unlocked	⇨, ⇧, ⇩, ⇧, ⇧, ⇨, ■
Need For Speed Carbon Special Logo Vinyls Unlocked	⇧, ⇧, ⇩, ⇩, ⇦, ⇨, ⇧, ■

Need for Speed Hot Pursuit 2

Enter these codes at the Main menu.

Aston Martin V12 Vanquish	R2, ⇨, R2, ⇨, ▲, ⇦, ▲, ⇦
BMW Z8	■, ⇨, ■, ⇨, R2, ▲, R2, ▲
Cheat Mode	L2, R2, L2, R2, ▲, ■, ▲, ■
Ferrari F550	L1, ■, L1, ■, ⇨, R1, ⇨, R1
HSV Coupe GTS	L1, L2, L1, L2, R1, ▲, R1, ▲

DS
GBA
PSP
PS2
PS3
Wii
Xbox
Xbox 360
Index

Need for Speed Hot Pursuit 2 (continued)

Lamborghini Diablo 6.0 VT	→, [R2], →, [R2], [R1], [L1], [R1], [L1]
Lotus Elise	▲, [R2], ▲, [R2], ←, ■, ←, ■
McLaren F1 LM	■, [L1], ■, [L1], ▲, →, ▲, →
Porsche Carrera GT	←, →, ←, →, [R1], [R2], [R1], [R2]

Need for Speed Most Wanted

All codes should be entered at the Start screen.

Unlockable	Code
Unlocks Burger King Challenge Event (#69)	⇧, ⇩, ⇩, ⇩, ⇩, ⇨, ⇦, ⇨
Unlocks Free Engine Upgrade Bonus Marker (Can be used in the backroom of the customization shops)	⇧, ⇧, ⇩, ⇩, ⇦, ⇨, ⇧, ⇩
Unlocks Special Edition Castrol Ford GT (Which is added to your bonus cars)	⇦, ⇨, ⇨, ⇨, ⇧, ⇩, ⇧, ⇩

Need for Speed Underground

At the Main menu:

Unlockable	Code
Drift Physics in All Modes	[R1], ↑, ↑, ↑, ↓, ↓, ↓, [L1]
Level 1 Performance Parts	[R2], [R2], [R1], [R1], ←, →, ←, →
Level 2 Performance Parts	[R1], [R1], [R1], [R1], [R2], [R2], ←, →
Level 2 Visual Parts	↓, ←, ↑, ↓, [R1], [R2], [R2], ■
Acura Integra	[R2], [R2], [R1], [R2], [L2], [L1], ↓, ↑
Acura RSX	[R1], [R2], ↓, ←, ↑, →, ←, →
Ford Focus	←, →, ↑, [R1], [R2], [R1], [R2], ↑
Honda S2000	↑, ↑, ↓, ↓, ↑, ←, ■, [R2]
Hyundai Tiburon	←, →, ←, →, ↑, ↓, ↑, ↓
Lost Prophets Car	↑, ↑, ↑, →, ↓, ↓, ↑, →
Mitsubishi Lancer	←, ←, ←, [R1], [R1], [R2], [R2], [L2]
Mystikal Car	↑, →, ↑, ↑, ↑, ↓, →, →
Nissan Nismo	↑, ↓, ↑, ←, ↓, ↓, ↑, →
Nissan 240SX	↑, ↓, ←, →, ■, [R1], [L2], [R1]
Nissan 350Z	→, →, ↓, ↑, ■, [L1], [R1], [L2]
Nissan Sentra	→, →, →, [L2], [L2], [R2], [R2], ↑
Nissan Skyline	↓, ↓, [L1], [L2], [L1], [L2], [L1], ↓
Petey Pablo Car	↑, ↑, ↑, ↑, ↓, ↑, ↑, →
Rob Zombie Car	↑, ←, ↑, ↑, ↓, ←, ↑, →
Subaru Impreza	↑, ↓, ↓, ↑, [L2], ↑, [L2], ↓
Toyota Supra	[R1], [R1], [R2], [R1], [R2], [R1], [L2], [L1]
All Circuit Tracks	↓, [R1], [R1], [R1], [R2], [R2], [R2], ■
All Drag Tracks	→, ■, ←, [R1], ■, [L1], [L2], [R2]
All Drift Tracks	←, ←, ←, ←, →, [R2], [R1], [L2]
All Sprint Tracks	↑, [R2], [R2], [R2], [R1], ↓, ↓, ↓

Need for Speed Underground 2

Enter these codes at the Title screen.

Unlockable	Code
$1000	←, ←, →, ■, ■, →, [L1], [R1]
All Circuit Tracks	↓, [R1], [R1], [R1], [R2], [R2], [R2], ■
Best Buy Vinyl	↑, ↓, ↑, ↓, ↓, ↑, →, ←
Burger King Vinyl	↑, ↑, ↑, ↑, ↓, ↑, ↑, ←

Need for Speed Underground 2 (continued)

D3 GTO	↑, ↓, →, ↑, ←, ↓, →, →
Hummer H2 Capone	↑, ←, ↑, ↑, ↓, ←, ↓, ←

Neo Contra

Enter this code at the Title screen.

Unlockable	Code
19 Lives	↑, ↑, ↓, ↓, L1, R1, L1, R1, L3, R3

NFL Blitz 2003

Unlockable	Code
All Stadiums	L1, L1, L1, R1, ×, ×, ×, ×, →
Allow Out of Bounds	L1, L1, R1, ×, ←
Always QB (Two Humans on Team)	L1, L1, R1, R1, ×, ×, ←
Always Receiver (Two Humans on Team)	L1, L1, R1, R1, ×, ×, →
Arctic Station	R1, R1, R1, ×, ×, ×, ×, ↓
Armageddon Team	L1, L1, L1, L1, L1, R1, R1, R1, R1, ×, ×, ×, →
Auto-Passing Icon	×, ×, ×, ↑
Big Feet	R1, R1, ×, ×, ×, ×, ×, ←
Big Head Teams	L1, L1, ×, ×, ×, →
Big Heads	L1, L1, →
Bilders Team	L1, L1, L1, R1, ↑
Brew Dawgs Team	L1, L1, L1, L1, R1, R1, R1, ×, ×, ↓
Central Park	R1, R1, R1, ×, ×, ×, →
Chimp Mode	R1, R1, ×, ×, ×, ×, ×, ↑
Chrome Ball	R1, R1, R1, ↓
Classic Ball	R1, R1, R1, ←
Clear Weather	L1, R1, R1, ×, ×, ×, →
Crunch Mode Team	L1, L1, L1, L1, ×, ×, ×, →
Disable Auto-Passing Icon	×, ×, ×, ↓
Extra Play for Offense	L1, L1, L1, L1, R1, R1, ×, ×, ×, ↓
Extra Time	×, →
Fast Passes	L1, L1, R1, R1, R1, R1, ←
Faster Running	R1, R1, R1, ×, ×, ←
Ground Fog	L1, L1, R1, R1, R1, ×, ×, ↓
Gsmers Team	L1, L1, L1, L1, L1, ×, ↑
Huge Heads	L1, R1, R1, R1, R1, ×, ×, ×, ×, ←
Midway Team	L1, L1, R1, R1, R1, R1, R1, ×, ×, ×, →
More Code Entry Time	L1, L1, R1, ×, ×, →
More Fumbles	L1, L1, R1, R1, R1, R1, ×, ×, ×, ×, ×, ↑
Neo Tokyo Team	L1, L1, L1, R1, R1, ×, ×, ×, ×, ↓
No CPU Assist	L1, L1, L1, L1, L1, L1, L1, L1, L1, L1, ×, ×, ↓
No First Downs	L1 x (12), R1, ↑
No Highlighting Receivers	L1, L1, L1, R1, ×, ↓
No Interceptions	L1, L1, L1, R1, R1, R1, R1, R1, ×, ×, ×, ×, ×, ↑
No Punting	L1, R1, R1, R1, R1, ×, ↑
No Random Fumbles	L1 x (15), R1, R1, R1, R1, R1, ↓
No Replays	L1, L1, L1, L1, L1, R1, R1, R1, R1, ×, ×, ×, ×, →
Noftle Mode	L1, L1, L1, R1, R1, ×, ×, ×, ×, ×, ↑
Power Loader	R1, R1, ×, ×, ×, ×, ×, →
Power-up Defense	L1, L1, L1, L1, R1, R1, ×, ↑
Power-up Linemen	L1, L1, L1, L1, L1, R1, ×, ↑
Power-up Offense	L1, L1, L1, L1, R1, ×, ×, ↑

DS · GBA · PSP · PS2 · PS3 · Wii · Xbox · Xbox 360 · Index

NFL Blitz 2003 (continued)

Unlockable	Code
Rollos Team	L1, L1, R1, R1, R1, R1, R1, X, X, X, X, ↑
Show More Field	L1 x (10), R1, R1, X, →
Showtime Mode	L1, L1, L1, R1, R1, R1, R1, R1, X, →
Smart CPU Teammates	L1, L1, L1, R1, X, X, X, X, ↓
Super Blitzing	R1, R1, R1, R1, R1, X, X, X, X, ↑
Super Field Goals	L1, R1, R1, X, X, X, ←
Tournament Mode	L1 x (11), R1, X, ↓
Training Grounds	R1, R1, R1, X, X, X, X, X, ↑
Unlimited Turbo	L1, L1, L1, L1, R1, X, X, X, X, X, ↑
Weather: Rain	L1, L1, L1, L1, L1, R1, R1, R1, R1, R1, X, X, X, X, X, →
Weather: Snow	L1, L1, L1, L1, L1, L1, R1, R1, R1, R1, R1, X, X, X, X, X, ←

NFL Street

Enter these codes at the User Name screen.

Unlockable	Code	Unlockable	Code
All 8 Division All-Star Teams	AW9378	KaySlay Team	KaySlay
		NFL Legends Team	Classic
All Stadiums	Travel	NFC West Team	NW9378
All Star Teams	AW9378	X-Ecutioners Team	Excellent

NFL Street 2

Create a profile then enter these case sensitive codes in the Cheats menu.

Unlockable	Code
AFC East All-Stars	EAASFSCT
AFC North All-Stars	NAOFRCTH
AFC South All-Stars	SAOFUCTH
AFC West All-Stars	WAEFSCT
All players will have a maxed out catching stat	MagnetHands
NFC East All Stars	NNOFRCTH
Unlockable	Code
NFC North All-Stars	NNAS66784
NFC South All Stars	SNOFUCTH
NFC West All Stars	ENASFSCT
EA Field	EAField
No Fumble Mode (Quick Game)	GlueHands
Reebok Team	Reebok

NHL 2001

Unlock	Code
Super Defense Players	Enter Sandis Ozolinsh or Chris Pronger as a name in the Create-a-Player screen. Choose "Yes" to use his ratings (you can still adjust them with NHL Challenge bonus points). Return to the previous screen and you can change his name to whatever you want, but don't change any other settings.

NHL 2001 (continued)

Unlock	Code
Super Forwards	Enter Peter Forsberg, Jaromir Jagr, Keith Tkachuk, Pavel Bure, Steve Yzerman, Owen Nolan, Olaf Kolzig, Nicklas Lidstrom, or Rob Blake as a name in the Create-a-Player screen. Choose "Yes" to use his ratings (you can still adjust them with NHL Challenge bonus points). Return to the previous screen and you can change his name to whatever you want, but don't change any other settings.
Super Goalies	Enter Patrick Roy, Dominik Hasek, or Ed Belfour as a name in the Create-a-Player screen. Choose "Yes" to use his ratings (you can still adjust them with NHL Challenge bonus points). Return to the previous screen and you can change his name to whatever you want, but don't change any other settings.
Taunts	Hold ▲ after you score a goal, win a fight, win a game, or the opposing team gets a penalty.
The Dude	Enter Bruce Willis as a name in the Create-a-Player screen. The announcer will call that player "The Dude" during the game.
The Hammer	Enter Hammer as a name in the Create-a-Player screen. The announcer will call that player "The Hammer" during the game.

NHL 2003

Unlockable	Code
Bonus Players	Create a player and enter one of the following names. The game completes his abilities and stats. Some players also have a portrait: Adam Hall, Alfie Michaud, Barry Richter, Ben Simon, Blake Bellefeuille, Brad Moran, Brian Sutherby, Chris Ferraro, Corey Hirsch, Dave Morisset, David Nemirovsky, Derek Mackenzie, Eric Fichaud, Evgeny Konstantinov, Greg Crozier, Greg Pankewicz, Guy Hebert, Ivan Huml, Jakub Cutta, Jason LaBarbera, Jason Zent, Johan Witehall, Kay Whitmore, Larry Murphy, Mark Fitzpatrick, Marquis Mathieu, Martin Brochu, Matt Herr, Matt Higgins, Michel Larocque, Raffi Torres, Rene Corbet, Rich Parent, Rick Tabaracci, Sascha Goc, Scott Fankhouser, Ty Jones, and Xavier Delisle.

NHL 2K6

Enter this as a profile name. Case Sensitive.

Unlockable	Password
Unlock everything	Turco813

NHL Hitz Pro

At the Choose Team screen, enter the following words as a profile name. Then go to Settings, Game Tuning, Visuals, then "Cheats" to activate the cheat.

Unlockable	Code	Unlockable	Code
Big Player Head	HERK	Different Puck Shadow	SASG
Big Team Heads	INGY	Glowing Puck	CARB
Different Puck Size	211S		

Nightshade

Unlockable	Objective
Hisu	Complete the game on Easy mode.
Hotsuma	Complete the game on Normal but be sure to have a Shinobi save on the same Memory Card.
Hibana's 2nd Costume	Complete the game on Normal mode.
Hibana's 3rd Costume	Complete the game on Hard mode.
Joe Musashi	Complete 88 Stages.

Nightshade (continued)

Unlockable	Objective	Unlockable	Objective
EX Mission Stage 1	3 Clan Coins	Survival Stage 5	52 Clan Coins
EX Mission Stage 2	14 Clan Coins	Survival Stage 6	64 Clan Coins
EX Mission Stage 3	24 Clan Coins	Survival Stage 7	76 Clan Coins
EX Mission Stage 4	35 Clan Coins	Survival Stage 8	88 Clan Coins
EX Mission Stage 5	45 Clan Coins	Time Attack Stage 1	7 Clan Coins
EX Mission Stage 6	56 Clan Coins	Time Attack Stage 2	17 Clan Coins
EX Mission Stage 7	68 Clan Coins	Time Attack Stage 3	28 Clan Coins
EX Mission Stage 8	80 Clan Coins	Time Attack Stage 4	38 Clan Coins
Hisui's 2nd Costume	88 Clan Coins	Time Attack Stage 5	49 Clan Coins
Survival Stage 1	10 Clan Coins	Time Attack Stage 6	60 Clan Coins
Survival Stage 2	21 Clan Coins	Time Attack Stage 7	72 Clan Coins
Survival Stage 3	31 Clan Coins	Time Attack Stage 8	84 Clan Coins
Survival Stage 4	42 Clan Coins		

Oni

For the following unlockables, press SELECT during gameplay, highlight the "Help" button, then enter code. A sound confirms correct code entry.

Unlockable	Code
Big Head Mode	L2, L1, L2, ■, ●, ■, START, ■, ●, START
Change the Character	L2, L1, L2, ■, ●, ■, L2, L2, L2, L2—do not move your cursor yet. Hit the L2 button until you select your character.
Extra Powerful Punches and Kicks	L2, L1, L2, ■, ●, ■, R3, L3, ●, ■
Godly Guns	L2, L1, L2, ■, ●, ■, L2, L2, L2, L1, L3—gives you unlimited ammo and you never have to reload.
Hard Mode	L2, L1, L2, ■, ●, ■, R3, L3, ●, ■
Huge Characters	L2, L1, L2, ■, ●, ■, R3, ■, ●, L3
Instant Level Completion	L2, L1, L2, ■, ●, ■, L3, R3, L2, L1
Itty Bitty Characters	L2, L1, L2, ■, ●, ■, L3, R3, ■, ●
One Shot, One Kill	L2, L1, L2, ■, ●, ■, L3, R3, ●, ■
Unlimited Health	L2, L1, L2, ■, ●, ■, R3, L3, R3, ●
Unlimited Phase Cloak	L2, L1, L2, ■, ●, ■, L1, R3, L2, L3—enables you to stay invisible for as long as you want

TIP

Here's an extra tip. To avoid fall damage, press ◄ to do a flip as you near the ground.

Onimusha: Blade Warriors

Unlockable	Objective
Blue Z-part	Beat Phantom Realm 2 using Megaman EXE.
Giramusaido	Musaido Reaches Level 3 Or Above.
Gogandantess	Clear the game with Samanosuke Akechi, Kaede, Normal Soldier, and Maeda Keijirou in Story Mode.
Green Z-part	Beat the Phantom Realm using Megaman EXE.
Jaido	Normal Genma/Sword foot light reaches Level 2 or above.

Onimusha: Blade Warriors (continued)

Unlockable	Objective
Jujudormah Ran	Clear the game with Jujudormah (Level 3 or above) in Story Mode.
Magoichi Saiga	Fight 200 battles in VS Mode.
Marcellus Modify P	Have Marcellus Reaches Level 2.
Marcellus Modify S	Have Marcellus Reaches Level 3 Or Above.
Miyamoto Musashi	Clear the game with Normal Soldier(Level 3 Or Above) in Story Mode.
Musaido	Three Eye reaches Level 2 or above.
Oda Nobunaga	Clear the game with all 12 Default characters in Story Mode.
Red Z-part	Beat Story mode using Megaman EXE.
Rockman EXE	Clear the game with Samanosuke Akechi in Story Mode.
Rockman EXE—Bug Style	Rockman EXE reaches Level 3 or above.
Rockman EXE—Grand Style	Rockman EXE reaches Level 2.
Rockman Zero	Use Rockman EXE to collect all 3 Z-Parts (Red, Blue, Green).
Rockman Zero—Proto Form	Rockman Zero reaches Level 2.
Rockman Zero—Ultimate Form	Rockman Zero reaches Level 3 or above.
Sasaki Kojirou	Clear the game with Miyamoto Musashi in Story Mode.
Zero	Have all 3 Z parts then beat him in VS mode.

Onimusha: Dawn of Dreams

Input these codes by going into the Special menu, highlighting exit, and entering a code.

Unlockable	Code
Gives Jubei a Racket	L1, R1, →, L2, ▲, →, L1, →, L3, R1
Gives Jubei Cammy's Costume	L2, L2, →, →, L3, ▲, ←, L1, L2, ■
Gives Ohatsu Chun-Li's Costume	R3, →, L2, ←, →, R3, L1, R1, →, R3
Gives Ohatsu a Piggy Bank	→, ▲, ←, L3, L1, ▲, ■, R2, ■, R2
Gives Roberto Boxing Gloves	▲, R3, ▲, →, R1, L3, ▲, L1, →, L3
Gives Roberto Guile's Costume	R2, L2, ←, L1, ←, →, R3, ■, ■, ▲
Gives Soki a Steel Pipe	L2, ■, ▲, R1, R1, R3, ←, ■, L1, ▲
Gives Soki Ryu's Costume	←, ▲, R2, R3, ■, R1, R1, ←, →, L2
Gives Tenkai a Microphone Stand	R2, R3, ■, ←, ←, →, L2, ←, R2, ←
Gives Tenkai Ken's Costume	L3, L3, R3, R3, R3, ←, R2, L1, ■, →

Onimusha: Warlords

Unlockable	Objective
Alternate Costumes	To make your character look different, complete the game one time, then start a new game after saving. You will see a "Normal/Special" option. If you select the Special option, you will appear in a special panda suit.

DS

GBA

PSP

PS2

PS3

Wii

Xbox

Xbox 360

Index

DS

GBA

PSP

PS2

PS3

Wii

Xbox

Xbox 360

Index

Onimusha: Warlords (continued)

Unlockable	Objective
Beat Oni Spirits/ Unlock An Arsenal	If you make it past all 12 levels of the challenging Oni Spirits mini-game, you unlock a gameplay option that allows you to start the regular game with a wonderful array of toys. Not only do you get to play through the game with the Bishamon Sword, but you get unlimited Arrows and Bullets, and begin with 99 Soul Absorbers in your inventory. In addition, any magic you use automatically respawns after the attack. With this at your disposal, beating the game again and unlocking everything else is a cinch!
Get the Bishamon Sword	Fight through all 20 levels of the Dark Realm. Kill all of the monsters on the 20th level, then open the treasure box to discover the Bishamon Ocarina. In the area just beyond the second Marcellus boss fight, use the Ocarina on the bone door to open it. Head inside and claim the prize: a sword with unlimited magic which kills any non-boss character in a single swipe. A powerful ally, indeed.
Preview for Onimusha 2	After you complete the game for the first time, it prompts you to save. Do so, then start a new game. View the "Special Report" to see a small preview of Onimusha 2, which takes place 10 years after the events in this game.
Unlock Easy Mode	There are two ways of unlocking the easy mode: 1. Beat the game 4 times to make the Easy Mode available. 2. If Osric beats you 5 times or more, the Easy Mode unlocks.
Unlock Oni Spirits	Collect all 20 Flourites and finish the game.
Unlock Onimusha 2 Trailer	Finish the game on any difficulty to unlock a sneak preview of Onimusha 2. When you go to the Main menu after saving, go to Special Feature to view the preview footage.
Unlock the Panda Suit	If you collect 10 or more Flurites during the course of the game and finish the game, there will be an extra costume available for Samanosuke when you begin a new game. When you restart, select Samanosuke-Extra to play as the big bear. Check out the daisy gauntlet and stuffed friend in the mucus pouch. During gameplay, use L2 to take the head on or off.

Onimusha 2: Samurai's Destiny

Unlockable	Objective
Critical Mode	Complete the game under the Hard difficulty setting.
Easy Mode	Start a game and die three times. A message appears to indicate that a new Easy difficulty setting is available. Note: You cannot achieve an Onimusha rank when playing in Easy mode.
Ending Bonuses	Complete the game to unlock the "Scenario Route" option, Man in Black mode, Team Onimusha mode, and an FMV preview of Onimusha 3.
Hard Mode	Complete the game under the Normal difficulty setting.
Issen Mode	Complete the Oni Organization minigame. You must hit with a One-Flash attack to damage opponents. The Issen Strike works on bosses. However, it does not kill them in one strike.
Jubei's Alternate Costume	Collect the Fashionable Goods item, and complete the game with an "S" rank. Enter the Special Features menu and enable the "Extra Jubei" option to dress her in leather and sunglasses (press L2 to toggle). In the Japanese version, complete the game with the Onimusha rank.
Mind Twister Mode	Complete the game with all Paintings.
Oyu's Alternate Costume	Get a 100 percent scenario completion by playing the game multiple times to make good alliances with all NPCs. After you unlock all scenarios in the "Scenario Route" viewer, enter the Special Features menu, and enable the "Extra Oyu" option to dress him in a 1970s style costume.
Team Onimusha One-Hit Kills	Complete the game in Team Onimusha mode to unlock an option to replay Team Onimusha with one-hit kills.

Onimusha 2: Samurai's Destiny (continued)

Unlockable	Objective
Ultimate Mode	Complete the game under the Hard difficulty setting. Enter the Special Features menu, and enable the "Ultimate Mode" option to begin a new game with the Rekka-Ken Sword, 20,000 in money, 30 Perfect Medicines, 10 Talismans, all Level 3 armors, unlimited ammunition, unlimited magic, and skill always full. Your NPCs also have unlimited subweapons.

Onimusha 3

Unlockable	Objective
The Adventures of Heihachi	Complete the game and this new mode will open up, enabling you to play as Heihachi.
Michelle's Wet Bathroom look	Complete the game with an S ranking on normal or higher difficulty.
Samanosuke and Jacque's Western Outfit	Score higher ending game points (Sum of Play Time points, Soul points, Enemies defeated points, Dark Realm "obtain points" and Critical Hit points.) when playing as Samanosuke vs. Jacques to unlock Samanosuke's special Western Outfit. On the flip side, score higher ending game points with Jacques than Samanosuke to unlock Jacques Western Outfit. These also become available if the game is completed wearing one of the two Western Outfits.
Samanosuke's Panda Suit	Complete the Oni Training mini game or have a Onimusha Blade Warrior save on your memory card. For added fun pressing L2 will flip the head on and off with different expressions each time.

The Operative: No One Lives Forever

In the Main menu, highlight Load Game, then enter the code.

Unlockable	Code
Level Select	Hold L3+R3, then press ✕.

Orphen: Scion of Sorcery

Unlockable	Objective
Restart the Battle	Pause the game and pick "Equip" before resuming the game at the start of the battle. All your energy will be restored.

Outlaw Golf 2

Unlockable	Objective
Everything unlocked	Enter I Have No Time as a profile name.

Outlaw Volleyball Remixed

Enter these codes at the Exhibition Court Select screen.

Unlockable	Code
Hell Pit court	Hold R1 and press ■, ■, ■, ■, ■, ■, ▲, ▲, ▲, ▲, ▲, ▲, L2, L2, L2, L2, L2, L2
Warehouse court	Hold L1 and press ⇧, ■, ■, ▲, ▲, ⇩

Enter this at the Character Select screen.

Unlockable	Code
Better Stats	Hold R1 and press ⇦, L2, ⇨, L2

Enter this code during gameplay.

Unlockable	Code
Big Heads	Hold L1 and press ●, ✕, ●, ▲

DS
GBA
PSP
PS2
PS3
Wii
Xbox
Xbox 360
Index

DS

GBA

PSP

PS2

PS3

Wii

Xbox

Xbox 360

Index

Pac-Man World 2

Unlockable	Objective
Ms. Pac-Man Mini-Game	Collect 180 tokens during gameplay to unlock the classic Ms. Pac-Man arcade game.
Music Test	Collect 60 tokens during gameplay to unlock the "Jukebox" option.
Pac-Attack Mini-Game	Collect 30 tokens during gameplay to unlock the classic Pac-Attack arcade game.
Pac-Man Mini-Game	Collect 10 tokens during gameplay to unlock the classic Pac-Man arcade game.
Pac-Mania Mini-Game	Collect 100 tokens during gameplay to unlock the classic Pac-Mania arcade game.
Pre-Production Art and Programmers	Collect 150 tokens during gameplay to unlock the "Museum" option.

Parappa The Rapper 2

Unlockable	Objective
Blue Hat	Beat the game once, and Parappa dons a snazzy blue hat.
Dog House	Beat each level while wearing the yellow hat and Parappa gets a new dog house. Go there to listen to some tunes. In the dog house, you can listen to tracks from any level on which you've earned a "Cool" rating.
Pink Hat	Beat each level while wearing the blue hat to give Parappa a new pink hat.
Yellow Hat	Beat each level while wearing the pink hat to give Parappa a new yellow hat.

Peter Jackson's King Kong

At the Main menu screen, hold ⌊1⌋+⌊R1⌋ and press ⇩, ✕, ⇧, ■, ⇩, ⇩, ⇧, ⇧, then release ⌊1⌋+⌊R1⌋. This opens the Cheat Menu. Now enter any of these case sensitive passwords.

Unlockable	Password	Unlockable	Password
999 ammunition	KK 999 mun	**One-hit kills**	GrosBras
Bonuses completed	KKmuseum	**Revolver**	KKtigun
God mode	8wonder	**Shotgun**	KKsh0tgun
Level select	KKst0ry	**Sniper rifle**	KKsn1per
Machine gun	KKcapone	**Unlimited spears**	lance 1nf

Pirates: The Legend of Black Kat

To access the following unlockables, hold ⌊R1⌋+⌊R2⌋, then enter code.

Unlockable	Code
Advance to Katarina's Next Sword	⌊R3⌋, ⌊SELECT⌋, ⌊L2⌋, ⌊L3⌋, ■, ✕, ⌊L1⌋, ●, ⌊L3⌋, ▲, ⌊L3⌋, ■, ✕, ⌊L1⌋, ●
All Treasure Chest Keys	●, ⌊SELECT⌋, ✕, ■, ⌊L3⌋, ⌊L1⌋, ⌊L3⌋, ⌊L2⌋, ▲, ⌊L3⌋
Alternate Glacial Gulf Music	Press ⌊L1⌋, ✕, ▲, ⌊L2⌋, ■, ●, ⌊L3⌋, ⌊SELECT⌋, ⌊R3⌋, ⌊L3⌋—you can now hear music from SSX when sliding down in Glacial Gulf.
Extra Gold	▲, ⌊R3⌋, ⌊L3⌋, ✕, ■, ⌊R3⌋, ⌊SELECT⌋, ⌊L1⌋, ●—you can now sail to another map to get the Galleon.
High-Pitched Voices	⌊R3⌋, ●, ⌊SELECT⌋, ✕, ⌊R3⌋, ▲, ⌊L1⌋, ■, ⌊L2⌋, ⌊L3⌋
Invincibility for Katarina	✕, ●, ⌊L3⌋, ▲, ⌊R3⌋, ⌊SELECT⌋, ⌊R3⌋, ⌊L1⌋, ⌊L2⌋, ■
Invincibility for the Wind Dancer	⌊SELECT⌋, ▲, ⌊L1⌋, ✕, ⌊R3⌋, ⌊L2⌋, ■, ⌊R3⌋, ●, ⌊L3⌋
Kane Poison Head	▲, ⌊L2⌋, ⌊L1⌋, ■, ⌊L3⌋, ✕, ⌊L3⌋, ●, ⌊R3⌋, ⌊SELECT⌋—the poison status will be indicated by the head of Kane from Command and Conquer.

Pirates: The Legend of Black Kat (continued)

To access the following unlockables, hold R1+R2, then enter code.

Unlockable	Code
Reveal All Treasure Chests	R3, ×, ▲, L3, ●, L1, SELECT, L3, ■, L2
Reveal Buried Treasure Chests	●, ×, ■, ▲, L1, SELECT, L3, L2, L3, R3—green Xs will appear on the captain's log maps to indicate the location of buried treasure chests.
Unlimited Items	▲, L1, SELECT, L2, R3, L3, ■, ×, L3, ●—once found, an item will be available in unlimited amounts.
Unlimited Wind Boost	SELECT, L1, R3, ●, L2, ▲, ×, L3
Wind Dancer	L2, ▲, R3, L3, ×, ■, R3, SELECT, L1, ●

To access alternate Karina costumes, please see table below. The following code requires two players and controllers. Simultaneously hold L1+L2+↑+SELECT+L3 on controller one and R1+R2+▲+START+R3 on controller two. A short sequence of music will confirm correct code entry. Click down on R3 on controller one to change the value of the numbers that appear on screen, then start a new game or resume a saved game to view the corresponding costume. The costumes that can be accessed are as follows:

Costume	Code
Blackbeard in Purple	00000001
Blonde Hair, Orange and Yellow Bikini	00000101
Blonde Hair, Pink Bikini	00000110
Blue Hair with Orange and Red Bikini	00000011
Blue Hair, Shiny Copper Body Suit	00001010
Blue Hair, Shiny Silver Bikini	00000111
Original Costume and Hair Color	00000000
Pink Hair, Shiny Black Body Suit	00001001
Purple Hair, Shiny Silver Body Suit	00001011
Red Hair with Red and Orange Bikini	00000010
Red Hair, Black Bikini, Black Stockings	00001000
Tan, Brown Hair, Orange and Yellow Bikini	00000100

Pitfall: The Lost Expedition

Enter the following codes at the Title Screen. If you entered the code correctly, a message will appear.

Unlockable	Code
Hyper Punch Mode	Hold L1+R1, then press →, ←, ●, ↑, ●, →, ←
Original Pitfall game	Hold L1+R1, then press ●, ●, ←, →, ●, ■, ×, ↑, ●
Original Pitfall 2: Lost Caverns game	Hold L1+R1, then press ←, →, ←, →, ▲, ▲, ▲
Play as Nicole	Hold L1+R1, then press ←, ↑, ↓, ↑, ●, ↑, ↑
Unlimited Water in Canteen	Hold L1+R1, then press ←, ■, ●, ↓, ■, ×, ■, ●

Prince of Persia: The Sands of Time

Unlockable	Code
Unlock the first	Start a new game and stay on the balcony, press L3 and Prince of Persia quickly enter ×, ■, ▲, ●, ▲, ×, ■, ●.

Pryzm Chapter 1: The Dark Unicorn

Unlockable	Code
Complete current level	←, →, ←, →, ↑, ↓, ↑, ↓
Invincibility, unlimited magic, and all levels	Start a new game and enter as your name SUPREMEMAGIC

DS

GBA

PSP

PS2

PS3

Wii

Xbox

Xbox 360

Index

DS

GBA

PSP

PS2

PS3

Wii

Xbox

Xbox 360

Index

Psi-Ops: The Mindgate Conspiracy

In Main menu, highlight Extra Content and press R1. Then enter these codes.

Unlockable	Code
All Powers	537893
Infinite Ammo	978945
Bulletproof	548975
Super Psi	456456
No Head	987978
Arcade mode	05051979
Co-op mode	07041979
Dark Mode	465486

Extra Missions	Code
Aura Pool	659785
Bottomless Pit	54897
Bouncy Bouncy	568789
Gasoline	9442662
Gearshift	154684
Gnomotron	456878
Panic Room	76635766
Pitfall	05120926
Psi Pool	565485
Stop Lights	945678
Survival	7734206
Tip the Buddha	428584
TK Alley	90702
Up and Over	020615

Skins	Code
Burned Soldier	454566
Dock Worker	364654
Edgar Barrett	497878
Edgar Barret (Training 1)	196001

Skins	Code
Edgar Barret (Training 2)	196002
Edgar Barret (Training 3)	196003
Edgar Barret (Training 4)	196004
Edgar Barret (Training 5)	196005
Edgar Barret (Training 6)	196006
The General	459797
The General (Clown)	431644
Jack	698798
Jov Leonov	468987
Marlena Kessler	489788
Marlena Kessler (Bikini)	135454
Marlena Kessler (Leather)	136876
MP1	321646
MP2	678999
MP3	654659
Nick Scryer (Stealth)	456498
Nick Scryer (Training)	564689
Nick Scryer (Urban)	484646
Nick Scryer (Wasteland)	975466
Sara Blake	135488
Sara Blake (Psi)	468799
Sara Blake (Suicide)	231644
Scorpion	546546
Tonya	678999
UN Soldier	365498
Wei Lu	231324
Wei Lu (Dragon)	978789
Wei Lu (Tranquility)	654654

The Punisher

Effect	Code
Everything Unlocked (except upgrades)	V Pirate as a Profile Name.

Quake III Revolution

Enter the following code during gameplay.

Unlockable	Code
Level Skip	Hold L1 + R1 + R2 + SELECT, then press ✕, ●, ■, ▲, ✕, ●, ■, ▲

Ratchet and Clank: Up Your Arsenal

Unlockable	Code
Duel Blade Laser Sword	Pause the game and press ●, ■, ●, ■, ↑, ↓, ←, ←.
Sly 2: Band of Thieves Demo	At the Title Screen, hold L1 + L2 + R1 + R2.

Rayman Arena

Enter these codes as a name, then press ⌊2⌋+●+■ to activate it.

Unlockable	Code
3D Mode	3DVISION
Every Battle Mode Unlocked	ALLFISH
Every Character Unlocked	PUPPETS
Every Mode Unlocked	ALLRAYMANM
Every Skin Unlocked	CARNIVAL
Every Battle Level Unlocked	ARENAS
Every Level Unlocked	FIELDS
Every Race Level Unlocked	TRACKS
Monochrome Mode	OLDTV

Ready 2 Rumble Boxing: Round 2

Unlockable	Code
Big Gloves	At the Character Selection screen, press ←,→,↑,↓, R1, R2. A sound confirms correct entry.
Fat Boxer	At the Character Selection screen, press →,→,↑,↓,→, R1, R1, R2. A sound confirms correct entry.
Play As Freak E. Deke and Michael Jackson	At the character selection screen, press R1 x (13), R2, R1 x (10), R2.
Skinny Boxer	At the Character Selection screen, press →,→,↑,↓,→, R1, R2. A sound confirms correct entry.
Undead Boxer	At the Character Selection screen, press ←,↑,→,↓, R1, R1, R2. A sound confirms correct entry.
Bill Clinton	Beat Arcade mode eight times.
Champion Costumes	Complete Championship mode.
Freak E. Deke	Beat Arcade mode once.
Freedom Brock	Beat Arcade mode six times.
G.C. Thunder	Beat Arcade mode three times.
Hillary Clinton	Beat Arcade mode nine times.
Michael Jackson	Beat Arcade mode twice.
Rocket Samchay	Beat Arcade mode seven times.
Rumbleman	Beat Arcade mode ten times.
Shaquille O'Neal	Beat Arcade mode five times.
Wild "Stubby" Corley	Beat Arcade mode four times.
Christmas Costume	Set the system date to December 25. Selene Strike will be in an elf costume and Rumbleman will be in a snowman costume.
Easter Costume	Set the system date to April 23. Mama Tua will be in a Playboy Bunny costume.
Fourth of July Costume	Set the system date to July 4. G.C. Thunder will be in an Uncle Sam costume.
Halloween Costume	Set the system date to October 31. J.R. Flurry will be in a skeleton costume.
New Year's Costume	Set the system date to January 1. Joey T will be in a baby costume.
St. Patrick's Day Costume	Set the system date to March 17. The referee will be in a leprechaun costume.
Valentine's Day Costume	Set the system date to February 14. Lulu will be in a sexy costume.

DS

GBA

PSP

PS2

PS3

Wii

Xbox

Xbox 360

Index

Red Card 2003

To access Cheat mode, enter BIGTANK as a name to unlock all teams, stadiums, and Finals mode.

Unlockable	Objective
Apes Team and Victoria Falls Stadium	Defeat the Apes team in World Conquest mode.
Dolphins Team and Nautilus Stadium	Defeat the Dolphins team in World Conquest mode.
Finals Mode	Win all matches in World Conquest mode.
Martians Team and USAFB001 Stadium	Defeat the Martians team in World Conquest mode.
Matadors Team and Coliseum Stadium	Defeat the Matadors team in World Conquest mode.
Samurai Team and Youhi Gardens Stadium	Defeat the Samurai team in World Conquest mode.
SWAT Team and Nova City Stadium	Defeat the SWAT team in World Conquest mode.

Red Dead Revolver

These are the rewards for each level. The first is for a Good rating and the second is for a Excellent rating.

Unlockable	Good rating	Excellent
Battle Finale	Focus (Dead-Eye) Max-Up	Mr. Kelley
Bear Mountain	Shadow Wolf	Focus (Dead-Eye) Max-Up
Bounty Hunter	"Bloody" Tom	"Big Oaf" Whitney
Bull's Eye	Old Pistol	Broken Creek
Carnival Life	Focus (Dead-Eye) Max-Up	"Pig" Josh
Cemetery	Ghost Town	Mr. Black
Devils & Angels	The Ranch	—
Fall From Grace	Scorpion Revolver	Governor Griffon
Fort Diego	Health Max-Up	Colonel Daren
Freak Show	Health Max-Up	Breech Loader
Hell Pass	Buffalo	Gabriel Navarro
The Mine	The Mine	"Smiley" Fawler
Railroaded	Owl Rifle	Rico Pedrosa
Rogue Valley	Cooper	Bad Bessie
Ugly Streetfight	"Ugly" Chris	Freak Show
Range War	The Ranch	Holstein Hal
Saloon Fight	Dan	Sam
The Siege	Mansion Grounds	Jason Cornet
Sunset Canyon	Twin Revolvers	Focus (Dead-Eye) Max-Up
The Traitor	The Bridge	Health Max-Up

Red Faction

Unlockable	Objective
Secret Roof Location in Lobby Multiplayer Map	You can get on the roof of the Lobby (where there is a giant skylight) to find a Fusion Rocket Launcher and a Rail Driver, as well as a great sniping spot. To get there, go up to the second level of the area where you are able to pick up the Rocket Launcher. Arm that weapon and aim for the corner of the wall where the skylight begins. Fire rockets to punch a hole into the ceiling and the wall. Continue to fire rockets until you form a small alcove where you can jump to, then up onto the roof. After you are there, grab a Fusion Rocket Launcher at one end of the skylight and a Rail Driver at the other end.

Red Faction II

Enter the following codes at the Cheats screen under the Options menu.

Unlockable	Code
Bouncy Grenades	●,●,●,●,●,●,●,●
Directors Cut	■,×,●,▲,●,×,■,▲
Gibby Bullets	●,●,●,●,▲,×,●,●
Gibby Explosions	▲,●,×,■,▲,●,×,■
Instagib Ammunition	×,×,×,×,■,●,×,×
Joke Message	■,×,■,×,■,×,■,×
Level Select	●,■,×,▲,■,●,×,×
Master Code unlocks all normal game options.	▲,▲,×,×,×,■,●,■,●

Unlockable	Code
Master Cheat Code	■,●,▲,●,■,×,▲,×
Rain of Fire	■,■,■,■,■,■,■,■
Rapid Rails	●,■,●,■,×,×,▲,▲
Super Health	×,×,■,▲,■,▲,●
Unlimited Ammunition	■,▲,×,●,■,●,×,▲
Unlimited Grenades	●,×,●,■,×,●,×,●
Wacky Deaths	▲,▲,▲,▲,▲,▲,▲,▲
Walking Dead	×,×,×,×,×,×,×,×

Reign of Fire

Unlockable	Code
Level Select	At Main menu, enter ↑, ←, ●, ●, ←, ←, ■, ↓, ↑, ●

Reservoir Dogs

Enter these codes in the Cheats menu under extras.

Unlockable	Code
All levels	L2, R2, L2, R2, L1, R1, START
Art gallery	●, ×, L2, R2, ●, ×, START
Movie gallery	L1, L1, ●, ×, L1, R1, START
Unlimited ammo	R2, L2, ●, L2, ×, R2, START

Resident Evil Code Veronica X

Unlockable	Objective
Get Special Journal	Go to the slot machine in the palace through the Battle Game (with the same character). On the third try, a special journal is there. It belongs to someone named D.I.J.
Unlock Linear Launcher for Battle Game	Get an A ranking with the two Claires, Steves, Chrises, and Weskers in the Battle Game to unlock the Linear Launcher. After you gain it, it automatically appears in your inventory when you begin the Battle Game again.
Unlock Rocket Launcher	Complete the main game with an "A" Ranking to earn the Rocket Launcher. To do this, do not use First Aid Spray, do not save your game, do not retry. You must save Steve from the Luger room quickly, give the Medicine to your jailer Rodrigo, and finish in under 4:30. When you begin another game, the Launcher will be available from the first Item Box you run across.
Unlock Steve for Battle Game	Solve a puzzle in the main game. In the underground Save Room in Chris's walkthrough, complete the drawer puzzle in the corner. Grab the Gold Luger to unlock Mr. Burnside.
Unlock the Battle Game	Beat the game once to unlock the Battle Game. Chris and Claire Redfield are now available as playable characters.
Unlock Wesker for Battle Game	Unlock Albert Wesker for use in the Battle Game by beating the Battle game with Chris Redfield.

DS

GBA

PSP

PS2

PS3

Wii

Xbox

Xbox 360

Index

Ridge Racer V

Unlockable	Objective
99 Lap Option	Get the top score in all the Time Attack GP races in Extra mode and finish in first place.
Changing Saved Game Icon	Beat the game with all secrets unlocked. The saved game icon will change from a car to Ai Fukami, a programmer.
Modifying the Intro Sequence	Press L1+R1 during the intro sequence with the girl. Press R1 once for black-and-white graphics. Press R1 a second time and the game will have a yellow tint. Press R1 a third time to add a blur effect. That blur effect eliminates the jaggies in the graphics. You can press L2 to cycle back through the various effects.
Onscreen Information	During a race, press and hold SELECT for a few seconds. A window shows up on the screen with various information. Press and hold SELECT again to make the information window go away.
Unlock 50's Super Drift Caddy	Place first in the Danver Spectra race in Duel mode to unlock this car in Free Run, Duel, and Time Attack modes.
Unlock a Beetle	Place first in the Solort Rumeur race in Duel mode to unlock this car in Free Run, Duel, and Time Attack modes.
Unlock a McLaren Type Car	Place first in the Kamata Angelus race in Duel mode to unlock this car in Free Run, Duel, and Time Attack modes.
Unlock Devil Drift	Place first in the Rivelta Crinale race in Duel mode to unlock this car in Free Run, Duel, and Time Attack modes.
Unlock Duel Mode	Enter Standard Time Attack GP and finish first in lap and overall time.
Unlock Pac-Man Mode	Race more than 3,000 kilometers in total distance. The Pac-Man race becomes available. Beat the Pac-Man race and the Pac-Man car and the ghosts on scooters become unlocked.
Unlocking Bonus Cars	Beat each of the Grand Prix circuits, or break the Time Attack high scores.

Rise of Kasai

Enter the following codes at the Press Start screen.

Unlockable	Code
Invincible Rau	■, ●, ✕, ■, ●, ■, ✕, ●, ✕, ■, ●, ✕
Infinite Ammunition	✕, ●, ■, ■, ✕, ■, ●, ●, ✕, ■, ■, ✕
Weaker Enemies	✕, ●, ●, ■, ✕, ■, ■, ●

Rise to Honor

Unlockable	Objective
Extra Costumes	Complete the game.
Hard Mode	Complete the game on Normal.
Kit Yun and Michelle's FMV	Complete the game.

Roadkill

Pause the game on the Map screen then enter the following codes.

Unlockable	Code
All Weapons	▲, ✕, ✕, ▲, ■, ●, ●, ■, ✕, ■, ●, ▲
All Vehicles	↑, ↓, ↑, ↓, ▲, ✕, ▲, ✕, ■, ●, ●, ■
Health	■, ●, ■, ●, ■, ●, ■, ●
Infinite Ammo	▲, ■, ■, ●, ▲, ■, ■, ●
More Money	▲, ●, ▲, ●, ■, ✕, ■, ✕, ↓, ↑

Robotech: Battlecry

To access Cheat mode, enter the New Game or Load Game screen. Hold L1+L2+R1+R2, then press ←, ↑, ↓, ✕, →, ▲, START to display the Code Entry screen. Enter one of the following codes to activate the corresponding cheat function.

Unlockable	Code
All Models and Awards	WHERESMAX
All Multiplayer Levels	MULTIMAYHEM

Robotech: Battlecry (continued)	
Unlockable	Code
Alternate Paint Schemes	MISSMACROSS
Disable Active Codes	CLEAR
Gunpod Ammunition Refilled Faster	SPACEFOLD
Gunpod and Missiles Refilled Faster	MIRIYA
Invincibility	SUPERMECH
Level Select	WEWILLWIN
Missiles Refilled Faster	MARSBASE
One-Shot Kills	BACKSTABBER
One-Shot Kills in Sniper Mode	SNIPER
Upside-Down Mode	FLIPSIDE

Robotech: Invasion

From Options, select Extras. Enter the following:

Unlockable	Code
1 Hit Kill	DUSTYAYRES
All Levels	RECLAMATION
Invincibility	SUPERCYC
Lancer's Multiplayer Skin	YLLWFLLW
Rand's Multiplayer Skin	KIDGLOVES
Rook's Multiplayer Skin	BLUEANGLS
Scott Bernard's Multiplayer Skin	LTNTCMDR
Unlimited Ammo	TRGRHPY

Rocky

Enter the following codes in the Main menu while holding R1:

Unlockable	Code
All Default Boxers and Arenas	→, ↓, ↑, ←, ↑, L1
All Default Boxers, Arenas, and Rocky Statue	→, →, →, ←, →, L1
All Default Boxers, Arenas, Rocky statue, and Mickey	↑, ↓, ↓, ←, ←, L1
Double Punch Damage	→, ↓, ←, ↑, ←, L1
Double Speed Boxing	↓, ←, ↓, ↑, →, L1
Max Stats for Movie Mode	→, ↓, ↓, ↑, ←, L1
Max Stats for Tournament and Exhibition Modes	←, ↑, ↑, ↓, →, L1
Win Movie Mode (During a fight, press R2+L2 to win!)	→, →, ←, ←, ↑, L1

Rogue Ops

At any time in the game pause and enter the following codes.

Unlockable	Code
God Mode	←, →, →, ←, ←, →, →, ←, ←, →, →, ←, ■, ■
Level Skip	L2, ■, L2, ●, L2, ←, L2, →, L2, R2, R2, ■, R2, ●, R2, ←, R2, →, ■
Unlimited Ammo	■, ●, ■, ●, ■, ●, ■, ●, ←, ●, ■, ●, ■, ●, ■, ●, ■

Rogue Trooper

Enter these codes in the Extras menu.

Unlockable	Code
Extreme Ragdoll Physics	⇧, ⇧, ⇧, R2, R2, ⇧
Hippy Blood	L2, ⇨, ●, ⇩, R1, SELECT
Infinite Health	⇦, ⇨, ⇧, ⇩, L3, ■
Infinite Supplies	SELECT, R1, L1, SELECT, R3, L1
Low Gravity Ragdoll Physics	■, ■, ●, ●, ⇧, ⇩

DS

GBA

PSP

PS2

PS3

Wii

Xbox

Xbox 360

Index

DS

GBA

PSP

PS2

PS3

Wii

Xbox

Xbox 360

Index

Romance of the Three Kingdoms VIII

Unlockable	Objective
Better Created Characters	100% item completion.
Extra Created Character Portraits	100% event completion.
Pre-Made Characters	Create an officer with one of the names below for a hidden pre-made character: *Abraham Lincoln, *Albert Einstein, *Ben Franklin, *Benedict Arnold, *Davy Crockett, *Jebidiah Smith, *Jim Bridger, *John Adams, *John Henry, *Kit Carson, *Patrick Henry, *Paul Bunyan, *Paul Revere, *Pecos Bill, *Red Cloud, *Sam Houston, *Sitting Bull, *Thomas Edison, *William Cody, *William Seward.

Romance of the Three Kingdoms IX

Unlockable	Objective
Bai Qi	New Officer with name "Bai" "Qi"
Change Kingdoms in Mid-game	Leave all forces under computer control, then during the action phase, press start to "go to main-menu." Press ✕ and the game will resume, then press SELECT. (You may also press the shoulder buttons and it will say "Select Force or Forces to play as" and at the end of the action phase you can choose up to eight new forces to play as.)
Chen Qingzhi	New Officer with name "Chen" "Qingzhi"
Chengji Sihan	New Officer with name "Chengji" "Sihan"
Da Qiao	Load Dynasty Warriors 4 Data
Emperor Xian	Unlock all sages and pick He Jin in 281 "Hero" scenario
Fan Zeng	New Officer with name "Fan" "Zeng"
Guan Yiwu	New Officer with name "Guan" "Yiwu"
Han Xin	New Officer with name "Han" "Xin"
Huang Yueying	Beat Tutorial Mode
Huo Qubing	New Officer with name "Huo" "Qubing"
Japan Tribe	Search near Bei Hai when warlord tells you to. You must have Bei Hai to do this.
Japan Tribe	Search Langxie while controlling two provinces and with 700 reputation or higher.
Kong Qiu	New Officer with name "Kong" "Qiu"
Li Ji	New Officer with name "Li" "Ji"
Li Si	New Officer with name "Li" "Si"
Lin Xiangru	New Officer with name "Lin" "Xiangru"
Liu Bang	New Officer with name "Liu" "Bang"
Lu Ling Qi	Load Dynasty Tactics 2 Data
Ma Yunlu	Beat Tutorial Mode
Mistress Zhen	Get Good Ending with Yuan Shang on Inheritance Wars challenge scenario.
Mistress Zhen	In Inheritance Wars, get event where Mistress Zhen gives Yuan Xi a carp charm, then beat the scenario.
Mistress Zou	In Defense of Nan Yang Scenario, get event where Jia Xu offers Mistress Zou up for Cao Cao, then beat the scenario.
Nanman Tribe	Beat Nanman Barbarians in scenario then beat game.
Qiang Tribe	Beat Qiang Barbarians in scenario then beat game.
Qin Liangyu	New Officer with name "Qin" "Liangyu"
Shan Yue Tribe	Beat Shen Yue Barbarians in scenario, then beat game.
Sun Bin	New Officer with name "Sun" "Bin"
Wang Jian	New Officer with name "Wang" "Jian"
Wu Wan Tribe	Beat Wu Wan Barbarians in scenario, then beat game.
Xiang Ji	New Officer with name "Xiang" "Ji"

Romance of the Three Kingdoms IX (continued)

Unlockable	Objective
Xiao He	New Officer with name "Xiao" "He"
Xiao Qiao	Load Dynasty Warriors 4 Extreme Legends Data
Yang Daiyan	New Officer with name "Yang" "Daiyan"
Ying Bu	New Officer with name "Ying" "Bu"
Ying Zheng	New Officer with name "Ying" "Zheng"
Yue Fei	New Officer with name "Yue" "Fei"
Yue Yi	New Officer with name "Yue" "Yi"
Zhang Liang	New Officer with name "Zhang" "Liang"
Zhang Yi	New Officer with name "Zhang" "Yi"
Zhen Ji	Beat Inheritance Wars Scenario.

RTX Red Rock

Unlockable	Code
Add Items	→,→,→,→,→,←,←,←,↑,↑
Difficult Mode	↓,↑,↑,↑,↑,↑,↑,↑,↑,↓
Easy Mode	↑,↓,↓,↓,↓,↓,↓,↓,↓,↑
Normal Mode	↑,↓,↑,↓,↑,↓,↑,↓,↑,↓
Old Soul Super Weapons	→,↑,↓,↓,↑,→,→,↑,↓,↓
Progressive Scan Mode	→,↑,→,→,↑,→,→,→,↑,→ (Note: You'll have to reboot your PS2 once the screen turns blue.)
Unlock All Levels	↓,←,←,↓,←,↓,↓,→,←,↓
Unlock All Special Features	←,↓,↑,←,↓,↑,↓,←,→,↓

R-Type Final

Pause the game and enter the following (you will hear a sound if you entered the code correctly):

Unlockable	Code
99.9% Charge Dose	Hold L2 and press R2, R2, ←,→,↑,↓,→,←,↑,↓,▲.
Curtain Call Ship (#100)	In the R's Museum, enter 1009 9201 as a password.
Full Blue Power, Missiles, and Bits	Hold L2 and press R2, R2, ←,→,↑,↓,→,←,↑,↓,●.
Full Red Power, Missiles, and Bits	Hold L2 and press R2, R2, ←,→,↑,↓,→,←,↑,↓,■.
Full Yellow Power, Missiles, and Bits	Pause the game, then hold L2 and press R2, R2, ←,→,↑,↓,→,←,↑,↓,✕.
Invincibility	Hold L2 and press →,→,←,→,←,←,→,←,L1,↑,↑,↓,↓,↑,↓, ↑,↓,L1.
Lady Love Ship (#3)	In the R's Museum, enter 5270 0725 as a password.
Mr. Heli Ship (#59)	In the R's Museum, enter 1026 2001 as a password.
Strider Ship (#24)	In the R's Museum, enter 2078 0278 as a password.

Rugby Challenge 2006

Unlockable	Code
Barbarian Ball	Win a match via a penalty shootout
British Isles Team	Score 10 tries in a match
Clowning Around Career Kit	Beat USA as Canada
Dimension Ball	Score 5 tries with one player in a game
England 2003 Team	Play a match with England against anyone
Girly Gang Career Kit	Beat New Zealand as Australia
Old Colour Vision	Complete Classic Match 1
Old Vision	Complete Classic Match 2
Revolution Ball	Big hit the referee 5 times in a match

DS
GBA
PSP
PS2
PS3
Wii
Xbox
Xbox 360
Index

DS

Rugby Challenge 2006 (continued)

Unlockable	Code
Sorted Career Kit	Beat England as Scotland
Tiger Bay Stadium	Hit the post in each half from a place kick
Vapour Ball	Score a try with a player who first gained possession in his own half

GBA

Samurai Warriors

Unlockable	Objective
Goemon Ishikawa	Complete Okuni Story.
Keiji Maeda	Complete Kenshin Story.
Kunoichi	Complete Shingen, Hanzo Stories.
Magoichi Saika	Complete any Story.
Masamune Date	Complete any two Stories.
Nobunaga Oda	Complete Noh, Oichi, Magoichi Stories.
Noh	Complete Ranmaru Story.
Okuni	Complete Keiji Story.
Ranmaru Mari	Complete Mitsuhide Story.
Shingen Takeda	Complete Yukimura Story.

PSP

Savage Skies

Enter these codes at the Main menu.

Unlockable	Code
All Creatures	⇦, ⇨, ⇦, ⇨, ⇦, ⇨, ⇨, ✕
All Multiplayer Maps	⇦, ⇨, ⇦, ⇦, ⇨, ⇦, ⇨, ✕

Enter these codes while the game is paused.

PS2

PS3

Unlockable	Code
Invulnerability	⇦, ⇦, ⇨, ⇨, ⇧, ⇧, ⇧, ⇧, ✕, ⇧, ✕
Unlock Crystal	⇦, ⇨, ⇨, ⇦, ⇦, ⇧, ⇧, ⇩, ⇦, ✕, ✕
Win Mission	⇦, ⇦, ⇨, ⇩, ⇩, ⇩, ⇧, ⇩, ⇩, ✕

Scarface

Enter these on the Cheats screen of the Pause menu.

Wii

Unlockable	Password	Unlockable	Password
1,000 Balls	FPATCH	Grey Suit	GREY
Antique Racer	OLDFAST	Grey Suit w/shades	GREYSH
Bacinari	666999	Increase Cop Heat	DONUT
Black Suit	BLACK	Increase Gang Heat	GOBALLS
Blue Suit	BLUE	Lightning	SHAZAAM
Blue Suit w/shades	BLUESH	Rain	RAINY
BReal "The World Is Yours" Music Track	TUNEME	Sandy Shirt	TANSHRT
		Sandy Shirt w/shades	TANSH
Bulldozer	DOZER	Stampede	BUMMER
Change Time of Day	MARTHA	Tiger Shirt	TIGSHRT
Decrease Cop Heat	FLYSTRT	Tiger Shirt w/shades	TIGERSH
Decrease Gang Heat	NOBALLS	Vehicle Repair	TBURGLR
Dump Truck	DUMPER	White Suit	WHITE
Fill Ammo	AMMO	White Suit w/shades	WHITESH
Fill Health	MEDIK		

Xbox

Xbox 360

Index

Scooby-Doo! Mystery Mayhem

Unlockable	Objective
Trap the Fake Ghost Mini Game	Collect all five sandwich ingredients in the first episode.
Monster Frenzy Mini Game	Collect all five sandwich ingredients in the second episode.
Mine Cart Mini Game	Collect all five sandwich ingredients in the third episode.
Trail Bike Mini Game	Collect all five sandwich ingredients in the fourth episode.
Spooky Science Mini Game	Collect all five sandwich ingredients in the fifth episode.

Scooby Doo: Night of 100 Frights

Pause the game and hold ⬜L1+⬜L2+⬜R1+⬜R2, then enter the following codes.

Unlockable	Code
All Power-Ups	●, ■, ●, ■, ●, ■, ■, ■, ●, ●, ■, ●, ●, ●
FMV Sequences	■, ■, ■, ●, ●, ●, ■, ●, ■
View Credits	■, ●, ●, ■, ●, ■

Change the date on the PlayStation 2 for some special holiday decorations:

Unlockable	Code
Assorted Fireworks	July 4
Fireworks	January 1
Giant Bats	October 31
Snow	December 25

Scorpion King: Rise of the Akkadian

Enter these codes while the game is paused. A sound will confirm if the code was entered correctly. You must have one handed class weapons enabled.

Unlockable	Code
Big Heads	↑, ↓, ←, →, ←, →, ●, R2
Enable All Bonuses	↑, ↓, ←, →, ←, →, ■, R2
Max Health And Weapons	↑, ↓, ←, →, ←, →, ■, ●
Small Enemies	↑, ↓, ←, →, ←, →, ●, ■
Unlock Meat Club	↑, ↓, ←, →, ←, →, ←, ←

Secret Weapons Over Normandy

At the Title screen (New Game or Continue), enter the following:

Unlockable	Code
All Levels in Instant Action	↑, ↓, ←, →, R1, R1, L1, R1
All Planes and Missions	▲, ▲, ▲, ■, ■, ■, L1, R1, R2, R2, L2, L2
Big Heads	→, ↑, ←, ↓, →, ↑, ←, ↓, →, L1, R1, L1, R1
Invulnerability	↑, ↓, ←, →, ←, →, →, →, L1, L1, R1, R1, L2, R2
Unlimited Ammo	↑, →, ↓, ←, ↑, →, ↓, ←, L1, R1

Sensible Soccer 2006

Unlockable	Code
Blue Boots for Custom-Made Players	Win the Scots Premier League
Golden Boots for Custom-Made Players	Win the European Cup
Green Boots for Custom-Made Players	Win the Portuguese 1st Div
Orange Boots for Custom-Made Players	Win the Dutch 1st Div

DS

GBA

PSP

PS2

PS3

Wii

Xbox

Xbox 360

Index

DS

GBA

PSP

PS2

PS3

Wii

Xbox

Xbox 360

Index

Sensible Soccer 2006 (Continued)

Unlockable	Code
Red Boots for Custom-Made Players	Win the French 1st Div
Silver Boots for Custom-Made Players	Win the EURO Cup (Uefa Cup)
White Boots for Custom-Made Players	Win the German Cup
All Star Ball	Win the Italian Cup
Bright Yellow Ball	Win the Spanish Cup
Classic Old Leather Football	Win the English Cup (FA Cup)
Retro Black-and-White Ball	Win the German 1st Div
Tournament Ball	Win the South American Cup
Afro Hair Style for Custom-Made Players	Win the German Shield
Aging Rocker Hairstyle for Custom-Made Players	Win the Portuguese Cup
Bouffant Hairstyle for Custom-Made Players	Win the Super Cup
Monk Spot Hairstyle for Custom-Made Players	Win the French League Cup
Mullet Hairstyle for Custom-Made Players	Win the English Shield (Community Shield)
Rasta Hairstyle for Custom-Made Players	Win the Dutch League Cup
Receding Hairstyle for Custom-Made Players	Win the Scots League Cup
String Band Hair Accessory for Custom-Made Players	Win the Italian Shield
Ponytail Hairstyle for Custom-Made Players?	Win the Spanish Shield
A Snowy Pitch	Win the Italian A Div
Icy Pitch Type	Win the European Cup (Champions League)
Muddy Pitch Type	Win the English Premiership
Synthetic Turf (Astroturf) Pitch Type	Win the World Cup
The Carpet Pitch Type	Win the Spanish Premier League
Codemasters Shirt	Win the English League (Championship)
Guerrilla Shirt	Win the Portuguese 2nd Div
Home and Away Shirt	Win the Spanish 2nd Div
Lederhosen Shirt	Win the German 2nd Div
Showtime Shirt	Win the Dutch 2nd Div
Tartan Shirt	Win the Scots League
Tropical Shirt	Win the African Cup
Tuxedo Shirt	Win the Italian B Div
"I Love Sensi" Shirt	Win the French 2nd Div
Guerrilla Shorts	Win the Portuguese League Cup
Hearts Shorts	Win the French Cup
Kinky Shorts	Win the Dutch Cup
Leather Shorts	Win the Italian League Cup
Lederhosen Shorts	Win the German League Cup
Tartan Shorts	Win the Scottish Cup
Tropical Shorts	Win the Asian Cup
Trunks Shorts	Win the Spanish League Cup
Union Jack Shorts	Win the English League Cup

DS

GBA

PSP

PS2

PS3

Wii

Xbox

Xbox 360

Index

Shadow of Destiny

Unlockable	Objective
Extra Ending	Complete the game five times and earn all of the Ending Files, then play through once more to get a special, extra ending.
Extra Option	When you beat the game, you are graded on how well you played. This leads to one of five endings. After you complete the game once and earn an ending, an "Extra" feature appears on the Main menu. Access it to see Movies, Ending Files, and the Result for each completed level.
Movies	Beat the game once and earn an Ending File, unlocking a Movie. Earn three Ending Files to unlock a movie from a European Konami show. Get the special "extra" ending to unlock a Movie from the Fall Tokyo Game Show.

Shark Tale

During gameplay, press ⊞, hold ⓵, and enter code. After you enter the code, release ⓵ to activate the cheat.

Unlockable	Code
Attack Mode	●,●,●,●,✕,●,●,●,●
Extra Clams and Fame	●,●,✕,✕,●,✕,●,●
Replace All Pearls with Fish King Coins	●,✕,●,●,●,✕,●,●

Shellshock: Nam '67

Enter the following codes at the Title screen (Press Start Button screen):

Unlockable	Code
Add Weapon Option	↑,↓,←,→,●,■,↑,↓,←,→,●,■
All Missions and Pictures	ⓛ2,ⓡ2,ⓛ1,ⓡ1,ⓛ1,ⓛ2,ⓛ2,ⓡ2,ⓛ1,ⓡ1,ⓡ1,ⓡ2
God Mode	ⓡ3,ⓛ3,→,←,ⓛ1,ⓡ1,ⓡ3,ⓛ3,→,←,ⓛ1,ⓡ1
Infinite Ammunition	ⓡ2,ⓡ1,▲,ⓛ2,ⓛ1,↑,ⓡ2,ⓡ1,▲,ⓛ2,ⓛ1,↑
Psychedelic Mode	↑,ⓡ2,●,←,▲,■,ⓛ2,ⓛ1,●,ⓡ1

Shinobi

Unlockable	Objective
Bonuses	Collect the gold Oboro Clan Coins during gameplay to unlock bonus options in the Extras menu, including level select and movies.
Hard Difficulty Setting	Complete the game under the Normal difficulty setting.
Play as Joe Musashi	Collect 40 Oboro Clan Coins during gameplay. Joe's sword damage does less than when playing as Hotsuma; however, his shurikens are unlimited in number and do more damage, but do not stun. Also, because he does not use the Akujiki sword, his energy does not drain constantly.
Play as Moritsune	Collect 30 Oboro Clan Coins during gameplay. Moritsune is Hotsuma's brother and is stronger and faster. However, the Akujiki sword drains him more.
Super Difficulty Setting	Successfully complete the game under the Hard difficulty setting.
VR Stage	Collect 50 Oboro Clan Coins during gameplay.

Shrek 2

During gameplay, pause the game. Then select the Scrapbook and enter the following:

Unlockable	Code
1,000 Coins	←,↑,✕,●,←,↑,✕,●,←,↑,✕,●,↑,→,↓,←,↑
Bonus Games	←,↑,✕,●,←,↑,✕,●,←,↑,✕,●,■,●,■,●,■,●
Full Health	←,↑,✕,●,←,↑,✕,●,←,↑,✕,●,↑,→,↓,←,↑
Level Select	←,↑,✕,●,←,↑,✕,●,←,↑,✕,●,↑,↑,↑,↑,↑

Sidebar tabs: DS | GBA | PSP | **PS2** | PS3 | Wii | Xbox | Xbox 360 | Index

Shrek Super Slam

Enter these codes at the Title screen.

Unlockable	Code
Pizza One mini game	⇧, ⇧, ▲, ▲, ⇨, ⇨, ●, ●, ⇩, ⇩, L1, R1, ⇦, ⇦, ■, ■, L1, R1
Pizza Two mini game	●, ●, ■, ■, ⇩, ⇨, ⇦, ⇨, L1, L1
Pizza Three mini game	⇩, ⇩, ⇨, ●, ⇧, ▲, ⇦, ■, L1, L1
Slammageddon	⇧, ⇧, ⇩, ⇩, ⇦, ⇨, ⇦, ⇨, ▲, ■, ■, L1, R1
Super Speed Modifier	L1, L1, R1, R1, L1, R1, L1, R1, ■, ●, ▲, ▲
Unlock All Challenges	▲, ▲, ▲, ●, ●, ●, ▲, ■, ●, ■, ■, ■, ⇧, ⇩, ⇦, ⇨, L1, R1

Silent Scope 3

Unlockable	Objective
Real-Time Window Option	Complete the indoor shooting range with an "S" or better rank to unlock the "Real-Time Window" option at the EX Options menu.

The Simpsons: Hit and Run

From the Main menu, go to Options. Hold L1+R1 and enter the following:

Unlockable	Code
Blurry View	▲, ●, ▲, ●
Explode on Impact Cars	▲, ▲, ■, ■
Fast Cars	■, ■, ■, ■
Grid View	●, ×, ●, ▲
Invincible Car	▲, ×, ▲, ×
Jumping Car	■, ■, ■, ▲
Speedometer	▲, ▲, ●, ■
Very Fast Cars	▲, ▲, ▲, ▲

> **TIP**
>
> *Change the date of the PlayStation 2 to Halloween, Thanksgiving, and Christmas to see new living room decorations.*

The Simpsons: Road Rage

Change the date of the PlayStation 2 to the following to unlock secret characters:

Unlockable	Code	Unlockable	Code
New Year's Barney	Jan 1	Thanksgiving Marge	Nov 22
Halloween Bart	Oct 31	Christmas Apu	Dec 25

The Simpsons Skateboarding

Enter these codes in the Character Selection screen while holding R1+R2+L1+L2.

Unlockable	Code
$99.00	▲, ×, ●, ■
Add Money	▲, ×, ●, ■
Ballerina Nelson	▲, ■, ×, ●
Big-Head Bart	×, ■, ●, ▲
Big-Head Frink	■, ×, ▲, ●
Big-Head Homer	●, ×, ▲, ■
Big-Head Lisa	■, ▲, ×, ●
Big-Head Nelson	▲, ■, ●, ×

The Simpsons Skateboarding (continued)

Unlockable	Code
Big-Head Wiggum	✕, ●, ■, ▲
Business Suit Krusty	●, ▲, ■, ✕
Demon Marge	✕, ■, ▲, ●
Fuzzy Skaters	✕, ▲, ■, ●
Gangsta' Bart	●, ✕, ■, ▲
Gangsta' Lisa	■, ▲, ●, ✕
Groovy Frink	✕, ●, ▲, ■
Man-Eater Wiggum	▲, ●, ■, ✕
Men in Black Otto	■, ✕, ●, ▲
Tightie-whitie Homer	▲, ●, ✕, ■
Transvestite Nelson	▲, ■, ✕, ●
Tuxedo Krusty	●, ▲, ■, ✕
Unlock All Boards	✕, ▲, ●, ■
Unlock All Levels	▲, ✕, ■, ●
Unlock All Skaters	●, ▲, ✕, ■

The Sims

To access the following unlockables, activate the Cheat mode by pressing
L1+R1+L2+R2 at the Main menu. You can then enter the following codes.

Unlockable	Code
Free Mode	FREEALL—all objects now cost 0 Simoleans. However, you can't sell any items for money. This has no effect on the cost of paying for bills and other services. Also, this code may cause some problems with saved games.
Midas Mode	MIDAS—begin the game in Get a Life mode, get into the hot tub with the girl, and press START to pause gameplay. Select "Quit" followed by "Just Quit." This mode unlocks all two-player games, all locked objects, and all locked skins.
Party Motel Mode	PARTY M—unlocks the Party Motel two-player game in Get a Life mode's bonus section.
Play the Sims Mode	SIMS—unlocks Play the Sims mode without going through the Get a Life Dream House. Players who have to play through the Dream House each time should find this useful.

The Sims Bustin' Out

Pause the game at any time and enter these codes.

Unlockable	Code
All Skins	L1, R2, ✕, ●, ↑, ↓
All Objects	L2, R2, ↑, ▲, L3
All Locations	R2, R2, L3, L2, R1, L1
Money	L1, R3, →, ■, L3

Sky Odyssey

Unlockable	Objective
A Tight Squeeze Card No. 16	Clear the A Tight Squeeze level two times. Pictures displayed are MS+Me262.
A Tight Squeeze Card No. 35	Clear the A Tight Squeeze level one time. Picture displayed is Mission Scenery.
Autogytro XG-1 Data Card No. 61	Get Autogytro. The picture displayed is of a CG Rendering.
Autogytro XG-1 Data Card No. 62	Get Autogytro. The picture displayed is of a Draft Illustration.

DS

GBA

PSP

PS2

PS3

Wii

Xbox

Xbox 360

Index

DS

GBA

PSP

PS2

PS3

Wii

Xbox

Xbox 360

Index

Sky Odyssey (continued)

Unlockable	Objective
Bf-109 Custom Data Card No. 47	Get Bf-109 Custom parts. The picture displayed is of a CG Rendering.
Bf-109 Custom Data Card No. 48	Get Bf-109 Custom parts. The picture displayed is of a Draft Illustration.
Bf-109 Customized Card No. 39	Clear the Maximus level with Bf-109. The picture displayed is of a customized craft.
Bf-109 Customized Card No. 40	Clear the Maximus level with Bf-109. The picture displayed is of a customized craft.
Blown Away Card No. 25	Clear the Blown Away level one time. Picture displayed is Mission Scenery.
Blown Away Card No. 6	Clear the Blown Away level two times. Pictures displayed are MS + Pulse Jet.
F117 Data Card No. 55	Get Stealth Jet. The picture displayed is of a CG Rendering.
F117 Data Card No. 56	Get Stealth Jet. The picture displayed is of a Draft Illustration.
F4U Corsair Data Card No. 53	Get F4U Corsair. The picture displayed is of a CG Rendering.
F4U Corsair Data Card No. 54	Get F4U Corsair. The picture displayed is of a Draft Illustration.
Great Divide Card No. 7	Clear the Great Divide level two times. Pictures displayed are MS+Shinden.
Heart of the Mine Card No. 11	Clear the Heart of the Mine level two times. Pictures displayed are MS+Bf-109.
Heart of the Mine Card No. 30	Clear the Heart of the Mine level one time. Picture displayed is Mission Scenery.
Hidden Plane	Right Wing: Land at the alternate landing strip in the Adventure Begins level.
Maximus Card No. 19	Clear the Maximus level two times. Pictures displayed are MS+Swordfish.
Maximus Card No. 38	Clear the Maximus level one time. Picture displayed is Mission Scenery.
Me262 Data Card No. 51	Get Me262. The picture displayed is of a CG Rendering.
Me262 Data Card No. 52	Get Me262. The picture displayed is of a Draft Illustration.
Mid-Air Rendezvous Card No. 10	Clear the Mid-Air Rendezvous level two times. Pictures displayed are MS+F117.
Mid-Air Rendezvous Card No. 29	Clear the Mid-Air Rendezvous one time. Picture displayed is Mission Scenery.
Movie Card No. 69	Earn 2,000 Acrobatic Points. The picture displayed is of a CG Movie.
Movie Card No. 70	Earn 3,000 Acrobatic Points. The picture displayed is of a CG Movie.
Movie Card No. 71	Earn 4,000 Acrobatic Points. The picture displayed is of a CG Movie.
Movie Card No. 72	Earn 5,000 Acrobatic Points. The picture displayed is of a CG Movie.
Movie Card No. 73	Earn 6,000 Acrobatic Points. The picture displayed is of a CG Movie.
Over the Falls Card No. 14	Clear the Over the Falls level two times. Pictures displayed are MS+Floatplane.
Over the Falls Card No. 33	Clear the Over the Falls level one time. Picture displayed is Mission Scenery.
Pontoon Plane Data Card No. 67	Get Pontoons. The picture displayed is of a CG Rendering.

Sky Odyssey (continued)

Unlockable	Objective
Pontoon Plane Data Card No. 68	Get Pontoons. The picture displayed is of a Draft Illustration
Pulse Jet Test Type Data Card No. 49	Get Pulse Jet Custom parts. The picture displayed is of a CG Rendering.
Pulse Jet Test Type Data Card No. 50	Get Pulse Jet Custom parts. The picture displayed is of a Draft Illustration.
Pulsejet Customized Card No. 43	Clear the Maximus level with Pulsejet. The picture displayed is of a customized craft.
Pulsejet Customized Card No. 44	Clear the Maximus level with Pulsejet. The picture displayed is of a customized craft.
Relief from Above Card No. 27	Clear the Relief from Above level one time. Picture displayed is Mission Scenery.
Relief from Above Card No. 8	Clear the Relief from Above level two times. Pictures displayed are MS+Shinden-kai.
S.O.S Card No. 13	Clear the S.O.S. level two times. Pictures displayed are MS+Shinden.
S.O.S Card No. 32	Clear the S.O.S. level one time. Picture displayed is Mission Scenery.
Shinden Data Card No. 57	Get Shinden. The picture displayed is of a CG Rendering.
Shinden Data Card No. 58	Get Shinden. The picture displayed is of a Draft Illustration.
Shinden-Kai Data Card No. 59	Get Shinden-kai. The picture displayed is of a CG Rendering.
Shinden-Kai Data Card No. 60	Get Shinden-kai. The picture displayed is of a Draft Illustration.
Special Card No. 74	All other cards earned. The picture displayed is of a Special Framed Card.
Special Card No. 75	All other cards earned. The picture displayed is of a Special Framed Card.
Special Card No. 76	All other cards earned. The picture displayed is of a Special Framed Card.
Storm Before the Calm Card No. 15	Clear the Storm Before the Calm level two times. Pictures displayed are MS+Swordfish.
Storm Before the Calm No. 34	Clear the Storm Before Calm level one time. Picture displayed is Mission Scenery.
Stormy Seas Card No 24	Clear the Stormy Seas level one time. Picture displayed is Mission Scenery.
Stormy Seas Card No. 5	Clear the Stormy Seas level two times. Pictures displayed are MS+F4U Corsair.
Swordfish Custom Data Card No. 45	Get Swordfish triple wing. The picture displayed is of a CG Rendering.
Swordfish Custom Data Card No. 46	Get Swordfish triple wing. The picture displayed is of a Draft Illustration.
Swordfish Customized Card No. 41	Clear the Maximus level with Swordfish. The picture displayed is of a customized craft.
Swordfish Customized Card No. 42	Clear the Maximus level with Swordfish. The picture displayed is of a customized craft.
Swordfish Triple Wing	Land at the alternative landing strip in the level Mid-Air Rendezvous. The alternate landing strip is easier to find after you earn the Special Radar by playing through the Target mode.
Take the Low Road Card No. 22	Clear the Take the Low Road level one time. Picture displayed is Mission Scenery.

DS

GBA

PSP

PS2

PS3

Wii

Xbox

Xbox 360

Index

DS
GBA
PSP
PS2
PS3
Wii
Xbox
Xbox 360
Index

Sky Odyssey (continued)

Unlockable	Objective
Take the Low Road Card No. 3	Clear the Take the Low Road level two times. Pictures displayed are MS+Pulse Jet.
The Adventure Begins Card No. 1	Clear the Adventure Begins level two times. Picture displayed is MS+Swordfish.
The Adventure Begins Card No. 20	Clear the Adventure Begins level one time. Picture displayed is Mission Scenery.
The Ancient Forest Card No. 28	Clear the Ancient Forest level one time. Picture displayed is Mission Scenery.
The Ancient Forest Card No. 9	Clear the Ancient Forest level two times. Pictures displayed are MS+Autogyro.
The Desert Express Card No. 2	Clear the Desert Express level two times. Pictures displayed are MS+Bf-109.
The Desert Express Card No. 21	Clear the Desert Express level one time. Picture displayed is Mission Scenery.
The Great Divide Card No. 26	Clear the Great Divide level one time. Picture displayed is Mission Scenery.
The Great Falls Card No. 18	Clear the Great Falls level two times. Pictures displayed are MS+Pulse Jet.
The Great Falls Card No. 37	Clear the Great Falls level one time. Picture displayed is Mission Scenery.
The Labyrinth Card No. 23	Clear the Labyrinth level one time. Picture displayed is Mission Scenery.
The Labyrinth Card No. 4	Clear the Labyrinth level two times. Pictures displayed are MS+Me262.
The Valley of Fire Card No. 17	Clear the Valley of Fire level two times. Pictures displayed are MS+Bf-109.
The Valley of Fire Card No. 36	Clear the Valley of Fire level one time. Picture displayed is Mission Scenery.
Towers of Terror Card No. 12	Clear the Towers of Terror level two times. Pictures displayed are MS+F4U Corsair.
Towers of Terror Card No. 31	Clear the Towers of Terror level one time. Picture displayed is Mission Scenery.
UFO Type Gold Data Card No. 63	Get UFO 2. The picture displayed is of a CG Rendering.
UFO Type Gold Data Card No. 64	Get UFO 2. The picture displayed is of a Draft Illustration.
UFO Type Silver Data Card No. 65	Get UFO 1. The picture displayed is of a CG Rendering.
UFO Type Silver Data Card No. 66	Get UFO 1. The picture displayed is of a Draft Illustration.
Custom Parts	Earn custom parts for your aircraft by earning grades of B or higher in the Adventure mode missions.
Emblems in Target Mode	Earn two silver medals. (Find the new emblems in the Customize Aircraft mode.)
Music Track in Target Mode	Earn one silver medal each (12 tracks total).
Radio in Target Mode	Earn four gold medals.
Special Radar in Target Mode	Earn two gold medals.
Auto Gyro Plane	Clear every stage of the Sky Canvas mode with a score of at least 90 Points.
Corsair	To unlock the Corsair you must be good enough at pulling acrobatic tricks to earn enough Acrobatic points in Adventure mode to get circles to appear around 10 of your mission grades.

Sky Odyssey (continued)

Unlockable	Objective
Gold UFO	To earn the gold UFO, get gold on every mission in Target mode.
ME 262	Beat the entire Adventure mode once (including the final level) to earn the ME 262, a very fast jet with two engines.
Pontoons	To earn a set of pontoons for your aircraft, allowing you to land in the water, complete the Stormy Seas level, landing on an aircraft carrier. The pontoons are required for a mission later in the game.
Silver UFO	Complete all Adventure mode missions with an A grade to unlock the silver UFO.
Stealth Jet	Complete every mission in Adventure mode with a total time of 10 minutes.
Unlimited Boost in Target Mode	Earn two gold medals. (Once equipped, all jet planes will have an infinite amount of boost, but must recharge after every use.)

Sled Storm

Enter the following codes at the Press Start screen while holding L1+R1.

Effect	Code	Effect	Code
All Characters	●,▲,●,▲,●,↓	Unlock Everything	●,■,↑,●,▲,↓
All Sleds	●,■,●,■,●,←	Unlock Hover Sled	●,▲,■,●,▲,→
All Tracks	●,←,●,→,●,↑		

Sly Cooper and the Thievius Raccoonus

Unlockable	Objective
Ending Bonuses	Get all the bottles hidden in a level to unlock an FMV sequence, special move, or background information.

Smuggler's Run

To access the following unlockables, pause the game, then enter code. A sound confirms correct entry.

Unlockable	Code
Invisibility	R1, L1, L1, R2, L1, L1, ↙
Less Time Warp	R2, L2, L1, R1, ←, ←, ←
Light Cars	L1, R1, R1, L2, R2, R2
More Time Warp	R1, L1, L2, R2, →, →, →
No Gravity	R1, R2, R1, R2, ↑, ↑, ↑

TIP

To unlock vehicles from Midnight Club: Street Racing, use a saved game from Midnight Club: Street Racing. Now you are able to use vehicles from that game.

Smuggler's Run 2 Hostile Territory

Enter these codes after pausing the game.

Unlockable	Code
Antigravity for ambient vehicles	R1, R2, R1, R2, ⇧, ⇧, ⇧
Double the frame rate	R3, L3, L3, R3, ⇦, ●, ⇦, ●
Fast Motion	R1, L1, L2, R2, ⇨, ⇨, ⇨
Glass Car	⇦, ⇧, ⇨, ⇩, ⇨, ⇧, ⇦, L2

DS
GBA
PSP
PS2
PS3
Wii
Xbox
Xbox 360
Index

DS

GBA

PSP

PS2

PS3

Wii

Xbox

Xbox 360

Index

Smuggler's Run 2 Hostile Territory (continued)

Unlockable	Code
Increase Speed	R1, L1, L2, R2, ⇨, ⇨, ⇨
Invisibility	R1, L1, L1, R2, L1, L1, L2
Level select and all cars	L2, R2, R2, L2, R1, L2, L1, ⇦, ⇨, L2, ⇩, R2
Low Gravity	L1, R1, R1, L2, R2, R2
Slow Motion	R2, L2, L1, R1, ⇦, ⇦, ⇦
Unlimited Countermeasures	R3, R3, R3, R1, R1, R2, R2

SOCOM: U.S. Navy SEALs

Unlockable	Objective
Admiral Difficulty	Complete the game under the Vice Admiral difficulty setting.
Captain Difficulty	Complete the game under the Commander difficulty setting.
Commander Difficulty	Complete the game under the Lieutenant Commander difficulty setting.
Level Select	Complete the game under the Lieutenant JG difficulty setting.
Lieutenant Commander Difficulty	Complete the game under the Lieutenant difficulty setting.
Lieutenant Difficulty	Complete the game under the Lieutenant JG difficulty setting.
Lieutenant JG Difficulty	Complete the game under the Ensign difficulty setting.
More Weapons	Complete the game under the Ensign difficulty setting to unlock terrorist weapons in the armory during Single-Player mode. Complete the game under the Lieutenant difficulty setting to unlock the MGL (Multiple Grenade Launcher).
Rear Admiral Difficulty	Complete the game under the Captain difficulty setting.
Vice Admiral Difficulty	Complete the game under the Rear Admiral difficulty setting.

SOCOM U.S. Navy SEALs: Combined Assault

Unlockable	Objective
ABOVE AND BEYOND BADGE	Complete all bonus objectives in campaign mode during your career
ANTI-ARMOR BADGE	Destroy at least 10 vehicles during your career
BASTILLE BADGE	Capture at least 40 enemies during your career
CAPTURE BADGE	Complete all CAPTURE Instant Action missions at any rank
COMMUNICATOR BADGE	Complete all SOCOM: Combined Assault crosstalk objectives in Campaign mode during your career
COVER OPS BADGE	Complete the campaign with a cumulative stealth score greater than 300,00 points
DEFUSE BADGE	Complete all DEFUSE Instant Action missions at any rank
DEMOLISH BADGE	Complete all DEMOLISH Instant Action missions at any rank
DODGER BADGE	Complete a mission with no team members downed and no medkit charges used
EFFICIENCY BADGE	Complete the campaign with an elapsed time less than 7:00:00
ESCORT BADGE	Complete all ESCORT Instant Action missions at any rank

SOCOM U.S. Navy SEALs: Combined Assault (continued)

Unlockable	Objective
EXEMPLARY RECORD BADGE	Complete the campaign with a cumulative performance score greater than 400,000 points
EXTRACT BADGE	Complete all EXTRACT Instant Action missions at any rank
FIRST AID BADGE	Use 40 medkit charges during your career
FROGMAN BADGE	Complete the campaign at the rank of Commander or Higher
GRENADIER BADGE	Neutralize at least 40 enemies with explosives during your career
LIQUIDATOR BADGE	Neutralize at least 600 enemies during your career
MARKSMANSHIP BADGE	Complete a mission with an accuracy rating greater than 85%
MELON HUNTER BADGE	Neutralize at least 150 enemies with headshots during your career
MERCY BADGE	Complete a mission without killing any enemies
OVER ACHIEVER BADGE	Complete all Instant Action missions on the rank of ADMIRAL
POQ BADGE	Complete the campaign with an elapsed time less than 4:30:00
RECOVER BADGE	Complete all RECOVER Instant Action missions at any rank
SAUSAGE BADGE	Obtain all sausages in Campaign mode during your career
SEAL BADGE	Complete the campaign at the rank of Admiral
SECURE BADGE	Complete all SECURE Instant Action missions at any rank
SHADOW OPERATOR BADGE	Neutralize at least 150 enemies undetected during your career
SUB-ROSA BADGE	Complete a mission with a stealth score greater than 30,000 points
SUPPORT BADGE	Complete all secondary objectives in Campaign mode during your career
TRIDENT BADGE	Complete the campaign with a total score greater than 1,200,000 points
TROPOLE BADGE	Complete the campaign at the rank of Ensign or higher
UNSEEN STRIKE BADGE	Neutralize at least 20 enemies with knife attacks during your career
ADJUSTABLE SCOPES	Badges needed: 06
DEFENSE FORCE WEAPON SET	Badges needed: 15
ENEMY EXPLOSIVES	Badges needed: 30
JUKEBOX BANG AND CLEAR	Badges needed: 21
JUKEBOX BOOMERS REPRISE	Badges needed: 15
JUKEBOX CATCH AND RELEASE	Badges needed: 15
JUKEBOX CREDITS	Badges needed: 21
JUKEBOX FIRE TEAM BRAVO	Badges needed: 21

DS

GBA

PSP

PS2

PS3

Wii

Xbox

Xbox 360

Index

DS

GBA

PSP

PS2

PS3

Wii

Xbox

Xbox 360

Index

SOCOM U.S. Navy SEALs: Combined Assault (continued)

Unlockable	Objective
JUKEBOX KARIMINAL	Badges needed: 15
JUKEBOX MAIN THEME	Badges needed: 15
JUKEBOX ROLL OVER ADJIKISTAN	Badges needed: 21
JUKEBOX THE INFINITE SOUL	Badges needed: 21
JUKEBOX URBAN DESTRUCTION	Badges needed: 21
MERCENARY WEAPON SET	Badges needed: 21
MM-I GRENADE LAUNCHER	Badges needed: 32
PARAMILITARY HEAVY WEAPON SET	Badges needed: 12
PARAMILITARY LIGHT WEAPON SET	Badges needed: 09
R44M GUN	Badges needed: 27
REBEL WEAPON SET	Badges needed: 18
SEAL WEAPON SET	Badges needed: 24
Credits	Complete the Socom Combined Assault campaign at the rank of Ensign or higher
Endgame	Complete the DARK HEART mission in Socom: Fireteam Bravo 2 at the rank of Ensign or higher
Envoy	Complete KINGFISHER in the campaign at the rank of Ensign or higher
Karim's Orders	Complete the RISING TIDE mission in Socom: Fireteam Bravo 2 at the rank of Ensign or higher
Polaris	Complete CHOKEHOLD in the campaign at the rank of Ensign or higher
Shadow Element	Sync with Socom: Fireteam Bravo 2
Stormsurge	Complete HIGHWIRE in the campaign at the rank of Ensign or higher
Turning Point	Complete TRAFFIC CONTROL mission in Socom: Fireteam Bravo 2 at the rank of Ensign or higher

Sonic Heroes

Unlockable	Code
2 Player Bobsled Race Mode	Collect 80 Emblems
2 Player Expert Race Mode	Collect 120 Emblems
2 Player Quick Race Mode	Collect 100 Emblems
2 Player Ring Race Mode	Collect 60 Emblems
2 Player Special Stage Mode	Collect 40 Emblems
2 Player Team Battle Mode	Collect 20 Emblems
Last Song and Movie	Complete the last story
Last Story Mode	Complete Story Mode with all four teams and all Choas Emeralds.
Metal Characters	Hold ✕+▲ once you pick a level in 2-Player mode.
Super Hard Mode	Collect 141 Emblems and have all A ranks.
Team Chaotix Song and Movie	Complete Story Mode with Team Chaotix
Team Dark Song and Movie	Complete Story Mode with Team Dark
Team Sonic Movie and Song	Complete Story Mode with Team Sonic
Team Rose Song and Movie	Complete Story Mode with Team Rose

The Sopranos: Road to Respect

Enter these codes while playing.

Unlockable	Code
Infinite Ammo	Hold L2 and R2 and press ●, ■, ✕, ■, ▲, ▲
Infinite Respect	Hold L2 and R2 and press ✕, ■, ✕, ■, ▲, ▲

Soul Calibur II

Unlockable	Objective
Money Pit	Beat Stage 1 of Chapter 4 in Weapon Master Mode.
Assassin	Beat Stage 2 of Subchapter 3 in Weapon Master Mode (Extra).
Astaroth—Soul Edge	Beat Stage 3 of Extra Chapter 1 in Weapon Master Mode.
Berserker	Beat Stage 1 of Subchapter 1 in Weapon Master Mode (Extra).
Cassandra—Soul Edge	Beat Stage 4 of Subchapter 2 in Weapon Master Mode.
Cassandra—Soul Edge	Beat Stage 5 of Subchapter 4 in Weapon Master Mode.
Cervantes	Beat Stage 4 of Chapter 3 in Weapon Master Mode.
Cervantes—Acheron	Beat Stage 5 of Chapter 3 in Weapon Master Mode.
Cervantes—Imitation Sword	Beat Stage 5 of Subchapter 4 in Weapon Master Mode.
Charade	Beat Stage 1 of Chapter 3 in Weapon Master Mode.
Unlock Egyptian Crypt	Beat Stage 5 of Chapter 8 in Weapon Master Mode.
Extra Arcade Mode	Either attempt Arcade Mode 10 times, or beat it once.
Extra Practice Mode	Beat Stage 1 of Chapter 1 in Weapon Master Mode.
Extra Survival Mode—Death Match	Beat Stage 3 of Subchapter 3 in Weapon Master Mode.
Extra Survival Mode—No Recovery	Beat Stage 2 of Extra Chapter 2 in Weapon Master Mode.
Extra Survival Mode—Standard	Beat Stage 5 of Chapter 6 in Weapon Master Mode.
Extra Team Battle Mode	Beat Stage 1 of Subchapter 1 in Weapon Master Mode.
Extra Time Attack—Extreme	Beat Stage 1 of Extra Chapter 1 in Weapon Master Mode.
Extra Time Attack Mode—Alternative	Beat Stage 4 of Chapter 9 in Weapon Master Mode.
Extra Time Attack Mode—Standard	Beat Stage 1 of Chapter 5 in Weapon Master Mode.
Extra VS Battle Mode	Either attempt Extra Arcade Mode 5 times, or beat it once.
Extra VS Team Battle Mode	Either attempt Extra VS Battle Mode 5 times, or beat it once.
Hwangseo Palace/Phoenix Court	Beat Stage 2 of Chapter 7 in Weapon Master Mode.
Ivy—Prototype Ivy Blade	Beat Stage 2 of Extra Chapter 2 in Weapon Master Mode.
Kilik—Bamboo Staff	Beat Stage 2 of Extra Chapter 1 in Weapon Master Mode.
Labyrinth	Beat Stage 6 of Chapter 6 in Weapon Master Mode.
Lakeside Coliseum	Beat Stage 3 of Chapter 1 in Weapon Master Mode.
Lizardman	Beat All Stages of Subchapter 2 in Weapon Master Mode (Extra).
Maxi—Fuzoroi	Beat Stage 5 of Chapter 3 in Weapon Master Mode.
Maxi—Termite Snack	Beat Stage 3 of Subchapter 4 in Weapon Master Mode.
Mitsurugi—Soul Edge	Beat Stage 5 of Subchapter 4 in Weapon Master Mode.

Sidebar tabs: DS · GBA · PSP · PS2 · PS3 · Wii · Xbox · Xbox 360 · Index

Soul Calibur II (continued)

Unlockable	Objective
Mitsurugi—Souvenir Gift	Beat Stage 3 of Subchapter 3 in Weapon Master Mode.
Necrid—Ethereal Edge	Beat Stage 5 of Chapter 8 in Weapon Master Mode.
Necrid—Soul Edge	Beat Stage 3 of Extra Chapter 2 in Weapon Master Mode.
Nightmare—Galley Oar	Beat Stage 3 of Extra Chapter 1 in Weapon Master Mode.
Nightmare—Soul Edge	Beat Stage 3 of Chapter 7 in Weapon Master Mode.
Raphael—Schweizer	Beat Stage 4 of Chapter 3 in Weapon Master Mode.
Seung Mina	Beat Stage 3 of Chapter 6 in Weapon Master Mode.
Seung Mina—Ambassador	Beat Stage 2 of Chapter 10 in Weapon Master Mode.
Seung Mina—Halberd	Beat Stage 6 of Chapter 6 in Weapon Master Mode.
Sophitia	Beat Stage 5 of Chapter 4 in Weapon Master Mode.
Sophitia—Memento	Beat Stage 3 of Extra Chapter 2 in Weapon Master Mode.
Sophitia—Synval	Beat Stage 2 of Chapter 10 in Weapon Master Mode.
Taki—Soul Edge	Beat Stage 3 of Subchapter 2 in Weapon Master Mode.
Talim—Double Crescent Blade	Beat Stage 2 of Chapter 3 in Weapon Master Mode.
Voldo—Soul Edge	Beat Stage 2 of Subchapter 2 in Weapon Master Mode.
Xianghua—Soul Calibur	Beat Stage 2 of Chapter 5 in Weapon Master Mode.
Xianghua—Soul Edge	Beat Stage 1 of Subchapter 2 in Weapon Master Mode.
Yoshimitsu	Beat Stage 3 of Chapter 2 in Weapon Master Mode.

Spawn: Armageddon

Pause the game and enter the following:

Unlockable	Code
All Comics	↑, ↓, ←, →, →, ←, ←, ↑
All Missions	↑, ↓, ←, →, ←, ←, →, →
All Weapons	↑, ↓, ←, →, ←, →, ←, ←
No Blood	↑, ↓, ←, →, ↑, ↑, ↑, ↑
Open Encyclopedia	↑, ↓, ←, →, ←, →, ↓, ↑
Unlimited Ammo	↑, ↓, ←, →, ↑, ←, ↓, →
Unlimited Health/ Necroplasm	↑, ↓, ←, →, →, ←, ↓, ↑
Unlimited Necroplasm	↑, ↓, ←, →, ↓, ←, ↑, →

Spider-Man

To access the following unlockables, enter the Specials menu to enter the sequence. A laugh will confirm a correct code entry. To return to normal, repeat the code entry.

Unlockable	Code
All Fighting Controls	KOALA
Big Head and Feet for Spider-Man	GOESTOYOURHEAD
Bonus Training Levels	HEADEXPLODY
Enemies Have Big Heads	JOELSPEANUTS
First-Person View	UNDERTHEMASK
Goblin-Style Costume	FREAKOUT
Level Select	IMIARMAS

DS
GBA
PSP
PS2
PS3
Wii
Xbox
Xbox 360
Index

Spider-Man (continued)

Unlockable	Code
Level Skip	Enter ROMITAS —after entering code, pause gameplay and select the "Next Level" option to advance to the next level.
Master Code	ARACHNID—unlocks all levels in the level warp option, all gallery options (movie viewer/production art), and combo moves.
Matrix-Style Attacks	DODGETHIS
Play as a Police Officer	REALHERO
Play as a Scientist	SERUM
Play as Captain Stacey (Helicopter Pilot)	CAPTAINSTACEY
Play as Shocker's Thug	THUGSRUS
Play as Skulls Gang Thug	KNUCKLES
Play as the Shocker	HERMANSCHULTZ
Small Spider-Man	SPIDERBYTE
Unlimited Green Goblin Glider Power	CHILLOUT
Unlimited Webbing	ORGANICWEBBING—you can also just accumulate 50,000 points during gameplay.

Unlockable	Objective
Alternate Green Goblin Costume	If you are using the Alex Ross Spider-Man, play any level with the Green Goblin in it and he will have an alternate costume that more closely resembles his classic costume.
Green Goblin FMV Sequence	Successfully complete the game under the Hero or greater difficulty setting.
Pinhead Bowling Mini-Game	Accumulate 10,000 points during gameplay to unlock the Pinhead bowling mini-game in the training menu.
Play as Alex Ross	Successfully complete the game under the Normal or higher difficulty setting to unlock the Alex Ross costume in the Specials menu.
Play as Peter Parker	Successfully complete the game under the easy or higher difficulty setting to unlock the Peter Parker costume in the Specials menu.
Play as the Green Goblin	Complete the game under the Hero or Superhero difficulty setting to unlock the Green Goblin costume option at the Specials menu. *(See below for more info)*
Play as Wrestler	Complete the game under the Easy or higher difficulty setting to unlock the wrestler costume in the Specials menu. To unlock this easily, first unlock the "Unlimited Webbing" cheat. When you get to the ring, zip to the top and keep on shooting Spidey Bombs.
Shocker FMV Sequence	Accumulate 30,000 points during gameplay to unlock a Shocker FMV sequence in the CG menu.
Vulture FMV Sequence	Accumulate 20,000 points during gameplay to unlock a Vulture FMV sequence in the CG menu.

DS

GBA

PSP

PS2

PS3

Wii

Xbox

Xbox 360

Index

DS

GBA

PSP

PS2

PS3

Wii

Xbox

Xbox 360

Index

Spider-Man (continued)

TIP

Unlocking the Green Goblin costume option allows you to play as Harry Osborn in the Green Goblin costume (complete with appropriate weapons) in an alternate storyline where he tries to correct the Osborn family's reputation. To unlock this easily, start a new game under the Hero or Superhero difficulty setting. At the first level, pause gameplay, then quit to the main menu. Enable the ARACHNID code, then go to the "Level Warp" option. Choose the "Conclusion" level (that features Norman revealing himself to Spider-Man followed by the glider sequence), then exit. This marks the game as completed under the selected difficulty setting. The Green Goblin costume option will be unlocked at the "Secret Store" screen.

Spider-Man 2

Start a New Game and enter HCRAYERT as a name. Go back and enter any name of your choice. This cheat will start in progress, with over 40% completion, 201,000 Hero points, upgrades, and other goodies!

Splashdown Rides Gone Wild

Enter codes in the Options menu screen.

Unlockable	Code
50,000 Warehouse Points	⇧, ⇧, ⇩, ⇩, ⇦, ⇨, ⇦, ⇨, ■, ●
All Warehouse Items	⇧, ⇩, ⇧, ⇩, ⇦, ⇨, ⇦, ⇨, ⇦, ⇩, ⇨, ⇧, ⇦, ⇩, ⇦, ⇧

Spyhunter

At the screen where you enter a name, enter this password. The sound of a chicken clucking will confirm that you have entered the code correctly.

Unlockable	Code
Unlock Saliva Video	GUNN
View Concept Art	SCW823
View Making of FMV	MAKING
View Spy Hunter Theme FMV	SALIVA
View Test Animatic FMV	WWS413

Spy Hunter 2

Unlockable	Code
All Missions and Weapons	In the Main Menu, press L1, R2, L2, R1, R1, L2, R2, L1.
Infinite Ammo	Pause the game and press R1, L1, R2, R2, L2, R1, L1, R2, L2. Enter the code again to deactivate it.
Invincibility	Pause the game and press L1, L1, L1, R2, L1, R1, R1, L1, R2. Enter the code again to deactivate it.

SSX

Unlockable	Code
Third Board	Obtain the Rookie rank.
Fourth Board	Obtain the Sensei rank.
Fifth Board	Obtain the Contender rank.
Sixth Board	Obtain the Natural rank.
Seventh Board	Obtain the Star rank.
Eighth Board	Obtain the Veteran rank.
Ninth Board	Obtain the Champ rank.
10th Board	Obtain the Superstar rank.
11th Board	Obtain the Master rank.

SSX (continued)

Unlockable	Code
Aloha Ice Jam Track	Get a medal on Tokyo Megaplex.
Hiro	Win four gold medals.
JP	Win two gold medals.
Jurgen	Win one gold medal.
Mercury City Meltdown Track	Get a medal on Elysium.
Mesablanca Track	Get a medal on Mercury City Meltdown.
Pipedream Track	Get a medal on Tokyo Megaplex.
Fourth Costume	Complete all blue square tricks.
Third Costume	Complete all green circle tricks.
Untracked Course	Get a medal on the Aloha Ice Jam.
Tokyo Megaplex Track	Get a medal on Mesablanca.
Zoe	Win three gold medals.

To access the following unlockables, go into the Options menu, hold R1 + R2 + L1 + L2, and enter code. A sound confirms correct code entry.

Unlockable	Code
All Courses, Costumes, Characters, and Boards	↓, ←, ↑, →, ×, ●, ▲, ■
All Course Hints	●, ×, ●, ×, ●, ×, ●, ×
Maximum Stats	×, ×, ×, ×, ×, ×, ×, ×, ■
Running Man	■, ▲, ●, ×, ■, ▲, ●, ×

SSX 3

From the Main menu, go to Options. Select "Enter Cheat" and enter the following codes (these codes are case-sensitive):

Unlockable	Code
All Artwork	naturalkoncept
All Boards	graphicdelight
All Peaks	biggerthank7
All Playlist Songs	djsuperstar
All Posters	postnobills
All Toys	nogluerequired
All Trading Cards	gotitgotitneedit
All Videos	myeyesaredim
Brodi	zenmaster
Bunny San	wheresyourtail
Canhuck	greatwhitenorth
Churchill	tankengine
Cudmore the Cow	milkemdaisy
Eddie	worm
Gutless	boneyardreject
Hiro	slicksuit
Lodge One Clothes	shoppingspree
Luther	bronco
Jurgen	brokenleg
Marty	back2future
North West Legend	callhimgeorge
Snowballs	betyouneverseen
Stretch	windmilldunk
Svelte Luther	notsosvelte
Unknown Rider	finallymadeitin

DS

GBA

PSP

PS2

PS3

Wii

Xbox

Xbox 360

Index

DS

GBA

PSP

PS2

PS3

Wii

Xbox

Xbox 360

Index

SSX On Tour

Enter these passwords at the Cheats menu.

Unlockable	Code	Unlockable	Code
All Clothing	FLYTHREADS	Unlock Characters	ROADIEROUNDUP
All Levels	BACKSTAGEPASS	Unlock Conrad (The MiniViking)	BIGPARTYTIME
All Movies	THEBIGPICTURE		
Extra Cash	LOOTSNOOT	Unlock Mitch Koobski (The Unicorn)	MOREFUNTHANONE
Infinite Boost	ZOOMJUICE		
Monster Tricks	JACKALOPESTYLE	Unlock Nigel (Rocker)	THREEISACROWD
Snowball Fight	LETSPARTY		
Stat Boost	POWERPLAY	Unlock Ski Patrol Character	FOURSOME

SSX Tricky

Unlockable	Objective
Alternate Costumes	To earn more costumes, complete all chapters in your trick book. To unlock the final chrome costume, complete World Circuit mode with a Master rank.
Fugi Board	Get a gold medal on every course with all boarders with their uberboard to unlock a Fugi board.
Pipedream Course	Win a medal on all Showoff courses.
Play as Brodi	Win a gold medal in World Circuit mode.
Play as JP	Win three gold medals in World Circuit mode.
Play as Kaori	Win four gold medals in World Circuit mode.
Play as Luther	Win eight gold medals in World Circuit mode.
Play as Marisol	Win five gold medals in World Circuit mode.
Play as Psymon	Win six gold medals in World Circuit mode.
Play as Seeiah	Win seven gold medals in World Circuit mode.
Play as Zoe	Win two gold medals in World Circuit mode.
Uberboards	Unlock all of the tricks for a character to get their uberboard, which is their best board.
Untracked Course	Win a medal on all Race courses.

To access the following unlockable, go to the Title screen and hold ⚫L1+⚫R1, enter code, then release ⚫L1+⚫R1. A sound will confirm correct code entry.

Unlockable	Code
Full Stat Points	↑, ↑, →, ↑, ↑, ↑, ↓, ✕, ✕, ✕, ←, ✕, ✕, ↑—all the boarders will have full stat points.
Mallora Board	✕, ✕, →, ●, ●, ↓, ↑, ↑, ←, ■, ■, ↑—choose Elise and start a track. Elise will have the Mallora Board and a blue outfit.
Master Code	✕, ↑, →, ●, ■, ↓, ↑, ▲, ■, ←, ●, ✕, ↑
Mix Master Mike	✕, ✕, →, ✕, ✕, ↓, ✕, ✕, ←, ✕, ✕, ↑— (See below for more info)
Running Man Mode	■, ↑, ●, ✕, ■, ↑, ●, ✕—enter at the Options screen.
Sticky Boards	■, ■, →, ↑, ↑, ↓, ●, ●, ←, ✕, ✕, ↑

NOTE

For the Mix Master Mike unlockable, once you've input the code, choose any boarder at the character selection screen and he or she will be replaced by Mix Master Mike on the course. He has decks on his back and a vinyl board. Repeat the code to disable its effect.

Star Wars Battlefront

Unlockable	Code
All Planets	Choose Historical Campaign, then press ■,●,■,● at the Planet Selection screen.

Star Wars Bounty Hunter

Enter the following sequences as codes.

Unlockable	Code	Unlockable	Code
Chapter 1	SEEHOWTHEYRUN	Mission 7	LOCKUP
Chapter 2	CITYPLANET	Mission 8	WHAT A RIOT
Chapter 3	LOCKDOWN	Mission 9	SHAFTED
Chapter 4	DUGSOPLENTY	Mission 10	BIGMOSQUITOS
Chapter 5	BANTHAPOODOO	Mission 11	ONEDEADDUG
Chapter 6	MANDALORIANWAY	Mission 12	WISHIHADMYSHIP
Concept Art	R ARTISTS ROCK	Mission 13	MOS GAMOS
Mission 1	BEAST PIT	Mission 14	TUSKENS R US
Mission 2	GIMMEMY JETPACK	Mission 15	BIG BAD DRAGON
Mission 3	CONVEYORAMA	Mission 16	MONTROSSISBAD
Mission 4	BIGCITYNIGHTS	Mission 17	VOSAISBADDER
Mission 5	IEATNERFMEAT	Mission 18	JANGOISBADDEST
Mission 6	VOTE4TRELL	TGC Cards	GO FISH

Star Wars: Episode III Revenge of the Sith

Enter the following codes in the Codes section of the Options menu.

Unlockable	Code
All Attacks and Force Power Upgrades Activated	JAINA
All Bonus Missions Unlocked	NARSHADDAA
All Concept Art Unlocked	AAYLASECURA
All Duel Arenas Unlocked	TANTIVEIV
All Duelist Unlocked	ZABRAK
All Story Missions Unlocked	KORRIBAN
Fast Force Energy and Health Regeneration Activated	BELSAVIS
Infinite Force Energy Activated	KAIBURR
Infinite Health Activated	XUCPHRA

Star Wars Jedi Starfighter

Enter the following in the Codes section of the Options menu.

Unlockable	Code
Invincibility	QUENTIN
Fly-By Mode	DIRECTOR
No Hud	NOHUD

Star Wars Starfighter

To access the following unlockables, go to the Code screen (via the Options menu) to enter the sequence.

Unlockable	Code
Default Message	SHOTS (or SIZZLE)
Director Mode	DIRECTOR
Hidden Christmas Video	WOZ
Hidden Message	LTDJGD
Invincibility	MINIME

DS

GBA

PSP

PS2

PS3

Wii

Xbox

Xbox 360

Index

DS

GBA

PSP

PS2

PS3

Wii

Xbox

Xbox 360

Index

Star Wars Starfighter (continued)

Unlockable	Code
Jar Jar Mode	JARJAR
My Day at Work (short slideshow)	JAMEZ
No Heads Up Display	NOHUD
Everything	OVERSEER
Experimental N-1 Fighter	BLUENSF
Multiplayer Mode	ANDREW
Gallery	SHIPS
View Character Sketches	HEROES
View Hidden Picture	SIMON—you'll see a picture of the LEC team.
View Planet Sketch-Work	PLANETS
View the Credits	CREDITS
View the Dev Team	TEAM

Unlockable	Objective
Burger Droid	Access this Easter Egg by typing the DIRECTOR code, then entering the Bonus Missions and selecting Fighter Training. After a few seconds you see an asteroid with an android on it barbecuing some hamburgers.
Grim Fandango Hotrod	Come in first in the Canyon Sprint Bonus Mission.
Outlaw Gallery	To view this Easter Egg, start the first level. Instead of following your instructor's ship, turn around and go the other way to fly into a large room and view artwork from a game called *Outlaw*.
Canyon Sprint Bonus Mission	Get silver in these six missions: Naboo Proving Grounds, the Royal Escort, Taking the Offensive, Midnight Munitions Run, Rescue On the Solleu, the Final Assault.
Charm's Way Bonus Mission	Get a bronze medal in these six missions: the Royal Escort, Contract Infraction, Piracy Above Lok, Taking the Offensive, the New Resistance, the Final Assault.
Darth Maul's Infiltrator	Get gold in every mission in the normal game.
Guardian Mantis	Get gold in these three missions: Contract Infraction, Secrets On Eos, The New Resistance.
Havoc	Get gold in these five missions using the Havoc in the normal game: Piracy Above Lok, Valuable Goods, Eye Of the Storm, the Crippling Blow, Last Stand On Naboo.
N-1 Starfighter	Get gold in these six missions using the N-1 in the regular game: Naboo Proving Grounds, the Royal Escort, Taking the Offensive, Midnight Munitions Run, Rescue on Solleu, the Final Assault.
Outpost Attack Bonus Mission	Get Bronze in all 14 missions of the normal game.
Space Sweep Bonus Mission	Get Silver in all 14 missions of the normal game.
Two-Player Canyon Race	Beat the normal game on any difficulty level. Once unlocked, get gold in every level of the normal game to play the bonus level.
Two-Player Capture the Flag	Beat the normal game on any difficulty level. Once unlocked, get gold in every level of the normal game to play the bonus level.

Star Wars: The Clone Wars

Enter the following as codes.

Unlockable	Code
Unlock Clone Trooper in Academy Geonosis Level	FAKE FETT
All FMV Sequences	12 PARSECS
Campaign Level Select	DOORDONOT
Invincibility	DARKSIDE
Multiplayer Level Select	JORG SACUL
Programming Team Photographs (viewable after Sketchbook open)	JEDICOUNCIL
Three Bonus Objectives for Current Mission Marked Complete	GIMME
Unlimited Secondary and Special Weapon	SUPERLASER
Battle Droid in Academy Geonosis Level	TRADEFED
Next Level	THRISNOTRY
Padme Amidala in Academy Geonosis Level	NATALIE
Wookie in Academy Geonosis Level	NERFHERDER

Starsky and Hutch

Type in VADKRAM as your Profile Name to unlock everything.

State of Emergency

To access the following unlockables, enter code during gameplay. A message will confirm correct code entry.

Unlockable	Code
AK47	←, →, ↓, R2, ▲
All Weapons	L1, L1, R2, R2, ×
Big Player	R1, R2, L1, L2, ▲
Bull	→, →, →, →, ×—enter in Kaos mode. Alternately, successfully complete the East Side level in Revolution mode to unlock Bull in Kaos mode.
Flame Thrower	←, →, ↓, R2, ●
Freak	→, →, →, →, ●—enter in Kaos mode. Alternately, successfully complete the Chinatown level in Revolution mode to unlock Freak in Kaos mode.
Grenade	←, →, ↓, R2, ■
Grenade Launcher	←, →, ↓, R1, ■
Invincibility	L1, L2, R1, R2, ×
Little Player	R1, R2, L1, L2, ×
Looting on the Rise	R1, L1, R2, L2, ▲
M16	←, →, ↓, R2, ●
Minigun	←, →, ↓, R1, ▲
Mission Select	L1, L2, L2, L2, L1, ×
Mission Skip	←, ←, ←, ←, ▲
Molotov Cocktail	←, →, ↓, R2, ×
Normal Player	R1, R2, L1, L2, ● Alternately, press R1, R2, L1, L2, ■.
Pepper Spray	←, →, ↓, L1, ■
Pistol	←, →, ↓, L1, ▲
Policeman	Hold L1, then press R2, R2, L2, R1
Punches Decapitate	L1, L2, R1, R2, ■
Rocket Launcher	←, →, ↓, R1, ×
Shotgun	←, →, ↓, L2, ▲

DS
GBA
PSP
PS2
PS3
Wii
Xbox
Xbox 360
Index

DS

GBA

PSP

PS2

PS3

Wii

Xbox

Xbox 360

Index

State of Emergency (continued)

Unlockable	Code
Spanky	→, →, →, →, ▲—enter in Kaos mode. Alternately, complete the Mall level in Revolution mode to unlock Spanky in Kaos mode.
Tazer	←, →, ↓, L1, ●
Tear Gas	←, →, ↓, L1, ✕
Unlimited Ammunition	L1, L2, R1, R2, ▲—enter without a weapon in your hands.
Unlimited Time in Kaos Mode	L1, L2, R1, R2, ●

Unlockable	Objective
Chinatown Level	Score 25,000 points in the Capitol City Mall level in Kaos mode.
Corporation Central Level	Score 100,000 points in the East Side level in Kaos mode.
East Side Level	Score 50,000 points in the Chinatown level in Kaos mode.
Last Clone Standing Levels	Successfully complete the three-minute and five-minute versions of a level to unlock the Last Clone Standing version of that map in Kaos mode.
Unlimited Kaos Mode Time	Successfully complete all Kaos levels in Arcade mode.

Street Fighter EX3

Unlockable	Objective
Bonus Characters	Beat the game on Normal difficulty without using a Continue to unlock one of the hidden characters. *(See below for more info)*
Evil Ryu	Beat Original mode eight times with Ryu and without continuing. Go to the Character Selection screen and highlight Ryu. Press ✕, ■, or ●.
M. Bison II	Beat Original mode eight times with M. Bison and without continuing. Go to the Character Selection screen and highlight M. Bison. Press ✕, ■, or ●.
Narrator Sakura	Beat Original mode eight times with Sakura and without continuing. Go to the Character Selection screen and highlight Sakura. Press SELECT.

NOTE

In order to unlock all the bonus characters, repeat the method described above nine times. However, each time you beat the game, you must use a different regular character. The order of bonus characters are: Sagat, Vega, Garuda, Shadow Geist, Kairi, Pullum, Area, Darun, and Vulcano.

Street Hoops

Go to Game Settings and choose "Cheats" to enter these codes.

Unlockable	Code
ABA Ball	●, R2, ■, R2
All Courts	■, ■, L1, R2, L1, ●, L2, ●
All Teams	■, ■, L1, R2, L1, ●, L2, ●
Black Ball	R2, R2, ●, L2
Blocking Galore	R1, ●, L2, R2
Faster Clock	●, ●, ●, ■, ■
Kung-Fu	●, ●, ■, L1, ■, L1, L2
Normal Ball	R1, ■, ■, L1

Street Hoops (continued)

Unlockable	Code
Super Steals	■, R2, ■, R1, ●, L1, ●, L2
Tuxedo	L2, L2, ●, ■

Street Racing Syndicate

At the Main menu, press ↑,↓,←,→. A code entry screen will appear. Enter the following:

Unlockable	Code
Free Car Repair	FIXITUP
Mazda RX-8	RENESIS
Mitsubishi Eclipse GS-T	IGOTGST
Only a warning for the first three busts	LETMEGO
Pac Man Vinyl	GORETRO
Police Car	GOTPOPO
Subaru Impreza S202 STI	SICKGDB
Toyota Celica GT-S Action Package	MYTCGTS
Toyota Supra RZ	SICKJZA

Stuntman

At the New Game menu, use the following codes as drivers' names. All of the codes for this game are case-sensitive—enter them exactly as you see them!

Unlockable	Code
All Cars	spiDER
All Driving Games, Cars, and Toys	BindI
All Toys	MeFf
Filmography Section (all trailers)	"fellA"

The Suffering

Unlockable	Objective
Alternate title sequence	Complete the game.
Director Commentary	In the Prelude level, wait for a crow to land next to the three inmates, then stand on top of the crow.
Prelude Level	Complete the game.

Enter the following codes during gameplay while holding L1 + R1 + X.

Unlockable	Code
All Items and Weapons except Gonzo Gun	↑,↓,↑,←,→,←, R2,↑,←,↓,→, ↑,↓,↑,↓,←, R2,↓,↓,↓,↓, R2, R2
Bloody Torque	↑,↓,←,→
Clean Torque	↓,↑,→,←
Dirty family picture	←,↓,←,↓,←,↓, R2
Full Health	↓,↓,↓, R2,↑,↑,↑,↑, R2
Full Xombium bottle	→,→,↓,↓, R2,←,→, R2,→,↑,→, R2
Gonzo Gun	←, R2, R2, R2,→,←,→,←,↑, R2, R2, R2,↓,↑,↓,↑, R2
Grenades	→,→,→,←,←,←
Increase Negative Karma	←,←,↓,↑, R2
Molotov Cocktails	↓,↓,↓,↑,↑,↑
New Family Picture	↑,→,↑,→,↑,→, R2
Overcome Insanity	→,→,→, R2,←,←,→,←, R2

DS
GBA
PSP
PS2
PS3
Wii
Xbox
Xbox 360
Index

DS GBA PSP PS2 PS3 Wii Xbox Xbox 360 Index

The Suffering (continued)

Unlockable	Code
Old Movie Mode	↑, R2, ←, R2, ↓, R2, →, R2
Psychedelic Mode	←, ←, R2, →, →, R2, ↑, ↑, R2, ↓, ↓, R2
Reload Ammunition for Current Gun	→, →, ↓, ↑, ←, →, ←, ←, R2
Refill Ranged Weapon Ammunition	←, ←, ↑, ↓, →, ←, →, →, R2
Shotgun with Full Ammunition	←, ←, ←, ↓, ↓, ↓
Wrinkled Family Picture	↑, ↑, →, ↑

The Suffering: Ties that Bind

While playing, enter the following codes while holding L1+R1+✕. Do not pause the game.

Unlockable	Code
All Items and Weapons Except the Gonzo Gun	⇓, ⇑, ⇐, ⇒, ⇐, R2, ⇑, ⇐, ⇓, ⇒, ⇑, ⇒, ⇓, ⇐, R2, ⇓, ⇐, ⇓, R2, R2
Arsenal	⇓, ⇑, ⇐, ⇒, R2, ⇐, ⇒, ⇒, ⇒, R2, ⇓, ⇑, ⇐, ⇒, R2
Dream State	⇐, ⇐, R2, ⇒, ⇒, R2, ⇑, ⇑, R2, ⇓, ⇓, R2
Full Bottles	⇒, ⇑, ⇐, ⇒, R2, ⇐, ⇒, ⇒, R2, ⇒, ⇑, ⇒, R2
Full Flashlight Power	⇑, ⇐, ⇓, ⇒, ⇑, ⇒, ⇐, R2
Full Health	⇓, ⇑, ⇐, ⇒, R2, ⇑, ⇑, ⇐, ⇑, R2
Full Insanity	⇒, ⇐, ⇒, ⇐, R2, ⇐, ⇐, ⇒, ⇒, R2
Gonzo Gun	⇐, R2, R2, R2, ⇒, ⇐, ⇐, ⇐, ⇑, R2, R2, R2, ⇓, ⇑, ⇐, ⇒, R2
Invincibility	⇓, ⇑, ⇐, ⇒
Max Evil Rep	⇐, ⇓, ⇐, ⇓, ⇐, ⇓, R2
Max Good Rep	⇑, ⇒, ⇑, ⇒, ⇑, ⇒, R2
Minus 50 Rep	⇐, ⇐, ⇑
Molotov Cocktails	⇓, ⇓, ⇐, ⇑, ⇑, ⇒
More Ammunition for Current Gun	⇒, ⇒, ⇓, ⇑, ⇒, ⇒, ⇐, ⇐, R2
More Ammo for Current Thrown Weapon	⇐, ⇐, ⇑, ⇐, ⇒, ⇓, ⇒, ⇒, R2
Plus 50 Rep	⇑, ⇑, ⇒
Projector State	⇑, R2, ⇐, R2, ⇑, R2, ⇒, R2
Shotgun & Ammo	⇐, ⇐, ⇐, ⇓, ⇓, ⇓
Shrapnel	⇒, ⇒, ⇒, ⇐, ⇐, ⇐
Suicide	⇓, ⇓, ⇐, ⇓
Zero Blood	⇓, ⇑, ⇒, ⇐

Summer Heat Beach Volleyball

Enter the following codes at the Cheat menu to unlock the bonus.

Unlockable	Code	Unlockable	Code
Disable Arrows	Whine	All Accessories	Werit
High Gravity	Zippy	All Beach House Bonuses	Mypad
High-pitched Voices	Mouse	All Characters	Peeps
Low Gravity	Space	All Difficulty settings	Champ
Low-pitched Voices	Horse	All Locations	80Day
Nails Mode	Nails	All Mini-games	Major
Spinning Heads	Exosz	All Movies	Musak

Summer Heat Beach Volleyball (continued)

Unlockable	Code	Unlockable	Code
All Swimsuits/Shorts	Greed	Nerd Ball	Golem
All Trailers	Gamon	Sun Ball	Hot 1
Coconut Ball	Milky		

Unlockable	Objective
Artemis	Beat Arcade Mode on Expert.
Dummy	Beat all the tournaments on Medium.
Enigma	Beat all the tournaments on Hard.
Hephestus	Beat Arcade Mode on Hard.
Incognito	Beat all the tournaments on Expert.
Mannequin	Beat all tournaments on Easy.
Tina	Complete Training Mode.

Supercar Street Challenge

Unlockable	Code
Additional colors for your car	Select change color in styling studio and press ↑, →, ↓, ←, ▲, ●, ✕, ■
Debug menu	At the main menu, enter ■, ■, ↑, →, ↓, ←, L2, R2, L1, R1

Surfing

Unlockable	Objective
Normal Boards and Riders	Beat the game on Normal difficulty to unlock Tyrone King, Lara Barcella, Gareos, and six new boards.
Pro Boards and Riders	Beat the game on Pro difficulty to unlock Largo, Lyco Sassa, Mikey Sands, and five new boards.
Semi-Pro Boards and Riders	Beat the game on Semi-Pro difficulty to unlock Jojo, Morsa, Serena Knox, and six new boards.
Master Boards and Riders	Beat the game on Master difficulty to unlock three new boards and Surfroid.

SWAT: Global Strike Team

These codes must be entered in the in game option screen.

Unlockable	Code
Infinite Ammo	←, →, ↑, ↓, ↑, ↓, R2, L2
God Mode	↑, ↓, ←, →, L2, R2

Tak and the Power of Juju

Enter these codes during gameplay then go into the Extra menu to activate them.

Unlockable	Code
100 Feathers	■, ▲, ●, ■, ▲, ●, ■, ▲
All Moonstones	▲, ▲, ■, ■, ●, ●, ←, →
All Plants	■, ▲, ●, ←, ↑, →, ↓, ↓
All Juju Powers	↑, →, ←, ↓, ▲, ●, ■, ↓
All Yorbels	↑, ▲, ←, ■, →, ●, ↓, ↑
Everything	←, →, ■, ■, ●, ●, ←, →

Side tabs: DS, GBA, PSP, PS2, PS3, Wii, Xbox, Xbox 360, Index

DS

GBA

PSP

PS2

PS3

Wii

Xbox

Xbox 360

Index

Teenage Mutant Ninja Turtles 2: Battle Nexus

From the Options menu, choose "Password" and enter the following:

***Key: M**=Michaelangelo **R**=Raphael **L**=Leonardo **D**=Donatello **S**=Shredder*

POWER UP CHEAT CODES:

Unlockable	Code
All Stamina Restore Items Are Upgraded to Pizza	M R L M R M R
Attack Power Doubled	S D L S R L L
Defense Power Doubled	L D R M R L M
Stamina Meter Gradually Restores Itself	D R M S R L R
Turtles No Longer Receive Damage	L S D R R D R
Turtles No Longer Suffer from Damage Effects	D S R D M R M
Unlimited Number of Shuriken	R S R L R S M

POWER DOWN CHALLENGE CODES:

Unlockable	Code
Any Damage is Fatal	L R S R D R D
Enemies' Attack Power Doubled	S L S D R D L
Enemies' Defense Power Doubled	R D S R M R L
No Falling Off	S D S D R L D
Shuriken No Longer Available	R L M R D S L
Stamina Restore Items No Longer Available	M R M D R M D
Turtles Suffer from Poisonous Effects	D R S L L S R

HUMOROUS CHEAT CODES:

Unlockable	Code
Attack Enemies to See What Happens	M L D S R D M
Walk About to Find Out the Effect	S S S M R D D

Tekken 4

Unlockable	Objective
Fight as Eddy Gordo	Successfully complete the game in Story mode as Christie Monteiro. Highlight Christie and press ▲ at the Character Selection screen. Eddy Gordo plays exactly like Christie.
Fight as Ling Xiaoyu in School Uniform	Complete the game in Story mode as Ling Xiaoyu. Highlight Ling Xiaoyu and press ▲ at the Character Selection screen.
Fight as Miharu	Complete the game in Story mode as Ling Xiaoyu. Highlight Ling Xiaoyu and press ● at the Character Selection screen. Miharu looks like Ling in her schoolgirl outfit from Tekken 3 and Tekken Tag Tournament and plays just like her.
Fight as Panda	Highlight Kuma at the Character Selection screen, then press ▲ or ●.
Fight as Violet	Highlight Lee at the Character Selection screen, then press ●.
Unlocking All Characters	Complete the game with the indicated character to unlock the corresponding fighter.

Tekken Tag Tournament

To unlock the different stages, first highlight Practice mode at the Main menu, then enter the code listed.

Unlockable	Objective
Eddy's Stage (Day)	Hold L2 and press R2 13 times.
Eddy's Stage (Sunset)	Hold L2 and press R2 ten times.
Heihachi's Stage	Hold L2 and press R2 12 times.

Tekken Tag Tournament (continued)

Unlockable	Objective
Hwoarang's Stage	Hold L2 and press R2, R2, R2, R2.
Jin's Stage (Day)	Hold L2 and press R2 17 times.
Jin's Stage (Night)	Hold L2 and press R2 eight times.
King's Stage	Hold L2 and press R2 11 times.
Law's Stage (New)	Hold L2 and press R2 once.
Law's Stage (Old)	Hold L2 and press R2 15 times.
Lei's Stage	Hold L2 and press R2, R2, R2, R2, R2.
Ling's Stage	Hold L2 and press R2, R2, R2.
Nina's Stage (Day)	Hold L2 and press R2 nine times.
Nina's Stage (Night)	Hold L2 and press R2 18 times.
Ogre's Stage	Hold L2 and press R2 six times.
Paul's Stage	Hold L2 and press R2 20 times.
School Stage (Day)	Hold L2 and press R2 16 times.
School Stage (Night)	Hold L2 and press R2 seven times.
Supercharging	During a match, press all buttons to charge up. Press ✕ + ● + ▲ + ■ if you kept the default buttons.
Unknown Stage	Hold L2 and press R2 14 times.
Yoshimitsu's Stage (Heavy Snow)	Hold L2 and press R2 19 times.
Yoshimitsu's Stage (Light Snow)	Hold L2 and press R2, R2.

Unlockable	Code
Bonus Characters	Beat Arcade mode with any character to unlock one of the hidden characters. A bonus character is revealed each time you beat the game. *(See more info below)*
Change Partners Before a Fight	Hold the tag button before a match begins to let your partner start first.
Extra Armor King Costume	Beat Arcade mode with Armor King. Go to the Character Selection screen and highlight Armor King. Press START to get his extra costume.
Extra Ling Ending	Beat Arcade mode with Ling. Then beat the game a second time with Ling in her school uniform.
Gallery Mode	Once you unlock Devil you can access Gallery mode.
Tekken Bowl Jukebox	Score higher than 200 in Tekken Bowl. Press START inside Tekken Bowl to access the Bowling menu. Choose "Bowling Options" and pick what song you want to listen to.
Tekken Bowl Mode	Once you unlock Ogre you have Tekken Bowl.
Theater Mode	Beat Arcade mode once.
Play As Angel	Highlight Devil at the Character Selection screen. Press START.
Play As Tiger	Highlight Eddy at the Character Selection screen. Press START.

NOTE

When unlocking the bonus characters, expect them to appear in this order: Kunimitsu, Bruce Irvin, Jack-2, Lee Chaolan, Wang Jinrey, Roger and Alex, Kuma and Panda, Kazuya Mishima, Ogre, True Ogre, Prototype Jack, Mokujin and Tetsujin, Devil and Angel, then Unknown.

Tenchu Fatal Shadows

While the game is paused, enter code on the second controller.

Unlockable	Code
View Score Status	■, ■, ⇩, ⇩, ⇧, ⇧

DS · GBA · PSP · PS2 · PS3 · Wii · Xbox · Xbox 360 · Index

DS

GBA

PSP

PS2

PS3

Wii

Xbox

Xbox 360

Index

Tenchu: Wrath of Heaven

Unlockable	Code
Increase Items	From the Items screen, hold R2+L2, then press ■, ■, ■, ↑, ←, ↓, →.
Play Demo Stage	From the title screen, press ↑, ↓, →, ←, X, X, X.
Portable Ninja Brainwipe Machine	Pause the game with the left controller. Using the same controller, press L2, R3, R2, L3, →, ■, ↑, ■, L2, ←, ■, ↓, R2. The game will unpause and you may control the nearest enemy using the left controller in Story mode.
Regain Health	Pause the game and press ↑, ↓, →, ←, ■, ■, ■.
Score Cheats	Pause the game and enter →, →, ←, ← on the left controller.
Special Move Cheat	Pause the game and hold L2+L2, press ↑, ↑, ↓, ↓ then release the L2+L2 and press ■, ■, R1, R2.
Stock Infinite Items	From the item selection screen, hold L2+L1+R1+R2 then press ■, ■, ■, ↑, ←, ↓, →, ■, ↑, →, ↓, ←.
All Characters	From the title screen, press L2, R2, L2, R1, →, ←, L3, R3.
All Items	From the Items screen, hold R1+L2, then press ↑, ■, ■, ←, ■, ■, ↓, ■, ■, ←, ■, ■.
All Layouts	From the Mission Select screen, press R3, L3, R2, L2, R1, L1.
All Missions	From the Mission Select screen, press L2, R1, L2, R2, →, ■, L3, R3.
All Stages (Multiplayer)	From the Mission Select screen for multiplayer, press L2, R1, L2, R2, →, ■, L3, R3.
Bonus Stage	From the title screen, press L2, ↑, R1, ↓, ↙, →, R2, ←.
Outtakes	From the title screen, hold L2+R2, then press ↓, ■, ↑, ■, →, ■, ←, ■. The choice will be listed as the "B-SIDE" under the Audio/Language menu.

Terminator 3: Rise of the Machines

From the Main menu, choose "Options," then select "Cheats." Enter the following:

Unlockable	Code
50% Less Health in Combat with TX	X, ▲, ■, ●, ▲, X, ■, ▲
50% More Health in Combat with TX	■, ▲, ■, ▲, ●, X, ●, X
All Future Weapons	X, X, X, ▲, ●, ●, ■, X
All Present Weapons	●, ●, ▲, ■, X, ▲, ▲, ■
Centipede (Located in Special Features)	●, ●, ●, ■, ■, ■, ▲, ■
Invincibility	■, ■, X, ▲, X, ●, X, ●
Missile Command (Located in Special Features)	●, ●, ●, ■, ■, ■, X, X
Unlimited Ammo	X, ▲, ▲, ▲, X, X, ●, X, ■

Terminator 3: The Redemption

In the Main menu, choose "Credits." While watching the credits, enter the following:

Unlockable	Code
All Levels	●+R2+▲
All Upgrades	●+▲+L1
Invincibility	●+R2+R1

Tiger Woods PGA Tour 2004

From the Options menu, choose "Passwords." (These are case-sensitive.)

Unlockable	Code
Ace Andrews	ACEINTHEHOLE
All Courses and Golfers	THEKITCHENSINK
All Courses	ALLTHETRACKS
All Golfers	CANYOUPICKONE
Cedric the Entertainer	CEDDYBEAR
Dominic "The Don" Donatello	DISCOKING
Edwin "Pops" Masterson	EDDIE
Erica "Ice" Von Severin	ICYONE
Felicia "Downtown Brown"	DTBROWN
Hamish "Mulligan" McGregor	DWILBY
Kellie Newman	TRAVELER
Melvin "Yosh" Tanigawa	THENEWLEFTY
Moa "Big Mo" Ta'a Vatu	ERUPTION
Solita Lopez	SHORTGAME
Sunday Tiger Woods	4REDSHIRTS
Takeharu "Tsunami" Moto	EMERALDCHAMP
Target World Challenge	SHERWOOD TARGET
Val "Sunshine" Summers	BEVERLYHILLS

Tiger Woods PGA Tour 2005

From the Options menu, choose "Passwords." (These are case-sensitive.)

Unlockable	Code
Adriana "Sugar" Dulce	SOSWEET
Alastair "Captain" McFadden	NICESOCKS
All Courses	THEWORLDISYOURS
All Golfers and Courses	THEGIANTOYSTER
Aphrodite Papadapolus	TEMPTING
Arnold Palmer	THEKING
Ben Hogan	PUREGOLF
Bev "Boomer" Bouchier	THEBEEHIVE
Billy "Bear" Hightower	TOOTALL
Bunjiro "Bud" Tanaka	INTHEFAMILY
Ceasar "The Emperor" Rosado	LANDOWNER
Gary Player	BLACKKNIGHT
Hunter "Steelhead" Elmore	GREENCOLLAR
Jack Nicklaus	GOLDENBEAR
Jeb "Shooter" McGraw	SIXSHOOTER
Justin Timberlake	THETENNESSEEKID
Kendra "Spike" Lovette	ENGLISHPUNK
Raquel "Rocky" Rogers	DOUBLER
Reginald	"Reg" Weathers REGGIE
Seve Ballesteros	THEMAGICIAN
Sunday Tiger Woods	4REDSHIRTS
The Roof	NIGHTGOLFER
Tiffany "Tiff" Williamson	RICHGIRL

DS

GBA

PSP

PS2

PS3

Wii

Xbox

Xbox 360

Index

DS

GBA

PSP

PS2

PS3

Wii

Xbox

Xbox 360

Index

Tiger Woods PGA Tour 2005 (continued)

Unlockable	Code	Unlockable	Code
All ADIDAS Items	91treSTR	All ODYSSEY Items	kjnMR3qv
All CALLOWAY Items	cgTR78qw	All PING Items	R453DrTe
All CLEVELAND Items	CL45etUB	All PRECEPT Items	BRi3498Z
All MAXFLI Items	FDGH597i	All TAG Items	cDsa2fgY
All NIKE Items	YJHk342B	All TourStage Items	TS345329

Tiger Woods PGA Tour 06

Go to the Options menu, then enter the Passwords menu to enter these passwords.

Unlockable	Code
All Clubs	CLUB11
All Courses	ITSINTHEHOLE
All Golfers	WOOGLIN
Tiger Woods with Alternate Old Golf Outfit	OLDSKOOL
Tiger Woods with Hat	GOLDENAGE
Tiger Woods with Old Striped Pants	TECHNICOLOR
Tiger Woods with Very Old Golf Outfit	THROWBACK

Tim Burton's The Nightmare Before Christmas: Oogie's Revenge

Enter this code while playing.

Unlockable	Code
Pumpkin Jack and Santa Jack costumes	⇦, ⇧, ⇨, ⇦, L3, R3

Time Crisis 2

Unlockable	Objective
Auto Bullets	Clear the Story mode twice at any difficulty level to be able to fire 20 bullets in one trigger.
Auto Reload	Clear the Story mode at any difficulty level using Auto Bullets to earn unlimited firepower with your gun.
Increase Your Credits in Arcade Mode	Receive extra credits if you clear the Story mode at any difficulty level. *(See below for more info)*
Mirror Mode	To activate the Mirror mode, clear the Story mode without using the "Continue" function.
Music Player	To access the Music Player, clear the final mission of the "Crisis" Mission.
Shoot Away 2 Arrange Mode	To access Arrange mode, score very high points in the Arcade Original mode (Retro). Hit two clay pigeons with one bullet to double your points for that shot.
Shoot Away 2 Extra Mode	To access Extra mode, score good points in the Arcade Original mode (Retro).
Stage Trial 2	To reach Stage Trial 2, clear Stage 1 of the Story mode at any difficulty level.
Stage Trial 3	To reach Stage Trial 3, clear Stage 2 of the Story mode at any difficulty level.
Wide Shots	Clear the Story mode at any difficulty level with the Auto Reload function to enable your firearm to shoot wide shots (shotgun type with nine bullets per reload).

NOTE

For the "Increase Your Credits in Arcade Mode" code, once you've cleared the mode several times, you are eventually entitled to "Free Play" and a maximum of nine lives that you can set in the "Game" options.

Timesplitters

Unlockable	Objective
Female Cyborg Bot Set	Beat the 2005 Cyberden level on Easy.
Siamese Cyborg Bots	Beat the 2005 Cyberden level on Easy.
Brick As an Arcade Mode Weapon	Complete challenge 4-C.
Challenge Mode	Beat Story mode at any difficulty to Challenge mode. Then defeat each successive Challenge to unlock the next.
Duckman Drake	Complete challenge 2-C.
Duckman Drake As a Bot	Complete challenge 2-A.
Enemy Bricks Cheat	Complete challenge 4-B.
Farrah Fun-Bunny	Complete challenge 8-C.
Fun-Bunny As a Bot	Complete challenge 8-A.
Gasmask SWAT	Complete challenge 6-B.
Ginger As a Bot	Complete challenge 7-A.
Gingerbread	Complete challenge 7-C.
Green and Brown Zombies	Complete challenge 1-B.
Gretel	Beat the 2020 Planet X level on Easy.
Hick Hyde and Insect Mutant Bots	Beat the 1965 Mansion level on Easy.
Jacques Misere	Beat the 2020 Planet X level on Easy.
Mary-Beth Casey and L208	Beat the 2020 Planet X level on Easy.
Olga Strom	Beat the 2020 Planet X level on Easy.
Overall Mutant and Girl Zombie Bots	Beat the 1965 Mansion level on Easy.
Paintball Mode	Unlock the Paintball mode by beating the 1935 Tomb level on Easy in under one minute.
Peekaboo Jones	Beat the 2020 Planet X level on Easy.
Police, Skull and Jacket Zombies	Complete challenge 1-C.
Robofish	Complete challenge 3-C.
Robofish As a Bot	Complete challenge 3-A.
1950 Village Arcade Level	Beat the 1950 Village level on Easy.
1965 Mansion Arcade Level	Beat the 1965 Mansion level on Easy.
1985 Chemical Plant Arcade Level	Beat the 1985 Chemical Plant level on Easy.
2000 Docks Arcade Level	Beat the 2000 Docks level on Easy.
2020 Planet X Arcade Level	Beat the 2020 Planet X level on Easy.
2035 Spaceways Arcade Level	Beat the 2035 Spaceways level on Easy.
All Enemies Are Bunnies Cheat	Complete challenge 8-B.
All Enemies Are Ducks Cheat	Complete challenge 2-B.
All Enemies Are Fish Cheat	Complete challenge 3-B.
All Enemies Are Gingerbreads Cheat	Complete challenge 7-B.
All Enemies Are Impersonators Cheat	Complete challenge 5-B.
Badass Cyborg Bot Set	Beat the 2005 Cyberden level on Easy.
Bank Arcade Level	Beat the 1985 Chemical Plant level on Normal.

DS

GBA

PSP

PS2

PS3

Wii

Xbox

Xbox 360

Index

DS

GBA

PSP

PS2

PS3

Wii

Xbox

Xbox 360

Index

Timesplitters (continued)

Unlockable	Objective
Castle Arcade Level	Beat the 1950 Village level on Normal.
Chinese Chef	Beat the 1970 Chinese level on Easy.
Compound Arcade Level	Beat the 2000 Docks level on Normal.
Cultist	Beat the 1935 Tomb level on Easy.
Eyes Mummy	Beat the 1935 Tomb level on Hard.
Fishwife Mutant Bot	Beat the 1965 Mansion level on Easy.
Gasmask Soldier, Male/Female SWAT Bots	Beat the 2000 Docks level on Easy.
Gasmask SWAT Bots	Beat the 2000 Docks level on Easy.
Graveyard Arcade Level	Beat the 1935 Tomb level on Normal.
Horror Shocker Bot Set	Beat the 1965 Mansion level on Easy.
Impersonator	Complete challenge 5-C.
Impersonator As a Bot	Complete challenge 5-A.
Law and Order Bot Set	Beat the 2000 Docks level on Easy.
Living Dead	Complete challenge 1-A.
Male and Female Soldier Bots	Beat the 2000 Docks level on Easy.
Malehood Bots	Beat the 1985 Chemical Plant level on Easy.
Mall Arcade Level	Beat the 1965 Mansion level on Normal.
Period Horror Bot Set	Beat the 1950 Village level on Easy.
Red and Green Alien Bots	Beat the 2020 Planet X level on Easy.
Site Arcade Level	Beat the 1970 Chinese level on Normal.
Space Opera Bot Set	Beat the 2020 Planet X level on Easy.
Space Opera Bot Set	Beat the 2035 Spaceways level on Easy.
Spaceship Arcade Level	Beat the 2020 Planet X level on Normal.
Streets Arcade Level	Beat the 2005 Cyberden level on Normal.
Suit Hoodlum	Beat the 1970 Chinese level on Easy.
Tuxedo Cyborg Bot	Beat the 2020 Planet X level on Easy.
Usual Suspects Bot Set	Beat the 1985 Chemical Plant level on Easy.
Waiter and Lumberjack Bots	Beat the 1985 Chemical Plant level on Easy.
Warzone Arcade Level	Beat the 2035 Spaceways level on Normal.
Timesplitter	Complete challenge 9-B.
Timesplitters As a Bot	Complete challenge 9-A.
Veiled SWAT	Complete challenge 6-C.

Timesplitters 2

Beat each level listed in Story mode under Medium difficulty to unlock its secret character. You'll be able to play these unlockable characters in Arcade mode.

Level	Playable Character
1853 Wild West Level Reward	The Colonel
1895 Notre Dame Paris Level Reward	Notre Dame
1920 Aztec Ruins Level Reward	Stone Golem
1853 Wild West Level Reward	The Colonel

Timesplitters 2 (continued)

Level	Playable Character
1895 Notre Dame Paris Level Reward	Notre Dame
1920 Aztec Ruins Level Reward	Stone Golem

NOTE

Beat the 2401 Space Station Level on "Easy" difficulty to unlock the ending sequence.

Tokyo Extreme Racer: Zero

Unlockable	Objective
Change Horn to Siren	Select rear spoiler type 5 for R30 and R30M.
Clean Pause Screen	When Pausing, press ▲+■ to remove the Pause menu. (See below for more info)
Driver View Replay	When viewing replay in "DRIVER VIEW," press L1+R1 to move the camera left/right.
Get a Special Nickname	Put a team sticker on the car you were driving for this team.
Manipulate Parts Camera	In the Parts Type select screen, selecting Aero parts or exhaust makes the camera move toward the car, but pressing ▲ will not cause the camera to move close to the parts (you'll see the entire car on your screen). Press ▲ again to see the close-up.
Reset Records	In Time Record screen, hold down L1+L2+R1+R2 with START. (This also resets the Quick race high score.) These will not be saved, though.
See Meters During Replay	When viewing replay, press SELECT.
See Other Car in One-on-One	When having one-on-one battle with a rival, hold down ■ on 1P's controller to show other cars on the course.
See Other Cars in Free Run	In "FREE RUN," press ■ on 1P's controller when you enter the course select.
Show Analyze Option	In Pause menu (except in the VS mode), hold ■ while you move the cursor to the bottom to show "ANALYZE."
Show Mirror Ornaments	Hold down L1+L2+R1+R2 when selecting the "Shift Assist" option.
Watch Replay with Regular Angle	When you're about to see the replay, hold ▲ on 1P's controller. (You can't switch camera angles when you do this.)

You can't unpause the game while removing the Pause menu; you'll have to press ▲+■ to show the Pause menu before unpausing.

Tom and Jerry War of the Whiskers

To enter these codes, go into Options then open Cheats menu.

Unlockable	Code
Auto Refill Health Bars	✕, ●, ✕, ▲, ▲, ■, ●, ▲
Infinite Ammo	●, ■, ●, ▲, ✕, ■, ✕, ✕
Unlock All Character Costumes	●, ●, ✕, ■, ●, ▲, ✕, ●

Tom Clancy's Ghost Recon

Enter the codes at the Title screen:

Unlockable	Code
All Missions	✕, L2, ▲, R2, SELECT
All Special Features	L1, L2, R1, R2, ✕, SELECT
Invincibility	Pause the game and press L1, R2, L2, R1, SELECT

DS
GBA
PSP
PS2
PS3
Wii
Xbox
Xbox 360
Index

Tom Clancy's Rainbow Six 3

Unlockable	Code
All Custom Mission maps	Press L1, R2, L2, R1, ←, →, ■, ● at the Main menu.

Tomb Raider: The Angel of Darkness

Unlockable	Code
Infinite Air	When Lara is swimming, save the game while underwater. When you load that save, the oxygen gauge will be restored to full.
Skip Level	Pause the game and press and hold L1 + R2 + ↓ + ▲ then press ●, ↑, ■, ▲, →, ↓.

Tomb Raider Legends

Enter these codes in game. Codes can not be used until they are unlocked.

Unlockable	Code
Bulletproof	Hold L1 press ✕, R1, ▲, R1, ■, L2
Draws Enemies Health	Hold L1 press ■, ●, ✕, L2, R1, ▲
Excalibur	Hold L2 press ▲, ✕, ● R1, ▲, L1
Infinite Assault Ammo	Hold L2 press ✕, ●, ✕, L1, ■, ▲
Infinite Grenade Launcher Ammo	Hold L2 press L1, ▲, R1, ●, L1, ■
Infinite Shotgun Ammo	Hold L2 press R1, ●, ■, L1, ■, ✕
Infinite SMG Ammo	Hold L2 press ●, ▲, L1, R1, ✕, ●
One Shot Kill	Hold L1 press ▲, ✕, ▲, ✕, L2, ●
Textureless Mode	Hold L1 press L2, ✕, ●, ✕, ▲, R1
Wield Soul Reaver	Hold L2 press ✕, R1, ●, R1, L1, ■

Tony Hawk's American Wasteland

Enter this code in the Cheats menu. (Note: case sensitive)

Unlockable	Code
Mat Hoffman	the_condor

Tony Hawk's Pro Skater 3

From the Options menu, choose "Cheats" and enter the following codes. (Cheats can be activated in the Pause menu.)

Unlockable	Code	Unlockable	Code
All Characters	YOHOMIES	Cheat Menu	backdoor
All FMV Movies	Peepshow	Lots of Stat Points	PUMPMEUP
All Levels	ROADTRIP		

Tony Hawk's Pro Skater 4

Go to the Options menu and choose "Cheats." Enter the following:

Unlockable	Code	Unlockable	Code
Cheat Mode	watch_me_xplode	Perfect Rail Balance	ssbsts
Daisy	(o)(o)	Matrix Mode	nospoon
Full Special Meter	doasuper	Moon Gravity	superfly
Hidden Skaters	homielist		
Perfect Manual	mullenpower		

At the Create a Skater screen, enter the following names to unlock hidden skaters:

#$%@!	Andy Marchal	Big Tex
Aaron Skillman	Angus	Brian Jennings
Adam Lippman	Atiba Jefferson	Captain Liberty
Andrew Skates	Ben Scott Pye	Chauwa Steel

Tony Hawk's Pro Skater 4 (continued)

Chris Peacock
ConMan
Danaconda
Dave Stohl
DDT
DeadEndRoad
Fakes the Clown
Fritz
Gary Jesdanun
Grjost
Henry Ji
Jason Uyeda
Jim Jagger
Joe Favazza
John Rosser

Jow
Kenzo
Kevin Mulhall
Kraken
Lindsey Hayes
Lisa G Davies
Little Man
Marilena Rixfor
Mat Hoffman
Matt Mcpherson
Maya's Daddy
Meek West
Mike Day
Mike Lashever
Mike Ward
Mr. Brad

Nolan Nelson
Parking Guy
Peasus
Pete Day
Pooper
Rick Thorne
Sik
Stacey D
Stacey Ytuarte
Stealing Is Bad
Team Chicken
Ted Barber
Todd Wahoske
Top Bloke
Wardcore
Zac ZiG Drake

Tony Hawk's Project 8

In the Options menu, select Cheats to enter these passwords.

Unlockable	Password
Big Realtor	shescaresme
Christian Hosoi	hohohosoi
Colonel and Security Guard	militarymen
Dad and Skater Jam Kid	strangefellows
Full Air Stats	drinkup
Grim Reaper	enterandwin
Inkblot Deck	birdhouse
Jason Lee	notmono
Kevin Staab	mixitup
Mascot	manineedadate
Most Decks	needaride
Nerd	wearelosers
Photographer and Cameraman	themedia
Travis Barker	plus44
Unlock Specials in Skate Shop	yougotitall

Tony Hawk's Underground

From the Options menu, choose "Cheat Codes" and enter the following:

Unlockable	Code	Unlockable	Code
All Thug Movies	digivid	Perfect Rail	letitslide
Moon Gravity	getitup	Perfect Skitch	rearrider
Perfect Manual	keepitsteady		

From the Options menu, choose "Cheat Codes" and enter the following:

1337
Akira2s
Alan Flores
Alex Garcia
Andy Marchel
arrr

Bailey
Big Tex
Chauwa Steel
Chris Rausch
ChrisP
CodePirate

crom
Daddy Mac
Dan Nelson
Dave Stohl
DDT
deadendroad

DS
GBA
PSP
PS2
PS3
Wii
Xbox
Xbox 360
Index

DS
GBA
PSP
PS2
PS3
Wii
Xbox
Xbox 360
Index

Tony Hawk's Underground (continued)

fatass	leedsleedsleeds	The Kraken
FROGHAM	MARCOS XK8R	The Swink
GEIGER	Mike Ward	THEDOC
Glycerin	moreuberthaned	Todd Wahoske
GMIAB	M'YAK	TOPBLOKE
Greenie	Noly	TSUEnami! (
grjost	NSJEFF	woodchuck
Guilt Ladle	POOPER	Y2KJ
Hammer	sik®	Yawgurt
Henry Ji	Skillzombie	ZiG
Jason Uyeda	Stacey D	
Jeremy Andersen	Steal2Liv	
Joel Jewett	tao zheng	
Johnny Ow		

Tony Hawk's Underground 2

Go to Cheat Codes and enter the following:

Unlockable	Code
All Levels	d3struct
All Movies	boxoffice
Always Special	likepaulie
Bonus Characters	costars
Infinite Rail	straightedge
Natas Kaupas	oldskool
Nigel Beaverhausen	sellout
Paulie	4-wheeler
Phil Margera	aprilsman

Transformers

Pause the game and enter any of the following codes:

Unlockable	Code
All Extras	Select Extras from the Main menu and press ■, ■, ●, ■, ■, ●, L1, L2
Invincibility	R1, ●, ●, R1, R2, L1, L1, L2
One Shot Kills	■, ●, ■, ●, L1, L1, L2, L1
Stealth Enemies	←, →, ←, R1, R2, R1, →, →

Enter the following codes at the Autobot HQ screen:

Unlockable	Code
All Mini-Cons	L1, L2, ●, ●, ■, ●, L2, L1
Big Head Mode	●, ●, ●, ■, L1, L1, L1, L2
Disable Mini Con Overload	R1, R1, L2, R1, R1, L2, ●, ●
Infinite Stealth	↑, ↑, ↓, ↓, L1, L2, L1, L2
Turbo Mode	L1, R2, R2, ■, ■, ■, ■, L1
Unlimited Powerlink	↑, ↓, ↑, ↓, ●, ■, ■, ●

At the Difficulty Select screen, enter the following:

Unlockable	Code
Alaska Level Complete	R1, ●, R1, ■, ←, ←, →, ←
Amazon Boss Fight	←, ←, →, L1, R2, ←, →, →
Amazon Level Complete	L1, L1, L2, ■, ■, ●, R1, R2
Antarctica Boss Fight	L1, ←, L2, →, ■, ■, ●, ●
Antarctica Level Complete	R1, R1, R2, L2, L1, L1, R1, R1
Cybertron	R2, R1, L1, L2, ■, ●, ■, ●
Deep Amazon Level Complete	←, →, ←, ←, →, R1, R2, ●
Mid-Atlantic Boss Fight	L2, ←, →, →, ←, L2, L2, L2
Mid-Atlantic Level Complete	●, ■, ●, ■, →, ←, ←, →
Starship Boss Fight	→, →, ■, R1, R2, ●, ←, ←
Starship Level Complete	←, ←, →, ●, ●, →, →, ←

True Crime: New York City

While on the Compstat/Map, hold ⬜L1⬜+⬜R1⬜ and enter these codes.

Unlockable	Code	Unlockable	Code
A Million Dollars	■, ■, ▲, ■, ▲, ■	Super Cop	▲, ✕, ▲, ✕, ▲, ▲
Double Damage	✕, ✕, ■, ✕, ✕, ✕	Ultra Easy Mode	●, ■, ✕, ✕, ▲, ●
Redman Gone Wild Mini-Game	▲, ✕, ✕, ●, ▲, ■	Unlimited Ammo	●, ■, ✕, ■, ■, ▲
		Unlimited Endurance	●, ■, ✕, ■, ✕, ●

True Crime: Streets of LA

Enter the following codes at the City Map screen:

Unlockable	Code	Unlockable	Code
All Driving Upgrades	←,→,←,→,✕	Bigger Vehicle	↓,↓,↓,✕
All Fighting Moves	↑,↓,↑,↓,✕	Nick Kang's Location	✕,●,■,▲
All Gun Upgrades	→,←,→,←,✕	Smaller Vehicle	↑,↑,↑,✕

Go to Create a License Plate and try the following codes:

Unlockable	Code	Unlockable	Code
Asian Worker	HARA	Lola Gees	B00B
Bartender	HAWG	Pimp	PIMP
Bum	B00Z	Policeman	FUZZ
Chief, The	B1G1	Rose in Lingerie	HURT M3
Commando	M1K3	Rosie	ROSA
Dirty Morales	BRUZ	Sewer Ghoul	J1MM
Donkey	JASS	Street Punk	MNKY
Gangsta	TFAN	SWAT Officer	5WAT
George	FATT	Tattoo Concubines	TATS
Jimmy Fu	MRFU	Triad Butcher	PHAM

Turok: Evolution

Enter the following codes at the Cheat menu.

Unlockable	Code
All Available Weapons	TEXAS
Big Head Mode	HEID
Demo Mode and Target Mini-Game	HUNTER
Invincibility	EMERPUS
Invisibility	SLLEWGH
Level Select	SELLOUT—after entering, load a saved game to unlock all levels.
Master Code	FMNFB
Unlimited Ammunition	MADMAN
Zoo Mode	ZOO—you can now kill any animal in the game with the war club as a weapon.

NOTE

There are two parts to the "Demo mode and Target Mini-Game" code. Besides starting Demo mode, you can also play the Target minigame at the main title screen. Use the D-pad to move the pointer and Fire to shoot.

DS
GBA
PSP
PS2
PS3
Wii
Xbox
Xbox 360
Index

DS
GBA
PSP
PS2
PS3
Wii
Xbox
Xbox 360
Index

Turok: Evolution (continued)

To access the following unlockables, pause gameplay, hold L1, then enter code. A message confirms correct code entry. Repeat the code to disable its effect.

Unlockable	Code
Invincible NPCs	■,●,▲,✕,■,●,▲,✕
Unlimited Ammunition	←,●,→,■,↑,▲,↓,✕
Unlimited Health	▲,■,▲,■,▲,●,▲,●
Unlimited Rage	←,↓,←,↓,→,↑,→,↑

Twisted Metal: Black

Unlockable	Code
Change Camera	To change the camera angle, press and hold SELECT, then press ↓. To switch between horizontal and vertical, hold SELECT, then press ←.
Convert Weapons into Health	During the game, hold down all four shoulder buttons, then press ▲,✕,■,●. Your weapons vanish and your health fills up a little.
Decipher Minion	To understand what Minion's numbered codes mean on the load screens (when playing as him), match the number with its corresponding letter. (A=1, B=2, and Z=26.)
Different Weapons Display	Press and hold SELECT, then press → during gameplay to change the weapons selection display.
Infinite Ammo	To have unlimited ammunition for your ride, press and hold the shoulder buttons, then press ↑,✕,←,●.
Invincibility	During gameplay (this includes story mode), press and hold the shoulder buttons, then press →,←,↓,↑.
Mega Machine Guns	To enable the Mega Machine Guns feature, press and hold the shoulder buttons, then press ✕,✕,▲.
One Hit Kills	During gameplay, hold the shoulder buttons and quickly press ✕,✕,↑. At the top of the screen, a message confirms correct code entry.
Unlock God Mode	During gameplay, hold the shoulder buttons and rapidly press ↑,✕,←,●. A message reading "God Mode On" appears at the top of the screen to confirm correct code entry.

Unlockable	Objective
Axel	After beating the first level, choose the Freeway level. Drive to the middle of the level, where an entrance to the construction lot and a Repair Station are located. There are two cranes; focus on the left one. Eliminate at least several enemies, then position your vehicle halfway up the ledge. If you've centered your vehicle in the middle of the construction site, use the middle ridge to a missile toward the orange control box near the center of the crane.
Downtown Jackpot	On one side of the river in the downtown level is the R&D Chemicals Plant. On the left side of the main building are three giant balls, like the ones in the highway loop level. Shoot the one closest to the sign with a gas can, and it rolls into a building, knocking it down and revealing three healths (which are supplied throughout the level at this location). Shoot the ball on the far left and it rolls into the building directly behind the previous one, giving you six power missiles.
Elevator in Downtown	Find this elevator to pick up power-ups. Find the Atom Bank and face it. To its left is a building with glass doors. Shoot them and they'll blow to pieces. Use the elevator to drive up to the higher reaches of the building. There's one health power-up up there, and it's a great view!

Twisted Metal: Black (continued)

Unlockable	Objective
Open Elevators Level	Go to the Highway Loop Level and kill off six or seven of the combatants. Drive to the raised, broken bridge (with the two health pick-ups and another pick-up in between), and find a power plant directly off the road. There are two or three giant steel balls there. Shoot the one closest to the bridge with a Gas Can, and it breaks off and rolls. Stay clear of its path, then follow the ball. When it crashes through a wall, go into the newly opened area and find the Black Cube, plus health and weapon pick-ups, inside.
Open Freeway Level	To open the Freeway for multiplayer action, get 10 Kills in Survival mode in the Snowy Roads arena.
Open Mini-Suburbs Level	To open the Mini-Suburbs for multiplayer action, get 10 Kills in Survival mode in the Drive-In arena.
Manslaughter	In the Prison Passage level, down on the docks to the starboard side of the landed ship, is a stack of crates holding a health power-up. Shoot the crates to blast open a ramp to the health, then shoot at the ship's hull above where the crates are stacked against it. A panel opens, and you can drive into a room inside the ship where Manslaughter is located. Destroy the control panel to unlock the new car.
Minion	Beat Story mode with every character, including those you unlock in the game (Manslaughter, Warthog, Yellow Jacket, and Axel).
Warhawk's Level	To open Warhawk's multiplayer level in the first level (Zorko Bros. Scrap and Salvage, a.k.a. the Junkyard), focus your efforts on the vertical crusher. Drive up the ramp to the broken freeway and drive halfway along it. Aim your car toward the Bob's Big Boy, and shoot it with a Power or a Fire, to avoid hitting any other cars. Once blown up, it creates a ramp to the vertical crusher. Drive down to the newly created green ramp and, when the crusher is down, drive onto it. Drive slowly onto it so you don't go over it. When it ascends, shoot the building on top of the deck, then drive onto the deck. On the left side is a Black Cube, which opens Warhawk's multiplayer level.
Warthog	In the Suburbia level, head to the carnival area. At the gate, take a left and head toward the smoke over the ridge. Speed up and ramp off the angled dirt ridge; you should land below on a building with a large hole in its roof. Go inside and look for a control panel in the corner. Shoot it to unlock Warthog.
Yellow Jacket	There is an airplane circling in the first level. Use a homing missile and shoot it down. After that's done, drive to the lower section of the level. The plane has crashed and you can drive in it. Go to the end, find the console and shoot it with machine gun fire. After four seconds, you can see Yellow Jacket's car lower down.

Ty the Tasmanian Tiger

Unlockable	Code
Aquarang, Elemental Boomerangs, Dive, and Swim Abilities	Press [L1], [R1], [L1], [R1], ▲, ▲, ■, ■, ▲, ■ during gameplay.
Show Objects	Press [L1], [R1], [L1], [R1], ▲, ▲, ●, ■, ■, ●, [R2], [R2] during gameplay.
Technorangs	Press [L1], [R1], [L1], [R1], ▲, ▲, ▲, ■, ▲, ■ during gameplay.
Unlimited Health	Quickly press [L1], [R1], [L1], [R1], ▲, ▲, ▲, ▲, ●, ● when "Press Start" appears.
Unlock Gallery and Movies	Quickly press [L1], [R1], [L1], [R1], ▲, ▲, ✕, ✕, [R2], ■, [R2], ■ when "Press Start" appears.

NOTE

To unlock an Ending Bonus, complete the game with all cogs, eggs, and opals collected for a 100 percent completion. The Ending Bonus includes a bonus level, an extra FMV sequence after the ending credits, and the "Movies" option at the Extras menu.

DS

GBA

PSP

PS2

PS3

Wii

Xbox

Xbox 360

Index

Ty the Tasmanian Tiger (continued)

> **NOTE**
>
> After you use the Show Objects code, the locations of hidden
> Opals, Bilbies, Golden Cogs, Rainbow Scales, and Thunder Eggs
> are shown with colored lines from the sky (Opals and Rainbow
> Scales with a green line, Golden Cogs with a gold line, Thunder
> Eggs with a purple line, and Bilbies with a whitish line).

Ultimate Spider-Man

Enter these codes in the Controller Setup screen.

Unlockable	Code
All Characters	⇨, ⇩, ⇨, ⇩, ⇦, ⇧, ⇦, ⇨
All Comic Covers	⇦, ⇦, ⇨, ⇦, ⇧, ⇦, ⇦, ⇩
All Concept Art	⇩, ⇩, ⇦, ⇧, ⇩, ⇧, ⇦, ⇦
All Landmarks	⇧, ⇨, ⇦, ⇩, ⇧, ⇨, ⇩, ⇦

Urban Reign

Enter these codes at the Title screen.

Unlockable	Code
All characters	R1, R2, ✕, ⇦, ⇨, ■, ■, ■, L1, ■, ▲, ●
All weapons	L1, R1, ✕, ✕, ▲, R1, R1, ▲, ■, ✕, R1
Bonus weapon in multi-player mode	L2, L2, ✕, ✕, ▲, R1, R1, ■, R1
Two players in story and free modes	L1, R2, ●, ●, ▲, L2, R1, ●, ▲, ●

Van Helsing

During gameplay, enter the following:

Unlockable	Code
Bonus Movie 1	↑, ↓, ↑, ↓, ←, ←, →, →, L1, L2, R3, R3
Bonus Movie 2	↑, →, ↓, ←, ↑, ←, ↓, →, ↑, R1, R2, R3
Bonus Movie 3	L1, L2, R2, R1, R2, L2, L1, ↑, ↑, ↓, ↓, SELECT
Bonus Movie 4	SELECT, L3, R3, SELECT, R1, L3, SELECT, ←, ←, ↑, →, →
Bonus Movie 5	L2, R2, L1, R1, SELECT, SELECT, L1, L1, R2, L2, L3, R3
Bonus Movie 6	R2, R1, R2, R1, L1, L2, L1, L2, ←, →, SELECT, SELECT
Bonus Movie 7	L3, ←, R3, →, L2, ↑, R2, ↓, L1, ←, R1, →

Viewtiful Joe

Unlockable	Objective
Unlock Dante	Beat game on any difficulty.
Unlock Sylvia	Beat game on Adult mode.

Virtua Fighter 4

Unlockable	Objective
Alternate Costumes	Hold START at the Character Selection screen. Press ✕ to select that character while holding START to wear the alternate costume.
Alternate Main Menu Background	Enter the Game Option menu, and press R1 to cycle forward or L1 to cycle backward through the list of backgrounds for the Main menu.

DS

GBA

PSP

PS2

PS3

Wii

Xbox

Xbox 360

Index

Virtua Fighter 4 (continued)

Unlockable	Objective
Classic Victory Poses	Use a created fighter to reach the Second Kyu level. Hold Punch + Kick + Guard during the replay to do a classic victory pose from Virtua Fighter 1.
Dural's Stage in Versus Mode	Use a created fighter to reach the Emperor or High King rank and unlock the hangar stage in Versus mode.
Fight as Dural	Defeat Dural in Kumite mode to unlock her in Versus mode.
Training Stage 1 in Versus Mode	Use a created fighter to reach the First Dan rank and unlock the first training stage in Versus mode.
Training Stage 2 in Versus Mode	Use a created fighter to reach the Fifth Dan rank and unlock the second training stage in Versus mode.
Training Stage 3 in Versus Mode	Use a created fighter to reach the Champion rank and unlock the third training stage in Versus mode.
Training Trophy	Complete the trial events in Training mode with a created fighter. A small trophy icon is displayed over your character's health bar.
Virtua Fighter 1 Fighter Model	Use a character fighter to reach at least the First Dan rank. Select that fighter and hold Punch + Kick until the match begins.

V-Rally 3

Unlockable	Objective
Extra Challenges	Win the Michelin Challenge in Challenge mode.
Mitsubishi Lancer Evolution VI	Select Career mode and win the 1.6L FWD championship in V-Rally mode.
Reversed Tracks	Four tracks exist in each country. Beat a track's record to unlock the next one. Unlock all of them to access the four reversed tracks for that country.
SEAT Cordoba Repsol	Win the Pirelli Challenge in Challenge mode.
Subaru Impreza 2000	Select Career mode and win the 2.0L 4WD championship in V-Rally mode.
Toyota Corolla V-Rally	Set a record time in all circuits.
Car Preview	At the Car Selection screen, hold → or ← to open either door; hold ↑ to open the hood; and hold ↓ to open the trunk.
Flat Cars	Enter 21051975 PTITDAV as a name.
Floating Cars	Enter 210741974 MARTY as a name.
Jelly Cars	Enter 07121974 FERGUS as a name.
Small Cars	Enter 01041977 BIGJIM as a name.
Small Cars with High-Pitched Commentary	Enter no first name and PALACH as a last name.
Smashed Cars	Enter 25121975 PILOU as a name.
Stretched Cars	Enter Gonzales SPEEDY as a name.

Wakeboarding Unleashed

Enter the following codes at the Main menu.

Unlockable	Code
Have All Gaps	(R1), (L2), (L2), (R2), (R1), (L2), (L2), (R2), (R1), (L2), (L2), (R2), (R1), (L2), (L2), (R2).
Level Select	■, ■, ■, ■, ●, ●, ●, ●, ▲, ▲, ▲, ▲, ■, ●, ▲.
Unlock Everything	↑, ↓, ↑, ↓, ↑, ↓, ↑, ↓, ↑, ↓, ←, →, ←, →, ←, →, ←, →.
Unlock Other Boards	↑, ↑, ←, ←, →, →, ↓, ↓, ↑, ←, →, ↓, ↑, ←, →, ↓.

Unlockable	Objective
All Boarders	Rotate the left analog stick clockwise fifteen times from the Main menu.

Wakeboarding Unleashed (continued)

Unlockable	Objective
Boarder Movies	Complete the game with a particular boarder to unlock his or her movie.
Credits	Beat the game once with any boarder.
Jordan	Collect every star in the Star Search Challenges.
Summer	Beat the game once with any boarder.

The Warriors

Enter codes during gameplay.

Unlockable	Code
200 Dollars, 3 Pieces of Flash, and Some Cans	R1, R2, L1, ✕, ⇩, L1
Bat	■, R2, ⇩, ⇩, L1, L1
Complete Current Mission	⇩, ■, ✕, SELECT, R1, ⇦
Finish with 100%	L1, SELECT, ■, ⇩, L2, ⇨
Infinite Rage	■, ●, ▲, SELECT, ✕, ⇦
Knife	⇩, ⇩, SELECT, ⇧, ⇧, L3
Lose Cops	⇧, SELECT, ✕, ▲, ▲, ■
Machete	L1, ✕, R1, R1, SELECT, R2
Pipe	R2, ●, SELECT, ⇧, L1, ⇨

Way of the Samurai

Unlockable	Code
Change Characters	In the New Game menu, press L1, R1, R1, L2, L2, L2, R2, R2, R2+■. To choose a character, press ← or →.
Full Health	Pause the game, hold L1+L2, and press ↓, ↑, ↓, ↑, →, ←, ●.
Increase Sword Toughness +1	Pause the game, hold R1+R2, and press →, →, ←, ←, ↓, ↑, ●.
Versus Mode	At the Title screen, hold L1+R1, and press ●+■.

Way of the Samurai 2

Unlockable	Code
All Characters	Select Character Customization, highlight name and press L1, R2, R1, L2, L1, R2, R1, L2, ■
More Store Items	In the Main Map, press L1, R1, L1, R1, R2, R2, ▲.

WDL: Warjetz

Unlockable	Code	Unlockable	Code
Add 10 Money	WNNNGS	Invincibility	DNGDM
All Codes	TWLVCHTS	Level Select	JMPTT
All Movies	GRTD	New York City 1	KKSPKRJHKBQN
Antarctica 1	CMPPLHJJNBQN	New York City 2	VBFKPLHBWZBQN
Antarctica 2	RKFPMYBZHBQN	New York City 3	WJYPLWFQGBQN
Antarctica 3	GNVPMQFSNBQN	Overlords Mode	VRLRDS
Australia 1	MHZKWTJMQBQM	Panama 2	JBVKWNBBCBQN
Australia 2	ZBCKXPBHNBQM	Panama 3	MDKKWYFTKBQN
Australia 3	LDRKXYFZTBQM	Plane Automatically Wins	SMSHNG
Double Money	TWFSTD		
Everything	SPRLZY	Rapid Fire	FRHS
Faster Jets	ZPPY	Rhine River 1	YJVPJCJGVBQN
Ghost mode	SNKY	Rhine River 2	FCNPKXBVWBQN
Huge Guns	QD	Rhine River 3	PGDPKGFPDBQN
Instantly Win	SMSHNG	San Francisco 1	TRLPMBJLVBQN

DS · GBA · PSP · PS2 · PS3 · Wii · Xbox · Xbox 360 · Index

WDL: Warjetz (continued)

Unlockable	Code	Unlockable	Code
San Francisco 2	SVMPNFBFVBQN	Thailand 2	TBPKYZBVHBQM
San Francisco 3	RXDPNHFYDBQN	Thailand 3	KFFPJRFNPBQN
Show All Boxes	BXDRW	Valhalla 1	XBXPNGKRKBQN
Spin Shots	DZZY	Valhalla 2	LPXKVMCQZBQM
Super Armor	MRRMR	Valhalla 3	QSMKVSGKHBQM
Thailand	ZHHKXJJTBBQM	View All FMV	GRTD

Whiteout

Unlockable	Code
10,000 Points	Hold L2 + ▲ and press ←, ←, ↑, ↓ during a race.
All Characters	Hold L1 + R1 and press ↓, ↓, ↓, ↓ at the Main menu.
All Parts	Hold L1 + R1 and press ←, ←, ←, ← at the Main menu.
All Tracks	Hold L1 + R1 and press ↑, ↑, ↑, ↑ at the Main menu.
Alternate View	Hold L2 + ▲ and press ↓, ↓, ←, ← during gameplay.
Master Code	Hold R1 + L1 and press →, →, →, → at the Main menu to unlock all tracks, characters, and snowmobiles.
Restore Stamina	Hold L2 + ▲ and press →, →, ←, ↓ during a race.
Win Race	Hold L2 + ▲ and press ↑, ↓, ←, → during a race.

Wild Wild Racing

Unlockable	Code
New Engines	Each country in Time Attack rewards you with an engine for one of the three initially-selectable buggies. Complete the three races per Time Attack (Uphill, Downhill, and Flat) to gain a new engine that ups the stats on your buggy.
Secret Menu and Top Secret Menu	At the Main menu, highlight and select Options. At the Options menu hold down ■ and press ↑, ●, ↓, ●, ←, ↑, ←, →, ●. This will open the Secret menu option on the Options screen. Enter Single Player and type your name as NORTHEND.

Winback Covert Operations

Enter these codes at the Start screen.

Unlockable	Code
All Versus Characters	⇧, ⇩, ⇩, ⇨, ⇨, ⇨, ⇦, ⇦, ⇦, then press ● + START
Max Power Mode	L1, R2, L2, R2, L2, ▲, ●, ▲, ●, then hold L1 and press START
Sudden Death Mode	L2, R2, L2, R2, ●, ▲, ●, ▲, then hold L1 and press START

Wipeout Fusion

Enter these codes in the Codes menu under Extras.

Unlockable	Code
Animal Ships	▲, ●, ●, ▲, ✕
Infinite Shield	▲, ▲, ■, ■, ■
Infinite Weapons	▲, ●, ✕, ●, ■
Mini Ships	●, ■, ■, ✕, ●
Retro Planes	✕, ●, ▲, ■, ✕
Super Fast ships	■, ✕, ✕, ✕, ▲
Unlock all Features	✕, ▲, ●, ▲, ●

DS · GBA · PSP · PS2 · PS3 · Wii · Xbox · Xbox 360 · Index

World Soccer Winning Eleven 7

Unlockable	Objective
Premier All Star Team	Win the LG Championship Cup.
World All Star Team	Win the Multi International Cup.

World Tour Soccer

At the Main menu, enter the following:

Unlockable	Code
All Bonuses	L2, L2, L1, R1, ←, ↑, ←, ↓
Infinite TIF Tokens	↑, ↓, ↑, ↓, R1, R1, R2, R2, ↑, ↓, ↑, ↓
QA Liverpool, TIF OldBoys, TIF Newbies, and Touchline Teams	↓, →, L2, R1, ←, R1
TimeWarp Teams	R2, L2, R2, L2, ↑, L1

Wrath Unleashed

Unlockable	Objective
Elephant Pool Arena	Win 20 Team Battles.
Metal Age Arena	Win 100 Arena Battles.

Wreckless

Unlockable	Objective
Alternate View	Press ↓ to cycle through different screen effects during gameplay and replays. To unlock more effects, complete Missions A-9, A-10, B-9, and B-10.
AUV	Complete Mission A-9.
Dragon-SPL Car	Complete Mission A-1.
Gold Rank on All Missions	Highlight the "Unlimited Time" option at the Main menu, then press L2+R1+→+● as the game loads.
Missions A-2 to A-4	Complete Mission A-1.
Missions B-2 to B-4	Complete Mission B-1.
Music Test	Complete all twenty missions to unlock the "Music Test" selection at the Options screen.
Super Car	Complete Mission B-1.
Tank-90	Complete Mission B-8.
Tiger-SPL	Complete Mission A-8 to unlock the car that Tiger Tagachi drives.
Yakuza Car	Complete Mission B-9.

WWE Crush Hour

Unlockable	Code
Special Meter Fills Quickly	Pause the game, hold L3, and press ▲, ●, ●, ●, ●.
Unlimited Turbo	Pause the game, hold L3, and press ✕, R1, R2.
All Levels and Vehicles	From the main menu, press ■, L2, R2, ●, ■, L2, L2, L2.
Kevin Nash	From the character select screen, press L2, ■, R2, ●.

Unlockable	Objective
All Levels	Beat Season mode with any character to unlock all levels.
Bradshaw	Beat Season mode with Brock Lesnar.
Christian	Beat Season mode with Chris Jericho.
D-Von Dudley	Beat Season mode with Bubba Ray Dudley.
Hulk Hogan	Beat Season mode with The Rock.

WWE Crush Hour (continued)

Unlockable	Objective
Lita	Beat Season mode with Matt Hardy.
Ric Flair	Beat Season mode with The Big Show, Rob Van Dam and Triple H.
Stephanie McMahon	Beat Season mode with Kurt Angle.
Vince McMahon	Beat Season mode, facing Vince in the final battle.

WWE SmackDown! vs. RAW 2007

Arenas

Unlockable	Objective
Backlash Arena	Win the Backlash Trophy in Season Mode
ECW One Night Stand Arena	Win Money in the Bank Ladder Match on Legend Difficulty
No Mercy Arena	Win the No Mercy Trophy in Season Mode
Saturday Night Main Event Arena	Win the Superstar Challenge Trophy
SummerSlam Arena	Win the SummerSlam Trophy in Season Mode
Unforgiven Arena	Win the Unforgiven Trophy in Season Mode
Vengeance Arena	Win the Vengeance Trophy in Season Mode
WrestleMania 22 Arena	Win the WrestleMania Trophy in Season Mode

Legend Championships

Unlockable	Objective
Million Dollar Championship	Complete The Legend Challenges
n.W.o. Championship	Win the SummerSlam Trophy and then you can buy it in the shop
Smoking Skull Championship	Win the Royal Rumble Trophy and then you can buy it in the shop
The Hardcore Championship Belt	Win the Superstar Challenge Trophy

Locker Room Shop Unlockables

Unlockable	Objective
Bret Hart Banner	Win the Survivor Series Trophy
Candice Banner	Win the No Mercy Trophy
D-X Banner	Win the Vengeance Trophy
Hulk Hogan Banner	Win the Wrestlemania Trophy
Lita Banner	Win the No Mercy Trophy
Melina Banner	Win the No Mercy Trophy
Mickie Banner	Win the No Mercy Trophy
Stone Cold Banner	Win the Royal Rumble Trophy
The Rock Banner	Win the Wrestlemania Trophy
Torrie Wilson Banner	Win the No Mercy Trophy
Trish Banner	Win the No Mercy Trophy
Chloe	Win the No Mercy Trophy
D-X Figure	Win the Vengeance Trophy
Edge and Lita Figure	Win the Legend Challenge Trophy
King's Crown	Win the No Way Out Trophy
Rock vs. Hogan Figure	Win the Wrestlemania Trophy
RVD's Money in the Bank	Win the Money in the Bank Trophy
Steveweiser	Win the Royal Rumble Trophy

DS

GBA

PSP

PS2

PS3

Wii

Xbox

Xbox 360

Index

DS

GBA

PSP

PS2

PS3

Wii

Xbox

Xbox 360

Index

WWE SmackDown! vs. RAW 2007 (continued)

Unlockable	Objective
Candice Cut-Out	Win the No Mercy Trophy
Diva Clock	Win the No Mercy Trophy
Hogan Trashcan	Win the Wrestlemania Trophy
Hogan's hanging boas	Win the Wrestlemania Trophy
Mickie Cut-Out	Win the No Mercy Trophy
Shane O'Mac Jersey	Win the Armageddon Trophy
Torrie Cut-Out	Win the No Mercy Trophy
Trish Cut-Out	Win the No Mercy Trophy
Chris Masters Statue	Win the Backlash Trophy
Pink Furry Couch	Win the No Mercy Trophy
Trucker Girl Rug	Win the No Mercy Trophy
Bret Hart	Win the Survivor Series Trophy
Cactus Jack	Win the SummerSlam Trophy
Candice Poster 1	Win the No Mercy Trophy
Candice Poster 2	Win the No Mercy Trophy
D-X Poster	Win the Vengeance Trophy
HulkMania Poster	Win the Wrestlemania Trophy
Jillian Poster	Win the No Mercy Trophy
Lita Poster 1	Win the No Mercy Trophy
Lita Poster 2	Win the No Mercy Trophy
Mankind	Win the SummerSlam Trophy
Melina Poster	Win the No Mercy Trophy
Melina Splits Poster	Win the No Mercy Trophy
Mickie James Poster 1	Win the No Mercy Trophy
Mickie James Poster 2	Win the No Mercy Trophy
Stone Cold 1	Win the Royal Rumble Trophy
Stone Cold 2	Win the Royal Rumble Trophy
The Rock	Win the Wrestlemania Trophy
Torrie Poster 1	Win the No Mercy Trophy
Torrie Poster 2	Win the No Mercy Trophy.
Trish Poster 1	Win the No Mercy Trophy
Trish Poster 2	Win the No Mercy Trophy
Divas Loading Screen	Win the No Mercy Trophy
DX tag entrance	Win the Vengeance Trophy
WWE Legends Loading Screens	Complete the Legend Challenge Mode
Unlimited CAW EXP Points	Become GM of the Year in GM mode
WWE Legends	
Unlockable	Objective
Bam Bam Bigelow	Win the Unforgiven Trophy
Bret Hart	Win the Survivor Series Trophy
Cactus Jack	Win the SummerSlam Trophy
Dude Love	Win the SummerSlam Trophy
Hulk Hogan	Win the WrestleMania Trophy
Jerry "the King" Lawler	Win the No Way Out Trophy

WWE SmackDown! vs. RAW 2007 (continued)

Unlockable	Objective
Mankind	Win the SummerSlam Trophy
Mr. Perfect	Win the Backlash Trophy
Shane McMahon	Win the Armageddon Trophy
Stone Cold Steve Austin	Win the Royal Rumble Trophy
Tazz	Win the No Way Out Trophy
The Anvil Jim Neidhart	Win the Survivor Series Trophy
The Rock	Win the WrestleMania Trophy

X2: Wolverine's Revenge

Unlockable	Code
All Cerebro Files and FMV Sequences	▲, ●, ▲, ■, ■, ■, R1 + R2
All Costumes	▲, ●, ▲, ■, ■, ■, L1 + L2
Cheat Menu	▲, ▲, ●, ●, ■, ■, ●, ●, L1 + R1 + L2 + R2
Level Select	▲, ●, ▲, ■, ▲, ●, L1 + R1

XG3 Extreme G Racing

Unlockable	Code
Unlimited Turbo	To get unlimited turbo, go to the title screen. Press R1 + L1, R2 + L2, R1 + L1, and R2 + L2. When the code is entered correctly, you get a message confirming entry.
All Tracks	Go to the Main menu and press L1, L1, L2, L2, R2, R2, R1, R1, then hold L1 + R1 + L2 + R2. If the code is entered correctly, a message appears.

X-Men Legends II: Rise of Apocalypse

Enter these codes on the Pause screen.

Unlockable	Code
God Mode	⇩, ⇧, ⇩, ⇧, ⇨, ⇩, ⇨, ⇦, START
Super Speed	⇧, ⇧, ⇧, ⇩, ⇧, ⇩, START
Unlimited Xtreme Tokens	⇦, ⇩, ⇨, ⇩, ⇧, ⇩, ⇩, ⇧, START

Enter this code at the Forge's or Beast's equipment screen.

Unlockable	Code
100,000 techbits	⇧, ⇧, ⇧, ⇩, ⇨, ⇨, START

Enter these codes on the Team Management screen.

Unlockable	Code
All skills	⇦, ⇨, ⇦, ⇨, ⇩, ⇩, START
Level 99	⇧, ⇩, ⇧, ⇩, ⇦, ⇨, ⇦, ⇨, START

Enter this code while playing. Do not pause.

Unlockable	Code
One hit kills	⇦, ⇦, ⇨, ⇦, ⇧, ⇧, START

Enter these codes while in the Review menu.

Unlockable	Code
All Comics	⇨, ⇦, ⇦, ⇨, ⇧, ⇩, ⇨, START
Game Cinematics	⇦, ⇨, ⇨, ⇦, ⇩, ⇩, ⇦, START

DS · GBA · PSP · PS2 · PS3 · Wii · Xbox · Xbox 360 · Index

X-Men The Official Game

Enter these codes in the Cerebro Files menu.

Unlockable	Code
Iceman's Danger Room	⇨, ⇨, ⇦, ⇦, ⇩, ⇧, ⇩, ⇧, START
Nightcrawler's Danger Room	⇧, ⇧, ⇩, ⇩, ⇦, ⇨, ⇦, ⇨, START
Wolverine's Danger Room	⇩, ⇩, ⇧, ⇧, ⇨, ⇦, ⇨, ⇦, START

Ys The Ark of Napishtim

To enter these codes, first select new game and then select cheat. Hit the crystals in this order: Red, Blue, Yellow, Red, Blue, and Yellow. Then do a downward strike on the center piece. This must be done before entering any of these codes.

Unlockable	Code
20 Item Tool Max Increase	Yellow, Yellow, Red, Red, Blue, Blue, Yellow, Red
All Items 1/2 Price	Yellow, Yellow, Blue, Blue, Red, Red, Red, Yellow, Yellow, Yellow, Red, Red, Blue, Blue
All Three Swords Maxed Out	Red, Red, Yellow, Blue, Yellow, Red, Blue, Blue, Blue, Red, Yellow, Yellow, Blue, Yellow, Red
Beach CG – English Voice with English Sub	Blue, Blue, Red, Yellow
Beach CG—English Voice with Japanese Sub	Blue, Blue, Blue, Red, Yellow
Beach CG Movie—Japanese Voice with English Sub	Blue, Red, Red, Yellow
Beach CG—Japanese Voice with Japanese Sub	Blue, Red, Yellow
Clearflag	Red, Red, Red, Red, Blue, Blue, Blue, Blue, Yellow, Yellow, Yellow, Yellow, Blue, Blue, Yellow, Yellow, Red, Red
Maxed Out Blirante Sword	Blue, Blue, Yellow, Yellow, Yellow, Red, Blue, Red, Red, Red, Yellow, Yellow
Maxed Out Ericcil Sword	Blue, Yellow, Yellow, Red, Red, Red, Blue, Blue, Blue, Red, Red, Yellow
Maxed Out Livart Sword	Blue, Blue, Blue, Yellow, Yellow, Red, Blue, Red, Red, Yellow, Yellow, Yellow
Napishtim Destroyed CG—English Voice with English Sub	Blue, Red, Yellow, Red, Red, Blue, Yellow, Yellow
Napishtim Destroyed CG—English Voice with Japanese Sub	Blue, Red, Yellow, Red, Red, Blue, Yellow, Yellow, Yellow
Napishtim Destroyed CG—Japanese Voice with English Sub	Blue, Red, Yellow, Red, Red, Blue, Yellow, Yellow, Yellow, Yellow
Napishtim Destroyed CG—Japanese Voice with Japanese Sub	Blue, Red, Yellow, Red, Red, Blue, Yellow
Ohla In A Bikini	Blue, Blue, Blue, Blue, Blue, Yellow, Yellow, Yellow, Red, Blue, Yellow, Yellow, Red, Red, Red
Olha Demo After Clearing Time Attack On Hard (Japanese)	Red, Red, Red, Red, Red, Blue, Blue, Blue, Yellow, Red, Blue, Blue, Yellow, Yellow, Yellow
Opening CG In English Voice with English Sub	Blue, Blue, Yellow, Red
Opening CG—English Voice with Japanese Sub	Blue, Blue, Blue, Yellow, Red
Opening CG—Japanese Voice with Japanese Sub	Blue, Yellow, Red
Romun Fleet Destroyed Anime	Blue, Red, Yellow, Red, Red, Yellow, Red, Red, Red

DS
GBA
PSP
PS2
PS3
Wii
Xbox
Xbox 360
Index

Ys The Ark of Napishtim (continued)

Unlockable	Code
Romun Fleet Destroyed CG	Blue, Red, Yellow, Red, Red, Yellow, Red
Romun Fleet Entrance Anime	Blue, Red, Yellow, Red, Red, Yellow, Blue, Blue, Blue
Romun Fleet Entrance CG	Blue, Red, Yellow, Red, Red, Yellow, Blue
Start at Level 10	Red, Blue, Blue, Red, Red, Blue
Start at Level 20	Red, Blue, Blue, Red, Red, Blue, Blue
Start at Level 30	Red, Red, Blue, Blue, Red, Red, Blue, Blue
Start at Level 40	Red, Red, Blue, Red, Red, Blue, Blue, Yellow
Start at Level 50	Red, Red, Blue, Red, Red, Blue, Blue, Yellow, Yellow
Start at Level 60	Red, Red, Blue, Blue, Yellow, Yellow, Red, Red, Blue, Blue, Yellow, Yellow
Unlock Nightmare Mode, Time Trial, And Red Spirit Monuments	Red, Red, Red, Red, Blue, Blue, Blue, Blue, Yellow, Yellow, Yellow, Yellow, Blue, Blue, Yellow, Yellow, Red, Red

Yu-Gi-Oh! The Duelist of the Roses

Press R3 at the Build Deck screen to enter a password for a card.

Unlockable	Password	Unlockable	Password
Ancient Tree of Enlightenment	EKJHQ109	Greenkappa	YBJMCD6Z
Aqua Dragon	JXCB6FU7	Harpie's Feather Duster	8HJHQPNP
Barrel Dragon	GTJXSBJ7	Horn of the Unicorn	S14FGKQ1
Beastking of the Swamp	QXNTQPAX	Left Arm of the Forbidden One	A5CF6HSH
Birdface	N54T4TY5	Magician of Faith	GME1S3UM
Black Hole	UMJ10MQB	Meteor Dragon	86985631
Blast Sphere	CZN5GD2X	Mimicat	69YDQM85
Change of Heart	SBYDQM8B	Mirror Wall	53297534
Crush Card	SRA7L5YR	Mystical Capture Chain	N1NDJMQ3
Dragon Seeker	81EZCH8B	Robotic Knight	S5S7NKNH
Earthshaker	Y34PN1SV	Royal Decree	8TETQHE1
Elf's Light	E5G3NRAD	Seiyaryu	2H4D85J7
Exodia the Forbidden One	37689434	Serpentine Princess	UMQ3WZUZ
Fairy King Truesdale	YF07QVEZ	Slate Warrior	73153736
Fairy's Gift	NVE7A3EZ	Swordsman from a Foreign Land	CZ81UVGR
Goblin Fan	92886423	Swordstalker	AH0PSHEB
Gravity Bind	0HNFG9WX	Tactical Warrior	054TC727

Yu Yu Hakusho: Dark Tournament

From the Options screen, choose "Cheats" and enter the following:

Unlockable	Code
All Cards	●, ■, ●, ■, ■, ↓
All Chapters	↑, ↓, ×, ●, ■, →
All Environments	↑, →, ←, →, ×, ×
All Fighters	■, ↑, ■, ●, ↓, ●
All Modes	←, →, ↓, →, ×, ●
No Damage to Player One	●, ■, ↓, ←, ●, ■
No Damage to Player Two	↑, ■, ←, ■, ●, ■

DS · **GBA** · **PSP** · **PS2** · **PS3** · **Wii** · **Xbox** · **Xbox 360** · **Index**

DS

GBA

PSP

PS2

PS3

Wii

Xbox

Xbox 360

Index

Yu Yu Hakusho: Dark Tournament (Continued)

Unlockable	Code
Player 1 Free Spirit Energy	■,×,●,■,×,●
Player 2 Free Spirit Energy	↓,↑,●,←,×,→
Turbo Mode	●,×,→,×,↑,■

Zapper

Enter these codes while the game is paused.

Unlockable	Code
Unlimited Lives	Hold L1 and press ⇧, ⇧, ⇦, ⇦, ⇨, ⇦, ⇨
Unlimited Shield	Hold L1 and press ⇧, ⇩, ⇧, ⇦, ⇨, ⇩, ⇧

Zone of the Enders

Press pause during gameplay, then enter this code.

Unlockable	Code
Full Health and Ammo	L1, L1, L2, L2, L1, R1, L1, R1, R2, R1

Unlockable	Objective
Alternate Ending	Complete all of the S.O.S calls, ranking A in each of them, and you see a different ending sequence.
Versus Mode	Complete the game to receive Versus mode. Your score (the amount of continues used, saves, and the amount of civilians you rescued) determines which frames you get to play.

Table of Contents - PS3

Armored Core 4

Hard Difficulty

Unlockable	How to Unlock
Hard Difficulty	Successfully complete any chapter on normal difficulty. Press ■ to toggle between difficulties.

Blazing Angels: Squadrons of WWII

Enter these codes while the game is paused.

Unlockable	Code
Increase Damage of Weapons	Hold L2 and quickly press L1, L1, R1; release L2, then hold R2 and quickly press R1, R1, L1
Invincibility	Hold L2 and press ■, ▲, ▲, ■; release L2, then hold R2 and quickly press ▲, ■, ■, ▲

Enter this code at the Title menu while holding L2 + R2

Unlockable	Code
All Campaign Missions and Planes	■, L1, R1, ▲, ▲, R1, L1, ■

Call of Duty 3

Enter this code in the Chapter Select screen.

Unlockable	Code
Unlock All Levels	Hold SELECT and press ⇨, ⇨, ⇦, ⇦, ■, ■

Call of Duty 4: Modern Warfare

Arcade and Cheat Options

These unlock automatically for completing *Call of Duty 4: Modern Warfare* on any difficulty level. During gameplay, find the Cheat menu in the Options menu.

Unlockable	How to Unlock
Arcade Mode	Complete game on any difficulty
Cheat Menu	Complete game on any difficulty

Easter Egg (Hidden Mission)

Beat the game on any difficulty and let the credits run all the way through. When they finish, you'll start another mission. This mission takes place on a plane that resembles Air Force One, wherein you must fight your way through a horde of baddies, save the V.I.P., and escape the plane in less than two minutes.

Cheats

Unlock cheats by collecting enemy intel (intelligence), which look like laptop computers that are hidden throughout the campaign. Note: Using cheats disables Achievements.

Unlockable Cheats

Unlockable	How to Unlock
A Bad Year: When you kill enemies, they explode into tires!	Collect 15 pieces of enemy intel.
Cluster Bombs: After one of your frag grenades explodes, four more explode in a cross-shaped pattern.	Collect 10 pieces of enemy intel.
CoD Noir: Turns all gameplay into black and white.	Collect 2 pieces of enemy intel.
Infinite Ammo: Weapons have unlimited ammo. Doesn't work with Perk 1 abilities such as C4 and Claymores.	Collect 30 pieces of enemy intel.
Photo-Negative: Inverses all of the game's colors.	Collect 4 pieces of enemy intel.
Ragtime Warfare: Gameplay goes black and white, dust and scratches fill the screen, it plays at 2x speed, and the music becomes piano music.	Collect 8 pieces of enemy intel.
Slow-Mo Ability: Use the melee button to change the game to slow-mo and play at half-speed.	Collect 20 pieces of enemy intel.
Super Contrast: Dramatically increases the game's contrast, making the darks much darker and the lights much lighter.	Collect 6 pieces of enemy intel.

DS

GBA

PSP

PS2

PS3

Wii

Xbox

Xbox 360

Index

Call of Duty 4: Modern Warfare (continued)

Golden weapons are a special camo (or skin) that you unlock when you fully complete all the challenges under the weapon subtype in the barracks (SMG, LMG, etc.). Access them by choosing the camo of the respective weapon. The effect is purely cosmetic and does not enhance the ability of the weapon in any way.

Golden Weapons

Unlockable	How to Unlock
Golden AK-47	Complete all Assault Rifle challenges.
Golden Desert Eagle	Get to Level 55.
Golden Dragunov	Complete all Sniper challenges.
Golden M1014	Complete all Shotgun challenges.
Golden M60	Complete all LMG challenges.
Golden Mini-Uzi	Complete all SMG challenges.

Multiplayer Unlockables

Unlockable	Unlocked at Rank
Assault Rifle (G3)	Rank 25
Assault Rifle (G36C)	Rank 37
Assault Rifle (M14)	Rank 46
Assault Rifle (M4)	Rank 10
Assault Rifle (MP44)	Rank 52
LMG (M60E4)	Rank 19
Pistol (Desert Eagle)	Rank 43
Pistol (Golden Desert Eagle)	Rank 55
Pistol (M1911)	Rank 16
Shotgun (M1014)	Rank 31
SMG (AK-74U)	Rank 28
SMG (Mini Uzi)	Rank 13
SMG (P90)	Rank 40
Sniper Rifle (Barret)	Rank 49
Sniper Rifle (Dragunov)	Rank 22
Sniper Rifle (M40)	Rank 04
Sniper Rifle (R700)	Rank 34

Calling All Cars!

Unlockable Vehicles

Complete the appropriate tasks in the correct game mode and difficulty to unlock extra vehicles.

Unlockable	How to Unlock
BLUE BOMBER	Win at the Trainyards on Captain difficulty, using only the helicopter to score in a single-level, 5-minute game
CHERRY PICKER	In a single-level, 5 minute-game on Chief difficulty, win at the Burbs with at least 20 points
DUMPER	On Sergeant difficulty, beat Tournament mode
FLEABAG	On Chief difficulty, beat Tournament mode
HIGHROLLER	Beat the Burbs on Captain difficulty without letting the opponent score in a single-level, 5-minute game
LITTER BOX	On Captain difficulty, beat Tournament mode
SHAMROCK	In a single-level, 5-minute game on Sergeant difficulty, beat any level without letting the opponent score

Calling All Cars! (continued)

SWEET CHEEKS	In a single-level, 2-minute game on Captain difficulty, win any level without letting the opponent score
YELLOW ROSE	On Rookie difficulty, beat Tournament mode
YELLOWJACKET	In a single-level, 5-minute game on Captain difficulty, win using only the 3-point ramp in the Alpine

The Darkness

Phone Numbers

Go to any phone and enter the 18 phone numbers, in no specific order, to unlock Keeper of Secrets accomplishment. Find these phone numbers throughout the game on posters, graffiti, etc. Out of the 25, you only need 18 to unlock the accomplishment.

Phone Number	Count	Phone Number	Count	Phone Number	Count
555-6118	1/18	555-4569	7/18	555-1206	13/18
555-9723	2/18	555-7658	8/18	555-9562	14/18
555-1847	3/18	555-9985	9/18	555-9528	15/18
555-5289	4/18	555-1233	10/18	555-7934	16/18
555-6667	5/18	555-1037	11/18	555-3285	17/18
555-6205	6/18	555-3947	12/18	555-7892	18/18

Def Jam: Icon

At the Press Start screen, enter these codes.

Unlockable	Code
It's Going Down music track	●, ⇧, ⇨, ⇦, ▲
Make It Rain music track	⇩, ●, ⇩, ⇨

Dynasty Warriors: Gundam

Extra Characters and Mobile Suits

Unlockable	How to Unlock
Any Mobile Suit for a Pilot	Finish a pilot's Story mode at least once
Char's Gelgoog	Complete Amuro Ray's Official mode
Char's Zaku II	Complete Char Aznable's Official mode
Gundam Mk-II (Black)	Complete Kamille Bidan's Official mode and Heero Yuy's Original mode
Gundam ZZ	Complete Judau Ashita's Official mode
Hyaku Shiki (Gold Gundam)	Complete Char Aznable's Official mode Mission 4
Master Asia and Master Gundam	Finish Domon Kasshu's Original mode
Milliardo Peacecraft and Epyon	Finish Heero's story in Original mode
Musha Gundam	Beat Original mode with all 6 protagonists: Amuro, Kamille, Judau, Domon, Heero, and Loran
Official: Char Aznable	Complete Amuro Ray's Official mode
Official: Haman Karn	Complete Kamille Bidan's Official mode
Official: Paptimus Scirocco	Complete Judau Ashita's Official mode
Original: Amuro Ray	Complete Amuro Ray's Official mode
Original: Char Aznable	Complete Char Aznable's Official mode
Original: Elpe Puru	Complete Judau Ashita's Official mode and Domon Kasshu's Original mode
Original: Emma Sheen	Complete Char Aznable's Official mode and Rolan Cehack's Original mode

DS
GBA
PSP
PS2
PS3
Wii
Xbox
Xbox 360
Index

DS

GBA

PSP

PS2

PS3

Wii

Xbox

Xbox 360

Index

Dynasty Warriors: Gundam (continued)

Original: Haman Karn	Complete Haman Karn's Official mode
Original: Jerid Messa	Complete Kamille Bidan's Official mode and Heero Yuy's Original mode
Original: Judau Ashita	Complete Judau Ashita's Official mode
Original: Kamille Bidan	Complete Kamille Bidan's Official mode
Original: Paptimus Scirocco	Complete Paptimus Scirocco's Official mode
Original: Puru Two	Complete Elpe Puru's Original mode
Original: Roux Louka	Complete Judau Ashita's Original mode and Haman Karn's Official mode
Qubeley	Complete Judau Ashita's Official mode
Qubeley Mk-II (Red)	Complete Elpe Puru's Original mode and Rolan Cehack's Original mode
Qubeley Mk-II (Black)	Complete Judau Ashita's Official mode and Domon Kasshu's Original mode
The O	Complete Kamille Bidan's Official mode

Fantastic 4: Rise of the Silver Surfer

Unlockables

Collect the indicated number of Tokens to unlock the corresponding bonus.

Unlockable	How to Unlock
1990's Fantastic Four	Collect 12 Tokens
2000's Fantastic Four	Collect 12 Tokens
Comic Covers #1	Collect 4 Tokens
Comic Covers #2	Collect 4 Tokens
Game Concept Art	Collect 4 Tokens
Ultimate Costumes	Collect 12 Tokens

Fight Night Round 3

Unlockable	Code
All Venues	newview

Unlockable	How To
Madison Square Garden	Win a match there in Career mode.
The Staples Center	Win a match there in Career mode.
"Hard Straights" Style	Win that style match in ESPN Classic Fights mode or Career mode.
"Hook Master" Style	Win that style match in ESPN Classic Fights mode or Career mode.
"Judge Jab" Style	Win that style match in ESPN Classic Fights mode or Career mode.
"Lethal Uppercuts" Style	Win that style match in ESPN Classic Fights mode or Career mode.
"Philly Shell" Style	Win that style match in ESPN Classic Fights mode or Career mode.
"Sinister Cross" Style	Win that style match in ESPN Classic Fights mode or Career mode.
"Slickster" Style	Win that style match in ESPN Classic Fights mode or Career mode.
"Smooth" Style	Win that style match in ESPN Classic Fights mode or Career mode.

Fight Night Round 3 (continued)

"Textbook" Style	Win that style match in ESPN Classic Fights mode or Career mode.
"Uptight" Style	Win that style match in ESPN Classic Fights mode or Career mode.
Ko Rey Mo	Defeat him in the Lightweight Career mode.
The Burger King (Trainer)	Finish the Burger King event in Career mode and select him as a trainer.

Full Auto 2: Battlelines

In the Option menu, select the Cheats option to enter these codes.

Unlockable	Code
Unlock Sceptre and Mini-Rockets	10E6CUSTOMER
Unlock Vulcan and Flamethrower	5FINGERDISCOUNT

The Godfather: The Don's Edition

Enter these codes while the game is paused.

Unlockable	Code
$5,000	■, ▲, ■, ■, ▲, L2
Full Ammo	▲, ⇦, ▲, ⇨, ■, R1
Full Health	⇦, ■, ⇨, ▲, ⇨, L2

Harry Potter and the Order of the Phoenix

Room of Rewards Trophies

Successfully complete the indicated task to unlock the corresponding trophy.

Unlockable	How to Unlock
Characters Cup	Meet all 58 characters in Hogwarts
Defense Against the Dark Arts Cup	Cast all defensive spells in 6 duels
House Ghost Cup	Find all 4 House Ghosts
Nature Trail Cup	Find all animal footprints

Lair

Passwords

Enter into the game's Cheat menu:

Password	Effect
chicken	Chicken Curry video
686F7420636F66666565	Hot Coffee video
koelsch	Unlocks Stable option for all levels on the Mission Select screen

DS · GBA · PSP · PS2 · PS3 · Wii · Xbox · Xbox 360 · Index

DS

GBA

PSP

PS2

PS3

Wii

Xbox

Xbox 360

Index

Madden NFL '07

CODES

Code	Effect
XL7SP1	Cannot throw an INT or Fumble the ball for 1 half
WROAOR	QB will have 100% accuracy for 1 half
5LAWOO	The opponent throws lob passes for 1 half
B57QLU	Unlock the 1958 Colts Gold card
1PL1FL	Unlock the 1966 Packers Gold card
MIE6WO	Unlock the 1968 Jets Gold card
CL2TOE	Unlock the 1970 Browns Gold card
NOEB7U	Unlock the 1972 Dolphins Gold card
YOOFLA	Unlock the 1974 Steelers Gold card
MOA11I	Unlock the 1976 Raiders Gold card
C8UM7U	Unlock the 1977 Broncos Gold card
VIU0O7	Unlock the 1978 Dolphins Gold card
NLAPH3	Unlock the 1980 Raiders Gold card
COAGI4	Unlock the 1981 Chargers Gold card
WL8BRI	Unlock the 1982 Redskins Gold card
H0EW7I	Unlock the 1983 Raiders Gold card
M1AM1E	Unlock the 1984 Dolphins Gold card
QOETO8	Unlock the 1985 Bears Gold card
ZI8S2L	Unlock the 1986 Giants Gold card
SP2A8H	Unlock the 1988 49ers Gold card
2L4TRO	Unlock the 1990 Eagles Gold card
J1ETRI	Unlock the 1991 Lions Gold card
W9UVI9	Unlock the 1992 Cowboys Gold card
DLA3I7	Unlock the 1993 Bills Gold card
DR7EST	Unlock the 1994 49ers Gold card
F8LUST	Unlock the 1996 Packers Gold card
FIES95	Unlock the 1998 Broncos Gold card
S9OUSW	Unlock the 1999 Rams Gold card
YI8P8U	Unlock the Aloha Stadium Gold card
RLA9R7	Unlock the Super Bowl XLI Gold card
WRLUF8	Unlock the Super Bowl XLII Gold card
NIEV4A	Unlock the Super Bowl XLIII Gold card
M5AB7L	Unlock the Super Bowl XLIV Gold card

Major League Baseball 2K7

To enter these codes select My 2K7. Then select Enter Cheat Code.

Unlockable	Code
Boosts a team's power rating by 25% for 1 inning	mightymick
Boosts the hitting of the 3, 4, 5 hitters in the lineup by 50% for 1 game	triplecrown
Boosts your ability to hit home runs during the game just like The Mick	m4murder
Mickey will pinch hit	phmantle
Unlocks everything	Derek Jeter
Unlocks Mickey Mantle in free agency	themick

Marvel Ultimate Alliance

Enter these codes while playing

Unlockable	Code
God Mode	⇧, ⇩, ⇧, ⇩, ⇧, ⇦, ⇩, ⇨, START
Super Speed	⇧, ⇦, ⇧, ⇨, ⇩, ⇨, START
Touch of Death	⇦, ⇨, ⇧, ⇩, ⇨, ⇦, START

Enter these codes at the Team menu.

Unlockable	Code
100K	⇧, ⇧, ⇨, ⇦, ⇨, ⇦, START
All Characters	⇧, ⇧, ⇩, ⇩, ⇦, ⇦, ⇦, START
All Costumes	⇧, ⇩, ⇧, ⇦, ⇨, ⇨, ⇦, ⇧, ⇩, START
All Powers	⇦, ⇨, ⇦, ⇨, ⇧, ⇩, ⇩, ⇦, ⇨, START
Level 99	⇧, ⇧, ⇩, ⇦, ⇩, ⇨, ⇨, START
Unlocks Daredevil	⇦, ⇦, ⇨, ⇧, ⇩, ⇩, ⇩, START
Unlocks Silver Surfer	⇩, ⇩, ⇦, ⇧, ⇩, ⇧, ⇦, START

Enter these codes at the Review menu.

Unlockable	Code
All Cinematics	⇧, ⇨, ⇦, ⇧, ⇨, ⇨, ⇧, START
All Comics	⇦, ⇨, ⇨, ⇦, ⇧, ⇧, ⇧, START
All Concept Art	⇩, ⇩, ⇩, ⇩, ⇨, ⇦, ⇩, START
All Wallpapers	⇧, ⇨, ⇨, ⇦, ⇧, ⇧, ⇩, START

Mobile Suit Gundam: Crossfire

Unlockable	Code
Amuro Ray	Beat EFF campaign on Very Hard mode once, and load the clear data
Char Aznable	Beat Zeon campaign on Very Hard mode once, and load the clear data
Fraw Bow	Beat any campaign on Very Hard and load the clear data
Gelgoog	Become Brigadier General and play on Very Hard mode, and just after you get the Hildolfr you should unlock the Gelgoog
Gundam	Reach the rank of Warrant General
Hildolfr	Become Brigadier General and play on Very Hard mode in early December before the unidentified enemy mission
Kai Shiden	Beat any campaign on Very Hard and load the clear data

Motorstorm

Enter this code at the main menu.

Unlockable	Code
Unlock Everything	Hold L1, L2, R1, R2, R2 pushed up, L2 pushed down

Enter this code while the game is paused.

Unlockable	Code
Big Head on ATVs and Bikes	Hold L1, L2, R1, R2, R2 pushed right, L1 pushed left

DS

GBA

PSP

PS2

PS3

Wii

Xbox

Xbox 360

Index

DS

GBA

PSP

PS2

PS3

Wii

Xbox

Xbox 360

Index

NASCAR 08

Passwords

Submit these cheats at the Cheat Code screen under Options at the main menu.

Password	Effect
checkered flag	Unlock all chase mode cars
EA SPORTS CAR	Unlock EA SPORTS CAR
race the pack	Unlock fantasy drivers
walmart everyday	Unlock Wal-Mart car and track

NBA 07

To enter these passwords, select Options, then Trophy Room and then select Team Jerseys. While in Team Jerseys, press ■ to enter these passwords.

Unlockable	Password
Charlotte Bobcats Secondary Road Uniform	JKL846ETK5
New Jersey Nets Secondary Road Uniform	NB79D965D2
Utah Jazz Secondary Road Uniform	228GG7585G
Washington Wizards Secondary Road Uniform	PL5285F37F

NBA 2K7

Enter these passwords in the Codes menu under Features.

Unlockable	Code
ABA Ball	payrespect
Defensive Awareness	getstops
Maximum Durability for One Game	ironman
Offensive Awareness	inthezone
Unlimited Stamina for One Game	norest
All-Star Uniforms	syt6cii
Bobcats Secondary	bcb8sta
Jazz Secondary	zjb3lau
Nets Secondary	nrd4esj
Wizards Secondary	zw9idla
St. Patrick Day Uniforms	tpk7sgn
International All-Stars	tns9roi
NBA 2K Team	bestsim
Superstar Team	rta1spe
Topps 2K Sports All-Stars	topps2ksports
2007 All-Star Ball	ply8mia
2007 All-Star Uniforms	syt6cii
New Orleans Hornets Uniforms (Valentine's Day)	vdr5lya

NBA Street Homecourt

Unlockable	Code
Brand Jordan Outfit 2	Get 10 blocks in a game
Brand Jordan Outfit 4	Get 10 steals in a game
Chicago All-Stars	Beat the Chicago Bulls in a Back to Basics game

NBA Street Homecourt (continued)

Detroit All-Stars	Defeat the Detroit Pistons in a GB Battle
Jordan 9.5 Team	Win 5 Back to Basics games
Jordan 9.5 Team	Win 5 GB Battles
Jordan Hoops Lo	Win 15 GB Battles
Jordan Hoops Lo	Win 15 Back to Basics games
Jordan Laney 23	Win 30 Back to Basics games
Jordan Show Em Lo	Win 30 GB Battles
Jordan XXI PE	Win 100 Pick Up games
Los Angeles All-Stars	Defeat the Los Angeles Lakers in a Pick Up game
New Jersey All-Stars	Defeat the New Jersey Nets in a Trick Battle
New York All-Stars	Defeat the New York Knicks in a GB Battle
Oakland All-Stars	Defeat the Golden State Warriors in a Trick Battle
Jordan 9.5 Team	Win 5 Pick Up games
Jordan 9.5 Team	Win 5 Trick Battles
Jordan Hoops Lo	Win 15 Pick Up games
Jordan Hoops Lo	Win 15 Trick Battles
Jordan Laney 23	Win 30 Pick Up games
Jordan Show Em Lo	Win 30 Trick Battles

Pirates of the Caribbean: At World's End

Characters

Successfully complete the indicated task to unlock the corresponding character.

Unlockable	How to Unlock
Ammand the Corsair	Successfully complete the Pirate Poker sub-mission in the Shipwreck City level
Black Bart	Successfully complete the Combat Challenge in the Maelstrom level
Bootstrap Bill Turner	Successfully complete the Defeat Enemies sub-mission in the Prison Fortress level
Cannon Arm	Successfully complete the Combat Challenge in the Pearl vs. Kraken level
Captain Barbossa	Successfully complete the Shipwreck City level
Captain Chevalle	Successfully complete the Port Royal level
Captain Elizabeth Swann	Successfully complete the Combo Challenge in the Davy Jones' Locker level
Captain Jack Sparrow	Successfully complete the Prison Fortress level
Captain Sao Feng	Successfully complete the Singapore level
Captain Teague	Successfully complete the Combat Challenge in the Prison Fortress level
Cotton	Successfully complete the Rescue sub-mission in the Isla de Pelegostos level
Davy Jones	Successfully complete Pearl vs. Dutchman level
Elizabeth Swann	Successfully complete the Tortuga level
Gentlemen Jocard	Successfully complete the Davy Jones' Locker level
Gibbs	Successfully complete the Combat Challenge in the Port Royal level
Governor Swann	Successfully complete the Combat Challenge in the Pearl vs. Dutchman level

DS

GBA

PSP

PS2

PS3

Wii

Xbox

Xbox 360

Index

DS
GBA
PSP
PS2
PS3
Wii
Xbox
Xbox 360
Index

Pirates of the Caribbean: At World's End (continued)

James Norrington	Successfully complete the Combat Challenge in the Tortuga level
Lian	Successfully complete the Combat Challenge in the Singapore level
Lord Cuttler Beckett	Successfully complete the Maelstrom level
Mercer	Successfully complete the Hit-Combo sub-mission in the Singapore level
Mistress Ching	Successfully complete the Jackanism sub-mission in the Tortuga level
Mordillah	Successfully complete the Combo Challenge in the Prison Fortress level
Pintel	Successfully complete the Isla Cruces level
Ragetti	Successfully complete the Combat Challenge in the Isla Cruces level
Sri Sumba Jee	Successfully complete the Combat Challenge in the Shipwreck City level
Tai Huang	Successfully complete the Sea Battle level
Tia Dalma	Successfully complete the Missing Person sub-mission in the Port Royal level
Villanueva	Successfully complete the Combo Challenge in the Tortuga level
Will Turner	Successfully complete the Isla de Pelegostos level

Swords

Successfully complete the indicated task to unlock the corresponding sword.

Unlockable	How to Unlock
Bone Sword	Successfully complete the Davy Jones' Locker level
Davy Jones' Sword	Successfully complete the Maelstrom level
Dutchman Sword	Successfully complete the Pearl vs. Dutchman level
Ghost Sword	Successfully complete the Hit Combo sub-mission on the Isla Cruces level
Gun Sword	Successfully complete the Sea Battle level
Legend Sword	Successfully complete the Hit Combo sub-mission on the Maelstrom level
Norrington Sword	Successfully complete the Isla Cruces level
Pirate King's Sword	Successfully complete the Shipwreck City level

Need for Speed Carbon

Enter at the main menu screen.

Unlockable	Code
10K Booster	⇩, ⇧, ⇦, ⇩, ⇨, ⇧, ■, ▲
Infinite Crew Charge	⇩, ⇧, ⇦, ⇨, ⇦, ⇦, ⇨, ■
Infinite Nitrous	⇦, ⇧, ⇦, ⇩, ⇦, ⇩, ⇨, ■
Infinite SpeedBreaker	⇩, ⇨, ⇨, ⇦, ⇨, ⇧, ⇩, ■
Unlock Logo Vinyls	⇨, ⇧, ⇩, ⇧, ⇦, ⇦, ⇨, ■
Unlock Special Logo Vinyls	⇧, ⇧, ⇩, ⇩, ⇦, ⇩, ⇧, ■

Ratatouille

Passwords

Load a saved profile or create a new profile. Then, select the "Extras" option at the main menu. Choose the "Gusteau's Shop" option, then select the "Secrets" option. Choose a "Code [number]" option and enter the corresponding cheat code to unlock that option. After a cheat option is unlocked, click on its name to enable it. Unlocked and enabled cheat options are saved with the current profile. However, some cheat options cannot be disabled.

* Codes marked with an asterisk cannot be unlocked until they are bought with Gusteau points earned during Story mode.

Password	Effect
Code 01 / Pieceocake	Very Easy difficulty *
Code 02 / Myhero	No impact or damage from enemies, but still take water and falling damage *
Code 03 / Shielded	No damage from enemies, but still take water and falling damage *
Code 04 / Spyagent	Move undetected by enemies *
Code 05 / Ilikeonions	Fart when jumping
Code 06 / Hardfeelings	Head butt when attacking instead of tailswipe
Code 07 / Slumberparty	Multiplayer mode
Code 08 / Gusteauart	All concept art
Code 09 / Gusteauship	All four championship modes
Code 10 / Mattelme	All single player and multiplayer minigames
Code 11 / Gusteauvid	All videos
Code 12 / Gusteaures	All bonus artworks
Code 13 / Gusteaudream	All Dream Worlds in Gusteau's Shop
Code 14 / Gusteauslide	All slides in Gusteau's Shop
Code 15 / Gusteaulevel	All single player minigames
Code 16 / Gusteaucombo	All items in Gusteau's Shop
Code 17 / Gusteaupot	+5,000 Gusteau points
Code 18 / Gusteaujack	+10,000 Gusteau points
Code 19 / Gusteauomni	+50,000 Gusteau points

Ridge Racer 7

Unlockable	How To
Auto Rocket Start System	100 Points with Zolgear
Collision Decreaser	100 Points with all tyre and suspension manufacturers
Down Force Control System	100 Points with Bosconian
Nitrous Tank 100	100 Points with all nitrous manufacturers
Over Limit Start System	100 Points all engine tune up manufacturers
Prize Money x2	100 Points with all manufacturers
Race Data Analyzer	100 Points with Galaxian
SS Booster	100 Points with Arkbird
SS Canceler	100 Points all exterior parts manufacturers
10&20% discount and special Age machine	Obtain 100 Manufacturer Points from Age
10&20% discount and special Assoluto machine	Obtain 100 Manufacturer Points from Assoluto

DS

GBA

PSP

PS2

PS3

Wii

Xbox

Xbox 360

Index

Ridge Racer 7 (continued)

10&20% discount and special Danver machine	Obtain 100 Manufacturer Points from Danver
10&20% discount and special Gnade machine	Obtain 100 Manufacturer Points from Gnade
10&20% discount and special Himmel machine	Obtain 100 Manufacturer Points from Himmel
10&20% discount and special Kamata machine	Obtain 100 Manufacturer Points from Kamata
10&20% discount and special Namco machine	Obtain 100 Manufacturer Points from Namco
10&20% discount and special SinseongMotors machine	Obtain 100 Manufacturer Points from SinseongMotors
10&20% discount and special Soldat machine	Obtain 100 Manufacturer Points from Soldat
10&20% discount and special Terrazi machine	Obtain 100 Manufacturer Points from Terrazi

Skate

Code

Enter code at main menu.

Code	Effect
⬇, ⬅, ⬇, ⬅, ■, R1, ▲, L1	Unlock Best Buy clothes in store

Sonic the Hedgehog

Unlockable	How To
Last Episode	Beat Sonic's Episode, Shadow's Episode, and Silver's Episode
Audio Room	Complete Sonic, Shadow, or Silver's story 100%
Theater Room	Complete Sonic, Shadow, or Silver's story 100%
Shadow the Hedgehog	Complete "Crisis City" with Sonic
Silver the Hedgehog	Complete "Silver the Hedgehog" boss battle with Sonic

Surf's Up

Passwords

Password	Effect
MYPRECIOUS	All Boards
FREEVISIT	All championship locations
GOINGDOWN	All leaf sliding locations
MULTIPASS	All multiplayer levels
NICEPLACE	Art gallery
ASTRAL	Astral board
TOPFASHION	Customizations for all characters
MONSOON	Monsoon board
IMTHEBEST	Plan as Tank Evans
TINYBUTSTRONG	Play as Arnold
SURPRISEGUEST	Play as Elliot
SLOWANDSTEADY	Play as Geek
KOBAYASHI	Play as Tatsuhi Kobayashi
THELEGEND	Play as Zeke Topanga

DS | GBA | PSP | PS2 | PS3 | Wii | Xbox | Xbox 360 | Index

Surf's Up (continued)

| TINYSHOCKWAVE | Tine shockwave board |
| WATCHAMOVIE | Video Gallery |

Tiger Woods PGA 07

Unlockable	How To
EA Black Series Clubs	Complete the game 100% to get the EA Black Series Clubs

Tiger Woods PGA Tour '08

Passwords

Go to the Password sub-menu from the EA Sports Extras menu and enter the following passwords to get the corresponding effects. Passwords are not case sensitive.

Password	Effect
Cream	Infinite money
PlayFIFA08	Unlock Wayne Rooney
Greensfees	Unlock all course
AllStars	Unlock all golfers

Tony Hawk's Project 8

In the Options menu, select Cheats to enter these passwords.

Unlockable	Password
Big Realtor	shescaresme
Christian Hosoi	hohohosoi
Colonel and Security Guard	militarymen
Dad and Skater Jam Kid	strangefellows
Full Air Stats	drinkup
Grim Reaper	enterandwin
Inkblot Deck	birdhouse
Jason Lee	notmono
Kevin Staab	mixitup
Mascot	manineedadate
Most Decks	needaride
Nerd	wearelosers
Photographer and Cameraman	themedia
Travis Barker	plus44
Unlock Specials in Skate Shop	yougotitall

Virtua Fighter 5

Unlockable	Code
DOJO training stages	Complete the Time Attack mode
Costume C	Reach the rank of 1st Dan
Costume D	Complete the first orb disc

DS

GBA

PSP

PS2

PS3

Wii

Xbox

Xbox 360

Index

Table of Contents - Wii

Side tabs: DS, GBA, PSP, PS2, PS3, **Wii**, Xbox, Xbox 360, Index

ActRaiser

Hidden Extra Lives

Do the following to find four hidden extra lives in the game's towns.

Town	Action
Fillmore	When you get the Compass, use it here.
Bloodpool	Make it rain over the big lake.
Kasandora	Cause an earthquake after uncovering the pyramid.
Northwall	Strike the town's shrine with a lightning bolt.

Professional Mode

Unlockable	How to Unlock
Professional Mode	First, beat the game. Then on the title screen, highlight "New Game" and press ✛ or SELECT.

DS

GBA

PSP

PS2

PS3

Wii

Xbox

Xbox 360

Index

DS
GBA
PSP
PS2
PS3
Wii
Xbox
Xbox 360
Index

Adventure Island

Passwords

Password	Effect
3WSURYXZY763TE	Advanced items/abilities
RMAYTJEOPHALUP	Disable sounds
NODEGOS0000000	Start the game as Hu man
3YHURYW7Y7LL8C	Start the game as Hawk man
3YHURYW7Y7LRBW	Start the game as Lizard man
3YHURYW7Y7LN84	Start the game as Piranha man
3YHURYW7Y7LK88	Start the game as Tiger man

Adventures of Lolo

Level Passwords

Password	Effect	Password	Effect	Password	Effect
BCBT	Level 1-2	CDZR	Level 4-4	DGYQ	Level 8-1
BDBR	Level 1-3	CGZQ	Level 4-5	DHYP	Level 8-2
BGBQ	Level 1-4	CHZP	Level 5-1	DJYM	Level 8-3
BHBP	Level 1-5	CJZM	Level 5-2	DKYL	Level 8-4
BJBM	Level 2-1	CKZL	Level 5-3	DLYK	Level 8-5
BKBL	Level 2-2	CLZK	Level 5-4	DMYJ	Level 9-1
BLBK	Level 2-3	CMZJ	Level 5-5	DPYH	Level 9-2
BMBJ	Level 2-4	CPZH	Level 6-1	DQYG	Level 9-3
BPBH	Level 2-5	CQZG	Level 6-2	DRYD	Level 9-4
BQBG	Level 3-1	CRZD	Level 6-3	DTYC	Level 9-5
BRBD	Level 3-2	CTZC	Level 6-4	DVYB	Level 10-1
BTBC	Level 3-3	CVZB	Level 6-5	DYVZ	Level 10-2
BVBB	Level 3-4	CYYZ	Level 7-1	DZVY	Level 10-3
BYZZ	Level 3-5	CZYY	Level 7-2	GBVV	Level 10-4
BZZY	Level 4-1	DBYV	Level 7-3	GCVT	Level 10-5
CBZV	Level 4-2	DCYT	Level 7-4		
CCZT	Level 4-3	DDYR	Level 7-5		

Level Skip

Unlockable	How to Unlock
Level Skip	This only works if you have a password that starts with A, B, C, or D and if the second letter in the password appears earlier in the alphabet than the fourth letter. If so, switch the second and fourth letters in the password. Use the new password to start at a level one higher than the original.

Adventures of Lolo 2

New Difficulty Levels

Password	Effect	Password	Effect
PPHP	Floor 01, Room 1	PZPC	Floor 02, Room 1
PHPK	Floor 01, Room 2	PGPG	Floor 02, Room 2
PQPD	Floor 01, Room 3	PCPZ	Floor 02, Room 3
PVPT	Floor 01, Room 4	PLPY	Floor 02, Room 4
PRPJ	Floor 01, Room 5	PBPM	Floor 02, Room 5

Adventures of Lolo 2 (continued)

Password	Effect	Password	Effect
PYPL	Floor 03, Room 1	HKKH	Floor 07, Room 2
PMPB	Floor 03, Room 2	QPKP	Floor 07, Room 3
PJPR	Floor 03, Room 3	QHDK	Floor 07, Room 4
PTPV	Floor 03, Room 4	QQDD	Floor 07, Room 5
PDPQ	Floor 03, Room 5	QVDT	Floor 08, Room 1
PKPH	Floor 04, Room 1	QRDJ	Floor 08, Room 2
HPPP	Floor 04, Room 2	QBDM	Floor 08, Room 3
HHKK	Floor 04, Room 3	QLDY	Floor 08, Room 4
HQKD	Floor 04, Room 4	QCDZ	Floor 08, Room 5
HVKT	Floor 04, Room 5	QGDG	Floor 09, Room 1
HRKJ	Floor 05, Room 1	QZDC	Floor 09, Room 2
HBKM	Floor 05, Room 2	QYDL	Floor 09, Room 3
HLKY	Floor 05, Room 3	QMDB	Floor 09, Room 4
HCKZ	Floor 05, Room 4	QJDR	Floor 09, Room 5
HGKG	Floor 05, Room 5	QTDV	Floor 10, Room 1
HZKC	Floor 06, Room 1	QDDQ	Floor 10, Room 2
HYKL	Floor 06, Room 2	QKDH	Floor 10, Room 3
HMKB	Floor 06, Room 3	VPDP	Floor 10, Room 4
HJKR	Floor 06, Room 4	VHTK	Floor 10, Room 5
HTKV	Floor 06, Room 5	VQTD	Last Level
HDKQ	Floor 07, Room 1		

Air Zonk

Codes

Unlockable	How to Unlock
Expert Mode	On the Configuration screen, hold ⬅ and press SELECT
Sound Test	Hold ① and ② and SELECT as you turn on the game

Alex Kidd in the Enchanted Castle

Skip Boss Sequences

Unlockable	How to Unlock
Skip Boss Sequences	Wait until the conversation with the boss has ended. After that, Press START to get to the Options screen, then press START again and you should skip the sequence.

Alien Crush

Bonus

Unlockable	How to Unlock
1 Million Points + Bonus Ball	Get to the bonus round with skulls and green aliens. Kill everything except for one skull. Keep going until a pterodactyl appears. Hit the pterodactyl with the ball to get a million points and a bonus ball once the stage is cleared.

DS
GBA
PSP
PS2
PS3
Wii
Xbox
Xbox 360
Index

Alien Soldier

Level Passwords

Password	Effect	Password	Effect	Password	Effect
1985	Level 1	8316	Level 10	9002	Level 19
3698	Level 2	6402	Level 11	2878	Level 20
0257	Level 3	9874	Level 12	3894	Level 21
3745	Level 4	1930	Level 13	4913	Level 22
7551	Level 5	2623	Level 14	2825	Level 23
8790	Level 6	6385	Level 15	7406	Level 24
5196	Level 7	7749	Level 16	5289	Level 25
4569	Level 8	3278	Level 17		
8091	Level 9	1039	Level 18		

Alien Syndrome

Unlock Extra Difficulties

Unlockable	How to Unlock
Unlock Expert Difficulty	Beat the game on Hard difficulty
Unlock Hard Difficulty	Beat the game on Normal difficulty

Altered Beast

Codes

Enter these on the title screen.

Unlockable	How to Unlock
Beast Select	Hold Ⓐ+Ⓑ+Ⓒ+✚ and then press START
Character Kicks Credits	When the credits are being displayed on the screen after you have beaten the game, you can control your character to kick away the credited names.
Continue from Last Stage Played	Hold Ⓐ and press SELECT after a Game Over
Level Select	Press Ⓑ and START
Sound Test	Hold Ⓐ+Ⓒ+✚ and then press START

Art of Fighting

Character Unlockables

Unlockable	How to Unlock
Mr. Big	Get to Mr. Big in 1-player mode and lose the match. Restart the game and Mr. Big will now be unlocked in 2-player mode.
Mr. Karate	Get to Mr. Karate in 1-player mode and lose the match. Restart the game and Mr. Karate will now be unlocked in 2-player mode.

Avatar: The Last Airbender

Passwords

Password	Effect	Password	Effect
37437	All treasure maps	24463	Unlimited chi
97831	Character concept gallery	23637	Unlimited copper
34743	Double damage	94677	Unlimited health
54641	One hit dishonor	53467	Unlimited stealth

Avatar: The Last Airbender (continued)

Unlockable Galleries

Unlockable	How to Unlock
Character Story Board Gallery	Collect all Set Items through level 6
Level Art Gallery	Collect all Set Items through level 3
Story Board Gallery	Collect all Set Items through level 5

Barnyard

Gameplay Cheat Codes

During gameplay hold ©+Ⓩ and enter codes.

Unlockable	How to Unlock
9,999 Gopher Bucks	⬇, ⬆, ⬇, ⬆, ⬇, ⬆, ⬇, ⬆
All Flower Pack and Knapsack Items	⬇, ⬇, ⬆, ⬆, ⬆, ⬆, ⬇, ⬇

Main Menu Cheat Codes

While on the main menu screen, hold ©+Ⓩ and enter codes.

Unlockable	How to Unlock
Unlock All Antics	⬆, ⬇, ⬆, ⬇, ⬆, ⬇, ⬆, ⬇
Unlock All Bonus Items	⬇, ⬆, ⬇, ⬆, ⬆, ⬆, ⬇, ⬆

Bases Loaded

Passwords

Password	Effect
LFBDJHE	Boston, one game away from the World Series
PFACNHK	DC, one game away from the World Series
CHXAACC	Game 162
LNADJPD	Hawaii, one game away from the World Series
CBIDNEP	Jersey, last game of the World Series
LFADNHH	Jersey, one game away from the World Series
PNCBNHD	Kansas, one game away from the World Series
PFBCNPD	LA, one game away from the World Series
PFCANHK	Miami, one game away from the World Series
PFDAJHH	New York, one game away from the World Series
LNDAJPD	Omaha, one game away from the World Series
JAELECO	Password for Pennant, must have selected "Pennant" option from menu
LFDBJHE	Philly, one game away from the World Series
Select Pennant Mode and Enter JALECO as Password	Skip to the last team
LNCBJPD	Texas, one game away from the World Series
LNBCJPD	Utah, one game away from the World Series

Other Actions

Action	How to Enact
Don't Get Ejected During a Fight	Continually press Ⓑ during the fight
Hitter Charges the Mound and Gets Ejected	After the 3rd inning, bean the 3rd or 4th hitter in the lineup

DS

GBA

PSP

PS2

PS3

Wii

Xbox

Xbox 360

Index

DS
GBA
PSP
PS2
PS3
Wii
Xbox
Xbox 360
Index

Battle City

Stage Select

Unlockable	How to Unlock
Stage Select	When you start the game and see the screen with "Stage 1," press Ⓐ and Ⓑ to choose any stage you want

Bionicle Heroes

Secret Character

Unlockable	How to Unlock
Vezon	Complete the game once

Blazing Angels: Squadrons of WWII

Unlockables

Unlockable	How to Unlock
All Aircraft/Missions/Paint Jobs	At the menu immediately following choose pilot, hold ⊖ and ⊕, then press ⬆, ⬇, ①, ②, ②, ①
B-17 Flying Fortress and Spitfire IX	Complete Campaign Mission 18—Counter Attack with at least a Veteran Pilot Ranking
B-25 Mitchell and Hs-129	Complete the Bombing Mini Campaign
Beaufighter and P-40C Warhawk	Complete Campaign Mission 6—Desert Rats with at least a Veteran Pilot Ranking
Boulton-Paul Defiant and Ki-43 Hayabusa (Oscar)	Complete Campaign Mission 10—Midway: Turning Point with at least a Veteran Pilot Ranking
De Havilland (DH) Mosquito and N1K Shiden (George)	Complete Campaign Mission 13—Rabaul Raid with at least a Veteran Pilot Ranking
Devastator and D3A1 Val	Complete Campaign Mission 7—Day of Infamy with at least a Veteran Pilot Ranking
Dornier Do-335 Pfeil (Arrow)	Complete Campaign mode
F2A Buffalo and B5N2 Kate	Complete Campaign Mission 8—Surprise Attack with at least a Veteran Pilot Ranking
Fw-190A and Me-109G	Complete Campaign Mission 14—Preemptive Strike with at least a Veteran Pilot Ranking
Hurricane I and Me-110C	Complete Campaign Mission 1—Training Day with at least a Veteran Pilot Ranking
Hurricane II and Me-110E	Complete Campaign Mission 5—Desert Recon with at least a Veteran Pilot Ranking
Me-262 Schwalbe (Sparrow) and Me-163 Komet	Complete the Dogfight Mini Campaign
Meteor and Kikka	Complete Campaign Mission 20—Berlin 1945 with at least a Veteran Pilot Ranking
P-51D Mustang and Me-109K	Complete Campaign Mission 16—D-Day Normandy with at least a Veteran Pilot Ranking
P-51H Mustang and Fw-190D-9	Complete Campaign Mission 19—Flying Fortress with at least a Veteran Pilot Ranking
P-82 Twin Mustang and J2M Raiden (Jack)	Complete Campaign Mission 12—The Battle of New Georgia with at least a Veteran Pilot Ranking
SB2C Helldiver and SB2A Buccaneer	Complete Campaign Mission 11—Holding Guadalcanal with at least a Veteran Pilot Ranking
SBD-3 Dauntless and A6M Zero	Complete Campaign Mission 9—Midway: Opening with at least a Veteran Pilot Ranking
Seafire and Ju-87 Stuka	Complete Campaign Mission 4—London 1940 with at least a Veteran Pilot Ranking

Blazing Angels: Squadrons of WWII (continued)

Unlockables

Unlockable	How to Unlock
Spitfire I and Me-109E	Complete Campaign Mission 2—Skies of Dunkirk with at least a Veteran Pilot Ranking
Swordfish and Spitfire V	Complete Campaign Mission 3—Dunkirk Evacuation with at least a Veteran Pilot Ranking
Tempest and A-1 Skyraider	Complete Campaign Mission 17—Paris: La Liberation with at least a Veteran Pilot Ranking
Typhoon and Me-110G	Complete Campaign Mission 15—Top Secret with at least a Veteran Pilot Ranking
Upgraded Bombs, Rockets, and Torpedos for All Aircraft	Complete the Bombing Mini Campaign
Upgraded Cannons and Machine Guns for All Fighters	Complete the Dogfight Mini Campaign

Bloody Wolf

Codes

Unlockable	How to Unlock
10 Flash Bombs	When your strength is at "1," climb a barricade and press ⬆+⬇+RUN+②
10 Super Grenades	When your strength is at "1," climb a barricade and press ⬆+⬇+RUN+②
50 Bazooka Rounds	When your strength is at "2," climb a fence and press ⬆+①+②
50 Flame Thrower Charges	Hold ⬆+①+② and press RUN when parachuting at the start of level 2 or level 5
50 Shotgun Rounds	When your strength is at "2," climb a fence and press ⬅+①+②
Fast Mode	At the title screen, press ⬆, ⬇, ⬆, ⬇, ①, ①, ② SELECT, RUN
Hover Mode (in game, press jump to hover)	At the title screen, press ⬆, ⬇, ⬅, ➡, ②, ②, ①, SELECT, RUN
Sound Test	At the title screen, press ⬆, then hold ①+②+SELECT

Level Select Codes

Press ②, ①, ①, ②, ①, ②, ②, ① at the title screen. Then press the following for the appropriate level.

Code	Effect	Code	Effect
Up	Level 1	Down	Level 5
Up/Right	Level 2	Down/Left	Level 6
Right	Level 3	Left	Level 7
Down/Right	Level 4	Up/Left	Level 8

Bonk's Revenge

Codes

Code	Effect
Bonus Levels	Press ①+② during the title screen
Clear Pause Screen	Pause the game and hold ①+②+SELECT
Ending Sequence Preview	First activate the "practice bonus rounds" code and then highlight the Exit option and press ②+RUN
Practice Bonus Rounds	Hold ② and then press RUN on the Difficulty Selection menu

Bonk's Revenge (continued)

Code	Effect
Remove Pause Text	Pause the game (by pressing RUN) and then press ①+②+SELECT
View Ending	Enable the Bonus Levels cheat, then Highlight "Exit" and press ②+RUN

Boogie

Unlockable Songs and Stages

Unlockable	How to Unlock
Song: Boogie Oogie Oogie	Beat Bubba's story
Song: Dancing in the Street	Beat Julius' story
Song: Love Shack	Beat Lea's story
Song: SOS (Rescue Me)	Beat Jet's story
Song: Tu y Yo	Beat Kato's story
Stage: Big Dub Hustle Club	Beat all 5 stories

Bratz: The Movie

Hidden Clothing Lines

To unlock these clothing lines, go to the small laptop near the computers in the Bratz Office and type in the following codes.

Code	Clothing Line
PRETTY	Feelin' Pretty Clothing Line
SCHOOL	High School Clothing Line
ANGELZ	Passion 4 Fashion Clothing Line
SWEETZ	Sweetz Clothing Line

Bravoman

Codes

Unlockable	How to Unlock
Bravo Kombat Minigame	Keep tapping ②, SELECT at the title screen
Continue Game	Press ②+RUN as Bravoman is dying
Unlimited Continues	Get 10,000 points, then lose and wait for the title screen to come up, then press ⬆, ⬇, ⬅, ➡, ②, SELECT, ②, SELECT

Breath of Fire II

Unlockable	How to Unlock
Old Friends	At Giant Island, in the northern area above the town gate, you'll find Bo and Karn from the first *Breath of Fire* game. They don't do anything, but you can talk to them. You need the whale or the bird to get there.

Bust-A-Move Bash!

More Stages

Unlockable	How to Unlock
250 More Stages	After completing the first 250 stages in Puzzle mode, return to the Select screen and press Ⓐ with the cursor hovering over Stage Select. The area should be mostly orange now instead of blue, and only the first stage will be available. This is how you access stages 251-500.

Call of Duty 3

Enter this code in the Chapter Select screen.

Unlockable	Code
Unlock All Levels	Hold ⊕ and press ⬅, ⬅, ⬅, ⬅, ②, ②
Unlock All Extras	At the Chapter Select screen, hold ⊕, and press ⬅, ⬅, ⬅, ⬅, ②, ②

Cars

Input codes in the password section under the Options menu.

Unlockable	Code
All Cars	YAYCARS
All Concept Art	CONC3PT
All Movies	WATCHIT
All Paint Jobs	R4MONE
All Races	MATTL66
All Tracks and Mini-games	IF900HP
Mater's Speedy Circuit and Mater's Countdown Clean Up	TRGTEXC
Super Fast Start	IMSPEED
Unlimited Boost	VROOOOM

Chew-Man-Fu

Codes

Unlockable	How to Unlock
Golden Balls	At the title screen, hold ①+SELECT and press ⬅+➡

Passwords

Password	Effect
573300	Area 1, Round 1 (2nd Playthrough)
344710	Area 1, Round 1 (3rd Playthrough)
274510	Area 1, Round 1 (4th Playthrough)
321310	Area 1, Round 1 (5th Playthrough)
536300	Area 1, Round 1 (6th Playthrough)
301710	Area 1, Round 1 (7th Playthrough)
231510	Area 1, Round 1 (8th Playthrough)
256310	Area 1, Round 1 (9th Playthrough)
441300	Area 1, Round 1 (10th Playthrough)
677261	Area 5, Round 50
075653	Fight enemy opponents only

China Warrior

Codes

Unlockable	How to Unlock
Enable Invincibility and Level Select	Press RUN+SELECT to reset the game, keep the buttons held, then release RUN and press ⬆ when the title screen is displayed. Release Select and press ⬆, ⬅, ⬆, ⬅, ⬇, ⬇, ➡, ⬇, ➡, ⬇, ⬇, ➡
Level Skip	Hold ⬆ then SELECT+①+② to skip the first level. For the other levels, hold ⬇ instead of ⬆.
Continue (up to three times) from the Start of the Last Level Played	Hold ①+②+⬆ and press RUN, RUN when the phrase "The End" appears after gameplay is over. Alternately, hold ①+2+⬆ and press RUN at the title screen after game play is over.

DS
GBA
PSP
PS2
PS3
Wii
Xbox
Xbox 360
Index

DS
GBA
PSP
PS2
PS3
Wii
Xbox
Xbox 360
Index

Comix Zone

Unlockables

Unlockable	How to Unlock
Fart	In some areas, press ✛.
Sega Plug	At any time during the main game, press START to pause. After a few seconds, Sketch will yell, "Sega!"
Stage Select	Go to the Jukebox mode and place the red checker on the following numbers in order, pressing ✛ at each one: 14, 15, 18, 5, 13, 1, 3, 18, 15, 6. Now, highlight a number from 1 to 6 and press ✛ to warp to the corresponding stage.
Unlimited Health	Go to Jukebox in the Options menu and push ✛ on these numbers: 3, 12, 17, 2, 2, 10, 2, 7, 7, 11. You hear Sketch say "oh yeah."
View Credits	At the Options mode, press Ⓐ+Ⓑ+Ⓒ.
Paper Airplane	During gameplay press and hold the Punch button. After a second or so Sketch will tear a piece of paper from the background and make a paper airplane out of it. The plane will travel to the edge of the panel and circle back around. The plane does massive damage to all enemies, objects, and Sketch himself, so be careful. You lose a considerable amount of health when creating the plane.

Cratermaze

Passwords

Password	Effect
Unlock All Normal Levels	Press RUN on the title screen and select Password. Enter this password, then use ① and ② to select a level before pressing RUN. Blue/Left, Blue/Left, Blue/Right, Red/Front
Expert Level Select	Blue/Back, Blue/Back, Red/Right, Blue/Forward

Cybernator

Codes

Unlockable	How to Unlock
Extra Continues	At the title screen, hold ✛+✛+✛and then press START.
Napalm Gun	Complete the first level without shooting anything except the boss, then complete level 2 without dying.
Secret Bad Ending	Go through the first level, and do not destroy the boss. Finish the rest of the game to see the failed ending.

Dance Dance Revolution Hottest Party

Unlockables

Unlockable	How to Unlock
Super Samurai—jun	Play 3 songs on Expert and get a AA or higher on the third song
tokyoEVOLVED—Naoki UNDERGROUND	Unlock all songs, then play 3 songs on Expert and get an AA or higher on the third song
Harmony's Alternate Outfit	Beat Harmony at the song Little Steps at the Genesis Venue
Root's Alternate Outfit	Beat Root at Break Down with a B ranking at the Tectonic Venue

Dead Moon

Unlockable

Unlockable	How to Unlock
Option Screen	Hold the following: ✛+①+② and press SELECT

Devil's Crush

Unlockable

Unlockable	How to Unlock
Sound Mode	Press ⬆, ⬇, ⬆ after pausing
Sound Test	Press RUN, SELECT during gameplay to display the High Score screen, then press ⬆, ⬆, ⬆, ⬆, ①

Passwords

Password	Effect
EFGHIJKLMB	924,000,000 points and 73 balls
AAAAAAAAAAAAAAAAAB	A 2-player game with unlimited balls
THECRUSHEL	Beat the game—launch the ball and once you hit something, the game ends
DAVIDWHITE	Beat the game—launch the ball and once you hit something, the game ends
FFFFFFFEEE	Beat the game—launch the ball and once you hit something, the game ends
NAXATSOFTI	Infinite balls, 206,633,300 points
AAAAAAHAAA	Infinite balls, 734,003,200 points
DEVILSATAN	Infinite balls, 955,719,100 points
THEDEVILSI	Over 145,000,000 points and 70 balls
ONECRUSHME	Over 594,000,000 points and 27 balls
AAAAAAAAAAAAAAABCE	2-player mode—gives player 1 unlimited balls and player 2 32 balls
PPPPPPPPPA	Unlimited balls
CKDEIPDBFM	25 balls and a score of 300,138,400
OJFJGDEJPD	34 balls and a score of 404,330,300
PNBIJOKJNF	38 balls and a score of 533,501,000
CGIAGPECGK	42 balls and a score of 610,523,600
OEHALCBGPF	45 balls and a score of 710,529,000
OLGGGEAPOF	52 balls and a score of 804,379,700
CBEOBLJGHA	62 balls and a score of 900,057,102
PFFMGHGOLK	65 balls and a score of 999,927,400
NLJBCFHGPO	65 balls and a score of 999,999,000
KGCMMCMLBN	65 balls and a score of 999,999,600
OMGANLOIJA	67 balls and a score of 976,769,800

Dewy's Adventure

Unlockables

Unlockable	How to Unlock
Character Gallery	Complete Groovy Grasslands
Hall of Records	Complete Groovy Grasslands
Music Gallery	Complete Groovy Grasslands
Photo Gallery	Complete Groovy Grasslands
Tips and Tricks	Complete Groovy Grasslands

DS

GBA

PSP

PS2

PS3

Wii

Xbox

Xbox 360

Index

Disney's Chicken Little: Ace in Action

Input the codes under Cheat option.

Unlockable	Code
All Levels Available	⇧, ⇧, ⇧, ⇧, ⇧
All Weapons Available	⇧, ⇩, ⇧, ⇩
Unlimited Shield Available	⇧, ⇧, ⇧, ⇧, ⇧

Double Dungeons

Passwords

At the Password screen, carefully enter the following passwords.

Password	Effect
cHR0EScxgoAq or iky7ihOfeBGe	In front of the last boss door
2R3KD4RG0J9D3YT0664LJ	Beginning of Level 22
YNzYSMChriGlgLV-ih0dfCGe	End of Level 22
Enter either Player01 or Player 02 as a password, with the remaining spaces filled in with either +'s or -'s	Get 65,535 HP
Enter any working password for player 1, then enter KKKKKKKKKKKKKKKKKKKKKKKKK as a password for player 2	Player 2 invincibility

Dr. Robotnik's Mean Bean Machine

Easy Mode Passwords

Password	Effect	Password	Effect
RRRH	Stage 2: Frankly	YPHB	Stage 8: Grounder
CPCG	Stage 3: Humpty	YPHB	Stage 9: Spike
RCHY	Stage 4: Coconuts	RYCH	Stage 10: Sir Fuzzy Logik
CBBP	Stage 5: Davy Sproket	GPBC	Stage 11: Dragon Breath
CRCP	Stage 6: Sqweel	RHHY	Stage 12: Scratch
PYRB	Stage 7: Dynamight	YHBB	Stage 13: Dr. Robotnik

Hard Mode Passwords

Password	Effect	Password	Effect
RRRH GCYY	Stage 2: Frankly	CYHY	Stage 8: Grounder
CPCG YPCP	Stage 3: Humpty	PBBG	Stage 9: Spike
RCHY BGCB	Stage 4: Coconuts	CGRY	Stage 10: Sir Fuzzy Logik
RPGG	Stage 5: Davy Sproket	BYYH	Stage 11: Dragon Breath
YYCG	Stage 6: Sqweel	GCCB	Stage 12: Scratch
PCBB	Stage 7: Dynamight	HCPH	Stage 13: Dr. Robotnik

Hardest Mode Passwords

Password	Effect	Password	Effect
BBGY	Stage 2: Frankly	CPHY	Stage 8: Grounder
GYGC	Stage 3: Humpty	PGHC	Stage 9: Spike
PPRH	Stage 4: Coconuts	GBYH	Stage 10: Sir Fuzzy Logik
GRPB	Stage 5: Davy Sproket	GPHR	Stage 11: Dragon Breath
PCGY	Stage 6: Sqweel	RGHB	Stage 12: Scratch
BPGH	Stage 7: Dynamight	RRCY	Stage 13: Dr. Robotnik

Dr. Robotnik's Mean Bean Machine (continued)

Unlockables

Unlockable	How to Unlock
Jumping Bean Title Screen	At the title screen, press Ⓐ, Ⓑ, or ✛ on controller 1 to make the "e," "a," and "n" in "Mean" jump. Press Ⓐ, Ⓑ, or ✛ on controller 2 to make the "e," "a," and "n" in "Bean" jump.
Last Boss	On Easy mode, enter Yellow Bean, Has Bean, Blue Bean, Blue Bean as your password. On Normal mode, enter Purple Bean, Yellow Bean, Has Bean, Clear Bean.

Scenario Mode Passwords—Normal Difficulty

Enter these passwords after selecting "Continue" to skip ahead to the desired level.

R = Red Bean

Y = Yellow Bean

G = Green Bean

B = Blue Bean

P = Purple Bean

C = Clear (Garbage) Bean

H = Has Bean (the little orange fellow)

Password	Effect	Password	Effect
HCYY	Stage 2: Frankly	GHCY	Stage 8: Grounder
BCRY	Stage 3: Humpty	BPHH	Stage 9: Spike
YBCP	Stage 4: Coconuts	HRYC	Stage 10: Sir Fuzzy Logik
HGBY	Stage 5: Davy Sprocket	CRRB	Stage 11: Dragon Breath
GPPY	Stage 6: Sqweel	GGCY	Stage 12: Scratch
PBGH	Stage 7: Dynamight	PYHC	Stage 13: Dr. Robotnik

Dragon Ball Z: Budokai Tenkaichi 2

"What If" Sagas

These special sagas become available when you win an "impossible" battle. Without these, you cannot attain 100% completion in Story mode. They're best attempted after you've run through Story mode and leveled up your characters.

Unlockable	How to Unlock
Beautiful Treachery	Defeat Dodoria with Gohan and Krillin in Mission 01 of the Frieza Saga "A Pursuer Who Calls Death"
Destined Rivals	Defeat Gohan with Goten in Mission 01 of the Majin Buu Saga "Training with Goten"
Fateful Brothers	Defeat Raditz with Piccolo in Mission 00 of the Saiyan Saga "Mysterious Alien Warrior" (first mission of the game)

Fight Intruders in Ultimate Battle Z

Some towers in the Ultimate Battle Z mode have hidden battles that require specific conditions to trigger. They are available only in difficulty level 3.

Unlockable	How to Unlock
Fight Broly Legendary SSJ in Saiyan Blood	Defeat Bardock with an Ultimate Blast
Fight Goku SSJ2 and Vegeta (Second Form) SSJ2 in Dragon Tag	Defeat any opponent with an Ultimate Blast
Fight Hercule in Unlimited	Defeat Gogeta SSJ4
Fight Omega Shenron in Ultimate Dragon	Defeat Syn Shenron with an Ultimate Blast

DS

GBA

PSP

PS2

PS3

Wii

Xbox

Xbox 360

Index

Dragon Ball Z: Budokai Tenkaichi 2 (continued)

Unlockable	How to Unlock
Fight SSJ3 Gotenks in Ultimate Children	Defeat Kid Goku with an Ultimate Blast
Fight Super Baby 2 in Normal-ism	Defeat Super 13 with an Ultimate Blast
Fight Tao Pai Pai in Assault Force!	Defeat any opponent with an Ultimate Blast
Fight Uub in Kakarot Road	Defeat Kid Buu with an Ultimate Blast

Unlockable Characters

Unlockable	How to Unlock
100% Full Power Frieza	Super Transformation + Final Form Frieza
Android 13	Computer + Hatred
Android 13 Fusion	Android 13 + Parts of 14 and 15
Baby Vegeta	Baby + Vegeta (second form)
Bardock	Defeat Lord Slug Saga
Bojack	Unsealed + Galactic Warrior
Broly	Son of Paragus + Hatred of Goku
Burter	Defeat Burter and Jeice with Goku
Cell	Defeat Cell with Piccolo and Android 17
Cell (2nd Form)	Defeat Cell (2nd Form) with Trunks and Vegeta
Cell (3rd Form or Perfect Form)	Defeat Cell (Perfect Form) with Gohan
Cell (Perfect or Perfect Cell)	Self Destruction + Cell Perfect Form
Cell Jr.	Defeat Cell Jrs. (5) with Gohan
Cooler	Frieza's Brother + Hatred of Goku
Cooler Final Form	Super Transformation + Cooler
Cui	Vegeta's Rival + Frieza's Soldier
Demon King Dabura	Defeat Dabura with Adult Gohan
Doboria	Defeat Doboria in Dragon Adventure
Dr. Gero	Defeat Dr. Gero with Krillin
Evil Buu	Evil Human Cannonball + Majin Buu
Full Power Bojak	Ultimate Transformation + Bojack
Garlic Jr.	Makyo Star + Dead Zone
General Tao	Bros. of Crane Hermit + Memorial Campaign
Giant Lord Slug	Slug + Giant Form
Ginyu	Defeat Ginyu (with Goku's body) and Jeice with Krillin, Vegeta, and Gohan
Gohan Super Buu	Gohan Absorbed + Evil Buu
Gotenks	Defeat Buu (Pure Evil) with Majin Buu and Hercule
Gotenks Super Buu	Gotenks Absorbed + Evil Buu
Grandpa Gohan	Master Roshi's Pupil + Fox Mask
Great Ape Baby	Super Baby 2 + Artificial Blutz Wave
Great Ape Bardock	Power Ball + Bardock
Great Ape Nappa	Power Ball + Nappa
Great Ape Raditz	Power Ball + Raditz
Great Ape Turles	Power Ball + Turles
Great Ape Vegeta	Power Ball + Vegeta (Scouter)
Great Saiyaman (Gohan)	Defeat Zangya and Bojack with Teen Gohan
Great Saiyaman 2 (Videl)	Defeat Broly with Goten and Adult Gohan

Dragon Ball Z: Budokai Tenkaichi 2 (continued)

Unlockable	How to Unlock
Guldo	Defeat Guldo with Vegeta, Krillin, and Gohan
Hercule	Defeat Perfect Cell with Super Trunks
Hirudegarn	Hirudegarn's Top Half + Hirudegarn's Lower Half
Janemba	Saike Demon + People's Bad Energy
Jeice	Defeat Jeice and Ginyu (with Goku's body) with Krillin, Vegeta, and Gohan
Kibitoshin	Kibito + Supreme Kai
Kid Buu	Defeat Kid Buu with Goku and Vegeta
Kid Goku	Defeat Grandpa Gohan
Legendary Super Saiyan Broly	Super Saiyan Broly + Breakthrough the Limit
Lord Slug	Namekian + Mutation
Majin Buu (Pure evil)	Human Gunman's Gun + Majin Buu
Majin Vegeta	Defeat Buu with Adult Gohan + Supreme Kai
Majin Vegeta	Defeat Majin Buu with Supreme Kai and Gohan
Majuub	Defeat Super Baby 2 with Pan and Uub
Master Roshi	Defeat Raditz with Goku
Master Roshi Full Power	Master Roshi + Seriousness
Mecha Frieza	Reconstructive Surgery + 100% Full Power Frieza
Metal Cooler	Big Gete Star + Cooler
Nappa	Defeat him in Dragon Adventure
Omega Shenron	Syn Shenron + Ultimate Dragon Ball
Pan	Defeat Hirudegarn with Tapion and Kid Trunks
Pikkon	Defeat Pikkon with Goku
Recoome	Defeat Recoome with Goku and Vegeta
Salza	Coolers Soldier + Armored Cavalry
Super Android 17	HFIL Fighter 17 + Android 17
Super Baby 1	Baby Vegeta + Lower Class Saiyan
Super Baby 2	Super Baby 1 + Power from Lower Class
Super Buu	Defeat Super Buu with Ultimate Gohan
Super Buu Gohan Absorbed	Absorb Gohan + Super Buu
Super Buu Gotenks Absorbed	Absorb Gotenks + Super Buu
Super Garlic Jr.	Garlic Jr. + Giant Form
Super Gogeta	Defeat Super Janemba with Pikkon + Buu
Super Gotenks	Defeat Pure Evil Buu with Buu + Hercule
Super Janemba	In item fusion combine Janemba + Ultimate Transformation
Super Perfect Cell	Suicide Bomb + Perfect Cell
Super Saiyan 1 Teen Gohan	Defeat Perfect Cell with Super Trunks
Super Saiyan 2 Goku	Defeat Majin Buu with Supreme Kai and Adult Gohan (Buu Saga)
Super Saiyan 2 Teen Gohan	Defeat Cell Jr. (5) with Super Saiyan 1 Gohan
Super Saiyan 2 Vegeta	Defeat Buu (Gotenks absorbed) with Goku
Super Saiyan 3 Goku	Defeat Majin Buu with Majin Vegeta
Super Saiyan 3 Gotenks	Defeat Super Buu with Gotenks

DS

GBA

PSP

PS2

PS3

Wii

Xbox

Xbox 360

Index

Dragon Ball Z: Budokai Tenkaichi 2 (continued)

Unlockable	How to Unlock
Super Saiyan 4 Gogeta	Defeat Omega Shenron with Super Saiyan 4 Goku and Vegeta
Super Saiyan 4 Goku	Defeat Super Baby with Majuub
Super Saiyan 4 Vegeta	Defeat Omega Shenron with Super Saiyan 4 Goku
Super Saiyan Broly	Broly + Super Saiyan
Super Saiyan Goku	Defeat Frieza Final Form with Piccolo, Krillin, and Kid Gohan (Frieza Saga)
Super Saiyan Goten	Defeat General Tao with Videl and Great Saiyaman
Super Saiyan Kid Trunks	Defeat General Tao with Videl and Great Saiyaman
Super Saiyan Trunks	Defeat Second Form Cell with Tien
Super Saiyan Trunks (Sword)	Defeat Androids 17 and 18 with Gohan
Super Saiyan Vegeta (Second Form)	Defeat Vegeta with Super Saiyan Teen Trunks (Buu Saga)
Super Trunks	Defeat Perfect Cell with Super Vegeta
Super Vegeta	Defeat Cell Form 2
Super Vegetto	Defeat Super Buu (Gohan Absorbed) with Goku and Vegeta
Supreme Kai	Defeat Android 18 with Hercule
Syn Shenron	Evil Dragon + Negative Energy
Tapion	Defeat Tapion with Trunks and Goten
Trunks	Unlock History of Trunks Saga
Turles	Lower-Class Saiyan Soldier + Fruit of the Gods
Ultimate Gohan (Mystic)	Defeat Buu with Piccolo or Super Saiyan 3 Gotenks
Uub	Defeat Hirudegarn with Super Saiyan 3 Goku
Vegeta (2nd Form)	Defeat Vegeta with Super Saiyan Teen Trunks (Buu Saga)
Vegeta (Post Namek)	Defeat Metal Cooler with Super Saiyan Goku (Return of Cooler Saga)
Vegetto	Defeat Super Buu + Gohan with Goku and Vegeta
Videl	Defeat Android 18 with Hercule (Buu Saga)
Videl	Defeat Bojack and Zangya with Piccolo + Gohan
Yajirobe	Defeat Great Ape Gohan with Piccolo
Zangya	The Fowers of Evil + Galactic Warrior
Zarbon Post-Transformation	Unsealed + Zarbon

Wii Exclusive Characters

In the European, Australian or Japanese versions of the game, you can unlock 6 extra secret characters by playing through Ultimate Battle Z mode.

Unlockable	How to Unlock
Appule	Complete Course 4
Cyborg Tao	Complete Course 6
Demon King Piccolo	Complete Course 8
Frieza Soldier	Complete Course 2
Pilaf Machine	Complete Course 10
Pilaf Machine Combined	Complete Course 10

Dragon Ball Z: Budokai Tenkaichi 2 (continued)

Easter Egg

Unlockable	How to Unlock
Bra in the Training Mode	Complete Basic Training

Dragon Blade: Wrath of Fire

Codes

At the Stage Select screen, Hold ⓩ and press ⊕ to start inputting the codes. To clear the codes, hold ⓩ and press ⊖. You will hear a confirmation when you do the combination to enter the codes, when you enter the codes, and when you clear them.

Unlockable	How to Unlock
Tail Power	Swing your Wii Remote Down, Up, Left, and Right
Double Fist Power	Swing your Nunchuk Right-> Swing your Wii Remote left-> Swing your Nunchuk right while swinging your Wii Remote left->Swing both Wii Remote and Nunchuk down

Unlockables

Unlockable	How to Unlock
Long Sword	Beat the game once

Dragon Spirit

Codes

Unlockable	How to Unlock
100 Continues	Press ⬆, ⬇, SELECT, ⬆, ②, ⬆, ①, ⬆, SELECT, ⬆, ①, ②, ① at the title screen
Arcade Mode Screen	Hold Select and press RUN 57 times to reset the game for a narrow screen
Sound Test	⬅, ⬇, ⬇, ⬆, SELECT, ⬆ at the title screen
Two Continues	Hold ① and press ② at the title screen

Dragon's Curse

Unlockable

Unlockable	How to Unlock
Full Life	After dying, use a potion while holding ②

Passwords

Password	Effect
3YHURYW7Y7LL8C	Start game at beginning with Max. Gold (983,040)/All Equipment/Full Health (8 Hearts)/Max. Stones (99)/All Items/Hawk-Man Status
3YHURYW7Y7LPBS	Start game at beginning with Max. Gold (983,040)/All Equipment/Full Health (8 Hearts)/Max. Stones (99)/All Items/Hu-Man Status
3YHURYW7Y7LRBW	Start game at beginning with Max. Gold (983,040)/All Equipment/Full Health (8 Hearts)/Max. Stones (99)/All Items/Lizard-Man Status
3YHURYW7Y7LM80	Start game at beginning with Max. Gold (983,040)/All Equipment/Full Health (8 Hearts)/Max. Stones (99)/All Items/Mouse-Man Status
3YHURYW7Y7LN84	Start game at beginning with Max. Gold (983,040)/All Equipment/Full Health (8 Hearts)/Max. Stones (99)/All Items/Piranha-Man Status

DS

GBA

PSP

PS2

PS3

Wii

Xbox

Xbox 360

Index

DS

GBA

PSP

PS2

PS3

Wii

Xbox

Xbox 360

Index

Dragon's Curse (continued)

Unlockable	How to Unlock
3YHURYW7Y7LK88	Start game at beginning with Max. Gold (983,040)/All Equipment/Full Health (8 Hearts)/Max. Stones (99)/All Items/Tiger-Man Status
W0CV5ATVKYR1SV	Start with all the necessary transformations and items to enter the final dungeon
MODE FOR 0000 000	Be Hu Man at Start (JP ONLY)
PLAY THE ONGA KUN	Disable door noise (JP ONLY)
NODEGOSO000000	Start as Be Hu Man
3WSURYXZY763TE	Start with advanced abilities and items
RMAYTJEOPHALUP	Take away the noises from doors
3ZHURYNZY726VH	Start as Hu-Man with 8 hearts, all equipment, all transformations unlocked, and only the final dungeon to beat

Driver: Parallel Lines

Password

Password	Effect
steelman	Invincibility

Collecting Stars

Collect the scattered golden stars throughout the map to unlock the following rewards. Note: Everything resets once you get to the 2006 era, and collecting another 50 Stars will unlock the same attributes. (There are 100 total in the game.)

Unlockable	How to Unlock
Double Ammunition Capacity	Collect 30 Stars
Double Car Durability	Collect 40 Stars
Free Vehicle Upgrades	Collect 50 Stars
Health Increase	Collect 10 Stars
Nitrous Increase	Collect 20 Stars

Unlockable Cars

Unlockable	How to Unlock
Andec Racer	Win the Jersey Racetrack race in 1978 on Hard
Bonsai Racer	Win the La Guardia race in 1978 on Medium
Brooklyn Racer	Win the Jersey Racetrack race in 1978 on Medium
Hot Rod	Win the Driver GP Long Island Race in 2006
Raven Racer	Win the Driver GP Long Island Race in 1978
San Marino Racer	Win the Hunts Points race in 1978 on Hard

Unlockables

Unlockable	How to Unlock
Far Out Mode	Reach 900 miles
Night Night Mode	Reach 700 miles
Play as a Pedestrian/Policeman	Reach 666 miles + melee attack the person you want to play as
Shortest Day Mode	Reach 800 miles

Drop Off

Unlockables

Unlockable	How to Unlock
Level Select	Press SELECT 16 times then press RUN
Sound Mode	Hold SELECT+①
Sound Test	Hold ② and press SELECT
Unlimited Continues	RUN+①, RUN+②

Dungeon Explorer

Passwords

Password	Effect
CHECK NAMEA	Change names
ADGDP-CJLPG	Final Dungeon is open
DEBDE DEBDA then press RUN+①	Invincibility
JBBNJ HDCOG	Play as Princess Aki
IMGAJ MDPAI	Play as the Hermit
HOMING AAAA	Precision guided weapons (smart weapons)

Level Select

Enable the "Invincibility" code. Enter one of the following 15 bushes in front of Axis castle to jump to the corresponding location. (Bush 1 is on the left end, bush 15 is on the right end.)

Bush	Location
1	Natas
2	Balamous Tower
3	Rotterroad (path to Judas)
4	Mistose Dungeon
5	Ratonix Dungeon
6	Reraport Maze
7	Rally Maze
8	Bullbeast
9	Melba Village
10	After Gutworm
11	Nostalgia Dungeon
12	Water Castle
13	Road to Cherry Tower
14	Stonefield
15	Karma Castle

Unlockables

Unlockable	How to Unlock
Secret Ending	Input the Invincibility code so you can pass through objects. When you take the ORA stone back to the King and he leaves, pass through the blockade to his throne, which initiates the secret ending.
Use the Harmit (Hermit) the hard way `	To use the Harmit (*sic*), level a Bard until you have at least 50 HP. Go into the second house to the west of Axis Castle.

Dynamite Headdy

Unlockables

Unlockable	How to Unlock
Head Animations	At the title screen select "Options" and press: ©, Ⓐ, ✛, ✛, Ⓑ. You hear "nice" when you've entered the code correctly. Then press START to view the head animations.
Stage Select	When the title screen appears, press START once. Leaving the cursor at Start Game, enter the code: ©, Ⓐ, ✛, ✛, Ⓑ. You hear a sound. Press START and you'll access the Stage Select. Choose your level and stage, then press START to play! (Note: This trick was done on an early version of the game. It may or may not work on later versions.)
Hard Mode (1-hit Death Mode)	At the title screen, press START once, then leave the cursor on "Start Game." Just like the Stage Select code, press ©, Ⓐ, ✛, ✛, Ⓑ. You hear Headdy say "Nice" when you've entered the code correctly. Then press and hold START. Continue holding START until you see the "Opening Demo" scene appear. Now release START and continue as normal. Be warned: 1 hit is all it takes to kill you now.
Secret Final Scene	After the end credits have finished rolling, you are prompted to enter a 4-digit secret code on a keypad. The code is different each time the game is played. Complete the basketball minigame four times while going through the game to determine your game's secret code.

Ecco the Dolphin

Unlockables

Unlockable	How to Unlock
Enable the Super Cheat Menu	Begin the game and move Ecco left and right. Press START to pause the game while Ecco is turning. You have to pause it when Ecco is directly facing you. When you do that, press ✛, Ⓑ, ©, Ⓑ, ©, ✛, ©, ✛. If you did it right, a Cheat menu appears that has options such as stage select, message test, sound test, and more.
Invincibility	Input a valid password, then press START, and wait for the screen that shows the name of the level you're currently in with your password. Next, hold Ⓐ and START. Keep hold of Ⓐ and START until Ecco appears on the screen. Now press START to unpause and you will be invincible.

Passwords

Level	Password		Level	Password
Final Level	KNLMLMLC		The Marble Sea	XAKUQQLS
The Undercaves	UYNAINCC		The Library	FDGXQQLC
The Undercaves 2	DQDIACCI		Deep City	ZUVPQQLU
The Vents	FKWLACCA		City of Forever	AABBRQLU
The Lagoon	NDRBRIKR		Jurassic Beach	PLABUNLI
Ridge Water	HYAUGFLV		Pteranodon Pond	FQREUNLI
Open Ocean	FNCQWBMT		Origin Beach	QXKIUNLX
The Ice Zone	DWFFZBMV		Trilobite Circle	OBEMUNLX
Hard Water Zone	QGDJRQLA		Dark Water	JNXPUNLA
Cold Water Zone	MCLFRQLW		Deep Water 2	WSGAKNLC
The Island Zone	UWXIOQLK		City of Forever 2	ZBPIGPLD
Deep Water Zone	EILQOQLC		The Tube	KUVEKMLK
			The Machine	SDDBKMLG

Ecco: The Tides of Time

Unlockables

Unlockable	How to Unlock
Debug Menu	Pause while Ecco is facing you. Once Ecco is facing you, press Ⓐ, Ⓑ, Ⓒ, Ⓑ, Ⓒ, Ⓐ, Ⓒ, Ⓐ, Ⓑ. If you entered the code correctly, a menu will pop up with all sorts of options such as a sound test, level select, tempo, etc. This code can be entered as many times as you'd like, as long as the game is paused while Ecco is facing you'd.
Hard Mode	In the starting area, break the two shells above you, and then swim through the tunnel to start the game in Hard mode.

Passwords

Level	Password	Level	Password
Crystal Springs	UEPMCVEB	Gateway	KDCGTAHB
Fault Zone	OZUNSKZA	Big Water	QQCQRDRA
Two Tides	KDKINTYA	Deep Ridge	UXQWJIZD
Skyway	SZXHCLDB	Hungry Ones	WBQHMIUE
Sky Tides	OZWIDLDB	Secret Cave	CHGTEYZE
Tube of Medusa	QSJRYHZA	Gravitorbox	UIXBGWXE
Skylands	MULXRXEB	Globe Holder	SBFPWWJE
Fin to Feather	YCPAWEXA	Dark Sea	MXURVMLA
Eagle's Bay	YCJPDNDB	Vortex Queen	OKIMTBPA
Asterite's Cave	AOJRDZWA	Home Bay	CSNCMRUA
Four Islands	UOYURFDB	Epilogue	CEWSXKPA
Sea of Darkness	UQZWIIAB	Fish City	SGTDYSPA
Vents of Medusa	MMVSOPBB	City of Forever	WSSXZKVA

Passwords for Hard Mode

* = New level found only in Hard mode

Level	Password	Moray Abyss	YCFSBRAB
Crystal Springs	WPHSAAFB	The Eye	AGNEXBTE
Fault Zone	CRNPTFZA	Big Water	YCBXONIA
Two Tides	QUKGZZYA	Deep Ridge	UPODMUQD
Skyway	MCMBPJDB	The Hungry Ones	YOHVUVLE
Sky Tides	OZMRKIDB	Secret Cave	SPKHKISE
Tube of Medusa	ODFADPYA	Lunar Bay	WTHXKISE
Aqua Tubeway*	KNHRKJYA	Black Clouds	USKIKDOE
Skylands	WXRDJYEB	GraviatorBox	WNQWZMME
Fin to Feather	UQTFBRXA	Globe Holder	MIPGDOME
Eagle's Bay	QSNVMMDB	New Machine*	GOSTCXJA
Asterite's Cave	EGAQRVXA	Vortex Queen	OOSFBXAA
Maze of Stone*	EUTQQQWA	Home Bay	QNSGAPGA
Four Islands	CZVQNHCB	Epilogue	AXBGKHBA
Sea of Darkness	WFMYIDAB	Fish City	WKGETHCA
Vents of Medusa	SHWZZNBB	City of Forever	WQHFTZHA
Gateway	QKLLFPHB	"Secret" Password	AVQJTCBA

DS
GBA
PSP
PS2
PS3
Wii
Xbox
Xbox 360
Index

DS
GBA
PSP
PS2
PS3
Wii
Xbox
Xbox 360
Index

Ecco: The Tides of Time (continued)

Unlockable

Unlockable	How to Unlock
Unlimited Air and Health	Turn Ecco left or right and pause the game while Ecco is facing the screen. Press Ⓐ, Ⓐ, ⬇, Ⓐ, ©, Ⓐ, ⬇, Ⓐ, Ⓐ, ⬇, Ⓐ and then unpause. You will now never die from lack of air or injuries.

Elebits

Unlockable	Code
Alpha Wave Unit	Beat 15 Missions in Challenge mode
Aroma Unit	Earn the title "King of Surveillance" after beating the last boss
Berserk Elebits	Earn the title "King of Capture" after beating the last boss
Extreme Silence	Earn the title "King of Noise" after beating the last boss
High Power Mode	Beat the third boss, then watch the cutscene at the beginning of the next level
Limit Release (Strongest Level Capture Gun)	Beat 25 Challenge Missions
Main Unit Only	Beat 5 Challenge Missions
Permanent Homing Laser (Deactivates Vacuum Laser)	Beat 20 Challenge Missions
Permanent Vacuum Laser (Deactivates Homing Laser)	Get 25 S ranks in Normal Mission
Worn Capture Gun	Beat 10 Missions in Challenge mode

Escape from Bug Island

Unlockable

Unlockable	How to Unlock
Samurai Sword and Death Scythe in Inventory	If you clear the game with either an "A" or "S" ranking, the next time you start the game, both the Samurai Sword and Death Scythe will be in your inventory.

ESWAT: City Under Siege

Unlockables

Unlockable	How to Unlock
Level Select	Start a game, and the Hero and Mission screen appears. Now hold down Ⓐ+Ⓑ+© and press ⬇, ⬇, ⬇, ⬇. Select the level by pressing ⬇/⬇. Then during the ending sequence, press and hold Ⓐ+Ⓐ+©+⬇+⬇. Keep holding these and press START until the Sound Test screen appears.

Fantastic 4: Rise of the Silver Surfer

Unlockables

Unlockable	How to Unlock
1990's Fantastic 4	12 Tokens
2000's Fantastic 4	12 Tokens
Comic Covers 1	4 Tokens
Comic Covers 2	4 Tokens
Concept Art	4 Tokens
Ultimate Costumes	12 Tokens

Far Cry Vengeance

Password

Password	Effect
GiveMeTheMaps	Unlock All Maps

Fatal Fury

Unlockable

Unlockable	How to Unlock
Good Ending	Beat the game on Normal or Hard without using a continue

Final Fight

Unlockable

Unlockable	How to Unlock
Secret Option Menu	Hold ⬇, press START (on title screen)

Final Soldier

Level Select

Unlockable	How to Unlock
Level Select	Before the demo starts, press ⬆, ⬆, ①, ⬇, ⬇, ②, ⬅, ⬅, ➡, ➡

Flappy

Passwords

Press Select on the title screen and then enter one of the following passwords. Note: each password allows you to chose your starting side (that's how levels are called in this game) from five corresponding levels. Just press ⬅ or ➡ after you input a password.

Password	Effect	Password	Effect
4NADA	Side 001-005	7GB17	Side 101-105
MATUI	Side 006-010	NZ100	Side 106-110
0MORI	Side 011-015	HINAM	Side 111-115
OK8MA	Side 016-020	K0D00	Side 116-120
YO4DA	Side 021-025	ATTAK	Side 121-125
MA2N0	Side 026-030	NO130	Side 126-130
MORII	Side 031-035	PAPAT	Side 131-135
KA582	Side 036-040	MAMAA	Side 136-140
H8SHI	Side 041-045	110NN	Side 141-145
MEGU3	Side 046-050	LUCKY	Side 146-150
EAMRA	Side 051-055	B5BAY	Side 151-155
KITA9	Side 056-060	EBIRA	Side 156-160
SAPP6	Side 061-065	YA3ZW	Side 161-165
CHUO9	Side 066-070	YA379	Side 166-170
KITA1	Side 071-075	WOMAN	Side 171-175
ZAXES	Side 076-080	00ZAR	Side 176-180
VOLGD	Side 081-085	B0KUD	Side 181-185
08ATA	Side 086-090	X3Y48	Side 186-190
OIKA8	Side 091-095	LAST1	Side 191-195
MRSRM	Side 096-100	O4MA5	Side 196-200

Gain Ground

Level Select

Unlockable	How to Unlock
Level Select	On the Options screen press Ⓐ, ©, Ⓑ, ©

Galaga '90

Unlockables

Unlockable	How to Unlock
Galactic Bonus	Just stand still (don't move) and don't shoot in the bonus stage.
Red Capsule	Hold ✛ and press RUN at the title screen. The capsule on the ship will turn red instead of blue to confirm code entry. Shoot the last target on the first level to capture the red capsule and power-up to a triple ship.

Gate of Thunder

Unlockables

Unlockable	How to Unlock
Hidden Bomberman Game	Press ✛, ✛, ✛, ✛, ②. You'll hear a sound and in a moment you'll be at the Bomberman title screen.
Stage Select	At the title screen press: ①, ②, ②, ①, SELECT, ①, ②, ①, ②, SELECT, SELECT, RUN.

Genpei Toumaden

Unlockable

Unlockable	How to Unlock
Options Menu	At the title screen, press ✛, ✛, ✛, ✛, ①, ②

Ghouls 'n Ghosts

Unlockables

Unlockable	How to Unlock
Japanese Mode	Enter the Options menu. Choose "26" for the music and "56" for sound selections, then hold ✛+ Ⓐ+Ⓑ+©+START.
Slow-Mo	At the title screen, press ✛, Ⓐ, ✛, Ⓐ, ✛, Ⓐ, ✛, Ⓐ. Begin the game, press START to pause, and hold Ⓑ and unpause.

Level Select

Press ✛, ✛, ✛, ✛ repeatedly at the title screen. You'll hear a harp if you did it right. Enter one of the following controller actions to select the corresponding level.

Effect	Code
The Execution Place	Press START
The Floating Island	Press Ⓐ, START
The Village of Decay	Press ✛, START
Town of Fire	Press ✛+Ⓐ, START
Baron Rankle's Tower	Press ✛, START
Horrible Faced Mountain	Press ✛+Ⓐ, START
The Crystal Forest	Press ✛, START
The Ice Slopes	Press ✛+Ⓐ, START
Beginning of Castle	Press ✛, START
Middle of Castle	Press ✛+Ⓐ, START
Loki	Press ✛, START

DS · GBA · PSP · PS2 · PS3 · Wii · Xbox · Xbox 360 · Index

Debug Mode

While "Press Start Button" is flashing at the title screen, input Ⓐ, Ⓐ, Ⓐ, Ⓐ, ⬇, ⬇, ⬇, ⬇ and you hear a chime. Start the game and you are in debug mode. Three functions can be accessed from the Pause menu now.

Code	Effect
Tap ⬇ During Pause	Frame Advance
Pause, Ⓐ, Pause	Invincibility Toggle (falling is still fatal)
Hold Ⓑ During Pause	Slow Motion

The Godfather: Blackhand Edition

Enter these codes while the game is paused. For the film clips, enter that clip in the Film Archives screen.

Unlockable	Code
$5,000	⊖, ②, ⊖, ⊖, ②, ⬇
Full Ammo	②, ⬇, ②, ⬇, ⊖, ⬇
Full Health	⬇, ⊖, ⬇, ②, ⬇, ⬇
Unlock Film Clips	②, ⊖, ②, ⊖, ⊖, ⬇

> **NOTE**
>
> *These codes may only be entered roughly every five minutes. If you really need the health or ammo before five minutes, pause and wait a few minutes, then enter the game.*

Golden Axe

Unlockables

Unlockable	How to Unlock
9 Continues	Hold ⬇+③+Ⓒ. Release and press START.
Level Select	Select Arcade mode. Hold ⬇+Ⓑ and press START at the Character Selection screen. A number that corresponds to the starting level appears in the screen's upper left. Use the D-pad to change it to the level you want.

Golden Axe II

Unlockables

Unlockable	How to Unlock
Level Select	While the opening screen scrolls, simultaneously hold down Ⓐ+Ⓑ+Ⓒ+START. Still holding Ⓐ, release Ⓑ+Ⓒ and press them again. This brings you to the Options screen. Still holding Ⓐ, let go of the other two, pick "exit," and press Ⓑ+Ⓒ once more. You'll be back at the main menu. Still holding Ⓐ, release Ⓑ+Ⓒ and hit them again to choose the number of players. Keep all the buttons down and press START. Release only START, select your character, then still holding down Ⓐ+Ⓑ+Ⓒ, press ⬇ and hit START. You can now select the level you want to play.
Level Select and 8 Credits (ultimate procedure)	With the cursor go to "Options" sign. Now press and hold Ⓐ+Ⓑ+Ⓒ. In the Options screen, release only Ⓑ+Ⓒ. Now configure the game if you want. Use Ⓑ to confirm successive selections, until the warrior selection. For the 8 credits, the cheat is identical, but release only Ⓐ and use START to confirm successive selections.

DS
GBA
PSP
PS2
PS3
Wii
Xbox
Xbox 360
Index

DS

GBA

PSP

PS2

PS3

Wii

Xbox

Xbox 360

Index

Gottlieb Pinball Classics

Passwords

Password	Effect
NYC	Unlock Central Park Table
LIS	Unlock Free Play in Black Hole table
PHF	Unlock Free Play in Goin' Nuts table
HOT	Unlock Free Play in Love Meter
HEF	Unlock Free Play in Playboy table
PBA	Unlock Free Play in Strikes 'N Spares table
PGA	Unlock Free Play in Tee'd Off table
BIG	Unlock Free Play in Xoltan

Unlockables

Unlockable	How to Unlock
Goin Nuts: Free Play Mode	Complete the table goal for El Dorado
Teed Off: Free Play Mode	Complete the table goal for Big Shot

Gradius

Unlockables

Unlockable	How to Unlock
10,000 Bonus Points	Get 6 power-ups so that the ? box is selected, then, when the thousands digit of your score is a 5, get a 7th power-up
Continue	At the Game Over Screen, press ⬆, ⬆, Ⓑ, Ⓐ, Ⓑ, Ⓐ, Ⓑ, Ⓐ, START (once per game)
Full Option Command	Press START during the game, then press ⬆, ⬆, ⬇, ⬇, ⬅, ➡, ⬅, ➡, Ⓑ, Ⓐ, START.
Warp to Level 3 (after defeating Core Fighter)	In level 1, when the thousands digit of your score is even, destroy 4 hatches
Warp to Level 4	Destroy Xaerous Core at end of level 2 within 2 seconds of its core turning blue
Warp to Level 5 (after beating level)	Destroy 10 stone heads in level 3

Gradius II

Unlockables

Unlockable	How to Unlock
30 Lives	At the title screen, press ⬆, ⬆, ⬆, ⬆, ⬆, ⬇, ⬇, ⬇, Ⓑ, Ⓐ
Max Out Abilities	During game, press ⬆, ⬆, ⬆, ⬆, ⬆, ⬇, ⬇, ⬇, Ⓑ, Ⓐ (once per level)
Sound Test Menu	Hold Ⓐ+Ⓑ and turn on. When the screen comes up, press START, hold Ⓐ+Ⓑ until title screen, then press START again.

Gradius III

Unlockables

Unlockable	How to Unlock
30 Extra Ships	At the title screen, hold ⬅Ⓒ and press Ⓧ, Ⓧ, Ⓧ, START
Arcade Mode	In the Options menu, highlight the Game Level, and rapidly tap Ⓐ until the level turns into ARCADE
Extra Credits	At the title screen, press ⬇ as many times as you can and then press START before the screen fades out

Gradius III (continued)

Unlockable	How to Unlock
Easy Final Boss	The final boss, Bacterion, will die whether or not you attack him. Just dodge his blasts, and in 15 or so seconds, he will spontaneously die. Even cheaper, park your ship in the screen's bottom center, and you can't be hit!
Extended Demo Mode	Continue to hold Ⓐ through the initial demo, and you'll see the entire first stage including the boss.
Full Power-Up	Pause the game and press ↑, ↑, ↓, ↓, ◁, ▷, ◁, ▷, Ⓑ, Ⓐ
Full Power-Up (without using the code)	Choose "speed down" for the "!" option in the Weapon Select screen. If you can get enough power-ups to highlight the last weapon, which will not be visible, and use it without powering up on speed up, you get all four options, missiles, and the shield. But if you have the laser already, it will be taken away.
Random Weapon Select	At the Weapon Select screen, press ▷ to enter Edit mode, then press ↓, Ⓑ, ↓, ↓, Ⓑ, Ⓑ, ↓, Ⓑ
Spread the Options	Activate the R-Option and collect enough power-ups that the option selection is highlighted. Now press and hold Ⓐ.
Suicide	Pause the game and press ↑, ↑, ↓, ↓, ◁, ▷, ◁, ▷, Ⓑ, Ⓐ, START

Bonus Stages

When you clear a bonus stage, you end up in the next level. That's right, you don't have to fight the boss of the level you were in previously. However, if you get killed in the bonus stage, you go back to the regular level, and cannot reenter the bonus stage.

Stage	How to Unlock
Stage 2	When you see a hole in the wall at the bottom of the screen, fly down there. Prerequisite: None.
Stage 3	When you reach the lower level, a platform in the ceiling drops down. Fly just below the part where the platform was. Prerequisite: Destroy all of the ground targets in the stage up to that point.
Stage 4	In the last set of Moai heads (they look like Easter Island heads), one that's lying down lifts up. Fly behind it. Prerequisite: Nothing must be highlighted on your power-up bar.
Stage 5	Fly just below the ceiling before the narrow corridor. Prerequisite: The hundreds digit of your score reads 5, 7, or 3.
Stage 7	Just after the long downward slope in the second half of the level, stay close to the ground and fly into the wall formation shaped like this: ..../ ....\ _____*/ (Key: dots are empty space, lines are walls, the asterisk is where your ship should be.) Prerequisite: Unknown.

The Grim Adventures of Billy and Mandy

View Concept Art Sketch

Enter this code at the main menu screen.

Unlockable	How to Unlock
Concept Art Sketch	Hold ①, press ⬦, ⬦, ⬦, ⬦, ⬦, ⬦, ⬦, ⬦, and release ①

The Grim Adventures of Billy and Mandy (continued)

Unlockables

Unlockable	How to Unlock
Extra Costume	Choose the character that you wish to have the extra costume and use him/her to clear Story mode
Unlock Boogey	In Mission mode, finish Mission 9 in Tier 4
Unlock Chicken	Finish Story mode with all characters on any difficulty with 10 hours of gameplay
Unlock Clown	Beat Story mode once with every character and fight a total of 100 Vs. mode matches
Unlock Dracula	In Mission mode finish Mission 5 in Tier 3
Unlock Eris	Finish Story mode once with either Billy, Mandy, Grim, or Irwin
Unlock Fred Fredburger	Finish Story mode once with either Billy, Mandy, Grim, or Irwin
Unlock General Skarr	In Mission mode finish Mission 6 in Tier 4
Unlock Hoss Delgado	Finish Mission 9 in Tier 1 in Mission mode
Unlock Jack O'Lantern	In Mission mode finish Mission 9 in Tier 2
Unlock Lord Pain	Finish Mission 9 in Tier 5
Unlock Mogar	Finish Story mode once with either Billy, Mandy, Grim, or Irwin
Unlock Nergal	Finish Story mode once with either Billy, Mandy, Grim, or Irwin
Unlock Nergal Jr.	In Mission mode finish Mission 9 in Tier 3
Unlock Nerglings	Finish Story mode with all characters on any difficulty
Unlock Pumpkin	Beat Story mode once with every character and accumulate a total of 100,000 damage in Vs. mode
Unlock Vikings	Finish Story mode with all characters and destroy every letter in the credits sequence

GT Pro Series

Unlockables

Unlockable	How to Unlock
Brake Street	Win Championship Race (Beginner)
Filter Grade-A	Win Enjoy Cup (Beginner)
Headlight Blue	Win 3 Door Cup (Beginner)
Highspeed Class	Win all cups in Intermediate Class
Intermediate Class	Win all cups in Beginner's Class
Mazda RX-7 Tune (FD3S)	Get at least a Great!, 20+ for max combo in Heights Mountain
Mazda RX-8	Win Championship Race (Beginner)
Nissan 180SX S13	Win Enjoy Cup (Beginner)
Nissan Silvia S14 Tune	Complete the first race in drift mode
Nissan Silvia Tune (S15)	Get at least a Good!, 15+ for max combo in Downtown Street
Professional Class	Win all cups in Highspeed Class
Toyota Celica LB TA27	Win 3 Door Cup (Beginner)

DS
GBA
PSP
PS2
PS3
Wii
Xbox
Xbox 360
Index

Gunstar Heroes

Unlockables

Unlockable	How to Unlock
Hidden Special Move	With either Gunstar Red or Gunstar Blue motion: ⬇, ⬇➡, ➡, ➡⬇, ⬇+shot button to execute a powerful standing slide.
Make the Logo Rotate	Hold ⬇ on controller 1 before the Gunstar Heroes logo appears on the screen in order to rotate it.
Timeron's Secret	During the second Timeron encounter (which is in the Space Battle stage) a timer begins ticking from 00'00"00. As the timer keeps going, the Timeron's attacks change, and every 20 minutes or so, a circular drone appears, accompanied by Smash Daisaku's laughter. Avoid this drone for about 2 minutes until it self-destructs, because a single hit will reduce your health to zero. At about 50'00"00 or so, large blue balls appear. These rebound once against the screen, and do 11 points of damage instead of the normal 10 points from the smaller ones. Once the timer gets up to 99'50"00 or so, don't destroy the Timeron yet. Instead, wait out the remaining 10 seconds while avoiding the Timeron's attacks, but don't stay too close to the Timeron, or you'll get killed by the drone. Once the timer reaches 00'00"00 again, you'll hear that nasty laughter again, but this time, "GIVE UP!!" appears in the middle of the screen, and the Timeron self-destructs, accompanied by the message, "YOU OPENED THE - SATORI MIND -." A bit more of that nasty laughter accompanies the next message, "REPROGRAMMED BY NAMI - 1993." Now, instead of getting a Timer Bonus as you usually would, a Soul Bonus of exactly 930,410 points is added to your score.

Happy Feet

Unlockables

Unlockable	How to Unlock
"All Together Now"	33 Gold Medals
"Amigo Racing"	15 Gold Medals
"Boogie Wonderland"	21 Gold Medals
"Driving Gloria Away"	26 Gold Medals
"Mumble the Outsider"	06 Gold Medals
"Out of the Egg"	01 Gold Medal
"Somebody to Love"	12 Gold Medals
"The Zoo"	31 Gold Medals

Heatseeker

Unlockables

Unlockable	How to Unlock
The Big One (SR-71 Blackbird's fourth Weapon Pack)	Successfully complete the Ace bonus objective
Top Secret plane (SR-71 Blackbird)	Successfully complete the Pilot bonus objective

DS
GBA
PSP
PS2
PS3
Wii
Xbox
Xbox 360
Index

DS

GBA

PSP

PS2

PS3

Wii

Xbox

Xbox 360

Index

Ice Age 2: The Meltdown

Codes

Pause the game and press the following codes.

Unlockable	How to Unlock
Unlimited Health	⬆, ⬆, ⬆, ⬆, ⬆, ⬆, ⬆, ⬆

Image Fight

Unlockables

Unlockable	How to Unlock
Arcade Mode	Do a reset (START+SELECT), then immediately hold ①
Mr. Heli mode	Highlight song C in Sound Test mode and press ⬆, SELECT, ②+①, then press ① on Mr. Heli and then press RUN
Sound Test	Press SELECT on the title screen

J.J. and Jeff

Unlockables

Unlockable	How to Unlock
Continue	When the Game Over screen appears, hold ①+②, then press RUN
Extra Lives	Stand at least five blocks away from a lamppost, then jump while kicking and hit the post perfectly.
Hidden Level Warps	Locate the brick bridge on level 1-4B. Kick the right corner of the bridge and underneath. This allows gameplay to continue in fields 2, 3, or 4. Locate the area halfway through level 3-3B where two rats begin to follow your character. Jump on top of them to reach the two bricks, then jump up. Gameplay resumes at 6-4.

Kid Chameleon

Unlockables

Unlockable	How to Unlock
5,000 Bonus Points	Complete any level without collecting any special items, or complete a stage without being hurt by an enemy.
10,000 Bonus Points	Complete Blue Lake Woods in less than 20 seconds
Last Boss Warp	At the end of Blue Lake Woods there is a series of blocks just above the flag. Jump to the last one and then press down and right, jump and special together. You get warped to Plethora, the last level.

Legend of Kage

Unlockables

Unlockable	How to Unlock
1-Up	If you stay in the water of the moat and kill seven ninjas with your sword, a blue creature flies across the screen. Catch him for a 1-Up. This works in all of the moat scenes.

Lode Runner

Unlockables

Unlockable	How to Unlock
Game Speed	Press SELECT to view current level. Hold SELECT and press Ⓑ to decrease game speed, or Ⓐ to increase game speed.
Level Select	Press select to view current level. Press SELECT then press Ⓐ to increase a level and Ⓑ to drop one.

Madden NFL 07

To enter these codes, select My Madden, then select Madden Cards, and then select Madden Codes.

Unlockable	Code
#220 Super Bowl XLI (Gold)	RLA9R7
#221 Super Bowl XLII (Gold)	WRLUF8
#222 Super Bowl XLIII (Gold)	NIEV4A
#223 Super Bowl XLIV (Gold)	M5AB7L
#224 Aloha Stadium (Gold)	YI8P8U
#225 '58 Colts (Gold)	B57QLU
#226 '66 Packers (Gold)	1PL1FL
#227 '68 Jets (Gold)	MIE6WO
#228 '70 Browns (Gold)	CL2TOE
#229 '72 Dolphins (Gold)	NOEB7U
#230 '74 Steelers (Gold)	YOOFLA
#231 '76 Raiders (Gold)	MOA11I
#232 '77 Broncos (Gold)	C8UM7U
#233 '78 Dolphins (Gold)	VIU007
#234 '80 Raiders (Gold)	NLAPH3
#235 '81 Chargers (Gold)	COAGI4
#236 '82 Redskins (Gold)	WL8BRI
#238 '84 Dolphins (Gold)	M1AM1E
#240 '86 Giants (Gold)	ZI8S2L
#241 '88 49ers (Gold)	SP2A8H
1985 Bears Gold card	QOETO8
1990 Eagles Gold card	2L4TRO
1991 Lions Gold card	J1ETRI
1992 Cowboys Gold card	W9UVI9
1993 Bills Gold card	DLA3I7
1994 49ers Gold card	DR7EST
1996 Packers Gold card	F8LUST
1998 Broncos Gold card	FIES95
1999 Rams Gold card	S9OUSW
Lame Duck card	5LAWOO
Mistake Free card	XL7SP1
QB On Target card	WROA0R
Pump up the crowd for the 49ers	KL0CRL
Pump up the crowd for the Bears	B1OUPH
Pump up the crowd for the Bengals	DRL2SW
Pump up the crowd for the Bills	1PLUYO
Pump up the crowd for the Broncos	3ROUJO
Pump up the crowd for the Browns	T1UTOA
Pump up the crowd for the Buccaneers	S9EWRI
Pump up the crowd for the Cardinals	57IEPI
Pump up the crowd for the Chargers	F7UHL8
Pump up the crowd for the Chiefs	PRI5SL

Madden NFL 07 (continued)

Unlockable	Code
Pump up the crowd for the Colts	1R5AMI
Pump up the crowd for the Cowboys	Z2ACHL
Pump up the crowd for the Dolphins	C5AHLE
Pump up the crowd for the Eagles	PO7DRO
Pump up the crowd for the Falcons	37USPO
Pump up the crowd for the Giants	C4USPI
Pump up the crowd for the Jaguars	MIEH7E
Pump up the crowd for the Jets	C0LUXI
Pump up the crowd for the Lions	3LABLU
Pump up the crowd for the Packers	4HO7VO
Pump up the crowd for the Panthers	F2IASP

Marvel Ultimate Alliance

Enter these codes while playing.

Unlockable	Code
God Mode	⇧, ⇧, ⇧, ⇧, ⇧, ⇧, ⇧, ⇧, ⊕
Fill Momentum	⇦, ⇦, ⇦, ⇦, ⇦, ⇦, ⇦, ⇦, ⊕
Super Speed	⇧, ⇦, ⇧, ⇦, ⇧, ⇦, ⊕
Touch of Death	⇦, ⇦, ⇧, ⇧, ⇦, ⇧, ⊕

Enter these codes in the Team menu.

Unlockable	Code
100k	⇧, ⇧, ⇧, ⇦, ⇦, ⇦, ⊕
Level 99	⇧, ⇦, ⇧, ⇦, ⇦, ⇧, ⇦, ⇧, ⊕

Enter these codes in the Team Selection screen.

Unlockable	Code
All Characters	⇧, ⇧, ⇦, ⇧, ⇦, ⇧, ⇦, ⊕
Unlock All Costumes	⇧, ⇧, ⇧, ⇧, ⇦, ⇦, ⇦, ⇦, ⇦, ⇦, ⊕
Unlock All Powers	⇦, ⇦, ⇦, ⇦, ⇦, ⇧, ⇧, ⇧, ⇦, ⇦, ⊕
Unlock Daredevil	⇦, ⇧, ⇦, ⇦, ⇧, ⇦, ⇧, ⇧, ⊕
Unlock Silver Surfer	⇧, ⇦, ⇦, ⇧, ⇦, ⇧, ⇦, ⇦, ⊕

Enter these codes in the Review menu.

Unlockable	Code
All Comics	⇦, ⇦, ⇦, ⇧, ⇧, ⇦, ⇦, ⊕
All Concept Art	⇧, ⇧, ⇧, ⇦, ⇦, ⇦, ⇦, ⊕
All Wallpapers	⇧, ⇧, ⇦, Z, ⇧, ⇦, ⇧, ⊕
All Cinematics	⇧, ⇦, ⇧, ⇦, ⇦, ⇦, ⇧, ⊕

Medal of Honor: Vanguard

Unlockable	Code
Cheat Menu (required for entering following codes)	In the pause menu, enter ⇧, ⇦, ⇧, ⇦
Extra Armor	⇦, ⇦, ⇧, ⇧, ⇧, ⇦
Invisibility	⇧, ⇧, ⇦, ⇧, ⇧, ⇧

Mega Man

Unlockables

Unlockable	How to Unlock
Select Trick	When using a weapon that goes through an enemy, press the SELECT button (this pauses the game without bringing up the weapon menu) when the weapon is making contact with the enemy. While the game is paused this way the enemy continues to flash. When the flashing has stopped, press the SELECT button again to un-pause the game and the weapon hits the enemy again, causing more damage. You can do this trick repeatedly with many of the bosses, making them very easy to beat.

Mercury Meltdown Revolution

Unlockables

Unlockable	How to Unlock
30mph Speed Limit Sign Skin	Collect the bonus points in each stage
Basketball Skin	Collect the bonus points in each stage
Black and White Cat's Face	Collect the bonus points in each stage
Brown and White Dog's Face	Collect the bonus points in each stage
Football Skin	Collect the bonus points in each stage
Smiley Face Skin	Collect the bonus points in each stage
Snooker Ball Skin	Collect the bonus points in each stage
Wheel Skin	Collect the bonus points in each stage

Metal Marines

Codes

Code	Effect	Code	Effect
Enter CSDV as a password	Start with more Money and Energy for each level	TRNS	Level 11
		RNSN	Level 12
		ZDCP	Level 13
HBBT	Level 02	FKDV	Level 14
PCRC	Level 03	YSHM	Level 15
NWTN	Level 04	CLPD	Level 16
LSMD	Level 05	LNVV	Level 17
CLST	Level 06	JFMR	Level 18
JPTR	Level 07	JCRY	Level 19
NBLR	Level 08	KNLB	Level 20
PRSC	Level 09		
PHTN	Level 10		

Metal Slug Anthology

Unlockables

Unlockable	How to Unlock
Special Music	Complete Metal Slug 1-5 and X on Hard with limited continues and also complete Metal Slug 6 with limited continues
Tonko Art Gallery	Complete Metal Slug 1-5 and X on Easy with limited continues and also complete Metal Slug 6 with limited continues

DS

GBA

PSP

PS2

PS3

Wii

Xbox

Xbox 360

Index

DS

GBA

PSP

PS2

PS3

Wii

Xbox

Xbox 360

Index

Mighty Bomb Jack

Unlockables

Unlockable	How to Unlock
Skip Levels	To perform this trick, get to the first treasure room in Round 1. Grab any of the bombs. Immediately you see another bomb light up with a sparkle. Grab the other bombs in the treasure room, making sure to grab the lit bomb last. You're transported to the Round 2 treasure room! Use this trick to skip as many of the normal stages as you wish. However, if you lose a life in one of the treasure rooms, you're transported back to the last level you were on before entering a treasure room.

Military Madness

Unlockables

Unlockable	How to Unlock
Alternate Colors	Power on the system, and hold SELECT to reset. While continuing to hold SELECT, choose the 1-player continue option and enter a map name.
Play as Axis	Select the new game or 1-player continue option on the title screen, then hold SELECT and press ①.
Switch Sides	Hold SELECT and press RUN before choosing the 1-player continue option.

Passwords

Password	Effect	Password	Effect
REVOLT	Level 01	IRAGAN	Level 18
ICARUS	Level 02	LIPTUS	Level 19
CYRANO	Level 03	INAKKA	Level 20
RAMSEY	Level 04	TETROS	Level 21
NEWTON	Level 05	ARBINE	Level 22
SENECA	Level 06	RECTOS	Level 23
SABINE	Level 07	YEANTA	Level 24
ARATUS	Level 08	MONOGA	Level 25
GALIOS	Level 09	ATTAYA	Level 26
DARWIN	Level 10	DESHTA	Level 27
PASCAL	Level 11	NEKOSE	Level 28
HALLEY	Level 12	ERATIN	Level 29
BORMAN	Level 13	SOLCIS	Level 30
APOLLO	Level 14	SAGINE	Level 31
KAISER	Level 15	WINNER	Level 32
NECTOR	Level 16	ONGAKU	Sound Test
MILTON	Level 17		

Milon's Secret Castle

Unlockables

Unlockable	How to Unlock
Continue Game	Hold down left and press START when you die after getting the first crystal

Monster 4X4: World Circuit

Unlockables

Unlockable	How to Unlock
Reverse Tracks	Get first place on a track to get the same track in reverse

Mortal Kombat: Armageddon

Krypt Kodes (Using a GameCube Controller)

Enter the following by choosing the "?" in the Krypt. Enter the Krypt and press L on the GameCube Controller 4 times and you'll see it in the bottom right corner.

Code	Effect
L, →, A, R, ↑, ↑	Unlock Alternate Costume: Drahmin
↓, ↑, R, L, Ⓨ, L	Unlock Alternate Costume: Frost
↓, L, ↑, L, L, →	Unlock Alternate Costume: Nitara
L, ←, ↑, Ⓨ, ↑, L	Unlock Alternate Costume: Shang Tsung
↑, Ⓨ, B, A, Ⓨ, Ⓩ	Unlock Arena: Falling Cliffs
↑, Ⓨ, R, ↑, A, A	Unlock Arena: General Reiko's Map Room
Ⓨ, L, ↑, B, Ⓨ, ↓	Unlock Arena: Krimson Forest
R, ←, ↑, ↓, L, B	Unlock Arena: Nethership Interior
R, L, B, A, ↑, ↑	Unlock Arena: Pyramid of Argus
←, ←, Ⓨ, ↑, Ⓩ, L	Unlock Arena: Shinnok's Spire
Ⓩ, B, ←, L, ←, Ⓨ	Unlock Character: Blaze
L, L, Ⓩ, ↓, ↓, B	Unlock Character: Daegon
↑, B, B, Ⓨ, Ⓨ, ↑	Unlock Character: Meat
L, ←, ↑, ↑, Ⓨ, ↓	Unlock Character: Taven
L, Ⓩ, L, L, R, B	Unlock Concept Art: Blaze
↑, A, ↑, ↓, L, A	Unlock Concept Art: Early Taven
↑, B, L, ↑, Ⓨ, L	Unlock Concept Art: Firewall Arena
R, →, ↑, R, Ⓩ, ↑	Unlock Concept Art: Mileena's Car Design
Ⓩ, ←, ←, A, ↓, Ⓨ	Unlock Concept Art: Pyramid Crack of Dawn
A, L, R, ↑, ↑, ↑	Unlock Concept Art: Pyramid of Argus
L, ←, ↑, Ⓨ, ↑, L	Unlock Concept Art: Scorpion Throw Sketch
R, L, ←, A, ↑, R	Unlock Concept Art: Sektor's 2 Handed Pulse Blade
Ⓨ, ↑, Ⓩ, ↓, Ⓨ, ←	Unlock Concept Art: Unused Trap in Konquest Mode
↑, ↑, ↓, ↑, L, A	Unlock Movie: Armageddon Promo
←, L, ↑, ↓, ↑, L	Unlock Movie: Cyrax Fatality Blooper
Ⓩ, ↑, ↑, L, R, ↑	Unlock Movie: Motor Gameplay
A, B, ←, Ⓩ, B, A	Unlock Tune: Armory
L, ←, Ⓨ, A, ↑, →	Unlock Tune: Lin Kuei Palace
↓, ←, ↑, L, ↑, L	Unlock Tune: Pyramid of Argus
↑, Ⓨ, L, R, R, A	Unlock Tune: Tekunin Warship

DS

GBA

PSP

PS2

PS3

Wii

Xbox

Xbox 360

Index

DS

GBA

PSP

PS2

PS3

Wii

Xbox

Xbox 360

Index

Mortal Kombat: Armageddon (continued)

Krypt Kodes (Using a Wii Remote)

Enter the following by choosing the "?" in the Krypt. Enter the Krypt and press ⬜ on the GameCube Controller 4 times and you'll see it in the bottom right corner.

Code	Effect
⬆, ➡, ⬆, Z, ◊, ◊	Unlock Alternate Costume: Drahmin
◊, Z, Z, ⬆, ⬆, ⬆	Unlock Alternate Costume: Frost
◊, ⬆, ◊, ⬆, ⬆, ➡	Unlock Alternate Costume: Nitara
⬆, ⬅, ◊, ⬆, ◊, ⬆	Unlock Alternate Costume: Shang Tsung
Z, ⬆, ⬆, ⬆, ⬆, ⬆	Unlock Arena: Falling Cliffs
Z, ⬆, Z, ◊, ⬆, ⬆	Unlock's Arena: General Reiko's Map Room
⬆, ⬆, ◊, ⬆, ⬆, ◊	Unlock Arena: Krimson Forest
Z, ⬅, ⬅, ◊, ◊, ⬆	Unlock Arena: Nethership Interior
Z, ⬆, ⬆, ⬆, Z, ◊	Unlock Arena: Pryamid of Argus
⬅, ⬅, ⬆, ◊, ⬆, ⬆	Unlock Arena: Shinnok's Spire
⬆, ⬆, ⬅, ◊, ⬅, ⬆	Unlock Character: Blaze
⬆, ⬆, ⬆, ◊, ◊, ⬆	Unlock Character: Daegon
◊, ⬆, ⬆, ⬆, ⬆, ◊	Unlock Character: Meat
⬆, ⬅, Z, ◊, ⬆, ◊	Unlock Character: Taven
⬆, ⬆, ⬆, ⬆, Z, ⬆	Unlock Concept Art: Blaze
◊, ⬆, Z, ◊, ⬆, ⬆	Unlock Concept Art: Early Taven
◊, ⬆, ⬆, Z, ⬆, ⬆	Unlock Concept Art: Firewall Arena
Z, ➡, ◊, Z, ⬆, ◊	Unlock Concept Art: Mileena's Car Design
⬆, ⬅, ⬅, ⬆, ◊, ⬆	Unlock Concept Art: Pyramid Crack of Dawn
⬆, ⬆, Z, Z, ◊, ◊	Unlock Concept Art: Pyramid of Argus
⬆, ⬅, ◊, ⬆, Z, ◊	Unlock Concept Art: Scorpion Throw Sketch
Z, ⬆, ⬅, ⬆, ◊, Z	Unlock Concept Art: Sektor's 2 Handed Pulse Blade
⬆, Z, ⬆, ◊, ⬆, ⬅	Unlock Concept Art: Unused Trap in Konquest Mode
◊, ◊, ◊, ◊, ⬆, ⬆	Unlock Movie: Armageddon Promo
➡, ⬆, Z, ◊, ◊, ⬆	Unlock Movie: Cyrax Fatality Blooper
⬆, ◊, Z, ⬆, Z, Z	Unlock Movie: Motor Gameplay
⬆, ⬆, ⬅, ⬆, ⬆, ⬆	Unlock Tune: Armory
⬆, ⬅, ⬆, Z, Z, ➡	Unlock Tune: Lin Kuei Palace
◊, ⬅, Z, ⬆, ◊, ⬆	Unlock Tune: Pyramid of Argus
◊, ⬆, ⬆, Z, Z, ⬆	Unlock Tune: Tekunin Warship

Alternate Costumes

Unlockable	How to Unlock
Ashrah's Alternate Costume	Defeat the Ice Beast you encounter in Arctika and open the chest that appears
Baraka's Alternate Costume	Kill all of the enemies in the final room of the Tekunin Warship and open the chest that appears
Bo'Rai Cho's Alternate Costume	Open the chest that appears after you defeat the Wraiths of Shinnok's Spire
Cyrax's Alternate Costume	Kill all of the enemies in the third room of the Tekunin Warship and open the chest that appears
Dairou's Alternate Costume	Open the chest at the end of the second ice hallway at the beginning of the Lin Kuei Temple Entrance
Darrius' Alternate Costume	In a chest behind a discolored wall at the beginning of the Lin Kuei Temple where you are attacked by Lin Kuei Archers
Drahmin's Alternate Costume	In the Netherrealm after you defeat Drahmin, shoot down the bat creature over the nearby cliff and open the chest that appears
Ermac's Alternate Costume	In a chest by the left wall in the room where you get attacked by the Red Commandos for the second time
Frost's Alternate Costume	Break all of the tombs lining the wall in the room where you meet Frost
Fujin's Alternate Costume	Defeat all of the Red Dragon Soldiers at the beginning of the Charred Mountain
Goro's Alternate Costume	In an invisible chest on the left side of the first area in Shao Khan's Fortress and directly to the right of a musical note
Havik's Alternate Costume	Defeat all of the demons in the second area of Shinnok's Spire
Hotaru's Alternate Costume	In a chest close to the wall in the second room of the Tekunin Warship
Hsu Hao's Alternate Costume	In a chest on the right walkway after you wake up on the Tekunin Warship
Jade's Alternate Costume	Defeat all of the Lin Kuei at the very beginning of the Lin Kuei Palace and open the chest that appears
Jarek's Alternate Costume	Open the right chest in the room where you fight with the Ice Scepter
Jax's Alternate Costume	Once you enter Arctika, turn around and go to the left to find an invisible chest
Johnny Cage's Alternate Costume	Defeat the Tengu Guards at the beginning of Arctika and open the chest that appears
Kai's Alternate Costume	In an invisible chest behind a breakable discolored wall to the right as you enter the third area of Lin Kuei Temple Entrance in Arctika

DS
GBA
PSP
PS2
PS3
Wii
Xbox
Xbox 360
Index

Mortal Kombat: Armageddon (continued)

Code	Effect
Kano's Alternate Costume	In an invisible chest to the left as you enter the last room of the Temple of Argus
Kenshi's Alternate Costume	Defeat all of the Tengu Ninjas with the given sword in Arctika
Kira's Alternate Costume	Step on the second Giant Spider in Botan Jungle and open the chest that appears
Kitana's Alternate Costume	Perform a Fatality on Wi Lae, leader of the Tengu Ninjas
Kobra's Alternate Costume	In an invisible chest behind the first monolith in the Botan Jungle
Kung Lao's Alternate Costume	Found in a chest to the right after you enter the Temple of Argus
Li Mei's Alternate Costume	In the second area of Shinnok's Spire, walk around the edge of the room until you find an invisible chest
Liu Kang's Alternate Costume	As you enter Shao Kahn's Fortress, turn around and run forward to find an invisible chest.
Mavado's Alternate Costume	Inside an invisible chest on the left part of the room where you do battle after you receive the Supermove: Time Stop
Mileena's Alternate Costume	After you defeat Mileena, hit the Ground Pound Switch in front of you and open the chest that appears
Motaro's Alternate Costume	After the third training obelisk, during the time you must gather crystals, go to the left side of this area and open the chest there
NightWolf's Alternate Costume	After you defeat the Giant Skulls in Edenia, travel up the path until all of the chests appear and open the first one on the right
Nitara's Alternate Costume	After you defeat the Undead Revenants for the first time in the Netherrealm, jump down the leftmost cliff instead of the right and open the nearby chest
Noob Saibot's Alternate Costume	Defeat all of the Shadow Ninjas the first time you encounter them in the Lin Kuei Palace and open the chest that appears
Quan Chi's Alternate Costume	Step on the rat in the tunnel after you travel through Door A1 in the Red Dragon Caverns and open the chest that appears
Raiden's Alternate Costume into the first room on the left	When or after fighting the Shao Khan Colossus, go
Rain's Alternate Costume	Open the chest at the end of the area in Arctika where you are attacked by Red Dragon Spies and before you meet Rain
Reiko's Alternate Costume	In a chest in Shao Khan's Fortress,; as you enter the first area with blades, travel down a hall to the left
Reptile's Alternate Costume	Defeat the Hybrid Dragons you encounter in the Red Dragon Caverns and open the chest
Sareena's Alternate Costume	Defeat Kai, Sareena, and Jataaka and open the chest that appears
Shang Tsung's Alternate Costume	At the beginning of Shao Khan's Fortress, hit the Ground Pound icon to the right and up the ramp
Shao Kahn's Alternate Costume	Open the chest that appears after you defeat Shao Khan's Statue

Mortal Kombat: Armageddon (continued)

Code	Effect
Shinnok's Alternate Costume	Once you get to the area in the Netherrealm with the falling rocks go to the leftmost side and open the chest
Shujinko's Alternate Costume	Hit the Ground Pound icon in one of the cells after you defeat The Executioner in Shao Khan's Dungeon
Sindel's Alternate Costume	Complete the third training obelisk
Smoke's Alternate Costume	Defeat Smoke and open the chest that appears
Sonya's Alternate Costume	In an invisible chest to the left of the gate in the area after you defeat Sonya
Stryker's Alternate Costume	Break the wall on the right of the hallway after the Shadow Stalkers, travel to the end of it, and open the chest in the left alcove
Sub-Zero's Alternate Costume	Open the chest to the right of the statue of your mother after your fight with Sub-Zero
Tanya's Alternate Costume	In Shao Khan's Dungeon, after you make it to the cell area, hit the Ground Pound icon and then go back to the third cell on the right
Taven's Alternate Costume	After you defeat the Giant Skulls in Edenia, travel up the path until all of the chests appear, and open the third one on the left

Characters

Unlockable	How to Unlock
Blaze	Obtain 50 relics in Konquest
Daegon	Obtain 30 relics in Konquest
Meat	Obtain 10 relics in Konquest
Taven	Finish the storyline in Konquest

Konquest Mode Unlockable

Unlockable	How to Unlock
+20,000 Koins	Obtain 20 relics in Konquest mode

Kreate-A-Kharacter Unlockables

The following parts for kreate-a-kharacter are unlocked in Konquest mode.

Unlockable	How to Unlock
Elder God Female Armor: Torso	Open the golden chest in the right path of the fork in the Red Dragon Caverns
Elder Gods Female Armor: Belt	Inside a golden chest in a locked gate in Arctika after the second obelisk that opens after you defeat the Tengu Ninjas
Elder Gods Female Armor: Boots	After the Shadow Stalkers, break the cracked wall to the left and travel down to the right alcove where you find the golden chest
Elder Gods Female Armor: Cape	Inside a golden chest in the area after you meet and defeat Sonya
Elder Gods Female Armor: Glove	Once you get to the flaming sword area of Shinnok's Spire, turn and run to your left and open the golden chest
Elder Gods Female Armor: Helmet	When or after fighting the Shao Khan Colossus, go into the second room on the right
Elder Gods Female Armor: Legs	Open the golden chest in the cave that gets opened after you defeat the undead of the Netherrealm after you get your gauntlets

DS

GBA

PSP

PS2

PS3

Wii

Xbox

Xbox 360

Index

DS

GBA

PSP

PS2

PS3

Wii

Xbox

Xbox 360

Index

Mortal Kombat: Armageddon (continued)

Unlockable	How to Unlock
Elder Gods Female Armor: Shoulders	In Shao Kahn's Dungeon, after you make it to the cell area, hit the Ground Pound icon and then go back to the first cell on the left
Elder Gods Male Armor: Belt	Inside of a golden chest to the right after you open the first door in the Tekunin Warship
Elder Gods Male Armor: Boots	After the Shadow Stalkers, break the second cracked wall on the right and travel down to the end and open the golden chest in the left alcove
Elder Gods Male Armor: Cape	When or after fighting the Shao Khan Colossus, go into the second room on the left
Elder Gods Male Armor: Glove	Inside of a golden chest after the second fallen log and to the right in Botan Jungle
Elder Gods Male Armor: Helmet	After you defeat the Giant Skulls in Edenia, travel up the path until you find a golden chest
Elder Gods Male Armor: Legs	In a golden chest in the left corner of the second area of Shinnok's Spire
Elder Gods Male Armor: Shoulders	Stand in the middle of the room after you free Shujinko, shoot a fireball at the nearby torch, and get the chest that appears
Elder Gods Male Armor: Torso	After you defeat the Tengu Leader, break open the discolored wall on the right in the blade trap area.

Soundtracks

All of the following soundtracks are unlocked in Konquest mode and found in the shape of a musical note.

Unlockable	How to Unlock
Arctika Tune	As you enter the second area of the Lin Kuei Temple Entrance, destroy the discolored wall on the right and open the chest
Bo'Rai Cho's Brewery Tune	Get the musical note after the bridge and in the cave to the right in Botan Jungle
Botan Jungle Track Tune	Get the musical note right before the second fallen log in Botan Jungle
Goro's Lair Fight Tune	In Shujinko's cell when you release him
Hell Fight Tune	In Shao Kahn's Dungeon, after you make it to the cell area, hit the Ground Pound icon and then go back to the second cell on the right
Konquest Final Battle Tune	In Shao Kahn's Fortress as you run up to the first area with the blades, travel to the right to find the musical note in the next room
Lin Kuei Palace Tune	Get the musical note in the Lin Kuei Palace directly to your left after you punch down the Ice Door
Lin Kuei Raceway Tune	Get the musical note near the entrance in the final area of Arctika after you defeat all of the Lin Kuei Warriors and Archers
Lumbermill Fight Tune	Get the musical note after the second crusher when you return to Arctika after the second obelisk
Meteor Storm Fight Tune	Get the musical note after you defeat the Undead Revenants for the first time in the Netherrealm, jump down the leftmost cliff instead of the right
Outworld Refinery Tune	Get the musical note behind you after you fight Drahmin in the Netherrealm

Mortal Kombat: Armageddon (continued)

Unlockable	How to Unlock
Outworld Spire Fight Tune	Get the musical note on the right side of the first room as you enter Shinnok's Spire
Pyramid of Argus Tune	After you defeat the Giant Skulls in Edenia, travel up the path and find the musical note to the right of a golden chest
Reptile's Lair Fight Tune	Get the musical note in the hallway right before the final room of the Red Dragon Caverns, behind a grouping of three blue barrels
Soul Chamber Fight Tune	Once you get to the flaming sword area of Shinnok's Spire, turn around and get the musical note
Subway Fight Tune	Get the musical note after you defeat Sonya Blade in A rctika
Tekunin Prison Fight Tune	In Shao Khan's Fortress, after you open the main door and enter the second area, go to the upper left side and get the musical note
Tekunin Warship Tune	Get the musical note in the area where you get attacked by Black Dragon Thug's in the Botan Jungle
The Lost Pyramid Tune	Behind an explosive barrel in the battle after you gain the Supermove: Time Stop
Wastelands Fight Tune	On the left of the elevator you get into at the end of Shao Khan's Dungeon

Unlockable Arenas

Unlockable	How to Unlock
Artika Arena	Beat all 7 trials in Artika Obelisk
Edenian Ruins	After you defeat the Giant Skulls in Edenia, travel up the path until all of the chests appear and open the second one on the left
Netherrealm Cliffs	Defeat Drahmin in Konquest mode
Pyramid of Argus Arena	Collect 40 Relics in Konquest mode
Scorpion's Lair	After you defeat the Giant Skulls in Edenia, travel up the path until all of the chests appear and open the third one on the right

Moto Roader

Unlockables

Unlockable	How to Unlock
Get $50,000	Hold SELECT and press ② on the Course Selection screen
Music Select	Hold SELECT and press ① or ② while the game is paused
See Winning Time	Hold SELECT and press ⬆ on the Course Selection screen
Special Course	Hold SELECT and press ⬆ on the Course Selection screen
Sound Test	Input MUSIC or ART88 as a player name

MySims

Unlock Special Outfits and Items

There is a hidden password system in MySims to unlock unique outfits and special furniture. To reach this password screen, do the following. While running around town, bring up the pause screen with the ⊖ button. Then input the following commands on the Wii Remote (not Nunchuk): ②, ①, ⬆, ⬆, ⬆, ⬆, ⬆, ⬆, ⬆, ⬆. A special keyboard to enter passwords now appears, allowing you to unlock clothes and furniture. The following passwords are case sensitive!

DS GBA PSP PS2 PS3 Wii Xbox Xbox 360 Index

DS

GBA

PSP

PS2

PS3

Wii

Xbox

Xbox 360

Index

MySims (continued)

Password	Effect
F3nevr0	Bunk bed (Furniture)
N10ng5g	Camouflage pants
Tglg0ca	Diamond vest (Outfit)
Gvsb3k1	Genie outfit
Ghtymba	Hourglass couch
I3hkdvs	Kimono dress (Outfit)
T7srhca	Modern couch
Ahvmrva	Racecar bed (Furniture)
Itha7da	Rickshaw bed
R705aan	White jacket

Unlockables

Once you reach a set level you'll receive a message telling you what new tool you've earned.

Unlockable	How to Unlock
Blow Torch	Have your town reach 4 stars
Crowbar	Have your town reach 1 star
Pickaxe	Have your town reach 3 stars
Saw	Have your town reach 2 stars
Town Monument Blueprint	Have a 5-star town

Unlockable Uber-Sims

After bringing your town's interest level to 100% in any of the six categories you receive a message telling you that a special guest will be waiting for you in the hotel. This Uber-Sim is waiting in the hotel the next day.

Unlockable	How to Unlock
Amazing Daryl	100% Fun Town
Chancellor Ikara	100% Tasty Town
Hopper	100% Cute Town
Mel	100% Spooky Town
Samurai Bob	100% Studious Town
Star	100% Geeky Town

Need for Speed Carbon

Unlockable	Code
Aston Martin DB9 (Exotic)	Defeat Wolf in Boss Battle mode
Dodge Charger RT Classic (Muscle)	Defeat the 21st Muscle Car Gang
Jaguar XK 2007 (Exotic)	Clear all three Turf War races
Mazda RX7 (Tuner)	Defeat Kenji in Boss Battle mode
Nissan 240SX (Tuner)	Clear all three Checkpoint challenges

Neutopia

Passwords

Password	Effect
5ltgaKyUFxsWssUkjzmVAkcQ	Begin game with 16 life bars
yP5ESDjsMwPB NDCYSzhXr%PP	End Level
KgKc%h5oFfep Qy1XwcjZXDVn	Level 4
rZtW68PjCG%L 1d9gSJ2uzn7r	Level 5
TQinHIUCDOQJ I$ZEhVQJNAwl	Super Password (5 medallions, 78 bombs)

Neutopia II

Everything Collected

Password	Effect
At the Password screen, enter the following passwords: IbnoBJt$ AyUkJ7Wa XACpGDjm q1j1uR1Q M8ozNOQa cPUM&XcX	Puts you in the Town of Oasis ready to tackle the last dungeon, The Atra Labyrinth
Music_From_Neutopia	Sound Test
Thats_Entertainment_Neutopia	View Enemies

New Adventure Island

Unlockables

Unlockable	How to Unlock
Level Select	Press ⬇, ➡, ①, ⬅, ⬆②, ⬆, ⬆, ⬆, ⬆
Level Skip	Insert a NEC Avenue 6 pad in 6-button mode into port 1

Ninja Gaiden

Unlockables

Unlockable	How to Unlock
Sound Test	When the screen says Techmo Presents 1989: Hold Ⓐ+Ⓑ+⬅+➡+SELECT, and press START
Extra Lives	In Area 5-3, there's a 1UP on the third floor of the tower. Go back down the ladder to the second floor, and then back up to the third floor. The 1UP has returned. You can do this as many times as you want.

One Piece: Unlimited Adventure

Unlockable Characters

Unlockable	How to Unlock
Unlock Survival Mode	Unlock the following characters in Vs. mode. All characters must be defeated to unlock them. All locations given are the first location you encounter each enemy.
Bazooka Marine	Defeat one in the Seaside Zone
Blue Demon General	Defeat one in the Cave Zone
Cluster Demon Soldier	Defeat one in the Cave Zone
Crimson Demon General	Defeat one in the Cave Zone
Knuckle Pirate	Defeat one in the Ruins Zone
Marine Corps Chief	Defeat one in the Jungle Zone
Normal Marine	Defeat one in the Seaside Zone
Pistol Pirate	Defeat one in the Jungle Zone
Sabre Pirate	Defeat one in the Jungle Zone

DS
GBA
PSP
PS2
PS3
Wii
Xbox
Xbox 360
Index

DS

GBA

PSP

PS2

PS3

Wii

Xbox

Xbox 360

Index

One Piece: Unlimited Adventure (continued)

Unlockable	How to Unlock
Sword Demon Soldier	Defeat one in the Cave Zone
World Government Agent	Defeat one in the Ruins Zone

Unlockables

Unlockable	How to Unlock
Transform into Overlimit Chopper in Story Mode	Defeat Overlimit Chopper in Story mode and create the Rumble Ball. You are now eligible to transform into Overlimit Chopper. To do so, you first must be in a boss fight. While in the fight you have to use two Rumble Balls (wait for one to run out, heal SP gauge, take another one). While you are using the second Rumble Ball, the enemy has to kill Chopper. Instead of dying, as he normally would, a cinema scene occurs. The scene shows Chopper taking a third Rumble Ball and he transforms into his Overlimit form. He gains a new HP and SP bar. He can't use items.

Open Season

Unlockable Minigames

Unlockable	How to Unlock
Duck Chorus	Complete "Crazy Quackers"
Flowers for My Deer	Complete "Meet the Skunks"
Rise, Rise to the Top!	Complete "Beaver Damage"
Shake That Butt!	Complete "Hunted"
Wild Memory	Complete "Shaw's Shack"

Ordyne

Unlockables

Unlockable	How to Unlock
Continue Game	While falling, hold ① and press RUN
Princess Mode	At the title screen, hold ① for about 10 seconds
Secret Test Mode	At the title screen, hold down RUN while pressing SELECT, SELECT, SELECT, SELECT, SELECT, SELECT, then release. Hold down ①+②+⬅+➡, then press RUN. Press SELECT and RUN simultaneously to reach each part of the Secret Test mode. You can access a Sound Test, select your starting stage and your starting number of ships, among other things.

Override

Levels

Enter the "Level Select mode" code before entering any of the level passwords.

Code	Effect
Level Select Mode	Hold RUN and press SELECT 10 times
Level 2	⬇, SELECT, RUN
Level 3	➡, SELECT, RUN
Level 4	⬆, SELECT, RUN
Level 5	⬅, SELECT, RUN
Level 6	⬆, ⬇, SELECT, RUN

Override (continued)

Unlockables

Unlockable	How to Unlock
Ending	Holding ✚+①+②+SELECT, press RUN
Invincibility	Press RUN, then quickly press and hold ①+②+SELECT+RUN
Sound Test	Hold SELECT and press RUN

Power Golf

Unlockables

Unlockable	How to Unlock
Left-handed Golfer	Hold ✚ and press ① when selecting a golfer

Prince of Persia Rival Swords

While in the Pause menu, use the d-pad to enter these codes.

Unlockable	Code
Unlock the Baby Toy Weapon	✚, ✚, ✚, ✚, ⓩ, Nunchuck down, Nunchuck down, ⓩ, ✚, ✚
Unlock Telephone Sword	✚, ✚, ✚, ✚, ✚, ✚, ✚, ✚, ⓩ, Nunchuck down, ⓩ, ⓩ, Nunchuck down, Nunchuck down
Unlock Swordfish Weapon	✚, ✚, ✚, ✚, ✚, ✚, ✚, ✚, ⓩ, Nunchuck down, ⓩ, Nunchuck down
Unlock Chainsaw	✚, ✚, ✚, ✚, ✚, ✚, ✚, ✚, ⓩ, Nunchuck down, ⓩ, Nunchuck down

Pro Wrestling

Unlockables

Unlockable	How to Unlock
Battle the Great Puma	Once you are VWA Champion, defend your title for 10 matches. Then you will have a match with the Great Puma.

Pulseman

Unlockables

Unlockable	How to Unlock
Level SELECT	At the Sega logo, press (in joystick 2): Ⓐ, Ⓑ, Ⓒ, Ⓒ, Ⓑ, Ⓐ. After this, go to Options and use the Map option.

R-Type

Unlockables

Unlockable	How to Unlock
Extra Credits	Set the turbo switch for I to full. Then, hold SELECT+① and press RUN on the title screen.

Passwords

Password	Effect
CPL-3590-CM	Hard mode

R-Type II

Passwords

Password	Effect
JJL-6589-MB	All items and 99 lives

R-Type III

Unlockables

Unlockable	How to Unlock
Level Select	At the continue screen, press ⬇, ⬇, ⬇, ⬇, ⬇, ⬇, ⬇, ⬇, ⬇, ⬆ then press ➡ one or more times, then press START (the number of times L is pressed dictates the level you skip to

Rampage: Total Destruction

At the main menu, press the ⊖+⊕ to open the Password screen.

Unlockable	Password
All Monsters Unlocked	141421
Demo Mode with Two Random Monsters	082864
Disable All Active Codes	000000
Display Game Version	314159
Instant Demo Mode with Two Random Monsters	874098
Invincible to Military Attacks, Bombers, Infantry, Tanks, Etc.	986960
Obtain All Ability Upgrades	011235
One Hit Destroys a Building	071767
Unlock All Cities	271828
View Credits	667302
View Ending Theme	667301
View Opening Theme	667300

Rapala Tournament Fishing

Unlockable	How To
DT Flat Sure Set Series	Correctly answer 20 questions
Glass Shad Rap Lure	Correctly answer 10 questions
Lauri Rapala 100th Anniversary Lure	Correctly answer 40 questions
X-Rap Jointed Shad Lure	Correctly answer 30 questions
Video 1	Answer 5 questions correctly
Video 2	Answer 15 questions correctly
Video 3	Answer 25 questions correctly
Video 4	Answer 35 questions correctly
Video 5	Answer every question correctly

Rayman Raving Rabbids

Unlockables

Unlockable	How to Unlock
Alternate Ending	Score at least 1,000,000 points in Score mode
Artwork 1	5,000 Points
Artwork 2	93,000 Points
Bunnies Can't Cook Eggs	84,000 Points
Bunnies Can't Infiltrate Games Convention	48,000 Points
Bunnies Can't Play Soccer	138,000 Points
Bunnies Don't Do Vacuum Cleaning	21,000 Points
Bunnies Don't Like Taking a Bath	9,000 Points
Bunnies Never Close Doors	111,000 Points

Rayman Raving Rabbids (continued)

Unlockable	How to Unlock
Bunny Costume	Clear all games on day 12
Bunny Hunt Survival Mode	Clear all games on Bunny Hunt Time mode at least once
Bunny Hunt Time Mode	Clear all games on Bunny Hunt Score mode at least once
Caramba Costume	Clear all games on day 08
Challenge Mode	Complete Story mode
"Dark Iron Bunnies" for the Jukebox	Clear all games on day 11
Dee-Jay Costume	Clear all games on day 02
French Bastille Day	57,000 Points
Gold Cow Trophy on Top of the Wardrobe	Clear all games on day 15
"Girls Just Want To Have Fun" for the Jukebox	Clear all games on day 05
"Good Time" for the Jukebox	Clear all games on day 03
Gothic Costume	Clear all games on day 04
"Hip Hop Hooray" for the Jukebox	Clear all games on day 07
"La Bamba" for the Jukebox	Clear all games on day 09
"Misirlou" for the Jukebox	Clear all games on day 01
Raymaninho Costume	Clear all games on day 10
Rock 'n Roll Costume	Clear all games on day 06
"The Butcher Deejay" for the Jukebox	Clear all games on day 13
"Ubisoft Montpellier Choir" for the Jukebox	Clear all games on day 14
US Independence Day	165,000 Points

Red Steel

Unlockables

Unlockable	How to Unlock
Secret Staff Photos	When you first find the geishas on the mission Reiko sends you on, you'll see some lockers near them. Open the one with a darker door to see photos of the developers wearing blonde wigs.

Ristar

Passwords

Password	Effect
STAR	A shooting star goes across the background (JP)
MUSEUM	Boss Rush mode
XXXXXX	Clears/Deactivates the current password
AGES	Copyright info is displayed
MIEMIE	Hidden items' grab points are shown with a blue star
FEEL	ILOVEU, MIEMIE, CANDY active all at once (JP)
CANDY	Invincibility (JP)
MACCHA	Mentions Miyake color (JP)
MASTER	Mentions next game (JP)
AAAAAA	No Continue limit (JP)
MAGURO	Onchi Music mode and credits music in sound test
HETAP	Reverses the high score in Demo mode (JP)

Sidebar tabs: DS, GBA, PSP, PS2, PS3, Wii, Xbox, Xbox 360, Index

DS

GBA

PSP

PS2

PS3

Wii

Xbox

Xbox 360

Index

Ristar (continued)

Password	Effect
VALDI	Shows the solar system (JP)
ILOVEU	Stage select
SUPERB	Super Difficulty mode
SUPER	Super Hard mode
DOFEEL	Time Attack mode

River City Ransom

Passwords

Password	Effect
XfMdZTHwiR3 jaj6jfRUDEt tilm2tWRo8b	Final Boss, with Max Stats, Dragon Feet, Stone Hands, Grand Slam, and Texas Boots
XfMdZTHUPR3 rztzPeQUCTt 61IxhtWRo2b	Final Boss, with Max Stats, Stone Hands, Dragon Feet, Acro Circus, Grand Slam, 4 Karma Jolts, and $999.99 cash
t1izvpdOZnZ JxNkJp7Cpub XMPQgXErSMF	Ivan Beaten, High School Open
w412ysgtMqc MUSjKm2PqtE UJMNdUTGOQC	Power Up
jrYplfTgbdj nOorLTlYXwR SjTuqpiIUHP	Start with all abilities and $500 in cash
fHUFBbvcnpa MS8iPpICZJP VKNOeVRQPDD	Strange item in inventory that gives stat increases

Unlockables

Unlockable	How to Unlock
Change Character Names	On the Character Select screen, press SELECT on the controller to go to a screen where you can change Alex and Ryan's names to whatever you want.
Merlin's Mystery Shop	To find Merlin's Mystery Shop go to the Armstrong Thru-Way. Once inside, press up at the top wall and the wall opens. Inside you can buy the best items in the game.

Romance of the Three Kingdoms IV: Wall of Fire

Unlockables

Unlockable	How to Unlock
Form Anti-Dong Zhuo Coalition	Select the first scenario (Dong Zhuo Triumphs in Luo Yang), then select Cao Cao as your leader. On your very first turn, move some generals and troops to Xu Chang. A few months later, Cao Cao will call a meeting, asking all the other leaders to form an alliance against Dong Zhuo. If Yuan Shao joins, he will become leader; otherwise, Cao Cao will become leader. This makes defeating Dong Zhuo a bit easier, depending on who joins you (such as Yuan Shao or Ma Teng).
Unlimited Soldiers	Use the War command and select a general to go into battle. Assign the maximum number of men to his unit. When they asked for confirmation of going to war select the "No" option. Remove the general from the list of commanders and reassign him to the post. Return to the troop assignment screen. The number of men available should be multiplied by the number that was assigned earlier. Repeat this process to increase the number of men, but don't go back to the main menu.

Scarface: The World Is Yours

Passwords

Password	Effect
OLDFAST	Antique racer
666999	Bacinari
BLACK	Black suit
BLUESH	Blue suit with shades
DOZER	Bulldozer
MARTHA	Change time of day
NOBALLS	Decrease Gang Heat
FLYSTRT	Decreases Cop Heat
DUMPER	Dump truck
FPATCH	Fill Balls Meter
GRAYSH	Gray suit Tony with sunglasses
HAWAII	Hawaii print shirt
HAWAIIG	Hawaii print shirt with sunglasses
DONUT	Increase Cop Heat
GOBALLS	Increase Gang Heat
AMMO	Max Ammo
TUNEME	Real "The World Is Yours" music track
MEDIK	Refill health
TBURGLR	Repairs car
BUMMER	Stampede
RAINY	Toggle rain
WHITE	White suit
WHITESH	White suit with shades

SD Gundam: Scad Hammers

Unlockables

Unlockable	How to Unlock
Unlock Turn A Gundam	Fill up the Data Accumulation gauge (the one with the picture of a mobile suit beside it) under the Educational Data/Analysis Situation menu to 100%, then beat the Side 3 stage (Lv. 10 Ki mama ni Hammer 50) to unlock the Turn A Gundam

Shadow Dancer

Unlockables

Unlockable	How to Unlock
Earning 200,000 points	When you battle any boss (except Stavros) reduce your foe to within a flame or two of destruction, then stay out of reach until the last 10 seconds. At the very last second, use ninja magic to destroy the boss.
Practice on Any Stage	Enter the following code at the Title screen: Ⓐ+Ⓑ+Ⓒ+START. A new option appears, allowing you to practice on any level.
Extra Life	In the bonus round where you have to shoot the ninjas, kill either all ninjas or none of them.

DS GBA PSP PS2 PS3 Wii Xbox Xbox 360 Index

Shadow Land

Secret Password Screen

Unlockable	How to Unlock
Password Screen	At the title screen hold ①+②+SELECT and press RUN

Passwords

Password	Effect
PC-ENGINE	(message)
NAMCO	(message)
NAMCOT	(message)
6502	(message)
6809	(message)
68000	(message)
756-2311	(message)
YAMASHITA	(message)
AKIRA	(message)
KOMAI	(message)
KAZUHIKO	(message)
KAWADA	(message)
SPEED-UP (4 way split screen)	Reset after entering the password
S.62.08.22 (Start from level 5)	Reset after entering the password

Shining in the Darkness

Unlockables

Unlockable	How to Unlock
Rename All Characters	At the Name Entry screen, input a name that takes up all the available spaces (5 letter spaces). Then, select the forward button and you can enter another name for the next character! This works for all the characters!

Shining Force

Unlockables

Unlockable	How to Unlock
Control All Opponents (JP Version Only)	When the battle begins, quickly tap Ⓐ, Ⓑ, Ⓒ, ✛, Ⓐ, Ⓒ, Ⓐ, Ⓑ, Ⓐ
Fight Any Battle (JP Version Only)	Hold START on controller 2 then reset the system. Let go of START and hold Ⓐ+Ⓑ on controller 2. Select continue and wait until the girl says good luck. At that instant hold Ⓐ on controller 1 while continuing to hold Ⓐ+Ⓑ on controller 2.
Name Characters	Start a new game (must have completed game first) and go to the Name Your Character screen. Put the cursor on end and hold START+Ⓐ+Ⓑ+Ⓒ on controller 2 while holding: START+Ⓐ+Ⓒ on controller 1. You will see another character. Continue this to name all characters.

Other Unlockables

Unlockable	How to Unlock
2 Jogurts	If you put jogurt in your army and kill an enemy with him, you get a jogurt ring item. Use this in battle on any character to make that character look like a jogurt! Repeat as many times as you want, but you will have to get another ring when it breaks.

DS

GBA

PSP

PS2

PS3

Wii

Xbox

Xbox 360

Index

Shining Force (continued)

Unlockable	How to Unlock
Anri's Alternate Costume	During the Laser Eye battle in Chapter 3, search to the left of the three dark elves. You'll receive a hidden item called Kitui Huku ("tight clothes" in Japanese). Give it to Anri and she'll have a new outfit.
Tao's Alternate Costume	In Chapter 3, after fighting the first battle to get the Moon Stone, go inside the cave and search the walls for a secret item called the Sugoi Mizugi. Give it to Tao and she will have an alternate costume.

Shinobi III: Return of the Ninja Master

Unlockables

Unlockable	How to Unlock
Bonus Points	Complete a level without throwing any shuriken to get 30,000 bonus points
Invincibility	Choose BMG selection on the options menu, then, press Ⓑ to select the following songs in order: He runs, Japonesque, shinboi walk, sakura, getufu
Unlimited Shuriken	Set the number of shuriken to 0 on the Options menu and set the sound effects option to Shuriken. Highlight the Shuriken option and keep it there, and the 0 will change into the symbol for infinity.

Shockman

Unlockables

Enter these cheats when the game is paused.

Unlockable	How to Unlock
Invincibility	⬆, ⬆, SELECT, ⬆, ②, SELECT
Level Skip	⬆, ⬆, SELECT, ⬅, ⬅, SELECT, SELECT
Refill Life Meter	⬅, SELECT, ②
Suicide	➡, SELECT, ⬆, SELECT, SELECT

Shrek the Third

Unlockables

Unlockable	How to Unlock
10,000 Bonus Coins	Press ⬆, ⬆, ⬇, ⬇, ⬅, ➡ at the Gift Shop
Bonus Damage	Buy at the Gift Shop for 10,500
Bonus Fairy Dust	Buy at the Gift Shop for 7,700
Academy Grounds Commentary	Buy at the Gift Shop for 1,500
Catacombs Commentary	Buy at the Gift Shop for 5,000
Docks Commentary	Buy at the Gift Shop for 1,000
Evil Queen's Castle Commentary	Buy at the Gift Shop for 5,000
Ice Lake Commentary	Buy at the Gift Shop for 3,000
Merlin's Hills Commentary	Buy at the Gift Shop for 4,000
Prison Cell Blocks Commentary	Buy at the Gift Shop for 2,000
Rundown Streets Commentary	Buy at the Gift Shop for 6,000
Stromboli's Workshop Commentary	Buy at the Gift Shop for 5,000
Donkey: Dragon Disguise	Buy at the Gift Shop for 3,650
Fiona: Funeral Dress	Buy at the Gift Shop for 2,150
Puss: Evil Knight Disguise	Buy at the Gift Shop for 2,850

DS

GBA

PSP

PS2

PS3

Wii

Xbox

Xbox 360

Index

DS

GBA

PSP

PS2

PS3

Wii

Xbox

Xbox 360

Index

Shrek the Third (continued)

Unlockable	How to Unlock
Shrek: Knight Armor	Buy at the Gift Shop for 3,500
Shrek: Pirate Outfit	Buy at the Gift Shop for 4,250
Shrek: Regal	Buy at the Gift Shop for 3,200
Shrek: Swim Trunks	Buy at the Gift Shop for 3,350
Sleeping Beauty: Gown	Buy at the Gift Shop for 2,500
Charming	Buy at the Gift Shop for 15,500
Grimm	Buy at the Gift Shop for 1,500
Cyclops (Character)	Buy at the Gift Shop for 1,500
Dragon Keep (Castle)	Buy at the Gift Shop for 1,600
Dragon Keep (Map)	Buy at the Gift Shop for 1,350
Dwarves (Character)	Buy at the Gift Shop for 2,400

SimCity

Unlockables

Unlockable	How to Unlock
$999,999	At any time while playing a city, spend all of your money. When the tax screen appears at the end of December, hold down L. Select "Go with Figures" and then go back to the tax screen. Turn all of the dues to 100% and exit still holding L. When you release L your money will be at $999,999.
999 Extra City Maps	Start a new city, and choose any map number, then start the game. Now select the "Go to Menu" icon at the screen's top, and choose Start New City without saving. After a short time, the map will change, but the number won't.
Freeland	Beat the Las Vegas scenario
Las Vegas Scenario	Beat the six game scenarios and have at least one city with over 100,000 citizens living in it saved to the game.

The Sims 2: Pets

Unlockables

Unlockable	How to Unlock
10,000 Simoleons	Hold ⒷB, press ⬆, ⬅, ⬇, ⬅
Advance 6 Hours	⬅, ⬅, ⬅, ⬅, ⬅, ⬅
Change Skills	⬆, ⬆, ⬆, ⬆, ⬆, ⬆

Soldier Blade

Codes

Code	Effect
Level Select	Hold ⬆, press SELECT, hold ⬇, press SELECT, hold ⬅, press SELECT, hold ➡, press SELECT

Solomon's Key

Unlockables

Unlockable	How to Unlock
Continue Game	At the "Game Deviation Value" screen, hold ⬆+Ⓐ+ⒷB

Sonic 3D Blast

Unlockables

Unlockable	How to Unlock
Level Select	Go to the Press Start screen and enter Ⓑ, Ⓐ, 🔼, Ⓐ, Ⓒ, 🔼, 🔼, Ⓐ (or baracuda). You're taken to the main screen. Press the Start option and the level select appears.
Quick Emerald Gain	Enter the Level Select code twice, and go to a level/act with Knuckles or Tails in it. Enter one of their bonus levels by collecting 50 rings. When the bonus level begins, press Ⓐ+START and you will receive the emerald for the bonus level.
Skip Levels	Do the Level Select code and start the game in any level. To skip levels, pause the game and press Ⓐ.
Stage Select (Alternative)	Beat the entire game with all the Chaos Emeralds. After the credits, the stage select is on.

Sonic and the Secret Rings

Unlockable	Code
Bookworm	Play a total time of 24 hours
Celebrity	Play attractions 35 times
Champion	Win 1st in 120 Party Games
Dark Master	Beat 20 missions using at least 5 Dark skills and no Wind/Fire skills
Dealer	Win World Bazaar 7 times
Explorer	Win at Treasure Hunt 7 times
Extreme Speeder	Use Speed Break 50 times
Flame Master	Beat 20 missions using at least 5 Fire skills and no Wind/Dark skills
Genie Buster	Defeat 1,000 Genies
Grind Performer	Grind a distance of 30 km (18.64 miles)
Hero	Defeat Erazor Djinn
Pirate	Win at Pirates Coast 7 times
Rebellion	Beat Erazor Djinn at level 25 or lower
Record Buster	Set records for all party games that have records
Ring Catcher	Collect 10,000 Rings
Skill Collector	Unlock every skill available
Skill Quinti	Beat 20 missions using 4 or fewer skills
Skill Saver	Beat 30 missions using fewer than 100 SP
Sonic Freak	Use Sonic 30 times in Party mode
Soul Collector	Collect every Fire Soul
Star	Play party games 200 times
Super	Reach level 99
The Ultimate	Collect all Gold Medals
Thief	Win at Genie's Lair 7 times
Time Controller	Use Time Break for 300 seconds
Trier	Win Tournament Palace 7 times
True Hero	Defeat Alf Layla wa Layla
Wind Master	Beat 20 missions using at least 5 Wind skills and no Fire/Dark skills
World Traveler	Travel 500 km (310.7 miles)

DS

GBA

PSP

PS2

PS3

Wii

Xbox

Xbox 360

Index

Sonic Spinball

Unlockables

Unlockable	How to Unlock
Level Select	Access the Options from the title screen, take controller 1, and press: Ⓐ, ⬇, Ⓑ, ⬇, Ⓒ, ⬇, Ⓐ, Ⓑ, ⬇, Ⓐ, Ⓒ, ⬇, Ⓑ, Ⓒ, ⬇. If you did it correctly, you hear a special sound. Go back to the title screen and hold Ⓐ and press START to begin on Level 2, Ⓑ and press START for Level 3, and ⬇ and press START for level 4.
Multi-Ball Stage	Collect every ring in any stage.
Stop the Platform in The Machine	In Level 3, The Machine, a moving platform takes you to either side of the area. Stand on the platform and press up or down to make the platform stop, allowing you to get a good look around or plan your jump carefully.

Sonic the Hedgehog

Unlockables

Unlockable	How to Unlock
Config Mode	There is a code called Control mode, which is required before activating this code. To activate Control mode, press ⬇, Ⓒ, ⬇, Ⓒ, ⬇, Ⓒ, ⬇, Ⓒ at the title screen, but before pressing START to begin the game, hold Ⓐ as you hit START. Now, rather than just being in Control mode, you can enable Config mode by pressing Ⓑ. Sonic will morph into a ring, and the arrows can move him anywhere, even in the air, or through obstacles such as walls, floors, or even ceilings. You can change the item Sonic appears as by hitting Ⓐ while in Config mode. Ⓑ makes Sonic normal again, and ⬇ will place the sprite that you have selected for Sonic to appear as. For example, you press Ⓑ, and Sonic becomes a ring, press ⬇ to make a ring appear exactly where the ring icon is. WARNING!: This distorts several different things, such as the score, time, and other various icons throughout the game such as the finish signs at the end of the first two acts of each zone that spin when Sonic shoots past them, and the small score icons that appear whenever Sonic jumps high enough after finishing a level.
Drunk Sonic	During the demo, hold ⬇. Sonic will crash into walls and get hit by enemies.
Level Select	At the title screen, press ⬇, ⬇, ⬇, ⬇. You should hear a noise like a ring being collected. Then, hold Ⓐ and press START for a level select!

Unlockables

Unlockable	How to Unlock
Secret Game Message	At the title screen, press Ⓒ, Ⓒ, Ⓒ, Ⓒ, Ⓒ, Ⓒ, ⬇, ⬇, ⬇, ⬇. When the demo starts, hold Ⓐ+Ⓑ+Ⓒ+⬇ then press START. Instead of the Sonic Team logo, you will see a list of the game's developers in Japanese. When the title screen appears, a flashing "Press Start Button" will be there under Sonic's head.
Different Ending	Beat game with all Chaos Emeralds.

Sonic the Hedgehog 2

Unlockables

Unlockable	How to Unlock
Level Select	Some other cheats require you to enable this one first. Go to the Options menu from the main screen. From there, head to the Sound Select menu and play the following sounds: 19, 65, 09, 17. Once you have played each (1 time only), press ⬆ and then press START to be brought back to the title screen. Now, when you see Sonic and Tails (Miles) appear on screen, hold Ⓐ and press START to finish off the code. You're brought to a menu where you have access to any level in the game, whether you've completed the level or not.
14 Continues	Go to the sound test (not the one on the level select) and put in 19, 65, 09, 17, 01, 01, 02, 04 (press Ⓐ after each one). There won't be a confirmation sound. Start the game by pressing START on the first option (character select) and you have 14 continues.
All 7 Chaos Emeralds	This code only works for Sonic. First, do the Level Select cheat. In the Level Select menu, go to Sound Test and play the sounds 04, 01, 02, 06. If done correctly, you'll hear a Chaos Emerald sound effect. Now, select any stage from this menu and you can turn into Super Sonic with 50 rings plus you'll get Sonic's second ending after beating Death Egg Zone.
Change Tails' Name to Miles	Press ⬆, ⬆, ⬆, ⬆, ⬆, ⬆, ⬆ at the title screen.
Debug Mode	First enter the Level Select code. Now, go to Sound Test option, and play the following tunes: 01, 09, 09, 02, 01, 01, 02, 04. It should make a ring sound when track 4 is played to signify you've entered it correctly. Now select the stage you want to go to, and press START while holding Ⓐ until the stage starts, and you'll have debug activated. Press Ⓑ to turn Debug on/off, Ⓐ to switch object, and ⬆ to put down object selected. Pressing Ⓐ while the game is paused will cause the game to reset.
Debug Mode (Alternate)	At Sound Test, enter: 19, 65, 09, 17, then press Ⓐ+START, then when Sonic and Tails pop up, press Ⓐ+START to go to the Level Select screen. On the Sound Test area, enter 01, 09, 09, 02, 01, 01, 02, 04, and then press Ⓐ+START.
Debug Mode and All Emeralds (when locked-on to Sonic and Knuckles)	First activate and go to the Stage Select. Play the following tracks in Sound Test with Ⓑ: 01, 09, 09, 04, 01, 00, 01, 08. This enables the Debug code, and you should hear a ring chime if the code is entered correctly. Start the selected level with Ⓐ+START. To get all 7 Chaos Emeralds, input this code the same way: 01, 06, 07, 07, 07, 02, 01, 06. You should hear the Emerald chime. Note: this code may not work without the Debug code.
Enable Super Sonic	First, head to the Options menu from the title screen, and then into the Sound Select menu from there. Play the following sounds in this order: 19, 65, 09, 17. After that, press ⬆, START. You will be taken back to the title screen. Now, when you see Sonic and Tails (Miles) appear on the screen, press and hold Ⓐ and press START to be taken to the Level Select menu. From this menu, enter the Sound Test feature, and play the following sounds: 04, 01, 02, 06. If done correctly, a familiar tune plays. Exit this menu and start the game as normal. Once you collect a minimum of 50 coins in any level, Jump (Press Ⓐ) to activate the Super Sonic code.

DS
GBA
PSP
PS2
PS3
Wii
Xbox
Xbox 360
Index

DS

GBA

PSP

PS2

PS3

Wii

Xbox

Xbox 360

Index

Sonic the Hedgehog 2 (continued)

Unlockable	How to Unlock
Get Super Sonic on Emerald Hill	First, enter the Stage Select code, shown above. Then you go into the Special Stage in the Stage Select menu. Every time you finish the special stage, press reset and go back to the special stage. Keep doing this until you get the sixth emerald. Then don't press reset. It zaps you with your 6 emeralds into Emerald Hill. Get the last emerald on Emerald Hill, get 50 rings, and jump to be Super Sonic. Don't run out of rings or you will change into Sonic again. The rings start disappearing when you are Super Sonic.
Infinite Lives	First, enable the Level Select cheat and the Debug mode. Choose Sonic and Tails as the players. After entering the codes, choose any stage from the Level Select menu (preferably stage 1). As soon as you can move Sonic, hold ⬇ and press Ⓐ (don't let go of down on the D-pad). This activates Sonic's spin; Tails will copy the Sonic spin also. Press Ⓑ and Sonic will become the Debug cursor. (Tails will be locked in the Sonic spin move). Press Ⓐ until the debug cursor displays an enemy sprite, like the monkey or that bee robot. Now that the debug cursor displays an enemy sprite, move the debug cursor to where Tails is, and repeatedly tap ⬇. This produces enemies where Tails is, and because Tails is locked in the Sonic spin move, he destroys the enemies. As Tails destroys enemies in this position, press ⬇ more until the score for destroying an enemy increases from 100 to 8,000 to a 1Up. Once you have enough 1Ups, press Ⓑ again to revert to Sonic.
Level Select (When Locked-On to Sonic and Knuckles)	At the title screen, press ⬇, ⬇, ⬇, ⬇, ⬇, ⬇, ⬆, ⬆, ⬆, ⬇. Then, hold Ⓐ and press START to be taken to the Level Select menu.
Night Mode	Activate level select and hold ⬇ while selecting a stage to darken the level. The effect wears off when you die or when you beat the level.
Level Select Screen	At the title screen, select Options. Highlight Sound Test then play the following music and sounds: 19, 65, 09, and 17. You hear a ring-collecting sound for correct code entry. Then press START to return to the title screen. Highlight 1-Player, hold Ⓐ, and press START. You are directed to Level Select screen. Choose a level then press START to begin.

Code	Effect
17	Play Invincibility Music
65	Plays a Shifting Sound
09	Plays Casino Night Zone 1-Player Music
19	Plays Sonic 2 Theme

Slow Motion	First, enter the Level Select code. Then start your game in any level. When you start, press pause. Then hold Ⓑ and try to do anything with Sonic. The game plays in slow motion as long as you hold down Ⓑ.
Oil Ocean Music Forever	Go to the Sound Test in the Options menu and put in the sounds, 02, 01, 02, 04, and hold Ⓐ and press START. The Oil Ocean music will now be playing constantly, no matter what stage.

Sonic the Hedgehog 2 (continued)

Unlockable	How to Unlock
Pseudo Super Sonic	In Oil Ocean Zone, if you manage to take a hit and end up landing in one of those green-and-gold checkered cannons, you'll fall right out, but you'll be moving at twice your normal speed as well as jumping twice your normal height (with twice as much gravity). A good place for doing this would be in Oil Ocean Zone, Act 2, near the first set of pop-tops and cannons. Just jump into the semi-hidden bed of spikes on the right and land in the cannon. Note: Moving at twice normal velocity can often get you stuck in a wall. Also, this wears off if you Super Spin Dash or Spin Dash. It also only lasts for that act.
Super Tails	Normally, when you turn into Super Sonic you lose Tails behind you all the time. Well, after you put in the debug cheat and have started a level (preferably Emerald Hill), turn yourself into a box and place it somewhere on the floor while you are Super Sonic. It should be a switch places box. Hit it and Tails has a permanent invincible circle around him. He stays like this through the whole level.
Unlimited Speed Shoes in 2-Player vs. Mode	In 2-Player vs. mode, get speed shoes and die (while you still have them) and you get to keep your speed shoes until the end of the level.

Sonic the Hedgehog 3

Unlockables

Unlockable	How to Unlock
All 7 Chaos Emeralds and Super Sonic	To get all 7 Chaos Emeralds without having to complete their Special Stages, first enter the Level Select and Sound Test codes. Go to the Sound Test and play the following tunes in order: 02, 04, 05, 06. You will hear an emerald sound if the code is entered correctly. To get Super Sonic after entering the previous code, just select any level from the level select and start it. Once you acquire 50 Rings, do a double-jump to become Super Sonic.
Control Tails in a 1-Player Game	Start a 1-player game with Sonic and Tails as the characters. With controller 2, you can take control of Tails while also using Sonic.
Hidden Special Stage	On the Level Select menu, play sounds 01, 03, 05, 07. Highlight Special Stage 2 and press Ⓐ+START.
Infinite Lives	Get up to Launch Base Zone. Sound any of the alarms, so that the Kamikaze birds come after you. Charge up a Super Sonic Dash in between the alarm, but do not let go of the button. The birds continually crash into you. After about 30 seconds, you have gained enough points to get an extra life. Continue the process for as many lives as you want.
Level Select (When Locked-On to Sonic and Knuckles)	Start a game and go to Angel Island Zone, Act 1. Go to one of the swings that you hang from and grab on. While Sonic is swinging, press ⬆️, ⬆️, ⬆️, ⬆️, ⬇️, ⬇️, ⬇️, ⬇️. You will hear a ring if you entered the code correctly. Pause the game and press Ⓐ to take you back to the title screen. Press ⬆️, ⬇️ to find the newly unlocked Sound Test menu. Enter it, where you can play all of the sounds/music in the game and warp to any level.
Turn into Super Sonic	After entering the Level Select and Debug code, you can use the debug to turn yourself into Super Sonic without getting all of the Chaos Emeralds. With the debug on, go into any level and press Ⓑ to turn yourself into a ring. Then press Ⓐ to turn yourself into a monitor. Now, press ⬆️ to duplicate the monitor, and then Ⓑ again to change back into Sonic. Jump on the monitor and you will become Super Sonic.

DS
GBA
PSP
PS2
PS3
Wii
Xbox
Xbox 360
Index

Sonic the Hedgehog 3 (continued)

Unlockables

Unlockable	How to Unlock
Level Select	When the "SEGA" screen fades, quickly press ⬆, ⬆, ⬇, ⬇, ⬆, ⬆, ⬆, ⬆. If you have done this right, you should be able to scroll down to "Sound Test" below "Competition."
Sonic and Knuckles Mini-Boss Music	Get to the end of Act 1 of Hydrocity Zone (Zone 2). When facing the mini-boss, keep yourself underwater until the water warning music plays. Then jump out of the water. The game should now be playing the mini-boss music from Sonic and Knuckles, which wasn't out at the time (the music was evidently included in *Sonic 3* to make the backward compatibility feature easier).
Walk Thru Walls	In the Icecap Zone, Act 1, when you come to a wall that only Knuckles can bust through, hold ⬆ until Sonic or Tails looks down, and the screen pans all the way down. Then press ⬆ and jump at the same time. The screen starts to rotate. Walk in the direction of the wall and you will walk right through it.
100,000 Points	Beat a stage at with your time at exactly 9:59.
Frame by Frame	When playing a level after enabling the Level Select cheat, pause the game, then press ⬆ to advance the game by one frame.
Slow Motion Mode	When playing any level that you have accessed using the Cheat menu, pause the game and hold Ⓑ. While Ⓑ is held down, the game plays in Slow Motion mode.

Codes

Code	Effect
Hold Ⓑ and press ⬆	Your character shows all of his sprite animations
Hold Ⓑ and press ⬆ again	Your character stops the sprite show if it is activated

Spider-Man 3

Unlockables

Unlockable	How to Unlock
Collect all 50 Spider Emblems	Unlock black suit Spider-man after you destroy the suit

Spider-Man: Friend or Foe

Codes

Code	Effect
5,000 Tech Tokens, One Time Only	⬆, ⬆, ⬆, ⬆, ⬆, ⬆
Unlock New Goblin	⬆, ⬆, ⬆, ⬆, ⬆, ⬆
Unlock Sandman	⬆, ⬆, ⬆, ⬆, ⬆, ⬆
Unlock Venom	⬆, ⬆, ⬆, ⬆, ⬆, ⬆

Splatterhouse

Unlockables

Unlockable	How to Unlock
Hard Mode	At the title screen, hold SELECT until "HARD" appears on the screen
Sound Test	First enter the code to access the Stage Select option. When the screen comes up and asks you to select what stage you want to start on, press and hold the select button. After a second or two, the Stage Select option becomes a Sound Test menu, allowing you to listen to various "songs" and sound effects. Hold select again to change it back to the Stage Select menu.

Splatterhouse (continued)

Unlockable	How to Unlock
Stage Select	When the prologue starts up and there's a house in the rain, press SELECT, SELECT, SELECT, hold ✛ and then press ① or ②. It brings up the option to select a level.

SpongeBob SquarePants: Creature from the Krusty Krab

Passwords

Password	Effect
ROCFISH	30,000 Z-Coins
HOVER	Alternate Plankton hovercraft
ROBOT	Astronaut suit for Plankton in Revenge of the Giant Plankton
LASER	Extra laser color in Revenge of the Giant Plankton level
ROCKET	Extra rocket for Patrick in Hypnotic Highway level
PILOT	Get Aviator SpongeBob costume
BRAIN	Get Exposed-Brain SpongeBob costume
INVENT	Get Inventor Plankton costume
SPIN	Get Patrick's different POW! effect
BUNRUN	Get Patrick's purple rocket
SAFARI	Get Safari Patrick costume
BONES	Get Skeleton Patrick costume
KRABBY	Get Skeleton SpongeBob costume
FLAMES	Get SpongeBob's flame effect color
HYPCAR	Get SpongeBob's Hypnotic car skin
DUCKGUN	Get SpongeBob's Squeaky Duck Gun
GASSY	Infinite Fuel (in Flying levels)
VIGOR	Infinite Health (in platforming levels)
SCOOTLES	Obtain all sleepy seeds
TISSUE	Obtain Sleepy Seed Detector
PIRATE	Play as Pirate Patrick in Rooftop Rumble level
SPONGE	Play as Punk SpongeBob in Diesel Dreaming level
PANTS	Play as SpongeBob Plankton in Super-Size Patty level
HOTROD	Unlock a bonus vehicle in the Diesel Dreaming level
PORKPIE	Unlock all bonus games
GUDGEON	Unlock all levels
SPACE	Unlock bonus ship in the Rocket Rodeo level
PATRICK	Unlock tuxedo for Patrick in Starfishman to the Rescue

SSX Blur

In the Options menu, select Cheat to enter this code.

Unlockable	Code
All Characters Unlocked	NoHolds

DS

Star Soldier

Unlockables

Unlockable	How to Unlock
Powered Up Ship	At the title screen, press SELECT 10 times on controller 1. Then, hold ⬆+⬇ on controller 2. Then, hold ⬆+⬇+Ⓐ+Ⓑ on controller 1, finally press START, START on controller 1.

GBA

Streets of Rage

Unlockables

Unlockable	How to Unlock
Bad Ending	Choose to be Mr. X's righthand man the first time you meet him. Then complete the game.
Extra Continues	Press ⬇, ⬇, Ⓑ, Ⓑ, Ⓑ, Ⓒ, Ⓒ, Ⓒ, START at the title screen.
Final Boss Duel	When you get to the final boss in 2-player mode, have one player choose "yes" and the other choose "no." You duel against each other.
Level and Lives Select	Go to the main menu. Hold Ⓐ+Ⓑ+Ⓒ+⬆ on controller 2 while selecting Options on controller 1 (best if done with two people). You can now select how many lives you start with and which stage to start on.

PSP
PS2

Streets of Rage 2

Unlockables

Unlockable	How to Unlock
Level and Lives Select	Go to the main menu. Hold Ⓐ+Ⓑ on controller 2 while selecting Options. Now select how many lives you start with (up to 9), choose your starting stage, and play at the Very Easy and Mania difficulty levels.
Same Character in 2 Player	At the title screen, hold ⬆+Ⓑ on controller 1 and hold ⬆+Ⓐ on controller 2. Press ⬆ on controller 2 with everything else still held down. Now both players can be the same person in 2 Player!

PS3
Wii

Streets of Rage 3

Unlockables

Unlockable	How to Unlock
Ending 1	Rescue the Chief in Stage 6 before his health runs out. Then, at the end of Stage 7, defeat Robot Y before the time limit runs out.
Ending 2	Rescue the Chief before his health runs out in Stage 6. Then, in Stage 7, defeat Robot Y but let the time limit run out.
Ending 3	Let the Chief's health run out in Stage 6. When you go to Stage 7, you will see that it is changed. Make it to the last boss and defeat him.
Ending 4	Set the difficulty to Easy and beat Robot X in Stage 5.
Extra Lives Select	Go to the Options screen and select the "Lives" option. Press and hold ⬆+Ⓐ+Ⓑ+Ⓒ on controller 2, and press ⬆ or ⬇ on controller 1 to select the number of lives you can start the game with. You can now select 9 lives, instead of the default max of 5.
Play as Ash	To select Ash, defeat him, then hold Ⓐ on controller 1. After losing all of your lives, continue, and you can choose Ash as your character.
Play as Roo	When you fight the clown and Roo, defeat the clown first and Roo should hop away off the screen. When you lose all your lives and continue, cycle through the characters and Roo is now available.

Xbox
Xbox 360
Index

Streets of Rage 3 (continued)

Unlockable	How to Unlock
Play as Roo	At the title screen, hold ⬇+Ⓑ, then press START. A kangaroo named Roo is now available at the Character Select screen.
Play as Shiva	After beating Shiva in the first stage when you get the last hit, hold Ⓑ+START. When the continue screen comes up, you can play as Shiva. (He is weaker than his *Streets of Rage 2* character).
Play as Super Axel	Press ⬇ to select a player, then quickly hold Ⓐ and sweep the D-pad in a clockwise circle until Axel appears. Then press Ⓐ.

This cheat is very hard to get working.

Play as Super Skate	Pick Skate. As the first level starts, lose your first life having 0 points. You will now be Super Skate, with a much more powerful combo.
Play as the Same Character	Hold ⬇+Ⓒ on controller 2 as you enter 2-player mode with controller 1.
Secret Items	In Stage 1, at the Warehouse area, go to the bottom-left region blocked by the crates in the background and press Ⓑ. You get 5,000 points and a 1-UP. Stage 7, (City Hall) also contains lots of hidden items. Search in areas blocked off by the background such as lampposts, flower pots, etc.
Secret Passageways	On Stage 5, in the first room with all the ninjas, there are three secret routes that you can access by killing all enemies here. These rooms have more items than the normal rooms. Route 1: Above the door where you follow your normal route, notice a white wall with cracks near the top. Punch it to access Secret Route 1. Route 2: Go to the bottom center of this room and punch a few times. You eventually bust a hole in the floor leading you to the basement of Stage 5 and also Secret Route 2. Route 3: Go to the top of the screen and go up to the red walls. A certain red wall has a few cracks in it. Punch it to access Secret Route 3. There are a lot of enemies here, so be careful.
Stage Select	Hold Ⓑ+⬇, then press START. Stage Select appears on the Options screen.

Super C

Unlockables

Unlockable	How to Unlock
10 Lives (Player 1)	On the title screen, press ⬇, ⬇, ⬇, ⬇, Ⓐ, Ⓑ, then START
10 Lives (Player 2)	On the title screen, press ⬇, ⬇, ⬇, ⬇, Ⓐ, Ⓑ, SELECT, then START
Access Sound Test	On the title screen, hold down Ⓐ+Ⓑ then press START
Retain Old Score and # of Lives on New Game	On the title screen, after you've beaten the game, press Ⓐ, and then START
Retain Old Score on New Game	On the title screen, after you've beaten the game, press Ⓐ, Ⓑ, then START

DS
GBA
PSP
PS2
PS3
Wii
Xbox
Xbox 360
Index

Super Castlevania IV

Unlockables

Unlockable	How to Unlock
Higher Difficulty	Heart, Axe, Space, Water. Axe, Space, Space, Heart. Space, Axe, Space, Space. Space, Heart, Space, Space.

Difficult Level Passwords

Use these passwords to get to stages on the Difficult setting. You need to use a blank name.

Password	Effect
Space, Axe, Space, Space. Water, Water, Space, Space. Space, Heart, Space, Axe. Water, Axe, Space, Space.	Difficult mode Stage 6 level 1
Space, Axe, Space, Heart. Water, Heart, Space, Space. Space, Space, Space, Water. Space, Axe, Space, Space.	Difficult mode Stage 7 level 1
Space, Axe, Space, Space. Water, Water, Space, Space. Space, Heart, Space, Water. Water, Water, Space, Space.	Difficult mode Stage 8 level 1

Stage Passwords

NOTE

When you come to "Enter your name," leave the space blank or these passwords won't work.

Password	Effect
Space, Space, Space, Space. Firebombs, Space, Space, Space. Space, Space, Space, Space. Firebombs, Space, Space, Space	Level 2
Sspace, Space, Space, Heart. Firebombs, Space, Space, Space. Space, Space, Space, Space. Heart, Space, Space, Space	Level 3
Space, Space, Space, Firebombs. Firebombs, Firebombs, Space, Space. Space, Firebombs, Space, Axe. Space, Space, Space, Space	Level 4
Space, Space, Space, Space. Firebombs, Space, Space, Space. Space, Space, Space, Axe. Firebombs, Axe, Space, Space	Level 5
Space, Space, Space, Space. Firebombs, Firebombs, Space, Space. Space, Firebombs, Space, Axe. Firebombs, Axe, Space, Space	Level 6
Space, Space, Space, Firebombs. Firebombs, Hart, Space, Space. Space, Heart, Space, Firebombs. Space, Heart, Space, Space	Level 7
Space, Space, Space, Space. Firebombs, Firebombs, Space, Space. Space, Firebombs, Space, Firebombs. Firebombs, Space, Space	Level 8
Space, Space, Space, Heart. Firebombs, Firebombs, Space, Space. Space, Firebombs, Space, Firebombs. Heart, Firebombs, Space, Space	Level 9
Space, Space, Space, Axe. Firebombs, Space, Space, Space. Space, Space, Space, Heart. Heart, Heart, Space, Space	Level B
Space, Space, Space, Firebombs. Firebombs, Firebombs, Space, Space. Space, Firebombs, Space, Space. Space, Heart, Axe, Space	Level B (Dracula)

Super Castlevania IV (continued)

Unlockables

Unlockable	How to Unlock
Full Arsenal	In the last stage, before you climb the stairs to Dracula, jump down to the left. You land on an invisible platform. Move all the way left and you will get full health, 99 hearts, a cross, a fully upgraded whip, and a III stone.

Hidden Routes

There are three hidden branches from the main path.

Unlockable	How to Unlock
Hidden Route 1	In stage 3-1, when you must descend a short vertical shaft, halfway down here is a wall of pillars to the left. Demolish these, and you find a small side room containing hearts, cash bags, and some Roast.
Hidden Route 2	The second secret, which is an actual hidden Block, is in stage 6-2. At the very beginning you pass a hallway with Axe Knights and falling chandeliers. The third archway has a chandelier but no guard. Hit the floor a couple of times and it'll crumble, revealing a stairwell into a secret area.
Hidden Route 3	The last one is in Block 9-2. You jump across a bed of spikes at the beginning. After this you see several whirlwind tunnels and some coffins. The last upper platform on the right has a coffin and a tunnel. Let the tunnel suck you in and you'll find a hidden area full of bonuses.

Super Ghouls 'N Ghosts

Unlockables

Unlockable	How to Unlock
Level Select	Highlight "Exit" on the Option screen with controller 1. Hold L + START on controller 2 and press START on controller 1.
Professional Mode	Beat the game on Normal mode.

DS

GBA

PSP

PS2

PS3

Wii

Xbox

Xbox 360

Index

Super Monkey Ball: Banana Blitz

Unlockables

Unlockable	How to Unlock
Baby Robo	To unlock the minigame version of Baby for the main game, play each minigame at least once (the game displays a play count on each minigame). After playing each minigame once, play one more minigame of your choice so that the game saves your stats. Baby Robo is now available in the main game. To select Baby Robo, you have to highlight Baby on the Character Select screen and press 1.
Staff Credits Game	Beat the first World
World 9	Complete Worlds 1-8 without continuing
World 10	Complete World 9 without continuing

Super Star Soldier

Cheat Menu

Following code unlocks a Cheat menu where you can mess with all the options for the game such as level selection and enemy difficulty. Input at the title screen.

Unlockable	How to Unlock
Unlock Cheat Menu	Press ✚, ②, ✚, ②, ✚, ②, ✚,②, ✚, ①, ✚, ①, ✚, ①, ✚, ①, ①+② x8, ①+SELECT x8

Super Swing Golf

Unlock Caddies

You unlock caddies by defeating the Pangya Festa with certain characters (except for Pipin). You must purchase them from the shop first just like the players. Outfits for the caddies will be unlocked and available for purchase when you unlock the caddies as well.

Unlockable	How to Unlock
Brie	Beat Arin's first Pangya Festa
Dolfini	Complete the first Pangya Storyline with Kooh
Lola	Complete the first Pangya Storyline with Uncle Bob
Pipin	Complete the Tutorial
Quma	Complete the first Pangya Storyline with Hana
Tiki	Complete the first Pangya Storyline with Max
TitanBoo	Beat Cecilia in Arin's first Pangya Festa

Unlockable Characters

To unlock a new character, beat Pangya Festa with another character. This means the first storyline of Pangya Festa, unless otherwise mentioned.

Unlockable	How to Unlock
Arin	Beat Pangya Festa with Kooh
Cecilia	Beat Pangya Festa with Hana or Uncle Bob
Kaz	Beat Arin's final storyline (to access this storyline, beat the first storyline with everyone but Kaz, and wear Arin's Magic School Uniform)
Kooh	Beat Pangya Festa with Max
Max	Beat Pangya Festa with Cecilia
Uncle Bob	Beat Pangya Festa with Scout

Super Thunder Blade

Level Select

Press these controller actions at the title screen to begin at the desired level.

Code	Effect
Press Ⓐ, ⬆, ⬆, ⬆, ⬆, ⬆, ⬆, ⬆, START	Level 2
Press Ⓐ, Ⓐ, ⬆, ⬆, ⬆, ⬆, ⬆, ⬆, ⬆, START	Level 3
Press Ⓐ, Ⓐ, Ⓐ, ⬆, ⬆, ⬆, ⬆, ⬆, ⬆, ⬆, START	Level 4
Press Ⓐ, Ⓐ, Ⓐ, Ⓐ, ⬆, ⬆, ⬆, ⬆, ⬆, ⬆, ⬆, ⬆, START	Level 5

Unlockables

Unlockable	How to Unlock
Avoid Enemy Fire	Begin the game with Hard difficulty. Stay in the upper right or left corners and fire your weapon continuously in levels 1 through 3.
Extra Lives	Enable the Level Select code and get a continue. Highlight "Option" and hold Ⓐ+Ⓑ+Ⓒ and press START. A picture of a panda appears on the "Player" selection to confirm the code.

Surf's Up

Passwords

Password	Effect
NICEPLACE	Unlocks all art galleries
MYPRECIOUS	Unlocks all boards
GOINGDOWN	Unlocks all leaf-sliding locations

DS

GBA

PSP

PS2

PS3

Wii

Xbox

Xbox 360

Index

DS

GBA

PSP

PS2

PS3

Wii

Xbox

Xbox 360

Index

Surf's Up (continued)

MULTIPASS	Unlocks all multiplayer levels
FREEVISIT	Unlocks all the locales
WATCHAMOVIE	Unlocks all video Galleries
TINYBUTSTRONG	Unlocks Arnold
ASTRAL	Unlocks Astral's board
DONTFALL	Unlocks bonus missions
TOPFASHION	Unlocks character customization
SURPRISEGUEST	Unlocks Elliot
SLOWANDSTEADY	Unlocks Geek
MONSOON	Unlocks Monsoon Board
IMTHEBEST	Unlocks Tank Evans
KOBAYASHI	Unlocks Tatsuhi Kobayashi
TINYSHOCKWAVE	Unlocks Tiny Shockwave board
THELEGEND	Unlocks Zeke Topanga

Unlockables

Unlockable	How to Unlock
Arnold	Obtain 30,000 points in Shiverpool 2
Big Z	Obtain 100,000 points in Legendary Wave
Elliot	Obtain 40,000 points in Pen Gu North 3
Geek	Obtain 60,000 points in Pen Gu South 4
Tank	Obtain 40,000 points in the Boneyards
Tatsuhi	Obtain 15,000 points in Pen Gu South 2

Sword of Vermilion

Unlockables

Unlockable	How to Unlock
Quick Cash	In Keltwick, when Bearwulf gives you the dungeon key to get to Malaga, sell it. It's worth 1,000 kims and Bearwulf has an unlimited number of them. Just go back, talk to him, and he'll say "Did you lose the key? I have another one." He'll give it to you, and you can repeat the process as much as you want.
Test Menu	Any time during the game, hold Ⓐ+Ⓑ+Ⓒ and press START on controller 2. A test menu appears with Input, Sound, and C.R.T. tests. And when you exit, it sends you back to the SEGA logo screen.

Teenage Mutant Ninja Turtles

Unlockables

Unlockable	How to Unlock
Restore Power	Find a doorway that has a pizza slice or full pizza right at the beginning. Enter, grab the pizza, and exit. The pizza regenerates when you reenter. Use this to restore power to all your turtles.
Remove Crushers in Level 3	Hop in the Party Wagon. Whenever you see a pesky Crusher, press SELECT. You exit the car, and the Crusher vanishes.
Share Boomerangs	When you get the boomerangs, throw up to 3 of them in the air, then switch turtles, and have the new turtle catch them. The new turtle can use those boomerangs without having picked up a boomerang icon.

Teenage Mutant Ninja Turtles II: The Arcade Game

Unlockables

Unlockable	How to Unlock
Extra Lives and Stage Select	At the title screen, press Ⓑ, Ⓐ, Ⓑ, Ⓐ, ⬆, ⬆, Ⓑ, Ⓐ, ⬆, ⬆, Ⓑ, Ⓐ, START
Extra Lives Without Stage Select	On the title screen, press ⬆, ⬆, ⬆, ⬆, ⬆, ⬆, ⬆, ⬆, ⬆, ⬆, Ⓑ, Ⓐ, START
Stage Select	On the title screen, press ⬆, ⬆, ⬆, ⬆, ⬆, ⬆, ⬆, ⬆, ⬆, ⬆, ⬆, ⬆, Ⓑ, Ⓐ, START
Easier Battle with Shredder	During the final battle against Shredder, Shredder splits up into two forms. They're identical in appearance, but only one is real and the other is fake. However, both forms use the lightning attack that instantly kills you by turning you into a normal turtle. However, when either form is weakened to near death, his helmet flies off. As you're beating up on the two forms of Shredder, one of them loses his helmet very quickly. When this happens, leave him alone. This Shredder is the fake, and he cannot use the lightning attack without his helmet on. Only the real Shredder can use the attack, but because it's only him using it, you can avoid it and slowly beat him down with ease. For the rest of the fight, ignore the fake. If you kill him, the real Shredder releases another fake.

TMNT

Unlockables

At the main menu, hold Ⓩ on the Nunchuk and enter the following codes. Release Ⓩ after each code to hear a confirmation sound.

Unlockable	Code
Unlock Don's Big Head Goodie	①, Ⓐ, ©, ②
Unlock Challenge Map 2	Ⓐ, Ⓐ, Ⓐ, ①, Ⓐ

Tiger Woods PGA Tour 07

Enter these codes under passwords in the Options menu.

Unlockable	Code
Acquire all Cobra gear	SnakeKing
Unlock all Adidas items	THREE STRIPES
Unlock all Bridgestone items	SHOJIRO
Unlock all Grafalloye items	JUST SHAFTS
Unlock all Level 3 EA Sports items	INTHEGAME
Unlock all Macgergor items	MACTEC
Unlock all Mizuno items	RIHACHINRZO
Unlock all Nike items	JUSTDOIT
Unlock all Oakley items	JANNARD
Unlock all PGA Tour items	LIGHTNING
Unlock all Ping items	SOLHEIM
Unlock all players in team play	GAMEFACE
Unlock all Taylormade items	MRADAMS

DS

GBA

PSP

PS2

PS3

Wii

Xbox

Xbox 360

Index

DS

GBA

PSP

PS2

PS3

Wii

Xbox

Xbox 360

Index

Tiger Woods PGA Tour 08

Passwords

Password	Effect
PROSHOP	All Clubs Unlocked
NOTJUSTTIRES	Unlock Bridgestone Items
THREESTRIPES	Unlock Buick Items
CLEVELAND	Unlock Cleveland Golf Items
SNAKEKING	Unlock Cobra Items
INTHEGAME	Unlock EA Items
JUSTSHAFTS	Unlock Grafalloy Items
JLINDEBERG	Unlock J.Lindeberg Items
RIHACHINRIZO	Unlock Mizuno Items
JUSTDOIT	Unlock Nike Items
GUYSAREGOOD	Unlock Precept Items

ToeJam and Earl

Unlockables

Unlockable	How to Unlock
Free Presents	Sneak up on Santa Claus before he takes off and he gives you a few presents.
Level 0	On Level 1, on the bottom left side, a small hole leads to level 0, which has hula dancers in a tub and a lemonade man who gives you another life.
Present Island	At the top right of the map on level 1, there is a hidden island with a load of presents for the taking. You need rocket skates, an inner-tube, or icarus wings to get there.
Ultimate Cheat	Pause the game, then press the following button combinations: ✛+Ⓐ+Ⓑ+ⓒ, ✛+Ⓐ, ✛+Ⓑ, ✛+Ⓠ. You hear a sound if you entered the code correctly. Unpause the game, and you have all but one of the ship pieces collected. The last piece will always be located on the next level.

ToeJam and Earl in Panic on Funkotron

Passwords

Password	Effect
R-F411W9Q986	Level 3
PJ04EK-5WT82	Level 5
MW0WEE6JRVF7	Level 7
VANDNEHF9807L	Level 9
MWAAK!8MDT76	Level 11
F!!NEHNW0Q73	Level 15
T0EJAMTEARL!	View Credits

High Funk Passwords

Enter these passwords at the password screen to go to your desired level with lots of Funk.

Password	Effect
RWJ21EW1R80X	Level 03 with 37 Funk
VJW6EK21-J07	Level 05 with 80 Funk
P0W09KAN-VQ	Level 07 with 95 Funk

DS

GBA

PSP

PS2

PS3

Wii

Xbox

Xbox 360

Index

ToeJam and Earl in Panic on Funkotron (continued)

VDJF7M2DyT6L	Level 09 with 99 Funk
VYJF73TH1PQQ	Level 11 with 99 Funk
DKYQHX4!EV!7	Level 13 with 89 Funk
J11L3R4C13H7	Level 15 with 49 Funk

Tom Clancy's Splinter Cell Double Agent

Unlockables

Unlockable	How to Unlock
Elite Mode	Clear the Solo mode once
Elite Mode (Co-op)	Beat the game in Co-op mode to unlock Co-op Elite mode

Tony Hawk's Downhill Jam

Enter these passwords in the Cheats menu.

Unlockable	Password	Unlockable	Password
Always Special	PointHogger	Perfect Manual	TightRopeWalker
Chipmunk Voices	HelloHelium	Perfect Rail	LikeTiltingAPlate
Demon Skater	EvilChimneySweep	Perfect Stats	IAmBob
Display Coordinates	DisplayCoordinates	Picasso Skater	FourLights
Enables Manuals	IMISSMANUALS	Power of the Fish!	TonyFishDownhillJam
Extreme Car Crashes	WatchForDoors	Shadow Skater	ChimneySweep
First Person Skater	FirstPersonJam	Tiny People	ShrinkThePeople
Free Boost	OotbaghForever	Unlock All Boards and Outfits	RaidTheWoodshed
Giganto-Skater	IWannaBeTallTall	Unlock All Events	AdventuresOfKwang
Invisible Skater	NowYouSeeMe	Unlock All Movies	FreeBozzler
Large Birds	BirdBirdBirdBird	Unlock All Skaters	ImInterfacing
Mini Skater	DownTheRabbitHole		

Tower of Druaga

Codes

Enter this code at the title screen. If entered properly, the word "DRUA-GA" will turn green. The game is now harder and the levels require different solutions.

Code	Effect
⇩, ⇩, ⇩, ⇩, ⇩, ⇩, ⇧, ⇩, ⇩, ⇩, ⇩, ⇩, ⇩, ⇩	Another Druaga (Second Quest)

Transformers: The Game

Codes

Enter the following codes at the Campaign/Bonus Features/Credits menu.

Code	Effect
⇩, ⇩, ⇩, ⇩, ⇩, ⇩, ⇩, ⇩	Unlock all missions
⇩, ⇩, ⇩, ⇩, ⇩, ⇩, ⇩	Infinite health—invincible
⇩, ⇩, ⇩, ⇩, ⇩, ⇩, ⇩	No vehicles running on the street and no tanks/cops attack
⇩, ⇩, ⇩, ⇩, ⇩, ⇩, ⇩	Unlock Cybertron missions
⇩, ⇩, ⇩, ⇩, ⇩, ⇩, ⇩	Unlock G1 Optimus Prime
⇩, ⇩, ⇩, ⇩, ⇩, ⇩, ⇩	Unlock Generation 1 Jazz Repaint
⇩, ⇩, ⇩, ⇩, ⇩, ⇩, ⇩	Unlock Generation 1 Starscream Repaint

DS
GBA
PSP
PS2
PS3
Wii
Xbox
Xbox 360
Index

Transformers: The Game (continued)

⬆, ⬆, ⬆, ⬆, ⬆, ⬆, ⬆	Unlock Robovision Optimus Prime
⬆, ⬆, ⬆, ⬆, ⬆, ⬆, ⬆	Unlock G1 Megatron

Unlockables

Unlockable	How to Unlock
G1 Jazz Repaint	Clear all sub-missions in Autobot and Decepticon Story modes
G1 Megatron	Collect all of the Decepticon icons on all of the maps
G1 Optimus Prime	Collect all of the Autobot Icons on all of the maps
G1 Starscream Repaint	Beat the Decepticon's Story mode
Robovision Optimus Prime	Beat the Autobot's Story mode

Trauma Center: Second Opinion

Unlockable	How To
X Missions for both doctors	Once unlocked, the first X mission will be available to both doctors. If you complete an X mission with one doctor, the next mission will be available to both doctors.
Episode 6	Complete all operations in episodes 1-5 and Z to unlock episode 6.

Vectorman

Unlockables

Unlockable	How to Unlock
Blow Up SEGA Logo	At the SEGA screen, move Vectorman slightly to the right of the logo. Aim upward and shoot. There is a hidden TV monitor there. Once it is broken, grab and use an orb power-up. The SEGA logo goes dark and the background stops moving.
Debug Mode	On the Options screen press Ⓐ, Ⓑ, Ⓑ, Ⓐ, ⬆, Ⓐ, Ⓑ, Ⓑ, Ⓐ. A menu then offers health, lives, level select, and weapon options.
Full Health	Pause the game and press Ⓐ, Ⓑ, ⬆, Ⓐ, Ⓒ, Ⓐ, ⬆, Ⓐ, Ⓑ, ⬆, Ⓐ.
Invisibility and Invincibility	First grab a bomb morph, and detonate Vectorman. Pause the game while Vectorman is still exploding and enter CALLACAB (Ⓒ, Ⓐ, ⬆, ⬆, Ⓐ, Ⓒ, Ⓐ, Ⓑ). Unpause the game. Pause again and enter the CALLACAB code. Unpause it, and Vectorman is invisible and invincible. Reenter the CALLACAB code to turn it off. No bomb morph is needed to disable it.
Level Warp	When you turn on the game, you can move Vectorman around on the SEGA screen. Shoot the SEGA logo 24 times, jump and hit the SEGA logo with Vectorman's head 12 times, and the letters S, E, G, and A start falling. Catch 90 to 110 letters to start on Stage 5, catch more than 110 letters to start on Day 10.
Light Bulbs	During gameplay, pause and enter Ⓐ, Ⓑ, Ⓐ, Ⓒ, Ⓐ, Ⓑ and press pause. A group of lights should be around you. The four lights that surround Vectorman indicate the field of collision detection. The light at the bottom indicates the collision detection of Vectorman's jets.

Vectorman (continued)

Slow Motion	This code slows down the game whenever you're hit. While playing, pause and press ⬇, ⬇, Ⓐ, Ⓒ, ⬇, ⬇, Ⓐ. Turn it off by entering the code again.
Stage Select	Ⓑ, Ⓐ, Ⓐ, Ⓑ, ⬇, Ⓑ, Ⓐ, Ⓐ, Ⓑ
Taxi Mode	Pause and press Ⓒ, Ⓐ, ⬇, ⬇, Ⓐ, Ⓒ, Ⓐ, Ⓑ (Call a Cab). You turn into a small cursor/arrow and can travel anywhere in the level. Enemies can also be killed by coming in contact with them. Bosses cannot be killed this way. To return to normal, pause and enter the code again.

Virtua Fighter 2

Unlockables

Unlockable	How to Unlock
Different Costumes	To play in a character's different costumes, Hold ⬇ and then select your character with Ⓐ or ⬇. Or hold ⬇ and select your character with Ⓐ, ⬇, or START.
Extra Character Selection Time	Press ⬇, ⬇, ⬇, Ⓐ+⬇ at the Character Selection Screen for 99 seconds of extra time.
Hidden Options	Enter the Options screen, highlight the "Exit" selection, and tap ⬇ until the hidden options are displayed.
No Damage	Hold Ⓑ while highlighting player 1's life selection at the Options screen, until the message "No Damage" appears. Then press START.
Play as Dural	Highlight Akira using controller 1 or Jacky using controller 2. Then press ⬇, ⬇. Repeat this a few times and Dural appears as a selectable character.

Wonder Boy in Monster World

Unlockables

Unlockable	How to Unlock
Stay at the Inn for Free	Any Inn throughout the game will let you spend the night, even if you don't have enough gold. They just take whatever you have, even if you don't have any gold at all.

World Series of Poker: Tournament of Champions

Unlockables

Unlockable	How to Unlock
All Locations	Input ⬇, ⬇, ⬇, ⬇, ⬇ at the main menu

Wrecking Crew

Unlockables

Unlockable	How to Unlock
Gold Hammer	In Phase 6, there are five bombs, 2 on the bottom, 2 in the middle of the level, and 1 on the top. Hit the 2 bombs on the bottom and then hit the middle left bomb. In a few seconds, a hammer appears. Hit it to obtain it. You now have the gold hammer. The music changes and you can hit enemies. You have the hammer until you die.

DS
GBA
PSP
PS2
PS3
Wii
Xbox
Xbox 360
Index

Table of Contents - Xbox

Sidebar tabs: DS, GBA, PSP, PS2, PS3, Wii, Xbox, Xbox 360, Index

Table of Contents - Xbox (con't.)

DS

GBA

PSP

PS2

PS3

Wii

Xbox

Xbox 360

Index

Table of Contents – Xbox (con't.)

Table of Contents - Xbox (con't.)

007: Agent Under Fire

Description	Objective
Alpine Guard Skin in Multiplayer Mode	Complete the Streets of Bucharest level with a "Platinum" rank and all 007 icons.
Calypso Gun in Multiplayer Mode	Complete the Fire and Water level with a "Platinum" rank and all 007 icons.
Carrier Guard Multiplayer Skin	Complete the Evil Summit level with a "Platinum" rank and all 007 icons.
Cyclops Oil Guard skin in Multiplayer Mode	Complete the Poseidon level with a "Platinum" rank and all 007 icons.

DS

GBA

PSP

PS2

PS3

Wii

Xbox

Xbox 360

Index

DS

GBA

PSP

PS2

PS3

Wii

Xbox

Xbox 360

Index

007: Agent Under Fire (continued)

Description	Objective
Full Arsenal in Multiplayer Mode	Complete the Forbidden Depths level with a "Platinum" rank and all 007 icons.
Golden Accuracy Power-Up (This cheat enables you to have greater auto-aim.)	Complete the Bad Diplomacy level with a "Gold" rank.
Golden Armor Power-Up	Complete the Forbidden Depths level with a "Gold" rank.
Golden Bullet Power-Up	Complete the Poseidon level with a "Gold" rank.
Golden CH-6 (This cheat gives you unlimited rockets.)	Complete the Precious Cargo level with a "Gold" rank.
Golden Clip Power-Up	Complete the Cold Reception level with a "Gold" rank.
Golden Grenade Power-Up	Complete the Night of the Jackal level with a "Gold" rank.
Golden Gun (Unlocks the Golden PK2)	Complete the Trouble in Paradise level with a "Gold" rank.
Golden Gun in Multiplayer Mode	Complete the Precious Cargo level with a "Platinum" rank and all 007 icons.
Gravity Boots in Multiplayer Mode	Complete the Bad Diplomacy level with a "Platinum" rank and all 007 icons.
Guard Skin in Multiplayer Mode	Complete the Cold Reception level with a "Platinum" rank and all 007 icons.
Lotus Esprit Car	Complete the Streets of Bucharest level with a "Gold" rank.
Poseidon Guard Skin in Multiplayer Mode	Complete the Mediterranean Crisis level with a "Platinum" rank and all 007 icons.
Rapid Fire Power-Up	Complete the Fire and Water level with a "Gold" rank.
Regenerative Armor Power-Up	Complete the Mediterranean Crisis level with a "Gold" rank.
Rocket Manor Multiplayer Level (This cheat unlocks a new multiplayer level, a large, open area. The map settings allow only rockets.)	Complete the Trouble in Paradise level with a "Platinum" rank and all 007 icons.
Stealth Bond Skin in Multiplayer Mode	Complete the Dangerous Pursuit level with a "Platinum" rank and all 007 icons.
Unlimited Car Missiles	Complete the Dangerous Pursuit level with a "Gold" rank.
Unlimited Golden Gun Ammunition	Complete the Evil Summit level with a "Gold" rank.
Viper Gun in Multiplayer Mode	Complete the Night of the Jackal level with a "Platinum" rank and all 007 icons.

TIP

Golden Gun Tip:

With this gun, you receive a silencer that the normal P2K doesn't have. To do this easily, get as much accuracy as you can, take as few hits as you can, and do all the Bond moves (shooting barrels to explode, shooting vital enemy characters, and finding secret areas).

007: Everything or Nothing

Unlockable	Objective	Unlockable	Objective
003	290 Points	Mya	14 Gold
All Weapons	17 Platinum	Nanotank Upgrade	24 Gold
Baron Samedi	50 Points	Odd Job	70 Points
Burn Chamber	370 Points	Platinum Gun	27 Platinum
Cayenne Upgrade	12 Gold	Production Stills 1	1 Gold
Cistern	30 Points	Production Stills 2	2 Gold
Cloak	13 Platinum	Production Stills 3	3 Gold
Diavolo Moscow	400 Points	Production Stills 4	4 Gold
Double Ammo	7 Platinum	Production Stills 5	5 Gold
Double Damage	9 Platinum	Production Stills 6	7 Gold
Egypt Commander	90 Points	Production Stills 7	9 Gold
Egypt Guard	180 Points	Production Stills 8	13 Gold
Full Ammo	11 Platinum	Production Stills 9	16 Gold
Full Battery	15 Platinum	Production Stills 10	18 Gold
Gallery	27 Gold	Production Stills 11	19 Gold
Golden Gun	1 Platinum	Production Stills 12	22 Gold
Hazmat Guard	110 Points	Production Stills 13	23 Gold
Helicopter Upgrade	6 Gold	Production Stills 14	25 Gold
Improved Battery	5 Platinum	Serena	350 Points
Improved Traction	3 Platinum	Serena	430 Points
Katya	20 Gold	Serena	8 Gold
Katya Jumpsuit	320 Points	Slow Motion Driving	25 Platinum
Le Rouge	260 Points	South Commander	210 Points
Moscow Guard	230 Points	Tank Upgrade	10 Gold
MI6 Combat Simulator	Complete all Missions	Test Lab	160 Points
MI6 Survival Test	Complete all Missions	Triumph Upgrade	21 Gold
Miss Nagai	450 Points	Underworld	11 Gold
Miss Nagai	17 Gold	Unlimited Ammo	23 Platinum
Mya	130 Points	Unlimited Battery	19 Platinum
		Vanquish Upgrade	15 Gold

007: Nightfire

Cheat Mode: For the following codes, select the "Codenames" option at the main menu. Select your character and enter one of the following codes at the Secret Unlocks screen. Save your Codename after entering the code. Then exit your Codename and begin gameplay.

Unlockable	Code
All Gadget Upgrades	Q LAB
All Multiplayer Options	GAMEROOM
Alpine Escape Level	POWDER
Bigger Clip for Sniper Rifle	MAGAZINE
Camera Upgrade	SHUTTER
Chain Reaction Level	MELTDOWN
Countdown Level	BLASTOFF
Decrypter Upgrade	SESAME

DS
GBA
PSP
PS2
PS3
Wii
Xbox
Xbox 360
Index

007: Nightfire (continued)

Unlockable	Code
Deep Descent Level	AQUA
Double Cross Level	BONSAI
Enemies Vanquished Level	TRACTION
Equinox Level	VACUUM
Golden P2K	AU P2K
Golden PP7	AU PP7
Grapple Upgrade	LIFTOFF
Island Infiltration Level	PARADISE
Laser Upgrade	PHOTON
Level Select	PASSPORT
Multiplayer Bond Spacesuit	ZERO G
Multiplayer Mode All Characters	PARTY
Multiplayer Mode Assassination Option	TARGET
Multiplayer Mode Baron Samedi	VOODOO
Multiplayer Mode Bond Tuxedo	BLACKTIE
Multiplayer Mode Christmas Jones	NUCLEAR
Multiplayer Mode Demolition Option	TNT
Multiplayer Mode Drake	NUMBER 1
Multiplayer Mode Elektra King	Enter SLICK
Multiplayer Mode Explosive Scenery Option	BOOM
Multiplayer Mode GoldenEye Strike Option	ORBIT
Multiplayer Mode Goldfinger	MIDAS
Multiplayer Mode Jaws	DENTAL
Multiplayer Mode Max Zorin	BLIMP
Multiplayer Mode Mayday	BADGIRL
Multiplayer Mode Nick Nack	BITESIZE
Multiplayer Mode Oddjob	BOWLER
Multiplayer Mode Protection Option	GUARDIAN
Multiplayer Mode Pussy Galore	CIRCUS
Multiplayer Mode Renard	HEADCASE
Multiplayer Mode Scaramanga	ASSASSIN
Multiplayer Mode Team King of the Hill Option	TEAMWORK
Multiplayer Mode Uplink Option	TRANSMIT
Vanquish Car Missile Upgrade	LAUNCH
Tranquilizer Dart Upgrade (Your tranquilizer darts are upgraded so enemies stay down longer.)	SLEEPY
Stunner Upgrade	ZAP
Rifle Scope Upgrade	SCOPE
Phoenix Fire Level	FLAME
P2K Upgrade	P2000
Night Shift Level	HIGHRISE
Multiplayer Mode Wai Lin	MARTIAL
Multiplayer Mode Xenia Onatopp	JANUS

DS
GBA
PSP
PS2
PS3
Wii
Xbox
Xbox 360
Index

007: Nightfire (continued)

Unlockable	Code
Berserk Racing	While racing on the Paris Prelude, Enemies Vanquished, Island Infiltration, or Deep Descent levels, press ⊘ to pause gameplay, hold ⓛ, press ✕, ⓨ, ⓨ, ✕, ⓨ, ⓑ, then release ⓛ.
Faster Gameplay	Press ⊘ to pause gameplay, hold ⓛ, press ✕, ⓨ, ⓑ, ⓦ, ✕, ⓨ, ⓑ, ⓦ, then release ⓛ.
Frantic Racing	While racing on the Paris Prelude, Enemies Vanquished, Island Infiltration, or Deep Descent levels, press ⊘ to pause gameplay, hold ⓛ, press ✕, ⓨ, ⓑ, ⓨ, ✕, then release ⓛ.
Drive a Shelby Cobra	While racing on the Enemies Vanquished level, press ⊘ to pause gameplay, hold ⓛ, press ◆, ◆, ◇, ◇, then release ⓛ. You can now use the Shelby Cobra from the Paris Prelude level in the race through the Alps.
Drive an SUV	While racing on the Enemies Vanquished level, press ⊘ to pause gameplay, hold ⓛ, press ✕, ⓑ, ⓨ, ✕, ⓨ, and then release ⓛ.
Double Armor during Racing	While racing on the Paris Prelude, Enemies Vanquished, Island Infiltration, or Deep Descent levels, press ⊘ to pause gameplay, hold ⓛ, press ⓑ, ⓨ, ✕, ⓑ, ⓑ, then release ⓛ.
Bonus Race in Alps	While racing on the Enemies Vanquished level, press ⊘ to pause gameplay, hold ⓛ, press ⓑ, ⓑ, ✕, ⓑ, ⓨ, then release ⓛ.
Quadruple Armor during Racing	While racing on the Paris Prelude, Enemies Vanquished, Island Infiltration, or Deep Descent levels, press ⊘ to pause gameplay, hold ⓛ, press ⓑ, ⓨ, ✕, ⓑ, ⓑ, ⓑ, then release ⓛ.
Super Bullets during Racing	While racing on the Paris Prelude, Enemies Vanquished, Island Infiltration, or Deep Descent levels, press ⊘ to pause gameplay, hold ⓛ, press ⓑ, ⓑ, ⓑ, ⓑ, then release ⓛ. Note: You can also do this when you fly the plane with Alura.
Trails during Racing	While racing on the Paris Prelude, Enemies Vanquished, Island Infiltration, or Deep Descent levels, press ⊘ to pause gameplay, hold ⓛ, press ✕, ⓑ, ⓑ, ✕, then release ⓛ.
Triple Armor during Racing	While racing on the Paris Prelude, Enemies Vanquished, Island Infiltration, or Deep Descent levels, press ⊘ to pause gameplay, hold ⓛ, press ⓑ, ⓨ, ✕, ⓑ, ⓑ, ⓑ, then release ⓛ.

4X4 Evolution 2

Enter these codes at the Main menu or Title screen.

Unlockable	Code
Extra Money in Career Mode	ⓨ, ✕, ⓦ, ⓨ, ✕, ⓦ, ✕, ⓨ, ✕, ⓦ, ✕, ⓨ
High Reputation (for team selection)	ⓨ, ⓨ, ⓦ, ✕, ✕, ⓦ, ⓨ, ⓨ, ✕, ✕, ✕
Mission Select	✕, ✕, ⓦ, ⓦ, ⓨ, ⓨ, ⓦ, ✕, ⓨ, ✕, ⓦ

50 Cent Bulletproof

To enter these passwords, pause the game. Go into Options, then enter the Cheat menu.

Unlockable	Password
Action 26	orangejuice
All Music Tracks	GrabAllThat50
All Music Videos	HookMeUp50
All Weapons	GotThemRachets
Bloodhound Counterkill	gunrunner
Bulletproof aka Invincible	ny'sfinestyo

DS

GBA

PSP

PS2

PS3

Wii

Xbox

Xbox 360

Index

DS

GBA

PSP

PS2

PS3

Wii

Xbox

Xbox 360

Index

50 Cent Bulletproof (continued)

Unlockable	Password
Empty n' Clips Counterkill	workout
"G'd Up" Counterkill	GoodDieYoung
"Guillotine" Counterkill	GettingDropped
Infinite Ammo	GrizzSpecial
Mike Mode	the hub is broken
My Buddy video	sayhellotomylittlefriend
So Seductive video	yayoshome Tony Yayo
"Wanksta" Counter-Kill	AintGotNothin

Advent Rising

Enter this code while the game is paused.

Unlockable	Code
Cheat menu	⚪, ⚪, ⚪, ⚪, ◀, ▶, ◀, ▶, 🄻🅃, 🅁🅃, ✕

To enter this code, select a spot for a 'new game'. After you do that, enter this code.

Unlockable	Code
Unlock all levels and cutscenes	🅁🅃, 🄻🅃, 🅁🅃, 🄻🅃, ✕

Aeon Flux

At the Main menu, press ❤, then go into the Enter Cheats menu to enter these passwords.

Unlockable	Password
Action Movie	BRAVO ALPHA GOLF MIKE ALPHA NOVEMBER
Action Movie	UNIFORM KILO GOLF ALPHA MIKE ECHO ROMEO
Free Fatalities	CHARLIE UNIFORM TANGO INDIA OSCAR NOVEMBER ECHO
God Mode	TANGO ROMEO INDIA ROMEO OSCAR XRAY
One Strike Kills	BRAVO UNIFORM CHARLIE KILO FOXTROT SIERRA TANGO
Restore Health	HOTEL ECHO ALPHA LIMA MIKE ECHO
Unlimited Ammo	FOXTROT UNIFORM GOLF
Unlimited Health	CHARLIE LIMA OSCAR NOVEMBER ECHO
Unlimited Power Strikes	LIMA CHARLIE VICTOR GOLF
Unlock All Replay Episodes	BRAVO ALPHA YANKEE OSCAR UNIFORM
Unlock All Slideshows	PAPA INDIA XRAY ECHO SIERRA
Unlock Bomber Jacket Outfit	JULIET ALPHA CHARLIE KILO ECHO TANGO
Unlock Fame Outfit	GOLF ROMEO ALPHA YANKEE
Unlock Monican Freya/Hostess Judy/Una/Fashion Una Outfits	CHARLIE LIMA OSCAR TANGO HOTEL ECHO SIERRA
Unlock Mrs. Goodchild Outfits	WHISKEY HOTEL INDIA TANGO ECHO
Unlock Revelation Outfits	ALPHA ROMEO MIKE SIERRA
Unlock Seed Outfits	MIKE OSCAR VICTOR INDIA ECHO
Unlock Seed Outfits	UNIFORM ROMEO BRAVO ALPHA NOVEMBER
Unlock War Outfits	BRAVO LIMA UNIFORM ROMEO

Aggressive Inline

Unlockable	Objective
Bonus Characters	Complete the normal and hidden challenges in a level to unlock a bonus character.
Cheats	Collect all juice boxes in a level to reveal a cheat code.
FMV Sequences	Complete the normal challenges in a level to unlock its FMV sequence.
Power Skates	Complete all challenges (normal and hidden) on every level. The Power Skates give you one blue stat point for every attribute.
Ultra Skates	Complete all the levels with 100 percent. The Ultra Skates give you the other blue stat point for every attribute.

AirForce Delta Storm

Unlockables

Unlockable	How to Unlock
Get More Planes	Beat any 2 levels in a row without returning to air base to get more planes.

Alias

Level select

Successfully complete the game, then enter the code below

Code	Effect
Hold (LT) + (RB) + (LB) + (WHT)	Level select

Alien Hominid

Passwords

Password	Effect
FBI	99 bombs and 10 lives

Unlockable Hats

Enter these as a player name. When you click submit, a foghorn sounds if the password was entered correctly.

Password	Effect
Grrl	Hat 11, top hat
Abe	Hat 12, diamond tiara
Betty	Hat 13, daisy headdress
Princess	Hat 13, daisy headdress
Dandy	Hat 14, Dick Tracy hat
TomFulp	Hat 2, Tom Fulp
Cletus	Hat 4, blonde hair
April	Hat 5, red hair
Superfly	Hat 7, Jheri curl
Goodman	Hat 8, pirate bandana

Other Unlockables

Unlockable	How to Unlock
Chicken Hat, Level 1-4	When you come across the Behemoth building, destroy it and a foghorn will sound
Curly Hair, Level 1-4	When you find the Fish Are Like Plants building, destroy it, and a foghorn will sound
Super Soviet Missile Master Minigame	Complete level 1-5

DS

GBA

PSP

PS2

PS3

Wii

Xbox

Xbox 360

Index

DS

Aliens vs. Predator: Extinction

Unlockable	Code
Cheats	Pause the game and press ⓇⓉ, ⓇⓉ, ⓁⓉ, ⓇⓉ, ⓁⓉ, ⓁⓉ, ⓇⓉ, ⓁⓉ, ⓇⓉ, ⓇⓉ, ⓁⓉ, ⓇⓉ, ⓁⓉ, ⓁⓉ, ⓇⓉ, ⓁⓉ. The cheats are now available via the Options menu.

GBA

Alter Echo

Enter these codes during gameplay.

Unlockable	Code
Remove Display	◊,◊,♀,♀,◁,▷,◁,♀+▼
Restore Health	◊,◊,♀,♀,◁,▷,◁,♀+▷
Restore Time Dilation	◊,◊,♀,♀,◁,▷,◁,♀+◊

PSP

Amped: Freestyle Snowboarding

Passwords

Select "Options" at the main menu, then "Cheats." Enter these codes as case-sensitive codes. A sound confirms correct code entry. Press ❽ to exit the Cheat menu.

Password	Effect
GimmeGimme	All Levels
BigLeg	Big Jumps
MegabOUnce	Bouncy Terrain
buzzsaW	Disable Tree Collisions
MegaLeg	Even Bigger Jumps
ZiPster	Go Faster (Even Uphill)
StickiT	Land All Jumps Perfectly
WhirlyGig	Major Spins
RidinwRaven	Play as Raven
ChillinwSteezy	Play as Steezy
KeepnReal	Realistic Mode
BigsteeZ	Super Snowboarder

PS2

PS3

Unlock Hidden Movie

Unlockable	How to Unlock
End Game Cinematic	Beat all the Pro Challenges, beat all the high scores, beat all the media challenges, and find all 8 snowmen on each level. (World Rank 1).

Wii

Amped 2

Go to Options and enter the following codes in the Cheats menu.

Xbox

Unlockable	Code	Unlockable	Code
All Courses Are Icy	AllIce	Open All Levels	AllLevels
All Secret Boarders	AllMyPeeps	Rider Moves Faster	FastMove
Cheats Are Deactivated	NoCheats	Rider Never Crashes	DontCrash
Low Gravity	LowGravity	Spin Faster	SuperSpin
Max Out Rider Stats	MaxSkills	Unlock a Pink Bunny	Bunny
No Collisions with Other Riders	NoCollisions		

Xbox 360

Index

Apex

Enter all codes as brand names in Dream mode.

Unlockable	Code
All Concept Cars in Arcade Mode	Dreamy
All Production Cars in Arcade Mode	Reality
All Tracks in Arcade Mode	World

Arctic Thunder

Enter these codes at the Mode Selection screen.

Unlockable	Code
All Atomic Snowballs	X, X, X, WHT, Y, START
All Boosts Mode	Y, BLK, BLK, Y, RT, START
All Grappling Hooks	Y, Y, LT, Y, Y, WHT, START
All Invisible	X, Y, X, RT, Y, Y, START
All Random Locations	BLK, RT, X, Y, BLK, RT, START
All Rooster Tails	BLK, RT, LT, WHT, X, START
All Snow Bombs	Y, Y, BLK, RT, START
Clone Mode	WHT, BLK, BLK, Y, WHT, Y, START
No Catch-Up Mode	Y, X, Y, Y, X, START
No Drones Mode	X, X, Y, Y, WHT, BLK, START
No Power-Up Mode	X, X, Y, Y, RT, X, START
Super Boost	4, WHT, X, RT, X, LT, START

Armed and Dangerous

Enter the following codes at the Cheats screen in the Options menu.

Unlockable	Code
Big Boots	RT, WHT, Y, A, LT, B, WHT, X
Big Hands	RT, WHT, X, LT, WHT, RT, RT, Y
Big Heads	LT, BLK, B, WHT, WHT, B, BLK, LT

Enter the following codes at the Cheats screen in the Options menu.

Unlockable	Code
Fill Ammo	BLK, B, A, RT, RT, A, LT, BLK
Fill Health Bar	X, RT, A, Y, BLK, B, A, RT
Invincible	X, X, X, RT, A, LT, LT, Y
Topsy Turvy	X, A, B, B, A, B, WHT, WHT

Azurik: Rise of Perathia

Unlockable	Code
Adjust Camera	Quickly press RT, Y, Ó, Y, Ó, click B, click L. The game stops, allowing you to alter the view. See Adjust Camera Tip for camera controls.
Adjust Lighting	Quickly press A, click B, B, click B, click L. Darker areas become easier to see, but at the expense of having less dramatic lighting. Repeat this code to return to normal.
Big Heads	Quickly click B, press RT, Y, Ó, A. A sound confirms correct code entry.
God Mode	Quickly press X, BLK, WHT, RT + LT, click L + B. A sound confirms correct code entry. Repeat this code to disable its effect.

Azurik: Rise of Perathia (continued)

Unlockable	Code
Level Select (This cheat also allows you to change your stats and view all FMV sequences.)	Press Ⓛ + Ⓡ, Ⓛ + Ⓡ, Ⓐ, Ⓑ, click Ⓝ, click Ⓛ. You must power off the Xbox to exit an FMV sequence.
Save at any point	Quickly press ⓦʜⓣ, Ⓨ, Ⓧ, Ⓐ, Ⓑ, click Ⓝ during the "swing" animation. A click confirms that the game has been saved.

TIP

Adjust Camera Tip: Camera Controls

Press Ⓛ or Ⓡ to move the view up or down. Press Ⓝ or Ⓝ to move the view forward and back. Press Ⓞ to zoom in and out. Press Ⓐ to view and remove the elemental power display. Press Ⓞ to resume the game.

CAUTION

Gem Mode Caution!

Do not create more gems than are supported! This will crash the game.

CAUTION

Save Point Caution!

While this may be done at any time during the game, remember to choose your save point carefully. Avoid saving on moving platforms, in areas where enemies respawn, while falling, or while dying.

Backyard Wrestling

Enter this code at the Main menu.

Unlockable	Code
All Wrestlers and Stages	Hold Ⓛ, then press Ⓐ, Ⓧ, Ⓨ, Ⓝ, Ⓐ, Ⓧ, Ⓨ, Ⓝ.

Bad Boys: Miami Takedown

Enter the code at the Title screen.

Unlockable	Code
Cheat Menu	Ⓑ, Ⓨ, Ⓧ, Ⓨ, Ⓞ, Ⓞ

Baldur's Gate: Dark Alliance

Unlockables

Unlockable	How to Unlock
The Gauntlet Mode	Complete the game on any difficulty
Unlock Extreme	Successfully complete The Gauntlet
Play as Drizzt	Import a standard player into Extreme mode and complete it with that character. Now you can import Drizzt (from your Gauntlet save file) into the main game.

The Bard's Tale

While playing, hold Ⓛ+Ⓡ, then enter the following codes.

Unlockable	Code
Damage x100	Ⓨ, Ⓞ, Ⓨ, Ⓞ, Ⓞ, Ⓞ, Ⓞ, Ⓞ
Full Mana and Health	Ⓞ, Ⓞ, Ⓞ, Ⓞ, Ⓨ, Ⓞ, Ⓨ, Ⓞ
Intangible	Ⓞ, Ⓞ, Ⓞ, Ⓞ, Ⓨ, Ⓞ, Ⓨ, Ⓞ
Invincible	Ⓞ, Ⓞ, Ⓞ, Ⓞ, Ⓨ, Ⓞ, Ⓨ, Ⓨ
Silver and Adderstones	Ⓨ, Ⓨ, Ⓞ, Ⓨ, Ⓞ, Ⓞ, Ⓞ, Ⓞ

DS GBA PSP PS2 PS3 Wii Xbox Xbox 360 Index

Batman: Rise of Sin Tzu

At the Mode Select screen, hold ⓛ+ⓡ, then enter the codes.

Unlockable	Code
All Rewards	◄, ♦, ◄, ►, ◄, ◄, ♦, ►
All Upgrades	♦, ♦, ►, ◄, ♦, ►, ♦, ♦
Dark Knight Mode	►, ♦, ♦, ◄, ►, ♦, ♦, ♦
Infinite Health	♦, ◄, ♦, ◄, ♦, ♦, ◄, ♦
Unlimited Combo Meter	◄, ►, ♦, ♦, ♦, ♦, ◄

Batman Vengeance

Input the following codes at the Main menu. Many of them will make a sound to confirm correct code entry.

Unlockable	Code
Bonus Characters	Press ◄, ►, ♦, ⓦ, ⓛ + ⓡ, then press Ⓧ
Master Code	Press ⓛ, ⓡ, ⓛ, ⓡ, Ⓧ, Ⓧ, Ⓨ, Ⓨ
Unlimited Batarangs	Press ⓛ, ⓡ, ⓦ, Ⓨ
Unlimited Electric Batarangs	Press ⓛ, ⓡ, Ⓑ, ⓦ, ⓛ

Battlefield 2: Modern Combat

Unlock All Weapons

Receive All Weapons Permanently
During gameplay, hold ⓦ+🔲 and press ►, ►, ♦, ♦, ◄, ◄

Battlestar Galactica

Enter the following codes in the Extras menu. A sound will confirm successful code entry.

Unlockable	Code
Wingmen, Starbuck and Apollo	♦, ♦, ◄, ♦, ♦, ♦, ◄, ►
Production Stills and Artwork	◄, ♦, ◄, ◄, ♦, ♦, ♦, ♦
	♦, ♦, ♦, ♦, ►, ♦, ◄, ♦
	♦, ♦, ♦, ♦, ◄, ◄, ◄, ◄
	♦, ♦, ♦, ♦, ♦, ♦, ◄, ►
	►, ►, ♦, ♦, ◄, ◄, ♦, ♦
	♦, ◄, ►, ►, ♦, ♦, ◄, ♦
	►, ◄, ♦, ♦, ◄, ◄, ♦, ♦
	♦, ◄, ♦, ►, ♦, ◄, ♦, ►

Big Mutha Truckers

Unlockable	Code
All Cheats	CHEATINGMUTHATRUCKER
Automatic Navigation	USETHEFORCE
Diplomatic Immunity	VICTORS
Evil Truck	VARLEY
Extra Money	LOTSAMONEY
Fast Truck	GINGERBEER
Infinite Time	PUBLICTRANSPORT
Level Select	LAZYPLAYER
Small Pedestrians	DAISHI
Toggle Damage	6WL

NOTE

You can also unlock Evil Truck by clearing the 60-Day Trial in Truckin'
mode and win the race to Big Mutha Trucking HQ.

Big Mutha Truckers 2

To enter these passwords, highlight "Trial by Trucking" and press ❂.

Unlockable	Code
$115,000	CASH
All Gallery Images	GALLERY
Invincible	NODAMAGE
Lots of Bikers	BIKERS
Lots of Cops	COPS
Opens All Bridges	BRIDGE
Removes All Police	NOCOPS
Unlocks All Missions	MISSIONS

Black

Enter this password as a profile name. Once it is entered you will be
asked to enter a real profile name.

Unlockable	Password
Start with the BFG	5SQQ-STHA-ZFFV-7XEV

Black Stone: Magic and Steel

Unlockable	Code
New Character Class	From the Class selection screen, press ℝⓉ as you highlight each of the following classes: Pirate, Thief, Warrior, Archer, Pirate, Warlock, Thief, Warlock, Thief.

Blade II

At the Main menu, hold down Ⓛ, then enter the following codes. Text
will appear upon successful code entry.

Unlockable	Code
All Weapons	❂,🅑,♀,◄,🅑,🅑,❖
Daywalker Difficulty	◄,🅑,🅑,♀,❂,🅑,◭
Level Select	♀,♂,◄,◄,🅑,▻,♀,❂

While paused, hold Ⓛ, then enter the following codes. Text will appear
upon successful code entry.

Unlockable	Code
Infinite Ammunition	◄,🅑,▻,❂,♂,❖,♀,◭
Infinite Health	❖,❂,❖,❂,❖,🅑,❖,🅑
Infinite Rage	◄,♀,◄,♀,▻,♂,▻,◄
Invincibility for NPCs during escort missions	❂,🅑,❖,◭,❂,🅑,❖,◭

Blazing Angels: Squadrons of WWII

Enter this code at the Main menu.

Unlockable	Code
All Planes and Missions	Hold Ⓛ + ℝⓉ and press ❂, ⓌⒽⓣ, ⓛⒷ, ❖, ❖, ⓛⒷ, ⓌⒽⓣ, ❂

Enter these codes while the game is paused.

Unlockable	Code
Extra Damage	Hold Ⓛ and press ⓌⒽⓣ, ⓌⒽⓣ, ⓛⒷ, then release Ⓛ. Then hold ℝⓉ and press ⓛⒷ, ⓛⒷ, ⓌⒽⓣ, then release ℝⓉ
God Mode	Hold Ⓛ and press ❂, ❖, ❖, ❂, then release Ⓛ. Then hold ℝⓉ and press ❖, ❂, ❂, ❖, then release ℝⓉ

Blinx

Unlockable	Objective
Bonus FMV Sequence	Complete Levels 1-1 through 8-4 with an "A+" or greater rank. (A game developers' FMV sequence unlocks in the "Collection" option for your prizes.)
Quick Level Completion	As soon as the level starts, quickly perform a low jump, and land back on the level start ring. The game is programmed to think that this is the finish ring. Note: This is very difficult to perform, but it is possible.
Ultimate Sweeper	Collect all 80 Cat Medals. (Now you can buy the Ultimate Sweeper for 90,000 at the last shop before the final boss. This Level 3 Sweeper can sweep any trash size and shoots fire and ice.)

Blitz: The League

From the Main menu, go to "Extras," then "Codes" and enter the following passwords.

Unlockable	Password
Ball Trail Always On	ONFIRE
Beach Ball	BOUNCY
Double Unleash Icons	PIPPED
Stamina Off	NOTTIRED
Super Clash	CLASHY
Super Unleash Clash	BIGDOGS
Two Player Co-op	CHUWAY

Blood Wake

Input the following codes at the Start screen. Listen for the sound to confirm correct code entry.

Unlockable	Code
All Battle Modes	Press ⓨ,ⓐ,ⓧ,ⓑ, click Ⓛ, click Ⓡ, ⓦⓗⓣ, ⓡⓣ, ⓡⓣ then press Ⓞⓢⓣⓐⓡⓣ.
All Boats	Press ⬆,ⓨ, ⬅,⬆, ⓛ, ⓑ, ⓧ, ⓧ, click Ⓡ, then press Ⓞⓢⓣⓐⓡⓣ.
All Levels	Press ⓧ,ⓨ,⬆,⬆, ⬆,ⓠ,⬆,⬆, click Ⓡ,ⓛ, then press Ⓞⓢⓣⓐⓡⓣ.
Blood Ball Mode	Press ⓧ,ⓨ, ⓦⓗⓣ, ⓛⓑ,ⓑ,ⓐ, ⬅,⬆,⬅,ⓠ, then press Ⓞⓢⓣⓐⓡⓣ.
Import Boat Mode	Press ⓨ,ⓑ,ⓧ,ⓐ, ⓛⓣ, ⓡⓣ, ⬅,⬆, click Ⓛ, click Ⓡ, then press Ⓞⓢⓣⓐⓡⓣ.
Invincibility	Click Ⓛ, click Ⓡ, press ⓠ,⬆,ⓠ,⬆,ⓑ,ⓨ, then press Ⓞⓢⓣⓐⓡⓣ.
Puffer Fish	Press ⓐ,ⓑ, ⓛⓑ, ⓦⓗⓣ,ⓨ,ⓧ, click Ⓡ,Ⓡ, click Ⓛ,Ⓛ, then press Ⓞⓢⓣⓐⓡⓣ.
Rubber Duck Mode	Click Ⓡ, click Ⓛ, ⓡⓣ, ⓛⓣ, ⓛⓑ, ⓦⓗⓣ,ⓠ,⬆,⬅,⬆, then press Ⓞⓢⓣⓐⓡⓣ.
Unlimited Ammunition	Press ⓛⓑ, ⓦⓗⓣ, ⓛⓣ, ⓡⓣ, click Ⓡ,ⓑ,ⓨ,ⓧ, then press Ⓞⓢⓣⓐⓡⓣ.
Unlimited Turbo	Press ⬆,⬆,ⓠ,ⓠ,⬅,⬆,⬅,⬆,ⓑ,ⓐ, then press Ⓞⓢⓣⓐⓡⓣ.

Unlockable	Objective
Basilisk	Complete the "Protection Racket" level under the captain difficulty setting.
Clanbake Battle Mode	Complete the "A Poke in the Eye" level under the ensign difficulty setting.
Fireshark	Complete the "Up the Nagau" level under the ensign difficulty setting.
Guncat Catamaran	Complete the "Protection Racket" level under the ensign difficulty setting.
Gunshark	Complete the "Ships in the Night" level under the ensign difficulty setting.
Hellcat Catamaran	Complete the "The Gauntlet" level under the ensign difficulty setting.

DS · GBA · PSP · PS2 · PS3 · Wii · Xbox · Xbox 360 · Index

Blood Wake (continued)

Unlockable	Objective
Hydroplane Switchblade	Complete the "Gladiator" level under the ensign difficulty setting.
Jackal	Complete the "Assault on Black Moon" level under the ensign difficulty setting.
Kingdom Come Battle Mode	Complete the "Baptism of Fire" level under the ensign difficulty setting.
Lightning	Complete the "A Friend in Need" level under the ensign difficulty setting.
Metal Massacre Battle Mode	Complete the "Hurricane of Fire" level under the ensign difficulty setting.
Pike	Complete the "Payment Is Due" level under the ensign difficulty setting.
Salamander	Complete the "Fish in a Barrel" level under the ensign difficulty setting.
Switchblade Hydroplane	Complete the "Gladiator" level under the ensign difficulty setting.
Tigershark	Complete the "Sampan Surprise" level under the ensign difficulty setting.

BloodRayne

From the Options screen, go to Enter Cheats and input the following.

Unlockable	Code
Fill Bloodlust	ANGRYXXXINSANEHOOKER
Freeze Enemies	DONTFARTONOSCAR
God Mode	TRIASSASSINDONTDIE
Gratuitous Dismemberment	INSANEGIBSMODEGOOD
Juggy Mode	JUGGYDANCESQUAD
Level Select	ONTHELEVEL
Restore Health	LAMEYANKEEDONTFEED
Secret Louisiana Level	BRIMSTONEINTHEBAYOU
Show Weapons	SHOWMEMYWEAPONS
Time Factor	NAKEDNASTYDISWASHERDANCE

Bloody Roar Extreme

Unlockable	Objective
Beast Mode	Beat the game fifteen times.
Big Kid Mode	Beat the game four times.
Break Walls Mode	Beat the game eight times.
Com Vs Com Battle Mode	Watch the computer spar against itself by clearing the game twice in Computer Vs Computer mode.
Corn Battle Mode	Beat the game twice.
Cronos	Beat the game twice.
Eliminate All Walls Mode	Beat the game six times.
Expert Mode	Beat the game twelve times.
Fang	Defeat Arcade Mode with all available characters, plus Uranus and Kohryu.
Ganesha	Beat the game once.
High Speed Mode	Beat the game ten times.
Human Mode	Beat the game fourteen times.
Kid Mode	Beat the game three times.
Knock Down Battle Mode	Beat the game thirteen times.

Sidebar tabs: DS, GBA, PSP, PS2, PS3, Wii, Xbox, Xbox 360, Index

Bloody Roar Extreme (continued)

Unlockable	Objective
Kohryu	Beat him in the Arcade Mode, then finish the Arcade Mode.
Low Speed Mode	Beat the game nine times.
Movie Player Option	Beat the game once.
No Blocking Mode	Beat the game eleven times.
Super Buff Mode	Beat the game five times.
Weaken All Walls Mode	Beat the game seven times.

Blow Out

Unlockable	Code
All Weapons	charliehustleoverdressedromeo
All Levels	coollevelcheatcode
God Mode	nopainnocane
Unlimited Ammo	fishinabarrel

BMX XXX

Passwords

Enter the following as your name to obtain the desired cheat:

Password	Effect
65 SWEET RIDES	All bikes
THISISBMXX	Bonus Movie 1 FMV sequence
KEEPITDIRTY	Bonus Movie 2 FMV sequence
FREESAMPLE	Bronx, NYC 3 FMV
BOING	Dam 1 FMV sequence
THONG	Dam 2 FMV
DDUULRRLDRSQUARE	Final movie
GHOSTCONTROL	Ghost control mode
MAKEMEANGRY	Green skin mode
FLUFFYBUNNY	Happy bunny mode
HIGHBEAMS	Las Vegas 1 FMV sequence
TASSLE	Las Vegas 2 FMV sequence
SHOWMETHEMONEY	Las Vegas level
IFLINGPOO	Launch Pad 69 1 FMV sequence
PEACH	Launch Pad 69 2 FMV sequence
SHOWMETHEMONKEY	Launch Pad 69 level
Z AXIS	More speed
3RD SOG	Night vision mode
BULLETPOINT	Park editor
BURLESQUE	Rampage Skatepark 2 FMV sequence
IOWARULES	Rampage Skatepark level
XXXINTRO	Random intro
UNDERGROUND	Rotts level
ONEDOLLAR	Sheep FMV
69	Sheep Hills 2 FMV sequence
BAABAA	Sheep Hills level

DS
GBA
PSP
PS2
PS3
Wii
Xbox
Xbox 360
Index

BMX XXX (continued)

Password	Effect
MASS HYSTERIA	Stage select
HEAVYPETTING	Super crash mode
FUZZYKITTY	Syracuse 1 FMV sequence
MICHAELHUNT	Syracuse 2 FMV sequence
BOYBANDSSUCK	Syracuse level
LAPDANCE	The Bronx, NYC 1 FMV sequence
STRIPTEASE	The Bronx, NYC 2 FMV sequence
THATDAMLEVEL	The dam level
BOOTYCALL	UGP Roots Jam 2 FMV sequence
XXX RATED CHEAT	Unlock All Levels
CHAMPAGNE ROOM	Unlock All Movies
ELECTRICITYBAD	Unlock Amish Boy
AMISHBOY1699	Unlock Amish Boy's Bikes
HELLKITTY487	Unlock Hellkitty's Bikes
ITCHI594	Unlock Itchi's Bikes
JOYRIDE18	Unlock Joyride's Bikes
KARMA311	Unlock Karma's Bikes
LATEY411	Unlock La'tey's Bikes
MANUEL415	Unlock Manuel's Bikes
MIKA362436	Unlock Mika's Bikes
NUTTER290	Unlock Nutter's Bikes
RAVE10	Unlock Rave's Bikes
SKEETER666	Unlock Skeeter's Bikes
TRIPLEDUB922	Unlock Tripledub's Bikes
TWAN187	Unlock Twan's Bikes
PARABOLIC	Visible gap mode

Unlockables

Unlockable	How to Unlock
Topless Girl Mode	Win first place in both competition levels.

Breakdown

Unlockable	Objective
Extreme Mode	Complete the game.
Gallery	Complete the game.
Music Player	Complete the game.
Trailer	Complete the game.

Brian Lara International Cricket 2005

Enter these passwords in the Cheat menu.

Unlockable	Password
Unlock All Classic Matches	BOWLEDHIM
Unlock All Teams	GOODLENGTH
Unlock All the Classic Players	GONEFORADUCK

DS

GBA

PSP

PS2

PS3

Wii

Xbox

Xbox 360

Index

Brian Lara International Cricket 2005 (continued)

Unlockable	Password
Unlock All Trophys	DOLLY
Unlock the Classic XI Challenge	STUMPED
Unlock the Picture Gallery	SLEDGING

Brothers in Arms: Road to Hill 30

Unlockable	Code
Unlock All Levels and Difficulties	BAKERSDOZEN

Bruce Lee: Quest of the Dragon

Enter this code at the Title screen.

Unlockable	Code
Bruce's Challenges	✪, ⓨ, ✪, ⓨ, ✪, ✪, ⓨ, ⓨ, Ⓛ, Ⓡ

Brute Force

Unlockable	Code
Better Aim	DEADAIM
Better Defense	ERINROBERTS
Cartoon Mode	HVYMTL
Harder Difficulty	BRUTAL
Quick Death	DBLDAY
Rapid Fire Weapons	RAPIDFIRE
Stupid AI	SPRAGNT
Tough Characters	MATTSOELL

Unlockable	Objective
Confed Marine	Find the DNA sequence in Mission 1 or Mission 6
Feral Colonist	Find the DNA sequence in Mission 2
Feral Outcast	Find the DNA sequence in Mission 3
Feral Shaman	Find the DNA sequence in Mission 9
Fire Hound	Find the DNA sequence in Mission 13
Gunthar Ghent	Find the DNA sequence in Mission 10
Hunter Lord	Find the DNA sequence in Mission 18
McTavish	Find the DNA sequence in Mission 14
Militia	Find the DNA sequence in Mission 5 or Mission 11
Outcast Shaman	Find the DNA sequence in Mission 7
Seer Follower	Find the DNA sequence in Mission 4
Seer Priest	Find the DNA sequence in Mission 8
Shadoon	Find the DNA sequence in Mission 12
Shrike Heavy	Find the DNA sequence in Mission 16
Shrike Hound	Find the DNA sequence in Mission 17
Shrike Soldier	Find the DNA sequence in Mission 15

Buffy the Vampire Slayer

Go to the Extras screen and input the following.

Unlockable	Code
All Four Multiplayer Arenas	⊗,⊗,⦾,⊞,⊞,⊗,⊗,⊗,⊗,⊗,⦾,⊞
Slayer Power	⊗,⊗,⊗,⊞,⊞,⊞,⊗,⦾,⊞,⊞,⦾,⊗
Unlimited Health	⊗,⦾,⊞,⊞,⦾,⊗,⊞,⊞,⊞,⊗,⊗,⊗

Buffy the Vampire Slayer: Chaos Bleeds

Unlockable	Objective
Abominator	Finish Mission 10 with Professional rating
Amber Benson Interview	Complete Mission 2
Amber Benson Voice Over Session	Complete Mission 8
Anthony Stewart Interview	Complete Mission 1
Anthony Stewart Voice Over Session	Complete Mission 7
Bat Beast	Finish Mission 4 with Professional rating
Cemetery	Finish Mission 2 with Slayer rating
Chainz	Finish Mission 10 with Slayer rating
Chaos Bleeds Comic Book	Complete Mission 5
Chris	Finish Mission 12 with Slayer rating
Faith	Finish Mission 8 with Professional rating
Female Vampire	Finish Mission 1 with Slayer rating
Initiative	Finish Mission 8 with Slayer rating
James Marsters Voice Over Session	Complete Mission 6
Joss Whedon	Finish Mission 12 with Professional rating
Joss Whedon Voice Over Session	Complete Mission 11
Kakistos	Finish Mission 9 with Slayer rating
Male Vampire	Finish Mission 1 with Professional rating
Materani	Finish Mission 5 with Professional rating
Nicholas Brendan Interview	Complete Mission 3
Nicholas Brendon Voice Over Session	Complete Mission 9
Out-Takes	Complete Mission 12
Psycho Patient	Finish Mission 6 with Professional rating
Quarry	Finish Mission 11 with Slayer rating
Robin Sachs Interview	Complete Mission 4
Robin Sachs Voice Over Session	Complete Mission 10
S&M Mistress	Finish Mission 7 with Slayer rating
S&M Slave	Finish Mission 7 with Professional rating
Sid the Dummy	Finish Mission 6 with Slayer rating
Tara	Finish Mission 3 with Slayer rating
Zombie Demon	Finish Mission 3 with Professional rating
Zombie Devil	Finish Mission 4 with Slayer rating
Zombie Gorilla	Finish Mission 11 with Professional rating
Zombie Skeleton	Finish Mission 2 with Professional rating
Zombie Soldier	Finish Mission 9 with Professional rating

Burnout 2:
Point of Impact–Developer's Cut

Unlockable	Objective
Cheat Mode Menu	Unlock any cheat and the Cheat Mode menu option will appear at the Options screen.
Classic 1970 Car	Destroy the car with a police car in Pursuit 2.
Custom Compact	Beat Custom Series Qualifier.
Custom Coupe	Get all gold medals at Split Second Grand Prix.
Custom Muscle Car	Beat Pursuit 6.
Custom Pickup Truck	Beat Pursuit 5.
Custom Roadster	Get all gold medals at the Point Of Impact Grand Prix.
Custom Series Championship	Earn gold medals in every race and complete Championship Mode.
Custom Sports Car	Get all gold medals at the Speed Streak Grand Prix.
Custom SUV	Beat Pursuit 4.
Drivers' Ed Car	Get all gold medals in Driving 101.
Freerun	Finish Custom Series Championship.
Gangster Car	Beat Pursuit 3.
Hot Rod Car	Beat Face Off 1.
Invulnerability Option	Finish the Grand Prix Championships with gold medals.
Japanese Muscle Car	Beat Face Off 2.
Oval Racer	Beat the car in Face Off 2.
Police Car	Beat Pursuit 1 and destroy the villain's car.
Super Car	Beat Face Off 4.

Burnout: Revenge

Have a *Madden NFL 06* and *Burnout 3: Takedown* saved before starting a new game. You will unlock two special cars for Crash mode.

Unlockable	Code
Dominator Assassin	Burnout 3 Save
Madden Challenge Bus	Madden 06 Save

Capcom Classic Collection

Enter this code at the Press Start screen.

Unlockable	Code
Unlock Everything	⬛, ⬛, ⬥, ◈ on right analog stick, ⬛, ⬛, ⬥, ◈ on left analog stick, ⬛, ⬛, ⬥, ◈ on the D-Pad.

Call of Cthulhu: Dark Corners of the Earth

Unlockables

Unlockable	How to Unlock
"A" ranking	All journal entries, get rifle at reception door, save Ruth, keep enough sailors in boat, and finish in under 3.5 hours, and less than 50 saves
"Craig Mullins" Gallery	Complete the game on Hardened Detective difficulty with any Mythos rank
Background Renders	Complete the game on Private Investigator difficulty with any Mythos rank

DS

GBA

PSP

PS2

PS3

Wii

Xbox

Xbox 360

Index

Call of Cthulhu: Dark Corners of the Earth (continued)

Unlockable	How to Unlock
Character Renders	Complete the game on Private Investigator difficulty with any Mythos rank
Concept Art	Complete the game on Private Investigator difficulty with any Mythos rank
Hardened Detective Difficulty	Complete the game on Private Investigator difficulty with any Mythos rank
Mythos Master Difficulty	Complete the game on Hardened Detective difficulty with any Mythos rank

Call of Duty 3

Enter this code in the Chapter Select screen.

Unlockable	Code
Unlock All Levels	Hold 🄻 and press 🟠, 🟠, 🔵, 🔵, ⊗, ⊗

Call of Duty Big Red One

To enter this code, go into the Chapter Selection menu.

Unlockable	Code
Level Select	Hold ⓛ+ⓡ and press 🔵, 🔵, 🟡, 🟡, 🔵, 🔵, 🟠, 🟠, ⊗, 🔵, ⊗, 🔵, ⊗

Cars

To enter these passwords, select Options, then select Cheat Codes.

Unlockable	Password
All cars	YAYCARS
All character skins	R4MONE
All tracks and mini games	MATTL66
Fast start	IMSPEED
Infinite boost	VROOOOM
Unlock art	CONC3PT
Unlock Master's speedy circuit and Master's countdown cleanup	TRGTEXC
Unlock movie clips	WATCHIT

Castlevania: Curse of Darkness

Unlockables

Unlockable	How to Unlock
Boss Rush Mode	Beat every boss in the game. Next time you go to a warp room, Boss Rush becomes a warp choice.
Complete Chair	Simply sit in the 23 other chairs in the game. Don't forget about Dracula's Throne during the final fight with him; it's your only chance to sit in it.
Crazy Mode	Beat the game once. Start a new game with @CRAZY as a name to play on an extreme difficulty.
Legion (optional boss)	To battle this floating mass of dead bodies, first obtain the 5th Innocent Devil, the Devil Type. With this, head back to Garibaldi Temple, and slide under the crack in the wall near the area with the four courtyards and Fencers. Travel down these hallways into the basement until you come to an area that seems to be "beating" like a human heart. Avoid the Evil Cores, and enter the boss door.
Moebius Brooch	Beat Crazy Mode and it becomes available in the shop. Equip it and Trevor can use sub-weapons without using hearts.

Castlevania: Curse of Darkness (continued)

Unlockable	How to Unlock
Sound Mode	Beat Boss Rush with Hector. You'll find a music box in the warp room. Now you can access sound mode from the title screen.
Tower of Evermore	To get to the Tower of Evermore, you'll need a bird-type Innocent Devil with the long glide ability. From the top of the Tower of Eternity, face the moon in the background and jump off the ledge, gliding all the way to the Tower of Evermore. The monsters here are much harder than the ones found in the Tower of Eternity.
Trevor Mode	Beat the game once. Start a new game with @TREVOR to play as Trevor Belmont.

Catwoman

Enter this code in the Vault menu.

Unlockable	Code
Extra Galleries	1941

Cel Damage

Enter these passwords as profile names.

Unlockable	Password
Unlock all Melee Weapons	MELEEDEATH
Unlock Everything	ENCHILADA!
Unlock Ranged Weapons	GUNSMOKE!

Chase Hollywood Stunt Driver

Enter these passwords as profile names.

Unlockable	Password
Unlock Everything	Dare Angel
All multiplayer levels	BAM4FUN

The Chronicles of Narnia: The Lion, The Witch, and The Wardrobe

To enter these codes, you must be at the title screen. Hold both ⓛ+ⓡ simultaneously and press ♀, ♀, ⬅, ⬆. The words "Please Press Start" should turn green. You will now be able to enter any of the following codes.

Unlockable	Code
Automatically Complete Level	While in-game hold ⓛ and press ♀, ⬅, ♀, ⬅, ♀, ⬅, ♀, ⬅, ⬆
Fill Combo Meter	While in-game hold ⓛ and press ⬆, ⬆, ⬅, ⬆
Receive 10,000 Coins	While in-game hold ⓛ and press ♀, ⬅, ⬅, ♀, ♀
Restore All Children's Health	While in-game hold ⓛ and press ♀, ⬅, ⬅, ⬅
Unlock All Abilities in Inventory	While in-game hold ⓛ and press ♀, ⬅, ⬅, ⬅, ⬆
Open All Levels	While on the Wardrobe screen hold ⓛ and press ⬆, ⬆, ⬅, ⬅, ⬆, ⬅, ♀
Unlock All Bonus Levels	While on the Bonus Drawer hold ⓛ and press ♀, ♀, ⬅, ⬅, ♀, ⬅, ⬆

The Chronicles of Riddick: Escape from Butcher Bay

Unlockables

Unlockable	How to Unlock
Cigarette List	Find Space Cowboy in Take off Platform
Game Concept Art 01	Find The Beetle Blend in Mainframe
Game Concept Art 02	Find OP in The Pit (Pope Joe)
Game Concept Art 02	Find Cone Puffs in Courtyard
Game Concept Art 03	Find Karavan in The Pit (Dark Tunnels)
Game Concept Art 04	Find 20 Musketeers in Container Route
Game Concept Art 05	Find Carl's Blend in Courtyard
Game Concept Art 06	Find Clemens in Tower 17 Base
Game Concept Art 07	Find Maestro in Container Route
Game Concept Art 08	Find CA Alderholm in Container Route
Game Concept Art 09, Riddick First Playable 4	Find Robot Smokes in Container Route
Game Concept Art 10, Starbreeze Motion Capture	Find Five Fingers in Courtyard
Game Concept Art 11	Find Pirate in Feed Ward
Game Concept Art 12	Find Yups in Showers
Game Concept Art 13	Find Mummy in Abandoned Equipment
Game Concept Art 14	Find Count Gunther in Abandoned Equipment
Game Concept Art 15	Find Iron Lungs in Feed Ward
Game Concept Art 16	Find Swift in Mining Core
Game Concept Art 17, TCoR Novelization	Find Mount Noir in The Pit
Game Concept Art 18	Find Enfermo in Central Storage
Game Concept Art 19	Find Charlie's in Tower 17
Game Concept Art 20	Find Yoyall in Tower 17 Base
Game Concept Art 21	Find Rolles Rok in Mine Entrance
Game Concept Art 22	Find Alunda Classics in Mainframe
Game Concept Art 23, Riddick First Playable 3	Find Space Jockey in Upper Mines
Game Concept Art 24	Find Voodoo in Prison Area
Game Concept Art 25	Find The Counts in Prison Area
Game Concept Art 26	Find Tiny Tims in The Work Pass
Game Concept Art 27	Find Jimboro in Mining Core
Game Concept Art 28	Find Old Timer in Courtyard
Game Concept Art 29, Riddick Prototype 4	Find Noname in Tower 17 Base
Game Concept Art 30	Find Nordqvist in Security Checkpoint
Game Concept Art 31	Find Q in Showers
Game Concept Art 32	Find Bloss in The Dream
Game Concept Art 33	Find Lungbusters in Courtyard
Game Concept Art 34, Starbreeze Technology Demo	Find Greas in Loading Docks
Game Concept Art 35	Find Habibs in Aquila Territory
Game Concept Art 36	Find MBryo in Aquila Territory

DS
GBA
PSP
PS2
PS3
Wii
Xbox
Xbox 360
Index

The Chronicles of Riddick: Escape from Butcher Bay (continued)

Unlockable	How to Unlock
Game Concept Art 37	Find Roulette in Feed Ward
Game Concept Art 38, Riddick First Playable 2	Find Sicher in Mine Entrance
Game Concept Art 39	Find Starlife in Tower 17 Base
Movie Concept Art 01, Game Concept Art 40	Find Gawd in Facility Control
Movie Concept Art 03	Find Candy Candy in Take Off Platform
Movie Concept Art 04, Riddick Prototype 2	Find JR Grass in Aquila Territory
Movie Concept Art 05	Find Cloud No. 17 in Abandoned Equipment
Movie Prop 01, Riddick Prototype 3	Find Gronkos Bar in Guard Quarters
Movie set 01	Find Dog Smokes in Feed Ward
Movie set 02	Find Black Death in Feed Ward
Movie set 03	Find Charlie's CC in Feed Ward
Movie Set 04	Find Red Frog in Work Pass
Movie Set 05	Find Yoshimi in Courtyard
Movie Set 06	Find Dr. Filur in Infirmary
Movie Set 07	Find Guards in Guard Quarters
Movie Set 08	Find 68th in Container Route
Movie Set 09	Find Painful in Courtyard
Movie Set 10	Find Addictive M in Cargo Transport
Movie still 01	Find Desert Air in The Dream
TCoR Combo trailer, Riddick Prototype 1	Find Hogdahl's Finest in The Dream
TCoR Movie Teaser, Riddick First Playable 1	Find Sensei in Feed Ward
Enclave Goblin in Butcher Bay	When you reach "Pigsville" (the guards quarters) after meeting Pope Joe, continue through the shower area. Once you leave it and step into the first corridor, turn right and go into the doorway at the end of the hall. These are the guards' individual quarters. Go to the first room on the right (the nameplate reads "Keenan") and ring the doorbell. You'll hear mostly gibberish, but also a mention of "Vatar." Vatar was the main villain of Enclave, another game made by Starbreeze (who are the developers of Escape from Butcher Bay), and the voice is that of the goblin character, a low-ranking enemy in Vatar's forces.
Get Gomer's Smoke Packs for Free	In the Double Max security level portion of the game, you meet a prisoner in the entrance hallway of the Feed Ward who's willing to sell you five packs of smokes for a high total price. After buying them, they will be saved to your game automatically. Load your latest checkpoint, and you'll still have the smokes AND the money you paid for them.

DS

GBA

PSP

PS2

PS3

Wii

Xbox

Xbox 360

Index

Cold War

Enter these codes while the game is paused.

Unlockable	Code
All items, gadgets, and tech points	⊗, Ⓦ, ⓨ, ⓛⓑ, ⓨ
Complete current level	⊗, Ⓦ, ⓨ, ⓛⓑ, ⊗
Invulnerability	⊗, Ⓦ, ⓨ, ⓛⓑ, ◐

Commandos Strike Force

Enter this password as a profile name.

Unlockable	Password
All Missions	TRUCO

Conflict: Desert Storm

Enter this code at the Main menu.

Unlockable	Code
Cheat Mode	⊗, ⊗, ⓨ, ⓨ, ⓛ, ⓛ, ⓑ, ⓑ, ⓛⓣ, ⓛⓣ, ⓡⓣ, ⓡⓣ

Conflict: Desert Storm II– Back to Baghdad

Unlockable	Code
Cheat Menu	At the Main menu, enter ⓛⓣ, ⓛⓣ, ⓡⓣ, ⓡⓣ, ⊗, ⊗, ⓨ, ⓨ, ⓑ, ⓑ. Go to Options and the Cheat menu will be at the bottom.

Conflict: Global Terror

Enter this code at the Main menu.

Unlockable	Code
Cheat Menu	ⓛⓣ, ⓡⓣ, ⓛⓣ, ⓡⓣ, ⊗, Ⓦ, ⓛⓑ, ⊗

Conflict: Vietnam

Enter this code at the Main menu.

Unlockable	Code
Cheat Menu	ⓡⓣ, ⓡⓣ, ⓛⓣ, ⓛⓣ, ⓑ, ⓑ, ⓨ, ⓨ, ⊗, ⊗, Ⓦ

Constantine

To enter these codes, press ⓠ to open your journal.

Unlockable	Code
Big Headed Demons	ⓛⓑ, ◐, ◑, ◐, ◐, ◑, ◐, ⓛⓑ
Big Weapon Mode	◐, ⊗, ⊗, ⊗, ⓨ, ⓨ, ⓨ
Explosive Holy Bomb	◑, ◐, ⊗, ⓨ, ⓨ, ◐, ◑
Rapid Fire Shotgun	Ⓦ, ◐, ⓛⓑ, ◐, ⓨ, ⓨ, ⓨ, ⊗
Shoot Fireballs	ⓨ, ⓨ, ⓨ, ◐, ◑, ◑, ◐, ◐, ◑

Corvette

In the Options menu, select "Change Name," then enter this code.

Unlockable	Code
All Cars and All Tracks	XOPENSEZ

Crash Bandicoot: The Wrath of Cortex

Unlockable	Code
Alternate Ending Sequence	Collect all 46 gems.

Crash Tag Team Racing

At the title screen, press and hold Ⓛ+Ⓡ, then enter the code.

Unlockable	Code
Chicken heads for characters	Ⓐ, Ⓑ, Ⓑ, Ⓧ
Disable HUD	Ⓐ, Ⓧ, Ⓨ, Ⓑ
Japanese-version characters	Ⓧ, Ⓑ, Ⓧ, Ⓑ
One-hit knockouts	Ⓐ, Ⓑ, Ⓑ, Ⓐ
No top speed on cars	Ⓑ, Ⓑ, Ⓨ, Ⓨ
Toy block cars	Ⓑ, Ⓑ, Ⓨ, Ⓧ

Crimson Skies: High Road to Revenge

Enter the following codes during gameplay.

Unlockable	Code
$5,000	Ⓐ, Ⓨ, Ⓐ, Ⓨ, Ⓛ
10 Tokens	Ⓑ, Ⓧ, Ⓧ, Ⓑ, Ⓛ
All Planes	Ⓨ, Ⓧ, Ⓑ, Ⓨ, Ⓛ
God Mode	Ⓨ, Ⓐ, Ⓧ, Ⓑ, Ⓛ
Super Primary Weapon	Ⓑ, Ⓧ, Ⓐ, Ⓑ, Ⓛ
Ultra Hard Mode	Ⓧ, Ⓑ, Ⓐ, Ⓧ, Ⓛ

The Da Vinci Code

Codes

Code	Effect
Et In Arcadia Ego	All bonuses Unlocked
Apocrypha	All Visual Database entries Unlocked
Sacred Feminine	Double Health
Vitruvian Man	God Mode (infinite health)
Clos Luce 1519	Level Select
Phillips Exeter	One Hit Fist Kill
Royal Holloway	One Hit Weapon Kill

Dai Senryaku VII
Modern Military Tactics

Enter these passwords in the Pass Code screen.

Unlockable	Password
Cobra (D7)	746C-3BBA-E396-9AFD AH-1S
Cobra (WT)	3D9A-D404-70E9-0162 AH-1S
Super Cobra	81FE-5327-CAD7-6500 AH-1W
Cyber Ninja	C554-D619-C0C7-33A9
SPRR (WT)	F4A3-6507-A7E5-E9CD Type 60
MBT (WT)	0993-4841-852E-14F9 Type 61
MBT (D7)	5285-2318-09F4-1DDC Type 74
MBT (WT)	6289-0549-0DF1-A797 Type 74
SPAAG (WT)	8399-71B4-500A-500A Type 87
MBT (D7)	B50A-6C45-CB7B-F94E Type 90
MBT (WT)	A124-2DC3-D9A6-D4F9 Type 90

DS

GBA

PSP

PS2

PS3

Wii

Xbox

Xbox 360

Index

Dakar 2

Enter these passwords in the Cheat menu under Extras.

Unlockable	Password
All Cars	SWEETAS
All Tracks	BONZER

Dance Dance Revolution Ultramix

Hook a controller to port 4. At the Main menu, go into options and select credits. Enter a code and you'll hear a sound if it was input correctly.

Unlockable	Code
All Music + Cleared Challenge Mode	⬧, ⬧, ⬥, ⬥, ◄, ►, ◄, ►, ®, Ⓐ

Dark Summit

Input each of the following codes at the Main menu. After inputting a code, listen for a sound to confirm correct code entry.

Unlockable	Code
Alien Unlocked (Challenges 43 (Race the Chief), 48 (Bomb #5), 49 (Alien Half Pipe), and 50 (Storm HQ) will be completed. You'll also have Bomb Piece #5.)	Hold 🄻 + 🄻 and press Ⓨ, Ⓛ, Ⓧ, Ⓑ, ®, Ⓐ, ®, Ⓧ.
All Boarders	Hold 🄻 + 🄻 and press Ⓨ, Ⓛ, Ⓧ, Ⓑ, ®, Ⓐ, ®, Ⓑ
Challenges Completed (All challenges except for 43 (Race the Chief), 48 (Bomb #5), 49 (Alien Half Pipe), and 50 (Storm HQ) will be completed. You'll also have all Bomb Pieces, with the exception of Bomb #5.)	Hold 🄻 + 🄻 and press Ⓨ, Ⓛ, Ⓧ, Ⓑ, ®, Ⓐ, ®, Ⓨ at the main menu.
Extra Points (You'll get 9,100,000 lift points, which unlock all lifts except for the Moon Gate. You'll also get 9,100,000 equipment points, which unlock all boards, accessories, and special tricks.)	Hold 🄻 + 🄻 and press Ⓨ, Ⓛ, Ⓧ, Ⓑ, ®, Ⓐ, ®, Ⓐ at the main menu.
Shoot Projectile	Hold 🄻 + 🄻 and press Ⓨ, Ⓧ, Ⓑ, ®. Press Ⓛ + ® to shoot a barrel with a projectile.
Slow Motion	Hold 🄻 + 🄻 and press Ⓨ, Ⓧ, Ⓑ, Ⓛ. Press Ⓛ + ® when in the air or during a railslide to activate Slow Motion mode. This mode automatically ends when you reach the ground.

Darkwatch

Unlockables

Unlockable	How to Unlock
Allies Art, Bosses Art	Complete Curse of the West on Shootist difficulty
Attract Mode Movie	Complete Dead Light Prism with 80 or more kills
Cowboy Animatic	Complete Torture Maze with 30 or more melee kills
Darkwatch Archives	Complete all Gunslinger levels on Deadeye
Enemies 1	Complete Boneyard with 65% or more accuracy
Enemies 2	Complete Showdown with 20 or more melee kills
Environments 1	Complete Darkwatch Outpost with no deaths
Environments 2	Complete Invasion on Deadeye difficulty
Environments 3	Complete Curse of the West in 10 minutes or less
Evolution of Jericho	Complete the Single Player Campaign on any difficulty

DS

GBA

PSP

PS2

PS3

Wii

Xbox

Xbox 360

Index

Darkwatch (continued)

Unlockable	How to Unlock
Highmoon Trailer	Complete Rescue in 15 minutes or less
Rescue Intro Movie	Complete Hangtown with 20 or more head shots
Showdown Animatic	Complete The Right Train on Shootist difficulty
Vehicles	Complete Deadfall with 20 or more head shots
Weapons	Complete Morning After with 70% or more accuracy
Wrong Train Animatic	Complete The Wrong Train with 65% or more accuracy

Dave Mirra Freestyle BMX 2

Enter all codes at the Main menu. If done correctly, a sound confirms correct code entry.

CHARACTER BIKES	CODE
Colin Mackay	↑, ↑, →, →, →, →, ↓, ⊗
Dave Mirra	↑, ↑, ↓, →, →, →, ↓, ↓, ⊗
Joey Garcia	↑, ↑, ↓, →, ←, ←, ↑, ↑, ⊗
John Englebert	↑, ↑, ↓, ↓, ←, ↓, ←, ←, ⊗
Kenan Harkin	↑, ↑, ↓, ↓, ↑, →, ↑, ↑, ⊗
Leigh Ramsdell	↑, ↑, ↓, ↓, ←, ←, ↑, →, ⊗
Mike Laird	↑, ↑, →, ←, ↑, ↓, ↓, ↓, ⊗
Rick Moliterno	↑, ↑, ↓, ←, ←, →, ←, ↓, ⊗
Ryan Nyquist	↑, ↑, ↑, ↑, ↑, →, ↓, ↑, ⊗
Scott Wirch	↑, ↑, →, ↓, ↑, ↑, →, ↑, ⊗
Tim Mirra	↑, ↑, →, ←, ↑, ↑, ↑, ↓, ⊗
Todd Lyons	↑, ↑, ↑, →, ↓, →, ←, ↑, ⊗
Troy McMurray	↑, ↑, →, ↓, →, ←, ↓, ←, ⊗
Zach Shaw	↑, ↑, ←, ↑, ↓, ↓, →, ↑, ↑, ⊗

LEVELS	CODE
Colin Mackay	↓, ↓, ←, ↑, ↓, ↓, →, →, ↓, ⊗
Dave Mirra	↓, ↓, ↓, →, ↓, ↓, ←, ↓, ↓, ⊗
Joey Garcia	↓, ↓, ↓, ↓, ↑, ↑, ↑, →, ⊗
John Englebert	↓, ↓, ←, ↑, ↓, ↑, ↓, ←, ↓, ⊗
Kenan Harkin	↓, ↓, ←, ↓, ↓, ↑, ↓, ↑, ↑, ⊗
Leigh Ramsdell	↓, ↓, ↓, ↑, ←, ↑, ↑, ↑, ⊗
Mike Laird	↓, ↓, →, ←, ↑, ↑, →, ↓, →, ⊗
Rick Molitero	↓, ↓, ↓, ↑, ↓, →, ←, ↓, ⊗
Ryan Nyquist	↓, ↓, ↑, ↑, ↓, ←, ↓, ↑, ⊗
Scott Wirch	↓, ↓, ↓, ↓, ←, ←, ←, ←, ⊗
Tim Mirra	↓, ↓, ↑, ↑, →, ←, ↑, ↓, ⊗

LEVELS	CODE
Todd Lyons	↓, ↓, ↑, ↓, →, →, →, ←, ↑, ⊗
Troy McMurray	↓, ↓, ←, ↓, ↓, ↓, ↓, ←, ↓, ⊗
Zach Shaw	↓, ↓, ←, ↑, →, ↑, ↑, →, ⊗

RIDER OUTFITS	CODE
Colin Mackay	→, ←, →, ←, ↑, →, ↓, ←, ↓, ⊗
Joey Garcia	→, ←, ↓, ↑, ↓, ↓, ←, ↑, →, ⊗
John Englebert	→, ←, ←, ↑, →, ↓, ↓, ←, ↓, ⊗
Kenan Harkin	→, ←, ←, ↑, ↑, ↓, ←, ↑, ↑, ⊗

Tabs (left margin): DS · GBA · PSP · PS2 · PS3 · Wii · **Xbox** · Xbox 360 · Index

Dave Mirra Freestyle BMX 2 (continued)

RIDER OUTFITS	CODE
Leigh Ramsdell	◄,►,♀,◄,♀,♀,◄,►,◄,⊗
Mike Laird	◄,►,◄,♀,◄,♀,♀,♀,►,⊗
Rick Moliterno	◄,►,◄,♀,♀,♀,►,◄,♀,⊗
Ryan Nyquist	◄,►,♀,♀,♀,◄,♀,♀,⊗
Scott Wirch	◄,►,◄,♀,◄,◄,◄,◄,⊗
Tim Mirra	◄,►,◄,♀,◄,♀,►,◄,►,⊗
Todd Lyons	◄,►,◄,◄,◄,◄,♀,►,⊗
Troy McMurray	◄,►,◄,►,♀,◄,♀,◄,⊗
Zach Shaw	◄,►,◄,◄,♀,♀,♀,►,♀,⊗

SIGNATURE TRICKS	CODE
Amish Air	◄,►,♀,♀,►,♀,♀,►,►,⊗
Colin Mackay	◄,►,►,◄,►,◄,◄,►,♀,⊗
Dave Mirra	◄,►,◄,♀,♀,►,♀,♀,♀,⊗
Joey Garcia	◄,►,◄,►,♀,♀,♀,♀,⊗
John Englebert	◄,►,◄,◄,♀,♀,♀,◄,◄,⊗
Kenan Harkin	◄,►,◄,►,♀,♀,♀,♀,⊗
Leigh Ramsdell	◄,►,◄,♀,♀,◄,◄,♀,►,⊗
Mike Laird	◄,►,◄,►,►,◄,◄,◄,♀,⊗
Rick Moliterno	◄,►,◄,♀,♀,♀,♀,►,♀,⊗
Ryan Nyquist	◄,►,◄,♀,♀,♀,♀,♀,♀,⊗
Scott Wirch	◄,►,◄,►,◄,♀,◄,►,◄,⊗
Slim Jim Guy	◄,►,♀,♀,►,♀,◄,◄,►,⊗
Tim Mirra	◄,►,◄,►,♀,♀,♀,♀,⊗
Todd Lyons	◄,►,♀,♀,♀,►,◄,►,◄,⊗
Troy McMurray	◄,►,◄,◄,♀,♀,♀,◄,⊗
Zach Shaw	◄,►,◄,►,◄,►,◄,►,♀,⊗

Dead or Alive 3

Unlockables

Unlockable	How to Unlock
Ayane's Schoolgirl (3rd) Costume	Get the silver Xbox item in Survival mode.
Change Colors	If you select your character and costume with ⊗, most will have an alternate color. Lei Feng has 3 different dress colors based on which button you press (⊗, ⊕, or ⊙).
Christie: Red Dress Costume	Choose "Time Attack" game mode with a tag team, then choose Christie and Helena as your characters, with their second costumes. Get an award (bronze, silver or gold cup). Her dress is now selectable. Press ⊗ when choosing her to have it be black.
Custom Weather for Snow Stage	Choose the weather for the snow stage in the Vs or Training mode by simply highlighting the snow stage on the stage selection. Press ⊗ for snowfall, ⊕ for snow storm, ⊙ for random.
Ein	Complete "Story Mode" with all characters. Then play either "Survival" or "Time Attack Mode" and get ranked in using HAYATE and then enter your nickname as EIN. After that, Ein will be playable in all modes except "Story mode."
Ein's 3rd Costume	Complete "Time Attack Mode" under 6 minutes with Ein. His 3rd costume is shirtless and red pants from *DOA 2 Hardcore*.

Dead or Alive 3 (continued)

Unlockable	How to Unlock
Gen Fu's 3rd Costume	Enter Gen Fu in the single Time Attack. Then complete it to obtain a gold cup and also the time must be 4 mins to at least 4 mins 18 seconds.
Hayate's 3rd Costume	Play Survival mode with Hayate until a silver Xbox appears from a defeated body. Pick it up and his 3rd costume is yours.
Kasumi's 3rd Costume	Complete "Exercise Mode" in "Sparring Mode" with Kasumi. This costume is her school outfit.
Kasumi's Braided Ponytail	When you select Kasumi, press ✗ to select her with a braided ponytail hairstyle. This works for all of her costumes including her secret school costume.
Kasumi's Loose Hair	When you select Kasumi, press ↗ to select her with loose hair. This works for all of her costumes, including her secret school costume.
Kasumi's Ninja Ponytail	When you select Kasumi, press Ⓐ to select her with a ninja ponytail hairstyle. This works for all of her costumes including her secret school costume.
Rotate Camera Angle	After winning a match and your character does their victory pose, you can press Ⓛ, then move it around to angle the camera differently. If you press Ⓡ then move it around, it zooms in and out.
Slow Mo Replay	Once you win a match, hold ✗+Ⓐ+Ⓑ until the replay starts. Then rewind/slow mo the action with Ⓨ.
Theater Mode	Complete "Story Mode" with a character to unlock "Theater Mode" and that ending movie will be available for that character. There are 16 ending movies. Each character has one ending movie.
Tina's 3rd Costume	To get Tina's cowgirl outfit just play Survival mode with her until a silver Xbox appears from a defeated player and collect it.
Toggle Ending Credits	Successfully complete the game with all fighters. An option to toggle the ending credits will be unlocked on the game settings screen.
Zack's 3rd Costume	To get Zack's third outfit (the silver outfit from *Dead or Alive 2*), defeat 20 opponents in Survival mode using Zack.
Zack's 4th Costume	Get the silver Xbox item in Survival mode.
Name Your Xbox	Place 1st in Single Survival mode. Whatever name you type in becomes the name of your Xbox.

Dead or Alive Xtreme Beach Volleyball

Unlockable	Objective
Bonus Music Tracks— "How Crazy Are You" (by Meja) and "Is This Love" (by Bob Marley).	Play through the game once. When you resume that saved game file, these two hidden songs are available in the Radio Station.
Ending Bonus	Complete the game. When you start a new game, you can immediately advance to the end. Select the "Leave Tomorrow" option at the Hotel or Pool menu to skip to the ending.
Ending Sequence	Wait for the credits to end to see an extra FMV sequence featuring Zack and the remains of his island.
Extra Items	Give many gifts to one character and complete that game. Start a new game with that saved game file, and choose to play as the character that received those gifts. Those items are available in your inventory in the new game.

DS

GBA

PSP

PS2

PS3

Wii

Xbox

Xbox 360

Index

DS
GBA
PSP
PS2
PS3
Wii
Xbox
Xbox 360
Index

Dead to Rights

Enter the code at the Main menu.

Unlockable	Code
Chapter Select	◊,♀,◊,♀,◄,◊,◄,◊,♥,⊗,⊗

Def Jam: Fight for NY

Enter these codes in the Cheat menu.

Unlockable	Code
100 Reward Points	NEWJACK
Anything Goes by CNN	MILITAIN
Bust by Outkast	BIGBOI
Comp by Comp	CHOCOCITY
Dragon House by Chiang	AKIRA
Koto by Chiang	GHOSTSHELL
Man Up by Sticky Fingaz	KIRKJONES
Move by Public Enemy	RESPECT
Original Gangster by Ice T	POWER
Take a Look at my Life by Fat Joe	CARTAGENA
Walk with Me by Joe Budden	PUMP

> **NOTE**
>
> *The following codes also yield the "100 Reward Points" unlockable:*
> *THESOURCE, CROOKLYN, DUCKET, GETSTUFF.*

Destroy All Humans

To activate these codes, pause the game and hold ⊕, then enter the code and release ⊕.

Unlockable	Code
Ammo-A-Plenty	◄,♥,ᵂᴴᵀ,◄,⊕,⊗

Unlockable	Code
Aware Like a Fox	◄,⊗,ᵂᴴᵀ,⊕,◄,ᵂᴴᵀ
Bulletproof Crypto	⊗,♥,◄,◄,♥,⊗
Deep Thinker	⊕,ᵂᴴᵀ,♥,◄,ᵂᴴᵀ,♥
Mmmm…Brains! (This code increases DNA.)	⊕,⊕,ᵂᴴᵀ,ᵂᴴᵀ,◄,◄,◄,◄,ᵂᴴᵀ,⊕ (You must be on the Mothership.)
Nobody Loves You	ᵂᴴᵀ,◄,ᵂᴴᵀ,⊕,⊗,◄

Destroy All Humans 2

Pause the game, go to archives, press and hold L3, and enter following cheats.

Unlockable	Code
Salad Days with Pox and Crypto Video	Ⓐ, ⊗, ♥, Ⓑ, ⊗, Ⓑ, ⊗, Ⓐ, Ⓐ

Disney's Extreme Skate Adventure

Enter these codes in the Cheats menu.

Unlockable	Code	Unlockable	Code
All Create-a-Skater Items	gethotgear	Special Meter always full	happyfeet
All Levels	frequentflyers	*Tarzan* Video	nugget
All Skaters	xtremebuddies	*Toy Story* Video	marin
Lion King Video	savannah		

Doom 3

These codes must be entered very quickly while playing.

Unlockable	Code
God Mode	Hold ⒧ and press ✕, ⓨ, ⓑ, ⓐ
Level Skip	Hold ⒧ and press ⓑ, ⓐ, ✕, ⓨ

Dr. Muto

In the Options menu, select "Cheats" to enter these codes.

Unlockable	Code
All Gadgets	TINKERTOY
All Morphs	EUREKA
Death No Touch	NECROSCI
Go Anywhere	BEAMMEUP
Never Take Damage	CHEATERBOY
Secret Morphs	LOGGLOGG
See all Movies	HOTTICKET
Super Ending Unlocked	BUZZOFF

Driv3r

Enter the following codes at the Main menu.

Unlockable	Code
All Missions	✕, ✕, ⓨ, ⓨ, ⓡⓣ, ⓡⓣ, ⒧
All Weapons	⒧, ⒧, ✕, ⓨ, ⓨ, ⓡⓣ, ⓡⓣ
Immunity	✕, ⓨ, ⓡⓣ, ⓡⓣ, ⒧, ⒧, ⓨ
Invincibility	✕, ⓨ, ⒧, ⓡⓣ, ⒧, ⓡⓣ, ⓡⓣ—(NOTE: Does not work in Story mode)
Unlimited Ammo	ⓡⓣ, ⓡⓣ, ⒧, ⒧, ✕, ⓨ, ⓨ
Unlock All Vehicles	✕, ✕, ⓨ, ⓨ, ⒧, ⓡⓣ, ⒧

Driver Parallel Lines

Enter these passwords in the Cheat menu.

Unlockable	Password
All Vehicles	CARSHOW
All Weapons in Your Time Zone	GUNRANGE
Indestructible Cars	ROLLBAR
Infinite Ammunition	GUNBELT
Infinite Nitro	ZOOMZOOM
Invincibility	IRONMAN
Weaker Cops	KEYSTONE
Zero Cost	TOOLEDUP

Dungeons and Dragons Heroes

To enter these codes, hold ⒧ and press ⓐ+ⓨ during gameplay.

Unlockable	Code	Unlockable	Code
10 Anti Venom	SPINRAD	10 Flash Freeze	ESKO
10 Berserker Brew	THOMAS	10 Globe Potions	WRIGHT
10 Fire Bomb	WEBER	10 Holy Water	CRAWLEY
10 Fire Flask	BROPHY	10 Insect Plagues	DERISO
10 Firey Oil	EHOFF	10 Keys	SNODGRASS

DS · GBA · PSP · PS2 · PS3 · Wii · Xbox · Xbox 360 · Index

DS

GBA

PSP

PS2

PS3

Wii

Xbox

Xbox 360

Index

Dungeons and Dragons Heroes (continued)

Unlockable	Code	Unlockable	Code
10 Large Healing Potions	THOMPSON	10 Thrown Viper Axe	HOWARD
10 Large Will Potions	GEE	10 Thunderstone	ELSON
10 Medium Potions of Will	LU	10 Tome of Apprentice	BILGER
10 Potions of Haste	UHL	10 Tome of Lessons	PAQUIN
10 Pyrokins	SMITH	10 Tome of Teacher	MEFORD
10 Rod of Destruction	AUSTIN	10 Tome of the Master	SPANBURG
10 Rod of Fire	DELUCIA	10 Warp Stones	HOPPENST
10 Rod of Miracles	JARMAN	10,000 XP Points	DSP633
10 Rod of Missiles	MILLER	500,000 Gold Pieces	KNE637
10 Rod of Reflection	WHITTAKE	Add 10 to Constitution	N STINE
10 Rod of Shadows	DINOLT	Add 10 to Dexterity	YAN
10 Thrown Axe of Ruin	RAMERO	Disable Cheats	UNBUFF
10 Thrown Daggers	MOREL	Invincibility	PELOR
10 Thrown Daggers of Stunning	BELL	Nightmare Setting	MPS LABS
10 Thrown Halcyon Hammer	PRASAD	Unlimited Mystical Will	OBADHI
		View Concept Art	CONCEPTS
10 Thrown Hammer	BRATHWAI	View Credits	Credits

EA Sports Bio Awards

Unlockable	Code	Unlockable	Code
2002 All-American Team	Level 18	Rose Bowl Pennant	Level 2
Butter Fingers Pennant	Level 4	Tostitos Bowl Pennant	Level 12
Orange Bowl Pennant	Level 8		

The Elder Scrolls III: Morrowind

During Gameplay, go to the Statistics page to enter the following codes. You can only enter one code at a time.

Unlockable	Code
Restore Fatigue	Highlight Fatigue and press 🎮, 🎮, 🎮, 🎮, 🎮, then hold Ⓐ to reach the desired level.
Restore Health	Highlight Health and press 🎮, 🎮, 🎮, 🎮, 🎮, then hold Ⓐ to reach the desired level.
Restore Magicka	Highlight Magicka and press 🎮, 🎮, 🎮, 🎮, 🎮, then hold Ⓐ to reach the desired level.

Enclave

Unlockable	Code
God Mode and Complete Mission	Pause the game and enter Ⓧ, Ⓨ, Ⓧ, Ⓧ, Ⓨ, Ⓨ, Ⓧ, Ⓧ, Ⓧ, Ⓧ, Ⓨ, Ⓨ.

Enter the Matrix

Enable Cheats: Enter the hacking system and enter cheat.exe from the A prompt. Then you can enter the codes below.

CAUTION

Warning! The game can crash with cheats enabled.

Enter the Matrix (continued)

Unlockable	Code	Unlockable	Code
All weapons	0034AFFF	Infinite Health	7F4DF451
Blind Enemies	FFFFFFF1	Invisibility	FFFFFFF1
Bonus level	13D2C77F	Low gravity	BB013FFF
Deaf Enemies	4516DF45	Multiplayer	D5C55D1E
Faster Logos	7867F443	Recover Focus Fast	FFF0020A
Faster Logos	7867F443	Taxi Driving	312MF451
Infinite ammo	1DDF2556	Turbo mode	FF00001A
Infinite focus	69E5D9E4		

Eragon

Passwords

Password	Effect
Hold all triggers down and press ✖, ✖, ⦵, ⦵	Unlocks Fury Mode

Secret Eggs Unlockables

There are 16 Secret Eggs in the game, one for each level of the game. Whenever you find a Secret Egg, it will unlock one of the following items. The unlockables are unlocked in the following order, regardless of which egg you've found first.

Unlockable	How to Unlock
Bonus Level: "Throne Room"	Find Secret Egg #16
Commentary—"Art Direction"	Find Secret Egg #03
Commentary—"Birth of a Game"	Find Secret Egg #04
Commentary—"Design"	Find Secret Egg #02
Commentary—"Edward John Speleers"	Find Secret Egg #01
Commentary—"Evolution of Games"	Find Secret Egg #14
Commentary—"Garrett Hedlund"	Find Secret Egg #13
Commentary—"Orchestra"	Find Secret Egg #06
Commentary—"Robert Carlyle"	Find Secret Egg #11
Commentary—"Saphira"	Find Secret Egg #07
Commentary—"Sienna Guillory"	Find Secret Egg #08
Commentary—"Sound Effects"	Find Secret Egg #12
Concept Art—"Beor & Varden"	Find Secret Egg #15
Concept Art—"Characters"	Find Secret Egg #09
Concept Art—"Gil'ead"	Find Secret Egg #10
Concept Art—"Spine, Carvahall & Daret"	Find Secret Egg #05

Secret Level: Throne Room

Unlockable	How to Unlock
Throne Room	Find all of the Secret Eggs in the game at any difficulty.

ESPN NBA 2Night 2002

Enter these passwords in the Cheats menu under Options.

Unlockable	Password
Ball Tails	BEFOREIMAGE
Basketball heads players	BALLHEAD
Better Performance	ABILITYBONUS
Big Feet	BIGFOOT
Big Hands	BIGHAND

DS

GBA

PSP

PS2

PS3

Wii

Xbox

Xbox 360

Index

DS

GBA

PSP

PS2

PS3

Wii

Xbox

Xbox 360

Index

ESPN NBA 2Night 2002 (continued)

Unlockable	Password
Big Heads	BIGHEAD
Easy Dunks	DUNKERS
Flat Mode	PANCAKE
Increased shooting percentage	EXCELLENT
No Fans	NOSPECTATOR
Small Mode	MINIMINI

ESPN NBA Basketball

Unlockable	Code
All 24/7 Items	Create a Player with the first name HUNT and the lastname 4TREASURE.

ESPN NFL 2K5

Get these unlockables by changing your VIP profile name to the following:

Unlockable	Profile Name
1,000,000 Crib Credits	PhatBank
All Crib items	CribMax
All Milestones complete (full trophy room)	MadSkilz

ESPN NHL 2K5

Unlockable	Code
All Skybox	Create a Profile with the name LuvLeafs.

Evil Dead: Fistful of Boomstick

Unlockable	Objective
Unlock Arcade Levels	Finish levels in story mode.
Unlock Gallery Art	Each time you finish a level, concept art for the level will be unlocked at the Extras menu.

Fantastic Four

Enter these codes quickly at the Main menu. You will hear a sound to confirm a correct entry.

Unlockable	Code
Barge Arena and Stan Lee Interview #1	⊗, ⓑ, ⊗, ♀, ♀, ⓑ, ⬧
Bonus Level Hell	◐, ◑, ⊗, ⓑ, ◐, ⬧, ♀
Infinite Cosmic Powers	⬧, ⊗, ⊗, ⊗, ◐, ◑, ⓑ

Far Cry Instincts

To enter these passwords, pause the game and select the Cheat menu. Note that these passwords are case sensitive.

Unlockable	Password
100 Health Points	GiveMeHealth
All Maps	TheWorldIsMine
Disables Auto-Aim	NotForSissies
Feral Attack Ability	PunchMeHard
Infinite Adrenaline	VitruviAnRush
Infinite Ammo	BulletsofHell

Enter this code after you select Map Maker.

Unlockable	Code
Secret Message	(LT), (RT), Ⓨ, Ⓑ, ⊗, (L3), (R3), Ⓐ

Fifa Street 2

Enter this code at the Main menu while holding ⓛ + Ⓨ.

Unlockable	Code
All stages unlocked	←, ↓, ↓, →, ♀, ♀, →, ♀

Fight Night 2004

Unlockable	Code
All Venues	At the Main menu, highlight My Corner and press ←, ←, ←, ←, ←, ←.
Big Tigger	In the Record Book menu, go to most wins and press ↓, ↓.
Miniature Fighters	At the Main menu, hightlight Play Now and press ←, ←, ←, ←, →, →, ←, △.

Fight Night Round 2

Unlockable	Code
All Venus	At the game mode select screen hold ← until you hear a bell.
Mini Fighters	At the choose Venue screen hold ↓ until you hear a bell ring.
Unlock Fabulous	Create a character with the first name GETFAB then cancel out and Fabulous will be available for Play Now and Career mode.

Fight Night Round 3

Unlockables

Unlockable	How to Unlock
ESPN Classic Fight	Clear the Underarmor Bout in Career mode to unlock the fight of Big E vs. Goliath
Judge Jab	Defeat Joe Frazier with Ali
King as Your Trainer	Win the BK event in Career mode. The next time you pick a trainer to train, the king will be a selectable trainer. And he gives you heart when you fight.
Ko Rey Mo	In the light heavy division, defeat him in Career mode
Lethal Uppercuts	Win a classic fight with Roberto Duran
Madison Square Garden Venue	Win a match at Madison Square Garden
Sinister Cross	Win a classic fight with Roy Jones Jr.
Smooth Style	Defeat Muhammed Ali in a challenge event
Textbook	Win a classic fight with Oscar De La Hoya

Finding Nemo

Enter all the codes at the Main menu and the word Cheat will show up if done correctly.

Unlockable	Code
Credits	Ⓨ, Ⓧ, Ⓑ, Ⓑ, Ⓨ, Ⓨ, Ⓧ, Ⓑ, Ⓨ, Ⓧ, Ⓑ, Ⓑ, Ⓨ, Ⓧ, Ⓧ, Ⓑ, Ⓨ, Ⓧ, Ⓑ, Ⓨ, Ⓧ, Ⓑ, Ⓑ, Ⓨ
Invincibility	Ⓨ, Ⓧ, Ⓧ, Ⓑ, Ⓑ, Ⓑ, Ⓨ, Ⓨ, Ⓧ, Ⓧ, Ⓧ, Ⓑ, Ⓑ, Ⓑ, Ⓑ, Ⓨ, Ⓨ, Ⓑ, Ⓑ, Ⓑ, Ⓧ, Ⓑ, Ⓨ, Ⓑ, Ⓑ, Ⓧ, Ⓑ, Ⓨ, Ⓧ, Ⓑ, Ⓧ, Ⓑ, Ⓑ, Ⓨ
Level Select	Ⓨ, Ⓨ, Ⓨ, Ⓧ, Ⓧ, Ⓑ, Ⓧ, Ⓨ, Ⓑ, Ⓨ, Ⓧ, Ⓨ, Ⓧ, Ⓨ, Ⓑ, Ⓨ, Ⓨ
Secret Level	Ⓨ, Ⓧ, Ⓑ, Ⓑ, Ⓧ, Ⓨ, Ⓨ, Ⓧ, Ⓑ, Ⓑ, Ⓧ, Ⓨ, Ⓨ, Ⓑ, Ⓧ, Ⓨ, Ⓧ, Ⓑ, Ⓑ, Ⓧ, Ⓨ

FlatOut

Create a profile using these passwords.

Unlockable	Passwords
Lots of Cash	GIVECASH
Unlock Everything	GIVEALL
Use the Shift Up Button to Launch the Driver	Ragdoll

DS

GBA

PSP

PS2

PS3

Wii

Xbox

Xbox 360

Index

Side tabs: DS, GBA, PSP, PS2, PS3, Wii, Xbox, Xbox 360, Index

FlatOut 2

Enter these passwords in the Cheats menu under extras.

Unlockable	Password
All Cars and 1 Million Credits	GIEVEPIX
All Tracks	GIVEALL
Big Rig	ELPUEBLO
Flatmobile Car	WOTKINS
Lots of Money	GIVECASH
Mob Car	BIGTRUCK
Pimpster Car	RUTTO
Rocket Car	KALJAKOPPA
School Bus	GIEVCARPLZ

Forza Motorsport

Start a new profile with this name. Note: the code is case sensitive.

Unlockable	Code
Start Career with 900,000,000 Credits	tEAm4za

Freaky Flyers

Unlockable	Objective
Pilot X	On the last level in Adventure mode, beat Pilot X by destroying his robot.

Freedom Fighters

Enter these codes during gameplay.

Unlockable	Code	Unlockable	Code
Change Spawn Point	Y, A, X, B, B, ↑	Ragdolls	Y, A, X, B, X, ↑
Fast Motion	Y, A, X, B, B, ↓	Rocket Launcher	Y, A, X, B, Y, ←
Heavy Machine Gun	Y, A, X, B, Y, ↓	Shotgun	Y, A, X, B, B, ↑
Infinite Ammo	Y, A, X, B, A, →	Slow Motion	Y, A, X, B, B, →
Invisibility	Y, A, X, B, B, ←	Sniper Rifle	Y, A, X, B, Y, →
Max Charisma	Y, A, X, B, A, ↓	Sub Machine Gun	Y, A, X, B, Y, ↑
Nail Gun	Y, A, X, B, A, ←		

Freestyle Metal X

Go to Options, then enter the following case-sensitive codes in the Cheat menu.

Unlockable	Code
$1,000,000	sugardaddy
All Bike Parts	garageking
All Costumes	johnnye
All FMV Sequences	watchall
All Levels and Events	universe
All Photos and Posters in the Gallery	seeall
All Riders and Bikes	dudemaster
All Songs	hearall
All Special Stunts	fleximan

Frogger Ancient Shadow

Art 1	Frogger, Frogger, Frogger, Frogger
Art 2	Finnus, Finnus, Finnus, Finnus
Art 3	Berry, Berry, Berry, Berry
Bird Nest Wig	Lily, Lily, Lily, Lily

<table>
<thead>
<tr><th colspan="2">Frogger Ancient Shadow (continued)</th></tr>
</thead>
<tbody>
<tr><td>Dev Picture 1</td><td>Wani, Frogger, Wani, Frogger</td></tr>
<tr><td>Dev Picture 2</td><td>Berry, Berry, Berry, Wani</td></tr>
<tr><td>Lobster Wig</td><td>Finnius, Wani, Lumpy, Frogger</td></tr>
<tr><td>Programmer Art 1</td><td>Wani, Wani, Wani, Wani</td></tr>
<tr><td>Programmer Art 2</td><td>Lumpy, Frogger, Berry, Lily</td></tr>
<tr><td>Programmer Art 3</td><td>Wani, Frogger, Lily, Finnius</td></tr>
<tr><td>Sail Boat Wig</td><td>Lumpy, Lumpy, Lumpy, Lumpy</td></tr>
<tr><td>Skull Wig</td><td>Frogger, Lumpy, Lily, Frogger</td></tr>
</tbody>
</table>

Full Spectrum Warrior

Enter the following codes at the Cheat menu.

Unlockable	Code
Big Head Mode	NICKWEST
Full Version of America's Army	ha2p1py9tur5tle
Play at a Harder Level with No HUD	SWEDISHARMY
Unlimited Ammo	MERCENARIES

Futurama

While playing, hold Ⓛ and enter the following codes.

Unlockable	Code
All Extras	Ⓐ, ⓇⓉ+Ⓧ, ⓇⓉ+Ⓨ, Ⓐ, ⓇⓉ+Ⓧ, ⓇⓉ+Ⓨ, ⓇⓉ+Ⓑ, ⓇⓉ+Ⓐ, ⓁⓉ, ⓇⓉ+Ⓑ, ⓇⓉ+Ⓠ
Full Charge	Ⓐ, ⓇⓉ+Ⓧ, ⓇⓉ+Ⓨ, Ⓐ, ⓇⓉ+Ⓧ, ⓇⓉ+Ⓨ, ⓇⓉ+Ⓑ, ⓇⓉ+Ⓐ, ⓁⓉ, Ⓧ, ⓇⓉ+Ⓠ
Full Health	Ⓐ, ⓇⓉ+Ⓧ, ⓇⓉ+Ⓨ, Ⓐ, ⓇⓉ+Ⓧ, ⓇⓉ+Ⓨ, ⓇⓉ+Ⓑ, ⓇⓉ+Ⓐ, ⓁⓉ, Ⓨ, ⓇⓉ+Ⓠ
Infinite Ammo	Ⓐ, ⓇⓉ+Ⓧ, ⓇⓉ+Ⓨ, Ⓐ, ⓇⓉ+Ⓧ, ⓇⓉ+Ⓨ, ⓇⓉ+Ⓑ, ⓇⓉ+Ⓐ, ⓁⓉ, Ⓑ, ⓇⓉ+Ⓠ
Invincibility	Ⓐ, ⓇⓉ+Ⓧ, ⓇⓉ+Ⓨ, Ⓐ, ⓇⓉ+Ⓧ, ⓇⓉ+Ⓨ, ⓇⓉ+Ⓑ, ⓇⓉ+Ⓐ, ⓁⓉ, ⓇⓉ+Ⓨ, ⓇⓉ+Ⓠ
Unlimited Lives	Ⓐ, ⓇⓉ+Ⓧ, ⓇⓉ+Ⓨ, Ⓐ, ⓇⓉ+Ⓧ, ⓇⓉ+Ⓨ, ⓇⓉ+Ⓑ, ⓇⓉ+Ⓐ, ⓁⓉ, Ⓐ, ⓇⓉ+Ⓠ
Bender's Breakout	Ⓐ, ⓇⓉ+Ⓧ, ⓇⓉ+Ⓨ, Ⓐ, ⓇⓉ+Ⓧ, ⓇⓉ+Ⓧ, ⓇⓉ+Ⓨ, ⓇⓉ+Ⓨ, Ⓨ, Ⓠ
Bogad Swamp Trail	Ⓐ, ⓇⓉ+Ⓧ, ⓇⓉ+Ⓨ, Ⓐ, ⓇⓉ+Ⓧ, ⓇⓉ+Ⓨ, ⓇⓉ+Ⓧ, Ⓧ, Ⓠ
Fry Fights Back	Ⓐ, ⓇⓉ+Ⓧ, ⓇⓉ+Ⓨ, Ⓐ, ⓇⓉ+Ⓧ, ⓇⓉ+Ⓨ, ⓇⓉ+Ⓨ, Ⓐ, Ⓠ
Inner Temple	Ⓐ, ⓇⓉ+Ⓧ, ⓇⓉ+Ⓨ, Ⓐ, ⓇⓉ+Ⓧ, ⓇⓉ+Ⓨ, ⓇⓉ+Ⓨ, Ⓐ, ⓇⓉ+Ⓠ
Leela's Last Laugh	Ⓐ, ⓇⓉ+Ⓧ, ⓇⓉ+Ⓨ, Ⓐ, ⓇⓉ+Ⓧ, ⓇⓉ+Ⓨ, ⓇⓉ+Ⓨ, ⓇⓉ+Ⓑ, Ⓠ
Left Wing	Ⓐ, ⓇⓉ+Ⓧ, ⓇⓉ+Ⓨ, Ⓐ, ⓇⓉ+Ⓧ, ⓇⓉ+Ⓨ, ⓇⓉ+Ⓨ, Ⓐ, Ⓑ, Ⓠ
Market Square	Ⓐ, ⓇⓉ+Ⓧ, ⓇⓉ+Ⓨ, Ⓐ, ⓇⓉ+Ⓧ, ⓇⓉ+Ⓨ, ⓇⓉ+Ⓨ, Ⓐ, Ⓨ, Ⓠ
Old New York	Ⓐ, ⓇⓉ+Ⓧ, ⓇⓉ+Ⓨ, Ⓐ, ⓇⓉ+Ⓧ, ⓇⓉ+Ⓨ, ⓇⓉ+Ⓨ, Ⓨ, Ⓨ, Ⓠ
Planet Express	Ⓐ, ⓇⓉ+Ⓧ, ⓇⓉ+Ⓨ, Ⓐ, ⓇⓉ+Ⓧ, ⓇⓉ+Ⓨ, ⓇⓉ+Ⓨ, Ⓨ, Ⓨ, Ⓠ
Red Light District	Ⓐ, ⓇⓉ+Ⓧ, ⓇⓉ+Ⓨ, Ⓐ, ⓇⓉ+Ⓧ, ⓇⓉ+Ⓨ, ⓇⓉ+Ⓨ, Ⓨ, Ⓨ, Ⓠ
Red Rock Creek	Ⓐ, ⓇⓉ+Ⓧ, ⓇⓉ+Ⓨ, Ⓐ, ⓇⓉ+Ⓧ, ⓇⓉ+Ⓨ, ⓇⓉ+Ⓨ, Ⓑ, Ⓧ, Ⓠ
Right Wing	Ⓐ, ⓇⓉ+Ⓧ, ⓇⓉ+Ⓨ, Ⓐ, ⓇⓉ+Ⓧ, ⓇⓉ+Ⓨ, ⓇⓉ+Ⓨ, Ⓐ, Ⓐ, Ⓠ
Rumble in the Junkyard	Ⓐ, ⓇⓉ+Ⓧ, ⓇⓉ+Ⓨ, Ⓐ, ⓇⓉ+Ⓧ, ⓇⓉ+Ⓨ, ⓇⓉ+Ⓨ, Ⓑ, ⓇⓉ+Ⓑ, Ⓠ
Run, Bender, Run	Ⓐ, ⓇⓉ+Ⓧ, ⓇⓉ+Ⓨ, Ⓐ, ⓇⓉ+Ⓧ, ⓇⓉ+Ⓨ, ⓇⓉ+Ⓧ, Ⓨ, Ⓑ, Ⓑ, Ⓠ
Sewers	Ⓐ, ⓇⓉ+Ⓧ, ⓇⓉ+Ⓨ, Ⓐ, ⓇⓉ+Ⓧ, ⓇⓉ+Ⓨ, ⓇⓉ+Ⓧ, Ⓨ, Ⓨ, Ⓠ
Subway	Ⓐ, ⓇⓉ+Ⓧ, ⓇⓉ+Ⓨ, Ⓐ, ⓇⓉ+Ⓧ, ⓇⓉ+Ⓨ, ⓇⓉ+Ⓧ, Ⓨ, Ⓑ, Ⓠ
Temple Courtyard	Ⓐ, ⓇⓉ+Ⓧ, ⓇⓉ+Ⓨ, Ⓐ, ⓇⓉ+Ⓧ, ⓇⓉ+Ⓨ, ⓇⓉ+Ⓧ, Ⓐ, Ⓧ, Ⓠ
The Junkyard	Ⓐ, ⓇⓉ+Ⓧ, ⓇⓉ+Ⓨ, Ⓐ, ⓇⓉ+Ⓧ, ⓇⓉ+Ⓧ, Ⓨ, Ⓑ, ⓇⓉ+Ⓨ, Ⓠ
The Mine Facility	Ⓐ, ⓇⓉ+Ⓧ, ⓇⓉ+Ⓨ, Ⓐ, ⓇⓉ+Ⓧ, ⓇⓉ+Ⓧ, Ⓨ, ⓇⓉ+Ⓧ, Ⓑ, Ⓐ, Ⓠ
Uptown	Ⓐ, ⓇⓉ+Ⓧ, ⓇⓉ+Ⓨ, Ⓐ, ⓇⓉ+Ⓧ, ⓇⓉ+Ⓨ, ⓇⓉ+Ⓧ, ⓇⓉ+Ⓨ, ⓇⓉ+Ⓑ, Ⓠ
Weasel Canyon	Ⓐ, ⓇⓉ+Ⓧ, ⓇⓉ+Ⓨ, Ⓐ, ⓇⓉ+Ⓧ, ⓇⓉ+Ⓨ, ⓇⓉ+Ⓨ, Ⓑ, Ⓨ, Ⓠ

Side tabs: DS · GBA · PSP · PS2 · PS3 · Wii · Xbox · Xbox 360 · Index

Future Tactics The Uprising

Enter these codes during gameplay—do not pause.

Unlockable	Code
Big heads	◊, ◁, ♀, ◁, ♀, ◊, ◊, ◁
Disco mode	(LT), ◁, (LT), ◁, (RT), ◁, (RT), ◁
Low gravity	◊, ◊, ◊, ◊, ◊, ◊, ♀, ◁, ◊

Fuzion Frenzy

Enter the following codes after pressing ⊙ to pause gameplay. Repeat each code to disable its effect.

Unlockable	Code
Enable "Real Controls"	Hold (LT) and press ❶, ❶, ❶, ❸.
First-Person Mode	Hold (LT) and press ❶, ❸, ❶, ❸.
Mutant Mode	Hold (LT) and press ❶, ❸, ❷, ❷. To get Mutant mode two, repeat the code. To return to Mutant mode, repeat the code again. To disable the code, repeat it one more time.
Squeaky Voices	Hold (LT) and press ❶, ❷, ❶, ❶.
Turbo Mode (during a mini-game)	Hold (LT) and press ❶, ❸, ❷, ❷.
Welsh Mode	Hold (LT) and press ❶, ❶, ❶, ❶.

Gauntlet: Dark Legacy

Enter the following codes as names to access these unlockables.

Unlockable	Name
10,000 Gold per Level	10000K
Always Have Nine Potions and Keys	ALLFUL
Dwarf in S&M Costume	NUD069
Dwarf Is a Large Jester	ICE600
Invincibility	INVULN
Jester Is a Stick Figure with Baseball Cap Head	KJH105
Jester Is a Stick Figure with Mohawk Head	PNK666
Jester Is a Stick Figure with Smiley Face	STX222
Knight Is a Bald Man in Street Clothes (Sean Gugler)	STG333
Knight Is a Ninja (Sword and Claws)	TAK118
Knight Is a Quarterback	RIZ721
Knight Is a Roman Centurion	BAT900
Knight Is an Orange-Skirted Waitress	KAO292
Knight Wears Black Karate Outfit with Twin Scythes	SJB964
Knight Wears Black Outfit and Cape	DARTHC
Knight Wears Street Clothes	ARV984
Knight Wears Street Clothes (Chris Sutton)	CSS222
Knight Wears Street Clothes and Baseball Cap	DIB626
Permanent Anti-Death	1ANGEL
Permanent Full Turbo	PURPLE
Permanent Invisibility	000000
Permanent Pojo the Chicken	EGG911
Permanent Reflect Shot	REFLEX
Permanent Shrink Enemy and Growth	DELTA1

Gladius

Enter these codes while paused in different locations.

Unlockable	Code
1,000 Dinars every time you input this code	Paused in the school ➡, ⬇, ⬅, ⬆, ⬅, ⬅, ⬅, ⬅, ⬇, ⬅
1,000 exp. points every time you input this code	Paused in the school ➡, ⬇, ⬅, ⬆, ⬅, ⬅, ⬅, ⬇, ➡
Control camera	Pause during combat ⬆, ⬅, ⬇, ➡, ⬅, ➡, ⬅, ➡, ⬆, ⬆, ⬆, ⬆
Higher level enemies	Pause at a league office ➡, ➡, ⬅, ⬆, ⬆, ⬅, ⬅, ⬅, ⬅, ➡, ⬆, ⬆, ⬆, ⬆, ⬇
Lower Level Enemies & Recruits	Pause at a league office ➡, ➡, ⬅, ⬆, ⬆, ⬅, ⬅, ⬅, ⬅, ➡, ⬇, ⬇, ⬇, ⬇, ⬆

Goblin Commander: Unleash the Horde

To access the following unlockables, hold the left and right triggers and ⬤ for three seconds during gameplay, then enter code.

Unlockable	Code
1,000 Gold and Souls	(RT), (RT), (LT), (RT), (RT), ⬤, ⬤, ⬤, (LT), (LT)
God Mode	(RT), (RT), (RT), (LT), (LT), (LT), (RT), ⬤, (RT)
Introduction Sequence	Press (LT) at the Midway Games screen to see how the story begins.
Permanent Super Shot with Large Crossbow	SSHOTS
Permanent Triple Shot	MENAGE
Permanent X-Ray Vision	PEEKIN
Run Quickly	XSPEED
Throw Quickly	QCKSHT
Valkyrie as a Cheerleader with Baton	CEL721
Valkyrie as a Japanese School Girl	AYA555
Valkyrie as the Grim Reaper with Bloody Scythe	TWN300
Warrior as an Orc Boss	MTN200
Warrior with a Rat Head	RAT333
Warrior with an Ogre Costume	CAS400
Wizard as a Pharaoh	DES700
Wizard as an Alien	SKY100
Wizard as an Undead Lich	GARM00
Wizard as Sumner	SUM224
Wizard with an Evil Appearance	GARM99

The Godfather

Unlockable	Code
$5,000	✕, ⬤, ✕, ⬤, ⬤, (L3)
Full Ammo	⬤, ⬅, ⬤, ➡, ⬇, (R3)
Full Health	⬅, ✕, ➡, ⬤, ➡, (L3)

Enter this code on the Join Family menu.

Unlockable	Code
Unlock All Movies	⬤, ✕, ⬤, ✕, ✕, (L3)

Side tabs: DS, GBA, PSP, PS2, PS3, Wii, Xbox, Xbox 360, Index

Godzilla: Destroy All Monsters Melee

Cheat List: At the main menu, highlight Versus mode. Then in order, press and hold ⓛ, ⓞ, and ⓡ. Then release them in this order: ⓞ, ⓡ, ⓛ. Then enter the following codes.

Unlockable	Code
Black and white mode	860475
Boxing Level	440499
Extra Military Damage	970432
Godzilla 2000	637522
Unlock All monsters	209697

Unlockable	Objective
Destroyah	Beat Adventure mode with Godzilla 2000.
Gigan	Beat Adventure mode with Aguirus.
Godzilla 2000	Complete the Adventure mode with Godzilla 90's.
King Ghidorah	Beat Adventure mode with Megalon.
Mecha Godzilla	Beat the Adventure mode with Destoroyah, Rodan and Mecha-King Ghidorah.
Mecha Godzilla 2	Beat adventure mode with all monsters, then beat it again with Mecha King Ghidrah.
Mecha Godzilla 3	Beat adventure mode with Orga on Hard.
Mecha-King Ghidora	Beat Adventure mode with King Ghidorah.
Mothership Level	Beat the game on adventure mode with Mecha Godzilla.
Orga	Beat Adventure mode with all the characters, then beat the mode once more on medium difficulty with Godzilla 2000.
Rodan	Complete Adventure mode with Gigan.
Vortaak Level	Beat adventure mode with Mecha Godzilla 3 on Medium.

Godzilla: Save the Earth

To activate the Cheat menu, press and hold ⓛ, then ⓞ, then ⓡ in that order, then release the keys starting with ⓞ, then ⓡ, then ⓛ.

Unlockable	Code
All Cities	659996
All Monsters	525955
Buildings are Indestructible	812304
Energy doesn't regenerate	122574
Health Regenerates	536117
Player 1 deals 4x damage	259565
Player 1 has Infinite Energy	819324
Player 1 is Invisible	531470
Player 1 is Invulnerable	338592
Player 2 deals 4x damage	927281
Player 2 has Infinite Energy	324511
Player 2 is Invisible	118699
Player 2 is Invulnerable	259333
Player 3 deals 4x damage	500494
Player 3 has Infinite Energy	651417
Player 3 is Invisible	507215
Player 3 is Invulnerable	953598

DS

GBA

PSP

PS2

PS3

Wii

Xbox

Xbox 360

Index

Godzilla: Save the Earth (continued)

Unlockable	Code
Player 4 deals 4x damage	988551
Player 4 has Infinite Energy	456719
Player 4 is Invisible	198690
Player 4 is Invulnerable	485542

Golden Eye: Rogue Agent

In the Extras menu, enter the following:

Unlockable	Code
Paintball Mode	▷, ◁, ▷, ◁, ▽, ▽, △, △
Unlock All Skins in Multiplayer	▽, ◁, △, ◁, ▷, ▽, ◁, △

Grabbed by the Ghoulies

Unlockable	Code
20 Challenges	Collect 100 Rare Bonus Books
21st Challenge	Get Gold on all 20 Challenges

Grand Theft Auto 3

Unlockable	Code
All Weapons	(LB), (RB), (LT), (RB), ◁, ▽, ▷, △, ◁, ▽, ▷, △
Full Health	(LB), (RB), (LT), (RT), ◁, ▽, ▷, △, ◁, ▽, ▷, △
Full Armor	(LB), (RB), (LT), WHT, ◁, ▽, ▷, △, ◁, ▽, ▷, △

Grand Theft Auto: San Andreas

Enter these codes during gameplay; do not pause the game.

Unlockable	Code
$250,000 Plus Full Health and Armor	(RT), (RB), (LT), (A), ◁, ▽, ▷, △, ◁, ▽, ▷, △
Adrenaline Mode	(A), (A), (X), (RT), (LT), (A), ▽, ◁, (A)
Aggressive Drivers	◁, (RB), ◁, △, △, (RB), (B), (X), (RB), (LT), ◁, ▽, (LT)
Aggressive Traffic	(RB), (B), (RT), WHT, ◁, (RT), (LT), (RB), WHT
Aiming while Driving	△, △, (X), WHT, ▷, (A), (RT), ▽, (RB), (B)
All Cars Are Pink	(B), (LT), ▽, WHT, ◁, (A), (RT), (LT), ▷, (B)
All Cars Fly Away When Hit	(X), (RB), ▽, ▽, ◁, ▽, ◁, ◁, WHT, (A)
All Cars Have Nitrous	◁, ▽, (RT), (LT), △, (X), ▽, ▽, (B), WHT, (LT), (LT)
All Cars Have Tank Properties	(LT), WHT, WHT, △, ▽, ▽, △, (RT), (RB), (RB)
All Cars You Drive Can Drive on Water	▷, (RB), (B), (RT), WHT, (X), (RT), (RB)
All Cars You Drive Can Fly	(X), ▽, WHT, △, (LT), (B), △, (A), ◁
All Vehicles Are Black	(B), WHT, △, (RT), ◁, (A), (RT), (LT), ◁, (B)
All Vehicles Are Farm Vehicles and Everyone Is Dressed Like Farmers	(LT), (LT), (RT), (RT), WHT, (LT), (RB), ▽, (A), △
All Vehicles Are Invisible (except motorcycles)	(Y), (LT), (Y), (RB), (X), (LT), (LT)
All Vehicles Are Junk Cars	WHT, ▷, (A), △, (A), (LT), WHT, (RB), (RT), (LT), (LT), (LT)
Always Midnight	(X), (LT), (RT), ▷, (A), △, (LT), ◁, ◁
Beach Mode	△, △, ▽, ▽, (X), (B), (LT), (RT), ▽, ▽
Better Car Suspension	(X), (X), (RB), ◁, △, △, (RB), (A), (A), (A)
Chaos Mode	WHT, ▷, ◁, (LT), (Y), ◁, ▷, (RT), (LT), ◁, (LT), (LT), (LT)
Cloudy	WHT, ▽, ▽, ◁, (X), ◁, (RB), (X), (A), (RT), (LT), (LT)
Clown Mode	(Y), (Y), (LT), (X), (X), (B), (X), ▽, (B)
Destroy All Cars	(RB), WHT, (RT), (LT), WHT, (RB), (X), (Y), (B), (Y), WHT, (LT)
Faster Cars	▷, (RT), △, WHT, WHT, ◁, (RT), (LT), (RT), (RT)

Grand Theft Auto: San Andreas (continued)

Unlockable	Code
Faster Clock	B, B, LT, X, X, X, X, LT, Y, B, Y
Faster Gameplay	Y, ◇, ◇, ◁, VIEW, LT, X
Flying Boats	LB, B, ◁, LT, ▷, RT, ▷, ◇, X, Y
Foggy Weather	LB, A, LT, LT, RT, VIEW, VIEW, A
Full Wanted Level	B, ▷, B, ◇, ◁, X, A, ▽
Hitman Rank (all weapons)	▽, X, A, ◁, RT, LB, ◁, ▽, ▽, LT, LT, LT
Increase Car Speed	◇, LT, RT, ◇, ▷, ◇, A, VIEW, A, LT
Infinite Air	▽, ◁, LT, ▽, ▽, LB, ▽, VIEW, ▽
Infinite Ammo	LT, RT, X, RT, ◁, LB, RT, ◁, X, ▽, LT, LT
Infinite Health	▽, A, ▷, ◁, ◁, RT, ▷, ▽, ◇, Y
Jetpack	◁, ▷, LT, VIEW, RT, LB, ◇, ▽, ◁, ▷
Lower Wanted Level	RT, RT, B, LB, ◇, ◇, ▽, ▽, ▽, ▽
Max Fat	Y, ◇, ◇, ◁, ◇, X, B, ▽
Max Muscle	Y, ◇, ◇, ◁, ◇, X, B, ▷
Max Respect	LT, RT, ▽, Y, LB, A, LT, ◇, VIEW, VIEW, LT, LT
Max Sex Appeal	B, Y, ▽, ◇, B, RT, VIEW, ▽, Y, LT, LT, LT
Max Stamina	◇, A, Y, ◇, Y, A, X, LB, ▷
Max Vehicle Stats	X, VIEW, A, RT, VIEW, VIEW, ▷, RT, ▷, LT, LT, LT
Morning	LB, A, LT, LT, VIEW, VIEW, VIEW, X
Never Hungry	X, VIEW, RT, ▽, ◇, X, VIEW, ◇, A
No Muscle and No Fat	Y, ◇, ◇, ◁, ◇, X, B, ▷
No Pedestrians and Low Traffic	A, ▽, ▽, LB, ▽, ▽, LT, Y, ◁
Noon	LB, A, LT, LT, VIEW, VIEW, VIEW, ▽
Orange Sky	◁, ◁, VIEW, RT, ▷, X, X, LT, VIEW, A
Overcast	LB, A, LT, LT, VIEW, VIEW, VIEW, X
Parachute	◁, ▷, LT, VIEW, RT, LB, LB, ◇, ▷, ◁, LT
Pedestrian Attack (This code cannot be turned off.)	▽, ◇, ◇, ◇, A, LB, RT, VIEW, VIEW
Pedestrian Riot Mode (This code cannot be turned off.)	▽, ◁, ◇, ◁, A, LB, RT, VIEW, LT
Pedestrians Dress Like Elvis	LT, B, Y, LT, LT, X, VIEW, ◇, ▽, ◁
Pedestrians Have Guns	A, LT, ◇, X, ▽, A, VIEW, Y, ▽, RT, LT, LT
Pedestrians Have Weapons	LB, RT, A, Y, A, Y, ◇, ▽
Perfect Handling in Vehicles	Y, RT, RT, ◁, RT, LT, LB, LT
Pimp Mode	X, ▷, X, X, VIEW, A, Y, A, Y
Prostitutes Pay You	▷, VIEW, VIEW, ▽, VIEW, ◇, ▽, VIEW, LB
Recruit Anyone (9mm)	▽, X, ◇, LB, LB, ◇, ▷, ◁, ◇
Recruit Anyone (rockets)	LB, LB, LB, A, VIEW, LT, LB, LT, ▽, A
Sand Storm	◇, ▽, LT, LT, VIEW, VIEW, LT, VIEW, RT, LB
Skinny	Y, ◇, ◇, ◁, ◇, X, B, ▷
Slow Down Gameplay	Y, ◇, ▷, ◁, X, LB, RT
Spawn Bloodring Banger	▽, RT, B, VIEW, A, RT, LT, ◁, ◁
Spawn Caddy	B, LT, ◇, RT, VIEW, A, RT, LT, B, A
Spawn Dozer	LB, LT, LT, ◁, ▷, ◇, ◇, A, LT, ◁
Spawn Hotring Racer #1	RT, B, LB, ▷, LT, VIEW, A, A, X, RT
Spawn Hotring Racer #2	LB, LT, B, ▷, LT, RT, ▷, ◇, B, LB

Grand Theft Auto: San Andreas (continued)

Unlockable	Code
Spawn Hunter	B, A, LT, B, B, LT, B, RT, BLK, WHT, LT, LT
Spawn Hydra	Y, Y, X, B, A, LT, LT, ◇, △
Spawn Monster	▷, △, RT, RT, RT, ▽, Y, Y, A, B, LT
Spawn Quadbike	◁, ◁, ▽, ▽, △, △, X, B, Y, RT, BLK
Spawn Rancher	△, ▽, ▷, LT, ◁, ◁, △, X, WHT
Spawn Rhino	B, B, LT, B, B, B, LT, WHT, RT, Y, B, Y
Spawn Stretch	BLK, △, WHT, ◁, ◁, RT, LT, B, ▷
Spawn Stunt Plane	B, △, LT, WHT, ▽, RT, LT, LT, ◁, ◁, A, Y
Spawn Tanker	RT, △, ◁, ▽, BLK, △, ▷, X, ▷, WHT, LT, LT
Spawn Vortex	Y, Y, X, B, A, LT, WHT, ▽, ◇
Stormy	BLK, A, LT, LT, WHT, WHT, WHT, B
Super Bike Jumps	Y, X, B, B, X, B, B, LT, WHT, RT, BLK
Super Jumps	△, △, Y, △, △, △, ◁, ▷, X, BLK, BLK
Super Punches	△, ◁, A, Y, RT, B, B, B, WHT
Traffic Lights Stay Green	▷, RT, △, WHT, WHT, ◁, RT, LT, RT, RT
Unlock Romero	▽, BLK, ▽, RT, WHT, ◁, RT, LT, ◁, ▷
Unlock Trashmaster	B, RT, B, RT, ◁, ◁, RT, LT, B, ▷
Weapon Set 1	RT, BLK, LT, BLK, ◁, ▽, ▷, △, ◁, ▽, ▷, △
Weapon Set 2	RT, BLK, LT, BLK, ◁, ▽, ▷, △, ◁, ▽, ▽, ◁
Weapon Set 3	RT, BLK, LT, BLK, ◁, ▽, ▷, △, ◁, ▽, ▽, ◁
Yakuza Mode	A, A, ▽, BLK, WHT, B, RT, B, X

Grand Theft Auto: Vice City

Enter these codes while playing; do not pause.

Unlockable	Code
Aggressive Drivers	BLK, B, RT, WHT, ◁, RT, LT, BLK, WHT
Bikini Girls with Guns	▷, LT, B, WHT, ◁, A, RT, LT, LT, A
Black Cars	B, WHT, △, RT, ◁, A, RT, LT, ◁, B
Blow Up Cars	BLK, WHT, △, LT, WHT, BLK, X, Y, B, Y, WHT, LT
Cars Can Drive on Water	▷, BLK, B, RT, WHT, X, RT, BLK
Change Clothes	▷, ▷, ◁, △, LT, WHT, ◁, △, ▽, ▷
Change Vehicle Wheel Size (Repeat to change again)	RT, A, Y, ▷, BLK, X, △, ▽, X
Cloudy Weather	BLK, B, LT, LT, WHT, WHT, WHT, Y
Dodo Cheat	▷, BLK, B, RT, WHT, ▽, LT, RT (Press the analog stick back to fly)
Foggy Weather	BLK, A, LT, LT, WHT, WHT, WHT, A
Higher Top Speed for Your Vehicle	▷, RT, △, WHT, WHT, ◁, RT, LT, RT, RT
Ladies Man (Certain women follow you)	B, A, LT, LT, BLK, A, A, B, Y
Pedestrians Hate You (code cannot be undone)	▽, △, △, △, A, BLK, RT, WHT, WHT
Pedestrians Have Weapons (code cannot be undone)	BLK, RT, A, Y, A, Y, △, ▽
Pedestrians Riot (code cannot be undone)	▽, ◁, △, ◁, A, BLK, RT, WHT, LT
Perfect Handling	Y, RT, RT, ◁, RT, LT, BLK, LT

Grand Theft Auto: Vice City (continued)

Enter these codes while playing; do not pause.

Unlockable	Code
Pink Cars	Ⓑ, ⓛⓣ, ♥, ⓦⓗⓣ, ◄, Ⓐ, ⓡⓣ, ⓛⓣ, ►, Ⓐ
Play As Candy Suxxx	Ⓑ, ⓛⓣ, ♥, ⓡⓣ, ◄, ►, ⓡⓣ, ⓛⓣ, Ⓐ, ⓦⓗⓣ
Play As Hilary King	ⓡⓣ, Ⓑ, ⓛⓣ, ⓛⓣ, ►, ⓡⓣ, ⓛⓣ, Ⓐ, ⓛⓣ
Play As Ken Rosenberg	►, ⓛⓣ, ♦, ⓦⓗⓣ, ⓛⓣ, ►, ⓡⓣ, ⓛⓣ, Ⓐ, ⓡⓣ
Play As Lance Vance	Ⓑ, ⓦⓗⓣ, ◄, Ⓐ, ⓡⓣ, ⓛⓣ, Ⓐ, ⓛⓣ
Play As Love Fist Guy #1	♥, ⓛⓣ, ♥, ⓦⓗⓣ, ◄, Ⓐ, ⓡⓣ, ⓛⓣ, Ⓐ, Ⓐ
Play As Love Fist Guy #2	ⓡⓣ, ⓦⓗⓣ, ⓛⓣ, ►, ►, ◄, ►, ◄, Ⓐ, Ⓧ, ⓛⓣ
Play As Mercedes	ⓛⓣ, ⓛⓣ, ♦, ⓛⓣ, ►, ⓡⓣ, ►, ♦, Ⓑ, Ⓨ
Play As Phil Cassady	►, ⓡⓣ, ♦, ⓛⓣ, ⓛⓣ, ◄, ⓡⓣ, ⓛⓣ, ►, Ⓑ
Play As Ricardo Diaz	ⓛⓣ, ⓦⓗⓣ, ⓡⓣ, ⓛⓣ, ♥, ⓛⓣ, ⓛⓣ, ⓦⓗⓣ
Play As Sonny Forelli	Ⓑ, ⓛⓣ, Ⓑ, ⓦⓗⓣ, ◄, Ⓐ, ⓡⓣ, ⓛⓣ, Ⓐ, Ⓐ
Police Return from Dead	Ⓑ, ⓛⓣ, ♥, ⓦⓗⓣ, ◄, Ⓐ, ⓡⓣ, ⓛⓣ, ►, Ⓐ
Raise Wanted Level	ⓡⓣ, ⓡⓣ, Ⓑ, ⓛⓣ, ◄, ►, ◄, ►, ◄, ►
Repair Vehicle Tires	ⓛⓣ, ⓦⓗⓣ, ⓛⓣ, Ⓑ, ◄, ♥, ◄, ♦, ◄, ♥, ◄, ♦
Slow Down Time	Ⓨ, ♦, ►, ♥, Ⓧ, ⓛⓣ, ⓡⓣ
Spawn A Bloodring Banger	♦, ►, ►, ⓛⓣ, ►, ♦, Ⓧ, ⓦⓗⓣ
Spawn A Bloodring Racer	♥, ⓡⓣ, Ⓑ, ⓦⓗⓣ, ⓦⓗⓣ, Ⓐ, ⓡⓣ, ⓛⓣ, ◄, ◄
Spawn A Caddie	Ⓑ, ⓛⓣ, ♦, ⓡⓣ, ◄, Ⓐ, ⓡⓣ, ⓛⓣ, Ⓑ, Ⓐ
Spawn A Hotring Racer #1	ⓡⓣ, Ⓑ, ⓛⓣ, ►, ◄, ⓛⓣ, ⓦⓗⓣ, Ⓐ, Ⓐ, Ⓧ, ⓡⓣ
Spawn A Hotring Racer #2	ⓛⓣ, ⓛⓣ, Ⓑ, ►, ►, ⓛⓣ, ⓡⓣ, ►, ♦, Ⓑ, ⓛⓣ
Spawn A Love Fist	ⓛⓣ, ♦, ►, ⓦⓗⓣ, ◄, ◄, ⓡⓣ, ⓛⓣ, Ⓑ, ►
Spawn A Rhino Tank	Ⓑ, Ⓑ, ⓛⓣ, Ⓑ, Ⓑ, Ⓑ, ⓛⓣ, ⓦⓗⓣ, ⓡⓣ, Ⓨ, Ⓑ, Ⓨ
Spawn A Romero's Hearse	♥, ⓛⓣ, ♥, ⓡⓣ, ⓦⓗⓣ, ◄, ⓡⓣ, ⓛⓣ, ◄, ►
Spawn A Sabre Turbo	►, ⓦⓗⓣ, ♥, ⓡⓣ, ⓦⓗⓣ, Ⓐ, ⓡⓣ, ⓛⓣ, Ⓑ, ◄
Spawn A Trashmaster	Ⓑ, ⓡⓣ, Ⓑ, ⓡⓣ, ◄, ►, ⓡⓣ, ⓛⓣ, Ⓑ, ►
Speed Up Time	Ⓑ, Ⓑ, ⓛⓣ, Ⓧ, ⓛⓣ, Ⓧ, Ⓧ, Ⓧ, ⓛⓣ, Ⓨ, Ⓑ, Ⓨ
Stormy Weather	ⓛⓣ, Ⓐ, ⓛⓣ, ⓛⓣ, ⓦⓗⓣ, ⓦⓗⓣ, ⓦⓗⓣ, Ⓑ
Suicide	►, ⓦⓗⓣ, ♥, ⓡⓣ, ◄, ◄, ⓡⓣ, ⓛⓣ, ⓦⓗⓣ, ⓛⓣ
Sunny Weather	ⓛⓣ, Ⓐ, ⓛⓣ, ⓛⓣ, ⓦⓗⓣ, ⓦⓗⓣ, ⓦⓗⓣ, ♥
Very Cloudy Weather	ⓛⓣ, Ⓐ, ⓛⓣ, ⓛⓣ, ⓦⓗⓣ, ⓦⓗⓣ, ⓦⓗⓣ, Ⓧ
Weapons #1	ⓡⓣ, ⓛⓣ, ⓛⓣ, ⓛⓣ, ◄, ♥, ►, ♦, ◄, ♥, ►, ♦
Weapons #2	ⓡⓣ, ⓛⓣ, ⓛⓣ, ⓛⓣ, ◄, ♥, ►, ♦, ◄, ♥, ►, ◄
Weapons #3	ⓡⓣ, ⓛⓣ, ⓛⓣ, ⓛⓣ, ◄, ♥, ►, ♦, ◄, ♥, ♥, ♥

Great Escape

Unlockable	Code
Restore Health	While playing, pause when you are equipping a gun and a health kit. Then press Ⓨ,Ⓧ,ⓛⓣ,ⓡⓣ,ⓛⓣ,ⓡⓣ,Ⓧ,Ⓨ,ⓛⓣ,Ⓨ,Ⓨ,ⓡⓣ,Ⓐ
Select Levels	From the Main menu, press Ⓨ,ⓡⓣ,Ⓨ,Ⓧ,Ⓨ,ⓡⓣ,Ⓧ,ⓛⓣ,Ⓧ,Ⓧ,Ⓧ,Ⓨ
Unlock All Movies	From the Main menu, press ⓛⓣ,ⓛⓣ,Ⓨ,Ⓧ,Ⓧ,ⓡⓣ,ⓡⓣ,Ⓨ,Ⓨ,Ⓧ,ⓛⓣ,ⓡⓣ

DS · GBA · PSP · PS2 · PS3 · Wii · Xbox · Xbox 360 · Index

Half-Life 2

Enter these codes while playing; do not pause the game.

Unlockable	Code
Restores 25 points of health (per use)	⬥, ⬥, ◗, ◗, ◖, ◗, ◖, ◗, ⓑ, ⓐ
Restores ammo for current weapon	ⓨ, ⓑ, ⓐ, ⓧ, WHT, ⓨ, ⓧ, ⓐ, ⓑ, WHT
Unlocks all chapters	◖, ◖, ◖, ◖, ⒝, ◗, ◗, ◗, ◗, WHT

Halo

Unlockable	Objective
Talking Grunt	During the last level, you'll come to a group of tunnels after the dropship pick up goes wrong. Take the tunnel on your right and there should be a fork leading to a dead end. If you head in that direction, you can hear a grunt talking about something phenomenally droll.

Halo 2

Skulls

Skull	Location/Effect
Angry Mode	When you are the Master Chief trying to recover the index from the Prophet of Truth on the Covenant Holy City, go until you reach the first outdoor area with dirt and vegetation. Take a right as you enter this room and run up to the wall past the gravity lift that leads up to the sniper point. Get on top of the wall by going up the dirt mound on your left. Follow the wall until you reach the floating skull called Angry. This skull makes enemies fire at a faster rate.
Assassins Mode	A skull similar to the one that activates Blind mode can be found if you start on "Regret." After the first lift ride (before the first underwater elevator), grenade jump from the front awning of the lift to the ledge in front of you (the one with two turrets). Grenade jump again onto the next ledge. Go to the back of the building. On Easy, you'll only find the skull. On Legendary, however, 2 invisible elites carrying swords just shake their heads wildly, ignoring you completely.
Blind Mode	At the beginning of Outskirts, crouch jump on top of the light over the door, then jump to the left platform. Turn to your left and go down the long dark corridor and pick up the skull; it says blind and your screen flashes black for a while. In this mode you can not see your weapon, body, shields, ammo, or radar. To get rid of this feature: 1. Turn off your Xbox or Save and Quit. 2. Go to Campaign and select level and choose Cairo Station. 3. Skip the cinematics and then Save and Quit. 4. Go Outskirt and your HUD is back.
Envy Mode	On the level Delta Halo on Legendary difficulty, progress until you reach the area during the "Push through the covenant held ruins" where you have to clear a Landing Zone for the Pelican to drop weapons. You will know you are in the right area when Cortana says, "They're pouring out of the center building." That area has plasma turrets along its borders. A little bit after the left side turret you see the outline of a door in a wall, but the door has a solid rock slab in it and a rock in front of it. Jump on the rock then jump to the ledge above the door then jump on the ledge to the left. Now jump onto the building with the sealed door using grenades. Atop the building you will find two dancing elites and the "Envy Skull." Pick up the Envy Skull and you can use Active Camouflage like the Arbiter.

DS

GBA

PSP

PS2

PS3

Wii

Xbox

Xbox 360

Index

Halo 2 (continued)

Skull	Location/Effect
Famine Skull	After you get off of the slowly descending elevator in The Oracle, you come to a hallway where you see a handful of dead bodies. Continue into the next room, and you will be on the second floor of a room with windows. When you enter this room, look to the right, and find the third pane of glass. It should be to the right of a wall that has some flood guts splattered on it. Shoot out this window, and either window directly across the room. If you look below you will see a platform that has four tall posts. On the room's far side is a column between the two windows. Turn on your active camo, and jump to the center platform. Jump on either of the posts on the far side of the platform and jump to the column between the windows. Jump through the window you shot out and make a left. Walk all the way to the end and you'll find four flood elites convulsing on the floor, with the Famine Skull in the middle of them. When you have this skull, all weapons will have less ammo.
Grunts' Birthday Party Mode	In the level Arbiter on Legendary, once you get to the first banshee section, immediately fly straight to the bottom of the map. In one of the cracks where the large cylinders connect to the station are a circle of grunts dancing around a skull. When you pick up the skull, it says Grunt Birthday Party on the screen. Now when you kill a enemy with a head shot, they blow up like a plasma grenade was stuck to them. To get rid of this feature use the same method as the Blind mode.
Iron Mode	On the last Master Chief level, on Legendary difficulty, when you enter the final Gravity Lift, look up. A skull passes through you extremely quickly, so start holding ⊗ a bit before you actually pass it to grab hold of it. Once you grab the Iron Skull, Iron mode will be activated. This skull causes you to go back to the last checkpoint when you die in co-op mode.
Mythic Mode	In Sacred Icon, there's a pair of semi-outdoor areas, each with a large sentinel in front. Go past this area and down the piston and you'll be in a very dark and dank flood infested area. Use the boxes to jump up to the landing above. A handful of alcoves are on your right. The skull is in the third alcove, floating above a dead human flood.
Sputnik Mode	At the start of Quarantine Zone on Legendary difficulty, turn directly around, and see a tunnel. Head through the tunnel. Go straight across the open area, and you'll come across a broken pipe tunnel on your right. Straight in front of you is a small ledge running across the wall, above the green pit. Carefully get onto that small ledge and walk to the end to find the Sputnik Skull. In this mode explosion force and melee force is greater.
Thunderstorm Mode	On the level Cario Station on Legendary, get to the "Priority Shift" checkpoint. Progress until the room with mounted plasma turrets, right after the armory with the elites. Clear out this room, and get on the raised area with the plasma turret on the side of the wall where the window curves. Look for two parallel beams on the ledge above. Climb up the supports for these beams and crouch jump up onto the upper ledge, then onto the beams themselves. Walk in the direction you came from, jump on a small ledge sticking out to the left, and pick up the Thunderstorm Skull from inside the trash container. This turns all Covenants into their spec ops rank.

DS

GBA

PSP

PS2

PS3

Wii

Xbox

Xbox 360

Index

Halo 2 (continued)

Skull	Location/Effect
Unknown Skull	At the beginning of Armory, wait in the room until the Sarge starts telling you to get into the elevator. You must wait for him to say "Would it help if I said please?" When he says this, get into the elevator and go down to the tram. Get on the tram and face the inside of the building. Press up against the glass doors toward the inside of the building. Hold ❌ and you should pick up the skull. It's on a stack of green crates, near the end of the tram ride.

Easter Eggs

Easter Egg	Description
Giant Soccer Ball	It's on the level Metropolis on any difficulty. Use the same method to get a Banshee through the tunnels as you would if you were getting the Scarab Gun. Now take your Banshee away from that half-dome thing and fly through the level using the same path you would as if you were walking. Once you get to the highway where the Warthogs are fighting the Ghosts, keep flying straight toward the half-demolished building. Fly into it and go to the bottom level. You find giant soccer ball! It's great fun to mess around with, especially if you have the Scarab Gun.
Messages on the Bomb	If you play multiplayer and hide with the bomb, then you probably have noticed this already. If you stand somewhere long enough, the Chief will start to toss the bomb up and catch it. Eventually he examines the bomb, and you can read what it says on the bottom. One message is "goodbye" and another is "xoxoxoxo".
Midship Bunny	On the level Midship, go to the top where the sword spawns. Now walk to the doorway that doesn't have a big roof. Look up and you should see an outline of a bunny!
Sign on Zanzibar	On the beach on Zanzibar, you will see signs that say NO SWIMMING. Go to your Xbox dashboard, go to the Settings, Clock, and change every number you can to 7 , then pop Halo 2 back into your Xbox and load it up. WARNING: Do not sign into XBoxLive, it resets your clock. Now go to Split-Screen and start a game on Zanzibar. Go to the beach and look at the sign. It mentions that something is missing, and there is a bloody dog's head.
Posters at the Old Mombassa Crash Landing after Cairo	After you crash land on Old Mombassa, you can see posters all around with the Master Chief from the demo and some grunt posters.
The Face of Chris	On the map Containment, get a sniper rifle and go anywhere where you can see the part of the Halo in the sky that's closest to the Sun Base (the base with orange-yellow glowing buildings). Zoom in with the sniper on the part of the halo that's just below where it begins to get dark. In the clouds you should be able to see the face of Chris Carney (grinning happily), one of Bungie's developers.
Rex in Outskirts	Head toward the Blind Skull way, but when you go up there, take a left instead of a right and jump on the ledge, then crouch jump on top of another ledge (which would be right above the wreckage). Jump on the ledge across the wreckage then continue the pathway until you reach the area with the sword sticking out of the ground (inside a broken rooftop). Right next to it is a rock with the word REX written on it.
Weird Window Reflections on Headlong	In Headlong, grab a Banshee and fly to the part of the level with water. On the same side as the Warthogs spawn, almost at the end of the level itself, there are some windows. Look closely at them, they aren't reflecting the other side of the level, but showing concept art for Halo 2.

DS

GBA

PSP

PS2

PS3

Wii

Xbox

Xbox 360

Index

DS

GBA

PSP

PS2

PS3

Wii

Xbox

Xbox 360

Index

Halo 2 (continued)

Easter Egg	Description
Why am I here? Message in Beaver Creek	This easter egg is very simple. Go to Beaver Creek. Run to where the sniper rifle spawns. Jump onto the ledge in front of you and push all of the rocks down. When you push the big rock down, look at the wall that was behind it. If you look carefully and you can see "Why am I here?" scratched in to the wall. (If you cannot see it, back away from the wall some and it should look much clearer.)
Zanibar Computer Screen	On Zanzibar, after you open the gate the computer screen (used to open the gate) changes. When you zoom in on the words, you can read how to fix your computer and some other gags.

Unlockables

Unlockable	How to Unlock
Banshee in the Control Room	To get a Banshee inside the room where you fight Tartarus, first get a Banshee. After the Scarab destroys the front door, fly inside and go straight up as soon as you enter. Get out of your Banshee and make the door open, then get back in your Banshee and fly through. When the Brutes come through the next door you can kill them or fly past them, but make sure you aren't in your Banshee when the cutscene starts.
Get a Scarab Gun	Do this on the level Metropolis. It's easiest when done on Co-op. When you start out, cross the bridge. Take out every enemy and even your marines. When you're near the end, Cortana says something about a "Welcome Party." Three Banshees and a few Ghosts appear. Take them all out. Then 2 Wraiths and 2 Banshees appear. Take out both Wraiths, and only one Banshee. Have Player 1 continue through the tunnel, but have Player 2 stay outside and distract the Banshee. Once Player 1 reaches the area with the circular opening (a Jackal with a Beam rifle is present), take out the Jackal and head back to where Player 2 is. Get the Banshee to follow both players into the tunnel. Do not board it yet! The first few times it will come at you and fly back out, but stay where you are. It should come back after you. (If it doesn't, go back outside and try again.) Eventually, you have to get it over two roadblocks. Once it is past the second one, have both players stand near the entrance of the room where Player 1 took out the Jackal. It should fly at you and get stuck. Shoot off both of its wings so it can fit through. Have Player 1 walk slowly in front of the Banshee, making it follow him. Player 2 should be behind it, gently pushing it. Take it to the left and get ready to board it. As soon as you hit the checkpoint, the Elite in the Banshee will disappear. You only have about a second to get in before the Banshee also disappears. Both players should press ⊗ quickly. If you do it right, one of the players will be driving the Banshee! Take it outside and directly up. Very high in the sky are two skyscrapers with two bridges connecting them. In the middle of the bridge closest to you, there is something that looks like a plasma rifle. It's actually a Scarab gun! It has infinite ammo, so have fun. Just don't aim at the ground.
Skip Banshee Flight in the Arbiter level	When you first get to fly the Banshee, zoom toward the tower to your right. When you get closer, a nav-point appears. Go to it and the game will automatically advance to that spot in the story. By doing this, you've skipped the grueling 20 minute-long Banshee flight. On the downside, however, you don't have much of a chance to grab a Fuel Rod Cannon.
Skip Fight around the Delta Halo tower	After the cutscene with the hologram regret telling you how he will start the ring in Delta Halo, continue until you see a crate. Then jump on it, then onto the ledge. Walk around until it loads the checkpoint. You have skipped the battle.

Haunted Mansion

To access the following unlockables, hold ⑪ on the D-Pad, then enter code.

Unlockable	Code
Level Select	Ⓑ, Ⓑ, Ⓧ, Ⓨ, Ⓨ, Ⓧ, Ⓐ
God Mode	Ⓧ, Ⓑ, Ⓑ, Ⓑ, Ⓧ, Ⓑ, Ⓨ, Ⓐ

Heroes of the Pacific

Enter these codes at the Main menu.

Unlockable	Code
Cheat Menu	Ⓨ, ⓁⓉ, ◄◊, ⓇⓉ, ◊►, WHT
Unlock All Planes and Missions	⬆, ⬇, WHT, BLK, ◄◉, ◉►
Unlock Japanese Planes	WHT, BLK, ⓁⓉ, ⓇⓉ, ⬆, ⬇
Upgrade Planes	ⓁⓉ, ◄◉, ⓇⓉ, ◉►, WHT, Ⓨ

Hitman 2: Silent Assassin

Unlockable	Code
All Weapons	Press ⓇⓉ, ⓁⓉ, ⬆, ⬇, Ⓐ, ⬇, Ⓧ, Ⓐ during gameplay.
Bomb Mode	Press ⓇⓉ, ⓁⓉ, ⬆, ⬇, Ⓐ, ⬇, ⬆ during gameplay.
Full Heal	Press ⓇⓉ, ⓁⓉ, ⬆, ⬇, Ⓐ, ⬇, ⬇ during gameplay.
God Mode	Press ⓇⓉ, ⓁⓉ, ⬆, ⬇, Ⓐ, ⓇⓉ, ⓁⓉ, BLK, WHT during gameplay.
Hitman AI	During gameplay press ⓇⓉ, ⓁⓉ, ⬆, ⬇, Ⓐ, ⬇, ⬆.
Lethal Charge	Press ⓁⓉ, ⓇⓉ, ⬆, ⬇, Ⓐ, BLK, BLK during gameplay.
Level Select	Press ⓇⓉ, ⓁⓉ, ⬆, ⬇, Ⓐ, Ⓑ at the main menu.
Level Skip	Press ⓇⓉ, ⓁⓉ, ⬆, ⬇, Ⓐ, Ⓧ, click Ⓛ, and press Ⓑ, Ⓐ, Ⓑ, Ⓐ during gameplay. Enable this code immediately after starting a level to complete it with a Silent Assassin rank.
Megaforce Mode	Press ⓇⓉ, ⓁⓉ, ⬆, ⬇, Ⓐ, ⓇⓉ, ⓇⓉ during gameplay. Restart the level to remove its effect.
Nailgun Mode (Weapons pin people to walls when you activate this code.)	Press ⓇⓉ, ⓁⓉ, ⬆, ⬇, Ⓐ, WHT, WHT during gameplay.
Punch Mode	Press ⓇⓉ, ⓁⓉ, ⬆, ⬇, Ⓐ, ⬇, ⬇ during gameplay.
Slow Motion	Press ⓇⓉ, ⓁⓉ, ⬆, ⬇, Ⓐ, ⬇, ⓁⓉ during gameplay.
SMG and 9mm Pistol SD	Press ⓁⓉ, ⓇⓉ, ⬆, ⬇, Ⓐ, ⬇, ⬆ during gameplay.
Toggle Gravity	Press ⓇⓉ, ⓁⓉ, ⬆, ⬇, Ⓐ, ⓁⓉ, ⓁⓉ during gameplay.

Hitman: Contracts

Enter the following codes at the Main menu.

Unlockable	Code
Level Select	Ⓧ, Ⓨ, Ⓑ, ◄◊, ⬇, ◊►, ⓁⓉ, ⓇⓉ
Level Skip and Silent Assasin Rating	ⓇⓉ, ⓁⓉ, ⬆, ⬇, Ⓧ, Ⓐ, ⓁⓉ, Ⓑ, Ⓐ, Ⓑ, Ⓐ

House of the Dead 3

Unlockable	Objective
Extra Items in Original Mode	Complete House of the Dead 3, and then go to House of the Dead 2, by taking an elevator down. On the way down, the door opens a couple of times. Shoot all the enemies as quickly and as accurately as possible to get items for Original mode in House of the Dead 2. Complete House of the Dead 3 again to repeat the process. Every time you do this, you get new items for Original mode. This works best if you unlocked the "Free-Play" option for House of the Dead 3.
Free Play	Complete the game with an "A" rank. Enter the Options screen, and select "House of the Dead 3." You can now increase the credits past nine until "Free Play" appears.
House of the Dead 2	Complete Survival mode in House of the Dead 3 to unlock House of the Dead 2.

The Hulk

Enter these cheats at the Code Input screen in the Options menu.

Unlockable	Code
Double Health for Enemies	BRNGITN
Double Health for Hulk	HLTHDSE
Full Rage Meter Cheat	ANGMNGT
Half Enemies' HP	MMMYHLP
High Score reset	NMBTHIH
Invincibility	GMMSKIN
Level Select	TRUBLVR
Play as Gray Hulk	JANITOR
Puzzle Solved Cheat	BRCESTN
Regenerator	FLSHWND
Unlimited Continues	GRNCHTR
Unlock Desert Battle art	FIFTEEN
Unlock Hulk Movie FMV art	NANOMED
Unlock Hulk Transformed art	SANFRAN
Unlock Hulk vs. Hulk Dogs art	PITBULL
Wicked Punch Cheat	FSTOFRY

I-Ninja

Codes

Unlockable	How to Unlock
Big Head Mode	Press START to pause gameplay, then hold RB and press Y, Y, Y, Y. Release RB, then hold L1 and press Y, Y. Hold RB+L1, then press Y, B, Y.
Level Skip	Press start to pause game, hold RT then press X, X, X, B. Release RT then hold LT and press Y, Y. Release LT then hold RT, X, X.

Unlockables

Unlockable	How to Unlock
Battle Arena	Collect all 64 Grades to unlock Battle Arena in Robot Beach

Ice Age 2: The Meltdown

Codes

Unlockable	How to Unlock
Unlimited Energy	↓, ←, →, ↓, ↓, →, ←, ↓
Unlimited Health	↑, →, ↓, ↑, ←, ↓, →, ←
Unlimited Pebbles	↓, ↓, ←, ↑, ↑, →, ↑, ↓

IHRA Drag Racing Sportsman Edition

Enter these case-sensitive passwords as profile names.

Unlockable	Password
$999,999	Loaded
All bonuses	IWantIt
All trophy room items	FilMeUp
Rocket cars	HotRodz

DS
GBA
PSP
PS2
PS3
Wii
Xbox
Xbox 360
Index

The Incredible Hulk: Ultimate Destruction

At the Code Input screen, enter the following codes.

Unlockable	Code
5,000 Smash Points	SMASH5
10,000 Smash Points	SMASH10
15,000 Smash Points	SMASH15
Abomination (must complete Story mode first)	VILLAIN
All Vehicles Become Taxis	CABBIES
American Flag Shorts	AMERICA
Black and White Graphics	RETRO
Canadian Flag Shorts	OCANADA
Cow Missiles	CHZGUN
Double Hulk's Damage Abilities	DESTROY
Double Value of Health Pickups	BRINGIT
French Flag Shorts	DRAPEAU
German Flag Shorts	DEUTSCH
Gorilla Invasion Mode	KINGKNG
Gray Hulk (without suit)	CLASSIC
Grey Hulk Mr. Fix It	SUITFIT
Italian Flag Shorts	Mutanda
Japanese Flag Shorts	FURAGGU
Low Gravity	PILLOWS
Mass Transit On/Off	TRANSIT
Sepia Mode	HISTORY
Spanish Flag Shorts	BANDERA
Union Jack Flag Shorts	FSHNCHP
Wild Traffic	FROGGIE

The Incredibles

Pause the game and go to the Secrets menu and enter the following codes.

Unlockable	Code
Big Heads	EINSTEINIUM
Credits	YOURNAMEINLIGHTS
Destroy All Enemies on Screen	SMARTBOMB
Eye Laser	GAZERBEAM
Feet of Fire	ATHLETESFOOT
One Hit Knockout	KRONOS
Restore Health	UUDDLRLRBAS
Slow down Gameplay	BWTHEMOVIE
Small Heads	DEEVOLVE
So many Colors	EMODE
Speed up Gameplay	SASSMODE
Turn off the HUD	BHUD
Unlimited Incredi-Power for Mr. Incredible	SHOWTIME
Unlimited Incredi-Power for Elastigirl	FLEXIBLE
Watch the Intro Again	HI

DS

GBA

PSP

PS2

PS3

Wii

Xbox

Xbox 360

Index

Indiana Jones and the Emperor's Tomb

Enter this code at the Main menu.

Unlockable	Code
God Mode	Hold ⓛ+ⓡ and press ⊙, ⊙, ♀, ⊙, ⊙, Ⓐ, ⓧ, Ⓐ, Ⓑ, ⊙, ♀, ▼, ♀

The Italian Job

Unlockable	Objective
All Bonus Content	Complete the story mode.
All Cars in Circuit Racing	Get an A ranking in every level.

Jade Empire

Unlockables

Unlockable	How to Unlock
Crimson Tears	To receive the upgraded dual sword Crimson Tears, climb the ranks in the Imperial Arena to the Bronze Division. When Cho comes and asks you to poison Crimson Khana, refuse, then find her and tell her about this. Once you defeat her in the ring she'll teach you Crimson Tears.
Minigame in Main Menu	To unlock the dragonfly minigame in the main menu, during the story choose attack instead of evade enemy between each chapters and complete the dragonfly missions.
New Title Screen	Finish the game, or at least get to the point where it auto-saves at the final boss. The title screen changes to Dirge. It will change back if you delete the auto-save created at the final boss.
Exploding Gambler	If you win 20 dice rolls in a row against the gambler in the Imperial Arena, he will explode.
Flawless Victory	If you can win the Imperial Arena without losing you will receive a new Technique from Sweet Poison Lyn.
Hilarious Dialogs/Audio	After finishing the game, don't skip the credits roll. Eventually after being half-done with it, you're treated to some funny dialog and voiceovers from several followers of yours.

Jaws Unleashed

Enter these passwords as Profile names.

Unlockable	Password
1 Million Points	Bloooood
Unlock All Bonuses	Shaaark

Juiced

Enter this passwords in the Password menu.

Unlockable	Password
All Cars in Arcade Mode	PINT

Jurassic Park: Operation Genesis

Codes

Unlockable	How to Unlock
$10,000	Press ⓛⒷ+⊙ and then ⓛⒷ+♀
All Dinosaurs have 55% DNA	⊙, ⊙, ⊙, ♀
All Missions, Exercises, and Sites	ⓡⒷ, ⊙, ⊙, ⊙, ⊙ ⓡⒷ
All Research	♀, ♀, ♀, ⊙, ⊙, ⓛⒷ, ♀, ⊙
Car Crash	Press ⓛ+ⓡⒷ, and repeatedly tap ⊙, ♀, w, ♀
Clear Storms	ⓡⒷ, ⓡⒷ, ⊙, ⊙, ⊙, ⊙

Side tabs: DS, GBA, PSP, PS2, PS3, Wii, Xbox, Xbox 360, Index

Jurassic Park: Operation Genesis (continued)

Unlockable	How to Unlock
Constant Rain	RB, LB, RB, ↓, ↑, ↓
Create a Heat Wave	Press RB+↓ (x2)
Create a Twister	←, ↑, →, ↓, and RB+LT
Create Stormy Weather	RB, RB, LB, RB, ↓, ↑, ↓
Damage All Paths	→, →, RB, RB, LB, ↓
Diseased Dinosaurs	↓, ↑, ↓, ←, RB, RB, RB
Destroy All Fences	↑, +, ↓, RB, ←, ←
Downgrade All Fences to Low Security	↓, ↓, ←, →, LB, LB, ↑, ↑
Extinction Event	LB, RB, ↓, RB, LB
Guaranteed Immunity	↑, ↑, RB, LB, ↑, ↑
Increase Park Budget by $250,000	LB, →, →, LB, RB, ↓
Increase Park Rating by 1 Star	→, LB, ↑, LB, LB, ↓
Kill All Tourists	→, ←, ↓, ←, ↓, RB
Make Visitors Happy	RB, ↓, LB, ↑, ↑, ↑
Make Your Finances Zero	RB+LT, ↓
No More Rampages	LB, ←, ↑, ←, ↑, ←, LB
No Red Tape	LB, RB, ←, ↓, ↓, ↓
No Twisters	LB+RT, release LB+RT, and then press LB+RT again.
Restock Your Market with Fossils	LB, RB, LB, RB, ↓, ↓
Set All Excavated Dinosaur DNA to 0%	LB, +, LB, →, ↓, RB
Set All Excavated Dinosaur DNA to 100%	RB, ↑, RB, →, LB, ↑
Shoot from Cars Using Camera	LT+RB, ←, ↓, ←, →
Stress Out All Carnivores	LB, LB, LB and ←, ←, ←
Three Stars	LB, RB, ↓, ↓, LB, →
Tourist Casualties Don't Affect Your Budget	RB, ←, ↓, ↓, ↓, ↓
Undead Dinosaurs	RB, RB, RB, LB, →
Upgrade all Fences to Maximum Security	LB, ←, ←, RB, RB →

Justice League Heroes

Codes

Code	Effect
All Cinematics	↓, →, ↓, ←
Get 20 Shields	↑, ↑, ↓, ↓
Gives 35 Random Boosts	←, →, ←, →
Infinite Energy	↓, ↓, →, →, ↑, ↑, ←, ←
Invincibility	←, ↓, →, ↑, ←, ↓, →, ↑
Maxes Out Abilities	→, ↓, →, ↓
One Hit Kills	↑, ↑, ↓, ←, ↑, ↓, ↓
Purchase All Heroes	→, ↓, ←, ↑
Take Less Damage	←, ↑, →, ↓
Unlock all Costumes	↓, ←, ↑, →

DS · GBA · PSP · PS2 · PS3 · Wii · Xbox · Xbox 360 · Index

DS

GBA

PSP

PS2

PS3

Wii

Xbox

Xbox 360

Index

Kelly Slater's Pro Surfer

Enter these passwords in the Options menu under cheats.

Unlockable	Password	Unlockable	Password
All Boards	619 555 4141	Max Stats	212 555 1776
All Levels	328 555 4497	Mega Cheat	714 555 8092
All Suits	702 555 2918	Pastrana	800 555 6292
All Surfers	949 555 6799	Perfect Balance	213 555 5721
All Tricks	626 555 6043	Play as Rainbow	213 555 5721
First-Person Mode	877 555 3825	Trippy	818 555 1447
Freak	310 555 6217	Unlock Tiki God	888 555 4506
High Jumps	217 555 0217	Unlock Tony Hawk	323 555 9787

Kill.switch

Unlockable	Code
Infinite Ammo	After completing the game, pause the game and press LT, RT, X, X

Kung-Fu Chaos

Enter these codes at the Main menu.

Unlockable	Code
All Available Costumes for Unlocked Characters	BADBABY
All Characters	BAWDYBALLAD
All Character Bios	BLARBDRAWL
All Island Scenes	BAYSAWAY
All Levels in the Style of a 1920's Movie	SALADDAYS
Play Ninja Challenge in Co-op	BUDDY
Unlock All Levels	LADYRADAR
Unlock Candi Roll	LADYSDAY
Unlock Captain Won	LARDYBUD
Unlock Championship Mode	SLAYDAY
Unlock Every Cheat	LUXURYLARD
Unlock Everything That Requires Rour Stars	ALLBRAWL
Unlock Miniseries Mode	SLYSUBURB
Unlock Shao Ting	WALRUSBALDY

Land of the Dead: Road to Fiddler's Green

Enter these codes during gameplay.

Unlockable	Code
All Weapons	Up, Down, Left, Right, A, B
God Mode	Up, Down, Left, Right, Up, Down, Left, Right
Kill All Spawned Enemies	A, B, Y, X, A, B, Y, X
Kungfu Fists	Right, Down, Left, A
Minigun	Up, Up, Down, Down, A, B, A, B
No Knockdown	Up, A, Up, B, Down, Y, Down, X

Legacy of Kain: Defiance

To access the following, pause the game any time and enter code.

Unlockable	Code
All Bonuses	LB, Down, White, RT, Left, White, Down, LT, Y
Infinite Reaver Charge	Down, Down, Up, Left, RT, LB, Down, Y, B
Card Board Tube Reaver	Up, Down, Left, Right, LB, White, Y, Down, B
God Mode	Up, Down, Right, Down, RT, LB, Down, Y, LT

Legends of Wrestling

Unlockable	Code
All Wrestlers	At the Main menu, press ⊕, ⊕, ⊙, ⊙, ⊲, ⊳, ⊲, ⊳, ⊗, ⊗, ⊗. The save prompt appears to let you know the code worked.

Legends of Wrestling II

Unlockables

Unlockable	How to Unlock
Andy Kaufman	Choose Jerry Lawler as your legend in Career mode, and when you face Andy Kaufman make sure to win. He is now unlocked for the shop.
Belle Jackson	Beat a storyline in the Southeast region to unlock her for purchase in the shop. To get her cheaper, continue completing storylines in the Southeast region.
Big John Studd	Go to Career mode with any wrestler. When you face Big John Studd, make sure to win by pinfall. He's now unlocked in the shop.
British Bulldog	Beat the entire Career mode with the Dynamite Kid.
Bruno Summartino	Beat Career mode using "Hollywood" Hulk Hogan.
Cheating Mode	Choose Career mode with any legend. During Career mode, enter one of each of the match types. After that, exit right away. After all match types have been entered, you get a message stating the cheats can now be purchased in the shop.
Hiro Natsume	Beat a storyline in the World Region to unlock him for purchase in the shop. To get him cheaper, continue completing storylines in the World Region.
Owen Hart	Beat the entire Career mode with his brother Bret Hart.
Randall Schmandall	Beat a storyline in the Pacific Region to unlock him for purchase in the shop. To get him cheaper, continue completing storylines in the Pacific region.
Scotty MacDougal	Beat a storyline in the Midwest region to unlock him for purchase in the shop. To get him cheaper, continue completing storylines in the Midwest region.
Tex McGraw	Beat a storyline in the Southwest region to unlock him for purchase in the shop. To get him cheaper, continue completing storylines in the Southwest region.
Tony "The Boss" Pavarotti	Beat a storyline in the Northeast region to unlock him for purchase in the shop. To get him cheaper, continue completing storylines in the Northeast region.
Unlimited Coins	Beat Career mode with every single wrestler.

LEGO Star Wars

To unlock characters for purchase in Free Play mode, go to Dexter's Diner, then the Codes menu, and enter the following.

Unlockable	Code	Unlockable	Code
Battle Droid	987UYR	Clone (Episode III)	ER33JN
Battle Droid (Commander)	EN11K5	Clone (Episode III, Pilot)	BHU72T
Battle Droid (Geonosis)	LK42U6	Clone (Episode III, Swamp)	N3T6P8
Battle Droid (Security)	KF999A	Clone (Episode III, Walker)	RS6E25
Big Blasters	IG72X4	Count Dooku	14PGMN
Boba Fett	LA811Y	Darth Maul	H35TUX
Brushes	SHRUB1	Darth Sidious	A32CAM
Classic Blasters	L449HD	Disguised Clone	VR832U
Clone	F8B4L6	Droideka	DH382U

Sidebar tabs: DS, GBA, PSP, PS2, PS3, Wii, Xbox, Xbox 360, Index

LEGO Star Wars (continued)

Unlockable	Code	Unlockable	Code
General Grievous	SF321Y	Padme	92UJ7D
Geonosian	19D7NB	PK Droid	R840JU
Gonk Droid	U63B2A	Princess Leia	BEQ82H
Grievous' Bodyguard	ZTY392	Purple	YD77GC
Invincibility	4PR28U	Rebel Trooper	L54YUK
Jango Fett	PL47NH	Royal Guard	PP43JX
Ki-Adi Mundi	DP55MV	Shaak Ti	EUW862
Kit Fisto	CBR954	Silhouettes	MS999Q
Luminara	A725X4	Silly Blasters	NR37W1
Mace Windu (Episode III)	MS952L	Super Battle Droid	XZNR21
Minikit Detector	LD116B	Tea Cups	PUCEAT
Moustaches	RP924W		

LEGO Star Wars II: The Original Trilogy

Enter these passwords in the Cantina.

Unlockable	Password	Unlockable	Password
Beach Trooper	UCK868	Imperial Spy	CVT125
Ben Kenobi (Ghost)	BEN917	Jawa	JAW499
Bespin Guard	VHY832	Lobot	UUB319
Bib Fortuna	WTY721	Palace Guard	SGE549
Boba Fett	HLP221	Rebel Pilot	CYG336
Death Star Trooper	BNC332	Rebel Trooper (Hoth)	EKU849
Ewok	TTT289	Sandtrooper	YDV451
Gamorrean Guard	YZF999	Skiff Guard	GBU888
Gonk Droid	NFX582	Snowtrooper	NYU989
Grand Moff Tarkin	SMG219	Stormtrooper	PTR345
Greedo	NAH118	The Emperor	HHY382
Han Solo (Hood)	YWM840	Tie Fighter	HDY739
IG-88	NXL973	Tie Fighter Pilot	NNZ316
Imperial Guard	MMM111	Tie Interceptor	QYA828
Imperial Officer	BBV889	Tusken Raider	PEJ821
Imperial Shuttle Pilot	VAP664	Ugnaught	UGN694

Links 2004

Unlockable	Code
80 Attribute Points	Create a new profile using the name SafariTK.
All courses	At the Main Menu, hold ⓛⒹ+ⓇⓉ and press ⊗+ⓥ

The Lord of the Rings: The Fellowship of the Ring

Input the following codes during gameplay.

Unlockable	Code
Infinite Ammo	3, 2, 4, 1, 3, 2.
Infinite Health	4, 1, 3, 2, 1, 4.
Infinite Ring Use	4, 2, 1, 2, 4, 3.

DS

GBA

PSP

PS2

PS3

Wii

Xbox

Xbox 360

Index

The Lord of the Rings: The Return of the King

To access the following unlockables, hold ⓛ+⟨RT⟩ and enter code.

Unlockable	Code
Legolas 1000 Exp Points	Ⓐ,▽,◇,Ⓐ
Gandalf 1000 Exp Points	Ⓑ,▽,◇,▽
Frodo 1000 Exp Points	▽,▽,◇,▽
Aragorn 1000 Exp Points	◇,⊗,◇,Ⓐ
Sam 1000 Exp Points	▽,Ⓐ,▽,Ⓐ
1000 Exp Points	Ⓑ,Ⓑ,▽,Ⓐ
Infinite Respawn in Co-Op Mode	Ⓑ,⊗,◇,Ⓑ

The Lord of the Rings: The Two Towers

Codes

The game must be completed first before these codes can be activated. Pause game play, then hold ⓛ+⟨RB⟩ and press the desired code. The sound of a sword confirms correct code entry.

Unlockable	How to Unlock
Add 1,000 Experience Points	Ⓐ,▽,▽,▽
All Combo Upgrades	▽,Ⓑ,▽,Ⓑ
Devastating Attack	⊗,⊗,Ⓑ,Ⓑ
Invincibility	▽,⊗,Ⓐ,Ⓑ
Level 2 Skills	Ⓑ,◁▷,Ⓑ,◁▷
Level 4 Skills	▽,◇,▽,◇
Level 6 Skills	⊗,◁▷,⊗,◁▷
Level 8 Skills	Ⓐ,Ⓐ,▽,▽
Restore Ammunition	Ⓐ,▽,▽,◇
Restore Health	▽,▽,Ⓐ,◇
Slow Motion	▽,Ⓑ,Ⓐ,⊗
Small Enemies	▽,▽,Ⓐ,Ⓐ
Unlimited Missiles	⊗,Ⓑ,Ⓐ,▽

Unlockables

Unlockable	How to Unlock
Concept Art	Complete Gates of Moria
Elijah Wood Interview	Complete Gates of Moria
Ian McKellen Interview	Complete Gates of Moria
Isildur	After Unlocking the Tower of Orthanic level, complete it with any character
John Rhys-Davis interview	Play with Gimli until he reaches level 5
Orlando Bloom Interview	Beat Helm's Deep: The Deeping Wall and reach level 10 with Legolas
Peter Jackson and Barrie Osborne Interview	Complete Gates of Moria
Play as Secret Character	Complete Secret Mission with any character
Production Photos	Complete Balin's Tomb
Production Photos, Fangorn Forest, and Orthanc	Complete Fangorn Forest
Production Photos, Rohan, and Helm's Deep	Complete Plains of Rohan

DS

GBA

PSP

PS2

PS3

Wii

Xbox

Xbox 360

Index

The Lord of the Rings: The Two Towers (continued)

Unlockable	How to Unlock
Secret Codes	Complete Secret Mission with Secret Character
Secret Mission as Aragorn	Beat Helms Deep: The Deeping Wall and reach level 10 with Aragorn
Secret Mission as Gimli	Beat Helms Deep: The Deeping Wall and reach level 10 with Gimli
Secret Mission as Legolas	Beat Helms Deep: The Deeping Wall and reach level 10 with Legolas
The Making of the Video	Complete Gates of Moria
Tower of Orthanc	Finish the game with any character at level 10
Viggo Mortensen Interview	Beat Helm's Deep: The Deepening Wall and reach level 10 with Aragorn

Madden NFL 2004

Unlockable	Objective
1990 Eagles Classic Team	Earn Level 4 EA Sports Bio
Bingo! Cheat	Earn Level 2 EA Sports Bio
Steve Spurrier Coach	Earn Level 6 EA Sports Bio

Madden NFL 2005

From My Madden menu, go to Madden Cards, Madden Codes, and enter the following:

Card	Password	Card	Password
Aaron Brooks Gold Card	_J95K1J	Casey Hampton Gold Card	Z11P9T
Aaron Glenn Gold Card	Q48E9G	Chad Johnson Gold Card	R85S2A
Adewale Ogunleye Gold Card	C12E9E	Chad Pennington Gold Card	B64L2F
Ahman Green Gold Card	T86L4C	Champ Bailey Gold Card	K89O9E
Al Wilson Gold Card	G72G2R	Charles Rogers Gold Card	E57K9Y
Alan Faneca Gold Card	U32S9C	Charles Woodson Gold Card	F95N9J
Amani Toomer Gold Card	Z75G6M	Chris Hovan Gold Card	F14C6J
Andre Carter Gold Card	V76E2Q	Corey Simon Gold Card	R11D7K
Andre Johnson Gold Card	E34S1M	Courtney Brown Gold Card	R42R75
Andy Reid Gold Card	N44K1L	Curtis Martin Gold Card	K47X3G
Anquan Boldin Gold Card	S32F7K	Dallas Coach Gold Card	O24U1Q
Antoine Winfield Gold Card	A12V7Z	Damien Woody Gold Card	F78I1I
Bill Cowher Gold Card	S54T6U	Dante Hall Gold Card	B23P8D
Brad Hopkins Gold Card	P44A8B	Dat Nguyen Gold Card	Q86I2S
Bret Favre Gold Card	L61D7B	Daunte Culpepper Gold Card	O62O9K
Brian Billick Gold Card	L27C4K	Dave Wannstedt Gold Card	W73D7D
Brian Dawkins Gold Card	Y47B8Y	David Boston Gold Card	A25I9F
Brian Simmons Gold Card	S22M6A	David Carr Gold Card	C16E2Q
Brian Urlacher Gold Card	Z34J4U	Dennis Erickson Gold Card	J83E3T
Brian Westbrook Gold Card	V46I2I	Dennis Green Gold Card	C18J7T
Bubba Franks Gold Card	U77F2W	Derrick Brooks Gold Card	P93I9Q
Butch Davis Gold Card	G77L6F	Derrick Mason Gold Card	S98P3T
Byron Leftwich Gold Card	C55V5C	Deuce McAllister Gold Card	D11H4J
Carson Palmer Gold Card	O36V2H	Dexter Coakley Gold Card	L35K1A

Madden NFL 2005 (continued)

Card	Password	Card	Password
Dexter Jackson Gold Card	G16B2I	Tony Gonzalez Gold Card	N46E9N
Dick Vermeil Gold Card	F68V1W	Torry Holt Gold Card	W96U7E
Dom Capers Gold Card	B97I6R	Travis Henry Gold Card	F36M2Q
Domanick Davis Gold Card	L58S3J	Trent Green Gold Card	Y46M4S
Donnie Edwards Gold Card	E18Y5Z	Ty Law Gold Card	F13W1Z
Donovin Darius Gold Card	Q11T7T	Walter Jones Gold Card	G57P1P
Donovon McNabb Gold Card	T98J1I	Washington Coach Gold Card	W63V9L
Donte Stallworth Gold Card	R75W3M	Will Shields Gold Card	B52S8A
Dre Bly Gold Card	H19Q2O	Zach Thomas Gold Card	U63I3H
Drew Bledsoe Gold Card	W73M3E	Jason Webster Gold Card	M74B3E
Dwight Freeney Gold Card	G76U2L	Jeff Fisher Gold Card	N62B6J
Edgerrin James Gold Card	A75D7X	Jeff Garcia Gold Card	H32H7B
Ed Reed Gold Card	G18Q2B	Jeremy Newberry Gold Card	J77Y8C
Eric Moulds Gold Card	H34Z8K	Jeremy Shockey Gold Card	R34X5T
Flozell Adams Gold Card	R54T1O	Jerry Porter Gold Card	F71Q9Z
Fred Taylor Gold Card	I87X9Y	Jerry Rice Gold Card	K34F8S
Grant Wistrom Gold Card	E46M4Y	Jevon Kearse Gold Card	A78B1C
Herman Edwards Gold Card	O19T2T	Jim Haslett Gold Card	G78R3W
Hines Ward Gold Card	M12B8F	Jim Mora Jr. Gold Card	N46C3M
Jack Del Rio Gold Card	J22P9I	Jimmy Smith Gold Card	I22J5W
Jake Delhomme Gold Card	M86N9F	Joe Horn Gold Card	P91A1Q
Jake Plummer Gold Card	N74P8X	Joey Harrington Gold Card	Z68W8J
Jamie Sharper Gold Card	W27I7G	John Fox Gold Card	Q98R7Y
Jason Taylor Gold Card	O33S6I	Jon Gruden Gold Card	H61I8A
Seattle Coach Gold Card	V58U4Y	Josh McCown Gold Card	O33Y4X
Shaun Alexander Gold Card	C95Z4P	Julian Peterson Gold Card	M89J8A
Shaun Ellis Gold Card	Z54F2B	Julius Peppers Gold Card	X54O4Z
Shawn Rogers Gold Card	J97X8M	Junior Seau Gold Card	W26K6Q
Shawn Springs Gold Card	Z28D2V	Kabeer Gbaja-Biamala Gold Card	U16I9Y
Simeon Rice Gold Card	S62F9T	Keith Brooking Gold Card	E12P4S
Stephen Davis Gold Card	E39X9L	Keith Bulluck Gold Card	M63N6V
Steve Mariucci Gold Card	V74Q3N	Kendrell Bell Gold Card	T96C7J
Steve McNair Gold Card	S36T1I	Kevan Barlow Gold Card	A23T5E
Steve Smith Gold Card	W91O2O	Kevin Mawae Gold Card	L76E6S
Takeo Spikes Gold Card	B83A6C	Kris Jenkins Gold Card	W63O3K
Tedy Bruschi Gold Card	K28Q3P	Kyle Boller Gold Card	A72F9X
Terence Newman Gold Card	W57Y5P	Kyle Turley Gold Card	Y46A8V
Terrell Suggs Gold Card	V71A9Q	LaDainian Tomlinson Gold Card	M64D4E
Tiki Barber Gold Card	T43A2V	LaVar Arrington Gold Card	F19Q8W
T.J. Duckett Gold Card	P67E1I	Laveranues Coles Gold Card	R98I5S
Todd Heap Gold Card	H19M1G	Lawyer Milloy Gold Card	M37Y5B
Tom Brady Gold Card	X22V7E	La'Roi Glover Gold Card	K24L9K
Tom Coughlin Gold Card	S71D6H	Lee Suggs Gold Card	Z94X6Q
Tony Dungy Gold Card	Y96R8V	Leonard Davis Gold Card	H14M2V

DS
GBA
PSP
PS2
PS3
Wii
Xbox
Xbox 360
Index

Madden NFL 2005 (continued)

Card	Password	Card	Password
Lovie Smith Gold Card	L38V3A	Norv Turner Gold Card	F24K1M
Marc Bulger Gold Card	U66B4S	Olin Kreutz Gold Card	R17R2O
Marcel Shipp Gold Card	R42X2L	Orlando Pace Gold Card	U42U9U
Marcus Stroud Gold Card	E56I5O	Patrick Surtain Gold Card	H58T9X
Marcus Trufant Gold Card	R46T5U	Peerless Price Gold Card	X75V6K
Mark Brunell Gold Card	B66D9J	Peter Warrick Gold Card	D86P8O
Marshall Faulk Gold Card	U76G1U	Peyton Manning Gold Card	L48H4U
Marty Booker Gold Card	P51U4B	Plaxico Burress Gold Card	K18P6J
Marty Schottenheimer Gold Card	D96A7S	Priest Holmes Gold Card	X91N1L
Marvin Harrison Gold Card	T11E8O	Quentin Jammer Gold Card	V55S3Q
Marvin Lewis Gold Card	P24S4H	Randy Moss Gold Card	W79U7X
Matt Hasselback Gold Card	R68D5F	Ray Lewis Gold Card	B94X6V
Michael Bennett Gold Card	W81W2J	Reggie Wayne Gold Card	R29S8C
Michael Strahan Gold Card	O66T6K	Rex Grossman Gold Card	C46P2A
Michael Vick Gold Card	H67B1F	Rich Gannon Gold Card	Q69I1Y
Mike Alstott Gold Card	D89F6W	Richard Seymour Gold Card	L69T4T
Mike Brown Gold Card	F12J8N	Ricky Williams Gold Card	P19V1N
Mike Martz Gold Card	R64A8E	Rod Smith Gold Card	V22C4L
Mike Mularkey Gold Card	C56D6E	Rodney Harrison Gold Card	O84I3J
Mike Rucker Gold Card	K89O6S	Ronde Barber Gold Card	J72X8W
Mike Shanahan Gold Card	H15L5Y	Roy Williams Gold Card	J76C6F
Mike Sherman Gold Card	F84X6K	Rudi Johnson Gold Card	W26J6H
Mike Tice Gold Card	Y31T6Y	Sam Madison Gold Card	Z87T5C
New England Coach Gold Card	N24L4Z	Samari Rolle Gold Card	C69H4Z
Nick Barnett Gold Card	X95I7S	Santana Moss Gold Card	H79E5B

Secret Teams

Card	Password	Card	Password
1958 Colts	_P74X8J	1982 Redskins	F56D6V
1966 Packers	G49P7W	1983 Raiders	D23T8S
1968 Jets	C24W2A	1984 Dolphins	X23Z8H
1970 Browns	G12N1I	1985 Bears	F92M8M
1972 Dolphins	R79W6W	1986 Giants	K44F2Y
1974 Steelers	R12D9B	1988 49ers	F77R8H
1976 Raiders	P96Q8M	1990 Eagles	G95F2Q
1977 Broncos	O18T2A	1991 Lions	I89F4I
1978 Dolphins	G97U5X	1992 Cowboys	I44A1O
1980 Raiders	K71K4E	1993 Bills	Y66K3O
1981 Chargers	Y27N9A		

Secret Stadiums

Stadium	Password	Stadium	Password
Pro Bowl Hawaii '05	G67F5X	Super Bowl XLII	T67R1O
Super Bowl XL	O85P6I	Super Bowl XXXIX	D58F1B
Super Bowl XLI	P48Z4D		

DS
GBA
PSP
PS2
PS3
Wii
Xbox
Xbox 360
Index

Madden NFL 2005 (continued)

Pump Up and Cheerleader Cards

Password	Card	Password	Card
49ers Cheerleader	_X61T6L	Jaguars Cheerleader	K32C2A
Bears Pump Up Crowd	K17F2I	Jets Pump Up Crowd	S45W1M
Bengals Cheerleader	Y22S6G	Lions Pump Up Crowd	C18F4G
Bills Cheerleader	F26S6X	Packers Pump Up Crowd	K26Y4V
Broncos Cheerleader	B85U5C	Panthers Cheerleader	M66N4D
Browns Pump Up Crowd	B65Q1L	Patriots Cheerleader	O59P9C
Buccaneers Cheerleader	Z55Z7S	Raiders Cheerleader	G92L2E
Cardinals Cheerleader	Q91W5L	Rams Cheerleader	W73B8X
Chargers Cheerleader	Q68S3F	Ravens Cheerleader	P98T6C
Chiefs Cheerleader	T46M6T	Redskins Cheerleader	N19D6Q
Colts Cheerleader	M22Z6H	Saints Cheerleader	R99G2F
Cowboys Cheerleader	J84E3F	Seahawks Cheerleader	A35T8R
Dolphins Cheerleader	E88T2J	Steelers Pump Up Crowd	C98I2V
Eagles Cheerleader	Q88P3Q	Texans Cheerleader	R74G3W
Falcons Cheerleader	W86F3F	Titans Cheerleader	Q81V4N
Giants Pump Up Crowd	L13Z9J	Vikings Cheerleader	E26H4L

Gold Cheat Cards

Card	Description	Code
3rd Down	For one half, your opponent has 3 downs to get a first down.	_Z28X8K
5th Down	For one half, you will have 5 downs to get a first down.	P66C4L
Bingo!	Your defensive interceptions increase by 75% for the game.	J33I8F
Da Bomb	You will receive unlimited pass range for one half.	B61A8M
Da Boot	You will receive unlimited field goal range for one half.	I76X3T
Extra Credit	Awards 4 points for every interception and 3 points for every sack.	M89S8G
1st and 15	Requires your opponent to get 15 yards to reach a first down for one half.	V65J8P
1st and 5	Your first down yards to go will be set to 5 for one half.	O72E9B
Fumblitis	Your opponent's fumbles will increase by 75% for the game.	R14B8Z
Human Plow	Your Broken Tackles will increase by 75% for the game.	L96J7P
Mr. Mobility	Your QB can't get sacked for one half.	Y59R8R
Super Dive	Your diving distance increases by 75% for the game.	D59K3Y
Lame Duck	Your opponent will throw a lob pass for one half.	D57R5S
Mistake Free	You can't fumble or throw an interception for one half.	X78P9Z
Tight Fit	Your opponent's uprights will be made very narrow for one half.	V34L6D
Unforced Errors	Your opponent will fumble every time he tries to juke for one half.	L48G1E

Madden NFL 06

To enter this code, go into My Madden, select Madden Cards, then select Enter Code.

Unlockable	Code
1st and 5 Bronze	2Y7L8B
1st and 15 Bronze	2W4P9T
3rd Down Bronze	3F9G4J
5th Down Bronze	3E9R4V
Da Boot Bronze	3J3S9Y

DS

GBA

PSP

PS2

PS3

Wii

Xbox

Xbox 360

Index

DS

GBA

PSP

PS2

PS3

Wii

Xbox

Xbox 360

Index

Madden NFL 06 (continued)

Unlockable	Code
Donovan McNabb Gold Card (alternate)	8Q2J2X
Extra Credit Bronze	3D3Q3P
Human Plow Bronze	3H3U7F
Super Dive Bronze	3H8M5U
Tight Fit Bronze	3D8X6T
Unforced Errors Bronze	2Z2F4H

Madden NFL 07

Under Madden Cards, select Madden Codes to enter these passwords. Passwords are case sensitive.

Unlockable	Password
When this card is played, you can't fumble or throw interceptions for one half	XL7SP1
When this card is played, your opponent will throw a lob pass for one half	5LAWO0
When this card is played, your QB accuracy will be 100% for one half	WROA0R

Mafia

Unlockable	Objective
Car Selection	Learn to break into cars during missions, which will allow you to use it in Free Ride.
City Selection	Progress through story mode to unlock more areas for Free Ride.
Monster Truck	Take first place in all of the races in Racing Championship mode.
Time of Day	Progress through story mode to unlock a Day/Night option for Free Ride.

Magic the Gathering: Battlegrounds

Unlockable	Code
All Quest	During the Quest select, press (LT)+(RT), ♦, ○, ●, (WH), ○, ♦, ◄, ○, ♦, (LT)+(RT).
Secret Level for Vs. Mode	At the Arena select, press (LT)+(RT), ◄, ○, ⊗, ♦, (RT), ♥, (LT)+(RT).
All Duelists in Arcade Mode	At the Character select screen, press (LT)+(RT), ♦, ○, ♦, (WH), ○, ♦, (L), ♦, ⊗, (LT)+(RT).

Major League Baseball 2K5: World Series Edition

Create a new profile and enter the following names.

Unlockable	Code
Unlock All Cheats	Ima Cheater
Unlock All Classic Teams	Old Timers
Unlock All Extras	Gimme Goods

Major League Baseball 2K7

Codes

Code	Effect
triplecrown	Increase ability of 3,4,5 hitters
Derek Jeter	Unlock everything (except the cheats you need special codes for)
themick	Unlock Mickey Mantle in free agency

Manhunt

In order to unlock these codes, you must complete each level with 3 stars or better. Then, once you unlock the codes, enter them at the main menu.

Unlockable	Objective	Code
Fully Equipped (All weapons in level and infinite ammo)	Beat Drunk Driving and Graveyard Shift	RT, WHT, LT, BLK, ○, ◇, ◁, ◇
God Mode	Complete whole game	○, ○, ⊖, ◇, ○, ○, ✕, WHT, ◇, ◇, LT
Helium Hunters (Explode when hit and speak with squeaky voices)	Beat Strapped for Cash and View of Innocence	RT, RT, ▽, ⊖, ✕, BLK, LT, ○
Invisibility (Hunters are blind)	Beat Trained to Kill and Border Patrol	✕, ✕, ✕, ○, ✕, ○, ⊖, ◇
Monkey Skin	Beat Press Coverage and Wrong Side of the Tracks	✕, ✕, WHT, ○, ▽, ✕, ⊖, ○
Piggsy Skin	Beat Key Personnel and Deliverance	◇, ○, ◁, ◁, RT, WHT, LT, LT
Rabbit Skin	Beat Kill the Rabbit and Divided They Fall	◁, RT, RT, ▽, RT, RT, ✕, LT
Regeneration (Cash's health regenerates)	Beat Fueled by Hate and Grounds for Assault	WHT, ▷, ⊖, WHT, BLK, ○, ⊖, ◁
Runner (Player has infinite stamina)	Beat Born Again and Doorway Into Hell	WHT, WHT, LT, WHT, ◁, ▷, ◁, ▷
Silence (Hunters are deaf)	Beat Road to Ruin and White Trash	RT, LT, WHT, LT, ▷, ◁, ◁, ◁
Super Punch	Beat Mouth of Madness and Doing Time	LT, ▽, ▽, ▽, ⊖, ⊖, ⊖, RT

Marc Ecko's Getting Up: Contents Under Pressure

Enter these passwords in the Cheats menu under Options.

Unlockable	Password
All Art	SIRULLY
All Black Book	SHARDSOFGLASS
All Characters in Versus Mode	STATEYOURNAME
All Combat	Upgrades DOGTAGS
All Legends	NINESIX
All Levels	IPULATOR
All Movies	DEXTERCROWLEY
All Ipod songs	GRANDMACELIA
All Versus Arenas	WORKBITCHES
Infinite Health	MARCUSECKOS
Infinite Skills	FLIPTHESCRIPT
Max Health	BABYLONTRUST
Max Skills	VANCEDALLISTER

Marvel Nemesis: Rise of the Imperfects

Enter these passwords in the Cheat menu under Options.

Unlockable	Password
All Fantastic Four comics	SAVAGELAND
All Tomorrow People comics	NZONE
Electra swimsuit card	THEHAND
Solara swimsuit card	REIKO
Storm's swimsuit card	MONROE

DS
GBA
PSP
PS2
PS3
Wii
Xbox
Xbox 360
Index

DS

GBA

PSP

PS2

PS3

Wii

Xbox

Xbox 360

Index

Marvel vs. Capcom 2

Unlockable	How to Unlock
Attack After Fight Is Finished	After you win a fight, press start to attack the other person until the end of the match
Choose Character to Start Match With	At the beginning of a battle, hold a character's assist button, and he/she will be first instead
Use the Same Character 3x Per Team	Unlock all hidden characters and all extra costumes

Mat Hoffman's Pro BMX 2

Enter these codes quickly at the "Press Start" screen. If done correctly you will hear a sound confirming the code worked.

Unlockable	Code
Adrenaline meter always full	♀, Ⓐ, Ⓐ, Ⓐ, RT, RT, RT
Big Foot's videos	RT, ○, ♀, ◁, Ⓐ, Ⓐ, Ⓐ, RT
BMX Costume	✕, Ⓑ, ◁, ▷, ◁, ✕
Boston (in Road Trip)	▼, ○, ♀, ♀, ○, ▼
Chicago (in Road Trip)	▼, ○, Ⓑ, ○, Ⓑ, ○, ▼
Cory's videos	RT, ▼, ✕, ✕, ▼, ▼, ▼, RT
Day Smith's videos	RT, ✕, ◁, ◁, ▼, ▷, ▷, RT
Fiery hands & feet	♀, Ⓑ, Ⓑ, Ⓐ, Ⓐ, RT, RT
Invisible Bikes	♀, ○, ◁, ♀, ▷, ♀, ◁, ○
Kevin's videos	RT, Ⓐ, Ⓑ, ♀, ○, RT
LA (in Road Trip)	▼, ◁, Ⓑ, Ⓑ, ◁, ▼
Mat's videos	RT, ◁, ✕, ◁, ✕, ◁, RT
Mike's videos	RT, ✕, Ⓐ, Ⓐ, Ⓐ, Ⓐ, Ⓐ, RT
Nate's videos	RT, ♀, Ⓑ, ✕, ♀, Ⓑ, ✕, RT

The Matrix: Path of Neo

Unlockables

Unlockable	How to Unlock
Bullet Reflection	Successful completion of The One difficulty
Consume/Drain Mode	Successful completion of Normal difficulty
God Mode	Successful completion of The One Difficulty
Infinite Ammo	Successful completion of Normal Difficulty
Start with Most Weapons	Successful completion of Easy difficulty
Unbreakable Melee Combat Weapons	Successful completion of Easy difficulty

Special Combos and their Locations

Combo	Code
The Codebreaker:	LB+Ⓑ, tap ▼, Ⓑ, tap ▼
Quick Kicks:	▼, 4, 4, ▼, LB+▼, Ⓑ+▼
Machine Gun Kick:	▼, 4, 4, 4, ▼, LB+▼, Ⓑ+▼, tap ▼
Ultimate Hyper Strike:	▼, 4, 4, ▼, LB+▼, Ⓑ+▼, LB+Ⓑ, ▼
The Beginning of the End:	▼, 4, 4, ▼, LB+▼, Ⓑ+▼, LB+Ⓑ, tap ▼
The One:	▼, 4, 4, 4, ▼, LB+▼, Ⓑ+▼, tap ▼, LB+Ⓑ, tap ▼, Ⓑ, tap ▼ press Ⓐ as Neo does the uppercut, spin ● 360 at peak of jump

The Matrix: Path of Neo (continued)

Unlockable	How to Unlock
Machine Gun Kick	Stage—The Chase "I Need an Exit." Find the briefcase in the corner of the market area behind the fruit stands. clear the stage.
Quick Kicks	Stage—Storming the Drain. In the second to last room, touch the top two platforms in the room and clear the stage.
The Beginning of the End	Stage—Seraph's Apology. After returning to the teahouse from the theater, destroy one of the tables and all eight support columns in the room.
The Codebreaker	Stage—Weapon Training. Find the briefcase among the operator's secret stash in the upstairs corridor, when returning to teahouse. Clear the stage.
The One	Stage—The Burly Brawl: Defeat 30 Smiths. A briefcase appears in the center of the level. Pick it up and clear the stage.
Ultimate Hyper Strike	Stage—Redpill Rescue: The Security Guard. Defeat the SWAT team on the stairs in the given time limit and clear the stage.

"The Making of..." Unlockables

Unlockable	How to Unlock
Storyboard Sequence 1	In the Red Pill level, select mission The Key and then complete the bonus objective in the second room without using any guns
Storyboard Sequence 2	In The Frenchman Level, kill the first few enemies. In the dungeon area, go to the red cross, go right and pick up the briefcase, then finish.
Storyboard Sequence 3	Distorted Dimension: Find the Face 2 area with three doors. Press Focus and move the block and open the gate to the center door to find the briefcase.
Storyboard Sequence 4	Distorted Dimension: In the Face 3 area, move directly ahead from the entrance. Drop a few levels down to find the hidden briefcase in a niche.
Storyboard Sequence 5	After finding the previous briefcase in a niche, find the big stained-glass window. Wallrun up it, then follow a ledge to another hidden briefcase.
View Hand-to-Hand Combos	Distorted Dimensions: In the Face 1 area, wallrun up the wall with the windows, then Focus Jump to the focus pack. Look to the left, then Focus Jump.
View Staff Combos	Kung Fu Training: Execute three silent takedowns on all three enemies in the tool shop.
View Sword Combos	Sword Training: Break the pot behind the waterfall.

Zion Archives

Unlockable	How to Unlock
Zion Archives	Choose the glyph in the 8 o'clock position in the Atman Principles

Maximum Chase

Go to Options, select Cheat Code, and enter the following.

Unlockable	Code
Black and white mode	9DE5
High Contrast mode	A8D7
Saturation mode	B6FC

DS

GBA

PSP

PS2

PS3

Wii

Xbox

Xbox 360

Index

DS

GBA

PSP

PS2

PS3

Wii

Xbox

Xbox 360

Index

Max Payne

Unlockable	Objective
Additional Difficulty Settings—"Dead on Arrival" and "New York Minute"	Complete the game under the "Fugitive" difficulty setting.
Bonus Level	Complete the game in New York Minute mode to unlock a new bonus level in which you have to kill a lot of enemies, all in bullet time.
Cheat Mode	Start a game. Press ⚙ during gameplay to display the main menu. Then, hold ⑴ + ⑬ + click ⬤ + click ⬤, and quickly press ⬜, ⬜, ⬜, ⬜, ⬜ at the main menu. A cheat option will appear.
Last Challenge Bonus Level	Complete the game under the "Dead on Arrival" difficulty setting.
Secret Programmer Room	Complete the Last Challenge level. The doors in the back of the room will open up to the Remedy Room.

Max Payne 2

Unlockable	Code
All Modes	At any time during the game, pause and enter ⚫, ⚫, ⚫, Ⓐ, ⑴, ⑬, ⑴, ⑬

Mech Assault

Unlockable	Code
Completion Bonuses	Complete the game to unlock Ragnarok in local multiplayer mode.

Medal of Honor: European Assault

Codes

To enter Cheat mode, hold ⑴+⑬ then ⚙, Ⓐ, ⚫, ⬜, ⑬, ⬅. Release ⑴+⑬ when entering the actual cheat.

Effect	Code
Disable Shell Shock	⚫, ⓨ, Ⓐ, ⑬, ⑴, ⚫
Find OSS Document	Ⓐ, ⑬, ⑬, ⬜, ⬜, ⑴
Full Adrenaline	⑬, ⓨ, ⬅, ⚫, Ⓐ, ⚫
God Mode	⬜, ⬜, ⓨ, ⬜, ⑴, ⑴
Kill Nemesis	⬅, ⬅, ⑬, ⑬, ⚫, ⓨ ↗
Suicide	⚫, ⑬, ⬜, ⓨ, ⑴, ⬜
Turn off HUD	⬜, ⑴, ⬜, ⑬, ⬆, ⓨ
Unlimited Ammo	⑴, ⓨ, ⑬, ⬆, Ⓐ, Ⓐ

Medal of Honor: Frontline

Enter these passwords in the Options menu.

Unlockable	Password
Achilles Mode	TODADOME
Bullet Shield	NUHITSFORU
Full Bonus Menu	ENCHILADA
Gold on Previous Level	SALMON
Invisible Enemies	GHOSTSHOTS
M.O.H.ton Torpedo	TONSOFUN
Men with Hats	MERCER
Perfectionist Mode	ONEPMPCHMP
Rubber Grenades	ELASTIC
Silver Bullet Mode	KILLERSHOT
Sniper Mode	LONGVIEW

Medal of Honor: Frontline (continued)

Pause the game to enter this code:

Unlockable	Code
Invincibility	✖, ⒧⒯, ⒝, ⒭⒯, ☲, ⓨ, ✖

Medal of Honor: Rising Sun

Unlockable	Code
God Mode	banner
Infinite Ammo	jawfish
All Missions	tuskfish

Metal Gear Solid 2: Substance

Unlockables

Unlockable	How to Unlock
Blue Raiden Title Screen	Beat the game (Tanker-Plant) on any difficulty.
Blue Wig (Infinite Oxygen)	Collect at least 200 dog tags on Plant mission and beat the game.
Boss Survival	Finish both the Plant and Tanker Missions on any difficulty. This works playing the Tanker and Plant separately or playing the Tanker/Plant as one game.
Brown Wig (Infinite Ammo)	Collect at least 70 dog tags in Plant mission and beat the game.
Casting Theater	Finish both the Plant and Tanker Missions on any difficulty. This works playing the Tanker and Plant separately or playing the Tanker/Plant as one game.
Extreme and European Extreme Difficulty Modes	Complete the game once.
Orange Wig (Infinite Grip)	Collect at least 160 dog tags on Plant mission and beat the game.
Photograph Mode (Snake VR Missions)	Complete all of the levels in Bomb Disposal mode, Eliminate mode and Hold Up mode (Alternative Missions).
Raiden with Orange Sunglasses	Beat Tanker-Plant on any difficulty, then Tanker on normal, then start Plantation on normal.
Snake with Sunglasses	Beat Plant and Tanker, then go back to Tanker again.
Stealth Camo (Invisibility)	Collect at least 110 dog tags in Plant mission and beat the game.
Unlock Bandana (Infinite Ammo for Tanker Chapter)	Collect 50 dog tags in the Tanker Chapter and finish the chapter. After viewing your Clear Code, you obtain the Bandana. Save, and then load your save data to start a new game with the Bandana in your inventory.
Unlock Stealth for Tanker Stage	Get 80 dog tags in Tanker stage.
Unlock the Digital Camera for Tanker-Plant	Beat the game (Tanker-Plant) on any difficulty level.
USP Suppresser	Beat the game and then save. Start a new game with the saved info. Go to the Navigation Deck after you defeat Olga. Go where you receive the Thermal Goggles and find this weapon on the middle platform.

Unlockable VR Characters

Unlockable	How to Unlock
Iroquois Pliskin	Complete 50% of the VR Training missions with Snake to play as this character in VR mode.
MGS1 Snake	Complete 100% Tuxedo Snake in VR.
Naked Raiden	Complete 100% of Raiden's (Ninja) VR Missions.

DS
GBA
PSP
PS2
PS3
Wii
Xbox
Xbox 360
Index

DS

Metal Gear Solid 2: Substance (continued)

Unlockable	How to Unlock
Ninja Raiden	Complete 50% of the VR Missions with Raiden.
Raiden X	Complete all of the VR missions while playing as Raiden.
Tuxedo Snake	Complete 100% of Pliskin's Missions in VR mode.

Easter Eggs

GBA

Easter Egg	Description
Alternate Snake Tales Endings	Complete a Snake Tale once and this unlocks the M9. Use the M9 to stun bosses rather than killing them. This gains you an alternate ending.
Control the Title Screen	On the title screen, press ⓦ and you should hear a gunshot and see a flash. Use the Right Analog stick to change the background color.
Emma's Codec Frequency	Her codec frequency is 141.52, which is the same frequency as Nastasha Romanenko from *Metal Gear Solid 1*. Call Emma a few times. Call Rose to save your game and after you save she will get all huffy about you being with another woman.
Hideo Kojima Status	When inputting your name into a node or into the VR training menu, enter HIDEO KOJIMA. His personal information is automatically inserted.
Internal Thoughts	When talking in the codec screen, press the ⓛⓣ or ⓡⓣ to hear Snake's or Raiden's thoughts on other characters in the game.
Picture of Game Creator Hideo Kojima in Tanker	In the Tanker chapter in Holds 2 where the marines are located, take a picture of the screen on the right, with the camera (not digital camera). A face flashes on the screen when you take a picture of it. When you upload the picture to otacon for his viewing, he will be scared. The picture is the face of the game creator Hideo Kojima of all the Metal Gear games.
Sea Lice Rank	At the start of the Plant chapter, crawl in the big patch of Sea Lice (the big tan spot on the ground), and a Sea Louse will appear in your inventory, slowly eating your Rations. If you keep it for the duration of the game, you will get the rank of Sea Lice at the end. To get rid of it, rapidly move the Item menu to eventually shake it out of your inventory.
Vulcan Raven Action Figure	In the engine room, there's a tiny Vulcan Raven doll lying on the ground. Shoot it and he'll say something repeatedly and shoot small balls everywhere.
Ken Ogasawra Dog Tag Info	When first playing as Raiden in the Plant chapter, enter the name Ken Ogasawra into the first node. It automatically puts in all of his statistics.
Yoji Shinkawa Tag Info	When first playing as Raiden in the Plant chapter, enter the name Yoji Shinkawa into the first node. It automatically puts in all of his statistics.

PSP

PS2

PS3

Wii

Xbox

Midnight Club II

Enter the following codes from the Cheat menu.

Unlockable	Code
All car abilities	greasemonkey
All cars	hotwired
All Locations	theworldismine
Change difficulty levels	howhardcanitbe0 (easiest)

Xbox 360

Index

Midnight Club II (continued)

Unlockable	Code
Change difficulty levels	howhardcanitbe1
Change difficulty levels	howhardcanitbe2
Change difficulty levels	howhardcanitbe3
Change difficulty levels	howhardcanitbe4
Change difficulty levels	howhardcanitbe5
Change difficulty levels	howhardcanitbe6
Change difficulty levels	howhardcanitbe7
Change difficulty levels	howhardcanitbe8
Change difficulty levels	howhardcanitbe9 (hardest)
Change Game Speed	howfastcanitbe0 (slowest)
Change Game Speed	howfastcanitbe1
Change Game Speed	howfastcanitbe2
Change Game Speed	howfastcanitbe3
Change Game Speed	howfastcanitbe4
Change Game Speed	howfastcanitbe5
Change Game Speed	howfastcanitbe6
Change Game Speed	howfastcanitbe7
Change Game Speed	howfastcanitbe8
Change Game Speed	howfastcanitbe9 (fastest)
Infinite Nitrous	zoomzoom4
Machine Gun and Rocket	lovenotwar
LAPD car in Arcade Mode	Beat all five circuit races for LA in Arcade mode.
Paris Cop Car	Beat all 6 of the Paris arcade circuit tracks.
SLF450X	Complete 100% of the game
Tokyo Cop Car	Beat all 7 Tokyo arcade circuit tracks.
Veloci	Beat all of the World Champion's races.

Midnight Club 3 Dub Edition

Enter these case sensitive passwords in the Cheats section under Options.

Unlockable	Password
All Cities Unlocked in Arcade Mode	crosscountry
Bunny Ears	getheadl
Chrome Body	haveyouseenthisboy
Faster Pedestrians/All Cities in Arcade Mode	urbansprawl
Flaming Head	trythisathome
Increase Car Mass in Arcade Mode	hyperagro
No Damage	ontheroad
Pumpkin Heads	getheadk
Skull Head	getheadn
Snowman Head	getheadm
Special Move Agro	dfens
Special Move Roar	Rjnr
Special Move Zone	allin
Unlock All Cities	roadtrip
Yellow Smile	getheadj

DS
GBA
PSP
PS2
PS3
Wii
Xbox
Xbox 360
Index

Midtown Madness 3

Unlockable	Objective
1959 El Dorado Seville	Complete the Washington Pizza Deliverer job.
1967 Ford Mustang	Complete the Washington Stunt Car Driver job.
All Cars	In the car select menu, click ❶ while entering the following commands: ⓛⓣ, ⓡⓣ, ⓛⓣ, ⓛⓣ, ⓛⓣ, ⓡⓣ, ⓡⓣ, ⓡⓣ, ⓛⓣ, ⓛⓣ, ⓡⓣ.
Ambulance	Complete the Paris Paramedic job.
Armored Car	Complete the Paris security guard job.
Audi S4 Avant	Complete the first six blitz races in Paris.
Audi TT	Complete the Paris Special Agent job.
Cadillac Escalade	Complete the Washington Limo Driver job.
Cement Truck	Win the first six checkpoint races in Washington.
Chevrolet Corvette Z06	Win the tenth checkpoint race in Washington.
Chevrolet SSR	Complete the first three blitz races in Washington.
Chrysler Crossfire	Win the tenth blitz race in Washington.
Chrysler PT Turbo	Complete the Washington Rental Car Driver job.
Dodge Viper SRT-10	Complete the Washington Private Eye job.
Fire Truck	Win the first six checkpoint races in Paris.
FLE	Complete the Paris Delivery Guy job.
Freightliner Century Class S/T	Complete the first six blitz races in Washington.
Hummer H2 SUV	Complete the Washington Salesman job.
Koenigsegg CC	Complete all the game.
Limousine	Complete the Paris chauffeur job.
Lotus Esprit V8	Win the tenth Paris Blitz race.
Mini Cooper S	Complete the first three blitz races in Paris.
Paris Bus	Win the first three checkpoint races in Paris.
Paris Police	Complete the Paris Police Officer job.
Saab 9-3 Turbo	Win the tenth checkpoint race in Paris.
Taxi	Complete the Paris Taxi Driver job.
Washington Bus	Win the first three checkpoint races in Washington.
Washington Police	Complete the Washington Police Officer job.

Minority Report

To enter these codes, select the Special menu, then select the Cheats menu.

Unlockable	Code	Unlockable	Code
All Combos	NINJA	Infinite Ammo	MRJUAREZ
All Movies	DIRECTOR	Invincibility	LRGARMS
All Weapons	STRAPPED	Level Warp	PASSKEY
Armor	STEELUP	Level Skip	QUITTER
Baseball Bat	SLUGGER	Lizard Skin	HISSSS
Bouncy Men	BOUNZMEN	Moseley Skin	HAIRLOSS
Clown Skin	SCARYCLOWN	Nara Skin	WEIGHTGAIN
Concept Art	SKETCHPAD	Nikki Skin	BIGLIPS
Convict Skin	JAILBREAK	Pain Arena	MAXIMUMHURT
Do Not Select	DONOTSEL	Rag Doll	CLUMSY
Dramatic Finish	STYLIN	Robot Skin	MRROBOTO
Ending	WIMP	Super Damage	SPINICH
First Person Mode	FPSSTYLE	Super John Skin	SUPERJOHN
GI John Skin	GNRLINFINTRY	Wreck the Joint	CLUTZ
Health	BUTTERUP	Zombie Skin	IAMSODEAD

Sidebar tabs: DS, GBA, PSP, PS2, PS3, Wii, Xbox, Xbox 360, Index

Mission Impossible: Operation Surma

Unlockable	Code
Level Select	In the Profiles menu, highlight Jasmine Curry and press ⓛ+ⓡ+Ⓨ+Ⓑ. You will be able to choose your level from the Main menu.

MLB Slugfest 2003

Cheat Mode: Press Ⓧ, Ⓨ, and Ⓑ to change the icons in the first, second, and third boxes respectively at the match-up screen. The numbers in the following list indicate the number of times you press each button. After the icons change, press the D-pad in the indicated direction to enable the code. For example, to enter 1-2-3 ⬅, press Ⓧ, Ⓨ, Ⓨ, Ⓑ, Ⓑ, Ⓑ, ⬅.

Unlockable	Code	Unlockable	Code
Mace Bat	0-0-4 ⬅	No Contact Mode	4-3-3 ⬅
Wiffle Bat	0-0-4 ➡	No Fatigue	3-4-3 ⬇
Big Heads	2-0-0 ➡	Pinto Team	2-1-0 ➡
Eagle Team	2-1-2 ➡	Rocket Park Stadium	3-2-1 ⬇
Extra Time after Plays	1-2-3 ⬇	Roman Coliseum Stadium	3-3-3 ⬇
Horse Team	2-1-1 ➡	Rubber Ball	2-4-2 ⬇
Lion Team	2-2-0 ➡	Small Heads	2-0-0 ⬅
Log Bat	0-0-4 ⬇	Softball	2-4-2 ⬇
Maximum Batting	3-0-0 ⬅	Terry Fitzgerald Team	3-3-3 ➡
Maximum Power	0-3-0 ⬅	Todd McFarlane Team	2-2-2 ➡
Maximum Speed	0-0-3 ⬅	Tournament Mode	1-1-1 ⬇
Monument Stadium	3-3-3 ⬇	Unlimited Turbo	4-4-4 ⬇

MLB Slugfest 2004

Unlockable	Code	Unlockable	Code
16" Softball	2, 4, 2, ⬇	Log Bat	0, 0, 4, ⬇
Alien Team	2, 3, 1, ⬇	Mace Bat	0, 0, 4, ⬅
Atlantis Stadium	3, 2, 1, ⬅	Max Batting	3, 0, 0, ⬅
Big Head	2, 0, 0, ➡	Max Power	0, 3, 0, ⬅
Blade Bat	0, 0, 2, ⬇	Max Speed	0, 0, 3, ⬅
Bobble Head Team	1, 3, 3, ⬇	Midway Park Stadium	3, 2, 1, ⬇
Bone Bat	0, 0, 1, ⬇	Minotaur Team	1, 1, 0, ⬇
Casey Team	2, 3, 3, ⬇	Monument Stadium	3, 3, 3, ⬇
Cheats Disabled	1, 1, 1, ⬇	Napalitano Team	2, 3, 2, ⬇
Coliseum Stadium	3, 3, 3, ⬇	Olshan Team	2, 2, 2, ⬇
Dolphin Team	1, 0, 2, ⬇	Pinto Team	2, 1, 0, ➡
Dwarf Team	1, 0, 3, ⬇	Rivera Team	2, 2, 2, ⬇
Eagle Team	2, 1, 2, ➡	Rocket Park Stadium	3, 2, 1, ⬇
Empire Park Stadium	3, 2, 1, ➡	Rodeo Clown	1, 3, 2, ⬇
Evil Clown Team	2, 1, 1, ⬇	Rubber Ball	2, 4, 2, ⬇
Extended Time for Codes	3, 0, 3, ⬇	Scorpion Team	1, 1, 2, ⬇
Forbidden City Stadium	3, 3, 3, ⬅	Spike Bat	0, 0, 5, ⬇
Gladiator Team	1, 1, 3, ⬇	Team Terry Fitzgerald	3, 3, 3, ➡
Horse Team	2, 1, 1, ➡	Team Todd McFarlane	2, 2, 2, ➡
Ice Bat	0, 0, 3, ⬇	Tiny Head	2, 0, 0, ⬅
Lion Team	2, 2, 0, ➡	Unlimited Turbo	4, 4, 4, ⬇
Little League	1, 0, 1, ⬇	Wiffle Bat	0, 0, 4, ➡

DS

GBA

PSP

PS2

PS3

Wii

Xbox

Xbox 360

Index

DS

GBA

PSP

PS2

PS3

Wii

Xbox

Xbox 360

Index

MLB SlugFest 2006

Bonus Stadiums

Hit an out of the park home run in the indicated location to unlock the corresponding bonus stadium.

Unlockable	How to Unlock
Atlantis	Hit a home run in AT&T Park
Coliseum	Hit a home run in Fenway Park
Empire	Hit a home run in Yankee Stadium
Forbidden City	Hit a home run in PetCo Park
Rocket Park	Hit a home run in Minute Made Park

Bonus Teams

Unlockable	How to Unlock
Bobble Head	Hit 10 home runs in one game.
Casey	Hit a triple in Wrigley Field.
Dolphins	Hit a home run in Atlantis.
Eagles	Walk 3 times in one game.
Gladiator	Hit a home run in Coliseum Park.
Horse	Steal 10 times in one game.
Lion	Hit a home run with the Lions in Comerica Park.
Martian	Hit a triple in Rocket Park.
Minotaur	Hit a home run in Forbidden City.
Pinto	Hit a home run at Busch Field.
Rodeo Clowns	Perform a double play.
Tame Evil Clown	Hit a home run with a Yankee in Empire Park.

MLB SlugFest Loaded

Unlockable	Code
Unlock Everything	At the Main Menu, hold +❤, then press the Right Trigger.

Mortal Kombat: Armageddon

Krypt Kodes

Enter at the ? in the krypt.

Unlockable	How to Unlock
Armageddon Promo Movie	◊, ◊, ♥, ◊, 𝖂𝖍𝖙, Ⓐ
Armory Music	Ⓐ, ✕, ◄, ♥, ✕, Ⓐ
Blaze	♥, ✕, ◄, ℝ𝕋, ◄, Ⓑ
Concept Art Blaze	ℝ𝕋, ♥, 𝖂𝖍𝖙, 𝖂𝖍𝖙, ℝ𝕋, ✕
Concept Art Early Taven	◊, Ⓐ, 𝖂𝖍𝖙, ♥, 𝖂𝖍𝖙, Ⓐ
Concept Art Ed Boon Drawing	ℝ𝕋, ◄, ◊, Ⓑ, 𝖂𝖍𝖙, ℝ𝕋
Concept Art Firewall Arena	◊, ✕, ℝ𝕋, 𝖂𝖍𝖙, Ⓑ, ℝ𝕋
Concept Art Mileena's Car Design	𝖂𝖍𝖙, ►, ◊, ℝ𝕋, ♥, ◊
Concept Art Pyramid of Argus	Ⓐ, ℝ𝕋, ℝ𝕋, 𝖂𝖍𝖙, ◊, ◊
Concept Art Pyramid of Argus	♥, ◄, ◄, Ⓐ, ♥, Ⓑ
Concept Art Sektor's Pulse Blade	𝖂𝖍𝖙, ℝ𝕋, ◄, Ⓐ, ◊, ℝ𝕋
Concept Art Unused Konquest Trap	Ⓑ, 𝖂𝖍𝖙, ♥, ♥, Ⓑ, ◄
Daegon	ℝ𝕋, ℝ𝕋, ♥, ♥, ♥, ✕
Drahmin's Alternate Costume	𝖂𝖍𝖙, ►, Ⓐ, 𝖂𝖍𝖙, ◊, ◊

Mortal Kombat: Armageddon (continued)

Unlockable	How to Unlock
Ed Boon Drawing	(RT), ◀, △, Ⓑ, WHT, (RT)
Falling Cliffs Arena	WHT, Ⓑ, Ⓧ, Ⓐ, Ⓑ, Ⓨ
Frost's Alternate Costume	◊, WHT, (RT), (RT), Ⓑ, WHT
General Reiko's Map Room Arena	WHT, Ⓥ, (RT), △, Ⓐ, Ⓐ
Lin Kuei Palace Tune	WHT, ◀, Ⓑ, Ⓐ, WHT, ▶
Meat	△, Ⓧ, Ⓧ, Ⓑ, Ⓑ, △
Motor Gameplay Movie	Ⓥ, △, WHT, (RT), (RT), WHT
Nethership Interior Arena	(RT), ◀, ◀, ◊, (RT), Ⓧ
Nitara's Alternate Costume	◊, (RT), △, (RT), (RT), ▶
Pyramid of Argus Arena	(RT), (RT), Ⓧ, Ⓐ, WHT, △
Pyramid of Argus Music	◊, ◀, WHT, WHT, △, △
Red Dawn Arena	Ⓑ, (RT), △, Ⓧ, Ⓑ, ◊
Shang Tsung's Alternate Costume	(RT), ◀, △, Ⓑ, △, WHT
Shinnok's Spire Arena	◀, ◀, Ⓑ, △, Ⓥ, (RT)
Taven	(RT), ◀, WHT, △, Ⓑ, ◊
Tekunin Warship Music	△, Ⓑ, (RT), (RT), Ⓐ

Alternate Costumes

All of the following are unlocked in Konquest mode, usually found in a hidden chest.

Unlockable	How to Unlock
Ashrah's Alternate Costume	Defeat the Ice Beast you encounter in Arctika and open the chest that appears.
Baraka's Alternate Costume	Kill all of the enemies in the final room of the Tekunin Warship and open the chest that appears.
Bo'Rai Cho's Alternate Costume	Open the chest that appears after you defeat the Wraiths of Shinnok's Spire.
Cyrax's Alternate Costume	Kill all of the enemies in the third room of the Tekunin Warship and open the chest that appears.
Dairou's Alternate Costume	Open the chest at the end of the second ice hallway at the beginning of the Lin Kuei Temple Entrance.
Darrius's Alternate Costume	Open the chest behind a discolored wall at the beginning of the Lin Kuei Temple where you are being attacked by Archers.
Drahmin's Alternate Costume	In the Netherrealm after you defeat Drahmin, shoot down the bat creature over the nearby cliff and open the chest that appears.
Ermac's Alternate Costume	Found in a chest by the left wall in the room where you get attacked by the Red Commandos.
Frost's Alternate Costume	Break all of the tombs lining the wall in the room where you meet Frost and open the chest that appears.
Fujin's Alternate Costume	Defeat all of the Red Dragon Ninjas at the beginning of the Charred Mountain.
Goro's Alternate Costume	In an invisible chest on the left side of the first area in Shao Khan's Fortress and directly to the right of a musical note.
Havik's Alternate Costume	Defeat all of the demons in the second area of Shinnok's Spire.
Hotaru's Alternate Costume	In a chest close to the wall in the second room of the Tekunin Warship.

DS | GBA | PSP | PS2 | PS3 | Wii | Xbox | Xbox 360 | Index

Mortal Kombat: Armageddon (continued)

Unlockable	How to Unlock
Hsu Hao's Alternate Costume	In a chest on the right walkway after you wake up on the Tekunin Warship.
Jade's Alternate Costume	Defeat all of the Lin Kuei at the very beginning of the Lin Kuei Palace and open the chest that appears.
Jarek's Alternate Costume	Open the right chest in the room where you fight with the Ice Scepter.
Jax's Alternate Costume	Once you enter Arctika, turn around and go to the left to find an invisible chest.
Johnny Cage's Alternate Costume	Defeat the Tengu Guards at the beginning of Arctika and open the chest that appears.
Kai's Alternate Costume	In an invisible chest behind a breakable discolored wall to the right as you enter the third area of the Lin Kuei Temple Entrance.
Kano's Alternate Costume	In an invisible chest to the left as you enter the last room of the Temple of Argus.
Kenshi's Alternate Costume	Defeat all of the Tengu Ninjas with the given sword in Arctika.
Kira's Alternate Costume	Step on the second Giant Spider in Botan Jungle and open the chest that appears.
Kitana's Alternate Costume	Perform a Fatality on Wi Lae, leader of the Tengu Ninjas.
Kobra's Alternate Costume	In an invisible chest behind the first monolith in the Botan Jungle.
Kung Lao's Alternate Costume	Found in a chest to the right after you enter the Temple of Argus.
Li Mei's Alternate Costume	In the second area of Shinnok's Spire, walk around the edge of the room until you find an invisible chest.
Liu Kang's Alternate Costume	As you enter Shao Kahn's Fortress, turn around and run forward to find an invisible chest.
Mavado's Alternate Costume	Inside an invisible chest on the left part of the room where you do battle after you receive the Supermove: Time Stop.
Mileena's Alternate Costume	After you defeat Mileena, hit the ground pound switch in front of you and open the chest that appears.
Motaro's Alternate Costume	After the third training obelisk, during the time you must gather crystals, go to the left side of this area and open the chest there.
NightWolf's Alternate Costume	After you defeat the Giant Skulls in Edenia, travel up the path until all of the chests appear. The first one on the right has this in it.
Nitara's Alternate Costume	After you defeat the Undead Revenants for the first time in the Netherrealm, jump down the left cliff instead of the right. Open the nearby chest.
Noob Saibot's Alternate Costume	Defeat all of the Shadow Ninjas the first time you encounter then in the Lin Kuei Palace and open the chest that appears.
Quan Chi's Alternate Costume	Step on the rat in the tunnel after you travel through Door A1 in the Red Dragon Caverns. Open the chest that appears.
Raiden's Alternate Costume	When or after fighting the Shao Khan Colossus, go into the first room on the left.

Mortal Kombat: Armageddon (continued)

Unlockable	How to Unlock
Rain's Alternate Costume	Open the chest at the end of the area in Arctika where you are attacked by Red Dragon Spies and before you meet Rain.
Reiko's Alternate Costume	In a chest in Shao Khan's Fortress, as you enter the first area with blades, travel down a hall to the left.
Reptile's Alternate Costume	Defeat the Hybrid Dragons you encounter in the Red Dragon Caverns and open the chest that appears.
Sareena's Alternate Costume	Defeat Kai, Serenna, and Jatakka and open the chest that appears.
Shang Tsung's Alternate Costume	At the beginning of Shao Khan's Fortress, hit the ground pound icon to the right and up the ramp.
Shao Kahn's Alternate Costume	Open the chest that appears after you defeat Shao Khan's Statue.
Shinnok's Alternate Costume	Once you get to the area in the Netherrealm with the falling rocks, go to the leftmost side and open the chest that you find there.
Shujinko's Alternate Costume	Hit the ground pound icon in one of the cells after you defeat The Executioner in Shao Khan's Dungeon.
Sindel's Alternate Costume	Complete the third training obelisk.
Smoke's Alternate Costume	Defeat Smoke and open the chest that appears.
Sonya's Alternate Costume	In an invisible chest to the left of the gate in the area after you defeat Sonya.
Stryker's Alternate Costume	Break the wall on the right of the hallway after the Shadow Stalkers. Travel to the end of it and open the chest in the left alcove.
Sub-Zero's Alternate Costume	Open the chest to the right of the statue of Taven's mother after your fight with Sub-Zero.
Tanya's Alternate Costume	In Shao Khan's dungeon, after you make it to the cell area, hit the ground pound icon and then go back to the third cell on the right.
Taven's Alternate Costume	After you defeat the Giant Skulls in Edenia, travel up the path until all of the chests appear. Open the third one on the left.

Konquest Mode Unlockable

Unlockable	How to Unlock
+20,000 Koins	Obtain 20 Relics in Konquest Mode

Kreate-A-Kharacter Unlockables

Each of the following are unlocked in Konquest mode.

Unlockable	How to Unlock
Elder Gods Female Armor: Belt	Inside a golden chest in a locked gate in Arctika after the second obelisk that opens after you defeat the Tengu Ninjas.
Elder Gods Female Armor: Boots	After the shadow stalkers, break the cracked wall to the left and travel down to the right alcove where you find the golden chest.
Elder Gods Female Armor: Cape	Inside a golden chest in the area after you meet and defeat Sonya.
Elder Gods Female Armor: Glove	Once you get to the flaming sword area of Shinnok's Spire, turn and run to your left and open the golden chest.
Elder Gods Female Armor: Helmet	When or after fighting the Shao Khan Colossus, go into the second room on the right.

DS
GBA
PSP
PS2
PS3
Wii
Xbox
Xbox 360
Index

Mortal Kombat: Armageddon (continued)

Unlockable	How to Unlock
Elder Gods Female Armor: Legs	Open the golden chest in the cave that gets opened after you defeat the undead of the Netherrealm after you get your gauntlets.
Elder Gods Female Armor: Shoulders	Found in Shao Kahn's dungeon, after you make it to the cell area. Hit the ground pound icon and then go back to the first cell on the left.
Elder Gods Female Armor: Torso	Open the golden chest in the right path of the fork in the Red Dragon Caverns.
Elder Gods Male Armor: Belt	Open a golden chest to the right after you open the first door in the Tekunin.
Elder Gods Male Armor: Boots	After the shadow stalkers, break the second cracked wall on the right and travel down to the end and open the golden chest in the left alcove.
Elder Gods Male Armor: Cape	When or after fighting the Shao Khan Colossus, go into the second room on the left.
Elder Gods Male Armor: Glove	Inside of a golden chest after the second fallen log and to the right in Botan Jungle.
Elder Gods Male Armor: Helmet	After you defeat the Giant Skulls in Edenia, travel up the path until you find a golden chest. Open it.
Elder Gods Male Armor: Legs	Open a golden chest in the left corner of the second area of Shinnok's Spire.
Elder Gods Male Armor: Shoulders	Stand in the middle of the room after you free Shujinko. Aim and shoot a fireball at the nearby torch and get the chest that appears.
Elder Gods Male Armor: Torso	After you defeat the Tengu Leader, go forward and break open the discolored wall on the right in the blade trap area.

Soundtracks

Find each of the following soundtracks in Konquest mode, in the shape of musical notes.

Unlockable	How to Unlock
Arctika Tune	As you enter the second area of the Lin Kuei Temple Entrance, destroy the discolored wall on the right.
Bo'Rai Cho's Brewery Tune	Find it after the bridge and in the cave to the right in the Botan Jungle.
Botan Jungle Track Tune	Get the musical note to the left before the second fallen log in Botan Jungle.
Goro's Lair Fight Tune	Find it in Shujinko's cell when you release him.
Hell Fight Tune	Find it in Shao Khan's Dungeon, after you make it to the cell area. You must hit the ground pound icon and then go back to the second cell on the right.
Konquest Final Battle Tune	In Shao Khan's Fortress as you run up to the first area with the blades, travel to the right to find the musical note in the next room.
Lin Kuei Palace Tune	Get the musical note the Lin Kuei Palace directly to your left after you punch down the Ice Door.
Lin Kuei Raceway Tune	Get the musical note near the entrance in the final area of Arctika after you defeat the Lin Kuei Warriors and Archers.
Lumbermill Fight Tune	Get the musical note after the second crusher when you return to Arctika after the second obelisk.
Meteor Storm Fight Tune	After you defeat the Undead Revenants for the first time in the Netherrealm, jump down the left cliff instead of the right.

Mortal Kombat: Armageddon (continued)

Unlockable	How to Unlock
Outworld Refinery Tune	Get the musical note behind you after you fight Drahmin in the Netherrealm.
Outworld Spire Fight Tune	Get the musical note on the right side of the first room as you enter Shinnok's Spire.
Pyramid of Argus Tune	After you defeat the Giant Skulls in Edenia, travel up the path until you find a golden chest. To the right of it is the musical note.
Reptile's Lair Fight Tune	Get the musical note in the hallway right before the final room of the Red Dragon Caverns. It is found behind a grouping of three blue barrels.
Soul Chamber Fight Tune	Once you get to the flaming sword area of Shinnok's Spire, turn around and get the musical note.
Subway Fight Tune	Get the musical note after you defeat Sonya Blade in Arctika.
Tekunin Prison Fight Tune	Found in Shao Khan's Fortress, after you open the main door and enter the second area, go to the upper left side and get the musical note.
Tekunin Warship Tune	Get the musical note in the area where you get attacked by Black Dragon Thugs in the Botan Jungle.
The Lost Pyramid Tune	Found behind an explosive barrel in the battle after you gain the Supermove: Time Stop.
Wastelands Fight Tune	On the left of the elevator you get into at the end of Shao Khan's dungeon.

Unlockable Arenas

Unlockable	How to Unlock
Artika Arena	Beat all 7 trials in Artika Obelisk.
Edenian Ruins	After you defeat the Giant Skulls in Edenia, travel up the path until all of the chests appear and open the second one on the left.
Netherrealm Cliffs	Defeat Drahmin in Konquest mode.
Pyramid of Argus Arena	Collect 40 Relics in Konquest mode.
Scorpion's Lair	After you defeat the Giant Skulls in Edenia, travel up the path until all of the chests appear. The third one on the right has this in it.
The Krypt	Collect 60 Relics in Konquest mode.

Unlockable Characters

The Relic items needed to unlock Meat, Daegon, and Blaze are found all throughout the Konquest mode.

Unlockable	How to Unlock
Unlock Blaze	Collect 50 Relic items in Konquest mode
Unlock Daegon	Collect 30 Relic items in Konquest mode
Unlock Meat	Collect 10 Relic items in Konquest mode
Unlock Taven	Complete Konquest mode

DS
GBA
PSP
PS2
PS3
Wii
Xbox
Xbox 360
Index

DS · **GBA** · **PSP** · **PS2** · **PS3** · **Wii** · **Xbox** · **Xbox 360** · **Index**

Mortal Kombat: Shaolin Monks

Enter to following codes for the fatalities for Kung Lao.

Unlockable	Code
Arm Cutter	←, →, ←, ↓, ⊗
Body Slice Fatality	←, →, →, →, ⊗
Buzzsaw Fatality	→, →, ↓, ↓, ⊗
Friendly Rabbit Fatality	↓, ↓, ↓, ↓, ⊗
Hat Control Mutality	←, →, →, ←, Ⓨ
Head Toss Fatality	←, →, →, →, ⊗
Headache Fatality	↓, ↓, ↓, →, ⊗
Many Chops Fatality	↓, ↓, ←, ↓, ⊗
Mid-Air Slice Fatality	↓, ↓, ↓, →, ⊗
Razor Edge Brutality	←, ←, ↓, ↓, Ⓑ
Tornado Mutality	↓, →, ↓, ←, Ⓨ

Enter to following codes for the fatalities for Liu Kang.

Unlockable	Code
Arm Rip Fatality	↓, ←, →, ↓, ⊗
Bonebreak Fatality	←, ↓, ↓, →, ⊗
Dragon Fatality	↓, →, ←, ←, ⊗
Dragon's Fury Mutality	←, →, ↓, ↓, Ⓨ
Fire Trails Mutality	↓, ↓, ↓, ↓, Ⓨ
Fire/Kick Combo Fatality	←, →, ↓, ↓, ⊗
Flipping Uppercut Fatality	↓, →, ↓, ←, ⊗
Headclap Fatality	→, ↓, ↓, ↓, ⊗
Rage Mode Brutality	→, ↓, ↓, ↓, Ⓑ
Shaolin Soccer Fatality	↓, ←, ↓, →, ⊗
Stomp Fatality	←, ←, ←, ↓, ⊗

Enter these codes at the Main menu.

Unlockable	Code
Mortal Kombat 2	⊗, ↓, ↓, →, ←, RT, ⊗
Scorpion	⊗, ↓, LT, RT, ←, →, ⊗
Sub-Zero	⊗, ↓, ↓, LT, LT, ↓, ⊗

Motocross Mania 3

Enter these codes at the Main menu.

Unlockable	Code
All bike upgrades	↓, ←, ↓, →, ↓, ↓, ↓, ←, ↓, ⊗
All bikes	↓, ←, ↓, →, ↓, ←, ↓, ↓, ⊗
All levels	↓, ←, ↓, →, ↓, ↓, →, ←, ↓, ⊗
All weapons	↓, ←, ↓, →, ↓, ←, ↓, ←, ↓, ⊗

Moto GP 2

Unlockable	Objective
Alex Barros	Earn 250,000 points in stunt mode.
Carlos Chera	Earn 100,000 points in stunt mode.
Edgy	Earn 325 championship points.
Floating bike mode	Enter kingpin as your custom bike name.
Legend difficulty	Win the championship on the champion difficulty setting.
Max Biaggi	Get an overall total of 500,000 points in stunt mode to unlock Max Biaggi.
Mini-Games	To get a few minigames, go to the options menu and go to the text credits. When you find the text for the minigames, press Ⓐ.

Moto GP 2 (continued)

Unlockable	Objective
Pop Video	Earn 375 championship points.
Saturate	Earn 300 championship points on rookie difficulty.
Season Highlights	Finish first in any track to see its highlight video.
Sheridan	Complete all the challenges in championship.
Tohru Ukawa	Earn 750,000 points in stunt mode.
Turbo	Earn 275 championship points.
Valentino Rossi	Earn 1000000 points in stunt mode.

MTX Mototrax

Unlockable	Objective
Officer Dick	Complete Free Ride in Career mode.
Police Bike	Complete all Freestyle Events.
Race as a Slipknot rider	Enter 86657457 at the Cheat Menu.
Sky view	HIC
Slipknot Bike	Complete Master Supercross.
Slipknot movie	Enter 23F7IC5 at the Cheat Menu.
Speed Demon	Complete Career mode.
Super Fast Acceleration	Enter JIH345 at the Cheat Menu.
Trick Bot	Complete Freestyle in Career mode.
Unlocks all Butter Finger gear	B77393
Unlocks all Sobe gear	5OB3
Unlocks Officer Dick	BADG3

MTX vs. ATV Unleashed

Enter the codes in the Cheat menu.

Unlockable	Code
50cc Bikes	Minimoto
All Freestyle Tracks	Huckit
Everything	Toolazy

Murakumo

Unlockable	Objective
Expert mission	Complete scenario mode with all missions at A rank.
Free mission	Beat Scenario mode.
Sound Test mode	Beat Expert mode all with double S ranks.
"Special Art"	Beat expert mode with any rank.

MVP Baseball 2003

Unlockable	Code
16:9 Anamorphic View	Press and hold the ⓛ and ⓡ for more than 3 seconds. Then, press ◁ to enable. Press ▷ to disable.
Easy Home Run	Create a player named Erik Kiss.
Lots of Broken Bats	Create a player named Keegn Patersn, Jacob Patersn, or Ziggy Patersn.

MVP Baseball 2004

Unlockable	Code
Horrible player	Enter Erik Kiss as a player name.
Huge Cap on your player	Enter john prosen as a player name.
Player will hold a huge bat	Enter jacob paterson as a player name.

DS

GBA

PSP

PS2

PS3

Wii

Xbox

Xbox 360

Index

MVP Baseball 2004 (continued)

Unlockable	Objective
Al Kaline	2500 MVP Points
Anahiem Angels 1986 Jersey	250 MVP Points
Astrodome	2500 MVP Points
Atlanta Braves 1974 Jersey	500 MVP Points
Babe Ruth	5000 MVP Points
Baltimore Orioles 1971 Jerseys	500 MVP Points
Billy Williams	2500 MVP Points
Bob Feller	3500 MVP Points
Bob Gibson	4500 MVP Points
Bob Lemon	3000 MVP Points
Boston Red Sox 1903 Jerseys	1000 MVP Points
Brooklyn Dodgers 1941 Jerseys	750 MVP Points
Brooks Robinson	3500 MVP Points
Catfish Hunter	3000 MVP Points
Chicago Cubs 1954 Jerseys	750 MVP Points
Chicago White Sox 1919 Jerseys	1000 MVP Points
Cincinatti Reds 1970 Jerseys	500 MVP Points
Cleveland Indians 1975 Jerseys	500 MVP Points
Crosley Field	2500 MVP Points
Cy Young	4500 MVP Points
Detroit Tigers 1906 Jerseys	750 MVP Points
Early Wynn	3500 MVP Points
Eddie Matthews	4000 MVP Points
Ferguson Jenkins	2500 MVP Points
Forbes Field	5000 MVP Points
Gaylord Perry	3500 MVP Points
Griffith Stadium	3000 MVP Points
Hal Newhouser	2500 MVP Points
Harmon Killebrew	3500 MVP Points
Honus Wagner	4500 MVP Points
Houston Astros 1986 Jerseys	250 MVP Points
Hoyt Wilhelm	3000 MVP Points
Jackie Robinson	5000 MVP Points
Jim Palmer	4000 MVP Points
Jimmie Foxx	4000 MVP Points
Joe Morgan	4000 MVP Points
Juan Marichal	3500 MVP Points
Kansas City Royals 1985 Jerseys	250 MVP Points
Larry Doby	3000 MVP Points
Lou Brock	3000 MVP Points
Lou Gehrig	4500 MVP Points
Luis Aprarico	3000 MVP Points
Mel Ott	3500 MVP Points
Mike Schmidt	4000 MVP Points
Milwaukee Brewers 1982 Jerseys	250 MVP Points
Minnesota Twins 1977 Jerseys	500 MVP Points
Montreal Expos 1981 Jerseys	350 MVP Points
New York Giants 1954 Jerseys	750 MVP Points
New York Mets 1986 Jerseys	350 MVP Points
New York Yankees 1927 Jerseys	1000 MVP Points
Nolan Ryan	4500 MVP Points

DS
GBA
PSP
PS2
PS3
Wii
Xbox
Xbox 360
Index

MVP Baseball 2004 (continued)

Unlockable	Objective
Oakland Athletics 1972 Jerseys	500 MVP Points
Orlando Cepeda	3500 MVP Points
Pee Wee Reese	3500 MVP Points
Phil Niekro	2500 MVP Points
Phil Rizzuto	3000 MVP Points
Philadelphia Phillies 1980 Jerseys	500 MVP Points
Pittsburgh Pirates 1916 Jerseys	750 MVP Points
Pittsburgh Pirates 1979 Jerseys	500 MVP Points
Ralph Kiner	2500 MVP Points
Reggie Jackson	4500 MVP Points
Richie Ashburn	2500 MVP Points
Robin Roberts	2500 MVP Points
Robin Yount	4000 MVP Points
Rod Carew	3500 MVP Points
Rollie Fingers	3500 MVP Points
Roy Campanella	4500 MVP Points
San Diego Padres 1984 Jerseys	350 MVP Points
Satchel Paige	4500 MVP Points
Seattle Mariners 1981 Jerseys	350 MVP Points
Shibe Park Stadium	4000 MVP Points
Sparky Anderson	4500 MVP Points
Sportsman's Park	4000 MVP Points
St. Louis Cardinals 1934 Jerseys	750 MVP Points
Texas Rangers 1976 Jerseys	500 MVP Points
The Polo Grounds	5000 MVP Points
Tiger Stadium	3000 MVP Points
Tom Seaver	4000 MVP Points
Tommy Lasorda	4500 MVP Points
Toronto Blue Jays 1992 Jerseys	250 MVP Points
Ty Cobb	5000 MVP Points
Walter Johnson	4500 MVP Points
Warren Spahn	4000 MVP Points
Washington Senators 1913 Jerseys	1000 MVP Points
Whitey Ford	3500 MVP Points
Willie McCovey	4500 MVP Points
Willie Stargell	4000 MVP Points
Yogi Berra	4500 MVP Points

MVP Baseball 2005

Create a character with these names.

Unlockable	Names
Everything	Katie Roy
Player Has a Huge Bat	Keegan Paterson
Player Has a Huge Bat	Jacob Paterson
Player Has a Huge Bat	Isaiah Paterson

MX Unleashed

Unlockable	Objective
All Bonuses	Enter clappedout under Career Completion in the cheats section.

Sidebar tabs: DS, GBA, PSP, PS2, PS3, Wii, Xbox, Xbox 360, Index

DS

Narc

Enter these codes while playing—do not pause the game.

Unlockable	Code
All Drugs and $10,000	Repeatedly press ⓛⓣ+ⓡⓣ+click ⬤.
All Weapons	Repeatedly press ⓛⓣ+ⓡⓣ+click ⓞ.
Infinite Ammo	Repeatedly press ⓛⓣ+ⓡⓣ+Ⓨ. (Only works for the weapon equipped.)
Invincibility	Repeatedly press ⓛⓣ+ⓡⓣ+Ⓐ.
The Refinery	Repeatedly press ⓛⓣ+ⓡⓣ+Ⓧ.

GBA

NASCAR 2005 Chase for the Cup

Enter these codes in the Edit Driver screen. The passwords need to be entered as a first name and a last name.

Unlockable	Code
2,000,000 Prestige Points	You TheMan
$10,000,000	Walmart Nascar
All Thunder Plates	Open Sesame
Dale Earnhardt	The Intimidator
Exclusive Race Track	Walmart Exclusive

PSP

NASCAR 06: Total Team Control

In Fight to the Top mode, go to the Edit Driver screen and enter the following passwords as your first and last names. (Note: case sensitive)

Unlockable	Password
$10,000,000	Walmart Money
Dale Jarett in the UPS "Big Brown Truck"	Race TheTruck
Max Fan Level	Super Star
Max Prestige	MeMyself AndI
Max Team Prestige	All ForOne
Unlock All Chase Plates	Gimme Gimme
Unlocks Dale Sr.	The Intimidator
Walmart Raceway, Walmart Cars, and Walmart Sponsorship for Custom Car	Walmart Exclusive

PS2

PS3

Wii

NASCAR 07

Passwords

Select the "Game Modes" option at the main menu. Then, select "Fight to the Top." Enter one of the following case-sensitive first and last names at the driver information screen to activate the corresponding cheat function.

Password	Effect
GiveMe More	$10 million
AllBow ToMe	10 million fans
ItsAll ForMe	All Chase plates
Walmart EveryDay	Exclusive
MoMoney BlingBling	Fills Prestige
Outta MyWay	Level 10 Prestige
Walmart NoCollision	No Collision Mode
KeepCool SmellGreat	Old Spice Fantasy track and all cars and drivers in all four divisions
TheMan InBlack	Unlock the Dale Earnhardt Platinum Chase Plate

Xbox

Xbox 360

Index

NASCAR Heat 2002

Enter these codes at the Main Menu. The screen will flash to indicate correct code entry.

Unlockable	Code
Credits	◊, ♀, ◄, ►, ☞, ◊, ♀
Hardcore Realism Mode	◊, ♀, ◄, ►, ☞, ◊, ♀
High Suspension	◊, ♀, ◄, ►, ☞, ◄, ►
Mini Cars	◊, ♀, ◄, ►, ☞, ♀, ◊
Paintball Mode for Single and Head to Head Race	◊, ♀, ◄, ►, ☞, ◊, ◊—while racing press ◊ to fire paintballs.
Wireframe Cars	◊, ♀, ◄, ►, ☞, ►, ◄

NASCAR Thunder 2002

Enter these codes at the main menu. The screen flashes to indicate correct code entry.

Unlockable	Code
Credits	◊, ♀, ◄, ►, ☞, ◊, ♀
Hardcore Realism mode	◊, ♀, ◄, ►, ☞, ◊, ♀
High Suspension	◊, ♀, ◄, ►, ☞, ◄, ►
Mini Cars	◊, ♀, ◄, ►, ☞, ♀, ◊
Paintball mode for Single and Head to Head Race	◊, ♀, ◄, ►, ☞, ◊, ◊—while racing press ◊ to fire paintballs
Wireframe Cars	◊, ♀, ◄, ►, ☞, ►, ◄

NBA 2K2

Cheat Menu: Enter the Options menu and select "Gameplay." Hold ◄ + ● and press ♀. The "Codes" selection is now unlocked at the Options menu.

Unlockable	Code
Airball	Select "Street" at the main menu. Press ☞, then hold ⬆ and press ♥, ♥. Press ♀ and "Airball" appears to confirm correct code entry.
Bonus Teams	Enter MEGASTARS as a case-sensitive code to unlock the Sega Sports, Visual Concepts, and Team 2K2 in Exhibition and Street modes.
Muhammad Ali and Michael Jackson	Press ♀ and hold ⬆ during an Exhibition game. The screen shakes to confirm correct code entry. Go onto the Sixers and they should be on the starting lineup.

Enter Options mode and choose the Game Play menu. Once in the menu, hold ◄, Left Analog Stick Right, Start. After you exit the Game Play menu, the Codes Entry screen selection is now available.

Unlockable	Password
NBA 2K2 Team, Sega Sports Team, Visual Concepts Team	MEGASTARS

NBA 2K6

From the Main menu, go to "Features," then "Codes" to enter the following codes.

Unlockable	Code
2005-2006 Pacers Uniform	31andonly
2K Sports Team	2ksports
Nike Up Tempo Pro Shoes	anklebreakers

DS
GBA
PSP
PS2
PS3
Wii
Xbox
Xbox 360
Index

DS

GBA

PSP

PS2

PS3

Wii

Xbox

Xbox 360

Index

NBA 2K6 (continued)

Unlockable	Code
Nike Zoom Kobe 1 Shoes	kobe

From the Main menu, go to "Features," then "THE CRIB." Go to the PowerBar vending machine and enter the following codes.

Unlockable	Code
+10 Bonus for Defensive Awareness	lockdown
+10 Bonus for Offensive Awareness	getaclue
Max Durability	noinjury
Powerbar Tattoo	pbink
Unlimited Stamina	nrgmax
Unlock All Items	criball

NBA 2K7

Passwords

Password	Effect
payrespect	ABA Ball Unlocked
ironman	Maximum Durability for one game
norest	Unlimited Stamina for one game
getstops	+10 Defensive Awareness
inthezone	+10 Offensive Awareness
vdr5lya	Hornets Valentine's Day Uniform
bcb8sta	New Bobcats Road Uniform
zjb3lau	New Jazz Road Uniform
nrd4esj	New Nets Road Uniform
zw9idla	New Wizards Road Uniform
syt6cii	Unlock 2007 All-Star Uniforms
tpk7sgn	Unlock 3 St. Patrick's Day jerseys for CHI, BOS, NY
topps2ksports	Topps 2K Sports All-Stars

NBA Ballers

The following cheats are entered at the Versus Screen, right before the match starts. ⓥ is the first number, ⓑ is the second number, and ⓧ is the third number. Press the corresponding button as many times as stated.

Unlockable	Code	Unlockable	Code
2X Juice Replenish	4 3 1	No Weather	1 1 2
Alley-Oop Ability	7 2 5	Paper Ballers	3 5 4
Alternate Gear	1 2 3	Perfect Free Throws	3 2 7
Baby Ballers	4 2 3	Play As Afro Man	5 1 7
Back-In Ability	1 2 2	Play As Agent	5 5 7
Back-In Ability	3 1 7	Play As BiznezMan-A	5 3 7
Big Head Mode	1 3 4	Play As BiznezMan-B	5 2 7
Expanded Move Set	5 1 2	Play As Coach	5 6 7
Fire Ability	7 2 2	Play As Secretary	5 4 7
Good Handling	3 3 2	Put Back Ability	3 1 3
Half House Meter	3 6 7	Pygmy	4 2 5
Hot Spot	6 2 7	R2R Mode	0 0 8
Kid Ballers	4 3 3	Rain	2 2 2
Legal Goal Tending	7 5 6	Random Moves	3 0 0

NBA Ballers (continued)

Unlockable	Code	Unlockable	Code
Shows Shot Percentage	012	Super Blocks	124
Snow	333	Super Push	315
Speedy Players	213	Super Steals	215
Stunt Dunk Ability	374	Tournament Mode	011
Super Back-Ins	235	Young Ballers	443

Go to "Inside Stuff" and select "Phrase-ology." Enter the following codes to unlock goodies:

Unlockable	Code
Allen Iverson's Alternate Gear	killer crossover
Allen Iverson's Studio	the answer
Alonzo Mourning	zo
Amare Stoudamire	rising sun
Baron Davis	Stylin & Profilin
Ben Wallace's alternate outfit	radio controlled cars
Bill Russell	celtics dynasty
Bill Walton	towers of power
Chris Webber	24 seconds
Clyde Drexler	clyde the glide
Darryl Dawkins	rim wrecker
Dikembe Mutumbo	in the paint
Dominique Wilkins	dunk fest
Elton Brand	rebound
George Gervin	the ice man cometh
Jalen Rose	bring it
Jason Kidd	pass the rock
Jason Williams	give and go
Jerry Stackhouse's Alt. Gear	Stop Drop and Roll
John Stockton	court vision
Julius Erving	one on one
Karl Malone	special delivery
Karl Malone's Devonshire Estate	ice house
Kevin Garnett's alternate outfit	boss hoss
Kevin McHale	holla back
Kobe Bryant's Alt. Gear	Japanese steak
Larry Bird	hoosier
Latrell Sprewell	spree
Lebron James	king james
Magic Johnson	laker legends
Manu Ginobili gear	manu
Michael Finley	student of the game
Nene Hilario	rags to riches
Oscar Robertson's Alt. Gear	Ain't No Thing
Pete Maravich	pistol pete
Rashard Lewis	fast forward
Rasheed Wallace	bring down the house

DS

GBA

PSP

PS2

PS3

Wii

Xbox

Xbox 360

Index

DS
GBA
PSP
PS2
PS3
Wii
Xbox
Xbox 360
Index

NBA Ballers (continued)

Unlockable	Code
Ray Allen	all star
Reggie Miller's Alt. Gear	From Downtown
Richard Hamilton	rip
Robert Parish's Alt. Gear	The Chief
Scottie Pippen	playmaker
Scottie Pippen's Yacht	nice yacht
Shaq's alternate outfit	diesel rules the paint
Special Movie #1	juice house
Special Movie #2	nba showtime
Special Shoe #1	dub deuce
Stephon Marbury	platinum playa
Steve Francis	ankle breaker
Steve Francis's Alt. Gear	Rising Star
Steve Nash	hair canada
Tim Duncan	make it take it
Tony Parker's Alt. outfit	run and shoot
Tracy McGrady	living like a baller
Wally Szczerbiak	world
Walt Frazier	Penetrate and Perpetrate
Wes Unseld	old school
Willis Reed	hall of fame
Wilt Chamberlain	wilt the stilt
Yao Ming	center of attention
Yao Ming's Grade School	prep school

NBA Inside Drive 2002

Enter the Options screen and select "Codes" to access the cheats menu. Repeat each code to disable its effect.

Unlockable	Code	Unlockable	Code
8-Ball	GAMEOVER	More Three Pointers	THREE4ALL
ABA Basketball	OLDSCHOOL	Soccer Ball	HOOLIGAN
Beach Ball	SANDINMYSHORTS	Unlimited Turbo	CARDIOMAN
Chicago Rooftop Court	WINDYCITY	Volleyball	SPIKEIT
Disable Trade Rules	GIMMETHAT	WNBA Basketball	GOTGAME
Little Players	SMALLSHOES	Xbox Ball	BACHMAN
More Alley-Oops	IGOTHOPS		

NBA Inside Drive 2004

In the Options screen, select Codes to enter these passwords.

Unlockable	Code	Unlockable	Code
8 Ball	CHALK	Small Player	MOONCHY
ABA Ball	FUNKY	Soccer Ball	DIEGO
All Trades Accepted	ARELESS	Unlimited Turbo	HOTSAUCE
Beach Ball	CONCERTSPIKE	Unlimited Create a Player Points	UNLIMITED
Chicago Skyline Stadium	DOWNTOWN	Volleyball	BAMBIBOOM
Easy 3 Pointers	RAINING3S	WNBA Ball	CHANGEBALL
Easy Alley-Oops	IMFLYING	Xbox Ball	XSNSPORTS

NBA Jam

Create a new profile using these names.

Unlockable	Code
Unlock Everything	-LPP-
Unlock the NBA Jam Development Team	CREDITS

NBA Live 2004

In the Create A Player screen, enter these passwords as last names to unlock the extra players.

Unlockable	Code	Unlockable	Code
Aleksander Pavlovic	WHSUCPOI	Air Foamposite 1 (White/Black/Red)	DOD843HH7F
Andreas Glyniadakis	POCKDLEK	Air Foamposite Pro (Blue/Black)	DG56TRF446
Carlos Delfino	SDFGURKL	Air Foamposite Pro (Black/Gray)	3245AFSD45
James Lang	NBVKSMCN		
Jermaine Dupri	SOSODEF	Air Foamposite Pro (Red/Black)	DSAKF38422
Kyle Korver	OEISNDLA	Air Force Max (Black)	F84N845H92
Malick Badiane	SKENXIDO	Air Force Max (White/Black/Blue)	985KJF98KJ
Mario Austin	POSNEGHX		
Matt Bonner	BBVDKCVM	Air Force Max (White/Red)	8734HU8FFF
Nedzad Sinanovic	ZXDSDRKE	Air Hyperflight (White)	14TGU7DEWC
Paccelis Morlende	QWPOASZX	Air Hyperflight (Black/White)	WW44YhU592
Remon Van De Hare	ITNVCJSD		
Rick Rickert	POILKJMN	Air Hyperflight (Blue/White)	A0K374HF8S
Sani Becirovic	ZXCCVDRI	Air Hyperflight (Yellow/Black)	JCX93LSS88
Sofoklis Schortsanitis	IOUBFDCJ		
Szymon Szewczyk	POIOIJIS	Air Jordan 11: (Black/Red/White)	GF64H76ZX5
Tommy Smith	XCFWQASE	Air Jordan 11: (Black/Varsity Royal/White)	HJ987RTGFA
Xue Yuyang	WMZKCOI		
15,000 Store Points	87843H5F9P	Air Jordan 11 (Cool Grey)	GF75HG6332
Air Bounds (Black/White/Blue)	7YSS0292KE	Air Jordan 11 (White)	HG76HN765S
Air Bounds (White/Black)	JA807YAM20	Air Jordan 11 (White/Black)	A2S35TH7H6
Air Bounds (White/Green)	84HHST61QI	Air Jordan 3 (White)	G9845HJ8F4
		Air Jordan 3 (White/Clay)	435SGF555Y
Air Flight 89 (Black/White)	FG874JND84	Air Jordan 3 (White/Fire Red)	RE6556TT90
Air Flight 89 (White/Black)	63RBVC7423	Air Jordan 3 (White/True Blue)	FDS9D74J4F
Air Flight 89 (White/Red)	GF9845JHR4		
Air Flightposite 2 (Blue/Grey)	2389JASE3E	Air Jordan 3 (Black/White/Gray)	CVJ554TJ58
Air Flightposite (White/Black/Gray)	74FDH7K945	Air Max2 CB (Black/White)	87HZXGFIU8
Air Flightposite (White/Black)	6HJ874SFJ7	Air Max2 CB (White/Red)	4545GFKJIU
Air Flightposite (Yellow/Black/White)	MN54BV45C2	Air Max2 Uptempo (Black/White/Blue)	NF8745J87F
Air Foamposite 1 (Blue)	0P5465UX12		

DS

GBA

PSP

PS2

PS3

Wii

Xbox

Xbox 360

Index

DS

GBA

PSP

PS2

PS3

Wii

Xbox

Xbox 360

Index

NBA Live 2004 (continued)

To enter these codes, go into the NBA Live menu, then enter the NBA Codes menu.

Unlockable	Code	Unlockable	Code
Air Max Elite (Black)	A4CD54T7TD	Nike Blazer (White/Orange/Blue)	4G66JU99XS
Air Max Elite (White/Black)	966ERTFG65	Nike Blazer (Black)	XCV6456NNL
Air Max Elite (White/Blue)	FD9KN48FJF	Nike Shox BB4 (Black)	WE424TY563
Air Zoom Flight (Gray/White)	367UEY6SN	Nike Shox BB4 (White/Black)	23ERT85LP9
Air Zoom Flight (White/Blue)	92387HD077	Nike Shox BB4 (White/Light Purple)	668YYTRB12
All Hardwood Classic Jerseys	725JKUPLMM	Nike Shox BB4 (White/Red)	424TREU777
All NBA Gear	ERT9976KJ3	Nike Shox VCIII (Black)	SDFH764FJU
All Team Gear	YREY5625WQ	Nike Shox VCIII (White/Black/Red)	5JHD367JJT
All Shoes	POUY985GY5	Zoom Generation (White/Black/Red)	23LBJNUMB1
Nike Blazer (Kaki)	W3R57U9NB2	Zoom Generation (Black/Red/White)	LBJ23CAVS1
Nike Blazer (Tan/White/Blue)	DCT5YHMU90		

NBA Live 2005

Go to My NBA Live, EA Sports Lounge, NBA Codes to enter these codes.

Unlockable	Code	Unlockable	Code
50,000 Dynasty Points	YISS55CZ0E	All Shoes	FHM389HU80
All Classics Hardwood Jerseys	PRYI234N0B	All Team Gear	1NVDR89ER2

Unlockable Team	Code
Atlanta Hawks 2004-05 Alternate	HDI834NN9N
Boston Celtics 2004-05 Alternate	XCV43MGMDS
Dallas Mavericks 2004-05 Alternate	AAPSEUD09U
Golden State Warriors 2004-05 Alternate	NAVNY29548

Unlockable Shoes	Code	Unlockable Shoes	Code
Nike Air Huarache	VNBA60230T	Nike Air Unlimited	XVLJD9895V
Nike BG Rollout	0984ADF90P	Zoom Lebron II Shoes	1KENZO23XZ
Nike Shox Elite	2388HDFCBJ	Zoom Generation Low	234SDJF9W4

NBA Live 06

Go to "My NBA Live," then "NBA Codes" and enter the following codes.

Unlockable	Code
Adidas A3 Garnett 3 Shoes	DRI239CZ49
S. Carter III LE Shoes	JZ3SCARTVY
TMac5 Black Shoes	258SHQW95B
TMac5 White Shoes	HGS83KP234P

NBA Live 07

Passwords

Password	Effect
99B6356HAN	Adidas Artillery II (black)
NTGNFUE87H	Adidas Artillery II (white)
7FB3KS9JQ0	Adidas BTB Low (St. Patty's edition)
BV6877HB9N	Adidas C-Billups (All-Star edition)
85NVLDMWS5	Adidas C-Billups (Vegas edition)
CLT2983NC8	Adidas Campus Lt (St. Patty's edition)
CC98KKL814	Adidas Crazy 8 (St. Patty's edition)
22OIUJKMDR	Adidas Equipment Bball (St. Patty's edition)
HYIOUHCAAN	Adidas Garnett Bounce (All-Star edition)
KDZ2MQL17W	Adidas Garnett Bounce (Vegas edition)
23DN1PPOG4	Adidas Gil-Zero (All-Star edition)
QQQ3JCUYQ7	Adidas Gil-Zero (Vegas edition)
369V6RVU3G	Adidas Gil-Zero Mid (Away)
1GSJC8JWRL	Adidas Gil-Zero Mid (Home)
FE454DFJCC	Adidas Stealth (All-Star edition)
MCJK843NNC	Adidas T-Mac 6 (All-Star edition)
84GF7EJG8V	Adidas T-Mac 6 (Vegas edition)
PNBBX1EVT5	Air Jordan V Black/White
VIR13PC451	Air Jordan V White/Blue/Grey
IB7G8NN91Z	Air Jordan V White/Red/Black
WOCNW4KL7L	East away uniform
5654ND43N6	East home uniform
JUL38TC485	Jordan Melo M3 Black
WEDX671H7S	New Bobcats road uniform
VCBI89FK83	New Jazz road uniform
D4SAA98U5H	New Nets road uniform
QV93NLKXQC	New Wizards road uniform
XX93BVL20U	West away uniform
993NSKL199	West home uniform

NBA Street Vol 2

Unlockable	Code/Objective
All Quicks	Hold LT and press ♦, ●, ♦, ✖.
Alternate Ball (NBA or ABA)	Hold LT and press ●, ✖, ●, ✖.
Always Legend Trails	Hold LT and press ♦, ♦, ♦, ✖.
Big Heads	Hold LT and press ●, ✖, ✖, ●.
Easy 2 pointers	Hold LT and press ♦, ●, ✖, ♦.
Explosive Rims	Hold LT and press ●, ●, ●, ♦.
Hard 2 Pointers	Hold LT and press ♦, ✖, ●, ♦.
Nelly and the St. Lunatics	Get 750 reward points or win 20 games in Pick Up.
No Counters	Hold LT and press ♦, ♦, ●, ●.
No HUD	Hold LT and press ✖, ●, ●, ●.
Street Kids	Hold LT and press ♦, ♦, ●, ✖.

DS
GBA
PSP
PS2
PS3
Wii
Xbox
Xbox 360
Index

NBA Street Vol 2 (continued)

Unlockable	Code/Objective
Unlimited Turbo	Hold Ⓛ and press Ⓧ, Ⓧ, Ⓨ, Ⓨ.
1985 Jordan	Collect the Street School trophy, NBA Challenge trophy and the Be A Legend trophy.
Biggie Little	Beat the tournament on Broad Street in Philly.
Bill Walton Jersey	Earn 1,000,000 trick points or more in a game.
Clyde Drexler Jersey	Collect 1 reputation star in Legend Mode.
Dime	Complete the tournament in Lincoln College.
Elgin Baylor Jersey	Get 20 or more blocks in a game.
Jerry West Jersey	Win a game without getting blocked.
Just Blaze	Get 500 Reward Points or win 15 games in Pick Up.
Osmosis	Win the Mosswood tournament in Legend mode.
Street Champ Costume	Complete *Be A Legend* by earning all 500/500 progress points.
Stretch	Beat the Soul in the Hole Tournament.
Whitewater	Complete the tournament in Green Lake to Whitewater.
WNBA Ball	Hold Ⓛ and press Ⓑ, Ⓨ, Ⓨ, Ⓑ.

NCAA Football 2005

All codes can be entered in the Pennant Collection Menu.

Unlockable	Code	Unlockable	Code
Unlockable	Code	Kansas State All Time	Victory
1st and 15	Thanks	Kentucky Mascot Team	On on uk
2003 All Americans	Fumble	LSU All Time	Geaux tigers
Alabama All Time	Roll tide	Miami All Time	Raising cane
Arizona Mascot Team	Bear down	Michigan All Time	Go blue
Arkansas All Time	Woopigsooie	Michigan State Mascot Team	Go green
Auburn All Time	War eagle		
Badgers All Time	U rah rah	Minnesota Mascot Team	Rah rah rah
Baylor Powerup	Sic em	Mississippi State All Time	Hail state
Blink	For	Missouri Mascot Team	Mizzou rah
Boing	Regi ering	Molasses Cheat	Home field
Clemson All Time	Death valley	NC State Mascot Team	Go cats
Colorado All Time	Glory	Nebraska All Time	Go big red
Crossed the Line	Tiburon	Norte Dame All Time	Golden domer
Cuffed Cheat	EA sports	North Carolina All Time	Rah rah
Florida All Time	Great to be	Ohio State All Time	Killer nuts
Florida State All Time	Uprising	Oklahoma All Time	Boomer
Georgia All Time	Hunker down	Oklahoma State All Time	Go pokes
Georgia Tech Mascot Team	Ramblinwreck		
		Ole Miss Mascot Team	Hotty totty
Illinois Team Boost	Oskee wow	Oregon All Time	Quack attack
Iowa All Time	On iowa	Penn State All Time	We are
Iowa St. Mascot Team	Red and gold	Pittsburgh All Time	Lets go pitt
Jumbalaya	Hike	Purdue All Time	Boiler up
Kansas Mascot Team	Rock chalk	QB Dud	Elite 11

NCAA Football 2005 (continued)

Unlockable	Code	Unlockable	Code
Stiffed	NCAA	Virginia All Time	Wahoos
Syracuse All Time	Orange crush	Virginia Tech Team Boost	Tech triumph
Take your Time	Football		
Tennessee All Time	Big orange	Wake Forest Mascot Team	Go deacs go
Texas A&M All Time	Gig em		
Texas All Time	Hook em	Washington All Time	Bowdown
Texas Tech Team Boost	Fight	West Virginia Mascot Team	Hail wv
Thread the Needle	2005		
UCLA All Time	Mighty	What a Hit	Blitz
USC All Time	Fight on	WSU Mascot Team	All hail

NCAA Football 06

Under MY NCAA, go into Pennant Collection. Click the Right Analog Stick to enter any of these passwords.

Unlockable	Password	Unlockable	Password
1ST and 15 mode-Opponent must gain 15 yards for 1ST down	THANKS	All-Washington Team	Bow Down
		Arkansas All-Time Team	WOOPIGSOOIE
2003 All Americans	FUMBLE	Arkansas Mascot	Bear Down
All Time Clemson Team	Death Valley	Baylor power-up	SIC EM
All Time Notre Dame	Golden Domer	Blink mode-ref spots the ball short for opponent	FOR
All Time Ohio State	Killer Nuts		
All Time Oklahoma State Team	Go Pokes	Boing Pennant; opponent drops passes more	REGISTERING
All Time Texas Team	Hook Em		
All-Colorado Team	Glory	Butter Fingers (#204)	With EA
All-Florida Team	Great To Be	Crossed The Line card	TIBURON
All-Kansas State Team	Victory	Cuffed mode	EA SPORTS
All-Michigan Team	Go Blue	Extra Credit; Gives 4 points per interception, 3 for each sack	TOUCHDOWN
All-Oklahoma Team	Boomer		
All-Oregon Team	Quack Attack	Free play pennant	IMPACT
All-Penn State Team	We Are	Gives you points when your player is injured (#211)	Heisman
All-Syracuse Team	Orange Crush		
All-Time Alabama	ROLL TIDE		
All-Time Auburn	WAR EAGLE	Hard to Tackle	Break Free
All-Time Florida State Team	UPRISING	Helium (#208)	In the Zone
		Illinois ratings boost	OSKEE WOW
All-Time Miami	RAISING CANE	Increased Pass Rush	Turnover
All-Time Mississippi State Team	HAIL STATE	Iowa All-Time Team	On Iowa
		Iowa State mascot team	RED AND GOLD
All-Time Nebraska	GO BIG RED		
All-Time Tennessee	BIG ORANGE	KU Mascot	Rock Chalk
All-Time Texas A&M Team	Gig Em	Makes wind go in your direction	Sideline
All-Time USC	FIGHT ON	Minnesota All-Time Team	Rah Rah Rah
All-UNC Team	Rah Rah	Mizzouri All-Time Team	Mizzou Rah
All-Virginia Tech Team	Tech Triumph	Molasses mode	HOME FIELD
		MSU Mascot	Go Green

DS

GBA

PSP

PS2

PS3

Wii

Xbox

Xbox 360

Index

DS

GBA

PSP

PS2

PS3

Wii

Xbox

Xbox 360

Index

NCAA Football 06 (continued)

Unlockable	Password	Unlockable	Password
NC State Mascot	Go Pack	Thread the needle mode	2006
NU Mascot	Go Cats	Tough as Nails (#226)	Offense
Pittsburgh All-Time Team	LETS GO PITT	Trip (#227)	Defense
Purdue All-Time Team	BOILER UP	UK Mascot	On On UK
QB dud mode	ELITE 11	Wake Mascot	Go Deacs Go
Stiffed mode	NCAA	What A Hit mode	BLITZ
Take Your Time (#223)	Football	WSU Mascot	All Hail
Texas Tech Boost	Fight		

NCAA Football '07

Passwords

At the Pennant Collection screen, press Back, then enter one of the following codes to activate the corresponding cheat function.

Unlockable	Code
2004 All-Americans #273	Fumble
Alabama All-Time Team	Roll Tide
Arizona Mascot Team	Bear Down
Arkansas All-Time Team	Woopigsooie
Auburn All-Time Team	War Eagle
Badgers All-Time Team	U Rah Rah
Clemson All-Time Team	Death Valley
Colorado All-Time Team	Glory
Cuffed #206	EA Sports
Florida All-Time Team	Great To Be
Florida State All-Time Team	Uprising
Georgia All-Time Team	Hunker Down
Georgia Tech Mascot Team	Ramblinwreck
Iowa All-Time Team	On Iowa
Iowa State Mascot Team	Red and Gold
Jumbalaya #211	Heisman
Kansas Mascot Team	Rock Chalk
Kansas State All-Time Team	Victory
Kentucky Mascot Team	On On UK
LSU All-Time Team	Geaux Tigers
Miami All-Time Team	Raising Cane
Michigan All-Time Team	Go Blue
Michigan State Mascot Team	Go Green
Minnesota Mascot Team	Rah Rah Rah
Mississippi State All-Time Team	Hail State
Mizzouri All-Time Team	Mizzou Rah
Nebraska All-Time Team	Go Big Red
North Carolina All-Time Team	Rah Rah
North Carolina State Mascot Team	Go Pack
Notre Dame All-Time Team	Golden Domer

NCAA Football '07 (continued)

Unlockable	Code
NU Mascot Team	Go Cats
Ohio State All-Time Team	Killer Nuts
Oklahoma All-Time Team	Boomer
Oklahoma State All-Time Team	Go Pokes
Ole Miss Mascot Team	Hotty Totty
Oregon All-Time Team	Quack Attack
Penn State All-Time Team	We Are
Pittsburgh All-Time Team	Lets Go Pitt
Purdue All-Time Team	Boiler Up
South Carolina Mascot Team	Go Carolina
Stiffed #222	NCAA
Syracuse All-Time Team	Orange Crush
Take Your Time #224	Football
Tennessee All-Time Team	Big Orange
Texas A&M All-Time Team	Gig Em
Texas Longhorns All-Time Team	Hook Em
Texas Tech #160	Fight
UCLA All-Time Team	Mighty
USC All-Time Team	Fight On
Virginia All-Time Team	Wahoos
Virginia Tech All-Time Team	Tech Triumph
Wake Forest Mascot Team	Go Deacs Go
Washington All-Time Team	Bow Down
Washington State Mascot Team	All Hail
West Virginia Mascot Team	Hail WV

Unlock Vince Young

Unlockable	How to Unlock
Vince Young	Beat Dynasty Mode with the Texas Longhorns

Need for Speed Carbon

Enter at the main menu.

Unlockable	Code
Extra Cash	↓, ↑, ←, ↓, →, ↑, ✕, Ⓑ
Infinite Crew Charge	↓, ↑, ↑, →, ←, ←, →, ✕
Infinite NOS	←, ↑, ←, ↓, ←, ↓, →, ✕
Infinite SpeedBreaker	↓, →, →, ←, →, ↑, ↓, ✕
Need For Speed Carbon Logo Vinyls Unlocked	→, ↑, ↓, ↑, ↓, ←, →, ✕
Need For Speed Carbon Special Logo Vinyls Unlocked	↑, ↑, ↓, ↓, ↓, ↓, ↑, ✕

Need for Speed: Hot Pursuit 2

Unlock All Tracks

Unlockable	How to Unlock
Unlock all tracks	⊗, ⓑ, ⓑ, ⓛⓑ, ⓛⓑ, ⬧, ♀, ⬥, ⬧

Unlockable Cars

Unlockable	How to Unlock
Dodge Viper GTS	2,000,000 points
Ferrari F50	Lead a single race with full grid and advanced for 8 laps
Ford Crown Victoria	Complete Hot Pursuit Event 5
Lamborghini Murcielago	3,000,000 points
Lamborghini Diablo 6.0 VT	2,500,000 points
McLaren F1	4,000,000 points
McLaren F1 LM	5 million points OR win world championship
Mercedes CLK GTR	4,500,000 points
Porsche 911 Turbo	800,000 points
Porsche Carrera GT	3,500,000 points
Vauxhall VX220	Win a single race with first place in all laps

Unlockable Tracks

Complete the following events to unlock the corresponding race tracks.

Unlockable	How to Unlock
Alpine Trail	Championship event 22
Ancient Ruins II	Ultimate racer event 12
Autumn Crossing	Ultimate racer event 17
Autumn Crossing II	Ultimate racer event 14
Calypso Coast	Ultimate racer event 10
Calypso Coast II	Ultimate racer event 26
Coastal Parklands	Championship event 4
Desert Heat II	Championship event 25
Fall Winds II	Championship event 24
Island Outskirts II	Championship event 8
Mediterranean Paradise II	Championship event 14
National Forest	Ultimate racer event 1
National Forest II	Ultimate racer event 6
Outback	Championship event 11
Outback II	Ultimate racer event 25
Palm City Island	Ultimate racer event 28
Palm City Island II	Ultimate racer event 29
Rocky Canyons	Championship event 27
Rocky Canyons II	Championship event 9
Scenic Drive II	Championship event 6
Tropical Circuit	Championship event 29
Tropical Circuit II	Championship event 28

DS

GBA

PSP

PS2

PS3

Wii

Xbox

Xbox 360

Index

Need for Speed Most Wanted

All codes should be entered at the Start screen.

Unlockable	Code
Unlocks Burger King Challenge Event (#69)	◌, ♀, ♀, ♀, ◌, ◌, ◌, ◌
Unlocks Free Engine Upgrade Bonus Marker (Can be used in the backroom of the customization shops)	◌, ◌, ♀, ♀, ◌, ◌, ◌, ♀
Unlocks Special Edition Castrol Ford GT (Which is added to your bonus cars)	◌, ◌, ◌, ◌, ◌, ♀, ◌, ♀

Need for Speed Underground

Enter the following codes at the Main menu.

Unlockable	Code
Circuit Tracks	♀, RT, RT, RT, LB, LB, Ⓧ
Drift Tracks	◌, ◌, ◌, ◌, ◌, LB, RT, WH
Drag Tracks	◌, Ⓧ, ◌, RT, Ⓧ, LT, WH, LB
Sprint Tracks	◌, LB, LB, LB, RT, ♀, ♀, ♀

Need for Speed Underground 2

Codes are entered at the Main menu.

Unlockable	Code
$1,000 for Career Mode	◌, ◌, ◌, Ⓧ, Ⓧ, ◌, LT, RT
Best Buy Vinyl	◌, ♀, ◌, ♀, ♀, ◌, ◌, ◌

NFL Fever 2002

Unlockable	Code
All Teams and Stadiums	Create a new Profile using the name Broadway.

NFL Fever 2003

To enter these codes you must make a user file using the following names.

Stadium Unlockable	Code	Stadium Unlockable	Code
Commandos	Barracks	DaRulas	Tut
Pansies	Flowery	Eruption	Lava
Pyramid	Sphinx	Firemen	Blazer
Samurai	Warrior	Gladiators	BigBack
Tumbleweeds	Dustball	Hackers	Axemen
64 Browns	Bigrun	King Cobras	Venom
67 Packers	Cheese	Mimes	Silence
72 Dolphins	Perfect	Monks	Robes
77 Cowboys	Thehat	Pansies	Viola
78 Steelers	Curtain	Polars	Igloo
83 Raiders	Outlaws	Samurai	Slasher
85 Bears	Sausage	Skeletons	Stone
89 49ers	Empire	Soldiers	Helmet
93 Cowboys	Lonestar	Sorcerers	Spellboy
96 Packers	Green	Spies	Target
98 Broncos	Milehigh	Thunder Sheep	Flock
Chromides	Regulate	Tumbleweeds	Dusty
Commandos	Camo	War Elephants	Horns
Cows	Milk	Wildcats	Kitty
Creampuffs	Cakewalk	Winged Gorillas	Flying
Crocs	Crykie		

NFL Street

Enter the following passwords as your User name.

Unlockable	Code
NFL Legends	classic
Xecutioner Team	excellent
Kay Slay Team	kayslay
All Stadiums	travel

NFL Street 2

Enter these codes in the Cheats menu.

Unlockable	Code
AFC East All-Stars	EAASFSCT
AFC North All-Stars	NAOFRCTH
AFC South All-Stars	SAOFUCTH
AFC West All-Stars	WAEFSCT
All players will have a maxed out catching stat	MagnetHands

NHL 2K6

Enter this as a profile name. Case Sensitive.

Unlockable	Password
Unlock everything	Turco813

NHL Hitz 2002

Activate Cheat Menu: Press ❽, ❿, and ❾ to change the icons in the first, second, and third boxes respectively at the Match-Up screen. The numbers in the following list indicate the number of times each button is pressed. After the icons have been changed, press the D-Pad in the indicated direction to enable the code. For example, to enter 1-2-3 ◎, press ❽, ❿(2), ❾(3), ◎.

Unlockable	Code	Unlockable	Code
Big Head Player	2-0-0 ▷	No Crowd	2-1-0 ▷
Big Head Team	2-2-0 ◁	No Fake Shots	4-2-4 ▽
Big Hits	2-3-4 ▽	No One-Timers	2-1-3 ◁
Big Puck	1-2-1 △	No Puck Out	1-1-1 ▽
Bulldozer Puck	2-1-2 ◁	Pinball Boards	4-2-3 ▷
Disable Previous Code	0-1-0 ▽	Rain Mode	1-4-1 ◁
Domino Effect	0-1-2 ◁	Show Shot Speed	1-0-1 △
First to Seven Wins	3-2-3 ▷	Show the Team's Hot Spot	2-0-1 △
Hitz Time	1-0-4 ▷	Skills Versus	2-2-2 ▷
Hockey Ball	1-3-3 ◁	Snow Mode	1-2-1 ◁
Huge Head Player	3-0-0 ▷	Tennis Ball	1-3-2 ▽
Huge Head Team	3-3-0 ◁	Turbo Boost	0-0-2 △
Huge Puck	3-2-1 △	Unlimited Turbo	4-1-3 ▷
Late Hits	3-2-1 ▽	Win Fights for Goals	2-0-2 ◁
More Time to Enter Codes	3-3-3 ▷		

NHL Hitz Pro

Enter these codes as User Names. To turn on these codes, pause the game and select Settings, then select Visuals, followed by Cheats.

Unlockable	Code	Different Puck Size	211S
Big Player Head	HERK	Different Puck Shadow	SASG
Big Team Heads	INGY	Glowing Puck	CARB
Unlockable	Code		

NHL Rivals 2004

To enter these codes, select Options, then select Unlocks.

Unlockable	Code	Unlockable	Code
All Agitators	PESTFEST	NHL Rivals West All Stars	CUJOWEST
All Balanced Players	EVENSTEVEN	No Bounce Dasherboards	DEADBOARDS
All Enforcers	BRUISERS	Microsoft All Stars	BLIBBET
All Snipers	SHOOTOUT	Small Players	TINYTYKES
Big Players	BIGDUDES	Unlimited Speed Burst	Caffeine
Big Puck	BIGBISCUIT		
Big Shot Mode	HOWITZER	XSN Sports East All Stars	XSNSPORTSEAST
Heavy Shot Trails	THESTREAK	XSN Sports West All Stars	XSNSPORTSWEST
Increase Gravity	HEAVYPUCK		
Invisible Players	INVISIBLEMAN	Zero Ice Friction	AIRHOCKEY
NHL Rivals East All Stars	CUJOEAST		

Ninja Gaiden

Unlockable	Objective
All Music and Sound Test	Complete the game.
Armlet of Benediction	Collect 15 Scarabs.
Armlet of Fortune	Collect 30 Scarabs.
Armlet of Tranquility	Collect 40 Scarabs.
Blue Ninja Outfit	At the Main Menu, highlight New Game, hold both ⊔+⊓ and press Ⓐ
Dabilahro	Collect 20 Scarabs.
Dark Dragon Blade	Complete the game. Then visit Muramasa's shop in chapter 13.
Evil Ryu	Complete the game on Very Hard.
Movie Gallery	Complete the game.
New Outfit and Sword	Once you complete the game, go to the Main Menu and highlight new game. Then hold ⊔ and press Ⓐ.
Ninja Gaiden 1	Collect 50 Scarabs.
Ninja Gaiden 2	Once you obtain Ninja Gaiden 1, shoot the clock tower near Muramasa's shop in Tairon.
Ninja Gaiden 3	In the Ceremonial room in the aquaducts, jump up the wall where you found the golden Scarab.
Very Hard	Complete the game.

Ninja Gaiden Black

Difficulty Levels

Unlockable	How to Unlock
Hard	Complete the game on Ninja Dog or Normal difficulty, or have a save file on your hard drive where you completed the original Ninja Gaiden on Xbox.
Master Ninja	Complete the game on Very Hard.
Ninja Dog	Die three times consecutively in Chapter 1, then accept the choices given to you.
Very Hard	Complete the game on Hard difficulty, or have a save file with the clear data of the Hurricane Pack 1.

DS
GBA
PSP
PS2
PS3
Wii
Xbox
Xbox 360
Index

Ninja Gaiden Black (continued)

DS

GBA

PSP

PS2

PS3

Wii

Xbox

Xbox 360

Index

Scarab Rewards in Ninja Dog (Easy) and Normal Mode

Select the "TALK" option at Muramasa's shop to give him Golden Scarabs. He keeps track of how many you have turned in and rewards you with items based upon your cumulative total.

Unlockable	How to Unlock
Arcade Ninja Gaiden	50 Scarabs
Armlet of Benediction	30 Scarabs
Armlet of Celerity	25 Scarabs
Armlet of Fortune	40 Scarabs
Armlet of Potency	5 Scarabs
Dabilahro	20 Scarabs
Great Sprit Elixir	35 Scarabs
Jewel of the Demon Seal	45 Scarabs
Life of a Thousand Gods	10 Scarabs
Life of the Gods	1 Scarab
Spirit of the Devils	15 Scarabs

Golden Scarab Rewards in Hard Mode

Select the "TALK" option at Muramasa's shop to give him Golden Scarabs. He keeps track of how many you have turned in and rewards you with items based upon your cumulative total.

Unlockable	How to Unlock
Armlet of Benediction	40 Scarabs
Armlet of Celerity	30 Scarabs
Armlet of Fortune	45 Scarabs
Dabilahro	25 Scarabs
Dark Dragon Blade	50 Scarabs
Plasma Saber Mk. II	49 Scarabs
Spear Gun	35 Scarabs
Technique Scroll—Counter Attacks	1 Scarab
Technique Scroll—Guillotine Throw	10 Scarabs
Technique Scroll—Izuna Drop	5 Scarabs
Windmill Shuriken	15 Scarabs
Wooden Sword	20 Scarabs

Golden Scarab Rewards in Very Hard Mode

Select the "TALK" option at Muramasa's shop to give him Golden Scarabs. He keeps track of how many you have turned in and rewards you with items based upon your cumulative total.

Unlockable	How to Unlock
Armlet of Fortune	30 Scarabs
Dark Dragon Blade	50 Scarabs
Jewel of the Demon Seal	35 Scarabs
Jewel of the Demon Seal	15 Scarabs
Jewel of the Demon Seal	25 Scarabs
Plasma Saber Mk.II	49 Scarabs
Spirit of the Devils	45 Scarabs
Spirit of the Devils	5 Scarabs

Ninja Gaiden Black (continued)

Unlockable	How to Unlock
Spirit of the Devils	20 Scarabs
The Art of the Ice Storm	10 Scarabs
The Art of the Inazuma	40 Scarabs
The Art of the Inferno	1 Scarab

Golden Scarab Rewards on Master Ninja Mode

Select the "TALK" option at Muramasa's shop to give him Golden Scarabs. He keeps track of how many you have turned in and rewards you with items based upon your cumulative total.

Unlockable	How to Unlock
Ayane's Ration Bundle	40 Scarabs
Ayane's Rations	30 Scarabs
Dark Dragon Blade	50 Scarabs
Elixir of Spiritual Life	5 Scarabs
Elixir of the Devil Way	15 Scarabs
Fragrance of Dayflower	35 Scarabs
Fragrance of Hydrangea	45 Scarabs
Great Devil Elixir	20 Scarabs
Great Spirit Elixir	10 Scarabs
Plasma Saber Mk. II	49 Scarabs
Smoke Bomb	1 Scarab, 25 Scarabs

Mission Mode Unlockables

Unlockable	How to Unlock
Mission Mode	Beat the game on any difficulty.
More Missions in Mission Mode	Beat five missions to unlock five more.
Play Missions on Multiple Difficulties	Beat a mission, and you unlock Hard for that mission. Beat Hard to unlock Very Hard, and Very Hard to unlock Master Ninja. Ninja Dog is not available.

Unlockable Armlets on Hard Mode

Unlockable	How to Unlock
Armlet of Benediction	Give Muramasa 30 Scarabs
Armlet of Celerity	Give Muramasa 25 Scarabs
Armlet of Fortune	Give Muramasa 40 Scarabs
Armlet of Potency	Beat clone Ryu in the archives room
Armlet of the Moon	Buy it for 5,000 essence
Armlet of the Sun	Buy it for 5,000 essence

Unlockables

Unlockable	How to Unlock
Arcade Ninja Gaiden	Complete the game on Ninja Dog or Normal difficulty with the "Ninja Gaiden Arcade" item, or complete the game on Hard
Ayane-themed Start Screen	Load a Ninja Dog save file, and reset the game (start+back)
Coming Attractions	Play the game for more than 1 hour
Movie Theater	Complete the game with any difficulty level

DS

GBA

PSP

PS2

PS3

Wii

Xbox

Xbox 360

Index

DS

GBA

PSP

PS2

PS3

Wii

Xbox

Xbox 360

Index

Ninja Gaiden Black (continued)

Unlockable	How to Unlock
Unlock All Music in "Sound Test"	Complete the game on any difficulty
DOA Throwback costume	Defeat Eternal Legends mission
The Ashtar Ryu Outfit (from the Hurricane Pack)	Defeat Ninja Dog/Normal
The Hotsuma Costume	Defeat Hard
The Ryuken (classic) Costume	Defeat Very Hard
Play Japanese Version of Arcade Ninja Gaiden	After unlocking the arcade Ninja Gaiden at the main menu, change both text and speech to Japanese

Unlockable	How to Unlock
Hidden Windmill Shuriken	Find this just outside Han's bar. If you are lucky enough, a hint in the form of a pink Kunai scroll will tell you to look for a special weapon left behind in an alley that "only a Ninja can get to." This "alley" is right outside Han's bar to the left. After defeating the ninjas outside, turn to the alley and look up. You will see a series of blue strips that you can use to run back and forth across the alley. Do this, starting with the first strip just outside of the alley, and then jump to the second and finally the third strip, all the while running along the wall. Once you hit the last strip, jump to the ledge right across from it. Here you find the Windmill Shuriken embedded in the wall, and an "Xbox" symbol that revives your KI energy and your life. Once you've taken the shuriken you can continue on with the mission with a new deadly weapon at your side. Doesn't work in Hard mode.

Oddworld Stranger's Wrath

Codes

This is all done in game, with no need to pause. Insert a second controller into port #2 on your Xbox. Remove the second controller. On controller 1, press ⊗, ⊗, ⊙, ⊙, Ⓑ, Ⓑ, Ⓐ, Ⓐ to activate Cheat mode. You hear a sound confirming that Cheat mode has been activated.

Unlockable	How to Unlock
1,000 Extra Moolah	Ⓛ, Ⓛ, Ⓛ, Ⓛ, Ⓛ, Ⓛ, Ⓡ, Ⓡ
Invincibility	⊗, ⊙, Ⓐ, Ⓑ, ⊗, ⊙
Level Select	Start a new game and enter the following Player Name: ©@®&
New Yolk City's Black Market	After bagging X'Plosives but before taking on a new bounty, Stranger can ask townfolk about where X got all his weapons. On the side of the road is a female clakker who knows about a black market in town, and she then tells you the password. The Black Market is located up a rope across from the Bounty Store. Go down the hallway, recite the password, and gain access. The store's items include: Bola Blasts, Wasps, Regen Upgrade, Stamina Upgrade, and Steel Knuckles.

Oddworld Stranger's Wrath (continued)

Unlockable	How to Unlock
Secret Grubb Statue	When you complete the Eugene Ius bounty you end up in a Grubb village. Proceed into the village by jumping across the rooftops. Turn right and keep going forward and you see a break to the right, leading to a little maze-like area. Turn right and there's a small forked path. Go left and you're right next to a rope. Climb it and jump on to the roof. You can see another rope that you have to jump onto. When you jump on it you can see a boarded-up window. Break it by shooting it or meleeing it. When you enter the room there is a shiny Grubb statue. It's worth a bit of moolah.
Sepia Graphics Filter	This code makes the graphics a brownish-yellow color that's synonymous with the western theme seen in Stranger's Wrath. While in-game and only one controller is plugged in (the first port), press ⓛ, ⓛ, ⓡ, ⓐ, ⓑ, ⓡⓣ, ⓑ, ⓐ, ⓡ, ⓛ, ⓛ After entering this, take a second controller, plug it into the fourth controller slot, then pull it back out. If done correctly, you will see the graphics filter change. To deactivate the code, repeat this process.

Oddworld: Munch's Oddysee

Unlock Alternate Endings

The game endings below can be obtained depending on your Quarma level near the end of the game. You can check your detailed Quarma level on the Quarma Bar in the Pause menu.

Unlockable	How to Unlock
Angelic Quarma Ending	Beat the game with the Quarma Bar filled higher that 75%
Bad Quarma Ending	Beat Level 23 with the Quarma Bar filled less than 50%
Neutral Quarma Ending	Beat the game with the Quarma Bar filled between 50% and 75%

Open Season

Unlockable Minigames

Unlockable	How to Unlock
Duck Chorus	Complete "Crazy Quackers"
Flowers for My Deer	Complete "Meet the Skunks"
Rise, Rise to the Top!	Complete "Beaver Damage"
Shake That Butt!	Complete "Hunted"
Wild Memory	Complete "Shaw's Shack"

Otogi: Myth of Demons

Unlockable	Objective
Black Swallow	Found behind the start point of Canyon of Death (Stage 23). Once the stage begins, turn around and head into the alcove. Kill the Death Serpent.
Butterfly Staff	Destroy the plants on the left side near the beginning of The Green Cave (Stage 10). One hides a secret hallway where the Butterfly Staff can be found.
Dragon Point	Kill 30 enemies in Restless Sea (Stage 7).
Dragon Staff	Finish Palace of Gold (Stage 5) with a time of 3:20 or better.
Golden Dragon	Found in the narrow passage near the beginning of Inner Sanctum (Stage 20).
Holy Staff	Beat Sea of Fire (Stage 15) with a time of 2:47 or better.
Jaws of Mountain	Found in Spirit Wood (Stage 11). Follow the narrow path to the right of the start point and cross the bridge to receive your prize.

Otogi: Myth of Demons (continued)

Unlockable	Objective
Moonlight Sword	Free 100% of all souls in first 28 stages.
Ogre's Horn	Defeat the Blaze Ogre near the beginning of Darkfire Cave (Stage 18).
Orchid Malevolence	Kill the Hydra in Stage 25.
Punisher	Found at the base of the hill to the right in A Clouded Moon (Stage 6).
Rune Scimitars	Perform a 20-hit combo (or greater) in Mountain Gates (Stage 3).
Skylarks	Beat Stage 14 in under 2 minutes.
Staff of Duality	Found in Forest of Wind (Stage 24). Look for the small passageway inside the tree stump.
Sword of Voracity	Kill 60 enemies in Stage 26, Valley of Prayer
Thunder	Found in Stage 22, Lair of Fire, underneath the bridge between the center island and the large statue.
Training Sword	Perform a 400-hit combo in Spirit Wood (Stage 11).

Outlaw Golf

Unlockable	Objective
Atlas Driver	Complete the Stroke Me event.
Atlas Fairway Woods	Complete the Not-So-Goodfellas event.
Atlas Irons	Complete the High Rollers event.
Atlas Putter (Black)	Complete the All the Marbles event.
Atlas Putter Gold	Complete the Suave's Revenge event.
Atlas Wedge	Complete the Pretty in Pink event.
Boiler Maker Fairway Woods	Complete the Hole Lotta Luv event.
Boiler Maker Irons	Complete the Jersey Ball Bash event.
Boiler Maker Putter	Complete the Sun Stroke event.
Boiler Maker Wedge	Complete the Back 9 Shuffle event.
Bonus Costumes	Hold ⓛⓣ and press ⓨ, ⓨ, ⓦⓑ, ⓨ, ⓛⓑ, ⓨ at the character selection screen.
C.C.	Complete the Hot, Hot, Hot event.
Cincinnati Balls	Complete the Rough Riders event.
Cincinnati Driver	Complete the Ol' Blood and Guts event.
Cincinnati Fairway Woods	Complete the Full Frontal event.
Cincinnati Irons	Complete the Stroke Me Again event.
Cincinnati Wedge	Complete the Blister in the Sun event.
Coiler Maker Driver	Complete the Money Talks event.
Distract Opponent	Start a game with two or more players. While the other person is hitting the ball, press ⓐ to say things to distract them.
Doc Diggler	Complete the Ladies Night event.
Ecstasy Balls	Complete the Scorched Earth Classic event.
Ecstasy Putter	Complete the Motley Crew event.
Killer Miller	Complete the Test Drive event.
Master Code	Start a new game and enter Golf_Gone_Wild as a case-sensitive name, including underscores, to unlock all characters, clubs, and stages.
Nelson Balls	Complete the Different Strokes event.
Python Driver	Complete the Heat Rash Invitational event.
Python Fairway Woods	Complete the Tough Crowd event.
Python Irons	Complete the A Hole in the Sun event.
Python Wedge	Complete the Garden State Stroke Fest event.
Scrummy	Complete the Odd Ball Classic event.

DS
GBA
PSP
PS2
PS3
Wii
Xbox
Xbox 360
Index

Outlaw Golf (continued)	
Unlockable	**Objective**
Suave's Balls	Complete the Garden State Menage a Trois event.
Suki	Complete the Baked on the Bone event.
Trixie	Complete the Chicks with Sticks event.

Outlaw Golf 2

Unlockable	Code
Big Head Mode	At any time during the game, hold ⓛ and press 🅑,🅐,🅑,🅨,🖓,🖘.
Everything	Enter I Have No Time as your name.

Outlaw Tennis

Unlockables

Unlockable	How to Unlock
Afrodite	Beat Vinny's tour
Apocalypse court	Beat Tour mode with all characters
Ball Boy	Beat all of the drills with every character including Heavy G
Bonus Movie 1	Beat Tour mode with Donna
Bonus movie 4	Beat the third event in Tour mode with Lizzie
Bruce	Beat Tour mode with Luther
Golf-ball Head for Ice Trey	Beat Tour mode with Ice Trey
Harley	Beat Tour mode with Afrodite
Heavy G	Beat Tour mode with every character
Ice Trey	Beat Shawnee's tour
Kiku	Beat Donna's tour
Lizzy	Beat Tour mode with Harley
Luther	Beat Tour mode with Ice Trey
Natasha	Beat Summer's tour
Shawnee	Beat or complete the tour with Sven
Slaughterhouse Court	Beat all drill events
Sven	Beat or complete the tour with Killer
Tennis-ball Head for Bruce	Beat Tour mode with Bruce
Tennis-ball Head for Luther	Beat Tour mode with Luther
Tennis-ball Hat for Killer	Complete the tour with Killer
Tennis-ball Hat for Sven	Complete the tour with Sven
Tommy	Beat the tour with Kiku
Unlock Everything	Create a profile using the name Cut To The Chase, then hold the Right and Left Triggers while you save the profile
Vinny	Beat El Suave's tour
Volley-ball Head for Shawnee	Beat Tour mode with Shawnee

DS

GBA

PSP

PS2

PS3

Wii

Xbox

Xbox 360

Index

DS

Outlaw Volleyball

Unlockable	Code
All Characters	At the character select screen, hold ⓛⓓ and press ◄, ⒲, ►, ⒲.
All Courts	On Court Selection Screen, hold ⓛⓓ and press ◊, ♀, ◊, ♀, ◄, ◄, ►, ►.
Big Head Mode	During gameplay, hold ⓛⓓ and press Ⓞ, Ⓐ, Ⓑ, Ⓥ.
Maximum Stats	In Exhibition mode, hold ⓡⓓ and press ◄, ⒲, ►, ⒲.
Time Bombs	In Exhibition mode, hold ⓛⓓ and press Ⓐ, Ⓑ, Ⓑ, Ⓥ, and Ⓐ+Ⓧ together.

GBA

Outrun 2

To enter these codes, select Outrun Challenge, then select Gallery, and last, select Enter Code.

Unlockable	Code
All Cars	DREAMING
All Mission Stages	THEJOURNEY
All Music	RADIOSEGA
Bonus Tracks	TIMELESS
Original Outrun	NINETEEN86
Reverse Tracks	DESREVER

PSP

Outrun 2006 Coast to Coast

To enter these passwords create a license. Then go into Edit License and change the name to the password. Do not press the Done button—instead, press the Ⓑ to back out of the screen.

Unlockable	Password
100% Complete	ENTIRETY
1,000,000 Outrun Miles	MILESANDMILES

PS2

PS3

Over the Hedge

Unlock Minigames and Attacks

Unlockable	How to Unlock
Unlock Attack: Finishing Moves	Complete 20 Objectives
Unlock Attack: Ground Pound	Complete 50 Objectives
Unlock Minigame: Bumper Carts 1	Complete 15 Objectives
Unlock Minigame: Bumper Carts 2	Complete 45 Objectives
Unlock Minigame: Race Track 1	Complete 25 Objectives
Unlock Minigame: Race Track 2	Complete 60 Objectives
Unlock Minigame: Range Driver 1	Complete 10 Objectives
Unlock Minigame: Range Driver 2	Complete 40 Objectives

Wii

Xbox

Panzer Dragoon Orta

Unlockable	Objective/Code
Box Game Mode	Complete the game under the Hard difficulty setting or accumulate fifteen hours of gameplay.
Flight Records Option	Complete the game under any difficulty setting or accumulate five hours of gameplay.
Pandora's Box Options	Accumulate twenty hours of gameplay to unlock most of the Pandora's Box Appendix options, including the Panzer Dragoon game.

Xbox 360

Index

Panzer Dragoon Orta (continued)

Unlockable	Objective/Code
Panzer Dragoon Dragon-Only Mode (Only the lock-on weapons are available with this code.)	Enable the "Power-ups" code, followed by ◁, ◁, ▷, ▷, ◇, ◇, ◇, (LT), (RT). The sound of the dragon being hit confirms correct code entry.
Panzer Dragoon Episode 0	Press ◇, ◇, ◇, ◇, ◇, ◇, ◁, ◁, ◁, ▷, ▷, ◁, ▷, (LT), (RT) at the Panzer Dragoon main menu. Shoot enemies to restore your health, which gradually decreases during gameplay.
Panzer Dragoon Episode Select	Press ◇, ◇, ◇, ◇, ◁, ▷, ◁, ▷, ✕, ✓, ◈ at the Panzer Dragoon main menu.
Panzer Dragoon Game	Complete the game or accumulate five hours of gameplay to unlock the original Panzer Dragoon game in the Pandora's Box Appendix.
Panzer Dragoon Invincible Mode	Press (LT), (LT), (RT), (RT), ◇, ◇, ◁, ▷ at the Panzer Dragoon main menu. The sound of the dragon being hit and the phrase "Invincible Mode" appears to confirm correct code entry.
Panzer Dragoon Power Ups	Press ◇, ✕, ▷, ✓, ◇, ◈, ◁, ✓, ◇, ✕ at the Panzer Dragoon Easy Game Options screen. The Sega logo turns into a polygon woman. This normally occurs after you complete the game without dying. Go to the Episodes screen, and hold ✕ for red lasers, ⬛ for missiles, ✓ for rapid fire, or ◈ for a wide-shot weapon.
Panzer Dragoon Red Sega Polygon Man	Press ◇, ✕, ▷, ✓, ◇, ◈, ◁, ✓, ◇, ✕ at the Panzer Dragoon main menu. The sound of the dragon being hit confirms correct code entry. After finishing the last continue, the polygon Sega figure is red instead of blue.
Panzer Dragoon Rolling Mode	Press ◱ at the Panzer Dragoon Title screen. Sweep the ◎ in three clockwise full circles when the screen with normal game and options appears. A sound and the phrase "Rolling Mode" appears to confirm correct code entry. Tap the ◎ twice to perform a roll during gameplay. To activate a smart bomb, begin a roll, and hold any button to highlight all enemy targets on the radar. Release the button to destroy the targets.
Panzer Dragoon Unlimited Continues	Press ◇, ✕, ▷, ✓, ◇, ◈, ◁, ✓, ◇, ✕ at the Panzer Dragoon main menu.
Panzer Dragoon View Hard Difficulty Ending Sequence	Press ◇, ◇, ◇, ◁, ◇, ◁, ◇, ◁, ◇, ◇, ◇, ◇, ▷, ▷, ◁, ▷ at the Panzer Dragoon main menu.
Panzer Dragoon View Normal Ending Sequence	Press ◇, ◇, ◇, ◇, ◁, ▷, ◁, ▷, ◇, ◇, ◇, ◇, ◁, ◁, ▷, ▷ at the Panzer Dragoon main menu.
Panzer Dragoon Wizard Mode	Press ◱ at the Title screen. Press (LT), (RT), (LT), (RT), ◇, ◇, ◇, ◇, ◁, ▷ at the Panzer Dragoon main menu. The phrase "Wizard Mode" appears to confirm correct code entry. Gameplay is very fast when you enable this mode.
White Dragonmare	Unlock the Dragonmare in Box mode. Highlight the "Dragon Select" option, hold ◈, and press ◱. Release ◈ when the game starts.

DS

GBA

PSP

PS2

PS3

Wii

Xbox

Xbox 360

Index

DS

Pariah

To enter these codes go to the Codes option.

Unlockable	Code
EB Games Multiplayer Level	⊞, 🅨, 🅧, ⊟
Gamestop Multiplayer Level	◌, ⊡, 🅧, ◌

Enter these codes in the Cheat Codes menu under "settings."

Unlockable	Code
All Ammo	◌, ◌, ◌, 🅨
God Mode	◌, ⊡, 🅧, ⊡

GBA

Peter Jackson's King Kong

At the Main menu screen, hold ⊞+⊞ and press 🅨, 🅧, ◌, 🅨, ◌, ◌, ◌, ◌, then release ⊞+⊞. This opens the Cheat menu. Now enter any of these case sensitive passwords.

Unlockable	Password
999 ammunition	KK 999 mun
Bonuses completed	KKmuseum
God mode	8wonder
Level select	KKst0ry
Machine gun	KKcapone
One-hit kills	GrosBras
Revolver	KKtigun
Shotgun	KKsh0tgun
Sniper rifle	KKsn1per
Unlimited spears	lance 1nf

PSP

PS2

PS3

Phantasy Star Online Episode I and II

Unlockable	Objective
Open the Dressing Room	Have 10,000 Meseta on your character (not in the bank) when you start the game.
Hard Mode (offline)	Beat Normal Mode.
Hard Mode (online)	Get to level 20.
Ultimate Mode (offline)	Beat Very Hard Mode.
Ultimate Mode (online)	Get to level 80.
Very Hard Mode (offline)	Beat Hard Mode.
Very Hard Mode (online)	Get to level 40.

Wii

Xbox

Pinball Hall of Fame

To enter these codes, go to Options, Code Entry.

Unlockable	Code	Unlockable	Code
Love Meter machine	LUV	Tournament mode	TMA
Playboy machine	PKR	Custom Balls option	BLZ
Xolton Fortune Teller machine	XTN	Infinite Final Ball option	INF
Payout mode	LAS	Unlock Gottlieb Tour	DGC

Xbox 360

Index

Pirates: The Legend of Black Kat

Unlockable	Code
Advance to Katarina's Next Sword	Hold ⓛ + ⓡ and click ⊙, press ⊙, ⊞, click ⊙, press ⊗, ⊙, ⊛, ⊙, click ⊙, press ⊙
All Treasure Chest Keys	Hold ⓛ + ⓡ and press ⊙, ⊙, ⊙, ⊗, click ⊙, press ⊛, click ⊙, press ⊞, ⊙, click ⊙.
Alternate Glacial Gulf Music	Hold ⓛ + ⓡ and press ⊛, ⊙, ⊙, ⊞, ⊗, ⊙, click ⊙, press ⊙, click ⊙, click ⊙ to hear music from SSX when sliding down in Glacial Gulf.
Alternate Katarina Costumes	Press ⓛ + ⓡ, click ⊙, press ⊙, ⊙. A short sequence of music confirms correct code entry. Click ⊙ to change the value of the numbers that appear on screen, then start a new game or resume a saved game to view the corresponding costume. The available costumes and their values are in the table below.
Extra Gold	Hold ⓛ + ⓡ and press ⊙, click ⊙, press ⊛, ⊗, ⊙, click ⊙, press ⊙, click ⊙, press ⊙, ⊞. Sail to another map to get the Galleon.
High-Pitched Voices	Hold ⓛ + ⓡ and click ⊙, press ⊙, ⊙, ⊙, click ⊙, press ⊙, ⊛, ⊗, ⊞, click ⊙.
Invincibility for Katarina	Hold ⓛ + ⓡ and press ⊗, ⊙, click ⊙, press ⊙, click ⊙, press ⊙, click ⊙, press ⊛, ⊞, ⊗.
Invincibility for the Wind Dancer	Hold ⓛ + ⓡ and press ⊙, ⊙, ⊛, ⊗, click ⊙, press ⊞, ⊗, click ⊙, press ⊙, click ⊙.
Kane Poison Head	Hold ⓛ + ⓡ and press ⊙, ⊞, ⊛, ⊗, click ⊙, press ⊗, click ⊙, press ⊙, click ⊙, press ⊙. The poison status will be indicated by the head of Kane from Command and Conquer.
Reveal All Treasure Chests	Hold ⓛ + ⓡ and click ⊙, press ⊗, ⊙, click ⊙, press ⊙, ⊛, ⊙, click ⊙, press ⊗, ⊞.
Reveal Buried Treasure Chests	Hold ⓛ + ⓡ and press ⊙, ⊗, ⊗, ⊙, ⊛, ⊙, click ⊙, ⊞, click ⊙, click ⊙. Green Xs appear on the captain's log maps to indicate the location of buried treasure chests.
Unlimited Items	Hold ⓛ + ⓡ and press ⊙, ⊛, ⊙, ⊞, click ⊙, click ⊙, press ⊗, ⊙, click ⊙, press ⊙. Once found, an item becomes available in unlimited amounts.
Unlimited Wind Boost	Hold ⓛ + ⓡ and press ⊙, ⊛, click ⊙, press ⊗, click ⊙, press ⊙, ⊞, ⊙, ⊙, click ⊙.
Wind Dancer	Hold ⓛ + ⓡ and press ⊞, ⊙, click ⊙, click ⊙, press ⊗, ⊗, click ⊙, press ⊙, ⊛, ⊙.

Alternate Costume	Numerical Value
Blackbeard in Purple	00000001
Blonde Hair, Orange and Yellow Bikini	00000101
Blonde Hair, Pink Bikini	00000110
Blue Hair with Orange and Red Bikini	00000011
Blue Hair, Shiny Copper Body Suit	00001010
Blue Hair, Shiny Silver Bikini	00000111
Original Costume and Hair Color	00000000
Pink Hair, Shiny Black Body Suit	00001001
Purple Hair, Shiny Silver Body Suit	00001011
Red Hair with Red and Orange Bikini	00000010
Red Hair, Black Bikini, Black Stockings	00001000
Tan, Brown Hair, Orange and Yellow Bikini	00000100

DS

GBA

PSP

PS2

PS3

Wii

Xbox

Xbox 360

Index

Sidebar tabs: DS, GBA, PSP, PS2, PS3, Wii, Xbox, Xbox 360, Index

Pirates of the Caribbean

Codes

Code	Effect
AXYBYBXBBA	+100,000 gold
AYXXYYBYXA	God Mode
ABYXYBBYBA	50 skill points
AXYXYBBYBA	Change your reputation back to neutral. This can only be done on land and no menus should be open at the start.

Easter Egg

Unlockable	How to Unlock
Portraits and AKELLA Logo	When you first enter the Labyrinth in the Incan Temple, Dannielle and Clement should make you go through the middle entryway. Keep going straight until you enter a different room. Go right. Keep an eye on the floor. You see a skull and a sun. Follow the sun. If you went the right way, you see a room with break in the wall. Look on the floor and you should see a sun and a skull. As you enter the room, run into the right wall. You go through the wall. Look at all of the portraits. Those are the crew who helped make the game. Look on the floor, you will see the AKELLA logo.

Pitfall: The Lost Expedition

Enter the following codes at the Main menu while holding ⒧+⒭.

Unlockable	Code
Bottomless Canteen	◀, ⊗, ⊕, ♥, ⊕, ♠, ⊗, ⊕
Original Pitfall	⊕, ⊕, ◀, ▶, ⊕, ⊗, ♠, ◆, ⊕
Play as Nicole	◀, ◆, ♥, ⊕, ♠, ◆, ◆
Punch Mode	◀, ▶, ⊕, ◆, ⊕, ▶, ◀

Prince of Persia

Unlockable	Objective
Original Prince of Persia	Complete the game and you will open up the very first Prince of Persia.

Prince of Persia: The Two Thrones

Extra Secondary Weapons

Pause the game while you have a secondary weapon equipped and ready.

Unlockable	How to Unlock
Chainsaw	◆, ◆, ♥, ♥, ◀, ▶, ◀, ▶, ♥, ⊗, ♥, ⊗
Phone	▶, ◀, ▶, ◀, ♥, ♥, ◆, ◆, ♥, ⊗, ♥, ⊗, ⊗
Rattle	◀, ◀, ▶, ▶, ♥, ⊗, ⊗, ♥, ◆, ♥
Swordfish	◆, ♥, ◆, ♥, ◀, ▶, ♥, ⊗, ♥, ⊗

Sand Gate Rewards

Unlockable	How to Unlock
100 Sand Credits	Deactivate Two Sand Gates
150 Sand Credits	Deactivate Five Sand Gates
200 Sand Credits	Deactivate Eight Sand Gates
Eye of the Storm Power	Deactivate Three Sand Gates
Fifth Sand Tank	Deactivate Four Sand Gates
Fourth Sand Tank	Deactivate One Sand Gate

DS
GBA
PSP
PS2
PS3
Wii
Xbox
Xbox 360
Index

Prince of Persia: The Two Thrones (continued)

Unlockable	How to Unlock
Sand Storm Attack	Deactivate Nine Sand Gates
Sixth Sand Tank	Deactivate Seven Sand Gates
Winds of Sand Attack	Deactivate Six Sand Gates
Video Gallery	Successfully complete the game

Prince of Persia: Warrior Within

Refill Sand Tanks

Code	Effect
Refills Sand Tanks	(Hold Left Analog Stick Down) Ⓑ, Ⓑ, Ⓐ, Ⓧ, Ⓧ, Ⓐ, Ⓨ, Ⓨ

Hidden Bonus: Indestructible Weapons

At certain points throughout the game you find Weapon Racks containing "unique" weapons. These weapons are indicated in the Secondary Weapon Display with a question mark icon and are indestructible, unlike other secondary weapons. There are five of these weapons in all. For all but the Giant Hand, you need the Scorpion Sword. The Garden Flamingo and Teddy Bear must be completed before you find the Mask, and require you to backtrack along the path you would take when trying to complete the towers in which they are located. The Teddy Bear also requires you to break a wall during the Dahaka chase zone in that area. You get one chance only to find the Giant Hand and Glowing Sword.

Unlockable	How to Unlock
Garden Flamingo	Hanging Garden (present)—Behind a wall in the first alcove you reach if you were trying to reach the giant ladder in the past.
Giant Hand (little damage, instant knock down)	During the escape from the Tomb, find it in a small alcove to your left during the second (or third) Dahaka chase (depending on how you play).
Glowing Sword (Very high stats, also damages Prince)	Behind a wall in a pit immediately after the room covered in fog.
Hockey Stick	Central Hall (past), rotate the switch toward the Hourglass Room. Use the new path to reach a breakable wall at the bottom of the room.
Teddy Bear (little damage, heals the Prince with each hit)	Mechanical Pit (present), in the area where you fought the second Brute, take the stairs up and look for a breakable wall in the water-filled pit.

Secret Ending

Unlockable	How to Unlock
Secret Ending	Collect all 9 life upgrades. Then go to the hourglass room as you would normally would, get the Water Sword from Kaileena, and beat a secret final boss.

DS

GBA

PSP

PS2

PS3

Wii

Xbox

Xbox 360

Index

Prisoner of War

At the Main menu, select Passwords to enter these codes.

Unlockable	Code
All Chapters	GER1ENG5
All Secrets	FARLEYMYDOG
Default Chapters	DEFAULTM
Defiance	FATTY
First Person Mode	BOSTON
Game Creation Date and Time	DT
Guard Perception	QUINCY
Guard Size	MUFFIN
Informed of all Events	ALLTIMES
Informed of Core Current Events	CORETIMES
Top Down Mode	FOXY
Unlimited Goodies	DINO

Project Gotham Racing

Unlockable	Code
All Cars and Courses	Enter the name Nosliw.

Project Gotham Racing 2

Bonus Cars

Unlockable	How to Unlock
Delfino Feroce	Beat Kudos Challenge on Steel
Ferrari 250 GTO	Beat Kudos Challenge on Bronze
Mercedes CLK-GTR	Beat Kudos Challenge on Gold
Porsche 911 GT1	Beat Kudos Challenge on Silver
TVR Cerbera Speed 12	Beat Kudos Challenge on Platinum

Unlockables

Unlockable	How to Unlock
Geometry Wars	Access this minigame by going into the Garage. While you're in Walk mode, go over to the arcade machine and press Ⓐ.
Reverse	On any track in online Xbox Live play, you can drive backward, but it takes 2 laps for every actual lap. So 3 laps is really 6 laps. Drive over the start line, do a U-turn, and go. Whoever crosses the finish line first, (sixth place) is first on the leaderboard and gets the bonus kudos as well.

Psi Ops: The Mindgate Conspiracy

At the Main menu, highlight Extra Content, press Ⓡ, and enter any of these codes.

Unlockable	Code	Unlockable	Code
All Powers from the start	537893	Dockworker	364654
Arcade Mode	05051979	Edgar Barret	497878
Bulletproof	548975	**Skin Unlockable**	**Code**
Co Op Play Mode	07041979	Edgar Barret	(Training 1) 196001
Dark Mode	465486		
Super Psi	456456	Edgar Barret	(Training 2) 196002
Unlimited Ammo	978945		
Crispy Soldier	454566	Edgar Barret	(Training 2) 196002

Psi Ops: The Mindgate Conspiracy (continued)

Skin Unlockable	Code	Skin Unlockable	Code
Edgar Barret	(Training 3) 196003	Sara Blake (Psi)	468799
		Sara Blake (Suicide)	231644
Edgar Barret	(Training 4) 196004	Scorpion	546546
		The General (Clown)	431644
Edgar Barret	(Training 5) 196005	The General (Default)	459797
		Tonya	678999
Edgar Barret	(Training 6) 196006	UN Soldier	365498
Jack	698798	Wei Lu	231324
Jov Leonov	468987	Wei Lu (Dragon)	978789
Kimiko Jones	978798	Wei Lu (Tranquility)	654654
Labcoat	998789	Aura Pool	659785
Marlena Kessler	489788	Bottomless Pit	154897
Marlena Kessler (Bikini)	135454	Bouncy, Bouncy	568789
Marlena Kessler (Leather)	136876	Floor of Death	05120926
Marlena Kessler (Saranae)	65496873	Gasoline	9442662
MP1	321646	Gearshift	154684
MP2	698799	Gnomotron	456878
MP3	654659	Panic Room	76635766
Nick Scryer (Stealth)	456498	Psi Pool	565485
Nick Scryer (Training)	564689	Survival Mode	7734206
Nick Scryer (Urban)	484646	Stoplights	945678
Nick Scryer (Wasteland)	975466	Tip the Idol	428584
No Head	987978	TK Alley	090702
Sara Blake	135488	Up and Over	020615

Psychonauts

During gameplay, hold ⓛⒹ+ⓇⓉ and enter the codes. A "you cheated" sound will confirm correct entry.

Unlockable	Code
9999 Ammo	▷, Ⓐ, ◁, ◁, ▽, Ⓨ, Ⓑ
9999 Arrow Heads	Ⓐ, ▷, ▷, ⓦⒽⓣ, Ⓨ, Ⓧ
9999 Lives	◁, ⓦⒽⓣ, ⓦⒽⓣ, Ⓑ, Ⓐ, ▷
All Items Except Dream Fluffs, Colorizer, and Psi-Ball	▷, Ⓑ, ⓦⒽⓣ, ⓦⒽⓣ, ◁, Ⓨ
All Powers and Max Rank	◁, ▷, ◁
All PSI Powers	Ⓑ, Ⓑ, Ⓨ, ⓦⒽⓣ, ◁, Ⓨ
Invincibility	Ⓑ, ⓦⒽⓣ, Ⓑ, Ⓑ, Ⓨ, ⓛⒹ, ⓦⒽⓣ, Ⓑ, ⓦⒽⓣ
Text Changes	ⓦⒽⓣ, Ⓐ, ◁, ⓦⒽⓣ, ⓦⒽⓣ, Ⓑ

The Punisher

Enter V Pirate as a Profile Name to unlock everything except Upgrades.

Quantum Redshift

Enter Cheat as your name, then in the Options menu, select the Cheats menu to enter these codes. Codes are case sensitive.

Unlockable	Code	Unlockable	Code
All Characters	Nematode	Infinite Shields	ThinkBat
All Speeds	zoomZOOM	Upgrade All Characters	RICEitup
Infinite Turbo	FishFace		

DS
GBA
PSP
PS2
PS3
Wii
Xbox
Xbox 360
Index

DS

GBA

PSP

PS2

PS3

Wii

Xbox

Xbox 360

Index

Rayman 3: Hoodlum Havoc

Unlockables

Unlockable	How to Unlock
Crush	Earn 4,000 game points
Racket Jump	Earn 3,000 game points
Rayman 2-D Madness	Earn 1,000 game points
Razzof Circus Mini-Game	Collect jewels and get 6,000 game points

Rayman Arena

Unlockables

Unlockable	How to Unlock
Dark Globox	Win the first cup in Obstacle Course
Dark Rayman	Beat every Master League challenge
Extreme Slide Bonus Map	Win the Beginner League under Time Attack
Future Bonus Map	Win the Pro League under Time Attack
Henchman 1000	Win the first circuit in Total Fight
Kurai Bonus Map	Win the Pro League under Freeze Combat
Low Gravity Arena Bonus Map	Win the Pro League under Total Fight
Master League	Earn every trophy in the game in Beginner and Pro Leagues
Master League	Obtain all the Beginner and Pro League trophies
Mrs. Razorbeard	Win the first circuit in Freeze Combat
Pac Arena Bonus Map	Win the Beginner League under Total Fight
Run, Run Bonus Map	Win the Pro League under Obstacle Racing
Speed Stress Bonus Map	Win the Beginner League under Obstacle Racing
Spooky Towers Bonus Map	Win the Beginner League under Freeze Combat
Tily	Win the first circuit in Time Attack

Red Card 2003

Unlockable	Objective
Apes Team and Victoria Falls Stadium	Defeat the Apes team in World Conquest mode.
Dolphins Team and Nautilus Stadium	Defeat the Dolphins team in World Conquest mode.
Finals Mode	Win all matches in World Conquest mode.
Martians Team and USAFB001 Stadium	Defeat the Martians team in World Conquest mode.
Matadors Team and Coliseum Stadium	Defeat the Matadors team in World Conquest mode.
Samurai Team and Youhi Gardens Stadium	Defeat the Samurai team in World Conquest mode.
SWAT Team and Nova City Stadium	Defeat the SWAT team in World Conquest mode.
Cheat Mode	Enter BIGTANK as a name to unlock all teams, stadiums, and finals mode.

Red Dead Revolver

These are the rewards for each level. The first is for a GOOD rating and the second is for a Excellent rating.

Unlockable	Good Rating	Excellent Rating
Battle Finale	Focus (Dead-Eye) Max-Up	Mr. Kelley
Bear Mountain	Shadow Wolf	Focus (Dead-Eye) Max-Up
Bounty Hunter	"Bloody" Tom	"Big Oaf" Whitney
Bull's Eye	Old Pistol	Broken Creek
Carnival Life	Focus (Dead-Eye) Max-Up	"Pig" Josh
Cemetery	Ghost Town	Mr. Black
Devils & Angels	The Ranch	—
Fall from Grace	Scorpion Revolver	Governor Griffon
Fort Diego	Health Max-Up	Colonel Daren
Freak Show	Health Max-Up	Breech Loader
Hell Pass	Buffalo	Gabriel Navarro
Railroaded	Owl Rifle	Rico Pedrosa
Range War	The Ranch	Holstein Hal
Rogue Valley	Cooper	Bad Bessie
Saloon Fight	Dan	Sam
Sunset Canyon	Twin Revolvers	Focus (Dead-Eye) Max-Up
The Mine	The Mine	"Smiley" Fawler
The Siege	Mansion Grounds	Jason Cornet
The Traitor	The Bridge	Health Max-Up
Ugly Streetfight	"Ugly" Chris	Freak Show

Red Faction II

Input the following codes at the Cheat menu.

Unlockable	Code
Bouncy Grenades	LT, LT, LT, LT, LT, LT, LT, LT
Bullet Gibs	LT, LT, LT, WHT, X, LT, LT
Bullets Instantly Gib	X, X, X, X, Y, LT, X, X
Directors Cut	Y, X, LT, WHT, LT, X, Y, WHT
Explosives Instantly Gib	WHT, LT, X, Y, WHT, LT, X, Y
Fat Mode	LT, LT, LT, LT, LT, LT, LT, LT
Fire Bullets	Y, Y, Y, Y, Y, Y, Y, Y
Hidden Message	Y, X, Y, X, Y, X, Y, X
Rapid Rails	LT, Y, LT, Y, X, X, WHT, WHT
Super Health	X, X, Y, WHT, Y, WHT, LT
Unlimited Ammo	Y, WHT, X, LT, Y, LT, X, WHT
Unlimited Grenades	LT, Y, LT, Y, X, WHT, Y, LT
Everything	WHT, WHT, X, X, Y, LT, Y, LT
Wacky Deaths	WHT, WHT, WHT, WHT, WHT, WHT, WHT, WHT
Zombie Walk	X, X, X, X, X, X, X, WHT

Reservoir Dogs

Codes

Unlockable	How to Unlock
Adrenaline Rush—Infinite Adrenaline	A, LT, Y, A, LT, A, START
Battering Ram—Instant Crash	LT, LT, A, A, Y, WHT, START
Bulletproof—Infinite Health	LT, RT, Y, Y, RT, WHT, START
Fully Loaded—Infinite Ammo	WHT, LT, Y, LT, A, WHT, START

Reservoir Dogs (continued)

Unlockable	How to Unlock
Magic Bullet—One Shot Kills	(RT), (LB), Y, A, (RT), A, (START)
Time Out—Infinite Timer	(RT), (RT), (WH), Y, A, (LB), (START)
Unlock All Levels	(LB), (WH), (LB), (WH), (LD), (RT), (START)
Unlock Art Gallery	Y, A, (LB), (WH), Y, A, (START)
Unlock Movie Gallery	(LD), (LD), Y, A, (LD), (RT), (START)

Unlockables

Unlockable	How to Unlock
Battering Ram	Successfully complete the game with the Professional ranking to unlock the Battering Ram cheat under the Extra menu.
Bulletproof	Successfully complete the game with the Professional ranking to unlock the Bulletproof cheat under the Extra menu.
Fully Loaded	Successfully complete the game with the Psychopath ranking to unlock the Fully Loaded cheat under the Extra menu.
Time Out	Successfully complete the game with the Career Criminal ranking to unlock the Time Out cheat under the Extra menu.

Return to Castle Wolfenstein: Tides of War

Unlockable	Code
Wolfenstein 3D	Beat the single player Campaign mode.

Roadkill

Enter the following codes at the map screen when paused.

Unlockable	Code
Restore Health	X, B, X, B, X, B, X, B
More Money	Y, B, Y, B, Y, A, A, Y, A, ○, ○
Infinite Ammo	Y, X, X, B, Y, X, X, B

Robotech: Battlecry

Cheat Mode: Start a new game or load a previous one. Highlight "Options," hold (LD) + (RT), and press ◄, ▲, ▼, ◄, ►, ●, Start to display the Code Entry screen. Enter one of the following codes to activate the corresponding cheat function.

Unlockable	Code
All Models and Awards	WHERESMAX
All Multiplayer Levels	MULTIMAYHEM
Alternate Paint Schemes	MISSMACROSS
Disable Active Codes	CLEAR
Gunpod Ammunition Refilled Faster	SPACEFOLD
Gunpod and Missiles Refilled Faster	MIRIYA
Invincibility	SUPERMECH
Level Select	WEWILLWIN
Missiles Refilled Faster	MARSBASE
One-Shot Kills	BACKSTABBER
One-Shot Kills in Sniper Mode	SNIPER
Upside-Down Mode	FLIPSIDE

Robotech: Invasion

In the Options menu, select Extras, then enter the following:

Effect	Password
1 Hit Kill	dustyayres
Access to all levels	reclamation

Robotech: Invasion (continued)

Effect	Password
Invincibility	supercyc
Lancer's Multiplayer Skin	yllwfllw
Rand's Multiplayer Skin	kidgloves
Rook's Multiplayer Skin	blueangls
Scott Bernard's Multiplayer Skin	ltntcmdr
Unlimited Ammo	trgrhpy

Robots

Pause the game to enter these codes.

Unlockable	Code
Give Rodney a Big Head	◊, ♀, ♀, ◊, ◒, ◒, ◒, ◒
Unlimited Health	◊, ◒, ♀, ◊, ◒, ♀, ◒, ◒
Unlimited Scrap	♀, ♀, ◒, ◊, ◊, ◒, ◊, ♀

Rocky

Unlockable	Code
All Default Boxers and Arenas	Hold ℞ and press ◒, ♀, ◊, ◒, ◊, 🄻 at the Main menu.
All Default Boxers, Arenas, and Rocky Statue	Hold ℞ and press ◒, ◒, ◒, ◒, ◒, 🄻 at the Main menu.
All Default Boxers, Arenas, Rocky Statue, and Mickey	Hold ℞ and press ◊, ♀, ♀, ◒, ◒, 🄻 at the Main menu.
Double Punch Damage	Hold ℞ and press ◒, ♀, ◒, ◊, ◒, 🄻 at the Main menu.
Double Speed Boxing	Hold ℞ and press ◊, ◒, ◊, ◒, ◒, 🄻 at the Main menu.
Full Stats in Movie Mode	Hold ℞ and press ◒, ♀, ♀, ◊, ◒, 🄻 at the Main menu.
Full Stats in Tournament and Exhibition Modes	Hold ℞ and press ◒, ◊, ◊, ♀, ◒, 🄻 at the Main menu.
Win Fight in Movie Mode	Hold ℞ and press ◒, ◒, ◊, ◒, ◒, ◊, 🄻 at the Main menu. Press ⦿ + 🆅ꜰ during a fight in Movie mode to win automatically.
Fight as Mickey Goldmill	Complete Movie mode under the Champ difficulty setting.
Gold Class Knockout Tournament	Win the silver class knockout tournament.
Rocky Statue	Complete Movie mode under the Contender difficulty setting.
Silver Class Knockout Tournament	Win the bronze class knockout tournament.

Rogue Ops

To enter these codes, just pause the game. If done correctly, the screen will flash.

Unlockable	Code
Big Feet	◒, ◒, ◒, ◒, ◒, ◒, ◒, ◒, ◒
Explosive Crossbow	◒, ◒, ◒, ◒, ◒, ♀, ⦿, 🆅ꜰ, ◒, ◒, ◒, ◒
Half Damage	⊗, ⊗, ♀, ♀, ◒, ◒, ◒, ◒, ♀, ♀, ⊗
Missile Sniper	⊗, ◒, ◒, ⦿, 🆅ꜰ, ◒, ⊗, 🆅ꜰ, 🆅ꜰ, ⦿, ◒, ◒
No Bullet Damage	◒, ◒, ◒, ◒, ⊗, ♀, ♀, ⊗
One Hit Kills	♀, ◒, ◒, ◒, ◒, ◒, ℞, 🄻, ♀, ♀, ⊗
Skeleton Mode	◒, ◒, ◒, ◒, ◒, ◒, ◒, ◒, ◒
Unlimited Bullets	⊗, ♀, ⊗, ♀, ⊗, ♀, ⊗, ♀, ◒, ♀, ⊗, ♀, ⊗, ♀, ⊗, ♀
Unlimited Health	◒, ◒, ◒, ◒, ◒, ◒, ◒, ◒, ◒, ◒, ⊗, ⊗
Unlimited Spy Cam	◒, ◒, ◒, ◒, 🆅ꜰ, 🆅ꜰ, ⦿, ⦿, ⊗, ⊗, ♀, ♀
Unlimited TOC	♀, ♀, ⊗, ⊗, ◒, ◒, ◒, ◒, ⦿, 🆅ꜰ, ⦿

Side tabs: DS · GBA · PSP · PS2 · PS3 · Wii · Xbox · Xbox 360 · Index

Sidebar tabs: DS | GBA | PSP | PS2 | PS3 | Wii | Xbox | Xbox 360 | Index

Rogue Trooper

Codes

To activate these codes, enter them while in the "Extras" Menu. You can then select them from the "Cheats" menu.

Unlockable	How to Unlock
Extreme Ragdoll	⬥, ⬥, ⬥, ⬛, ⬛, ⬛, ⬥
Hippy Blood	WHT, ◀, ⓑ, ♀, (RB), ♀
Infinite Health	◀, ▶, ⬥, ♀, ⓑ, ⊗
Infinite Supplies	♀, (RB), (LB), ♀, ⓑ, (LB)
Low Gravity Ragdoll	⊗, ⊗, ⊗, ⓑ, ⓑ, ⓑ, ⬥, ♀

Unlockables

Unlockable	How to Unlock
All Weapons and Upgrades	Complete the game. Instead of starting a new game, use the Level Select cheat and start on the first level to keep everything you unlocked.
Extreme Ragdoll	Complete the game on any difficulty, start a new game, enter the Options menu, select Cheats.
Hippy Blood (Changes blood into colorful flowers)	Complete the game on any difficulty, start a new game, enter the Options menu, select Cheats.
Level Select	Successfully complete a level to unlock it at the Cheats menu.
Low Gravity Ragdoll (Enemies fly away when killed)	Complete the game on any difficulty, start a new game, enter the Options menu, select Cheats.
Massacre Mode	Complete the game on any difficulty setting to unlock the Massacre difficulty setting.

Run Like Hell

Unlockable	Code
Breaking Benjamin Video	◀, ⓑ, Ⓐ, (LT), (RT), ⬥
Baby Nick	ⓑ, Ⓐ, ⓑ, ♥, ♀, ♀
Max Assault Rifle Damage	◀, ⓑ, ▶, ⊗, ♀, ♥, ⬥, Ⓐ
Max Bolt Thrower Damage	⊗, ♥, ⓑ, WHT, ⓑ, ♥, ⊗, ⬛
Max Pulse Rifle Damage	ⓑ, ♀, ◀, Ⓐ, WHT, ⬛, ⊗, ♥
Max Repeater Rifle Damage	◀, ♥, ▶, Ⓐ, ⬥, ⊗, ♀, ⓑ
Max Rifle Damage	ⓑ, ⓑ, ⊗, ♥, ⓑ, Ⓐ, ⓑ, ⓑ
Max Shotgun Damage	Ⓐ, Ⓐ, ⓑ, ⓑ, ⬥, ♀, ◀, ▶
Refill Armor	Ⓐ, ♥, ⓑ, ⊗, ♥, Ⓐ, (LT), (RT)
Refill Health	⬥, ♀, ◀, ▶, ◀, ▶, Ⓐ, ⓑ
Show Credits	⊗, ⓑ, Ⓐ, ⬥, ♀, ♥

Rugby 06

Unlockable	Code
South Africa Training Video	Complete the World Cup with South Africa
Wallabies at Play Video	Complete the Tri-Nations Tournament and the Bledisloe Cup with Australia or New Zealand
Wallabies at Work Video	Complete the World Cup with the New Zealand All Blacks

Samurai Warriors

Unlockable	Objective
Goemon Ishikawa	Complete Okuni Story.
Keiji Maeda	Complete Kenshin Story.
Kunoichi	Complete Shingen, Hanzo Stories.
Magoichi Saika	Complete any Story.
Masamune Date	Complete any two Stories.
Nobunaga Oda	Complete Noh, Oichi, Magoichi Stories.
Noh	Complete Ranmaru Story.
Okuni	Complete Keiji Story.
Ranmaru Mari	Complete Mitsuhide Story.
Shingen Takeda	Complete Yukimura Story.

Scaler

Enter these codes while the game is paused. Select Options, then Audio, and then enter these codes.

Unlockable	Code
200,000 Klokkies	Ⓛ, Ⓛ, Ⓡ, Ⓡ, Ⓨ, Ⓧ, Ⓨ
Full Health	Ⓡ, Ⓛ, Ⓡ, Ⓛ, Ⓨ, Ⓨ, Ⓧ, Ⓧ, Ⓡ, Ⓧ
Infinite Electric Bombs	Ⓡ, Ⓡ, Ⓛ, Ⓛ, Ⓨ, Ⓨ, Ⓧ

Scarface

Enter these on the Cheats screen of the Pause menu.

Unlockable	Password	Unlockable	Password
1,000 Balls	FPATCH	Grey Suit	GREY
Antique Racer	OLDFAST	Grey Suit w/shades	GREYSH
Bacinari	666999	Increase Cop Heat	DONUT
Black Suit	BLACK	Increase Gang Heat	GOBALLS
Blue Suit	BLUE	Lightning	SHAZAAM
Blue Suit w/shades	BLUESH	Rain	RAINY
BReal "The World Is Yours" Music Track	TUNEME	Sandy Shirt	TANSHRT
Bulldozer	DOZER	Sandy Shirt w/shades	TANSH
Change Time of Day	MARTHA	Stampede	BUMMER
Decrease Cop Heat	FLYSTRT	Tiger Shirt	TIGSHRT
Decrease Gang Heat	NOBALLS	Tiger Shirt w/shades	TIGERSH
Dump Truck	DUMPER	Vehicle Repair	TBURGLR
Fill Ammo	AMMO	White Suit	WHITE
Fill Health	MEDIK	White Suit w/shades	WHITESH

Scarface: The World Is Yours

Passwords

Password	Effect
BUMMER	4x4 Stampede vehicle
S13	Babylon Club Redux
DW_fron	Cabana Cigar/Oakly drive in
FLYSTRT	CHEAT: Decrease Cop Heat
NOBALLS	CHEAT: Decrease Gang Heat

DS
GBA
PSP
PS2
PS3
Wii
Xbox
Xbox 360
Index

DS

GBA

PSP

PS2

PS3

Wii

Xbox

Xbox 360

Index

Scarface: The World Is Yours (continued)

Password	Effect
FPATCH	CHEAT: Fill Balls Meter
DONUT	CHEAT: Increase Cop Heat
GOBALLS	CHEAT: Increase Gang Heat
KILLTONY	CHEAT: Kill Tony
AMMO	CHEAT: Max Ammo
MEDIK	CHEAT: Refill Health
BLACK	Clothing: Black Suit Tony
BLUESH	Clothing: Blue Suit Tony with Sunglasses
GRAY	Clothing: Gray Suit Tony
GRAYSH	Clothing: Gray Suit Tony with Sunglasses
S12	Deliver
S07A	Freedom town redux
F_M_SHA	Havana Storehouse
HAWAII	Hawaiian shirt Tony
HAWAIIG	Hawaiian shirt Tony w/shades
F_M_SHC	Leopard Storage
F_M_SHB	Marina Storage
TUNEME	Music Track: "The World Is Yours"
S09	Nacho Contreras
S10	Nacho's Tanker
DW_fron	Ogrady's
TBURGLR	Repair Tony's Vehicle
SANDY	Sandy shirt Tony
SANDYSH	Sandy shirt Tony w/shades
F_M_SHD	Shoreline Storage
A51	The Dock Boss
S18	The End
A22	The Plantation
A23	Tranquilandia
S11	Un-Load
OLDFAST	Vehicle: Spawn Ariel MK III
666999	Vehicle: Spawn Bacinari
DOZER	Vehicle: Spawn Bulldozer
MARTHA	Weather Modifier: Change Time of Day
SHAZAAM	Weather Modifier: Toggle Lightning
RAINY	Weather Modifier: Toggle Rain
WHITE	White suit Tony
WHITESH	White suit Tony w/shades

Scooby-Doo: Night of 100 Frights

To access the following unlockables, pause the game, hold ⓛ+®, then enter code.

Unlockable	Code
All Power Ups	Ⓑ,Ⓧ,Ⓑ,Ⓧ,Ⓑ,Ⓧ,Ⓧ,Ⓧ,Ⓑ,Ⓑ,Ⓧ,Ⓑ,Ⓑ,Ⓑ
All Warp Gates	Ⓧ,Ⓧ,Ⓑ,Ⓧ,Ⓧ,Ⓑ,Ⓧ,Ⓑ,Ⓑ,Ⓑ

Scooby-Doo: Night of 100 Frights (continued)

Unlockable	Code
View Credits	⊗, ⊕, ⊕, ⊗, ⊕, ⊗

Set the clock on your Xbox to the following dates and see what happens!

Holiday	Date
Christmas	December 25
Halloween	October 31
Independence Day	July 4
New Year's	January 1
New Year's Eve	December 31
St. Patrick's Day	March 17
Valentine's Day	February 14

Secret Weapons Over Normandy

Enter the following codes at the New Game/Continue screen.

Unlockable	Code
God Mode	⬆, ⬇, ⬅, ➡, ⬅, ⬅, ➡, ➡, LT, LT, RT, RT, WHT, BLK
Infinite Ammo	⬆, ➡, ⬇, ⬅, ⬆, ⬆, ➡, ⬅, LT, RT
All Planes and Levels	▼, ▼, ▼, ⊗, ⊗, ⊗, LT, RT, BLK, BLK, WHT, WHT

Sega Soccer Slam

Enter these codes at the Title screen.

Unlockable	Code
8-Ball	RT, ➡, ⬆, ⬆, ▼, ▼
All Player Items	⬅, ⊗, ⬅, ⊗, ⬅
All Stadiums	RT, RT, ➡, ➡, ⬆, ⬆, ⬆, ⬆, ⊗, ⊗
Alpen Castle	⬆, ⬆, ⬆, ⬇, ⊗, ⊗
Beachball	RT, ➡, ➡, ⬇, ▼, ⊗
Big Head Mode	RT, LT, ⬆, ⬆, ▼, ▼
Big Hits	LT, RT, ⬆, ⬆, ⊗, ▼
Black Box	RT, ⬅, ⬅, ⬇, ⊗, ⊗
Crate	RT, ⬅, ⬇, ➡, ▼, ⊗
Eyeball	RT, ➡, ⬇, ⬆, ⊗, ⊗
Get Unlimited Turbo	LT, RT, ➡, ⬆, ⊗, ⊗
Globe	RT, ➡, ➡, ⬅, ⊗, ⊗
Jungle Canopy	LT, RT, ⬆, ⬇, ⬅, ➡, ⊗, ▼
Kid's Block	RT, ⬅, ➡, ➡, ▼, ▼
Kid's Play (star)	RT, ➡, ⬆, ⬇, ⊗, ▼
Maximum Power	LT, RT, ⬅, ➡, ▼, ▼
Old-School	RT, ➡, ⬅, ⬅, ▼, ⊗
Pacific Atoll	⬆, ⬆, ⬅, ⬅, ▼, ▼
Reactor Core	⬆, ⬅, ⬅, ➡, ⊗, ▼
Riviera Ruins	⬆, ⬇, ⬇, ➡, ▼, ⊗
Rob's Head	RT, ⬅, ⬆, ⬅, ▼, ⊗
Rusty Can	RT, ⬅, ⬆, ⬆, ▼, ▼
Tribal Oasis	LT, RT, ⬆, ⬆, ⬇, ⬇, ⊗, ⊗
Unlimited Spotlight	LT, RT, ⬇, ➡, ▼, ⊗

DS

GBA

PSP

PS2

PS3

Wii

Xbox

Xbox 360

Index

Sensible Soccer 2006

Unlockable	Code
Blue Boots for Custom-Made Players	Win the Scots Premier League
Golden Boots for Custom-Made Players	Win the European Cup
Green Boots for Custom-Made Players	Win the Portuguese 1st Div
Orange Boots for Custom-Made Players	Win the Dutch 1st Div
Red Boots for Custom-Made Players	Win the French 1st Div
Silver Boots for Custom-Made Players	Win the EURO Cup (Uefa Cup)
White Boots for Custom-Made Players	Win the Gernam Cup
All Star Ball	Win the Italian Cup
Bright Yellow Ball	Win the Spanish Cup
Classic Old Leather Football	Win the English Cup (FA Cup)
Retro Black-and-White ball	Win the German 1st Div
Tournament Ball	Win the South American Cup
Afro Hairstyle for Custom-Made Players	Win the German Shield
Aging Rocker Hairstyle for Custom-Made Players	Win the Portuguese Cup
Bouffant Hairstyle for Custom-Made Players	Win the Super Cup
Monk Spot Hairstyle for Custom-Made Players	Win the French League Cup
Mullet Hairstyle for Custom-Made Players	Win the English Shield (Community Shield)
Rasta Hairstyle for Custom-Made Players	Win the Dutch League Cup
Receding Hairstyle for Custom-Made Players	Win the Scots League Cup
String Band Hair Accessory for Custom-Made Players	Win the Italian Shield
Ponytail Hairstyle for Custom-Made Players	Win the Spanish Shield
A Snowy Pitch	Win the Italian A Div
Icy Pitch Type	Win the European Cup (Champions League)
Muddy Pitch Type	Win the English Premiership
Synthetic Turf (Astroturf) Pitch Type	Win the World Cup
The Carpet Pitch Type	Win the Spanish Premier League
Codemasters Shirt	Win the English League (Championship)
Guerrilla Shirt	Win the Portuguese 2nd Div
Home and Away Shirt Type	Win the Spanish 2nd Div
Lederhosen Shirt	Win the German 2nd Div
Showtime Shirt	Win the Dutch 2nd div
Tartan Shirt	Win the Scots League
Tropical Shirt	Win the African Cup
Tuxedo Shirt	Win the Italian B Div
"I Love Sensi" Shirt	Win the French 2nd Div
Guerrilla Shorts	Win the Portuguese League Cup
Hearts Shorts	Win the French Cup
Kinky Shorts	Win the Dutch Cup
Leather Shorts	Win the Italian League Cup
Lederhosen Shorts	Win the German League Cup

Sensible Soccer 2006 (continued)

Unlockable	Code
Tartan Shorts	Win the Scottish Cup
Tropical Shorts	Win the Asian Cup
Trunks Shorts	Win the Spanish League Cup
Union Jack Shorts	Win the English League Cup

Serious Sam

Cheat Mode: Click and hold ⬤, and press ⬤, ⬤, ⬤ at the main menu. A "Cheats" option now appears at the main menu. After enabling Cheat mode, press ⬤ during gameplay to access the Cheat menu. You can restore lives and ammunition to avoid dying.

Unlockable	Objective
Hidden Level	Destroy all the statues in the "Valley of the Kings" level.
Mental Mode (Mental fades in and out under Serious. In Mental mode, all the enemies appear and disappear.)	Complete the game in Serious mode, and start a new game.

Serious Sam 2

Enter this code while the game is paused.

Unlockable	Code
Unlock Cheat Menu	Hold ⬤, then keep pressing ⬤, ⬤, ⬤, ⬤ until the Cheat menu appears at the bottom of the screen.

Shadow Ops: Red Mercury

Enter the following codes at the Password screen.

Unlockable	Objective
All Co-op Levels	wanderlust
All Single Player Missions	happycamper

Shadow the Hedgehog

Unlockables

Unlockable	How to Unlock
2 Turrets	Get all 5 keys in Black Comet
3 Extra Lives	Get all 5 keys in The ARK
Alternate Path to a Red Terminal	Get all 5 keys in Mad Matrix
Armored Car	Get all 5 keys in Lost Impact
Black Hawk	Get all 5 keys in Glyphic Canyon
Black Volt	Get all 5 keys in Sky Troops
Extra Shooting Gallery	Get all 5 keys in Circus Park
Large GUN Cannon	Get all 5 keys in Lethal Highway
Opens Cage (triggers shortcut to the end of the level)	Get all 5 keys in The Doom
Shortcut	Get all 5 keys in Cryptic Castle
Switch That Makes Ring Trails to the End of the Level	Get all 5 keys in Cosmic Fall
Turrets	Get all 5 keys in Final Haunt
Warp Hole	Get all 5 keys in Death Ruins
Warp Hole	Get all 5 keys in Space Gadget
Warp Portal	Get all 5 keys in The Last Way
Air Saucer	Get all 5 keys in Lava Shelter

DS

GBA

PSP

PS2

PS3

Wii

Xbox

Xbox 360

Index

Shadow the Hedgehog (continued)

Unlockable	How to Unlock
Air Saucer	Get all 5 keys in Central City
An Air Saucer	Get all 5 keys in Air Fleet
Armored car	Get all 5 keys in Westopolis
Black Arm's Vehicle	Get all 5 keys in Sky Troops
Black Arm's Vehicle	Get all 5 keys in Glyphic Canyon
GUN Vehicle	Get all 5 keys in Lost Impact
Military Vehicle	Get all 5 keys in GUN Fortress
Tank Cannon	Get all 5 keys in Prison Island
Tank cannon	Get all 5 keys in Iron Jungle
Warp Hole	Get all five 5 in Digital Circuit

Library Cutscenes

Complete a combination of levels to an ending boss to unlock the cutscenes used in that combination. They appear in Library mode, each numbered and named.

Unlockable	How to Unlock
001: Punishment, Thy Name is Ruin	6 Dark missions, Dark final boss
002: Prologue to World Conquest	All Dark, Hero ending
003: The March to a Darker World	Dark, Neutral, Dark, Neutral, Hero, Dark
004: The Ultimate Ego	Dark, Dark, Dark, Dark, Normal, Hero
005: Purification via Ruination	Dark, Dark, Dark, Hero, Dark, Hero
006: Apogee of Darkness	Dark, Dark, Dark, Hero, Dark, Dark
007: True Soldier of Destruction	Dark, Dark, Dark, Hero, Normal, Dark
008: Believe in Yourself	Dark, Dark, Dark, Hero, Normal, Hero boss
009: An Android's Determination	Dark, Dark, Dark, Hero, Hero, Dark
010: For Machine, By Machine...	Dark, Dark, Dark, Hero, Hero, Hero
011: Revenge at Last	2 Dark, 1 Neutral, 2 Dark, Dark ending
012: Ego's Awakening	Dark, Dark, Normal, Dark, Dark, Hero
013: Destruction and Scorn	Dark, Dark, Normal, Dark, Normal, Dark
014: The Last Remaining Purpose	Dark, Dark, Normal, Dark, Normal, Hero
015: The Nightmare's Insulation	Dark, Dark, Normal, Normal, Dark, Dark
016: The Nightmare's Sublimation	Dark, Neutral, Neutral, Neutral, Dark, Hero
017: The Loner's Choice	2 Dark, 3 Normal, 1 Dark
018: Subjugation in Black	Dark, 5 Normal
019: Replica's Depression	2 Dark, 2 Normal, Hero, Dark
020: Machine, Machine	2 Dark, 2 Normal, 2 Hero
021: Disciple from the Darkness	2 Dark, Normal, Hero, 2 Dark
022: Beloved Clone	2 Dark, Normal, Hero, Dark, Hero
023: Revenge Upon the Doctor	2 Dark, Normal, Hero, Normal, Dark
024: The Ultimate Replica	2 Dark, Normal, Hero, Normal, Hero
025: Sanction's Demise	Dark, Dark, Normal, Hero, Hero, Dark
026: Along With My Home	Dark, Dark, Normal, Hero, Hero, Hero
027: The Cleansing of Darkness	2 Dark, Hero, 3 Dark
028: Birth of a God	Dark, Dark, Hero, Dark, Dark, Hero
029: The Last Soldier's Grim Fate	2 Dark, Normal, Hero, 2 Dark

Shadow the Hedgehog (continued)

Unlockable	How to Unlock
030: Isolation and Solitude	2 Dark, Hero, Dark, Normal, Dark
031: Archimedes and the Tortoise	2 Dark, Hero, Dark, Normal, Hero
032: Where Is My Happiness?	2 Dark, Hero, Dark, 2 Hero
033: Seduced by Taste of Blood	2 Dark, Hero, Dark, Hero, Dark
034: A Machine Made for War	2 Dark, Hero, Normal, Dark, Hero
035: Original Definition	2 Dark, Hero, Normal, Normal, Dark
036: Machine Paradise	2 Dark, Hero, 2 Normal, Hero
037: Last Will and Testament	2 Dark, Hero, 2 Normal, Dark
038: Enveloped in Solitude	2 Dark, Hero, 2 Normal, Hero
039: Parricidal Savior	2 Dark, Hero, Normal, Hero, Dark
040: Copy of a Savior	2 Dark, 2 Hero, Dark, Hero
041: Excess of Intellect	2 Dark, 2 Hero, Normal, Dark
042: Crystallization of Intellect	Dark, Dark, Hero, Hero, Normal, Hero
043: The Ultimate Confrontation	Dark, Dark, Hero, Hero, Hero, Dark
044: Miracle of Love	Dark, Neutral, Hero, Hero, Hero, Hero
045: The World's Demise	dark, hero, dark, dark, dark, dark ending
046: The Ultimate Power	Dark, Hero, Dark, Dark, Dark, Hero
047: Dyed in Lovely Darkness...	Dark, Hero, Dark, Dark, Hero, Dark
048: Vainglory or Abandonment?	Dark, Hero, Dark, Dark, Neutral, Hero ending
049: Messenger of Ruination	Dark, Hero, Dark, Normal, Dark, Dark
050: Standing at the Summit	Dark, Hero, Dark, Neutral, Dark, Hero
051: Controller from the Capsule	Dark, Hero, Dark, Normal, Normal, Dark
052: Beyond One's Own Power...	Dark, Hero. Dark, Neutral, Neutral, Good.
053: A Clone's Determination	Dark, Hero, Dark, Neutral, Hero, Dark
054: Machine Utopia	Dark, Hero, Dark, Neutral, Hero, Hero
055: A Toast to the Ruler	Dark, Hero, Dark, Hero, Dark, Dark
056: Answer from the Black Comet	Dark, Hero, Dark, Hero, Dark, Hero
057: Transcendentalism	Dark, Hero, Dark, Hero, Neutral, Dark
058: Imperialism	Dark, Hero, Dark, Hero, Neutral, Hero
059: The Weight of One's Crimes	Dark, Hero, Dark, Hero, Hero, Dark
060: Imprisonment by the Past	Dark, Hero, Dark, Hero, Hero, Hero
061: The Ultimate World Conquest	Dark, Hero, Neutral, Dark, Dark, Dark
062: Black Angel	Dark, Hero, Neutral, Dark, Dark, Hero
063: Under Darkness's Control	Dark, Hero, Neutral, Dark, Neutral, Dark
064: To Love One's Self	Dark, Hero, Neutral, Dark, Neutral, Hero
065: Revenge and Determination	Dark, Hero, Neutral, Dark, Hero, Dark
066: Birth of the Robot Empire	Dark, Hero, Neutral, Dark, Hero, Hero
067: Shadow, the Black Android	Dark, Hero, Neutral, Neutral, Dark, Dark
068: A Solitary Android	Dark, Hero, Neutral, Neutral, Dark, Hero
069: Over the Original	Dark, Hero, Neutral, Neutral, Neutral, Dark
070: Machine Sunshine	Dark, Hero, Neutral, Neutral, Neutral, Hero
071: Life Is Guilty	Dark, Hero, Neutral, Neutral, Hero, Dark
072: Fallen Angel of Despair	Dark, Hero, Neutral, Neutral, Hero, Hero

DS

GBA

PSP

PS2

PS3

Wii

Xbox

Xbox 360

Index

Shadow the Hedgehog (continued)

Unlockable	How to Unlock
073: An Eternal Rival...	Dark, Hero, Neutral, Hero, Dark, Dark
074: This Is Just the Beginning	Dark, Hero, Neutral, Hero, Dark, Hero
075: Crystal of Tragic Knowledge	Dark, Hero, Neutral, Hero, Neutral, Dark
076: Shadow's Second Death...?	Dark, Hero, Neutral, Hero, Neutral, Hero
077: The Legend of Shadow	Dark, Hero, Neutral, Hero, Hero, Dark
078: Power of Love	Dark, Hero, Neutral, Hero, Hero, Hero
079: Deep Black	Dark, Hero, Hero, Dark, Dark, Dark
080: Walk My Way	Dark, Hero, Hero, Dark, Dark, Hero
081: This Is Shadow's Way of Life	Dark, Hero, Hero, Dark, Neutral, Dark
082: A Monarch's Style	Dark, Hero, Hero, Dark, Neutral, Hero
083: In the Gap of Sadness	Dark, Hero, Hero, Dark, Hero, Dark
084: To Be Ignorant of the Past	Dark, Hero, Hero, Dark, Hero, Hero
085: At Vengeance's End	Dark, Hero, Hero, Neutral, Dark, Dark
086: Machine Boys	Dark, Hero, Hero, Neutral, Dark, Hero
087: Reborn Along with Sorrow	Dark, Hero, Hero, Neutral, Neutral, Dark
088: With a Fate of Self-Denial	Dark, Hero, Hero, Neutral, Neutral, Hero
089: I Am Shadow	Dark, Hero, Hero, Neutral, Hero, Dark
090: Shining Within Memory	Dark, Hero, Hero, Neutral, Hero, Hero
091: The Rise and Fall of the ARK	Dark, Hero, Hero, Hero, Dark, Dark
092: Requiem for a Fallen Angel	Dark, Hero, Hero, Hero, Neutral, Hero
093: Ultimate Shadow	Dark, Hero, Hero, Hero, Hero, Dark
094: For Love's Sake	Dark, Hero, Hero, Hero, Hero, Hero
095: A Heart Awoken from Darkness	Neutral, Dark, Dark, Dark, Dark, Dark
096: Destruction from Perfection	Neutral, Dark, Dark, Dark, Dark, Hero
097: Darkness' Strongest Soldier	Neutral, Dark, Dark, Dark, Neutral, Dark
098: Severing Chains	Neutral, Dark, Dark, Dark, Neutral, Hero
099: Retribution Against Humanity	Neutral, Dark, Dark, Hero, Dark, Dark
100: To Be Known as "Ultimate"	Neutral, Dark, Dark, Hero, Dark, Hero
101: Dark Warrior's Advent	Neutral, Dark, Dark, Hero, Neutral, Dark
102: Arriving at the Ego	1 Neutral, 2 Dark, 1 Hero, 1 Neutral, Hero ending
103: Determination of a Fake	Neutral, Dark, Dark, Hero, Hero, Dark
104: Path to the Machine Empire	Neutral, Dark, Dark, Hero, Hero, Hero
105: Demise Wrought by Tragedy	Normal, Dark, Normal, Dark, Dark, Dark boss
106: Turning Sorrow into Strength	Neutral, Dark, Neutral, Dark, Dark, Hero
107: The Liberated Soldier	Neutral, Dark, Neutral, Dark, Neutral, Dark
108: Stupefaction's End	Neutral, Dark, Neutral, Dark, Neutral, Hero
109: Humanity's Folly	Neutral, Dark, Neutral, Neutral, Dark, Dark
110: Surpassing All Else	Neutral, Dark, Neutral, Neutral, Dark, Hero
111: Soldier of Grief	Neutral, Dark, Neutral, Neutral, Neutral, Dark
112: Reclaimed Heart	Neutral, Dark, Neutral, Neutral, Neutral, Hero
113: Fighting Spirit of Steel	Normal, Hero, 2 Normal, 2 Dark
114: Machine Soldier Uprising	Neutral, Dark, Neutral, Neutral, Hero, Hero
115: The Devil Born from Betrayal	Neutral, Dark, Neutral, Hero, Dark, Dark

Shadow the Hedgehog (continued)

Unlockable	How to Unlock
116: Beyond the Truth of Impact	Neutral, Dark, Neutral, Hero, Dark, Hero
117: The Immortal Android	Neutral, Dark, Neutral, Hero, Neutral, Dark
118: The New, Coldhearted Empire	Neutral, Dark, Neutral, Hero, Neutral, Hero
119: Singular Atonement	Neutral, Dark, Neutral, Hero, Hero, Dark
120: Spawn of the Devil	Neutral, Dark, Neutral, Hero, Hero, Hero
121: Black Doom's Scheme	Neutral, Dark, Hero, Dark, Dark, Dark
122: Subjugating Heaven and Earth	Normal, Dark, Hero, Dark, Dark, Hero boss
123: Road of the Dark Soldier	Neutral, Dark, Hero, Dark, Neutral, Dark
124: Dark Finale	Neutral, Dark, Hero, Dark, Neutral, Hero
125: Realization While on Board	Neutral, Dark, Hero, Dark, Hero, Dark
126: Birth of a Champion	Normal, Dark, Hero, Dark, 2 Hero
127: With the Black Arms	Neutral, Dark, Hero, Neutral, Dark, Dark
128: The Road to Self-Assurance	Normal, Dark, Hero, Normal, Dark, Hero
129: The Pursuit of Dr. Eggman	Neutral, Dark, Hero, Neutral, Neutral, Dark
130: Surpassing His Creator	Neutral, Dark, Hero, Neutral, Neutral, Hero
131: ARK, Colony of Pathos	Neutral, Dark, Hero, Neutral, Hero, Dark
132: Perfection Lost to Darkness	Neutral, Dark, Hero, Neutral, Hero, Hero
133: A New Challenge	Neutral, Dark, Hero, Hero, Dark, Dark
134: The Machine's Coup d'Etat	Neutral, Dark, Hero, Hero, Dark, Hero
135: A Vow for the Victims	Neutral, Dark, Hero, Hero, Neutral, Dark
136: The Truth of Sadness	Neutral, Dark, Hero, Hero, Neutral, Hero
137: The Destined Sonic Showdown	Neutral, Dark, Hero, Hero, Hero, Dark
138: The Black Hero's Rebirth	Neutral, Dark, Hero, Hero, Hero, Hero
139: Truth, Thy Name is Vengeance	Neutral, Neutral, Dark, Dark, Dark, Dark
140: Searching for "Ultimate"	Neutral, Neutral, Dark, Dark, Dark, Hero
141: Reborn Hatred for Humanity	Neutral, Neutral, Dark, Dark, Neutral, Dark
142: A Future Taken from the Past	Neutral, Neutral, Dark, Dark, Neutral, Hero
143: The Devil's Victory Song	Neutral, Neutral, Dark, Neutral, Dark, Dark
144: One to Succeed a God	Neutral, Neutral, Dark, Neutral, Dark, Hero
145: Disappointed in Humanity	Neutral (x2), villain, neutral (x2), villain.
146: Faith Taken from Solitude	2 Normal, 1 Dark, 3 Normal, Hero final boss
147: Planted Memories	Neutral, Neutral, Dark, Neutral, Hero, Dark
148: To Unite Humanity	Neutral, Neutral, Dark, Neutral, Hero, Hero
149: Isolated Soldier Shadow	Neutral, Neutral, Dark, Hero, Dark, Dark
150: Answer Derived from Truth	Neutral, Neutral, Dark, Hero, Dark, Hero
151: A Fake's Disposition	Neutral, Neutral, Dark, Hero, Neutral, Dark
152: A New World without Betrayal	Neutral, Neutral, Dark, Hero, Neutral, Hero
153: Together with Maria...	Neutral, Neutral, Dark, Hero, Hero, Dark
154: The Tragedy's Conclusion	Neutral, Neutral, Dark, Hero, Hero, Hero
155: The Day That Hope Died	3 Neutral, 3 Dark
156: Dark Destroyer	Neutral, Neutral, Neutral, Dark, Dark, Hero
157: Diabolical Power	Neutral, Neutral, Neutral, Dark, Neutral, Dark
158: For Freedom	Neutral, Neutral, Neutral, Dark, Neutral, Hero

DS

GBA

PSP

PS2

PS3

Wii

Xbox

Xbox 360

Index

Shadow the Hedgehog (continued)

Unlockable	How to Unlock
159: At Least, Be Like Shadow...	Neutral, Neutral, Neutral, Dark, Hero, Dark
160: Seeking a Silent Paradise	Neutral, Neutral, Neutral, Dark, Hero, Hero
161: The Lion's Awakening	4 Neutral, 1 Dark, Dark ending
162: Identity	Neutral, Neutral, Neutral, Neutral, Dark, Hero
163: An Android's Rebellion	Neutral (5x), then villain
164: A New Empire's Beginning	6 Normal, Hero final boss
165: Bullets from Tears	4 Neutral, 1 Hero, Dark ending
166: Journey to Nihility	Neutral, Neutral, Neutral, Neutral, Hero, Hero
167: Shadow Surpassing Shadow	Neutral, Neutral, Neutral, Hero, Dark, Dark
168: Dr. Eggman's Miscalculation	Neutral, Neutral, Neutral, Hero, Dark, Hero
169: Along with the ARK	Neutral, Neutral, Neutral, Hero, Neutral, Dark
170: Requiem for the Heavens	Neutral, Neutral, Neutral, Hero, Neutral, Hero
171: Sonic Dethroned	Neutral, Neutral, Neutral, Hero, Hero, Dark
172: Justice Reborn	Neutral, Neutral, Neutral, Hero, Hero, Hero
173: Steel Ruler	Neutral, Neutral, Neutral, Dark, Dark, Dark
174: For Sake of Self	Neutral, Neutral, Neutral, Dark, Dark, Hero
175: Farewell to the Past	2 Neutral, 1 Hero, 1 Dark, 1 Neutral, Dark ending
176: Steel Paradise	Neutral, Neutral, Hero, Dark, Neutral, Hero
177: The Guardian with No Past	Neutral, Hero, Dark, Hero, Dark
178: The Ultimate Atonement	Neutral, Neutral, Hero, Dark, Hero, Hero
179: A Fake's Aspiration	Neutral, Neutral, Hero, Neutral, Dark, Dark
180: Machine World	Neutral, Neutral, Hero, Neutral, Dark, Hero
181: Twilight ARK	Neutral, Neutral, Hero, Neutral, Neutral, Dark
182: Compensation for a Miracle	2 Normal, 1 Hero, 3 Normal, Hero final boss
183: The Strongest Hedgehog	2 Normal, Hero, Normal, Hero, Dark
184: The Ultimate Punisher	Neutral, Neutral, Hero, Neutral, Hero, Hero
185: Voyage of Reminiscence	2 Normal, 2 Hero, 2 Dark
186: Wandering's End	2 Normal, 2 Hero, Normal, Hero
187: The Ultimate Proof	Neutral, Neutral, Hero, Hero, Hero, Dark
188: Punisher of Love	Neutral, Neutral, Hero, Hero, Hero, Hero
189: Messenger from the Darkness	Normal, Hero, 4 Dark
190: The New Ruler	Normal, Hero, 3 Dark, Hero
191: Dark Soldier	Normal, Hero, 2 Dark, Normal, Dark
192: Road of Light	Neutral, Hero, Dark, Dark, Neutral, Hero
193: The Machine-Laden Kingdom	Normal, Hero, 2 Dark, Hero, Dark
194: New Determination	Neutral, Hero, Dark, Dark, Hero, Hero
195: Birth of the Dark Soldier	Neutral, Hero, Dark, Neutral, Dark, Dark
196: A New Journey	Neutral, Hero, Dark, Neutral, Dark, Hero
197: The Android's Opposition	Neutral, Hero, Dark, Neutral, Neutral, Dark
198: Founding of the Robot Empire	Neutral, Hero, Dark, Neutral, Neutral, Hero
199: The Eternal Protector	Neutral, Hero, Dark, Neutral, Hero, Dark
200: The Sinner's Repose	Neutral, Hero, Dark, Neutral, Hero, Hero
201: A Hero's Resolution	Normal, Hero, Dark, Hero, 2 Dark

Shadow the Hedgehog (continued)

Unlockable	How to Unlock
202: The Weapon's Empire	Neutral, Hero, Dark, Hero, Dark, Hero
203: Perpetual Voyage	Neutral, Hero, Villain, Hero, Neutral, Villain
204: A Hero's Atonement	Neutral, Hero, Dark, Hero, Neutral, Hero
205: Dark Hegemony	Neutral, Hero, Dark, Hero, Hero, Dark
206: And the Dream Continues	Normal, Hero, Dark, 3 Hero
207: Fighter for Darkness	Neutral, Hero, Neutral, Dark, Dark, Dark
208: The Path I Believed In	Normal, Hero, Normal, 2 Dark, Hero
209: Determination's Daybreak	Neutral, Hero, Neutral, Dark, Neutral, Dark
210: Machine Kingdom at Dawn	Neutral, Hero, Neutral, Dark, Neutral, Hero
211: Sinful Protector	Neutral, Hero, Neutral, Dark, Hero, Dark
212: At the End of the Journey	Neutral, Hero, Neutral, Dark, Hero, Hero
213: Surmounting the Nightmare	Neutral, Hero, Neutral, Neutral, Dark, Dark
214: Dawn of the Machines	Neutral, Hero, Neutral, Neutral, Dark, Hero
215: Wandering for Eternity	Neutral, Hero, Neutral, Neutral, Neutral, Dark
216: At Vagrancy's End	1 Neutral, 1 Hero, 3 Neutral, Hero ending
217: The Summit of Power	Neutral, Hero, Neutral, Neutral, Hero, Dark
218: Under the Name of Love	Neutral, Hero, Neutral, Neutral, Hero, Hero
219: Eternally Drifting	Neutral, Hero, Neutral, Hero, Neutral, Dark
220: The Importance of Truth	Neutral, Hero, Neutral, Hero, Neutral, Hero
221: The Beginning of Judgment	Neutral, Hero, Neutral, Hero, Hero, Dark
222: The World's Guardian	Neutral, Hero, Neutral, Hero, Hero, Hero
223: Light Born from Darkness	Neutral, Hero, Hero, Dark, Dark, Dark
224: The Order of Steel	Neutral, Hero, Hero, Dark, Dark, Hero
225: Solitary Journey	Neutral, Hero, Hero, Dark, Neutral, Dark
226: The Fall Home	Normal, Dark, Dark, Hero, Normal, Hero boss
227: Sovereign of All Creation	Neutral, Hero, Hero, Dark, Hero, Dark
228: I Shall Be One to Judge	Neutral, Hero, Hero, Dark, Hero, Hero
229: Gone with the Darkness	Neutral, Hero, Hero, Hero, Neutral, Dark
230: The Ultimate Choice	Neutral, Hero, Hero, Neutral, Dark, Hero
231: I Am the Strongest!	Normal, 4 Hero, Dark
232: Justice's Awakening	Normal, 5 Hero
233: Prelude to Ruination	Hero, 5 Dark
234: A World United by Darkness	Hero, 4 Dark, Hero
235: The Pulse of Darkness	Hero, 3 Dark, Normal, Dark
236: To Just Be Myself	Hero, 3 Dark, 2 Hero
237: Punishment in Jet Black	Neutral, Dark, Dark, Neutral, Dark, Dark
238: The Ruler's First Cry	Hero, Dark, Dark, Neutral, Dark, Hero
239: Darkness' Conspiracy	Hero, Dark, Dark, Neutral, Neutral, Dark
240: The Faint Light of Tomorrow	Hero, Dark, Dark, Neutral, Neutral, Hero
241: Time of Departure	Hero, Dark, Dark, Neutral, Hero, Dark
242: Rise of the Machine Kingdom	Hero, Dark, Dark, Neutral, Hero, Hero
243: Despair's Quickening	Hero, Dark, Dark, Hero, Dark, Dark
244: The Beginning	Hero, Dark, Dark, Hero, Dark, Hero

DS

GBA

PSP

PS2

PS3

Wii

Xbox

Xbox 360

Index

Shadow the Hedgehog (continued)

Unlockable	How to Unlock
245: Setting Out in the Morning	Hero, Dark, Dark, Neutral, Dark, Dark
246: The Weapon's Dawn	Hero, Dark, Dark, Hero, Neutral, Hero
247: Pure ARK	Hero Dark, Dark, Hero, Hero, Dark
248: Making Up for It in the End	Hero, Dark, Dark, Hero, Hero, Hero
249: The Coming of the Dark Time	Hero, Dark, Neutral, Dark, Dark, Dark
250: The Throne of God	Hero, Dark, Neutral, Dark, Dark, Hero
251: God of War	Hero, Dark, Neutral, Dark, Neutral, Dark
252: Howl of Solitude	Hero, Dark, Normal, Dark, Normal, Hero
253: Howl of Solitude	Hero, Dark, Neutral, Dark, Neutral, Hero
254: Ardent View	Hero, Dark, Neutral, Dark, Hero, Hero
255: A Deal with the Devil	Hero, Dark, Neutral, Neutral, Dark, Dark
256: A Reason to Life	Hero, Dark, Neutral, Neutral, Dark, Hero
257: Induplicable Thoughts	Hero, Dark, Neutral, Neutral, Neutral, Dark
258: Steel Struck with Flame	Hero, Dark, Neutral, Neutral, Neutral, Dark
259: A Heart Bound to the ARK	Hero, Dark, Neutral, Neutral, Hero, Dark
260: Tears Shed by the Stars	Hero, Dark, Neutral, Neutral, Hero, Hero
261: Imitation Complex	Hero, Dark, Neutral, Hero, Dark, Dark
262: Steel Combat Boots	1 Hero, 1 Dark, 1 Neutral, 1 Hero, 1 Dark, Dark ending
263: Protector of the Ashen Moon	Hero, Dark, Neutral, Hero, Neutral, Dark
264: A Demon Drifting	Hero, Dark, Neutral, Hero, Neutral, Hero
265: The Ultimate Pride	Hero, Dark, Neutral, Hero, Hero, Dark
266: I Know the Will of Heaven	Hero, Dark, Neutral, Hero, Hero, Hero
267: Ego Dyed in Black	Hero, Dark, Hero, Dark, Dark, Dark
268: Isolation by Choice	Hero, Dark, Hero, Dark, Dark, Hero
269: Faith without Falsehood	Hero, Dark, Hero, Dark, Neutral, Dark
270: Machine Kingdom	Hero, Dark, Hero, Dark, Neutral, Hero
271: The Eternally Closed Door	Hero, Dark, Hero, Dark, Hero, Dark
272: The Sealed-Away ARK of Sin	Hero, Dark, Hero, Dark, Hero, Hero
273: Silver Emergence	Hero, Dark, Hero, Neutral, Dark, Dark
274: Pulsating Black Comet	Hero, Dark, Hero, Neutral, Dark, Hero
275: The Reason I Was Born	Hero, Dark, Hero, Normal, Normal, Dark
276: The Dark Part of the Galaxy	Hero, Dark, Hero, Neutral, Neutral, Hero
277: The View from Atop the World	Hero, Dark, Hero, Neutral, Hero, Dark
278: Maria's Testament	Hero, Dark, Hero, Neutral, Hero, Hero
279: A Genius Scientist's Lineage	Hero, Dark, Hero, Hero, Dark, Dark boss
280: Distorted Truth	Hero, Dark, Hero, Hero, Neutral, Hero
281: A Counterfeit Existence	Hero, Dark, Hero, Hero, Hero, Dark
282: Beloved Memories	Hero, Dark, Hero, Hero, Hero, Hero
283: Birth of a Devil	Hero, Hero, Dark, Dark, Dark, Dark
284: A Dark Myth's Beginning	Hero, Hero, Dark, Dark, Dark, Hero
285: Black Thunder	Hero, Hero, Dark, Dark, Neutral, Dark
286: The Torn-away Necklace	Hero, Hero, Dark, Dark, Neutral, Hero
287: A Soul Sheltered by Iron	Hero, Hero, Dark, Dark, Hero, Dark

Shadow the Hedgehog (continued)

Unlockable	How to Unlock
288: Steel Nation's Decree	Hero, Hero, Dark, Dark, Hero, Hero
289: Coronation of Darkness	Hero, Hero, Dark, Neutral, Dark, Dark
290: Opened Eyes	Hero, Hero, Dark, Neutral, Dark, Hero
291: The Doctor's Lie	Hero, Hero, Dark, Neutral, Neutral, Dark
292: The Uninvited Successor	Hero, Hero, Dark, Normal, Normal, Hero boss
293: The Closed Pandora's Box	Hero, Hero, Dark, Neutral, Hero, Dark
294: A Heart Bound by Sin	Hero, Hero, Dark, Neutral, Hero, Hero
295: Courage from Turning Gears	Hero, Hero, Dark, Hero, Dark, Dark
296: Fullmetal Prince	Hero, Hero, Dark, Hero, Dark, Hero
297: Time's Watchman	Hero, Hero, Dark, Hero, Neutral, Dark
298: Galaxy's Requiem	Hero, Hero, Dark, Hero, Neutral, Hero
299: Charm of the Chaos Emeralds	Hero, Hero, Dark, Hero, Hero, Dark
300: Promise of a Far-Off Day	2 Hero, Dark, 3 Hero
301: The Grim Reaper's Horn	Hero, Hero, Neutral, Hero, Dark, Dark
302: A Flame Extinguished by Fate	Hero, Hero, Neutral, Dark, Dark, Hero
303: Shouting at the Morning Sun	Hero, Hero, Neutral, Dark, Neutral, Dark
304: Iron Ambition	Hero, Hero, Neutral, Dark, Neutral, Hero
305: Sleeping on Hallowed Ground	Hero, Hero, Neutral, Dark, Hero, Dark
306: Explanation of the Truth	Hero, Hero, Neutral, Dark, Hero, Hero
307: An Android's Dream	Hero, Hero, Neutral, Neutral, Dark, Dark
308: Metallic Quickening	Hero, Hero, Neutral, Neutral, Dark, Hero
309: Funeral Procession in Space	Hero, Hero, Neutral, Neutral, Neutral, Dark
310: Lost to the Universe's Abyss	2 Hero, 3 Neutral, Hero
311: Destiny for Two	2 Hero, 2 Normal, Hero, Dark
312: The Spun Threads of Fate	Hero, Hero, Neutral, Neutral, Hero, Hero
313: Ark of the Heavens	Hero, Hero, Neutral, Hero, Neutral, Dark
314: Ghost of the ARK	Hero, Hero, Neutral, Hero, Neutral, Hero
315: A Pair of Shooting Stars	Hero, Hero, Neutral, Hero, Hero, Dark
316: The One Who Maria Entrusted	3 Hero, Neutral, then Hero all the way through.
317: A.I.'s Enlightenment	Hero, Hero, Hero, Dark, Dark, Dark
318: A Dying Empire's Cry	3 Hero, 2 Dark, Hero
319: Moon of Atonement	Hero, Hero, Hero, Dark, Neutral, Dark
320: Tear-Soaked Hometown	3 Hero, Dark, Normal, Hero
321: Sparks on the horizon	3 hero, 1 dark, 1 hero, dark ending
322: A Use for a Saved Life	Dark, Neutral, Dark, Hero, Dark
323: Coffin of Memories	Hero, Neutral, Hero, Neutral, Dark, Dark
324: The Self-Imposed Seal	4 Hero, Neutral, Hero
325: Pretense in the Mirror	5 Hero, Dark on the last one
326: A Missive from 50 Years Ago	6 Hero, Hero final boss

Unlockable Songs

Unlockable	How to Unlock
Air Fleet Theme	Play this level at least once
All Hail Shadow	Beat the pure good side

Shadow the Hedgehog (continued)

Unlockable	How to Unlock
All of Me (full version)	Beat the last story
Almost Dead	Beat any of the evil sides
Black Bull Boss Theme	Beat this boss
Black Comet Theme	Play this level at least once
Black Doom Boss Theme	Beat this boss
Central City Theme	Play this level at least once
Chosen One	Beat the slightly good side
Circus Park Theme	Play this level at least once
Cosmic Fall Theme	Play this level at least once
Cryptic Castle Theme	Play this level at least once
Death Ruins Theme	Play this level at least once
Devil Doom (I am [Full])	Beat the last story
Devil Doom Boss Theme	Play this boss and defeat him once
Diablon and Sonic Boss Theme	Beat this boss
Digital Circuit Theme	Play this level at least once
Egg Breaker Boss Theme	Beat this boss
Egg Dealer Theme	Beat Egg Dealer after going Neutral all the way
Ending	Defeat Devil Doom
Event 1 Theme	Listen to this theme at least once in Story mode
Event 2 Theme	Listen to this theme at least once in Story mode
Event 3 Theme	Listen to this theme at least once in Story mode
Event 4 Theme	Listen to this theme at least once in Story mode
Event 5 Theme	Listen to this theme at least once in Story mode
Event 6 Theme	Listen to this theme at least once in Story mode
Final Haunt Theme	Play this level at least once
Glyphic Canyon Theme	Play this level at least once
Gun Fortress Theme	Play this level at least once
Heavy Dog/Blue Falcon Remixed Boss Theme	Beat these bosses
Iron Jungle Theme	Play this level at least once
Lava Shelter Theme	Play this level at least once
Lethal Highway Theme	Play this level at least once
Mad Matrix Theme	Play this level at least once
Never Turn Back	Beat the last story
Prison Island Theme	Play this level at least once
Sky Fleet Theme	Play this level at least once
Space Gadget Theme	Play this level at least once
The Ark Theme	Play this level at least once
The Doom Theme	Play this level at least once
The Last Way	Listen to this theme at least once in Story mode
Waking Up	Beat the game after clearing Lava Shelter (neutral story)
Westopolis Theme	Play this level at least once

DS
GBA
PSP
PS2
PS3
Wii
Xbox
Xbox 360
Index

Shadow the Hedgehog (continued)

Unlockable Weapons

To make the weapons level 2, beat the story that you unlocked it from.

Unlockable	How to Unlock
Egg Vacuum	Beat the neutral story
Heal Gun	Beat the pure good side
Omochao Gun	Beat the slightly good side
Samurai Sword	Beat the pure evil side
Satellite Laser	Beat the bad side
Shadow Rifle	Beat the last story

Unlockables

Unlockable	How to Unlock
Expert Mode	Get all 71 "A" rankings
Last Story	Beat every 6th stage in Story mode, and see the Hero and Dark endings for each (10 endings in all)

Shattered Union

To enter these codes, press the start button to bring up the menu during Campaign mode. Once the menu is up, select cheat and enter your code.

Unlockable	Code
$100,000 into your Treasury	X, X, A, A, Y
Arcadia Plains	B, X, X, X, A
Arizona Territory	B, X, X, A, X
Carolinas	B, X, Y, X, A
Central Cascades	B, X, X, X, Y
Central Heartland	B, X, X, B, Y
Cumberlands	B, X, Y, X, Y
Dakotas	B, X, X, B, X
Eastern Shenandoah	B, X, Y, Y, B
Florida	B, X, Y, X, B
Great Basin	B, X, X, Y, A
Great Lakes	B, X, X, B, A
Great Plains	B, X, X, B, B
Mississippi Delta	B, X, Y, X, X
New Mexico	B, X, X, Y, B
New York	B, X, Y, Y, Y
Northern California	B, X, X, Y, X
Northern Cascades	B, X, X, X, B
Northern New England	B, X, Y, Y, A
Northern Texas	B, X, X, A, A
Ohio Valley	B, X, Y, X, X
Oklahoma Grasslands	B, X, X, A, Y
Southeastern Cascades	B, X, X, X, X
Southern California	B, X, X, Y, Y
Southern Texas	B, X, X, A, B

Shrek 2

Codes

Press Start during game play to access the Scrapbook, enter a code here.

Code	Effect
◑, ◐, ⓐ, ⓑ, ◑, ◐, ⓐ, ⓑ, ◑, ◐, ⓐ, ⓑ, ⓑ, ⓑ, ⓑ, ⓑ	1,000 Coins
◑, ◐, ⓐ, ⓑ, ◑, ◐, ⓐ, ⓑ, ◑, ◐, ⓐ, ⓑ, ⓧ, ⓑ, ⓧ, ⓑ, ⓧ, ⓑ	Bonus game (Found under "bonus")

Unlockable Bonuses

The following bonuses will be unlocked depending on the number of missions you have completed in *Shrek 2*.

Unlockable	How to Unlock
Cage Drop	59 missions completed
Cloud Maze	45 missions completed
Floating Floor	31 missions completed
Movie Stills and Crash Coliseum	70 missions completed
Ring Coliseum	21 missions completed

Shrek Super Slam

Enter these codes at the Title screen.

Unlockable	Code
Pizza One mini game	◐, ◐, ⓥ, ⓥ, ◑, ◑, ⓑ, ⓑ, ◕, ◕, ⓛⓣ, ⓡⓣ, ◑, ◑, ⓧ, ⓧ, ⓛⓣ, ⓡⓣ
Pizza Two mini game	◕, ◕, ◑, ⓑ, ◐, ◐, ◑, ⓧ, ⓛⓣ, ⓛⓣ
Pizza Three mini game	ⓑ, ⓑ, ⓧ, ⓧ, ⓡⓣ, ⓡⓣ, ◑, ◑, ⓛⓣ, ⓛⓣ
Slammageddon	◐, ◐, ◕, ◕, ◑, ◑, ◑, ◑, ⓥ, ⓧ, ⓧ, ⓛⓣ, ⓡⓣ
Super Speed Modifier	ⓛⓣ, ⓛⓣ, ⓡⓣ, ⓡⓣ, ⓛⓣ, ⓡⓣ, ⓛⓣ, ⓡⓣ, ⓧ, ⓑ, ⓥ, ⓥ
Unlock All Challenges	ⓥ, ⓥ, ⓥ, ⓑ, ⓑ, ⓑ, ⓥ, ⓧ, ⓑ, ⓧ, ⓧ, ⓧ, ◐, ◕, ◑, ◕, ⓛⓣ, ⓡⓣ

Sid Meier's Pirates

Enter these as names for the desired effects.

Unlockable	Password
Begin game with the best ship in the game and a full crew	D.Gackey
Bonus Frag	Snappy Dresser
Dueling Invincibility	Dragon Ma
Food Never Dwindles	Sweet Tooth
Invincibility in Ship Battles	Bloody Bones Baz
The Governor's daughters always love you no matter how badly you dance	Scooter
Your crew is always at highest possible morale	B.Caudizzle
Your fleet sails twice as fast	Sprinkler

Silent Hill 2

Completion Bonuses: Complete the game. Start another game and enter the Extra Options menu to access new features. You can set a "Bullet Adjust" option, allowing the normal amount of ammunition found at a location to double or triple. You can toggle a "Noise Effect" option. Another new option you can toggle allows you to view scenes without distortion.

Silent Hill 2 (continued)

Unlockable	Objective
Additional Riddle Difficulty	Complete the game under the Easy, Normal, and Hard riddle difficulty settings. Select the Hard riddle difficulty again, and begin a new game with a new combination of riddles.
Book of Lost Memories	Complete the game. Start a new game and look for the newspaper stand near the Texxon Gas Station. Find the Book of Lost Memories inside.
Book of the Crimson Ceremony	Find this book in the reading room on the second floor of the Nightmare hotel.
Chainsaw	Complete the game under the Normal difficulty and Normal riddle difficulty settings. Start a new game to find the Chainsaw among logs before the cemetery.
Dog Key	Complete the game with the "Rebirth" ending. Start a new game and a doghouse appears near Jack's Inn and the gas station. Look inside the doghouse to find the Dog Key. Use it to open the observation room in the Nightmare hotel.
Hyper Spray	Complete the game two times. Start a new game to find the Hyper Spray on the south side of the motor home.
Introduction FMV Sequence Audio	If you wait at the title screen for a while, the introduction FMV sequence begins. In some scenes, there will be no audio. Complete the game one time to restore the audio to those.
Joke Ending	To view the sixth secret joke ending, use the Blue Gem at Alternate Brook Haven Hospital's garden, the dock before getting on the boat, and room 312 in the Lakeview Hotel. Once you use it in room 312, the game ends and the joke ending appears.
Obsidian Goblet	Complete the game. Start a new game, and enter the Historical Society building. Find the Obsidian Goblet on a shelf.
Reveal Signs	Unlock all five endings, and start a new game. All signs are now revealed.
White Chrism	Complete the game. Start a new game to find the White Chrism vial in the kitchen of apartment 105 in Blue Creek Apartments.

Silent Hill 4: The Room

Alternate Endings

Unlockable	How to Unlock
21 Sacraments	Disregard both Eileen and your room
Eileen's Death	Disregard Eileen but take care of your room
Escape	Look after Eileen and your room
Mother	Look after Eileen but not your room

Misc. Unlockables

Unlockable	How to Unlock
10-Star Rating	Finish the game on Hard difficulty before 120 mins (2 hours), kill 150 or more monsters, collect all notes/memos (52/52), and don't save. The ending doesn't matter.
Alternate Cynthia Costume	Unlock all 4 endings and Eileen's alternate costume on 1 game save. Start a new game and select Eileen's alternate costume. Cynthia will wear her alternate costume.
Brand New Fear Mode	Complete the game on any difficulty setting. Save the game after the credits complete to unlock the "Brand New Fear" option.
Eileen Nurse Outfit	Finish the game once and save. Start a new game using that save and go to room 302 to find the outfit. It can be picked up on the 3rd time through

DS
GBA
PSP
PS2
PS3
Wii
Xbox
Xbox 360
Index

DS

GBA

PSP

PS2

PS3

Wii

Xbox

Xbox 360

Index

Silent Hill 4: The Room (continued)

Unlockable	How to Unlock
Locate Chainsaw	After finishing the game once, save and then reload the save. Go to Forest World and look for the cut tree and the chainsaw will be there.
Submachine Gun	Complete the game with a rank of at least 9 big stars. Start a game in "Brand New Fear" mode and look in Room 202 in the Apartment World.
Unlock All Weapons Mode	Finish One Weapon mode.
Unlock One Weapon Mode	Get 10 stars using Hard mode.

The Simpsons Hit and Run

Pause the game and enter the Option menu, then hold ⓛ+® and enter the code.

Unlockable	Code
All cars for new game (must be typed in with complete save loaded)	Ⓐ, Ⓑ, Ⓐ, Ⓑ
One hit kills (all cars will explode if you ram them or if they ram you, including cops and bosses)	Ⓨ, Ⓨ, Ⓧ, Ⓧ
Press your horn for high flying jumps	Ⓧ, Ⓧ, Ⓧ, Ⓨ
Secret cars replaced by red box racer	Ⓑ, Ⓑ, Ⓨ, Ⓧ
Show grid view	Ⓑ, Ⓐ, Ⓑ, Ⓨ
Show speedometer	Ⓨ, Ⓨ, Ⓑ, Ⓧ
Super fast Cars	Ⓧ, Ⓧ, Ⓧ, Ⓧ
Your car is invincible	Ⓨ, Ⓐ, Ⓨ, Ⓐ
Your cars are 5 times faster than normal	Ⓨ, Ⓨ, Ⓨ, Ⓨ

The Simpsons Road Rage

Codes

In the Options menu, hold both triggers and press the following buttons:

Code	Effect
Ⓧ, Ⓧ, Ⓧ, Ⓧ	2D Cardboard People
Ⓨ, Ⓨ, Ⓨ, Ⓨ	Cars in Slow Motion
Ⓑ, Ⓑ, Ⓧ, Ⓑ	Christmas Apu
Ⓑ, Ⓑ, Ⓐ, Ⓐ	Debug Mode
Ⓐ, Ⓐ, Ⓐ, Ⓐ	Drive at Night
Ⓑ, Ⓑ, Ⓨ, Ⓐ	Drive Nuclear Bus
Ⓑ, Ⓑ, Ⓧ, Ⓧ	Drive Red Soapbox Car
Ⓑ, Ⓑ, Ⓧ, Ⓐ	Halloween Bart
Ⓑ, Ⓑ, Ⓧ, Ⓨ	Happy New Year Krusty!
Ⓑ, Ⓑ, Ⓧ, Ⓧ	Marge's Thanksgiving Car
Ⓨ, Ⓨ, Ⓨ, Ⓨ	More Camera Views
Ⓧ, Ⓧ, Ⓧ, Ⓨ	Overhead View
Ⓑ, Ⓑ, Ⓨ, Ⓨ	Play as Smithers
Ⓧ, Ⓑ, Ⓨ, Ⓐ	Stop Watch Mode

Unlockable	How to Unlock
New Car for Homer	Play through and complete all missions and you get "The Car Built for Homer" from the episode where Danny DeVito was Homer's brother and Homer designed a car for his company.
Play as Frankenstein Bart	Set the system date/clock to Halloween (October 31st).

The Simpsons Road Rage (continued)

Play as Pilgrim Marge	Set the system date/clock to Thanksgiving (3rd Thursday of November).
Play as a Santa Apu	Set the system date/clock to Christmas (December 25th).
Play as Tuxedo Krusty	Set the system date/clock to New Year's Day (January 1st).
Skip Missions	Skip every mission (play the mission by trying it 5 times) and then beat the 10th mission. Then you will have beaten every mission and get the car built for Homer.

The Sims

Press both ⓛ + ⓡ to call up a cheat menu, then enter the codes below.

Unlockable	Code
2 Player mode	MIDAS
First person View (press Black)	FISH EYE
Free Items	FREEALL
Party Motel in 2 Player Mode	PARTY M
Play the Sims Mode	SIMS

The Sims 2

Codes

Enter these codes in game. Most codes require the player to enter the master code (ⓛⒷ, ⓇⒷ, ⚫, ⚫, ⚫) first.

Code	Effect
ⓛⒷ, ⓇⒷ, ⚫, ⚫, ⚫	Master code
⚫, ⚫, ⚫, ⚫, 🎮	Max all motives
⚫, ⚫, ⚫, ⚫, ⚫, ⚫, ⚫, ⚫	Remove messages
⚫, ⚫, ⚫, 🎮, ⚫	Change any Sim's skill
ⓇⒷ, ⓛⒷ, 🎮, ⚫, ⚫	Give the household §10,000
⚫, ⚫, ⓛⒷ, ⚫, ⚫	Go six hours forward in time
⚫, 🎮, ⚫, ⚫, ⚫	Unlock all Story mode locations
⚫, 🎮, ⚫, ⚫, ⚫	Unlock all clothes
🎮, ⚫, ⚫, ⚫, ⚫	Unlock all objects
🎮, ⚫, ⚫, ⚫, ⚫, ⚫	Unlock all recipes
⚫, 🎮, ⚫, ⚫, ⚫, ⚫	Unlocks all lots/locations

Unlock Locations

To Unlock New Locations, complete all of your Gold and Platinum goals. Do not worry too much with the Green ones. You also need to complete your roommates' Gold and Platinum goal.

Unlockable	How to Unlock
Alien Crash Site	Help XY-XY. Fulfill all Aspirations and become friends with Jonas.
Bio Dome	Have Noelle complete one full career.
Cliffside Retreat	Fulfill all of Isabella's Wants, but it might take a while for her to make a sandwich.
HMS Armore	Fulfill all of Betty's Wants until she is in a Platinum mood. Then marry Captain Nelson.
Jugen House	Fulfill Toothless Joe's Aspirations until your Sim gets "Visit New Location" as an Aspiration. Go back to Tranquility Falls, and help Chantel
Mesa Gallery	Help Hector complete his goals at HMS Amore.

DS   GBA   PSP   PS2   PS3   Wii   Xbox   Xbox 360   Index

DS

GBA

PSP

PS2

PS3

Wii

Xbox

Xbox 360

Index

The Sims 2 (continued)

Orbit Room	Become friends with Red S. and serve him food. Move back to Sunset Canyon and make Red S. and Helga get married and get Red S. in Platinum mood.
Rockwall Acres	Follow instructions on what it says
Shoreline Trails	Buy a foosball table and defeat Torin
Sunset Canyon	Bring Helga, Billy, and Sheila back to life, make a kitchen, clean up mess, buy them beds, and build bathroom
Tranquility Falls	Fulfill Larry's Want and put him in Platinum mood, same with Chantel.

The Sims Bustin' Out

Enter the following codes any time during the game (when paused).

Unlockable	Code
The Gnome	®, ⒧, ♥, ⒝, ◄ (This must be entered first before any of the other codes.)

Unlockable	Code
All Locations	⒝, ♥, ®, ⒧, ♥
All Objects	⒝, ♠, ♥, ♥, ®
All Socials	⒧, ®, ♠, ♥, ⒝
Money	⒧, ⒝, ►, ✕, ◄

Smashing Drive

Unlockable Shift	Objective
Dusk and Wired Shift	Complete the Night Owl shift.
Night Owl Shift	Complete the Rush Hour shift.
Rush Hour Shift	Complete the Early Bird shift.

Soldier of Fortune II: Double Helix

While playing, click in the left analog stick, then enter these codes.

Unlockable	Code
All Weapons	✕, ♥, ♠, ⒝
God Mode	⒝, ♠, ♥, ✕
Level select	⒝, ⒝, ♠, ⒲
Unlimited Ammo	⒝, ♠, ♥, ⒲

Sonic Heroes

Unlockable	Objective
2 Player Team Battle Mode	Collect 20 Emblems.
2 Player Special Stage Mode	Collect 40 Emblems.
2 Player Ring Race Mode	Collect 60 Emblems.
2 Player Bobsled Race Mode	Collect 80 Emblems.
2 Player Quick Race Mode	Collect 100 Emblems.
2 Player Expert Race Mode	Collect 120 Emblems.
Last Song and Movie	Complete the Last Story.
Last Story Mode	Complete Story Mode with all four teams and all Choas Emeralds.
Metal Characters	Press ♠+♥ after you chose a level for 2 players.
Super Hard Mode	Collect 141 Emblems and have all A ranks.

Team Chaotix Song and Movie	Complete Story Mode with Team Chaotix.
Team Dark Song and Movie	Complete Story Mode with Team Dark.
Team Rose Song and Movie	Complete Story Mode with Team Rose.
Team Sonic Movie and Song	Complete Story Mode with Team Sonic.

Soul Calibur II

Unlockable	Objective
Assassin	Beat Stage 2 of Subchapter 3 in Weapon Master Mode (Extra)
Astaroth—Soul Edge	Beat Stage 3 of Extra Chapter 1 in Weapon Master Mode
Berserker	Beat Stage 1 of Subchapter 1 in Weapon Master Mode (Extra)
Cassandra—Soul Edge	Beat Stage 4 of Sub chapter 2 in Weapon Master Mode
Cassandra—Soul Edge	Beat Stage 5 of Subchapter 4 in Weapon Master Mode
Cervantes	Beat Stage 4 of Chapter 3 in Weapon Master Mode
Cervantes—Acheron	Beat Stage 5 of Chapter 3 in Weapon Master Mode
Cervantes— Imitation Sword	Beat Stage 5 of Subchapter 4 in Weapon Master Mode
Charade	Beat Stage 1 of Chapter 3 in Weapon Master Mode
Egyptian Crypt	Beat Stage 5 of Chapter 8 in Weapon Master Mode
Extra Arcade Mode	Either attempt Arcade Mode 10 times, or beat it once
Extra Practice Mode	Beat Stage 1 of Chapter 1 in Weapon Master Mode
Extra Survival Mode— Death Match	Beat Stage 3 of Subchapter 3 in Weapon Master Mode
Extra Survival Mode— No Recovery	Beat Stage 2 of Extra Chapter 2 in Weapon Master Mode
Extra Survival Mode— Standard	Beat Stage 5 of Chapter 6 in Weapon Master Mode
Extra Team Battle Mode	Beat Stage 1 of Subchapter 1 in Weapon Master Mode
Extra Time Attack— Extreme	Beat Stage 1 of Extra Chapter 1 in Weapon Master Mode
Extra Time Attack Mode—Alternative	Beat Stage 4 of Chapter 9 in Weapon Master Mode
Extra Time Attack Mode—Standard	Beat Stage 1 of Chapter 5 in Weapon Master Mode
Extra VS Battle Mode	Either attempt Extra Arcade Mode 5 times, or beat it once
Extra VS Team Battle Mode	Either attempt Extra VS Battle Mode 5 times, or beat it once
Hwangseo Palace/ Phoenix Court	Beat Stage 2 of Chapter 7 in Weapon Master Mode
Ivy—Prototype Ivy Blade	Beat Stage 2 of Extra Chapter 2 in Weapon Master Mode
Kilik—Bamboo Staff	Beat Stage 2 of Extra Chapter 1 in Weapon Master Mode
Labyrinth	Beat Stage 6 of Chapter 6 in Weapon Master Mode
Lakeside Coliseum	Beat Stage 3 of Chapter 1 in Weapon Master Mode
Lizardman	Beat All Stages of Subchapter 2 in Weapon Master Mode (Extra)
Maxi—Fuzoroi	Beat Stage 5 of Chapter 3 in Weapon Master Mode
Maxi—Termite Snack	Beat Stage 3 of Subchapter 4 in Weapon Master Mode
Mitsurugi—Soul Edge	Beat Stage 5 of Subchapter 4 in Weapon Master Mode
Mitsurugi—Souvenir Gift	Beat Stage 3 of Subchapter 3 in Weapon Master Mode
Money Pit	Beat Stage 1 of Chapter 4 in Weapon Master Mode
Necrid—Ethereal Edge	Beat Stage 5 of Chapter 8 in Weapon Master Mode

Soul Calibur II (continued)

Unlockable	Objective
Necrid—Soul Edge	Beat Stage 3 of Extra Chapter 2 in Weapon Master Mode
Nightmare—Galley Oar	Beat Stage 3 of Extra Chapter 1 in Weapon Master Mode
Nightmare—Soul Edge	Beat Stage 3 of Chapter 7 in Weapon Master Mode
Raphael—Schweizer	Beat Stage 4 of Chapter 3 in Weapon Master Mode
Seung Mina	Beat Stage 3 of Chapter 6 in Weapon Master Mode
Seung Mina—Ambassador	Beat Stage 2 of Chapter 10 in Weapon Master Mode
Seung Mina—Halberd	Beat Stage 6 of Chapter 6 in Weapon Master Mode
Sophitia	Beat Stage 5 of Chapter 4 in Weapon Master Mode
Sophitia—Memento	Beat Stage 3 of Extra Chapter 2 in Weapon Master Mode
Sophitia—Synval	Beat Stage 2 of Chapter 10 in Weapon Master Mode
Taki—Soul Edge	Beat Stage 3 of Subchapter 2 in Weapon Master Mode
Talim—Double Crescent Blade	Beat Stage 2 of Chapter 3 in Weapon Master Mode
Voldo—Soul Edge	Beat Stage 2 of Subchapter 2 in Weapon Master Mode
Xianghua—Soul Calibur	Beat Stage 2 of Chapter 5 in Weapon Master Mode
Xianghua—Soul Edge	Beat Stage 1 of Subchapter 2 in Weapon Master Mode
Yoshimitsu	Beat Stage 3 of Chapter 2 in Weapon Master Mode

Spawn: Armageddon

Enter the following codes any time during the game (when paused).

Unlockable	Code
All Comics	◊,♀,◁,▷,◁,▷,◁,◊
All Weapons	◊,♀,◁,▷,◁,◁,◁,▷
Infinite Health and Necroplasm	◊,♀,◁,▷,▷,◁,♀,◊
Infinite Ammo	◊,♀,◁,▷,◊,◁,♀,▷

Spider-Man

Enter the following codes at the Specials menu. Listen for the laugh to know you entered it correctly. Repeat code entry to return to normal.

Unlockable	Code
All Fighting Controls	KOALA
Big Head and Feet for Spider-Man	GOESTOYOURHEAD
Bonus Training Levels	HEADEXPLODY
Enemies Have Big Heads	JOELSPEANUTS
First-Person View	UNDERTHEMASK
Goblin-Style Costume	FREAKOUT
Level Select	IMIARMAS
Level Skip	ROMITAS (Pause gameplay and select the "Next Level" option to advance to the next level.)
Master Code	ARACHNID (All levels in the Level Warp option, all Gallery options (movie viewer/production art), and combo moves are unlocked.)
Matrix-Style Attacks	DODGETHIS
Play as a Police Officer	REALHERO
Play as a Scientist	SERUM
Play as Captain Stacey (Helicopter Pilot)	CAPTAINSTACEY

Spider-Man (continued)

Unlockable	Code
Play as Mary Jane	GIRLNEXTDOOR
Play as Shocker's Thug	THUGSRUS
Play as Skulls Gang Thug	KNUCKLES
Play as the Shocker	HERMANSCHULTZ
Play as Uncle Ben's Killer	STICKYRICE
Small Spider-Man	SPIDERBYTE
Unlimited Green Goblin Glider Power	CHILLOUT
Unlimited Webbing	ORGANICWEBBING

Unlockable	Code
Alternate Green Goblin Costume	If you're using the Alex Ross Spider-Man, play any level with the Green Goblin in it and he'll have an alternate costume that more closely resembles his classic costume
Green Goblin FMV Sequence	Complete the game under the hero or greater difficulty setting.
Pinhead Bowling Mini-Game	Accumulate 10,000 points during gameplay to unlock the Pinhead bowling mini-game in the Training menu.
Play as Alex Ross	Complete the game under the normal or higher difficulty setting to unlock the Alex Ross costume in the Specials menu.
Play as Peter Parker	Complete the game under the easy or higher difficulty setting to unlock the Peter Parker costume in the Specials menu.
Play as Wrestler	Complete the game under the easy or higher difficulty setting to unlock the wrestler costume in the Specials menu. To unlock this easily, first unlock the Unlimited Webbing cheat. When you get to the ring, zip to the top and keep on shooting Spidey Bombs.
Shocker FMV Sequence	Accumulate 30,000 points during gameplay to unlock a Shocker FMV sequence in the CG menu.
Unlimited Webbing	Accumulate 50,000 points during gameplay.
Vulture FMV Sequence	Accumulate 20,000 points during gameplay to unlock a Vulture FMV sequence in the CG menu.

TIP

Play as Green Goblin!

Complete the game under the hero or superhero difficulty setting to unlock the Green Goblin Costume option at the Specials menu. Select that option to play as Harry Osborn in the Green Goblin costume, including his weapons, in an alternate storyline in which he tries to correct the Osborn family's reputation. To unlock this easily, start a new game under the hero or superhero difficulty setting. At the first level, pause gameplay, then quit to the main menu. Enable the ARACHNID code, then go to the Level Warp option. Choose the Conclusion level (that features Norman revealing himself to Spider-Man followed by the glider sequence), then exit. This marks the game as completed under the selected difficulty setting. The Green Goblin costume option will be unlocked at the Secret Store screen.

Spider-Man 2

Type in HCRAYERT as a name to gain upgrades, a lot of Hero Points, and 44% game completion.

DS

GBA

PSP

PS2

PS3

Wii

Xbox

Xbox 360

Index

Left margin tabs: DS, GBA, PSP, PS2, PS3, Wii, Xbox, Xbox 360, Index

Splashdown

On the option screen, hold down (RT). Then press ◊, ◊, ♀, ♀, ◁, ▷, ◁, ▷, ⊗, ⊜, ⊗, ⊜. Once this is done, you can enter these passwords.

Unlockable	Password
All Stages	Passport
Cannot be knocked off your SeaDoo	TopBird
Expert AI	AllOutAI
Max Out Performance Meter	PMeterGo
Race against an F-18 Jet in Time Trials	F18
Race against the Ghost of the currently selected Character	SEADOO
Race against a UFO in Time Trials	IBelieve
Unlock all characters	AllChar
Unlock all endings	Festival
Unlock hard tracks with normal AI difficulty	Hobble
Unlock all wetsuits	LaPinata

SpongeBob SquarePants Battle for Bikini Bottom

Pause the game and hold (LT)+(RT), then input the code. You must do this quickly. You'll hear a sound if you entered the code correctly.

Unlockable	Code
10 Spatulas	⊗, ⊙, ⊙, ⊗, ⊗, ⊙, ⊙, ⊗
1000 Shiny Objects	⊙, ⊗, ⊗, ⊙, ⊙, ⊗, ⊗, ⊙
All monsters in Monster Gallery (Police Station)	⊗, ⊙, ⊗, ⊙, ⊗, ⊙, ⊗, ⊙
Big Plankton	⊙, ⊙, ⊙, ⊙, ⊙, ⊙, ⊙, ⊙, ⊗, ⊗, ⊗
Bubble Bowl Power Up	⊗, ⊗, ⊙, ⊗, ⊗, ⊙, ⊗, ⊙
Cruise Bubble Bowl Power Up	⊙, ⊗, ⊙, ⊙, ⊙, ⊙, ⊗, ⊗
Cruise Bubble has Cruise Control	⊗, ⊗, ⊙, ⊙, ⊙, ⊙, ⊗, ⊗, ⊙, ⊙
Invert Camera Controls (Left/Right)	⊙, ⊙, ⊗, ⊗, ⊙, ⊗, ⊙, ⊙
Invert Camera Controls (Up/Down)	⊙, ⊗, ⊗, ⊗, ⊗, ⊙, ⊗, ⊙
Restore health	⊗, ⊗, ⊗, ⊗, ⊗, ⊙, ⊗, ⊙, ⊙, ⊙
Small Patrick, Mr. Crab, Squidword, Squirrel Girl in Astronaut Costume	⊙, ⊙, ⊗, ⊙, ⊙, ⊗, ⊙, ⊙, ⊙, ⊙
Small Towns People	⊙, ⊙, ⊙, ⊙, ⊙, ⊙, ⊙, ⊗, ⊗, ⊗
Sponge Bob No Pants	⊗, ⊗, ⊙, ⊗, ⊙, ⊙, ⊗, ⊙, ⊗, ⊗
Townspeople are Thieves (Shiny Objects)	⊙, ⊙, ⊙, ⊙, ⊙, ⊙, ⊗, ⊙, ⊙, ⊗, ⊗
Unlock Art Gallery (Theatre)	⊙, ⊗, ⊙, ⊗, ⊗, ⊙, ⊗, ⊙

SpongeBob SquarePants: Lights, Camera, Pants!

Passwords

Password	Effect
893634	Hook, Line and Cheddar
486739	Silver Story mode challenges

Action Figures

Unlockable	How to Unlock
1. Patrick Star	Get a 20-Patty Combo on Flippin' Out in Bronze Story mode

SpongeBob SquarePants: Lights, Camera, Pants! (continued)

Password	Effect
2. Mr. Eugene Krabs	Hit no more than 10 Nets on Inflatable Pants in Bronze Story mode
3. Sandy Cheeks	Get a Bumper Bonus on Goo-Ladiators in Bronze Story mode
4. SpongeBob SquarePants	Make perfect repetition more than 5 times on Beats Me in Bronze Story mode
5. Squidward Tentacles	Never have a breakdown on Machine Meltdown in Bronze Story mode
6. SpongeBob SquarePants	Get a 5-Jelly Combo on Jellyfish Jamboree in Bronze Story mode
7. Patrick Star	Release 3 Prisoners at the same time on Breakin' Out in Bronze Story mode
8. Sandy Cheeks	Get "Blisterin'" at least once on Blisterin' Barnacles in Bronze Story mode
9. Patrick Star	Get a Perfect Round on Flippin' Out in Silver Story mode
10. Mr. Eugene Krabs	Hit no more than 3 obstacles on Inflatable Pants in Silver Story mode
11. Sandy Cheeks	Get a 5-In-A-Row Bonus on Goo-Ladiators in Silver Story Mode
12. Sheldon Plankton	Be in the lead by the end of the first Up-Tempo on Beats Me in Silver Story mode
13. SpongeBob SquarePants	Never fall under 25% efficiency on Machine Meltdown in Silver Story mode
14. Man Ray	Get two 5-Jelly Combos on Jellyfish Jamboree in Silver Story mode
15. Barnacleboy	Get caught by the searchlights no more than 2 times on Breakin' Out in Silver Story mode
16. The Dirty Bubble	Scrape off the Big Barnacle before the other team on Blisterin' Barnacles in Silver Story mode
17. Mermaidman	Get an Atomic Wedgie on Hook, Line, and Cheddar in Silver Story mode
18. Bubble Bass	Catch no more than 3 Chum Bucket patties on Flippin' Out in Gold Story mode
19. Larry the Lobster	Make it first across 10 Nets on Inflatable Pants in Gold Story mode
20. Mrs. Puff	Get two "5-In-A-Row"s on Goo-Ladiators in Gold Story mode
21. Squilliam	Never make a mistake on Beats Me in Gold Story mode
22. Karen the Computer	Make more than 160 Chum Bucket Meals on Machine Meltdown in Gold Story mode
23. Kevin C. Cucumber	Get more than three 5-Jelly Combos on Jellyfish Jamboree in Gold Story mode
24. Don the Whale	Get caught by the searchlights no more than once on Breakin' Out in Gold Story mode
25. Cannonball Jenkins	Get Blisterin' more than 3 times on Blisterin' Barnacles in Gold Story mode
26. Gill Hammerstein	Get 3 Double Wedgies on Hook, Line, and Cheddar in Gold Story mode

DS
GBA
PSP
PS2
PS3
Wii
Xbox
Xbox 360
Index

DS
GBA
PSP
PS2
PS3
Wii
Xbox
Xbox 360
Index

SpongeBob SquarePants: Lights, Camera, Pants! (continued)

Artwork

Unlockable	How to Unlock
1. The Birth of SpongeBob	Get 1,000 Points or more on The Bouncers in Bronze Story mode
2. Abstract-Bob	Get 1,500 Points or more on Surf Resc-Goo in Bronze Story mode
3. Beware the Hooks	Get 1,000 Points or more on Pedal of Honor in Bronze Story mode
4. Cubist Bob	Get 500 Points or more on Rock Bottom in Bronze Story mode
5. The Chum Bucket! of Dr. P	Get 4,000 Points or more on Surface Tension in Bronze Story mode
6. Spatula!	Get 250 Points or more on Jellyfish Swish in Bronze Story mode
7. Spondrian	Get 800 Points or more on Rubble Rabble in Bronze Story mode
8. Creature with 6 Tentacles	Get 500 Points or more on Flingin' and Swingin' in Bronze Story mode
9. Sponge Van Gogh	Get 250 Points or more on Mother of Pearl in Bronze Story mode
10. Bacon Bob	Get 1,200 Points or more on The Bouncers in Silver Story mode
11. Bat-Sponge	Get 2,000 Points or more on Surf Resc-Goo in Silver Story mode
12. Rock Bottom	Get 1,300 Points or more on Pedal of Honor in Silver Story mode
13. Spongebrandt	Get 850 Points or more on Rock Bottom in Silver Story mode
14. Patrick's Secret Box	Get 5,000 Points or more on Surface Tension in Silver Story mode
15. Orb of Confusion	Get 300 Points or more on Jellyfish Swish in Silver Story mode
16. Rock Sponge Face	Get 950 Points or more on Rubble Rabble in Silver Story mode
17. Sunday in Jellyfish Fields	Get 800 Points or more on Flingin' & Swingin' in Silver Story mode
18. I Was a Teenage Gary	Get 300 Points or more on Mother of Pearl in Silver Story mode
19. Robot Chef	Get 1,500 Points or more on The Bouncers in Gold Story mode
20. The Flying Dutchman	Get 3,000 Points or more on Surf Resc-Goo in Gold Story mode
21. Vitruvian Sponge	Get 2,000 Points or more on Pedal of Honor in Gold Story mode
22. Gothic Sponge	Get 1,000 Points or more on Rock Bottom in Gold Story mode
23. PicassoBob	Get 5,000 Points or more on Surface Tension in Gold Story mode
24. The Hash-Slinging Slasher	Get 200 Points or more on Jellyfish Swish in Gold Story mode
25. The Chaperone	Get 1,000 Points or more on Rubble Rabble in Gold Story mode
26. She Came from Texas!	Get 900 Points or more on Flingin' and Swingin' in Gold Story mode
27. The Persistence of SpongeBob	Get 350 Points or more on Mother of Pearl in Gold Story mode

Mermaidman Movies

Unlockable	How to Unlock
Bronze Mermaidman Movie	Successfully beat the Bronze Story mode
Gold Mermaidman Movie	Successfully beat the Gold Story mode
Make-Your-Own-Movie	Successfully beat the Gold Story mode
Silver Mermaidman Movie	Successfully beat the Silver Story mode

SpongeBob SquarePants: Lights, Camera, Pants! (continued)

Unlockable Auditions

Unlockable	How to Unlock
Hook, Line, and Cheddar	Complete Silver Story mode
Loot Scootin'	Complete Gold Story mode with all action figures unlocked
Mother of Pearl	Complete Bronze Story mode
Tethered and Weathered	Complete Gold Story mode

Unlockable story modes

Unlockable	How to Unlock
Gold Story Mode	Complete Silver Story mode
Silver Story Mode	Complete Bronze Story mode

SpongeBob SquarePants: The Movie

Pause the game, hold ⓛ+ⓡ to enter the following codes.

Unlockable	Code
All Health	⍐,⍐,⍐,⍐,⍇,⍐,⍐,⍐
All Moves	⍇,⍇,⍐,⍐,⍐,⍐,⍐,⍇
All Moves to Macho	⍇,⍇,⍐,⍐,⍐,⍐,⍐,⍐
All Tasks	⍐,⍇,⍐,⍐,⍐,⍐,⍐,⍇

Spy Hunter

Cheat Grid: Cheats are unlocked by completing all mission objectives (not just the primary objectives) within a set amount of time. To activate the cheats, enter "System Options," then choose "Extras," and "Cheat Grid." To play the FMV sequences unlocked in the Cheat menu, choose the Movie Player option that is above "Cheat Grid."

Unlockable	Objective
Camera Flip	Complete Level 11 in 310.
Concept Art Video	Complete Level 9 in 345.
Early Test Animatic FMV Sequence	Choose an agent at the start of the game and select an empty slot. Enter WOODY or WWS413 as a name. The name disappears and a clucking sound confirms correct code entry. Next, enter your own name and start the game.
Early Test Animatic Video	Complete Level 5 in 325.
Extra Cameras	Complete Level 6 in 345.
Fisheye View	Complete Level 10 in 315.
Green HUD	Complete Level 2 in 335.
Hover Spy	Complete the entire game.
Inversion Camera	Complete Level 8 in 305.
Making of Video	Complete Level 13 in 215.
Night Vision	Complete Level 4 in 315.
Puke Camera	Complete Level 12 in 330.
Rainbow HUD	Complete Level 7 in 310.
Saliva Spy Hunter Them FMV Sequence	Choose an agent at the start of the game and select an empty slot. Enter GUNN as a name. The name disappears and a clucking sound confirms correct code entry. Next, enter your own name and start the game.
Saliva Spy Hunter Video	Complete Level 1 in 340.

Spy Hunter (continued)

Unlockable	Objective
Saliva Your Disease FMV Sequence	Choose an agent at the start of the game and select an empty slot. Enter SALIVA as a name. The name disappears and a clicking sound confirms correct code entry. Next, enter your own name and start the game.
Saliva Your Disease Video	Complete Level 3 in 240.
Spy Hunter Concept Art FMV Sequence	Choose an agent at the start of the game and select an empty slot. Enter SHAWN or SCW823 as a name. The name disappears and a clicking sound confirms correct code entry. Next, enter your own name and start the game.
Super Spy (Unlimited ammunition and invincibility for your car)	Complete all 65 objectives in the game.
The Making of Spy Hunter FMV Sequence	Choose an agent at the start of the game and select an empty slot. Enter MAKING or MODEL as a name. The name disappears and a clicking sound confirms correct code entry. Next, enter your own name and start the game.
Tiny Spy	Complete Level 14 in 510.

TIP

Classic Spy Hunter Mini-Game

Choose an agent at the start of the game and select an empty slot. Enter OGSPY as a name. The name disappears and a clicking sound confirms correct code entry. Next, enter your own name and start the game.

Spy Hunter 2

To access the following codes, pause gameplay at any time during the game and enter code.

Unlockable	Code
God Mode	(LT), (LT), (LT), ⬅, (LT), (RT), (RT), (LT), ⬅
Infinite Ammo	(RT), (LT), ⬅, ⬅, (WH), (RT), (LT), ⬅, (WH)

Spy vs. Spy

Go to the Extras menu, then enter the following codes in the Cheats menu.

Unlockable	Code
All Modern Maps	PROHIAS
All Multiplayer Maps	MADMAG
All Spy Attachments	DISGUISE
All Story Maps	ANTONIO
Invulnerability	ARMOR
Permanent Fairy	FAIRY

SSX 3

Unlockable	Code	Unlockable	Code
Snow Boards	graphicdelight	Hiro	slicksuit
Videos	myeyesaredim	Stretch	windmilldunk

SSX 3 (continued)

Unlockable	Objective
Alternate Costumes	To earn more costumes, complete all chapters in your trick book. To unlock the final chrome costume, complete World Circuit mode with a "Master" rank.
Fugi Board	Get a gold medal on every course with all boarders with their überboards to unlock a Fugi board.

SSX On Tour

Enter these passwords at the Cheats menu.

Unlockable	Password
All Clothing	FLYTHREADS
All Levels	BACKSTAGEPASS
All Movies	THEBIGPICTURE
Extra Cash	LOOTSNOOT
Infinite Boost	ZOOMJUICE
Monster Tricks	JACKALOPESTYLE
Snowball Fight	LETSPARTY
Stat Boost	POWERPLAY
Unlock Characters	ROADIEROUNDUP
Unlock Conrad (the MiniViking)	BIGPARTYTIME
Unlock Mitch Koobski (the Unicorn)	MOREFUNTHANONE
Unlock Nigel (Rocker)	THREEISACROWD
Unlock Ski Patrol Character	FOURSOME

SSX Tricky

Unlockable	Objective
Pipedream Course	Win a medal on all Showoff courses.
Play as Brodi	Win a gold medal in World Circuit mode.
Play as JP	Win three gold medals in World Circuit mode.
Play as Kaori	Win four gold medals in World Circuit mode.
Play as Luther	Win eight gold medals in World Circuit mode.
Play as Marisol	Win five gold medals in World Circuit mode.
Play as Psymon	Win six gold medals in World Circuit mode.
Play as Seeiah	Win seven gold medals in World Circuit mode.
Play as Zoe	Win two gold medals in World Circuit mode.
Überboards	Unlock all of the tricks for a character to get his or her überboard, which is that character's best board.
Untracked Course	Win a medal on all Race courses.

Input these codes at the main options screen, with the "Start Game" and "DVD Extras" option. Listen for the sound to confirm correct code entry.

Unlockable	Code
Annette Board	Hold ⒧ + ⑧ and press ✪, ✪, ⬦, ✪, ✪, ♀, ✪, ✪, ⬦, ✪, ✪, ⬧, then release ⒧ + ⑧. Choose Kaori and start a track. Kaori will have a full Tricky meter, and a faster board.
Full Stat Points	Hold ⒧ + ⑧ and press ♥, ♥, ⬦, ♥, ♥, ♀, ✪, ✪, ⬦, ✪, ✪, ⬧. (All the boarders will have full stat points.)

DS
GBA
PSP
PS2
PS3
Wii
Xbox
Xbox 360
Index

SSX Tricky (continued)

Unlockable	Code
Mallora Board	Hold LT + RT and press A, A, ➪, B, B, ♀, ♀, ♥, ◅, ✖, ✖, ◊, then release LT + RT. Choose Elise and start a track. Elise will have the Mallora Board and a blue outfit. This code only works for Elise.
Master Code	Hold LT + RT and press A, ♥, ➪, B, ✖, ♀, ♀, ✖, ◅, B, A, ◊, then release LT + RT.
Mix Master Mike	Hold LT + RT and press A, A, ➪, A, A, ♀, A, A, ◅, A, A, ◊, then release LT + RT. Choose any boarder at the character selection screen, and he or she will be replaced by Mix Master Mike on the course, with the number of the character that was originally selected. He has decks on his back and a vinyl board. Repeat the code to disable its effect.
Sticky Boards	Hold LT + RT and press ✖, ✖, ➪, ♥, ♥, ♥, B, B, ◅, A, A, ◊, then release LT + RT.

Star Trek: Shattered Universe

Enter these codes at the Main Menu.

Unlockable	Code
All Medals and Ranks Awarded	LB, LT, RT, B, RT, Y, LT, WHT
All Missions Open	LB, RT, RT, B, ✖, LT, RT, Y, WHT
All Ships Open	LB, LT, ✖, LT, ✖, RT, RT, B, WHT
Invincibility	LB, LT, B, LT, RT, Y, Y, B, WHT
Kobayashi Maru Open	LB, LT, Y, LT, LT, ✖, Y, Y, RT, WHT

Star Wars Battlefront

Unlockable	Code
All Missions	In Historical Campaign, press ✖, ♥, ✖, ♥ at the Level Select screen.

Star Wars Battlefront II

During gameplay, pause the game. Enter the following codes. There will be a sound if done correctly.

Unlockable	Code
Disable HUD	◊, ◊, ◊, ◊, ◅, ◊, ◊, ◊, ♀, ◅, ♀, ◊, ◊, ◅, ➪
Lower Resolution Soldiers	♀, ♀, ♀, ◊, ◅, ◊, ♀, ♀, ♀, ♀, ♀, ◅, ◊, ◊, ◊, ◅, ➪
Invulnerable	◊, ◊, ◊, ◅, ♀, ♀, ♀, ◅, ◊, ◊, ◊, ◅, ➪
Slow Motion Sound Effects	◊, ◊, ◊, ◅, ◊, ♀, ♀, ◊, ◊, ♀, ◅, ◊, ◊, ♀, ♀, ◅, ➪
Weird Captions	◊, ♀, ◅, ♀, ◅, ➪

Star Wars: Episode I Obi-Wan

Unlockable	Code
Additional Versus Mode Characters	Defeat a character in the Jedi Arena during gameplay to unlock him or her in Versus mode.
All levels until Darth Maul	Enter M1A2U3L4!? as a saved game name
Battle Royal Mission (You have to fight eight other Jedi Masters in the Saber Arena.)	Defeat Darth Maul in Level 25.
Level Select (All levels, including the bonus levels, will be unlocked.)	Select the "New Game" option at the main menu, then enter GREYTHERAT as saved game name.

DS · GBA · PSP · PS2 · PS3 · Wii · Xbox · Xbox 360 · Index

Star Wars: Episode III Revenge of the Sith

These codes can be entered in the Codes section of the Options menu.

Unlockable	Code
All Attacks and Force Power Upgrades Activated	JAINA
All Bonus Missions Unlocked	NARSHADDAA
All Concept Art Unlocked	AAYLASECURA
All Duel Arenas Unlocked	TANTIVEIV
All Duelist Unlocked	ZABRAK
All Story Missions Unlocked	KORRIBAN
Fast Force Energy and Health Regeneration Activated	BELSAVIS
Infinite Force Energy Activated	KAIBURR
Infinite Health Activated	XUCPHRA

Star Wars Jedi Knight II: Jedi Outcast

Passwords

Password	Effect
DINGO	All Levels
BUBBLE	God Mode
BISCUIT	Infinite Ammo
PEEPS	Multiplayer Characters
DEMO	Play Bonus Level
Fudge	Start With Lightsaber
SCOOTER	Unlimited Force
CHERRY	Unlock First Seven Levels

Unlockable	How to Unlock
Fight Desann Twice	When you are in Yavin Courtyard, run as fast as you can to the room with the Seeker Drones. Push the red button on the right wall 5 times and Desann appears. He is easier to fight right now than when you fight him at Yavin Final Conflict.

Star Wars Knights of the Old Republic

Unlock the Hidden Ending: Before the final battle with Darth Malak press ⒧ + ⒭ + ❤ on all controllers (you need to have more than one) that you have plugged into the Xbox. This must be done before you enter the door to face Darth Malak. If you did it right, your Jedi takes out her/his lightsaber. Then open the door and walk up to Malak and talk to him.

Star Wars Republic Commando

Enter this code while the game is paused.

Unlockable	Code
Refill Ammo (refills the weapon equipped)	❤,❤,⊗,♀,ⓇⓉ,⒧,ⓇⓉ,♢

Star Wars Starfighter: Special Edition

Enter the following as codes to access the specified unlockable.

Unlockable	Code
Alternate Camera Angles	DIRECTOR—the message "Director Mode" confirms correct code entry.
Bruiser Gun	BRUISER
Default Screen	SIZZLE
Disable Cockpit Displays	NOHUD
Enemy Ship Gallery	SHIPS

DS
GBA
PSP
PS2
PS3
Wii
Xbox
Xbox 360
Index

DS

GBA

PSP

PS2

PS3

Wii

Xbox

Xbox 360

Index

Star Wars Starfighter: Special Edition (continued)

Invincibility	EARCHIPS—the message "Invincibility" confirms correct code entry.
Master Code (Everything except the multiplayer levels will be unlocked.)	EUROPA
Pre-Production Art	PLANETS
Programmer FMV Sequence	LATEAM
Reversed Controls	JARJAR—the message "Jar Jar Mode" confirms correct code entry.
Secret Level Programmers	SLTEAM
Secret Spaceship for Bonus Missions (Unlock the Experimental N-1 Fighter.)	FSNEULB
Spaceship and Cast Pictures	HEROES
Trade Federation Freighter	UTILITY
View Credits	CREDITS

Unlockable	Code
Canyon Sprint Mission	Earn a silver medal in the Naboo Proving Grounds, the Royal Escort, Taking the Offensive, Midnight Munitions Run, Rescue on the Solleu, and the Final Assault missions.
Charm's Way Mission	Earn a bronze medal in the Royal Escort, Contract Infraction, Piracy above Lok, Taking the Offensive, the New Resistance, and the Final Assault missions.
Darth Maul's Infiltrator Ship	Earn a gold medal in all default missions.
Guardian Mantis Ship	Earn a gold medal in the Contract Infraction, Secrets on Eos, and the New Resistance missions.
Havoc Ship	Earn a gold medal in the Piracy above Lok, Valuable Goods, Eye of the Storm, the Crippling Blow, and Last Stand on Naboo missions.
Outpost Attack Mission	Earn a bronze medal in all default missions.
Secret Spaceship for Bonus Missions (Unlock the Experimental N-1 Fighter.)	Earn a gold medal in the Naboo Proving Grounds, the Royal Escort, Taking the Offensive, Midnight Munitions Run, Rescue on the Solleu, and the Final Assault missions.
Space Sweep Mission	Earn a silver medal in all default missions.

Star Wars: The Clone Wars

Unlockable	Code
All Bonus Menu Items	IGIVEUP
All Multiplayer Levels	LETSDANCE
Earn the three bonus objectives	ALITTLEHELP
Get All FMV Movies	GOTPOPCORN
Invincibility	LORDOFSITH
Team Photos	YOURMASTERS
Unlimited Ammo	NOHONOR

Starsky and Hutch

Unlockable	Code
Everything	Enter VADKRAM as a profile name.

State of Emergency

Unlockable	Code
AK47	◄, ►, ○, (RT), Ⓥ
All Weapons Cheat	While playing, press ⓦ, ⓦ, (RT), (RT).
Flamethrower	◄, ►, ○, ⬤, Ⓑ
God Mode	While playing, press ⓦ, (LT), ⬤, (RT), Ⓐ.
Grenade	◄, ►, ○, (RT), Ⓧ
Grenade Launcher	◄, ►, ○, ⬤, Ⓧ
Looting Cheat	While playing, press ⬤, ⓦ, (RT), (LT), Ⓥ⬤
M16	◄, ►, ○, (RT), Ⓑ
Minigun	◄, ►, ○, ⬤, Ⓥ
Molotov Cocktail	◄, ►, ○, (RT), Ⓐ
Pepper Spray	◄, ►, ○, ⓦ, Ⓧ
Pistol	◄, ►, ○, ⓦ, Ⓥ
Rocket Launcher	◄, ►, ○, ⬤, Ⓐ
Select a Level	ⓦ, (LT), (LT), (LT), ⓦ, Ⓐ
Shotgun	◄, ►, ○, (LT), Ⓥ
Skip Level	◄, ◄, ◄, ◄, Ⓥ
Tazer	◄, ►, ○, ⓦ, Ⓑ
Tear Gas	◄, ►, ○, ⓦ, Ⓐ
Unlimited Ammunition	While playing, press ⓦ, (LT), ⬤, (RT), Ⓥ.
Unlimited Time	While playing, press ⓦ, (LT), ⬤, (RT), Ⓑ.
Unlock Bull	While playing KAOS Mode, press ►, ►, ►, ►, Ⓐ.
Unlock Freak	While playing KAOS Mode, press ►, ►, ►, ►, Ⓑ.
Unlock Spanky	While playing KAOS Mode, press ►, ►, ►, ►, Ⓥ.

Stolen

Enter this code in the Equipment screen.

Unlockable	Code
99 of all equipment items	(RT), (LT), ►

Street Hoops

In the Setting menu, select Cheats to enter these codes.

Unlockable	Code
ABA Ball	Ⓥ, ⓦ, Ⓧ, ⓦ
Black Ball	ⓦ, ⓦ, Ⓥ, ⬤
Block Party (easier to block)	(RT), Ⓥ, ⬤, ⓦ
Brick City Clothing	(RT), ⬤, (RT), (LT), Ⓥ, Ⓧ, (RT), (LT)
Clown Uniform	Ⓧ, (LT), Ⓧ, Ⓥ
Cowboy Uniform	Ⓥ, ⓦ, ⓦ, (RT)
Elvis Uniform	Ⓥ, ⬤, ⓦ, ⬤, ⬤, ⓦ, (LT), ⬤
Kung Fu Uniforms	Ⓧ, Ⓥ, Ⓧ, (LT)
Normal Ball	(RT), Ⓧ, Ⓧ, (LT)
Pimp Uniforms	(RT), Ⓧ, Ⓥ, ⬤
Power Game	ⓦ, Ⓥ, ⬤, Ⓥ
Santa Uniform	ⓦ, ⬤, ⓦ, ⬤
Tuxedo Uniform	⬤, ⬤, Ⓥ, Ⓧ
Theft Mode (easier to steal)	(RT), Ⓧ, Ⓧ, Ⓧ, (RT), ⬤, Ⓥ, ⓦ

DS · GBA · PSP · PS2 · PS3 · Wii · Xbox · Xbox 360 · Index

Street Racing Syndicate

Press ⬒, ⬓, ⬔, ⬕ at the Main menu to enter these codes.

Unlockable	Code
1996 Supra RZ	SICKJZA
1999 Mitsubishi Eclipse GS-T	IGOTGST
2004 Toyota Celica GT-S Action Package	MYTCGTS
Free car repair	FIXITUP
Mazda RX-8	RENESIS
Pac Man Vinyl	GORETRO
Police Car	GOTPOPO
Subaru Impreza Sti	SICKGDB
The first three times you are pulled over in street mode, you will be released with a warning.	LETMEGO

The Suffering

Unlockable	Objective
Alternate title sequence	Complete the game.
Director Commentary	In the Prelude level, wait for a crow to land next to the three inmates, then stand on top of the crow.
Prelude Level	Complete the game.

Enter the following codes during gameplay while holding ⓛ+⒭+⊗.

Unlockable	Code
All Items and Weapons except Gonzo Gun	⬓,⬒,⬓,⬔,⬕,⬔,Ⓐ,⬒,⬔,⬓, ⬔,⬒,⬕,⬓,Ⓐ,⬔,Ⓐ,⬓,⬓,⬓,Ⓐ,Ⓐ
Bloody Torque	⬒,⬓,⬔,⬕
Clean Torque	⬓,⬒,⬕,⬔
Dirty Family Picture	⬔,⬓,⬔,⬓,⬔,⬓,Ⓐ
Full Health	⬓,⬓,⬓,Ⓐ,⬒,⬒,⬒,Ⓐ
Full Xombium bottle	⬕,⬕,⬒,⬒,Ⓐ,⬔,⬕,⬒,Ⓐ,⬒,⬔,⬕,Ⓐ
Gonzo Gun	⬔,Ⓐ,Ⓐ,Ⓐ,⬔,⬕,⬔,⬕,⬔,⬒,Ⓐ,Ⓐ,Ⓐ,⬔,⬒,⬕,⬒,Ⓐ
Grenades	⬕,⬔,⬕,⬔,⬕,⬔
Increase Negative Karma	⬔,⬔,⬓,⬒,Ⓐ
Molotov Cocktails	⬓,⬓,⬕,⬒,⬒,⬒
New Family Picture	⬒,⬕,⬒,⬔,⬒,⬕,Ⓐ
Overcome Insanity	⬕,⬔,⬕,Ⓐ,⬔,⬕,⬕,⬔,Ⓐ
Old Movie Mode	⬒,Ⓐ,⬔,⬒,⬓,Ⓐ,⬕ Press Start to disable this effect.
Psychedelic Mode	⬔,⬔,Ⓐ,⬕,⬔,⬕,Ⓐ,⬒,⬔,⬓,⬓,Ⓐ
Refill Ranged Weapon Ammunition	⬔,⬔,⬒,⬔,⬓,⬕,⬔,⬕,⬒,Ⓐ
Reload Ammunition for Current Gun	⬕,⬔,⬓,⬒,⬔,⬔,⬕,⬔,⬕,Ⓐ
Shotgun with Full Ammunition	⬔,⬔,⬕,⬓,⬓,⬓
Wrinkled Family Picture	⬒,⬒,⬕,⬒

The Suffering: Ties that Bind

Enter these codes while playing; do not pause.

Unlockable	Code
All Weapons and Items	Hold 🢤 + ⒭ + ⊗, then press ⬓, ⬒, ⬓, ⬔, ⬕, ⬔, Ⓐ, ⬒, ⬔, ⬕, ⬔, ⬒, ⬕, ⬓, ⬔, Ⓐ, ⬓, ⬓, ⬓, Ⓐ, Ⓐ
Full Ammunition for Equipped Gun	Hold ⓛ + ⒭ + ⊗, then press ⬕, ⬕, ⬓, ⬒, ⬔, ⬕, ⬔, ⬕, Ⓐ
Refill Health	Hold ⓛ + ⒭ + ⊗, then press ⬓, ⬓, ⬓, Ⓐ, ⬒, ⬒, ⬓, ⬒, Ⓐ
Shotgun with Full Ammo	Hold ⓛ + ⒭ + ⊗, then press ⬔, ⬔, ⬔, ⬓, ⬓, ⬓

Superman: The Man of Steel

Pause the game to enter these codes.

Unlockable	Code
All Levels and Bonuses	(RT), (LB), (Y), (LB), (LT), (WHT)
Unlimited Health	(LB), (WHT), (LT), (Y), (LT), (WHT)

SWAT: Global Strike Team

Enter these codes at the Mission Selection screen in either Single Player or Cooperative mode.

Unlockable	Code
All Missions	○, (LT), ○, (RT), ○, (LT), ○, (RT)

Tao Feng: Fist of the Lotus

Unlockable	Objective
Unlock Extra Stage	Clear advance training.
Unlock Zhao Yen	Beat Quest Mode with every member of the Black Mantis and Pale Lotus and beat Zhao Yen with both factions.

Teenage Mutant Ninja Turtles 2: Battle Nexus

In the Options menu, select Passwords to enter any of these codes. When selecting a turtle, hold the (LT) button to pick his New Nexus Outfit.

Unlockable	Code
Challenge Code Abyss	SDSDRLD
Challenge Code Endurance	MRMDRMD
Challenge Code Fatal Blow	LRSRDRD
Challenge Code Lose Shuriken	RLMRDSL
Challenge Code Nightmare	SLSDRDL
Challenge Code Poison	DRSLLSR
Challenge Code Super Tough	RDSRMRL
Cheat Code All You Can Throw Shuriken	RSRLRSM
Cheat Code Health	DSRDMRM
Cheat Code Mighty Turtle	LSDRRDR
Cheat Code Pizza Paradise	MRLMRMR
Cheat Code Self Recovery	DRMSRLR
Cheat Code Squeaking	MLDSRDM
Cheat Code Super Defense Power	LDRMRLM
Cheat Code Super Offense Power	SDLSRLL
Cheat Code Toddling	SSSMRDD
New Nexus Outfit for Donatello	DSLRDRM
New Nexus Outfit for Leonardo	LMRMDRD
New Nexus Outfit for Michelangelo	MLMRDRM
New Nexus Outfit for Raphael	RMSRMDR
Playmates Added to Bonus Materials	SRMLDDR

DS
GBA
PSP
PS2
PS3
Wii
Xbox
Xbox 360
Index

DS

GBA

PSP

PS2

PS3

Wii

Xbox

Xbox 360

Index

Teenage Mutant Ninja Turtles 3: Mutant Nightmare

Passwords

Password	Effect
MSRLSMML	2x Enemy Attack
SLRMLSSM	2x Enemy Defense
DMLDMRLD	Endurance—No health pickups available on map
LDMSLRDD	Instant Death—Die in 1 hit
MDLDSSLR	Invincibility—Never die or even lose health!
RRDMLSDL	Max Ougi—Unlimited Ougi!
LLMSRDMS	Shuriken loser—Shurikens no longer available on maps
SLLMRSLD	Sushi Party—All Health pickups become Sushi!
LMDRRMSR	Unlimited shuriken—Unlimited shuriken

TMNT: Mutant Melee

Extra Modes and Stages

Unlockable	How to Unlock
April's Adventure Mode	As Donatello, successfully complete the Ghetto level
April's Apartment Stage	As Donatello, successfully complete the April's Apartment 2 level
April's Melee Mode	As Casey Jones, successfully complete Adventure mode
Autumn Stage	As Michelangelo, successfully complete The Dojo level
Casey Jones's Adventure Mode	As Raphael, successfully complete the Subway level
Casey Jones's Jacket Costume	As April, successfully complete her adventure mode
Casey Jones's Melee Mode	As Casey Jones, successfully complete Adventure mode
Casey Jones's Red Shorts	As Casey Jones, successfully complete the Ghetto level
Dojo Complete Stage Costume	As Casey Jones, successfully complete the Turtle's Lair level
Foot Soldier's Adventure Mode	As Raphael, successfully complete his Adventure mode
HUN 2's Melee Mode	As HUN, successfully complete his Adventure mode
HUN's Adventure Mode	As Michelangelo, successfully complete his Adventure mode
Monster's Melee Mode	As HUN, successfully complete the Sewer Canal level
Sewer Falls Stage	As Raphael, successfully complete the Sewer Falls level
Sewers Stage	As Leonardo, successfully complete the Sewers level
Shredder's Adventure Mode	As Donatello, successfully complete his Adventure mode
Shredder's Gold Costume	As Shredder, successfully complete his Adventure mode
Shredder's Palace Exterior stage	As Leonardo, successfully complete The Lab 12 level
Splinter's adventure mode	As Leonardo, successfully complete his adventure mode
Subway Stage	As Leonardo, successfully complete the Sparring with Splinter level
Tech Foot's Melee Mode	As Foot Soldier, successfully complete Adventure mode
Waterfall Stage	As April, successfully complete the Turtle's Lair level

Tenchu: Return from Darkness

Unlockable	Objective
All Characters	At the Start screen, hold WHT+BLK and press ↑,→,←,↑,↓. Release WHT+BLK and press LT,RT.
All Enemy Locations	At the Mission Select screen, press →,←,LT,RT,WHT,BLK.
All Items	At the Item Selection screen, hold LT+RT and press ↑,↓,↑,⊗,⊗,⊗,←,→,←,→,⊗,⊗,⊗.
All Missions	At the Mission Select screen, press WHT,WHT,LT,RT,→,⊗,←,→.
Bonus Mission	At the Title screen, press WHT,↑,BLK,↓,LT,→,RT,←.
B-Side Voices	At the Title screen, hold LT+RT and press ↓,⊗,⊗,↑,←,→,⊗,⊗,⊗.
Fill the Kuji Meter	During a mission, pause and hold LT+RT, then press ←,←,←,↓,⊗.
Increase Items	At the Item Selection screen, hold LT+RT and press ↑,←,↓,→,⊗,⊗,⊗.
Increase Offensive Power	During a mission, pause and hold RT+WHT and press ↑,↓,↑,↓, then release RT+WHT and press ⊗,⊗,⊗.
Increase Score	During a mission, pause and hold WHT+BLK and press →,←,→,←.
New Ability	During a mission, pause and hold RT+BLK and press ↑,↑,↓,↓, then release RT+BLK and press ⊗,⊗,LT,RT.
One Kanji	During a mission, pause and press ←,←,←,↓,⊗.
Restore Health	During a mission, pause and press ↑,↓,↑,↓,⊗,⊗,⊗.
Score	During a mission, pause and press →,→,→,←.
Unlimited Item Capacity	At the Item Selection screen, hold LT+RT+WHT and press ↑,↓,↓,↓,←,→,←,→, then release WHT and press ⊗,⊗,⊗.

Terminator 3: Rise of the Machines

Enter these codes in the Cheats menu under "Options."

Unlockable	Code
All Future Weapons	ⓐ,ⓐ,ⓐ,⊗,ⓑ,⊗,ⓑ,ⓑ
All Present Day Weapons	ⓨ,ⓑ,ⓐ,ⓑ,ⓐ,⊗,ⓨ,⊗
Invincibility	ⓨ,⊗,ⓑ,ⓑ,ⓐ,ⓐ,ⓑ,⊗
T-850's Hit Points Increased by 50 Percent	ⓐ,ⓨ,ⓐ,ⓨ
T-850's Hit Points Reduced by 50 Percent	ⓑ,ⓨ,ⓐ,ⓐ
T-X Hit Points Increased by 50 Percent	ⓑ,⊗,⊗,⊗,ⓑ,ⓐ,ⓨ,ⓐ
T-X Hit Points Reduced by 50 Percent	ⓑ,ⓑ,⊗,⊗,⊗,ⓑ,ⓐ,ⓨ
Unlimited Ammo	⊗,ⓐ,ⓨ,ⓨ,ⓨ,ⓐ,⊗,ⓑ
Unlimited Continues	ⓑ,ⓑ,ⓑ,⊗,ⓑ,ⓐ,ⓨ,ⓐ
Unlock All Exclusive Movie Scenes	ⓑ,ⓑ,ⓑ,ⓐ,⊗,ⓨ,⊗,ⓨ
Unlock All Game Scenes	ⓑ,ⓑ,ⓑ,⊗,ⓑ,ⓨ,ⓑ,ⓑ
Unlock All Levels	⊗,ⓨ,ⓨ,⊗,ⓑ,ⓐ,ⓐ,ⓑ
Unlock Centipede	ⓐ,ⓑ,ⓑ,ⓑ,⊗,ⓨ,ⓑ,ⓐ
Unlock Missile Command	ⓐ,ⓑ,ⓑ,ⓑ,⊗,ⓨ,ⓐ,ⓑ

Terminator 3: The Redemption

Unlockable	Code
All Upgrades	Highlight Credits and press ⓑ+ⓨ+LT

DS

GBA

PSP

PS2

PS3

Wii

Xbox

Xbox 360

Index

Test Drive

Passwords

Password	Effect
Unlock 2 Jaguars and an Aston Martin Vanquish	Set a new record on the drag racing level in Story mode and enter SOUNDMAX
Unlock the G4TV Viper	Set a new record on any track and Enter KQXYKGVY as the name

Unlock Cars and Tracks

Unlockable	How to Unlock
Aston Martin DB7 Vantage Police Car, Lotus Espirit V8 Police Car, and Jaguar XK-R Police Car in cop chase mode	Win all races in Story mode for London
Aston Martin DB7 Vantage, Chevrolet Corvette Z06, TVR Cebera Speed 12, and Ford SVT Mustang Cobra R	Win all races in Story mode for Monte Carlo
Chevrolet Chevelle SS 454 and Skeeter's Pontiac GTO	Win all races in Story mode for London
Jaguar XJ220 Police Car, Chevrolet Corvette Z06 Police Car, and TVR Cebera Speed 12 Police Car on the Monte Carlo	Win all races in Story mode for Monte Carlo
Jaguar XK-R "SoundMAX SPX," Jaguar XK-R "Analog Devices," and the Aston Martin DB7 "SoundMAX SPX"	Unlock all of the other cars in the game. Select the San Francisco Drag Race and use the Dodge Concept Viper to set a new time record. Then, enter SOUNDMAX as a name at the high score screen.
London Tracks in Single Race and Cop Chase Modes	Win all races in Story mode for London
Monte Carlo Tracks in Single Race and Cop Chase Modes	Win all races in Story mode for Monte Carlo
Nissan Skyline GT-R V-Spec Police Car, Subaru Impreza 22B Police Car, and Toyota Supra Police Car	Win all races in Story mode for Tokyo
Never Get Busted	When the word "busted" appears at the top of your screen hit "R" until it goes away
Nissan Skyline GT-R V-Spec, Dodge Charger, Subaru Impreza 22B, and Shelby Series 1	Win all races in Story mode for Tokyo
San Francisco Tracks in Single Race and Cop Chase Modes, as well as the Chevrolet Corvette L-88, Jaguar XK-R, Lotus Elise	Win all races in Story mode
Tokyo Tracks in Single Race and Cop Chase Modes	Win all races in Story mode for Tokyo

DS

GBA

PSP

PS2

PS3

Wii

Xbox

Xbox 360

Index

Test Drive Off-Road: Wide Open

Unlockable	Objective
Dodge T-Rex	Finish in first place in season four of Career mode in the power division.
Humvee	Finish in first place in the first three seasons of Career mode in all divisions.
Monster Truck	Complete the 27 tracks in Single Race mode in first place.
Moon Level and Moon Buggy	Collect all nine Blue Moon cafe signs in Free Roam or Career mode. There are three signs in each level.
Pro Class Trucks	Complete the first nine tracks in single-race mode.
Rod Hall Hummer	Finish in first place in all divisions in Career mode.
Shelby Dodge Durango	Finish in first place in season four of Career mode in the speed division.
Unlimited Class Trucks	Complete the first of 27 tracks in Single Race mode.

NOTE

The Rod Hall Hummer is good for speed. It handles poorly and is average in climbing. It can be a power vehicle if needed and it works well for single race on the blitz races. The Moon Buggy, however, is the best all-around vehicle and can reach speeds of 132 mph. It's the vehicle to use on all the other races in single race.

Tiger Woods PGA Tour 2003

Unlockable	Code	Unlockable	Code
All Courses	14COURSES	Mark Calcavecchia	CALCULATE
All Golfers and Courses	ALLTW3	Notah Begay III	NOTABLY
All Golfers Except Josey Scott	ALL28G	Mark Omeara	TB
Brad Faxon	XON	Melvin "Yosh" Tanigawa	YOYOYO
Cedric Ace Andrews	IAM#1	Solita Lopez	SOLITARY1
Charles Howell III	BANDPANTS	Steve Stricker	SS
Dominic "The Don" Donatello	GODFATHER	Stewart Cink	SINK
Hamish Character	MCRUFF	Stuart Appleby	ORANGES
Jim Furyk	THESWING	Super Tiger Woods	SUNDAY
Josey "Superstar" Scott	SUPERSTAR	Takeharu "Tsunami" Moto	2TON
Justin Leonard	JUSTINTIME	Ty Tyron	TYNO
Kellie Newman	COWGIRL	Val "Sunshine" Summers	VALENTINE
		Vijay Singh	VJSING

Tiger Woods PGA Tour 2004

Go to the Options menu, select "Passwords," and enter any of these passwords.

Unlockable	Password
Ace Andrews	ACEINTHEHOLE
All Courses	ALLTHETRICKS
All Courses and Golfers	THEKITCHENSINK
All Golfers	CANYOUPICKONE
Cedric The Entertainer	CEDDYBEAR
Dominic "The Don" Donatello	DISCOKING
Downtown Brown	DTBROWN
Edwin "Pops" Masterson	EDDIE
Erica Ice	ICYONE

DS
GBA
PSP
PS2
PS3
Wii
Xbox
Xbox 360
Index

DS

GBA

PSP

PS2

PS3

Wii

Xbox

Xbox 360

Index

Tiger Woods PGA Tour 2004 (continued)

Unlockable	Password
Hamish "Mulligan" McGregor	DWILBY
Moa "Big Mo" Ta'a Vatu	ERUPTION
Solita Lopez	SHORTGAME
Sunday Tiger	4REDSHIRTS
Takehuru "Tsunami" Moto	EMERALDCHAMP
Target World Championship 3 Hole Shootout	SHERWOOD TARGET
Val Summers	BEVERLYHILLS
"Yosh" Tanegawa	THENEWLEFTY

Tiger Woods PGA Tour 2005

In the Options menu, select Cheats to enter these passwords.

Unlockable	Code
Adriana "Sugar" Dolce	SOSWEET
Alastair "Captain" McFadden	NICESOCKS
All Accessories	TIGERMOBILE
All Courses	THEWORLDISYOURS
All Courses and Golfers	THEGIANTOYSTER
Aphrodite Papadapolus	TEMPTING
Arnold Palmer	THEKING
Ben Hogan	PUREGOLF
Bev "Boomer" Bouchier	THEBEEHIVE
Billy "Bear" Hightower	TOOTALL
Bunjiro "Bud" Tanaka	INTHEFAMILY
Ceasar "The Emperor" Rosado	LANDOWNER
Dion "Double D" Douglas	DDDouglas
Gary Player	BLACKKNIGHT
Hunter "Steelhead" Elmore	GREENCOLLAR
Jack Nicklaus	GOLDENBEAR
Jeb "Shooter" McGraw	SIXSHOOTER
Justin Timberlake	THETENNESSEKID
Kendra "Spike" Lovette	ENGLISHPUNK
Raquel "Rocky" Rogers	DOUBLER
Reginald "Reg" Weathers	REGGIE
Roof in the Skillzone Game Mode	NIGHTGOLFER
Seve Ballesteros	THEMAGICIAN
Sunday Tiger Woods	NEWLEGEND
The Hustler	ALTEREGO
Tiffany "Tiff" Williams	RICHGIRL

Item Unlockable	Code	Item Unlockable	Code
ADIDAS Items	91treSTR	ODYSSEY Items	kjnMR3qv
CALLOWAY Items	cgTR78qw	PING Items	R453DrTe
CLEVELAND Items	CL45etUB	PRECEPT Items	BRi3498Z
MAXFLI Items	FDGH597i	TAG Items	cDsa2fgY
NIKE Items	YJHk342B	TourStage Items	TS345329

Tiger Woods PGA Tour 06

Go to the Options menu, then enter the Passwords menu to enter these passwords.

Unlockable	Code
All Clubs	CLUB11
All Courses	ITSINTHEHOLE
All Golfers	WOOGLIN
Tiger Woods with Alternate Old Golf Outfit	OLDSKOOL
Tiger Woods with Hat	GOLDENAGE
Tiger Woods with Old Striped Pants	TECHNICOLOR
Tiger Woods with Very Old Golf Outfit	THROWBACK

Tiger Woods PGA Tour 07

Passwords

Password	Effect
ELDRICK	Unlocks 20+ golfers and 30+ course memberships
THREE STRIPES	Unlocks the Adidas sponsorship
JUSTDOIT	Unlocks the Nike sponsorship (Does not unlock the Nike TW items, only the regular Nike items)

Timesplitters 2

Complete these levels in Story mode under the Medium difficulty setting to access the playable characters.

Level Reward	Playable Character
1853 Wild West	The Colonel
1895 Notre Dame Paris	Notre Dame
1920 Aztec Ruins	Stone Golem
1932 Chicago	Big Tony
1972 Atom Smasher	Khallos
1990 Oblask Dam Siberia	The Mutant TimeSplitter
2019 NeoTokyo	Sadako
2280 Return to Planet X	Ozor Mox
2315 Robot Factory	Machinist
2401 Space Station	Reaper Splitter See Tip

TIP

Complete the 2401 Space Station level under the Easy difficulty setting to unlock the ending sequence.

TimeSplitters: Future Perfect

Platinum Awards

Platinum awards are unlockable in Arcade by beating the gold requirements and going beyond as much as possible.

Unlockable	How to Unlock
A Pox of Mox Platinum-Honorary-Dead Weight	Get 36 points in 2:30 or less
Astro Jocks Platinum-Amateur-Smash 'N Grab	Kill all in 2 minutes or less
Bag Slag Platinum-Honorary-Fever Pitch	Hold the bag for 3:15 or more
Big Game Hunt Platinum-Amateur-One Gun Fun	Get at least 45 kills
Commuting Will Kill You Platinum-Amateur-Nightstick	Kill all within 2:20
Dam Cold Out Here Platinum-Amateur-Nightstick	Get 41 points in 2 minutes 45 seconds or less

Sidebar tabs: DS, GBA, PSP, PS2, PS3, Wii, Xbox, Xbox 360, Index

TimeSplitters: Future Perfect (continued)

Unlockable	How to Unlock
Divine Immolation's Platinum Medal: Amateur Arcade—One Gun Fun	Get 1st Place and at least 22 kills before time runs out
Freak Unique Platinum-Honorary-Dead Weight	Get 30 kills in 2:45 or less
Front Loaded Platinum-Elite-Group Therapy	10 kills in under 1:30
I Like Dead People Platinum-Honorary-Mode Madness	Get 44 kills or more before the time runs out
Lip Up Fatty Platinum-Honorary-Mode Madness	Complete all goals in 3:30 or less
Missile Bunker-Honorary-Fever Pitch	Don't get touched at all
Oh Shoal-O-Mio Platinum-Elite-Smash'N Grab	40 kills in under 2 minutes
Old Blaggers Platinum-Elite-Group Therapy	Score 5 times
Outbreak Hotel Platinum-Honorary-Fever Pitch	Stay Alive for 3 minutes
Pirates Gold Platinum-Amateur-On the Take	Get 12 coins in under 2 minutes
Rockets 101 Platinum-Amateur-One Gun Fun	Get at least 23 kill and 1st
Screw Loose Platinum-Elite-Smash'N Grab	Get 25 points in 2:30 or less
Sock It to 'Em-Elite-Retro Chique	Complete all goals in under a minute
Toy Soldiers Platinum-Amateur-Nightstick	At least 34 kills and 1st
Vamping in Venice Platinum-Amateur-On the Take	Kill all within 2 minutes
Virtual Brutality Platinum-Amateur-On the Take	Complete all tasks in under 2 and a half minutes
Zany Zepplin Platinum-Honorary-Mode Madness	Get 30 kills before the time runs out

Unlock Items

Unlockable	How to Unlock
Anya and The General Characters	Beat first Story mission on Hard
Arthur Aching	Complete "Mansion of Madness" on Easy difficulty
Aztec Warrior	Beat Super Smashing Great Challenge, "Avec Le Brique"
Badass Cyborg	Beat Cut-Out Shoot-Out Challenge "Balls of Steel"
Berserker Splitter	Finish "The Hooded Man" under Easy difficulty or higher
Big Hands Cheat	Complete the Challenge "Cortez Can't Jump" with a bronze medal or higher
Big Heads Cheat	Complete "Outbreak Hotel" with a bronze medal or higher
Booty Guard	Beat Arcade Level "Zany Zeppeling"
Braces	Complete the Arcade League match "Old Blaggers" with at least a bronze medal
Brains	Beat Behead the Undead Challenge, "Brain Drain"
Brick Weapon	Beat Super Smashing Great Challenge, "Queen of Hearts"
Bricks	Complete "Don't Lose Your Bottle" challenge
Candi Skyler	Complete League Challenge "Screw Loose" with a bronze or higher
Captain Ed Shivers	Beat Arcade Level "Pirate Gold"
Cardboard Characters	Beat Cut-Out Shoot-Out Challenge, "Hart Attack"
Carrion Carcass	Beat Behead the Undead Challenge, "Rare or Well Done?"
Cascade Cheat	Complete "Zone Control" with a bronze medal or higher
Changeling	Complete Honorary League with golds
Chinese Chef	Complete "Ninja Garden" with a bronze medal or higher

DS
GBA
PSP
PS2
PS3
Wii
Xbox
Xbox 360
Index

TimeSplitters: Future Perfect (continued)

Unlockable	How to Unlock
Comrade Papadov	Complete the Challenge "Lap it Up" with a bronze medal or higher
Corporal Hart	Complete all Story Levels on Normal or Hard difficulty
Daisy Dismay	Beat all Story missions in co-op
Deadwina	Beat Arcade Level "I Like the Dead People"
Deep Diver	Complete "Oh Shoal-o-Mio" with a bronze medal or higher
Dozer	Beat Arcade Level "Lip Up Fatty"
Dr. Amy	Complete "U Genius, U-Genix" on Easy difficulty
Dr. Cortez	Complete "U Genius, U-Genix" on Normal difficulty
Dr. Lancet	Complete "What Lies Below" on Easy difficulty
Dr. Peabody	Get all golds or higher in Amateur League
Elite Henchman	Complete the Challenge "Melon Heist" with a bronze medal or higher
Elite Henchwoman	Complete "The Khallos Express" on Normal difficulty
Fat Characters Cheat	Complete "Commuting Will Kill You" with a bronze medal or higher
Fergal Stack	Beat Arcade Level "Virtual Brutality"
Gaston Boucher	Complete Story Level "Mansion of Madness" on normal or higher
Ghengis Kant	Complete Story Level "Machine Wars" on Easy or higher
Gideon Gout	Complete Amateur League with at least silvers
Gilbert Gastric	Complete challenge "The Cat's Pajamas" with a bronze or higher
Goddard	Beat Cut-Out Shoot-Out Challenge, "Come Hell or High Water"
GOLIATH SD/9	Complete Story Level "Something to Crow About" on Easy or higher
Hans	Beat Arcade Level "Freak Unique"
Henchman Cortez	Beat level 3 on Normal
Henchman Harry Tipper	Beat level 3 on Easy
Human Gun Sounds cheat	Earn bronze, silver, or gold in Cat's Out of the Bag challenge
Inceptor	Complete "Breaking and Entering" on Easy difficulty
Insetick SK/10	Complete Elite League with golds
Jack Sprocket	Complete "Breaking and Entering" on Normal difficulty
Jacob Crow	Complete "Future Perfect" on Easy difficulty
Jacque de la Morte	Beat Arcade Level "Vamping in Venice"
Jared Slim	Complete "The Dead, the Bad and the Silly" with a bronze medal or higher
Jed	Complete all Challenges with golds
Jim Smith	Beat all Story missions in co-op
Jo-Barf Creepy	Complete the Story Level "What Lies Below" on at least Normal difficulty
Jungle Queen	Complete "Scotland the Brave" on Easy difficulty
Karma Crow	Beat last Story mission on Hard mode
Kitten Celeste	Complete "The Khallos Express" on Easy difficulty
Koozer Mox	Beat Arcade Level "A Pox of Mox" with at least a bronze medal

DS

GBA

PSP

PS2

PS3

Wii

Xbox

Xbox 360

Index

TimeSplitters: Future Perfect (continued)

Unlockable	How to Unlock
Leo Krupps	Beat Arcade Level "Rumble in the Jungle"
Leonid	Beat Arcade Level "Commanding Will Kill You"
Monkey Gun	Complete "Electro Chimp Discomatic" challenge
Mordecai Jones	Complete "Mordecai Jones" on Easy difficulty
Mr. Fleshcage	Get a bronze or better on all challenges
Mr. Socky	Complete "Sock It To Them" with a bronze or better
Mr. Underwood	Complete the Challenge "Glimpse of Stocking" with a bronze medal or higher
Neophyte Constance	Beat Arcade Level "Freak Unique"
Neophyte Constance	Complete "The Freak Unique" with at least a bronze medal
Neophyte Lucian	Complete "Zone Control" with a bronze medal or higher
Nobby Peters	Beat Arcade Level "Toy Soldiers"
Nurse Sputum	Beat Arcade Level "Missile Bunker"
Oleg	Beat the TSUG: Timesplitters Underground challenge with a bronze or higher
Paintball Cheat	Beat Super Smashing Great Challenge, "Absolutely Potty"
Prison Officer	Complete "Screw Loose" with at least a bronze medal
Private Jones	Complete "Something to Crow About" on Normal difficulty
Prometheus SK/8	Beat Arcade Level "Virtual Brutality"
Pulov Yuran	Beat the challenge Plainly Off His Rocker with a bronze or higher
Robot Louis Stevenson	Complete "You Take the High Road" on Easy difficulty
Rotating Heads	Beat Behead the Undead Challenge, "Brain Drain"
Sapper Johnson	Complete the Challenge "Sammy Hammy Namby Pamby" with a bronze medal or higher
Sewer Zombie	Complete all Challenges with at least silvers
Sister Faith	Complete Elite League with at least silvers
Slow Motion Deaths	Complete the Arcade level "Rockets 101"
Small Heads Cheat	Complete "A Pox of Mox" with at least a bronze medal
Snowman	Beat Arcade Level "Damn Cold Out Here"
Stumpy	Complete "Front Loaded" with a bronze medal or higher
Swinging Tipper	Complete Story Level "The Russian Connection" on Easy or higher
The General	Complete Story Level "Time to Split" on Easy or higher
The Master	Beat Arcade Level "Divine Immolation"
Time Assassin	Beat level 12 on Normal
Time Assassin Cortez	Complete "You Take the High Road" on Normal difficulty
Timesplitter	Beat level 12 on easy
Tin-Legs Tommy	Beat Behead the Undead Challenge "Boxing Clever"
Tommy Jenkins	Complete all Elite League Arcade with bronze or higher
Venus	Beat Arcade Level "Bag Slag"
Victorian Crow	Complete all Story Levels on Normal or Hard difficulty
Viola	Beat Cut-Out Shoot-Out Challenge, "Hart Attack"
Vlad the Installer	Beat Arcade Level "Big Game Hunt"
Warrant Officer Cain	Complete "Scotland the Brave" on Normal difficulty

TimeSplitters: Future Perfect (continued)

Unlockable	How to Unlock
Warrant Officer Keely	Complete Honorary League with at least silvers
Zombie Monkey	Earn bronze, silver, or gold in Brain Drain Challenge

Extras

Unlockable	How to Unlock
Anaconda Music	In mission 2, find an organ somewhere in the mansion. Press the Activate button near it to make it play the Anaconda game music from *Time Splitters 2*.
Build Your Own Zombie!	When you reach the second part of the 1994 level, where you are inside the lab, turn on the two computers running the classic Mac screen saver. Wiggle the control stick to activate, then turn the Xboxes white and mess with the bars next to them. The man in the adjacent cell will become whatever you want him to be—a pancake zombie, an electric zombie, a midget flaming zombie, etc! Mix and match and knock yourself out.

Tom Clancy's Ghost Recon: Island Thunder

To unlock more "ghosts" to join your squad, complete the special objectives in the following missions on the required difficulty setting.

Unlockable Ghost	Objective
A. Galinsky	Campaign Mission 1 on Recruit during a Quick Mission in Mission Mode
B. Gordon	Campaign Mission 6 on any difficulty
D. Munz	Campaign Mission 2 on Veteran during a Quick Mission in Mission Mode
G. Osadze	Campaign Mission 5 on Veteran during a Quick Mission in Mission Mode
H. Ramirez	Campaign Mission 2 on any difficulty
J. Stone	Campaign Mission 4 on any difficulty
K. Henkel	Campaign Mission 3 on any difficulty
L. Cohen	Campaign Mission 4 on Recruit during a Quick Mission in Mission Mode
N. Tunny	Campaign Mission 3 on Elite during a Quick Mission in Mission Mode
S. Grey	Campaign Mission 5 on any difficulty
S. Ibrahim	Campaign Mission 6 on Elite during a Quick Mission in Mission Mode
W. Jacobs	Campaign Mission 1 on any difficulty

Tom Clancy's Ghost Recon 2: Summit Strike

Pause the game during gameplay, choose "In Game Options," then choose "Enter Cheats."

Unlockable	Code
Complete Current Mission	Ⓑ, Ⓑ, Ⓧ, Ⓨ
Refill Ammo	Ⓑ, Ⓑ, Ⓧ, Ⓧ
Superman (Player Invincibility)	Ⓑ, Ⓑ, Ⓧ, Ⓐ
Team Superman (Team Invincibility)	Ⓑ, Ⓑ, Ⓧ, Ⓑ

Tom Clancy's Rainbow Six 3: Black Arrow

Unlockable	Code
Guns fire lasers instead of bullets	Enter ⬆,⬇,⬆,⬇,(RT),(RT)
God Mode	Enter ⬆,⬆,⬇,⬇,⬅,➡,⬅,➡,Ⓑ,Ⓐ during gameplay.

DS
GBA
PSP
PS2
PS3
Wii
Xbox
Xbox 360
Index

Tom Clancy's Rainbow Six 4

This code only works in single player mode.

Unlockable	Code
God mode	Press ⬡, ⬡, ⬡, ⬡, ◁, ▷, ◁, ▷, Ⓑ, Ⓐ

Tomb Raider Legends

Enter these codes in game. Codes can not be used until they are unlocked.

Unlockable	Code
Bulletproof	Hold ⓛ press Ⓐ, Ⓡ, Ⓨ, Ⓡ, Ⓧ, ⓛ
Draw enemies' health	Hold ⓛ press Ⓧ, Ⓑ, Ⓐ, ⓛ, Ⓡ, Ⓨ
Excalibur	Hold ⓛ press Ⓨ, Ⓐ, Ⓑ, Ⓡ, Ⓨ, ⓛ
Infinite Assault Ammo	Hold ⓛ press Ⓐ, Ⓑ, Ⓐ, ⓛ, Ⓧ, Ⓨ
Infinite Grenade Launcher Ammo	Hold ⓛ press ⓛ, Ⓨ, Ⓡ, Ⓑ, ⓛ, Ⓧ
Infinite Shotgun Ammo	Hold ⓛ press Ⓡ, Ⓑ, Ⓧ, ⓛ, Ⓧ, Ⓐ
Infinite SMG Ammo	Hold ⓛ press Ⓑ, Ⓨ, ⓛ, Ⓡ, Ⓐ, Ⓑ
One Shot Kills	Hold ⓛ press Ⓨ, Ⓐ, Ⓨ, Ⓧ, ⓛ, Ⓑ
Soul Reaver	Hold ⓛ press Ⓐ, Ⓡ, Ⓑ, Ⓡ, ⓛ, Ⓧ
Textureless Mode	Hold ⓛ press ⓛ, Ⓑ, Ⓑ, Ⓐ, Ⓨ, Ⓡ

Tony Hawk's American Wasteland

Enter this code at the Cheats menu. (Note: case sensitive)

Unlockable	Code
Mat Hoffman	the_condor

Tony Hawk's Project 8

In the Options menu, select Cheats to enter these passwords.

Unlockable	Password
Big Realtor	shescaresme
Christian Hosoi	hohohosoi
Colonel and Security Guard	militarymen
Dad and Skater Jam Kid	strangefellows
Full Air Stats	drinkup
Grim Reaper	enterandwin
Inkblot Deck	birdhouse
Jason Lee	notmono
Kevin Staab	mixitup
Mascot	manineedadate
Most Decks	needaride
Nerd	wearelosers
Photographer and Cameraman	themedia
Travis Barker	plus44
Unlock Specials in Skate Shop	yougotitall

Tony Hawk's Pro Skater 2X

Unlockable	Code
All Cheats	While playing, pause the game and hold the ⓛ, then press ⬅, Ⓐ, ⬇, ⬆, ➡, ⬆, Ⓐ, Ⓨ, Ⓑ, Ⓐ, Ⓑ, Ⓨ.

Tony Hawk's Pro Skater 3

To enter these codes, select Cheats in the Options menu.

Unlockable	Code	Unlockable	Code
All Characters	teamfreak	Complete game with selected Character	stiffcomp
All Decks	neverboard		
All Movies	rollit	Max Stats	juice4me

Tony Hawk's Pro Skater 4

To enter these codes, select Cheats in the Options menu.

Unlockable	Code	Unlockable	Code
Always Special	i'myellow	Perfect Manuals	freewheelie
Daisy	(o)(o)	Perfect Rails	belikeeric
Everything	watch_me_xplode	Perfect Skitch	bumperrub
Matrix Mode	fbiagent	Stats 13	4p0sers
Moon Gravity	moon$hot		

Tony Hawk's Underground

Unlockable	Code
Moon Gravity	getitup
Perfect Manuals	keepitsteady
Perfect Rails	letitslide

Tony Hawk's Underground 2

To enter these codes, select Cheats in the Options menu.

Unlockable	Code
Paulie Ryan	4wheeler
Perfect Rails	straightedge

Toxic Grind

Enter these codes at the main menu. To enter them, you will need to hold ⓛⓣ+ⓡⓣ.

Unlockable	Code
All Bikes	♀, ⬗, ⬥, ⬥, ⬥, ⬥, ⬥, ⬥, ⬥, ⓛ③
All Levels	♀, ⬗, ⬥, ⬥, ⬗, ⬥, ⬥, ⬥, ⓛ③
All Music Tracks	⬥, ⬥, ⬥, ⬥, ⬥, ⬥, ⬗, ♀, ⓛ③
All Riders	⬥, ⬗, ♀, ⬗, ♀, ⬥, ⬥, ⓛ③
Unlock All Movies	⬥, ⬗, ♀, ♀, ⬗, ⬥, ♀, ♀, ⓛ③

True Crime: New York City

While on the Compstat/Map, hold ⓛⓣ+ⓡⓣ and enter these codes.

Unlockable	Code
A Million Dollars	Ⓧ, Ⓧ, Ⓨ, Ⓧ, Ⓨ, Ⓧ
Double Damage	Ⓐ, Ⓐ, Ⓐ, Ⓐ, Ⓐ, Ⓐ
Redman Gone Wild Mini Game	Ⓨ, Ⓐ, Ⓐ, Ⓐ, Ⓐ, Ⓧ
Super Cop	Ⓨ, Ⓐ, Ⓨ, Ⓐ, Ⓨ, Ⓨ
Ultra Easy Mode	Ⓑ, Ⓧ, Ⓐ, Ⓐ, Ⓨ, Ⓑ
Unlimited Ammo	Ⓑ, Ⓧ, Ⓐ, Ⓧ, Ⓧ, Ⓨ
Unlimited Endurance	Ⓑ, Ⓧ, Ⓐ, Ⓧ, Ⓐ, Ⓑ

DS
GBA
PSP
PS2
PS3
Wii
Xbox
Xbox 360
Index

DS

GBA

PSP

PS2

PS3

Wii

Xbox

Xbox 360

Index

True Crime: Streets of LA

Enter the following codes on the Map screen.

Unlockable	Code
All Driving skills	◀,▶,◀,▶,Ⓐ
All Gunplay Skills	▶,◀,▶,◀,Ⓐ
All Fighting Skills	▼,▲,▼,▲,Ⓐ

Turok: Evolution

Go to the Cheats menu and enter the following codes.

Unlockable	Code	Unlockable	Code
All Cheats	FMNFB	Invisible	SLLEWGH
All Weapons	TEXAS	Level Select	SELLOUT
Big Head Mode	HEID	Opens All Codes	FMNFB
Demo Mode/Mini-Game	HUNTER	Unlimited Ammo	MADMAN
Invincible	EMERPUS	Zoo Level	ZOO

Ty the Tasmanian Tiger 2: Bush Rescue

Enter these codes during gameplay.

Unlockable	Code
100,000 Opals	▲start, ▲start, Ⓨ, ▲start, ▲start, Ⓨ, Ⓑ, Ⓐ, Ⓑ, Ⓐ
All Bunnyip Licenses	▲start, ▲start, Ⓨ, ▲start, ▲start, Ⓨ, Ⓧ, Ⓑ, Ⓧ, Ⓐ
All Level One Rangs	▲start, ▲start, Ⓨ, ▲start, ▲start, Ⓨ, Ⓧ, Ⓧ, Ⓑ, Ⓧ
All Level Two Rangs	▲start, ▲start, Ⓨ, ▲start, ▲start, Ⓨ, Ⓧ, Ⓧ, Ⓑ, Ⓨ

UFC: Tapout 2

Unlock Fighters: Win five matches in a row to unlock new fighters from the list below. Each time you win five in a row, you unlock a new fighter of this list. Robbie Lawler, Tsuyoshi Kosaka, Vitor Belfort, Pat Miletich, John Lewis, Dan Severn, Jeremy Horn, Hayato Sakurai, Maurice Smith, Mark Coleman, Mikey Burnett, Bas Rutten, Gary Goodridge, Frank Shamrock, Marco Ruas.

Unlockable	Objective
Bruce Buffer	Win 33 matches in a row in Arcade Mode.
Frank Fertitta	Lose a total of 66 matches in Arcade mode.
Skyscrape	Beat Legend Mode with all default characters.

Ultimate Spider-Man

Enter these codes in the Controller Setup menu. A sound confirms a correct entry.

Unlockable	Code
Unlock All Characters	▶,▼,▶,▼,◀,▲,◀,▶
Unlock All Comic Covers	◀,◀,▶,◀,▲,◀,◀,▼
Unlock All Concept Art	▼,▼,▼,▲,▲,◀,◀
Unlock All Landmarks	▲,◀,▼,◀,▼,▲,◀,◀

Unreal Championship

Unlockable	Code
Agility Power-up	When your adrenaline reaches 100 and starts to flash, quickly tap ▼, ▼, ▼, ▲.
Berserk Power-up	When your adrenaline reaches 100 and starts to flash, quickly tap ▲, ▲, ▲, ▲.
Invincibility Power-up	When your adrenaline reaches 100 and starts to flash, quickly tap ▶, ▶, ◀, ◀.
Regeneration Power-up	When your adrenaline reaches 100 and starts to flash, quickly tap ▼, ▼, ▼, ▼.
Wall Jump	If a wall exists to your right, jump up and to the right, and then jump off the wall to your left.

Unreal Championship 2: The Liandri Conflict

Unlockable	Code
Cheat Menu	Pause, then hold down ⓛ+ⓇⓉ and press ⓦⓗⓣ. Turn on any of the cheats you want.

Urban Chaos Riot Response

At the Main menu, enter ◐, ◐, ◑, ◑, ◒, ◑, ◐, ◒ to open the Cheat menu. Then input these passwords.

Unlockable	Password
All Levels and Emergencies	KEYTOTHECITY
Assault Rifle Mk3 with Infinite Shells	ULTIMATEPOWER
Disco Mode	DANCINGFEET
Enhanced (Longest Ranged) Stun Gun Unlocked	FRYINGTIME
Headless Enemies	KEEPYOURHEAD
Mini-Gun Unlocked	MINIFUN
Pistol Mk4. Unlocked	ZEROTOLERANCE
Shot Sets Enemy on Fire	BURNINGBULLET
Squeaky Voices	WHATWASTHAT
Terror Difficulty Unlocked	BURNERSREVENGE

Van Helsing

During gameplay, enter the following. Access the movies in the Gallery.

Unlockable	Code
Bonus Movie 1	◐, ◑, ◐, ◑, ◅, ◅, ▷, ▷, ⓛ, ⓛ, Ⓡ, ⓇⓉ
Bonus Movie 2	◐, ▷, ◑, ◐, ◅, ◅, ◑, ◐, ◑, ⓇⓉ, ▣, Ⓡ
Bonus Movie 3	ⓛ, ⓦⓗⓣ, ▣, ⓇⓉ, ▣, ⓦⓗⓣ, ⓛ, ◐, ◐, ◑, ◑, ◑
Bonus Movie 4	◑, ⓑⓐⓒⓚ, ⓛ, Ⓡ, ⓑⓐⓒⓚ, ▣, ⓛ, ⓑⓐⓒⓚ, ◑, ◅, ◅, ◐, ▷
Bonus Movie 5	ⓦⓗⓣ, ▣, ⓛ, ⓇⓉ, ◑, ◑, ⓑⓐⓒⓚ, ⓛ, ⓛ, ▣, ▣, ⓛ, Ⓡ
Bonus Movie 6	▣, ⓇⓉ, ▣, ⓇⓉ, ⓛ, ⓦⓗⓣ, ⓛ, ⓦⓗⓣ, ◅, ▷, ⓑⓐⓒⓚ, ⓑⓐⓒⓚ
Bonus Movie 7	ⓛ, ◅, Ⓡ, ⓇⓉ, ⓦⓗⓣ, ◐, ▣, ◑, ⓛ, ◅, ⓇⓉ, ▷

Wakeboarding Unleashed

Unlockable	Code
All Boarders	Rotate ⊙ clockwise fifteen times at the Main menu.
Boarder Movies	Complete the game with that character.
Credits	Beat the game once with any boarder.
Jordan	Collect every star in the Star Search Challenges.
Level Select	Go to the Main menu and enter: ✕, ✕, ✕, ✕, ⓑ, ⓑ, ⓑ, ⓑ, ⓥ, ⓥ, ⓥ, ⓥ, ✕, ⓥ.
More Boards	Enter this code at the Main menu: ◐, ◐, ◅, ◅, ▷, ▷, ◑, ◑, ◐, ◅, ◅, ◑, ◐, ◅, ▷, ◑.
Summer	Beat the game once with any boarder.
Unlock Everything	Enter this code at the Main menu: ◐, ◑, ◐, ◑, ◐, ◐, ◑, ◑, ◐, ◑, ◅, ▷, ◅, ◅, ▷, ◅, ◅, ▷, ◅, ▷.

World Series Baseball

Unlockable	Objective
Batting Champ Medal	Complete Franchise mode in the top three teams in batting averages.
Big Spender Medal	Complete Franchise mode in the top three teams in BP spent.
Cellar Dweller Medal	Complete Franchise mode in the bottom three teams in wins.
Dominant Team Medal	Complete Franchise mode in the top three teams in wins.

DS
GBA
PSP
PS2
PS3
Wii
Xbox
Xbox 360
Index

DS

GBA

PSP

PS2

PS3

Wii

Xbox

Xbox 360

Index

World Series Baseball (continued)

Unlockable	Objective
Golden Slugger Medal	Complete Franchise mode in the top three teams in homeruns.
Great Glove Medal	Complete Franchise mode in the top three teams in fielding percentages.
Pitching Ace Medal	Complete Franchise mode in the top three teams in earned run averages.
Speed Demon Medal	Complete Franchise mode in the top three teams in stolen bases.
Strikeout King Medal	Complete Franchise mode in the top three teams in strikeouts.
Tightwad Medal	Complete Franchise mode in the bottom three teams in BP spent.

Wrath Unleashed

Unlockable	Code
Big World Map Critters	◇, ⊗, ◇, ▽, ▷, ⊕, ▽, ⊟
Extended Fighting	▽, ▽, ◇, ▽, ◁, ▷, ▽, ◇, ◇, ◇, ▷, ◁, ⊗
Team Fighter Character Variation	LT, LT, ▽, ▽, BK, WHT, BK, WHT, RT, LT, BK, RT, RT, RT, WHT
Versus Character Variations	LT, LT, ▽, ▽, BK, WHT, BK, WHT, RT, LT, BK, RT, RT, WHT

Wreckless

Unlockable	Objective
Alternate View	Press Down to cycle through different screen effects during gameplay and replays. To unlock more effects, complete missions A-9, A-10, B-9, and B-10.
AUV	Complete mission A-9.
Dragon-SPL Car	Complete mission A-1.
Missions A-2 to A-4	Complete mission A-1.
Missions B-2 to B-4	Complete mission B-1.
Music Test ("Options" screen)	Complete all 20 missions.
Super Car	Complete mission B-1.
Tank-90	Complete mission B-8.
Tiger-SPL (Tiger Tagachi's car)	Complete mission A-8.
Yakuza Car	Complete mission B-9.

WWE Raw

Unlockable	Objective
Bubba Ray Dudley's Glasses	Attack Bubba Ray Dudley during his entrance.
Christian's Glasses	Fight Christian during his entrance. Keep hitting him until his glasses fall off.
Crash Holly's Hat	Fight Crash Holly during his entrance.
D-Von Dudley's Glasses	Attack D-Von Dudley during his entrance.
Edge's Glasses	Attack Edge during his entrance.
Fred Durst	Win all the championship belts.
Fred Durst's Hat	Fight Fred Durst in a one-on-one hardcore match and knock it off. Play as Fred Durst and let another wrestler knock your hat off. Pick it up and you'll have the item.
K-Kwik's Mic	Attack K-Kwik during his entrance.
Kurt Angle's Real Gold Medals	Fight Kurt Angle during his entrance and steal his medals after they fall off his head. Hit him with them 64 times, and the real medals appear. They're gold and have a green band.
Perry Saturn's Moppy	Attack Perry Saturn during his entrance. Alternately, fight Perry Saturn in a one-on-one hardcore match.
Shane McMahon	Win the Hardcore title.

WWE Raw (continued)

Unlockable	Objective
Spike Dudley's Glasses	Choose a one-on-one match and fight with Spike Dudley during his entrance.
Stephanie McMahon-Helmsley	Win the Women's title.
Tazz's Glasses	Fight Tazz during his entrance until his glasses fall off.
Triple H's Water Bottle	Fight Triple H during his entrance.
Undertaker's Bandanna	Fight Undertaker during his entrance until he drops his bandana.
Undertaker's Glasses	Fight Undertaker during his entrance until his glasses fall off.
Vince McMahon	Win the WWF Heavyweight title.
X-Pac's Bandanna	Fight X-Pac during his entrance until he drops his bandana.

WWE Wrestlemania 21

Enter the code at the Title screen.

Unlockable	Code
All items in the Shop Zone unlocked	Hold Ⓛ+Ⓡ, and then press Ⓐ+Ⓑ+Ⓧ+Ⓨ

X2: Wolverine's Revenge

Cheats Option: On the main menu, press Ⓧ, Ⓧ, Ⓛ, Ⓛ, Ⓛ, Ⓛ, Ⓧ, Ⓧ, Ⓛ. The cheats option should now be available when you pause the game.

Unlockable	Code
All Cerebro Files and Movies	On the main menu, press Ⓧ,Ⓛ,Ⓧ,Ⓛ,Ⓧ,Ⓧ,Ⓡ,Ⓛ.
Level Select and All Challenges	On the main menu, press Ⓧ,Ⓛ,Ⓧ,Ⓛ,Ⓧ,Ⓧ,Ⓛ,Ⓛ,Ⓡ.
Unlock Everything	Press Ⓧ, Ⓛ, Ⓧ, Ⓛ, Ⓧ, Ⓧ, Ⓛ, Ⓡ at the title screen. Repeat the code a few times to unlock absolutely everything.

XGRA: Extreme-G Racing Association

Go to Options, select the Cheat menu, and enter the following.

Unlockable	Code
All Tracks	WIBBLE
All Racing Levels	FREEPLAY
O2 Liveried	UCANDO

X-Men Legends 2: Rise of Apocalypse

Enter these codes in the Review menu.

Unlockable	Code
Unlocks All Comics	◷, ◶, ◷, ◷, ◊, ◊, ◷, ◷, Ⓢ
Unlocks Game Cinematics	◶, ◷, ◷, ◶, ◊, ◊, ◷, ◶, Ⓢ

X-Men The Official Game

Enter these codes in the Cerebro Files menu.

Unlockable	Code
Iceman's Danger Room	◷, ◷, ◶, ◷, ◊, ◊, ◷, ◊, Ⓢ
Nightcrawler's Danger Room	◊, ◊, ◊, ◊, ◷, ◶, ◷, ◷, Ⓢ
Wolverine's Danger Room	◊, ◊, ◊, ◊, ◷, ◶, ◷, ◷, Ⓢ

Table of Contents - XBOX 360

2006 FIFA World Cup

Unlockable	Code
Beat the Host Nation	Beat the host nation Germany in a full match
Complete a Scenario	Complete any Challenge in Global Challenge
Complete all Scenarios	Complete all the Challenges in Global Challenge
Qualify for the World Cup	Qualify for the World Cup in 2006 FIFA World Cup mode
Win the World Cup	Win the World Cup in 2006 FIFA World Cup mode

Alien Hominid HD

Unlockable Hats

To unlock each hat do the following. Note: you must finish the level for it to unlock. Just doing the task isn't enough.

Unlockable	How to Unlock
Area 51 Agent Hat	Beat 3-2
Black Afro	Beat 1-5
Blond Wig/Pearls	Beat 1-2
Brown Hair	On Hard, jump off the spaceship before the screen fades after beating the final boss
Brown Hat	In 2-5, kill 7 birds
Brown Wig/Pearls	Beat 1-3
Chef Hat	Beat 1-3
Conical Purple Hat	In 1-3, destroy "Castle of Crap" building
Crown of Flowers	1-1 with gore off
Daisy-petal	Beat 2-3
Jester's Cap	Beat 3-4 on Hard
Jheri Curl	In 1-4 destroy "fish are like plants" building
KGB Agent Hat	Beat 2-1
Nurse Cap	In 3-5, get to final boss (don't have to win)
Pirate Hat	1-1 destroy "Hairy Mommy Daycare"
Private Eye hat	Beat 3-2 on Hard
Red Bandana	Beat 1-4
Rooster Hat	In 1-4 destroy the Behemoth-logo building (must be out of tank)
Stove Pipe Hat	1-1 with gore off
Tiara	2-2 on Hard
Yellow Shark Fin	In 2-4 dig/suffocate before riding snowmobile

Amped 3

At the Main menu, go into Options, then into the Cheats menu to enter this code.

Unlockable	Code
All Sleds	(RT), ⊗, (LT), ♀, ↻, (LB), (LT), (RT), ♥, ⊗

Assassin's Creed

Achievements

Complete each achievement to get the allotted gamerscore.

Unlockable	How to Unlock
Absolute Symbiosis (45)	Have a complete Synchronization bar.
Blade in the Crowd (30)	Kill one of your main targets like a true assassin.

DS GBA PSP PS2 PS3 Wii Xbox Xbox 360 Index

Assassin's Creed (continued)

Unlockable	How to Unlock
Conversationalist (20)	Go through every dialog with Lucy.
Defender of the People: Acre (20)	Complete every free mission in Acre.
Defender of the People: Damascus (20)	Complete every free mission in Damascus.
Defender of the People: Jerusalem (20)	Complete every free mission in Jerusalem.
Disciple of the Creed (30)	Assassinate all your targets with a full DNA bar.
Eagle's Challenge (20)	Defeat 25 guards in a single fight.
Eagle's Dance (10)	Perform 50 leaps of faith.
Eagle's Dive (20)	Perform 50 combo kills in fights.
Eagle's Eye (15)	Kill 75 guards by throwing knives.
Eagle's Flight (20)	Last 10 minutes in open conflict.
Eagle's Prey (20)	Assassinate 100 guards.
Eagle's Swiftness (20)	Perform 100 counter kills in fights.
Eagle's Talon (15)	Perform 50 stealth assassinations.
Eagle's Will (20)	Defeat 100 opponents without dying.
Enemy of the Poor (5)	Grab and throw 25 harassers.
Fearless (25)	Complete all reach high points.
Gifted Escapist (5)	Jump through 20 merchant stands.
Hero of Masyaf (20)	You've protected Masyaf from the Templar invasion.
Hungerer of Knowledge (20)	See 85% of all the memory glitches.
Keeper of the 8 Virtues (10)	Find all Hospitalier flags in Acre.
Keeper of the Black Cross (10)	Find all Teutonic flags in Acre.
Keeper of the Creed (10)	Find all flags in Masyaf.
Keeper of the Crescent (20)	Find all flags in Damascus.
Keeper of the Four Gospels (20)	Find all flags in Jerusalem.
Keeper of the Lions Passant (25)	Find all of Richard's flags in the kingdom.
Keeper of the Order (10)	Find all Templar flags in Acre.
March of the Pious (5)	Use scholar blending 20 times.
Personal Vendetta (40)	Kill every Templar.
The Blood of a Corrupt Merchant (25)	You've slain Tamir, Black Market Merchant in Damascus.
The Blood of a Doctor (25)	You've slain Garnier de Naplouse, Hospitalier Leader in Acre.
The Blood of a Liege-Lord (25)	You've slain William of Montferrat, Liege-Lord of Acre.
The Blood of a Nemesis (25)	You've slain Robert de Sable, but there is one more.
The Blood of a Regent (25)	You've slain Majd Addin, Regent of Jerusalem.
The Blood of a Scribe (25)	You've slain Jubair, the Scribe of Damascus.
The Blood of a Slave Trader (25)	You've slain Tatal, Slave Trader of Jerusalem.
The Blood of a Teutonic Leader (25)	You've slain Sibrand, the Teutonic Leader of Acre.
The Blood of the Merchant King (25)	You've slain Abul Nuqoud, Merchant King of Damascus.

Sidebar tabs: DS, GBA, PSP, PS2, PS3, Wii, Xbox, Xbox 360, Index

Assassin's Creed (continued)

Unlockable	How to Unlock
The Eagle and the Apple—1191 (100)	Complete *Assassin's Creed*.
The Hands of a Thief (15)	Pickpocket 200 throwing knives.
The Punishment for Treason (20)	You have found the traitor and have brought him before Al Mualim.
Visions of the Future (50)	After the credits roll, walk back into Desmond's bedroom and activate Eagle Vision by pressing Ⓥ and look at the wall above the bed.
Welcome to the Animus (20)	You've successfully completed the Animus tutorial.

Battlefield 2: Modern Combat

Unlock All Weapons (Campaign)

Code	Effect
Hold the ⓛⒷ and ⓡⒷ and press ➪ ➪ ♀ ♂ ➪ ➪ on the d-pad	Unlock all Weapons

Multiplayer ranks

To advance in rank in multiplayer you must get the right number of Medals, Points, and PPH (points per hour).

Unlockable	How to Unlock
Brigadier General	12 Medals, 19,390 Points, 85 PPH
Captain	8 Medals, 8,430 Points, 65 PPH
Chief Warrant Officer	5 Medals, 3,700 Points, 50 PPH
Colonel	11 Medals, 16,070 Points, 80 PPH
Commanding Sergeant Major	3 Medals, 1,820 Points, 40 PPH
Corporal	0 Medals, 70 Points, 15 PPH
First Lieutenant	7 Medals, 6,560 Points, 60 PPH
Five Star General	15 Medals, 32,000 Points, 100 PH
Lieutenant Colonel	10 Medals, 13,150 Points, 75 PPH
Lieutenant General	14 Medals, 27,330 Points, 95 PH
Major	9 Medals, 10,620 Points, 70 PPH
Major General	13 Medals, 23,150 Points, 90 PPH
Master Sergeant	1 Medal(s), 720 Points, 30 PPH
Private	0 Medals, 0 Points, 0 PPH
Private First Class	0 Medals, 20 Points, 10 PPH
Second Lieutenant	6 Medals, 4,900 Points, 55 PPH
Sergeant	0 Medals, 190 Points, 20 PPH
Sergeant First Class	0 Medals, 390 Points, 25 PPH
Sergeant Major	2 Medals, 1,180 Points, 35 PPH
Warrant Officer	4 Medals, 2,650 Points, 45 PPH

Battlestations: Midway

Enter this code at the mission select screen.

Unlockable	Code
Unlock All Levels	Hold ⓡⒷ, ■, ↑, ↖ and push ↘

DS

GBA

PSP

PS2

PS3

Wii

Xbox

Xbox 360

Index

Bejeweled 2 Deluxe

Mode Unlockables

Unlockable	How to Unlock
Remove Background Grid	Hold (LB) (LT) (RB) (RT) then press (B)
Change Jewel Types	Hold (LB) (LT) (RB) (RT) then press (A)
Unlock Cognito Mode	Finish all the puzzles in Puzzle mode. It is okay to look at hints constantly to solve all the puzzles. Cognito mode is basically Puzzle mode with no hints.
Finity Mode	Complete 280 levels of Endless mode
Hyper Mode	Complete 8 levels of Action mode
Twilight Mode	Complete 17 levels of Classic mode
Original Mode	Go into Play Game when you first load up the game. Select the Classic, Action, Endless, and Puzzle mode buttons (in that order) at the menu screen repeatedly (so you're basically maneuvering the cursor across the screen clockwise). After several rounds, a window will come up saying "Please Wait," and Original mode will load up.

Blazing Angels: Squadrons of WWII

Enter these codes while the game is paused.

Unlockable	Code
Firepower Increased	Hold (LT), press (LT), (LT), (RB), release (LT), hold (RT), and then press (RB), (RB), (LT)
God Mode	Hold (LT), press (X), (Y), (Y), (X), release (LT), hold (RT), and then press (Y), (X), (X), (Y)

Enter this code at the Main menu.

Unlockable	Code
Unlock all campaign levels and planes	Hold (LT)+(RT), then press (X), (LT), (RB), (Y), (Y), (RB), (LT), (X)

Blitz: The League

Enter these passwords in the Code menu under Extras.

Unlockable	Password
Ball Trail Always On	ONFIRE
Beach Ball	BOUNCY
Double Unleash Icons	PIPPED
Stamina Off	NOTTIRED
Two Player Co-op	CHUWAY
Unlimited Clash Icons	CLASHY
Unlimited Unleash	BIGDOGS

Bullet Witch

Unlockable	Code
Hell Mode	Beat Chaos and Hard modes

Burnout Revenge

Unlock Special Cars Offline

Unlockable	How to Unlock
Black Elite Racer	Gain the "Elite" Ranking
Criterion GT Racer	Complete Central Route's Challenge Sheet

Burnout Revenge

Custom Classic	Complete Sunshine Keys' Challenge Sheet
EA GT Racer	Complete White Mountain's Challenge Sheet
Etnies Racer	Complete Motor City's Challenge Sheet
Euro Classic LM	Complete Eternal City's Challenge Sheet
Hot Rod	Complete Lone Peak's Challenge Sheet
Logitech World Racer	Complete Rank 10 Ultimate Revenge Grand Prix
Low Rider	Complete Angel Valley's Challenge Sheet
Nixon Special	Complete Eastern Bay's Challenge Sheet
Revenge Racer	Gain "100% Complete" Status
Unlock the Madden Van	Open Options, then Special Features, and bring up the Madden 06 preview

Call of Duty 2

Enter this code on the Mission Select screen.

Unlockable	Code
Unlock all levels	Hold both the left and right bumpers, then quickly input ⊙, ⊙, ⊙, ⊙, ⓥ, ⓥ

Call of Duty 3

Enter this code at the Chapter Select screen.

Unlockable	Code
Unlock All Levels and Pictures	Hold ◯ then press ⊙, ⊙, ⊙, ⊙, ⊗, ⊗

Call of Duty 4: Modern Warfare

Arcade and Cheat Options

These unlock automatically for completing *Call of Duty 4: Modern Warfare* on any difficulty level. During gameplay, find the Cheat menu in the Options menu.

Unlockable	How to Unlock
Arcade Mode	Complete game on any difficulty
Cheat Menu	Complete game on any difficulty

Cheats

Unlock cheats by collecting enemy intel (intelligence), which look like laptop computers that are hidden throughout the campaign. Note: Using cheats disables Achievements.

Unlockable Cheats

Unlockable	How to Unlock
A Bad Year: When you kill enemies, they explode into tires!	Collect 15 pieces of enemy intel.
Cluster Bombs: After one of your frag grenades explodes, four more explode in a cross-shaped pattern.	Collect 10 pieces of enemy intel.
CoD Noir: Turns all gameplay into black and white.	Collect 2 pieces of enemy intel.
Infinite Ammo: Weapons have unlimited ammo. Doesn't work with Perk 1 abilities such as C4 and Claymores.	Collect 30 pieces of enemy intel.
Photo-Negative: Inverses all of the game's colors.	Collect 4 pieces of enemy intel.
Ragtime Warfare: Gameplay goes black and white, dust and scratches fill the screen, it plays at 2x speed, and the music becomes piano music.	Collect 8 pieces of enemy intel.

DS

GBA

PSP

PS2

PS3

Wii

Xbox

Xbox 360

Index

DS

GBA

PSP

PS2

PS3

Wii

Xbox

Xbox 360

Index

Call of Duty 4: Modern Warfare (continued)

Unlockable	How to Unlock
Slow-Mo Ability: Use the melee button to change the game to slow-mo and play at half-speed.	Collect 20 pieces of enemy intel.
Super Contrast: Dramatically increases the game's contrast, making the darks much darker and the lights much lighter.	Collect 6 pieces of enemy intel.

Golden weapons are a special camo (or skin) that you unlock when you fully complete all the challenges under the weapon subtype in the barracks (SMG, LMG, etc.). Access them by choosing the camo of the respective weapon. The effect is purely cosmetic and does not enhance the ability of the weapon in any way.

Golden Weapons

Unlockable	How to Unlock
Golden AK-47	Complete all Assault Rifle challenges.
Golden Desert Eagle	Get to Level 55.
Golden Dragunov	Complete all Sniper challenges.
Golden M1014	Complete all Shotgun challenges.
Golden M60	Complete all LMG challenges.
Golden Mini-Uzi	Complete all SMG challenges.

Multiplayer Unlockables

Unlockable	Unlocked at Rank:
AK-74U Submachine Gun	28
Bandolier Perk Class 1	32
Barret Sniper Rifle	49
Bomb Squad Perk Class 1	13
Boot Camp Challenges 1	08
Boot Camp Challenges 2	14
Boot Camp Challenges 3	17
Clan Tag	11
Claymore Perk Class 1	23
Commander Prestige Mode	55
Create a Class	03
Dead Silence Perk Class 3	44
Demolitions Class Weapon Class	01
Desert Eagle Pistol	43
Double Tab Perk Class 2	29
Dragunov Sniper Rifle	22
Eavesdrop Perk Class 3	35
Elite Challenges	51
Elite Challenges 2	53
Elite Challenges 3	54
Frag x 3 Perk Class 1	41
G3 Assault Rifle	25
G36C Assault Rifle	37
Golden Desert Eagle	55
Gun Challenges	04
Humiliation Challenges	42

Call of Duty 4: Modern Warfare (continued)

Unlockable	Unlocked at Rank:
Humiliation Challenges 2	45
Humiliation Challenges 3	47
Humiliation Challenges 4	48
Humiliation Challenges 5	50
Iron Lungs Perk Class 3	26
Killer Challenges	30
Killer Challenges 2	33
Killer Challenges 3	36
Killer Challenges 4	39
Last Stand Perk Class 3	07
M1014 Shotgun	31
M14 Assault Rifle	46
M1911 Pistol	15
M4 Carbine Assault Rifle	09
M40 Sniper Rifle	06
M60E4 Light Machine Gun	18
Martyrdom Perk Class 2	16
Mini Uzi Submachine Gun	12
MP44 Assault Rifle	52
New Playlists	05
Operations Challenges	20
Operations Challenges	21
Operations Challenges 2	24
Operations Challenges 3	27
Overkill Perk Class 2	38
P90 Submachine Gun	40
R700 Sniper Rifle	34
Sleight of Hand Perk Class 2	19
Sniper Class Weapon Class	02
UAV Jammer Perk Class 2	10

Cars

Passwords

Password	Effect
CONC3PT	All art concept
WATCHIT	All movies
R4MONE	All paint jobs
IMSPEED	Super fast start
VROOOOM	Unlimited boost
YAYCARS	Unlock all cars
MATTL66	Unlock all races
IF900HP	Unlock everything in the game

DS

GBA

PSP

PS2

PS3

Wii

Xbox

Xbox 360

Index

DS

GBA

PSP

PS2

PS3

Wii

Xbox

Xbox 360

Index

Castlevania: Symphony of the Night

Play as Other Characters and Extras

You must complete the game as Alucard with 180% or more and have a "CLEAR" Save.

Password	Effect
Enter AXEARMOR as your name	Alucard with Axelord armor
Enter RICHTER as your name	Play as Richter Belmont
Enter X-X!V"Q as your name	Alucard with lower stats and MAX Luck

Cloning Clyde

Unlock Mutant Clyde

Unlockable	How to Unlock
Mutant Clyde	Beat all levels under par time

College Hoops 2K6

Unlockable Alternate Team Jerseys

These jerseys are unlockable via the Campus Store under the Extras menu. All items are unlockable using points you earn during game play.

Unlockable	How to Unlock
Arizona Wildcats Alternate Jersey (red)	45 points
Duke Blue Devils Alternate Jersey (black)	45 points
Florida Gators Alternate Jersey (black)	45 points
Illinois Fighting Illini Alternate Jersey (orange)	45 points
Michigan Wolverines Alternate Jersey (yellow)	45 points
Missouri Tigers Alternate Jersey (yellow gold)	45 points
Notre Dame Fighting Irish Alternate Jersey (gold)	45 points
Oregon Ducks Alternate Jersey (bright yellow)	45 points
Pittsburgh Panthers Alternate Jersey (navy blue)	45 points

Condemned: Criminal Origins

All Levels and Content

Code	Effect
Enter ShovelFighter as a case-sensitive profile name	Unlocks all levels and all additional content usually unlocked through earning achievements

Achievement	How to Achieve	Reward
Bird Bath Xbox 360	Find hidden Xbox 360 with the Bird Bath TV in Chapter 7	Initial crawler grabbing animation video
Bronze Detective Badge	Find hidden Bronze Detective Badge TV in Chapter 1	Video of some early forensic tool testing
Bronze Melee Master Award	Complete a single chapter with only melee weapons (no firearms)	Stick-fighting animation video with special performance by Detective Dickenson
Chapter 1 Bronze Bird Award	Find a dead bird in Chapter 1	Concept artwork of addicts
Chapter 1 Completion Award	Finish Chapter 1	Concept artwork for Weisman Office Building
Chapter 1 Silver Bird Award	Find all six birds in Chapter 1	Concept artwork of police officers
Chapter 2 Bronze Bird Award	Find a dead bird in Chapter 2	Concept artwork of the Glassman character (who was cut from the final game)

Condemned: Criminal Origins (continued)

Achievement	How to Achieve	Reward
Chapter 2 Completion Award	Finish Chapter 2	Concept artwork for Central Metro Station
Chapter 2 Silver Bird Award	Find all six birds in Chapter 2	Concept artwork and character model of Detective Dickenson
Chapter 3 Bronze Bird Award	Find a dead bird in Chapter 3	Concept artwork of the Sandhog (burly enemy in fireman-style uniform)
Chapter 3 Completion Award	Finish Chapter 3	Concept artwork of the subway tunnels
Chapter 3 Silver Bird Award	Find all six birds in Chapter 3	Concept artwork and character model of Officer Becker
Chapter 4 Bronze Bird Award	Find a dead bird in Chapter 4	Concept artwork of vagrant characters (and others)
Chapter 4 Completion Award	Finish Chapter 4	Additional concept artwork for the subway tunnels
Chapter 4 Silver Bird Award	Find all six birds in Chapter 4	Concept artwork of Agent Ethan Thomas (you)
Chapter 5 Bronze Bird Award	Find a dead bird in Chapter 5	Concept artwork of mannequins
Chapter 5 Completion Award	Finish Chapter 5	Concept artwork for Bart's Department Store
Chapter 5 Silver Bird Award	Find all six birds in Chapter 5	Concept artwork of Vanhorn
Chapter 6 Bronze Bird Award	Find a dead bird in Chapter 6	Concept artwork and character models of the Rejects (the weakest crawlers)
Chapter 6 Completion Award	Finish Chapter 6	Concept artwork of the first crime scene
Chapter 6 Silver Bird Award	Find all six birds in Chapter 6	Concept artwork of Rosa
Chapter 7 Bronze Bird Award	Find a dead bird in Chapter 7	Concept artwork of the Trespassers
Chapter 7 Completion Award	Finish Chapter 7	Concept artwork for Metro City Library
Chapter 7 Silver Bird Award	Find all six birds in Chapter 7	Additional character concept artwork
Chapter 8 Bronze Bird Award	Find a dead bird in Chapter 8	Concept artwork and character models of the crawlers
Chapter 8 Completion Award	Finish Chapter 8	Concept artwork for St. Joseph's Secondary School
Chapter 8 Silver Bird Award	Find all six birds in Chapter 8	Character model images for Samuel Tibbits
Chapter 9 Bronze Bird Award	Find a dead bird in Chapter 9	Additional character concept artwork
Chapter 9 Completion Award	Finish Chapter 9	Concept artwork for the Apple Seed Orchard
Chapter 9 Silver Bird Award	Find all six birds in Chapter 9	Concept artwork and character model of the Match Maker
Chapter 10 Bronze Bird Award	Find a dead bird in Chapter 10	Lunch lady concept artwork and character model
Chapter 10 Silver Bird Award	Find all six birds in Chapter 10	Concept artwork, character model, and screenshots of Serial Killer X
Chief Investigator Award	Find every crime scene clue in the game	Concept artwork of Dark enemies
Compassion Award	Let Serial Killer X live	Final pull video

DS

GBA

PSP

PS2

PS3

Wii

Xbox

Xbox 360

Index

Condemned: Criminal Origins (continued)

DS
GBA
PSP
PS2
PS3
Wii
Xbox
Xbox 360
Index

Achievement	How to Achieve	Reward
DUO Report	Discover 29 metal pieces	Deep Undercover Operative Report & related evidence photos
Firearm Freedom Award	Wield every type of firearm in the game	Concept artwork of Dark enemies
Gold Detective Badge	Find hidden Gold Detective Badge TV in Chapter 9	Filipino stick-fighting video
Gold Game Completion Award	Finish entire game	Concept artwork for the different weapons in the game
Gold Melee Master Award	Complete game without using any firearms	Second prototype trailer video
Golden Bird Award	Find all birds in the game	Condemned E3 Trailer Video
Internal Affairs Report	Discover 20 metal pieces	Report that sheds light on current events/background
Melee Mayhem Award	Wield every type of debris and entry tool weapon in the game	Video of metal reduction animations (and some finishing moves)
Propaganda Report #1	Discover 9 metal pieces	Initial propaganda report and translated findings
Propaganda Report #2	Discover 20 metal pieces	Secondary propaganda report and additional translations
Propaganda Report #3	Discover 29 metal pieces	Third propaganda report and additional translations
Propaganda Report #4	Discover 30 metal pieces	Fourth propaganda report and a clue to shed additional light on the mystery
Revenge Award	Kill Serial Killer X	Serial Killer X wire-frame speech video
Ripple Xbox 360	Find hidden Xbox 360 with the Ripple TV in Chapter 2	Video of further concept artwork
Silver Detective Badge	Find hidden Silver Detective Badge TV in Chapter 6	Video of further concept artwork
Silver Melee Master Award	Complete three chapters without using any firearms	Crawler animation video
Static Xbox 360	Find hidden Xbox 360 with the Static TV in Chapter 4	A headless Ethan Thomas video
Test Pattern Xbox 360	Find hidden Xbox 360 with the Test Pattern TV in Chapter 8	Condemned credits video
Propaganda Report #2	Discover 20 metal pieces	Secondary propaganda report and additional translations
Propaganda Report #3	Discover 29 metal pieces	Third propaganda report and additional translations
Propaganda Report #4	Discover 30 metal pieces	Fourth propaganda report and a clue to shed additional light on the mystery
Revenge Award	Kill Serial Killer X	Serial Killer X wire-frame speech video
Ripple Xbox 360	Find hidden Xbox 360 with the Ripple TV in Chapter 2	Video of further concept artwork
Silver Detective Badge	Find hidden Silver Detective Badge TV in Chapter 6	Video of further concept artwork
Silver Melee Master Award	Complete three chapters without using any firearms	Crawler animation video
Static Xbox 360	Find hidden Xbox 360 with the Static TV in Chapter 4	A headless Ethan Thomas video
Test Pattern Xbox 360	Find hidden Xbox 360 with the Test Pattern TV in Chapter 8	Condemned credits video

Contra

Codes

Code	Effect
🔼🔼🔽🔽◀▶◀▶🅱🅰	Start game with 30 lives. Your score is not eligible for the High Score Leader Board.

The Darkness

Special Darklings

At any in-game phone, enter the number and you will unlock a special Darkling

Password	Effect
555-GAME	Unlocks Special 2K Darkling
555-5664	Unlocks the European Retailer (Golfer) Special Darkling

Dead Rising

Ending Requirements

These are the requirements needed in 72 hour mode to unlock different endings, with A the best and F the worst.

Unlockable	How to Unlock
Ending A	Solve all cases, talk to Isabella at 10 am, and return to the heliport at 12 pm on the 22nd
Ending B	Don't solve all cases and be at the heliport on time
Ending C	Solve all cases but do not talk to Isabella at 10 am on the last day
Ending D	Be a prisoner of the special forces at 12 pm on the 22nd
Ending E	Don't be at the heliport and don't solve all cases
Ending F	Fail to collect all of Carlito's bombs on act 7-2

Unlock Weapon: Molotov Cocktail

Unlockable	How to Unlock
Molotov Cocktail (infinite supply)	Use fire extinguisher to save Paul, then bring him to the security room.

Unlockables

A handful of the Achievements have Unlockable content that becomes available once they've been activated. These, rewards, which include special costumes and items, can be found inside Shopping Bags behind the air duct in the Security Room after you've finished the game.

Unlockable	How to Unlock
Ammo Belt	Perfect Gunner
Arthur's Boxers	7 Day Survivor
Cop Hat	Saint
Hockey Mask	PP Collector
Laser Sword	5 Day Survivor
Mall Employee Uniform	Transmissionary
Mega Man Boots	Unbreakable
Mega Man Tights	Punisher
Prisoner Garb	Carjacker
Pro Wrestling Boots	Item Smasher
Pro Wrestling Briefs	Karate Champ
Real Mega Buster	Zombie Genocide

DS
GBA
PSP
PS2
PS3
Wii
Xbox
Xbox 360
Index

Dead Rising (continued)

Unlockable	How to Unlock
Special Forces Boots	Legendary Soldier
Special Forces Uniform	Hella Copter
White Hat	Census Taker

Unlockable Modes

Unlockable	How to Unlock
Infinity Mode	Complete Overtime mode
Overtime Mode	Complete all missions in 72 mode, talk to Isabella at 10am, and return to the helipad by noon on the 22nd

Def Jam: Icon

Enter these codes at the Press Start screen.

Unlockable	Code
"It's Going Down" Music Track	Ⓑ, ◍, ◌, ◌, Ⓨ
"Make It Rain" Music Track	◍, Ⓑ, Ⓐ, ◌

Doom

Gamer Pics

Unlockable	How to Unlock
Secret Gamer Pic of a Demon	Beat any level on Nightmare difficulty
Secret Gamer Pic of a Doom Marine	Get a 100% kill rating on any level with a "Hurt Me Plenty" or higher difficulty level

Dynasty Warriors 5 Empires

Unlockables

Unlockable	How to Unlock
1,000 K.O Ribbon	Defeat 1,000 enemies in one battle. You also must win the battle.
All Created Officer Attire	Create an officer, then complete the Yellow Turban campaign.
Extra Models (Unique Characters only)	Reach the maximum number of Experience Points (60,000) with any unique character to unlock all of their models.
A Divided Land Scenario	Successfully complete the Dong Zhou in Luo Yang scenario to unlock the A Divided Land scenario.
Battle of Guan Du Scenario	Successfully complete the A Divided Land scenario to unlock the Battle of Guan Du scenario.
Dong Zhou in Luo Yang Scenario	Successfully complete The Yellow Turban Rebellion scenario to unlock the Dong Zhou in Luo Yang scenario.
Flames over Chi Bi scenario	Successfully complete the Battle of Guan Du scenario to unlock the Flames over Chi Bi scenario.
Level 4 weapons	Raise a weapon type to maximum, then get 500 kills with the person who you want to get the 4th weapon.
Executions/Old Age Death	Beat Empire mode once.
Isolate	Beat Empire mode once.
Unlimited Time	Beat Empire mode once.

Unlockable Ending Events

All endings must be unlocked on Empire mode using any difficulty and on any era.

Dynasty Warriors 5 Empires (continued)

Unlockable	How to Unlock
Death	Fail to conquer all 25 territories when the campaign time limit runs out. Campaign time limit option must be on.
Unification (Evil Ruler)	Continuously use evil deeds such as Despotism and become Emperor. Then conquer all 25 territories without committing a good deed.
Unification (Good Ruler)	Continuously use good deeds such as Philanthropy and become Emperor. Then conquer all 25 territories without committing a evil deed.
Unification (Neutral)	Conquer all 25 territories without being extremely good or evil.

Dynasty Warriors: Gundam

Unlockable Characters and Pilots

Unlockable	How to Unlock
Char Aznable and Char's Gelgoog	Complete Amuro Ray's Story mode on any difficulty in Official mode
Char's Zaku II	Complete Char Aznable's Story mode on any difficulty in Official mode
Elpe Ple and Qubeley Mk-II (Black)	Complete Both Judau Ashita and Domon Kasshu's Story modes on any difficulty
Emma Sheen	Complete Both Char Aznable and Rolan Cehack's Story modes on any difficulty
Haman Karn, Judau Ashita, Qubeley Gundam, and Gundam ZZ	Complete Judau Ashita's Story mode on any difficulty in Official mode
Hyaku Shiki	Complete Mission 4 of Char Aznable's Official mode on any difficulty
Jerid Messa and Gundam Mk-II (Black)	Complete Both Kamille Bidan and Heero Yuy's Story modes on any difficulty
Master Gundam/Master Asia	Beat Domon/Burning Gundam's Story mode on any difficulty
Milliardo Peacecraft and Gundam Epyon	Complete Heero Yuy's Story mode on any difficulty in Original mode
Musha Gundam	Complete Story mode for Amuro Ray, Kamille Bidan, Judau Ashita, Domon Kasshu, Heero Yuy, and Rolan Cehack on any difficulty
Paptimus Scirocco and The O	Complete Kamille Bidan's Story mode on any difficulty in Official mode
Ple Two	Complete Elpe Ple's Story mode on any difficulty in Original mode
Qubeley Mk-II (Red)	Complete Both Elpe Ple and Rolan Cehack's Story modes on any difficulty
Roux Louka	Complete Both Judau Ashita and Haman Karn's Story mode on any difficulty

Earth Defense Force 2017

Unlockable Bonus Weapons

Beat every mission on a certain difficulty to unlock the corresponding weapon.

Unlockable	How to Unlock
Genocide Gun	Beat all missions on Inferno
PX50 Bound Shot	Beat all missions on Hardest
Y20 Impulse	Beat all missions on Hard

DS

GBA

PSP

PS2

PS3

Wii

Xbox

Xbox 360

Index

Earth Defense Force 2017 (continued)

Unlockable	How to Unlock
ZE Launcher	Beat all missions on Normal
Zero Laser Rifle	Beat all missions on Easy

Ecco the Dolphin

Level Passwords

Password	Effect	Password	Effect
UYNAINCC	The Undercaves	ZUVPQQLU	Deep City
DQDIACCI	The Undercaves 2	AABBRQLU	City of Forever
FKWLACCA	The Vents	PLABUNLT	Jurassic Beach
NDRBRIKR	The Lagoon	FQREUNLI	Pteranodon Pond
HYAUGFLV	Ridge Water	QXKIUNLX	Origin Beach
FNCQWBMT	Open Ocean	OBEMUNLX	Trilobite Circle
DWFFZBMV	The Ice Zone	JNXPUNLA	Dark Water
QGDJRQLA	Hard Water Zone	WSGAKNLC	Deep Water 2
MCLFRQLW	Cold Water Zone	ZBPIGPLD	City of Forever 2
UWXIOQLK	The Island Zone	KUVEKMLK	The Tube
EILQOQLC	Deep Water Zone	SDDBKMLG	The Machine
XAKUQQLS	The Marble Sea	AJPPOWAX	Last Fight
FDGXQQLC	The Library		

Eragon

Unlimited Fury Mode

Pause the game while in a level.

Unlockable	How to Unlock
Unlimited Fury Mode	Hold ⓛ + ⓛⓣ + ⓡ + ⓡⓣ and press ⓧ ⓑ ⓑ ⓑ (Note: This makes magic cooldown go much faster.)

Far Cry Instincts Predator

To enter these passwords, pause the game and select the Cheat menu. Note that these passwords are case sensitive.

Unlockable	Password
Enable Evolutions	FeralAttack
Evolution Game	GiveMeItAll
Heal Yourself	ImJackCarver
Infinite Adrenaline	Bloodlust
Infinite Ammo	UnleashHell
Unlock All Maps	GiveMeTheMaps

F.E.A.R.

To unlock all levels but disable achievements, enter F3ARDAY1 as a profile/gamertag.

FIFA 06

Bonus Team, Kits, and Balls

Unlockable	How to Unlock
Adidas Etrusco Ball	Win an 8 (or more) Team Custom Knockout Tournament
Adidas Tango Espana Ball	Win a 16 (or more) Team Custom Knockout Tournament
Adidas Tricoloure Ball	Win a 5 (or more) Team Custom League
Classic 11 Team	Qualify for the World Cup in Road to the World Cup Mode

FIFA 06 (continued)

| England 1966 World Cup Kit | Win the International Masters Tournament with England in Road to the World Cup mode |
| England 1990 World Cup Kit | Win the International Open Tournament with England in Road to the World Cup mode |

Fight Night Round 3

Create a new boxer with this first name.

Unlockable	Code
All Venues	newview

FlatOut: Ultimate Carnage

Unlock Vehicles

Perform well enough to get a Bronze medal or better in each stage of three/four races to unlock the following cars. Please note that to unlock the cars, you don't need to complete the other objectives such as Time Trial, only races count. Also note that one or two of each class are unlocked in the Carnage mode. You'll have to earn gold to unlock them.

Unlockable	How to Unlock
Bonecracker (Derby)	Get Gold in the Bonecracker Demolition Derby
Bullet, Lentus, and Ventura (Race)	Complete the Race Class Stage 2
Canyon (Street)	Get Gold in the Canyon, beat the Bomb Race
Crusader (Street)	Get Gold in the Crusader Deathmatch Derby
Flatmobile (Special)	Get Gold in the Flatmobile, beat the Bomb Race
Grinder (Derby)	Get Gold in the Grinder Demolition Derby
Insetta (Race)	Get Gold in the Insetta Carnage Race
Lancea, Daytona, and Fortune (Race)	Complete the Race Class Stage 1
Mob Car (Special)	Get Gold in the Mob Car Carnage Race
Road King (Street)	Get Gold in the Road King, beat the Bomb Race
Shaker, Blaster XL, and Banger (Derby)	Complete the Derby Class Stage 1
Sparrowhawk, CTR Sport, and Vexter XS (Street)	Complete the Street Class Stage 1
Speedshifter, Terrator, Speeddevil, Bullet GT, and Sunray (Street)	Complete the Street Class Stage 2
Splitter, Switchblade, and Venom (Derby)	Complete the Derby Class Stage 2
Truck (Special)	Get Gold in the Truck Deathmatch Derby

Forza Motorsport 2

Amateur Race Series

Get first place in all the races in the series.

Unlockable	How to Unlock
#22 3R-Racing Viper Competition Coupe	Complete 5X5 V10 Super Sprint
1973 Porsche 911 Carrera RS	Complete Sports Car Classic
1992 Toyota Do-Luck Supra	Complete Boosted Shootout
2000 Acura VIS Racing Integra Type-R	Complete Inline 4 Showcase
2002 Chevrolet Lingenfelter 427 Corvette	Complete Big Block Shootout
2002 Nissan Tommy Kaira Skyline GT-R R34	Complete 6-Cylinder Showoff
Corvette Goldstrand Edition	Complete American Iron Runoff
ME Four-Twelve Concept	Complete Extreme Performance Shoot-Out

DS
GBA
PSP
PS2
PS3
Wii
Xbox
Xbox 360
Index

DS

GBA

PSP

PS2

PS3

Wii

Xbox

Xbox 360

Index

Forza Motorsport 2 (continued)

Unlockable	How to Unlock
Mugen S2000	Complete Free-Breathing Challenge
VeilSide Supra Fortune 99	Complete 20th Century Supercar Invitational

Asia Level Reward Cars

Reach these levels in Asia to unlock the cars.

Unlockable	How to Unlock
1969 Nissan Fairlady Z 432R	Reach Level 5
2004 Mitsubishi Lancer Evolution VIII MR	Reach Level 10
1998 Subaru Impreza 22B STi	Reach Level 15
2002 Nissan Skyline GT-R V-Spec II Nur	Reach Level 20
2002 Mazda RX-7 Spirit R Type-A	Reach Level 25
2005 Honda NSX-R GT	Reach Level 30
2003 Subaru #77 CUSCO SUBARU ADVAN IMPREZA	Reach Level 35
2006 Toyota #25 ECLIPSE ADVAN SUPRA	Reach Level 40
1998 Nissan #32 NISSAN R390 GTI	Reach Level 45
1999 Toyota #3 Toyota Motorsports GT-ONE TS020	Reach Level 50

Europe Level Reward Cars

Reach these levels in Europe to unlock the cars.

Unlockable	How to Unlock
1961 Jaguar E-type S1	Reach Level 5
1974 Lancia Stratos HF Stradale	Reach Level 10
1982 Porsche 911 Turbo 3.3	Reach Level 15
1989 Lotus Carlton	Reach Level 20
1987 Porsche 959	Reach Level 25
1998 Ferrari F355 Challenge	Reach Level 30
2005 Porsche #3 Lechner Racing School Team 1 911 GT3 Cup	Reach Level 35
2005 BMW Motorsport #2 BMW Motorsport M3-GTR	Reach Level 40
McLaren #41 Team McLaren F1 GTR	Reach Level 45
Audi #1 Infineon Audi R8	Reach Level 50

Manufacturer Club Races

Get first place in all the races in the series.

Unlockable	How to Unlock
1967 Ferrari 330 P4	Complete Club Ferrari
1995 Toyota VIS Racing MR2 Turbo T-bar	Complete MR2 Cup
1999 Lamborghini Diablo GTR	Complete Running of the Bulls
2000 Audi AWE S4 Tuning Silver Bullet S4	Complete Audi Cup
2000 Dodge Hennessey Viper 800TT	Complete Viper Performance Cup
2000 Nissan Top Secret D1-Spec S15	Complete Nissan Racing Club
2002 Honda Mugen Integra Type-R	Complete Integra Cup
2003 Volkswagen Golf R32	Complete Volkswagen Driver's Club
2005 Chevrolet #99 Tiger Racing Corvette Z06	Complete Corvette Touring Cup
2006 Porsche #82 Red Bull 911 GT3 Cup	Complete Porsche Sports Car Club

North America Level Reward Cars

Reach these levels in North America to unlock the cars.

Unlockable	How to Unlock
1968 Shelby Mustang GT-500KR	Reach Level 5
1969 Dodge Charger R/T-SE	Reach Level 10
1970 Chevrolet Chevelle SS-454	Reach Level 15
2000 Ford Mustang Cobra R	Reach Level 20
1996 Chevrolet Corvette Grand Sport	Reach Level 25
1999 Dodge Viper GTS ACR	Reach Level 30
2005 Chevrolet #31 Whelen Engineering Corvette Z06	Reach Level 35
2005 Panoz #51 JML Team Panoz Esperante GTLM	Reach Level 40
2002 Saleen #11 Graham Nash Motorsport S7R	Reach Level 45
2002 Cadillac #6 Team Cadillac NorthStar LMP-02	Reach Level 50

Proving Grounds Unlockable Cars

Get first place in all the races in the series.

Unlockable	How to Unlock
1969 Chevrolet Camaro Z28	Complete North American Open
1970 Porsche 914/6	Complete European Open
1985 Toyota AE86 Sprinter Trueno	Complete Asian Open
1992 Lancia Delta Integrale EVO	Complete RWD Shootout
1994 Honda Do-Luck NSX	Complete Flyweight Invitational
1995 Toyota Border MR2 Turbo T-bar	Complete Mid-Engine Challenge
2001 Mazda Mazdaspeed Roadster	Complete FWD Shootout
2003 Renault Sport Clio V6 RS	Complete Hot Hatch Runoff
2004 Honda Wings West Civic Si	Complete AWD Shootout
2007 Shelby GT500	Complete Heavyweight Open

Semi-Pro Races

Get first place in all the races in the series.

Unlockable	How to Unlock
1995 Mazda AB Flug RX-7	Complete Kumho 250HP
1998 Nissan R390	Complete Nissan 350HP
1998 Subaru Tommy Kaira Impreza M20b	Complete Goodyear 150HP
2003 Dodge #23 Viper Comp Coupe	Complete Stoptech 400HP
2003 Mitsubishi Sparco Lancer Evo VIII	Complete Sparco 200HP
2004 Volvo #24 At-Speed S60-R	Complete Toyo 450HP
2005 Maserati #35 Risi Comp MC12	Complete Risi Comp 600HP
2006 Audi #2 FSI Champion Racing R8	Complete K&N 700HP
2006 Panoz #81 Team LNT Esperante GTLM	Complete Panoz 500HP
2007 Peugeot 207 Super 2000	Complete Castrol 300HP

DS

GBA

PSP

PS2

PS3

Wii

Xbox

Xbox 360

Index

DS

GBA

PSP

PS2

PS3

Wii

Xbox

Xbox 360

Index

Frogger

Make Frogger Bigger

Unlockable	How to Unlock
Make Frogger Bigger	At the screen where you are selecting to choose One or Two players, enter ⬆ ⬆ ⬇ ⬇ ⬅ ➡ ⬅ ➡ Ⓑ Ⓐ

Full Auto

To unlock everything, you must make a new profile from the Xbox 360 dashboard.

Unlockable	Password
Unlock everything	magicman

Gauntlet

Walls Become Exits

Unlockable	How to Unlock
Walls Become Exits	On any level, all players must stand still for 200 seconds. After 200 seconds, all the walls in the level will become exit doors. If players wish to, they can shoot enemies, and change the direction of their shooting, just as long as they do not move. This works on single and multiplayer.

Gears of War

Unlockable	How To
Insane Difficulty	Complete the game on either Casual or Hardcore difficulty.
Secret Gamer Pic	Complete the game on Insane difficulty to unlock a secret gamer picture.
Secret Gamer Pic #2	Unlock the "Seriously…" achievement by getting 10,000 kills in ranked multiplayer matches to get that respective GamerPic.

The Godfather

Cheat Codes

Code	Effect
Ⓨ ⬅ Ⓨ ➡ Ⓧ ➡	Full Ammo
⬅ Ⓧ ➡ Ⓨ ➡ ⓁⒷ	Full Health
Ⓨ Ⓧ Ⓧ Ⓧ Ⓨ ⓁⒷ (click)	Film Clips

Infinite Ammo

Unlockable	How to Unlock
Infinite Ammo	Become Don of NYC

Guitar Hero II

Codes

Enter code at the main menu screen where it shows "Career" and "Quick Play."

Unlockable	How to Unlock
Air Guitar	Y, B, Y, O, Y, B
Enables Hyperspeed	B, O, Y, O, B, O, Y, Y
Eyeball Head Crowd	Y, O, B, B, B, O, Y
Flaming Heads	O, Y, Y, O, Y, Y, O, Y, Y, B, Y, Y, B, Y, Y
Monkey Head Crowd	O, Y, B, B, Y, O, B, B
Performance Mode	B, B, Y, B, B, O, B, B
Unlock All Songs	B, Y, O, R, Y, O, B, Y, B, Y, B, Y, B, Y, B, Y

Guitar Hero II (continued)

Unlockable Guitars

Unlockable	How to Unlock
"The Log" Guitar	5 Star every song on Expert mode
Axe Guitar	Beat Expert mode
Casket Guitar	Beat Medium mode
Eyeball Guitar	5 Star every song on Hard mode
Fish Guitar	Beat Easy mode
Snaketapus Guitar	Beat Hard mode
USA Guitar	5 Star every song on Easy mode
Viking Guitar	5 Star every song on Medium mode

Extra Bass Guitars Unlockable in Co-Op

NOTE

"Extra" songs do not count toward these unlockables.

Cream SG	Get 5 stars on 20 Co-Op songs
Gibson Grabber	Beat 20 Co-Op songs
Gibson SG Bass	Beat 10 Co-Op songs
Gibson Thunderbird	Beat 30 Co-Op songs
Hofner Bass	Beat all Co-Op songs
Lava Pearl Musicman Stingray	Get 5 stars on 10 Co-Op songs
Natural Maple Gibson Grabber Bass	Get 4 stars on all Co-Op songs
Natural Sunburst Gibson Thunderbird Bass	Get 5 stars on all Co-Op Songs

Guitar Hero III: Legends of Rock

Enter the following in the Cheats menu under Options. You must strum every note/chord. The letters correspond to colored frets G=Green, R=Red, Y=Yellow, B=Blue, O=Orange

Code	Effect
(BY) (GY) (GY) (RB) (RB) (RY) (RY) (BY) (GY) (GY) (RB) (RB) (RY) (RY) (GY) (GY) (RY) (RY)	Air guitar
(GR) (GR) (GR) (GB) (GB) (GB) (RB) R R R (RB) R R R (RB) R R R	Bret Michaels singer
(GR) (GY) (YB) (RB) (BO) (YO) (RY) (RB)	Easy Expert
O, B, O, Y, O, B, O, Y	Hyperspeed
(GR) (B) (GR) (GY) (B) (GY) (RY) (O) (RY) (GY) (Y) (GY) (GR)	No fail (does not work in Career mode)
RY, RB, RO, RB, RY, GB, RY RB	Performance mode
GR, GR, GR, RY, RY, RB, RB, YB, YO, YO, GR, GR, GR, RY, RY, RB, RB, YB, YO, YO	Precision mode
YO, RB, RO, GB, RY, YO, RY, RB, GY, GY, YB, YB, YO, YO, YB, Y, R, RY, R, Y, O	Unlock all songs
(GR_BO) (GRYB_) (GRY_O) (G_BYO) (GRYB_) (_RYBO) (GRYB_) (G_YBO) (GRYB_) (GRY_O) (GRY_O) (GRYB_) (GRY_O)	Unlock everything (no sound plays when you enter these chords)

Unlockable	How to Unlock
Lou	Defeat this boss and you can buy him for $15,000
Slash	Defeat this boss and you can buy him for $10,000
Tom Morello	Defeat this boss and you can buy him for $10,000

Guitar Hero III: Legends of Rock (continued)

After unlocking these guitars, you can buy them in the shop.

Unlockable Guitars

Unlockable	How to Unlock
Assassin Bass	5-star Co-op Expert mode.
Bat Guitar	5-star all songs in Easy mode.
Beach Life Bass	Complete Co-Op Career Hard mode.
El Jefe Guitar	5-star all songs in Expert mode.
Jolly Roger Guitar	5-star all songs in Medium mode.
Moon Guitar	Complete Easy mode.
Pendulaxe Blade Bass	Complete Co-op Expert mode.
Risk Assessment Guitar	Complete Expert mode.
Rojimbo! Guitar	Complete Hard mode.
Saint George Guitar	Complete Medium mode.
Tiki Face Guitar	5-star all songs in Hard mode.
Tiki Fortune 4 Bass	Complete Co-op Easy mode.

Gun

Unlockables

Unlockable	How to Unlock
Magruder's Seven Barrel Nock Gun	Successfully complete the Story mode
Reed's Horse and Magruder's Cannon Nock Gun	Get 100% completion in the Story mode
.69 Ferguson Rifle	Defeat Hollister
Apache Shirt	Successfully complete the Hunting Missions
Cavalry Sword	Defeat Reed
Dual Peacemakers	Defeat Hoodoo
Magruder's Seven Barrel Nock Gun	Successfully complete Story mode
Reed's Armored Horse	Complete the game and get 100%
Silver Spurs	Successfully complete the Pony Express Missions

Half-Life 2: The Orange Box

Half-Life 2 *Codes*

Enter the code while playing *Half Life 2*. No specific requirements other than the game. Can be entered at any time on any level. Using cheats does not disable Achievements.

Code	Effect
LB, ⬆, RB, ⬆, LB, ⬆, RB, RB, ⬆	Invincibility
⬆, ⬆, ⬇, ⬇, ⬅, ➡, ⬅, ➡, B, A	Restores health by 25 points
Y, B, A, X, RB, Y, X, A, B, RB	Restores ammo for current weapon
⬅, ⬅, ⬅, ⬅, P, ➡, ⬅, ➡, ⬅, ➡, RB	Unlocks all levels, which can then be accessed from the new game window

Portal Codes

Enter these codes anytime during gameplay.

Code	Effect
⬆, B, A, B, Y, ⬆, B, A, B, Y	Create box
LB, ⬆, RB, ⬆, LB, LB, ⬆, RB, RB, ⬆	Enables invincibility
⬆, A, Y, Y, X, X, A, A, B, B, ⬆	Fire energy ball
Y, A, B, A, B, Y, Y, A, ⬅, ➡	Portal placement anywhere
X, B, LB, RB, ⬅, ➡, LB, RB, LT, RT	Upgrade Portalgun

Halo 3

Armor Permutations Unlockables

Body Pieces: Spartan marked with (S) and Elite marked with (E).

Unlockable	How to Unlock
(E) Ascetic Body	Unlock "Up Close and Personal" Achievement
(E) Ascetic Head	Unlock "Steppin' Razor" Achievement
(E) Ascetic Shoulders	Unlock "Overkill" Achievement
(E) Commando Body	Unlock "Triple Kill" Achievement
(E) Commando Head	Unlock "Overkill" Achievement
(E) Commando Shoulders	Unlock "Killing Frenzy" Achievement
(E) Flight Body	Complete Tsavo Highway on Heroic or Legendary
(E) Flight Head	Complete Campaign mode on Heroic
(E) Flight Shoulders	Complete The Ark on Heroic difficulty or higher
(S) EOD Body	Complete Tsavo Highway on Legendary
(S) EOD Head	Complete Campaign mode on Legendary
(S) EOD Shoulders	Complete The Ark on Legendary
(S) EVA Body	Complete Tsavo Highway on Normal or higher
(S) EVA Head	Complete Campaign mode on Normal
(S) EVA Shoulders	Complete The Ark on Normal difficulty or higher
(S) Hayabusa Chest	Collect 5 hidden skulls
(S) Hayabusa Helmet	Collect 13 hidden skulls
(S) Hayabusa Shoulders	Collect 9 hidden skulls
(S) Mark V Head	Unlock "UNSC Spartan" Achievement
(S) ODST Head	Unlock "Spartan Graduate" Achievement
(S) Rogue Head	Unlock "Spartan Officer" Achievement
(S) Scout Body	Unlock "Too Close to the Sun" Achievement
(S) Scout Head	Unlock "Used Car Salesman" Achievement
(S) Scout Shoulders	Unlock "Mongoose Mowdown" Achievement
(S) Security Head	Earn 1,000 Gamerscore points
(S) Security Shoulders	Earn 850 Gamerscore points
Katana	Complete all Achievements (1,000/1,000)

BLACK-EYE SKULL

Effect: Melee hits instantly recharge your shield.

Level: Crow's Nest

Location: As soon as you start the level, head straight up to the higher level. Head toward the door with the red light, then turn around. Jump onto the racks, onto the red metal light holders, then onto the ventilation tube. The skull spawns at the end.

BLIND SKULL

Effect: "Shoot from the hip."

Level: First Stage

Location: When you get to the area where you see the Phantom overhead (one of the marines points it out) jump over the rocks and keep following the path on the right. When you get to the cliff, there's a rock over on the side. The skull is on the end of the rock. Note: This skull has to be activated before you start a Campaign map.

CATCH SKULL

Effect: all enemies have 2 grenades, throw more grenades.

Level: The Storm

DS
GBA
PSP
PS2
PS3
Wii
Xbox
Xbox 360
Index

Location: From the start, go through until you go outside again. Outside, look straight across to a small round building. The skull is on top. To get up there, either use a warthog as a platform or grenade-jump. DO NOT destroy the wraith near the door or the skull will disappear.

COWBELL SKULL

Effect: Explosive force increased (sputnik from H2).

Level: The Ark

Location: First pick up a grav lift from the small building near where you fight the scarab. Now proceed through the level until you reach the second sloping hallway (stairway). You should see some partitioned risers (platforms) halfway down. The skull is on the top level. Toss the grav-lift on the right side of the hall so it lands on the fourth little green dot from the door. Then run, jump, and use the grav-lift to propel you to the top. You reach a checkpoint just as you enter the room, so if you miss, just try again.

FAMINE SKULL

Effect: "Trust us. Bring a magazine." Dropped weapons have very little ammo compared to normal.

Level: The Ark

Location: When you first go into the valley to the right after the wrecked phantom, look left to see a huge boulder. Use a ghost and get to the side of the boulder closest to the bridge overhead. It is easy to pilot the ghost up the side of the wall using the thrust. To get the skull, pilot 2 ghosts up the wall to the top of the bridge and stack them one on top of another next to the beam where the skull is placed. Simply jump from the top of the ghosts toward the skull and land on the beam.

FOG SKULL

Effect: "You'll miss those eyes in the back of your head." Your motion sensor disappears.

Level: Floodgate

Location: As you are walking down from the anti-air gun you destroyed in the previous mission, you encounter a ramp (next to a missile launcher). Around this ramp, you hit a checkpoint. At this point, you should also hear a marine yelling, "There! Over There!" Look up and to the right, directly at the roof of the building next to the missile launcher. A single flood form (not to be mistaken for the two other flood forms jumping in front of you) holds the skull. Kill him before he jumps, and he drops the skull down to the ground where you can retrieve it. If you shoot too early, and the skull gets stuck on the roof.

GRUNT BIRTHDAY PARTY SKULL

Effect: Headshots on grunts cause heads to explode with confetti.

Level: Crow's Nest

Location: Right after the first objective, while en route to the barracks, you fall onto a pipe. At the end of this pipe, look over the edge to see a small space a few feet below you. Drop over and as quickly as you can, pull back to land under the floor you were just on. The skull is at the end.

IRON SKULL

Effect: When either player dies in Co-Op on any difficulty both players restart at last checkpoint. In single player, you restart the level if you die.

Level: Sierra 117

Location: In the area where you rescue Sarge, behind the prison cell is a large ledge. Go to the far right side and jump on the boxes, then onto the pipes to get up on the ledge. Go to the far end of the ledge, turn two corners, and the skull is at the far end.

IWHBYD SKULL

Effect: "But the dog beat me over the fence." Unlocks bonus dialogue throughout the game. For most, this is the last skull, so this gives you the Hayabusa Helmet as well.

Level: The Covenant

Location: To get this, get to the room where you "fight" the Prophet of Truth. Let the Arbiter kill him, turn around, and kill all the flood here as well. This makes it a lot easier. Then jump through the Halo holograms in this order: 4 6 5 4 5 3 4. When you jump through the final hologram, they all light up in a sequential pattern. The skull is at the end, right before the energy bridge leading to Truth's corpse.

MYTHIC SKULL

Effect: Every enemy on the field now has double the normal amount of health.

Level: Halo

Location: As soon as the mission starts, walk up the hill in front of you and into the cave. Hug the right side of the cave, and after a large boulder you see a path on your right. Take the short path and find it at the end.

THUNDERSTORM SKULL

Effect: "Field promotions for everyone!" Upgrades enemies to their stronger versions.

Level: The Covenant

Location: After you shut down tower 1 and get access to the hornet, fly to tower 2 (the one the Arbiter shut down). While walking up the stairs, go to the middle part that connects both. A stair leads up to a platform where the skull is.

TILT SKULL

Effect: "What was once resistance is now immunity." Enemies have different body parts that may be resistant to certain bullet types.

Level: Cortana

Location: When in the circular type room with all the flood, look for a small structure piece next to two archways. Jump on top of it and up on the rocks to the top left, turn left and jump up again, then do a 180 and jump to the rocks across from you. Follow the rock sticking out and leading up on top of the original circular room. The skull is in a pile of blood.

TOUGH LUCK SKULL

Effect: Enemies do saving throws.

Level: Tsavo Highway

Location: On Tsavo Highway, about halfway through the mission (right after you are forced to walk through a large blue barrier), you will come out of a tunnel on the highway, and see a large pipeline on your left. Drop down in between the two, and run to the wall in front of you. Follow the wall all the way to where it connects with the cliff on your right, and turn to the left. There should be a few ledges—simply crouch-jump from ledge to ledge, and the last one should have the "Tough Luck" skull on it.

THE SEVEN TERMINALS

The Ark:

1. Start the mission and once you enter the first building, take a left into another door and emerge in a curved corridor. On the inside is a Terminal.

2. After activating the bridge to let your comrades across the gap, do a 180 and you should see it. (It does not open until you activate the bridge.)

3. In the third building after defeating the scarab, kill the group of sleeping covenant, then follow the corridor downward. Once you reach a door in front that is locked, immediately on the left there's an open door. Go through and walk straight, then do a 180 to find a secret room. It is in there.

The Covenant:

1. When in the first tower standing on the lift, face the access panel and turn left. Jump over and it's right there.

DS

GBA

PSP

PS2

PS3

Wii

Xbox

Xbox 360

Index

DS

GBA

PSP

PS2

PS3

Wii

Xbox

Xbox 360

Index

Halo 3 (continued)

2. Land your hornet on the second tower, walk toward the entrance, but when you see the locked door, do a 180.

3. When in the third tower standing on the lift, face the access panel and turn right. Jump over.

Halo:

1. After reaching the end of the first cave, hug the right wall and you see a building. Jump up onto the walkway and hang a left once inside.

Harry Potter and the Order of the Phoenix

Room of Rewards Trophies

Unlockable	How to Unlock
Characters Cup	Meet all 58 characters in Hogwarts
Defense Against the Dark Arts Cup	Cast all defensive spells in six duels
House Ghost Cup	Find all four House Ghosts
Nature Trail Cup	Find all animal footprints

Jetpac Refuelled

Pictures and Dashboard

Unlockable	How to Unlock
Two Gamer Pictures and Dashboard Theme	Beat level 64. You can download these items in the Help and Options menu.

Kameo: Elements of Power

Thorn's Castle

Unlockable Required	Description	Pts.
Audio—The Troll Song	You have to hear it to believe it.	1,000,000
Cheats #1	Big Troll heads, Big Kameo head	2,500,000
Classic Kameo Skin	Have Kameo don her original purple outfit!	100,000
Video—Cutscene Style Test	A test clip of an early cutscene.	2,000,000
Video—Making Backgrounds	Shows how the background were made.	500,000
Video—Trailer Concept	An insight into the development process of the trailer.	1,500,000

Forgotten Forest

Unlockable Required	Description	Pts.
Cheats #2	Warrior Vision, Screen FX	2,000,000
FMV Player	The Story Begins, Kameo Meets Thorn, Pummel Weed Evolves, Rubble Evolves, Major Ruin Evolves, Deep Blue Evolves, Flex Evolves, 40 Below Evolves, Thermite Evolves, Shadow Troll Vision, Halis Vision, Lenya Vision, Yeros Vision, Airship, Warp, Death, The End…, Credits.	1,600,000
Pummel Weed Skin	Enable a new skin for Pummel Weed!	400,000
Rubble Skin	Enable a new skin for Rubble!	1,200,000
Video—Animation Creation	The magic of animation.	200,000
Video—The Wotnot Book	Learn more about the ancient tome.	800,000

Kameo: Elements of Power (continued)

Water Temple

Unlockable Required	Description	Pts.
Ash Skin	Enable a new skin for Ash!	1,000,000
Boss Battles	Old Mawood, Corallis, Queen Thyra, Lord Cheats #3	3,000,000
Drok, Thorn	Retro FX, Hard Trolls (disables Battle Points)	2,500,000
Cutscene Extras	Bonus bits for cutscene aficionados.	1,500,000
Gothic Kameo Skin	Kameo goes goth.	500,000
Major Ruin Skin	Enable a new skin for Major Ruin!	2,000,000

Snow Temple

Unlockable Required	Description	Pts.
Bonus Music Player	Bonus Tune #1—Umchacka, Bonus Tune #2—Alternative Theme	1,500,000
Cheats #4	Fire Proof (disables Battle Points), Troll Traitors—flip-kick a Troll to turn it against the others! (disables Battle Points), Scaredy-Trolls (disables Battle Points)	3,000,000
Chilla Skin	Enable a new skin for Chilla!	2,000,000
Deep Blue Skin	Enable a new skin for Deep Blue!	1,000,000
Group Shot Movie Player	An evolution of the group; Group Shot—2003, Group Shot—2004 #1, Group Shot—2004 #2	500,000
Video—Model Gallery	Check out the different character models.	2,500,000

Thorn's Pass

Unlockable Required	Description	Pts.
Animatic Player #1	Kameo Meets Thorn, Pummel Weed Evolves, Flex Evolves, 40 Below Evolves, Thermite Evolves, Transform Animatic	4,500,000
Cheats #5	Max Health (disables Battle Points), Elemental Override: fire (disables Battle Points), Elemental Override: ice (disables Battle Points)	5,000,000
Coyote Kameo Skin	Kameo blends in with the animals.	2,500,000
Flex Skin	Enable a new skin for Flex! .	4,000,000
Old Evolve Sequences Player	Video—Evolving Rubble, Video—Evolving 40 Below, Video—Evolving Pummel Weed, Video—Evolving Deep Blue	3,500,000
Video—Old Chars. & Moves	View some old character and moves.	3,000,000

DS
GBA
PSP
PS2
PS3
Wii
Xbox
Xbox 360
Index

DS
GBA
PSP
PS2
PS3
Wii
Xbox
Xbox 360
Index

Kameo: Elements of Power (continued)

Thorn's Airship

Unlockable Required	Description	Pts.
40 Below Skin	Enable a new skin for 40 Below!	1,500,000
Video—Airship Concept	Working on Thorn's Airship.	2,000,000
Cheats #6	Easy Trolls (disables Battle Points), One-Hit Kills (disables Battle Points), Invulnerable (disables Battle Points), Upgrade All Warriors (disables Battle Points)	3,000,000
Other Deleted Scenes Player	Video—Kalus Attacks!, Video—Evolving Cloud Monster, Video—Kameo Rare Logo, Video—Vortex Capture	1,000,000
Video—Early Years	Check out footage of a very early version of Kameo.	500,000
Video—Ending Concept	An early idea for the ending sequence.	2,500,000

Overall Score

Unlockable Required	Description	Pts.
Animatic Player #2	The Release of Thorn, Cailem Goes to the Citadel, Cailem Leads the Trolls, Tree Monster Evolves, Cloud Monster Evolves, Whirly Bird Evolves, Death Animatic	18,000,000
Concept Art Gallery #1	Concept art straight from the designers.	9,000,000
Concept Art Gallery #2	More awesome concept art.	12,000,000
Snare Skin	Enable a new skin for Snare!	15,000,000
Video—Deleted Cutscenes	See what didn't make the cut.	21,000,000
Thermite Skin	Enable a new skin for Thermite!	24,000,000

LEGO Star Wars II: The Original Trilogy

Different Characters

Password	Effect	Password	Effect
Beach Trooper	UCK868	Palace Guard	SGE549
Ben Kenobi's Ghost	BEN917	Rebel Pilot	CYG336
Bespin Guard	VHY832	Rebel Trooper from Hoth	EKU849
Bib Fortuna	WTY721	Red Noses on All Characters	NBP398
Boba Fett	HLP221	Santa Hat and Red Clothes	CL4U5H
Death Star Trooper	BNC332	Skiff Guard	GBU888
Emperor	HHY382	Snowtrooper	NYU989
Ewok	TTT289	Stormtrooper	PTR345
Gamorean Guard	YZF999	TIE Fighter	HDY739
Gonk Droid	NFX582	TIE Fighter Pilot	NNZ316
Grand Moff Tarkin	SMG219	TIE Interceptor	QYA828
Han Solo with Hood	YWM840	Ugnaught	UGN694
IG-88	NXL973	Unlock Greedo	NAH118
Imperial Guard	MMM111	Unlock Jawa	JAW499
Imperial Officer	BBV889	Unlock Sandtrooper	YDV451
Imperial Shuttle Pilot	VAP664	Unlock Tusken Raider	PEJ821
Imperial Spy	CVT125	White Beard Extra	TYH319
Lobot	UUB319		

The Lord of the Rings, The Battle for Middle-Earth II

Unlockable Heroes

Unlockable	How to Unlock
Avatan	Win 10 capture and hold games
Brerthor	Complete the whole good campaign
Celebrim	Win 10 resource race games
Felek	Win 10 hero vs. hero games
Fhaleen	Win 10 king of the hill games
Hadhood	Complete level 1 of good campaign with all bonus objectives
Idrial	Complete level 8 of good campaign with all bonus objectives
Krashnack	Complete level 1 of dark campaign with all bonus objectives
Maur	Complete level 4 of the dark campaign with all bonus objectives
Mektar	Complete good campaign with no heroes dying
Ohta	Win 10 versus games
Olog	Complete level 8 of the dark campaign with all bonus objectives
Thrugg	Complete level 4 of the dark campaign with all bonus objectives
Tumna	Complete the whole bad campaign
Urulooke	Complete dark campaign with no heroes dying

Lost Planet: Extreme Condition

Enter these codes when the game is paused. They can be used only on Easy mode.

Unlockable	Code
500 Thermal Energy	↑, ↓, ↑, ↓, ↓, ←, →, ←, →, X, Y, RB, LB
Infinite Ammunition	LB, LT, RT, RB, Y, X, ←, ↓, ←, LB, LT, RT, LT, LB, RB, X, ←, ↓, X, RB, LB
Infinite Health	↓, ↓, ↓, ↑, Y, ↑, ↓, ↑, Y, ↑, ↓, ↑, ↓, ↓, X, ↓, X, ←, Y, X, ←, Y, →, X, RB, LB
Infinite Ammunition	RT, RB, Y, X, ←, →, ↓, ←, LB, LT, RT, RB, Y, X, →, ↓, ←, LB, LT, RT, LT, LB, RB, X, ←, ↓, X, RB, LB

Major League Baseball 2K6

To enter these passwords, go into My 2K6, then select Enter Codes. Note that passwords are case sensitive.

Unlockable	Password
Bouncy Ball	Crazy Hops
Crazy Pitches	Unhittable
Rocket Arms	Gotcha
Super Wall Climbs	Last Chance
Topps 2k6 All-Stars	Dream Team
Unlock All Cheats	Black Sox
Unlock All Extras	Game On
Unlock Everything	Derek Jeter

DS GBA PSP PS2 PS3 Wii Xbox Xbox 360 Index

DS

GBA

PSP

PS2

PS3

Wii

Xbox

Xbox 360

Index

Major League Baseball 2K7

To enter these codes select My 2K7. Then select Enter Cheat Code.

Unlockable	Code
Boosts a team's power rating by 25% for 1 inning	mightymick
Boosts the hitting of the 3, 4, 5 hitters in the lineup by 50% for 1 game	triplecrown
Boosts your ability to hit home runs during the game just like The Mick	m4murder
Mickey will pinch hit	phmantle
Unlocks everything	Derek Jeter
Unlocks Mickey Mantle in free agency	themick

Marvel: Ultimate Alliance

These codes need to be entered in different areas of the game.

Enter these in the Team menu.

Unlockable	Code
100k	↑, ↑, ↓, ↓, ←, →, ←, ☺
Level 99	↑, ←, ↑, ←, ↓, ↓, ↓, →

Enter these in the Character Selection screen.

Unlockable	Code
All Character Code	↑, ↑, ↓, ↓, ↓, ←, ←, →, ☺start
All Costumes	↑, ↓, ↑, ↓, ←, →, ←, →, ↑, ↓, ☺start
All Powers	←, →, ←, →, ↑, ↓, ↑, ↓, ←, →, ☺
Unlock Daredevil	←, ←, ↓, →, ↑, ↓, ↑, ↓
Unlock Silver Surfer	↓, ←, ←, ↑, ↑, ↓, ↓, ←

Enter these codes in the Review menu.

Unlockable	Code
All Cinematics	↑, ←, ←, ↑, ↑, →, ↑
All Comics	←, →, →, ←, ↑, ↑, →
All Concept Art	↓, ↓, ↓, →, →, ←, ↓
All Wallpapers	↑, ↓, →, ←, ↑, ↑, ↓

Enter these codes while playing.

Unlockable	Code
Filler	←, →, →, ←, ↑, ↓, ↓, ↑
God mode	↑, ↓, ↑, ↓, ↑, ←, →, ↓, →
Super Speed	↑, ↑, ↑, ↑, ↓, →
Touch of Death	←, ↑, ↓, ↓, →, ←, ←

Enter this code on the Comic Book missions.

Unlockable	Code
The Courses	↑, →, ←, ↓, ↑, ←, →

Mass Effect

Achievements

Complete each of the following achievements to get the allotted gamerscore.

Unlockable	How to Unlock
AI Hacking Specialist (15)	Use AI hacking 75 times.
Asari Ally (20)	Complete the majority of the game with the Asari squad member.
Assault Rifle Expert (15)	Register 150 assault rifle kills.

Mass Effect (continued)

Unlockable	How to Unlock
Barrier Mastery (15)	Use Biotic Barrier 75 times.
Charismatic (10)	Use Charm or Intimidate to resolve an impossible situation.
Completionist (25)	Complete the majority of the game.
Council Legion of Merit (25)	Complete Virmire.
Damping Specialist (15)	Use Damping Field 75 times.
Distinguished Combat Medal (25)	Complete one Mass Effect playthrough on the Hardcore difficulty setting.
Distinguished Service Medal (25)	Complete Eden Prime.
Dog of War (25)	Register 150 organic enemy kills.
Extreme Power Gamer (50)	Reach 60th level with one character.
First Aid Specialist (15)	Use medi-gel 150 times.
Geth Hunter (25)	Register 250 synthetic enemy kills.
Honorarium of Corporate Service (25)	Complete Noveria.
Krogan Ally (20)	Complete the majority of the game with the Krogan squad member.
Lift Mastery (15)	Use Biotic Lift 75 times.
Long Service Medal (25)	Complete two playthroughs on any setting.
Medal of Exploration (50)	Land on an uncharted world.
Medal of Heroism (25)	Complete Feros.
Medal of Honor (100)	Complete one playthrough on any difficulty setting.
Medal of Valor (50)	Complete one playthrough on the Insanity difficulty setting.
Neural Shock Specialist (15)	Use Neural Shock 75 times.
Overlord Specialist (15)	Use Shield Overload 75 times.
Paragon (15)	Accumulate 75% of total Paragon points.
Paramour (10)	Complete any romance subplot.
Pistol Expert (10)	Register 150 pistol kills.
Power Gamer (20)	Reach 50th level with one character.
Quarian Ally (20)	Complete the majority of the game with the Quarian squad member.
Renegade (15)	Accumulate 75% of total Renegade points.
Rich (25)	Exceed 1,000,000 Credits.
Sabotage Specialist (15)	Use Sabotage 75 times.
Scholar (25)	Find all primary aliens: Council Races, Extinct Races, and Non-Council Races codex entries.
Search and Rescue (10)	Locate Dr. T'Soni in the Artemis Tau cluster.
Sentinel Ally (20)	Complete the majority of the game with the Alliance sentinel squad member.
Shotgun Expert (15)	Register 150 shotgun kills.
Singularity Mastery (15)	Use Biotic Singularity 75 times.
Sniper Expert (15)	Register 150 sniper rifle kills.
Soldier Ally (20)	Complete the majority of the game with the Alliance soldier squad member.
Spectre Inductee (15)	Become a Spectre.
Stasis Mastery (15)	Use Biotic Stasis 75 times.

DS

GBA

PSP

PS2

PS3

Wii

Xbox

Xbox 360

Index

DS

GBA

PSP

PS2

PS3

Wii

Xbox

Xbox 360

Index

Mass Effect (continued)

Unlockable	How to Unlock
Tactician (25)	Complete playthrough with shield damage greater than health damage.
Throw Mastery (15)	Use Biotic Throw 75 times.
Turian Ally (20)	Complete the majority of the game with the Turian squad member.
Warp Mastery (15)	Use Biotic Warp 75 times.

Character Benefit Unlockables

Attain certain achievements to gain benefits on future playthroughs.

Unlockable	How to Unlock
+10% Experience Bonus	Complete 75% of game.
+10% Hardening Bonus	Complete 75% of game with Ashley in squad.
+10% Health Bonus	Kill 150 organic beings.
+10% Shield Bonus	Kill 250 synthetics.
+25% Marksman Cooldown Bonus	Attain 150 kills with pistol.
10% Reduced Cooldown for Barrier and Stasis	Complete 75% of game with Liara in squad.
10% Reduced Cooldown for Lift and Throw	Complete 75% of game with Kaiden in squad.
10% Reduced Cooldown for Overload and Damping	Complete 75% of game with Garrus in squad.
10% Reduced Cooldown for Sabotage and AI Hacking	Complete 75% of game with Tali in squad.
10% Shield Increase	Sustain more shield damage than health damage during one playthrough.
5% Increase in Weapon Damage	Complete the game twice on any difficulty.
Assault Rifle Skill for New Characters	Attain 150 kills with assault rifle.
Barrier Skill for New Characters	Use Barrier 75 times.
Decryption Skill for New Characters	Use Sabotage 75 times.
Electronics Skill for New Characters	Use Overload 75 times.
First Aid Skill for New Characters	Use medi-gel 150 times.
Hacking Skill for New Characters	Use AI Hacking 75 times.
Lift Skill (for non-biotics)	Use Lift 75 times.
Medicine Skill for New Characters	Use Neural Hacking 75 times.
Regenerate 1 Health per Second	Complete 75% of game with Wrex in squad.
Shielding Skill for New Characters	Use Dampening 75 times.
Shotgun Skill for New Characters	Attain 150 kills with shotgun.
Sniper Rifle Skill for New Characters	Attain 150 kills with sniper rifle.
Spectre Grade Weapons for Purchase	Attain 1,000,000 credits in your wallet.
Singularity Skill for New Characters	Use Singularity 75 times.
Statis Skill for New Characters	Use Statis 75 times.
Throw Skill for New Characters	Use Throw 75 times.
Warp Skill for New Characters	Use Warp 75 times.

Unlockable Gamer Pics

Complete the game on the Hardcore and Insanity difficulties to unlock two special gamer pics for your profile.

Mass Effect (continued)

Unlockable	How to Unlock
"N7" Gamer Pic	Gain the Medal of Valor achievement.
Saren Gamer Pic	Gain the Distinguished Combat Medal achievement.

Unlockables

Complete the game on Normal to unlock the secrets.

Unlockable	How to Unlock
Hardcore Mode	Complete the game once.
Increased Level Cap (51–0)	Complete the game once.
Insane Difficulty	Beat the game on the Hardcore difficulty without changing the difficulty.
New Game +	Start a New Game, then select existing Career. You'll be playing with your older character (with all items and skills intact).

Medal of Honor: Airborne

Codes

Unlockable	How to Unlock
Enter Cheat menu	Press ⏺+⏺, then press ⊗,⏺,⏺,Ⓐ,Ⓐ
Full Ammo	Press and hold ⏺+⏺ then press ⏺,⏺,⏺,⊗,Ⓐ,Ⓨ
Full Health	Ⓨ,⊗,⊗,Ⓨ,Ⓐ,⏺

Monster Madness: Battle for Suburbia

At the pause screen press: ⬆,⬆,⬇,⬇,⬅,➡,⬅,➡,⏺,Ⓐ. The typing console appears. Then type in the cheat.

Code	Effect
patrickdugan	Animal sounds
ihatefunkycameras	Disable special tracking cameras
upthejoltcola	Faster music
MorgyTheMole	First person/headless
ArieannDeFazioWithFlair	Increase the size of Jennifer's chest
stevebrooks	Infinite secondary items
SouthPeak	Push objects away from player
reverb	Remove film grain
chipmunks	Squeaky voices

NASCAR 08

Passwords

Password	Effect
checkered flag	All Chase mode cars unlocked
ea sports car	Unlocks the EA Sports car
race the pack	Unlocks the fantasy drivers
Walmart Everyday	Unlocks the Walmart car and track

NBA 2K6

Enter these passwords in the Codes menu from the Features menu.

Unlockable	Password
2K Sports Team	2KSPORTS
Air Zoom Kobe 1 Shoes	KOBE
Alt. All-Star Team Jerseys	fanfavorites

DS

GBA

PSP

PS2

PS3

Wii

Xbox

Xbox 360

Index

NBA 2K6 (continued)

Unlockable	Password
Boston, New York and Chicago St. Patricks Day Jerseys	gogreen
Celebrity Players Unlocked in 24/7 Mode	ballers
Champagne Uniform	sac 2nd
Dark Blue Uniform	den 2nd
Green Uniform	bos 2nd
Lebron James Summer Shoes	lebronsummerkicks
Lebron's Allstar shoes	lb allstar
Lebron's Birthday Shoes	lb bday
Lebron's Black and Crimson shoes	lb crimsonblack
Lebron's White and Gold shoes	lb whitegold
Navy Blue Uniform	cle 2nd
NBA 2K6 Team	NBA2K6
New Indiana Pacers Jerseys	31andonly
Nike Shoes	anklebreakers Uptempo
Red Pistons Uniform	det 2nd
Unlocks Chicago Bulls Throwback	chi retro
Unlocks Houston Rockets Throwback	hou retro
Unlocks L.A. Clippers Throwback	lac retro
Unlocks Memphis Grizzlies Throwback	mem retro
Unlocks Miami Heat Throwback	mia retro
Unlocks New Jersey Nets Throwback	nj retro
Unlocks New Orleans Hornets Throwback	no retro
Unlocks New York Knicks Throwback	ny retro
Unlocks Orlando Magic Throwback	orl retro
Unlocks Phoenix Suns Throwback	phx retro
Unlocks Seattle Sonics Throwback	sea retro
Unlocks Shawn Marions signature shoes "MTX"	crazylift
Unlocks Washington Wizards Throwback	was retro
Visual Concepts Team	vcteam

Enter these passwords at the Vending Machine located in "The Crib".

Unlockable	Password
+10 defensive awareness	lockdown
+10 offensive awareness	getaclue
No quick game fatigue	nrgmax
No quick game injuries	noinjury
Power bar tattoo in the create player mode	pbink

NBA 2K7

Enter these passwords in the Codes menu under Features.

Unlockable	Code
ABA Ball	payrespect
Defensive Awareness	getstops
Maximum Durability for One Game	ironman
Offensive Awareness	inthezone
Unlimited Stamina for One Game	norest
All-Star Uniforms	syt6cii
Bobcats Secondary	bcb8sta
Jazz Secondary	zjb3lau

DS

GBA

PSP

PS2

PS3

Wii

Xbox

Xbox 360

Index

NBA 2K7 (continued)

Unlockable	Code
Nets Secondary	nrd4esj
Wizards Secondary	zw9idla
St. Patrick Day uniforms	tpk7sgn
International All-Stars	tns9roi
NBA 2K Team	bestsim
Superstar Team	rta1spe
Topps 2K Sports All-Stars	topps2ksports
2007 All-Star Ball	ply8mia
2007 All-Star Uniforms	syt6cii
New Orleans Hornets Uniforms (Valentine's Day)	vdr5lya

NBA Street Homecourt

Enter these codes at the main menu.

Unlockable	Code
All Courts	Hold ⓛⒷ and ⓡⒷ and press ⬆, ➡, ⬇, ⬅
Virtual Ball	Hold ⓛⒷ and ⓡⒷ and press ⬆, ⬇, ⬅, ➡

Need for Speed Carbon

Enter at the main menu.

Unlockable	Code
Infinite Crew Charge	⬇, ⬆, ⬆, ➡, ⬅, ⬅, ➡, ✕
Infinite NOS	⬅, ⬆, ⬅, ⬇, ⬅, ⬇, ➡, ✕
Infinite SpeedBreaker	⬇, ➡, ➡, ⬅, ⬇, ⬆, ⬇, ✕
Need For Speed Carbon Logo Vinyls Unlocked	➡, ⬆, ⬇, ⬆, ⬇, ⬅, ⬅, ✕
Need For Speed Carbon Special Logo Vinyls Unlocked	⬆, ⬆, ⬇, ⬇, ⬇, ⬇, ⬆, ✕

Need for Speed Most Wanted

All codes should be entered at the Start screen.

Unlockable	Code
Unlocks Burger King Challenge Event (#69)	⬆, ⬇, ⬆, ⬇, ⬅, ➡, ⬅, ➡
Unlocks Free Engine Upgrade Bonus Marker (Can be used in the backroom of the customization shops)	⬆, ⬆, ⬇, ⬇, ⬅, ➡, ⬆, ⬇
Unlocks Special Edition Castrol Ford GT (Which is added to your bonus cars)	⬅, ➡, ⬅, ➡, ⬆, ⬇, ⬆, ⬇

NHL 2K6

Enter this as a profile name. Case Sensitive.

Unlockable	Password
Unlock everything	Turco813

NHL 08

RBK Edge Jersey

Password	Effect
h3oyxpwksf8ibcgt	Unlock RBK Edge Jerseys

DS
GBA
PSP
PS2
PS3
Wii
Xbox
Xbox 360
Index

DS

GBA

PSP

PS2

PS3

Wii

Xbox

Xbox 360

Index

Ninety-Nine Nights

Unlockables

Unlockable	How to Unlock
Character Profiles	Clear all of a character's missions to unlock his or her profile
Special Stage	Complete each character's story and then play Inphyy's last stage again and you will travel to fight the King of Nights
Character: Aspharr	Clear Fort Wyandeek with Inphyy
Character: Dwingvatt	Clear all of Inphyy, Aspharr, and Myifee's missions
Character: Klarrann	Clear all of Dwingvatt's missions
Character: Myifee	Clear the Pholya Flatlands with Inphyy
Character: Tyurru	Clear all of Dwingvatt's missions
Character: Vigk Vagk	Clear all of Tyurru and Klarrann's missions

Peter Jackson's King Kong

At the Main menu screen, hold LT+RT+RB+LB, and press ❑, ◉, ❑, ⊗, ❑, ❑, ❑, ❑. This opens the Cheat Menu. Now enter any of these case sensitive passwords.

Unlockable	Password	Unlockable	Password
999 ammunition	KK 999 mun	Machine gun	KKcapone
Bonuses completed	KKmuseum	One-hit kills	GrosBras
God mode	8wonder	Sniper rifle	KKsn1per
Level select	KKst0ry	Unlimited spears	lance 1nf

Prince of Persia Classic

Passwords

Password	Effect	Password	Effect
73232535	Level 2	51139315	Level 9
96479232	Level 3	53246739	Level 10
53049212	Level 4	32015527	Level 11
51144526	Level 5	44153123	Level 12
18736748	Level 6	96635134	Level 13
42085223	Level 7	75423134	Level 14
98564243	Level 8	89012414	End

Project Gotham Racing

From the simple to the complex, these badges are your rewards for what you can accomplish as a driver.

Race Craft Badges

Unlockable Badge	Objective
3 Back-to-Back Wins	Successfully complete three races in a row.
5 Back-to-Back Wins	Successfully complete five races in a row.
10 Back-to-Back Wins	Successfully complete ten races in a row.
10 Races with No Penalties	Keep it clean by completing 10 races in a row without hitting another car or the barrier.
20m Power Slide	Complete a 20 meter powerslide anywhere on the track.
30m Power Slide	Complete a 30 meter powerslide anywhere on the track.
50m Power Slide	Complete a 50 meter powerslide anywhere on the track.

Project Gotham Racing (continued)

Unlockable Badge	Objective
All Kudos Maneuvers in Game	In a single race, complete every type of Kudos maneuver there is!
All Slide Types in Race	Perform every type of slide-based Kudo maneuver there is in a race.
Big Air	Hit an incline and stay in the air for two seconds or more.
Millionaire Badge	Spend one million credits on cars.
My First Win	Finish in first place in any street race.
No Penalties	Successfully complete a race without smashing into either the barriers or another car.
X3 Combo	Complete three Kudos maneuvers in a row.
X5 Combo	Complete five Kudos maneuvers in a row.
X10 Combo	Perform 10 Kudos maneuvers in a row to earn this badge.

Career Badges focus on your victories in Gotham Career mode.

Career Badges

Unlockable Badge	Objective
All Bronze	Win every match in Gotham Career mode on Easy difficulty.
All Gold	Win every match in Gotham Career mode on Hard difficulty.
All Platinum	Win every match in Gotham Career mode on Hardcore difficulty.
All Silver	Win every match in Gotham Career mode on Medium difficulty.
All Steel	Win every match in Gotham Career mode on Novice difficulty.
Complete a Championship in Manual	Drive a stick for an entire tournament.
First Medal	Earn your first medal in Gotham Career mode.
First Platinum Medal	Earn one platinum medal.
First Platinum Trophy	Complete every race in a tournament on Hardcore difficulty.
First Trophy	Win your first championship in Career mode.
Own a Car from Each Group	Buy a car from each of the five car classes.
Own All Cars	Collect every car in the game.
Pro Racer	Complete any championship on Hardcore difficulty using only a car with a manual transmission.
Race King	Complete all the wheel-to-wheel championships.
Style King	Complete all the style-based championships.
Time King	Complete all the time-based championships.

Online badges are rewarded based on your performance in Online Career mode.

Online Badges

Unlockable Badge	Objective
Clean Racer	Complete a race in Online Career mode without hitting another car or a barrier.
Complete 25 Races	Complete 25 races in Online Career mode.
Complete 50 Races	Complete 50 races in Online Career mode.

DS

GBA

PSP

PS2

PS3

Wii

Xbox

Xbox 360

Index

Project Gotham Racing (continued)

Unlockable Badge	Objective
Complete 100 Races	Complete 100 races in Online Career mode.
Earn 250 Kudos in One Race	Earn 250 Kudos in a single online race.
Earn 500 Kudos in One Race	Earn 500 Kudos in one race while in Online mode.
Earn 1,000 Kudos in One Race	Earn 1,000 Kudos in a single race in Online mode.
Earn 10,000K Online	Gather more than 10,000 Kudos in the Online Career mode.
Earn 25,000K Online	Gather more than 25,000 Kudos in the Online Career mode.
Earn 100,000K Online	Gather more than 100,000 Kudos in the Online Career mode.
First Online Win	Win one race on Xbox Live.
Start Last, Finish First	Overcome your tragic handicap to win this badge.
Win in Each Online Scenario	Try all of the Online Career scenarios and win at least once each.
Winning Streak X3	Win three races in a row.
Winning Streak X5	Win five races in a row.
Winning Streak X10	Win ten races in a row.

Quake 4

To enter these codes, press the Back button while playing.

Unlockable	Code
Ammo Refill for All Weapons	Ⓑ, Ⓐ, Ⓧ, Ⓨ, ◁, ▷, ◁
Full Health Refill	Ⓑ, Ⓐ, Ⓑ, Ⓐ, △, △, ▽, Ⓧ

Ratatouille

Passwords

Password	Effect
SPEEDY	Unlimited running
MATTELME	Unlock all single player and multiplayer minigames

Rock Band

Unlock All

Enter quickly at the "Rock Band" title screen (disables saving).

Code	Effect
Red, Yellow, Blue, Red, Red, Blue, Blue, Red, Yellow, Blue	Unlock All Songs

Rush 'n Attack

Codes

A meow confirms that the code was entered correctly.

Code	Effect
At the main menu, using the D-pad, press △/△/▽/▽/◁/▷/◁/▷/Ⓑ/Ⓐ	Alternate Sound FX

Saint's Row

Pause the game and select your phone to enter these codes.

Unlockable	Password
Ambulance (Restores Health)	911
Ambulance in Your Garage	#262852623
Anchor in Your Garage (Newsvan)	#Anchor
Ant	#268
Aqua Car	#AQUA
Ar-40 Xtnd Rifle	#27409863
Baron	#22766
Baron in Your Garage	#Baron
Baseball Bat	#BaseBall
Best Car in the Game	#337 335 2623
Betsy in Your Garage	#BETSY
Big Willy's Cab	(555) 819 8415
Brown Baggers	555 3765
Bulldog	#2855364
Bulldozer	#bulldozer
Cavallaro in Your Garage	#CAVALLARO
Chicken Ned	555 2445
Clear Skies	#sunny
Compton in Your Garage	#Compton
Cosmos in Your Garage	#267667
Crash Landing	555 MART
Destiny	#3378469
Eagleline Yellow (Taxi Service)	555 018 0174
Enables .44 Shepherd	#Shepherd
Enables 12 Gauge	#12Gauge
Enables AS12 Riot	#AS12Riot
Enables GDHC .50	#GDHC50
Enables Hand Grenade	#Grenade
Enables Knife	#Knife
Enables Molotov Cocktail	#Molotov
Enables Nightstick	#Nightstick
Enables NR4	#NR4
Enables Pipe Bomb	#Pipebomb
Enables Rattler	#728 8537
Enables RPG Launcher	#Rocket
Enables T3K Urban	#T3KUrban
Enables Tombstone	#Tombstone
Enables Vice 9	#Vice9
Enables Zenith	#936484
Eye for an Eye Voodoo	555 5966
FBI	#FBI
Five-O	#34836
Full Health	#fullhealth

DS
GBA
PSP
PS2
PS3
Wii
Xbox
Xbox 360
Index

OS

GBA

PSP

PS2

PS3

Wii

Xbox

Xbox 360

Index

Saint's Row (continued)

Unlockable	Password
God's Wrath	#10
Grounds for Divorce	555 9473
Gunslinger in Your Garage	#Gunslinger
Halberd in Your Garage	#HALBERD
"Hammerhead" in Your Garage	#Hammerhead
Hollywood in Garage	#hollywood
Impressions Clothing	555 3248
Infinite Ammo	#AMMO
Infinite Sprint	#SPRINT
Justice in Your Garage	#5878423
K6Krukov	#K6Krukov
Keystone in Your Garage	#KEYSTONE
Komodo in Your Garage	#566636
Legal Lee's	555 9467
Lik-a-Chick	555 3863
Mag in Garage	#mag
McManus Sniper Rifle	#Macmanus
Money	#66639
Newman in Your Garage (Mail Truck)	#Newman
No Cop Notoriety	#nocops
No Gang Notoriety	#nogangs
Nordberg in Your Garage	#66732374
On the Fence (Pawn Shop)	555 7296
On The Rag Clothing	555 5926
On Thin Ice	555 2564
Pimpcane Shotgun	#pimpcane
Quasar in Your Garage	#Quasar
Quota	#78682
Rattler	#7288537
Reaper (Hurst)	#732737
Rim Jobs	555 3493
Shogun in Garage	#shogun
Spawns Taxi in Your Garage	#TAXI
Special GameStop T-Shirt	#42637867
Stocks	555 2626
Suicide Hotline	1 555 ITS OVER
The Dead Cow	555 6238
The Job	#843562
Titan	#84816
TNA Taxi	555 455 8008
TraxxMaster in Your Garage	#TRAXXMASTER
Tuasar in Your Garage	#882727

Saint's Row (continued)

Unlockable	Password
Vortex in Your Garage	#867839
Voxel	#87935
Xenor	#14333
Zenith in Your Garage	#936484

Shrek the Third

Gold

Code	Effect
○ ⓑ, ♀, ○, ○, ○	Receive 10,000 gold coins

Skate

Best Buy Clothes

Code	Effect
○, ♀, ○, ○, ⊗, ⓡⓑ, ♥, ⓛⓑ	Unlock exclusive Best Buy clothes

Unlock Dem Bones Character

Unlockable	How to Unlock
Dem Bones	Break each bone in your body at least 3 times

Small Arms

Unlockables

Unlockable	How to Unlock
Shooting Range Practice	Beat Mission mode
Billy Ray Logg	Beat him in Mission mode with any character
ISO-7982	Complete Mission mode
Mousey McNuts	Beat him in Mission mode with any character
Professor Von Brown	Beat him in Mission mode with any character

Smash TV

Invincibility

Code	Effect
Press ⓐ+♥	Become invincible. This code must be entered in every room. You can move around and change the angle of your shooting. If you stop shooting, the code deactivates. Don't stop shooting unless you want to pick up a new weapon or prize.

Sonic the Hedgehog 2

Code	Effect
17	Play Invincibility Music
65	Plays a Shifting Sound
09	Plays Casino Night Zone 1-Player Music
19	Plays Sonic 2 Theme

Space Giraffe

Super Ox Mode

Do this after finishing the game once, when the game asks you to choose between tutorial or main game mode.

Code	Effect
Hold ♥, then push ⓐ	Play an extra 100 levels

DS

GBA

PSP

PS2

PS3

Wii

Xbox

Xbox 360

Index

DS

GBA

PSP

PS2

PS3

Wii

Xbox

Xbox 360

Index

Spider-Man: Friend or Foe

Codes

Venom and new Green Goblin (from the movie) can be unlocked by entering the following codes using the d-pad when standing in the Helicarrier in between levels. You hear a tone if you entered the code correctly, and they are then be selectable from the sidekick select console.

Code	Effect
↑, ↑, ↓, ↓, ←, →	Gain 5,000 upgrade points
←, ↓, →, →, ↓, ←	New Green Goblin
←, ←, →, ↑, ↓, ↓	Venom

Star Trek: Legacy

Unlockable	How to Unlock
Unlock the U.S.S. Legacy	To unlock the secret ship (and receive the achievement), beat the game once on any difficulty, then load your game. When you do, you should be on the ship buying screen right before the final mission. From there; sell and/or buy ships to make sure you have 3 Sovereign-class ships. The final ship you buy will be the U.S.S. Legacy.

Stuntman Ignition

Passwords

Password	Effect
COOLPROP	3 props in Stunt Creator mode
NOBLEMAN	All items unlocked for Construction mode
GFXMODES	Several new camera effects and styles
Kungfoopete	Unlock all cheats
IceAge	Unlock Ice Wheels cheat
TheDuke	Unlock Nitro Addiction cheat
Imtarex	Unlock Touchable cheat
Wearefrozen	Unlock Vision Switcher cheat
fastride	Unlocks the MVX Spartan

Super Contra

Unlockable	How to Unlock
Unlimited Lives and Super Machine Gun	On the main menu, select Arcade Game, and then enter the following code: (Using the D-Pad) ↑, ↑, ↓, ↓, ←, →, ←, →, Ⓑ, Ⓐ. If done correctly, the game will start up instead of backing out to the main menu. You will begin with 5 lives that never decrease when killed, and you will have a super machine gun weapon equipped at all times! Using this code disables all Achievements and you cannot upload scores to Xbox Live Leaderboards. The code remain active until you exit the game using the Exit Game option in the Pause menu.

Super Puzzle Fighter II Turbo HD Remix

Hidden Characters

Unlockable	How to Unlock
Akuma	Press ↓, while having Hsien-Ko highlighted on the Player Select screen
Anita	Press Ⓛ or Ⓡ on Donovan, then press Ⓐ
Bat	Press Ⓛ or Ⓡ on Morrigan then press Ⓐ
Dan Hibiki	Press ↓, while having Donovan highlighted on the Player Select screen

Alternate Finishing Moves

Devilot	Press ◎, while having Morrigan highlighted on the Player Select screen
Mei-Ling	Hold the ⓛⒷ or ⓡⒷ button on Hsien-Ko, then press ◎

Unlockable	How to Unlock
Ken's Alternate Finishing Move	Hold ⓛⒷ or ⓡⒷ during selection of Ken
Ryu's Alternate Finishing Move	Hold ⓛⒷ or ⓡⒷ during selection of Ryu

Superman Returns

Cheat Codes

Anytime during gameplay after the Gladiator Battle first set, pause the game. Enter the following buttons to unlock the cheats. A chime confirms that the code has been entered correctly.

Unlockable	How to Unlock
Infinite Health (Metropolis)	◉, ◒, ◉, ◒, ◌, ◒, ◒, ◉
Infinite Stamina	◌, ◌, ◉, ◉, ◒, ◒, ◒, ◒, ◉, ⊗
Unlock All Costumes, Trophies, and Theater Items	◒, ◌, ◒, ◉, ◉, ⊗, ◉, ◌, ◒, ⊗
Unlock All Moves	◒, ◉, ◒, ⊗, ◉, ◉, ◌, ◉, ⊗, ◉, ⊗

Unlockables

Unlockable	How to Unlock
Bizarro	◌,◒,◉,◒,◌,◉,◉,◒,◌ (Enter it when you load your game, at the menu that lets you choose Metropolis or Fortress of Solitude before you start the game you loaded.)
Golden Age Superman Suit	Save Metropolis from the tornadoes
Pod Suit	Beat Bizarro

Surf's Up

Passwords

Password	Effect
MYPRECIOUS	All Boards unlocked
GOINGDOWN	All Leaf Slide stages unlocked
WATCHAMOVIE	Unlocks all videos
TINYBUTSTRONG	Unlocks Arnold
THELEGEND	Unlocks Big Z
SURPRISEGUEST	Unlocks Elliot
SLOWANDSTEADY	Unlocks Geek
KOBAYASHI	Unlocks Kobayashi
IMTHEBEST	Unlocks Tank Evans

Thrillville: Off the Rails

In-Park Cheats

To enter cheats, quickly enter the following button presses while you're in any park. For most, you won't see any changes, but you will get results if you entered them correctly.

Effect	Code
$50,000	⊗,Ⓑ,◉,⊗,Ⓑ,◉,Ⓐ
500 Thrill Points	Ⓑ,⊗,◉,Ⓑ,⊗,◉,⊗
Activate Mission Unlock	⊗,Ⓑ,◉,⊗,Ⓑ,◉,Ⓑ

DS

GBA

PSP

GC

PS2

PS3

Wii

Xbox

Xbox 360

Thrillville: Off the Rails (continued)

Effect	Code
Unlock All Minigames in Party Play	✕,🅱,🅨,✕,🅱,🅨,◁
Unlock All Parks	✕,🅱,🅨,✕,🅱,🅨,✕
Unlock All Rides in Current Park	✕,🅱,🅨,✕,🅱,🅨,🅨

Achievements

Complete each achievement to get the allotted gamerscore.

Unlockable	How to Unlock
Bandito Beater (20)	Complete Bandito Chinchilla.
Casanova (10)	Become sweethearts with 10 park guests.
Challenge Champ (10)	Win 10 challenges with park guests on any minigames.
Chatter Box (10)	Fill your MyCrowd list.
Coaster Boaster (10)	Design a rollercoaster.
Coaster Dropper (10)	Build a coaster with a drop height of more than 300 ft.
Coaster Speedster (10)	Build a coaster with a top speed over 80 mph.
Crackshot (10)	Get a X5 combo multiplier in a shooting gallery.
Critics (30)	Complete the "Bribery 101!" mission in Thrillville Stunts.
Disc Jockey (10)	Collect all the Hypnodiscs.
Flippin' Great (10)	Perform a 720 backflip in Stunt Rider.
Fore! (10)	Complete a round of timed minigolf on Hard difficulty.
Games Master (40)	Complete all arcade games.
Hypnosis (30)	Complete the "Trance-Cendtal" mission in Thrillville Giant.
Karting Krazy (10)	Finish first in 20 races.
King of the Ring (15)	Win a match by knockout on Robo K.O. without losing any health.
Lunar Lunatic (15)	Complete Event Horizon 2 on Hard difficulty.
Money Maker (10)	Achieve a combined park value of $100,000.
Party Dude (10)	Play 20 party games with your friends.
Party Host (10)	Complete a four-player battle or co-op game in party play.
Perfect Clearance (15)	Pocket all the balls in one turn at the table.
Propaganda (10)	Collect all the anti-Thrillville propaganda boards.
Putt Putt Power (10)	Design a minigolf course.
Robots (30)	Complete the "Clearance Sale" mission in Thrillville Otherworlds.
Sabotage (30)	Complete the "Alien Antics" mission in Thrillville Explorer.
Sideshow Superstar (20)	Get a 5-star rating score on all sideshow games.
Smooth Move (10)	Get a 60-note combo in the entertainer minigame.
Sparkling Secret (10)	Discover all the secret areas on Sparkle Quest level 1.
Spoon Time (15)	Get 30,000 points in three moves on trampolines.
Sprint King (15)	Get a best lap time under 4'90" seconds on the first track on Autosprint 2.
Squadron Ace! (20)	Complete Squadron Ace.
Stunt Rider! (20)	Complete Stunt Rider.
Super Sparkler (20)	Complete Sparkle Quest.
Tank Commander (20)	Complete Tank Frenzy.

DS
GBA
PSP
PS2
PS3
Wii
Xbox
Xbox 360
Index

Thrillville: Off the Rails (continued)

Unlockable	How to Unlock
Teamwork (10)	Complete a minigame in co-op mode.
The Green (10)	Find all Mortimer's cash drops hidden in all parks.
The Rainbow (10)	Collect all the Nano Paint Sprayers.
Thrillville Explorer (40)	Unlock Thrillville Explorer.
Thrillville Giant (40)	Unlock Thrillville Giant.
Thrillville Holiday (50)	Unlock Thrillville Holiday.
Thrillville Otherworlds (40)	Unlock Thrillville Otherworlds.
Thrillville Phenomenon (60)	Reach park owner level 10.
Thrillville Sensation (40)	Reach park owner level 5.
Thrillville Superstar (50)	Rank in the top 10 on any online leaderboard for *Thrillville: Off the Rails*.
Thrillville Talent (20)	Reach park owner level 2.
Traitor (30)	Complete the "Traitors Arena" mission in Thrillville Holiday.
UFO Survivor (15)	Survive without being knocked out of the arena in Saucer Sumo on normal difficulty.
White Knuckle Ace (10)	Build all WHOA pieces.
Whoa (10)	Finish a coaster using a WHOA piece.
Winner! (20)	Successfully win 20 multiplayer battle games.

Tiger Woods PGA Tour 07

Enter this password in the Passwords menu under options.

Unlockable	Code
Crowd has big heads	tengallonhat

Tiger Woods PGA Tour 08

Passwords

Password	Effect
cream	Unlimited money
allstars	Unlock all golfers
playfifa08	Unlock Wayne Rooney
greensfees	Unlocks All Courses

TMNT

Codes

At the main menu screen, hold Ⓛ and enter the code, then release Ⓛ. You should hear a sound to confirm you entered the code right.

Code	Effect
AABA	Unlocks challenge map 2
BYAX	Unlocks Don's big head goodie

DS

GBA

PSP

PS2

PS3

Wii

Xbox

Xbox 360

Index

Tom Clancy's Ghost Recon Advanced Warfighter

When the game is paused, enter these codes while holding 🔘, ⓛ, ⓡ.

Unlockable	Code
Full Life	ⓛ, ⓛ, ⓡ, ⊗, ⓡ, ⓨ
Scott Mitchell Invincible	ⓨ, ⓨ, ⊗, ⓡ, ⊗, ⓛ
Team Invincible	⊗, ⊗, ⓨ, ⓡ, ⓨ, ⓛ
Unlimited Ammo	ⓡ, ⓡ, ⓛ, ⊗, ⓛ, ⓨ

Enter this code on the Mission Select screen while holding 🔘, ⓛ, ⓡ.

Unlockable	Code
All Levels	ⓨ, ⓡ, ⓨ, ⓡ, ⊗

Tom Clancy's Ghost Recon Advanced Warfighter 2

Enter this password as a name.

Unlockable	Code
FAMAS in Quick Missions Only (works in Australian version only)	GRAW2QUICKFAMAS

Tom Clancy's Rainbow Six Vegas

Unlockable	How To
01 Private 2nd Class	All Starting Equipment
02 Private 1st Class	Headgears 1: Tactical Helm, Balaclava
03 Specialist	Rainbow Weapons: MP7A1, SIG552, USP40
04 Corporal	Camo 1: Desert, Urban, Russian, Guerrilla, Fall, Desert 2
05 Sergeant	Tactical Armor: Raven Recon Armor, Vulture Combat Armor, Falcon Assault Armor
06 Staff Sergeant	Headgears 2: 3 Hole Balaclava, Baseball Cap, Breathing Mask
07 Sergeant First Class	Camo 2: Flecktarn, Orange, Swedish, War2k5, Alpen, White
08 Master Sergeant	Freedom Fighter weapons: AK47, Raging Bull, SV98
09 First Sergeant	Headgears 3: Bonnie Hat, Beret, Tinted Goggles
10 Sergeant Major	Black Market Armor: Typhoon Recon Armor, Cyclone Combat Armor, Hurricane Assault Armor
11 2nd Lieutenant	Camo 3: Pink, Blue, Woodland, Wasp, Sand, Crimson
12 1st Lieutenant	Headgears 4: Half-Face Mask, Reinforced Helm, Tactical Goggles
13 Captain	Merc Weapons: MG36, SPAS12, Deagle
14 Major	Military Armor: Vier Recon Armor, Diamondback Combat Armor, Anaconda Assault Armor
15 Lt. Colonel	Camo 4: Yellow Urban, Red Urban, Tiger, Rust, Urban 2, Grey
16 Colonel	Headgears 5: Ballistic Face Mask, Riot Helm, NVGs
17 Elite	Camo 5: Custom 1, Custom 2, Custom 3

Tom Clancy's Splinter Cell Double Agent

Unlockables

Unlockable	How to Unlock
Spy—Second Skin	Achieve RECRUIT level (with a general average higher that 1%)
Spy—Third Skin	Achieve SPECIAL AGENT level (with a general average higher than 45%)

Tom Clancy's Splinter Cell Double Agent (continued)

Unlockable	How to Unlock
Uspilon Forces—Second Skin	Achieve FIELD AGENT level (with a general average higher than 20%)
Upsilon Forces—Third Skin	Achieve COMMANDER level (with a general average higher than 95%)
Unlock All Multiplayer maps	Win 6 games as a Spy, 6 games as a UPSILON Force member, and play 25 games overall.
Electric Lock Pick	Complete the primary objectives in JBA HQ 1
EMP Device—Enhanced	Complete the primary objectives in JBA HQ 1
EMP Grenade	Complete the secondary objectives in the Iceland Assignment
EMP Grenade Attachment	Complete the secondary objectives in the Cozumel Assignment
Explosive Sticky Camera Attachment	Complete the secondary objectives in the Iceland Assignment
Frag Grenade Attachment	Complete the primary objectives in JBA HQ 3
Gas Grenade	Complete the primary objectives in JBA HQ 1
Gas Grenade Attachment	Complete the secondary objectives in the Cozumel Assignment
Hacking Device— Force Hack Upgrade	Complete the primary objectives in JBA HQ 2
Hacking Device— Software Upgrade	Complete the secondary objectives in the Shanghai Assignment
Night Vision—Enhanced	Complete the primary objectives in JBA HQ 3
Shotgun Shell Attachment	Complete the secondary objectives in the Okhotsk Assignment
Smoke Grenade - Attachment	Complete the secondary objectives in the Shanghai Assignment
Sonic Grenade Attachment	Complete the primary objectives in JBA HQ 2
Ultrasonic Emitter	Complete the secondary objectives in the Ellsworth Assignment
Wall Mine—Flash	Complete the secondary objectives in the Okhotsk Assignment
Wall Mine—Stun	Complete the secondary objectives in the Ellsworth Assignment
Ending A: Good	NSA trust above 33%, and you managed to save at least two of the three targets.
Ending B: Normal	NSA trust below 33%, but you managed to save the three targets. Or destroy two of the three targets, and NSA trust above 33%.
Ending C: Bad	Destroy/Kill all three targets. Or Destroy/Kill two of the targets, and NSA trust below 33%.

Tomb Raider Legends

Enter these codes in game. Codes can not be used until they are unlocked.

Unlockable	Code
Bulletproof	Hold ⓛⓣ press Ⓐ, ⓇⓉ, Ⓨ, ⓇⓉ, Ⓧ, ⓁⒷ
Draw enemies' health	Hold ⓛⓣ press Ⓧ, Ⓑ, Ⓐ, ⓁⒷ, ⓇⓉ, Ⓨ
Excalibur	Hold ⓛⒷ press Ⓨ, Ⓐ, Ⓑ, ⓇⓉ, Ⓨ, ⓛⓣ
Infinite Assault Ammo	Hold ⓛⒷ press Ⓐ, Ⓑ, Ⓐ, ⓛⓣ, Ⓧ, Ⓨ
Infinite Grenade Launcher Ammo	Hold ⓛⒷ press ⓛⓣ, Ⓨ, ⓇⓉ, Ⓑ, ⓛⓣ, Ⓧ

DS
GBA
PSP
PS2
PS3
Wii
Xbox
Xbox 360
Index

Tomb Raider Legends (continued)

Unlockable	Code
Infinite Shotgun Ammo	Hold (LB) press (RT), ⊕, ⊗, (LT), ⊗, ⊕
Infinite SMG Ammo	Hold (LB) press ⊕, ⊛, (LT), (RT), ⊕, ⊕
One Shot Kills	Hold (LT) press ⊛, ⊕, ⊛, ⊗, (LB), ⊕
Soul Reaver	Hold ⊛ press ⊕, (RT), ⊕, (RT), (LT), ⊗
Textureless Mode	Hold (LT) press ⊛, ⊕, ⊕, ⊕, ⊛, (RT)

Tony Hawk's American Wasteland

In the Options menu, select the Cheats menu and enter these passwords. (Note: case sensitive)

Unlockable	Password
Matt Hoffman	the_condor
Perfect Grinds	grindXpert
Perfect Manuals	2wheels!

Tony Hawk's Project 8

Enter these passwords in the Cheats menu.

Unlockable	Password
All decks unlocked and free except for inkblot deck and Gamestop deck	needaride
All specials in shop	yougotitall
Travis Barker	plus44
Grim Reaper (Freeskate)	enterandwin
Jason Lee	notmono
Anchor Man	newshound
Big Realtor	shescaresme
Christian Hosoi	hohohosoi
Colonel and Security Guard	militarymen
Inkblot Deck	birdhouse
Kevin Staab	mixitup
Nerd	wearelosers
Photographer Girl and Filmer	themedia
Zombie	suckstobedead
Dad and Skater Jam Kid	strangefellows

Transformers: The Game

Codes

Enter codes at the "Campaign/Bonus Features" main menu. Enter codes for each character during one of their missions. This changes the character's appearance to their Generation 1 skin. Note: Using these cheats prevents you from achieving gamerscore!

Code	Effect
◇, ◁, ◁, ◇, ◁, ◁, ◇	Generation 1 Skin Megatron
◇, ▷, ◁, ◇, ◇, ◇, ◇	Generation 1 Skin Prime
◁, ◇, ◇, ◇, ◁, ◁, ◇	Generation 1 Skin Jazz
◇, ◇, ◇, ◇, ◁, ◁, ▷	Generation 1 Skin Optimus Prime
▷, ◇, ◁, ◁, ◇, ◇, ◇	Generation 1 Skin Starscream
◁, ◁, ◇, ◁, ◁, ◇, ▷	Infinite Health—Invincible
◇, ◇, ◁, ◇, ◇, ◇, ◇	No Ammo Reload

Transformers: The Game (continued)

Code	Effect
◇,◇,◇,◇,◇,◇,◇	No Military or Police
♀,♦,◇,◇,◇,◇,♦,♀	Unlock All mission including 2 special mission
◇,♦,♦,♀,◇,◇,◇	Unlocks the two Cybertron missions.

Unlockables

Unlockable	How to Unlock
G1 Megatron	Collect all the Transformer Shields in the Decepticons Story mode
G1 Optimus Prime (Cartoon Model)	Find all the Autobot faction symbols during the Autobot campaign.
G1 Robo-vision Optimus	Finish the Autobot campaign.
Jazz G1 Repaint	Complete all of the "challenge" sub-missions in both Autobot and Decepticon campaigns.
Starscream G1 repaint	Complete Decepticon Story mode.

Two Worlds

Codes

Note that Bonus codes do NOT stop you from getting achievements. But all other codes DO. To open the code menu hold down ⒧ + ⒭ and hit Ⓐ. A small text box appears. Now hit Ⓧ to open up the keyboard menu. Remember, only codes that start with "Bonuscode" will not affect your achievements. All codes other than the Bonuscodes require you to put in "twoworldscheats 1" first before entering the code. This permanently disables achievements for this character.

Code	Effect
ec.dbg addskillpoints	Add skill points
AddGold XXXX	Adds gold, where XXXX is the amount of gold added
AddParamPoints	Adds Param Points, where X is the number of points added
AddSkillPoints X	Adds Skill Points, where X is the number of skill points added
AddExperiencePoints XXX	Adds XXX amounts of experience
Bonuscode 9728-1349-2105-2168	Armor of Darkness
BonusCode 9470-4690-1542-1152	Aziraal's Sword of Fire
Create Lockpick	Creates a lockpick
Create Personal_Teleport	Creates a Teleport Stone
Bonuscode 9470-6557-8820-9563	Great Shield of Yatolen
ec.dbg levelup	Level Up
ec.dbg skills	Makes all skills available
Create Teleport_Activator	Recover lost teleport activator
ResetFog	Reveal map
ec.dbg levels X	Sets you to level 'X'
Bonuscode 9144-3879-7593-9224	Spear of Destiny
Bonuscode 9447-1204-8639-0832	The Great Bow of Heaven's Fury
Jump2	Transports player to where mouse is pointing
PhysX.Door.RemoveAll 1	Walk through doors and walls

DS · GBA · PSP · PS2 · PS3 · Wii · Xbox · Xbox 360 · Index

Ultimate Mortal Kombat 3

Codes

Enter codes at the VS screen.

Code	Effect
Player 1: LPx9, BLx8, LKx7; Player 2: LPx6, BLx6, LKx6	"Hold Flippers During Casino Run" Message
Player 1: LPx7, BLx1, LKx1; Player 2: LPx3, BLx1, LKx3	"Rain Can Be Found in the Graveyard" Message
Player 1: LPx1, BLx2, LKx3; Player 2: LPx9, BLx2, LKx6	"There Is No Knowledge That Is Not Power" Message
Player 1: LKx4; Player 2: LPx4	"Whatcha Gun Do?" Message
Player 1: BLx2; Player 2: BLx2	Blocking Disabled
Player 1: LPx6, BLx8, LKx8; Player 2: LPx6, BLx8, LKx8	Dark Kombat
Player 1: LPx1, BLx2, LKx2; Player 2: LPx2, BLx2, LKx1	Display "Skunky !!" Message
Player 1: LPx4, BLx4, LKx8; Player 2: LPx8, BLx4, LKx4	Don't Jump at Me
Player 1: LPx2, BLx2, LKx7; Player 2: LPx2, BLx2, LKx7	Explosive Combat (2 on 2 only)
Player 1: LPx6, BLx8, LKx8; Player 2: LPx4, BLx2, LKx2	Fast Uppercut Recovery Enabled
Player 1: BLx9, BLx1; Player 2: LPx1, BLx9	Kombat Zone: Bell Tower
Player 1: LPx3, BLx3; Player 2: BLx3, LKx3	Kombat Zone: Jade's Desert
Player 1: LKx4; Player 2: BLx7	Kombat Zone: Kahn's Kave
Player 1: LPx8, BLx8; Player 2: LPx2, BLx2	Kombat Zone: Kahn's Tower
Player 1: LPx6; Player 2: BLx4	Kombat Zone: Kombat Temple
Player 1: BLx5; Player 2: BLx5	Kombat Zone: Noob Saibot Dorfen
Player 1: LKx2; Player 2: LKx3	Kombat Zone: River Kombat
Player 1: LPx3, BLx4, LKx3; Player 2: LPx3, BLx4, LKx3	Kombat Zone: Rooftop
Player 1: LPx9, BLx3, LKx3	Kombat Zone: Scislac Busorez
Player 1: LPx6, BLx6, LKx6; Player 2: LPx4, BLx4, LKx4	Kombat Zone: Scorpion's Lair
Player 1: LPx1, BLx2, LKx3; Player 2: LPx9, LKx1	Kombat Zone: Soul Chamber
Player 1: BLx7, LKx9; Player 2: BLx3, LKx5	Kombat Zone: Street
Player 1: LPx8, BLx8; Player 2: BLx8, LKx8	Kombat Zone: Subway
Player 1: BLx7, LKx7; Player 2: BLx2, LKx2	Kombat Zone: The Bridge
Player 1: LPx6, BLx6, LKx6; Player 2: LPx3, BLx3, LKx3	Kombat Zone: The Graveyard
Player 1: LPx8, BLx2; Player 2: BLx2, LKx8	Kombat Zone: The Pit 3
Player 1: LPx2, BLx8, LKx2; Player 2: LPx2, BLx8, LKx2	No Fear = EB Button, Skydive, Max Countdown
Player 1: LPx9, BLx8, LKx2; Player 2: LPx1, BLx2, LKx3	No Powerbars
Player 1: BLx3, LKx3	Player 1 Half Power
Player 1: LPx7, LKx7	Player 1 Quarter Power
Player 2: BLx3, LKx3	Player 2 Half Power
Player 2: LPx7, LKx7	Player 2 Quarter Power
Player 1: LPx4, BLx4, LKx4; Player 2: LPx4, BLx4, LKx4	RandPer Kombat (Method 1)
Player 1: LPx4, BLx6; Player 2: LPx4, BLx6	RandPer Kombat (Method 2)
Player 1: LPx9, BLx9, LKx9; Player 2: LPx9, BLx9, LKx9	Revision
Player 1: LPx5, BLx5; Player 2: LPx5, BLx5	See the Mortal Kombat Live Tour !!
Player 1: LPx3; Player 2: LPx3	Silent Kombat
Player 1: LPx1; Player 2: LPx1	Throwing Disabled

DS
GBA
PSP
PS2
PS3
Wii
Xbox
Xbox 360
Index

Ultimate Mortal Kombat 3 (continued)

Code	Effect
Player 1: LPx6, BLx4, LKx2; Player 2: LPx4, BLx6, LKx8	Two-Player Minigame of Galaga
Player 1: BLx4, LKx4; Player 2: LPx4, BLx4	Unikoriv Referri: Sans Power
Player 1: LPx4, BLx6, LKx6 - Player 2: LPx4, BLx6, LKx6	Unlimited Run
Player 1: LPx9, BLx6, LKx9; Player 2: LPx1, BLx4, LKx1	Winner of this round battles Motaro
Player 1: BLx3, LKx3; Player 2: LPx5, BLx6, LKx4	Winner of this round battles Shao Kahn
Player 1: LPx2, LKx5; Player 2: LPx2, LKx5	Winner of this round battles Smoke
Player 1: LPx7, BLx6, LKx9; Player 2: LPx3, BLx4, LKx2	Winner of this round battles Noob Saibot

Unlock and Save Hidden Characters

Choose Arcade mode, lose a match. Then let the timer run out. You have 10 seconds to enter the ultimate kombat code for the character, one at a time. After unlocking them in Arcade mode, get to the Character Select screen. Pause, then exit the game. You'll have them for the rest of that play session. Now, very important, when you start the game up the next time around, you need to first go to the Arcade mode. This loads the characters you unlocked. Just wait and get to the Character Select screen, then exit. Now you can play with the characters online. If you do not go to the Arcade mode first, you will erase the characters. Just load and exit, then play online.

Virtua Tennis 3

Enter these codes at the main menu.

Unlockable	Code
Unlock All Courts	⇧, ⇧, ⇩, ⇩, ⇦, ⇨, ⇦, ⇨
Unlock King & Duke	⇧, ⇧, ⇩, ⇩, ⇦, ⇨, ⇦, ⇨
Unlock All Gear	⇦, ⇨, ↓, ⇨, ⇨, ↓, ⇧, ⇩
Test End Sequence (win one match to win tournament)	↓, ⇦, ↓, ⇨, ↓, ⇧, ↓, ⇩

Viva Piñata

Enter these passwords as names for your garden.

Unlockable	Password
Five Extra Accessories at the Pet Shop	chewnicorn
Items for Your Piñatas to Wear	goobaa nlock
Items for Your Piñatas to Wear	Bullseye
YMCA Gear	Kittyfloss

DS
GBA
PSP
PS2
PS3
Wii
Xbox
Xbox 360
Index

Index

Side tabs: DS · GBA · PSP · PS2 · PS3 · Wii · Xbox · Xbox 360 · Index

DS
GBA
PSP
PS2
PS3
Wii
Xbox
Xbox 360
Index

DS

GBA

PSP

PS2

PS3

Wii

Xbox

Xbox 360

Index

Side tabs: DS · GBA · PSP · PS2 · PS3 · Wii · Xbox · Xbox 360 · Index

DS

GBA

PSP

PS2

PS3

Wii

Xbox

Xbox 360

Index

DS
GBA
PSP
PS2
PS3
Wii
Xbox
Xbox 360
Index

DS

GBA

PSP

PS2

PS3

Wii

Xbox

Xbox 360

Index

Index

DS

GBA

PSP

PS2

PS3

Wii

Xbox

Xbox 360

DS

GBA

PSP

PS2

PS3

Wii

Xbox

Xbox 360

Index

DS
GBA
PSP
PS2
PS3
Wii
Xbox
Xbox 360
Index

DS

GBA

PSP

PS2

PS3

Wii

Xbox

Xbox 360

Index

DS

GBA

PSP

PS2

PS3

Wii

Xbox

Xbox 360

Index

DS

GBA

PSP

PS2

PS3

Wii

Xbox

Xbox 360

Index

DS

GBA

PSP

PS2

PS3

Wii

Xbox

Xbox 360

Index

DS

GBA

PSP

PS2

PS3

Wii

Xbox

Xbox 360

Index

DS

GBA

PSP

PS2

PS3

Wii

Xbox

Xbox 360

Index

DS | GBA | PSP | PS2 | PS3 | Wii | Xbox | Xbox 360 | Index

DS

GBA

PSP

PS2

PS3

Wii

Xbox

Xbox 360

Index

DS

GBA

PSP

PS2

PS3

Wii

Xbox

Xbox 360

Index

DS

GBA

PSP

PS2

PS3

Wii

Xbox

Xbox 360

Index

GAME TITLE	PLATFORM	PAGE
Sky Odyssey	PS2	277
Sled Storm	PS2	281
Sly Cooper and the Thievius Raccoonus	PS2	281
Small Arms	Xbox 360	617
Smash TV	Xbox 360	617
Smashing Drive	Xbox	546
Smuggler's Run	PS2	281
Smuggler's Run 2 Hostile Territory	PS2	281
SOCOM: U.S. Navy SEALs	PS2	282
SOCOM: U.S. Navy SEALs Fireteam Bravo 2	PSP	110
SOCOM: U.S. Navy SEALs: Combined Assault	PS2	282
Soldier Blade	Wii	388
Soldier of Fortune II: Double Helix	Xbox	546
Solomon's Key	Wii	388
Sonic 3D Blast	Wii	389
Sonic Advance	GBA	55
Sonic Adventure 2	GBA	56
Sonic and the Secret Rings	Wii	389
Sonic Heroes	PS2	284
Sonic Heroes	Xbox	546
Sonic Rivals	PSP	112
Sonic Spinball	Wii	390
Sonic the Hedgehog	PS3	334
Sonic the Hedgehog	Wii	390
Sonic the Hedgehog 2	Wii	391
Sonic the Hedgehog 2	Xbox 360	617
Sonic the Hedgehog 3	Wii	393
Sopranos, The: Road to Respect	PS2	285
Soul Calibur II	PS2	285
Soul Calibur II	Xbox	547
Space Giraffe	Xbox 360	617
Spawn: Armageddon	PS2	286
Spawn: Armageddon	Xbox	547
Spider-Man	GBA	56
Spider-Man	PS2	286
Spider-Man	Xbox	548
Spider-Man 2	PS2	288
Spider-Man 2	PSP	113
Spider-Man 2	Xbox	549
Spider-Man 3	Wii	394
Spider-Man: Friend or Foe	Wii	394
Spider-Man: Friend or Foe	Xbox 360	618
Splashdown	Xbox	550
Splashdown Rides Gone Wild	PS2	288
Splatterhouse	Wii	394
SpongeBob SquarePants: Battle for Bikini Bottom	Xbox	505
SpongeBob SquarePants: Creature from the Krusty Krab	Wii	395
SpongeBob SquarePants: Lights, Camera, Pants!	Xbox	550

DS

GBA

PSP

PS2

PS3

Wii

Xbox

Xbox 360

Index

DS

GBA

PSP

PS2

PS3

Wii

Xbox

Xbox 360

Index

DS

GBA

PSP

PS2

PS3

Wii

Xbox

Xbox 360

Index

DS

GBA

PSP

PS2

PS3

Wii

Xbox

Xbox 360

Index